ABORIGINAL PEOPLES
AND
THE LAW

ABORIGINAL PEOPLES AND THE LAW:

Indian, Metis and Inuit Rights in Canada

EDITED BY

Bradford W. Morse

CARLETON UNIVERSITY PRESS
OTTAWA, CANADA
1989

© Carleton University Press Inc., 1985
ISBN 0-88629-019-8 (paperback)

Printed and bound in Canada
Reprinted 1989
Canadian Cataloguing in Publication Data

Main entry under title:
  Aboriginal people and the law

(Carleton library series; no. 131)
ISBN 0-88629-019-8

1. Indians of North America — Canada— Legal status,
laws, etc. — History — Addresses, essays, lectures.
2. Inuit — Canada — Legal status, laws, etc. —
History — Addresses, essays, lectures. I. Morse,
Bradford W. (Bradford Wilmot), 1950- II. Series:
The Carleton library; no. 131

KE7709.5.A26   1984   342.71'0872   C84-090160-7

Distributed by:
  Oxford University Press Canada
  70 Wynford Drive
  DON MILLS, Ontario, CANADA, M3C 1J9
  (416) 441-2941

ACKNOWLEDGEMENT

Carleton University Press gratefully acknowledges the support extended to its
publishing programme by the Canada Council and the Ontario Arts Council.

Acknowledgements

Indian and the Law by the Canadian Corrections Association (Copyright 1967 by Canadian Corrections Association). Permission to quote granted by its successor organization, the Canadian Association for the Prevention of Crime.

Permission to quote granted by the Government of Canada for the following:

A Survey of the Contemporary Indians of Canada: Economic, Political, Educational Needs and Policies by H.B. Hawthorn, ed., (Copyright 1967 by Queen's Printer).

Canadian Indian Treaties and Surrenders. From 1680 to 1890 (Copyright 1891 by Queen's Printer and reprinted in 1971 by Coles Publishing Co.). Permission also granted by Coles Publishing Co., Coles Canadiana Series.

Handbook of Indians of Canada by F.W. Hodge (Copyright 1913 by King's Printer).

The James Bay Treaty: Treaty No. 9 (Copyright 1964 by Queen's Printer).

1845 Report on Indian Affairs.

P.A.C. R.G. 10, Vol. 5, Kempt to Colbourne, May 16, 1829.

Legal Aspects of Economic Development on Reserve Lands
By D. Sanders (Copyright 1976 by Department of Indian Affairs and Northern Development).

Indian Conditions: a Survey (Copyright 1980 by Department of Indian Affairs and Northern Development).

"Statement of the Government of Canada on Indian Policy", 1969.

Native Claims: Policy, Processes and Perspectives by the Office of Native Claims (Copyright 1978 by Supply and Services Canada).

Circular of Office of Native Claims, July 1980. *A Report: Statements and Conclusions* by the Commissioner on Indian Claims (Copyright 1977 by Supply and Services Canada).

In All Fairness — A Native Claims Policy — Comprehensive Claims (Copyright 1981 by Supply and Services Canada).

Outstanding Business — A Native Claims Policy — Specific Claims (Copyright 1982 by Supply and Services Canada).

Foster Care and Adoption in Canada by Philip Hepworth (Copyright 1980 by Canadian Council on Social Development). Permission granted to quote by the Canadian Council on Social Development.

Manual for Clerks and Staff of the Ontario Provincial Courts (Family Division) on the Child Welfare Act, 1978, Part II: Protection and Care of Children by Roman N. Komar (Copyright 1979 by the Ministry of Community and Social Services). Permission granted to quote by the Ministry of Community and Social Services.

"The Spanish Origins of Indian Rights in the Law of the United States" by Felix S. Cohen (1942) 31 *Georgetown Law Journal 17*. Reprinted with the permission of the publisher, (c) 1942 by the Georgetown Law Journal Association.

"The Concept of Aboriginal Rights in the Early Legal History of the United States" by H. Berman, (1978) 27 *Buffalo Law Reivew* 637. Permission granted to quote by the Buffalo Law Review.

First Nations: Indian Governments in the Community of Man by Delia Opekokew (Copyright 1982 by Federation of Saskatchewan Indian Nations). Permission to quote from this book and the Statement contained therein by Chief Sol Sanderson granted by the Federation of Saskatchewan Indian Nations.

"Principles of Indian Government" (Copyright 1977 by Federation of Saskatchewan Indians). Permission to quote granted by the Federation of Saskatchewan Indian Nations.

First Nations: Indian Government and the Canadian Confederation (Copyright 1980 by the Federation of Saskatchewan Indians). Permission to quote granted by Federation of Saskatchewan Indian Nations.

"Sovereignty and Self-Determination: The Rights of North Americans Under International Law" by Clinebell and Thompson, (1978) 27 *Buffalo Law Review* 669. Permission to quote granted by the Buffalo Law Review.

"Aboriginal Rights: Indian Tribes and Constitutional Renewal" by R. Barsh and J. Henderson, (1982) 27 *Buffalo Law Review* 617. Permission to quote granted by the Buffalo Law Review.

Together Today for our Children Tomorrow (Copyright 1973 by the Yukon Native Brotherhood). Permission to quote granted by the Council for Yukon Indians.

The Fourth World: An Indian Reality by George Manuel and Michael Posluns (Copyright 1974 by Collier-MacMillan Canada Ltd). Permission to quote granted by Collier-MacMillan Canada Ltd.

We are Metis: A Metis View of the Development of a Native Canadian People by Duke Redbird (Copyright 1980 by the Ontario Metis and Non-Status Indian Association). Permission to quote granted by the author and OMNSIA.

"A Concept of Native Title" by Leroy Littlebear (Copyright 1976 by the Canadian Association in Support of Native People. Permission to quote granted by CASNP.

"A Dene's View on the Pipeline (a presentation to the Berger Commission)" by Phillip Blake (Copyright 1976 by Canadian Association in Support of Native People). Permission to quote granted by CASNP.

Native Rights in Canada by P.A. Cumming and N.H. Mickenberg, eds., (Copyright 1972 by Indian-Eskimo Association). Permission to quote granted by Peter Cumming and CASNP.

"Baker Lake and the Concept of Aboriginal Title" by D. Elliott, (1980) 4 *Osgoode Hall Law Journal* 653. Permission to quote granted by the author and the Osgoode Hall Law Journal.

The Treaties of Canada with the Indians of Manitoba and the Northwest Territories by Alexander Morris (Copyright 1862 by P.R. Randall; reprinted 1971 by Coles Publishing Company). Permission to quote granted by Coles Publishing Company, Coles Canadiana Series.

"Native Rights" by Doug Sanders in *Report of Discussions on the Legal Status of Indians in the Maritimes,* October 16, 1970. Permission to quote granted by the author.

"Indian Hunting Rights: Constitutional Considerations and the Role of Indian Treaties in British Columbia" by K. Lysyk, (1966) 2 *University of British Columbia Law Review* 401. Permission to quote granted by the University of British Columbia Law Review.

Micmacs and Colonists: Indian-White Relations in the Maritimes 1713-1867 by L.F.S. Upton (Copyright 1979 by *U.B.C. Press*). Permission to quote granted by the University of British Columbia Press.

"Aboriginal Peoples and the Constitution" by D.E. Sanders, (1981) 19 *Alberta Law Review* 410. Permission to quote granted by the author and the Alberta Law Review.

"He Makes the Best Use of His Opportunities" by Charles B. Blackmar (1968-69) 21 *Journal of Legal Education* 499. Permission to quote granted by the Journal of Legal Education.

"Development of an Indian Reserve Policy in Canada" by R.J. Surtees, *Ontario History*, Vol. CXI, p. 82. Permission granted to quote by the author.

"Indian Lands and Canada's Responsibility" (Copyright 1979 by the Government of Saskatchewan). Permission to quote granted by the Government of Saskatchewan.

The Struggle for Survival by F.E. LaViolette (Copyright 1961 by University of Toronto Press). Permission to quote granted by University of Toronto Press.

"Survey of Canadian Law: Indian and Native Law" by R. Bartlett, (1983) 15 *Ottawa law Review* 431. Permission to quote granted by the author and the Ottawa Law Review.

"Indian Act of Canada" by R. Bartlett, (1978) 27 *Buffalo Law Review* 581 and 1980 by the Native Law Centre. Permission to quote granted by the Buffalo Law Review and the author.

"Indian and Native Rights in Uranium Development in Northern Saskatchewan" by R. Bartlett, (1980) 45 *Saskatchewan Law Review* 13. Permission to quote granted by the author and the Saskatchewan Law Review.

"Indian Water Rights on the Prairies" by R. Bartlett, (1980) 11 *Manitoba Law Journal* 59. Permission granted by the author.

CONTENTS

Preface

Since this book is somewhat unusual in its development and purpose, I think it is appropriate to discuss these matters in a Preface, as well as to express my appreciation to certain individuals and organizations essential to its creation.

The idea of a book containing cases and material on the original inhabitants of Canada and the law was first suggested to me four years ago by the Native Law Centre of the University of Saskatchewan. I declined their very kind offer to publish the materials that I had developed for my own teaching purposes, believing that it was far preferable to foster a collaboration among all those people who offer law school and undergraduate courses on this subject. In this case, the result would represent the sum of the knowledge and talents of the group and would constitute more than a simple casebook.

After contacting all people known to me who were teaching such courses, a proposal was presented to and approved by the Indian and Native Law Section of the Canadian Association of Law Teachers in June 1981. I am happy to say that this project has received the active support and participation of most of the people who teach this subject, and has been encouraged by members of the Canadian Indian Lawyers Association.

The book is designed to meet several objectives. It is primarily intended for use in law schools and in undergraduate departments of law and Native studies. My hope is that it will promote the establishment of new courses by universities and colleges that do not presently include a course on aboriginal people and the law in their curriculum. Moreover, since the book contains a great deal of original material we trust that it will be a useful resource for Indian, Metis and Inuit organizations, as well as for lawyers and government officials who work in this field.

The preparation of this book has been made easier by the financial assistance for travel and editorial research provided by the Department of Indian and Northern Affairs (DINA) and the Canadian Association of Law Teachers. In this regard, I would particularly like to thank Lizzie Fraitkin, Director of Research and Evaluation for DINA, and her predecessor, Dr Katie Cook, for their patience and unflagging support.   I would also like to express my appreciation to Dr. Margaret H. Ogilvie, the law books editor of Carleton University Press. Her help, effort and understanding have been invaluable in ensuring that the manuscript was completed and published.

I wish to thank my colleagues and fellow contributors for their continued interest, cooperation and responsiveness to my many, and seemingly unending, requests and suggestions for revisions. This collection of essays reflects the law as of July 1983, with minor revisions and amendments during the publication process, wherever possible, up to May 1984. I would like particularly to express my gratitude to Noel Lyon, whose work on the project, especially while I was away from Canada on sabbatical leave, was vital.

Thanks also are owed to the many secretaries of the University of Ottawa and the University of New South Wales, who cheerfully and excellently complied with all my urgent demands for aid, and to Miss Joan Steegstra who prepared tables. We hope that this volume will eventually be revised and updated and I would welcome all comments, criticisms and suggestions from readers in order to improve the quality and breadth of a second edition.

Bradford W. Morse,
Faculty of Law,
Common Law Section,
University of Ottawa.

Preface to the Revised First Edition

There has been an incredible level of activity in the field of aboriginal law over the last five years in terms of litigation, land claims settlements, constitutional negotiations, the development of First Nations and off-reserve self-government negotiations, the drafting of new international covenants, the passage of significant amendments to the *Indian Act*, and major reviews of how the justice system affects Aboriginal Peoples, as well as a number of other topics. In this revised edition, a modest supplement has been added, which includes extracts from a few of the most important judgments and statutory changes over the past few years. Chapters 1 to 13 have been left untouched. A completely revamped second edition is currently under way that will be more expansive in scope as well as thoroughly overhauling the contents of this edition. Your suggestions in this regard and your criticisms of this book are most welcome.

I would like to take this opportunity formally to thank the contributors to the first edition once again, as well as Ms. Mona Carkner for her excellent word processing assistance on the Supplement, and my wife.

This revised first edition is dedicated to the memory of Sam Odjick of the River Desert Reserve who died tragically while in his third year of law school at the University of Ottawa. All royalties, from the date of initial publication of this book in 1985, onward are being donated to the Sam Odjick Fund to provide scholarships to Aboriginal students in this Faculty and to encourage writing by law students on Aboriginal legal issues.

Bradford W. Morse
July 1989

Introduction

BRADFORD W. MORSE

The position in Canadian law of the Indian, Inuit and Metis peoples (hereinafter referred to collectively as the ''Aboriginal Peoples'') is a unique one. More importantly, their experience with colonialism and their relationship to white society occupies a central role in the political, social, military, and economic history of the territory now known as Canada.[1]

That the Aboriginal Peoples are still a force in present Canadian society was shown by the patriation process, the terms of the Canadian Constitution,[2] the First Ministers and Aboriginal leaders constitutional conferences of March 1983 and 1984,[3] the special 1982-83 inquiry of the Parliamentary Standing Committee on Indian Affairs concerning self-government, and the continuing dispute over land rights. The latter issue frequently raises broad social and economic questions about the potential dichotomy between the perceived resource needs of an energy-hungry industrialized society in southern Canada versus the conservationist, communal Indian and Inuit societies in the North. Aboriginal Peoples are experiencing the tensions inherent in a traditional, subsistence economy which is in contact with, and partially incorporated within, a wage economy that emphasizes individual income, materialism, and industrial development. Whether or not the dominant society is prepared to allow the Aboriginal Peoples of northern Canada to set their own pace for development and to create their own style of adopting and adapting modern technology to coincide with their current and future objectives is an issue that will probably be discussed for decades to come. The same is true of the drive of indigenous people for full self-government and the recognition of their continuing sovereignty *within* the modern Canadian nation-state.[4]

This is a field of domestic and international law that is heavily influenced by the history of the last five centuries. During this period, European settlement has slowly moved inland and northwards from the coast, transforming the cultures of indigenous societies. Indian and Inuit communities have moved gradually from self-sufficiency and complete sovereignty as independent nations to a state of partial (and in some cases almost total) dependency upon external governments and what is now the dominant society. The original inhabitants had their own governments, laws, systems for resolving disputes, cultures, religions, and languages — in short, their own civilization — but now these aspects of nationhood are viewed by some as continuing only at the pleasure of the immigrant majority. Fortunately, some of the traditional society has survived all attempts to change it. In recent years the vitality of some of these communities has been revived. It is essential to know something of this in order to understand the law currently in force and the goals of indigenous organizations.

The existence of an indigenous population in Canada with its own system of law and government has presented, and still presents, fundamental issues with which the common law and civil law systems have had to grapple. The common law, in particular, has itself evolved from customary law in England and had only this experience, plus exposure to the civil law approach of continental Europe, before colonization. The presence of Aboriginal Peoples provokes all sorts of questions, such as: do they as occupiers of the land own it just as much as, for example, British and French titleholders own land in their home countries? Are the laws of Aboriginal Peoples to be recognized as regulating their own affairs? Are their laws to be recognized as the *lex loci*, or local law, governing the affairs of all Canadians, including the settlers? Are their sovereign governments to be recognized on the same or similar terms as European governments? When, on what basis, and to what extent is the common law received into Canada (different rules apply under the common law doctrine of reception depending on whether conquest, cession, peaceful annexation or settlement has occurred)?[5]

Modern Canada has been considerably affected by the way in which these issues have been addressed, ignored, or inadequately answered. Gaps in logic and theory exist in our current legal regime. New "compromises" or principles have been developed by the judiciary in response to the inconvenience of some interpretations and to reflect historical events occurring before such questions were raised before the courts. It must be remembered that this is a field where the elaboration of the law by Canadian courts and the Privy Council has followed long after government-to-government relations commenced and the European policies (British as well as French, being most relevant in Canada) were articulated. Judges have often relied upon assumptions regarding this indigenous-settler relationship current at the time of judgment which were neither historically accurate nor reflected the basis of European policy and international law on these matters. The judiciary and the legal profession have generally been ignorant of indigenous life, government and law.

Today, this field of law is the one sphere in which Canada can be said to engage in legal pluralism, at least informally, because a separate legal system still functions outside the general courts and laws.[6] Furthermore, the common law has absorbed certain aspects of indigenous law in whole (for instance, family law and estates)[7] or in part (though modifying traditional land law into what is now described as aboriginal title). In addition, many areas of law must be examined in light of the special considerations and rules that apply only to Aboriginal Peoples and their assets as a result of federal, provincial or territorial legislation, executive acts, or the Canadian Constitution. This means that constitutional, family and international law, as well as the law concerning taxation, estates, real property, personal property, trusts, and civil procedure, to name only some of the areas, must be analyzed carefully in cognizance of the differences that exist in relation to members of the indigenous population in certain circumstances.

Therefore, to understand the applicable law on a given topic requires expert knowledge of this special area of law in combination with expertise in other legal fields. Standard legal approaches often may be inappropriate. For example, incorporating a company to operate an enterprise is normal practice; but this will attract tax liability for a business functioning on an Indian reserve when a partnership, co-operative or business trust would not.[8] Another example is in the area of matrimonial property and divorce, where special considerations arise in the division of family assets, orders of partition and enforcement of financial awards regarding on-reserve residents.

The law pertaining to Aboriginal Peoples is not disappearing; rather, it is expanding and evolving. The new Constitution, along with recent and future comprehensive land claims agreements, should cause a further expansion of this branch of the law, into wildlife management, environmental protection, education law, language rights, and so on.

Anthropologists and geographers are often called upon to serve as expert witnesses in litigation involving land ownership or land use patterns. Historians are regularly called upon to document the history of land management and its maladministration by government officials as part of the claims process. Lawyers are often sought to assist in negotiations unrelated to threatened civil litigation regarding intergovernmental agreements (for example, Canada-Ontario-Indian Policing Agreement, or Canada-Manitoba-Indian Child Welfare Agreement), land claims, funding agreements, and economic development projects. Of course, lawyers also act as solicitors and barristers in this field on behalf of corporations, governments, organizations and individuals.

It is not possible to include all portions of human knowledge relevant to this field in one book. The reader must rely upon the wealth of literature in the arts and social sciences, particularly in history and anthropology, for a more thorough understanding of what is the essential background to the law.[9] This book does not intend to represent or describe the demands, needs or goals of the Indian, Metis and Inuit peoples. That is the task of their regional and national organizations (the respective political representatives in Ottawa are the Assembly of First Nations, the Native Council of Canada, the Metis National Council, the Native Womens Association of Canada, and the Inuit Tapirisat of Canada).

This volume does not encompass all relevant aspects of the law, since it was not possible to include chapters on indigenous government and sovereignty, customary law, Indian Act government, specialized legal services and courts, the criminal justice system, sentencing law, some special facets of civil law, and unique aspects of the law relating to the Metis and the Inuit. This book is not intended to be definitive and further readings are suggested in each chapter.

The book attempts to provide a basic resource: excerpts of selected materials and original text regarding certain of the critical issues within this field. After a chapter describing the general position of the indigenous population today, the book considers five basic themes. Maureen Davies analyzes the historic importance of international law to the development of aboriginal and treaty rights, and in the book's final chapter examines the impact of modern international law concepts on our domestic legal thinking, as well as the increasing ''internationalization'' of the concerns of indigenous peoples around the world.

Chapters 3, 4 and 5, by David Elliott, Bruce Wildsmith and Norman Zlotkin respectively, are all concerned directly with the substantive Canadian law on aboriginal and treaty rights. The chapters by Noel Lyon and Douglas Sanders are intended to introduce the reader to constitutional issues. The two chapters by Richard Bartlett provide an extensive consideration of selected matters affected by the Indian Act, namely, reserve lands and taxation.

The final themes addressed concern the details and impact of land rights and the land claims process. This part of the book begins with a chapter concerning the land claims process in Canada as it has developed over the last fifteen years, with a brief look at different approaches in the United States and Australia. The next chapter, by Wendy Moss, is something of a case study of the land claims experience in that it focuses upon the development of the James Bay and Northern Quebec Agreement and its aftermath. In the penultimate chapter, Peter Cumming analyzes land rights and economic development in the North.

It is the general hope of all the contributors that this collection will aid in the understanding of this complex area of law and human relations, as well as foster further interest, communcation, cooperation and research in the field of Aboriginal People and the law. The authors' royalties are being donated to promote research and discussion on these subjects.

Endnotes

1. See, for example, E. Palmer Patterson, *A History of Canadian Indians Since 1500,* Collier-Macmillan, 1972.
2. This includes ss. 25 and 35 of the Constitution Act, 1982; British North America Act, 1867, RSC 1970, Appendix II, s. 91(24); British North America Act, 1930, RSC 1970, App. II; Royal Proclamation of 1763, RSC 1970, App. II; and many others.
3. This occurred as a result of a requirement in the new Constitution, s. 37.
4. For further information on these issues, see, for example, Mel Watkins (ed.), *The Dene Nation — The Colony Within,* University of Toronto Press, 1978; and Boyce Richardson, *Strangers Devour the Land,* Macmillan, 1976.
5. For a consideration of some of these questions, see Brian Slattery, *The Land Rights of Indigenous Canadian Peoples as Affected by the Crown's Acquisition of their Territories,* 1979, DPhil, Thesis, (Oxford University), Native Law Centre, University of Saskatchewan, 1979. Jack Stagg, *Anglo-Indian Relations in North America to 1763 and*

an Analysis of the Royal Proclamation of 7 October 1763, DIAND, Government of Canada, 1981. Geoffrey Lester, *The Territorial Rights of the Inuit of the Canadian Northwest Territories: A Legal Argument*, 1981, DJur Thesis, (York University, Toronto).

6. For some further discussion on this point, see two publications of Bradford W. Morse: *Indian Tribal Courts in the US — A Model for Canada?*, Native Law Centre, University of Saskatchewan, 1980; and "Section 107 of the Indian Act: A Unique Court System," (1982) 5 *Canadian Legal Aid Bulletin*, Nos. 2 and 3, 131.

7. Bradford W. Morse, "Indian and Inuit Customary Family Law in Canada," (1980) 8 *American Indian Law Review*, 199.

8. This is discussed in the chapter on taxation by Richard Bartlett, pp. 569-616.

9. For an excellent survey of historical events that are especially important to this area of law, see Peter Cumming and Neil Mickenberg, *Native Rights in Canada*, 2d ed., General Publishing Co., 1972.

TABLE OF CASES

TABLE OF STATUTES

NOVA SCOTIA

ONTARIO

QUEBEC

SASKATCHEWAN

AUSTRALIA

UNITED KINGDOM

USA

INTERNATIONAL

Chronology of Key Events

1497	John Cabot claims Newfoundland for King Henry VII of England.
1514	Bartolome de las Casas renounces his *encomienda* (a grant of land and compulsory Indian labour) in Cuba and preaches his first sermon against the Spanish colonial system. These events begin his career as champion of Indian rights and lead to his monumental *History of the Indies*.
1532	Francisco de Vitoria, Spanish international lawyer, gives two lectures on the rights of Indians in North America.
1534	Jacques Cartier, at Gaspe, claims the new land for King Francis I of France.
1537	Pope Paul III issues the Papal Bull *Sublimis Deus*, stating that Indians are men and should be protected in their liberty and property.
1606	Establishment of Port Royal in Acadia.
1609	Hostilities begin between Samuel de Champlain and the Iroquois.
1670	Charles II grants the charter to the Company of Adventurers trading into Hudson Bay (Hudson's Bay Company).
1713	The Treaty of Utrecht, ceding Acadia to England from France, contains special provisions for the five Nations of Indians.
1713-60	Treaties of Peace and Friendship in Nova Scotia.
1749	The appointment of Sir William Johnson as Superintendent of Indian Affairs for the northern region, based in what is now New York State.
1760	The Articles of Capitulation of Montreal. The Indian allies of France to be maintained in the lands they inhabit.
1763	Chief Pontiac creates an alliance of Indian tribes on the frontier and lays siege to the fort at Detroit.
1763	The Royal Proclamation of 1763 of George III, following the Treaty of Paris.
1763-1850	Land cession treaties and surrenders in Upper Canada (now Ontario).
1772	The Somerset case: slavery is not recognized in England.
1778	Captain Cook explores the coast of British Columbia.
1783	The Treaty of Paris formally ends the American Revolutionary War.
1784	The North West Company is established.
1787	The Northwest Ordinance is passed by the United States Congress: "The utmost good faith shall always be observed towards the Indians: their land and property shall never be taken from them without their consent. . . ."
1791	The Constitutional Act divides Quebec into Upper and Lower Canada.

1794	The Jay Treaty settles the United States-Canada border and provides for Indian custom and immigration rights.
1807	Britain abolishes the slave trade.
1823	The Anti-Slavery Society is formed in England.
1823	The United States Supreme Court decides *Johnson* v. *McIntosh*.
1832	The United States Supreme Court decides *Worcester* v. *Georgia*.
1833	Salvery is abolished in the British colonies.
1835	The Aborigines Protection Society is formed in England.
1837	Report of the Select Committee of the British House of Commons on Aborigines.
1840	The New Zealand Treaty of Waitangi recognizes Maori land rights.
1840	Upper and Lower Canada unite to form the Province of Canada.
1849	Vancouver Island is granted to the Hudson's Bay Company for purposes of settlement and a colony is established on the Island.
1850	The Robinson Treaties are signed in north-western Upper Canada.
1850	Indians are defined for the first time in colonial legislation.
1850-53	Fourteen treaties are signed on Vancouver Island, covering one-fortieth of the land area of the island.
1860	Jurisdiction over Indian policy is transferred from the Imperial Parliament to Upper Canada.
1867	Confederation. Jurisdiction over "Indians, and Lands reserved for the Indians" is given to the federal government under s. 91(24) of the British North America Act.
1869	The Riel Rebellion begins in Red River.
1870	Rupert's Land and the Northwestern Territory are transferred to Canada by Britain after the termination of the Hudson's Bay Company Charter. Canada accepts full responsibility to settle all Indian claims in the area.
1870	The Manitoba Act is passed: 1,400,000 acres are to be allotted to "half-breeds" in settlement of their "Indian title".
1871	British Columbia enters Confederation. The Terms of Union provide that Canada will follow a policy as "liberal" in relation to Indians as that followed by the government of British Columbia before Union.
1871	Treaties 1 and 2 are signed in Manitoba.
1871	The United States Congress decrees that there are to be no more Indian treaties in that country. Previously, the House of Representatives played no role in the treaties, which needed only to be approved by the Senate. Future dealings to be formalized by legislation, not treaties.
1873	Treaty 3 is signed at the Lake of the Woods.
1874	Treaty 4 is signed for southern Saskatchewan and portions of Manitoba and Alberta.
1875	Treaty 5 is signed for the remainder of Manitoba.

1876	Treaty 6 is signed for mid-Alberta and Saskatchewan.
1877	Treaty 7 is signed in southern Alberta.
1879	The Dominion Lands Act provides for "half-breed" allotments in the Northwest.
1885	The Northwest Rebellion is put down in Saskatchewan. Riel is tried and hanged in Regina.
1887	The United States Congress passes the Dawes Allotment Act designed to individualize the ownership of Indian reservations and sell all "surplus" lands to non-Indians.
1899	Treaty 8 is signed. It covers north-east British Columbia, northern Alberta and Saskatchewan, and part of the Northwest Territories.
1905	The Alberta and Saskatchewan Acts are passed by the Canadian Parliament.
1906-07	Treaty 10 is signed for northern Saskatchewan.
1912	The Quebec and Ontario Boundaries Extension Acts are passed. Those provisions are required to enter into treaties with the Indians in the areas added, such treaties to be subject to federal approval.
1912	The federal government abandons the idea of a reference to the courts on the aboriginal title question in British Columbia. The federal and provincial governments sign the McKenna-McBride agreement establishing a joint royal commission dealing only with the Indian reserve questions.
1917	The Migratory Birds Convention Act is passed by the Parliament of Canada. Later it will feature in Indian hunting rights litigation.
1921	Treaty 11 is signed, the last numbered treaty.
1923	The last treaties are signed, with members of the Mississaugas and Chipewas in Ontario.
1951	The Indian Act is completely revised for the first time in decades. It has not been revised since then.
1966	The Hawthorn Report, the first major study on Indians is commissioned by the federal government, is released.
1967	*Indians and the Law*, a major study on legal and justice issues regarding Indians commissioned by the federal government, is released.
1967-69	Cross-Canada consultations between the federal government and Indian people regarding the future of government-Indian relations is conducted.
1969	The federal government releases its White Paper to resolve Indian "problems".
1973	The Yukon Native Brotherhood presents *Together Today For Our Children Tomorrow* to the federal cabinet. Negotiations begin with the status and non-status people in the Yukon to settle the land claim.
1973	The new Labour Government in Australia appoints the Woodward

Commission to recommend the proper means of recognizing aboriginal land rights in the Northern Territory of Australia.

1973   The *Calder* and *Lavell* cases are decided by the Supreme Court of Canada.

1973   Indian Affairs Minister Jean Chrétien announces that the federal government will negotiate settlements of claims based on the loss of traditional rights to use land in certain non-treaty areas of Canada.

1973   Mr Justice Morrow of the Northwest Territories Supreme Court rules in the *Paulette* case that the Dene people can protect their aboriginal rights land claim by filing a caveat in the land titles registry. The actual filing of the caveat is delayed pending a completion of appeals in the case.

1973   Mr Justice Malouf of the Quebec Superior Court rules in the *Kanatewat* case that the James Bay project must be halted because of native land claims. One week later, the Quebec Court of Appeal lifts the injunction order pending a hearing of the appeal. The Supreme Court of Canada later refuses leave to appeal (3-2).

1973   The New Zealand government issues a white paper on the Maori Affairs Act and other New Zealand legislation affecting Maori land.

1974   The Quebec court of Appeal reverses the substance of the Malouf decision in *Kanatewat*.

1975   The World Council of Indigenous People is created at an international indigenous peoples conference in Port Alberni, British Columbia. George Manuel, President of the National Indian Brotherhood of Canada, heads the new world organization.

1975   The final agreement settling the James Bay claim is signed by representatives of the Cree, Inuit and the provincial and federal governments.

1975   Minister of Indian Affairs, Warren Almand, approaches three western provinces for assistance in meeting treaty obligations to provide lands.

1976   Negotiations begin between the Nishga Tribal Council and the federal and provincial governments to resolve the Nishga land claim.

1976   Inuit Tapirisat of Canada presents their land claims proposal to establish Nunavut in the eastern arctic.

1976   The Berger Commission on the Mackenzie Valley pipeline finishes its hearings.

1976   Land claims are presented in the Northwest Territories.

1977   The Supreme Court of Canada holds British Columbia provincial law to override aboriginal fishing rights in *Derriksan* and hunting rights in *Kruger and Manuel*.

1977   The Berger Commission report is presented on 15 April. It recommends a 10-year moratorium on the construction of the Mackenzie Valley Pipeline to permit the just resolution of Indian and Inuit land claims.

1977   The Alaska Highway Pipeline Inquiry is established with Kenneth Lysyk as chairman. It completes a quick investigation of the issues involved and presents its recommendations on 29 July 1977. It recommends approval-in-principle for this route, but that land claims should be settled before construction. The federal government gives the go-ahead for this route.

1977   The James Bay Settlement Acts are proclaimed by the federal and Quebec governments.

1977   The Polar Gas consortium files its application to bring natural gas from the high Arctic to the South.

1977   The Canadian Indian Rights Commission is established jointly by the federal government and the National Indian Brotherhood.

1977   Preliminary agreement is reached on compensation for flooding reserve lands in northern Manitoba with the five bands affected by the hydro project.

1977   The Royal Commission on the Northern Environment is established under Mr Justice Hartt to investigate all development north of the 50th parallel in Ontario.

1977   Preliminary agreement is reached on the treaty Indian land entitlement issue in Saskatchewan by adoption of the ''Saskatchewan Formula''.

1978   Negotiations resume on the Nishga claim.

1978   The Northern Pipeline Act is passed by Canada's Parliament.

1978   The Northeastern Quebec Agreement is signed with the Naskapis de Schefferville Band, Hydro-Quebec, and the governments of Quebec and Canada.

1978   Preliminary agreement is reached between Committee for Original Peoples' Entitlement and the federal government on land claims.

1978   The Canadian Indian Rights Commission is dissolved.

1978   The Indian Commission of Ontario is established by the federal and Ontario governments and the Chiefs of Ontario, to facilitate the resolution of land claims and other issues.

1979   The first specific claims are presented through the Indian Commission of Ontario.

1979   The Federal Court decides the *Baker Lake* case.

1979   The federal government presents its proposal on a new constitution.

1979   The first land transfers begin in Saskatchewan to fulfil outstanding treaty promises.

1980   Joint Parliamentary Hearings begin on the Constitution.

1981   The United Nations Human Rights Committee finds Canada and the Indian Act in violation of international law for a breach of Article 27 of the International Covenant on Civil and Political Rights in the *Lovelace* case.

1981   The Canada Act is passed, despite the opposition of the Indian people.

1981   The Government of Canada issues a "new" policy on comprehensive land claims.

1981   The Stony Rapids band becomes the first band to have its outstanding Treaty Indian Land Entitlement fulfilled pursuant to the "Saskatchewan Formula".

1982   Passage of the Canada Act by the British Parliament is fought unsuccessfully in the British courts.

1982   The federal government releases a new specific land claims policy.

1982   The Constitution Act is proclaimed by Queen Elizabeth II.

1982   The result of a plebiscite favours the division of the Northwest Territories into Denendeh and Nunavut.

1982   The first claim of Indian bands in British Columbia regarding the "cut-off" lands is settled with the Penticton Band for $14.2 million and 4,855.2 hectares of land. The Osoyoos Band later settles its "cut-off" land claim for $1 million.

1982   The first specific claim in the Atlantic Provinces is settled with the Wagmatcook Band in Nova Scotia for $1.2 million.

1982   A Parliamentary Sub-committee on Indian Women and the Indian Act releases its Report.

1983   The first Constitutional Conference is held as required by s. 37 of the Constitution Act. Several specific amendments to the Constitution are agreed upon as is an increased schedule of future such conferences.

1983   The Clinton Band's "cut-off" claim in British Columbia is settled for $150,000 and the return of almost 70 of the original 90 hectares of reserve land removed in 1916.

1983   The Oromocto Band of New Brunswick settles its specific claim for $2.5 million.

1983   The Parliamentary Committee on Indian Self-Government releases its Report.

1983   The governments of Canada and the Yukon Territory sign an agreement-in-principle with the Council of Yukon Indians for the latter's comprehensive claim.

1984   Final agreement is reached on the comprehensive claim of the Committee of Original People's Entitlement.

1984   The second Constitutional Conference is held in Ottawa.

1984   B.C. "Cut-off" Indian land claims legislation enacted by

Parliament and three more claims — Westbank, Squamish and Okanagan — are settled.

1984   Blackfoot Band claim for cattle promised under Treaty 7 in 1877 is settled for $1.675 million.

1984   The comprehensive claim for the Inuvialuit of the Western Arctic (COPE) is ratified by Parliament through the passage of a special statute.

1984   The Indians of Conne River, Newfoundland, are finally recognized as an Indian band under the Indian Act.

1984   Legislation to amend the Indian Act to remove sexual discrimination and reinstate many, but not all people disenfranchised due to these provisions is introduced in Parliament.

1984   Federal legislation to provide a limited form of self-government to Indian Nations is introduced.

1984   Special legislation to expand the powers of Cree and Naskapi governments under the James Bay and Northeastern Quebec Agreements is enacted by Parliament.

1. Aboriginal Peoples and the Law

BRADFORD W. MORSE

1. The Aboriginal Peoples in Canada

(a) Who Are The Aboriginal People?

Although this subheading appears to pose a very simple question, it cannot be answered without a definition of the term "Aboriginal People". A lack of precision and consistency in the use of this term has created a continual problem and source of confusion. This author is using the phrase "Aboriginal People" to encompass all people who trace their ancestors in these lands to time immemorial. This means that the term subsumes all Indians, whether registered under the Indian Act[1] or not, the Metis, and all Inuit (also known as "Eskimos").

The Government of Canada has received the authority under s. 91(24) of the Constitution Act, 1867,[2] to legislate in relation to "Indians, and Lands reserved for the Indians." This power has been exercised in the passage of special legislation called the Indian Act. This statute sets forth a complex system for registering Indians, administering their lands and regulating their lives. The idea of such a definitional system has existed since the early legislation concerning Indians was enacted in 1850[3] and has been maintained in all subsequent statutes.[4]

The registration system was implemented by sending an Indian agent, appointed by the government, to the Indian nations to enumerate persons in order to develop treaty payment lists or band lists.[5] If people were away on hunting parties, out on their traplines, or off fishing, or if bands were in remote areas, then they simply were not registered under the Indian Act.[6]

Many Indians who were once registered, or who are the descendants of people who were registered, are no longer legally considered to be Indians under the Act.[7] Over the years, thousands were persuaded by local Indian agents to become enfranchised under the provisions in the Act. There were obvious attractions to doing so — for instance, until 1960 only enfranchised Indians could vote in federal elections. For many years, status Indians could not send their children to public schools, enjoy the provincially managed social welfare programs, or join a profession such as law.[8]

Indian people were told that they had to become enfranchised and leave the reserves if they wanted to join the mainstream of society and enjoy its advantages. The federal government's philosophy toward the Indian nations reflected the beliefs commonly shared by the dominant society. Lacking an understanding of the ways of Indian culture and suspicious of the

1

non-Christian genesis of their religion, successive governments made negative value judgments about Indian lifestyles, attitudes and customs.[9]

The government sought to implement these value judgments through a persistent and pervasive effort to persuade Indian people that they were in fact maintaining an inappropriate way of life. They were told that they should feel ashamed of their traditions and values. This message was repeated in the schools and churches, and was disseminated by Indian agents.

As a result of this procedure of enfranchisement, many Indian people gave up their status under the Indian Act. They were then paid a lump sum, representing any treaty annuities they would have received over the next twenty years, along with one per capita share of any band funds held on trust by the Crown in right of Canada. Many people needed the money to survive and did not understand the effects of enfranchisement. They generally did not realize that they were selling their legal right to be considered as an ''Indian''; and they did not appreciate that the stroke of a pen would alter their life and their racial status. There was clearly no parallel in their culture or their experience.

Indian people still can apply to Ottawa for enfranchisement, if they are willing to renounce their birthright. If this is done by a male, then he and his spouse, any minor children (if the family is living together) and all heirs are permanently excluded from being Indians. All rights and obligations of Indian status are lost.[10] Although voluntary enfranchisement has practically disappeared in recent years, from 1955 to 1975 some 2,666 adults and children gave up their position as legally recognized Indians.[11]

Another method by which people are enfranchised, which has received considerable publicity in the *Lavell*[12] and *Bedard*[13] cases and the Sandra Lovelace complaint,[14] occurs when a registered Indian woman marries a non-registered man.[15] She and her minor unmarried children will lose their status as registered Indians by virtue of s. 109(2) of the Indian Act. Apparently, between 1955 and 1975 10,484 Indian women and children ''forfeited'' their status because of this procedure.[16] The fact that an Indian woman may be marrying a full-blooded, yet non-registered, Indian man or one of aboriginal ancestry is considered to be irrelevant.

Another group that involuntarily loses status under the Indian Act consists of those who are included within the so-called ''double-mother rule''. Section 12(1)(a)(iv) results in an individual being involuntarily enfranchised upon reaching the age of twenty-one if his or her mother and the father's mother gained Indian status through marriage, providing that the parents' marriage occurred after 4 September 1951.[17] This is a particularly common event in the St Regis Reserve on the banks of the St Lawrence, which extends across the border into the United States, since the community is divided into Canadian and American Indians and the latter are not legally considered to fall within the scope of the Indian Act.

Children of enfranchised parents often live in a blatant contradiction. They may be full-blooded Indian people, yet be denied the right to live on a reserve, receive educational assistance, or participate in fishing or hunting privileges, through no fault or decision of their own, while still suffering from the racial prejudice that all Aboriginal People receive.

There is a necessity for some form of a status definition or membership system to determine *who* possesses the special rights of residency on or ownership of reserve lands and *who* will be treated differently by the courts, the laws and the governments of Canada as a result of the unique legal, constitutional and political position of at least some of the Aboriginal Peoples within the territory now called Canada. The need to make a distinction does not automatically determine the nature of the status system that must be implemented. There are at least four basic kinds of status definition systems from which to choose: blood; kinship; style of life; a charter group.

Most such systems in Africa and the United States rely upon a set minimum percentage of blood for an individual to be included within the membership of a particular aboriginal tribe. Indian tribes in the USA have control over membership and generally use a one-quarter blood rule: any person who possesses one-fourth or more blood from that Indian nation will be entitled to be a member of the tribe.

A kinship system focuses upon the individual's family connection to existing members of the group. That is, all children of the selected parent, either the father (patrilineal) or the mother (matrilineal), will automatically receive status upon birth, but no non-member will be included by virtue of marrying a member.

A third approach is to concentrate upon the beliefs or lifestyle of individuals to determine who is a member of the group. For example, someone who adopts a particular philosophy or joins a religious group becomes a member of that community and can be treated separately in law. The same is true by defining a "style of life," such as a nomadic one that survives through hunting, fishing and trapping. A person who adopts this mode of living or a child who is adopted by a group member can then be regarded as having this status.

Finally, one can use a charter group system. In other words, all people who possess essential criteria on a set date are considered to have status. The essential criteria could be geographic, such as residency on reserves; or based on community acceptance; or it might be determined through individual choice, such as a person taking half-breed land scrip or signing a treaty roll. These people then belong to the special group. Unless their descendants also become members, which leads us into a kinship system, the group is fixed and will slowly disappear through attrition.

Over the years the Canadian system has used all four of these approaches, although not at the same time. The "style of life" criterion was dropped in the 1951 revision of the Indian Act when a charter group factor was added. Possession of Indian blood has always been an important element but it has never been decisive; for example, a non-Indian wife of an Indian man has been considered to be an Indian since the first definition system was introduced in 1850. Kinship also plays a role but not a conclusive one due to the "double mother rule" and the fact that marriage can give or remove status.

The net result is that the present Indian Act contains a hybrid status definition system that precludes any Indian control over the decision-making process.

The term "Metis" is often used to describe all those people who have a "mixed" ancestry. "Initially the title meant a half 'mixture' of French and Indian, although it has not been broadened to include almost all people with at least some Indian ancestry."[18] A related label was the term "halfbreed," which was usually used to denote children of mixed English-Indian marriages. This group now includes many of the descendants of the enfranchised Indians, as well as those whose families were never registered, or who had been alloted half-breed lands or money scrip rather than receiving treaty payments and the right to live on reserves. Although the terms "non-status Indian" and "non-registered Indian" are becoming more common today in lieu of the word "Metis," the Metis represented a uniquely Canadian culture developed in the Prairies through blending the French *coureur des bois* and the Indian, creating a strongly Catholic community with many Indian values.

To further confuse matters, some Aboriginal People are referred to as "treaty Indians" and "non-treaty Indians," yet both groups are status Indians under the Indian Act. Roughly 50 percent of the registered Indian population are non-treaty Indians, residing primarily in Quebec, the Atlantic Provinces, parts of the Northwest Territories and most of British Columbia. Residence on a reserve is not a factor in differentiating between treaty Indians and non-treaty Indians, nor does it affect the status issue. Some of the former were never given the reserves promised to them in the treaties, yet many of the latter were granted reserves while the rest of their land was taken without agreement or compensation.[19] Roughly 30 percent of the Indians who could live on a reserve do not reside there anyway, largely due to the absence of employment opportunities.[20]

To summarize: the Indian population of Canada is described in a variety of ways. They are called treaty Indians; non-treaty Indians; non-registered or non-status Indians; and registered or status Indians. They are all Indians; yet the result of this process of registration has been to divide the Indian people. That is, the dominant white society has decided which Indians it is willing to consider as being legal "Indians" for the purposes of receiving the benefits which flow from that status — special federal programs, tax exemptions, residence on reserves, treaty rights, and so on. The procedure has been amazingly successful in fostering division and competition between the status and non-status Indians of Canada. Its effect is just beginning to lessen as Indian people in some parts of Canada, particularly in the Yukon and the

Northwest Territories, are uniting by adopting their own political and social definitions.

Historically, the federal government had ignored the Inuit and had not attempted to interfere in their daily lives in a substantial way until after World War II. They were not affected by the early Indian legislation and are explicitly excluded in the present Act.[21] This occurred as a result of the desultory contact between society at large and the Inuit, and the absence of any need for or value placed upon the lands of these people until recent decades.

Therefore, the Inuit have no reserves, no significant treaties with the Crown, and no legislative guarantees to protect them, other than some limited hunting rights under federal and territorial legislation. They do fall within the federal jurisdiction, since the Supreme Court of Canada held *In re Eskimos*[22] that the Inuit are included within the meaning of the word "Indians," in s. 91(24) of the Constitution Act, 1867. The federal government has responded with a number of social and economic programs administered by the Department of Indian Affairs and Northern Development (hereinafter referred to as DIAND). These programs extend to the Inuit in the Yukon, the Northwest Territories and Quebec,[23] although the James Bay Agreement has changed things for the Inuit in Quebec.[24]

(b) Demographic and Economic Information[25]

Society generally does not understand the position of Aboriginal People in Canada, mainly because of the shortage or complete absence of critical information. Although there are a number of historical and anthropological studies available on American Indians, and a growing collection of similar studies on Aboriginal People in Canada, these studies mainly tend to refer to individual bands or tribes. There is very little general information that can help society understand the position of Aboriginal People and that might be adduced to bring about reforms in the system of justice.

A simple illustration of this fact is that no one knows exactly how many Aboriginal People there are in Canada. DIAND states that in 1979 there were just over 300,000 registered Indians in Canada, belonging to some 573 bands.[26] Yet, in an earlier report, DIAND mentions the existence of only 565 Indian bands.[27] Most of the band members reside on 2,242 reserves with a total area of 10,021 square miles.[28]

The exact number of non-status Indians (a term used herein as encompassing both "non-registered Indians" and "Metis") is unknown. James Frideres quotes estimates ranging from 260,000 to 850,000 people;[29] Douglas A. Schmeiser places the number at 570,438,[30] but this apparently precise figure is based upon broad estimates. The Inuit population is estimated to be about 25,000, resulting in the Native population being somewhere between 585,000 and 1,175,000. The official 1981 census, however, records only 75,110 non-status Indians and 98,260 Metis resulting in a total population of 491,460 Aboriginal People. These figures have been criticized as not reflecting the true total due to alleged missed people and refusal to identify under these criteria.

The present social, economic, educational and health conditions of the indigenous peoples of Canada is a national disgrace.[31] Despite a 64 percent increase in Indian reserve housing since 1958, at least one-third of all Indian families live in crowded conditions, and some 18.8 percent of reserve homes have two or more families as occupants. In 1977, approximately 11,000 new houses were needed and 24 percent of existing homes required major repairs. Less than 40 percent of rural and remote reserve housing had running water, sewage and indoor plumbing. Lack of running water and poor quality housing results in an extraordinarily high number of fires; the fire death rate is six times the national average.

The health situation of registered Indians is even more startling. Indian children can expect an average life span of ten years less than that of the national population, while the death rates range from two to four times the national average, with violent deaths and suicides occurring three times more than among the non-Indian public. Although there have been significant improvements in health care, such as a reduction in infant mortality from six times the national rate in 1963 to twice the average in 1977, there is clearly no cause for rejoicing over the present situation. There is also some suggestion that recent improvements in health care face a reversal due to industrial pollution: a minimum of twenty Indian communities, involving some 10,000 Indians, are confronted by severe environmental hazards.

Indians also suffer heavily from the 'last hired, first fired' syndrome within the Canadian economy. The most optimistic figures place on-reserve Indian participation in the labour force at only two-thirds of the national rate, whereas the other estimates of Indian unemployment run from 35 percent to 75 percent. On many reserves, unemployment is a fact of life for almost everyone. Those who can find work are often limited to seasonal employment. Although recent income data are unavailable, it appears that the position of status Indians has not significantly improved from what it was in 1970 when over 80 percent were below the national poverty line, and some 62 percent of employed Indians earned less than $2,000 per year.

The position of Aboriginal People within the criminal justice system is also disheartening. They are three times more likely than others to spend time in federal penitentiaries and represent over 40 percent of the provincial prison population in some provinces and the two territories. The Indian juvenile delinquency rate is also three times higher than their numbers warrant and Indians generally are much more likely than other groups to spend time in prison.[32]

The only aspect of this review that demonstrates some promise of hope is education. Even here, however, the high school "drop-out" rate is still extremely high: only 20 percent of registered Indians complete grade 12. Although the presence of poverty, allegedly inferior quality education, racism, the irrelevance of a school system that fosters middle-class goals, and the conflict between the values and beliefs of Indian culture and those held by the dominant society tend to explain these unsatisfactory statistics, one must be impressed with the determination and drive of those Indians who instituted a jump in university enrollment from almost zero in 1957 to over 2,500 students in 1979. There are, however, worrisome signs here too, because the data indicates that in recent years there has been a decline in secondary school participation, pre-vocational training, vocational training and adult education.

The preceding data do not paint an attractive picture of the life of Aboriginal People. The following statements, made in a 1967 government-commissioned study entitled *Indians and the Law*, are still sadly true today:

> It is accurate to say that the Indian and Eskimo people of Canada are in cultural, social and economic isolation from the rest of the population. This situation is aggravated by their geographic isolation which compounds the difficulty in providing adequate levels of service. The majority of them lack such basic necessities as running water, electricity, plumbing, telephones, roads and other transportation facilities. The cost of bringing these services to them is substantially higher than to other groups because they are scattered thinly throughout the rural and remote sections of the country. Access to sophisticated services such as employment counselling and placement, child and family services and recreation, is even more limited for many of them, and in some areas not available at all.[33]

(c) The Position of Aboriginal Families

The dimensions of the tragedy indicated by the preceding data are clearly apparent when one examines the condition in which Aboriginal families find themselves. Indian, Metis, and Inuit families across Canada live in a state of crisis. The situation is so serious, and the statistics so alarming, that one might be tempted to say that Aboriginal families are in a state of siege. Although there is always cause for hope, and there have been a few positive developments recently that might fuel some guarded optimism, the stability of Aboriginal families is crumbling as social conditions deteriorate both within Aboriginal communities and in urban centres.

The destabilization of Aboriginal families and communities is in large part a result of federal and provincial social services policies, provincial family legislation, and the administration of Canadian justice. The courts, the statutes, and the policies all tend to reflect a common perception: that the Aboriginal People are unable adequately to meet their own family needs through their own policies, programmes and laws. An attitude, based on notions of guardianship and superiority, has been adopted by Canadian society that has justified, if not necessitated, the intervention of the state and its agents into the indigenous family structure. Although this intervention has been well intentioned, it has been misguided and has had disastrous consequences. The interventionist approach of the social service agencies has been supplemented by the legal system's general lack of regard for the rights of Aboriginal People and the validity of their traditional family laws.

A substantial amount of public attention has been focussed of late upon the burgeoning political aspirations of Native People in Canada for the rights of self-government and self-determination. The constitutional debate has provided a forum for Native People to pursue their desire for sovereignty and the recognition of treaty and aboriginal rights. These goals are seen as prerequisite for the redevelopment and reinforcement of Indian, Inuit and Metis cultural values and community life. The desire to break the vicious cycle of dependence is now beginning to have its effect on family law and the child welfare system, with the call for the transfer of control over services, resources and the law to Aboriginal People so that they can be created by, controlled by and made accountable to Aboriginal communities.[34]

Aboriginal People are the victims of a major dilemma. Although registered Indians and Inuit are regarded as being within the jurisdiction of the federal government, which has resulted in the passage of the Indian Act to deal with a number of aspects of Indian life and government, there is no federal legislation that directly addresses the relationship between status Indians and most aspects of the general law, such as family law, criminal law, torts and others let alone the position of other Aboriginal People. Provincial legislation and the common law are generally relied upon to fill this gap by providing general statutes and jurisprudence dealing with the law regarding trusts, contracts, consumer protection, marriage, child welfare and matrimonial property,[35] among others, while federal legislation — for example, the Divorce Act, Criminal Code and Fisheries Act — deals with matrimonial affairs, crime and fisheries. This approach means that legislation is applied to Aboriginal People that is not tailored to meet their particular needs and values, but rather is enacted to cover the entire population.

Status Indians are caught in a financial squeeze and a jurisdictional conflict. For political and administrative reasons, a number of provinces have been unwilling to extend social services to status Indians. This situation was summarized in a 1967 government-commissioned report as follows:

> . . . the special status of Indians, and more importantly the policies and practices which have affixed themselves to that status, have had the effect of placing barriers between an underprivileged ethnic minority and welfare services which they need. The assumption that Indians were "wards" of the federal government, and that reserves were federal islands in the midst of provincial territory has had the unfortunate effect

that basic provincial welfare activities have ignored and bypassed reserve Indians. Indians have also been excluded from a number of shared cost programs operated by the provinces which received federal financial support. In general, the major barrier has been the unwillingness of provincial and municipal governments to provide services or expend monies on a minority group regarded as the exclusive responsibility of the federal government.[36]

Although strides have been made in extending provincial services to status Indians over the last few decades, largely as a result of arranging "bill-back", or cost-sharing, agreements with provincial governments, status Indians are still not eligible for all provincial services and benefits.[37] Some provinces, such as Saskatchewan and Manitoba, have been exceedingly reluctant to provide services in any but life-or-death situations.[38]

The arrangements between the federal and provincial governments for the provision of child welfare services to status Indian children are remarkably varied and at the level of official policy bespeak tremendous arbitrariness and variability; at the level of actual service delivery the policies of provincial and local child welfare agencies are even more variable and whether services are delivered or not depends on the availability of local resources and the personal judgment of local personnel. These circumstances are likely to hold even in Ontario where there is a formal agreement with the federal government.[39]

The situation regarding service delivery is less confusing for other Aboriginal People. Historically, non-status Indians and Metis have been viewed as a provincial responsibility, whereas the Inuit and other residents in the far North are serviced by the federal government through the Northern Affairs branch of DIAND.

This dilemma also extends to the type of service delivered. Aboriginal People must accept the existing, professionalized services, if they exist, or do without. These services focus upon individual problems and do not make connections between the individual, the family and the community.

Divergent cultural values also lead to different perceptions of problems and how to resolve them. This is particularly evident in the child welfare system. The legislation in this field, and the guidelines developed for children's aid staff in implementing it, are very broad and flexible. This gives the professional staff considerable latitude in interpreting specific provisions relating to child neglect in the light of their own cultural values and biases. Unfortunately, this sometimes leads to unnecessary and insensitive interventions in Aboriginal families, poorer communication and a lower quality of services. Roman Komar, an advisor to the Ontario government, has warned child care workers that:

. . . they can, consciously or unconsciously become the vehicle for the imposition of North American middle-class standards of child care upon people whose social and cultural standards happen to be different. Thus, the poor, immigrants and native peoples seem to be singled out for special attention and it is here that Courts must be vigilant to prevent misuse of the law by agencies.[40]

Even the most conservative figures, which will omit many Metis and non-status Indian children, demonstrate that in "1977 about 20% of all children in care in Canada, that is 15,500 children, were native children."[41] Depending upon one's sources, the rate of status Indian children in the care of child welfare agencies is approximately two[42] to five times the national average.[43] The statistics in some provinces are frightening. The number of Indian and Metis children in care range as high as 39 percent in British Columbia to 44 percent in Alberta to 51.5 percent in Saskatchewan and 60 percent in Manitoba. Even in Ontario, where the rate is only 9 percent, it does run as high as 19 percent in the north of the province,[44] and as large as 85 percent in the Kenora district.[45]

These figures are even more startling when one realizes that the divorce rates of status Indians are only half the national average, and the proportion of children released for adoption at birth, or thereafter, by unmarried Indian and Metis women is dramatically less than the national pattern. Despite the fivefold increase in child care expenditures by DIAND over the last two decades, family conditions on reserves are deteriorating. The increase in the federal financial commitment to child care expenses for status Indians has neither minimized this distressful state of affairs nor has provided any tangible benefits to Indian communities.

Indian, Inuit and Metis families are isolated from all parts of the legal system, including child welfare legislation and the family courts. When Aboriginal People attempt to resolve social problems through the traditional approach of the extended family, by which grandparents, aunts, or uncles step in to assist families in crisis, they encounter further problems with social service agencies. Relatives generally will not qualify for financial assistance as foster parents, and, even an unrelated adult who wishes to be a foster or adoptive parent is evaluated according to criteria that emphasize material wealth rather than cultural suitability. Similar problems are encountered when Aboriginal communities attempt to redress juvenile delinquency and criminality through traditional means and under traditional law.

Years of domination and dependence render Aboriginal People less likely to contest actions through the courts. In addition, the procedures for seeking out available services and demanding those services and rights are alien to traditional native ways of dealing with life. This can lead to tragic consequences and misunderstandings on the part of the white professional:

Thus native parents who have had their children taken into care may not make persistent demands for the return of the children or continued contact with them. This can easily be misinterpreted as constituting abandonment, and reinforces whatever negative images were formed about the parents initially. In turn this can reinforce the native sense of futility in making any impact on decisions made by white social workers and white judicial officers.[46]

This conflict in cultures and cultural values is particularly evident in decisions on adoption placements. Indian and Metis children are far less likely to be adopted than other children,[47] and therefore will stand a greater chance of remaining within the care of the child welfare authorities until they reach adulthood. This often means that these children will endure a number of placements in non-aboriginal foster and group homes during their formative years. Adoption of Aboriginal children is on the rise, however, and the adoption of status Indian children has increased by almost 500 percent since 1962. This dramatic increase does not mean that these children are returning to Indian homes, since it mainly reflects an increase in adoptions by non-Indian parents.

The net result of these events has been to foster frustration and futility in many Indian, Inuit, and Metis communities. Very little has been done by social service and criminal justice agencies, or by DIAND, to mitigate the effect of cultural assimilation or to counteract it. Some Aboriginal People are beginning to say that the situation reflects a policy of cultural genocide.

Indian communities have started to overcome despair and pain by beginning to demand changes in the present system.[48] Certain communities have assumed control over child welfare law and services, while others have established their own courts, police forces, schools, fire departments, businesses and social service programs. These efforts and others give vivid expression to the desire by Aboriginal People to regain control over their fate and their future so as to strengthen their communities and protect their resources.

(d) Conclusion

The writer has attempted to describe who the original peoples of Canada are, what their lives are like, and what crises confront them. But it must be stated that this represents only a part of the total picture. There has been no discussion of the lengthy history of the indigenous peoples, either before or after contact with the colonizers, nor has there been any description of the varied and rich cultures possessed by the aboriginal population.

Writing about the condition of Aboriginal People in broad terms fails to disclose the brutal impact of the processes of colonization, economic destabilization and acculturation. Statistics do not bleed or feel pain, frustration and hopelessness.

Generalities also mask the diversities that exist, as well as the cultural, political and economic revival that has begun in aboriginal communities.

Aboriginal People are not all the same nor do they all face the same problems. There are at least eleven major linguistic groups (Algonquin, Iroquois, Sioux, Athabasca, Kootenay, Salish, Wakash, Tsimish, Haida, Tlingt and Inuktituk) and dozens of different dialects. Anthropologists recognize at least seven major cultural areas (Algonquin, Iroquois, Plains, Plateaus, Pacific Coast, McKenzie River and the Arctic), within each of which there is considerable variety of lifestyle, governmental system, laws, religion and culture.[49]

Although many of these differences have been minimized or obliterated by the conduct of the dominant society, their psychological and practical importance remains. It is a grave mistake to expect all Aboriginal People to speak in a single voice, to seek the same objectives, or to have one vision for their future. Furthermore, it is an error to presume that one can establish a particular type of programme or deliver a service or enact one general statute that will meet the needs of all Indian, Metis and Inuit peoples. Only they, through their own communities, institutions and governments, can determine how best to serve their own needs. With that in mind, the dominant society, including students and lawyers, can be of considerable assistance in promoting the economic, social and political revitalization of the original peoples of Canada.

Endnotes

*This chapter is based upon an article that appeared under the title, "The Original Peoples of Canada" (1982), 5 *Canadian Legal Aid Bulletin*, No. 1, 1-16.

[1] RSC 1970, c. I-6.
[2] RSC 1970, App. II, No. 5.
[3] The term "Indians" was first defined in An Act for the Better Protection of the Lands and Property of the Indians in Lower Canada, SC 1850, c. 42, 13 & 14 Vic., s. 5.
[4] For the complete text of all Indian legislation, both pre- and post-Confederation, see the briefs of the various counsel filed with the Supreme Court of Canada in Gail Hinge (ed.), *Consolidation of Indian Legislation Vol. I: United Kingdom and Canada* (unpublished, available from the Department of Indian and Northern Affairs).
[5] This procedure was used only for Indians and not for the Inuit or the Metis.
[6] For a more complete view of Indian history, see E. Palmer Patterson, *The Canadian Indians: A History Since 1500* (Don Mills: Collier-Macmillan Ltd., 1972), or, *The Historical Development of the Indian Act* (Ottawa: Department of Indian and Northern Affairs, 1978).
[7] This is the effect of ss. 7-12 of the Indian Act.
[8] James S. Frideres, *Canada's Indians: Contemporary Conflicts* (Scarborough: Prentice-Hall of Canada Ltd., 1974), p. 3.
[9] Waubageshig, "The Comfortable Crisis" in Waubageshig (ed.) *The Only Good Indian*, (Toronto: New Press, 1970), p. 74.
[10] This occurs through the operation of ss. 109-110, s. 12(1)(a)(iii), and s. 15 of the Indian Act. The Indian wife and minor unmarried children are automatically enfranchised with the husband, unless she and the children are living apart from the husband and she does not apply in her own right.
[11] Frideres, *supra*, note 8, p. 4; and Kathleen Jamieson, *Indian Women and the Law in Canada: Citizens Minus* (Ottawa: Minister of Supply and Services Canada, 1978), p. 64.

[12] *Attorney General of Canada* v. *Lavell,* [1974] SCR, 1349.

[13] *Isaac* v. *Bedard,* [1974] SCR, 1349.

[14] Sandra Lovelace is from Tobique Reserve in New Brunswick, whose complaint of sexual discrimination against the Government of Canada under the Optional Protocol to the International Covenant on Civil and Political Rights was upheld by the United Nations Human Rights Committee in July 1981. For further information, see William Pentney, *Lovelace v. Canada: A Case Comment,* (1982) 5 *Canadian Legal Aid Bulletin,* Nos. 2 and 3, 259.

[15] S. 12(1)(b) and s. 8(1), Indian Act. For greater information on the history and consequences of this process, see K. Jamieson, *supra,* note 11.

[16] K. Jamieson, *supra,* note 11.

[17] For a discussion of the "double-mother rule" and status systems in general, see Douglas Sanders, "The Bill of Rights and Indian Status," (1972), 7 UBCL Review, 81.

[18] Frideres, *supra,* note 8.

[19] For a more complete history of the treaty process, see Peter Cumming and Neil Mickenberg, *Native Rights in Canada,* 2nd ed. (Toronto: Indian-Eskimo Association, 1972) and Patterson, *supra,* note 6.

[20] For more information on this point, see W.T. Stanbury, *The Social & Economic Conditions of Indian Families in British Columbia,* (unpublished, November 1974), p. 1, and *Indian Conditions: A Survey* (Ottawa: Ministry of Indian Affairs and Northern Development, 1980).

[21] This is the indirect effect of ss. 5-13, and the direct result of s. 4(1), of the Indian Act.

[22] [1939] SCR, 104; 2 DLR, 417.

[23] See the Annual Report of DIAND for a description of these programmes.

[24] *The James Bay and Northern Quebec Agreement* (Quebec: Editeur officiel du Quebec, 1976).

[25] For more detailed information, see authorities cited in note 20, *supra,* and Frideres, note 8, *supra,* pp. 13-58.

[26] *Indian Conditions: A Survey,* note 20, *supra,* pp. 3 and 10.

[27] *DIAND Annual Report 1973-1974* (Ottawa: Queen's Printer, 1974), p. 38. However, Frideres, *supra,* note 8, p. 11, refers to 576 bands.

[28] *Indian Conditions: A Survey,* note 20, *supra,* p. 3. However, Frideres, *supra,* note 8, p. 11, refers to 2,281 separate parcels of reserve land.

[29] Frideres, note 8, *supra,* p. 11.

[30] Douglas A. Schmeiser, *Native Offenders and the Law* (Ottawa: Information Canada, 1974), pp. 1-16.

[31] The following categories refer only to registered Indians, unless otherwise specified. The statistics are generally not available for non-registered Indians, the Inuit, and the Metis. The information all stems from *Indian Conditions: A Survey,* note 20, *supra,* unless otherwise noted.

[32] See, for example, Schmeiser, note 30, *supra;* and Native Council of Canada, *Metis and Non-Status Indian Crime and Justice Commission Report* (Ottawa: Native Council of Canada, 1977), for statistics that indicate upwards of 90 percent of the inmate population of certain institutions are of Indian ancestry. For further information on this general area, see two special issues on Native People and Justice in Canada in 5 *Canadian Legal Aid Bulletin,* Nos. 1 and 2.

[33] *Indians and the Law* (Ottawa: The Canadian Corrections Association, 1967), p. 26.

[34] See, for example, Tripartite Task Group on Social Services, *Community Care: Toward Indian Control of Indian Social Services* (unpublished, December 1980, available from the Indian Commission of Ontario).

[35] This is by virtue of s. 88 of the Indian Act, which states:

88. Subject to the terms of any treaty and any other Act of Parliament of Canada, all laws of general application from time to time in force in any province are applicable to

and in respect of Indians in the province, except to the extent that such laws are inconsistent with this Act or any order, rule, regulation or by-law made thereunder, and except to the extent that such laws make provision for any matter for which provision is made by or under this Act.

See, for example, *Natural Parents* v. *Superintendent of Child Welfare et al.,* [1976] 2 SCR 751, 6 NR 491, 60 DLR (3d), 148; *Nelson et al.* v. *Children's Aid Society of Eastern Manitoba* (1975), 56 DLR (3d) 567 (Man. CA); *Re Ranville et al.* v. *Attorney General of Canada* (1979), 26 OR (2d) 271.

[36] H.B. Hawthron (ed.), *A Survey of the Contemporary Indians of Canada: Economic, Political, Educational Needs and Policies,* Vols. I and II (Ottawa: Queen's Printer, 1967), p. 316.

[37] *Community Care,* note 34, *supra*.

[38] Canadian Council on Children and Youth, *Legislation Related to the Needs of Children* (Toronto: Carswell Co. Ltd., 1979), pp. 107-08.

[39] H. Philip Hepworth, *Foster Care and Adoption in Canada* (Ottawa: Canadian Council on Social Development, 1980), p. 111.

[40] Roman N. Komar, *Manual for Clerks and Staff of the Ontario Provincial Courts (Family Division) on the Child Welfare Act, 1978; Part II: Protection and Care of Children* (Toronto: Ministry of Community and Social Services, 1979).

[41] Hepworth, note 39, *supra*, p. 111.

[42] ibid., p. 112.

[43] *Indian Conditions: A Survey,* note 20, *supra*, p. 24.

[44] Hepworth, note 39, *supra*, p. 115.

[45] Patrick Johnston, "Planting the roots for Indian social services," (1981), 5 *Perception* (No. 2) 18, p. 33.

[46] Michael Jackson and Bradford Morse, "Summary of Prince George Native People's Conference" (unpublished, 1974), quoted in Royal Commission on Family and Children's Law of British Columbia, Tenth Report, *Native Families and the Law* (Victoria: Queen's Printer, 1975), p. 16.

[47] Hepworth, note 39, *supra*, pp. 118-19.

[48] For further information, see Johnston, note 45, *supra*, p. 32 and John A. MacDonald, "The Spallumcheen Indian Band By-law and its Potential Impact on Native Indian Child Welfare Policy in British Columbia" (unpublished, 1981).

[49] See, for example, Diamond Jenness, *The Indians of Canada*, 6th ed., (Ottawa: Queen's Printer, 1967).

2. Further Reading

Harold Cardinal, *The Unjust Society* (Edmonton: Hurtig, 1977).

──────────, *The Rebirth of Canada's Indians* (Edmonton: Hurtig, 1977).

Keith J. Crowe, *A History of the Original Peoples of Northern Canada* (Montreal: McGill-Queen's University Press, 1974).

Department of Indian Affairs and Northern Development, *Indian Conditions: A Survey* (Ottawa: Ministry of Indian Affairs and Northern Development, 1980).

James S. Frideres, *Canada's Indians: Contemporary Conflicts* (Scarborough: Prentice-Hall of Canada Ltd., 1974).

René Fumoleau, *As Long as This Land Shall Last: A History of Treaty Eight and Treaty Eleven, 1870-1939* (Toronto: McClelland and Stewart, 1973).

Ian A.L. Getty and Donald B. Smith (eds.), *One Century Later: Western*

Canadian Reserve Indians since Treaty Seven (Vancouver: University of British Columbia Press, 1978).

Charles E. Hendry, *Beyond Traplines* (Toronto: Anglican Church of Canada, 1969).

Kathleen Jamieson, *Indian Women and the Law in Canada: Citizens Minus* (Ottawa: Supply and Services Canada, 1978).

Diamond Jenness, *The Indians of Canada*, 7th ed. (Toronto: University of Toronto Press, 1977).

E. Palmer Patterson, *The Canadian Indians: A History Since 1500* (Don Mills: Collier-Macmillan Ltd., 1972).

Richard Price (ed.), *The Spirit of the Alberta Indian Treaties* (Montreal: Institute for Research on Public Policy, 1979).

Heather Robertson, *Reservations Are for Indians* (Toronto: James Lorimer, 1970).

Robert J. Surtees, *The Original People* (Toronto: Holt, Rinehart and Winston, 1971).

2. Aspects of Aboriginal Rights in International Law

MAUREEN DAVIES

We the Indigenous Peoples of the world, united in this corner of our Mother the Earth in a great assembly of men and wisdom, declare to all nations:

We glory in our proud past:
*   when the earth was our nurturing mother,*
*   when the night sky formed our common roof,*
*   when Sun and Moon were our parents,*
*   when all were brothers and sisters,*
*   when our chiefs and elders were great leaders,*
*   when justice ruled the Law and its execution.*

Then other peoples arrived:
*   thirsting for blood, for gold, for land and all its wealth,*
*   carrying the cross and the sword, one in each hand,*
*   without knowing or waiting to learn the ways of our worlds,*
*   they considered us to be lower than the animals,*
*   they stole our lands from us and took us from our lands,*
*   they made slaves of the Sons of the sun.*

However, they have never been able to eliminate us,
*   nor to erase our memories of what we were,*
*   because we are the culture of the earth and the sky,*
*   we are of ancient descent and we are millions,*
*   and although our whole universe may be ravaged,*
*   our people will live on*
*   for longer than even the kingdom of death.*

Now, we come from the four corners of the earth,
*   we protest before the concert of nations*
*   that, ''we are the Indigenous Peoples, we who*
*   have a consciousness of culture and peoplehood*
*   on the edge of each country's borders and*
*   marginal to each country's citizenship.''*

And rising up after centuries of oppression,
*   evoking the greatness of our ancestors,*
*   in the memory of our Indigenous martyrs,*
*   and in homage to the counsel of our wise elders:*

16

We vow to control again our own destiny and
recover our complete humanity and
pride in being Indigenous People.[1]

1. Introduction

For centuries the problem of regulating relations between the so-called "civilized" and "uncivilized" societies has been the subject of international concern. This simple fact has often been conveniently overlooked by various governments in their desire to confine the "native question" to a municipal context. The fact that, until recently, indigenous peoples have not had an effective voice in the international process has perpetuated the exclusively domestic approach. Recent developments, including internationalization by indigenous peoples through such organizations as the World Council of Indigenous Peoples and through making use of the burgeoning international fora for redress of human rights grievances, indicate that this will not continue to be the case.

In spite of the historical inaccessibility of the international arena, recognition of certain fundamental Aboriginal rights has existed in international law and practice since the dawn of the era of discovery itself. That the law of nations properly concerns itself with this question has never been seriously challenged, as was noted by A. H. Snow in 1921:

> . . . the dealings of individual civilized states with Aborigines under their respective sovereignties are matters of common interest to *All Nations*, and the law and practice of Nations properly concerns itself with the common and international aspects of such rational relations.[2]

The direction and content of this concern have, of course, varied over the centuries but a consistent thread of recognition has always existed.

2. International Legal Principles

Before attempting an overview of aboriginal rights within the context of international law, it is essential to clarify at least some of the basic features of that system.

(a) Sources of International Law

It is generally recognized that the acceptable sources of international law are set out in the Statute of the International Court of Justice.[3] Article 38.1 of the Statute provides that:

> The Court, whose function is to decide in accordance with international law such disputes as are submitted to it, shall apply:
> a. international conventions, whether general or particular, establishing rules expressly recognized by the contesting states;

  b. international custom, as evidence of a general practice accepted as law;

  c. the general principles of law recognized by civilized nations;

  d. subject to the provisions of Article 59, judicial decisions and the teachings of the most highly qualified publicists of the various nations, as subsidiary means for the determination of rules of law.[4]

Unlike municipal law, international law cannot rely on a legislative body to promulgate binding principles of law. It is further hampered by a lack of courts with compulsory jurisdiction extending to all disputes and an inability to enforce its rules. Of course, international law is further clouded by political considerations.

In the absence of a law-making body, it is not always easy to determine the existence and nature of an international rule of law. Article 38 of the Statute of the Court of Justice identifies for the court the sources from which it is to ascertain the law in a given dispute. The court's first task is to determine whether there is a treaty which is applicable between the parties (38.1.a.).[4] Where there is no such express agreement, the court is to look to custom. In making a determination, the court looks primarily to state practice. To constitute custom, the practice must be viewed as obligatory and not merely as a matter of convenience. Thus, to be binding, the practice must be both uniform and obligatory.

The court examines a number of factors when making its assessment of these points. One element to be considered is the duration of the practice, but it is not always necessary to show that the practice has been in existence for a long time. In some cases, a practice which has come into existence very recently will be accepted as "customary" if it has been uniformly accepted.[5] When considering the issue of the uniformity of the practice, it is possible that a customary rule of law may emerge where only a few states actually follow a practice, providing that there is no conflicting practice.[6]

The court will also look at the practice of international institutions, the resolutions of international organizations such as the General Assembly of the United Nations, the decisions of national and international courts and tribunals, and the existence of treaties, patterns of treaties and other international instruments.[7]

State practice appears to include what states actually do, what states say, what states omit to do, and why states behave in a certain way (*opinio juris sive necessitatis*).

If a situation arises where the court is unable to apply either treaty or custom, the Statute provides for a third alternative. Overall, Article 38.1.c. was intended to be a stop-gap provision, and there is little consensus about its meaning. Does it refer to general principles of international law, to national law, or to both? Perhaps, as Akehurst suggests, in view of the nature of the provision, the most appropriate interpretation is the one which gives maximum flexibility.[9]

Article 38.1.d. provides for subsidiary means of determining "rules of law". These include judicial decisions and "the teachings of the most highly qualified publicists of the various nations."

It is important to note that the decisions of international courts and tribunals are *not* binding except "between the parties and in respect of a particular case."[10] The decisions of these bodies are therefore of persuasive value only. Nevertheless, in practice these decisions are generally taken into consideration. In addition, previous decisions may be used as evidence of customary law.

The decisions of municipal courts may also have some persuasive value either with reference to the statement of an international rule of law or as evidence of state practice.

Article 38.1.d. also includes the pronouncements of international writers among its subsidiary sources. The work of various scholars may be used either as a statement which clarifies the legal rule in question or as evidence of state practice. When modern international law was in its infancy, the writers such as Victoria, Grotius and Pufendorf were particularly influential. Their works are regarded as classics of international law, and are still considered to be important.[11]

(b) The Hierarchy of Sources[12]

Where rules of law derived from a treaty or treaties conflict with rules derived from custom, the former takes precedence over the latter. It is possible, however, for a treaty that has been repeatedly ignored to fall into desuetude and thereby to be superseded by a new rule of customary international law. General principles of law are clearly subordinate to both custom and treaty.

(c) International Law and Domestic Law[13]

The Canadian courts can and do apply rules of international law. In some cases they apply rules of customary international law:

> . . . customary rules of international law are adopted automatically into our law amid a few caveats about sovereignty, and then directly applied unless they conflict with statute or some fundamental constitutional principle.[14]

The courts will also apply the provisions of international treaties where these have been implemented by legislation. Where an ambiguity exists, the courts may use customary and treaty law as guides to interpretation.[15]

3. Historical Roots of Aboriginal Rights in International Law

It is often thought that discussion of Aboriginal rights is a recent phenomenon, a product of the post-World War II climate that generally has been favourable to human rights. In fact, the discussion of fundamental rights in relation to Aboriginal peoples is contemporaneous with the "Age of Discovery" itself. One of the fathers of modern international law can, with justification, also be labelled the father of European Aboriginal rights theory. In addition, subsequent publicists of renown referred in their classic treatises to the rights of Indians with a remarkable degree of consistency.

The thread of discussion of Aboriginal rights thus reaches back to the sixteenth century and may be said to begin, from the European perspective, with the Spanish scholastic theologians and continues through Hugo Grotius, and Pufendorf, whose work is described below.

A Spanish theologian, Francisco de Vitoria, may be said to be one of the fathers of both international law and Aboriginal rights theory:

> In the first place, we must recognize that [our] Indian law originated and can still be most clearly grasped, as a branch of international law, and that in the field of international law the basic concepts of Modern doctrine were all hammered out by the Spanish theological jurists of the sixteenth and seventeenth Centuries. . . .[16]

Vitoria's sixteenth-century treatise, *De Indis Et De Jure Belli*, outlined basic concepts of the rights of indigenous peoples that have survived the rigours of time practically intact.[17]

Vitoria was appointed to the *prima* chair of theology at the University of Salamanca in 1526. His lectures reflected a genuine personal and contemporary interest in the native populations being "discovered" by the Spanish adventurers. Reports of abuses, enslavement and massacres of the "newly discovered" peoples found their way back to Spain, with the result that those in the seats of power became embroiled in debates concerning the rights of the indigenous populations and the duties owed to them.[18]

Both the Crown of Spain and the papacy consistently decried such abuses and through a series of cedulas and papal bulls sought to ensure that certain basic rights were recognized.[19] These measures ultimately proved ineffective, primarily because the central authorities were unable to control the outposts in the New World, and were unwilling to give up the riches of empire that such exploitation provided.[20]

Vitoria is recognized as one of the most important thinkers of this period. His work had a tangible influence on the policies and attitudes of the powers of the day, as well as on pupils such as Domingo de Soto and Melchior Cano, who went on to become well-known scholars in their own right.[21]

Vitoria's concept of the Law of Nations recognized that certain rights inhere in men as men and that state equality was applicable to *all* states, not merely to those that were Christian or European:

> Vitoria's teaching marks an important step in the expansion of international law into a world system; for it meant that a law which had

its rise among the few princes of European Christendom was not to be limited to them or to their relations with one another but was universally valid, founded as it was on a natural law applying equally to all men everywhere.[22]

Vitoria lectured extensively on the subject of "The Indians Lately Discovered" and these lectures, carefully recorded by his students, were published posthumously as the *Relictiones*.

In *The First Relictio*, Vitoria dealt with the important issue of ownership.[23] He states that since the indigenous peoples were in "peaceable possession of their goods both publicly and privately," they ought not to be deprived of this possession unless just cause be advanced by the Spaniards for so doing. It was frequently suggested that the lack of Christianity constituted such a cause. Vitoria rejects this proposition totally. He states that it is no less theft to take Indian possessions than it is to take from Christians.

Another argument being advanced was that the Indians were of "unsound mind." Vitoria answers this allegation by comparing the Indians with Spanish peasants; he concludes that even if they were in fact "as inept and stupid as alleged, still dominion could not be denied to them."

In section 2 Vitoria dealt systematically with the titles being advanced by the Spaniards. The first title was based on the premise that the Emperor was "Lord of the World" and therefore of the Indians. Vitoria unequivocally rejects this proposition. In similar fashion, he disposes of the claims made by the papacy to supreme jurisdiction, temporal as well as spiritual, stating that the Pope may not justify exploitation of the Indians on the ground that they refused to accept his "lordship."

Another claim advanced at the time, and one which continued to be advanced by the competing European powers, was title by right of discovery:

> . . . and no other title was originally set up, and it was in virtue of this title alone that Columbus the Genoan first set sail. And this seems to be an adequate title because those regions which are deserted become, by the law of nations and the natural law, the property of the first occupant. Therefore, as the Spaniards were the first to discover and occupy the provinces in question, they are in lawful possession thereof, just as if they had discovered some lonely and hitherto uninhabited region.

Vitoria rejected this proposition outright:

> Not much, however, need be said about this third title of ours, because, as proved above, the barbarians were true owners, both from the public and from the private standpoint. Now the rule of the law of nations is that what belongs to nobody is granted to the first occupant. . . . And so, as the object in question was not without an owner, it does not fall under the title which we are discussing. Although, then, this title, when conjoined with another, can produce some effect here (as will be said

below), yet in and by itself it gives no support to a seizure of the aborigines any more than if it had been they who had discovered us.
. . .

Vitoria concludes section 2 with a strong statement on the subject of the Spaniards' attempts to justify exploitation on the ground that the indigenous population had rejected Christianity. He states that for a just war, there must be a just cause. Since the Indians were "innocent," no such cause existed:

> . . . although the Christian faith may have been announced to the Indians with adequate demonstration and they have refused to receive it, yet this is not a reason which justifies making war on them and depriving them of their property.

In section 3 Vitoria outlines the nature of legitimate contacts with the Indian nations. He deals first with the concept of *jus gentium* under which "all nations [reckoned that it was] inhumane to treat visitors and foreigners badly."

If after legitimate attempts at demonstrating that they are "peaceful guests," the Indians used force against the Spaniards, the latter were justified in defending themselves. Again, however, Vitoria qualified this statement by suggesting that the Indians were naturally timid and understandably fearful of the "men in strange garb and armed." If, however, the Spaniards were forced to protect themselves, they were exhorted to do so "as far as possible with the least damage to the natives."

Vitoria concludes on a pragmatic note, stating that commerce between the Spaniards and the natives was justifiable and that

> . . . there are already so many native converts that it would be neither expedient nor lawful for our sovereign to wash his hands entirely of the administration of the lands in question.

Although Vitoria's influence was considerable during his lifetime, his impact as an international scholar derives perhaps most directly from his influence on later scholars. The principles he expounded, mirrored to a greater or lesser degree in the official cedulas and papal bulls, found their way into the texts of subsequent writers on international law.

Writing a full century after the Spaniard, the great Dutch scholar Hugo Grotius drew extensively on his works and on numerous occasions referred to Vitoria by name. A few examples from his early classic, *De Jure Praedae Commentarius*,[24] will serve to demonstrate Vitoria's profound influence on Grotius and his acceptance of Vitoria's principles relating to Aboriginal Peoples.

In the most famous chapter, "On the justness of private war," Grotius refers to Vitoria's belief that the Spaniards were entitled by the "law of nations" to travel and reside among the American Indians:

. . . or if they should be prevented from sharing in those things which are common property under the law of nations or by custom — if, in short, they should be debarred from the practice of commerce — these causes might serve them as just grounds for war against the Indians and indeed as grounds more plausible than others.

However Grotius goes on to say that ownership of property and possessions of the Indians cannot be taken without just cause and that infidelity does not constitute such cause:

> Vitoria correctly maintains that the Spaniards acquired no greater right over the American Indians in consequence of that defect of faith, than the Indians would have possessed over the Spaniards if any of the former had been the first foreigners to come to Spain.

He also says, again in specific agreement with Vitoria, that

> The Hispanic peoples did not carry with them to still more distant regions, any right to take possession of the lands to which they sailed.
> . . .

Furthermore, Grotius relies upon the pronouncements by the Spanish Senate and by the theologians, who held that the American Indians should be converted to the faith not through war but solely through the preaching of the Word, and that ''the liberty taken from them on the pretext of conversion should be restored to them.'' He also reiterates Vitoria's conclusion that an Emperor ''could not convert the provinces of the empire to his own uses'' and that ''all the pretexts advanced in connection with the Indian questions are seized upon unjustly.''

Grotius had accepted the principles enunciated a century earlier regarding Spain's dealings in the Americas and had applied them specifically to matters of Dutch interest.

A German contemporary of Grotius, Samuel Pufendorf, who achieved some renown for his work *De Jure Naturae et Gentium,*[25] criticised Vitoria and Grotius for failing to recognize that indigenous nations might not be obligated to accept the visiting Spaniards. According to Pufendorf, no nation is required to admit visiting foreign peoples. As ''property holders,'' the Indians would be within their rights to consider the purpose and length of the visit as well as the number of visitors involved. In addition, Pufendorf suggests that, even where the Indian peoples had granted certain privileges of travel and commerce, they had a concomitant right to withdraw such privileges. He concludes that it is untenable to suggest that Indian nations be forced to receive ''a great multitude, armed, and with hostile intent . . . especially since it [was] hardly possible that the native inhabitants [ran] no danger from such a host.''

It is clear, from the foregoing, that the most influential and respected founding fathers of modern international law regarded the question of aboriginal rights as important and that strong arguments were adduced to recognize certain basic rights. This fact may prove significant if judicially applied by the court in light of Section 38.1.d. of the Statute of the Court of Justice as outlined above.[26]

The work of these scholars is important for other reasons too. If the issues raised within the context of Aboriginal rights are to be dealt with satisfactorily, it is important to understand the origin, nature and impact of concerns in this field of law. Modern scholars are looking to history to substantiate and exemplify concepts of discovery and settlement.[27] The work of Vitoria and subsequent writers in articulating contemporary concerns and legal principles provides a frame of reference that is essential to an understanding of subsequent developments.

4. The Question of Status in International Law

Although it has long been considered a legitimate concern of international law, the exact nature of the legal status of Aboriginal Peoples in their dealings with European powers and under international law has yet to be resolved. The issues tend to be clouded by conflicting notions of "sovereignty" and "dependency." On the one hand, it is clear that relations between the so-called civilizing powers and the Aboriginal populations were very often regulated by the use of treaties. On the other hand, the doctrine of guardianship became firmly entrenched in international law to the extent that some scholars suggest that it has attained the status of customary international law.[28]

(a) Sovereignty

The concept of sovereignty is a far from static one. Its different meanings and implications have prompted some international scholars to say that the term has outlived its usefulness. Nevertheless, it is a term invoked to such a great extent that it cannot be ignored. Perhaps the most common application is derived from linking notions of "independence" and "statehood". The state is one of the fundamental units in international law. A sovereign state is an independent state. For the purpose of international considerations, this independence is *de jure* not *de facto*. In other words, a sovereign state may exercise its power to create for itself a voluntary state of dependence through, for example, the exercise of its treaty-making powers.[29] This appears to be a possible interpretation of the relationship that existed between certain aboriginal nations and European powers:

> Since a treaty is a consensual alteration of the rights and status that exist in all states under international law, failure to delegate an incident of sovereignty leaves it undisturbed.

At one extreme a treaty might acknowledge the constitutional supremacy of Parliament in so many words, or the inhabitants might incorporate themselves completely with Britain. The result would be a country abroad peopled by free British subjects, and generally controlled by the same rules as a chartered settlement, the treaty being the charter. The 1707 Act of Union with Scotland is illustrative. This compact declares "fundamental and essential conditions" of association, and has been considered an entrenched constitutional instrument by the courts. In all other respects the constitutional status of Scots and of other Britons has merged. As "conquests," by comparison, Wales and Ireland traditionally have been considered subject to parliamentary control without the benefit of entrenched limitations.

Alternatively, a treaty might confer upon the Crown alone the powers of a military protector, diplomatic representative, or civil judge, and no more. Without words of cession, or dissolution of the protected state's own government, such a treaty simply establishes a new extraterritorial branch of prerogative which the Sovereign presumably has undertaken for his own honour and advantage, and for the advantage and safety of his subjects. The effect of limited association would be to unite two states under one Crown but not under one law. It would be neither just nor constitutional for treaties establishing free, amicable associations to be construed later as abject surrenders, for to do so implies that the Crown wilfully deceived its allies. Nothing could be less compatible with the respect owing the Crown in its sovereign actions.

The relationship of "protection" was well known to Georgian lawyers as an ancient principle of the law of nations. The eighteenth-century jurist Emmerich Vattel explained in his *Droit des Gens*:

> We ought, therefore, to account as sovereign states those which unite themselves to another more powerful, by an unequal alliance, in which, as Aristotle says, to the more powerful, is given more honour, and to the weaker, more assistance. . . .
>
> Consequently a weak state, which in order to provide for its safety, places itself under the protection of a more powerful one, and engages, in return, to perform several offices equivalent to that protection, without however divesting itself of the right of government and sovereignty — that state, I say, does not, on this account, cease to rank among the sovereigns who acknowledge no other law than that of nations.

In 1832, the United States Supreme Court relied on Vattel in concluding that the Indian nations of North America had been protectorates of the British Crown:

> . . . a weak power does not surrender its independence — its right to self-government, by associating with a stronger and taking its protection. A weak state, in order to provide for its safety, may

place itself under the protection of one more powerful without stripping itself of the right of government and ceasing to be a State.[30]

The classical criteria for statehood are contained in Article 1 of the Montevideo Convention of 1933.[31] These are (a) a permanent population; (b) a defined territory; (c) a government; and (d) the capacity to enter into relations with other states.

Indigenous nations have consistently maintained that they constitute sovereign independent states within these criteria. One of the most interesting cases in this field is *The Cherokee Nations* vs. *The State of Georgia* (30 US (5 Pet.)1), a decision of the American Supreme Court under Chief Justice Marshall, in 1831. The key question addressed by the court was whether the Cherokee nation constituted a foreign state. The court maintained that the situation of Indians in relation to the United States was probably unique:

> The condition of the Indians in relation to the United States is perhaps unlike that of any other two people in existence. In general, nations not owing a common allegiance are foreign to each other. The term *foreign nation* is, with strict propriety, applicable by either to the other. But the relation of the Indians to the United States is marked by peculiar and cardinal distinctions which exist nowhere else. (p. 17)

According to Marshall CJ, the Indians acknowledged within their treaties that they were under the protection of the United States. Thus, although "the Indians are acknowledged to have an unquestionable, and heretofore, unquestioned right to the lands they occupy", since they resided within the boundaries of the United States, they did not constitute foreign nations. Marshall characterised them as ". . . domestic dependent nations." He went on to say that the United States might assert a title "independent" of the will of the Cherokee people, but he failed to explain or justify this tentative assertion. It is also quite clear that the court recognized that the Cherokee people constituted a "state".

Perhaps most telling is the following passage:

> *The Cherokees are a state*. They have been uniformly treated as a state since the settlement of our country. The numerous treaties made with them by the United States recognize them as a people capable of maintaining the relations of peace and war; of being responsible in their political character for any violation of their engagements, or for any aggression committed on the citizens of the United States by any individual of their community. Laws have been enacted in the spirit of these treaties. The acts of our government plainly *recognize the Cherokee nation as a state*; and the courts are bound by those acts.[32] (p. 17) (emphasis added)

The Marshall court addressed this issue once again in *Worcester* v. *Georgia*

(1832) 31 US (6 Pet.) 515. In this case, again involving the Cherokee nation, Marshall refers to "the settled doctrine of the law of nations . . . that a weaker power does not surrender its independence, its right to self-government, by associating with a stronger, and taking its protection" (pp. 560-61).

The indigenous nations of many countries, including Canada and the United States, have continued to assert their sovereign status, including by implication, the right to cede various aspects of that sovereignty to another state.

The international Non-Governmental Organizations Conference on Discrimination Against Indigenous Populations in the Americas (Geneva, 1977) produced a Declaration of Principles For the Defense of the Indigenous Nations and Peoples of the Western Hemisphere.[33] The Declaration sets out in Article 1 the criteria for recognition of indigenous nations as contained in the Montevideo Convention. A recent article by Clinebell and Thompson attempts to apply these criteria to the indigenous peoples of the United States:[34]

> Native Americans have stressed for many years that they are sovereign peoples who were originally and now should be recognized as independent, self-governing nations. That plea today falls on deaf ears in the United States. Indians are therefore turning to the international community and asking the nations of the world to recognize the right of Native Americans to be judged by the same standards as other countries.

Clinebell and Thompson suggest that there is no serious dispute as to the existence of permanent populations within the scope of Article 1(a) of the Convention:

> Indians constitute a separate racial group, as well as distinct political groups under their own laws and federal law. Before the European invasion they were organized in bands and villages, and to some extent tribes. The size of the native population has of course varied, but has always been defined by birth into one of those bands or groups. Indian population is specifically counted today both by tribe and as a total. The United States counted not quite 800,000 Native Americans in its 1970 census. One writer has stated that in order to fulfill the requirement of a permanent population a people must be sufficient in number to maintain and perpetuate itself. If Native Americans can survive and maintain their identity in the face of the destructive policies of the United States government, they certainly have permanent and durable populations.

When addressing Article 1(b) of the Convention — the question of a defined territory — Clinebell and Thompson point out that there are 267 reservations in the United States containing over 51 million acres. Certain of the Native American Nations are, in fact, larger than some states recognized as independent by the international community. The authors cite in this regard the Navajo nation, which they point out is larger than forty self-governing foreign nations.

With regard to criterion (c), government, the authors conclude that:

The United States recognizes and encourages tribal government, albeit not in the way most conducive to tribal sovereignty. The Supreme Court has repeatedly and consistently recognized the authority of Indian tribes on reservations.

They also state that the fact that some governmental functions on Indian reservations are performed by the government is a manifestation of the state's sovereign right to delegate certain of its powers.

The final criterion — capacity to carry on foreign relations — needs little commentary in light of the long history of native peoples' dealings with European and other foreign states:

For centuries Native Americans have entered into treaties with the United States and other countries. Native Americans have the skills and experience to act in the international community. The desire and need to protect their rights, resources and authority has led them to develop expertise in business, law, government and diplomacy with which they can quite adequately protect their interests at the international level.

Similar arguments are being advanced by indigenous peoples in Canada:

By our own efforts, over the last decade, we have successfully reasserted our sovereignty as Indian Nations in our own homelands and have begun to re-establish our international personality in the courts and political assemblies of the world. . . .[35]

In the last ten years we have begun to take back control of Indian education, we have re-organized our political institutions and begun the drive to recover our land and natural resources and to generate the economic strength necessary for survival and development. There is still much work to be done here in Canada. But the recognition and exercise of our rights is not a matter for Canada alone. As Indian Nations who have never been conquered and who have never surrendered sovereignty, we are entitled to the recognition and protection of the world community and of the laws and conventions which govern its relationships.[36]

Indigenous nations in both the United States and Canada are striving to make use of various international instruments in an effort to make governments recognize various aspects of their sovereign status.[37]

(b) Treaties

Clearly, one of the compelling indications that Aboriginal nations were indeed sovereign has been the extensive use of treaties to order relations with the European powers.

The word "treaty" is an international legal term meaning "an international agreement concluded between States in written form and governed by international law, whether embodied in a single instrument or in two or more related instruments and whatever its particular designation."[38] The question as to whether agreements made between Aboriginal Peoples and European or "civilizing" powers constitute "treaties" in this sense is one which has been the subject of a great deal of litigation.

In 1926, the American-British Claims Commission addressed this issue, among others, in the *Cayuga Indians Case* ((1926) 6 RIAA 173). The tribunal held that treaties between the Cayugas and the State of New York were in the nature of contracts:

> We must ask whether the United States would be liable directly and immediately on the basis of the Treaty of 1795. . . . Neither in form nor in substance was the Treaty of 1795 a Federal treaty; it was a contract of New York with respect to a matter as to which New York was fully competent to contract. In form it is exclusively a New York contract. The negotiators derived their authority from the State Legislature and purported to represent the State only. The United States does not appear anywhere in the negotiations nor in the treaty. . . . Nor was the subject-matter one of Federal cognisance. . . .
>
> We must hold that the Treaty of 1795 was a contract of the State of New York . . . the United States would not be liable merely on the basis of a failure of New York to perform a covenant to pay money.

Two years later, the Permanent Court of Arbitration dealt with the question in similar fashion in the *Island of Palmas Case* ((1928) 2 RIAA 829).

This approach has been cited most recently in the judgement of Kerr L.J. in *the Queen* v. *The Secretary of State for Foreign and Commonwealth Affairs:* ((1982), 2 WLR 641):

> Although the relevant agreements with the Indian peoples are known as "treaties" they are not treaties in the sense of public international law. They were not treaties between sovereign states. . . .

Yet, in spite of bald assertions of this nature, a certain resistance to such an interpretation has always existed.

In his text, *Great Britain and the Law of Nations* (1935), H.A. Smith took a less restrictive approach:

> From mediaeval times to the present day there has been constant controversy as to how far the law of nations is applicable to the relations between European powers and communities outside the range of European civilization. In the earlier stages of this discussion the

question took the form of asking whether international law was confined to Christian states or whether it extended also to infidels and pagans. In later times the question at issue has rather been that of the degree of civilization and stability necessary for the due functioning of regular international relations. The modern practice of Great Britain makes it clear that in her view this is the real test. The facts of particular cases vary greatly, and the cases are too numerous even to be summarised within the limits of the present chapter. A large number of treaties have been made by Great Britain with native rulers in various parts of the world, and in many cases it is clear that these treaties are regarded as sources of international obligations in the strict sense. Many of these treaties are acts of cession, which extinguish the independence of the native community and in such cases the subsequent relations between Great Britain and the native inhabitants fall within the scope of municipal law.[39]

An interesting contrast with this view is that of the American author A.H. Snow, writing in 1921:

The practice of regulating by treaty the relations between a civilized State exercising sovereignty over a region and the aboriginal tribes inhabiting the region, though permissible when these relations can not be regulated by the legislative, executive, and judicial action of the State, is recognized as *undesirable*.

In the report of the British Parliamentary Committee of 1837 on Aboriginal Tribes, it was said:

As a general rule . . . it is inexpedient that treaties should be frequently entered into between the local governments and the tribes in their vicinity. Compacts between parties negotiating on terms of such entire disparity are rather the preparatives and the apology for disputes than securities for peace; as often as the resentment or cupidity of the more powerful body may be excited, a ready pretext for complaint will be found in the ambiguity of the language in which their agreements must be drawn up, and in the superior sagacity which the European will exercise in framing, interpreting, and in evading them.[40]

The Marshall Court lends further support to the international connotation of treaties in its landmark decision in *Worcester* v. *Georgia* (1832) discussed above:

The very term ''nation,'' so generally applied to them, means ''a people distinct from others.'' The constitution, by declaring treaties already made, as well as those to be made to be the supreme law of the land, has adopted and sanctioned the previous treaties with the Indian nations, and, consequently, admits their rank among those powers who are capable of making treaties. The words "treaty" and "nation" are words of our own language, selected in our diplomatic and legislative proceedings, by ourselves, having such a definite and well understood meaning. We have applied them to Indians, as we have applied them to the other nations of the earth. They are applied to all in the same sense. (No. 559)

The position outlined by the Marshall Court in the *Worcester* Case finds support in the judgment of the Judicial Committee of the Privy Council in the case of in *Re Southern Rhodesia* ([1919] AC 211.) Here the court recognized the sovereignty of King Lobengula, Chief of Matabeleland, in a dispute relating to a grant made by the chief to the British South Africa Company:

. . . about 1888 Her Majesty Queen Victoria recognized Lobengula as Sovereign of both peoples. The British Government stated to the Portuguese Government that he was "an independent King," "undisputed ruler over Matabeleland and Mashonaland," who had not parted with his sovereignty though his territory was under British influence, and in 1889 the Colonial Secretary wrote Lobengula himself saying that he, Lobengula, "is king of the country," and no one can exercise jurisdiction in it without his permission. "Lobengula's sovereignty over what is now Southern Rhodesia is therefore the starting point of the history of the land question there." (p. 214)

Essentially there appears to be no uniform view as to whether agreements with indigenous peoples are treaties in the classical international legal sense. Perhaps the view which most closely approximates the historical, legal and sociological exigencies is one that allows flexibility, recognizing that the legal characterization of the arrangement might vary with circumstances, and keeping in mind that:

. . . a Country embarrasses itself by trying to define away tribes' treaty rights semantically. As Sir William Blackstone remarked, "there are some oppressions so great that men will not be reasoned out of them." To what avail is it for . . . jurists to argue that Indian treaties really are not treaties; that treaties of peace and unity are really abject surrenders of all rights; or that reservations of absolute territoriality really are merely acknowledgments of a tenancy at will? No injustice ever was righted by calling it just. We recall the words of Levi General, then Deskaheh (Speaker) of the Six Nations, in 1925:

If this must go on to the bitter end, we would rather that you come with your guns and poison gases and get rid of us that way. Do it openly and aboveboard. Do away with the pretence that you have the right to subjugate us to your will.[41]

Regardless of the approach taken, however, it is clear that treaties create binding legal obligations between the parties and that certain rules of construction favourable to the indigenous party apply in the interpretation of such treaties.[42]

(c) The Concept of Guardianship

The concept of sovereignty normally implicit in the treaty process was perhaps undermined in certain cases by the subsequent application by "civilizing" powers of notions of guardianship to indigenous peoples.

Although this idea professed concern for the protection and welfare of such peoples, it was based squarely on the belief that European society was superior, culturally, technologically and intellectually. As a result, indigenous peoples were to be treated as "children" or "wards" of the civilized powers which purported to exert dominion over them. Chief Justice Marshall's statements in *Cherokee Nation* v. *Georgia* (30 US (5 Pet.)1.) are typical of this approach.

> [The Cherokees] occupy a territory to which we assert a title independent of their will, which must take effect in point of possession when their right of possession ceases — meanwhile they are in a state of pupilage. Their relations to the United States resemble that of a ward to his guardian. They look to our government for protection; rely upon its kindness and its power; appeal to it for relief to their wants; and address the President as their great father. (no. 17)

The concept dates from the earliest contact with indigenous peoples. Even Vitoria appears to formulate his theories on the premise that the "newly discovered Indians" are less mature and intelligent than their Spanish "discoverers" and require protection from the abuses of the "superior" European power. During this period, Las Casas, the Dominican friar who was largely responsible for the initial revelation of abuses against indigenous peoples, was made "General *Protector* of All Indians". It became apparent that those who manifested an interest in the welfare of indigenous peoples felt that European society had a civilizing mission to carry out, in an attempt to bring the "benefits" of the "superior" culture and religion to peoples who were perceived to be in varying stages of "savagery".

Illustrative of the attitude underlying the concept is the following excerpt from a letter sent by Lord John Russell to Sir George Gipps, governor of New South Wales in 1840:

> . . . we indeed, who come into contact with these various races, have one and the same duty to perform toward them all, but the manner in which this duty is to be performed must vary with the varying materials upon which we are to work. . . .
>
> There appears to be great difficulty in making reserves of land for the natives which shall be really beneficial to them. Two sources of

mischief mar the most benevolent designs of this nature; the one arising from the inaptitude of the natives to change their desultory habits and learn those of settled industry; the other from the constant inroad of Europeans to rob, corrupt and destroy them. Between the native, who is weakened by intoxicating liquors, and the Europeans, who have all the strength of Superior Civilization and is free from its restraint the unequal context is generally of no long duration; the natives decline, diminish and finally disappear. . . .

The best chance of preserving the unfortunate race . . . lies in the means employed for training their children. The education given to such children should consist in a very small part of reading and writing. Oral instruction in the fundamental truths of the Christian religion will be given by the missionaries themselves. The children should be taught early; the boys to dig and plough, and the trades of shoemakers, tailors, carpenters and masons; the girls to sew and cook and wash linen and keep clean the rooms and furniture. . . .[43]

The concept became accepted as official colonial policy and subsequently found its way into international law theory as the doctrine of guardianship.[44]

While the proposed aim of the doctrine was one of "protection," its effect was to deny the intrinsic worth and validity of indigenous societies and culture, undercutting the very elements that, from the point of view of European legal institutions, might have afforded some degree of actual protection. At the same time, the doctrine largely failed to create any legally enforceable rights.[45]

The doctrine of guardianship is based squarely on the premise that European civilization is superior and that there exists a recognizable — indeed, measurable — distinction between "civilized" and "uncivilized" peoples. The dearth of evidence to support this assumption is an indication of the extent to which it was considered to be self-evident.

It is clear that ultimately the doctrine worked to the disadvantage of indigenous populations, which, given the underlying impetus for its development, is not surprising. Whatever the exact nature of the status of Aboriginal nations *vis-à-vis* European powers, there seems little doubt that tribal groups have for the most part been the objects rather than the subjects of international law. Under classic international law, only states were recognized as having legal personality within the international area. Indigenous peoples were denied this status.

The landmark decision in this regard is the *Cayuga* case of 1926:

. . . a tribe is not a legal unit of international law. The American Indians have never been so regarded. . . . from the time of the discovery of America the Indian tribes have been treated as under the exclusive protection of the power which by discovery or conquest or cession held the land which they occupied. . . . So far as an Indian tribe exists as a legal unit, it is by virtue of the domestic law of the sovereign nation within whose territory the tribe occupies the land, and so far only as that law recognizes it. (pp. 65-66)[46]

Aboriginal Peoples are at present engaged in an effort to change this status. For example, the Declaration of Principles For the Defense of the Indigenous Nations and Peoples of the Western Hemisphere states:

Article 2: Subjects of International Law

Indigenous groups not meeting the requirements of nationhood are hereby declared to be subjects of international law and are entitled to the protection of this Declaration, provided they are identifiable groups having bonds of language, heritage, tradition, or other common identity.[47]

Subsequent developments in this field have afforded varying degrees of international personality to individuals, companies and international organizations.[48] Coupled with an evolving recognition of the special position of Aboriginal Peoples within the international context, it is conceivable that an accommodation on this point will be reached.[49]

5. The Question of Territorial Rights[50]

Central to any consideration of sovereignty and Aboriginal rights is the issue of territoriality. Since the dawn of the era of discovery, "European" civilization has engaged in the relentless practice of divesting indigenous peoples of their land. It is a practice that continues unabated. Deprived of a land base, Aboriginal nations have little hope of survival. Examples of the resulting disintegration and its intolerable human consequences are everywhere apparent. Many of the concepts that underly discussions of "land title" within the municipal context derive from international law. For the most part, these international legal concepts have been inappropriately applied by municipal courts in an effort to justify early claims to territorial sovereignty.

Among the more important doctrines advanced to legitimatize "European" acquisition of native lands are: (a) Discovery, (b) Occupation, (c) Conquest, and (d) Cession.

(a) Discovery

The doctrine of discovery, advanced with vigour by the western European powers whenever it is expedient, was unequivocally rejected by Vitoria in his treatise *De Indis*.[51] To invoke the doctrine, Vitoria points out, it is necessary to demonstrate that the territory is uninhabited: *terra nullius*. Since clearly the lands in question *were* already occupied, the doctrine could not be applied.

Vitoria's views on the matter represent the position in international law at that time, that "discovery" of an inhabited area was not a claim which could be seriously maintained. If anyone had "discovered" the lands in question, it would have been the peoples already there!

In spite of subsequent attempts to put forward such claims, it is very doubtful whether the doctrine was even accepted by the competing states themselves. Discovery, by itself, was for the most part not considered sufficient to establish a valid claim.[52]

In what is considered to be one of the landmark municipal cases in this field, *Johnson* v. *McIntosh* (1823), 21 US (8 Wheat.) 543), the Supreme Court of the United States ruled that the principle of discovery was acknowledged by all Europeans because it was in the interest of all to acknowledge it, and "gave the nation making the discovery the sole right of acquiring the soil and establishing settlements on it." It was, the court held, a rule which regulated the competing interests of the European powers *inter se*, and was subject to the right of original inhabitants to retain possession of their land. The Court went on to say however that indigenous peoples' power to dispose of the soil at their own will, to whomsoever they pleased, was denied *"by the original fundamental principle that discovery gave exclusive title to those who make it."* (emphasis added) This statement certainly does not reflect the international reality either theoretically or in terms of the state practice of the time.[53]

The doctrine of discovery was considered and rejected by the Permanent Court of Arbitration in the *Island of Palmas Case* (1928).

> . . . discovery alone, without any subsequent act, cannot at the present time suffice to prove sovereignty over the Island of Palmas or Miangas.
> . . .
> If on the other hand the view is taken that discovery does not constitute a definite title of sovereignty, but only an "inchoate" title, such a title exists, it is true, without external manifestation. However, according to the view that has prevailed at any rate since the nineteenth century, an inchoate title of discovery must be completed within a reasonable period by the effective occupation of the region claimed to be discovered. (p. 425)

It is apparent that "discovery" alone was not a tenable claim in international law with reference either to inhabited or to uninhabited lands.[54]

(b) Occupation

If discovery, by itself, was never considered a legitimate title in international law, did "discovery plus" confer such a right?

The decision in the *Island of Palmas* Case indicates that "an inchoate title of discovery must be completed, within a reasonable period, by the effective occupation of the region claimed to be discovered."

The elements of "effective occupation" include "uninterrupted and permanent possession."[55]

The doctrine of occupation also requires that the lands so occupied be *terra nullius* — uninhabited. The definition of *terra nullius*, however, has created certain practical difficulties.

Claims were often advanced that lands occupied by certain tribal populations properly fell within the scope of the term. Judgments of this kind were based on the supposed inferiority of such societies and their inability or unwillingness to exploit the land in a "civilized" way. Nomadic peoples who inhabited vast tracts of land were particularly vulnerable. The present position, however, clearly favours a restrictive view of this interpretation.

The International Court of Justice in the *Western Sahara Case* (1975) held that "the presence of nomadic tribes with a degree of political and social organization precluded the territory from being regarded as *terra nullius*."

> Whatever differences of opinion there may have been among jurists, the State practice of the relevant period indicates that territories *inhabited by tribes or peoples having a social and political organization were not regarded as terra nullius*. It shows that in the case of such territories the acquisition of sovereignty was not generally considered as effected unilaterally through 'occupation' of *terra nullius* by original title but through agreements concluded with local rulers. On occasion, it is true, the word "occupation" was used in a non-technical sense denoting simply acquisition of sovereignty; but that did not signify that the acquisition of sovereignty through such agreements with authorities of the country was regarded as an "occupation" of a "*terra nullius*" in the proper sense of these terms. On the contrary, such agreements with local rulers, whether or not considered as an actual "cession" of the territory, were regarded as derivative roots of title, and not original titles obtained by occupation of *terra nullius* (p. 31) (emphasis added)

The separate opinion of Judge Ammoun in this regard is worth noting:

> In short, the concept of *terra nullius*, employed at all periods, to the brink of the twentieth century, to justify conquest and colonization, stands condemned. It is well known that in the sixteenth century, Francisco de Vitoria protested against the application to the American Indians in order to deprive them of their lands, of the concept of *res nullius*.
>
> This approach by the eminent Spanish Jurist and Canonist, which was adopted by Vattel in the nineteenth century, was hardly echoed at all at the Berlin Conference of 1885. It is however the concept which should be adopted today. (p. 78)

Claims advanced on the basis of acquisition through occupation clearly cannot apply to areas already inhabited by indigenous peoples. It appears that the only peoples who might have a sound claim on the basis of this doctrine are, again, Aboriginal Peoples themselves.

(c) Conquest

The international legal concept of "conquest" was central to the Marshall thesis in *Johnson* v. *McIntosh*. In his decision, Marshall in effect equates discovery and conquest:

> We will not enter into the controversy whether agriculturists, merchants, and manufacturers have a right, on abstract principles, to expel hunters from the territory they possess, or to contract their limits. Conquest gives a title which the courts of the conqueror cannot deny, whatever the private and speculative opinions of individuals may be, respecting the original justice of the claim which has been successfully asserted. (p. 588)

Marshall does not explain the conquest theory until later when he equates it with discovery:

> However extravagant the pretension of converting the discovery of an inhabited Country into Conquest may appear if the principle has been asserted in the first instance, and afterwards sustained; if a country has been acquired and held under it; if the property of the great mass of the community originates in it, it becomes the law of the land, and cannot be questioned. (p. 591)

Clearly, as Berman points out, "the equation of discovery to conquest amounts to a nimble transmutation of definition that itself stands as a conquest by judicial *fiat*." From an international perspective, the doctrine of conquest is quite distinct from that of discovery:

> Title to lands in North America was rooted in the European discovery. This "*doctrine of discovery*" provided an organizing principle through which the European nations articulated claims against each other to spheres of control within the western hemisphere.
>
> This principle was, that discovery gave title to the government by whose subjects, or by whose authority, it was made, against all other European governments, which title might be consummated by possession.
>
> The exclusion of all other Europeans necessarily gave to the nation making the discovery the sole right of acquiring the soil from the natives, and establishing settlements upon it.
>
> The nature of the titles thus established included the right of European nations to grant the soil.
>
> While the different nations of Europe respected the rights of the natives, as occupants, they asserted the ultimate dominion to be in themselves; and claimed and exercised, as a consequence of this ultimate dominion, a power to grant the soil, while yet in possession of the natives. These grants have been understood by all to convey a

title to the grantees, subject only to the Indian right of occupancy.

At this stage of the Court's reasoning, the doctrine of discovery amounted to no more than a distributional principle that created a potential interest in the lands. This interest has been termed a "perfectable entitlement" that could be made complete only by extinguishing the Indian title through a purchase or conquest. As a regulating principle for the conduct of European nations, the doctrine recognized the Indian title and provided a mechanism by which that title might be acquired by the Europeans.

This principle was adequate to establish a framework for the orderly derivation of land titles in the United States. The right of exclusion against European nations could be readily traced through a chain of sovereign succession beginning with the British Crown and culminating with the formation of the United States. The exclusive right to extinguish the Indian title, combined with the now judicially recognized sovereign power to establish land titles coterminous with the Indian title, set forth sufficient grounds to determine the validity of land holdings within the United States.

Marshall was not content to rest the Court's decision solely on these grounds. He proceeded to explore the nature of the relationship that discovery created between the Indian nations and the United States. It is here that "principles of abstract justice" are left behind. As a judicial principle derived from the conduct of nations, discovery concerned only the European nations. The occurrence of discovery, however, created a continuing relationship with the indigenous peoples of the continent, the legal consequences of which remained to be mapped.

Discovery, then, must be viewed in its dual aspects: first as a rule of exclusivity to determine which European nation was entitled to acquire the Indian title through a purchase or conquest, and second as an event that established a relationship between the European nations and the Indian nations. Surprisingly, it is under the first aspect of discovery that the only concrete expression of a limitation on Indian sovereignty occurs. Under the rule of exclusivity, "their power to dispose of the soil at their own will, to whomsoever they pleased, was denied by the original fundamental principle, that discovery gave exclusive title to those who made it." Thus the Indian sovereignty, which was complete before the European discovery, was qualified in this case only by the limitation on the scope of alienability.

It is strange that Marshall should analyze the Indian-European relationship under the rights adhering to discovery. An extensive literature on the law of nations existed concerning the rights of non-European peoples. It cannot be assumed that Marshall was ignorant of the law of nations as it had been conceived up to his time. The writings of such classical publicists as Vattel, Grotius, Pufendorf, and others were introduced in the pleadings of *Fletcher* v. *Peck* and *Johnson* v. *McIntosh* to argue the validity of Indian sovereignty. Moreover, these writings were well known to legal scholars of his day. It is clear that this omission was by deliberate choice and reflected his intention to base his analysis on other grounds.

At the outset, Marshall announced his intention to ratify a specific historical process that resulted in the transfer of vast areas of land to the jurisdiction of the United States. He ruled that ''those relations which were to exist between the discoverer and the natives were to be regulated by themselves.'' The actual historical record of the relationship as memorialized in the treaty process provided ample opportunity to derive legal principles. Moreover, the Chief Justice revealed more than a passing familiarity with the historical antecedents of the controversies before the Court in the texts of his decisions. He chose, however, also to omit the treaty process from his analysis. Instead he presented what might be termed a political standard based on the creation of a myth of conquest that was rooted in the judicial power to define, rather than in historical reality. It is on this point that the opinion becomes confusing and occasionally incoherent.

In the middle of the opinion Marshall restated the doctrine of discovery, but with an important addition. He stated that ''discovery gave an exclusive right to extinguish the Indian title of occupancy, either by purchase or conquest; and gave also a right to such a degree of sovereignty, as the circumstances of the people would allow them to exercise.'' While this assertion of sovereignty is given without explanation and is otherwise left undefined, it hints at a political standard that would make Indian lands vulnerable to forced extinguishment. The restatement is followed in the text by a disclaimer that the issues were not being decided according to theories of cultural superiority, but that the Court was bound to ratify the end results of the political process whatever its ideological roots.

We will not enter into the controversy, whether agriculturists, merchants, and manufacturers, have a right, on abstract principles, to expel hunters from the territory they possess, or to contract their limits. Conquest gives a title which the Courts of the conqueror cannot deny, whatever the private and speculative opinions of individuals may be, respecting the original justice of the claim which has been successfully asserted.

The Court here introduced the language of conquest for the first time, combined with perhaps the earliest articulation of the ''political question'' doctrine as applied to the issue of aboriginal rights. There is no immediate hint in the text as to the source of the conquest theory. The description of British claims to a right of extinguishments that ''have been maintained and established as far west as the river

Mississippi, by the sword'' quite apparently refers to the war with the French, and does not provide a basis for a theory of conquest of the Indian nations.

It is only later in the opinion that the source of the conquest theory is revealed to lie in the mere act of discovery. . . .[56]

In international law, the use of force has generally been subject to certain limitations. Vitoria's comments in this regard have already been noted above. Vattel and Grotius held similar views:

The right of employing force, or making war, belongs to nations no farther than is necessary for their own defense and for the maintenance of their rights . . . a nation is not allowed to attack another with a view to aggrandize itself by subduring and giving law to the latter. This is just the same as if a private person should attempt to enrich himself by seizing his neighbour's property.[57]

In addition, the Conquest doctrine was only applicable where "the conquered territory was effectively reduced to possession and annexed by the conquering state."[58] It is questionable to what extent the acquisition of indigenous lands would conform to this definition.[59]

The *Status of Eastern Greenland Case* (3 World Court Reports, 151) a decision of the Permanent Court of International Justice, 1933, held that:

Conquest only operates as a cause of loss of sovereignty when there is war between two states and by reason of the defeat of one of them sovereignty over territory passes from the loser to the victorious state. The principle does not apply in a case where a settlement has been established in a distant country and its inhabitants are massacred by the aboriginal population. (pp. 171-72)

By implication, then, one might argue that the piecemeal annihilation of indigenous groups by encroaching powers would similarly not amount to "conquest" in the sense indicated by the court.

The conquest doctrine, when applied to acquisition of Aboriginal lands, seems to be, at the very least, inappropriate. In many cases lands have been acquired, not through open warfare, but through the treaty process. Where force has been employed, it has tended to conform more to the *Eastern Greenland* model.

(d) Cession

A necessary precondition to the legitimate acquisition of ihhabited territories, then, appears to be the consent of the peoples thus affected. The process involved here is the signing of treaties. As discussed below, the very nature of the treaty concept seems to imply a sovereign capacity in those engaged in the undertaking. Conflicting views with regard to the status of those indigenous parties involved create a climate of uncertainty, which extends not only to the status of the parties concerned but also to the subsequent effects of such arrangements.

Certainly in many cases one is led to question the voluntary nature of such cessions. The surrounding circumstances of the agreements involving, as history reveals, elements of undue influence, fraud and misunderstanding, tend to undermine the legitimacy of claims made on that basis by the non-aboriginal party. For example:

> . . . the American Indians' understanding of the treaties was consistent with Vattel's and Marshall's descriptions of "unequal alliances." As Marshall discussed in *Worcester* v. *Georgia*, the Indians perceived the treaties as a promise of protection, and not as any surrender of sovereignty, except in the particulars agreed in the treaties. The Indians regarded land as available for the use of all members of the group. They often thought that the treaties entitled whites to come into their area; they did not agree or understand that they were to be excluded from land they had traditionally inhabited. And regardless of the various understandings and misunderstandings as to the use of land, they certainly did not knowingly relinquish any of their sovereignty.
>
> As Vitoria stated, fear and ignorance vitiate any consent to be governed. In short, the United States explained the treaties to the Indians in one way, and now claims a quite different interpretation.
>
> Native Americans have ceded and sold a great deal of land to the United States and to private purchasers. Many of those sales were not voluntary. They were often made after persuasion or promises from government officials, "trustees" appointed for "incompetent" Indians (a common fiction used to ease land away from natives), and other Indians whom the government had pressured or bribed into advocating the non-Indian cause. Sales were often made without the consent of the Indian owner (his signature was forged or one signature would be obtained for a parcel with many joint owners); many times he was coerced and threatened until he agreed. But even if some of the land sales and cessions were considered valid, they would not change the fact that Indian tribes have retained millions of acres of land under their control and jurisdiction, land that is a more than adequate basis for their sovereignty. Further, even if the treaties could in some way be considered a surrender of sovereignty, any such grant would have to be considered long ago rescinded by virtue of the wholesale violation of the treaties by the United States. The United States cannot ignore its treaty obligations, and then insist that concessions made by the Indians are still binding.[60]

In any event, it is important to note that an act of cession or conquest does not disturb the rights of private owners:

The generally accepted modern rule is that, whatever the degree of development of the territory concerned, privately owned property within a region which has been acquired by Conquest or Cession remains unaffected by the transfer of sovereignty unless and until the new sovereign brings about some alteration in its condition by means of his municipal law.[61]

This clearly has implications for the survival of Aboriginal title in terms of municipal law.[62] The fact of "possession since time immemorial" is the fundamental basis of Aboriginal title from the perspective of international law:

The notion that long occupation is to be deemed lawful, in the absence of proof to the contrary, is as ancient as the concept of property itself; indeed the right to use that which one has created, possessed or occupied without wrongfully taking from another is fundamental to any legal system.[63]

Respect for this doctrine has been the cornerstone of almost all legal systems.

As noted above, if occupation is a valid claim *vis-à-vis* encroaching states, it must *a fortiori* apply to indigenous peoples.

The Marshall Court recognized the legitimacy of Aboriginal rights founded on possession in *Johnson* v. *McIntosh* and in *Worcester* v. *Georgia*.

[The original inhabitants] were admitted to be the rightful occupants of the soil, with a legal as well as a just claim to retain possession of it, and use it according to their own discretion.

This is a view that echoes the writings of Vitoria and others, and one which finds confirmation in subsequent decisions of the court. However, the issue has yet to find resolution in other municipal jurisdictions, including Canada.[64]

Under international law it is possible to acquire territory belonging to another state through effective occupation of that territory with the acquiescence of the original owner-state.[65] It has been argued that the doctrine is inapplicable to indigenous peoples since they are the original occupants and therefore the element of adversity of possession is lacking.

The recognition in most municipal legal systems of the doctrine of adverse possession and of acquisitive prescription in international law indicates the importance attached to the concept. It seems more than ironic, therefore, that the same municipal systems that have no difficulty supporting such a doctrine find it difficult to accommodate the concept of Aboriginal title based on "possession since time immemorial" which would, *prima facie,* imply an even stronger claim.

The acceptable sources of international law, as outlined in Article 38 of the Statute of the International Court of Justice, include "international custom as evidence of a general practice accepted as law." It appears feasible to argue that "possession" in this context has been accorded a degree of recognition in "the custom and practice" of nations (both municipally and internationally) such that it may fall within this category.

In addition, the growing application of principles contained in the various covenants and declarations to the question of land rights indicate an increasing awareness of the importance of employing standards derivable from international sources, whether they have been crystallised into law or not.

6. Conclusion

The brief survey presented here raises a number of difficult and important issues. Definitive resolutions to the questions implied have not, as yet, been formulated.

Traditionally, Aboriginal Peoples have been considered to be the objects rather than the subjects of international law. European powers were directly responsible for the content and direction of this facet of law, and it is therefore not surprising that the interests of Aboriginal Peoples have not found adequate representation and protection at this level. In spite of this fact, even a cursory analysis of the principles pertaining to "sovereignty" and "status" in international law reveal that the inadequate protection stems not so much from the principles of law themselves but rather from incorrect interpretation and application of these principles by the European powers and their courts. Difficulties in this regard also stem in part from inaccurate assumptions about the social and political institutions of the various Aboriginal Peoples and the circumstances surrounding agreements made between them and the European powers.

A fair and accurate analysis of this branch of law will be possible only when certain basic issues raised here have been resolved. One thing, at least, is clear. The international legal context for indigenous rights issues is not a recent phenomenon. It is the context within which most of the issues central to Aboriginal rights have their foundation. Significant discussion of such issues at the municipal level will depend on the extent to which this fact is recognized.

Endnotes

[1] D.E. Sanders, "The Formation of the World Council of Indigenous Peoples," unpublished paper, 1975.

[2] A.H. Snow, *The Question of Aboriginals in the Law and Practice of Nations* (New York: Putnam, 1921), p. 4, emphasis added.

[3] Statute of the International Court of Justice, 59 Stat. 1055, TS No. 993, 3 Bevans 1153, 1976 TBUN 1052.

[4] Note that the term "convention" means "treaty". For a discussion of terminology in this field, see M. Akehurst, *A Modern Introduction to International Law,* (London: Allen and Unwin, 1982), pp. 23-24; and D.W. Grieg, *International Law* (London: Butterworths, 1976), pp. 5-10.

[5] For a general discussion of this, see *supra*, footnote 4, M. Akehurst, pp. 17-30; D.W. Grieg, pp. 19-20, pp. 25-34.

[6] M. Akehurst, *supra*, footnote 4, p. 31.

[7] I. Brownlie, *Principles of Public International Law*, 3rd ed., (Oxford: Clarendon Press, 1979), p. 6. J. Brierly, *The Law of Nations* 6th ed., (Oxford: Clarendon Press, 1963), pp. 59-62. With regard to treaties, note *caveat* by Akehurst, *supra*, footnote 4., p. 28.

[8] See M. Akehurst, *supra*, footnote 4, p. 28.

[9] For a discussion of this, see M. Akehurst, *supra*, footnote 4, pp. 34-36; and D.W. Grieg, *supra*, footnote 4, pp. 31-38.

[10] Article 59 of the Statute of the International Court of Justice.

[11] For a discussion of these points, see D.W. Grieg, *supra*, footnote 4, pp. 45-49.

[12] For a general discussion of this, see M. Akehurst, *supra*, footnote 4, pp. 39-40.

[13] For a general discussion of the position vis-à-vis Canada, see J. Claydon, "The International Law of Human Rights and Canadian Courts" in, *Proceedings of the 1981 Conference of the Canadian Council on International Law.*
R. St J. Macdonald, "The Relationship between International Law and Domestic Law in Canada", in Macdonald, Morris and Johnston, *Canadian Perspectives on International Law and Organization,* (Toronto: University of Toronto Press, 1974).

[14] R. St J. Macdonald, *supra*, footnotes 13, 88, 111.

[15] J. Claydon, *supra*, footnotes 13, 2, 9.

[16] F. Cohen, "The Spanish Origins of Indian Rights in the Law of the United States," (1942) 31 *Geo. LJ1*, p. 17.

[17] E. Nys, *Relictiones: De Indis et De Jure Belli* (Washington: Carnegie Classics of International Law, 1917).
J.B. Scott, *The Spanish Origin of International Law, Part 1, Francisco de Vitoria and his Law of Nations,* Carnegie Classics of International Law, (Oxford: Clarendon Press, 1934).

[18] One of the key figures in this process was Fra Bartalome de Las Casas, a Dominican who participated in the conquest of the Caribbean and, as a result of witnessing the brutal destruction of the native populations, became a fervent advocate of the native cause.

[19] For example, *The Bull Sublimus Deus,* (issued by Pope Paul in 1537); cited in Cohen, *supra*, footnote 16 at 12:

> We, who, though unworthy, exercise on earth the power of our Lord and seek with all our might to bring those sheep of His flock who are outside into the fold committed to our charge, consider, however, that the Indians are truly men and that they are not only capable of understanding the catholic faith, but, according to our information, they desire exceedingly to receive it. Desiring to provide ample remedy for these evils, We define and declare by these our letters, or by any translation thereof assigned by any notary public and sealed with the seal of any ecclesiastical dignitary, to which the same credit shall be given as to the originals, that, notwithstanding whatever may have been or may be said to the contrary, the said Indians and all other people who may later be discovered by Christians, are by no means to be deprived of their liberty or the possession of their property, even though they be outside the faith of Jesus Christ, and that they may and should, freely and legitimately, enjoy their liberty and the possession of their property; nor should they in any way be enslaved; should the contrary happen it shall be null and of no effect.

[20] For a general discussion of this, see L. Hanke, *All Mankind is One* (DeKalb: Northern Illinois University Press, 1974); L. Hanke, *Aristotle and the American Indians* (London: Hollis and Carter, 1959); and J.B. Scott, *supra*, footnote 17.

[21] See J. Brierly, *supra*, footnote 7, p. 26; B. Hamilton, *Political Throught in Sixteenth-Century Spain*, (Oxford: Clarendon Press, 1963); E. Nys, *supra*, footnote 17.

[22] E. Nys, *supra*, footnote 17, p. 119.
De Indis was followed by a second relectio, *De Jure Belli*, which he gave "so as to give

more completeness'' to the discussion of ''titles'' in the first relectio. In it he sets out the ''laws of war'' upon which subsequent writers, such as Grotius, have built.

[23] *supra*, pp. 119-62.

[24] J.B. Scott, *The Classics of International Law, De Jure Praedae Commentarius*, Vol. 1 (Oxford: Clarendon Press, 1950), pp. 219-26.

[25] J.B. Scott, *De Jure Naturae et Gentium Libri Octo*, Carnegie Classics of International Law Vol. 2 (Oxford: Clarendon Press, 1934), pp. 364-66.

[26] The recent decision of Judge Ammoun in the *Western Sahara Case,* (ICJ Report 1975, p. 4), in which he refers in a positive way to the writing of Vitoria, gives some impetus in this direction.

[27] See G. Lester, *The Territorial Rights of the Inuit of the Canadian Northwest Territories,* 1981, D. Jur. Thesis (York University, Toronto); B. Slattery, *Land Rights of Indigenous Canadian Peoples*, University of Saskatchewan, 1979.

[28] See G. Bennett, *Aboriginal Rights in International Law*, (Royal Anthropological Institute of Great Britain and Ireland, Occasional Paper No. 37, 1978).

[29] See the judgment, *per curiam*, in the *Lotus* case, Permanent Court of International Justice (1927), series A, No. 10 (2 WCR 20).

[30] R. Barsh and J. Henderson, ''Aboriginal Rights, Treaty Rights and Human Rights: Tribes and Constitutional Renewal,'' (1982) 17 *Journal of Canadian Studies,* No. 2, 55, 58, 59.

[31] For a general discussion see J. Crawford, *The Creation of States in International Law*, (Oxford: Clarendon Press, 1979) pp. 36-128.

[32] The Court at this point avoided the political implications of the dispute by deciding that the Cherokee State was not ''foreign'' and that therefore the court had no jurisdiction to hear the case.

[33] See G. Bennett, *supra*, footnote 28, p. 85.

[34] J. Clinebell and J. Thomson, ''Sovereignty and Self-Determination: The Rights of Native Americans under International Law,'' (1978) 27 *Buffalo Law Review*, 669.

[35] D. Opekokew, Statement by Chief S. Sanderson, in *The First Nations: Indian Governments in the Community of Man,* Federation of Saskatchewan Indian Nations, 1982.

[36] ibid., p. 10.

[37] See Chapter 10, *infra*, for a discussion of this.

[38] Vienna Convention on the Law of Treaties, 1969, UN Doc. 81,LM.

[39] (London: P.S. King & Son Ltd., 1932) at 30.

[40] A.H. Snow, *supra*, footnote 2 (emphasis added).

[41] Barsh and Henderson, *supra*, footnote 30, pp. 68-69.

[42] For a fuller discussion of this, see chapter 5, *infra*. See also: *Manuel et al* v. *AG,* [1982] 3 All E.R. 786.

[43] A.H. Snow, *supra*, footnote 2, chapter III.

[44] See, for example, The Berlin Africa Treaty (1885), The Brussels Act (1892), The Convention of St Germain (1991), The League of Nations Covenant, Article 22.

[45] Note, for example, *Tito* v. *Waddell* (No. 2) [1977] 2 WLR 496. See also Bennett, *supra*, footnote 28, pp. 7-11.

[46] It ought to be noted, however, that while the tribunal held that a tribe was not a legal unit of international law, it went on to award the Cayugas a lump sum payment, which was to be held in trust for them by Canada.

[47] Bennett, *supra*, footnote 28, p. 86.

[48] See Akehurst, *supra*, footnote 4, p. 69.

[49] For a discussion of this, see chapter 13.

[50] For a general discussion of Territorial Acquisition in International Law, see Akehurst, *supra*, footnote 4, Chapter 11. J. Crawford, *supra*, footnote 31.

[51] G. Bennett, *supra*, footnote 28, p. 86.

[52] Note, in particular, studies by Slattery and Lester which deal in detail with this point (*supra*, footnote 27).

[53] There is a school of thought which suggests that the court was, in fact, aware of the departure from international law in this respect and that it felt compelled to do so rather reluctantly, as a result the necessity of applying the "law of the land" i.e., The United States.) (See: H. Berman, "The Concept of Aboriginal Rights in the Early Legal History of the United States," (1979) 27 *Buffalo Law Review* 637.)

Note, in particular, Marshall's comment at p. 591:

". . . with respect to the concomitant principle that the Indian inhabitants are to be considered merely as occupants, to be protected, indeed, while in peace, in the possession of their lands, but to be deemed incapable of transferring the absolute title to others. However, this restriction may be opposed to the usages of civilized nations, yet, if it be indispensable to that system under which the country has been settled . . . it certainly cannot be rejected by Court of Justice."

[54] For further discussion see B. Slattery, *The Land Rights of Indigenous Canadian Peoples*, DPhil Thesis, Oxford, 1979.

[55] G.H. Hackworth, *Digest of International Law*, Vol. 1 (Washington: US Government Printing Office, 1940), p. 406.

[56] H. Berman, "The Concept of Aboriginal Rights in the Early Legal History of the United States," (1978) 27 *Buffalo Law Review*, 637 at 648.

[57] Vattel, *The Law of Nations*, bk 3, No. 26 (J. Chitty trans. 1852).

[58] Hackworth, *supra*, footnote 55, p. 427.

[59] See Clinebell and Thomson, *supra*, footnote 33, for a discussion of this point with reference to the American Indian.

[60] Clinebell and Thomson, *supra*, footnote 33, p. 695.

[61] M.F. Lindley, *The Acquisition and Government of Backward Territory in International Law* (London: Longmans, Green & Co., 1926).

[62] See chapter 3.

[63] G. Bennett, "Aboriginal Title in the Common Law: A Stony Path through Feudal Doctrine," (1978) 27 *Buffalo Law Review* 617, at pp. 618, 619.

[64] See chapter 3.

[65] For a discussion of this doctrine, see M. Akehurst, footnote 4, *supra*, pp. 144-45.

7. Questions

Consider the following questions:

1. What was and/or is the status of Aboriginal Peoples or nations in their relations with European (i.e., Non-Aboriginal) states such as, for example, Canada and the United States?

2. How and by whom is/was/ought this status to be defined?

3. Are municipal courts the appropriate fora for the resolution of this and other key issues in this field of law?

4. Is it possible to discuss the territorial rights of indigenous peoples within the municipal context without first resolving the key issues of sovereignty and status?

8. Further Reading

(a) Books

G. Bennett, *Aboriginal Rights in International Law*, Royal Anthropological Institute of Great Britain, occasional paper no. 37, 1978.

J. Crawford, *The Creation of States in International Law*, (Oxford: Clarendon Press, 1979).

G. Lester, *The territorial Rights of the Inuit of the Canadian Northwest Territories,* 1981, (DJur Thesis. Toronto: York University).

D. Opekokew, *The First Nations: Indian Governments in the Community of Man*, Federation of Saskatchewan Indians, 1982.

B. Slattery, *The Land Rights of Indigenous Canadian Peoples as affected by the Crown's Acquisition of Their Territories,* 1979, DPhil Thesis (Oxford University), University of Saskatchewan, Native Law Centre, 1979.

A. H. Snow, *The Question of Aboriginals in the Law and Practice of Nations,* (New York, Putnam, 1921).

(b) Articles

E. Anderson, "The Saskatchewan Indians and Canada's New Constitution," (1982-83) 36 *Col. Journal of International Affairs* 125.

R. Barsh and J. Henderson, "Aboriginal Rights, Treaty Rights and Human Rights: Tribes and Constitutional Renewal," (1982) 17 *Journal of Canadian Studies*, No. 2, 55.

G. Bennett, "Aboriginal Title in the Common Law: A Stoney Path through Feudal Doctrine," (1978) 27 *Buffalo Law Review* 617.

H. Berman, "The Concept of Aboriginal Rights in the Early Legal History of the United States," (1978) 27 *Buffalo Law Review* 637.

J.H. Clinebell & J. Thomson, "Sovereignty and Self-Determination: The Rights of Native Americans under International Law," (1978) 27 *Buffalo Law Review* 669.

F. Cohen, "Original Indian Title," (1947) 32 *Minnesota Law Review* 28.

F. Cohen, "The Spanish Origin of Indian Rights in the Law of the United States," (1942) 31 *Georgetown LJ1*.

J. Ryan, "Indian Nations Compared to Other Nations," (1977) 3 *American Indian Journal* 2.

3. Aboriginal Title*

DAVID W. ELLIOTT

1. Introduction

Long before the arrival of John Cabot on the shores of eastern North America in the late fifteenth century, the native people were here. They had been here for many thousands of years. Recent excavations in the extreme north-western parts of Canada are providing evidence that indigenous people used and occupied this continent at least 80,000 years ago.**

The fact that the Aboriginal People were here first is at the core of the notion of aboriginal rights or aboriginal title. Building on this idea of original use and occupancy, Peter A. Cumming has defined aboriginal rights in "Native Rights and Law in an Age of Protest" (1973) 11 *Alberta Law Review* 238, 239 as "those property rights which native peoples retain as the result of their original use and occupancy of lands." Similarly, in their text *Native Rights in Canada* (1972), P.A. Cumming and N.H. Mickenberg defined aboriginal rights as "those property rights which inure to aboriginal peoples by virtue of their occupation upon certain lands from time immemorial."

Logically, "aboriginal title" is the basic interest from which aboriginal rights are derived. Nevertheless, the two terms are often used interchangeably, together with "native title," "Indian title," and similar expressions.

2. Some Aboriginal Peoples' Concepts of Aboriginal Title

Despite some variations in emphasis, there are a number of common themes running through concepts of aboriginal title expressed by indigenous writers. Most of these writers emphasize the importance of the land and its resources to their traditional way of life. They describe a relationship to the land different from standard European concepts of ownership or title, but no less crucial to their society and generally stress the communal, holistic character of their traditional relationship to the land.

---

* The writer acknowledges with thanks the permission of the Government of the Yukon Territory to adapt portions of his study, *The Development of Greater Self-Government in the Yukon Territory: Legal and Constitutional Provisions Affecting Yukon Indian People*, 1979, to parts of this chapter.

** B. Estabrook, "Bone Age Man," *Equinox*, March/April 1982, pp. 84-96. In the summer of 1981 the Toronto archaeologist William Irving discovered remnants of a human encampment in the Old Crow area of northern Yukon. Irving claims that this site may be up to 150,000 years old.

(a) Yukon Native Brotherhood, *Together Today for our Children Tomorrow*, 1973, pp. 5-6, 63.

For many years before we heard about the Whiteman our people who lived in what is now called Yukon lived a different way. We lived in small groups and moved from one place to another at different times of the year. Certain families had boundaries which they could not cross to hunt, because that area was used by other Indians. Sometimes we gathered together in larger groups in the summer to fish and relax after a hard winter.

We had our own God and our own Religion which taught us how to live together in peace. This Religion also taught us how to live as a part of the land. We learned how to practice what is now called multiple land use, conservation, and resource management. We have much to teach the Whiteman about these things when he is ready to listen.

Our family was the centre of "The Indian Way." The man was head of the family and was the provider of food, clothing, housing and protection. The mother was the centre of the family and the children took her name.

Marriage, adoption and care of older people were all regulated by custom. These were many generations old and were adapted to the way of life.

Education was handled by our parents and was done by children watching and copying what they saw. It was the method of learning by doing. A child was considered an adult, when he proved that he could handle adult responsibilities.

People were busy supplying the needs of the community. All possessions belonged to the group and individuals did not suffer unless the whole group was in need. This required planning, organization and leadership. These three were carried out without a formal organized system, which is one of the reasons why we are finding it difficult to adopt the Whiteman's way.

(b) George Manuel, Michael Posluns, *The Fourth World: An Indian Reality,* 1974, p. 6.

. . . wherever I have travelled in the Aboriginal World, there has been a common attachment to the land.

This is not the land that can be speculated, bought, sold, mortgaged, claimed by one state, surrendered or counter-claimed by another. These are things that men do only on the land claimed by a king who rules by the grace of God, and through whose grace and favour men must make their fortunes on this earth.

The land from which our culture springs is like the water and the air, one and indivisible. The land is our Mother Earth. The animals who grow on that land are our spiritual brothers. We are a part of that Creation that the Mother Earth brought forth. More complicated, more sophisticated than the other creatures, but no nearer to the Creator who infused us with life.

(c) Duke Redbird, *We are Metis: A Metis View of the Development of a Native Canadian People,* 1980, p. 39.

The concept of "title to land" was alien to the native consciousness, except as a natural birthright. The emphasis, in native culture, was on use of land, not formal possession, a cultural manifestation the eastern land grabbers were quick to exploit in Manitoba and Saskatchewan. The Metis assumed title in the traditional way of the Indian, by reason of their occupation and use.

(d) Leroy Little Bear, "A Concept of Native Title," CASNP Bulletin, December 1976, p. 33.

. . . if one attempts to trace the Indian's source of title, one will quickly find the original source is the Creator. The Creator, in granting land, did not give the land to human beings only but gave it to all living beings. This includes plants, sometimes rocks, and all animals. In other words, deer have the same type of estate or interest as any human being. This concept of sharing with fellow animals and plants is one that is quite alien to Western society's concept of land. To Western society, only human beings have a right to land, and everything else is for the convenience of human beings. . . .

An observation about the Indians' concept of land title includes a reference back to the basic philosophy. Indian property concepts are wholistic. Ownership does not rest in any one individual, but belongs to the tribe as a whole, as an entity. The land belongs not only to people presently living, but it belongs to past generations and to future generations. Past and future generations are as much a part of the tribal entity as the living generation.

Little Bear says that the philosophical differences in European and aboriginal approaches to ownership of land do not prevent the drawing of analogies between the two. In "A Concept of Native Title," he suggests that communal Indian ownership is akin to a joint tenancy, and, by virtue of its restriction to Indian people, somewhat less than a fee simple interest.

Aboriginal writers have questioned the fairness or legitimacy of non-native displacement or erosion of aboriginal title. In the article referred to above, Little Bear suggests that in light of the historical fact of prior aboriginal occupancy, the onus should be on governments, not the Aboriginal People, to establish the validity of their claim to the land:

> When the courts and the government say that the Indians' title is dependent on goodwill of the sovereign, and that the Indians' interest is a mere burden on the underlying title of the Crown, the question to ask is, "What did the Crown get its title from? And how?"

In its *Statement on Aboriginal Title*, presented to the Standing Committee on Indian Affairs and Northern Development on 29 March 1973, the National Indian Brotherhood argued that colonial governments arbitrarily imposed their own property concepts on indigenous people and severely limited aboriginal rights in the process. The feeling underlying these views is expressed in the following extract:

(e) Phillip Blake, "A Dene's Views on the Pipeline (a Presentation to the Berger Commission)," CASNP Bulletin, March 1976, p. 25.

> White people came as visitors to our land. Suddenly they claim it as their land. They claim that we have no right to call it Indian land, land that we have occupied and used for thousands of years. . . .
> Is this the great system of justice, which your nation is so proud of?

3. Aboriginal Title and the Law

Although Aboriginal People have long been regarded as having some kind of interest in lands in North America, it is only in recent times that Canadian courts have recognized interests in terms that approximate the definitions referred to in Part 1 above. Many aspects of aboriginal title and the aboriginal rights derived from it remain to be clarified and defined.

The concept of aboriginal title involves four basic sets of questions:

i) *A question of legal status:* To what extent is aboriginal title recognized in law? To what extent has aboriginal title received recognition in the various sources (prerogative, judicial, legislative, or other) of law? What status has been accorded aboriginal title in relation to ordinary legislation?

ii) *A question of scope and content:* What is the actual scope and content of the rights derived from aboriginal title?

iii) *A question of termination or restriction:* What, if anything, can put an end to aboriginal title or restrict the rights derived from it? and

iv) *A question of compensation:* To what extent, if any, is there a legal obligation on government to pay compensation for termination or restriction of aboriginal title?

4. Legal Status of Aboriginal Title

Before the coming of the Europeans as well as after, the Aboriginal People of what is now Canada undoubtedly had close relations with the land. From anthropological accounts and current indigenous writings, it appears that many of the traditional systems of occupation and use were as distinct and patterned in their own way as the English common law notion of property. However, over the past two centuries, it has been the English system of law, not aboriginal or other systems, that has been imposed over the area now comprising Canada.

The English legal system recognizes three "direct" sources of law: (a) the royal prerogative; (b) the common law; and (c) statutes, including constitutional enactments and subordinate legislation. In addition, there are a variety of phenomena relevant to the formation of the common law. These include custom, official government practice, international law, and resemblance to established common law rules. To the extent that these phenomena are not incorporated in one or more of the sources above, they do not give rise to legally enforceable interests. Nevertheless, they are capable of supporting interests or aspects of interests which may gain explicit judicial recognition at some future date. The common law is continually developing and changing.

Aboriginal rights in Canada have been constitutionally recognized and affirmed in the Constitution Act, 1982. However, as will be seen in Part 4(c)(i), below, the provisions which recognize and affirm these rights are less than clear. Moreover, they refer not simply to aboriginal rights but to "existing" aboriginal rights. For these reasons, it is useful to look at the status of aboriginal rights and aboriginal title in some of the other possible sources of law and related phenomena before proceeding directly to the Constitution Act, 1982.

(a) The Royal Prerogative

(i) *The Royal Proclamation of 1763* [reprinted in RSC 1970, Appendices, p. 125]. See also discussions of *St Catharine's* Case.

The most significant prerogative instrument respecting the status of aboriginal title is the Royal Proclamation of 7 October 1763 issued by King George III of Britain with respect to the governing of British North America. The section of the Proclamation dealing with Indian people is as follows:

> And whereas it is just and reasonable, and essential to our Interest, and the security of our Colonies, that the several Nations or Tribes of Indians with whom We are connected, and who live under our protection, should not be molested or disturbed in the Possession of such Parts of Our Dominions and Territories as, not having been ceded

to or purchased by Us, are reserved to them or any of them, as their Hunting Grounds — We do therefore, with the Advice of our Privy Council, declare it to be our Royal Will and Pleasure, that no Governor or Commander in Chief in any of our Colonies of Quebec, East Florida, or West Florida, do presume, upon my Pretence whatever, to grant Warrants of Survey, or pass any Patents for Lands beyond the Bounds of their respective Governments, as described in their Commissions; as also that no Governor or Commander in Chief in any of our other Colonies or Plantations in America do presume for the present, and until our further Pleasure be Known, to grant warrants of Survey, or pass Patents for any Lands beyond the Heads or Sources of any of the Rivers which fall into the Atlantic Ocean from the West and North West, or upon any Lands whatever, which, not having been ceded to or purchased by Us as aforesaid, are reserved to the said Indians, or any of them.

And We do further declare it to be Our Royal Will and Pleasure, for the present as aforesaid, to reserve under our Sovereignty, Protection, and Dominion, for the use of the said Indians, all the Lands and Territories not included within the Limits of Our Said New Governments, or within the Limits of the Territory granted to the Hudson's Bay Company, as also all the Lands and Territories lying to the Westward of the Sources of the Rivers which fall into the Sea from the West and North West as aforesaid:

And We do hereby strictly forbid, on Pain of our Displeasure, all our loving subjects from making any Purchase or Settlements whatever, or taking Possession of any of the Lands above reserved, without our especial leave and Licence for the Purpose first obtained.

And, We do further strictly enjoin and require all Persons whatever who have either wilfully or inadvertently seated themselves upon any Lands within the Countries above described, or upon any other Lands which, not having been ceded to or purchased by Us, are still reserved to the said Indians as aforesaid, forthwith to remove themselves from such Settlements.

And Whereas Great Frauds and Abuses have been committed in purchasing Lands of the Indians, to the Great Prejudice of our Interests, and to the Great Dissatisfaction of the said Indians; In Order, therefore, to prevent such Irregularities for the future, and to the End that the Indians may be convinced of our Justice and determined Resolution to remove all reasonable Cause of Discontent, We do, with the Advice of our Privy Council, strictly enjoin and require, that no private Person do presume to make any Purchase from the said Indians of any Lands reserved to the said Indians, within those parts of our Colonies where, We have thought proper to allow Settlement; but that, if at any Time any of the said Indians should be inclined to dispose of the said Lands, the same shall be Purchased only for Us, in our Name, at some public Meeting or Assembly of the said Indians, to be held for the Purpose of the Governor or Commander in Chief of our Colony respectively within which they shall lie; and in case they shall lie within the limits of any Proprietary Government, they shall be purchased only for the Use and in the name of such Proprietaries, conformable to such Directions and Instructions as We or they shall think proper to give for the Purpose; And We do, by the Advice of our Privy Council, declare and enjoin, that the Trade with the said Indians shall be free and open to all our Subjects whatever, provided that every Person who may incline to Trade with the said Indians do take out a Licence for carrying on such Trade from the Governor or Commander in Chief of any of our Colonies respectively where such Person shall reside, and also give Security to observe such Regulations as We shall at any Time think fit, by ourselves or by our Commissaries to be appointed for this Purpose, to direct and appoint for the Benefit of the said Trade:

And We do hereby authorize, enjoin, and require the Governors and Commanders in Chief of all our Colonies respectively, as well those under Our immediate Government as those under the Government and Direction of Proprietaries, to grant such Licences without Fee or Regard, taking especial care to insert therein a Condition, that such Licence shall be void, and the Security forfeited in the case the Person to whom the same is granted shall refuse or neglect to observe such Regulations as We shall think proper to prescribe as aforesaid.

And We do further expressly enjoin and require all Officers whatever, as well Military as those Employed in the Management and Direction of Indian Affairs, within the Territories reserved as aforesaid for the Use of the said Indians, to seize and apprehend all Persons whatever, who standing charged with Treason, Misprisons of Treason, Murders, or other Felonies or Misdemeanors, shall fly from Justice and take Refuge in the said Territory, and to send them under a proper Guard to the Colony where the Crime was committed of which they stand accused, in order to take their Trial for the same.

> Given at our Court at
> St James' the 7th Day
> of October 1763, in the
> Third Year of our Reign.

GOD SAVE THE KING

EASTERN NORTH AMERICA AFTER THE ROYAL
PROCLAMATION OF 1763*

* Based on map in P.A. Cumming and N.H. Mickenberg (eds.) *Native Rights in Canada* 2d ed.,
1972, and modified in respect of Labrador, Nova Scotia, and Cape Breton Island pursuant to
discussion in B. Slattery, *The Land Rights of Indigenous Canadian Peoples, as Affected by the
Crown's Acquisition of their Territories,* 1979, pp. 277-81 and G.S. Lester, *The Territorial
Rights of the Inuit of the Canadian Northwest Territories: A Legal Argument,* 1981, pp.
1,182—86. These latter authorities differ as to whether the Proclamation extended to Labrador
and to Nova Scotia other than Cape Breton Island.

Note the size and location of the tract of land reserved to the Indian people "as their Hunting Grounds." Note the prohibition on grants or purchases of this land, or settlement of this land, without a licence, and the requirement that all non-Indians on the land without a licence must leave. There are separate but similar stipulations affecting Indian reserve lands *within* British colonies or proprietary governments. These latter lands can be purchased only by the Crown after a public meeting or by a proprietary government acting on instructions of the Crown. Finally, the section contains a general provision permitting trade with the Indians only by licence.

Today, in Canada, that part of the Royal Proclamation of 1763 which deals with Indian people has the force of a statute. There is a well-established common law principle that instruments issued under the royal prerogative in British colonial possessions lacking representative legislative assemblies have the force of statutes in these areas. That part of the Proclamation which deals with Indian people has never been repealed by a Canadian statute.

Because of its force as a statute, the Proclamation unquestionably resulted in legal interests for the Indians to which it applied. As a result, some have regarded the Proclamation as a major support for the contention that occupancy-based aboriginal rights have legal status.

In support of the argument that the Proclamation confirms a pre-existing title, it can be noted that the document reserves the lands to the Indians after describing them as "not having been ceded to or purchased by Us." This might suggest that the Indians had an interest capable of cession or sale.

On the other hand, other aspects of the Proclamation may detract from its strength as a confirmation of a general occupancy-based aboriginal title. First, the document makes no *express* reference to any pre-existing interest. Second, the Proclamation does not apply to land belonging to the Hudson's Bay Company, a vast tract of the Canadian north. Third, it is unclear from the text whether the Proclamation is intended to apply to the far western regions of northern North America. (See also B. Slattery, *The Land Rights of Indigenous Canadian Peoples as Affected by the Crown's Acquisition of their Territories*, 1979, Parts I and II; J. Stagg, *Anglo-Indian Relations in North America to 1763 and An Analysis of the Royal Proclamation of 7 October, 1763*, 1981; and G.S. Lester, *The Territorial Rights of the Inuit of the Canadian Northwest Territories: A Legal Argument*, 1981, Chapter XIX.)

(b) The Common Law

The second major direct source of law is the decisions of the courts of law — the common law. For many years the common law appeared to offer two different and potentially conflicting notions of the status of aboriginal title in Canada. The first was the idea that aboriginal title is rooted exclusively in the Royal Proclamation of 1763. The second was the notion that aboriginal title was derived originally from the fact of aboriginal occupation and use of land from earliest times and that it survived the settlement or conquest of North America by European states. For convenience, the narrower concept can be referred to as ''Proclamation-based'' title and the broader concept can be referred to as ''occupancy-based'' aboriginal title.*

> (i) *St Catharine's Case* [*St Catharine's Milling and Lumber Company* v. *The Queen* (1889) 14 App. Cas. 46 (JCPC, aff'g. (1887) 13 SCR 577 (SCC); which aff'd. (1887) 13 OAR 148 (OCA); which aff'd. (1886) 10 OR 196 (Chancery Div.)]. See also parts 5(c)(i) and 5(g)(i), *infra*.

The major early Canadian case on the question of the legal status of aboriginal title is *St Catharine's Milling and Lumber Company* v. *The Queen*. In this case, the province of Ontario challenged the federal government's right to grant a timber licence to the St Catharine's Milling and Lumber Company. Because of a complex combination of legal provisions and historical developments, the province of Ontario could succeed in its claim *if* the Indian interest which had existed earlier in the land in question were an interest less than the full fee simple interest* of English property law. The Judicial Committee of the Privy Council decided that this interest *had* been less than a full fee simple interest, and so the province succeeded in its claim.

Speaking for the Judicial Committee, Lord Watson started his discussion of the general character and status of the Indian title with a description of the Royal Proclamation of 1763 (pp. 53-54) and continued:

> The territory in dispute has been in Indian occupation from the date of the Proclamation until 1873. During that interval of time Indian affairs have been administered successively by the Crown, by the Provincial Governments, and (since the passing of the British North America Act, 1867) by the Government of the Dominion. The policy of these administrations has been all along the same in this respect, that the Indian inhabitants have been precluded from entering into any transaction with a subject for the sale or transfer of their interest in the land, and have only been permitted to surrender their rights to the Crown by a formal contract, duly ratified in a meeting of their chiefs or head men convened for the purpose. Whilst there have been changes in the administrative authority, there has been no change since the year 1763 in the character of the interest which its Indian inhabitants had in the lands surrendered by the treaty. Their possession, such as it was, can only be ascribed to the general provisions made by the royal

---

* Cf. the distinction drawn between ''recognized'' and ''aboriginal'' rights in G.S. Lester, *The Territorial Rights of the Inuit of the Canadian Northwest Territories: A Legal Argument*, pp. 19-26.
* Or, possibly, the freehold interest: see Part 5(g)(i), *infra*.

proclamation in favour of all Indian tribes then living under the sovereignty and protection of the British Crown. It was suggested in the course of the argument for the Dominion, that inasmuch as the proclamation recites that the territories thereby reserved for Indians had never "been ceded to or purchased by" the Crown, the entire property of the land remained with them. That inference is, however, at variance with the terms of the instrument, which show that the tenure of the Indians was a personal and usufructuary right, dependent upon the good will of the Sovereign. The lands reserved are expressly stated to be "parts of Our dominions and territories"; and it is declared to be the will and pleasure of the sovereign that, "for the present," they shall be reserved for the use of the Indians, as their hunting grounds, under his protection and dominion. There was a great deal of learned discussion at the Bar with respect to the precise quality of the Indian right, but their Lordships do not consider it necessary to express any opinion upon the point. It appears to them to be sufficient for the purposes of this case that there has been all along vested in the Crown a substantial and paramount estate, underlying the Indian title, which became a plenum dominion whenever that title was surrendered or otherwise extinguished.

For the present purposes, the key features of the *St Catharine's* case are the fact that the Privy Council recognized the existence at law of an Indian interest in the land in question and attributed the interest solely to the provisions of the Royal Proclamation of 1763. (See, further, Parts 5(c)(i) and 5(g)(i), *infra*, and the references to this case in the passages from *Calder* quoted in Part 4(b)(iii), *infra*.)

What, though, did Lord Watson mean by the passage commencing "Their possession, such as it was . . .," in the above quotation? It is possible that by this statement he did not intend to exclude other possible kinds of aboriginal title, such as that derived from occupancy since time immemorial. It is also possible that Lord Watson saw the Royal Proclamation interest as merely recognizing and formalizing a wider occupation-based aboriginal title. However, Lord Watson did not address himself to these questions. In the circumstances of this case, the Privy Council had only to determine (a) whether there had indeed been an Indian interest (however derived) in the lands in question, and (b) whether or not this interest was sufficiently large to amount to the equivalent of a fee simple interest.*

(ii) Some Early British and American Colonial Cases of Relevance to Occupancy-Based Title. [See also the survey of early American cases in Part 5(g)(iii), *infra*.]

In *Johnson and Graham's Lessee* v. *McIntosh* 21 US (8 Wheat) 543 (1823),

---

* Or, possibly, a freehold interest: see Part 5(g)(i), *infra*.

Marshall CJ of the United States Supreme Court recognized an aboriginal title in eastern North America and made it clear that this title existed independently of the Proclamation. Marshall CJ's references (for example, at p. 588) to the Indian right of "occupancy" pointed to the Indians' first occupation of the land as the basis of their title, but he did not elaborate. Marshall CJ did make it clear that he considered this right to be a legal right (p. 574):

> They [the aboriginal inhabitants] were admitted to be the rightful occupants of the soil, with a legal as well as a just claim to retain possession of it, and to use it according to their own discretion . . . [but their sovereignty was diminished and their powers of disposition of the soil were restricted].

Early British colonial decisions tended to focus less on the origin of occupancy-based title and more on a second question relevant to the nature of this title in Canada — the question of the legal effect of British acquisition of territory. Here there appears to have been a movement from the very early view that the rights of non-Christians do not survive acquisition to a view closer to the general international law principle* that a change of sovereignty does not automatically terminate existing rights.

In *Calvin's Case* (1608) 7 Co. Rep. la, 17a-17b; 77 ER 377, 397-8, Coke CJ said that the laws of a conquered country remain in place until they are altered by the conquering monarch, unless the inhabitants of the conquered country are "infidels," in which case the infidels' laws cease automatically at the time of conquest. Coke CJ's exception regarding infidels was qualified and then entirely rejected in *Blankard* v. *Galdy* (1963) Holt 341; 90 ER 1089 (KB) and *Campbell* v. *Hall* (1774) 1 Cowp. 204; 98 ER 1045 (KB), respectively; see the quotation from *Campbell* v. *Hall* in the judgment of Hall J in the *Calder* decision, reproduced in Part 4(b)(iii), *infra*. However, in *Blankard* v. *Galdy*, Holt CJ drew another distinction, which was to complicate the question of whether aboriginal rights survived an acquisition of territory by or in the name of the British Crown:

> In case of an uninhabited country newly found out by British subjects, all laws in force in England, are in force there: but Jamaica being conquered, and not pleaded to be parcel of the kingdom of England, but part of the possessions and revenue of the Crown of England; the laws of England did not take place there, 'til declared so by the conqueror or his successors.

In *The Land Rights of Indigenous Canadian Peoples, as Affected by the Crown's Acquisition of their Territories*, 1979, Brian Slattery has pointed out (p. 27) that the distinction in *Blankard* v. *Galdy* did not allow for the common colonial situation — and one occurring in many parts of the region now

---

* See D.P. O'Connell, *International Law for Students*, 1971, p. 161, and Chapter Two, *supra*.

comprising Canada — "where British settlers establish autonomous communities in already inhabited lands held by the Crown." For this situation, the key question is whether or not the antecedent rights of the aboriginal inhabitants could survive the fact of acquisition in some legally significant form. Although the case law is hardly clear, there is some evidence that by the late nineteenth century British colonial law was moving toward the position that they could.* In regard to the status of antecedent rights, then, British colonial law arguably was on the way to assimilating the general legal consequences of the conquest (or cession) and peaceful settlement doctrines.

Meanwhile, the United States Supreme Court appeared to be moving in the same general direction. In *Johnson and Graham's Lessee* v. *McIntosh* 21 US (8 Wheat) 543, 587-88 (1823), Marshall CJ said that European title in North America was based on a principle of "discovery". He added that the practical situation here did not really fit the standard categories of acquisition, but had been treated more or less (and, in his view, inappropriately) as if it were conquest (p. 591):

> However extravagant the pretension of converting the discovery of an inhabited country into conquest may appear, if the principle has been asserted in the first instance, and afterwards sustained; if a country has been acquired and held under it; if the property of the great mass of the community originates in it, it becomes the law of the land, and cannot be questioned.

In Marshall CJ's view, the Europeans had been less than consistent with the spirit of the conquest doctrine by driving many of the Indians from their lands and stipulating that Indian rights could be alienable only to the Crown (pp. 589-92). Moreover, Marshall CJ's affirmation that Indian lands were in the same position as vacant lands in regard to the Crown's power to grant title (pp. 595-97) might appear to imply settlement rather than conquest. Nevertheless, he considered that the conquest doctrine's corollary that "the rights of the conquered to property remain unchanged" (p. 589) applied.

---

* See B. Slattery, *The Land Rights of Indigenous Canadian Peoples*, pp. 27-30. In *The Territorial Rights of the Inuit of Canadian Northwest Territories*, 1981, pp. 166-67, G.S. Lester criticizes Slattery's use of examples from British India, but the language of decisions such as *Freeman* v. *Fairlie* (1828) 1 Moo. Ind. App. 305 (Ch.) is in general terms applicable beyond that particular colony. Although their analyses differ widely, both Slattery (e.g., pp. 354-56) and Lester (e.g., p. 1,416) conclude that antecedent rights can survive acquisition by peaceful settlement. In *Milirrpum* v. *Mabalco Pty*. [1971] 17 FLR 141 (Northern Territory Supreme Court) Blackburn J concluded, after an extensive examination of British and other case law, that without special government recognition or policy there is no principle of communal native title in a settled colony (p. 223). However, Blackburn J's concern in *Milirrpum* was whether or not there was a communal native title which — under normal circumstances — could be enforced legally against the Crown (e.g., pp. 198, 213 and 217). In Part 5(g), *infra*, there are suggestions that aboriginal rights are *not* normally enforceable against the Crown. *Contra*, Slattery, p. 356, and Lester, p. 1,445.

Whatever the difficulties in labelling the acquisition process, then, and despite some qualifications, the original rights survived the fact of acquisition.*

In *Worcester* v. *State of Georgia* 31 US (6 Pet.) 515, 543-44 (1832), Marshall CJ departed further from the "conquest" terminology. He said that after a discovery (presumably whether followed by settlement *or* conquest) the legal effect was not to annul the rights of the original inhabitants of the discovered territory but to confer a title to the territory on the government of the discoverer *vis-à-vis* other European governments and to give this government the exclusive right to purchase land from the original inhabitants:

> This principle [discovery], acknowledged by all Europeans, because it was the interest of all to acknowledge it, gave to the nation making the discovery, as its inevitable consequence, the sole right of acquiring the soil and of making settlements on it. It was an exclusive principle which shut out the right of competition among those who had agreed to it; *not one which could annul the previous rights of those who had not agreed to it*. It regulated the right given by discovery among the European discoverers, *but could not affect the rights of those already in possession, either as aboriginal occupants, or as occupants by virtue of a discovery made before the memory of man*. It gave the exclusive right to purchase, but did not found that right on a denial of the right of the possessor to sell. (Emphasis added)

(iii) *Calder* [*Calder et al.* v. *Attorney General of British Columbia*, [1973], SCR 313 (SCC); aff'g. (on technical grounds) (1971), 13 DLR (3d) 64 (BCCA); which aff'd. (1969), 8 DLR (3d) 59 (BCSC)]. See also parts 5(f)(ii), 5(g)(iv), 6(a), and 7(a), *infra*.

By January 1973, the Canadian common law position on the question of the legal status of aboriginal title was little different from that resulting from the *St Catharine's* case eighty-four years earlier. Canadian courts recognized a Proclamation-based title. Although this title had legal status, it was subject to all the geographical and other uncertainties of the Proclamation. There was no clear indication from the courts as to whether the broader concept of an occupancy-based right had any status at common law.

This was the context in which the Supreme Court of Canada rendered its judgment in *Calder* v. *Attorney General of British Columbia*. In *Calder*, the Nishga people of northwestern British Columbia had sought a declaration that they had aboriginal title to their land, and that this title had not been terminated. The Nishgas based their claim to the land on the fact that their ancestors had been occupying and using the land from time immemorial. Hall

---

* In *The Territorial Rights of the Inuit of the Canadian Northwest Territories*, G.S. Lester argues that the thirteen colonies were originally acquired by conquest, and that the discovery principle was an *ex post facto*, unhistorical judicial construct: see, for example, pp. 197-205. (Lester also argues that on a proper view of peaceful settlement, original inhabitants' rights survive the settlement: see, for example, pp. 1,412-45.)

J, speaking for three members of the Supreme Court of Canada, agreed that the Nishgas had an existing aboriginal title derived from original occupancy and use. The argument of these three judges on this question might be summarized as follows:

1. There is "a wealth of jurisprudence affirming common law recognition of aboriginal rights to possession and enjoyment of lands of aborigines precisely analogous to the Nishga situation here". (p. 376) In support of this proposition, Hall J quoted, *inter alia*, from the judgments of Strong J (dissenting, in the Supreme Court of Canada) and Lord Watson in the *St Catharine's* case; Chief Justice Marshall in *Johnson* v. *McIntosh* and *Worcester* v. *State of Georgia* 6 Peters 515, 31 US 530 (1832); Norris JA in *R.* v. *White and Bob* (1965), 52 WWR 193 (BCCA); Lord Summer in *Re Southern Rhodesia*, [1919] AC 211 (JCPC); and others and from the *Commentaries on American Law*, 1889, Vol. 3, by Chancellor Kent.
2. The conquest doctrine's principles respecting prior rights "must apply to lands which become subject to British sovereignty by discovery or by declaration". (p. 389) Hall J did not elaborate on this suggestion.
3. "The aboriginal Indian title does not depend on treaty, executive order or legislative enactment". (p. 391) Hall J cited in support of this contention cases such as *Cramer* v. *United States* 261 US 219 (1923); *United States* v. *Sante Fe Ry Co.* 314 US 339 (1941); and *Lipan Apache Tribe* v. *United States* 180 Ct. Cl. 487 (1967).
4. The Act of State doctrine has never been considered applicable to aboriginal title in the traditional case law, and in any event it merely bars procedural remedies in some cases: it does not negate substantive rights. (p. 405)
5. "Surely the Canadian Indian treaties, made with much solemnity on behalf of the Crown, were intended to extinguish the Indian title. What other purpose did they serve? If they were not intended to extinguish the Indian right, they were a gross fraud and that is not to be assumed". (p. 394)
6. The claim to common law occupancy-based rights is paralleled and supported by the Royal Proclamation of 1763. (pp. 394-401)

The following extract from the judgment of Hall J (pp. 376-89, footnotes omitted) contains most of the authorities he relied on in support of the first three propositions above:

Strong J (later CJC) in *St Catharine's Milling and Lumber Company* v. *The Queen,* said at p. 608:

In the Commentaries of Chancellor Kent and in some decisions of the Supreme Court of the United States we have very full and clear accounts of the policy in question. *It may be summarily stated as consisting in the recognition by the Crown of a usufructuary title in the Indians to all unsurrendered lands. This title, though not perhaps susceptible of any accurate legal definition in exact legal terms, was one which nevertheless sufficed to protect the Indians in the absolute use and enjoyment of their lands, whilst at the same time they were incapacitated from making any valid alienation otherwise than to the Crown itself, in whom the ultimate title was, in accordance with the English law of real property, considered as vested.* This short statement will, I think, on comparison with the authorities to which I will presently refer, be found to be an accurate description of the principles upon which the Crown invariably acted with reference to Indian lands, at least from the year 1756, when Sir William Johnston was appointed by the Imperial Government superintendent of Indian Affairs in North America, being as such responsible directly to the Crown through one of the Secretaries of State, or the Lords of Trade and Plantation, and thus superseding the Provincial Governments, down to the year 1867, when the confederation act constituting the Dominion of Canada was passed. So faithfully was this system carried out, that I venture to say that there is no settled part of the territory of the Province of Ontario, except perhaps some isolated spots upon which the French Government had, previous to the conquest, erected forts, such as Fort Frontenac and Fort Toronto, which is not included in and covered by a surrender contained in some Indian treaty still to be found in the Dominion Archives. These rules of policy being shown to have been well established and acted upon, and the title of the Indians to their unsurrendered lands to have been recognized by the Crown to the extent already mentioned, it may seem of little importance to enquire into the reasons on which it was based. (Emphasis added)

and at p. 610:

The American authorities, to which reference has already been made, consist (amongst others) of passages in the commentaries of Chancellor Kent, [Kent's Commentaries 12 ed. by Holmes, Vol. 3, p. 379 *et seq.* and in editor's notes] in which the whole doctrine of Indian titles is fully and elaborately considered, and of several decisions of the Supreme court of the United States, from which three, *Johnston* v. *McIntosh*, 8 Wheaton 543, *Worcester* v. *State of Georgia*, 6 Peters 515, and *Mitchell* v. *United States*, 9 Peters 711, may be selected as leading cases. *The value and importance of these authorities is not merely that they show that the same doctrine as that already propounded regarding the title of the Indians to unsurrendered lands prevails in the United States, but, what is of vastly greater importance, they without exception refer its origin to a date anterior to the revolution and recognize it as a continuance of that established by the British Government, and therefore identical with those which have also continued to be recognized and applied in British North America.* Chancellor Kent, referring to the decision of the Supreme Court of the United States, in *Cherokee Nation* v. *State of Georgia*, 5 Peters 1, says:

> The court there held that the Indians were domestic, dependent nations, and their relations to us resembled that of a ward to his guardian; and they had an unquestionable right to the lands they occupied until that right should be extinguished by a voluntary cession to our government, 3 Kent Comms. 383 (Emphasis added.)

It thus appears, that in the United States, a traditional policy, derived from colonial times, relative to the Indians and their lands has ripened into well established rules of law, and that the result is that the lands in the possession of the Indians are, until surrendered, treated as their rightful though inalienable property, so far as the possession and enjoyment are concerned; in other words, that the *dominium utile* is recognized as belonging to or reserved for the Indians, though the *dominium directum* is considered to be in the United States. Then, if this is so as regards Indian lands in the United States, which have been preserved to the Indians by the constant observance of a particular rule of policy acknowledged by the United States courts to have been originally enforced by the Crown of Great Britain, how is it possible to suppose that the law can, or rather could have been, at the date of confederation, in a state any less favorable to the Indians whose lands were situated within the dominion of the British Crown, the original author of this beneficient doctrine so carefully adhered to in the United States from the days of the colonial governments? *Therefore, when we consider that with reference to Canada the uniform practice has always been to recognize the Indian title as one which could only be dealt with by surrender to the Crown,* I maintain that if there had been an entire absence of any written legislative act ordaining this rule as an express positive law, we ought, just as the United States courts have done, to hold that it nevertheless existed as a rule of the unwritten common law, which the courts were bound to enforce as such, and consequently, that the 24th sub-section of section 91, as well as the 109th section and the 5th sub-section of section 92 of the British North America Act, must all be read and construed upon the assumption that these territorial rights of the Indians were strictly legal rights which had to be taken into acocunt and dealt with in that distribution of property and proprietary rights made upon confederation between the federal and provincial governments. (Emphasis added) . . .

To summarize these arguments, which appear to me to possess great force, we find, that at the date of confederation the Indians, by the constant usage and practice of the Crown, were considered to possess a certain proprietary interest in the unsurrendered lands which they occupied as hunting grounds; that this usage had either ripened into a rule of the common law as applicable to the American Colonies, or that such a rule had been derived from the law of nations and had in this way been imported into the Colonial law as applied to Indian Nations; that such property of the Indians was usufructuary only and could not be alienated, except by surrender to the Crown as the ultimate owner of the soil. . . .

Strong J, with whom Gwynne J agreed, was dissenting in the case, but the dissent was on the question of whether the Dominion or Provincial Government acquired title when the Indian title was extinguished as it had been in that case by treaty. The majority held that the Crown in the right of the Province became the owner, and Strong and Gwynne JJ held that the Dominion became the owner. However, on the point of Indian title there was no disagreement between the majority and minority views. Ritchie CJ for the majority agreed substantially with Strong J in this respect, saying at pp. 559-60:

I am of opinion, that all ungranted lands in the Province of Ontario belong to the Crown as part of the public domain, subject to the *Indian right of occupancy in cases in which the same has not been lawfully extinguished,* and when such right of occupancy has been lawfully extinguished absolutely to the Crown, and as a consequence to the Province of Ontario. I think the Crown owns the soil of all the unpatented lands, the Indians possessing only the right of occupancy, and the Crown possessing the legal title subject to that occupancy, with the absolute exclusive right to extinguish the Indian title either by conquest or by purchase. . . . (Emphasis added)

The *St Catharine's Milling* case was affirmed in the Privy Council. The judgment was given by Lord Watson who, in referring to Indian aboriginal interests, said at p. 54:

[Here Hall J quoted from the passage reproduced in Part 4(b)(i), *supra*, commencing with the words, "It was suggested in the course of the argument for the Dominion," and ending with the words "wherever that title was surrendered or otherwise extinguished." Hall J added emphasis of his own to the last two sentences of the passage he quoted. He then continued as follows]:

The case most frequently quoted with approval dealing with the nature of aboriginal rights is *Johnson* v. *McIntosh*. It is the *locus classicus* of the principles governing aboriginal title. Gould J in his reasons said of this case at p. 514:

The most cogent one of these is the argument based upon a classsic and definitive judgement of Chief Justice Marshall of the United States, in 1823, in the case of *Johnson* v. *McIntosh*, (1823) 8 Wheaton, p. 541, wherein that renowned jurist gave an historical account of the British Crown's attitude towards the rights of aboriginals over land originally occupied by them, and an enunciation of the law of the United States on the same subject.

and on p. 518 he said:

For more than 150 years this strong judgement has at various times been cited with approval by such authorities as the House of Lords (*Tamaki* v. *Baker* [1901] AC 561 at 580); the Supreme Court of Canada (*St Catharine's Milling* v. *The Queen* (1886) 13 SCR 577, Strong J at 610); Court of Appeal for Ontario, (in the same case, (1886) — 13 OAR 148, Burton, JA, at 159-60); Ontario High Court, Chancery Division (in the same case, 10 OR 196, Boyd, J, at 209); Court of Appeal for British Columbia (*White and Bob, supra,* p. 230); Supreme Court of New Brunswick (*Warman* v. *Francis* (1958) — 20 DLR (2d) 627, Anglin J, at 630).

Chief Justice Marshall said in *Johnson* v. *McIntosh:*

On the discovery of this immense continent, the great nations of Europe were eager to appropriate to themselves so much of it as they could respectively acquire. Its vast extent offered an ample field to the ambition and enterprise of all; and the character and religion of its inhabitants afforded an apology for considering them as a people over whom the superior genius of Europe might claim an ascendency. The potentates of the old world found no difficulty in convincing themselves that they made ample compensation to the inhabitants of the new, by bestowing on them civilization and Christianity, in exchange for unlimited independence. But, as they were all in pursuit of nearly the same object, it was necessary, in order to avoid conflicting settlements, and consequent war with each other, to establish a principle which all should acknowledge as the law by which the right of acquisition, which they all asserted, should be regulated as between themselves. This principle was that discovery gave title to the government by whose subjects, or by whose authority, it was made, against all other European governments, which title might be consummated by possession.

The exclusion of all other Europeans necessarily gave to the nation making the discovery the sole right of acquiring the soil from the natives, and establishing settlements upon it. It was a right which all asserted for themselves, and to the assertion of which, by others, all assented.

Those relations which were to exist between the discoverer and the natives, were to be regulated by themselves. The rights thus acquired being exclusive, no other power could interpose between them.

In the establishment of these relations, the rights of the original inhabitants were, in no instance, entirely disregarded: but were necessarily, to a considerable extent, impaired. *They were admitted to be the rightful occupants of the soil, with a legal as well as just claim to retain possession of it, and to use it according to their own discretion;* but their rights to complete sovereignty, as independent nations, were necessarily diminished, and their power to dispose of the soil at their own will to whomsoever they pleased, was denied by the original fundamental principle that discovery gave exclusive title to those who made it.

While the different nations of Europe respected the right of the natives, as occupants, they asserted the ultimate dominion to be in themselves; and claimed and exercised, as a consequence of this ultimate dominion, a power to grant the soil, while yet in possession of the natives. These grants have been understood by all to convey a title to the grantees, subject only to the Indian right of occupany. (Emphasis added)

It is pertinent to quote here what Norris JA said of *Johnson* v. *McIntosh* in *R.* v. *White and Bob*, pp. 212-13:

. . . the judgment in *Johnson* v. *McIntosh, supra,* was delivered at an early stage of exploration of this continent and when controversy as to those rights was first becoming of importance. Further, on the consideration of the subject matter of this appeal, it is to be remembered that it was delivered only five years after the Convention of 1818 between Great Britain and the United States (erroneously referred to by counsel as the *Jay Treaty*) providing that the northwest coast of America should be free and open for the term of ten years to the vessels, citizens, and subjects of both powers in order to avoid disputes between the powers. The rights of Indians were naturally an incident of the implementation of a common policy which was perforce effective as applying to what is now Vancouver Island and the territory of Washington and Oregon, all of which were then Hudson's Bay territories. For these reasons and because the judgment in *Johnson* v. *McIntosh* was written at a time of active exploration and exploitation of the West by the Americans, it is of particular importance.

The dominant and recurring proposition stated by Chief Justice Marshall in *Johnson* v. *McIntosh* is that on discovery or on conquest the aborigines of newly found lands were conceded to be the rightful occupants of the soil with a legal as well as a just claim to retain possession of it and to use it according to their own discretion, but their rights to complete sovereignty as independent nations were necessarily diminished and their power to dispose of the soil on their own will to whomsoever they pleased was denied by the original and fundamental principle that discovery or conquest gave exclusive title to those who made it.

Chief Justice Marshall had occasion in 1832 once more to adjudicate upon the question of aboriginal rights in *Worcester* v. *State of Georgia*. He said at pp. 542-44:

America, separated from Europe by a wide ocean, was inhabited by a distinct people, divided into separate nations, independent of each other and of the rest of the world, *having institutions of their own, and governing themselves by their own laws*. It is difficult to comprehend the proposition that the inhabitants of either quarter of the globe could have rightful original claims of dominion over the inhabitants of the other, or over the lands they occupied; or that the discovery of either by the other should give the discoverer rights in the country discovered which annulled the pre-existing rights of its ancient possessors.

After laying concealed for a series of ages, the enterprise of Europe, guided by nautical science, conducted some of her adventurous sons into this western world. They found it in possession of a people who had made small progress in agriculture or manufactures, and whose general employment was war, hunting and fishing.

Did these adventurers, by sailing along the coast and occasionally landing on it, acquire for the several governments to whom they belonged, or by whom they were commissioned, a rightful property in the soil from the Atlantic to the Pacific; or rightful dominion over the numerous people who occupied it? Or has nature, or the great Creator of all things, conferred these rights over hunters and fishermen, on agriculturalist and manufacturers?

But power, war, conquest, give rights, which after possession, are conceded by the world; and which can never be controverted by those on whom they descend. We proceed, then, to the actual state of things, having glanced at their origin, because holding it in our recollection might shed some light on existing pretensions.

The great maritime powers of Europe discovered and visited different parts of this continent at nearly the same time. The object was too immense for anyone of them to grasp the whole, and the claimants were too powerful to submit to the exclusive or unreasonable pretensions of any single potentate. To avoid bloody conflicts, which might terminate disastrously to all, it was necessary for the nations of Europe to establish some principle which all would acknowledge, and which should decide their respective rights as between themselves. This principle, suggested by the actual state of things, was "that discovery gave title to the government by whose subjects or by whose authority it was made, against all other European governments, which title might be consummated by possession.''

The principle, acknowledged by all Europeans, because it was the interest of all to acknowledge it, gave to the nation making the discovery, as its inevitable consequence, the sole right of acquiring the soil and of making settlements upon it. It was an exclusive principle which shut out the right of competition among those who had agreed to it; not one which could annul the previous rights of those who had not agreed to it. It regulated the right given by discovery among the European discoverers, *but could not affect the rights of those already in possession, either as aboriginal occupants, or as occupants by virtue of a discovery made before the memory of man. It gave the exclusive right to purchase, but did not found that right on a denial of the right of the possessor to sell.* (Emphasis added)*

The view that the Indians had a legal as well as a just claim to the territory they occupied was confirmed as recently as 1946 by the Supreme Court of the United States in the case of *United States* v. *Alcea Band of Tillamooks*. In that case it was held that the Indian claims legislation of 1935 did not confer any substantive rights on the Indians; that is, it did not convert a moral claim for taking their land without their consent and without compensation into a legal claim, and there was no necessity to create one. The statute simply removed the necessity that previously existed for the Indians to obtain the consent of the Government of the United States to sue for an alleged wrongful taking. The judgment is based squarely on the recognition by the Court of "original Indian title" founded on their previous possession of the land. It was held that "the Indians have a cause of action for compensation arising out of an involuntary taking of lands held by original Indian title." Vinson CJ said at p. 45:

The language of the 1935 Act is specific, and its consequences are clear. By this Act Congress neither admitted or denied liability. The Act removes the impediments of sovereign immunity and lapse of time and provides for judicial determination of the designated claims. No new right or cause of action is created. A merely moral claim is not made a legal one.

It has long been held that by virtue of discovery the title to lands occupied by Indian tribes vested in the sovereign. This title was deemed subject to a right of occupancy in favour of Indian tribes, because of their original and previous possession. It is with the

---

* See also Chancellor Kent in his *Commentaries on American Law*, (1839), Vol. 3, p. 411.

content of this right of occupancy, this original Indian title, that we are concerned here.

As against any but the sovereign, original Indian title was accorded the protection of complete ownership but it was vulnerable to affirmative action by the sovereign, which possessed exclusive power to extinguish the right of occupancy at will. Termination of the right by sovereign action was complete and left the land free and clear of Indian claims. Third parties could not question the justness or fairness of the methods used to extinguish the right of occupancy. Nor could the Indians themselves prevent a taking of tribal lands or forestall a termination of their title. However, it is now for the first time asked whether the Indians have a cause of action for compensation arising out of an involuntary taking of lands held by original Indian title.

. . . . .

A contrary decision would ignore the plain import of traditional methods of extinguishing original Indian title. The early acquisition of Indian lands, in the main, progressed by a process of negotiation and treaty, the first treaties reveal the striking deference paid to Indian claims, as the analysis in *Worcester* v. *Georgia, supra,* clearly details. It was usual policy not to coerce the surrender of lands without consent and without compensation. *The great drive to open western lands in the 19th century, however productive of sharp dealing, did not wholly subvert the settled practice of negotiated extinguishment of original Indian title. In 1896, this Court noted that "nearly every tribe and band of Indians within the territorial limits of the United States was under some treaty relations with the government." Marks v. United States, 161, US 297, 302 (1896). Something more than sovereign grace prompted the obvious regard given to original Indian title.* (Emphasis added)

The same considerations applied in Canada. Treaties dealing with enormous tracts of land were made with the Indians of the Canadian West. See Kerr's *Historical Atlas of Canada* (1961), p. 57 (map no. 81). These treaties were a recognition of Indian title.

In *Re Southern Rhodesia,* Lord Sumner said at p. 233:

In any case it was necessary that the argument should go the length of showing that the rights, whatever they exactly were, belonged to the category of rights of private property, such that upon a conquest it is to be presumed, in the absence of express confiscation or of subsequent expropriatory legislation, that the conqueror has respected them and forborne to diminish or modify them.

The estimation of the rights of aboriginal tribes is always inherently difficult. Some tribes are so low in the scale of social organization that their usages and conceptions of rights and duties are not to be reconciled with the institutions or the legal ideas of civilized society. Such a gulf cannot be bridged. It would be idle to impute to such people some shadow of the rights known to our law and then to transmute it into the substance of transferable rights of property as we know them. In the present case it would make each and every person by a fictional inheritance a landed proprietor "richer than all his tribe." *On the other hand, there are indigenous peoples whose legal conceptions, though differently developed, are hardly less precise than our own. When once they have been studied and understood they are no less enforceable than rights arising under English Law.* (Emphasis added)

Chief Justice Marshall in his judgment in *Johnson* v. *McIntosh* referred to the English case of *Campbell* v. *Hall*. This case was an important and decisive one which has been regarded as authoritative throughout the Commonwealth and the United States. It involved the rights and status of residents of the island of Grenada which had recently been taken by British Arms in open war with France. The judgment was given by Chief Justice Mansfield. In his reasons he said at p. 1,047:

A great deal has been said, and many authorities cited relative to propositions, in which both sides seem to be perfectly agreed; and which, indeed are too clear to be controverted. The stating of some of those propositions which we think quite clear, will lead us to see with greater perspicuity, what is the question upon the first point, and upon what hinge it turns. I will state the propositions at large, and the first is this:

A country conquered by the British arms becomes a dominion of the King in the right of his Crown; and, therefore, necessarily subject to the Legislature, the Parliament of Great Britain.

The 2d is, that the conquered inhabitants once received under the King's protection, become subjects, and are to be universally considered in that light, not as enemies or aliens.

The 3d, that the articles of capitulation upon which the country is surrendered, and the articles of peace by which it is ceded, are sacred and inviolable according to their true intent and meaning.

The 4th, that the law and legislative government of every dominion, equally affects all persons and all property within the limits thereof; and is the rule of decision for all questions which arise there. Whoever purchases, lives, or sues there, puts himself under the law of the place. An Englishman in Ireland, Minorca, the Isle of Man, or the plantations, has no privilege distinct from the natives.

The 5th, that the laws of a conquered country continue in force, until they are altered b the conqueror: the absurd exception as to pagans, mentioned in *Calvin's case*, shows the universality and antiquity of the maxim. For that distinction could not exist before the

Christian era; and in all probability arose from the mad enthusiasm of the Crusades. In the present case the capitulation expressly provides and agrees, that they shall continue to be governed by their own laws, until His Majesty's further pleasure be known.

The 6th, and last proposition is, that if the King (and when I say the King, I always mean the King without the concurrence of Parliament) has a power to alter the old and to introduce new laws in a conquered country, this legislation being subordinate, that is, subordinate to his own authority in Parliament, he cannot make any new change contrary to fundamental principles: he cannot exempt an inhabitant from that particular dominion; as for instance, from the laws of trade, or from the power of Parliament, or give him privileges exclusive of his other subjects, and so in many other instances which might be put. *A fortiori,* the same principles, particularly Nos. 5 and 6, must apply to lands which become subject to British sovereignty by discovery or by declaration.

Judson J, speaking for three other members of the court, held that whatever title the Nishgas may have had, had since been terminated. Before considering the questions of extinguishment and compensation, and arriving at this conclusion, Judson J referred to some of the authorities respecting the general nature and status of aboriginal title (pp. 320-23, footnotes omitted):

Any Canadian inquiry into the nature of the Indian title must begin with *St Catharine's Milling and Lumber Co.* v. *The Queen.* This case went through the Ontario Courts, the Supreme Court of Canada and ended in the Privy Council. The Crown in right of the Province sought to restrain the Milling Company from cutting timber on certain lands in the District of Algoma. The company plkeaded that it held a licence from the Dominion Government which authorized the cutting. In 1873, by a treaty known as the North-West Angle Treaty No. 3, the Dominion had extinguished the Indian title.

The decision throughout was that the extinction of the Indian title enured to the benefit of the Province and that it was not possible for the Dominion to preserve that title so as to oust the vested right of the Province to the land as part of the public domain of Ontario. It was held that the Crown had at all times a present proprietary estate, which title, after confederation, was in the Province, by virtue of s. 109 of the *BNA Act.* The Indian title was a mere burden upon that title which, following the cession of the lands under the treaty, was extinguished.

The reasons for judgment delivered in the Canadian Courts in the *St Catharine's* case were strongly influenced by two early judgments delivered in the Supreme Court of the United States by Chief Justice Marshall — *Johnson* v. *McIntosh,* and *Worcester* v. *State of Georgia.* In *Johnson* v. *McIntosh* the actual decision was that a title to lands, under grants to private individuals, made by Indian tribes or nations northwest of the river Ohio, in 1773 and 1775, could not be recognized in the Courts of the United States. In *Worcester* v. *Georgia*, the plaintiff, who was a missionary, was charged with residing among the Cherokees without a licence from the State of Georgia. His defence was that his residence was in conformity with treaties between the United States and the Cherokee nation and that the law under which he was charged was repugnant to the constitution, treaties and laws of the United States. The Supreme Court made a declaration to this effect. Both cases raised the question of aboriginal title to land. The following passages from 8 Wheaton, pp. 587-88, give a clear summary of the views of the Chief Justice:

The United States, then, have unequivocally acceded to that great and broad rule by which its civilized inhabitants now hold this country. They hold, and assert in themselves, the title by which it was acquired. They maintain, as all others have maintained, that discovery gave an exclusive right to extinguish the Indian title of occupancy, either by purchase or by conquest; and gave also a right to such a degee of sovereignty as the circumstances of the people would allow them to exercise.

The power now possessed by the government of the United States to grant lands, resided, while we were colonies, in the Crown, or its grantees. The validity of the titles given by either has never been questioned in our courts. It has been exercised uniformly over territory in possession of the Indians. The existence of this power must negative the existence of any right which may conflict with, and control it. An absolute title to lands cannot exist, at the same time, in different persons, or in different govenrments. An absolute, must be an exclusive title, or at least a title which excludes all others not compatible with it. All our institutions recognize the absolute title of the Crown, subject only to the Indian right of occupancy; and recognized the absolute title of the Crown to extinguish that right. This is incompatible with an absolute and complete title in the Indians.

The description of the nature of Indian title in the Canadian Courts in the *St Catharine's* case is repeated in the reasons delivered in the Privy Council. I quote from 14 App. Cas. at pp. 54-55:

[Judson J here quoted the entire passage reproduced in Part 4(b)(i), *supra*. He then continued as follows]:

There can be no doubt that the Privy Council found that the Proclamation of 1763 was the origin of the Indian title — "Their possession, such as it was, can only be ascribed to the Royal Proclamation in favour of all Indian tribes then living under the sovereignty and protection of the British Crown."

I do not take these reasons to mean that the Proclamation was the exclusive source of Indian title. The territory under consideration in the *St Catharine's* appeal was clearly within the geographical limits set out in the Proclamation. It is part of the appellants' case that the Proclamation does apply to the Nishga territory and that they are entitled to its protection. They also say that if it does not apply to the Nishga territory, their Indian title is still entitled to recognition by the Courts. These are two distinct questions.

I say at once that I am in complete agreement with judgements of the British Columbia Courts in this case that the Proclamation has no bearing upon the problem of Indian title in British Columbia. I base my opinion upon the very terms of the Proclamation and its definition of its geographical limits and upon the history of the discovery, settlement and establishment of what is now British Columbia.

[After examining the terms of the Royal Proclamation of 1763 and the history of the discovery and settlement of British Columbia, Judson J made the following comment on the claim being advanced by the Nishga Indians (p. 328)]:

Although I think that it is clear that Indian title in British Columbia cannot owe its origin to the Proclamation of 1763, the fact is that when the settlers came, the Indians were there, organized in societies and occupying the land as their forefathers had done for centuries. This is what Indian title means and it does not help one in the solution of this problem to call it a "personal or usufructuary right." What they are asserting in this action is that they had a right to continue to live on their lands as their forefathers had lived and that this right has never been lawfully extinguished. There can be no question that this right was "dependent on the goodwill of the Sovereign."

Judson J and the two other judges he represented also agreed with the reasons of a seventh judge, Pigeon J. However, Pigeon J's only reason for dismissing the Nishgas's application was that the Nishgas had failed to comply with a British Columbia statute requiring the Lieutenant Governor's consent where litigation involved the Crown's own title to land. Because of the 3-3 stalemate between the other judges on the substantive issues, Pigeon J's procedural argument is the sole reason for which the *Calder* decision is binding authority in law.

As a legal precedent, the Supreme Court's *Calder* decision did little to clarify the status of aboriginal title. Three judges explicitly recognized, as a legal concept, an aboriginal title based on occupancy and use of land from time immemorial. However, because of the result in *Calder*, the reasons of these judges were technically dissents. Three other judges (represented by Judson J) stated that Indian title in British Columbia was not based on the

Proclamation and suggested that any title which might exist was based on occupancy since time immemorial. On this basis, of the six judges in *Calder* considering occupancy-based title, none rejected the proposition that this title may have legal status at common law. But Judson J may have been simply pointing out that what the *Nishgas* were claiming were not Proclamation rights but occupancy-based rights. Moreover, the reasons of Judson J and the two others for whom he spoke were not majority reasons in this or any other substantive issue in *Calder*. As has been shown, the only majority reason for which *Calder* is authority in law is the procedural reason of Pigeon J.

The real significance of *Calder* lies in its strong suggestion that aboriginal title is not necessarily limited to the confines of the Royal Proclamation of 1763, but may be based on the concept of prior occupation of lands. On the other hand, *Calder* made little more than a start at answering some of the many questions surrounding that status of occupancy-based aboriginal title.

In the first place, while it is important to bear in mind the warning in *Amodu Tijani* v. *Secretary, Southern Nigeria*, [1921] 2 AC 399, 402-03 (JCPC) not to attempt to redefine aboriginal title in terms appropriate only to the common law, it is still necessary to have some kind of conceptual bridge between the two if the common law is to be able to accommodate aboriginal title as a fully recognized and enforceable legal right.

Hall J said in *Calder* that possession — a central element of aboriginal title — is itself proof of ownership at common law (p. 375), but it would have been useful to have more exploration of the analogies between the derivation of aboriginal title and the modes of acquisition of property in Western legal systems. What, for example, are the merits of the suggested analogy in *R.* v. *Isaac* (1975) 13 NSR (2d) 460, 469 (NSSCAD) between aboriginal title and a profit à prendre? Hall J did say in *Calder*, p. 353, that the claimed aboriginal interest was not prescriptive in origin "because a prescriptive right presupposes a prior right in some other person or authority." While it is true that prescriptive rights normally arise in the context of prior rights of others, is not the element of long use a central ingredient of prescription?

A concept with more resemblance than most to the occupancy-based aboriginal title is the Roman law idea of *occupatio* or occupancy. In his work, *Ancient Law* (1917), Sir Henry Maine says (p. 144) that:

> Occupancy is the advisedly taking possession of that which at the moment is the property of no man, with the view (adds the technical definition) of acquiring property in it for yourself. The objects which Roman lawyers called *res nullius* — things which have not or have never had an owner — can only be ascertained by enumerating them. Among things which *never had* an owner are wild animals, fishes, wild fowl, jewels disinterred for the first time, and lands newly discovered or never before cultivated.

In the second place, although Hall J suggested in *Calder* that the conquest doctrine's principles respecting prior rights must also apply to British acquisition of territory by discovery or declaration, he did not say why this was so. As was seen in part (ii), *supra*, there is room for a re-examination of colonial case law along these lines.

Finally, *Calder* gave little express indication of the status of an occupancy-based title *vis-à-vis* otherwise competent legislation, although the implication of common law recognition would be common law status *vis-à-vis* statutes.

(iv) Some Post-Calder Canadian Decisions

Has the case law subsequent to *Calder* produced a general legal recognition of occupancy-based title in Canada? In the sample of post-*Calder* cases examined below, note whether or not a decision supporting this kind of aboriginal title has been reversed or qualified on appeal. Are there any unreversed or unqualified recognitions of occupancy-based title among the cases? If so, at what level and in what jurisdiction are they found? Do any of the cases say anything about the status of aboriginal rights in relation to legislation? Because of the doctrine of the sovereignty of Parliament, ordinary common law rights are subordinate to statutory provisions to the extent of a conflict. Are there indications here that the courts might be considering treating aboriginal rights like common law rights, at least in regard to their relationship with statutes?

In *R.* v. *Isaac* (1975), 13 NSR (2d) 460 (NSSCAD), an Indian on a reserve was convicted of possessing a rifle contrary to the Nova Scotia Lands and Forests Act. A four-judge Appeal Division of the Nova Scotia Supreme Court quashed the conviction. MacKeigan CJNS held that Indian hunting on an Indian reserve is a use of reserve land, and that provincial legislation purporting to regulate the use of reserve land is constitutionally invalid. To help support his proposition that hunting is a use of land rather than a merely personal act, MacKeigan CJNS undertook a discussion of aboriginal and reserve rights. MacKeigan CJNS placed considerable weight on his view that in *Calder*:

> Both Mr Justice Judson and Mr Justice Hall agreed that "Indian title" or rights flowed from basic principles authoritatively expressed by Chief Justice Marshall of the United States Supreme Court in *Johnson and Graham's Lessee* v. *McIntosh* . . . and *Worcester* v. *Georgia* . . ., and adopted by many other American, Canadian and English courts. (p. 475)

MacDonald JA agreed with MacKeigan CJNS. He said that:

> Prior to their conquest the Indians possessed this province. After conquest and with the expansion of the White immigrant population the position of the Indians was compromised and as a result of treaties and

governmental policy they were literally forced to live in and on certain designated tracts of lands which were called reserves.

This action resulted in the Indians being stripped of many of their rights, but the one right that was never taken away from them by treaty, or otherwise, was the right to hunt and fish on reserve land. (p. 498)

Cooper JA felt that hunting is a personal act, not a use of land. On the other hand, he found (p. 496) that the Indians on the reserve had a right to hunt "pursuant to the terms of the *Royal Proclamation*," which was itself "declaratory of the aboriginal rights of Indians" (p. 497). Coffin JA agreed with the Chief Justice on the constitutional question but expressed no opinion on aboriginal title.

Of the three decisions in *Isaac* which lend support to the notion of an occupancy-based aboriginal title, that of Cooper JA is perhaps the least unqualified. The Chief Justice was concerned primarily to show that hunting is a use of land. He noted that his discussion of aboriginal title was perhaps unnecessary to confirm this proposition. Although Cooper JA saw the Proclamation as declaratory of aboriginal rights, his discussion of these rights was limited to the observation that they included the right to hunt. Of a legal basis for these rights apart from the Proclamation, Cooper JA said nothing.

In *Re Paulette et al. and Registrar of Titles (No. 2)*, 42 DLR (3d) 8 (NWTSC), rev'd. in NWTCA and SCC, Morrow J of the Northwest Territories Supreme Court held that the Indian people of the western Northwest Territories had aboriginal rights over 400,000 square miles of the Northwest Territories. In Morrow J's opinion, the aboriginal rights derived from the fact that these Indian people were:

. . . present-day descendants of those distinct Indian groups who, organized in societies and using the land as their forefathers had done for centuries, [had] since time immemorial used the land [in question] as theirs. (p. 39)

Morrow J found support for this conclusion in the *Calder* case, saying (pp. 26-27) that:

In the *Calder* case it would appear that both Mr Justice Judson and Mr Justice Hall in writing the two opposing judgements agree that even without the Royal Proclamation of 1763 there can be such a legal concept as Indian title or aboriginal rights in Canadian law.

Morrow J felt that the occupancy-based title of the native people of this region might be reinforced at the constitutional level. The joint address from the Canadian federal houses of Parliament seeking the transfer of Rupert's Land and the North-Western Territory to Canada promised that:

. . . upon the transference of the territories in question to the Canadian Government, the claims of the Indian tribes to compensation for lands required for the purposes of settlement will be considered and settled in conformity with the equitable principles which have uniformly governed the British Crown in its dealings with the aborigines. [Address to Her Majesty the Queen from the Senate and House of Commons of the Dominion of Canada, 16 and 17 December 1867, reprinted in RSC 1970, Appendices, 8].

This address was incorporated into the Imperial Order in Council transferring the northern territories to Canada. By virtue of section 146 of the British North America Act, 1867, the joint address may have the same effect as if it were enacted pursuant to this act. Morrow J observed (p. 29) that:

> To the extent, therefore, that the above assurances represent a recognition of Indian title or aboriginal rights, it may be that the Indians living within that part of Canada covered by the proposed caveat may have a constitutional guarantee that no other Canadian Indians have.

Morrow J concluded that the aboriginal title of the Indian people in question constituted an interest in land that could be protected by a caveat under the Land Titles Act, RSC 1970, c. L-4.

In the decision of the Northwest Territories Court of Appeal, reported in (1976), 63 DLR (3d) 1, the majority avoided all discussion of the legal status and character of aboriginal title, and reversed Morrow J's decision on a technicality. To the majority, the provisions of the Land Titles Act did not permit the filing of a caveat against unpatented Crown land. Since the land in question here was unpatented, no caveat could be filed, no matter what the nature of aboriginal title.

In its decision reported in [1977] 2 SCR 628, the Supreme Court of Canada took a similar view, and upheld the majority decision of the Northwest Territories Court of Appeal. Laskin CJC said that:

> The course of proceedings . . . made it clear . . . that it was unnecessary to determine the character or extent of the asserted aboriginal rights but only whether the *Land Titles Act* permitted the lodging of a caveat where, *ex facie*, an interest in land was claimed thereunder. (p. 6)

In *Kanatewat et al.* v. *The James Bay Development Corporation and Attorney General (Quebec)*, [1974] RP 38 (CS), Indian and Inuit people affected by the James Bay Hydro development sought an interim injunction to prevent the James Bay Development Corporation from proceeding with work on the giant power project until a court decision was reached on their earlier application for a permanent injunction. They based their application on the claim that the development was prejudicing the hunting, trapping, fishing, and other rights derived from their aboriginal title to the land affected. Malouf J of the Quebec Superior court granted the interim injunction. He found in part (p. 76) that:

. . . at the very least the Cree Indians and Eskimo have been exercising personal and usufructuary rights over the territory and the lands adjacent thereto. They have been in possession and occupation of these lands and exercising fishing, hunting and trapping rights thereon from time immemorial [Translation].

In support of his finding that the Indians and Inuit of the region had occupancy-based rights that were cognizable at common law, Malouf J referred, *inter alia*, to two decisions (*R. v. Wesley*, [1932] 4 DLR 774 (ASCAD) and *R. v. Sikyea* (1964) 43 DLR (2d) 150 (NWTCA), aff'd. in [1964] SCR 642, at 646 (SCC)) which stressed that the Canadian government had traditionally treated Indians in areas excluded from the Royal Proclamation of 1763 as having rights comparable to those guaranteed to Indians under the Proclamation. Malouf J cited the decision of Hall J in *Calder* and noted (p. 75) that the decision of Judson J in *Calder*:

. . . did not say that the Nishgas tribe had never had title to the land, but simply that whatever title they had, was extinguished when the government decided to exercise its sovereign authority over the lands in question. [Translation]

To Malouf J, the occupancy-based aboriginal title in this region was reinforced by the Quebec Boundaries Extension Act of 1912. Like comparable Ontario legislation, section 2(c) of this Act made the extension of Quebec's boundaries conditional on the undertaking that:

. . . the Province of Quebec will recognize the rights of the Indian inhabitants in the territory above described to the same extent, and will obtain surrenders of such rights in the same manner, as the Government of Canada has heretofore recognized such rights and has obtained surrender thereof, and the said Province shall bear and satisfy all charges and expenditures in connection with or arising out of such surrenders.

In the view of Malouf J (p. 39):

This legislation clearly shows that the Province of Quebec agreed to recognize the rights of the Indian inhabitants in the territory described in the said Act to the same extent and in the same manner that the Government of Canada had prior thereto recognized such rights and obtained surrender thereof. [Translation]

The government of Canada, said Malouf J, had recognized Indian title across the country: otherwise, why were the Indian treaties negotiated?

A week later it had been issued by Malouf J, the interim injunction was suspended mainly on procedural grounds by the Quebec Court of Appeal, and the Quebec Court of Appeal's suspension decision was upheld in the Supreme

Court of Canada: QCA decision of 15 November 1973, unreported; SCC decision reported in (1974), 41 DLR (3d) 1 (SCC).

A year later, in [1975] CA 166, the Quebec Court of Appeal reversed the decision of Malouf J. The Quebec Court of Appeal felt that it was doubtful that there were any legally enforceable aboriginal rights in the region in question and that, in any event, such rights as might exist were too vague to justify the issuing of an interim injunction. Turgeon JA, with whom the other four judges expressed general agreement, said that it had been the traditional approach of the European nations not to recognize any aboriginal title. He said (p. 172) that:

> The case law [at the time of the granting of the Hudson's Bay Charter] shows that English public law [in regard to Aboriginal People] subjected indigenous people to English law and denied them any sovereignty. [Translation]

Turning to section 2(c) of the Quebec Boundaries Extension Act, 1912, Turgeon JA noted that there had been little consistency in the Canadian government's treaty and surrender policy before the passing of this Act: in some areas it had negotiated treaties and in other areas it had not. He said (p. 175) that the meaning of section 2(c) was less than clear:

> Was it simply a question of a moral and political obligation or was it a provision conferring some kind of right on the Indians of the territory ceded in 1912?

Because of his finding that any aboriginal rights which might have existed were extinguished, Turgeon JA found it unnecessary to decide finally on the question of the legal status of such rights, with or without the help of the 1912 Act. He made it clear, though, that he regarded the existence of any such rights as doubtful.

In *Kruger and Manuel* v. *The Queen,* a post-*Calder* case from British Columbia, two Indians were convicted of hunting deer contrary to the British Columbia Wildlife Act. The County Court judge discharged the conviction on the ground that Kruger and Manuel's aboriginal rights were protected by the Royal Proclamation, which prevailed over the provincial game legislation: (1975), 51 DLR (3d) 435. The British Columbia Court of Appeal reversed this decision, primarily on the ground that the Proclamation did not prevail over the wildlife statute: (1975), 60 DLR (3d) 144.

As it had done in the similar case of *R.* v. *Derriksan,* reported in (1977), 71 DLR (3d) 159, the Supreme Court of Canada upheld the conviction: (1977), 75 DLR (3d) 434. Once again, the highest court avoided making an explicit and definitive commitment as to the legal status and character of aboriginal title. The wildlife statute, said the Court, was constitutionally valid. That being so, the statute could restrict any pre-existing rights in the course of regulating wildlife management. As a result, the Court found it unnecessary to consider the questions of the nature of aboriginal title, whether it had been extinguished, and the effect of the Proclamation.

As it had in *Derriksan,* the Supreme Court of Canada treated aboriginal rights as subject to the general rule that governs the relationship between competent legislation and ordinary common law rights: the rule that in the event of a conflict, the legislation prevails. However, in neither decision did the Court explicitly accord legal status to the aboriginal rights themselves, or to the aboriginal title from which they are derived.

The cases considered above suggest that for the most part higher Canadian courts have failed to give clear legal recognition to an occupancy-based aboriginal title. The Supreme Court of Canada has subjected aboriginal rights to the same upper limit in relation to legislation as ordinary common law rights, but has not yet explicitly equated them with common law rights. Higher courts have shown an apparent preference for resolving issues on the basis of more procedural or technical issues, rather than undertaking a comprehensive examination of aboriginal title.

This approach may be more than merely accidental. Consider, for example, the following passage from the judgment of Dickson J in *Kruger and Manuel:*

> Before considering the two other grounds of appeal, I should say that the important constitutional issue as to the nature of aboriginal title, if any, in respect of lands in British Columbia, the further question as to whether it had been extinguished, and the force of the Royal Proclamation of 1763 — issues discussed in *Calder* v. *Attorney General of British Columbia* [1973] SCR 313 — will not be determined in the present appeal. They were not directly placed in issue by the appellants and a sound rule to follow is that questions of title should only be decided when title is directly in issue. Interested parties should be afforded an opportunity to adduce evidence in detail bearing upon the resolution of the particular dispute. Claims to aboriginal title are woven with history, legend, politics and moral obligations. If the claim of any Band in respect of any particular land is to be decided as a justiciable issue and not a political issue, it should be so considered on the facts pertinent to that Band and to that land, and not on any global basis. (pp. 108-09)

> (v) *Baker Lake* [*Hamlet of Baker Lake et al.* v. *Minister of Indian Affairs and Northern Development* (1980), 107 DLR (3d) 513 (FCTD)]. See also Parts 5(f)(iii) and 6(b), *infra*.

In the *Baker Lake* case, Mahoney J of the Federal Court of Canada, Trial Division, decided that the Inuit of the Baker Lake area of the Northwest Territories had an occupancy-based aboriginal title, cognizable at common law, to the Baker Lake area, although they acknowledged that the rights pursuant to this title could be validly abridged by competent legislation. Mahoney J's decision was not appealed.

How did Mahoney J arrive at his conclusion that the Inuit had a common law occupancy-based aboriginal title? The main elements of his reasoning on this point are contained in the following passages (pp. 522 and 542-44 footnotes omitted):

> The Baker Lake area lies within the former proprietary colony of Rupert's Land, the territory granted to the Hudson's Bay Company by Royal Charter of Charles II May 2, 1670. It is common ground that Rupert's Land was a settled colony, rather than a conquered or ceded colony. It is to be noted that the particular legal consequences of settlement, as distinct from conquest or cession, insofar as the domestic laws of a colony were concerned, was [sic] not articulated in a reported case until 1693. The distinction developed in response to the needs of the English settlers and was not, in its early development, extended to the resolution of disputes involving the indigenous population. I am bound to hold that *The Royal Proclamation* of 1763 does not and never did apply to Rupert's Land. (p. 532)
>
> While *The Royal Proclamation* of 1763, various statutes and almost all the decided cases refer to Indians and do not mention Inuit or Eskimos, the term "Indians", in Canadian constitutional law, includes the Inuit. In the absence of their exclusion from that term, either expressly or by compelling inference, decisions relevant to the aboriginal rights of Indians in Canada apply to Inuit. In light of the *Sigeareak* decision, *The Royal Proclamation* must be dismissed as a source of aboriginal title in Rupert's Land. However, the Proclamation is not the only source of aboriginal title in Canada.
>
> In *Calder* v. *Attorney General of British Columbia,* the six members of the Supreme Court who found it necessary to consider the substantive issues, which dealt with territory outside the geographic limits of the Proclamation, all held that an aboriginal title recognized at common law had existed. Judson J, with Martland and Ritchie JJ concurring, put it, (p. 328), as follows:
>
> Although I think it clear that Indian title in British Columbia cannot owe its origin to the Proclamation of 1763, the fact is that when the settlers came, the Indians were there, organized in *societies* and occupying the land as their forefathers had done for centuries. This is what Indian title means and it does not help one in the solution of this problem to call it a "personal or usufructuary right". What they are asserting in this action is that they had a right to continue to live on their lands as their forefathers had lived and that this right has never been lawfully extinguished. There can be no question that this right was "dependent on the goodwill of the Sovereign".
>
> The emphasis is mine. In the result, he held that "Indian title" to have been extinguished. The dissenting judgement, which held the

aboriginal title, with certain exceptions, not to have been extinguished, was delivered by Hall J, with Spence and Laskin JJ concurring. Pigeon J disposed of the matter exclusively on the procedural ground that the plaintiffs had not obtained the required fiat to sue the Crown in right of British Columbia, a conclusion concurred in by Judson, Martland and Ritchie JJ. While it appears that the judgment of Pigeon J embodies the *ratio decidendi* of the Supreme Court, the clear agreement of the other six judges on the point is solid authority for the general proposition that the law of Canada recognizes the existence of an aboriginal title independent of *The Royal Proclamation* or any other prerogative act or legislation. It arises at common law. Its recognition by the Supreme Court of Canada may well be based upon an acceptance of the reasoning of Chief Justice Marshall in *Worcester* v. *The State of Georgia*, a decision referred to in both their judgements by Judson and Hall JJ:

> America, separated from Europe by a wide ocean, was inhabited by a distinct people divided into separate nations, independent of each other and of the rest of the world, *having institutions of their own, and governing themselves by their own laws.* It is difficult to comprehend the proposition that the inhabitants of either quarter of the globe could have rightful original claims of dominion over the lands they occupied; or that the discovery of either by the other should give the discoverer rights in the country discovered which annulled the pre-existing rights of its ancient possessors.

The emphasis was included in the passage when it was quoted by Mr Justice Hall. (p. 383)

The decision of the Supreme Court of the Northern Territory of Australia in *Milirrpum* v. *Nabalco Pty. Ltd.* is most useful in its exhaustive compilation and analysis of pertinent authorities from numerous common law jurisdictions. It is, however, clear in that portion of the judgement dealing with Australian authorities, pages 242 to 252, that Blackburn J found himself bound to conclude that the doctrine of communal native title had never, from Australia's inception, formed part of its law. If I am correct in my appreciation of the authority of the *Calder* decision, that is not the law of Canada. The *Calder* decision renders untenable, insofar as Canada is concerned, the defendant's arguments that no aboriginal title exists in a settled, as distinguished from a conquered or ceded, colony and that there is no aboriginal title unless it has been recognized by statute or prerogative act of the Crown or by treaty having statutory effect. (pp. 542-44)

In many respects, *Baker Lake* can be seen as a logical extension of the judgment of Hall J in *Calder* and of the Supreme Court's decisions in *Derriksan* and *Kruger and Manuel*. Hall J held that aboriginal rights could be recognized independently of support from the Proclamation while *Derriksan* and *Kruger and Manuel* subjected aboriginal rights to the same upper limit *vis-à-vis* competent legislation as ordinary common law rights: *Baker Lake* has recognized aboriginal rights as a form of common law right.

Will *Baker Lake* lead the way to a general recognition at common law of occupancy-based aboriginal rights? As a matter of strict precedent, it could be argued that *Baker Lake* relies too heavily on the result in *Calder* for support for the notion of a common law, occupancy-based title. If in the passage from the reasons of Judson J cited above, Judson J may have been doing no more than saying (a) that Indian title in British Columbia cannot be based on the Proclamation and (b) that the Nishgas' claim was an occupancy-based title. If so, then *Calder* is neither "solid authority" for an occupancy-based title, nor does it render "untenable" settled/conquered colony distinction.

If occupancy-based aboriginal title is to achieve general common law recognition in the higher Canadian courts, the reasoning on which it is built will likely have to go beyond the inconclusive collective result in *Calder*. Similarly, it will have to do more than rely on the Royal Proclamation, on the joint address requesting a transfer of North-Western Territory and Ruperts' Land, on the Quebec Boundaries Extension Act, on the treaties or on other examples of government "recognition". Formal government recognition alone cannot create a doctrine cognizable at common law.

What may be required is a creative re-examination of the nature of the origin of aboriginal title in terms that the English property law system can cope with. If, as will be seen later, the English property system is flexible enough to accommodate the Roman law concept of usufruct in regard to the content of aboriginal title, it should be flexible enough to accommodate a notion similar to occupation in regard to its origin and status. What may also be needed is a re-examination of the direction of the early colonial law of Britain and the United States in regard to the special case of settlement of inhabited lands and the maintenance of the rights of their inhabitants.

(c) Legislation: The Constitution

There is no general legislation of the Parliament of Canada expressly recognizing or affirming aboriginal title. On the other hand, there are a great number of enactments which arguably are consistent with the existence of such a title. Among these are the Manitoba Act of 1870, the Dominion Lands Act from 1872 to 1908; and the Ontario and Quebec Boundaries Extensions Acts of 1912. (Other quasi-legislative or official government documents which, it may be contended, support such a title include Article 40 of the Articles of Capitulation of Quebec of 1760, the Royal Proclamation of 1763, the land cession treaties, and the documents initiating and implementing the transfer of Rupert's Land and the North-Western Territory into Canada in 1980.) All are discussed in P.A. Cumming and N.H. Mickenberg (eds.), *Native Rights in Canada*, 1972.

i) Sections 35 and 37(1) and (2) of the Constitution Act, 1982

    35. (1) The existing aboriginal and treaty rights of the aboriginal peoples of Canada are hereby recognized and affirmed.

    (2) In this act, "aboriginal peoples of Canada" includes the Indian, Inuit and Metis peoples of Canada.

    37. (1) A constitutional conference composed of the Prime Minister of Canada and the first ministers of the provinces shall be convened by the Prime Minister of Canada within one year after this part comes into force.

    (2) The conference convened under Subsection (1) shall have included in its agenda an item respecting constitutional matters that directly affect the aboriginal peoples of Canada, including the identification and definition of the rights of those peoples to be included in the Constitution of Canada, and the Prime Minister of Canada shall invite representatives of those peoples to participate in the discussions on that item.

These provisions, and the constitutional framework in which they are set, invite a multitude of questions. Only a few will be noted here.

If the conference contemplated in section 37 does result in a definition of aboriginal rights, will the definition be added to the Constitution Act by means of constitutional amendment? If the conference fails to produce a definition, will not this responsibility revert to the courts of law? If so, how will the courts construe the meaning of section 35?

To what aboriginal rights will they apply the section: Proclamation-based rights or occupancy-based rights? Will they apply it to aboriginal rights or occupancy-based rights? Will they apply it to aboriginal rights in regions "acquired" by European colonists, regardless of whether these were conquered or settled? What is the significance of the inclusion of the word "Metis" in section 35(2)? What aspect of section 35 (if any) will be given super-legislative status in the event of a conflict between the section and ordinary legislation? Will the aboriginal rights themselves prevail over legislation in the event of a conflict, or is it only their recognition and affirmation which cannot be removed by ordinary statute? Does the affirmation of aboriginal rights give them a stronger constitutional foundation than a mere recognition would have done?

What is the effect of the word "existing"? Does the constitutional recognition and affirmation of "existing" aboriginal rights elevate these rights to super-legislative status while preserving their "existing" scope (i.e., hunting, fishing, trapping, and so on) intact, or does it preserve their existing status *vis-à-vis* legislation as well? If the latter is correct, then what *is* the existing status of aboriginal rights? Are they to be considered as common law rights, as *Baker Lake* would suggest? Or is their status at common law to be regarded as dubious, as the Quebec Court of Appeal suggested in *Kanatewat*? Does section 35 preserve the "existing" scope of aboriginal rights, while elevating the status of these rights to the common law level, for all jurisdictions in which common law status had not yet been attained? Does the provision freeze the status of aboriginal rights in each region according to the last judicial pronouncement relevant to that jurisdiction before the section came into force? Does it freeze the scope of aboriginal rights in each jurisdiction according to the degree these rights were abridged by competent legislation in effect at the time the section came into force? Does section 35 preclude future judicial findings that aboriginal rights exist in regions where they have not been found previously? Alternatively, are future findings of this kind possible on the ground that aboriginal rights declared at some future date to exist would have practically always been "existing" rights at the time section 35 came into force?

If section 35 gives aboriginal rights more than common law status, so that they are immune to statutory change, is a constitutional amendment required to give effect to all aboriginal land claims settlements concluded after section 35 comes into force? Does section 35 subordinate all future federal and provincial legislation to aboriginal rights in the event of a conflict? What is the status of existing federal and provincial legislation which conflicts with aboriginal rights?

Finally, what impact will section 35 have on the general pattern of judicial interpretation of aboriginal rights? If the status of aboriginal rights is regarded as having been elevated substantially by virtue of the section, will this encourage a more restrictive judicial approach to their scope? Or will the fact of constitutional recognition and affirmation serve as the springboard for broad judicial interpretaitons of all aspects of aboriginal title?

5. Content of Aboriginal Title

Assuming the existence of an occupancy-based aboriginal title, what is its content? In exploring this question, it is useful to bear in mind a number of preliminary considerations.

First, the content and extent of an interest in property can be measured in many different ways. It can be measured in terms of the degree to which the land in question can be used and enjoyed; the duration of the interest (i.e., for a fixed period of years or for an indefinite period); the restrictions, if any, on the capacity of the owner of the interest to alienate it to another; and the restrictions, if any, on those eligible to inherit the interest.

In English common law, the largest recognized private property interest is the fee simple absolute. Subject to any legislative restrictions or reservations from the original grant, the fee simple absolute gives the owner an unlimited right of use and enjoyment of his land. The interest lasts for an indefinite period, rather than the fixed term of years of a lease. There are no restrictions on the owner's capacity to alienate a fee simple absolute interest. Nor are there any restrictions on who may inherit this kind of interest. Another way of describing a property interest is to determine whether it is individually or communally owned. Practically all ordinary English property interests are individually owned; as will be seen, the same is not true of aboriginal interests.

A property interest can also be described in terms of its relationship to the title of the Crown in the land in question. In English property law, for example, the Crown has the ultimate ownership of all land, although this is a relatively nominal ownership in cases where an extensive private interest has been granted in the land in question.

Second, in the modern case law, Canadian courts have not differentiated between Proclamation-based interests and occupancy-based interests in describing the content of aboriginal title. In the *St Catharine's Milling* case, for example, Lord Watson purported to concern himself only with the Royal Proclamation. He said that the terms of that instrument show that:

> . . . the tenure of the Indians was a personal and usufructuary right, dependent upon the good will of the Sovereign. (p. 54)

These words have been quoted or paraphrased in decisions describing both Proclamation-based rights and Indian title not based on the Proclamation: see, for example, the passages referred to in the following citations: [1903] AC 73, 79 (JCPC); [1921] AC 401, 410-11 (JCPC); (1959) 28 WWR 379, 385 (NWTTC); [1973] SCR 313, 380 (SCC); and [1974] RP 38, 70 (QSC).

Third, there are a variety of opinions as to just how precisely defined the content of aboriginal title is. On the one hand, Morrow J said in *Re Paulette* that ''I conclude that there are certain well-established charactersitics of Indian legal title if the Indians or aborigines were in occupation of the land prior to colonial entry'' (p. 27). On the other hand, Turgeon JA took a less sanguine view of the clarity of the content of the title in the *Kanatewat* case:

> Indian title, if it exists, has never been clearly defined. There are many theories on the subject, based on hypotheses and doctrines which vary according to their authors. Some maintain that it yields only a right to hunt and fish. Others see it as a vague right of occupation, and even as a personal usufructuary right. . . . (p. 175: translation).

(a) Degree of Enjoyment

In almost all cases, aboriginal title appears to involve a right of occupancy of the land over which the title was claimed. Describing the right claimed by the Nishgas people in the *Calder* case, Judson J said: ''What they were asserting in this section is that they had a right to continue to live on their lands as their forefathers had lived. . . .'' (p. 328).

What is usually less clear is how much *more* than occupancy can be supported by aboriginal title. In the statement quoted earlier, Lord Watson described the Indian interest concerned in the *St Catharine's* case as a "usufructuary" right. In *Native Rights in Canada,* P.A. Cumming and N.H. Mickenberg noted that "usufruct" is a term of Roman law origin, little known in the common law. They continued:

> The usufruct developed as a form of trust, often created by will. It has been defined as a "right of enjoying a thing, the property of which is vested in another, and to draw from the same all the profit, ultility, and advantage which it may produce, provided it be without altering the substance of the thing." The usufruct was a personal and inalienable right which terminated upon the death of its holder. (p. 40)

Cumming and Mickenberg pointed out that the description above does not coincide in several respects with the aboriginal title of Indian tribes. They concluded that "it is apparent that the term has been applied by the court as a guide or analogy rather than by a strict definition" [p. 40]. If this is so, "usufructuary" probably means little more than "use" and the questions "what kind of use?"; "how extensive a use?" still remain to be answered [see also Part 5(g)(i), *infra*].

As well as occupancy, aboriginal title has been regarded as including a right to hunt, fish, and carry on related subsistence activities. The Royal Proclamation itself reserved the tract of land for the Indians "as their Hunting Grounds."

In a judgment affirmed by the Supreme Court of Canada (in [1964] SCR 642), Johnson JA said in *R.* v. *Sikyea* (1964), 43 DLR (2d) 150 (NWTCA) that:

> The right of Indians to hunt and fish for food on unoccupied Crown lands has always been recognized in Canada — in the early days as an incident of their 'ownership' of the land, and later by the treaties by which the Indians gave up their ownership right in these lands [p. 152].

See also *R.* v. *Isaac* (1975) 13 NSR (2d) 460, 478 (NSSCAD)

Hall J took a somewhat broader view of the content of aboriginal title in *Calder*, describing it as:

> . . . a usufructuary right and a right to occupy the lands and to enjoy the fruits of the soil, the forest and of the rivers and streams. . . . (p. 352)

A third possible view is that aboriginal rights are no more and no less than a reflection of the traditional use of the land which gave rise to them in the first place. Because in most cases aboriginal peoples traditionally carried on hunting, fishing and trapping, this is reflected in their aboriginal rights. This would not preclude the content of the aboriginal rights from differing with the usual content where the traditional use of the land was different. In support of this view, an analogy might be drawn with use-derived rights in English property law. Here, for example, continuous passage over a portion of the property of another may result in an acquired right of passage over that portion, but not in some greater right, or in some other right unrelated to the original action. (See P.V. Baker (ed.), *Megarry's Manual of the Law of Real Property*, 5th ed., 1975, p. 421, discussing rights of way, a species of easement.)

(b) Duration

When Lord Watson described the Indian interest in the *St Catharine's* case as a "personal" right, it might have been thought that what was meant was a right which terminated with the death of the holder of the right. However, in the *Star Chrome* case of 1921, the Privy Council defined "personal" as meaning "inalienable except by surrender to the Crown": *Attorney General (Quebec)* v. *Attorney General (Canada)*, [1921] AC 401, 410-11 (JCPC). No other case has prescribed any fixed period for aboriginal title; its duration would therefore appear to be indefinite.

On the other hand, the Indian interest in the *St Catharine's* case is described as existing "for the present," and as being "dependent on the good will of the Sovereign." Presumably, it can be revoked at any time by the Crown: see part 5(g)(i), *infra*.

(c) Alienation

(i) *St Catharine's Case* [*St Catharine's Milling and Lumber Company* v. *The Queen* (1889) 14 App. Cas. 46 (JCPC)]. See also part 4(b)(i), *supra*, and part 5(g)(i), *infra*.

The Royal Proclamation of 1763 stipulated that land reserved for Indians within colonies could be alienated only to the Crown, by a Crown representative, after a public meeting with the Indians for that purpose. For the area outside the colonies and proprietary governments, most of which constituted the tract of land reserved for the Indians "as their Hunting Grounds," cession to or purchase by the Crown was made practically the only way in which the Indian interest could be alienated.

In the *St Catharine's* case, Lord Watson commenced the main portion of his reasons for judgment with a brief general description of the Royal Proclamation, noting, *inter alia*, that the Indian "reserve" lands protected and set apart there could be alienated only to the Crown. Turning to the land in question in the *St Catharine's* case, Lord Watson referred again (p. 54) to the restriction on alienation:

The territory in dispute has been in Indian occupation from the date of the proclamation until 1873. During that interval of time Indian affairs have been administered successively by the Crown, by the Provincial Governments, and (since the passing of the British North America Act, 1867), by the Government of the Dominion. The policy of these administrations has been all along the same in this respect, that the Indian inhabitants have been precluded from entering into any transaction with a subject for the sale or transfer of their interest in the land, and have only been permitted to surrender their rights to the Crown by a formal contract, duly ratified in a meeting of their chiefs or head men convened for the purpose. Whilst there have been changes in the administrative authority, there has been no change since the year 1763 in the character of the interest which its Indian inhabitants had in the lands surrendered by the treaty. Their possession, such as it was, can only be ascribed to the general provisions made by the royal proclamation in favour of all Indian tribes then living under the sovereignty and protection of the British Crown.

Evidently, the Judicial Committee saw the restriction permitting alienation of Proclamation-based Indian title only to the Crown as a key characteristic of this form of title. As will be seen in Part 5(g)(i), *infra*, it was one of the features which distinguished the Indian interest in this case from a full fee simple interest.

Since the *St Catharine's* case, there has been no doubt that Proclamation-based interests can be alienated only to the Crown. As was indicated in Part (b) above, the Privy Council explained in the 1921 *Star Chrome* case that this restriction on alienation was what was meant when the Indian right was described as a "personal" right.

There seems little question that this restriction on alienation would also apply to occupancy-based title. Marshall CJ saw it as a restriction on the occupancy-based title in *Johnson* v. *McIntosh* (and as a qualification on the full operation of the conquest doctrine presumption in favour of existing rights). Moreover, there is a general tendency in Canadian case law to assimilate the features of occupancy-based title to Proclamation-based title: see, for example, *R.* v. *Wesley*, [1932] 4 DLR 774 (ASCAD); (1964), 43 DLR (2d) 150, 152 (NWTCA); and the judgment of Hall J in *Calder* v. *AG (BC)*, [1973] SCR 313 (SCC).

Since the aboriginal title can be alienated only to the Crown (when it then ceases to be aboriginal title, and becomes an interest of the Crown), it follows that occupancy-based aboriginal title can be possessed or owned only by the aboriginal people from whom it originated: the ancestors of those Indian or Inuit people who had occupied the region in question from time immemorial. Both the restriction on alienation of aboriginal title and this consequence of the restriction distinguish aboriginal title from the fee simple interest, which can be alienated to any person and owned by any person.

(d) Inheritance

Just as aboriginal title cannot be alienated to individuals who lack aboriginal ancestry, so too these individuals cannot inherit aboriginal title. This restriction also distinguishes aboriginal title from the fee simple interest, which has no inherent restrictions on those eligible to inherit it.

(e) Individual or Communal Ownership

i) *Amodu Tijani [Amodu Tijani* v. *Secretary, Southern Nigeria,* [1921] 2 AC 399, 403-4 (JCPC)].

The title, such as it is, may not be that of the individual, as in this country [Britain] it nearly always is in some form. The title, such as it is, may not be that of the individual, but may be that of a community. Such a community may have the possessory title to the common enjoyment of a usufruct, with customs under which its individual members are admitted to enjoyment. . . .

ii) J. Cruikshank, *Through the Eyes of Strangers: A Preliminary Survey of Land Use History in the Yukon During the Late Nineteenth Century,* 1974.

In general terms . . . the land was owned not by individuals but by collective groups related by ties of kinship. These were not territorial groups but lineage-based moieties (Crow, Wolf, and their various clans) at least in the southern Yukon.

The passage from *Amodu Tijani* was quoted by Hall J in the *Calder* case [p. 355]. In *Re Paulette*, Morrow J characterized the aboriginal title as a communal right (p. 27).

(f) Proof

The matter of proof of aboriginal title involves three main and interrelated questions: (a) how, in technical terms, is aboriginal title to be ascertained?; (b) is evidence of anything more than mere occupancy required, and if so, that?; and (c) how strict should standards of proof be? As well, there are numerous difficult "sub-questions". For example, how far back must the evidence of traditional occupancy, and so forth extend — to the advent of the arrival of the Europeans or further back in time? Would a temporary departure from the region in question break the continuity of the claim? Must the occupancy or other use of the traditional region have been exclusive of all other traditional societies? Conversely, are joint aboriginal titles between two or more different traditional societies possible? How should a court deal with a "nomadic" claim to aboriginal title in which an aboriginal society can show continuous occupancy and other use of a succession of different regions?

(i) *Milirrpum [Milirrpum et al.* v. *Nabalco Pty. Ltd. and Common-*

wealth of Australia, [1971] 17 FLR 141 (Northern Territory Supreme Court)]. See also Part 5(g)(iii), *infra*.

In his decision in the *Milirrpum* case, Blackburn J of the Supreme Court of the Northern Territory found that the claimants had occupied the land claimed at least from the time of the advent of the Europeans, and that the traditional aboriginal community had been governed by a system of law. On the other hand, Blackburn J was unable to find that the clans themselves were sufficiently closely associated with specific parts of the land claimed, or that the relationship of the clans to the land could be described as proprietary. The *Milirrpum* case provides an instructive example of many of the practical and legal problems of proof that can arise in conjunction with aboriginal title claims.

ii) *Calder* [*Calder et al.* v. *Attorney General of British Columbia,* [1973] SCR 313 (SCC)]. See also part 4(b)(iii), *supra,* and parts 5(g)(iv), 6(a) and 7(a), *infra*.

Although Judson J did not expressly accord legal status to occupancy-based title in *Calder*, the following passage from his judgment is suggestive of the elements of proof which may have been significant to him had he done so [1973] SCR 513 372:

> Although I think it is clear that Indian title in British Columbia cannot owe its origin to the Proclamation of 1763, the fact is that when the settlers came, the Indians were there, organized in societies and occupying the land as their forefathers had done for centuries.

In the same decision, Hall J characterized a line of questions by the trial judge attempting to relate the evidence of Nishga concepts of ownership of real property as "interesting and apt", but concluded (p. 372) that "the trial judge's consideration of the real issue was inhibited by a preoccupation with the traditional *indicia* of ownership." Hall J continued (p. 375):

> In enumerating the *indicia* of ownership the trial judge overlooked that possession is of itself proof of ownership. *Prima facie*, therefore, the Nishgas are the owners of the lands that have been in their possession from time immemorial. . . .
>
> What emerges from the foregoing evidence is the following: the Nishgas in fact are and were from time immemorial a distinctive cultural entity with concepts of ownership indigenous to their culture and capable of articulation under the common law. . . .

iii) *Baker Lake* [*Hamlet of Baker Lake et al.* v. *Minister of Indian Affairs and Northern Development et al.* (1980), 107 DLR (3d) 513 (FCTD)]. See also Part 4(b)(v), *supra*, and Part 6(b), *infra*.

One of the most recent and comprehensive discussions of the requirements of proof of aboriginal title is contained in the judgment of Mahoney J in the *Baker Lake* case, (pp. 542-45):

> The elements which the plaintiffs must prove to establish an aboriginal title cognizable at common law are:
>
> 1. That they and their ancestors were members of an organized society.
> 2. That the organized society occupied the specific territory over which they asserted the aboriginal title.
> 3. That the occupation was to the exclusion of other organized societies.
> 4. That the occupation was an established fact at the time sovereignty was asserted by England.

Decisions supporting these propositions include those of the Supreme Court of Canada in *Kruger and Manuel* v. *The Queen* (1977), 75 DLR (3d) 434, 34 CCC (2d) 377, [1978] SCR 104, and the *Calder* case and those of the United States Supreme Court in *Johnson and Graham's Lessee* v. *McIntosh* (1823), 8 Wheaton 543, 21 US 240, 5 LEd 681; *Worcester* v. *Georgia, supra;* and *United States* v. *Santa Fe Pacific R. Co.* (1941), 314 US 339, 62 Sct 248, 86 LEd 260.

Proof that the plaintiffs and their ancestors were members of an organized society is required by the authorities. In quoting Mr Justice Judson's *Calder* judgement, I emphasized the phrase "organized in societies" and I repeated the emphasis Mr Justice Hall had included in quoting the passage from *Worcester* v. *Georgia*: "having institutions of their own, and governing themselves by their own laws." The *rationale* of the requirement is to be found in the following *dicta* of the Privy Council in *Re Southern Rhodesia,* [1919] AC 211 (pp. 233-34):

> The estimation of the rights of aboriginal tribes is always inherently difficult. Some tribes are so low in the scale of social organization that their usages and conceptions of rights and duties are not to be reconciled with the institutions or the legal ideas of civilized society. Such a gulf cannot be bridged. It would be idle to impute to such people some shadow of the rights known to our law and then to transmute it into the substance of transferable rights of property as we know them. In the present case it would make each and every person by a fictional inheritance a landed proprietor "richer than all his tribe." On the other hand, there are indigenous peoples whose legal conceptions, though differently developed, are hardly less precise than our own. When once they have been studied and understood they are no less enforceable than rights arising under English law. Between the two there is a wide tract of much ethnological interest, but the position of the natives of Southern Rhodesia within it is very uncertain; clearly they approximate rather to the lower than to the higher limit.

Their Lordships did not find it necessary to pursue the question further since they found that the aboriginal rights, if any, that might once have existed had been expressly extinguished by the Crown.

It is apparent that the relative sophistication of the organization of any society will be a function of the needs of its members, the demands they make of it. While the existence of an organized society is a prerequisite to the existence of an aboriginal title, there appears no valid reason to demand proof of the existence of a society more elaborately structured than is necessary to demonstrate that there existed among the aborigines a recognition of the claimed rights, sufficiently defined to permit their recognition by the common law upon its advent in the territory. The thrust of all the authorities is not that the common law necessarily deprives aborigines of their enjoyment of the land in any particular but, rather, that it can give effect only to those incidents of that enjoyment that were, themselves, given effect by the regime that prevailed before: *Amodu Tijani* v. *Secretary, Southern Nigeria,* [1921] 2 AC 399.

The fact is that the aboriginal Inuit had an organized society. It was not a society with very elaborate institutions but it was a society organized to exploit the resources available on the barrens and essential to sustain human life there. That was about all they could do: hunt and fish and survive. The aboriginal title asserted here encompasses only the right to hunt and fish as their ancestors did.

The organized society of the Caribou Eskimos, such as it was, and it was sufficient to serve them, did not change significantly from well before England's assertion of sovereignty over the barren lands until their settlement. For the most part, the ancestors of the individual plaintiffs were members of that society; many of them were members of it themselves. That their society has materially changed in recent years is of no relevance.

The specificity of the territory over which aboriginal title has heretofor been claimed in the reported cases appears not to have been a disputed issue of fact. In the *Calder* case, *supra*, the subject territory was agreed between the parties. In the *Kruger* case, the Court did not find it necessary to deal with the questions of aboriginal title and extinguishment and disposed of the appeal on other grounds to which I will return. It did, however, give a clear signal as to what its approach would be in the future. Mr Justice Dickson, for the Court, (p. 437) DLR, (p. 109) SCR said:

Claims to aboriginal title are woven with history, legend, politics and moral obligations. If the claim of any Band in respect of any particular land is to be decided as a justiciable issue and not a political issue, it should be so considered on the facts pertinent to that Band and to that land, and not on any global basis.

There were obviously great differences between the aboriginal societies of the Indians and the Inuit and decisions expressed in the context of Indian societies must be applied to the Inuit with those differences in mind. The absence of political structures like tribes was an inevitable consequence of the *modus vivendi* dictated by the Inuit's physical environment. Similarly the Inuit appear to have occupied the barren lands without competition except in the vicinity of the tree line. That, too, was a function of their physical environment. The pressures of other peoples, except from the fringes of the boreal forest, were non-existent and, thus, the Inuit were not confined in their occupation of the barrens in the same way Indian tribes may have confined in their occupation of the barrens in the same way Indian tribes may have confined each other elsewhere on the continent. Furthermore, the exigencies of survival dictated the sparse, but wide-ranging, nature of their occupation.

In *Mitchell* v. *United States* (1835), 9 Peters 711 (p. 746), Mr Justice Baldwin, delivering the opinion of the Court, said:

Indian possession or occupation was considered with reference to their habits and modes of life; their hunting-grounds were as much in their actual possession as the cleared fields of the Whites; and their rights to its exclusive enjoyment in their own way and for their own purposes were as much respected, until they abandoned them, made a cession to the government, or an authorized sale to individuals. . . .

The merits of this case do not make it necessary to inquire whether the Indians within the United States had any other rights of soil or jurisdiction; it is enough to consider it as a settled principle that their right of occupancy is considered as sacred as the fee-simple of the Whites.

The value of early American decisions to a determination of the common law of Canada as it pertains to aboriginal rights is so well established in Canadian courts, at all levels, as not now to require rationalization. With respect, the American decisions seem considerably more apposite than those Privy Council authorities which deal with aboriginal societies in Africa and Asia at the upper end of the scale suggested in *Re Southern Rhodesia, supra*. American decisions as to the existence of aboriginal title, rendered since creation of the Indian Claims Commission (Public Law 79-959, August 13, 1946), must be approached with considerable caution. The Commission, whose decisions are the subject of most recent American jurisprudence, is authorized, *inter alia*, to determine "claims based upon fair and honorable dealings that are not recognized by any rule of law or equity", a jurisdiction well beyond any Parliament has yet delegated to any Canadian tribunal.

The nature, extent or degree of the aborigines' physical presence on the land they occupied, required by the law as an essential element of their aboriginal title, is to be determined in each case by a subjective test. To the extent human beings were capable of surviving on the barren lands, the Inuit were there; to the extent the barrens lent themselves to human occupation, the Inuit occupied them.

The occupation of the territory must have been to the exclusion of other organized societies. In the *Sante Fe* case, *supra*, (p. 345), Mr Justice Douglas, giving the opinion of the court, held:

> Occupancy necessary to establish aboriginal possession is a question of fact to be determined as any other question of fact. If it were established as a fact that the lands in question were, or were included in, the ancestral home of the Walapais in the sense that they constituted definable territory occupied exclusively by the Walapais (as distinguished from lands wandered over by many tibes), then the Walapais had "Indian title" which, unless extinguished, survived the railroad grant of 1866.

Mahoney J concluded that, "on a balance of probabilities on the evidence before me," the Inuit were the exclusive occupants of all the region claimed except the southwesterly portion, which had been occupied by Chipewyan Indians in the early historic period (pp. 546-47).

(g) Relationship with Crown Interest in Land

i) *St Catharine's Case* [*St Catherine's Milling and Lumber Company* v. *The Queen* (1888) 14 App. Cas. 46 (JCPC)]. See also Part 4(b)(i) and Part 5(c)(i), *supra*.

The *St Catharine's* case touched on three important questions respecting the relationship between aboriginal title and the Crown's interest in land. Although the *St Catharine's* decision assumed that the basis of the title was the Proclamation, Canadian courts have tended subsequently to take a similar general approach in regard to occupancy-based title.

First, was the Indian title subject to the ultimate ownership of the Crown? In the opinion of the Judicial Committee, it was. In their view, "there has been all along vested in the Crown a substantial and paramount estate, underlying the Indian title. . . ." (p. 55). What was the basis of this ultimate ownership? The Judicial Committee did not find it necessary to advert to a doctrine of settlement, conquest or discovery (see part 4(b)(ii), *supra* and Chapter Two, *supra*). They noted simply that by its terms the Royal Proclamation extended to all Indian tribes who then lived "under the sovereignty and protection of the British Crown" (p. 54) and that the Indians' rights were reserved in that document "under his [the Sovereign's] protection and dominion" (p. 55: "dominium" appears to be used in the sense of "sovereignty" rather than "ownership" in this particular phrase).

Second, since the Indian title was subject to the ultimate dominium of the Crown, did the Crown possess any special privileges in regard to the Indian title? The Crown's exclusive right to purchase the Indian title has been considered above (in Part 5(c)(i), *supra*). Another Proclamation-based Crown right implied in the *St Catharine's* decision was the Crown's right to terminate the Indian title at will. Lord Watson said (pp. 54-55) that:

> . . . the tenure of the Indians was a personal and usufructuary right, dependent upon the good will of the Sovereign . . . it is declared [in the Proclamation] to be the will and pleasure of the sovereign that 'for for the present' they [the "reserve" lands] shall be reserved for the use of the Indians.

Third, how did the Indian title and the Crown interest in land subject to this title coexist? For an indication of the Judicial Committee's approach to this question, it is useful to consider two longer extracts, which include some of the passages quoted above. After stressing the fact that the Indian title could be alienated only to the Crown (p. 54; see Part 5(c)(i), *supra*), Lord Watson continued (p. 54-55):

> It was suggested in the course of the argument for the Dominion, that inasmuch as the proclamation recites that the territories thereby reserved for Indians had never "been ceded to or purchased by" the Crown, the entire property of the land remained with them. That inference is, however, at variance with the terms of the instrument, which show that the tenure of the Indians was a personal and usufructuary right, dependent upon the good will of the Sovereign. The lands reserved are expressly stated to be "parts of Our dominions and territories"; and it is declared to be the will and pleasure of the sovereign that, "for the present," they shall be reserved for the use of the Indians, as their hunting grounds, under his protection and dominion. There was a great deal of learned discussion at the Bar with respect to the precise quality of the Indian right, but their Lordships do not consider it necessary to express any opinion upon the point. It appears to them to be sufficient for the purposes of this case that there has been all along vested in the Crown a substantial and paramount estate, underlying the Indian title, which became a plenum dominium whenever that title was surrendered or otherwise extinguished.

At p. 58, Lord Watson said that:

> Had its Indian inhabitants been the owners in fee simple of the territory which they surrendered by the treaty of 1873, *Attorney General of Ontario* v. *Mercer* might have been an authority for holding that the Province of Ontario could derive no benefit from the cession, in respect that the land was not vested in the Crown at the time of the union. But

that was not the character of the Indian interest. The Crown has all along had a present proprietary estate in the land, upon which the Indian title was a mere burden. The ceded territory was at the time of the union, land vested in the Crown, subject to "an interest other than that of the Province in the same," within the meaning of section 109; and must now belong to Ontario in terms of that clause, unless its rights have been taken away by some provision of the Act of 1867 other than those already noticed [footnote omitted].

In Lord Watson's view, the Indian title was less than a full fee simple interest because it contained restrictions not found in the full fee simple interest. While the fee simple interest is fully alienable, the Indian title could be alienated only to the Crown. While the fee simple interest cannot be unilaterally revoked by the Crown, the Indian title could. While the fee simple interest is freely inheritable, the Indian title could pass only to other Indians.

Because the Indian interest was less extensive than a full fee simple (or possibly because it was less extensive than a freehold interest in land — the Judicial Committee did not articulate the precise criterion used*), the land subject to it could not be regarded as "private" land. It remained Crown land, subject to a private interest — the Indian title.

Since the land was Crown land, it was subject to the provisions of the British North American Act, 1867, which distributed Crown land of the Province of Canada to the Canadian provinces created in 1867. These provinces were given ownership of this land, subject to any private or other non-provincial interest in it.

In the *St Catharine's* case, the Indian people had surrendered their interest in the Crown land to the Crown in 1873. As a result, when the federal government purported to grant a timber licence on the land ten years later, they were granting an interest they did not have. As a result of the 1873 surrender, the land had reverted to the province of Ontario [technically, to the Crown in right of Ontario] in much the same way that a tenant's lease reverts to the landlord on its expiry.

Although the reasoning above was sufficient to enable the Judicial Committee to dispose of the case, it is unfortunate that they did not attempt a more precise description of the character of the Indian title and its relation to

---

* Lord Watson did not make it clear whether he regarded the boundary between private and public land as lying between fee simple interests and all lesser interests, respectively, or at some other point. In the latter case, the boundary would probably lie between freehold interests on one hand and interests less than freeholds on the other, since leaseholds have never been regarded as ending the public or Crown status of the lands on which they have been granted. In the former case, the restrictions on the alienability and inheritance and the ability of the Crown to revoke the title would all be relevant to the conclusion in *St Catharine's* that the land was Crown land in 1867. In the latter case, only Crown revocability would be relevant to this condition.

the interest of the Crown and third parties. For example, is the Proclamation-based Indian title enforceable against the Crown and third parties claiming an interest by virtue of a Crown grant? It has been pointed out that in a subsequent decision Lord Watson said that the word "interest" in section 109 of the British North America Act, 1867 connoted an interest "capable of being vindicated in competition with the beneficial interest of the old province": G.S. Lester, *The Territorial Rights of the Inuit of the Canadian Northwest Territories: A Legal Argument,* 1981, pp. 83-84, referring to *AG (Canada)* v. *AG (Ontario),* 1897 AC 199, 210-11 (JCPC). In the *St Catharine's* case itself, though, where the nature of the Indian title is being directly addressed, the Indian title is said to depend on the good will of the Sovereign. Could an interest dependent on the good will of another be enforced against the other, without the other's consent?

It is at least arguable, though, that the Indian interest in the *St Catharine's* case may have a proprietary character *vis-à-vis* interests other than that of the Crown or those derived from the Crown. In the absence of legislation to the contrary, for example, it might support a trespass action against third parties other than the Crown or those claiming under the Crown. Although the Judicial Committee described the Indian interest as "personal", a later decision makes it clear that this term is to be taken to mean "alienable only to the Crown" (and "non-proprietary"): *AG (Quebec)* v. *AG (Canada),* [1921] AC 401, 410-11 (JCPC); see part 5(b) *supra.* In the *St Catharine's* case, the Judicial Committee said that the Indian interest fell within section 109 of the British North America Act. This provision contemplates only interests in land. The Judicial Committee also described the Indian interest as "usufructuary". Roman law put the holder of a usufruct in a stronger position than the holder of an ordinary common law licence. It afforded the usufruct holder certain protections against third parties by means of possessory interdict: see G.A. Grove and J.F. Garner, *Hargreaves on Land Law*, 4th ed., 1963, p. 44). (Note, though, that the recent *Baker Lake* decision referred to at the end of part 5(g)(iv), below, would apparently deny the Indian interest any proprietary character.)

(ii) *R.* v. *Symonds* (1847) NZPCC 387 (NZSC).

As will be seen, both Judson and Hall JJ in *Calder* have used the *St Catharine's* decision as a starting point for their respective analyses of the relationship between aboriginal title and the Crown's interest in land which is subject to this title. First, however, it is interesting to look at some comments in a New Zealand decision which suggest quite a different relationship from that outlined by the Privy Council in the *St Catharine's* case.

In *R.* v. *Symonds*, a Mr McIntosh obtained a certificate from the Governor of New Zealand purporting to waive the Crown's exclusive right of acquiring Maori land. McIntosh then purchased some of this land from the Maoris. Later the Crown granted some of the same land to a Mr Symonds. McIntosh sought to have the grant to Symonds set aside. The New Zealand Supreme Court held that the Governor's certificate was ineffective as a waiver because it was unauthorized (per Martin CJ) and because it was not in the correct form for conveying a Crown interest (per Chapman J and Martin CJ). In the course of his decision, Chapman J said (p. 390) that:

> The practice of extinguishing Native titles by fair purchases is certainly more than two centuries old. It has long been adopted by our government in our American colonies, and by that of the United States. It is now part of the law of the land, and although the Courts of the United States, in suits between their own subjects, will not allow a grant to be impeached under pretext that the Native title has not been extinguished, yet they would not hesitate to do so in a suit by one of the Native Indians. . . . Whatever may be the opinion as to the strength or weakness of the Native title . . . it cannot be too solemnly asserted that it is entitled to be respected, that it cannot be extinguished (at least in times of peace) otherwise than by the free consent of the Native occupiers. But for their protection, and for the sake of humanity, the government is bound to maintain, and the courts to assert, the Queen's exclusive right to extinguish it.

Chapman J went on to say (p. 391) that:

> The assertion of the Queen's pre-emptive right [the Crown's exclusive right of extinguishing the Native title] supposes only a modified dominium as residing in the Natives. But it is also a principle of our law that the freehold never can be in abeyance; hence the full recognition of the modified title of the Natives, and its most careful protection, is not theoretically inconsistent with the Queen's seisin in fee as against her European subjects. This technical seisin against all the world except the Natives is the strongest ground whereon the due protection of their qualified dominium can be based.

Chapman J's comments on the nature of Native title and its relationship to the Crown's interest have been controversial. The statement that the free consent of the Native occupiers is required before extinguishment can occur, at least in peacetime, was cited with evident approval in *Nireaha Tamaki* v. *Baker,* [1901] AC 561, 579 (JCPC). See also *Calder* v. *AG (BC),* [1973] SCR 313, 403-04 (SCC). Chapman J's comments have been vigorously supported by G.S. Lester in *The Territorial Rights of the Inuit of the Canadian Northwest Territories*, 1981, pp. 764-88 (although see his criticism, at pp. 139-46, of the argument that the treaty-making process necessarily implies legally enforceable rights or has developed into a requirement of law). Chapman J's comments were criticized at length in *Milirrpum et al.* v. *Nabalco Pty. Ltd. et al.,* [1971] 17 FLR 141, 236-40 (Northern Territory Supreme Court). Chapman J himself conceded that it was "not at all necessary'' for the purposes of this decision to decide the nature of the Crown's interest in the land (p. 391) and that his own remarks on this topic represented an "extreme view" (p. 391) which, apart from one dissenting judgment, had not been supported by any colonial or American court (pp. 391-92).

> (iii) *Milirrpum [Milirrpum et al.* v. *Nabalco Pty. Ltd. and Common-*
> *wealth of Australia,* [1971] 17 FLR 141 (Northern Territory
> Supreme Court)]. See also part 5(f)(i) and 5(g)(ii), *supra*.

The plaintiffs in the *Milirrpum* case argued that their aboriginal title was a legal right that could be terminated only by the Crown with the consent of the aboriginal occupants themselves or perhaps by explicit legislation. Until that time, they contended, their aboriginal rights were rights of property, enforceable against the Crown itself. After a long examination of the authorities, Blackburn J concluded that this claim could not be sustained. Some extracts from Blackburn J's analysis of the American authorities are set out below:

> I turn now to the cases decided in the United States of America after the Revolution. Less than twelve years elapsed from the beginning of the Revolution (4th July, 1776) to the foundation of New South Wales in January 1788. Before I deal with the United States cases, I mention a matter of historical significance. From its earliest times the Government of the United States continued the policy, which was of such long standing in the colonies, of "purchasing" lands occupied by Indians. After the Revolution these transactions often took the form of treaties to which the parties were the United States of the one part and a tribe or tribes of Indians of the other part. No less than 242 such treaties were made between 1778 and 1842; a list is given in *United States Statutes at Large*, Vol. VII, p. iii. There is an enlightening article by F.S. Cohen, (1947) 32 *Minnesota Law Review* 28, in which the learned author surveys the history of the matter and shows that it was the persistent policy of the United States to make bargains, for proper compensation, with the Indian tribes for the cession of land occupied by them. According to him, most of the land of the continental United States (apart from Alaska) was bought from the Indians in this way — a statement which takes into account both pre-Revolutionary and post-Revolutionary history.
>
> The learned author goes on to survey the later developments of United States case law, his general theme being that what began as a matter of practice, as distinct from law, developed into a doctrine of law, that the courts must recognize and enforce Indian communal title, even against the United States or a person deriving title from them. I have followed his argument closely, and with respect and with some

diffidence I must say that some of his authorities in my opinion do not support the doctrinal burden which he puts upon them. But what is of more importance is that the United States Supreme Court has, since the publication of that article, denied its principle contention: *Tee-Hit-Ton Indians* v. *United States* [p. 209].

. . . . .

The next case is *Fletcher* v. Peck, decided by the Supreme Court of the United States. The question which is material for the present purposes was whether certain land, which had been part of the Indian reserve created by the Royal Proclamation of 1763, between the Alleghany Mountains and the Mississippi River, in the State of Georgia, was vested in that State or the United States. It was suggested by one party that the effect of the Proclamation of 1763 had been to disannex the land from the State of Georgia, and that the United States thereafter acquired title to it by virtue of the treaty with Great Britain at the end of the Revolutionary War. The Court rejected this argument and held, just as was held years later by the Judicial Committee in the *St Catharine's Milling Co.* case, that the land of the great Indian reserve was after 1763 none the less land of the Crown. At the end of his judgement Marshall CJ said this (p. 142): "It was doubted whether a state can be seized in fee of lands subject to the Indian title, and whether a decision that they were seized in fee might not be construed to amount to a decision that their grantee might maintain an ejectment for them, notwithstanding that title. The majority of the Court is of opinion that the nature of the Indian title, which is certainly to be respected by all courts, until it be legitimately extinguished, is not such as to be absolutely repugnant to seisin in fee on the part of the State." The last part of this is of course entirely consistent with what the plaintiffs are saying in the case before me, that the doctrine of communal native title is not inconsistent with the ultimate or radical title being in the Crown. But the language of Marshall CJ in *Fletcher* v. *Peck* is interesting as showing the tendency to emphasize the status of native occupancy, even to the stage of using the word "title" in relation to the communal occupation of Indian lands, which by custom had to be extinguished by purchase, but which in law had no significance as against a properly constituted title to the land. In a dissenting judgement Johnson J went even further, and asserted in effect that everything but full ownership was in the Indians, while only a bare residual right was in the sovereign: "If the interest in Georgia was nothing more than a pre-emptive right, how could that be called a fee-simple, which was nothing more than a power to acquire a fee-simple by purchase, when the proprietors should be pleased to sell?" (p. 147).

Mr Woodward's contention was that the language used in these early cases represents the birth, or perhaps a sign of the incipient birth, of the doctrine upon which he relied.

Next is the case of *Johnson and Graham's Lessee v. McIntosh*. This has been quoted and referred to many times, and the plaintiffs relied strongly on it. An action of ejectment was brought for land in the State of Illinois which had been in the great Indian reserve set up by the Royal Proclamation of 1763. The plaintiffs claimed under a purchase and conveyance from Indians and the defendant under a grant from the United States. The court below gave judgement for the defendant, upon a case stated which set out the facts in very great detail; the whole case is set out in the report. On a writ of error, the Supreme Court affirmed the judgement of the court below.

The plaintiffs claimed under two conveyances made in 1773 and 1775 by Indian chiefs on behalf of their tribes. The land was conquered from the British in the Revolutionary War, and in 1784 was duly made over by the State of Virginia to the United States, which in 1818 granted it to the defendant. Marshall CJ (p. 572) described the principal question before the Court as the power of Indians to give, and of private individuals to receive, a title which could be sustained in the courts of the United States. He began by setting out first the conquest of land on the American Continent by European powers and the principle of title through discovery. He went on (p. 574): ". . . the rights of the original inhabitants were, in no instance, entirely disregarded; but were necessarily, to a considerable extent, impaired. They were admitted to be the rightful occupants of the soil, with a legal as well as just claim to retain possession of it, and to use it according to their own discretion; but their rights to complete sovereignty, as independent nations, were necessarily diminished, and their power to dispose of the soil at their own will, to whomsoever they pleased, was denied by the original fundamental principle, that discovery gave exclusive title to those who made it. While the different nations of Europe respected the right of the natives, as occupants, they asserted the ultimate dominion to be in themselves, and claimed and exercised, as a consequence of this ultimate dominion, a power to grant the soil, while yet in possession of the natives. These grants have been understood by all, to convey a title to the grantees, subject only to the Indian right of occupancy."

The Chief Justice proceeded to give a historical account which showed in detail how all the colonizing powers of Europe had adopted these principles in North America. He went on (p. 579): "Thus has our whole country been granted by the Crown while in the occupation of the Indians. These grants purport to convey the soil as well as the right of dominion to the grantees. . . . It has never been objected to this, or to any other similar grant, that the title as well as possession was in the Indians when it was made, and that it passed nothing on that account."

Later (p. 583) he referred to "the principle, that discovery gave a title to lands still remaining in the possession of the Indians. Whichever title prevailed, it was still a title to lands occupied by the Indians, whose right of occupancy neither controverted, and neither had then extinguished." The word "neither" here refers to England and France; the Chief Justice had been referring to the dispute which resulted in the Seven Years' War and the extinction of French sovereignty over a large part of the American Continent. He went on to give an account (p. 584) of the treaty which ended the War of the American Revolution, pointing out that as a result of it the rights to the soil which had previously been in Great Britain "passed definitively to these States."

At this point he said: "It has never been doubted that either the United States, or the several States, had a clear title to all the lands within the boundary lines described in the treaty, subject only to the Indian right of occupancy, and that the exclusive power to extinguish that right was vested in that government which might constitutionally exercise it." At p. 588 he said: "All our institutions recognize the absolute title of the Crown, subject only to the Indian right of occupancy, and recognize the absolute title of the Crown to extinguish that right. This is incompatible with an absolute and complete title in the Indians." He repeatedly used similar words. For example (p. 588): "The British Government . . . asserted . . . a limited sovereignty over [the Indians] and the exclusive right of extinguishing the title which occupancy gave to them." Again (p. 592): ". . . the principle which has been supposed to be recognized by all European governments, from the first settlement of America. The absolute ultimate title has been considered as acquired by discovery, subject only to the Indian title of occupancy, which title the discoverers possessed the exclusive right of acquiring. Such a right is no more incompatible with a seisin in fee, than a lease for years, and might as effectually bar an ejectment." Again (p. 603): "It has never been contended that the Indian title amounted to nothing. Their right of possession has never been questioned. The claim of government extends to the complete ultimate title, charged with this right of possession, and to the exclusive power of acquiring that right."

In my most respectful opinion, these statements of law by the great Chief Justice do not affirm the principle that the Indian "right of occupancy" was an interest which could be set up against the sovereign, or against a grantee of the sovereign, in the same manner as an interest arising under the ordinary law of real property. In the first place, the case does not raise that issue; the Indians were not parties to the action and the question was not the validity of the Indian title against the United States or its grantees, but the validity of an alienation by Indians to subjects of the Crown. No doubt, the Chief Justice was deeply concerned to emphasize the practical value to the Indians of the common custom of "extinguishing Indian title." He was concerned to stress the propriety of respecting the Indian occupancy, and he must have been mindful of the existence since 1763 of the great Indian reserve and that, in general, land in it had been acquired by the Whites from the Indians by treaty or purchase. He was concerned to uphold the value of Indian occupancy because, I venture to suggest, he was obliged to state its weakness — its incapacity to be alienated save to the sovereign. His judgement, in short, may, in my opinion, be regarded as an eloquent exposition of the soundness of the practice applicable to the relations between Whites and Indians in respect of Indian land, but not as an encroachment upon the rigour of the law. That law was well settled, and contained no doctrine of communal native title.

It would be an over-simplification to classify these statements of the Chief Justice as *obiter dicta*, on the ground that the ratio of the case was simply that a title derived from a United States grant was superior to one derived from an Indian grant. What he said may well have been directed at the first argument for the plaintiffs, which is reported at pp. 562-63. This was that the Indians were the owners of the land in dispute at the time of executing the deed of 1775, and had power to sell, and that the United States had purchased the same lands of the same Indians and that therefore both parties claimed from the same source, namely the Indians. This argument, of course, elevates communal native title to a height from which the Chief Justice was concerned to bring it down, and perhaps this too helps to explain his emphasis on the value and status of the Indian right of occupancy.

I have shown what seems to me to be the true explanation of what Marshall CJ said in *Johnson* v. *McIntosh*, but I concede that there is one passage which is not consistent with my explanation. I have already quoted it: "The absolute ultimate title has been considered as acquired by discovery, subject only to the Indian title of occupancy, which title the discoverers possessed the exclusive right of acquiring. Such a right is no more incompatible with a seisin in fee, than a lease for years, and might as effectually bar an ejectment" (p. 502). The "right" referred to in the last sentence in this passage must, I think, refer, not to the word "right" at the end of the preceding sentence, but to the "Indian title of occupancy." The Chief Justice seems to be saying that just as seisin in fee in one person is compatible with a lease for years in another, so the ultimate title to the land in the sovereign is compatible with the Indian title of occupancy. He goes on to say that the latter would be an effective defence to an action of ejectment. If this is what the Chief Justice really meant, one can only say that the statement appears not to be borne out by any other authority. It would be surprising, if there were such a case, that it was not mentioned in F.S. Cohen's article to which I have already referred — or by Mr Woodward in this case. None such was cited to me, and notwithstanding Mr Woodward's weighty submissions, I am clear that *Johnson* v. *McIntosh* does not support the view that communal native title, not extinguished by consent or legislation, prevails over a title derived from the sovereign having the ultimate title.

The matter next came before the Supreme court of the United States in two cases relating to a dispute between the Cherokee Indians and the State of Georgia. In the first, *Cherokee Nation* v. *State of Georgia*, the complainants were described in their own bill as ''the Cherokee Nation of Indians, a foreign state, not owing allegiance to the United States, nor to any State of this Union, nor to any prince, potentate or State, other than their own.'' Their complaint was that the State of Georgia had passed certain enactments which were unjust and oppressive to them in various respects, and in particular in denying their right to occupy their land. They sought an injunction to restrain the State and its officers from executing and enforcing the laws of Georgia within the Cherokee territory, as designated by treaty between the United States and the Cherokee Nation. An injunction was refused, on the ground that the matter was not within the court's jurisdiction. Article III, s. II, of the United States Constitution extends the judicial power of the United States to cases ''between a State or the citizens thereof and foreign States, citizens, or subjects.'' On the short ground that the Cherokee Indians were not a foreign State, nor were they foreign citizens or foreign subjects, the Supreme Court refused the injunction. Marshall CJ described the position of Indian tribes in relation to the United States thus: ''Though the Indians were acknowledged to have an unquestionable and, heretofore, unquestioned right to the lands they occupy, until that right shall be extinguished by a voluntary cession to our government, yet it may well be doubted whether those tribes which reside within the acknowledged boundaries of the United States can, with strict accuracy, be denominated foreign nations. They may, more correctly, perhaps, be denominated domestic dependent nations. They occupy a territory to which we assert a title independent of their will, which must take effect in point of possession when their right of possession ceases'' (p. 17).

The second case was *Worcester* v. *State of Georgia*. The plaintiff in error, a missionary from Vermont, went to live in the Cherokee territory, in Georgia, without a licence, contrary to a penal provision enacted by the legislature of Georgia. He was convicted and imprisoned. His defence, and his argument in the Supreme Court, was that the Georgia enactment was void as repugnant to the several treaties which had been entered into by the United States with the Cherokee Nation. By *art. VI* of the United States Constitution treaties made under the authority of the United States ''shall be the supreme law of the land;

and the judges in every State shall be bound thereby, anything in the Constitution or laws of any State to the contrary notwithstanding.'' On this ground the plaintiff in error was successful. The opinion of the Court was delivered by Marshall CJ, who once again surveyed the history of colonization on the North American Continent, and once again stated the position of the Indians in relation to their land in strong and eloquent terms. What, he said, was conveyed by the charters given by European sovereigns to grantees of land in North America was ''the exclusive right of purchasing such lands as the natives were willing to sell. The Crown could not be understood to grant what the Crown did not affect to claim; nor was it so understood.'' His judgement as a whole makes it quite clear, however, and he emphasizes (p. 560), that the decision in the case was based on the invalidity of the Georgia enactment. That invalidity did not rest upon any ground other than the incompatibility between the enactment and the treaties, which the Court held to be binding on the State of Georgia (pp. 210-15).

. . . . .

The high water mark of support for the status of Indian occupancy occurred in the following passage, on which Mr Woodward placed great reliance: ''The merits of this case do not make it ncessary to inquire whether the Indians within the United States had any other rights of soil or jurisdiction; it is enough to consider it as a settled principle that their right of occupancy is considered as sacred as the fee simple of the Whites'' (p. 746). But where are the cases which show the Indians upholding their right as if it were an estate in fee simple?

I am well aware of my inexperience in American law, yet I cannot help concluding that despite the force and eloquence of the dicta in them, none of these cases is authority for the proposition that the mere fact of communal occupancy gives a title enforceable in the sovereign's courts against the sovereign or one claiming under him. I do not think it necessary to discuss several later United States cases which were cited to me, since none of them either contains such strong dicta as those I have cited or is authority for Mr Woodward's contention. I set apart a long line of cases exemplified by *United States* v. *Alcea Band of Tillamooks*, in which, under special statutory provisions, rights had been created to compensation for the taking of Indian-occupied lands. To establish the existence of his doctrine Mr Woodward must show it put into force without the command of statute.

The earlier cases which I have cited undoubtedly show a growing tendency to elevate the status of native occupancy. There is debate between the judges as to the respective qualities of the sovereign's title and of the Indian title, which, it is agreed, are not inconsistent with each other. Yet native occupancy never achieves the status of being unequivocally defined as a proprietary interest in relation to proprietary interests derived from the sovereign. One might think that even though it failed to gain acceptance in this respect, it might eventually have been held to be a right enjoying the protection of the Constitution. But what has emerged has been not the affirmation of that principle, but the denial of it.

The case in *Tee-Hit-Ton Indians* v. *United States*. The importance of this case is that the claim was made under the Fifth Amendment and not under any special statutory provision. The petitioners, an identifiable group of Indians, contended that their tribal predecessors had continually claimed, occupied and used certain land in Alaska from time immemorial, and that the Russian Government of Alaska before 1867 had never interfered with them. They claimed that the United States Government, by taking and selling timber from the land, was acting in violation of their constitutional rights under the Fifth Amendment. The opinion of the court, delivered by Reed J, included this passage on the subject of "Indian title" (p. 279): "It is well settled that in all the States of the Union the tribes who inhabited the lands of the States held claim to such lands after the coming of the White man, under what is sometimes termed original Indian title or permission from the Whites to occupy. That description means mere possession not specifically recognized as ownership by Congress. After conquest they were permitted to occupy portions of territory over which they had previously exercised "sovereignty," as we use that term. This is not a property right but amounts to a right of occupancy which the sovereign grants and protects against intrusion by third parties fully disposed of by the sovereign itself without any legally enforceable obligation to compensate the Indians." And later (p. 231): "No case in this Court has ever held that taking of Indian title or use by Congress required compensation."

Having distinguished the *Tillamooks'* case as one of compensation under a special statute, the opinion proceeded: "This leaves unimpaired the rule derived from *Johnson* v. *McIntosh* that the taking by the United States of unrecognized Indian title is not compensable under the Fifth Amendment. This is true, not because an Indian or an Indian tribe has no standing to sue or because the United States has not consented to be sued for the taking of original Indian title, but because Indian occupation of land without government recognition of ownership creates no rights against taking or extinction by the United States protected by the Fifth Amendment or any other principle of law." It is surprising, at any rate to one not well versed in United States law, to find *Johnson* v. *McIntosh* cited as authority for this proposition; but the case must amount to a total denial that communal Indian occupancy of lands gives a proprietary right. If the doctrine of communal native title ever existed in the United States, it does no longer (pp. 217-18).

(iv) *Calder* [*Calder et al.* v. *Attorney General of British Columbia,* [1973] SCR 313 (SCC). See also Parts 4(b)(iii) and 5(f)(ii), *supra,* and Parts 6(a) and 7(a), *infra*.

In *Calder*, both Judson and Hall JJ appeared to regard the principles articulated in the *St Catharine's* decision as applicable to occupancy-based aboriginal title as well as that based on the Royal Proclamation of 1763. Judson J, for example, said (p. 320) that "Any inquiry into the nature of the Indian title must begin with *St Catharine's Milling and Lumber Co.* v. *The Queen*". He quoted extensively from the passages in the earlier decision respecting the relationship of aboriginal title with the Crown's interest in land, even though it was his view that the Royal Proclamation does not extend to British Columbia. Judson J quoted (p. 344) with apparent approval from *Tee-Hit-Ton Indians* v. *United States* (1955), 348 US 272, 279 (US Supreme Court):

> This is not a property right but amounts to a right of occupancy which the sovereign grants and protects against intrusion by third parties but which right of occupancy may be terminated and such lands fully disposed of by the sovereign itself without any legally enforceable obligation to compensate the Indians.

It is unclear as to whether Judson J felt that the *courts* might be able to protect the aboriginal interest against intrusion by third parties: his support of the blanket assertion that this is "not a property right" suggests that he did not.

Although Hall J did think that the Royal Proclamation extends to British Columbia, he, too made no differentiation between Proclamation-based title and occupancy-based title. Like Judson J, Hall J quoted extensively from the Privy Council's decision in the *St Catharine's* case. In regard to the Nishga claim itself, Hall J said (p. 352) that:

> This is not a claim to title in *fee* but is in the nature of an equitable title or interest . . . a usufructuary right and a right to occupy the lands and to enjoy the fruits of the soil, the forest and of the rivers and streams which does not in any way deny the Crown's paramount title as it is recognized by the law of nations. Nor does the Nishga claim challenge the federal Crown's right to extinguish that title. Their position is that they possess a right of occupation against the world except the Crown and that the Crown has not to date lawfully extinguished that right.

Hall J was quite convinced that the aboriginal title was a legal right of ownership in the lands concerned (see, for example, pp. 375, 383 and 385). He specifically rejected the contention that aboriginal rights must first be "recognized" by the legislative or executive branch of government before they can be recognized and enforced by the courts (pp. 404-06). Although Hall J quoted at one point from a passage from *R. v. Symonds* suggesting that in peacetime aboriginal rights can be surrendered only by the voluntary consent of the occupants (pp. 403-04), Hall J's own view appeared to be that the sovereign *could* unilaterally extinguish aboriginal rights as long as it showed a "clear and plain" intention to do so (p. 404).

Although Judson J did not specifically address the question of prior legislative or executive recognition, his apparent willingness (p. 328) to contemplate an aboriginal interest based simply on traditional use and occupancy seems inconsistent with this requirement in regard to recognition by the courts. On the other hand, he did appear to support the proposition that there can be no legal right to compensation for claims arising out of an aboriginal title in the absence of a statutory direction to pay (pp. 339-44).

(See, further, *Hamlet of Baker Lake et al. v. Minister of Indian Affairs and Northern Development* (1980), 107 DLR (3d) 513, 568 (FCTD).)

(v) Other Authorities

Clearly, many aspects of the common law relationship between aboriginal title and the Crown's interest in land which is subject to this title require further exposition in the courts. The question of enforceability at common law is particularly unclear, although it may be that the existing authorities provide the basis for an answer.

Brian Slattery in *The Land Rights of Indigenous Canadian Peoples,* and Geoffry S. Lester in *The Territorial Rights of the Inuit of the Canadian Northwest Territories: A Legal Argument,* both conclude (by quite different reasoning) that aboriginal rights in a peaceful settlement are capable of being enforced against the Crown, without any prior requirement of executive or legislative recognition.

The Lester thesis is especially concerned with the question of enforceability. In Lester's view, where the constitutional situation is one of peaceful settlement, it properly applies to inhabited as well as uninhabited lands, and in the former case the existing rights of the original inhabitants not only continue, but cannot be unilaterally terminated by the Sovereign (see, for example, pp. 1,412-45). Where the situation is one of conquest, however, Lester feels that the enforceability of the rights of original inhabitants depends strictly on what has or has not been recognized by the conquering Sovereign (pp. 75-81).

Lester's conclusions, then, posit two potentially different enforceability levels, depending on whether the original inhabitants' land was subject to conquest or peaceful settlement. Contrast Lester's "two level" approach with the apparent tendency noted (a) in part 4(b)(ii), above, toward assimilating conquest and peaceful settlement consequences and (b) in parts 5(g)(i) and

5(g)(iv), above, toward assimilating Proclamation and occupancy-based rights. Compare Lester's approach to that in *R*. v. *Symonds,* considered in part 5(g)(ii), above. Are the criticisms of *Symonds* in *Milirrpum* (see Part 5(g)(iii), above) applicable to Lester's approach? Has Lester provided a full answer to the *Milirrpum* criticisms? (see Chapter XV of Lester, especially pp. 736-37, 781-82, 785-88, 809 and 845). Is Lester right in arguing that the American decisions of Marshall CJ are irrelevant to peaceful settlements? (see Chapters IX to XIII). Does the considerable controversy as to whether many areas are in fact peaceful settlements or conquests (see, for example, Slattery, pp. 34-35 and Lester, Chapters IX to XIII; pp. 727-34; and Chapter XX) have implications for the practical workability of the Lester approach?

The judicial and academic authorities above are all concerned with the common law situation before the enactment of section 35 of the Constitution Act, 1982. *Quaere*, whether, and if so, how, this constitutional provision alters the situation at common law?

Of the two views expressed at the beginning of part 5, which correctly describes the state of Canadian law regarding the content of aboriginal title? Was Morrow J correct in saying that aboriginal title has certain characteristics which are "well-established"? Was Turgeon JA correct in saying that the law regarding the content of aboriginal title is vague and imprecise? Is it possible that both judges were correct?

It is true that some of the basic characteristics of aboriginal title — alienability only to the Crown, certain aspects of its relationship to the interest of the Crown, and so on — are fairly well established. Nevertheless, many unanswered questions remain. *Is* the content of the Proclamation interest identical to that of occupancy-based title? Precisely how great a degree of enjoyment and use does aboriginal title permit? Need this enjoyment and use be related to traditional activities? To what extent is it enforceable?

The judicial statements in this area are tentative and incomplete. Most of the modern pronouncements are from lower court decisions. Many of these were subsequently reversed on other grounds. Some pronouncements occur in *obiter dicta*. Some are from dissenting judgments. There is a great need for more clarification and more certainty.

6. Extinguishment of Aboriginal Title and Abridgment of Aboriginal Rights

Assuming that there was at one time an aboriginal title in the region now comprising Canada, has this title been subsequently extinguished or abridged?

Extinguishment is government action that terminates aboriginal rights. Abridgment is government action that diminishes or otherwise restricts aboriginal rights but falls short of terminating the aboriginal title.

The existing case law recognizes several main forms of extinguishment.

The simplest and perhaps least controversial of these is an Indian land cession treaty negotiated for the express purpose of surrendering the Indian title in the land concerned. The power of the appropriate government to terminate Indian title by treaty (in accordance, presumably, with the general procedure contemplated in the Royal Proclamation of 1763: see part 4(a)(i), *supra*) was one of the few questions upon which there was little disagreement in the Supreme Court's decision in *Calder*.

On the other hand, there has been considerable uncertainty regarding the scope of the extinguishment effected by treaty. For example, does extinguishment by treaty terminate the rights of all Indians in regard to a given area of land? Or does the treaty leave open the question of aboriginal claims made by Indians whose ancestors were not parties to the treaty, but may nevertheless have traditionally used and occupied the land in question? Proponents of the second view might use the analogy of the contract and argue that a treaty no less than a contract must be ineffective to dispose of the rights of third parties not subject to it. They might argue, too, that a treaty which purported to extinguish or override the aboriginal titles of Indian people not parties to it would be, at the very least, extremely unfair.

Another problem relates to the effect of a waiver or defect on the capacity of an Indian treaty to effect extinguishment. Can a treaty, once signed, be treated subsequently as ineffective to effect extinguishment because the parties have waived its application, or because of ambiguity, misunderstanding, or mistake? If this were the case, the question of claims based on aboriginal title would presumably remain open in the area covered by the purported treaty.

The decision of the Northwest Territories Supreme Court in the *Paulette* case supported the view that ambiguity resulting in misunderstanding can have this effect. Morrow J found evidence of "haste and perhaps irregularities" in Treaties 8 and 11 (p. 34). He suggested that this, and the inadequate character of the land granted, gave some reason to suspect the *bona fides* of the negotiations leading to the signing of these treaties. Morrow J cited evidence of oral assurances given by the negotiators as a reason for suspecting that what was said (that the treaty was no more than a "peace treaty" preserving all existing rights of the Indians and serving only to reaffirm the dominant interest of the Crown) and what was signed (a full surrender of existing Indian rights in return for benefits granted under the terms of the treaties) conflicted. Accordingly, in the view of Morrow J, there was room for an argument that aboriginal title in the lands concerned had not been validly surrendered.

If it were followed in later decisions, the approach taken by Morrow J in *Paulette* could conceivably support decisions questioning the effectiveness of "defective" treaties to extinguish title in other parts of Canada. For the present, however, the authority of Morrow J's statements regarding aboriginal title is uncertain. As noted earlier, Morrow J's decision in *Paulette* was reversed by the Northwest Territories Court of Appeal and the Supreme Court of Canada, on purely technical and procedural grounds.

The entire question of the capacity of treaties to extinguish Indian title may be subject to reassessment in light of section 35 of the Constitution Act, 1982, discussed in part 4(c), *supra*. One possible construction of section 35 is that it will require formal constitutional amendment for any future extinguishment. This construction could have far-reaching effects. It could put an end to the capacity of government to extinguish aboriginal title by treaty alone. It could put an end to the second major form of explicit extinguishment, extinguishment by legislative provisions of the appropriate level of government expressly terminating aboriginal title. Because of the uncertainty as to the legal effect of section 35, the important question of its effect on extinguishment will have to be resolved at a future constitutional conference or by the courts of law.

The difficulties surrounding the existing case law on extinguishment increase when the government action in question lacks express provisions purporting to extinguish the Indian title. This situation has been discussed more frequently in the American case law, but the net result of the American decisions is somewhat unclear.

On one hand, there are sweeping dicta suggesting that extinguishment can be carried out by almost any official means at all. In *United States* v. *Santa Fe Pacific Railroad Co.,* 314 US 339, 347 (1941), Douglas J of the United States Supreme Court said that:

> As stated by Chief Justice Marshall in *Johnson* v. *McIntosh, supra*, p. 586, "the exclusive right of the United States to extinguish" Indian title has never been doubted. And whether it be done by treaty, by the sword, by purchase, by the exercise of complete dominion adverse to the right of occupancy, or otherwise, its justness is not open to inquiry in the courts.

On the other hand, later in the *Sante Fe* case, Douglas J said (p. 354) that:

> . . . an extinguishment cannot be lightly implied in view of the avowed solicitude of the federal government for the welfare of its Indian wards.

In *Lipan Apache Tribe* v. *United States*, 180 Ct. Cl. 487, 492 (1967), the American Court of Claims said that the act of extinguishment must be "plain and unambiguous".

>   (a) *Calder* [*Calder et al.* v. *Attorney General of British Columbia,* [1973] SCR 313 (SCC)]. See also parts 4(b)(iii), 5(f)(ii) and 5(g)(iv), *supra*, and part 7(a), *infra*.

This apparent difference of emphasis as to what is required before a general government action can constitute an extinguishment of Indian title is reflected in the leading judgments in the *Calder* decision. What were in question in this case were legislative enactments and executive instruments:

(a) declaring that all lands belonged to the Crown in fee, and
(b) providing for the disposition of lands without regard to Indian claims asserted over them.

In the view of Judson J, these general legislative enactments were sufficient to extinguish any Indian title claimed in regard to the lands in question. In the view of Hall J, they were insufficient to result in extinguishment.

(b) Case Comment on *Baker Lake* [D.W. Elliott, "*Baker Lake* and the Concept of Aboriginal Title," (1980) 4 Osgoode Hall LJ 653, 658-59 (footnotes omitted). See also parts 4(b)(v) and 5(f)(iii), *supra*.

Had the Inuit title been extinguished? Here Mahoney J was faced with an apparently divided view from the Supreme Court of Canada on the proper test for legislative extinguishment of aboriginal title. The plaintiffs, relying on the judgment of Hall J in *Calder*, argued that to extinguish aboriginal title legislation must contain express words stating this object. The defendants, relying on the judgment of Judson J in *Calder* argued that extinguishment could occur as a necessary result of legislation, even where no such intention was expressed in it.

Mahoney J disagreed with the contention that Hall J had gone so far as to say that Parliament must state its intention to extinguish explicitly in the statute itself. He said that this requirement would be contrary to the basic principle that:

Once a statute has been validly enadcted, it must be given effect. If its necessary effect is to abridge or entirely abrogate a common law right, then that is the effect that the courts must give it. That is as true of an aboriginal title as of any other common law right.

The true test, concluded Mahoney J, is whether or not the legislator has expressed a clear and plain intention to extinguish the aboriginal title. In his view, the legislation by the Parliament of Canada since 1870 had not expressed such an intention in relation to the aboriginal title of the Inuit. Examining the charter granting Rupert's Land (of which the Baker Lake area is now a part) to the Hudson's Bay Company in 1670 and the order-in-council admitting Rupert's Land to Canada in 1870, Mahoney J found that there had been no intention to extinguish the aboriginal title. Since there had been no surrender of the title either, the title continued.

Whether, as Mahoney J suggested, the "clear and plain intention" test was effectively the test of both Hall and Judson JJ in *Calder*, or whether it represents a compromise between the tests of these two judges, it is not without merit. If aboriginal title is to be a concept cognizable generally at common law, then it must be subject to the same general limitations as are other common law rights, and one of these limitations is subordination to statute by virtue of the principle of parliamentary sovereignty. On the other hand, the requirement of a clear and plain intention to extinguish aboriginal title raises a form of presumption against extinguishment that should provide at least some protection against cases of "extinguishment by oversight."

Can the rights enjoyed pursuant to aboriginal title be abridged? This question had already been answered for Mahoney J by the decisions of the Supreme Court of Canada in *Derriksan* v. *The Queen* and *Kruger* v. *The Queen*. Mahoney J summarized the answer as follows: "There can, however, be no doubt as to the effect of competent legislation and that, to the extent that it does diminish the rights comprised in an aboriginal title, it prevails."

In the view of Mahoney J, extinguishment can be effected only by the Parliament of Canada, whereas abridgment may be possible by other legislatures or through delegated legislation. In the case at hand, Mahoney J held that to the extent that the aboriginal rights of the Inuit had been abridged by federal mining legislation, this abridgment was not valid.

As with extinguishment, it is difficult to argue with a legal capacity conferred pursuant to the parliamentary sovereignty doctrine, assuming the absence of impediments in the written part of our constitution. Nevertheless, it would seem inconsistent if on one hand the law imposed special requirements before permitting extinguishment by parliament, while, on the other hand, it permitted all legislatures to override aboriginal rights at will by way of abridgment.

Apart from the fact that an abridged right, unlike an extinguished right, presumably "revives" once the offending legislation is repealed or amended, the present law appears to contain no definite limit to the extent of possible federal abridgment. Provincial abridgment is subject to two additional constraints, although they are indirect in nature. Provincial abridgment is invalid if it constitutes legislation directed at Indians or lands reserved for the Indians, or if it is found to have the effect of paralyzing the status and capacities of Indians.

It might be asked whether the existing common law constraints on abridgment are adequate. Thought might be given in a subsequent case to articulating a simple presumption against abridgment. Such a presumption would involve no challenge to parliamentary sovereignty: it would apply to communal rights a well-established common law tradition used to safeguard rights considered important to individuals. It would provide some balance to the presumption already in place in regard to extinguishment.

Note that *Calder* and *Baker Lake* predate the Constitution Act, 1982 (see discussion in part 4(c), *supra*). If section 35 of the Constitution Act is not construed as requiring formal constitutional amendment for all forms of extinguishment, how will it affect implied extinguishment, if at all? Will section 35 incline the courts closer to the approach of Hall J in *Calder*? Will it persuade them that implied extinguishment is now impossible? What effect will current judicial approaches to extinguishment have on the construction given to section 35? What effect, if any, will section 35 have on abridgment? Whatever the answers to these questions, they will be fundamental to the relationship between government and aboriginal title in the future.

7. Compensation for Extinguishment of Aboriginal Title or Abridgment of Aboriginal Rights

The last part of the Fifth Amendment to the American constitution stipulates that:

> . . . nor shall private property be taken for public use without just compensation.

Before the 1955 *Tee-Hit-Ton* case, 348 US 272 (1955), it was thought that this provision supplied American Indians with a constitutional guarantee of compensation for the extinguishment of aboriginal title. See, for example, *United States* v. *Alcea Band of Tillamooks et al.*, 329 US 40, 51 (1946). In the *Tee-Hit-Ton* case, the Supreme Court of the United States held that aboriginal title is not a property right but a right of occupancy, and thus not subject to the Fifth Amendment. Judson J in the *Calder* decision summed up the American situation as follows:

> The last word on the subject [of compensation] from the United States is, therefore, that there is no right to compensation for such claims in the absence of a statutory direction to pay. (p. 344)

In Canada, although many statutes provide for compensation for expropriation of property (see, for example, legislation surveyed in Law Reform Commission of Canada, *Working Paper No. 9, Expropriation*, 1975), there is no general constitutional right to compensation where property has been taken. The Canadian Bill of Rights asserts:

> . . . the right of the individual to life, liberty, security of the person and enjoyment of property, and the right not to be deprived thereof except by due process of law.

In the case of *National Capital Commission* v. *Lapointe*, however, it was held that due process under the Canadian Bill of Rights is a guarantee of natural justice and other procedural safeguards, not of fair compensation: [1972] FC 568 (FCTD). In a comparable provision in the Constitution Act, 1982, the phrase "by due process of law" has been replaced with "in accordance with the principles of fundamental justice."

The general common law position in Canada regarding compensation for the taking of private property interests is simple to state and difficult to apply. On one hand, the common law imposes no automatic, overriding obligation on government to provide compensation for private property taken. On the other hand, there is a common law presumption that the government will provide compensation for the expropriation or other taking of private property unless the relevant legislation or other enactment indicates clearly to the contrary.

> (a) *Calder* [*Calder et al.* v. *Attorney General of British Columbia,*
> [1973] SCR 313 (SCC)]. See also parts 4(b)(iii), 5(f)(ii), 5(g)(iv)
> and 6(a), *supra*.

In the decision of the Supreme Court of Canada in *Calder*, Judson and Hall JJ arrive at opposite conclusions regarding the requirement of compensation for the extinguishment of aboriginal title by emphasizing different aspects of the common law situation. Judson J summarizes the current American case law as permitting no right to compensation for extinguishment of title in the absence of a statutory direction to pay. Judson J implies that the same rule should apply in Canada, but makes no mention of the common law presumption in favour of compensation. Hall J, on the other hand, places great stress on the presumption, and implies that nothing but an explicit statement in the enactment can enable the government to escape its overriding duty to compensate:

> . . . according to common law, the expropriation of private rights by the
> government under the prerogative necessitates the payment of
> compensation. . . . Only express words to that effect in an enactment
> would authorize a taking without compensation. (p. 1277)

The position of Hall J seems somewhat closer to the general Canadian common law position described above than that of Judson J. Nevertheless, a presumption is no more than a presumption, a fact which at least the first statement of Hall J quoted above obscures. As on so many issues in *Calder*, the opposing views of Judson J and Hall J on compensation for extinguishment of title resulted in an apparent stalemate. As indicated earlier, Judson J spoke for three judges, Hall J spoke for three judges, and the opinion of Pigeon J decided the case solely on a procedural point.

> (b) *Address of 16 and 17 December 1867* [Address to Her Majesty the
> Queen from the Senate and Dominion of Canada, 16 and 17
> December 1867, reprinted in RSC 1970, Appendices, p. 8].

The indigenous people in northern Canada may be able to rely on a constitutional or quasi-constitutional enactment in support of claims they may have for compensation for any aboriginal title extinguished, or about to be extinguished, as a result of settlement requirements. As was indicated in the discussion of the legal status of aboriginal title, earlier the Canadian government obtained Rupert's Land and the North-Western territory in return for, *inter alia*, a promise that:

> . . . upon the transference of the territories in question to the Canadian Government, the claims of the Indian tribes to compensation for lands required for the purposes of settlement will be considered and settled in conformity with the equitable principles which have uniformly governed the British Crown in its dealings with the aborigines.

Although the constitutional status and specific content of this enactment are not entirely clear, it is certainly an argument in favour of compensation not available to indigenous people in southern Canada.

(c) *Kruger and Manuel* [*Kruger and Manuel v. The Queen*, [1978] 1 SCR 104 (SCC); aff'g. (1975), 60 DLR (3d) 144 (BCCA); which rev'd. (1975), 51 DLR (3d) 435 (British Columbia County Court)].

Assuming that there is a general common law presumption in favour of compensation for the expropriation or other extinguishment of aboriginal title by government, does this presumption apply where certain of the aboriginal rights are abridged by legislation? On one hand, it might be argued that the same considerations of equity that would govern the application of the presumption in the case of complete termination of the title, should apply when interests derived from that title are interfered with. On the other hand, to apply the presumption to all cases where aboriginal title benefits are abridged could be detrimental to effective government regulation. It would confer on aboriginal title a protection not accorded to any other private property interest. Owners of fee simple estates and leasehold interests are subjected to a multitude of statutes, bylaws and regulations that effectively limit the use and enjoyment of the property concerned, but permit the owners to claim compensation. In none of these cases need the statutes, bylaws or regulations contain express exemption clauses to free the government from any general presumptions in favour of compensation.

In *Re Derriksan*, the Supreme Court of Canada held that expressly worded federal legislation (but legislation containing no clause exempting the government from any requirement to pay compensation) was effective to restrict any Indian fishing rights claimed to be derived from aboriginal title: *R. v. Derriksan* (1977), 75 DLR, (3d) 159; aff'g. (1976), 60 DLR (3d) 140 (BCCA); which aff'd. (1975), 52 DLR (3d) 744 (BCSC).

Kruger and Manuel v. The Queen, [1978] 1 SCR 104, involved a somewhat similar situation to *Derriksan*. Kruger and Manuel, two non-treaty Indians living in British Columbia, killed four deer for food during the closed season, contrary to the British Columbia Wildlife Act. As was pointed out by

Dickson J, "The acts of hunting took place upon unoccupied Crown land which was and is the traditional hunting ground of the Penticton Indian Band." Kruger and Manuel were convicted before a British Columbia Provincial Court judge, but the conviction was set aside in the County Court, which found that:

(1) the Indians in question had aboriginal rights that had not been extinguished and were protected by the Royal Proclamation of 1763.

and

(2) the Royal Proclamation had the force of a statute, and thus prevailed over provincial legislation by vritue of section 88 of the *Indian Act,* which subordinated such legislation to "the terms of any treaty and any other Act of the Parliament of Canada . . ." [(1975), 51 DLR (3d) 435].

The British Columbia Court of Appeal disagreed. It said that while the Proclamation may have had the *force* of statute, it was not a statute of Canada: (1975), 60 DLR (3d) 144. Thus, section 88 of the Indian Act had no application to it. Consequently, the Wildlife Act, whose application was not otherwise restricted, applied.

The lawyers for Kruger and Manuel argued before the Supreme Court of Canada that, among other things, the British Columbia Court of Appeal was wrong:

(3) In ruling, in effect, that aboriginal hunting rights could be expropriated without compensation and without explicit federal legislation. (p. 437)

Dickson J, for the Supreme Court of Canada, replied to this argument as follows:

The third point can be disposed of shortly. The British Columbia Court of Appeal was not asked to decide, nor did it decide, as I read its judgement, whether aboriginal hunting rights could be expropriated without compensation. It is argued that the loss of compensation supports the proposition that there had been no loss or regulation of rights. That does not follow. Most regulation imposing negative prohibitions affects previously enjoyed rights in ways not deemed compensatory. The *Wildlife Act* illustrates the point. It is aimed at wildlife management and to that end it regulates the time, place and manner of hunting game. It is not directed to the acquisition of property. (p. 437)

Ultimately, the Supreme Court of Canada upheld the British Columbia Wildlife Act on the ground that it was a law of general application and was valid either as a provincial law in its own right, or as a provincial law that had been referentially incorporated as federal legislation by virtue of section 88 of the Indian Act. As a result, the conviction was upheld.

Generally, then, the Supreme Court of Canada has upheld legislation abridging any aboriginal title benefits which may exist in the area concerned, and has done so without applying a special presumption in favour of compensation. Whether the Constitution Act, 1982 will change this approach remains to be seen.

8. Questions

1. What is the difference, if any, between aboriginal title and aboriginal rights?

2. To what extent have the concepts quoted in part 2 been incorporated into our law?

3. Should the onus be on governments, not the Aboriginal People, to establish the validity of their claim to the land?

4. What is the more satisfactory basis for aboriginal title: the Royal Proclamation of 1763 or the notion of traditional occupancy and use? Why?

5. Is Proclamation-based aboriginal title significantly different in content from occupancy-based aboriginal title?

6. Has the British and American colonial case law followed the general principle that a change of sovereignty does not automatically affect existing rights?

7. Have the Canadian courts accorded aboriginal title general recognition as a common law right?

8. Has aboriginal title a fixed content, or does it vary according to the nature of the traditional use?

9. Is aboriginal title finite or indefinite in duration? Can it be revoked? Is it fully alienable? Who can inherit it? Is it individually or communally owned? What is necessary to prove aboriginal title?

10. Compare and contrast aboriginal title and the fee simple interest. What other common law interest(s) does aboriginal title resemble? How? How does it differ?

11. What is the nature of the Crown's interest in Crown lands subject to aboriginal title? How do the aboriginal title and the Crown's interest coexist?

12. Is aboriginal title a common law "proprietary" interest? Can it be enforced in any way against third parties other than the Crown? Can it be enforced against the Crown?

13. What is (a) extinguishment and (b) abridgment? Will section 35 of the Constitution Act, 1982 affect either, or both? If so, how? Will the Constitution Act, 1982 make any other changes in the law respecting aboriginal title? What changes, if any, should be made in this law?

9. Further Reading

P.A. Cumming and N.H. Mickenberg (eds.), *Native Rights in Canada,* 1972, 2nd ed.

G.S. Lester, *The Territorial Rights of the Inuit of the Canadian Northwest Territories: A Legal Argument,* 1981, unpublished DJur thesis (York University).

K. Lysyk, "The Indian Title Question in Canada: An Appraisal in the Light of Calder," (1973) 51 *Canadian Bar Review* 450.

K. Lysyk, "The Rights and Freedoms of the Aboriginal Peoples of Canada (Ss. 25, 35 and 37)," in W. Tarnopolsky and G.-A. Beaudoin (eds.), *The Canadian Charter of Rights and Freedoms: Commentary,* 1982, p. 467.

B. Slattery, *The Land Rights of Indigenous Canadian Peoples as Affected by the Crown's Acquisition of their Territories,* 1979, DPhil thesis (Oxford University), published by University of Saskatchewan, Native Law Centre.

J. Stagg, *Anglo-Indian Relations in North America to 1763 and An Analysis of The Royal Proclamation of 7 October, 1763,* 1981, published by Department of Indian Affairs and Northern Development, Government of Canada.

Yukon Native Brotherhood, *Together Today for Our Children Tomorrow,* 1973.

4. Pre-Confederation Treaties

BRUCE H. WILDSMITH

Chronology of Indian Treaties to Confederation

Year	Name or Place Made
1693	Massachusetts Bay (USA)
1713	Saint John River, New Brunswick
1725	Boston, Mass.
1725	No. 239 (Boston, Mass.)
1727	Casco Bay, Mass.
1728	Ratification at Annapolis Royal, Nova Scotia
1749	Chebucto Harbour, NS
1752	Halifax, NS
1761	Draft Proclamation from Court of St James
1762	Actual Proclamation at Halifax
1763	Royal Proclamation from Court of St James
1778	NB — NS
1779	Windsor, NS
1779	Halifax, NS
1784	The Haldimand Proclamation
1784	Haldimand Grant
1784	Southern Ontario
1790	Southern Ontario
1792	Southern Ontario
1793	Southern Ontario
1793	The Simcoe Patent
1794	Miramichi, NB
1796(2)	Southern Ontario
1798	Southern Ontario
1805	Southern Ontario
1806	Southern Ontario
1815	Southern Ontario
1817	The Selkirk Treaty
1818(3)	Southern Ontario
1822(2)	Southern Ontario
1827	Southern Ontario
1836	Southern Ontario

1850	The Robinson Superior Treaty
1850	The Robinson Huron Treaty
1850	Sooke Treaty, BC
1852	Sanitch Treaty, BC
1854	Southern Ontario
1854	Saalequun Treaty, BC
1850-54	Other Vancouver Island Treaties
1862	The Manitoulin Island Treaty

1. The Nature of Indian Treaties

Indian treaties are written documents. Although they may be incomplete in the sense that all spoken promises, representations and interpretations may not have been reduced to writing, in the final analysis words were committed to paper and signed by British colonial or Canadian federal government representatives, and Indian representatives. Bodies of law have been developed which apply to written documents, and in some respects different principles or rules apply, depending upon how the document in question is classified. What is the nature of or classification applying to Indian treaties?

Excerpt from P.A. Cumming and N.H. Mickenberg (eds.), *Native Rights in Canada* (2nd ed., Toronto: Indian-Eskimo Association of Canada, 1972), pp. 54-58 [Footnotes deleted].

1. International Treaties. Both historically and legally, it seems that the Indian treaties are not international treaties in the sense of agreements between two or more independent nations. In *Regina* v. *White and Bob,* Davey, JA, stated clearly that an Indian treaty is not an "executive act establishing relationships between what are recognized as two or more independent states acting in sovereign capacities." Historically, it also seems clear that the Government did not consider the Indians to be independent nations at the time the original treaties were made, and in the Commissioner's reports on the post-Confederation treaties, both the Government representatives and the Indian negotiators indicate that they considered the Indian peoples to be subjects of the Queen.

The Indian treaties made by Canada and those made by the United States differ in several respects. In the United States, the Federal power to make treaties was the basis for both international treaties and agreements with the Indians. During the treaty-making period, American Indian tribes were described as dependent nationalities and a tribal Indian was a legal alien. In 1828, the United States Attorney-General examined the contention that the treaties between the Indians and the United States were ineffective because they were not treaties with an independent nation. In his opinion, he concluded that the Indian tribes had sufficient independence for the purpose of entering into treaties. The limitations on their independence in other spheres of competence were not directly on point and hence were irrelevant in determining the legal capacity of the Indian tribes to enter into binding compacts with the American government. Although this argument assumes the existence of the very point at issue (i.e., that the Indian tribes possessed the necessary degree of independence), it seems to have settled the question in the United States.

In American law, the ratification of a treaty involves both executive action and approval by the United States Senate. Having the same legal status as Congressional legislative action, it can override previous legislation and can be annulled by subsequent enactments. In 1871, the United States Congress prohibited further treaties with the Indians, and later dealings with native Americans have taken the form of specific legislation.

In Canada, the power of the Dominion Government to enter into treaties with the Indians does not appear to have been questioned. By virtue of the British North America Act, the Federal Government has authority over "Indians, and Lands reserved for the Indians." Consequently, there has been no need to justify the Federal authority to engage in agreements with the Indians under its power to enter into international treaties.

In Canadian law, the "ratification" of an international treaty is procedurally and legally distinct from the "implementation" of the treaty. The completion of a treaty constitutes the legitimate exercise of the prerogative power. The concurrence of Parliament or the provincial legislative bodies is not required. On the other hand, domestic law is not affected by the provisions of a treaty until the treaty agreements are formally implemented by legislation. This distinction was made explicit by the Supreme Court in *Francis* v. *The Queen*. The accused in this case was an Indian charged with importing goods from the United States without paying the requisite customs duty. The defence relied upon the partial exemption from import duties granted to Indians by the Jay Treaty of 1794. The Court, however, held that since the provisions of the Jay Treaty were never enacted by legislation, the accused could not rely upon the exemptions contained in that agreement:

> The *Jay Treaty* was not a Treaty of Peace and it is clear that in Canada such rights and privileges as are here advanced of subjects of a contracting party to a treaty are enforceable by the Courts only where the treaty has been implemented or sanctioned by legislation.

The reasoning of this argument would be of some importance in regard to the binding effect of Indian treaties, if the analogy between international agreements and the Indian treaties were carried to its logical extreme. The Indian treaties have not formally been implemented by the appropriate provincial or Federal legislation, as would be required to make effective an international agreement. Notwithstanding this non-implementation, the Canadian courts have considered the various treaties with the Indians to constitute obligations enforceable at law. Therefore, in this fundamental way, Canadian law considers Indian treaties different from international treaties.

Whether or not other rules respecting international treaties can be applied to Indian treaties is an issue which remains unresolved in Canadian law. Further, the question of whether an Indian treaty can be attacked as based on fundamental mistake and lack of comprehension by the Indian signatories, cannot be answered because no treaty has ever been challenged in the courts on this ground. The possible range of methods by which the legality of treaties is challengeable in Canada is a field of law which is largely unexplored.

2. Contracts. In certain situations, the courts have viewed Indian treaties as analogous to private agreements or contracts. Indeed, the available, but admittedly limited, judicial authority implicitly supports the application of the contractual model to the Indian treaties.

In *Attorney General for Canada* v. *Attorney General for Ontario*, for example, the Privy Council suggested that the duty to compensate under the Indian treaty in question constituted a "personal obligation" between the Indians and the Governor:

> Their Lordships have had no difficulty in coming to the conclusion that, under the treaties, the Indians obtained no right to their annuities, whether original or augmented, beyond a promise and agreement, which was nothing more than a personal obligation by its governor, as representing the old province, that the latter should pay the annuities as and when they became due. . . .

The reasoning of the Court in this case was that the treaty in question, having been entered into under the prerogative or executive power, was not formally authorized by a body competent to authorize the expenditure of public funds. Therefore, the obligation to compensate the Indians, which was not denied by either party to the action, was described as a personal obligation of one of the Governors, although formal payment was to come from the old Province of Canada.

The question of the legal nature of treaties was also raised in *Rex* v. *Wesley*, where the Supreme Court of Alberta accepted the contract analogy as used by the Privy Council: "In Canada the Indian treaties appear to have been judicially interpreted as being mere promises and agreements." The court carefully noted that the obligation on the Government to carry out its treaty agreements was still binding, even though the treaties were held to constitute "mere promises and agreements":

Assuming as I do that our treaties with Indians are on no higher plane than other formal agreements yet this in no wise makes it less the duty and obligation of the Crown to carry out the promises contained in those treaties with the exactness which honour and good conscience dictate and it is not to be thought that the Crown has departed from those equitable principles which the Senate and the House of Commons declared in addressing Her Majesty in 1867, uniformly governed the British Crown in its dealings with the aborigines.

The Government of Canada has also indicated that it considers Indian treaties to be analogous to contracts. In a speech given in Vancouver, British Columbia, Prime Minister Trudeau made the following comments:

. . . the way we propose it, we say we won't recognize aboriginal rights. We will recognize treaty rights. We will recognize forms of contract which have been made with the Indian people by the Crown and we will try to bring justice to that area and this will mean that perhaps the treaties shouldn't go on forever. It's inconceivable, I think, that in a given society one section of the society have a treaty with the other section of the society.

If Canadian courts were to consistently and logically view the treaties with the Indians as contracts, then a number of sources of litigation are possible. Assuming that the problems inherent in the applicable limitation statutes can be avoided, then questions of duress, undue influence, mistake, and reality of consent could be raised in the courts.

3. Legislation. Because the Indian treaties predated legislation such as the Indian Act as a means of legally arranging relations between the Government and the Indian peoples, the treaties could be seen as analogous to legislation. It is arguable that by interpreting s. 88 of the Indian Act in such a manner that Federal legislation prevails over conflicting treaty provisions, while treaty provisions prevail over conflicting provincial legislation, the courts, by applying the rules of statutory interpretation, have viewed Indian treaties as a form of legislation. In the United States, a committee of Congress in 1830 described Indian treaties as being "but a mode of government, and a substitute for ordinary legislation. . . ." A.H. Snow, an American scholar of Indian law, further states:

It is thus evident that the term "treaty" as applied to an agreement between a civilized state and an aboriginal tribe is misleading, and that such an agreement is, according to the law of nations, a legislative act on the part of the civilized state, made upon conditions which it is bound to fulfil since it insists that the aboriginal tribes shall be bound in its part.

4. Summary. Since the case law developed by Canadian courts in dealing with the Indian treaties is exceptionally sparse, the rules which will be applied by the judiciary in dealing with these treaties cannot be stated definitively. The courts have ruled that the provisions of the treaties may be overriden by Federal legislation but not by provincial legislation. The cases which have interpreted and applied treaty provisions make it clear that the Indian treaties constitute legally enforceable obligations. Unfortunately, the extent to which treaty obligations are enforceable, and perhaps more importantly, the extent of compensation which would be accorded breaches of treaty obligations is unclear. Although some preliminary work in this area has been initiated, the courts have yet to rule on any litigation directly raising these issues.

It seems certain that both the Government and the Indians entered into the various treaties with the intention of creating mutually binding obligations. In the course of Canadian history, these treaties have been acted and relied upon by both parties as inherently legal documents. As a result, it would seem that a court would consider both parties bound by the terms of the agreements, regardless of any formal difficulties in fitting the Indian treaties into a traditional legal framework:

> What is important in cases of this kind is the intention of the parties at the date of the agreement, the recognition that they and others give to their agreement, and the legal consequences that they afford it during the years following its signature. In so far as the Indian treaties are concerned, there is little doubt that, at the time of signing, both parties were using terms that they thought covered their relationship, that both intended to create legal obligations of a permanent character and that both carried out the terms of the agreement for many years. These practices confirm that, whether or not they are treaties, they constitute mutually binding arrangements which have hardened into commitments that neither side can evade unilaterally.

Notes

/ 1 Is an existing category adequate to take account of the uniqueness of the colonist-aboriginal relationship? Should Indian treaties be regarded as *sui generis*, as constituting a class alone?

2 If Indian treaties are to be regarded as *sui generis*, what principles of interpretation and rules of evidence ought to be developed in applying them?

2. Why are there Treaties?

(a) *St Catharine's Milling and Lumber Company* v. *The Queen* (1887), 13 SCR 577.

This case, on a 4-2 split, held that the underlying title to lands in relation to which Indian claims had been surrendered or extinguished by the North West Angle Treaty of 1873 belonged to the Crown in right of Ontario, and not to the Dominion. Ritchie CJ, with whom Fournier J concurred, formed part of the majority and delivered the following judgment.

Sir W.J. Ritchie CJ — I am of opinion, that all ungranted lands in the province of Ontario belong to the crown as part of the public domain, subject to the Indian right of occupancy in cases in which the same has not been lawfully extinguished, and when such right of occupancy has been lawfully extinguished absolutely to the crown, and as a consequence to the province of Ontario. I think the crown owns the soil of all the unpatented lands, the Indians possessing only the right of occupancy, and the crown possessing the legal title subject to that occupancy, with the absolute exclusive right to extinguish the Indian title either by conquest or by purchase; that, as was said by Mr Justice Story (1), [Story on the Constitution 4th Ed. ss. 687]

It is to be deemed a right exclusively belonging to the Government in its sovereign capacity to extinguish the Indian title and to perfect its own dominion over the soil and dispose of it according to its own good pleasure. The crown has the right to grant the soil while yet in possession of the Indians, subject, however, to their right of occupancy.

That the title to lands where the Indian title has not been extinguished is in the crown, would seem to be clearly indicated by Dominion legislation since confederation. See 31 Vic. ch. 42; 33 Vic. ch. 3; 43 Vic. ch. 36.

I agree that the whole course of legislation in all the provinces before, and in the Dominion since, confederation attaches a well understood and distinct meaning to the words ''Indian reserves or lands reserved for the Indians,'' and which cover only lands specifically appropriated or reserved in the Indian territories, or out of the public lands, and I entirely agree with the learned Chancellor that the words ''lands reserved for Indians,'' were used in the BNA Act in the same sense with reference to lands specifically set apart and reserved for the exclusive use of the Indians. In no sense that I can understand can it be said that lands in which the Indian title has been wholly extinguished are lands reserved for the Indians.

The boundary of the territory in the north west angle being established, and the lands in question found to be within the Province of Ontario, they are necessarily, territorially, a part of Ontario, and the ungranted portion of such lands not specifically reserved for the Indians, though unsurrendered and therefore subject to the Indian title, forms part of the public domain of Ontario, and they are consequently public lands belonging to Ontario, and as such pass under the British North

America Act to Ontario, under and by virtue of sub-sec. 5 of sec. 92 and sec. 109 as to lands, mines, minerals and royalties, and sec. 117 by which the Provinces are to retain all their property not otherwise disposed of by that act, subject to the right of the Dominion to assume any lands or public property for fortifications, etc., and therefore, under the British North America Act, the Province of Ontario has a clear title to all unpatented lands within its boundaries as part of the Provincial public property, subject only to the Indian right of occupancy, and absolute when the Indian right of occupancy is extinguished.

I am therefore of opinion, that when the Dominion Government, in 1873 extinguished the Indian claim or title, its effect was, so far as the question now before us is concerned, simply to relieve the legal ownership of the land belonging to the Province from the burden, incumbrance, or however it may be designated, of the Indian title. It therefore follows that the claim of the Dominion to authorize the cutting of timber on these lands cannot be supported, and the Province has a right to interfere and prevent their spoliation.

Mr Justice Henry, part of the majority in result, commented:

In 1873 the crown, in its wisdom, decided to hold these lands as a hunting ground for the Indians. In the first settlement of the country to assert sovereignty and to put that assertion into operation would have caused war, and it was necessary to treat with the Indians from time to time in order to facilitate settlement. They were, therefore, dealt with in such a manner that they were not asked to give up their lands without some compensation. The treaty in question was made when the Dominion Government claimed that the lands in question were not a part of Ontario, and many years before the Privy Council decided that they were. The Dominion Government, asserting that it was a portion of the territory of Manitoba over which they had jurisdiction (for, by arrangement, all the crown lands and timber in Manitoba were reserved to the Dominion), entered into negotiations with the Indians for the extinguishment of their title. That being done we have to inquire what was the operation, in law, of that extinguishment.

Mr Justice Taschereau supported the result of the majority, but was of the view that the claim of the Indians to a title to a beneficial interest in the soil was without legal foundation. To the extent that Indian claims have been recognized, this has been "for obvious political reasons, and motives of humanity and benevolence."

Mr Justice Strong, who dissented in result, put the issue most graphically. He was consistent with the majority viewpoint on this issue:

In the Commentaries of Chancellor Kent and in some decisions of the Supreme Court of the United States we have very full and clear accounts of the policy in question. It may be summarily stated as consisting in the recognition by the crown of a usufructuary title in the Indians to all unsurrendered lands. This title, though not perhaps susceptible of any accurate legal definition in exact legal terms, was one which nevertheless sufficed to protect the Indians in the absolute use and enjoyment of their lands, whilst at the same time they were incapacitated from making any valid alienation otherwise than to the crown itself, in whom the ultimate title was, in accordance with the English law of real property, considered as vested. This short statement will, I think, on comparsion with the authorities to which I will presently refer, be found to be an accurate description of the principles upon which the crown invariably acted with reference to Indian lands, at least from the year 1756, when Sir William Johnston was appointed by the Imperial Government superintendent of Indian affairs in North America, being as such responsible directly to the crown through one of the Secretaries of State, or the Lords of Trade and Plantation, and thus superseding the provincial Governments, down to the year 1867, when the confederation act constituting the Dominion of Canada was passed. So faithfully was this system carried out, that I venture to say that there is no settled part of the territory of the Province of Ontario, except perhaps some isolated spots upon which the French Government had, previous to the conquest, erected forts, such as Fort Frontenac and Fort Toronto, which is not included in and covered by a surrender contained in some Indian treaty still to be found in the Dominion Archives. These rules of policy being shown to have been well established and acted upon, and the title of the Indians to their unsurrendered lands to have been recognized by the crown to the extent already mentioned, it may seem of little importance to enquire into the reasons on which it was based. But as these reasons are not without some bearing on the present question, as I shall hereafter shew, I will shortly refer to what appears to have led to the adoption of the system of dealing with the territorial rights of the Indians. To ascribe it to moral grounds, to motives of humane consideration for the aborigines, would be to attribute it to feelings which perhaps had little weight in the age in which it took its rise. Its true origin was, I take it, experience of the great impolicy of the opposite mode of dealing with the Indians which had been practised by some of the Provincial Governments of the older colonies and which had led to frequent frontier wars, involving great sacrifices of life and property and requiring an expenditure of money which had proved most burdensome to the colonies. That the more liberal treatment accorded to the Indians by this system of protecting them in the enjoyment of their hunting grounds and prohibiting settlement on lands which they had not surrendered, which it is now contended the British North America Act has put an end to, was successful in its results, is attested by the historical fact that from the memorable year 1763, when Detroit was besieged and all the Indian tribes were in revolt, down to the date of confederation, Indian wars and massacres entirely ceased in the British possessions in North America, although powerful Indian nations still continued for some time after the former date to inhabit those territories. That this peaceful conduct of the Indians is in a great degree to be attributed to the recognition of their rights to lands unsurrendered by them, and to the guarantee of their protection in the possession and enjoyment of such lands given by the crown in the proclamation of October, 1763, hereafer to be more fully noticed, is a well known fact of Canadian history which cannot be controverted. The Indian nations from that time became and have since continued to be the firm and faithful allies of the crown and rendered it important military services in two wars — the war of the Revolution and that of 1812.

The American authorities, to which reference has already been made, consist (amongst others) of passages in the commentaries of Chancellor Kent[1], in which the whole doctrine of Indian titles is fully and elaborately considered, and of several decisions of the Supreme Court of the United States, from which three, *Johnston* v. *McIntosh*[2], *Worcester* v. *State of Georgia*[3], and *Mitchell* v. *United States*[4], may be selected as leading cases. The value and importance of these authorities is not merely that they show that the same doctrine as that already propounded regarding the title of the Indians to unsurrendered lands prevails in the United States, but, what is of vastly greater importance, they without exception refer its origin to a date anterior to the revolution and recognise it as a continuance of the principles of law or policy as to Indian titles then established by the British government, and therefore identical with those which have also continued to be recognized and applied in British North America. Chancellor Kent, referring to the decision of the Supreme Court of the United States, in *Cherokee Nation* v. *State of Georgia*[5], says:

> The court there held that the Indians were domestic, dependent nations, and their relations to us resembled that of a ward to his guardian; and they had an unquestionable right to the lands they occupied until that right should be extinguished by a voluntary cession to our government[1].

On the same page the learned commentator proceeds thus:

> The Supreme Court in the case of Worcester reviewed the whole ground of controversy relative to the character and validity of Indian rights within the territorial dominions of the United States, and especially with reference to the Cherokee nation within the limits of Georgia. They declared that the right given by European discovery was the exclusive right to purchase, but this right was not founded on a denial of the Indian possessor to sell. Though the right of the soil

was claimed to be in the European governments as a necessary consequence of the right of discovery and assumption of territorial jurisdiction, yet that right was only deemed such in reference to the whites; and in respect to the Indians it was always understood to amount only to the exclusive right of purchasing such lands as the natives were willing to sell. The royal grants and charters asserted a title to the country against Europeans only, and they were considered as blank paper so far as the rights of the natives were concerned. The English, the French and the Spaniards were equal competitors for the friendship and aid of the Indian nations. The Crown of England never attempted to interfere with the national affairs of the Indians further than to keep out the agents of foreign powers who might seduce them into foreign alliances. The English Government purchased the alliance and dependence of the Indian Nations by subsidies, and purchased their lands when they were willing to sell at a price they were willing to take, but they never coerced a surrender of them. The English Government considered them as nations competent to maintain the relations of peace and war and of governing themselves under her protection. The United States, who succeeded to the rights of the British Crown in respect of the Indians, did the same and no more; and the protection stipulated to be afforded to the Indians and claimed by them was understood by all parties as only binding the Indians to the United States as dependent allies.

Again the same learned writer says[2]:

The original Indian Nations were regarded and dealt with as proprietors of the soil which they claimed and occupied, but without the power of alienation, except to the Governments which protected them and had thrown over them and beyond them their assumed patented domains. These Governments asserted and enforced the exclusive right to extinguish Indian titles to lands, enclosed within the exterior lines of their jurisdictions, by fair purchase, under the sanction of treaties; and they held all individual purchases from the Indians, whether made with them individually or collectively as tribes, to be absolutely null and void. The only power that could lawfully acquire the Indian title was the State, and a government grant was the only lawful source of title admitted in the Courts of Justice. The Colonial and State Governments and the government of the United States uniformly dealt upon these principles with the Indian Nations dwelling within their territorial limits.

Further, Chancellor Kent, in summarising the decision of the Supreme Court in *Mitchell* v. *United States*, states the whole doctrine in a form still more applicable to the present case. He says:

The Supreme Court once more declared the same general doctrine, that lands in possession of friendly Indians were always, under the

colonial governments, considered as being owned by the tribe or
nation as their common property by a perpetual right of possession;
but that the ultimate fee was in the crown or its grantees, subject to
this right of possession, and could be granted by the crown upon that
condition; that individuals could not purchase Indian lands without
license, or under rules prescribed by law; that possession was
considered with reference to Indian habits and modes of life, and the
hunting grounds of the tribes were as much in their actual occupation
as the cleared fields of the whites, and this was the tenure of Indian
lands by the laws of all the colonies.

It thus appears, that in the United States a traditional policy derived
from colonial times, relative to the Indians and their lands has ripened
into well established rules of law, and that the result is that the lands in
the possession of the Indians are, until surrendered, treated as their
rightful though inalienable property, so far as the possession and
enjoyment are concerned; in other words, that the *dominium utile* is
recognized as belonging to or reserved for the Indians, though the
dominium directum is considered to be in the United States. Then, if this
is so as regards Indian lands in the United States, which have been
preserved to the Indians by the constant observance of a particular rule
of policy acknowledged by the United States courts to have been
originally enforced by the crown of Great Britain, how is it possible to
suppose that the law can, or rather could have been, at the date of
confederation, in a state any less favorable to the Indians whose lands
were situated within the dominion of the British crown, the original
author of this beneficent doctrine so carefully adhered to in the United
States from the days of the colonial governments? Therefore, when we
consider that with reference to Canada the uniform practice has always
been to recognize the Indian title as one which could only be dealt with
by surrender to the crown, I maintain that if there had been an entire
absence of any written legislative act ordaining this rule as an express
positive law, we ought, just as the United States courts have done, to
hold that it nevertheless existed as a rule of the unwritten common law,
which the courts were bound to enforce as such, and consequently, that
the 24th sub-section of section 91, as well as the 109th section and the
5th sub-section of section 92 of the British North America Act, must all
be read and construed upon the assumption that these territorial rights of
the Indians were strictly legal rights which had to be taken into account
and dealt with in that distribution of property and proprietary rights
made upon confederation between the federal and provincial governments.

The voluminous documentary evidence printed in the case contains
numerous instances of official recognition of the doctrine of Indian title
to unceded lands as applied to Canada. Without referring at length to

this evidence I may just call attention to one document which, as it contains an expression of opinion with reference to the title to the same lands part of which are now in dispute in this cause by a high judicial authority, a former Chief Justice of Upper Canada, is of peculiar value. In the appendix to the case for Ontario laid before the Judicial Committee in the Boundary Case[1] we find a letter dated 1st of May 1819 from Chief Justice Powell to the Lieutenant Governor, Sir Peregrine Maitland, upon the subject of of the conflict then going on between the North West and Hudson's Bay Companies, and of which the territory now in question was the scene. The Chief Justice, writing upon the jurisdiction of the Upper Canada Courts in this territory and of an act of Palriament relating thereto, says:

> The territory which it affects is in the crown and part of a district, but the soil is in the aborigines and inhabited only by Indians and their lawless followers.

There cannot be a more distinct statement of the rights claimed by the appellants to have existed in the Indians than this, and if the soil, *i.e.* the title to the soil, was in the Indians in 1819 it must have so remained down to the date of the North West Angle Treaty No. 3 made in 1873.

To summarize these arguments, which appear to me to possess great force, we find, that at the date of confederation the Indians, by the constant usage and practice of the crown, were considered to possess a certain proprietary interest in the unsurrendered lands which they occupied as hunting grounds; that this usage had either ripened into a rule of the common law as applicable to the American Colonies, or that such a rule had been derived from the law of nations and had in this way been imported into the Colonial law as applied to Indian Nations; that such property of the Indians was usufructuary only and could not be alienated, except by surrender to the crown as the ultimate owner of the soil

A like view is expressed by Gwynne J, also in dissent on the ultimate issue of whether the title underlying the Indian's usufructuary interest was provincial or federal:

> The inviolable manner in which the Indian title as declared by the Proclamation of 1763 has been recognized amply justifies the language of the commissioners appointed by the crown to report upon Indian affairs in the Province of Upper Canada in 1842 and 1856. The former commissioners in their report say:
>
> > The Proclamation of His Majesty George the third issued in 1763 furnished the Indians with a fresh guarantee for the possession of their hunting grounds and the protection of the crown. This document the Indians look upon as their charter. They have preserved a copy of it to

the present time, and have referred to it on several occasions in their representations to the Government.

And again:

Since 1763 the Government, adhering to the Royal Proclamation of that year, have not considered themselves entitled to dispossess the Indians of their lands without entering into an agreement with them and rendering them some compensation.

The commissioners of 1856 in their report say:

By the Proclamation of 1763 territorial rights, akin to those asserted by Sovereign Princes, are recognised as belonging to the Indians, that is to say, that none of their land can be alienated save by treaty made publicly between the crown and them. Later, however, as this was found insufficient to check the whites from entering into bargains with the Indians for portions of their lands or for the timber growing thereon, it has been found necessary to pass stringent enactments for the protection of the Indian Reserves.

After the most explicit recognition by the crown of the Indian title for upwards of a century in the most solemn manner — by treaties entered into between the crown and the Indian nations in council assembled according to their national custom, and by deeds of cession to the crown and of purchase by the crown, prepared by officers of the crown for execution by the Indians — it cannot, in my opinion, admit a doubt that at the time of the passing of the British North America Act the Indians in Upper Canada were acknowledged by the crown to have, and that they had, an estate, title and interest in all lands in that part of the Province of Canada formerly constituting Upper Canada for the cession of which to the crown no agreement had been made with the nations or tribes occupying the same as their hunting grounds, or claiming title thereto, which estate, title and interest could be divested or extinguished in no other manner than by cession made in the most solemn manner to the crown. These cessions were made sometimes upon purchases made by the crown for the use of the public, in which case the lands so acquired became *"Public lands,"* because the revenue to be derived from their sale was appropriated for the benefit of the public and was paid into the Provincial Treasury. Sometimes the cessions were made to the crown upon trust for sale and investment of the proceeds for the benefit of the Indians themselves, and sometimes upon trust to grant to some person upon whom the Indians desired to confer a benefit for special services rendered to them; but all such lands, until the cession thereof should be made by the Indians to the crown, constituted what were known as and designated "Indian Reserves," "Lands reserved for the Indians," or "Indian lands." It is the lands *not ceded to* or *purchased by* the crown which are spoken of in the proclamation of 1763 as *the lands reserved to* the Indians for their hunting ground — and the unceded lands have ever since been known by the designation "Lands reserved for the Indians" or "Indian Reserves."

When the Indians in the deeds or treaties by way of cession of land to the crown reserved from out of the general description of the lands given in the instruments of cession, as they often did, certain particularly described portions of the lands so generally described, for the special uses, occupation or residence of particular bands, the parts so reserved did not come under the operation of the deed or treaty of cession, but were reserved and excepted out of it and so continued to be just as they were before, lands not ceded to, or purchased by, the crown, and therefore remained still within the designation of "Lands reserved for the Indians," or "Indian Reserves."

It was not the exception of the particular parcels from the operation of the instrument of cession which made such parts come within designation of "Lands reserved for Indians" or "Indian Reserves," but because, being so excepted, they remained in the position they were before, namely, lands not yet ceded to or purchased by the crown.

Note

[1.] This case was affirmed on appeal (1889), 14 App. Cas. 46 by the Judicial Committee or the Privy Council. The Privy Council version is included in chapter 3, Sec. 4(b)(i), *supra*.

(b) *Johnson and Graham's Lessee* v. *McIntosh* (1823), 21 US (8 Wheaton) 543.

In the course of holding that the title to certain lands granted by Indian tribes to private individuals could not be recognized in the courts of the United States, Chief Justice Marshall, for the full court, made the following remarks:

On the discovery of this immense continent, the great nations of Europe were eager to appropriate to themselves so much of it as they could respectively acquire. Its vast extent offered an ample field to the ambition and enterprise of all; and the character and religion of its inhabitants afforded an apology for considering them as a people over whom the superior genius of Europe might claim an ascendancy. The potentates of the old world found no difficulty in convincing themselves that they made ample compensation to the inhabitants of the new, by bestowing on them civilization and Christianity, in exchange for unlimited independence. But, as they were all in pursuit of nearly the same object, it was necessary, in order to avoid conflicting settlements, and consequent war with each other, to establish a principle, which all should acknowledge as the law by which the right of acquisition, which they all asserted, should be regulated as between themselves. This principle was, that discovery gave title to the government by whose subjects, or by whose authority, it was made, against all other European governments, which title might be consummated by possession.

The exclusion of all other Europeans necessarily gave to the nation making the discovery the sole right of acquiring the soil from the natives, and establishing settlements upon it. It was a right with which no Europeans could interfere. It was a right which all asserted for themselves, and to the assertion of which, by others, all assented.

Those relations which were to exist between the discoverer and the natives, were to be regulated by themselves. The rights thus acquired being exclusive, no other power could interpose between them.

In the establishment of these relations, the rights of the original inhabitants were, in no instance, entirely disregarded; but were necessarily, to a considerable extent, impaired. They were admitted to be the rightful occupants of the soil, with a legal as well as just claim to retain possession of it, and to use it according to their own discretion; but their rights to complete sovereignty, as independent nations, were necessarily diminished, and their power to dispose of the soil at their own will, to whomsoever they pleased, was denied by the original fundamental principle, that discovery gave exclusive title to those who made it.

While the different nations of Europe respected the right of the natives, as occupants, they asserted the ultimate dominion to be in themselves; and claimed and exercised, as a consequence of this ultimate dominion, a power to grant the soil, while yet in possession of the natives. These grants have been understood by all, to convey a title to the grantees, subject only to the Indian right of occupancy.

The history of America, from its discovery to the present day, proves, we think, the universal recognition of these principles.

The United States, then, have unequivocally acceded to that great and broad rule by which its civilized inhabitants now hold this country. They hold, and assert in themselves, the title by which it was acquired. They maintain, as all others have maintained, that discovery gave an exlcusive right to extinguish the Indian title of occupancy, either by purchase or by conquest; and gave also a right to such a degree of sovereignty, as the circumstances of the people would allow them to exercise. . . .

According to the theory of the British constitution, the royal prerogative is very extensive, so far as respects the political relations between Great Britain and foreign nations. The peculiar situation of the Indians, necessarily considered, in some respects, as a dependent, and in some respects as a distinct people, occupying a country claimed by Great Britain, and yet too powerful and brave not to be dreaded as formidable enemies, required, that means should be adopted for the preservation of peace; and that their friendship should be secured by quieting their alarms for their property. This was to be effected by restraining the encroachments of the whites; and the power to do this was never, we believe, denied by the colonies to the crown. . . .

(c) *Worcester* v. *The State of Georgia* (1832), 31 US (6 Peters) 515.

This case involved an indictment for residing within the limits of the Cherokee nation without a license or permit from the Governor of Georgia, contrary to a statute passed by that state. The Supreme Court held "that the act of the legislature of the State of Georgia, upon which the indictment in this case is founded, is contrary to the constitution, treaties, and laws of the United States." In the course of delivering the opinion of the majority, Chief Justice Marshall stated:

America, separated from Europe by a wide ocean, was inhabited by a distinct people, divided into separate nations, independent of each other and of the rest of the world, having institutions of their own, and governing themselves by their own laws. It is difficult to comprehend the proposition, that the inhabitants of either quarter of the globe could have rightful original claims of dominion over the inhabitants of the other, or over the lands they occupied; or that the discovery of either by the other should give the discoverer rights in the country discovered, which annulled the pre-existing rights of its ancient possessors.

After lying concealed for a series of ages, the enterprise of Europe, guided by nautical science, conducted some of her adventurous sons into this western world. They found it in possession of a people who had made small progress in agriculture or manufactures, and whose general employment was war, hunting, and fishing.

Did these adventurers, by sailing along the coast, and occcasionally landing on it, acquire for the several governments to whom they belonged, or by whom they were commissioned, a rightful property in the soil, from the Atlantic to the Pacific; or rightful dominion over the numerous people who occupied it? Or has nature, or the great Creator of all things, conferred these rights over hunters and fishermen, on agriculturists and manufacturers?

But power, war, conquest, give rights, which, after possession, are conceded by the world; and which can never be controverted by those on whom they descend. We proceed, then, to the actual state of things, having glanced at their origin; because holding it in our recollection might shed some light on existing pretensions.

The great maritime powers of Europe discovered and visited different parts of this continent at nearly the same time. The object was too immense for any one of them to grasp the whole; and the claimants were too powerful to submit to the exclusive or unreasonable pretensions of any single potentate. To avoid bloody conflicts, which might terminate disastrously to all, it was necessary for the nations of Europe to establish some principle which all would acknowledge, and which should decide their respective rights as between themselves. This principle, suggested by the actual state of things, was, "that discovery gave title to the government by whose subjects or by whose authority it was made, against all other European governments, which title might be consummated by possession." 8 Wheat. 573.

This principle, acknowledged by all Europeans, because it was the interest of all to acknowledge it, gave to the nation making the discovery, as its inevitable consequence, the sole right of acquiring the soil and of making settlements on it. It was an exclusive principle which shut out the right of competition among those who had agreed to it; not one which could annul the previous rights of those who had not agreed to it. It regulated the right given by discovery among the European discoverers; but could not affect the rights of those already in possession, either as aboriginal occupants, or as occupants by virtue of a discovery made before the memory of man. It gave the exclusive right to purchase, but did not found that right on a denial of the right of the possessor to sell.

The relation between the Europeans and the natives was determined in each case by the particular government which asserted and could maintain this pre-emptive privilege in the particular place. The United States succeeded to all the claims of Great Britain, both territorial and political; but no attempt, so far as is known, has been made to enlarge them. So far as they existed merely in theory, or were in their nature only exclusive of the claims of other European nations, they still retain their original character, and remain dormant. So far as they have been practically exerted, they exist in fact, are understood by both parties, are asserted by the one, and admitted by the other.

Soon after Great Britain determined on planting colonies in America, the king granted charters to companies of his subjects who associated for the purpose of carrying the views of the crown into effect, and of enriching themselves. The first of these charters was made before possession was taken of any part of the country. They purport, generally, to convey the soil, from the Atlantic to the South Sea. This soil was occupied by numerous and warlike nations, equally willing and able to defend their possessions. The extravagant and absurd idea, that the feeble settlements made on the sea coast, or the companies under whom they were made, acquired legitimate power by them to govern the people, or occupy the lands from sea to sea, did not enter the mind of any man. They were well understood to convey the title which, according to the common law of European sovereigns respecting America, they might rightfully convey, and no more. This was the exclusive right of purchasing such lands as the natives were willing to sell. The crown could not be understood to grant what the crown did not affect to claim; nor was it so understood.

These motives for planting the new colony are incompatible with the lofty ideas of granting the soil, and all its inhabitants from sea to sea. They demonstrate the truth, that these grants asserted a title against Europeans only, and were considered as blank paper so far as the rights of the natives were concerned. The power of war is given only for defence, not for conquest.

The charters contain passages showing one of their objects to be the civilization of the Indians, and their conversion to Christanity — objects to be accomplished by conciliatory conduct and good example; not by extermination.

The actual state of things, and the practice of European nations, on so much of the American continent as lies between the Mississippi and the Atlantic, explain their claims, and the charters they granted. Their pretensions unavoidably interfered with each other; though the discovery of one was admitted by all to exlcude the claim of any other, the extent of that discovery was the subject of unceasing contest. Bloody conflicts arose between them, which gave importance and security to the neighbouring nations. Fierce and warlike in their character, they might be formidable enemies, or effective friends. Instead of rousing their resentments, by asserting claims to their lands, or to dominion over their persons, their alliance was sought by flattering professions, and purchased by rich presents. The English, the French, and the Spaniards were equally competitors for their friendship and their aid. Not well acquainted with the exact meaning of words, nor supposing it to be material whether they were called the subjects, or the children of their father in Europe; lavish in professions of duty and affection, in return for the rich presents they received: so long as their actual independence was untouched, and their right to self-government acknowledged, they were willing to profess dependence on the power which furnished supplies of which they were in absolute need, and restrained dangerous intruders from entering their country: and this was probably the sense in which the term was understood by them.

Certain it is, that our history furnishes no example, from the first settlement of our country, of any attempt on the part of the crown to interfere with the internal affairs of the Indians, farther than to keep out the agents of foreign powers, who, as traders or otherwise, might seduce them into foreign alliances. The king purchased their lands when they were willing to sell, at a price they were willing to take; but never coerced a surrender of them. He also purchased their alliance and dependence by subsidies; but never intruded into the interior of their affairs, or interfered with their self government, so far as respected themselves only.

The general views of Great Britain, with regard to the Indians, were detailed by Mr Stuart, superintendent of Indian affairs, in a speech delivered at Mobile, in presence of several persons of distinction, soon after the peace of 1763. Towards the conclusion he says, "lastly, I inform you that it is the king's order to all his governors and subjects, to treat Indians with justice and humanity, and to forbear all encroachments on the territories allotted to them; accordingly, all inividuals are prohibited from purchasing any of your lands; but, as you know that, as your white brethren cannot feed you when you visit them unless you give them ground to plant, it is expected that you will cede lands to the king for that purpose. But, whenever you shall be pleased to surrender any of your territories to his majesty, it must be done, for the future, at a public meeting of your nation, when the governors of the provinces, or the superintendent shall be present, and obtain the consent of all your people. The boundaries of your hunting grounds will be accurately fixed, and no settlement permitted to be made upon them. As you may be assured that all treaties with your people will be faithfully kept, so it is expected that you, also, will be careful strictly to observe them."

The proclamation issued by the king of Great Britian, in 1763, soon after the ratification of the articles of peace, forbids the governors of any of the colonies to grant warrants of survey, or pass patents upon any lands whatever, which, not having been ceded to, or purchased by, us (the king), as aforesaid, are reserved to the said Indians, or any of them.

The proclamation proceeds: "and we do further declare it to be our royal will and pleasure, for the present, as aforesaid, to reserve, under our sovereignty, protection, and dominion, for the use of the said Indians, all the lands and territories lying to the westward of the sources of the rivers which fall into the sea, from the west and northwest as aforesaid: and we do hereby strictly forbid, on pain of our displeasure, all our loving subjects from making any purchases or settlements whatever, or taking possession of any of the lands above reserved, without our special leave and license for that purpose first obtained.

"And we do further strictly enjoin and require all persons whatever, who have, either wilfully or inadvertently, seated themselves upon any lands within the countries above described, or upon any other lands which, not having been ceded to, or purchased by us, are still reserved to the said Indians, as aforesaid, forthwith to remove themselves from such settlements."

A proclamation, issued by Governor Gage, in 1772, contains the following passage: "whereas many persons, contrary to the positive orders of the king, upon this subject, have undertaken to make settlements beyond the boundaries fixed by the treaties made with the Indian nations, which boundaries ought to serve as a barrier between the whites and the said nations; particularly on the Ouabache." The proclamation orders such persons to quit those countries without delay.

Such was the policy of Great Britain towards the Indian nations inhabiting the territory from which she excluded all other Europeans; such her claims, and such her practical exposition of the charters she had granted: she considered them as nations capable of maintaining the relations of peace and war; of governing themselves, under her protection; and she made treaties with them, the obligation of which she acknowledged.

This was the settled state of things when the war of our revolution commenced. The influence of our enemy was established; her resources enabled her to keep up that influence; and the colonists had much cause for the apprehension that the Indian nations would, as the allies of Great Britain, add their arms to hers. This, as was to be expected, became an object of great solicitude to congress. Far from advancing a claim to their lands, or asserting any right of dominion over them, congress resolved "that the securing and preserving the friendship of the Indian nations appears to be a subject of the utmost moment to these colonies."

The Indian nations had always been considered as distinct, independent political communities, retaining their original natural rights, as the undisputed possessors of the soil, from time immemorial, with the single exception of that imposed by irresistible power, which excluded them from intercourse with any other European potentate than the first discoverer of the coast of the particular region claimed: and this was a restriction which those European potentates imposed on themselves, as well as on the Indians. The very term "nation," so generally applied to them, means "a people distinct from others." The constitution, by declaring treaties already made, as well as those to be made, to be the supreme law of the land, has adopted and sanctioned the previous treaties with the Indian nations, and consequently admits their rank among those powers who are capable of making treaties. The words "treaty" and "nation" are words of our own language, selected in our diplomatic and legislative proceedings, by ourselves, having each a definite and well understood meaning. We have applied them to Indians, as we have applied them to the other nations of the earth. They are applied to all in the same sense.

Mr Justice McLean, who concurred with the Chief Justice, also delivered an opinion, in the course of which he remarked:

The abstract right of every section of the human race to a reasonable portion of the soil, by which to acquire the means of subsistence, cannot be controverted. And it is equally clear, that the range of nations or tribes, who exist in the hunter state, may be restricted within reasonable limits. They shall not be permitted to roam, in the pursuit of game, over an extensive and rich country, whilst in other parts, human beings are crowded so closely together, as to render the means of subsistence precarious. The law of nature, which is paramount to all other laws, gives the right to every nation, to the enjoyment of a reasonable extent of country, so as to derive the means of subsistence from the soil.

In this view perhaps, our ancestors, when they first migrated to this country, might have taken possession of a limited extent of the domain, had they been sufficiently powerful, without negotiation or purchase from the native Indians. But this course is believed to have been nowhere taken. A more conciliatory mode was preferred, and one which was better calculated to impress the Indians, who were then powerful, with a sense of the justice of their white neighbours. The occupancy of their lands was never assumed, except upon the basis of contract, and on the payment of a valuable consideration.

This policy has obtained from the earliest white settlements in this country, down to the present time. Some cessions of territory may have been made by the Indians, in compliance with the terms on which peace was offered by the whites; but the soil, thus taken, was taken by the laws of conquest, and always as an indemnity for the expenses of the war, commenced by the Indians.

At no time has the sovereignty of the country been recognized as existing in the Indians, but they have been always admitted to possess many of the attributes of sovereignty. All the rights which belong to self government have been recognized as vested in them. Their right of occupancy has never been questioned, but the fee in the soil has been considered in the government. This may be called the right to the ultimate domain, but the Indians have a present right of possession.

Notes

[1] Is it not fair to conclude that the treaties are premised upon the recognition of Indian rights which pre-existed colonialization? If so, do these rights not continue until extinguished? For further details see Chapter 3, Sec. 4(b), which deals with cases on the legal status of aboriginal rights.

[2] War, conquest and the subsequent imposition of a new legal regime could extinguish Indian rights. Was this the methodology adopted? Was the technique of negotiating treaties not adopted to minimize hostilities and secure both peace and land by agreement? If so, are treaties not fundamental documents governing the relationship between the white colonists and their successors, and the aboriginal inhabitants and their successors?

3. An Indian View on the Treaties

Excerpts from Harold Cardinal, *The Unjust Society* (Edmonton: M.C. Hurtig Ltd., 1969), pp. 28-43.

To the Indians of Canada, the treaties represent an Indian Magna Carta. The treaties are important to us, because we entered into these negotiations with faith, with hope for a better life with honour. We have survived for over a century on little but that hope. Did the white man enter into them with something less in mind? Or have the heirs of the men who signed in honour somehow disavowed the obligation passed down to them? The Indians entered into the treaty negotiations as honourable men who came to deal was equals with the queen's representatives. Our leaders of that time thought they were dealing with an equally honourable people. Our leaders pledged themselves, their people and their heirs to honour what was done then.

Our leaders mistakenly thought they were dealing with an honourable people who would do no less than the Indians were doing — bind themselves, bind their people and bind their heirs to honourable contracts.

Our people talked with the government representatives, not as beggars pleading for handouts, but as men with something to offer in return for rights they expected. To our people, this was the beginning of a contractual relationship whereby the representatives of the queen would have lasting responsibilities to the Indian people in return for the valuable lands that were ceded to them.

The treaties were the way in which the white people legitimized in the eyes of the world their presence in our country. It was an attempt to settle the terms of occupancy on a just basis, legally and morally to extinguish the legitimate claims of our people to title to the land in our country. There never has been any doubt in the minds of our people that the land in Canada belonged to them. Nor can there have been any doubt in the mind of the government or in the minds of the white people about who owned the land, for it was upon the basis of white recognition of Indian rights that the treaties were negotiated. Otherwise, there could have been nothing to negotiate, no need for treaties. In the language of the Cree Indians, the Indian reserves are known as *the land that we kept for ourselves* or *the land that we did not give to the government.* In our language, *skun-gun.* . . .

By and large, the articles of all written treaties between the Indians of Canada and the government of Canada must be considered misleading because they omitted substantial portions of what was promised verbally to the Indian. Additionally, they carry key phrases that are not precise, or they state that certain things were ceded that, in actual fact, were never considered or granted by the Indians who signed the treaties. Nevertheless, the government, although not willing even to begin to honour its side of the partnership, holds Indians to the strictest letter of the treaties. According to government interpretation, the following outline represents the sum total of its commitment to the Indians involved in one particular, but typical treaty.

Under Treaty Six, the Indians involved (the Plain and Wood Cree tribes in Saskatchewan and Alberta) surrendered land comprising an approximate area of 121,000 square miles. Concerning land, written reports of the treaty make the following commitment: "And Her Majesty, the Queen, hereby agrees and undertakes to lay aside reserves for farming lands, due respect being had to lands at present cultivated by the said Indians, and other reserves for the benefit of the said Indians, to be administered and dealt with for them by Her Majesty's Government of the Dominion of Canada; provided all such reserves shall not exceed in all one square mile for each family of five or in that proportion for larger or smaller families. . . . The Chief Superintendent of Indian Affairs shall depute and send a suitable person to determine and set apart the reserves for each band, after consulting with the Indians thereof as to the locality which may be found to be most suitable for them."

In the field of education, Treaty Six states: "Her Majesty agrees to maintain schools for instruction in such reserves hereby made as to Her Government of the Dominion of Canada may deem advisable, whenever the Indians of the reserve shall desire it."

The government also promised under treaty to give the Indians "the right to pursue their avocations of hunting and fishing throughout the tract surrendered as herintofor described, subject to such regulations as may from time to time be made by Her Government of Her Dominion of Canada." The formal statement on aboriginal rights also outlines hunting restrictions in areas of settlement, mining or lumbering.

Surprisingly, many non-Indian people believe that the Indians receive all the money they need from the government throughout the year. In the Prairie provinces, the Indians were promised that the government would "pay to each Indian person the sum of $5.00 per head yearly."

In order to assist the Indians to make a beginning in farming, the government made the following commitment: "four hoes for every family actually cultivating; also, two spades per family aforesaid; one plough for every three families as aforesaid; one harrow for every three families as aforesaid; two scythes and one whetstone, and two hay forks and two reaping hooks, for every family aforesaid and also two axes; and also one crosscut saw, one hand-saw, one pit-saw, the necessary files, one grindstone and one auger for each band; and also for each chief for the use of his band, one chest of ordinary carpenter's tools; also, for each band, enough of wheat, barley, potatoes and oats to plant the land actually broken up for cultivation by such band; also for each band four oxen, one bull and six cows; also one boar and two sows and one hand-mill when any band shall raise sufficient grain therefor.''

Recognition of leadership was given: chiefs were to be paid an ''annual salary of twenty-five dollars per annum and each subordinate officer, not exceeding four for each band, shall receive fifteen dollars per annum . . . shall receive once every three years a suitable suit of clothing and each chief shall receive in recognition of the closing of the treaty a suitable flag and medal and also as soon as convenient, one horse, harness and wagon.''

The promise of medical care was contained in the following phrase: ''A medicine chest shall be kept at the house of each Indian agent for the use and benefit of the Indians at the direction of such agent.''

Under Treaty Six, welfare or social assistance was promised under the phrase, ''In the event hereafter of the Indians comprised within this treaty being overtaken by any pestilence or by a general famine, the Queen, on being satisfied and certified thereof by Her Indian agent or agents will grant to the Indians assistance of such character and to such extent as Her Chief Superintendent of Indian Affairs [the minister] shall deem necessary and sufficient to relieve the Indians from the calamity that shall have befallen them.''

These pledges are typical, if not all-inclusive, of the promises that were made to the Indians by the government, although the cautionary phrase, ''Her Majesty reserves the right to deal with. . .,'' appearing commonly throughout the treaty, would have alerted a more sophisticated people to possible loopholes and pitfalls. There are many other aspects of the written treaties that are questionable. Generally, the treaties are outstanding for what they *do not* say rather than what they do say.

In spite of their admissions and omissions the treaties are doubly significant and important because they represent or imply principles that are intrinsically part of the concept of justice and respect for other men's property. They have a symbolic importance to Indians that cannot be ignored.

Many people, including the prime minister, have suggested that treaties are problems of yesteryear. They suggest that Indian treaties are irrelevant to life in the twentieth century and that to consider them important now is to look at life backwards, that we should forget the past and the treaties and look only toward the future. This position was put forward by Mr Chrétien at the national consultation meetings (between the government and representatives of all Canada's Indians) held in Ottawa April 28-May 2, 1969. It is difficult to understand how this government or any government could adopt such a position. For the Trudeau government, preoccupied as it has been with language rights, the Canadian constitution, the criminal code and the concept of human rights, it becomes doubly a paradox.

Once our rights are guaranteed, there will be less need for our people to emphasize their sovereignty. The question of Indian rights is the paramount question for all Indian people from the vantage point of the past, the present and the future.

While we find much to quarrel with in the treaties as they were signed, they are, we contend, important, not so much for their content as for the principles they imply in their very existence.

The Manitoba Indian Brotherhood, under its progressive and capable president, David Courchene, made the following observations about the treaties during their regional consultation meetings in December 1968.

"From reading these treaties it is apparent that:

1. The officials representing the Government full well knew the value of the land requested to be ceded to the Crown;
2. . . . they were aware that the Indian was not able to communicate with them;
3. . . . the Indian had no counsel;
4. . . . the Indian was impressed by the pomp and ceremony and the authority of the officials;
5. . . . they [the officials] were dealing with uneducated people;
6. . . . the respect and ceremony with which the officials were dealing with the Indians lulled the Indians into a passive mood;
7. . . . a father image was being advanced by the authorities;
8. . . . the Indians, although it is alleged were explained the terms of the Treaties, really did not know or understand fully the meaning and implications;
9. . . . the alleged consideration that was being advanced by the Government to the Indians in exchange for the ceded land was not totally appreciated by the Indians, nor could they understand the concept of binding their heirs and executors, administrators and assigns to these documents;
10. . . . forever and a day it will be obvious to all who read the said Treaties and the history of their making, that the officials of Her Majesty the Queen committed a legal fraud in a very sophisticated manner upon unsophisticated, unsuspecting, illiterate, uninformed natives."

Manitoba's Indians, taking for the first time a hard look at the past, said, "These treaties must be renegotiated." Their study of the past pointed the way to the future.

We can brook no argument that the treaties are not relevant to the present. They are related in a very direct way to the hunting, trapping and fishing rights of our people because, even today, a large portion of the Indian people still depend upon these rights for their livelihood. Our rights are today's problem, for upon them the education of our people rests. Access to medical services, upon which our people depend, proportionately, more than any other Canadians for their health and well-being, is entirely at the pleasure of the government. Our rights are even more relevant today when one considers the need for land and the need for future economic development.

The future of the Indian in Canada lies in the area of education, proper medical services, land and economic development. There is no future for our people if the government does not respect and protect our rights.

The Indians of Alberta made their position clear to the government when they demanded that legislation be passed to protect:

1. hunting, trapping and fishing rights,
2. the right of education,
3. the right of full and free medical services,
4. the right of land,

and to encourage

5. economic development on reserves.

"The terms of the treaties," insisted the Manitoba Indian Brotherhood, "must be extended and interpreted in light of present social and economic standards. To renegotiate the treaties does not necessarily mean to rewrite the treaties, nor does it mean to repudiate the treaties."

It was recognized at the Manitoba meeting that the importance of the treaties lies in the recognition and acceptance of the true spirit of the treaties rather than studied adherence to archaic phraseology.

The brotherhood noted: "A promise by the Government and a carrying out of that promise to give economic and financial assistance to the Indian so that he may better be able to advance his economic position in the community, would be a carrying out of one of the terms of the treaties. A promise and a carrying out of that promise by the Government that every child will have the right to a full education with all facilities made available to him for that purpose, is a carrying out of one of the terms of the treaties. A guarantee that every Indian will have full and adequate and immediate medical treatment as and when required, is a carrying out of one of the terms of those treaties.

"To renegotiate those treaties means to reach agreement, to carry out the full meaning and intent of the promises given by the representatives of the Queen, as interpreted, and as understood by the Indians. To successfully renegotiate those treaties is to being about a legal commitment by the Government that the true intent and tenure of those treaties will be carried out."

The Indian people cannot be blamed for feeling that not until the sun ceases to shine, the rivers cease to flow and the grasses to grow or, wonder of wonders, the government decides to honour its treaties, will the white man cease to speak with forked tongue.

Not only was much of what was written in the treaties written without the full understanding of the Indians involved; much more which the Indian expected to be in the treaties never was written. Preceding the writing of the treaties, the white man and the Indian talked and what the white man said was reassuring. His promises and reassurances without doubt helped to convince the Indian leaders they could and should sign the treaties.

Obviously, both in the case of mineral rights and in the sub-surface water rights, vast amounts of money could be involved. Opportunities for Indians to advance their own economic development could be at stake.

Treaty Eight in many ways exemplifies the manner in which the government representatives worked legally to swindle our people. They promised everything. They wrote bloody little.

The report of the commissioners states: "We promised that supplies of medicines, would be put in the charge of persons selected by the Government at different points, and would be distributed free to those of the Indians who might require them. . . . We assured them . . . that the Government would always be ready to avail itself of any opportunity of affording medical service just as it provided that the physician attached to the Commission should give free attendance to all Indians whom he might find in need of treatment as he passed through the country." Yet the main articles of the treaty do not in any way refer to medical services or rights to free medical attention.

The commissioner admits on record that the Indians were assured of medicine and medical treatment. The Indians expected this to be in the treaty. They were not told it was not there. Legally, the commitment is not there in the treaty. Legally, the white man clearly won that round. Ethically, it is damned comforting to be Indian.

In relation to education the government representatives made the following observation: "They seemed desirous of securing educational advantages for their children, but stipulated that in the matter of schools there should be no interference with their religious beliefs. . . . As to education, the Indians were assured that there was no need of any special stipulation, as it was the policy of the Government to provide in every part of the country, as far as circumstances would permit, for the education of Indian children, and that the law, which was as strong as a treaty, provided for non-interference with the religion of the Indians in schools maintained or assisted by the Government."

The main article of the treaty simply states: "Further, Her Majesty agrees to pay the salaries of such teachers to instruct the children of said Indians as to her Majesty's Government of Canada may seem advisable."

The Indian people clearly understood that free education would be provided. This they were promised verbally — if the commissioners' report can be taken at face value. Yet the written guarantee in the treaty stipulated no such thing. Deceived again by the noble white man.

Much research must be done to trace and pin down all such examples of moral lapse. Much work must be done to alleviate the immoral situation created by such double-dealing. However, inadequate and highly questionable as the treaties are, they are important, for they symbolize the commitment of the government to our people.

4. A Legal Distinction Between Pre- and Post-Confederation Treaties?

Pre-Confederation treaties were made with the Crown acting through representatives of the British government; post-Confederation treaties were made with the Crown acting through representatives of the Canadian government. Does Britain retain any obligation directly to Indians because of the agreements entered into on its behalf? May Canadian Indians enforce those obligations, in British courts or otherwise, directly against Britain?

(a) *The Queen (ex parte The Indian Association of Alberta, Union of New Brunswick Indians, Union of Nova Scotia Indians) v. Secretary of State for Foreign and Commonwealth Affairs, ex parte Indian Association of Alberta and others*, [1982] 2 All ER 118 (CA)

Appeal
The applicants, the Indian Association of Alberta, the Union of New Brunswick Indians and the Union of Nova Scotia Indians, appealed with the leave of the Court of Appeal granted on 21 December 1981 against the decision of Woolf J, hearing the Crown Office List, on 9 December 1981 whereby he refused the applicants leave to apply for judicial review by way of declarations (i) that the decision of the respondent, the Secretary of State for Foreign and Commonwealth Affairs, that all relevant treaty obligations entered into by the Crown with the Indian peoples of Canada in so far as they still subsisted became the responsibility of the government of Canada with the attainment of independence, at the latest with the Statute of Westminister 1931, was wrong in law and (ii) that treaty and other obligations entered into by the Crown to the Indian peoples of Canada were still owed by Her Majesty in right of her government in the United Kingdom. The government of Canada appeared as intervener. The facts are set out in the judgment of Lord Denning MR.

Louis Blom-Cooper QC and *Richard Drabble* for the applicants.
Robert Alexander QC and *Simon D Brown* for the Secretary of State.
Andrew Morritt QC and *Peter Irvin* for the Canadian government.

Cur adv vult

28 January. The following judgments were read.

LORD DENNING MR

1. *The Indian peoples come here*

Over 200 years ago, in the year 1763, the King of England made a royal proclamation under the Great Seal. In it he gave solemn assurances to the Indian peoples of Canada. These assurances have been honoured for the most part ever since. But now the Indian peoples feel that the assurances are in danger of being dishonoured. They are anxious about the Canada Bill which is now before the Parliament of the United Kingdom. Under it there is to be a new constitution for Canada. The Indian peoples distrust the promoters of the Bill. They feel that, if it is passed, their own special rights and freedoms will be in peril of being reduced or extinguished. They have not gone to the courts of Canada for redress. They have come to this court. They say that the assurances which were given 200 years ago, and repeated in treaties 100 years later, were binding on the Crown of the United Kingdom. So they come to the courts of this country to plead their case. They come in particular from Alberta, Nova Scotia and New Brunswick. But the other Indian peoples from the other provinces are watching closely too. They want to see what happens. Seeing that their claim is against the Crown in respect of the United Kingdom, they are entitled, I think, to come here to put their case. They ask this court to make a declaration ''that treaty or other obligations entered into by the Crown to the Indian peoples of Canada are still owed by Her Majesty in right of Her Government in the United Kingdom''.

This is disputed by the Department of State in the United Kingdom. When the matter was under consideration by the Foreign Affairs Committee of the House of Commons, the question was put to the Foreign and Commonwealth Office (Foreign Affairs Committee minutes of evidence (HC Papers (1979-80) no 362-xxi) p. 63): ''Has the UK any treaty or other responsibilities to Indians in Canada?'' The answer given by that office on 11 November 1980 was: ''No. All relevant treaty obligations insofar as they still subsisted became the responsibility of the Government of Canada with the attainment of independence, at the latest with the Statute of Westminster 1931.''

The Indian peoples dispute that answer. In order to challenge it, they have brought these proceedings for judicial review. They seek declarations (i) that the answer is wrong in law, (ii) ''that treaties or other obligations entered into by the Crown to the Indian peoples of Canada are still owed by Her Majesty in right of Her Government in the United Kingdom''.

In order to decide the case we have had to look into the constitutional law affecting the colonies of the United Kingdom, just as Lord

Mansfield CJ did years ago. He had to consider this very royal proclamation of 1763. He did it in 1774 in the great case of *Campbell* v. *Hall* (1774) 1 Cowp 204, [1558-1774] All ER Rep 252, which has been ever since a landmark in the law. So I will try to trace the history of the rights and freedoms of the aboriginal peoples of Canada.

2. *Aboriginal rights and freedoms*

The Indian peoples of Canada have been there from the beginning of time. So they are called the ''aboriginal peoples''. In the distant past there were many different tribes scattered across the vast territories of Canada. Each tribe had its own tract of land, mountain, river or lake. They got their food by hunting and fishing and their clothing by trapping for fur. So far as we know they did not till the land. They had their chiefs and headmen to regulate their simple society and to enforce their customs. I say ''to enforce their customs'', because in early societies custom is the basis of law. Once a custom is established it gives rise to rights and obligations which the chiefs and headmen will enforce. These customary laws are not written down. They are handed down by tradition from one generation to another. Yet beyond doubt they are well established and have the force of law within the community.

In England we still have laws which are derived from customs from time immemorial. Such as rights of villagers to play on the green; or to graze their cattle on the common: see *New Windsor Corp.* v. *Mellor* [1975] 3 All ER 44, [1975] 1 Ch 380. These rights belong to members of the community and take priority over the ownership of the soil.

3. *The coming of the English*

To return to primitive societies, their solitude was disturbed by the coming of the English from across the seas. They came as explorers, like Captain Cook in 1774, or Captain Vancouver in 1792; or as traders, like the East India Company, or the Hudson's Bay Company; or as colonists, like those who sailed across the ocean to found Virginia and Massachusetts. Wherever the English came, they came as representatives of the Crown of England. They carried with them the rights of Englishmen. They were loyal to the Crown and acted with the direct authority of the Crown under royal charter. Thus in 1600 there was the charter of the East India Company. In 1606 the first charter of Virginia drawn by Sir Edward Coke. In 1629 the charter of Massachusetts Bay. In 1670 the charter of the Hudson's Bay Company. In 1681 Pennsylvania. And so on.

Our long experience of these matters taught us how to treat the indigenous peoples. As matter of public policy, it was of the first importance to pay great respect to their laws and customs, and never to interfere with them except when necessary in the interests of peace and good order. It was the responsibility of the Crown of England, and those representing the Crown, to see that the rights of the indigenous people were secured to them, and that they were not imposed on by the selfish or the thoughtless or the ruthless. Witness the impeachment of Warren Hastings in Westminster Hall for his conduct of affairs as Governor General of Bengal.

4. *The unity of the Crown*
In all these matters in the eighteenth and nineteenth centuries it was a settled doctrine of constitutional law that the Crown was one and indivisible. The colonies formed one realm with the United Kingdom, the whole being under the sovereignty of the Crown. The Crown had full powers to establish such executive, legislative and judicial arrangements as it thought fit. In exercising these powers, it was the obligation of the Crown (through its representatives on the spot) to take steps to ensure that the original inhabitants of the country were accorded their rights and privileges according to the customs coming down the centuries, except in so far as these conflicted with the peace and good order of the country or the proper settlement of it. This obligation is evidenced most strikingly in the case of Canada by the royal proclamation of 1763.

5. *The royal proclamation of 1763*
You will all recall the events which preceded this proclamation. In the year 1759 James Wolffe [*sic*] with his redcoats crept stealthily and silently by night up the St Lawrence River and scaled the Heights of Abraham. It was the turning-point in the Seven Years War between England and France. It was followed in 1763 by the Treaty of Paris, under which the French surrendered all the rights which they had previously held or acquired in Canada. England gained dominion over Quebec. Later in that very same year, on 7 October 1763, the Crown made this solemn proclamation:

> And whereas it is just and reasonable, and essential to our Interest, and the Security of our Colonies, that the several Nations or Tribes of Indians with whom We are connected, and who live under our Protection, should not be molested or disturbed in the Possession of such Parts of Our Dominions and Territories as, not having been ceded to or purchased by Us, are reserved to them, or any of them, as their Hunting Grounds — We do therefore, with the Advice of our Privy Council, declare it to be our Royal Will and Pleasure . . .

Then followed detailed assurances by which the Crown bound itself to reserve "under our Sovereignty, Protection and Dominion, for the use of the said Indians, all the lands and territories" thereafter described.

The royal proclamation superseded earlier agreements for other territories. Thus in 1752 in Nova Scotia a treaty had been made with the Indians by which it was agreed:

That all Transactions during the late War shall on both sides be buried in Oblivion with the Hatchet, And that the said Indians shall have all favour, Friendship & Protection shewn them from this His Majesty's Government.

I cannot forbear from mentioning also that in 1794 in New Brunswick there was this delightful little treaty with the Micmacs:

And the English King said to the Indian King "Henceforth you will teach your children to maintain peace and I give you this paper upon which are written many promises which will never be effaced." Then the Indian King, John Julian with his brother Francis Julian begged His Majesty to grant them a portion of land for their own use and for the future generations. His Majesty granted their request. A distance of six miles was granted from Little South West on both sides and six miles at North West on both sides of the rivers. Then His Majesty promised King John Julian and his brother Francis Julian "Henceforth I will provide for you and for the future generation so long as the sun rises and river flows."

The effect of the royal proclamation

The royal proclamation of 1763 had great impact throughout Canada. It was regarded as of high constitutional importance. It was ranked by the Indian peoples as their Bill of Rights, equivalent to our own Bill of Rights in England 80 years before. It came under the close consideration of Lord Mansfield CJ himself in the great case of *Campbell* v. *Hall* (1774) 1 Cowp 204, [1558-1774] All ER Rep 252. That case came from the island of Grenada in the West Indies which we conquered from the French during the war. It was one of the places to which the 1763 proclamation expressly applied. Lord Mansfield CJ emphasised that by it the King made an immediate and irrevocable grant to all who were or should become habitants. Lord Mansfield CJ took the opportunity to lay down five fundamental propositions, of which I would quote two 1 Cowp 204 at 208, 209, [1558-1774] All ER Rep 252 at 254:

A country conquered by the British arms becomes a dominion of *the King in the right of his Crown;* and, therefore, necessarily subject to the Legislature, the Parliament of *Great Britain* . . . that the laws of a conquered country continue in force, until they are altered by the conqueror . . .

To my mind the royal proclamation of 1763 was equivalent to an entrenched provision in the constitution of the colonies in North America. It was binding on the Crown "so long as the sun rises and the river flows". I find myself in agreement with what was said a few years ago in the Supreme Court of Canada in *Calder* v. *A-G of British Columbia* (1973) 34 DLR (3d) 145 at 203, in a judgment in which Laskin J concurred with Hall J and said:

> This Proclamation was an Executive Order having the force and effect of an Act of Parliament and was described by Gwynne J., . . . as the "Indian Bill of Rights" . . . its force as a statute is analogous to the status of Magna Carta which has always been considered to be the law throughout the Empire. It was a law which followed the flag as England assumed jurisdiction over newly-discovered or acquired lands or territories . . . In respect of this Proclamation, it can be said that when other exploring nations were showing a ruthless disregard of native rights England adopted a remarkably enlightened attitude towards the Indians of North America. The Proclamation must be regarded as a fundamental document upon which any just determination of original rights rests.

The 1763 proclamation governed the position of the Indian peoples for the next hundred years at least. It still governs their position throughout Canada, except in those cases when it has been supplemented or superseded by a treaty with the Indians. It still is the basis of the rights of the aboriginals in those provinces of Nova Scotia and New Brunswick. That is shown by the decision of the Supreme Court of Nova Scotia in *R* v. *Isaac* (1975) 9 APR 175, and of the Provincial Court of New Brunswick in *R* v. *Polchies* (2 December 1981, unreported).

But I must say that the proclamation is most difficult to apply so as to enable anyone to say what lands are reserved to the Indians and what are not. It contains general statements which are wanting in particularity. In this respect it is like other Bills of Rights. The details have to be worked out by the courts or in some other way. To this I will return.

6. *The British North America Act 1867*

This brings me to the British North America Act 1867. It proclaimed the union of the provinces of Ontario, Quebec, Nova Scotia and New Brunswick into one dominion under the name of Canada. It contained powers to admit other colonies later into the union. It was the result of consultation over many years before. It set up a federal government. It contained a written constitution which was to last for over 100 years and more. It declared in s. 9 that the executive government and authority of and over Canada was "to continue and be vested in the Queen". That is, in the Crown of England. The Governor General was her representative. It set up a Dominion parliament with its own legislative powers. It refashioned the provincial governments with their own Lieutenant Governors and their own parliaments. It set out detailed provisions, in ss. 91 and 92, distributing legislative powers between the

Dominion parliament and the provincial legislatures. It delegated, by ss. 12 and 65, executive authority in similar respects to the Governor General and Lieutenant Governors respectively. It provided for a judicature and it contained detailed provisions about revenue, debts, assets and taxation.

The effect on the Indians

How did this Act affect the Indians? Section 91(24) gave the Dominion parliament the exclusive power to legislate for "Indians, and lands reserved for the Indians". The 1867 Act contained nothing specific about the executive power, but I think it mirrored the legislative division so that the executive power in regard to the "Indians, and lands reserved for the Indians" was vested in the Governor General of the Dominion, acting through his representative; and he in turn represented the Queen of England, that is the Crown, which, as I have said, was in our constitutional law at that time regarded as one and indivisible.

Save for that reference in s. 91(24), the 1867 Act was silent on Indian affairs. Nothing was said about the title to property in the "lands reserved for the Indians", nor to the revenues therefrom, nor to the rights and obligations of the Crown or the Indians thenceforward in regard thereto. But I have no doubt that all concerned regarded the royal proclamation of 1763 as still of binding force. It was an unwritten provision which went without saying. It was binding on the legislatures of the Dominion and the provinces just as if there had been included in the statute a sentence: "The aboriginal peoples of Canada shall continue to have all their rights and freedoms as recognised by the royal proclamation of 1763."

No power to alter the 1867 Act

There is this other important point. The 1867 Act could not be altered either by the Dominion parliament or by the provincial legislatures. There was no provision in the statute for any means of altering it. This was, no doubt, at the wish of the provinces. They did not want the Dominion parliament to alter it to their prejudice. If it was to be altered at all, it could only be done by the Parliament of the United Kingdom. This shows to my mind, quite conclusively, that the Crown of the United Kingdom was regarded at that time as still the Crown of the Dominion and of the provinces of Canada. It was all one Crown, single and indivisible. As Lord Haldane said in *Theodore* v. *Duncan* [1919] AC 696 at 706: "The Crown is one and indivisible throughout the Empire, and it acts in self-governing States on the initiative and advice of its own Ministers in those States."

7. *The making of the treaties*

After the 1867 Act was passed, there were a series of important treaties made with the Indian peoples across the greater part of Canada affecting all the provinces. They follow the same pattern but suffice it to state as an example a treaty made in 1873 between "The Queen of Great Britain and Ireland, by Her Commissioners" and "The Saulteaux Tribe of the Ojibbeway Indians by their Chiefs".

After describing a tract of land, the treaty goes on to provide that the tribe and all other Indians —

do hereby cede, release, surrender and yield up to the Government of the Dominion of Canada for Her Majesty the Queen and Her successors forever, all their rights, titles and privileges whatsoever, to the lands. . . . To have and to hold the same to Her Majesty the Queen, and Her successors forever.

In return Her Majesty the Queen entered into several obligations to the Indians, of which I select some as illustrations:

And Her Majesty the Queen hereby agrees and undertakes to lay aside reserves for farming lands, due respect being had to lands at present cultivated by the said Indians, and also to lay aside and reserve for the benefit of the said Indians, to be administered and dealt with for them by Her Majesty's Government of the Dominion of Canada, in such a manner as shall seem best, other reserves of land in the said territory hereby ceded . . . And further, Her Majesty agrees to maintain schools for instruction in such reserves hereby made as to Her Government of Her Dominion of Canada may seem advisable whenever the Indians of the reserve shall desire it . . . Her Majesty further agrees with Her said Indians that they, the said Indians, shall have right to pursue their avocations of hunting and fishing throughout the tract surrendered as hereinbefore described, subject to such regulations as may from time to time be made by Her Government of Her Dominion of Canada, and saving and excepting such tracts as may, from time to time, be required or taken up for settlement, mining, lumbering or other purposes by Her said Government of the Dominion of Canada, or by any of the subjects thereof duly authorized therefor by the said Government.

Then follow the signatures from which you can get the charming scene:

IN WITNESS WHEREOF, Her Majesty's said Commissioners and the said Indian Chiefs have hereunto subscribed and set their hands at the North-West Angle of the Lake of the Woods this day and year herein first above named.

The effect of the treaties

That treaty gave rise to a most important case. It is *St Catharine's*

Milling and Lumber Co. v. *R* (1889) 14 App Cas 46. The Dominion asserted that it had the right to the produce of the Indian lands. It granted a licence to a milling company to cut and carry away one million feet of timber. The Province of Ontario disputed it. The Privy Council decided in favour of the province. It was the province, and not the Dominion government, which was entitled to the revenues from the sale of timber. The Privy Council considered the rights of the various persons in the Indian lands. The judgment was given by Lord Watson, who, being bred in Scots law, expressed himself in the concepts of Roman law. He said that the Indian tribes had a "personal and usufructuary right" in the lands reserved to the Indians, by which he meant that they had a right to use and take the fruits and products of these lands and to hunt and fish thereon. Underneath the Indian title, there had been —

> all along vested in the Crown a substantial and paramount estate, underlying the Indian title, which became a plenum dominium whenever that title was surrendered or otherwise extinguished.

(See 14 App Cas 46 at 55.)

By the treaty the Indians ceded and surrendered much of their lands to the Crown and in return the Crown undertook the obligations to the Indians specified in the treaty.

So the Crown by the treaty obtained a "plenum dominium" in the lands. That "plenum dominium" was distributed between the Dominion and the province. By reason of s. 109 of the 1867 Act the revenues from timber, mines and so forth belonged to the Province of Ontario. But the administration of the lands was left to the Dominion. The obligations under the treaty remained the obligations of the Crown.

That judgment was given at a time when, in constitutional law, the Crown was single and indivisible. In view of it, and later cases, I think that the Indian title (by which I mean "the personal and usufructuary right" of the Indians in respect of "lands reserved to the Indians") was a title superior to all others save in so far as the Indians themselves surrendered or ceded it to the Crown. That title was guaranteed to them by the Crown. Then by treaties which covered much of Canada the Indians did cede and surrender their right in some lands to the Crown and in return the Crown undertook to fulfil the obligations set out in the treaties. Those treaty obligations were obligations of the Crown, the single and indivisible Crown, which was at that time the Crown of the United Kingdom.

Apart from the ceded lands, ceded under the treaties, there were Indian reserves, not ceded to the Crown, in which the Indian peoples still retained their "personal and usufructuary right" to the fruits and produce of the lands and to hunt and fish thereon.

8. *The British North America Act 1930*

Similar treaties were made in 1876, 1877 and 1899 with the Indian tribes who were living in what is now Alberta, with which we are here particulary concerned. The Province of Alberta was formed in 1905 and joined the union. In 1929 an agreement was made between the Dominion government and the provincial government of Alberta. Similar agreements were made with the provinces of Manitoba, British Columbia and Saskatchewan. The agreements were in every case "subject to approval by the Parliament of Canada and by the Legislature of the Province and also to confirmation by the Parliament of the United Kingdom".

In 1930, by the British North America Act 1930, the United Kingdom Parliament gave the force of law to those agreements. It recognised that Canada was bound "to fulfil its obligations under the treaties with the Indians of the Province" and that —

> the said Indians shall have the right, which the Province hereby assures to them, of hunting, trapping and fishing game and fish for food at all seasons of the year on all unoccupied Crown lands and on any other lands to which the said Indians may have a right of access.

This 1930 Act seems to me to recognise that the Crown had subsisting obligations to the Indians under the treaties. That is why it was necessary to have the agreements confirmed by the Parliament of the United Kingdom with the assent of the Queen.

The division of the Crown

Hitherto I have said that in constitutional law the Crown was single and indivisible. But that law was changed in the first half of this century, not by statute, but by constitutional usage and practice. The Crown became separate and divisible, according to the particular territory in which it was sovereign. This was recognised by the Imperial Conference of 1926 (Cmd 2768). It framed the historic definition of the status of Great Britain and the dominions as —

> autonomous Communities within the British Empire, equal in status, in no way subordinate one to another in any aspect of their domestic or external affairs, though united by a common allegiance to the Crown, and freely associated as members of the British Commonwealth of Nations.

It was also agreed that —

> the Governor-General in a Dominion is the representative of the Crown holding in all essential respects the same position in relation to the administration of public affairs in a Dominion as is held by His Majesty the King in Great Britain and that he is not the representative or agent of His Majesty's Government in Great Britain or of any Department of that Government.

(See Cmd 2768, pp 14, 16.)

Thenceforward the Crown was no longer single and indivisible. It was separate and divisible for each self-governing dominion or province or territory. Thus in 1968 it was held in this court that the Queen was the Queen of Mauritius, and the Crown in right of Mauritius could issue passports to its citizens: see *R* v. *Secretary of State for the Home Dept, ex p Bhurosah* [1967] 3 All ER 831, [1968] 1 QB 266: and in 1971 it was held, again in this court, that the Queen was the Queen of the Province of New Brunswick, and that province was entitled to state immunity: see *Mellenger* v. *New Brunswick Development Corp* [1971] 2 All ER 593, [1971] 1 WLR 604.

As a result of this important constitutional change, I am of opinion that those obligations which were previously binding on the Crown simpliciter are now to be treated as divided. They are to be applied to the dominion or province or territory to which they relate: and confined to it. Thus the obligations to which the Crown bound itself in the royal proclamation of 1763 are now to be confined to the territories to which they related and binding only on the Crown in respect of those territories; and the treaties by which the Crown bound itself in 1875 are to be confined to those territories and binding on the Crown only in respect of those territories. None of them is any longer binding on the Crown in respect of the United Kingdom.

9. *The Statute of Westminster 1931*

The Statute of Westminster 1931 gave considerable independence to the dominions. By s. 4 it was enacted that no Act of Parliament of the United Kingdom was to extend to a dominion as part of the law of the dominion unless "it is expressly declared in that Act that that Dominion has requested, and consented to, the enactment thereof".

But, at the same time, there was an express limitation in s. 7(1): "Nothing in this Act shall be deemed to apply to the repeal, amendment or alteration of the British North America Acts, 1867 to 1930 . . ."

That provision shows that the Parliament of the United Kingdom has still the power to repeal, amend or alter the British North America Acts 1867 to 1930 and that the Dominion parliament has no such power. No doubt the Parliament of the United Kingdom would not exercise this power except at the request of the Dominion itself and the consent of the majority of the provinces. But still in point of law the power still rests in the Parliament of the United Kingdom to repeal, amend or alter the British North America Acts 1867 to 1930. To my mind this shows that, in strict constitutional law, the Dominion of Canada is not completely independent. It is still tied hand and foot by the British North America Acts 1867 to 1930. The Dominion itself cannot alter one jot or title of those Acts.

But the Crown, as I have said already, was separate and divisible.

10. *The Crown Proceedings Act 1947*

In order that proceedings should be brought against the Crown in this country, it is necessary that the liability of the Crown should be a liability "in respect of Her Majesty's Government in the United Kingdom": see 40(2)(c) of the Crown Proceedings Act 1947.

Now, at the time when the Crown entered into the obligations under the 1763 proclamation or the treaties of the 1870s, the Crown was in constitutional law one and indivisible. Its obligations were obligations in respect of the government of the United Kingdom as well as in respect of Canada: see *Williams* v. *Howarth* [1905] AC 551. But, now that the Crown is separate and divisible, I think that the obligations under the proclamation and the treaties are obligations of the Crown in respect of Canada. They are not obligations of the Crown in respect of the United Kingdom. It is, therefore, not permissible for the Indian peoples to bring an action in this country to enforce these obligations. Their only recourse is in the courts of Canada.

11. *The Canada Bill 1982*

This brings me to the Canada Bill. It is designed to give complete independence to Canada. It is to be done by "patriating" the constitution, to use a coined word. It is to be done by the Constitution Act 1982. No longer will the United Kingdom Parliament have any power to pass any law extending to Canada. No longer will it have power to repeal, amend or alter the British North America Acts 1867 to 1930. But the Dominion parliament will have power to do so. This is to be done by setting out a new constitution for Canada to be enacted by the United Kingdom Parliament. This new constitution contains a charter of rights and freedoms. It specifically guarantees to the aboriginal peoples the rights and freedoms which I have discussed earlier. These are the relevant sections:

25. The guarantee in this Charter of certain rights and freedoms shall not be construed so as to abrogate or derogate from any aboriginal, treaty or other rights or freedoms that pertain to the aboriginal peoples of Canada, including (a) any rights or freedoms that have been recognized by the Royal Proclamation of October 7, 1763; and (b) any rights or freedoms that may be acquired by the aboriginal peoples of Canada by way of land claims settlement.

35.—(1) The existing aboriginal and treaty rights of the aboriginal peoples of Canada are hereby recognized and affirmed.

(2) In this Act, "aboriginal peoples of Canada" includes the Indian, Inuit and Métis peoples of Canada.

It also provides for a constitutional conference to be called within one year. That conference is to consider—

an item respecting constitutional matters that directly affect the aboriginal peoples of Canada, including the identification and definition of the rights of those peoples. . .

(See 37(2).)

Conclusion

It seems to me that the Canada Bill itself does all that can be done to protect the rights and freedoms of the aboriginal peoples of Canada. It entrenches them as part of the constitution, so that they cannot be diminished or reduced except by the prescribed procedure and by the prescribed majorities. In addition, it provides for a conference at the highest level to be held so as to settle exactly what their rights are. That is most important, for they are very ill-defined at the moment.

There is nothing, so far as I can see, to warrant any distrust by the Indians of the government of Canada. But, in case there should be, the discussion in this case will strengthen their hand so as to enable them to withstand any onslaught. They will be able to say that their rights and freedoms have been guaranteed to them by the Crown, originally by the Crown in respect of the United Kingdom, now by the Crown in respect of Canada, but, in any case, by the Crown. No parliament should do anything to lessen the worth of these guarantees. They should be honoured by the Crown in respect of Canada "so long as the sun rises and river flows". That promise must never be broken. There is no case whatever for any declaration. I would dismiss the appeal accordingly.

KERR LJ In connection with the "repatriation" of the Canadian constitution, a number of statements have been made on behalf of Her Majesty's government in Parliament to the effect that all treaty obligations entered into by the Crown with the Indian peoples of Canada became the responsibility of the government of Canada with the attainment of independence, at latest with the Statute of Westminster 1931. The repatriation of the Canadian constitution is now proposed by means of the Canada Bill which is awaiting its second reading in the House of Commons. By ss. 25 and 35 of the annexed Constitution Act 1982 the rights of the aboriginal peoples of Canada, including in particular of the Indian peoples, are expressly preserved. However, various Canadian Indian organisations, and perhaps all of them, are dissatisfied with the present situation. They contend that the government's conclusion as to the legal position is wrong. The applicants accordingly seek a declaration by way of judicial review to the effect that this conclusion is wrong in law and that all "treaty and other obligations entered into by the Crown to the Indian peoples of Canada are still owed by Her Majesty in right of Her Government in the United Kingdom''.

We are here only directly concerned with the Indian organisations in the provinces of Alberta, New Brunswick and Nova Scotia. But on the voluminous material placed before us it is clear that the same considerations apply throughout Canada. Thus, the applicants rely on the royal proclamation of 1763 which purported to extend to the Indian peoples beyond those parts of eastern Canada, the Maritime Provinces and parts of Quebec, which had by then been opened up for settlement. They also rely on the pattern of the so-called ''treaties'' concluded between the Crown and many Indian ''bands'', which ultimately covered most of the territory of Canada, and to which most or all of the remaining Indians subsequently adhered. They contend that under all of these, whether made before or after the British North America Act 1867 which set up the Dominion of Canada, as well as under the royal proclamation, the Crown assumed obligations to the Indians in return for formal concessions-of-territory by the Indians, and that these obligations still subsist and have never been transferred to Canada.

As to the subsistence of these rights, we have been referred to many legislative enactments and decisions of the courts in Canada in which the continuing binding effect of the proclamation and treaties has been recognised. Their binding effect has also been accepted before us by counsel on behalf of the Secretary of State and of the government of Canada as interveners in the proceedings, as well as in the Canada Bill mentioned above. However, the Indian peoples wish to achieve certain political objectives, viz, a greater degree of recognition, and the right of consultation on those aspects of the constitution of Canada resulting from its ''repatriation'' which may affect them. This is the object of these proceedings and of the declarations which they seek.

However great may be one's sympathy with the grievances and aspirations of the Indian peoples of Canada, this court can only concern itself with the decision of justiciable issues on the basis of law. The issue raised in the declarations which are sought, quite apart from any question whether this should be dealt with by any formal declaration, is in my view only justiciable as a matter of concession by the court, faced with the wish of the applicants to have it decided and of the respondents' non-objection to its decision. The reason is that the applicants are not asserting any breach of any of the obligations on the part of the Crown, and are a fortiori not asking for any relief or remedy in respect of such obligations. Indeed, it has been virtually conceded by counsel on behalf of the applicants, rightly in my view, that no such relief or remedy could be obtained in our courts; and for the reasons explained hereafter this factor is in itself a crucial pointer to the decision. In effect, however, the parties are agreed that this could should determine the abstract and bare issue as to the situs of obligations which are ultimately owed by the Crown, whether in right or respect of the United Kingdom on the one hand or of the Dominion or provinces of Canada on the other. Since we have heard full argument on this issue over several days, whereas the position in this respect was different before Woolf J who dismissed the application for other reasons, I think that we should express our views on this issue.

It is settled law that, although Her Majesty is the personal Sovereign of the peoples inhabiting many of the territories within the Commonwealth, all rights and obligations of the Crown, other than those concerning the Queen in her personal capacity, can only arise in relation to a particular government within those territories. The reason is that such rights and obligations can only be exercised and enforced, if at all, through some governmental emanation or representation of the Crown. Thus, the Crown Proceedings Act 1947 distinguishes between liabilities in respect of, and proceedings in right of, Her Majesty in the United Kingdom on the one hand and outside the United Kingdom on the other. In relation to the latter class, it is open to the Secretary of State under s. 40(3) to issue a certificate which is conclusive for the purposes of that Act. This has not been done in the present case, though without prejudice to the Secretary of State's contention that the legal position of the Indian peoples of Canada has no connection with the Crown in right of the United Kingdom. It is accordingly necessary to examine the constitutional principles which determine the situs of the Crown's rights and obligations in this regard, but bearing in mind that, although the relevant agreements with the Indian peoples are known as 'treaties', they are not treaties in the sense of public international law. They were not treaties between sovereign states, so that no question of state succession arises.

The principles which govern the situs of rights and obligations of the Crown are conveniently summarised in 6 Halsbury's Laws (4th ed) para 820, under the heading 'Unity and Divisibility of the Crown'. For present purposes it is sufficient to refer to two passages and to a number of authorities cited in support of these.

First, as there stated, it is clear that —

on the grant of a representative legislature, and perhaps even as from the setting up of courts, legislation council and other such structures of government, Her Majesty's government in a colony is to be regarded as distinct from Her Majesty's government in the United Kingdom.

Thus, in *R* v. *Secretary of State for the Home Dept, ex p Bhurosah* [1967] 3 All ER 831, [1968] 1 QB 266 an issue arose as to passports issued in Mauritius, which was then a dependent British colony, on behalf of the Governor. The passports were issued "in the name of Her Majesty" to persons who were British subjects and citizens of the United Kingdom and Colonies under s. 1 of the British Nationality Act 1948. The issue was whether they were "United Kingdom passports" within the Commonwealth Immigrants Act 1962. It was held that they were not, because, in effect, they had been issued in the name of Her Majesty in right of the government of Mauritius and not of the United Kingdom.

This being the position in relation to a dependent colony, the government of a dominion is clearly in a an fortiori position, and neither of these forms of established government within the Commonwealth presents any constitutional problem for present purposes. In times long past there was such a problem, when many of the territories which are now within the Commonwealth had not yet been opened up for settlement, or even fully discovered, and there was no established government on behalf of the Crown. Thus, the royal charter of 1670, granting Rupert's Land to the Hudson's Bay Company, described the territory as "one of our Plantacions or Colonyes in America" and conveyed it "as of our Mannor of East Greenwich in our County of Kent in free and common Soccage." This was clearly a Crown grant in right of the government here. Subsequently, as the overseas territories gradually came to be settled and colonised, there may have been an indeterminate and intermediate stage of constitutional development in many cases, when it was uncertain whether rights and obligations concerning the overseas territory arose in right of respect of the Crown here or of the emerging forms of local administration overseas. This may still have been the position at the time of the eighteenth century "Maritime Treaties" and of the royal proclamation of 1763, although all these contain references to the then emerging colonial governments of what later became the eastern provinces of Canada and the eastern states of America. However, for the reasons explained hereafter, it is unnecessary to determine what was the resulting situs of the rights and obligations of the Crown in these territories at that time, since the subsequent constitutional development of Canada in my view puts the present issue beyond doubt.

The second relevant principle stated in the same passage in Halsbury's Laws is that —

> the liabilities of the Crown in right of, or under the laws of, one of the Crown's territories can be satisfied only out of the revenues, and by the authority of the legislature, of that territory.

In effect, the situs of obligations on the part of the Crown is to be found only in that territory within the realm of the Crown where such obligations can be enforced against a local administration. A nineteenth century illustration of this principle in relation to Canada, which is interesting because the case was decided before the British North America Act 1867, was *Re Holmes* (1861) 2 John & H 527, 70 ER 1167. This concerned disputes arising out of certain lands vested in the Crown, in the then Province of Upper Canada, in relation to which a petition of right was brought in the Court of Chancery here. It was held by Page Wood VC that, whether or not the Crown was a trustee of the land, the situs of any resulting rights and obligations lay in Canada and that these were only enforceable there. He said (2 John & H 527 at 543, 70 ER 1167 at 1174): ". . . as the holder of Canadian land for the public purposes of Canada, the Queen should be considered as present in Canada, and out of the jurisdiction of this Court." In other words, any resulting rights and obligations existed only in right or respect of the Crown in what was then Upper Canada, and not in right or respect of what was then Great Britain.

An even more important illustration for present purposes of the same principle is to be found in the decision of the House of Lords in *A-G* v. *Great Southern and Western Rly Co. of Ireland* [1925] AC 754, which has been followed in the Australian courts in relation to similar problems as between Australia and Papua in *Faithorn* v. *Territory of Papua* (1938) 60 CLR 772 and as between the rights of the Crown in respect of the Commonwealth of Australia and the State of New South Wales in *Federal Comr of Taxation* v. *Official Liquidator of EO Farley Ltd.* (1940) 63 CLR 278. The importance of this case for present purposes is that it shows that there may be a devolution of rights and obligations of the Crown in respect of the government of Great Britain to another government within the Commonwealth without any express statutory or other transfer, but merely by virtue of the creation of the new government and of the assignment to it of responsibilities which relate to the rights and obligations in question. This was a point on which counsel for the applicants strongly sought to rely in relation to the Crown obligations arising out of the royal proclamation and the various Indian treaties, particularly those before 1867, which he contended had never been formally transferred to the federal or provincial governments in Canada.

The facts of that case were briefly as follows. By agreements made in 1917 and 1918 between the President of the Board of Trade in Britain, which were subsequently transferred to the Minister of Transport, and a railway company in what was then Southern Ireland, certain rights of compensation were conferred on the company in consideration of the company taking up the rails and sleepers on portions of their line, since these were required for public purposes in the war effort. Thereafter the Irish Free State was created with —

the same constitutional status in the Community of Nations known as the British Empire as the Dominion of Canada, the Commonwealth of

Australia, the Dominion of New Zealand, and the Union of South
Africa . . .

and a provisional government was established. Then, by an Order in
Council which recited that a Ministry of Economic Affairs had been set
up within the provisional government, responsible for, inter alia,
transport, including functions hitherto performed by the Minister of
Transport and the Board of Trade, the corresponding functions were
transferred to the provisional government together with (purportedly)
"any property, rights and liabilities" connected with those functions.
The company thereupon brought a petition of right, contending that,
notwithstanding those enactments, the responsibility for the obligations
under the original agreement remained with the British government.
The company's contention in relation to the purported transfer of
liabilities under the Order in Council was that those had not been
effectively transferred, either on the true construction of the order, or
because the order was ultra vires and to that extent void. This contention
failed.

Although most of the speeches proceeded on the basis of the
construction of the order, it is clear that in the view of the House the
same result also followed from the mere devolution of governmental
responsibility for the matters to which the obligations related. In
particular, the following passage is worth citing from the speech of
Viscount Haldane in which Lord Dunedin and Lord Carson concurred
([1925] AC 754 at 773-774):

In the present case Parliament transferred the duty of producing the
fund out of which the liability in question, when it accrued, should be
met to the Irish Parliament. It thereby declared its intention not itself
to provide the money required out of its own Consolidated Fund. It
does not matter whether the liability was in terms transferred to the
Irish Government. By its very character it would cease when it
became operative to be a liability of the British Consolidated Fund
and become one of the Irish Legislature Central Fund, if they chose to
so provide.

This is a clear illustration, of the highest authority, of the second of
the principles concerning the situs of Crown obligations to which I have
referred. Its effect is that such obligations exist only in respect of that
government within the realm of the Crown against which such
obligations can be enforced.

In the light of the foregoing principles, I return to the position in
relation to all obligations assumed by the Crown under the royal
proclamation and the various treaties with the Indian peoples of Canada.
The treaties fall into two parts: the Maritime Treaties, which also
covered what is now part of the Province of Quebec, and which were
made before the British North America Act 1867, and the subsequent

treaties numbered 1 to 11 which were thereafter made in relation to what became parts of the Prairie Provinces, the North Western Territory and British Columbia. For this purpose it is unnecessary to review the historical and constitutional development in Canada, which has extended into the present century. It is also irrelevant to consider whether, as maintained by the applicants but denied on behalf of the Secretary of State and the government of Canada, the pre-1867 treaties were mere treaties of peace, or whether these also gave rise to Crown obligations concerning "personal and usufructuary" rights of the Indian peoples, in particular in relation to hunting and fishing. I am content to assume this in favour of the applicants for present purposes. Finally, it is irrelevant to consider whether any Crown obligations under these treaties arose in respect of the Crown in Great Britain or whether, as I am inclined to think, they would already have arisen in respect of the developing governments of the Maritime Provinces and Quebec. It is sufficient to turn directly to the British North America Act 1867.

This Act created the Dominion of Canada, then constituted by the four provinces of Ontario, Quebec, Nova Scotia and New Brunswick. By s. 146 it provided for the admission of Newfoundland, Prince Edward Island, British Columbia, Rupert's Land and the North Western Territory by Order in Council, as subsequently happened. It set up the structure of the Dominion and provincial legislatures and executive governments in Canada. The executive power was to remain vested in the Crown, to be exercised for the Dominion by the Governor General appointed by the Sovereign, in certain cases in conjunction with the newly created Queen's Privy Council of Canada. Executive power within the provinces was vested in Lieutenant Governors to be appointed by the Governor General and responsible to him. A Consolidated Reserve Fund for Canada was created, and it was provided that the Dominion was to be liable for the debts and liabilities of each province.

This Act was subsequently extended by amendment and by other Acts until 1930 to the whole of the present territory of the Dominion and provinces of Canada.

The effect of the 1867 Act and its successors, up to the Statute of Westminster 1931, was accordingly to create an all-embracing federal governmental structure for Canada, which, subject to one point discussed hereafter, was wholly independent and autonomous in relation to all internal affairs. For present purposes only a few of its provisions require to be mentioned specifically. First, ss. 91 and 92 conferred exclusive legislative powers on the Dominion and the provinces respectively in relation to the matters therein mentioned. By s. 91(24), the Dominion government was invested with exclusive powers in relation to "Indians, and lands reserved for the Indians".

Second, however, by s. 109 all lands, mines, minerals and royalties belonging to the provinces were expressly declared to continue to belong to them.

Since the passing of this Act there have been numerous cases, many of which reached the Privy Council, concerning the respective rights and obligations as between the Dominion and the provinces. In the present context the most important ones arose out of the dichotomy between ss. 91(24) and 109: whereas the Dominion government was vested with exclusive legislative power concerning the Indian peoples and the lands reserved for them, the lands themselves, and the usufructuary rights arising out of them, were vested in the provinces. The problem was that large parts of those lands were subsequently ceded by the Indians under the treaties nos 1 to 11 and accordingly accrued to the provinces. This dichotomy gave rise to a number of disputes, of which *St Catharine's Milling and Lumber Co.* v. *R* (1888) 14 App Cas 46 is the leading authority. The issue concerned the right to timber growing on land covered by the royal proclamation of 1763 and ceded on behalf of the Salteaux Tribe of Ojibbeway Indians under treaty no. 3 of 1873, subject to certain privileges of hunting and fishing. It was held by the Privy Council that the Indian usufructuary rights were preserved and did not fall within s. 109, but that this section, and the cession under the treaty, vested the whole of the beneficial interest in the land (including its timber etc) in the Province to the exclusion of the Dominion, notwithstanding the legislative power of the Dominion under s. 91(24).

This decision was followed in many subsequent cases to which we were referred. It is unnecessary to discuss these further, other than to mention that I cannot accept that it follows from one sentence in the judgment of Lord Watson in the *St Catharines's* case 14 App Cas 46 at 60 that any right or obligation in relation to the Indian peoples remained vested in the Crown in respect of what was then Great Britain. On the contrary, subsequent decisions of the Privy Council have authoritatively established that the effect of the 1867 Act and of its successors was to transfer to Canada, as between the governments of the Dominion and of the provinces, every aspect of legislative and executive power in relation to Canada's internal affairs. Thus in *A-G for Ontario* v. *A-G for Canada* [1912] AC 571 at 581, Earl Loreburn LC said:

> It would be subversive of the entire scheme and policy of the Act to assume that any point of internal self-government was withheld from Canada . . . For whatever belongs to self-government in Canada belongs either to the Dominion or to the provinces, within the limits of the British North America Act.

(I return to the reference to the limits under the Act hereafter.)

Similarly, in *Bonanza Creek Gold Mining Co. Ltd.* v. *R* [1916] 1 AC

566 at 579, [1916-17] All ER Rep 999 at 1005 Viscount Haldane stated:
It is to be observed that the British North America Act has made a
distribution between the Dominion and the provinces which extends
not only to legislative but to executive authority.

We are here not concerned with the many difficult and complex
problems concerning the distribution of power and responsibility as
between the Dominion and the provinces, which have given rise to so
much litigation. We are only concerned with the question whether any
of these still remain vested in the Crown in right or respect of the United
Kingdom. On the basis of the principles discussed earlier in this
judgment, and of the British North America Act 1867 and its
successors, there can in my view be no doubt that the answer to this is in
the negative. So far as rights and obligations in relation to the Indian
peoples of Canada are concerned, the entire devolution of these from the
Crown in right of what is now the United Kingdom to the Crown in right
of the Dominion or provinces of Canada, is further confirmed by
numerous Canadian enactments, both federal and provincial, culminating in the consolidated Indian Act 1970. This derives its ultimate
constitutional authority under the Crown from s. 91(24) of the 1867
Act, as mentioned above, and deals comprehensively with all matters
concerning the Indian peoples. The devolution to Canada of all
legislative and executive powers in this regard is therefore complete.

It then only remains to deal with one further argument put forward by
counsel on behalf of the applicants. This is that, by virtue of ss. 55 to 57
of the British North America Act 1867, the Crown, in right of what is
now the United Kingdom, retained the ultimate power over all
legislation enacted by the Dominion of Canada. On this basis it is said
that the Crown in right of the United Kingdom also indirectly
maintained ultimate power over the enactments of the provincial
legislatures, but it is unnecessary further to consider the constitutional
complexities in relation to this latter aspect apart from mentioning that
the independence of the provinces under the Crown, in the same way as
that of the Dominion, was recognised by the Privy Council in
Liquidators of Maritime Bank of Canada v. *Receiver-General of New
Brunswick* [1892] AC 437. The argument, however, is that Canada has
never been, and still is not, wholly independent, since there is an
ultimate power to deny royal assent to Canadian legislation. The fact
that it has become an established constitutional convention not to invoke
this ultimate power is said to be irrelevant, since this derives from
convention and not from law. Further, the fact that the entire
independence and self-government of the Dominion of Canada in all
matters, both internal and external, was recognised or affirmed by the
Statute of Westminster 1931 is also said to be irrelevant, since s. 7 of
the 1931 Act expressly provides that nothing in that Act —

shall be deemed to apply to the repeal, amendment or alteration of the British North America Acts, 1867 to 1930, or any order, rule or regulation made thereunder.

What is contended, in other words, is that Canada is still not wholly independent from the Crown in right of the United Kingdom, and that its total independence will only be achieved by the enactment of the Canada Bill, which has not yet taken place.

With respect, in my judgment, this argument is wholly fallacious. As shown by the basic constitutional principles discussed at the beginning of this judgment, it is perfectly clear that the question whether the situs of rights and obligations of the Crown is to be found in right or respect of the United Kingdom, or of other governments within those parts of the Commonwealth of which Her Majesty is the ultimate sovereign, has nothing whatever to do with the question whether those governments are wholly independent or not. The situs of such rights and obligations rests with the overseas governments within the realm of the Crown, and not with the Crown in right of respect of the United Kingdom, even though the powers of such governments fall a very long way below the level of independence. Indeed, independence, or the degree of independence, is wholly irrelevant to the issue, because it is clear that rights and obligations of the Crown will arise exclusively in right or respect of any government outside the bounds of the United Kingdom as soon as it can be seen that there is an established government of the Crown in the overseas territory in question. In relation to Canada this had clearly happened by 1867.

It follows in my judgment that the declarations sought by the applicants have no foundation in law, and that this appeal must be dismissed.

MAY LJ   The application in this case is for two declarations: first, that the decision of the Secretary of State for Foreign and Commonwealth Affairs that all treaty obligations entered into by the Crown with the Indian peoples of Canada became the responsibility of the government of Canada with the attainment of independence, at the latest with the Statute of Westminster 1931, is wrong in law; and, second, that treaty and other obligations entered into by the Crown to the Indian peoples of Canada are still owed by Her Majesty in right of her government in the United Kingdom.

There is no question that the decision is one that has been come to by the Secretary of State for Foreign and Commonwealth Affairs and which has been communicated in the various ways to which Lord Denning MR and Kerr LJ have referred. Indeed it is quite clear that the decision is one on which the governments of both the United Kingdom and Canada are agreed.

These applications therefore raise three specific questions. First, with what treaty or other obligations are we concerned? Second, were these or any of them ever owed to the persons with whom they were made by Her Majesty or the Crown in the right of the United Kingdom? Third, are they or any of them still so owed?

Before seeking to answer these three questions, however, I think that it is first necessary to consider and reach a clear understanding of the constitutional questions and law involved. Whilst, like Lord Denning MR and Kerr LJ, I have every sympathy for the interests of the Indian peoples of Canada and understand why they come to the courts of England at this time when the Canada Bill is before the Parliament of the United Kingdom, I also feel that there is at the root of their application and the arguments in support of it a fundamental misunderstanding of the constitutional position.

Although at one time it was correct to describe the Crown as one and indivisible, with the development of the Commonwealth this is no longer so. Although there is only one person who is the Sovereign within the British Commonwealth, it is now a truism that in matters of law and government the Queen of the United Kingdom, for example, is entirely independent and distinct from the Queen of Canada. Further, the Crown is a constitutional monarchy and thus when one speaks today, and as was frequently done in the course of the argument on this application, of the Crown "in right of Canada", or of some other territory within the Commonwealth, this is only a short way of referring to the Crown acting through and on the advice of her ministers in Canada or in that other territory within the Commonwealth.

Another consequence of this process of evolution from a single individual imperial Crown, to which counsel for the applicants frequently but as I think erroneously referred in the course of his submissions, to the multi-limbed Crown of the British Commonwealth is that as different territories within the Commonwealth attained self-government to a greater or less extent, acquired the right to legislate on some and ultimately all matters within and affecting that territory, and thus to raise the finance to enable them to manage their own affairs, so pro tanto did any rights or obligations of what had been the Imperial Crown, that is to say the Crown in right of the United Kingdom, devolve on the Crown in right of the particular territory concerned.

This divisibility of the Crown was recognised by the courts in this country at a relatively early stage in the evolution from Empire to Commonwealth. In *Re Holmes* (1861) 2 John & H 527, 70 ER 1167 the Court of Chancery was asked to entertain a petition of right presented under the then recent Petitions of Right Act 1860 claiming the restoration of certain lands taken for a canal by an Act of the provincial legislature of Canada and vested in the Queen. This was before the

British North America Act 1867 at a time when the then Province of Canada comprised the two provinces of what had been Upper Canada and Lower Canada respectively. In fact three provincial Acts were concerned: two of the provincial parliament of Upper Canada, before the merger, and the third of the provincial parliament of the merged Province of Canada itself. In essence the argument on behalf of the suppliants was that, although the land concerned was land in Canada and the relevant statutes had been passed by the Canadian legislatures, nevertheless the Queen in her person was within the United Kingdom and that accordingly a petition of right under the new Act would lie. In rejecting that claim Page Wood V-C said (2 John & H 527 at 543-544, 70 ER 1167 at 1174):

> Now it is said that the Queen is present here, and therefore amenable (by virtue of the recent Act) to the jurisdiction of this Court. But it would be at least as correct to say that, as the holder of Canadian land for the public purposes of Canada, the Queen should be considered as present in Canada, and out of the jurisdiction of this Court. This alone supplies a sufficient answer to the argument of the suppliants; and, without entering into a number of other questions which the case involves, it is enough to say that, when land in Canada is vested in the Queen, not by prerogative, but under an Act of the Provincial Legislature, for the purposes of the province, and subject to any future directions which may be given by the Provincial Legislature, I hold that, for the purpose of any claims to such land made under the provincial statutes, the Queen is not to be regarded as within the jurisdiction of this Court. I wish to rest my decision on the broadest ground, that it was not the object of the Petitions of Right Act, 1860, to transfer jurisdiction to this country from any colony in which an Act might be passed vesting lands in the Crown for the benefit of the colony; and upon that ground I allow the demurrer . . . I prefer to rest upon the higher ground that this land cannot be withdrawn from the control of the Canadian Legislature, and brought within the jurisdiction of this Court, merely on the technical argument that the Queen, in whom it is vested for Canadian purposes, is present in this country.

That the duties and liabilities of the Crown in right of the United Kingdom in respect of another territory or its peoples within the Commonwealth should devolve in this way on the Crown in right of that territory as the latter attained its own legislature, and with that its own revenue and Consolidated Fund, was itself merely a natural consequence of that progress of self-government and ultimately independence. It necessarily followed from the political concept, convention or, in some cases, specific legislation which realised, accepted or enacted that Parliament in the United Kingdom would not thereafter interfere with or derogate from laws passed by the legislature in the self-governing territory on any subject which had in truth been left to its jurisdiction. To contemplate any other result would be to contemplate legislative and inter-governmental chaos.

On this point, however, I do not have to rest solely on political theory. There is in my judgment good support for it in the speeches of their Lordships' House in *A-G* v *Great Southern and Western Rly Co of Ireland* [1925] AC 754. By agreements made in 1917 and 1918 the President of the Board of Trade in the United Kingdom agreed that, if the Irish railway company took up the rails and sleepers on parts of their line and transferred them to the British government to enable them to construct certain other lines to help their transport of coal for local use during the 1914-18 war, then after the war the latter government would pay the railway company the cost of new rails and sleepers and of reconstructing their previous railway line. The company duly transferred the rails and sleepers to the government. Subsequently by legislation and an Order in Council the liabilities so incurred by the Board of Trade were transferred to the British Minister of Transport. There followed in 1922 two further Acts of the Parliament at Westminster creating the Irish Free State and an Order in Council transferring relevant functions from certain British ministers to Irish ones. The railway company claimed a declaration on a petition of right that notwithstanding those statutes and orders the liability of the British government under the 1917 and 1918 agreements still subsisted. The decision in the House of Lords that the liability had been transferred to and vested in the government of the Irish Free State rested principally on the proper construction and effect of the statutes and orders involved, but having so held that that was their result Viscount Cave LC continued (at 765-766):

That this conclusion is in accordance, not only with the terms of the several Acts and Orders, but with the reason of the case, is (I think) plain. The Free State Government now holds the branch lines to which the rails and sleepers were transferred. That Government alone can sanction the replacement of the lines removed from the respondents' railway and can regulate the method of replacement and control the expense incurred. The lines when replaced will be for the benefit of the surrounding population, and the betterment of the respondents' line (for which under the terms of the Castlecomer Agreement the respondents are to make an allowance) will proceed from that population. At the time when the Acts and Orders were passed, it was plain that the administration of all the railways in Southern Ireland would pass out of the jurisdiction and control of the British Ministry of Transport and would become a function of the

Free State; and it was natural that the assets and future liabilities connected with that function should at the same time be transferred to the Government of that State. I think that on the true construction of the Acts and Orders this was their effect, and accordingly that this appeal should succeed.

Viscount Haldane, with whose speech Lord Carson concurred, having considered the point of construction and then referred to three cases concerning Newfoundland, New Zealand and England respectively, said (at 773-774):

My Lords, I am of opinion that the judgments in these three cases illustrate a principle which is definitely recorded in our textbooks of constitutional law. However clear it may be that before the Revolution Settlement the Crown could be taken to contract personally, it is equally clear that since that Settlement its ordinary contracts only mean that it will pay out of funds which Parliament may or may not supply. In the present case Parliament transferred the duty of producing the fund out of which the liability in question, when it accrued, should be met to the Irish Parliament. It thereby declared its intention not itself to provide the money required out of its own Consolidated Fund. It does not matter whether the liability was in terms transferred to the Irish Government. By its very character it would cease when it became operative to be a liability of the British Consolidated Fund and become one of the Irish Legislature Central Fund, if they chose to so provide.

Finally Lord Phillimore in his speech said (at 779-780):

So far then it is merely a departmental question whether a particular property is stated to be vested in one Minister or another. But when it becomes a question of a transfer from the Home Government to the Irish Free State or to any other Dominion, it is necessary to look into it somewhat more closely. The property of the Crown in the Dominion is held for the purposes of that Dominion. Its benefits accrue to the Dominion Exchequer, and liabilities in connection with it must be discharged out of the same Exchequer. His Majesty has separate Attorney-Generals to sue and be sued in respect of each Dominion . . . In these circumstances I am of opinion that no petition of right can be brought in the High Court of Justice of England which has for its object a judgment against the Crown which is to be satisfied out of the Exchequer of a Dominion, and that no judgment can be obtained on a petition of right so brought in respect of liabilities incident to the Ministry of a Dominion, because such liabilities are not to be satisfied out of the Exchequer of the United Kingdom.

It was in these circumstances, and as a part of the evolutionary and and devolutionary process to which I have referred, that the British North America Act 1867 was passed. I will myself refer to a few specific sections in a moment, but its general effect has been described in two judgments of the Privy Council. In *Liquidators of the Maritime Bank of Canada* v *Receiver-General of New Brunswick* [1892] AC 437 at 441-442. Lord Watson said:

> The object of the Act was neither to weld the provinces into one, nor to subordinate provincial givernments to a central authority, but to create a federal government in which they should all be represented, entrusted with the exclusive administration of affairs in which they had a common interest, each province retaining its independence and autonomy. That object was accomplished by distributing between the Dominion and the provinces, all powers executive and legislative, and all public property and revenues which had previously belonged to the provinces; so that the Dominion Government should be vested with such of these powers, property, and revenues as were necessary for the due performance of its constitutional functions, and that the remainder should be retained by the provinces for the purposes of provincial government. But, in so far as regards those matters which, by sect. 92, are specially reserved for provincial legislation, the legislation of each province continues to be free from the control of the Dominion, and as supreme as it was before the passing of the Act. In *Hodge* v *The Queen* ((1883) 9 App Cas 117 at 132), Lord Fitzgerald[1], delivering the opinion of this Board, said: ''When the British North America Act enacted that there should be a legislature for Ontario, and that its legislative assembly should have exclusive authority to make laws for the province and for provincial purposes in relation to the matters enumerated in sect. 92, it conferred powers not in any sense to be exercised by delegation from or as agents of the Imperial Parliament, but authority as plenary and as ample within the limits prescribed by sect. 92 as the Imperial Parliament in the plenitude of its power possessed and could bestow. Within these limits of subjects and area the local legislature is supreme, and has the same authority as the Imperial Parliament, or the Parliament of the Dominion.'' The Act places the constitutions of all provinces within the Dominion on the same level; and what is true with respect to the legislature of Ontario has equal application to the legislature of New Brunswick.

Secondly, in *A-G for Ontario* v *A-G for Canada* [1912] AC 571 at 581 Earl Loreburn LC said:

> In 1867 the desire of Canada for a definite Constitution embracing the

entire Dominion was embodied in the British North America Act. Now, there can be no doubt that under this organic instrument the powers distributed between the Dominion on the one hand and the provinces on the other hand cover the whole area of self-government within the whole area of Canada. It would be subversive of the entire scheme and policy of the Act to assume that any point of internal self-government was withheld from Canada. Numerous points have arisen, and may hereafter arise, upon those provisions of the Act which draw the dividing line between what belongs to the Dominion or to the province respectively. An exhaustive enumeration being unattainable (so infinite are the subjects of possible legislation), general terms are necessarily used in describing what either is to have, and with the use of general terms comes the risk of some confusion, whenever a case arises in which it can be said that the power claimed falls within the description of what the Dominion is to have, and also within the description of what the province is to have. Such apparent overlapping is unavoidable, and the duty of a Court of law is to decide in each particular case on which side of the line it falls in view of the whole statute.

For our present purposes it is sufficient to recall that s 3 of the 1867 Act enacted that the Queen by proclamation might constitute the three then provinces of Canada, Nova Scotia and New Brunswick into the Dominion of Canada. The Province of Canada, which had earlier been formed by the joinder of Upper and Lower Canada, became the two new provinces of Ontario and Quebec. The Act then created separate self-governing constitutions for the Dominion and each of the four provinces. Sections 91 and 92 laid down the classes of subject which were to be within the exclusive legislative powers of the Dominion parliament and provincial legislatures respectively. Among these, by s 91(24), the power to legislate in respect of 'Indians, and lands reserved for the Indians' was given to the Dominion parliament. By s 109 all lands, mines, minerals and royalties belonging to the three existing provinces were to continue to belong to the four provinces thereafter to form the Dominion, subject to any trusts existing in respect thereof and to any interest other than that of the provinces in the same. The effect of this section was considered in *St Catharine's Milling and Lumber Co* v *R* (1888) 14 App Cas 46, in which the Privy Council held that lands ceded by Indians under treaties made with the Crown after federation became vested in the relevant province. Section 132 provided that the parliament and government of the Dominion should have all the necessary powers to enable it to perform the obligations of Canada or any province, as part of the British Empire, towards foreign countries arising under treaties between the Empire and such foreign countries.

Finally, s 146 gave power to admit to the Dominion, inter alia, what was then Rupert's Land and the North Western Territory, which were each then vested in the Hudson's Bay Company under the latter's charter.

By the 1867 Act, therefore, the Dominion and the provinces acquired a substantial degree of self-government and their own treasuries. Between then and the Imperial Conferences of 1926 and 1930 the Dominion acquired, largely by agreement and convention, increasing independence over and above that given it by the 1867 Act from the United Kingdom and its Parliament until, by the Statute of Westminster 1931, it and the other Dominions referred to in that statute attained complete independence subject, in the case of Canada, to s 7, which, as it was put in argument, entrenched the constitution of Canada and its provinces in Westminster, subject to this, that such constitution can only be amended at the request and with the consent of the Dominion.

As a result of this process and on the authorities to which I have referred, I have no doubt that any treaty or other obligations which the Crown had entered into with the Indian peoples of Canada in right of the United Kingdom had become the responsibility of the government of Canada with the attainment of independence, at the latest with the Statute of Westminster 1931. I therefore think that this application must fail.

However, as counsel have dealt with the general facts and merits of this case, I shall do so shortly myself. As will finally appear, however, I do not think that it is the function of this court in all the circumstances to do so.

It is a matter of history, in so far as is material in this case, that the royal charter granting Rupert's Land to the Hudson's Bay Company was made in 1670. Thereafter, as a result of the Treaty of Utrecht 1713, Hudson Bay, Nova Scotia and Newfoundland passed to England and ultimately the rest of the territory claimed by France in North America was ceded to England in 1763 by the Treaty of Paris.

In that same year George III issued a proclamation with which I shall have to deal in a moment. However, prior to this and to the formal hostilities between Great Britain and France called the Seven Years War, a number of treaties were entered into between the local Indian communities and the English Crown or representatives of it. These are what have been described as the Maritime Treaties in this case and are the first class of documents under which it is alleged that the Indian peoples of Canada obtained rights against the English Crown. I do not agree. I think that if one looks at these treaties as they have been shown to us, they were merely articles of submission. The Indians concerned had been engaging in hostilities against the English Crown. By these treaties they agreed to cease to do so and in the main to trade and treat with the British rather than with the French. Only two of these treaties, namely those of 1752 and 1794, both with the Micmac Indians, could in any way be said to have granted anything to the Indians, but even then this was in such general terms that it is impossible to say to what, if anything, they relate in a context 200 years after they were made.

There was then the royal proclamation of 1763. It is agreed on both sides that this had and continues to have the effect at least of secondary legislation, if not of a statute. After setting up the four self-governing colonies of Quebec, East Florida, West Florida and Grenada, it reserved under the Crown's sovereignty, protection and dominion, for the use of the Indian inhabitants of such land, substantial parts of the territories recently ceded to England by France, but not including the four colonies I have mentioned, or lands within the limits of the territory earlier granted to the Hudson's Bay Company under its charter.

From some of the Canadian decisions which have been shown to us it seems that the Canadian courts have held that the provisions of the royal proclamation did and do extend to the provinces of Nova Scotia and New Brunswick, subject to the terms of any cessions of land to the Crown by Indians in those provinces which have been made since 1763. From the arguments addressed to us I would respectfully agree with this view of the Canadian courts. As I shall indicate, however, I do not think that it is competent for this or any English court to pronounce definitively on the point and had I disagreed with the Canadian judges I would not have thought it correct for me to say so.

Of the many Canadian cases we have seen, I think that it is sufficient for present purposes to refer to *R* v *Isaac* (1975) 9 APR 175, a decision of the Nova Scotia Supreme Court, as an authority for the existence of an aboriginal or Canadian common law right possessed by Indians to hunt and fish over their lands. Were it within my jurisdiction now to do so, I would hold that this right was confirmed to the Indians by the proclamation and, save to the extent where it has been extinguished by the cession of Indian lands or a Dominion statute pursuant to s 91(24) of the British North America Act 1867, is still an Indian right over relevant land. This was the decision not only in *R* v *Isaac* but also in a number of the other Canadian cases to which our attention was directed.

It is a right which the Indians possess against the Crown, but for the reasons I have given against the Crown in right of Canada and not in right of the United Kingdom.

I turn finally to the post-federation treaties, those which have been described in this case as the Prairie Treaties, and in particular to treaty no 6 of 1876, which is the one relating to the Alberta Indians, whose association was the first of the applicants in these proceedings.

I shall refer to the terms of the treaty shortly, but, in addition to the general reasons which I have already given for my conclusion that any rights owed today by the Crown to the Indian population of Canada are owed by the Crown in right of Canada, the history of Alberta, and for that matter Manitoba and Saskatchewan, is also relevant. The territory of what is now the Province of Alberta was part of Rupert's Land, which was granted to the Hudson's Bay Company by its charter of 1670. As such the Indians occupying it were expressly excluded from the reservation of sovereignty in the proclamation of 1763 to which I have referred. The Hudson's Bay Company surrendered Rupert's Land to the Crown in November 1769 and by an Order in Council pursuant to s 146 of the British North America Act 1867 the Crown admitted Rupert's Land into the Dominion the same year. At that stage Rupert's Land and the power to legislate for it was given to the Dominion government. However, by the Alberta Act 1905, the relevant part of Rupert's Land was established as the Province of Alberta and a system of local self-government set up as in the other provinces. The land itself, however, still remained vested in the Dominion. Nevertheless by the schedule to the British North America Act 1930 the land constituting Alberta was transferred from the Dominion to the province, except for the lands included in the Indian Reserves, which, because of the responsibility of the Dominion government for Indians and their lands, under s 91(24) of the 1867 Act, remained vested in the Dominion.

Thus, at least in so far as Alberta itself was concerned, at the date of the treaty which we have been asked to consider its land was vested in the Dominion. Then, understandably, when the lands constituting Alberta were vested in the province, so as to put it in the same position as other provinces, that land which by the treaties had been reserved to the Indians was still kept vested in the Dominion government, which had the responsibility for these people.

Further, although treaty no 6 was expressed to have been made by Her Majesty the Queen of Great Britain and Ireland with the Indians, it was nevertheless made by her through commissioners, including the Lieutenant Governor of the relevant lands. In addition the cession of lands by the Indians, in exchange for which the Crown granted them certain rights and privileges, was to the government of the Dominion of Canada for Her Majesty the Queen. Next, when the Crown in the treaty agreed to lay aside reserves for the Indians, they were to be administered and dealt with for them by Her Majesty's government of the Dominion of Canada.

On both the general and also these particular grounds, therefore, I think that the rights granted to the Alberta Indians by the relevant treaty were granted to them by the Crown in right of Canada and not by the Crown in right of the United Kingdom.

In essence, the argument of counsel for the applicants was that, because at least some element of sovereignty over the Canadian constitution remained in Westminster, this necessarily carried with it at least some obligation in the Crown in the right of the United Kingdom to the Indian peoples of Canada under the royal proclamation of 1763 and the Prairie Treaties to which I have referred. As a matter of construction, clearly s 7 of the Statute of Westminster 1931 did retain a limited sovereignty of the Crown in right of the United Kingdom over the Dominion. But, in my opinion, on both the general and particular considerations to which I have referred, I do not think that this in any way means that any treaty or other obligations into which the Crown may have entered with its Indian peoples of Canada still ensure against the Crown in right of the United Kingdom. Quite clearly, to the extent that these still continue, and I think that it is clear that the Canadian courts have held that they do, they are owed by the Crown in right of the Dominion or in right of the particular province.

As I have said earlier, the Crown is a constitutional monarchy, acting only on the advice of its relevant ministers. Two hundred years ago, in so far as North America was concerned, these were clearly the ministers of the United Kingdom government. Equally clearly, in 1982 and in the events which have occurred, notwithstanding s 7 of the 1931 statute, the relevant ministers on whose advice the Crown acts in relation to Canada and its provinces are those of her government in the Dominion and those provinces.

In the course of his argument counsel for the applicants referred to s 7(1)(*b*) of the India Independence Act 1947, relating to India in Asia, and the corresponding provision in s 1(3) of the Burma Independence Act 1947. By these legislative provisions the Crown's suzerainty of the Indian states and the Karenni states respectively was to lapse on the appointed day and with it, inter alia, all obligations of the Crown to these various states and their rulers at the same time. Counsel for the applicants argued that the absence of any similar provision in the British North America Act 1867, the Statute of Westminster 1931 or the present Canada Bill relating to the Crown's suzerainty of and obligations to the Indian peoples of Canada clearly meant that these were to continue and remain the responsibilities of the Crown in right of the United Kingdom. It is always dangerous to argue from default in this way: circumstances vary so much from case to case and Parliamentary draftsmen in the nineteenth century may have adopted a very different approach from their successors in the twentieth century. In any event, if, for instance, one looks at s 6 and analagous sections (as to India) and s 320 (as to Burma) of the Government of India Act 1935, one can see there were substantial formal relationships between the Crown in right of the United Kingdom and local rulers in India and Burma which had to be set aside when those two countries obtained their independence. Further, this was obtained by these two countries once and for all by their respective Acts of 1947. Similar independence for Canada, and within her for the provinces, was not the result of one simple legislative act of the United Kingdom Parliament at Westminster, either in 1867 or 1931. It was a gradual process which, save for the entrenched constitution, had been effected by 1931.

For these reasons, the comparative argument of counsel for the applicants relating to India and Burma is, in my opinion, of little, if any, force.

Finally, counsel on behalf of the Crown in right of the United Kingdom, in particular the Foreign and Commonwealth Office, and counsel on behalf of the Crown in right of Canada, each argue that the issues raised by these applications are outside the jurisdiction of the English courts, that they ought not to be considered by them, and that in any event it is inappropriate to grant any declaration in this or any other similar application. With all respect to these arguments, I think that the last is dependent on our decision on the first two. If the issues raised in this case are within this court's jurisdiction, then I see no reason why we should not make an appropriate declaration on the application of one side or the other. On the other hand, if the issues raised are not within this court's jurisdiction, then not only should we in truth not hear them but certainly we should make no declaration, in favour of either side.

On the authority of the decisions of this court in such cases as *Mellenger v New Brunswick Development Corp* [1971] 2 All ER 593, [1971] 1 WLR 604, I do not think that this court has any jurisdiction to consider the issues raised by this application, and not merely no jurisdiction, but that it would be contrary to the comity existing between independent nations were we to do so. The rights and obligations on which we have been asked to adjudicate are said to be enjoyed by and owed to citizens of Canada in respect of land which is itself within the Dominion. Further, any enforcement of these rights and obligations could ex hypothesi only be carried out within Canada and would have to be subject to the relevant provisions of Canadian law. We have only heard the arguments on the merits de bene esse and out of consideration of those who have travelled 4,000 miles and further to hear their cause pleaded before us. We appreciate their anxieties; we have done all that we can relevant to this application to learn about their history and understand the arguments put before us on their behalf.

In the end, however, I am quite satisfied both, on general constitutional grounds as well as on the construction of the relevant instruments and the history of the relevant provinces themselves, that any treaty or other other obligations still owed by the Crown to the Indian peoples of Canada are owed by the Crown in right of the Dominion of Canada and not in the right of the United Kingdom. If such obligations still exist, and, if they do, their extent, is, in my opinion, not a matter for this court: it is a matter for the courts of Canada.

I, too, would therefore refuse this application.

Application for judicial review refused; application for leave to appeal to the House of Lords refused.

11 March. The Appeal Committee of the House of Lords (Lord Diplock, Lord Fraser of Tullybelton, Lord Russell of Killowen, Lord Scarman and Lord Bridge of Harwich) heard a petition by the applicants for leave to appeal.

Louis Blom-Cooper QC for the applicants.
Robert Alexander QC for the Secretary of State.
Andrew Morritt QC for the Canadian government.

LORD DIPLOCK. Their Lordships do not grant leave to appeal in this case. They wish to make it clear that their refusal of leave is not based on any technical or procedural grounds, although it is not to be taken as their view that there is jurisdiction to entertain an application for judicial review in such a case as this. Their refusal of leave is because in their opinion, for the accumulated reasons given in the judgments of the Court of Appeal, it simply is not arguable that any obligations of the Crown in respect of the Indian peoples of Canada are still the responsibility of Her Majesty's government in the United Kingdom. They are the responsibility of Her Majesty's government in Canada, and it is the Canadian courts and not the English courts that alone have jurisdiction to determine what those obligations are.

Petition dismissed.

5. The Treaties, Including Proclamations and Other Documents

(a) The Maritime Treaties

(i) From Peter A. Cumming and Neil H. Mickenberg (eds.), *Native Rights in Canada* (2d ed., Toronto: General Publishing Co. Ltd. for Indian-Eskimo Association of Canada, 1972).

**The Submission and Agreement
of the
Delegates of the Eastern Indians
(December 15, 1725, Boston, New England, British Possession)**

WHEREAS the Severall Tribes of Eastern Indians vis: The Penobscot, Maridgwalk, St John, Cape Sables and other tribes Inhabiting within

His Majesty's Territories of New England and Nova Scotia who have been engaged in the present War from whom Wesauguaaram alias Loron Arexus Francois Xavier and Meganumoe are delegated and fully impowred to enter into Articles of Pacification with his Majesty's Governments of the Mass Bay New Hampshire and Nova Scotia, Have contrary to the several Treaties they have Solemnly intered into with the said Governments made an open rupture and have continued some years in Acts of Hostility against the subjects of His Majesty King George within the said Governments. They being now sensible of the miseries and troubles they have involved themselves in, and being desirous to be restored to His Majesty's Grace and favour and to live in peace with all His Majesty's Subjects of the said Three Governments, The Province of New York and Colonys of Connecticutt and Rhod Island and that all former acts of injury be forgotten. Have concluded to make and we Do by these presents in the name and behalf of the said Tribes make our Submission unto his most Excellent Majesty George by the Grace of God of Great Britain, France and Ireland, King Defender of the faith in as full and ample manner as any of our Predecessors have heretofore done.

And we do hereby promise and engage with the Honourable William Dummer Esq; as he is Lieutenant Governour and Commander in Chief of His Majesty's Province of the Massachusetts Bay And with the Governours or Commanders in Chief of the said Province for the time being. That is to say.

We the said Delegates for and in behalf of the several Tribes abovesaid Do promise and engage that at all times forever from and after the date of these presents We and They will Erase and for bear all Acts of Hostility, Infuries and discords towards all the Subjects of the Crown of Great Britain and not offer the least hurt, violence or molestation to them or any of them in their persons or Estates, But will hence forward hold and maintain a firm and Constant Amity and Friendship with all the English, and will never confederate or combine with any other nation to their prejudice.

That all the Captives taken in the present War shall at or before the time of the further Ratification of this Treaty be restored without any ransom or payment to be made for them or any of them.

That His Majesty's Subjects the English Shall and may peaceably and quietly enter upon Improve and forever enjoy all and singular their Rights of God and former Settlements properties and possessions within the Eastern parts of the said province of the Massachusetts Bay Together with all Islands, inletts Shoars Beaches and Fishery within the same without any molestation or claims by us or any other Indian and be in no ways molested interrupted or disturbed therein.

Saving unto the Penobscot, Naridgwalk and other Tribes within His

Majesty's province aforesaid and their natural Descendants respectively all their lands, Liberties and properties not by them convey'd or sold to or possessed by any of the English Subjects as aforesaid. As also the priviledge of fishing, hunting, and fowling as formerly.

That all trade and Commerce which hereafter may be allowed betwixt the English and Indians shall be under such management and Regulations as the Government of the Mass. Province shall direct.

If any Controversy or difference at any time hereafter happen to arise between any of the English and Indians for any reall or supposed wrong or injury done on either side no private Revenge shall be taken for the same but proper application shall be made to His Majesty's Government upon the place for Remedy or induse there of in a due course of Justice. We Submitting ourselves to be ruled and governed by His Majesty's Laws and desiring to have the benefit of the same.

We also the said Delegates in behalf of the Tribes of Indians Inhabiting within the French Territories who have assisted us in this war for a term we are fully Impowered to Act in this present Treaty. Do hereby promise and ingage that they and every of them shall henceforth cease and forbear all acts of Hostility force and violence towards all and every the Subjects of His Majesty the King of Great Britain.

We do further in behalf of the Tribe of the Penobscot Indians promise and engage that if any of the other Tribes intended to be included in this Treaty that notwithstanding Refuse to confirm and ratifie this present Treaty entered into on their behalf and continue or renew Acts of Hostility against the English. In such case the said Penobscot Tribe shall join their young men with the English in reducing them to reason.

In the next place We the aforenamed Delegates. Do promise and engage with the Honourable John Wentworth Esq; as he is Lieutenant Governour and Commander in Chief of His Majesty's Province of New Hampshire and with the Governour and Commanders in Chief of the said province for the time being that we and the tribes we are deputed from will henceforth erase and for bear all Acts of Hostility Injuries and discords towards all the Subjects of His Majesty King George within the said province And we do understand and take it that the said Government of New Hampshire is also included and excepting that respecting the regulating the trade with us.

And further we the aforenamed Delegates do promise and ingage with the Honourable Lawrence Armstrong; Lieutenant Governour and Commander in Chief of His Majesty's Province of Nova Scotia or Acadie to live in peace with His Majesty's Good Subjects and their Dependants in the Government according to the Articles agreed on with Major Paul Makarene commissioned for that purpose and further to be Ratified as mentioned in the said Articles.

That this present Treaty shall be accepted Ratified and confirmed in a public and solemn manner by the Chiefs of the several Eastern Tribes of Indians included Therein at Talmouth in Casco Bay sometime in the month of May next. In Testimony whereof we have signed these presents and affixed our Seals.

[Signatures Deleted]

Note

1. A Treaty of 13 July 1713 was made with Indians situate on the Saint John River in New Brunswick, then part of the province of New Hampshire, and other Indians south to the Merrimack River. This document saved unto the Indians "their own grounds, and free liberty for hunting, fishing, fowling, and all other of their Lawful Liberties and privileges," as on 11 August 1693. The Treaty of 1713 and one of 11 August 1693 are reproduced in Cumming and Mickenberg, *supra*, pp. 295-99.

(ii) From *Canada Indian Treaties and Surrenders. From 1680 to 1890* (Original Ottawa: Queen's Printer, 1891; reprint Toronto: Coles Publishing Co., 1971).

No. 239.

ARTICLES OF SUBMISSION AND AGREEMENT made at Boston, in New England, by Sanquaaram *alias* Loron Arexus, François Xavier and Meganumbe, delegates from Pebonscott, Naridgwack, St Johns, Cape Sables and other tribes inhabiting within His Majesty's territories of Nova Scotia or New England.

Whereas His Majesty King George by concession of the Most Christian King, made at the Treaty of Utrecht, is become the rightful possessor of the Province of Nova Scotia or Acadia according to its ancient boundaries: We, the said Sanquaaram *alias* Loron Arexus, François Xavier and Meganumbe, delegates from the said tribes of Penobscott, Naridgwack, St Johns, Cape Sables and other tribes inhabiting within His Majesty's said territories of Nova Scotia or Acadia and New England, do, in the name and behalf of the said tribes we represent, acknowledge His said Majesty King George's jurisdiction and dominion over the territories of the said Province of Nova Scotia or Acadia, and make our submission to His said Majesty in as ample a manner as we have formerly done to the most Christian King.

And we further promise on behalf of the said tribes we represent that the Indians shall not molest any of His Majestie's subjects or their dependants in their settlements already made or lawfully to be made, or in their carrying on their traffick and other affairs within the said Province.

That if there happens any robbery or outrage committed by any of the Indians, the tribe or tribes they belong to shall cause satisfaction and restitution to be made to the parties injured.

That the Indians shall not help to convey away any soldiers belonging to His Majestie's forts, but on the contrary shall bring back any soldier they shall find endeavouring to run away.

That in case of any misunderstanding, quarrel or injury between the English and the Indians no private revenge shall be taken, but application shall be made for redress according to His Majestie's laws.

That if the Indians have made any prisoners belonging to the Government of Nova Scotia or Acadie during the course of the war they shall be released at or before the ratification of this treaty.

That this treaty shall be ratified at Annapolis Royal.

Dated at the Council Chamber in Boston, in New England, this fifteenth day of December, *Anno Domini* one thousand seven hundred and twenty-five, *Annoq. Regni Regis Georgii, Magna Britannia, &c., Duodecimo.*

[Signatures Deleted]

From *Indian Treaties and surrenders*

(iii) Ratification at Annapolis Royal, 1728

We the underwritten Chiefs and others of the St Johns, Cape Sables and other tribes of Indians inhabiting within this His Majestie's Province of Nova Scotia or Acadia having had the several articles of the within written Instrument (being a true copy of what was signed in our behalf by Sanquaaram *alias* Loron Arexus, François Xavier and Meganumbe, our delegates at the Treaty of Peace concluded at Boston) distinctly read over, faithfully interpreted and by us well understood, do hereby for ourselves and in behalf of our respective tribes consent to ratifie and confirm all the within mentioned articles and that the same shall be binding to us and our heirs forever to all intents and purposes.

IN WITNESS WHEREOF, we have signed, sealed and delivered these presents to the Honourable Lieut. Governor in the presence of several officers belonging to His Majestie's troops and other gentlemen underwritten.

Done at the Fort of Annapolis Royal in Nova Scotia, this thirteenth day of May, in the first year of the reign of Our Sovereign Lord, George the Second, by the Grace of God, of Great Britain, France and Ireland, King, Defender of the Faith, &c., *Annoq. Domini*, 1728.

[Signatures Deleted]

(iv) From *Indian Treaties and Surrenders*

Casco Bay Articles, 1727

By the parties to these Articles: the following Article is unanimously and reciprocally agreed upon for the more effectual preservation of the peace: That if any hostility shall be committed or offered to be committed by any Indians on any of the English subjects the Tribes who have enter'd into and ratified the treaty shall furnish and supply fifty Indians with a Captain of their own and the English two hundred and fifty, and so in proportion a greater or lesser number as the occasion shall require. The forces to be paid and subsisted by the English and under the conduct of such a General Officer as the English Governour may judge proper to pursue such refractory Indians either by sea or land and compell them to live peaceably and quietly with their neighbours. And if any other Tribes of Indians shall make warr upon any of the Tribes now enter'd into peace, in such a case the English shall assist them att their own cost and charge with the like proportion of men as may be necessary.

Done at the Conference att Casco Bay, this twenty-fifth day of July, in the thirteenth year of the reign of Our Sovereign Lord King George, *Annoque Domini.* 1727.

[Signed on behalf of Colonies of Massachusetts Bay, New Hampshire and Nova Scotia — Signatures deleted.]

[Chebucto Harbour Ratification, 1749]

I, Joannes Pedousaghtigh, Chief of the Tribe of Chinecto Indians, for myself and in behalf of my Tribe, my heirs and their heirs for ever, and we, François Aurodowish, Simon Sactawino and Jean Battiste Maddouanhook   *   *   *   * deputys from the Chiefs of the St Johns Indians, and invested by them with full power for that purpose, do in the most solemn manner renew the above articles of agreement and submission, and every article thereof, with His Excellency Edward Cornwallis, Esquire, Capt. Gener'l and Governor in Chief in and over His Majestie's Province of Nova Scotia or Accadie, Vice-Admiral of the same, Colonel in His Majestie's service and one of His bed chamber. In wittness whereof, I, the said Joannes Pedousaghtigh, have subscribed this treaty and affixed my seal, and we, the said François Aurodowish, Simon Sactawino and Jean Battiste Maddouanhook   *   *   *   * in behalf of the chiefs of the Indian Tribes we represent, have subscribed and affixed our seals to the same, and engage that the said Chief shall ratifie this treaty at St Johns. Done in Chebucto Harbour the fifteenth of August, one thousand seven hundred and forty-nine.

[Signatures deleted]

The Articles of Peace on the other side, concluded at Chebucto, the fifteenth of August, one thousand seven hundred and fourty-nine, with His Excellency Edward Cornwallis, Esqr., Capt. General, Governor and Commander in Chief of His Majesty's Province of Nova Scotia or Accadie, and signed by our deputies, having been communicated to us by Edward How, Esqr., one of His Majesty's Council for said Province, and faithfully interpreted to us by Madame De Bellisle, inhabitant of this river, nominated by us for that purpose. We the Chiefs and Captains of the River St. Johns and places adjacent do for ourselves and our different Tribes conform and ratefy the same to all intents and purposes. Given under our hands at the River St. Johns this fourth day of September, one thousand seven hundred and forty-nine, in the presence of the under written witnesses.

[Signatures deleted]

(v) From Cumming and Mickenberg, *supra*

Enclosure in letter of Governor Hopson
to the
Right Honourable The Earl of Holdernesse 6th of Dec. 1752

Treaty or
Articles of Peace and Friendship Renewed
between

His Excellency Peregrine Thomas Hopson Esquire Captain General and Governor in Chief in and over His Majesty's Province of Nova Scotia or Acadie Vice Admiral of the same & Colonel of One of His Majesty's Regiments of Foot, and His Majesty's Council on behalf of His Majesty.

AND

Major Jean Baptist Cope chief Sachem of the Tribe of Mick Mack

Indians, Inhabiting the Eastern Coast of the said Province, and Andrew Hadley Martin, Gabriel Martin and Francis Jeremiah members & Delegates of the said Tribe, for themselves and their said Tribe their heirs and the heirs of their heirs forever. Begun made and Concluded in the manner form & Tenor following, viz.

1. It is agreed that the Articles of Submission & Agreements made at Boston in New England by the Delegates of the Penobscot Norridgwolk & St John's Indians in the Year 1725 Ratifyed and Confirmed by all the Nova Scotia Tribes at Annapolis Royal in the Month of June 1726 and lately Renewed with Governor Cornwallis at Halifax and Ratifyed at St John's River, now read over Explained & Interpreted shall be and are hereby from this time forward renewed, reiterated and forever Confirmed by them and their Tribe, and the said Indians for themselves and their Tribe and their Heirs aforesaid do make and renew the same Solemn Submissions and promises for the strict Observance of all the Articles therein Contained as at any time heretofore hath been done.

2. That all Transactions during the late War shall on both sides be buried in Oblivion with the Hatchet, And that the said Indians shall have all favour, Friendship & Protection shewn them from His Majesty's Government.

3. That the said Tribe shall use their utmost Endeavours to bring in the other Indians to Renew and Ratify this Peace, and shall discover and make known any attempts or designs of any other Indians or any Enemy whatever against his Majesty's Subjects within this Province so soon as they shall know thereof and shall also hinder and Obstruct the same to the utmost of their power, and on the other hand if any of the Indians refusing to ratify this Peace shall make War upon the Tribe who have now Confirmed the same; they shall upon Application have such aid and Assistance from the Government for their defence as the Case may require.

4. It is agreed that the said Tribe of Indians shall not be hindered from, but have free liberty of hunting and Fishing as usual and that if they shall think a Truck house needful at the River Chibenaccadie, or any other place of their resort they shall have the same built and proper Merchandize, lodged therein to be exchanged for waht the Indians shall have to dispose of and that in the mean time the Indians shall have free liberty to bring to Sale to Halifax or any other Settlement within this Province, Skins, feathers, fowl, fish or any other thing they shall have to sell, where they shall have liberty to dispose thereof to the best Advantage.

5. That a Quantity of bread, flour, and such other Provisions, as can be procured, necessary for the Familys and proportionable to the

Numbers of the said Indians, shall be given them half Yearly for the time to come; and the same regard shall be had to the other Tribes that shall hereafter Agree to Renew and Ratify the Peace upon the Terms and Conditions now Stipulated.

6. That to Cherish a good harmony and mutual Correspondence between the said Indians and this Government His Excellency Peregrine Thomas Hopson Esq. Capt. General & Governor in Chief in & over His Majesty's Province of Nova Scotia or Accadie Vice Admiral of the same & Colonel of One of His Majesty's Regiments of Foot hereby promises on the part of His Majesty that the said Indians shall upon the first day of October Yearly, so long as they shall Continue in Friendship, Receive Presents of Blankets, Tobacco, some Powder & Shott, and the said Indians promise once every year, upon the said first of October, to come by themselves or their Delegates and Receive the said Presents and Renew their Friendship and Submissions.

7. That the Indians shall use their best Endeavors to save the Lives & Goods of any People Shipwrecked on this Coast where they resort and shall Conduct the People saved to Halifax with their Goods, and a Reward adequate to the Salvadge shall be given them.

8. That all Disputes whatsoever that may happen to arise between the Indians now at Peace and others His Majesty's Subjects in this Province shall be tryed in His Majesty's Courts of Civil Judicature, where the Indians shall have the same benefits, Advantages & Priviledges as any others of His Majesty's Subjects.

In Faith & Testimony whereof the Great Seal of the Province is hereunto appended, and the Partys to these Presents have hereunto interchangeably Set their Hands in the Council Chamber at Halifax this 22nd day of Nov. 1752 in the 26th Year of His Majesty's Reign.

[Signatures deleted]

(vi) From Cumming and Mickenberg, *supra*

Proclamation of 1761

Draft of an Instruction for the Governors of Nova Scotia, New Hampshire, New York, Virginia, North Carolina, South Carolina, and Georgia forbidding them to Grant Lands or make Settlements which may interfere with the Indians bordering on those Colonies.

WHEREAS the peace and security of Our Colonies and Plantations upon the Continent of North America does greatly depend upon the

Amity and Alliance of the several Nations or Tribes of Indians bordering upon the said Colonies and upon a just and faithful Observance of those Treaties and Compacts which have been heretofore solemnly entered into with the said Indians by Our Royall Predecessors Kings and Queens of this Realm, And whereas notwithstanding the repeated Instructions which have been from time to time given by Our Royal Grandfather to the Governors of Our several Colonies upon this head the said Indians have made and do still continue to make great complaints that Settlements have been made and possession taken of lands, the property of which they have by Treaties reserved to themselves by persons claiming the said lands under pretence of deeds of Sale and Conveyance illegally, fraudulently and surreptitiously obtained of the said Indians; And whereas it has likewise been represented unto Us that some of Our Governors or other Chief Officers of Our said Colonies of the Duty they owe to Us and of the Welfare and Security of our Colonies have countenanced such unjust claims and pretensions by passing Grants of the Lands so pretended to have been purchased of the Indians. We therefor taking this matter into Our Royal Consideration, as also the fatal Effects which would attend a discontent amongst the Indians in the present situation of affairs, and being determined upon all occasions to support and protect the said Indians in their just Rights and Possessions and to keep inviolable the Treaties and Compacts which have been entered into with them, Do hereby strictly enjoyn & command that neither yourself nor any Lieutenant Governor, President of the Council or Commander in Chief of Our said Colony/Province of   do upon any pretence whatever upon pain of Our highest Displeasure and of being forthwith removed from your or his office, pass any Grant or Grants to any persons whatever of any lands within or adjacent to the Territories possessed or occupied by the said Indians or the Property Possession of which has at any time been reserved to or claimed by them. And it is Our further Will and Pleasure that you do publish a proclamation in Our Name strictly enjoining and requiring all persons whatever who may either willfully or inadvertently have seated themselves on any lands so reserved to or claimed by the said Indians without any lawfull Authority for so doing forthwith to remove therefrom And in case you shall find upon strict enquiry to be made for the purpose that any person or persons do claim to hold or possess any lands within Our said Colony/Province upon pretence of purchases made of the said Indians without a proper licence first had and obtained either from Us or any of Our Royal Predecessors or any person acting under Our or their Authority you are forthwith to cause a prosecution to be carried on against such person or persons who shall have made such fraudulent purchases to the end that the land may be recovered by due Course of Law And whereas the wholesome Laws that have at different times been passed in several of our said Colonies and the instructions which have been given by Our Royal Predecessors for restraining persons from purchasing lands of the Indians without a Licence for the purpose and for regulating the proceedings upon such purchases have not been duly observed, It is therefore Our express Will and Pleasure that when any application shall be made to you for licence to purchase lands of the Indians you do forebear to grant such Licence untill you shall have first transmitted to Us by Our Commissioners for Trade and Plantations the particulars of such applications as well as in respect to the situation as the extent of the lands so proposed to be purchased and shall have received Our further directions therein; And it is Our further Will and Pleasure that you do forthwith cause this Our Instruction to you to be made Publick not only within all parts your said Colony/Province inhabited by Our Subjects, but also amongst the several Tribes of Indians living within the same to the end that Our Royal Will and Pleasure in the Premises may be known and that the Indians may be apprized of Our determin'd Resolution to support them in their just Rights, and inviolably to observe Our Engagements with them.

(vii) Letter of Jonathan Belcher to the Lords of Trade, 2 July 1762

Halifax,
Nova Scotia
2nd July 1762

My Lords,

I have received from Mr Secretary Pownall His Majesty's Additional Instructions directed to His Excellency Governor Ellis, or the Commander in Chief, of this Province and dated the 9th of December 1761, respecting the Appointment of Judges in this Province, and the Incroachments upon the possessions and Territories of the Indians in the American Colonies, to the interruption of their hunting Fowling and Fishing.

Inobedience to this Royal Instruction from His Majesty, I caused a Proclamation to be published in His Majesty's name injoining all Persons against any Molestation of the Indians in the Claims. Lest any difficulties might arise, it appeared advisable, previous to the proclamation, to inquire into the Nature of the Pretensions of the Indians for any part of the Lands within this Province. A return was accordingly made to me, from a Common-right to the Sea Coast from Cape Fronsac onwards for Fishing without disturbance or Opposition by any of His Majesty's Subjects. This claim was therefore inserted in the Proclamation, that all persons might be notified of the Reasonableness of such a permission, whilst the Indians themselves should continue in Peace with Us, and that this Claim should at least be entertained by the Government, till His Majesty's pleasure should be signified. After the Proclamation was issued no Claims for any other purposes were made. If the Proclamation had been issued at large, the Indians might have been incited by the disaffected Acadians and others, to have made extravagant and unwarrantable demands, to the disquiet and perplexity of the New Settlements in the Province. Your Lordships will permit me humbly to remark that no other Claim can be made by the Indians in this Province, either by Treaties or long possession (the Rule, by which the determination of their Claims is to be made, by Virtue of this His Majesty's Instructions) since the French derived their Title from the Indians and the French ceded their Title to the English under the Treaty of Utrecht. The issuing of this proclamation, My Lords, was seasonable and of moment, as some little time before, disquiets and complaints had been occasioned among the Indians, by interruptions in their hunting grounds, which the Government upon inquiry had the satisfaction of finding, was commited by some of the Acadians, and not by any of the inhabitants of the province. Other applications have been made to the Government from supposed Violences upon the personal property of the Indians, which it was judged best to accomodate in a private way, rather than to hazard a decision in the courts, where the verdicts if found against them for want of sufficient evidence or otherwise, might have discontented their Tribes, and have been of disagreeable consequences in the present situation of affairs. It could be wished, My Lords, that some measures might be pursued for removing the Acadians whose members are this summer increasing by the resort to Cumberland from Restigouche and Miramichi, of such as had made their submission to Captain McKenzie last Year, as the firmness of the peace with the Indians so considerably depends upon their being separated from the Acadians, who are incessant in their endeavours for alienating the Savages from His Majesty's Government. The necessary reduction of the Troops and of the Fleets for other services (having at presently only a single Man of War in the harbour and not a thousand regular troops, and those in the several Forts having been greatly reduced) adds weight to the applications for removing the Acadians.

Jonathan Belcher

The Rt. Honorable The Lords
Commissioners for Trade & Plantation

(viii) Proclamation issued in Nova Scotia, 1762

His Majesty by His Royal Instruction, Given at the Court of St James, the 9th day of December, 1761 having been pleased to Signify,

THAT the Indians have made, and still do continue to make great Complaints, that Settlements have been made, and Possessions taken, of Lands, the Property of which they have by Treaties reserved to themselves, by Persons claiming the said Lands, under Pretence of Deeds of Sale & Conveyance, illegally, Fraudulently, and surreptitiously obtained of said Indians.

AND THAT His Majesty had taken this Matter into His Royal Consideration, is also the fatal Effects which would attend a Discontent among the Indians in the Present Situation of Affairs.

AND BEING determined upon all Occasions to support and protect the Indians in their just Rights and Possessions and to keep inviolable the treaties and Compacts which have been entered into with them, was pleased to declare His Majesty's further Royal Will and Pleasure, that His Governor or Commander in Chief in this Province should publish a Proclamation in His Majesty's Name, for this special purpose;

WHEREFORE in dutiful Obedience to His Majesty's Royal Orders I do accordingly publish this proclamation in His Majesty's Royal Name, strictly injoining and requiring all Persons what ever, who may either willfully or inadvertently have seated themselves upon any Lands so reserved to or claimed by the said Indians, without any lawful Authority for so doing, forthwith to remove therefrom.

AND, WHEREAS Claims have been laid before me in behalf of the Indians for Fronsac Passage and from thence to Nartigonneich, and from Nartigonneich to Piktouk, and from thence to Cape Jeanne, from thence to Emchih, from thence to Ragi Pontouch, from thence to Tedueck, from thence to Cape Rommentin, from thence to Miramichy, and from thence to Bay Des Chaleurs, and the environs of Canso. From thence to Mushkoodabwet, and so along the coast, as the Claims and Possessions of the said Indians, for the more special purpose of hunting, fowling and fishing, I do hereby strictly injoin and caution all persons to avoid all molestation of the said Indians in their said claims, till His Majesty's pleasure in this behalf shall be signified.

AND if any person or persons have possessed themselves of any part of the same to the prejudice of the said Indians in their Claims before specified or without lawful Authority, they are hereby required forthwith to remove, as they will otherwise be prosecuted with the utmost Rigour of the Law.

Given under my Hand and Seal at Halifax this Fourth Day of May, 1762, and in the Second Year of His Majesty's Reign.

(ix) **The Royal Proclamation of 1763, RSC 1970, Appendices, 123-29. The relevant portions of this Proclamation are reproduced in chapter 3, *supra*.**

Notes

1. The Royal Proclamation of 1763 was held in *R. v. Tennisco* (1981), 131 DLR (3d) 96 (Ontario High Court) not to constitute a "treaty" within the meaning of s. 88 of the Indian Act so as to exclude the application of the Game and Fish Act (Ont.).
2. A Treaty of 24 September 1778 with the "Malacete Indians of the River St John", the "Micmacks of Richibuctou", the "Micmacks of Mirimichi", the "Micmacks of Chignectou", the "Micmacks of Poqmousche" and the "Micmacks of the Basin of Minas" is referred to and relied upon in *R. v. Polchies* (1981), 37 NBR (2d) 546 (Provincial Court "to render inapplicable at least most of the provisions of the Fish and Wildlife Act[N.B.]. . . .")

(x) **From *Indian Treaties and Surrenders***

No. 152.

NOVA SCOTIA S. S.,
    Rd. Hughes.

TO ALL WHOM THESE PRESENTS SHALL COME, GREETING:

KNOW YE, that I, Richard Hughes, Esquire, Lieutenant-Governor and Commander-in-Chief in and over His Majesty's Province of Nova Scotia and its dependencies, &c., &c., &c.

By virtue of the power and authority to me given by His present Majesty King George the Third, under the great seal of Great Britain, have given, granted and confirmed, and do by these presents, by and with the advice and consent of His Majesty's Council for the said Province, give, grant and confirm unto Michael Francklin, Esquire, Superintendent of Indian Affairs for the Province aforesaid; Pierre Thomas, Chief Sachem; Francis Zavier or Xavier; Nicholas Ackmobishe; Francis Joseph Mezentwite; Francis Joseph La Belmite and Zackareen, Captains, in trust, for and in behalf of the Malecite Indians, inhabitants of the River St Johns, — a tract of land situate, lying and being:

Beginning at the creek eastward of the burying ground of Ekougrahag, and to run south eleven degrees, west one hundred and twenty-five chains; thence north seventy-nine degrees, west forty chains; thence north eleven degrees, east till it meets the River St. John;

thence the course of the said river to the first mentioned bounds — containing five hundred acres. Also, the island commonly called Indian Island, lying in front of said tract, containing about two hundred acres. Also, a piece of ground at Ste. Ann's Point, containing about four acres, in which piece is comprehended the Indian burying ground and the ground on which the chapel, and the priest's house formerly stood, containing in the whole by estimation seven hundred and four acres, more or less, with all and all manner of mines unopened, excepting mines of gold and silver, lead, copper and coals.

To have and to hold the said granted premises, with all privileges, profits, commodities and appurtenances thereunto belonging, unto the said Michael Francklin, Pierre Thomas, Francis Zavier or Xavier, Nicholas Ackmobishe, Francis Joseph Mezentwite, Francis Joseph La Belmite, and Zackareen, their heirs and assigns, in trust, for and in behalf of the said Malecite Indians, inhabiting as aforesaid, their heirs forever, yielding and paying by the said grantees, and their heirs, which, by the acceptation hereof, they bind and oblige themselves and their heirs, to pay to His Majesty King George the Third, His heirs and successors, or to any person lawfully authorized to receive the same for His Majesty's use, a free yearly quit rent of one farthing per acre, for every acre so granted — the first payment of the same to be made on Michaelmas Day next after the expiration of ten years from the date hereof; and so to continue payable yearly hereafter forever — on default thereof this grant to be null and void.

And provided also that no part of the lands hereby granted shall at any time hereafter be sold or disposed of in any manner or form, or for any consideration whatever, without the consent of the Governor or Commander-in-Chief being first had and obtained under the seal of the Province for that purpose; otherwise, the said lands to become thereby forfeited to the King, and this grant to be void and of none effect.

And provided further, that this grant shall be registered in the Register's office, and docquet thereof entered at the Auditor's office within six months from the date, and the land hereby granted to become forfeited as aforesaid.

IN WITNESS WHEREOF, I have signed these presents, and caused the seal of the Province to be hereunto affixed, at Halifax, this second day of August, in the nineteenth year of the reign of our Sovereign Lord, George the Third, by the Grace of God, of Great Britain, France and Ireland, King, Defender of the Faith, and so forth; and in the year of Our Lord, one thousand seven hundred and seventy-nine.

By command of the Lieutenant-Governor, with the advice and consent of His Majesty's Council.

NOVA SCOTIA., HALIFAX, S.S.
Registered the 2nd day of August, 1779.
Lib. 6, Page 106.

ARTHUR GOOLD, *Registrar*.
RD. BULKLEY.

Entered in the Auditor's Office, at Halifax,
5th August, 1779.

JNO. BREYNTON,
Deputy Auditor.

(xi) Treaty of 1779
From *R*. v. *Francis*, [1970] 3 CCC 165
(NBSC, AD), at 167-69.

Whereas in May and July last a number of Indians at the Instigation of the Kings disaffected subjects did Plunder stok Mr John Cort and several other other English Inhabitants at Mirimichy of the principal part of their effects in which transaction, we the undersigned Indians had no concern, but nevertheless do blame ourselves, for not having exerted our Abilitys more Effectually than we did to prevent it, being now greatly distressed and at a loss for the necessary supplys to keep us from the Inclemency of the Approaching winter and to Enable us to Subsist our familys, And Whereas Captain Augustus Hervey Commander of His Majestys Sloop Niper did in July last (to prevent further Mischeif) Seize upon (in Mirimichy River) Sixteen of the said Indians one of which was killed, three released and Twelve of the most Atrocious have been carried to Quebec, to be dealt with, as His Majesty's Government of this Province, shall in future Direct, which measure we hope will tend to restore Peace and good Order in that Neighbourhood.

Be it Known to all men, that we John Julien, Chief, Antoine Arneau Captain, Francis Julien and Thomas Demagonishe Councillors of Mirimichy, and also Representatives of, and Authorized by, the Indians of Pogmousche and Restigousche, Augustine Michel Chief, Louis Augustine Cobaise, Francis Joseph Arimph Captains, Antoines, and Guiaume Gabelier Councillors of Richebouctou, and Thomas Tanas Son and Representative of the Chief of Iedyac, do for ourselves and in behalf of the several Tribes of Mickmack Indians before-mentioned and all others residing between Cape Tormentine and the Bay DeChaleurs in the Gulph of St. Lawrence inclusive, Solemnly Promise and Engage to and with Michael Francklin Esq., the King's Superintendant of Indian Affairs in Nova Scotia.

That we will behave Quietly and Peaceably towards all his Majesty King George's good Subjects treating them upon every occasion in an honest friendly and Brotherly manner.

That we will at the Hazard of our Lives defend and Protect to the utmost of our power, the Traders and Inhabitants and their Merchandize and Effects who are or may be settled on the Rivers Bays and Sea Coasts within the forementioned Districts against all the Enemys of His Majesty King George whether French, Rebells or Indians.

That we will whenever it shall be required apprehend and deliver into the Hands of the said Mr. Francklin, to be dealt with according to his Deserts, any Indian or other person who shall attempt to Disturb the Peace and Tranquillity of the said District.

That we will not hold any correspondance or Intercourse with John Allen, or any other Rebell or Enemy to King George. Let his Nation or Country be what it will.

That we will use our best Endeavours to prevail with all other our Mickmack Brethern throughout the other parts of the Province, to come into the like measures with us for their several Districts.

And we do also by these presents for ourselves, and in behalf of our several Constituents hereby Renew, Ratify and Confirm all former Treatys, entered into by us, or any of us, or them heretofore with the late Governor Lawrence, and others His Majesty King George's Governors, who have succeeded him in the Command of this Province.

In Consideration of the true performance of the foregoing Articles, on the part of the Indians, the said Mr. Francklin as the King's Superintendant of Indian Affairs doth hereby Promise in behalf of Government.

That the said Indians and their Constituents shall remain in the Districts beforementioned Quiet and Free from any molestation of any of His Majesty's Troops or other his good Subjects in their Hunting and Fishing.

That immediate measures shall be taken to cause Traders to supply them with Ammunition, clothing and other necessary stores in exchange for their Furrs and other Commoditys. In Witness whereof we the abovementioned have Interchangeably set our hands and Seals at Windsor in Nova Scotia this Twenty Second day of September 1779.

[Signatures deleted]

(xii) From Cumming and Mickenberg, *supra*.

Treaty Made with Micmacs on Miramichi, 1794

By Governor William Milan and Micmac King John Julian on June 17th, 1794.

The following copy of the Treaty made with the Micmac Indians of the Miramichi and the representative of King George III was translated from the original treaty written in Micmac.

The Treaty made with the Micmac Indians and the representative of King George III of England on June 17, 1794.

Thus was agreed between the two Kings — The English King George III and the Indian King John Julian in the presence of the Governor, William Milan of New Brunswick, and Francis Julian (Governor) the brother of said John Julian, on board His Majesty's ship, that henceforth to have no quarrel between them.

And the English King said to the Indian King 'Henceforth you will teach your children to maintain peace and I give you this paper upon which are written many promises which will never be effaced.'

Then the Indian King, John Julian with his brother Francis Julian begged His Majesty to grant them a portion of land for their own use and for the future generations. His Majesty granted their request. A distance of six miles was granted from Little South West on both sides and six miles at North West on both sides of the rivers. Then His Majesty promised King John Julian and his brother Francis Julian 'Henceforth I will provide for you and for the future generation so long as the sun rises and river flows.'

(Sgd)   KING JOHN JULIAN

KING GEORGE III per

GOVERNOR WM. MILAN

Notes

1. The treaties made with respect to the Maritime Provinces are generally distinguished from those in the rest of Canada because they are not expressed in terms of the surrender of land by the Indians. Rather they are political in nature, acknowledging British sovereignty and protection. Their purpose seems aimed at ending then-existing hostilities between the Indians and the English and setting up terms governing their relationship in the future.

2. Acknowledging British sovereignty is not incompatible with retaining native title. Cumming and Mickenburg, *supra*, p. 98, comments:

> From a legal standpoint the simple acknowledgment of British sovereignty in the treaties could not be held to extinguish native title, for British sovereignty is assumed in all discussions of the recognition of native rights by English law. The maximum effect that the treaties could have on native title would be to cede to the English the lands they had settled on in the areas covered by, and at the times of, the treaties of 1713, 1725 (No. 239) and 1752. [Notes deleted].

See also *R*. v. *Isaac*, *infra*.

3. The Treaty of 1779 was first considered in *R*. v. *Francis*, [1970] 3 CCC 165 (NBSC, AD), where Hughes, JA, for the Court, stated, at 169: ". . . I find it impossible to construe the treaty as conferring, either expressly or impliedly, any right of hunting and fishing." The Treaty, as well as those of 1725 and 1752, was again considered in *R*. v. *Paul* (1980), 30 NBR (2d) 545 (CA), where Hughes, CJNB (Bugold, JA concurring) acknowledged that while the Treaty could not be construed as the grant of a right to hunt and fish, "it could and probably should, in the circumstance, be interpreted as a recognition of a pre-existing right" (p. 554) and hence a treaty right within s. 88 of the Indian Act, making provincial game regulations inapplicable.

(b) The Ontario Treaties

(i) From Alexander Morris, *The Treaties of Canada with the Indians of Manitoba and the North-West Territories* (Toronto: Coles Publishing Co., 1971, reprint of Toronto: P.R. Randall, 1862), pp. 299-300.

THE SELKIRK TREATY.

THIS INDENTURE, made on the eighteenth day of July, in the fifty-seventh year of the reign of our Sovereign Lord King George the Third, and in the year of our Lord eighteen hundred and seventeen, between the undersigned Chiefs and warriors of the Chippeway or Saulteaux Nation and of the Killistine or Cree Nation, on the one part, and the Right Honorable Thomas Earl of Selkirk, on the other part:

Witnesseth, that for and in consideration of the annual present or quit rent hereinafter mentioned, the said Chiefs have given, granted and confirmed, and do, by these presents, give, grant and confirm unto our Sovereign Lord the King all that tract of land adjacent to Red River and Ossiniboyne River, beginning at the mouth of Red River and extending along same as far as Great Forks at the mouth of Red Lake River, and along Ossiniboyne River, otherwise called Rivière des Champignons, and extending to the distance of six miles from Fort Douglas on every side, and likewise from Fort Doer, and also from the Great Forks and in other parts extending in breadth to the distance of two English statute miles back from the banks of the said rivers, on each side, together with all the appurtenances whatsoever of the said tract of land, to have and to hold forever the said tract of land and appurtenances to the use of the said Earl of Selkirk, and of the settlers being established thereon, with the consent and permission of our Sovereign Lord the King, or of the said Earl of Selkirk. Provided always, and these presents are under the express condition that the said Earl, his heirs and successors, or their agents, shall annually pay to the Chiefs and warriors of the Chippeway or Saulteaux Nation, the present or quit rent consisting of one hundred pounds of weight of good and merchantable tobacco, to be delivered on or before the tenth day of October at the forks of Ossiniboyne River — and to the Chiefs and warriors of the Killistine or Cree Nation, a like present or quit rent of one hundred pounds of tobacco, to be delivered to them on or before the said tenth day of October, at Portage de la Prairie, on the banks of Ossiniboyne River. Provided always that the traders hitherto established upon any part of the above-mentioned tract of land shall not be molested in the possession of the lands which they have already cultivated and improved, till His Majesty's pleasure shall be known.

In witness whereof the Chiefs aforesaid have set their marks, at the Forks of Red River on the day aforesaid.

[Signatures deleted]

Notes

1. Two earlier documents entitled The Haldimand Proclamation, 1784 and The Simcoe Patent, 1793 are set out and considered in *Isaac et al.* v. *Davey et al.* (1974), 5 OR (2d) 610 (CA). The Supreme Court of Canada dealt with this case: *Davey et al.* v. *Isaac et al.* (1977), 77 DLR (3d) 481.
2. F.W. Hodge, *Handbook of Indians of Canada* (Ottawa: King's Printer, 1913) provides the following information on other Ontario pre-Confederation Treaties, at p. 472:

    The Indian title to the portion of southern Ontario that had not previously been acquired by the French was extinguished by a series of purchases of which the following are the most important:
    A. Mississauga.—Lands purchased prior to 1784.
    B. Chippewa.—May 19, 1790, for £1,200 cy.
    C. Chippewa.—Purchased in 1785; northern and eastern boundaries doubtful.
    D. Mississauga.—Dec. 7, 1792, for £1,180-7-4 stg.

E. Chippewa.—Sept. 7, 1796, for £800 cy.

F. Chippewa.—Sept. 7, 1796, for £1,200 cy.

G. Chippewa.—May 22, 1798, confirming surrender of May 19, 1795; for £101 cy.; 28,000 acres.

H. Mississauga.F—Aug. 1, 1805, confirming surrender of Sept. 23, 1787; for 10s. 'and divers good and valuable considerations given on 23rd September, 1787.''

I. Mississauga.—Sept. 5-6, 1806, confirming the surrender of Aug. 2, 1805; for £1,000 cy.; 85,000 acres.

J. Chippewa.—Nov. 17-18 1815, for £4,000 cy.; 250,000 acres.

K. Chippewa.—Oct. 17, 1818, for £1,200 cy.; 1,592,000 acres.

L. Mississauga.—Oct. 28, 1818 for annuity of £522-10 cy.; 648,000 acres.

M. Mississauga.—Nov. 5, 1818, for annuity of £740 cy.; 1,951,000 acres.

N. Mississauga.—Nov. 28, 1822, confirming surrender of May 31, 1819; for annuity of £642-10 cy.; 2,748,000 acres.

O. Chippewa.—July 8, 1822, confirming surrenders of Mar. 8, 1819 and May 9, 1820; for annuity of £600 cy.; 580,000 acres.

P. Chippewa.—July 10, 1827, confirming surrender of April 26, 1825; for annuity of £1,100 cy.; 2,200,000 acres.

Q. Chippewa (Saugeens).—Aug. 9, 1836, for annuity of £1,250 cy.; 1,500,000 acres.

R. Chippewa.—Oct. 13, 1854; for "interest of principal sum arising out of the sale of our lands."

In addition to the above, a map following page 632 and titled "Surrenders of Indian Lands in Southern Ontario Prior to 1854" contains in the "Legend" the following two items:

S. SIX NATIONS—Oct. 25, 1784, granted by Gov. Haldimand; confirmed by Lt.-Gov. Simcoe, Jan. 14, 1793; 17 townships; strip "six miles deep from each side of the (Grand River)," in "consideration of the early attachment to his cause." This tract was purchased from the Mississaugas for £2,000, by the crown.

T. MOHAWKS—April 1, 1793, grant by Lt.-Gov. Simcoe, of Tyeudiuaga township.

3. Item P in Note 2, the Chippewa Treaty of 10 July 1827 was involved in *R. v. George* (1966), 55 DLR (2d) 386 (SCC). This case involved the application of the *Migratory Birds Convention Act*, RSC 1952, c. 179. The majority simply said that s. 87 of the *Indian Act*, RSC 1952, c. 149 (the predecessor to the present s. 88) did not make the *Migratory Birds Convention Act* subject or subordinate to the 1827 Treaty. Only provincial laws were, in their application to Indians, subject to such treaties. Cartwright J alone dissented from this view. Interestingly, he also adopts the view of the majority in the Ontario Court of Appeal that a reservation of land to the Indians in the 1827 Treaty for their "exclusive use and enjoyment" included by implication "the right to hunt and fish thereon which they had enjoyed from time immemorial" (p. 389).

4. A Treaty of 1818, known as Treaty No. 20 and entered into on 5 November 1818 at what

is believed now to be Port Hope, Ontario, with six chiefs of the Chippewa Nation, was the subject of *R.* v. *Taylor and Williams* (1981), 34 OR (2d) 360 (CA), *infra*.

(ii) From Morris, supra, pp. 302-04.

THE ROBINSON SUPERIOR TREATY.

THIS AGREEMENT, made and entered into on the seventh day of September, in the year of Our Lord one thousand eight hundred and fifty, at Sault Ste Marie, in the Province of Canada, between the Honorable William Benjamin Robinson, of the one part, on behalf of Her Majesty the Queen, and Joseph Peandechat, John Iuinway, Mishe-Muckqua, Totomencie, Chiefs, and Jacob Warpela, Ahmutch-iwagabou, Michel Shelageshick, Manitoshainse, and Chiginans, principal men of the Ojibewa Indians inhabiting the Northern Shore of Lake Superior, in the said Province of Canada, from Batchewananng Bay to Pigeon River, at the western extremity of said lake, and inland throughout the extent to the height of land which separates the territory covered by the charter of the Honorable the Hudson's Bay Company from the said tract, and also the islands in the said lake within the boundaries of the British possessions therein, of the other part, witnesseth:

That for and in consideration of the sum of two thousand pounds of good and lawful money of Upper Canada, to them in hand paid, and for the further perpetual annuity of five hundred pounds, the same to be paid and delivered to the said Chiefs and their tribes at a convenient season of each summer, not later than the first day of August at the Honorable the Hudson's Bay Company's Posts of Michipicoton and Fort William, they the said Chiefs and principal men do freely, fully and voluntarily surrender, cede, grant and convey unto Her Majesty, Her heirs and successors forever, all their right, title and interest in the whole of the territory above described, save and except the reservations set forth in the schedule hereunto annexed, which reservations shall be held and occupied by the said Chiefs and their tribes in common, for the purposes of residence and cultivation, — and should the said Chiefs and their respective tribes at any time desire to dispose of any mineral or other valuable productions upon the said reservations, the same will be at their request sold by order of the Superintendent-General of the Indian Department for the time being, for their sole use and benefit, and to the best advantage.

And the said William Benjamin Robinson of the first part, on behalf of Her Majesty and the Government of this Province, hereby promises and agrees to make the payments as before mentioned; and further to allow the said Chiefs and their tribes the full and free privilege to hunt over the territory now ceded by them, and to fish in the waters thereof as they have heretofore been in the habit of doing, saving and excepting only such portions of the said territory as may from time to time be sold or leased to individuals, or companies of individuals, and occupied by them with the consent of the Provincial Government. The parties of the second part further promise and agree that they will not sell, lease, or otherwise dispose of any portion of their reservations without the consent of the Superintendent-General of Indian Affairs being first had and obtained; nor will they at any time hinder or prevent persons from exploring or searching for minerals or other valuable productions in any part of the territory hereby ceded to Her Majesty as before mentioned. The parties of the second part also agree that in case the Government of this Province should before the date of this agreement have sold, or bargained to sell, any mining locations or other property on the portions of the territory hereby reserved for their use and benefit, then and in that case such sale, or promise of sale, shall be perfected, if the parties interested desire it, by the Government, and the amount accruing therefrom shall be paid to the tribe to whom the reservation belongs. The said William Benjamin Robinson on behalf of Her Majesty, who desires to deal liberally and justly with all here subjects, further promises and agrees that in case the territory hereby ceded by the parties of the second part shall at any future period produce an amount which will enable the Government of this Province without incurring loss to increase the annuity hereby secured to them, then, and in that case, the same shall be augmented from time to time, provided that the amount paid to each individual shall not exceed the sum of one pound provincial currency in any one year, or such further sum as Her Majesty may be graciously pleased to order; and provided further that the number of Indians entitled to the benefit of this treaty shall amount to two-thirds of their present numbers (which is twelve hundred and forty) to entitle them to claim the full benefit thereof, and should their numbers at any future period not amount to two-thirds of twelve hundred and forty, the annuity shall be diminished in proportion to their actual numbers.

Schedule of Reservations made by the above named and subscribing Chiefs and principal men.

First — Joseph Pean-de-chat and his tribe, the reserve to commence about two miles from Fort William (inland), on the right bank of the River Kiministiquia; thence westerly six miles, parallel to the shores of the lake; thence northerly five miles, thence easterly to the right bank of the said river, so as not to interfere with any acquired rights of the Honorable Hudson's Bay Company.

Second — Four miles square at Gros Cap, being a valley near the Honorable Hudson's Bay Company's post of Michipicoton, for Totominai and tribe.

Third — Four miles square on Gull River, near Lake Nipigon, on both sides of said river, for the Chief Mishimuckqua and tribe.

[Signatures deleted]

(iii) From Morris, *supra*, pp. 305-09.

THE ROBINSON HURON TREATY.

THIS AGREEMENT, made and entered into this ninth day of September, in the year of our Lord one thousand eight hundred and fifty, at Sault Ste Marie, in the Province of Canada, between the Honorable William Benjamin Robinson, of the one part, on behalf of Her Majesty the Queen, and Shinguacouse Nebenaigoching, Keokouse, Mishequonga, Tagawinini, Shabokishick, Dokis, Ponekeosh, Windaw-tegowinini, Shawenakeshick, Namassin, Naoquagabo, Wabakekik, Kitchepossigun, by Papasainse, Wagemaki, Pamequonaisheung, Chiefs; and John Bell, Paqwatchinini, Mashekyash, Idowekesis, Waquacomick, Ocheek, Metigomin, Watachewana, Minwawapenasse, Shenaoquom, Oningegun, Panaissy, Papasainse, Ashewasega, Kageshewawetung, Shawonebin; and also Chief Maisquaso (also Chiefs Muckata, Mishoquet, and Mekis), and Mishoquetto and Asa Waswanay and Pawiss, principal men of the Ojibewa Indians, inhabiting and claiming the eastern and northern shores of Lake Huron, from Penetanguishene to Sault Ste Marie, and thence to Batchewanaung Bay, on the northern shore of Lake Superior, together with the Islands in the said Lakes, opposite to the shores thereof, and inland to the height of land which separates the territory covered by the charter of the Honorable Hudson's Bay Company from Canada; as well as all unconceded lands within the limits of Canada West to which they have any just claim, of the other, witnesseth:

That for and in consideration of the sum of two thousand pounds of good and lawful money of Upper Canada, to them in hand paid, and for the further perpetual annuity of six hundred pounds of like money, the same to be paid and delivered to the said Chiefs and their tribes at a convenient season of each year, of which due notice will be given, at such places as may be appointed for that purpose, they the said Chiefs and principal men, on behalf of their respective tribes or bands, do hereby fully, freely and voluntarily surrender, cede, grant, and convey unto Her Majesty, here heirs and successors forever, all their right, title, and interest to, and in the whole of, the territory above described, save and except the reservations set forth in the schedule hereunto annexed; which reservations shall be held and occupied by the said Chiefs and their tribes in common, for their own use and benefit.

And should the said Chiefs and their respective tribes at any time desire to dispose of any such reservations, or of any mineral or other valuable productions thereon, the same will be sold or leased at their request by the Superintendent-General of Indian Affairs for the time being, or other officer having authority so to do, for their sole benefit, and to the best advantage.

And the said William Benjamin Robinson of the first part, on behalf of Her Majesty and the Government of this Province, hereby promises and agrees to make, or cause to be made, the paymenets as before mentioned; and further to allow the said Chiefs and their tribes the full and free privilege to hunt over the territory now ceded by them, and to fish in the waters thereof, as they have heretofore been in the habit of doing; saving and excepting such portions of the said territory as may from time to time be sold or leased to individuals or companies of individuals, and occupied by them with the consent of the Provincial Government.

The parties of the second part further promise and agree that they will not sell, lease, or otherwise dispose of any portion of their Reservations without the consent of the Superintendent-General of Indian Affairs, or other officer of like authority, being first had and obtained. Nor will they at any time hinder or prevent persons from exploring or searching for minerals, or other valuable productions, in any part of the territory hereby ceded to Her Majesty, as before mentioned. The parties of the second part also agree, that in case the Government of this Province should before the date of this agreement have sold, or bargained to sell, any mining locations, or other property, on the portions of the territory hereby reserved for their use; then and in that case such sale, or promise of sale, shall be perfected by the Government, if the parties claiming it shall have fulfilled all the conditions upon which such locations were made, and the amount accruing therefrom shall be paid to the tribe to whom the Reservation belongs.

The said William Benjamin Robinson, on behalf of Her Majesty, who desires to deal liberally and justly with all her subjects, further promises and agrees, that should the territory hereby ceded by the parties of the second part at any future period produce such an amount as will enable the Government of this Province, without incurring loss, to increase the annuity hereby secured to them, then and in that case the same shall be augmented from time to time, provided that the amount paid to each individual shall not exceed the sum of one pound Provincial currency in any one year, or such further sum as Her Majesty may be graciously pleased to order; and provided further that the number of Indians entitled to the benefit of this treaty shall amount to two-thirds of their present number, which is fourteen hundred and twenty-two, to entitle them to claim the full benefit thereof. And should they not at any future period amount to two-thirds of fourteen hundred and twenty-two, then the said annuity shall be diminished in proportion to their actual numbers.

The said William Benjamin Robinson of the first part further agrees, on the part of Her Majesty and the Government of this Province, that in consequence of the Indians inhabiting French River and Lake Nipissing having become parties to this treaty, the further sum of one hundred and sixty pounds Provincial currency shall be paid in addition to the two thousand pounds above mentioned.

————

Schedule of Reservations made by the above-named subscribing Chiefs and Principal Men.

First — Pamequonaishcung and his band, a tract of land to commence seven miles, from the mouth of the River Maganetawang, and extending six miles east and west by three miles north.

Second — Wagemake and his band, a tract of land to commence at a place called Nekickshegeshing, six miles from east to west, by three miles in depth.

Third — Kitcheposkissegan (by Papasainse), from Point Grondine westward, six miles inland, by two miles in front, so as to include the small Lake Nessinassung — a tract for themselves and their bands.

Fourth — Wabakekik, three miles front, near Shebawenaning, by five miles inland, for himself and band.

Fifth — Namassin and Naoquagabo and their bands, a tract of land commencing near Quacloche, at the Hudson Bay Company's boundary;

thence westerly to the mouth of the Spanish River; then four miles up the south bank of said river, and across to the place of beginning.

Sixth — Shawenakishick and his band, a tract of land now occupied by them, and contained between two rivers, called Whitefish River, and Wanabitaseke, seven miles inland.

Seventh — Windawtegawinini and his band, the Peninsula east of Serpent River, and formed by it, now occupied by them.

Eighth — Ponekeosh and his band, the land contained between the River Mississaga and the River Penebewabecong, up to the first rapids.

Ninth — Dokis and his band, three miles square at Wanabeyakokaun, near Lake Nipissing and the Island near the Fall of Okickandawt.

Tenth — Shabokishick and his band, from their present planting grounds on Lake Nipissing to the Hudson Bay Company's post, six miles in depth.

Eleventh — Tagawinini and his band, two miles square at Wanabitibing, a place about forty miles inland, near Lake Nipissing.

Twelfth — Keokouse and his band, four miles front from Thessalon River eastward, by four miles inland.

Thirteenth — Mishequanga and his band, two miles on the lake shore east and west of Ogawaminang, by one mile inland.

Fourteenth — For Shinguacouse and his band, a tract of land extending from Maskinongé Bay, inclusive, to Partridge Point, above Garden River on the front, and inland ten miles, throughout the whole distance; and also Squirrel Island.

Fifteenth — For Nebenaigoching and his band, a tract of land extending from Wanabekineyunnung west of Gros Cap to the boundary of the lands ceded by the Chiefs of Lake Superior, and inland ten miles throughout the whole distance, including Batchewanaunng Bay; and also the small island at Sault Ste. Marie used by them as a fishing station.

Sixteenth — For Chief Mekis and his band, residing at Wasaquesing (Sandy Island), a tract of land at a place on the main shore opposite the Island; being the place now occupied by them for residence and cultivation, four miles square.

Seventeenth — For Chief Muckatamishaquet and his band, a tract of land on the east side of the River Naishconteong, near Pointe aux Barils, three miles square; and also a small tract in Washauwenega Bay — now occupied by a part of the band — three miles square.

[Signatures Deleted]

Note

1. The Robinson Treaty, 1850 (probably the Superior Treaty) was considered and held to provide a defence to a charge under the Game and Fish Act (Ont.) relating to the sale of yellow pickerel without a commercial licence in *R.* v. *Penasse and McLeod* (1971), 8 CCC (2d) 569 (Ontario Provincial Court). See also *R.* v. *Moses*, [1970] 3 OR 314, 13 DLR (3d) 50 (Dist. Ct.); *R.* v. *Wesley* (1975), 9 OR (2d) 524 (Dist. Ct.). The liability to pay the annuities contained in the Robinson Treaties was the subject of a federal-provincial dispute in *AG Can.* v. *AG Ont.*, [1897] AC 199 (PC). These treaties also appear to be involved in a case still under litigation — *AG Ont.* v. *Bear Island Foundation et al.* The result of two motions in this case are reported at (1982) 13 ACWS (2d) 522, No. 1136. An old and previously unreported decision involving the Robinson Huron Treaty and its interpretation has recently been published: *AG Ont.* v. *Francis et al.*, [1980] 4 CNLR 1 (Ont. H. Ct., Ch. D.).

(iv) From Morris, *supra*, pp. 309-13.

THE MANITOULIN ISLAND TREATY.

ARTICLES OF AGREEMENT AND CONVENTION made and concluded at Manitowaning, on the Great Manitoulin Island, in the Province of Canada, the sixth day of October, Anno Domini 1862, between the Hon. William McDougall, Superintendent-General of Indian Affairs, and William Spragge, Esquire, Deputy Superintendent of Indian Affairs, on the part of the Crown and Government of said Province, of the first part, and Mai-she-quong-gai, Oke-mah-be-ness, J.B. Assiginock, Benjamin Assiginock, Mai-be-nesse-ma, She-no-tah-gun, George Ah-be-tos-o-wai, Paim-o-quo-waish-gung, Abence, Tai-bose-gai, Ato-wish-cosh, Nai-wan-dai-ge-zhik, Wan-kan-o-say, Keesh-kewan-bik, Chiefs and principal men of the Ottawa, Chippewa, and other Indians occupying the said Island, on behalf of the said Indians, of the second part:

Whereas, the Indian title to said Island was surrendered to the Crown on the ninth August, Anno Domini 1836, under and by virtue of a treaty made between Sir Francis Bond Head, then Governor of Upper Canada, and the Chiefs and principal men of the Ottawas and Chippewas then occupying and claiming title thereto, in order that the same might "be made the property (under their Great Father's control) of all Indians whom he should allow to reside thereon;"

And whereas, but few Indians from the mainland whom it was intended to transfer to the Island, have ever come to reside thereon;

And whereas, it has been deemed expedient (with a view to the improvement of the condition of the Indians, as well as the settlement and improvement of the country), to assign to the Indians now upon the Island certain specified portions thereof, to be held by patent from the Crown, and to sell the other portions thereof fit for cultivation to settlers, and to invest the proceeds thereof, after deducting the expenses of survey and management, for the benefit of the Indians;

And whereas, a majority of the Chiefs of certain bands residing on that portion of the Island easterly of Heywood Sound and the Manitoulin Gulf have expressed their unwillingness to accede to this proposal as respects that portion of the Island, but have assented to the same as respects all other portions thereof; and whereas the Chiefs and principal men of the bands residing on the Island westerly of the said Sound and Gulf have agreed to accede to the said proposal:

Now this agreement witnesseth that in consideration of the sum of seven hundred dollars now in hand paid (which sum is to be hereafter deducted from the proceeds of lands sold to settlers), the receipt whereof is hereby acknowledged, and in further consideration of such sums as may be realized from time to time as interest upon the purchase money of the lands to be sold for their benefit as aforesaid, the parties hereto of the second part have and hereby do release, surrender and give up to Her Majesty the Queen, all the right, title, interest and claim of the parties of the second part, and of the Ottawa, Chippewa and other Indians in whose behalf they act, of, in and to the Great Manitoulin Island, and also of, in and to the Islands adjacent, which have been deemed or claimed to be appertinent or belonging thereto, to have and to hold the same and every part thereof to Her Majesty, her heirs and successors forever.

And it is hereby agreed by and between the parties hereto as follows:

Firstly. A survey of the said Manitoulin Island shall be made as soon as conveniently may be, under the authority of the Department of Crown Lands.

Secondly — The Crown will, as soon as conveniently may be, grant by deed for the benefit of each Indian being the head of a family and residing on the said Island, one hundred acres of land; to each single person over twenty-one years of age, residing as aforesaid, fifty acres of land; to each family of orphan children under twenty-one years of age, containing two or more persons, one hundred acres of land; and to each single orphan child under twenty-one years of age, fifty acres of land; to be selected and located under the following rules and conditions: Each Indian entitled to land under this agreement may make his own selection of any land on the Great Manitoulin Island:

Provided, 1st. That the lots selected shall be contiguous or adjacent to each other, so that Indian settlements on the Island may be as compact as possible. 2nd. That if two or more Indians claim the same lot of land, the matter shall be referred to the Resident Superintendent, who shall examine the case and decide between them. 3rd. That selections for orphan children may be made by their friends, subject to the approval of the Resident Superintendent. 4th. Should any lot or lots, selected as aforesaid, be contiguous to any bay or harbor, or any stream of water, upon which a mill site shall be found, and should the Government be of opinion that such lot or lots ought to be reserved for the use of the public, or for village or park lots, or such mill site be sold with a view to the erection of a mill thereon, and shall signify such its opinion through its proper agent, then the Indian who has selected, or who wishes to select such lot, shall make another selection; but if he has made any improvements thereon, he shall be allowed a fair compensation therefor. 5th. The selections shall all be made within one year after the completion of the survey, and for that purpose plans of the survey shall be deposited with the Resident Superintendent as soon as they are approved by the Department of Crown Lands, and shall be open to the inspection of all Indians entitled to make selections as aforesaid.

Thirdly — The interests which may accrue from the investment of the proceeds of sales of lands as aforesaid, shall be payable annually, and shall be apportioned among the Indians now residing westerly of the said Sound and Gulf, and their descendants *per capita*, but every Chief lawfully appointed shall be entitled to two portions.

Fourthly — So soon as one hundred thousand acres of the said land is sold, such portion of the salary of the Resident Superintendent, and of the expenses of his office as the Government may deem equitable, shall become a charge upon the said fund.

Fifthly — The deeds or patents for the lands to be selected as aforesaid, shall contain such conditions for the protection of the grantees as the Governor in Council may, under the law, deem requisite.

Sixthly — All the rights and privileges in respect to the taking of fish in the lakes, bays, creeks and waters within and adjacent to the said Island, which may be lawfully exercised and enjoyed by the white settlers thereon, may be exercised and enjoyed by the Indians.

Seventhly — That portion of the Island easterly of Heywood Sound and Manitoulin Gulf, and the Indians now residing there, are exempted from the operation of this agreement as respects survey, sale of lots, granting deeds to Indians, and payment in respect of moneys derived from sales in other parts of the Island. But the said Indians will remain under the protection of the Government as formerly, and the said easterly part or division of the Island will remain open for the occupation of any Indians entitled to reside upon the Island as formerly, subject, in case of dispute, to the approval of the Government.

Eighthly — Whenever a majority of the Chiefs and principal men at a council of the Indians residing easterly of the said Sound and Gulf, to be called and held for the purpose, shall declare their willingness to accede to the present agreement in all respects and portions thereof, and the Indians there shall be entitled to the same privileges in every respect from and after the date of such approval by the Government, as those residing in other parts of the Island.

Ninthly — This agreement shall be obligatory and binding on the contracting parties as soon as the same shall be approved by the Governor in Council.

In witness whereof the said Superintendent-General of Indian affairs, and Deputy Superintendent, and the undersigned Chiefs and principal men of the Ottawa, Chippewa and other Indians have hereto set their hands and seals at Manitowaning, the sixth day of October, in the year first above written.

[Signatures Deleted]

(c) The Vancouver Island Treaties

(i) Sooke Treaty of 1850

From *R.* v. *Cooper* (1968), 1 DLR (3d) 113, at 114-15.

SOOKE TRIBE — NORTH-WEST OF SOOKE INLET

KNOW all men, We the chiefs of the family of Sooke, acting for and on behalf of our people, who being here present have individually and collectively ratified and confirmed this our act. Now know that we, who have signed our names and made our marks to this deed on the first day of May, one thousand eight hundred and fifty, do consent to surrender, entirely and forever, to James Douglas, the agent of the Hudson's Bay Company in Vancouver Island, that is to say, for the Governor, Deputy Governor, and Committee of the same, the whole of the lands situate and lying between the Bay of Syusung, or Sooke Inlet, to the Three Rivers beyond Thlowuck, or Point Shirringham, on the Straits of Juan de Fuca, and the snow covered mountains in the interior of Vancouver Island.

The condition of or understanding of this sale is this, that our village sites and enclosed fields are to be kept for our own use, for the use of our children, and for those who may follow after us; and the land shall be properly surveyed hereafter. It is understood, however, that the land itself, with these small exceptions, becomes the entire property of the white people for ever; it is also understood that we are at liberty to hunt over the unoccupied lands, and to carry on our fisheries as formerly.

We have received, as payment, Forty-eight pounds six shillings and eight pence.

In token whereof, we have signed our names and made our marks, at Fort Victoria, on the first day of May, One Thousand eight hundred and fifty.

(Signed)   Wanseea his X mark
Tanasman his X mark
Chysimkan his X mark
Yokum his X mark

Chiefs commissioned by and respresenting the Sooke Tribe here assembled.

(ii) Sanitch Treaty of 1852

From *R.* v. *Bartleman*, [1981] 1 CNLR 83 (British Columbia County Court), at 84.

Know all men that we Chiefs and people of the Sanitch Tribe, who have signed our names and made our marks to this Deed, on the 11th day of February 1852, do consent to surrender entirely and for ever, to James Douglas the Agent of the Hudson's Bay Company, in Vancouver's Island, that is to say for the Governor, Deputy Governor and Committee of the same, the whole of the lands situate and lying as follows, viz. commencing at Cowitchan Head and following the coast of the Canal de Arro north west nearly to Sanitch Point or Qua-na-sung from thence following the course of the Sanitch Arm to the point where it terminates and from thence by a straight line across country to said Cowitchan Head the point of commencement; so as to include all the country and lands, with the exceptions hereafter named, within those boundaries.

The condition of or understanding of this sale, is this that our village sites and enclosed fields are to be kept for our own use for the use of our children and for those who may follow after us, and the lands shall be properly surveyed hereafter; it is understood however that the land itself with these small exceptions, becomes the entire property of the white people for ever, it is also understood that we are at liberty to hunt over the unoccupied lands, and to carry on our fisheries as formerly. We have received as payment . . . .

(iii) Saalequun Treaty of 1854

From *R.* v. *White and Bob* (1964), 50 DLR (2d) 613 (BCCA), at 622.

The practice was to pay the Indians the purchase price against their signature by mark on blank paper to be filled in later as a deed. In 1854 the Saalequun tribe so surrendered their lands on Commercial Inlet, 12 miles up the Nanaimo River. For that surrender no deed was made up but the signatures or marks were obtained on blank paper against payment (ex. 8). Had the deed been completed it would have been substantially in the following form (ex. 8):

> Know All men that we the Chiefs and people of the . . . Tribe who have signed our names and made our marks to this deed, on the . . . day of . . . do consent to surrender entirely and forever, to James Douglas the Agent of the Hudsons Bay Company, in Vancouver Island that is to say for the Governor, Deputy Governor and Committee of the same, the whole of the lands situate and lying between . . .
>
> The condition of, or understanding of this sale, is this, that our village sites and enclosed fields, are to be kept for our own use, for the use of our children, and for those who may follow after us, and the lands shall be properly surveyed hereafter; it is understood however, that the land itself with these small exceptions, becomes the entire property of the white people forever, it is also understood that we are at liberty to hunt over the unoccupied lands, and to carry on our fisheries as formerly. We have received as payment . . .

The accused contend that this arrangement was acted on throughout and therefore is binding, although the deed has not been drawn, and that the agreement so read is a Treaty between the band and Governor Douglas as the Governor of Vancouver Island and representing the Crown, whereby the Crown granted to the Indians the right "to hunt over the unoccupied lands, and to carry on our fisheries as formerly".

Notes

1. The document between the Saalequun tribe and James Douglas of 1854 and that between the Sooke Tribe and James Douglas of 1850 are treaties within the meaning of s. 88 of the Indian Act. See *R.* v. *White and Bob* (1965), 52 DLR (2d) 481n (SCC); *R.* v. *Cooper* (1968), 1 DLR (3d) 113 (BCSC). The 1852 treaty with the Sanitch tribe was considered in *R.* v. *Bartleman*, [1981] 1 CNLR 83 (BC Co Ct), but its application was rejected because the land on which the hunting took place was not covered by the treaty.
2. As to the balance of treaties on the west coast, Professor K. Lysyk notes in "Indian Hunting Rights: Constitutional Considerations and the Role of Indian Treaties in British Columbia" (1966), 2 *UBCL Review* 401 that "only a small part of British Columbia was ever surrendered to the Crown through treaties made with the Indians" and in footnote 1 states:

> From 1850 to 1854, fourteen agreements or treaties were concluded with Indian tribes

on the southern half of Vancouver Island. The only treaty area on mainland British Columbia is that part of the Province to which Treaty No. 8 extends. The latter treaty, made on June 21, 1899, embraces the Peace River district in northeastern British Columbia as well as parts of Alberta, Saskatchewan and the Northwest Territories. Unlike the Vancouver Island Treaties, Treaty No. 8 was made with the Crown in right of Canada.

3. For background information placing these treaties into their historical setting, see *The Canadian Indian: Quebec and the Atlantic Provinces* (Ottawa: Department of Indian Affairs and Northern Development, 1973) pp. 18-31 (Atlantic Provinces) and Morris, *supra*, pp. 13-24 (Ontario).

6. An Integrating Overview

Excerpts from Doug Sanders, "Native Rights," in *Report of Discussions Legal Status of Indians in the Maritimes*, held 16 October 1970. Halifax, Nova Scotia, Indian-Eskimo Association of Canada under the sponsorship of Union of Nova Scotia Indians and Union of New Brunswick Indians, pp. 7-20.

By about 1700 the control of Indian policy in New France was in the hands of the Church. The early reserves in New France were established when the Church made requests to France for grants of land to be used for their work with Indian people. The title to the reserve land varies depending on the particular grant to each reserve. Of great importance to the Indian people of Quebec, is the fact that you do not have any treaties in the way that we generally think of treaties. You had political alliances but you did not have written treaties which dealt with the tribal territories of the Indian people. If treaties are necessary to terminate tribal rights to tribal territories, why was it never done in New France? An explanation can be found not in legal principle but in the kind of situations both the colonialists and the Indians were in. New France never engaged in extensive settlement; right up to capitulation there was still a fairly small land area which was in settled occupation by the colonialists. There was no major conflict in relation to land. In addition, the Indians of the area had a small population and were of a roaming nature. Thus, the loss of certain lands (a certain limited amount of land) was not viewed as being a terribly serious matter. The overriding factors include the economic role the Indians were playing in the fur trade life of Montreal and the political alliances of the Hurons and Algonkians and New France with this common enemy, the Iroquois. For these reasons, the French never felt it necessary to enter into treaties to ensure peaceful settlement by the colonial power and to settle any native land claims.

Many unsettled questions in relation to Indian claims in Quebec persist to this day. At present, a commission in Quebec is examining the territorial integrity of the province. Their report should be coming out soon and will have a fairly extensive amount of material on native land claims in Quebec.

The Maritimes presents a rather different history, but with some similarities because of periods of French sovereignty in Acadia. The French were sovereign from 1605 to 1621 when James I of England granted the area to Sir William Alexander. Between 1621 and 1710 political control changed hands about six times with the French enjoying sovereignty for about 61 years and England for about 28 years. In 1725 when there were negotiations by the Indians from this area in Boston the Indian representatives said to the English "We shall neither hear nor listen to anything but what the Indians shall say, and that what they say is from their hearts, and we shall stop our ears from hearing anything to the contrary . . . by stopping our ears we mean that we will not be prevented from a peace by any unknown tongue, that is the French." One factor that led to a fair amount of political instability in Acadia (the Maritimes) after the Treaty of Utrecht in 1713 down to about 1763 was the suspicion that the Indian had stronger political allegiance to the French than to the English. 1713, the Treaty of Utrecht, marks the period of English sovereignty in the Maritimes and in the period from 1713 up until the Proclamations of 1762 and 1763, there were a series of treaties of Peace and Friendship. During a lull in hostilities, a Treaty of Peace would be made, then broken, more hostilities, another Treaty of Peace, and so forth. These treaties are unique in Canada because they most reflect the character of international treaties. As far as these treaties were concerned the major issues were peace and political alliance rather than lands. Some of the treaties would conform to the English lands that they had already encroached upon, but none of them deal with land claims on any large scale.

In southern Ontario a new pattern emerged in which land claims of native people are dealt with for the first time. Between 1764 and 1850 a complex series of treaties and surrenders, often covering very small areas, were entered into over most of southern Ontario. In 1850 the Robinson/Huron and Robinson/Superior Treaties (the first of the major treaties) were made in regard to extensive areas of land. As the record indicates, the government sought to obtain surrenders in those areas because of the discovery of minerals. Some treaties entered into during this period were so imprecise in their boundaries that they really could not be upheld as legal documents. In 1923 an attempt was made to clean up some of the loopholes that had been left in southern Ontario. For instance, one complaint relating to part of the Robinson/Treaty was brought forward by some Indians who said "These were our tribal territories and no representative of our group participated in the signing of the treaty, and therefore the treaty cannot be effective to extinguish our claim." Thus, in 1923 a commission was appointed and instructed to find out if there were gaps and if there were gaps then clearly should be treaties.

In 1951 there was a special committee of the House of Commons to look into the Indian Act and there were some exchanges which related to the Maritimes. A Mr Hatfield, a Member of Parliament, I gather, from the Maritimes, suggested that all Indians should be treated the same, and questioned why the Indians in the Maritimes did not get treaty payments although Indians in other parts of Canada did. He said "I'm not trying to do anything but to put every Indian in Canada in the same position." But the then Minister of Citizenship and Immigration said, "You mean we should pay treaty money to the other half of the Indians who have no treaty requiring it?" (Only about one-half of the Indian population in Canada is covered by treaty.) Mr Hatfield said, "Sure!". The Minister said, "Well, you are a minority in this room if you want to propose something like that." Mr Hatfield said, "Where do you get the money to pay treaty money? Was it out of the sale of lands in the west?" But the Minister says, "It was for the purpose of obtaining from them a surrender of their interest in the land." So Mr Hatfield said, "Right! How did not the Indians in the east surrender their lands long before the Indians in the west?" The Minister said, "Well, that's a historical question which the province of New Brunswick could probably answer better." This seems to represent the attitude of the Federal Government. But Mr Hatfield's question keeps coming back — why no treaty payments; why no land cession treaties in the Maritimes?

The treaties that we noted earlier were clearly political — the main issue being peace and cessation of hostility.

In the 1725 negotiations reference was made to a hostage being kept during the negotiations by the English and the explanation given to the hostage was, "You are a hostage and therefore according to the laws of nations must tarry until peace be concluded." The reference to the laws of nations is a reference to international law. The early treaties in the Maritimes were seen much in the terms of international treaties. One explanation of why the treaty making process in the Maritimes never dealt with the land claims of the native people is that they were handled separately and were considered essentially private dealings. Gradually the government and the trading companies came to realize that this led to problems. There were many disputes and accusations of sharp, unfair or illegal dealings, by the whites in acquiring lands from the Indians. Thus a pattern developed by legislation which created a government monopoly in the acquiring of lands from the Indians.

Another factor which must be considered is what had been happening to the Indian population in the Maritimes during the early, fairly crucial period of negotiations. In 1746 the records indicate that one-third of the population of the Micmac Indians in Acadia had died as a result of typhus. Joseph Howe, first commissioner for Indian Affairs in Nova Scotia reported in 1843 on the decrease in population that with the existing rate of decrease the whole race would be extinct in 40 years, and "half a century hence the very existence of the tribe would be as a dream and a tradition to our grandchildren who would find it as difficult to imagine the features or dwelling of the Micmac as we do to realize those of an ancient Briton." In a later report Commissioner Gesner noted that the population in Nova Scotia had declined from 15,000 in 1745 to 1,461 in 1847 commenting:

"Melancholy indeed, is the reflection arising from these details but still more painful is the consideration that the destruction of the whole Micmac race, the ejected owners of the country, is still advancing with fearful rapidity, for they are falling like leaves of their native forests before the withering autumnal frost. If Her Majesty's and the Provincial Government desire to save this small remnant of the Aborigines, the work of justice and humanity must be commenced immediately. The efforts of the Micmacs to resist the invaders of their lands and liberties, were just and natural. Without religion or civilization they practiced their peculiar mode of warfare, and its barbarities were increased by the merciless and wanton cruelties of the early European voyageurs. They were exposed to the most vindictive ferocities. In Nova Scotia the soldiers were ordered to spare the disaffected Acadians but to give the Indians no quarter. They were hunted like the wild animals of the forest and the Caughnawaga (the place where Christians live), was to them the place of destruction. To these painful scenes the inhabitants now ever avert but in sorrow. The small presents made to them by the grants of the Legislature, they consider as testimonies of respect and they pride themselves upon such bounties rather than consider them in any way humiliating. For the lands, forest and fisheries, long since taken from them, they are of the opinion the Government should make a far greater compensation than they have ever received, for the permanent protection contemplated by the Chief at that time they laid down their arms and smoked the pipes of peace."

And again: "The scattered remnants of this once brave and patriotic people is now utterly degraded and overwhelmed in misery. They have been supplanted by civilized inhabitants and in return for the lands of which they were the rightful owners, they have received loathsome diseases, alcoholic drink, the destruction of their game and threatened extermination. More than once I have seen the tears trickle down the cheeks of aged Indians as they recounted the losses of their tribe by what they always called an impolitic treaty."

Thus in the Maritimes we find a pattern of private dealings taking place, the Belcher Proclamation in 1762 which tried to regularize dealings with Indians, and the famous Royal Proclamation in 1763 which was designed to deal with Indian unrest and to try and establish a pattern of dealings with native people in relation to their land claims. Even after the Royal Proclamation of 1763, however, there were still individual dealings going on in the Maritimes. For instance, New Brunswick was formed in 1784 and in 1884 passed an Act to regulate the management and disposal of the Indian reserves in the province. It provided that the lands were to be surveyed and any land which was unimproved land could be sold by the government at public auction without requiring the consent of the native people. The revenues from these sales were to be applied for the benefit of the Indians but first the government deducted the cost of the surveys, the auction, plus a 5% commission. This legislation, permitting the sale of reserve lands without Indian consent, continued right up until Confederation.

7. The Cases

(a) *R. v. Isaac* (1975), 13 NSR (2d) 460 (SCAD).

This case held that s. 150(1)(b) of the Lands and Forests Act (Nova Scotia), a provincial provision characterized as regulating the hunting of game, did not apply to an Indian while present on an Indian reserve. While MacKeigan CJ based his decision upon the ground that game laws on reserves are laws relating to "lands reserved for the Indians," an exclusively federal domain under s. 91(24) of the Constitution Act, 1867, he also made the following remarks:

> In Part II of these reasons I conclude that Indians on Nova Scotia reserves have a usufructuary right in the reserve land, a legal right to use that land and its resources, including, of course, the right to hunt on that land. In my opinion that right arises in our customary or common law, was confirmed by the *Royal Proclamation* of 1763 and other authoritative declarations, was preserved in respect of reserve lands when they were originally set apart for the Indians, and is implicit in the *Indian Act* which continues reserves "for the use and benefit of the respective bands" (s. 18(1)). That legal right is possibly a supervening law which in itself precludes the application of provincial game laws in a reserve, but it is, I think, more properly considered as an "Indian land right" which is inextricably part of the land to which the provincial game law cannot extend.
>
> That right, sometimes called "Indian title" is an interest in land akin to a *profit à prendre*. It arose long before 1867 but has not been extinguished as to reserve land and, being still an incident of the reserve land, can be controlled or regulated only by the federal government. This stresses legalistically the perhaps self-evident proposition that hunting by an Indian is traditionally so much a part of his use of his land and its resources as to be for him, peculiarly and specially, integral to that land.
>
> We need not, however, rely on aboriginal right theories or "Indian title" concepts to establish that hunting is a use of land and its resources. To shoot a rabbit, deer or grouse on land especially Indian reserve land, is as much a use of that land as to cut a tree on that land, or to mine minerals, extract oil from the ground, or farm that land, or, as in the *Peace Arch* case, supra, erect a building on that land — all of which are activities unquestionably exclusively for the federal government to regulate.

PART II

This Part is a historical review which assembles and summarizes data from many sources not readily available. It will confirm, perhaps unnecessarily, that an Indian has a special right to hunt on reserve lands.

The review begins with the original rights of Indians to the use of the land when the white man came, and then examines to what degree those rights have been modified, affirmed or extinguished in Nova Scotia.

Calder et al. v. *The Attorney General of British Columbia,* [1973] SCR 313, confirmed that such rights existed in law and that ''Indian title'' to land was a legal reality. The Nishga Indians of British Columbia sought a declaration ''that the aboriginal title, otherwise known as the Indian title, of the Plaintiffs to their ancient tribal territory . . . has never been lawfully extinguished''. The provincial Court of Appeal held (13 DLR (3d) 64) that no Indian title could be recognized unless it had been incorporated into provincial law by executive or legislative authority, and that no such incorporation could be found. The Supreme Court of Canada, on equal division on this issue, dismissed the appeal, three of seven judges per Judson J finding that any Indian title that existed originally had been extinguished and three other judges per Hall J finding that title had existed but that it had not been extinguished.

Both Mr Justice Judson and Mr Justice Hall agreed that the ''Indian title'' or rights flowed from basic principles authoritatively expressed by Chief Justice Marshall of the United States Supreme Court in *Johnson and Graham's Lessee* v. *McIntosh* (1823), 8 Wheaton 543 (21 US), and *Worcester* v. *Georgia* (1832), 6 Peters 515 (31 US), and adopted by many other American, Canadian and English courts. Those rights were rights to use and occupy the land, rights which overlay the basic Crown title but which could be extinguished by the Crown.

Mr Justice Hall at pp. 381-82 quoted at length from Chief Justice Marshall's opinion in the *Johnson* case, including the following at p. 574:

> . . . they were admitted to be *the rightful occupants of the soil, with a legal as well as just claim to retain possession of it, and to use it according to their own discretion* . . . (italics added)

Mr Justice Judson at p. 321 also quoted extensively from *Johnson*, including the following at p. 588:

> . . . all our institutions recognize the absolute title of the crown, *subject only to the Indian right of occupancy*: and recognize the absolute title of the crown to extinguish that right. (italics added)

It will be noted that the Indian title or right could be extinguished by the sovereign power. Statements are found in some of the cases (notably in *Worcester* v. *Georgia* and see Hall J in *Calder* at p. 389) implying that the extinction of the right could only occur with the consent of the Indians, by purchase, treaty or otherwise. Bearing in mind the scant evidence in Nova Scotia, or indeed in New England, Quebec or New Brunswick, of any recorded transaction or explicit consent, I must prefer Mr Justice Judson's view (p. 329) that extinction may occur by prerogative acts, e.g., by setting apart reserves and opening the rest of the land for homestead grants and settlement, however unfair that may sometimes have been. He quoted (p. 334) the United States Supreme Court in *United States* v. *Santa Fe Pacific Ry. Co.* (1941), 314 US 339, at 347, as follows:

> As stated by Chief Justice Marshall in *Johnson* v. *McIntosh*, 'the exclusive right of the United States to extinguish' Indian title has never been doubted. And whether it be done by treaty, by the sword, by purchase, by the exercise of complete dominion adverse to the right of occupancy, or otherwise, its justness is not open to inquiry in the courts.

Calder adopted *St Catharine's Milling and Lumber Company* v. *The Queen* 1889), 14 App. Cas. 46 (PC), which was greatly influenced by the Marshall judgments which were discussed at length in the courts below (13 SCR 577 (SCC), 13 Ont. App. R. 148 (Ont. CA), and 10 Ont. R. 196 (Boyd C)). *St. Catharine's* held that lands originally occupied by Indians became completely owned by the Provincial Crown, after the Indian right had been extinguished by an 1873 treaty between the tribe and the federal government. The Privy Council held that once the lands were by the surrender "disencumbered of the Indian title" (p. 59), they became again fully provincial Crown property, subject only to the federal government's "exclusive power to regulate the Indians' privilege of hunting and fishing" (p. 60).

The Judicial Committee per Lord Watson at p. 54 held that "the tenure of the Indians was a personal and usufructuary right, dependent upon the good will of the Sovereign", and said:

> There was a great deal of learned discussion at the Bar with respect to the precise quality of the Indian right, but their Lordships do not consider it necessary to express any opinion upon the point. It appears to them to be sufficient for the purposes of this case that there has been all along vested in the Crown a substantial and paramount estate, underlying the Indian title, which became a plenum dominion whenever that title was surrendered or otherwise extinguished.

And at p. 58 stated:

> The Crown has all along had a present proprietary estate in the land, upon which the Indian title was a mere burden.

In 1921 the Privy Council (per Duff J as he then was) applied the *St Catharine's* case to an Indian reserve which in 1882 had been surrendered by the Indians to the federal government. The title was held to be vested in the provincial Crown "freed from the burden" of the Indian interest, which was described as:

> . . . a usufructuary right only and a personal right in the sense that it is in its nature inalienable except by surrender to the Crown.
>
> (*Attorney General for Quebec* v. *Attorney General for Canada*, [1921] AC 401 at p. 408 — the *Silver Chrome* case).

(The *St Catharine's* and *Silver Chrome* cases are doubtless the two Privy Council cases referred to in the Canada-Nova Scotia agreement of April 14, 1959, whereby the province transferred to Canada all its interest in "reserve lands", consisting of the existing Nova Scotia reserves, including the Chapel Island reserve. The agreement also confirmed any grants previously made by the federal government to any person of former reserve lands surrendered by the Indians since 1867. The agreement was ratified by Statutes of Canada, 1959, c. 50, and Statutes of Nova Scotia.

A "usufructurary right" to land is, of course, merely a right to use that land and its "fruit" or resources. It certainly must include the right to catch and use the fish and game and other products of the streams and forests of that land. For the primitive, nomadic Micmac of Nova Scotia in the 18th Century, no other use of land was important.

The original Indian rights as defined by Chief Justice Marshall were not modified by any treaty or ordinance during the French regime which lasted until 1713 in Acadia, and until 1758 in Cape Breton, and must be deemed to have been accepted by the British on their entry. Such acceptance is shown by the British *Royal Proclamation* of October 7, 1763, (RSC 1970, Appendices, pp. 123-29), which has been perhaps a little extravagantly termed the "Indian Bill of Rights" (Gwynne J in *St Catharine's*, 13 SCR at p. 652), or the "Charter of Indian Rights" (McGillivray, JA, in *Rex* v. *Wesley*, [1932] 4 DLR 774 (Alta. CA) at p. 784). It had, however, the legislative effect of a statute. Hall J in *Calder*, *supra*, at p. 394 said:

> This Proclamation was an Executive Order having the force and effect of an Act of Parliament . . ..

Maclean J (as he then was) in *The King* v. *Lady McMaster*, [1926] Ex. C.R. 68 at p. 72 said the Proclamation "has the force of a statute, and . . . has never been repealed".

The Proclamation was clearly not the exclusive source of Indian rights (Judson J in *Calder* at p. 322) but rather was "declaratory of the aboriginal rights" (Hall J in *Calder* at p. 397).

I am of the opinion that the Proclamation in its broad declaration as to Indian rights applied to Nova Scotia including Cape Breton. Its recital

(p. 127) acknowledged that in all colonies, including Nova Scotia, all land which had not been "ceded to or purchased by" the Crown was reserved to the Indians as *"their Hunting Grounds"*. Any trespass upon any lands thus reserved to the Indians was forbidden (p. 127).

A long provision (p. 128) prohibited any purchase of land by whites from Indians or any sale by Indians of their land except by a public assembly of Indians and then only to the Crown. It applied to "Lands reserved to the said Indians, within those parts of our Colonies where, We have thought proper to allow Settlement."

The "lands reserved" apparently included all lands in Nova Scotia which the Indians had not ceded or sold to the Crown. "Ceded" land presumably included lands then occupied with the assumed or forced acquiescence of the Indians, such as those at Halifax, Lunenburg, Liverpool and Yarmouth and the former Acadian lands taken over by New England "planters". Later the "lands reserved" as "Hunting Grounds" were, of course, gradually restricted by occupation by the white man under Crown grant which extinguished the Indian right on the land so granted. Indeed, the land where that right exists may have in time become restricted in Nova Scotia to the reserved lands which we now know as "Indian reserves".

I shall now review how the Indian land rights, confirmed by the Proclamation of 1763, were further confirmed, modified or extinguished in Nova Scotia between 1713 and 1867.

A basic distinction exists between treaty Indians and non-treaty Indians. In most of Ontario, the Prairies, the Northwest Territories, and eastern British Columbia, treaties were made with Indian tribes, in the west between 1871 and 1921, and earlier in Ontario, whereby the Indians formally ceded lands to the Crown, which in return set aside specific lands as "reserves" for the Indians. The Indians often retained a specific right to hunt and fish on the land they had ceded, so long as it remained unoccupied Crown land. (Examples of such treaties are Treaty No. 3, in the *St Catharine's* case, and Treaty No. 8, in *Regina* v. *White and Bob* (1964), 50 DLR (2d) 613. See, generally, *Native Rights in Canada*, 2nd ed., by P. Cumming and N. Mickenberg (Eds.) 1972, chapters 9 and 14.)

In the rest of Canada, including Nova Scotia, the treaties or arrangements were quite different. No Nova Scotia treaty has been found whereby Indians ceded land to the Crown, whereby their rights on any land were specifically extinguished, or whereby they agreed to accept and retire to specified reserves, although thorough archival research might well disclose record of informal agreements especially in the early 1800's when reserves were established by executive order.

Agreements with the Indians in the Maritimes were primarily treaties of peace, informal and sometimes oral. They were pledges of peace, often soon broken prior to 1758, and between 1775 and 1784 when many Indians in New Brunswick fought for the American rebels. They usually provided for exchange of prisoners. They often acknowledged gifts to the Indians and sometimes specifically assured hunting and fishing rights to the Indians.

The Micmacs of Nova Scotia, like related tribes in New Brunswick and Maine, were not highly developed socially and politically. The tribe consisted of many loose clans and nomadic groups, over which the so-called chiefs had little authority, and which had no clear territorial jurisdictions. They were a poor, disorganized race, decimated by disease and famine in 1746, and demoralized after the fall of Louisbourg in 1758 (As to the nature of the early Micmac society, see: *The Native Peoples of Atlantic Canada*, H.F. McGee (ed.), 1974, Carleton Library, No. 72: *"The Micmac Indians of Eastern Canada"*, W.D. and R.S. Wallis, 1955: Reports of Joseph Howe, as Commissioner for Indian Affairs, 1843-4, Appendices to Journal, Nova Scotia Legislative Assembly.)

Nova Scotia until 1784 included New Brunswick and much of Maine and from 1763 to 1784 included Prince Edward Island and Cape Breton Island. The latter was a separate colony from 1784 to 1824.

The earliest treaty was made in 1713 with Indians of the eastern part of the then Massachusetts Bay Colony, including tribes in most of what is now New Brunswick. The treaty (*Native Rights in Canada, supra*, pp. 296-98) promised peace and confirmed to the English rights of land in their settlements, "saving unto the said Indians their own Grounds, & free liberty for Hunting, Fishing, Fowling. . . ."

A treaty of December 15, 1725 (*Native Rights, supra*, pp. 300-06) purportedly covered all tribes of Nova Scotia, but specifically named only the Cape Sable Indians. It pledged peace and saved unto the Indians all lands "not by them convey'd or sold or possessed by" the English, "As also the privilege [*sic*] of fishing, hunting, and fowling as formerly."

Next is the treaty of November 22, 1752, made by Governor Hopson of Nova Scotia with representatives purportedly acting for all Micmacs on the eastern coast of Nova Scotia, and in the Shubenacadie area. It was agreed "the said Tribe of Indians shall . . . have free liberty of hunting and Fishing as usual." (*Native Rights, supra*, pp. 307-08).

The 1752 treaty was held in *Rex* v. *Syliboy* (1928), 50 CCC 389 (Nova Scotia County Court), not to apply to Cape Breton or to protect a Cape Breton Micmac from conviction for having muskrat skins in his possession contrary to provincial law (apparently not on a reserve); aboriginal rights were not mentioned and the 1763 Proclamation was, wrongly in my opinion, held not applicable to Cape Breton.

Both the 1725 and 1752 treaties were found in *Regina* v. *Simon*

(1958), 124 CCC 110 (NBCA), and *Regina* v. *Francis* (1969), 10 DLR (3d) 189 (NBCA), not to apply to Micmac Indians from the parts of New Brunswick involved. The treaties were unsuccessfully invoked to avoid application of regulations under the federal *Fisheries Act*. The courts properly held that valid federal law may override any Indian "rights".

Many other "treaties" of peace were made with groups of Nova Scotia Micmacs of which no copies have been produced. Beamish Murdoch, Q.C., in his *History of Nova Scotia*, 1866, Vol. 2, refers to many, including April 1753 for LaHave (p. 219); November 1753 for Cape Sable (p. 225); February 1755 for the Amherst area (p. 257); February 1760 for LaHave, Shubenacadie and Musquodoboit (p. 385); October 15, 1761, for Pictou and Merigomish (p. 407); November 9, 1761, for LaHave (p. 407); and August 1763 again for LaHave (p. 431).

Murdoch refers also to treaties during the American Revolution, when Michael Francklyn reported in June 1779 (p. 599) that he had succeeded in re-establishing peace with "all the tribes who inhabit this province". This probably referred mainly to New Brunswick Indians who had been supporting the American rebels (p. 595). Francklyn, who was the Nova Scotia deputy of Sir William Johnson, who was then Indian Commissioner for all the colonies north of Virginia, worked assiduously to maintain peace, meeting with and writing many groups of Indians.

In the meantime, important "Royal Instructions" were issued on December 9, 1761, to the Governor of Nova Scotia. I assume they were in the form of the draft instructions printed in *Native Rights in Canada*, *supra*, pp. 285-86, and there erroneously called a Proclamation, but I note Lieutenant-Governor Belcher in his 1762 report describes them (p. 286) as dealing with encroachments upon the Indians, "to the interruption of their hunting, Fowling and Fishing", a subject not specifically mentioned in the draft.

The draft instruction anticipated the 1763 Proclamation in directing the governor to protect the Indians "in their just Rights and Possessions", to prevent persons buying lands from the Indians, and to require trespassers to vacate any land "reserved to or claimed by the said Indians".

Belcher on May 4, 1762, issued a proclamation (*idem*, pp. 287-88). He recited the Indian claim of land along the relatively unsettled eastern coast "for the more special purpose of hunting, fowling and fishing". He enjoined all persons to avoid molestation of the Indians, and to vacate any lands possessed "to the prejudice of the said Indians in their Claims."

Belcher in a report of July 2, 1762 (*idem*, pp. 286-87) explained why he had implied that the coastal claim of the Indians was the only one about which anyone need be concerned. He said the only complaint received from the Indians had been respecting interference with fishing along the coast. He said:

> This claim was therefore inserted in the Proclamation, that all persons might be notified of the Reasonableness of such a permission, whilst the Indians themselves should continue in Peace with Us, and that this Claim should at least be entertained by the Government, till his Majesty's pleasure should be signified. After the Proclamation was issued no Claims for any other purposes were made. If the Proclamation had been issued at large, the Indians, might have been incited by the disaffected Acadians and others, to have made extravagant and unwarrantable demands, to the disquiet and perplexity of the New Settlements in the Province. Your Lordships will permit me humbly to remark that no other Claim can be made by the Indians in this Province, either by Treaties or long possession (the Rule, by which the determination of their Claims is to be made, by Virtue of this His Majesty's Instructions) since the French derived their Title from the Indians and the French ceded their Title to the English under the Treaty of Utrecht.

Belcher, of course, was right as to basic title to the land having been received by Britain from France, but erred in not recognizing the "burden of Indian rights" overlying that title. Neither the French nor British had extinguished the Indian rights in Nova Scotia. Belcher, although not recognizing that Indians had a general right to use land not occupied by settlement, did recognize the "reasonableness" of the Indian claim to hunt and fish freely, at least in most of the province, and recognized that Indians justly complained about "interruptions in their hunting grounds" by Acadians.

I have been unable to find any record of any treaty, agreement or arrangement after 1780 extinguishing, modifying or confirming the Indian right to hunt and fish, or any other record of any cession or release of rights or lands by the Indians.

The history of the next eighty-seven years discloses little concern for the Indians. The incoming settlers pushed them back to poorer land in the interior of the province. The government gradually herded them into reserves and made sporadic and unsuccessful attempts to convert them into an agricultural people.

In 1773 the Executive Council had issued a proclamation forbidding land negotiations with Indians and stating that tracts of land would be set aside for their use (*Indians of Quebec and the Maritime Provinces: An Historical Review*, Department of Indian Affairs, Ottawa, 1971, p. 12). A two mile square reserve was established at Shubenacadie in 1779 (*idem*). The Crown in 1786 granted 500 acres to Indians in St

Margaret's Bay ("Indian Affairs in Nova Scotia, 1760-1834," by Elizabeth A. Hutton, in *The Native Peoples of Atlantic Canada*, *supra*, p. 76). (See also, *The Canadian Indian — A History Since 1500* by E. Palmer Patterson, 1972, pp. 62-65.)

During 1819 and 1820 eight additional reserves of 1,000 acres each were established in mainland Nova Scotia. They were placed in trust for the Indians "to whom they are to be hereafter considered as exclusively belonging" (*idem*, p.78). The separate colony of Cape Breton had by 1824, when it rejoined Nova Scotia, similarly set aside six Indian reserves, totalling over 12,000 acres.

The Indian problem was first given statutory attention by c. 16 of the Statutes of 1842, which provided for a Commissioner for Indian Affairs, who was to survey the reserves, and "preserve them for the use of the Indians". He was "to put himself in communication with the Chiefs of the different tribes of the Micmac Race throughout the Province . . . and to invite them to co-operate in the permanent settlement and instruction of their people".

The Indian Commissioner for the first two years was the Honourable Joseph Howe. His first report (Assembly Journal, 1843, Appendix No. 1) spoke eloquently of the neglected condition of the Micmacs. He found not more than 1,300, of whom 500 lived in Cape Breton, a drastic decrease since 1798. He inspected most reserves and found the land "sterile and comparatively valueless". In this and his 1844 report (Assembly Journal, 1844, Appendix No. 50) he gave many instances of extreme poverty and of reserve land being taken by white trespassers.

A few years later Commissioner Crawley complained in his 1849 report about Scots settlers trespassing on the reserves at Margaree and Whycocomagh (MG 15, Vol. 4, No. 70):

> Under the present circumstances no adequate protection can be obtained for the Indian property. It would be in vain to seek a verdict from any jury in this Island against the trespassers on the reserves: nor perhaps would a member of the Bar be found willingly and effectually to advocate the cause of the Indians, inasmuch as he would thereby injure his own prospects, by damaging his own popularity.

Apparently little improvement was effected before 1867. Howe himself in 1873 condemned policies in the Maritimes as compared to those in Ontario and Quebec, where the "crowning glory" was the treatment of Indians. (Sess. Papers, 1873, Vol. 6, No. 5, Paper No. 23, quoted by Boyd, C in the *St Catharine's Milling* case, 10 Ont. Rep. at p. 216) (See *The Canadian Indian — A History Since 1500*, *supra*, pp. 115-19.)

Pre-Confederation fish and game laws occasionally recognized that

Indians were in a special position. The first game act, providing for closed seasons for partridge and black duck, 1794, c. 4, exempted "any Indian or other poor settler who shall kill any partridge or black duck . . . for his own use". A like exemption respecting snipe and woodcock appeared 1816, c. 5, and, as to trout, in 1824, c. 36. An Act of 1843, c. 19, prohibiting the use of moose snares, did not specifically exempt Indians, but seemed to presume they were excluded. It noted that the use of snares would "lead to the destruction of all the Moose . . . thereby depriving the Indians and poor Settlers of one of their means of subsistence."

The exemptions as to partridge, duck, snipe and woodcock were continued in the Revised Statutes of 1851 (c. 92) and 1859 (c. 92), but were dropped by the commissioners compiling the Revised Statutes of 1864. Similarly, no exemptions as to Indians appeared in the consolidations respecting river fishing which appeared in the Revised Statutes of 1851 and subsequently.

The pre-Confederation statutory record as to the application of fish and game laws to the Indians is thus spotty and ambiguous and we do not know how they were in fact administered. The legislature at no time, however, either revoked any Indian exemption or dealt specifically with the use of reserve land.

I would here apply the comments of Norris JA in *Regina* v. *White and Bob*, who, referring to colonial game laws in British Columbia, said ((1964) 50 DLR (2d) at p. 662):

> In none of these statutes was there any prohibition applying specifically to Indians. It would have required specific legislation to extinguish the aboriginal rights, and it is doubtful whether Colonial legislation, even of a specific kind, could extinguish these rights in view of the fact that such rights had been confirmed by the *Royal Proclamation of 1763*.

This Part has established that Indians in Nova Scotia had a usufructuary right to the use of land as their hunting grounds. That right was not extinguished for reserve land before Confederation by any treaty, or by Crown grant to others or by occupation by the white man. It has not been extinguished or modified since 1867 by or under any federal Act. (We are not concerned whether the right may still exist for any land other than reserves. It would appear that in Nova Scotia, apart from reserves, only a few thousand widely scattered acres have never been granted, placed under mining or timber licences or leases, set aside as game preserves or parks, or occupied prescriptively.)

The review has confirmed that Indians have a special relationship with the lands they occupy, not merely a quaint tradition, but rather a right recognized in law. Hunting by Indians is and always has been a use of land legally integral to the land itself. A provincial law purporting to regulate that use on a reserve must be therefore *pro tanto* constitutionally ineffective.

Cooper JA also stated, *inter alia*,

> There do not appear to have been any land cession treaties in Nova Scotia but rather "treaties" or agreements of another character — see App. III to *Native Rights in Canada*, 2nd ed., Cumming and Mickenberg (eds.). These have been comprehensively reviewed by the Chief Justice in his reasons for judgment. I will not repeat that review. It is sufficient for me to say that I do not find in any of them hunting rights reserved to the Indians on Cape Breton Island so as to overcome the application of s. 88 in respect of the appellant. I should perhaps mention the "Treaty or Articles of Peace and Friendship Renewed" of 1752. It does state that the Tribe of Indians there referred to "shall not be hindered from, but have free liberty of hunting and fishing as usual . . ." Cape Breton Island was held by the French in 1752 and the Tribe of Micmac Indians referred to in the *Treaty* are those inhabiting the eastern coast of Nova Scotia. The *Treaty of 1752* was considered in *Rex v. Syliboy* (1928), 50 CCC page number 389. It was there held by Patterson, Acting CCJ, that it did not extend to Cape Breton Indians and further that it was not in reality a treaty. I have doubt as to the second finding and express no opinion on it, but I have no doubt as to the correctness of the first finding.
>
> I now turn to my reason for agreeing that this appeal should be allowed. Following the *Treaty of Paris* in 1763 there was issued on October 7, 1763 a *Royal Proclamation* — see RSC 1970, appendices 123-129. This *Proclamation*, as pointed out by the Chief Justice, has been held to have the legislative effect of a statute — see *The King* v. *Lady McMaster*, [1926] ExCR 68, where Maclean J said at p. 72:

> > The proclamation of 1763, as has been held, has the force of a statute, and so far therein as the rights of the Indians are concerned, it has never been repealed.

and see also *Regina* v. *White and Bob* (1965), 50 DLR (2d) 613 at p. 616 and *Calder* v. *Attorney General of B.C.*, [1973] SCR 313 at p. 394. The *Proclamation* has also been held in *Calder* at pp. 396-97 to have been declaratory of the aboriginal rights of Indians and it is beyond dispute that such rights included the right to hunt.

The *Proclamation* recites that:

> And whereas it is just and reasonable, and essential to our Interest, and the Security of our Colonies, that the several Nations or Tribes of Indians with whom We are connected, and who live under our

Protection, should not be molested or disturbed in the Possession of such Parts of Our Dominions and Territories as, not having been ceded to or purchased by Us, are reserved to them, or any of them, as their Hunting Grounds.

and declares, *inter alia*, that no Governor or Commander in Chief ''do presume for the present, and until our further Pleasure be known'' to grant Warrants of Survey or pass any Patents ''upon any Lands whatever, which, not having been ceded to or purchased by Us as aforesaid, are reserved to the said Indians, or any of them.''

I respectfully agree with the Chief Justice that the *Proclamation* extended to and included the Indians on Cape Breton Island. There is no evidence before us that the rights of the Indians to the reserve lands here in question have been surrendered to or purchased by the Crown. The Federal Crown holds legal title to the lands in trust for the use and benefit of the Indians concerned but their interest remains. That interest has been characterized as a personal and usufructuary right which in my opinion must include the right to hunt. It remains until it has been surrendered to the Crown or otherwise extinguished by the federal power: neither of which has happened — see *St Catharine's Milling and Lumber Company* v. *The Queen* (1888), 14 App. Cas. 46 at pp. 54-55. Section 88 does not have the effect of converting the *Lands and Forests Act* into federal legislation by referential incorporation. That Act remains provincial legislation and as such cannot be held to have extinguished hunting rights of the Indians confirmed by the *Royal Proclamation* — see *Natural Parents* v. *The Superintendent of Child Welfare et al.* (SCC) October 7, 1975, as yet unreported, [Now reported 6 NR 491.]

I conclude, therefore, that s. 150 of the *Lands and Forests Act* in the circumstances of this case does not apply to the appellant on the ground that he had, pursuant to the terms of the *Royal Proclamation*, the right to hunt and this right has not been surrendered or extinguished. It follows that this appeal should be allowed. I respectfully agree, however, with the Chief Justice that the question should be amended to encompass s. 150(1)(b) of the *Lands and Forests Act* only.

MacDonald JA agreed with the conclusions of the Chief Justice and delivered some remarks of his own, concurring that hunting and fishing on reserves were land use rights that had never been taken away. He did believe, however, that as a result of conquest and being forced onto reserves, Indians had lost the right to hunt and fish on non-reserve land, and could by appropriate federal legislation be deprived of that right upon reserve lands. Coffin JA also delivered reasons, agreeing with his three brethren on the result of this case.

Note

1. Section 91(24) of the Constitution Act 1867 gives exclusive legislative jurisdiction over Indians and lands reserved for the Indians to the federal government. It is clear that this exclusive power means that the provinces cannot legislate in relation to the essential status and capacities of Indians. Are Indian hunting and fishing activities so intimately tied to Indian economic, cultural and recreational traditions as to be part of Indians' essential status and capacities? Whether this is so in relation to fishing is not important, the courts have said, because fisheries regulation is an exclusive federal jurisdiction under s. 91(12) — sea coast and inland fisheries. Thus, whether as Indian legislation or as fisheries legislation, the federal government can deal with Indian fishing rights.

   However, hunting regulation, with such limited exceptions as in respect of migratory birds and on federally owned lands like national parks, is a provincial subject area under s. 92(13) and s. 92(16). The provinces have asserted this jurisdiction by enacting general hunting regulations applying to all persons. Whether the effect of these hunting regulations on Indians is so unique as to affect their essential status and capacities has not been clearly resolved by the courts. In any event, the application of such general provincial hunting regulations to Indians is by s. 88 of the Indian Act "subject to the terms of any treaty". A frequent issue therefore in Indian hunting rights cases is whether a treaty has conferred rights which conflict with provincial hunting regulations. See *Kruger and Manuel* v. *The Queen*, [1978] 1 SCR 104, at 110, [1977] 4 WWR 300, at 305; *R.* v. *White and Bob* (1965), 52 DLR (2d) 481 (SCC), affirming (1964), 50 DLR (2d) 613 (BCCA) at 618; *R.* v. *Frank*, [1978] 1 SCR 95, at 99, 34 CCC (2d) 209, at 212; *R.* v. *Paul* (1980), 30 NBR (2d) 545 (CA); *R.* v. *George*, [1966] 3 CCC 137 at 150-51, 55 DLR (2d) 386 at 397-98 (SCC); *Moosehunter* v. *The Queen*, [1981] 9 CNLR 61 (SCC) at 68; D. Knoll, *Treaty and Aboriginal Hunting and Fishing Rights*, [1979] CNLR 1; K. Lysyk, *Indian Hunting Rights: Constitutional Considerations and the Role of Indian Treaties in British Columbia* (1966), 2 *UBCL Review* 401; *R.* v. *Tennisco* (1981), 131 DLR (3d) 96 (Ontario High Court); *R.* v. *Paul and Copage* (1977), 24 NSR (2d) 313 (SCAD) at 320.

(b) *R.* v. *Cope* (1981), 49 NSR (2d) 555 (SC, AD)

COFFIN, HART and MACDONALD, JJA, concurred with MACKEIGAN, CJNS

MACKEIGAN CJNS: This is an appeal by stated case from the conviction of the accused William Raymond Cope on a charge of possessing more trout than permitted by the limit set by the "Nova Scotia Fishing Regulations". The question stated for our opinion by Judge C.W. Archibald, of the Provincial Magistrate's Court, is:

> Did I err in holding that the Treaty of 1752, made between Thomas Hopson, Governor of Nova Scotia, and Jean Baptiste Cope, did not exempt the accused Micmac Indian from the Nova Scotia Fishery Regulations made pursuant to the Fisheries Act, RSC 1970, c. F-14, section 34?

The appellant is a Micmac Indian and a descendant of the Indians on whose behalf the Treaty of 1752 was purportedly made. The offence here alleged was not committed on Indian reserve land.

The appellant contends that the 1752 Treaty is a treaty "unique in North America" and that it conferred on all Micmacs in Nova Scotia a "vested property right or franchise" to fish and hunt. Such rights, so it is argued, cannot be affected by federal legislation, such as the federal fishing regulations in issue here, unless such legislation is specifically made applicable to Indians, which there regulations are not.

We are not in this appeal concerned with the argument that the 1752 Treaty would also be a "treaty" within the meaning of s. 88 of the *Indian Act* so as to exclude the application of the provincial game laws to all Micmacs, whether on reserves or not.

This court in *Isaac* v. *The Queen* (1975), 13 NSR (2d) 460; 9 APR 460 (NSCA), held that the Nova Scotia provincial game laws did not apply to an Indian hunting on an Indian reserve. The principal *ratio decidendi*, as I conceive it, was that Indians had a personal and usufructuary right to hunt, a right historically associated with their lands, and that that aboriginal right had been affirmed by various treaties (including the 1752 Treaty now in issue per MacKeigan CJNS, at p. 480), and especially affirmed by the *Royal Proclamation of 1763* (MacKeigan) CJNS, at p. 469 and Cooper JA, at pp. 496-97). We held that the lands in Nova Scotia where that aboriginal right must still be enjoyed were essentially limited to Indian reserve land. We thus concluded that the aboriginal right to hunt, which impliedly included a right to fish, had been preserved for the Indians on reserve land and could not be affected by provincial laws, having regard to the exclusive federal power in respect of Indians and lands reserved for the Indians.

In the course of my opinion in *Isaac*, I reviewed (in 13 NSR (2d), 9 APR at pp. 478-83) the history of Indian treaty arrangements affecting Nova Scotia. At pp. 479-80 I said:

> . . . no Nova Scotia treaty has been found whereby Indians ceded land to the Crown, whereby their rights on any land were specifically extinguished, or whereby they agreed to accept and retire to specified reserves, although thorough archival research might well disclose record of informal agreements especially in the early 1800s when reserves were established by executive order.
>
> Agreements with the Indians in the Maritimes were primarily treaties of peace, informal and sometimes oral. They were pledges of peace, often soon broken prior to 1758, and between 1775 and 1784 when many Indians in New Brunswick fought for the American rebels. They usually provided for exchange of prisoners. They often acknowledged gifts to the Indians and sometimes specifically assured hunting and fishing rights to the Indians.
>
> The Micmacs of Nova Scotia, like related tribes in New Brunswick and Maine, were not highly developed socially and politically. The

tribe consisted of many loose clans and nomadic groups, over which the so-called chiefs had little authority, and which had no clear territorial jurisdictions.

See also Macdonald JA, at pp. 498-99, who emphasized the historical Indian usufructary right to use their hunting and fishing grounds.

I reviewed many treaties made between 1713, when Britain took over Acadia (mainland Nova Scotia and southern New Brunswick) and 1763. I treated the few that referred to hunting and fishing as merely affirmations of native rights or, perhaps more accurately, as acquiescence in the Indians' exercise of their historical rights. (Indeed, what alternative did the British have but to acquiesce? Britain until 1755 or so had little control of any land area except the Annapolis Valley and, after 1749, around Halifax. Until the conquest of Louisbourg in 1758, minor Indian raids harassed the settlements despite any treaties. Thus, in 1751 and again in May, 1753, Indians killed settlers at Dartmouth: Beamish Murdoch, *History of Nova Scotia*, Vol. II, pp. 200, 208, 219).

In *Isaac*, after reviewing treaties of 1713 and 1725 and the Treaty of 1752 now before us, I commented (at p. 481):

> Both the 1725 and 1752 treaties were found in *Regina* v. *Simon* (1958), 124 CCC 110 (NBCA), and *Regina* v. *Francis* (1969), 10 DLR (3d) 189 (NBCA), not to apply to Micmac Indians from the parts of New Brunswick involved. The treaties were unsuccessfully invoked to avoid application of regulations under the federal *Fisheries Act*. The courts properly held that valid federal law may override any Indian 'rights'.

Many other 'treaties' of peace were made with groups of Nova Scotia Micmacs of which no copies have been produced. Beamish Murdoch, QC, in his *History of Nova Scotia*, 1866, vol. 2, refers to many, including April 1753 for LaHave (p. 219); November 1753 for Cape Sable (p. 225); February 1755 for the Amherst area (p. 257); February 1760 for LaHave, Shubenacadie and Musquodoboit (p. 385); October 15, 1761, for Pictou and Merigomish (p. 407); November 9, 1761, for LaHave (p. 407); and August 1763 again for LaHave (p. 431).

The appellant disavows any reliance on mere aboriginal rights, but claims immunity from the federal fishery regulations because of the unique and "specifically expressed negotiated rights contained in a Treaty", viz., the 1752 Treaty. Were it otherwise, the appellant would be conclusively met by the judgment of the Supreme Court of Canada in *R.* v. *Derriksan* (1977), 16 NR 231, affirming the judgment of the British Columbia Court of Appeal (1975), 16 NR 233; 60 DLR (3d) 140, which held that the fishery regulations here in issue overrode the aboriginal right to fish in an area of British Columbia. Chief Justice Laskin orally dismissed the appeal, saying (16 NR at 232):

> On the assumption that Mr. Sanders is correct in his submission (which is one which the Crown does not accept) that there is an aboriginal right to fish in the particular area arising out of Indian occupation and that this right has had subsequent reinforcement (and we express no opinion on the correctness of this submission), we are all of the view that the *Fisheries Act* and the Regulations thereunder which, so far as relevant here, were validly enacted, have the effect of subjecting the alleged right to the controls imposed by the Act and Regulations. The appeal is accordingly dismissed.

Mr Justice Robertson for the British Columbia Court of Appeal placed strong reliance (16 NR at p. 236) on the opinion of Hughes JA (as he then was) in *R. v. Francis* (1969), 10 DLR (3d) 189 (NBCA), and especially the following (p. 195):

> There can be no doubt that since the decisions of the Supreme Court of Canada in *Sikyea* v. *The Queen*, 50 DLR (2d) 80; [1965] 2 CCC 129; [1964] SCR 642, and *R.* v. *George*, *supra*, legislation of the Parliament of Canada and Regulations made thereunder, properly within s. 91 of the BNA Act, 1867, are not qualified or in any way made unenforceable because of the existence of rights acquired by Indians pursuant to treaty. It follows that even if the appellant had established that a right to fish salmon in the Richibucto River had been conferred by an Indian Treaty, the benefit of which he was entitled to claim, such right could afford no defence to the charge on which he was convicted.

The appellant's counsel contends, as I understand his argument, that the Treaty of 1752 was a special royal grant to all Micmacs of the privilege or franchise of hunting and fishing free of any restriction. He claims that this royal grant is an unique and immutable constitutional document in full force since 1752. He contends that, if it could be changed at all, which he denies, it could not be modified or extinguished by the federal fishery regulations, which do not specifically mention or apply to Micmacs or any other Indians.

Even if the so-called treaty had conferred the special rights which counsel for the appellant claims, the reasoning of cases such as *Derriksan*, *Sikyea*, *George* and *Francis* would have compelled us to reject his argument. Review of the actual agreement shows, however, that it was in any event a mere acknowledgment of aboriginal rights indistinguishable from the many other temporary Indian peace "treaties" of that period.

The minutes of a council meeting presided over by the Governor of

Nova Scotia, attended by five other members of the council, and held at Halifax on November 22, 1752, record the following:

The following Treaty of peace was signed and ratified and exchanged with the Mick Mack Tribe of Indians, inhabiting the Eastern part of this province, and it was resolved that Mr. Saul should be ordered to issue provisions according to the allowances of the Troops for six months for ninety of said Indians being the computed numbers of that tribe.

Then follows a copy of the Treaty.

The Treaty, as executed in the same form, is printed in *Native Rights in Canada* by Cumming and Mickenberg (2nd Ed.), App. III, at pp. 307-08, and is as follows:

[Treaty deleted, see *supra*]

The only words in the Treaty that have any conceivable bearing on the question of rights of hunting and fishing are the first few words of clause 4, which I repeat:

It is agreed that the said Tribe of Indians shall not be hindered from, but have full liberty of hunting and fishing as usual . . ..

These words are clearly a promise by the British not to interfere with or "hinder" the Indians, "usual" right or "liberty" to hunt and fish, coupled with an affirmation of that right or "full liberty of hunting and fishing *as usual*" (emphasis added).

By these words the British merely affirmed the Indians' already existing "full liberty of hunting and fishing *as usual*" (emphasis added) and specifically promised not to "hinder" or interfere with the Indians' exercise of that right. This clause is no more than a general affirmation of the aboriginal right. It falls very far short in words and substance from being a grant by the Crown of a special franchise or privilege replacing the more nebulous aboriginal rights.

Having reached the conclusion that the Treaty is no more than a general affirmation of the Indians' traditional hunting and fishing rights, we need not dwell on other reasons why this document cannot be considered a treaty granting or conferring new permanent rights. It was made for a "tribe" consisting of about ninety persons, obviously only a small portion of the Micmac nation. It does not define any land or area where the rights are to be exercised; specific references are made only to the Shubenacadie River and generally to the "Eastern Coast" of the province. (Murdoch, *supra*, vol. II, pp. 222-23, states Cope's headquarters in June, 1753, were at Jeddore on the eastern coast.) I agree with the New Brunswick Court of Appeal which described this document as follows (*Regina* v. *Simon* (1958), 124 CCC 110, per McNair CJNB, at p. 113):

Having regard to the language of the treaty, we are satisfied with the correctness of the view taken by Patterson, acting county court judge, that the treaty was not made with the Micmac Nation or Tribe as a whole but only with a small group of Micmac Indians inhabiting the eastern part of what is now the Province of Nova Scotia with their habitat in or about the Shubenacadie area.

Chief Justice McNair was referring to *R.* v. *Syliboy*, 50 CCC 389, where Patterson, Co. Ct. J, had dealt with the Treaty more summarily (p. 396):

In my judgment the Treaty of 1752 is not a treaty at all and is not to be treated as such; it is at best a mere agreement made by the Governor and council with a handful of Indians giving them in return for good behaviour food, presents, and the right to hunt and fish as usual — an agreement that, as we have seen, was very shortly after broken.

In my opinion, the Treaty of 1752 cannot be given the effect for which the appellant strives. The learned trial judge did not err in finding that the Treaty did not exempt the appellant from the federal fisheries regulations. The question asked in the stated case should be answered in the negative.

The appeal should be dismissed.

JONES JA: The simple issue raised on this appeal is whether the trial judge was precluded from entering a conviction against the appellant under the *Nova Scotia Fishery Regulations* made under the *Fisheries Act*, RSC 1970, c. F-14, because of the existence of a treaty made in 1752 with a band of Micmac Indians, reserving to the Indians "full liberty of hunting and fishing as usual . . . ."

With respect, this issue has been determined by the decisions of the Supreme Court of Canada in *Sikyea* v. *The Queen* and *R.* v. *George*. The effect of those decisions, it seems to me, was appropriately summarized by Hughes JA, speaking for New Brunswick Court of Appeal in *R.* v. *Francis* (1970), 10 DLR (3d) 189, at p. 195, where he stated:

There can be no doubt that since the decisions of the Supreme Court of Canada in *Sikyea* v. *The Queen*, 50 DLR (2d) 80, [1965] 2 CCC 129, [1964] SCR 642, and *R.* v. *George*, *supra*, legislation of the Parliament of Canada and regulations made thereunder, properly within s. 91 of the *BNA Act*, 1867, are not qualified or in any way made unenforceable because of the existence of rights acquired by Indians pursuant to treaty. It follows that even if the appellant had established that a right to fish salmon in the Richibucto River had been conferred by an Indian treaty, the benefit of which he was entitled to claim, such right could afford no defence to the charge on which he was convicted.

I find confirmation of that view as to the effect of the *Fisheries Act* and *Regulations* in the decision of the Supreme Court of Canada in *R.* v. *Derriksan* (1977), 16 NR 231. It becomes unnecessary, therefore, to comment on the nature and extent of any treaty rights which may exist in Nova Scotia. I agree with the Chief Justice that the appeal should be dismissed.

Appeal dismissed.

Notes

1. Leave to appeal in *Cope* was refused by the Supreme Court of Canada on 5 April 1982. The panel hearing the application was of the view that *R.* v. *Derriksan*, an aboriginal rights case, decided the point at issue in *Cope*. This is clearly consistent with the general proposition that the power unilaterally to extinguish treaty rights resides in Parliament. Accepting this proposition, ought it to be applied to extinguish treaty rights by implication, rather than openly and explicitly? See D.E. Sanders, "Indian Hunting and Fishing Rights" (1973-74), 38 *Sask. L. Rev.* 45, at 46; L.C. Green, "Legal Significance of Treaties Affecting Canada's Indians" (1972), 1 *Anglo-Am. L. Rev.* 119, at 134.

2. If the effect of legislation is to extinguish treaty rights, are the affected Indians entitled as a matter of law to compensation? Is the deprivation of hunting and fishing rights, arguably part of a usufructuary interest in land, any different than the expropriation of land, or the injurious affection of an interest in land, for which compensation is prescribed by federal and provincial statutes? This issue was raised in relation to aboriginal hunting rights, but not decided in *Kruger and Manuel* v. *The Queen*, [1977] 4 WWR 300, 75 DLR (3d) 434 (SCC) at 302-03 [WWR]. See *R.* v. *Bob*, [1979] 4 CNLR 71 (British Columbia County Court). The issue is also discussed in *Pawis* v. *the Queen* (1979), 102 DLR (3d) 602 (Fed. Ct., TD), *infra*.

3. It appears to have been a consistent practice from about the time of Confederation to express in land cession treaties a limitation upon the Indian hunting and fishing rights guaranteed. For example,

    (a) The Manitoulin Island Treaty, of 1862, *supra*, provided: "All the rights and privileges in respect to the taking of fish in the lakes, bays, creeks and waters within and adjacent to the said Island, which may be lawfully exercised and enjoyed by the white settlers thereon, may be exercised and enjoyed by the Indians";

    (b) The North-West Angle Treaty, Number Three, of 1873, Morris, *supra*, p. 320, provides, at p. 323;

      Her Majesty further agrees with her said Indians, that they, the said Indians, shall have right to pursue their avocations of hunting and fishing throughout the tract surrendered as hereinbefore described, subject to such regulations as may from time to time be made by her Government of her Dominion of Canada, and saving and excepting such tracts as may from time to time be required or taken up for settlement, mining, lumbering or other purposes, by her said Government of the Dominion of Canada, or by any of the subjects thereof duly authorized therefore by the said Government;

    (c) The Qu'Appelle Treaty, Number Four, of 1874, Morris, *supra*, p. 330, provides, at p. 333;

      And further, Her Majesty agrees that her said Indians shall have right to pursue their avocations of hunting, trapping and fishing throughout the tract surrendered, subject to such regulations as may from time to time be made by the Government of the country acting under the authority of Her Majesty, and saving and expecting such traits as may be required or taken up from time to time for settlement, mining or other purposes under grant, or other right given by Her Majesty's said Government;

(d) The Lake Winnipeg Treaty, Number Five, of 1875, Morris, *supra*, p. 342, at p. 346, and The Treaties at Forts Carlton and Pitt, Number Six, of 1876, Morris, *supra*, p. 351,at p. 353, each contain a provision identical to that in The North-West Angle Treaty;

(e) The Treaty with the Black feet, Number Seven, of 1877, Morris, *supra*, p. 368, provides, at p. 369:

And Her Majesty the Queen hereby agrees with her said Indians, that they shall have right to pursue their vocations of hunting throughout the tract surrendered as heretofore described, subject to such regulations as may, from time to time, be made by the Government of the country, acting under the authority of Her Majesty; and saving and excepting such tracts as may be required or taken up from time to time for settlement, mining, trading or other purposes by her Government of Canada or by any of her Majesty's subjects duly authorized therefor by the said government.

See also D. Knoll, "Treaty and Aboriginal Hunting Rights", [1979] 1 CNLR 1 at 7.

How ought we to treat the fact of explicit limitations of the hunting and fishing (and trapping) rights being guaranteed in later treaties? Do they just represent an abundance of caution on the part of their drafters? Or are they a recognition of the need expressly to state such limitations if they are to be relied upon? Thus, does the absence of express qualifications in documents like the Treaty of 1752 mean that no qualifications or limits apply?

4. Note that the classic case cited for the proposition that federal legislation supercedes Indian treaty rights, *Sikyea* v. *The Queen*, [1964] SCR 642, adopting the reasoning of the NWTCA, [1964] 2 CCC 325, involved a 1921 treaty under which the Indian right "to pursue their usual vocations of hunting, trapping and fishing" was expressly "subject to such regulations as may from time to time be made by the Government of the Country . . .." The application of the same federal statute as was in issue in *Sikyea*, the *Migratory Birds Convention Act*, to Indians in Manitoba was analyzed and seemingly justified by an interpretation of a provincial-federal agreement in 1929 that concerned Indian hunting, trapping and fishing and treaties containing the like proviso as *Sikyea, Daniels* v. *White and The Queen*, [1968] SCR 517.

5. Like decisions to *Cope*, applying federal fisheries regulations to Indians, were rendered in *R.* v. *Nicholas et al.* (1979), 26 NBR (2d) 54, [1981] 2 CNLR 114 (SCAD), (leave to appeal to SCC refused); *R.* v. *Sacobie* (1980), 30 NBR (2d) 70, [1981] 2 CNLR 115 (SC); *R.* v. *Saulis* (1980), 30 NBR (2d) 147, [1981] 2 CNLR 121 (SC).

6. The term ". . . we are at liberty . . . to carry on our fisheries as formerly . . .", an expression similar to that in the Treaty of 1752, was used in the Sooke Treaty of 1850 and interpreted in *R.* v. *Cooper* (1968), 1 DLR (3d) 113 (British Columbia Supreme Court) at 115 as "describing the extent of fishing reserved to the tribe (presumably unlimited) rather than the method." This sounds like something more than simple confirmation of pre-existing aboriginal rights.

(c) *R.* v. *Simon* (1982) 49 NSR (2d) 566 (SC, AD)

HART JA concurred with MACDONALD JA

MACDONALD JJA: The appellant is an Indian within the meaning of s. 2(1) of the *Indian Act*, RSC 1972 c. I-6. He was convicted by His

Honour Judge R.E. Kimball, a judge of the Provincial Magistrate's Court, of two violations of s. 150(1) of the *Lands and Forests Act*, RSNS 1967, c. 151, namely, that on September 21, 1980:

(1)   at West Indian Road, Hants County, Nova Scotia (he) did unlawfully commit the offence of illegal possession of shotgun cartridge loaded with shot larger than AAA, and

(2)   at West Indian Road, Hants County, Nova Scotia (he) did unlawfully commit the offence of illegal possession of rifle during closed season.

The appellant now appeals against these convictions by way of stated case.

The relevant portions of the case stated by Judge Kimball are:

FACTS

At the trial on March 18, 1981, the defence admitted the following facts:

1.   That James Matthew Simon, the accused herein is a registered Indian under the Indian Act and is an adult member of the Shubenacadie — Indian Brook Band of Micmac Indians and is a member of the Shubenacadie Band Number 02 at all relevant times hereto.

2.   That James Matthew Simon was, on September 21st, 1980, at or about three-thirty, p.m., the driver of a Chevrolet one-half ton four wheel drive truck, Nova Scotia license plate number 85192A and was the only occupant therein and was driving on the West Indian Road, a public highway in Colchester County, Province of Nova Scotia, which road is not in an Indian reserve, but is adjacent to the Shubenacadie Indian Reserve.

3.   That James Mathew Simon was found in possession of an operable .243 calibre rifle with scope and a leather shell container with six live and two spent .243 calibre shells and two live twelve guage shotgun shells loaded with shot, larger than size AAA and during closed season, all within the meaning of section 150(1) of the Lands and Forests Act, RSNS all other provisions of the said act and the regulations made pursuant to the said act.

4.   It is also agreed that the rifle and all shells have been in the continuous and exclusive possession of the RCMP from September 21st, 1980 to the date of trial inclusive.

5.   That the rifle was test fired by Corporal Phillip Campbell, of the RCMP, a firearm expert, and was found to be operable.

6.   That the live shells were also examined by Corporal Phillip Campbell and were found to be operable and that all shells were so examined and were found to have been ejected from the rifle

chamber and not its magazine, and that the two spent shells had been fired from the rifle.

7. That James Matthew Simon had no license or other authority, permitting him to be in possession of the rifle and shells and shotgun cartridges, under the *Lands and Forest Act*.

8. That the said West Indian Road passes through or by a forest, wood, or other resource frequented by moose or deer.

9. That all the essential elements of the charges herein are admitted by the defendant.

The defendant relied on the terms of the *Treaty of 1752* arguing that paragraph 4 thereof granted to him immunity from prosecution from the provisions of section 150

(1) of the *Lands and Forest Act*.

I assumed that the *Treaty of 1752* was a valid Treaty and that the defendant, James Matthew Simon, is a direct descendant of the parties to the *Treaty of 1752*.

My decision, based largely on *R.* v. *Isaac* (1975), 13 NSR (2d) 460; 9 APR 460 (NSCA) concluded:

I am satisfied that any right which the defendant may have to hunt off the reserve is not applicable to the area where the offence took place. It is my opinion that any right which the defendant may have to hunt on that said land has been extinguished "by Crown grant to others or by occupation by the white man." There is little evidence as to the nature of the area in question, but the admitted facts establish that the defendant was at the material time the only occupant driving on the West Indian Road, a public highway in Colchester County, Province of Nova Scotia and that the road is not in an Indian Reserve but adjacent to the Shubenacadie Indian Reserve. I am satisfied that the area in question is an area which has been occupied extensively by the white man for farming as a rural mixed-farming and dairy-farming area. I am prepared to take judicial notice of the fact that the area is made up of land where the right to hunt no longer exists because the land has been settled and occupied by the white man for purposes of farming and that the Crown grants have been extended to farmers for some considerable length of time so that any right which might have at one time existed to the defendant or his ancestors, to use or occupy the said lands for purposes of hunting, has long since been extinguished.

The question stated for our opinion is:

Did I err in law in holding that the *Treaty of 1752* did not exempt the accused Micmac Indian from the provisions of section 150(1) of the *Lands and Forest Act*.

Section 150(1) of the *Lands and Forests Act* is contained in Part III thereof. In *R.* v. *Paul and Copage* (1977), 24 NSR (2d) 313; 35 APR 313, I said on behalf of the court (pp. 319, 320):

> In my view Part III of the *Lands and Forests Act* is valid provincial legislation as being designed basically for the protection of game within the province and thus comes within s. 92(13) and (16) of the *British North America Act*, its effect upon Indians, *off a reserve*, over whom the Parliament of Canada has exclusive jurisdiction under s. 91(24) of the *British North America Act*, being only incidental to its true object. Therefore, Indians on lands other than 'Indian lands' are subject to the *Lands and Forests Act*, such legislation not being a law that deals with Indians *qua* Indians.

See also *R.* v. *Julian* (1978), 26 NSR (2d) 156; 40 APR 156.

Counsel for the appellant however says that the foregoing authorities are not conclusive of the issue here, because the appellant is protected against the *Lands and Forests Act* and other provincial acts of general application by a so-called Treaty of Peace and friendship entered into on November 22, 1752 by Governor Hopson of the Province of Nova Scotia and His Majesty's Council and Major Jean Baptiste Cope, Chief Sachem of the tribe of Mick Mack Indians inhabiting the eastern coast of Nova Scotia and Andrew Halley Martin and Francis Jeremiah, members and delegates of the same tribe. Article 4 of this Treaty stated that "the said tribe of Indians shall not be hindered from, but have free liberty to hunt and fish as usual."

Counsel for the appellant contends that this is a treaty within the meaning of s. 88 of the *Indian Act* and that it consequently renders the appellant immune from the provisions of the *Lands and Forests Act*.

Section 88 of the *Indian Act* reads as follows:

> 88 Subject to the terms of any treaty and any other act of the Parliament of Canada, all laws of general application from time to time in force in any province are applicable to and in respect of Indians in the province, except to the extent that such laws are inconsistent with this act or any order, rule, regulation or bylaw made thereunder, and except to the extent that such laws make provision for any matter for which provision is made by or under this act.

Since the judgment of the Supreme Court of Canada in *R.* v. *George*, [1966] SCR 267; [1966] 3 CCC 137, it is clear that s. 88 refers only to provincial laws of general application and that federal legislation can override the terms of any Indian treaty.

Provincial laws of general application thus cannot affect treaty protected rights provided the treaty is one within the meaning of s. 88. If it is not, then provincial laws of general application will prevail against it.

In *R.* v. *Syliboy*, [1929] 1 DLR 307; 50 MPR 389, Acting County Court Judge Patterson held that the *Treaty of 1752* was not in reality a treaty not being made between competent contracting parties. At p. 396 of the MPR he said:

> . . . in my judgment the Treaty of 1752 is not a treaty at all and is not to be treated as such; it is at best a mere agreement made by the Governor and council with a handful of Indians giving them in return for good behaviour, food, presents, and the right to hunt and fish as usual — an agreement that, as we have seen, was very shortly after broken.

The correctness of Judge Patterson's characterization of the 1752 Treaty as being at best simply an agreement he had some doubt case upon it by the British Columbia Court of Appeal in *R.* v. *White and Bob* (1965), 50 DLR (2d) 613, affirmed 52 DLR (2d) 481. In that case a broad interpretation was given to the word treaty in s. 88 of the *Indian Act*. The document was informal and unclear as to the exact capacity of its signatory; by such document Indians sold lands to the Hudson Bay Company on the understanding *inter alia* that "we are at liberty to hunt over the unoccupied lands, and to carry on our fishing as formerly." The court held that it was a s. 88 treaty even though it possibly only recognized pre-existing privileges. Chief Justice Davey said at p. 616:

> . . . in my opinion an exception, reservation or confirmation is as much a term of a Treaty as a grant, (I observe parenthetically that a reservation may be a grant), and the operative words of the section will not extend general laws in force in any Province to Indians in derogation of rights so excepted, reserved or confirmed.

The *1752 Treaty* was commented upon by this court in *Isaac* v. *The Queen* (1975), 13 NSR (2d) 460; 9 APR 460, and in *R.* v. *Cope*. [Excerpts from *Isaac* and *Cope* deleted.]

How can the Treaty of November 22, 1752 continue to have any effect after May 1753 when Jean Baptiste Cope and his band flagrantly breached it by killing six Englishmen at Jeddore? Beamish Murdoch: *History of Nova Scotia*, vol. II, pp. 222-23 states:

> On the 16 May, 1753, at the request of Joseph Cope, the son of J.B. Cope, the Indian who called himself major, a small sloop was sent by the government to convey them home, and to remove the provisions given them from Jeddore. In this vessel were Mr Bannerman, Mr Samuel Cleveland, one Anthony Casteel, and four bargemen. They

sailed accordingly at once, and arrived at Isidore (Jeddore) the next day. There they were civilly treated by the Indians, major Cope telling them he would write to his brother, the governor. When they had near finished the business they were sent upon, Mr Bannerman, with four hands, went ashore in his boat, and was surprized and taken prisoner with his people. Immediately afterwards the Indians came on board the sloop, after firing several shots at them. They then seized Mr Cleveland and Casteel. They decided to spare Casteel, who called himself a Frenchman. The others they killed with their hatchets and took off their scalps. Cope boasting of his being a good soldier, in conducting this enterprise and distressing the English. Casteel was carried by the Indians by the river Shubenacadie to Cobequid, thence to Tatamagouchie and Remsek; thence they were carred to by Verte, at a French fort there called Gasparo. He was examined as to the state of the English settlements at Halifax and Lunenburg. Casteel was after this ransomed for 300 livres, from the Indians, by Jacques Morris, a French inhabitant, and sent to Louisbourg, where he arrived 16 June. There he was closely examined by the governor, count Raymond, and after that subjected to interrogatories by M. Loutre, who treated him with very abusive language, and inveighed bitterly against Mr. Cornwallis, and said that if the English governor wanted a peace, he ought to write to him, and not treat with the tail of Indians, — that the English might build forts but he would torment them with his Indians. Casteel got a pass from the governor, and was allowed to return to Halifax. The vessel in which Bannerman, Cleveland and others, were sent to Jeddore, was destroyed by the Indians. This vessel had belonged to one Henry Ferguson and Cleveland. The council gave £25 to Ferguson, and the same sum to the widow, Sarah Cleveland, for their interests in the vessel. They also voted £30 to the widow Cleveland and her children, as a gratuity, and £30 to the two sisters of Mr James Bannerman, who was murdered at the same time, and £30 to Anthony Casteel who went in the vessel by the governor's orders.

In *R.* v. *Syliboy*, *supra*, Judge Patterson said (p. 393 MPR):

. . . the ink was not much more than dry on the Treaty when Indians led by a son of Cope (let us hope not that son to whom the complacent Governor had sent a laced hat as a present) were carrying on in the characteristic Indian way a war against Britain. It was the very Indians who were parties to the Treaty that were responsible for the repeated raids upon Dartmouth, (2 Murdoch's History, p. 231), and it is a well-known and established fact that right down until the Treaty of Paris put an end to the war between England and France the

Indians were on the side of France and were carrying on way in her behalf.

Would that clause in the Treaty guaranteeing them the right to hunt be in consequence put an end to, or would it be merely suspended? Mr. McLennan as I have pointed out argues it would put an end to, but I am inclined to hold it would only be suspended.

In commenting on Judge Patterson's conclusion that the actions of the Indians would only suspend the operation of the treaty, N.A.M. MacKenzie in an article published in (1929) 7 CBR 561 said at pp. 565-66:

The effect of a subsequent war on the terms of a treaty depends, as His Honour correctly states, on the kind of treaty it is. Some treaties are abrogated by war. Others are merely suspended. In this case as the hunting concession was granted the Indians in return for their good behaviour their breach of its terms would seem to terminate, automatically, the obligation of the other party and John Cope's heirs would not have any valid claim under it.

Mr MacKenzie relied on the statement in *Hall-International Law* (8th Ed.), p. 379 *et seq*, and quoted as follows: "A treaty becomes void when an express condition, upon which the continuance of the obligation of the treaty is made to depend, ceases to exist". With such proposition I agree.

There can be no doubt that the *Treaty of 1752* was one of peace. In my opinion, the resumption of hostilities by the Indians in Nova Scotia terminated automatically and for all time any and all obligations to them under such peace treaty.

If I am wrong in my conclusion that the *Treaty of 1752* was terminated by the actions of the Indians, then I am of the opinion that in order for the respondent here to claim its protection he would have to establish a connection by descent or otherwise with the original group of Indians with whom the treaty was made. This he has not done; although Judge Kimball said he assumed Mr Simon "was a direct descendant of the parties to the Treaty". When one considers the number of regional treaties entered into with the Indians in Nova Scotia before and after 1752, it certainly is a valid requirement to demand proof of an ancestral connection between those claiming protection under the treaty and the signatories thereto. In *Simon* v. *The Queen* (1958), 124 CCC 110 (NBCA), McNair, CJNB, said at p. 113 in referring to the *Treaty of 1752*:

. . . having regard to the language of the Treaty, we are satisfied with the correctness of the view taken by Patterson, acting County Court

Judge, that the Treaty, was not made with the Micmac Nation or Tribe as a whole but only with a small group of Micmac Indians inhabiting the eastern part of what is now the Province of Nova Scotia with their habitat in or about the Shubenacadie area . . . The appellant made no effort to establish any connection, by descent or otherwise, with the original group of Indians with whom the 1752 Treaty was made.

I would summarize my conclusions as follows:

1.   This court held in *R.* v. *Paul and Copage* (1977), 24 NSR (2d) 313; 35 APR 313, that Indians on lands other than "Indian Lands" are subject to the *Lands and Forests Act* — I am not in the least persuaded that such position is incorrect.
2.   It is extremely doubtful whether the *Treaty of 1752* is one within the meaning of s. 88 of the *Indian Act* — assuming it is it was terminated in 1753 by the Indians with whom it was made by their resumption of hostilities against the English.
3.   In any event the *Treaty of 1752* cannot be called in aid by the respondent because he has not established any connection by descent or otherwise with the original group of Indians with whom the treaty was made.

I would accordingly answer the question submitted for our opinion in the negative, dismiss the appeal and affirm the convictions.

JONES JA: I have had the privilege of reading the decision of Mr Justice Macdonald. It is clear from the cases to which he has referred, and having regard to the history and development of the Province, that any rights of Indians to hunt and fish under the terms of any treaty or otherwise have been restricted to reserve lands as stated in *Isaac* v. *The Queen*, 13 NSR (2d) 460. Certainly no such rights have been recognized since the decision in *R.* v. *Syliboy*, 50 MPR 389.

As pointed out by Mr Justice Macdonald, under s. 88 of the *Indian Act* the *Lands and Forests Act* applies to Indians subject to the terms of any treaty. In claiming exemption from the general law the burden was on the defendant. There was absolutely no evidence to show that the appellant was entitled to or was exercising "the free liberty to hunt and fish as usual" under the terms of the treaty of 1752 when he was apprehended.

I would accordingly dispose of the appeal as proposed by Macdonald JA.

Appeal dismissed.

Notes

1. Leave to appeal was granted by the Supreme Court of Canada on 10 May 1982. The case is not expected to be heard until the Fall of 1984.
2. Macdonald JA notes the reference by MacKeigan, CJNS in *Isaac* to a series of treaties from April 1753 to August 1763 with other Micmac groups in Nova Scotia. He does not attach any significance to these documents, even though they postdate the 22 November, 1752 treaty. A suggestion raised by the Nova Scotia Micmacs is that the 1752 treaty might be a "head" treaty to which the series of documents from 1753 to 1763 are adhesions. MacKeigan CJNS's source, Beamish Murdock, *A History of Nova Scotia or Acadia* (Halifax: James Barnes, 1866) is silent on any connection between these later treaties and that of 1752, although the 1760 treaty for LaHave, Shubenacadie and Musquodoboit is said to be "based on those of 1725 and 1749." Further archival research would be useful. How should we treat the fact that the English continued to deal with groups of Nova Scotia Micmacs after the so-called "resumption of hostilities"?
3. The value of accurate historical information is again shown by Macdonald JA's reliance upon Murdock's description of the May 1753 killing by Cope of six Englishmen at Jeddore. Murdock presents this Indian action as unprovoked. Another source, L.F.S. Upton, *Micmacs and Colonists: Indian-White Relations in the Maritimes 1713-1867* (Vancouver: University of B.C. Press, 1979) presents a different summary, at pp. 54-55:

> The first apparent break in Micmac resistance came shortly after Peregrine Hopson succeeded Cornwallis as governor. On 14 September 1752 Major Jean-Baptiste Cope of the Shubenacadie band appeared before the council and proposed that "the Indians should be paid for the land the English had settled upon in this Country." He spoke, he said, for the forty men he had under him and offered to contact other bands to bring about a full-scale conference at Halifax. Two days later the council replied, studiously ignoring any question of paying for the land. They pointed out instead that they were all the children of King George and that the Indians had acknowledged him as their great chief and father. The English promised not to interfere with the Indians' hunting and fishing and said they would not "meddle with the lands where you are." If Cope wished to settle at Shubenacadie, he was free to do so. The governor would open a truckhouse where his band could trade at fair prices. Cope should spread this good news around and would receive handsome presents on his return; indeed, there would be annual presents for all the Indians as long as they behaved themselves.
>
> Governor Hopson expected little to come of this conference, but Cope returned in November to conclude a formal agreement. The treaty of 1726 was confirmed and all recent warlike events "buried in Oblivion with the Hatchet." The English gave their friendship and protection, and presents of blankets, tobacco, powder and shot were promised for each October first "so long as they Continue in Friendship." The band was to enjoy "free Liberty of Hunting & Fishing as usual," and the Indians were invited to come to Halifax at any time for trade. The *Treaty or Articles of Peace and Friendship* was quickly embodied in a printed proclamation to ensure the widest distribution. Hopson gave the band, now ninety persons strong, provisions for six months, a costly business, he admitted to his superiors, "but as the French have done it we cannot be behind hand with them, when indeed we ought to outbid." The Lords of Trade expressed great satisfaction and entirely agreed that presents were necessary. The money would have to come from economies elsewhere in the province, such as taking the soldiers off rations during the summer months.
>
> News of the treaty naturally provoked French indignation. Maillard wrote of the

"faux frères," and Prevost at Louisbourg denounced the "mauvais Micmac" named Cope and the "mauvais sujets" who had ratified the treaty. But these worries proved premature; the treaty was soon wiped out by a deed of revenge. On 15 April 1754 two sailors arrived at Halifax carrying six Indian scalps. The men said that they were the survivors of a ship's crew that had been seized by Indians and that they had escaped when they caught their captors off guard. The truth was totally different, for the two men had been on a schooner that had robbed the Indians of forty barrels of government provisions at Jeddore. A short while later the crew was shipwrecked, and the two survivors were taken in and cared for by friendly Indians whom they murdered for the scalp money. Such treachery required vengeance. On 16 May Cope's son requested the use of a government ship to move provisions given the Indians from Jeddore. A sloop was accordingly sent, and the crew was civilly received ashore by Cope. Then, without warning, the whole party was seized and killed with the exception of the Acadian pilot. He was taken to Cobequid where Cope threw his copy of last year's treaty into the fire "telling him that was the way they made Peace with the English." The first exercise in Anglo-Micmac peacemaking had come to a dramatic end.

In November, 1754, Charles Lawrence succeeded Hopson as governor. His attitude was soon put to the test, for two Cape Sable Indians came to Halifax to say that their band, sixty in number, was in great distress since their friendship with the English meant they got no supplies from the French. Despite the Cope débacle, the council decided to send them food, blankets, powder, and shot. The fact that the English were still ready to treat with the Indians and at last had presents to back up their words continued to worry the French. Governor Duquesne at Quebec decided that he must see to it that negotiations were broken off, that the Indians were pushed "à frapper sans qu'il paraisse que cela vienne de moy." But the time for French leadership was fast running out. [Footnotes deleted]

Murcock, *supra*, vol. II, pp. 19-20, presents only the view of the two sailors, Connor and Grace, that they had been attacked by the Indians first.

4. In addition to the fact that the English continued to solicit Indian friendship and entered into the treaties of peace referred to, what is the effect on the Treaty of 1752 of the statement in the Belcher Proclamation of 1762, *supra*, that His Majesty is "determined upon all Occasions to support and protect the Indians in their just Rights and Possessions and to keep inviolable the treaties and Compacts which have been entered into with them?"
5. What is the effect of the statement in the Royal Proclamation of 1763 that "it is just and reasonable, and essential to an Interest, and the Security of our Colonies, that the several Nations or Tribes of Indians, with whom We are connected, and who live under our Protection, should not be molested or disturbed in the Possession of such Parts of Our Dominions and Territories as, not having been ceded to or purchased by Us are reserved to them, or any of them, as their Hunting Grounds . . .?"
6. In *R*. v. *Paul* (1980), 30 NBR (2d) 545, [1981] 2 CNLR 83 (CA), a case that considered the treaties of 1725, 1752 and 1779, Ryan JA, dissenting in part, was of the view that the Treaty of 1752 was available to render the appellant immune from prosecution for an offence under the Game Act (New Brunswick), Hughes, CJNB (Bugold JA concurring) held that the Treaty of 1779 recognized pre-existing hunting and fishing rights, which continue today, beyond provincial control, on Micmac reserves between Cape Tormentine and Bay De Chaleur. *R*. v. *Atwin and Sacobie*, [1981] 2 CNLR 99 (New Brunswick Provincial Court) applied the Treaty of 1752 to acquit the two accused of offences under the Game Act (NB) related to hunting muskrat for food about one-quarter mile off a reserve. A similar and very extensive decision was rendered in *R*. v. *Polchies* (1981), 37 NBR (2d) 546 (Prov. Ct.) where Harper J at p. 587 held that because of such

things as the Royal Proclamation of 1763 and the treaties of 24 September 1778 and 1779 the accused Maliseet Indians could hunt for food upon all undeveloped land in New Brunswick upon which any ordinary hunter would have the right to enter for the purpose of hunting. In *obiter*, Harper J said that this right would apply equally to Micmacs as well as Maliseets and to "any other North American Indian of any tribal origin who choose to hunt within the borders of the Province of New Brunswick." Compare these two recent off-reserve cases with *R*. v. *Perley* (1982), 37 NBR (2d) 591 (Prov. Ct.), where Tomlinson J at p. 600 held that the "right to hunt or fish by Indians is restricted to the right to hunt and fish for food on Reserve lands only, subject to any legislative controls that the Parliament of Canada may impose."

7. Two other decisions of the Nova Scotia Supreme Court, Appeal Division, decided in the period between the *Isaac* and the *Simon* cases, deal with off-reserve hunting rights: *R*. v. *Paul and Copage* (1977), 24 NSR (2d) 313 and *R*. v. *Julian*, [1977] 1 CNLR 66, 26 NSR (2d) 156. Both cases hold that the Indians accused were, in their off-reserve activities, subject to the provisions of the Lands and Forests Act (Nova Scotia). Neither case, however, deals with treaty rights or the relationship between treaties in Nova Scotia and s. 88 of the Indian Act.

(d) *R*. v. *Taylor and Williams* (1981), 34 OR (2d) 360 (CA).

The judgment of the Court was delivered by

MACKINNON ACJO: — The respondents, Indians by definition under the *Indian Act*, RSC 1970, c. I-6, s. 2(1), were charged and convicted of taking bullfrogs during the closed season established under provincial legislation of general application. The respondents successfully argued on appeal to the Divisional Court [55 CCC (2d) 172] that by virtue of s. 88 of the *Indian Act* and a treaty that the Chiefs of their tribe had entered into with His Majesty The King in 1818, the provincial legislation did not apply to them. Section 88 reads:

88. Subject to the terms of any treaty and any other Act of the Parliament of Canada, all laws of general application from time to time in force in any province are applicable to and in respect of Indians in the province, except to the extent that such laws are inconsistent with this Act or any order, rule, regulation or bylaw made thereunder, and except to the extent that such laws make provision for any matter for which provision is made by or under this Act.

The Divisional Court were also of the view that a 1923 treaty may have extinguished all fishing, hunting and trapping rights of the Indians in Ontario, and, accordingly, while agreeing with the respondents on the major issue before them, sent the matter back for a new trial to deal with the effect of the 1923 treaty. Counsel for the Crown advised us that if we agreed with the Divisional Court as to the effect of the 1818 treaty, he was not requesting a new trial to consider the effect of the 1923 treaty.

I

Ontario Reg. 576 of 1976 [now RRO 1980, Reg. 406] passed pursuant to s. 74 [rep. & sub. 1980, c. 47, s. 27] of the *Game and Fish Act*, RSO 1970, c. 186 [now RSO 1980, c. 182], for the first time introduced throughout Ontario a closed season on the hunting of bullfrogs, commencing October 16, 1976 and ending June 30, 1977. The closed season thereafter ran from October 16th of one year until June 30th of the following year.

On June 11, 1977, the respondents took 65 bullfrogs from the waters of Crowe Lake in the Township of Belmont in the County of Peterborough. It is agreed that the bullfrogs were taken from unoccupied Crown lands being the navigable waters of Crowe Lake. It is also agreed that the respondents took the bullfrogs for food for their families and not for any commercial purposes.

II

The respondents are descendants and members of the Indian tribes who were parties to Articles of Provisional Agreement (as it was described in its opening words) entered into at what is believed now to be Port Hope, Ontario on November 5, 1818, between the Honourable William Claus, Deputy Superintendent General of Indian Affairs, on behalf of His Majesty, and six chiefs of the Chippewa Nation, inhabiting the back parts of the New Castle District. The document is known as Treaty No. 20. By this Provisional Agreement the Indians ceded a tract of land containing about 1,951,000 acres to the Crown. The bullfrogs taken by the respondents were within the area covered by this treaty. After setting out the names of the parties and describing the lands to be surrendered, the treaty went on to say:

> And the said Buckquaquet, Pishikinse, Pahtosh, Cahgahkishinse, Cahgagewin and Pininse, as well for themselves as for the Chippewa Nation inhabiting and claiming the said tract of land as above described, do freely, fully and voluntarily surrender and convey the same to His Majesty without reservation or limitation in perpetuity.

The consideration for the conveyance was "yearly, and in every year, forever, the said sum of seven hundred and forty pounds currency in goods at the Montreal price, which sum the said Chiefs and Principal People, parties hereunto, acknowledge as a full consideration for the lands hereby sold and conveyed to His Majesty". In 1821 the consideration was restated as "being at the rate of ten dollars for each individual now living". The payments have long since ceased. The question is whether there was other, and for the Indians, more material consideration given to them, namely the reservation to them and their descendants of their aboriginal fishing and hunting rights.

A council meeting between the Deputy Superintendent of Indian Affairs and the chiefs of the six tribes who were parties to the Provisional Agreement was held the same day as the Provisional Agreement. The council meeting both preceded and followed the signing of the Provisional Agreement. Counsel for both parties to this appeal agreed that the minutes of this council meeting recorded the oral portion of the 1818 treaty and are as much a part of that treaty as the written articles of the Provisional Agreement. As these minutes are central to the issue of this appeal, they must be recited in whole:

> Minutes of a Council held at Smiths Creek, in the Township of Hope on Thursday the 5th of November 1818, with the Chippewa Nation of Indians, inhabiting & claiming a Tract of Land situate between the Western Boundary Line of the Midland District & the Eastern Boundary Line of the Home District, & extending Northerly to a Bay at the Northern Entrance of Lake Simcoe in the Home District
> Present
> The Honbl W. Claus Dep. Supt. General of Indian Affairs
> I. Givins Esq. Supt. of Indian Affairs for the Port of York
> W. Hands, Clerk Indn. Dept.
> W. Gruet, Interpreter
> After the usual ceremonies the Dep. Supt. General addressed the Chiefs as follows:
> Children. I salute you in behalf of your Great Father & condole with you for the loss you have met with since I last met you — it is the will of the Great Spirit to remove our nearest & dearest connexions, we must submit to his will & not repine.
> I should have seen you before this, but I have had business with others of your Nation which has kept me until this day. My errand is, to put at rest the doubts with respect to the Lands in the back parts of this Country which you seem to think were never disposed of to the King, & hope that hereafter none of your young men will be so idle as to remove the Posts or marks which will be put up by the Kings Surveyors. Your Great Father has directed me to lay before you a sketch of the Country in the back of this & you will point out to me the Land as far as the last purchase was, from the Waters edge from the Great lake.
> Children. You must perceive the number of your Great Fathers children about here have no home, & out of pity for them, he wishes to acquire Land to give to them — He is charitable to all, does not like to see his Children in distress. Your Land is not all that he has been purchasing, he has looked to the setting of the Sun, as well as to the rising, for places to put his Children, & when he asked your Country from you, he does not mean to do as formerly, to pay you at once, but as long as any of you remain on

the Earth to give you Cloathing [*sic*] in payment every year, besides the presents he now gives you. You will go to your Camp & consult together & when you have made up your minds come & let me hear what it is

Buckquaquet, Principal Chief addressing the Dept. Supt. general, said

Father. We have heard your words, & will go to our Camp & consult & give your an answer to the request of our Great Father — But, Father, our Women & Children are very hungry, and desired me to ask you to let them taste a little of our Fathers Provisions & Milk —

After their return, Buckquaquet continued

Father. You see me here, I am to be pitied, I have no old men to instruct me. I am the Head Chief, but a young man. You must pity me, all the old people have gone to the other world. My hands are naked, I cannot speak as our Ancestors were used to.

Father. If I was to refuse what our Father has requested, our Women & Children would be more to be pitied. From our Lands we receive scarcely anything, & if your words are true we will get more by parting with them, than by keeping them — our hunting is destroyed, & we must throw ourselves on the compassion of our Great Father the King.

Father. Our young People & Chief have always thought of not refusing our Father any request he makes to us, & therefore do what he wishes.

Father. If it was not for our Brethren the Farmers about the Country we should near starve for our hunting is destroyed.

Father. *We hope that we shall not be prevented from the right of Fishing, the use of the Waters, & Hunting where we can find game. We hope that the Whites who are to come among us will not treat us ill*, some of young men are giddy, but we hope they will not hurt them.

Father. *The young men. I hope you will not think it hard at their requesting, that the Islands may be left for them that when we try to scratch the Earth, as our Brethren the Farmers do, & put any thing in that it may come up to help our Women & Children*

Father. *We do not say that we must have the Islands, but we hope our Father will think of us & allow us this small request* — this is all we have to say —

To which the Dept. Supt. general replied

Children — I have heard your answer, & in the name of your Great Father thank you for the readiness with which you have complied with his desire. Your words shall be communicated to him. *The request for the Islands, I shall also inform him of, & have no doubt*

*but that he will accede to your wish. The Rivers are open to all &
you have an equal right to fish & hunt on them.* I am pleased to
learn from you, that your Brothers the Whites have been so kind to
you & hope those that will come among you will be as charitable.
Keep from Liquor, & your young men will not be giddy. It is the
ruin of your Nation. As soon as I get your Numbers you shall get
something to eat, & some Liquor. Do not expect much, for I have
so great a dread of it that I am at all times disinclined to give you
any. We will now sign the Paper, it is merely to shew your Great
Father our work, & when he agrees to our proceeding, you will
then have to sign another paper which Conveys the Country we
now talk about to him, & the first payment will be made, an equal
quantity of which you will receive every year —————

(Emphasis added.)

III

Cases on Indian or aboriginal rights can never be determined in a
vacuum. It is of importance to consider the history and oral traditions of
the tribes concerned, and the surrounding circumstances at the time of
the treaty, relied on by both parties, in determining the treaty's effect.
Although it is not possible to remedy all of what we now perceive as
past wrongs in view of the passage of time, neverthless it is essential
and in keeping with established and accepted principles that the courts
not create, by a remote, isolated current view of past events, new
grievances.

In the instant appeal, both counsel were in agreement that we could,
and indeed should, look at the history of the period and place, and at the
Papers and Records of the Ontario Historical Society dealing with this
particular treaty and the persons involved in it. The Crown was of the
view that a historical analysis of the times and conditions supported its
position that the Indians intended to surrender their hunting and fishing
rights. Counsel for the respondents took the contrary view.

IV

In interpreting the treaty, accordingly, it is appropriate to have regard to
the following matters. First, the tribes who were parties to the treaty had
hunted and fished in the area covered by the treaty, and had taken
bullfrogs for food there since earliest memory. It is part of the oral
tradition of the tribes that this right was not only recognized at the time
of the treaty, but that they continued to exercise the right without
interruption up until the present. The respondents' evidence as to the
oral traditions of the Indian tribes concerned was accepted by the trial
judge and was not disputed by the Crown.

Secondly, it appears that one of the reasons for the Crown entering into the treaty was to facilitate Crown grants of land to settlers who were arriving in the county in 1818. From the histories of the period, it is clear that the early settlers in the area were in difficult material circumstances. Edwin Guillet in his book *Early Life in Upper Canada* (1933), in describing the conditions at the time of the treaty wrote at p. 62:

> The first in Peterborough County to be surveyed was Smith, in 1818, and in that year a number of English immigrants from Cumberland made their way thither via Rice Lake and the Otonabee River. They erected a temporary log house near the site of the city of Peterborough, and all lived in it until a small shanty had been built on each lot. They suffered great privations before they were able to grow potatoes and wheat on a few small patches of cleared land.

That the early settlers found themselves in adverse circumstances is also evident from the minutes of the council metting quoted above wherein Mr Claus addressed the Indian chiefs as children and advised them that the "Great Father" wished to acquire land for the settlers who had no home and were in distress.

The minutes also make it clear that the Indians were equally suffering great privation at the time. The chiefs, through their spokesman, addressed Claus as "Father" and before they retired to consider the request of their Great Father, advised Claus that their women and children were very hungry and desired some of their "Fathers Provisions & Milk". We were advised that, historically, the Indian used the word "milk" to mean rum. Claus, in his reply, advised them that he would give them some liquor but also told them not to expect much as he dreaded the effect on them. After the Indians returned from their consultation, the spokesman said he was a head chief but a young man with his "hands naked", which could be taken to mean that he had no wampum which was a further indication of the dire circumstances of the Indians. The histories of the period indicate that the beaver hunting in the area had been destroyed and the Indians greatly relied on beaver skins for trading. As a result, as he said, they received scarcely anything from the lands and "we must throw ourselves on the compassion of our Great Father the King . . . Our young People & Chief have always thought of not refusing our Father any request he makes to us, & therefore do what he wishes."

Finally, it should be noted that William Claus, who represented The King, is described in vol. XXV of the Papers and Records of the Ontario Historical Society published by the society in 1929 as "a valuable and highly esteemed public servant" who "made at least seven of the treaties of surrender of lands with the Indians from 1798 to 1818'', and who ''because of his familiarity with the Indians in all their ways and with their language, and his kindly attitude toward them, was trusted by them and exceptionally successful in dealing with them for the Crown''.

V

The respondents argue that a proper interpretation of the treaty, when the relationship between the Crown and the Indians and their necessitous circumstances at the time is considered, is that the agreement and reassurance contained in the minutes was a clear reservation to the Indians of their time-honoured rights to hunt and fish over the lands now conveyed to the Crown — certainly so long as they were held by the Crown. If that is so then it follows, they submit, that the treaty comes within the opening words of s. 88 of the *Indian Act*.

The words that have caused the difficulty and which have to be interpreted in deciding whether the treaty reserved to the Indians the right to hunt and fish are the following (emphasized in the earlier quotation):

The Indian spokesman said:

Father. We hope that we shall not be prevented from the right of Fishing, the use of the Waters, & Hunting where we can find game

. . .

Father. The young men, I hope you will not think it hard at their requesting, that the Islands may be left for them that when we try to scratch the Earth, as our Brethren the Farmers do, & put any thing in that it may come up to help our Women & Children.

Father. We do not say that we must have the Islands, but we hope our Father will think of us & allow us this small request. . . .

To these particular requests, Claus replied:

The request for the Islands, I shall also inform him of, & have no doubt but that he will accede to your wish. The Rivers are open to all & you have an equal right to fish & hunt on them.

The request and the assurance were given before the treaty was signed. From the treaty it can be seen that there was no reservation established for the Indians. It is clear, on the other hand, that both parties expected the Indians to remain on the lands conveyed as the Indian spokesman said, ''We hope that the Whites who are to come among us will not treat us ill, some of [the Indian] young men are giddy, but we hope they will not hurt them.'' No exception was taken to this statement by Claus but rather he said, ''I am pleased to learn from you, that your Brothers the Whites have been so kind to you & hope *those that will come among you* will be as charitable.'' (Emphasis added.)

If the Indians were to remain in the area one wonders how they were to survive if their ancient right to hunt and fish for food was not continued. Be that as it may, the question to be answered is whether this treaty can be interpreted so as to limit the applicability of the Ontario *Game and Fish Act* which, it is agreed, is a law of general application.

The principles to be applied to the interpretation of Indian treaties have been much canvassed over the years. In approaching the terms of a treaty quite apart from the other considerations already noted, the honour of the Crown is always involved and no appearance of "sharp dealing" should be sanctioned. Mr Justice Cartwright emphasized this in his dissenting reasons in *R. v. George*, [1966] SCR 267 at p. 279, 55 DLR (2d) 386, [1966] 3 CCC 137, where he said:

> We should, I think, endeavour to construe the treaty of 1827 and those Acts of Parliament which bear upon the question before us in such manner that the honour of the Sovereign may be upheld and Parliament not made subject to the reproach of having taken away by unilateral action and without consideration the rights solemnly assured to the Indians and their posterity by treaty.

Further, if there is any ambiguity in the words or phrases used, not only should the words be interpreted as against the framers or drafters of such treaties, but such language should not be interpreted or construed to the prejudice of the Indians if another construction is reasonably possible: *R. v. White and Bob* (1964), 50 DLR (2d) 613 at p. 652, 52 WWR 193 (BCCA); affirmed [1965] SCR *vi*, 52 DLR (2d) 481*n* (SCC).

Finally, if there is evidence by conduct or otherwise as to how the parties understood the terms of the treaty, then such understanding and practice is of assistance in giving content to the term or terms. As already stated, counsel for both parties to the appeal agreed that recourse could be had to the surrounding circumstances and judicial notice could be taken of the facts of history. In my opinion, that notice extends to how, historically, the parties acted under the treaty after its execution.

In my view, all the principles recited lead to the conclusion that the terms of the treaty, which include the oral terms recorded in the minutes, preserve the historic right of these Indians to hunt and fish on Crown lands in the lands conveyed and fall under the exception established by the opening words of s. 88 of the *Indian Act*.

The Crown's position was simply that "the terms of the treaty" did not preserve or grant the right to fish and hunt on Crown lands inconsistent with the application of provincial laws. The surrender of the Indian lands to the Crown, counsel submitted, included a surrender of their aboriginal hunting and fishing rights. Once it is accepted that the minutes of the council meeting between the representative of the Crown on the one hand and the Indian chiefs on the other is part of the treaty, it cannot be successfully argued that Treaty No. 20 is "silent" on the question of the right to hunt and fish.

With respect to the oral representation made in answer to the "hope" expressed by the Indians that they would not be prevented from hunting and fishing, it is argued that that representation was only to advise the Indians that they were to have an equal right with all others and was not a preservation of special rights. The transcript of the minutes cannot and should not be analyzed in minute detail. The use of certain words and their conciliatory tone only serve to emphasize the disparity in the positions of the two parties to the treaty, but do not lessen the force of the request nor the right to be attached to the assurance — quite the contrary.

The Indians' request for the continued right to hunt and fish was put on a higher plane than their request for the islands. In making their request for the islands their spokesman said "We do not say that we *must* have the Islands". (Emphasis added.) No such qualification or limitation was put on their request that their traditional and historic right to hunt and fish for food continue. The representative of the Crown was clearly not intending to put any limitation on the rights of the Indians by saying that the rivers were open to "all" and that the Indians had an "equal" right to fish and hunt. These words immediately follow his dealing with the Indians' request for the islands to which he replied that no doubt "[your Great Father] will accede to your wish." It seems to me that rather than putting a limitation on the Indians' ancient right, William Claus, whose integrity was respected by the Indians, was emphasizing that that right would continue. The accepted evidence was that this understanding of the treaty has been accepted and acted on for some 160 years without interruption. In my view, it is too late now to deprive these Indians of their historic aboriginal rights: *R.* v. *White and Bob* at pp. 648-49 DLR.

VI

The Divisional Court held, as secondary support for its conclusion, that the native hunting and fishing rights were confirmed by the *Royal Proclamation of 1763* [reprinted in RSC 1970, Appendices, p. 123]. Their conclusion was that for the Indians to lose those rights, they had to be taken away by the specific terms of a treaty. The Court [at p. 179] concluded that the provincial laws of general application dealing with hunting and fishing do not apply to Indians "because of the Royal

Proclamation which preserves those rights independent of s. 88.''

In view of my conclusion on the other aspect of this appeal, it is not necessary for me to come to any final conclusion on this secondary ground used by the Divisional Court to support its conclusion. However, I must say that I have serious reservations as to the correctness of their view of the *Royal Proclamation* and its relationship to s. 88 of the *Indian Act* and I am not to be taken as agreeing with the members of the Divisional Court on this particular point.

VII

As noted at the beginning of these reasons, there no longer is any request that consideration be given to the 1923 treaty and, accordingly, the appeal is dismissed without any reference back to the County Court as directed by the Divisional Court. I think it is appropriate in this type of case to ask the Crown to pay the costs of the respondents on a solicitor-and-client basis.

Appeal dismissed.

Note

1. Leave to appeal to the Supreme Court of Canada was refused on 21 December 1981.

(e) *Pawis* v. *The Queen* (1979), 102 DLR (3d) 602 (Fed. Ct., TD)

MARCEAU J: — These four actions were heard together, on common evidence. Not only are they related, they are identical as to their significant facts (which are uncontested), the legal issues involved (breach of contract, breach of trust, negligent misrepresentations) and the reliefs sought (general, special and punitive damages).

Each plaintiff is an Ojibway Indian, a registered member of a Band of Ojibways and a resident of an Indian reservation. Lawrence Pawis belongs to the Shawanaga Band and lives on the Shawanaga Reserve; Clarence E. Boyer is a Mississaugi Band member and resides on the Mississaugi #8 Reserve; Eli and Godfrey McGregor, uncle and nephew, are both of the Whitefish River Band and both reside on the Whitefish River Reserve.

During the years 1975 and 1977, at different dates and places, the four plaintiffs went through similar unfortunate experiences. While fishing on the waters bordering their respective reserves, they were apprehended by fishery officers and charged under various sections of the *Ontario Fishery Regulations*, SOR/63-157 [now CRC 1978, c. 849], enacted pursuant to the *Fisheries Act*, RSC 1970, c. F-14. They were later convicted by a Provincial Court, their equipment was

confiscated and they were fined. Pawis had breached s-s. 4(5) [enacted
SOR/68-135, s. 2 (now s-s. 4(6)] of the said Regulations by fishing
yellow pickerel with a spear during a closed season, while the others
had contravened s-s. 12(1) [rep. & sub. SOR/68-135, s. 5] by using a
gill net without the authority of a licence. At the time of their offences,
the plaintiffs were fishing for food for themselves and other members of
their respective bands, at a place where they had often fished in the past
and in a manner which was customary to them. Of course, the
experience was determinative for each of them: since their convictions,
the plaintiffs have abided by the Regulations.

The plaintiffs, however, did not see fit to leave things as they stood.
They thought that they had always had the right to fish where they were
and as they pleased. Their convictions under the *Ontario Fishery
Regulations* convinced them that that right had somehow been taken
away from them. They decided to seek relief in Court and commenced
the present proceedings by filing their respective statements of claim in
March, April and May, 1978.

The plaintiffs are not acting in a representative capacity nor are their
actions class actions. Each one is individually and personally suing the
defendant, Her Majesty the Queen in right of Canada, claiming for
himself, general, special and punitive damages. The four actions are,
however, based on the same alleged causes and the paragraphs relating
thereto are identically framed in the four declarations. I think it proper
to reproduce these paragraphs *verbatim* (with the numbering used in the
Pawis and McGregor actions):

3. On the 9th day of September, 1850, at Sault Ste. Marie, in the
Province of Canada, an agreement was entered into between the
Honorable William Benjamin Robinson, of the one part, on behalf of
Her Majesty the Queen, and Shinguacouse Nebenaigoching,
Keokouse, Mishequonga, Tagawinini, Shabokishick, Dokis,
Ponekeosh, Windawtegowinini, Shawenakeshick, Namassin,
Naoquagabo, Wabakekik, Kitchpossigun by Papasainse, Wagemaki,
Pamequonaisheung, Chiefs; and John Bell, Paqwatchinini,
Mashekyash, Idowekesis, Waquacomick, Ocheek, Metigomin,
Watachewana, Minwawapenasse, Shenaoquom, Oningegun,
Panaissy, Papasainse, Ashewasega, Kageshewawetung, Shawone-
bin; and also Chief Maisquaso (also Chiefs Muckata, Mishoquet, and
Mekis), and Mishoquetto and Asa Waswanay and Pawiss, principal
men of the Ojibewa Indians, inhabiting and claiming the Eastern and
Northern Shores of Lake Huron, from Pentanguishine to Sault Ste.
Marie, and thence to Batchewanaung Bay, on the Northern Shore of
Lake Superior; together with the Islands in the said Lakes, opposite to
the Shores thereof, and inland to the Height of land which separates
the Territory covered by the charter of the Honorable Hudson Bay

Company from Canada; as well as all unconceded lands within the limits of Canada West to which they have any just claim, of the other part, which agreement expressly provided the following.

That for, and in consideration of the sum of two thousand pounds of good and lawful money of Upper Canada, to them in hand paid, and for the further perpetual annuity of six hundred pounds of like money, the same to be paid and delivered to the said Chiefs and their Tribes at a convenient season of each year, of which due notice will be given, at such places as may be appointed for that purpose, they the said Chiefs and Principal men, on behalf of their respective Tribes or Bands, do hereby fully, freely, and voluntarily surrender, cede, grant, and convey unto Her Majesty, her heirs and successors for ever, all their right, title, and interest to, and in the whole of, the territory above described, save and except the reservations set forth in the schedule hereunto annexed; which reservations shall be held and occupied by the said Chiefs and their Tribes in common, for their own use and benefit . . ..

. . . . .

"And the said William Benjamin Robinson of the first part, on behalf of Her Majesty and the Government of this Province, hereby promises and agrees to make, or cause to be made, the payments as before mentioned; and further to allow the said Chiefs and their Tribes the full and free privilege to hunt over the Territory now ceded by them, and to fish in the waters thereof, as they have heretofore been in the habit of doing . . ..

4.   The Honourable William B. Robinson, signatory to said Treaty on behalf of Her Majesty the Queen, submitted a report to the Honourable Colonel Bruce, Superintendent-General of Indian Affairs dated September 24, 1850, wherein it was stated:

In allowing the Indians to retain reservations of land for their own use I was governed by the fact that they in most cases asked for such tracts as they had heretofore been in the habit of using for purposes of residence and cultivation, and by securing these to them and the right of hunting and fishing over the ceded territory, they cannot say that the Government takes from their usual means of subsistence and therefore have no claims for support, which they no doubt would have preferred, had this not been done.

6.   The Agreement or the Treaty entered into on September 9, 1850, and referred to in paragraph 3 herein is binding on the Crown.

7.   The Agreement or the Treaty dated September 9, 1850, and referred to in paragraph 3 herein has not been repudiated or renegotiated by the Crown.

8.   The Crown, through Ministers of the Crown, has on a number of occasions recognized the lawful obligations imposed on the Crown by treaties entered into with the Indian people such as the one set out in paragraph 3 herein.

9.   On or about the 8th day of August, 1973, the then Minister of Indian Affairs and Northern Development published the following statement in Ottawa:

> Many Indian groups in Canada have a relationship with the Federal Government which is symbolized in Treaties entered into by those people with the Crown in historic times. As the Government pledged some years ago, lawful obligations must be recognized. This remains the basis of Government policy.

10.   On or about January 21, 1976, the then Minister of Indian Affairs and Northern Development in a letter to Chief Flora Tabobondung of Parry Island Indian Band in reply to a petition presented to His Excellency the Governor General by 15 Indian Chiefs from the Lake Huron area stated as follows:

> While the Federal Government's policy is to honour the spirit and the letter of all its treaty obligations towards the Indian people, we have concluded that we cannot open the treaties to renegotiation.

15.   By enacting the Ontario Fishery Regulations under the Fisheries Act, the Crown breached and contravened treaty and contractual obligations which were solemnly undertaken and entered into in the Lake Huron Treaty of 1850 referred to in paragraph 3 herein.

16.   The Plaintiff has suffered damage resulting from the interference with his right of fishing by reason of the actions of the Crown.

17.   The Plaintiff relied to his detriment on the statements made by the authorized representatives of the Crown set out in Paragraphs 8, 9 and 10.

18.   The actions by the Crown constitute a breach of the contractual and trust obligations toward the Ojibway people solemnly undertaken in the Lake Huron Treaty of 1850.

Before embarking upon an analysis of the claims, I wish to repeat here what I had occasion to say in open Court at the closing of the hearing, however obvious it may be. This is a Court of law. As a Judge of this Court, I am not called upon to pass judgment on the legitimacy of the Indian people's grievances as these have been lately so often formulated. I must leave to others the task to deal properly and fairly with the so-called "Indian cause" in all its political and social aspects. The question for me today is not whether the Indians have been unfairly treated; it is whether, on the facts herein alleged, judicial redress can be had against the federal Crown. My responsibility is strictly to dispose of the four actions as they stand and to do so I cannot go beyond asking whether there is a legal and enforceable obligation on the part of the defendant to make good the claims for damages asserted therein.

There is one cause of action clearly pleaded: breach of contract. The plaintiffs say that, by enacting the *Ontario Fishery Regulations* under the *Fisheries Act* without exempting the Ojibway Indians from their application, the Crown breached the contractual obligations it had undertaken in the Lake-Huron Treaty of 1850. A second cause of action is brought in to supplement the first one: breach of trust. The plaintiffs say that the Crown in the Lake-Huron Treaty took upon itself trust obligations respecting the privilege granted to the Ojibway Indian people, which obligations it failed to perform. A third and subsidiary cause of action is said to flow from the allegations contained in paras. 8, 9, 10 and 17 of the declarations: negligent misrepresentation. The plaintiffs say that they acted to their detriment on statements made by authorized representatives of the Crown.

Obviously these three causes of action are linked to one another, so in dealing at length with the first one I will be led to make comments which will apply to the others. Nevertheless, since they bring into play different legal rules and principles, they must be considered separately.

1. *The issue of breach of contractual obligations*

Some preliminary remarks ought to be made to clarify and circumscribe the issue here.

(i) It is obvious that the Lake-Huron Treaty, like all Indian treaties, was not a treaty in the international law sense. The Ojibways did not then constitute an ''independent power'', they were subjects of the Queen. Although very special in nature and difficult to precisely define, the Treaty has to be taken as an agreement entered into by the Sovereign and a group of her subjects with the intention to create special legal relations between them. The promises made therein by Robinson on behalf of Her Majesty and the ''principal men of the Ojibewa Indians'' were undoubtedly designed and intended to have effect in a legal sense and a legal context. The agreement can therefore be said to be tantamount to a contract, and it may be admitted that a breach of the promises contained therein may give rise to an action in the nature of an action for breach of contract.

(ii) It is common ground that the Lake-Huron Treaty is still binding on the Crown: it has not been renegotiated or repudiated by the Crown.

(iii) Section 91(12) of the *British North America Act, 1867* assigned to the federal Crown control over and responsibility for inland fisheries. The first *Fisheries Act* was enacted by Parliament in 1868 (RSC 1886,

c. 95). Pursuant to the provisions of that Act, the Governor in Council was given the authority and the duty to make Regulations for the purpose of management and conservation of fisheries within the limits of the various Provinces. The *Ontario Fishery Regulations* are the regulations which were thus adopted under the authority of the *Fisheries Act* for the purpose of management and conservation of fisheries within the limits of of Province of Ontario. These Regulations were first enacted in 1889; they have been revised several times since, the last revision having occurred on May 9, 1963 (PC 1963-709, SOR/63-157). It must be noted that the provisions of the *Ontario Fishery Regulations* enacted in 1963 under which the plaintiffs were charged and convicted — namely, s. 12 thereof which prohibits certain types of fishing except under a licence and s. 4(5) which establishes closed seasons — were not new: all of the previous sets of Regulations contained provisions substantially to the same effect. The fishery officers responsible for the enforcement of the Regulations are employed by the provincial Government but are of course acting as agents of the federal Crown. Although the Regulations have always been formally made applicable to the Indians (definition of "person" in s. 3 (VA)), prior to their apprehension the plaintiffs themselves, and the members of their respective bands, had not been disturbed by fishery officers with respect to their way of fishing.

(iv) The plaintiffs do not challenge the validity of the *Fisheries Act* or its *Ontario Fishery Regulations*. They readily admit that the power of Parliament to legislate could not be impeded by the terms of any treaty or agreement entered into by the executive branch of the State. They do not overlook the well-known basic constitutional principle that the sovereignty of Parliament cannot be fettered: *A-G BC* v. *Esquimalt & Nanaimo R. Co.*, [1950] 1 DLR 305, [1950] AC 87, [1949] 2 WWR 1233 (P.C.).

With these precisions in mind, the legal reasoning on which the actions rest, in so far as they are based on an alleged breach of contract, is easier to understand. It can be formulated as follows. While the fisheries legislation is undoubtedly valid, the passing of such legislation by the federal Crown and its implementation against the Indians were made contrary to an obligation undertaken in the Treaty and constituted therefore a breach of contract for which the plaintiffs themselves are personally entitled to damages. Three propositions are put forward in that reasoning, to wit: (a) that the Crown assumed in the Treaty an obligation not to regulate the fishing of the Ojibway Indians; (b) that the passing of the Regulations constituted a breach of that obligation for which damages are recoverable in a Court of law by the other party to the contract; and (c) that, as a result of such a breach, the plaintiffs, who are "the other party to the contract", have suffered a loss and are personally entitled to be indemnified therefor. Each of these three propositions must of course be verified in order for the reasoning as a whole to be acceptable. I will therefore consider them in order.

(a) The first proposition implies that, by granting the Indians "the full and free privilege to hunt over the territory now ceded by them, and to fish in the waters thereof, as they have heretofore been in the habit of doing", the Crown was, as a consequence, assuming formally the obligation not to regulate in any way the manner in which such fishing was to be done. This I cannot accept.

First, I do not think that, properly understood, the words used convey the broad and unlimited meaning that would otherwise be necessary. I agree that the word "full", in the context, is difficult to define; but if it seems to connote a plenary quality, a completeness of the right, it is, in my view, strictly as regards the right of the owner or possessor of the land. As to the word "free", to me it simply means that no consideration is to be exacted from those entitled to hunt and fish in exercise of the right. In fact, it is not so much the words "full and free' than the expression "as they have heretofore been in the habit of doing" that was invoked by counsel in support of the plaintiffs' basic contention. But the expression, as I understand it, does not refer to the methods used but to the purpose for which the activity was carried on. It refers to the extent of the hunting and fishing. The right is not restricted to hunting and fishing for sport. Nor are there words expressly referring to it as hunting and fishing commercially. The right is defined by reference to what the tribes had theretofore been in the habit of doing. What that may have been may be lost in obscurity but it is nevertheless the extent of the right. The words have nothing to do with the manner of fishing. Such interpretation, it seems to me, is the most reasonable one since any other would have the effect of limiting the Indians, in the exercise of their privilege, to the means of fishing and hunting that were theirs in 1850. And it is the interpretation that is in better conformity with the statements made by the signatory to the Treaty in his report referred to in para. 4 of the plaintiffs' declaration reproduced above. In brief, I agree with counsel for the defendant that the wording does not import any intention that there be unrestricted rights and perpetuity to fish regardless of the general laws regulating the means of hunting and fishing.

But, be that as it may, even if the wording were taken as conveying an unambiguous unlimited meaning, leaving no room for interpretation, I would still believe that a restriction with respect to eventual general regulations would have to be inferred and supplied, in like manner that clauses that are customary or necessary are supplied in ordinary contracts between individuals. Since it is clear that, in 1850, the Crown could not legally bind itself to not enact legislation regulating methods of fishing, the promises made in the Treaty, so far as they were intended to have effect in a legal sense and a legal context, could not legally be made otherwise than subject to possible future regulations. Counsel for the plaintiffs made a great deal of the fact that in subsequent treaties, especially the so-called "numbered treaties", entered into by the Crown with other Indian Bands, the similar granting of hunting and fishing privileges was always expressly made "subject to such regulations as may from time to time be made by Her Government of Her Dominion of Canada": in my view, such a proviso had the great advantage of expressing clearly the rule of law and avoiding all possible misunderstanding or eventual impression of deceit, but legally speaking it did not add anything. The right acquired by the Indians in those treaties was, in the Canadian legal system, necessarily subject in its exercise to restriction through acts of the Legislature, just as the person who acquires from the Crown a grant of land is subject in its enjoyment to such legislative restrictions as may later be passed as to the use which may be made of it.

In brief, I do not think that in the Lake-Huron Treaty, the Crown undertook an obligation to keep the privilege of hunting and fishing granted to the Indians immune from any general regulations governing the exercise thereof.

(b) The second proposition raises the question of whether, assuming that the Treaty was meant to confer a privilege of hunting and fishing that could not be restricted by any laws relating to management and conservation, the enactment of the fisheries legislation amounted in law to a breach of contract giving rise to an action for damages sustainable in a Court of law?

My answer to this question is simple. I cannot understand how the legal enactment by Parliament of a particular piece of legislation can give rise to an action for damages against the Crown for breach of contract. How can a legal act be at the same time an act to be sanctioned as an illegal breach of contract? If a debtor is liable to pay damages when he fails to perform his contractual obligation, it is because the law does not approve of such conduct and forces him to pay the loss resulting from his failure. The debtor brought upon himself the reprobation of the law. He will not be so liable if the inexecution of the obligation was caused by an unavoidable and irresistible force, independent of his own conduct, for instance supervening illegality, unless he has obliged himself thereunto by the special terms of the contract. The Crown cannot be treated here as having brought upon itself the reprobation of the law.

The cause of action I am dealing with here, must it be reminded, is that of breach of contract. The plaintiffs are not claiming that they are entitled to compensation because the legislation had the effect of taking away their property. That would be a completely different matter, although I doubt that such a claim could have been sustained since the mere regulating of the exercise of the privilege to fish and hunt does not result in the taking away of the privilege itself amounting to a dispossession of property. As was said by Wright J, in *France Fenwick & Co. Ltd.* v. *The King*, [1927] 1 KB 458 at p. 467, in a passage that was cited with approval by the majority of the Judicial Committee in *Government of Malaysia* v. *Selanger Pilot Ass'n*, [1977] 2 WLR 901 at p. 909:

> I think, however, that the rule can only apply (if it does apply) to a case where property is actually taken possession of, or used by, the Government, or where, by the order of a competent authority, it is placed at the disposal of the Government. A mere negative prohibition, though it involves interference with an owner's enjoyment of property, does not, I think, merely because it is obeyed, carry with it at common law any right to compensation. A subject cannot at common law claim compensation merely because he obeys a lawful order of the State.

In my view, the enactment of the fisheries legislation may perhaps have been invoked by the Ojibway Indians as calling for a renegotiation of the Lake-Huron Treaty, but it could not give rise to an action for damages in a Court of law for breach of contract.

(c) Coming to the last proposition on which the plaintiffs' legal reasoning relies, I find it likewise unacceptable. Even if it could have been said that the enactment of the *Fisheries Act* and the Regulations applicable to Ontario amounted to a breach of contract for which the Crown is liable in damages, the plaintiffs, in my view, would not have been individually and personally entitled to obtain the relief they seek today. My reasons here are twofold.

On the one hand, the plaintiffs would not, it seems to me, have had the status to sue as individuals. The Treaty, by its terms, is made with the Ojibway people collectively. Those Indians who signed the Treaty are referred to in it as "principal men of the Ojibewa Indians". The Treaty provides for the annuity payments to be made "to the said Chiefs and Tribes". The surrender is referred to in the Treaty as being by the "the said Chiefs and Principal men, on behalf of their respective Tribes or Bands". It is stated that the lands reserved "shall be held and occupied by the said Chiefs and their Tribes in common, for their own use and benefit". The Treaty allows "the said Chiefs and their Tribes the full and free privilege to hunt over the Territory now seeded [*sic*] by them, and to fish in the waters thereof, as they have heretofore been in the habit of doing". The Schedule of Reservations describes each as being for one of "the Chiefs or Principal men and his Band". Although each individual Ojibway Indian was to benefit from the Treaty, it seems to me that the language used therein precludes the idea that each individual was a party to the contract and had therefore the status to sue personally and individually for an alleged breach thereof. Since the Treaty was negotiated and entered into with the Ojibway Indians taken as a group, it seems to me that an action based on the Treaty, alleging breach of the promises subscribed therein toward the group, could only be instituted by the contracting party itself, that is to say, the group. Of course, I am not saying that the collectivity of all living Ojibway Indians can be as such the owner of rights; I am not overlooking the fact that it has no legal personality. What I mean is that, the Treaty having been negotiated and entered into with the Chiefs in the name of all of the members of their bands, it could not then be contemplated that a right of action for eventual breach thereof was to accure to each Ojibway Indian, and each of his descendants, individually and personally.

On the other hand, the Court cannot entertain today an action whose cause occurred as far back as 1868, when the first *Fisheries Act* was enacted, or 1889 when the first *Ontario Fishery Regulations* were made. The plaintiffs contend that their actions were commenced within the time limited by law (namely, the *Limitations Act*, RSO 1970, c. 246), since they were denied the privilege allegedly granted to them by the Treaty and suffered the damage for which they seek compensation, only when they were apprehended by the fishery officer, charged, and finally convicted. Such a contention is unacceptable. If it can be argued that the privilege granted by the Treaty was intended to be unconditional, it certainly cannot be denied that from the moment the legislation was passed the situation changed. The act complained of which removed the privilege occurred at that moment, and the limitation period therefore started then. The Indians were legally bound to abide by the Regulations regardless of the inaction of the fishery officers. The plaintiffs themselves never enjoyed that "unconditional privilege" to fish they say their forefathers had been given by the Treaty. The breach of contract they allege, and the damage they say was thereby caused to the Ojibways, occurred long before they were born.

From the foregoing discussion, one can only conclude that on the basis of breach of contract, the actions are ill-founded. Indeed, there was no breach of a contractual obligation, such a breach, if it had occurred, would not have given rise to a right of action for damages and, in any event, if the right existed, the plaintiffs would not have been personally entitled to exercise it.

2. *The issue of breach of trust obligations*

The basic suggestion here is that the Lake-Huron Treaty of 1850 created a trust, the subject-matter of which was the "full and free privilege to hunt over the territory now ceded by them and to fish in the waters thereof as they have heretofore been in the habit of doing''. It is, however, a suggestion that I am again unable to accept.

There is no doubt that the Crown can take upon itself trust obligations which are enforceable in a Court of Equity: *Tito* v. *Waddell (No. 2)*, [1977] 3 All ER 129. It is equally true that no specific form of words is necessary to create a trust, and that a treaty of that nature ought to be liberally construed. But I fail to see how one can find here the prerequisites for the existence of a proper trust that may be the subject-matter of an action before a Court. As was said by Cannon, J., in *M.A. Hanna Co.* v. *Provincial Bank of Canada*, [1935] 1 DLR 545 at p. 565, [1935] SCR 144 at p. 167:

> To completely constitute a trust, four elements are required:
> (a) A trustee;
> (b) A beneficiary;
> (c) Property the subject-matter of the trust;
> (d) An obligation enforceable in Court of Equity on the trustee to administer or deal with the property for the benefit of the beneficiary. There must be an equitable interest based on a conscientious obligation which can be enforced against the legal owner of the property alleged to be the subject-matter of the trust. Otherwise there is no trust.

How can the privilege to hunt and to fish be the ''property of a trust''? There is no subject-matter here capable of being ''held'' or ''administered'' by a trustee for the benefit of a beneficiary. Unless the lands said to be ceded, were to be considered as being the trust property? That suggestion, however, cannot hold since there never has been any doubt that the title to the lands was already vested in the Crown before 1850, and the Treaty cannot be construed as purporting to recognize in favour of the Indians a right different in nature than that of a licensee.

In *A.G. Can.* v. *A.G. Ont; A.G. Que.* v. *A.G. Ont.*, [1897] AC 199, the Judicial Committee of the Privy Council, in deciding questions that turned upon the construction of the very treaty which forms the subject-matter of this trial, and its sister-treaty, the Lake-Superior Treaty, arrived at the following conclusion [at p. 213]:

> Their Lordships have had no difficulty in coming to the conclusion that, under the treaties, the Indians obtained no right to their annuities, whether original or augmented, beyond a promise and agreement, which was nothing more than a personal obligation by its governor, as representing the old province, that the latter should pay the annuities as and when they became due; that the Indians obtained

no right which gave them any interest in the territory which they surrendered, other than that of the province; and that no duty was imposed upon the province, whether in the nature of a trust obligation or otherwise, to apply the revenue derived from the surrendered lands in payment of the annuities.

That case was concerned with the payment of the annuities promised in the treaties but it seems to me that the same reasoning must apply with respect to the other promise contained therein, that is the promise of a licence to fish and hunt.

In my view, it cannot be said that, by entering into the Lake-Huron Treaty, the Crown took upon itself a trust obligation. I mean, of course, a trust obligation in the technical sense. The expression "trust obligations" is sometimes used to refer to "governmental obligations" and in that sense it may perhaps be properly applied to the obligations created by the Treaty. But "trust obligations" of that type are not enforceable as such. The distinction between trust obligations enforceable in the Courts of Chancery and these governmental or trust obligations in the higher sense is referred to by Lord Selborne, LC, in *Kinloch* v. *Secretary of State for India* (1882), 7 App. Cas. 619 at pp. 625-6:

> Now the words "in trust for" are quite consistent with, and indeed are the proper manner of expressing, every species of trust — a trust not only as regards those matters which are the proper subjects for an equitable jurisdiction to administer, but as respects higher matters, such as might take place between the Crown and public officers discharging, under the directions of the Crown, duties or functions belonging to the prerogative and to the authority of the Crown. In the lower sense they are matters within the jurisdiction of, and to be administered by, the ordinary Courts of Equity; in the higher sense they are not.

(See also *Tito* v. *Waddell (No. 2)* referred to above.)

In any event, assuming that true trust obligations were in fact created by the Treaty, the problem would remain as to the content thereof and the nature of the duties imposed on the Crown as trustee. Much of what I said in analyzing the contractual obligation of the Crown would simply have to be repeated, and the conclusion would be the same. The facts do not support the allegation of a breach of trust giving rise to an action for damages.

3. *The issue of negligent misrepresentation*

In four paragraphs of their declarations (8, 9, 10 and 17) the plaintiffs state that they relied to their detriment on statements made in 1973 and 1977 by former Ministers of Indian Affairs to the effect that the policy of the Government was to "recognize the lawful obligations imposed on the Crown by treaties entered into with the Indian people".

I do not accept the contention of counsel for the plaintiffs that these allegations raised a third and different cause of action, that of negligent misrepresentation by authorized representatives of the defendant. It is not pleaded that the statements were made either negligently or with intention to deceive but only that the statements were made and relied upon with resulting detriment and that, in my view, was not sufficient to properly raise the issue. But, in any event, it is clear to me that the actions would have had no chance of success on that basis. Leaving aside the question of whether the Crown can be held vicariously liable for allegedly negligent political statements made by its Ministers, I simply believe that the statements referred to were not misrepresentations. They were not inaccurate nor were they misleading. They could not be taken as overriding a legislation that had been in existence for so long, and they were not meant to, nor could they be construed as, inducing the Indians to disobey the law. Besides, as mentioned above, it was part of the plaintiffs' cases that they had always fished the way they were fishing when they were apprehended: they can hardly pretend that they were really influenced by the statements, and were then behaving as they were in view of what they had been told to be the policy of the Government.

I can see no substance whatever in the contention that an action for damages against the Queen could lie as a result of the above-mentioned statements referred to in the declaration.

For all the foregoing reasons, I must conclude that none of the three causes of action alleged by the plaintiffs can be sustained. Counsel for the plaintiffs presented the cases as being novel in the long series of unsuccessful attempts made by the Indians in their quest to seek judicial redress for the allegedly unfair treatment to which they have been subjected in the past. Unfortunately, he failed to convince me that the new approach adopted had any more merit in law.

The actions will therefore be dismissed. I see no reason why the defendant should be deprived of her costs, if she demands them, although of course, there shall be only one set of Court costs for the four actions.

Actions dismissed.

Endnotes

1. An appeal was filed with the Federal Court of Appeal. No date has been set for hearing the appeal and the case is inactive.
2. Section 35(1) of the Constitution Act, 1982 provides: "The existing aboriginal and

treaty rights of the aboriginal peoples of Canada are hereby recognized and affirmed.'' What meaning does this constitutional statement have? Does the existence of federal legislation that the courts have held to supercede treaty rights, like the Fisheries Act, mean that treaty rights to this extent are not ''existing'' as of April 1982? Can new encroachments on treaty rights be now effected by simple federal legislation? Or are Indian treaty rights as they existed in April 1982 now entrenched from unilateral federal action without a constitutional amendment? See K.M. Lysyk, ''The Rights and Freedoms of the Aboriginal Peoples of Canada'' in W.S. Tarnopolsky and G-A. Beaudoin (eds.), *The Canadian Charter of Rights and Freedoms: Commentary* (Toronto: The Carswell Co. Ltd., 1982).

8. Further reading

The Canadian Indian: Quebec and the Atlantic Provinces (Ottawa: Department of Indian Affairs and Northern Development, 1973).

Green, L.C., ''Legal Significance of Treaties Affecting Canada's Indians'' (1972), 1 *Anglo-Am. L. Rev.* 119.

Green, L.C., ''Canada's Indians: Federal Policy, International and Constitutional Law'' (1970), 4 *Ottawa Law Rev.* 101.

Knoll, D., ''Treaty and Aboriginal Hunting and Fishing Rights'', [1979] 1 CNLR 1.

Lysyk, K.M., ''The Rights and Freedoms of the Aboriginal Peoples of Canada'' in W.S. Tarnopolsky and G.-A. Beaudoin (eds.), *The Canadian Charter of Rights and Freedoms: Commentary* (Toronto: The Carswell Co. Ltd., 1982).

Lysyk, K.M., ''Indian Hunting Rights: Constitutional Considerations and the Role of Indian Treaties in British Columbia'' (1966), 2 *UBCL Rev.* 401.

McGee, H.F. (ed.), *The Native Peoples of Atlantic Canada* (Ottawa: Carleton Library, 1974).

Murdock, B., *A History of Nova Scotia or Acadia* (Halifax: James Barnes, 1866).

Sanders, D.E. ''Native Rights,'' in *Report of Discussions Legal Status of Indians in the Maritimes* (Halifax: Indian-Eskimo Association of Canada, 1970).

Sanders, D.E., ''Indian Hunting and Fishing Rights'' (1973-74), 38 *Sask. L. Rev.* 45.

Sanders, D.E., ''Aboriginal Peoples and The Constitution'' (1981), 19 *Alta. Law Rev.* 410.

Upton, L.F.S., *Micmacs and Colonists: Indian-White Relations in the Maritimes 1713-1867* (Vancouver: U. of B.C. Press, 1979).

5. Post-Confederation Treaties

NORMAN K. ZLOTKIN

1. The Treaty-Making Process

(a) Introduction: The "Numbered" Treaties

After the Treaty of Paris of February 1763 which confirmed Britain's acquisition from France of Canada, Florida, and the Ohio Valley, the British Government set about pacifying the Indian Tribes. On 7 October, King George III issued the Royal Proclamation of 1763, establishing governments in Quebec and Florida, and outlining future methods of dealing with Indian nations. No settlement was to be allowed west of the American colonies "on pain of our Displeasure". These "Lands and Territories" were to be reserved to the Indians. Within the various "Colonies," lands could only be acquired from the Indian tribes at a public meeting of the tribes in question, which would be conducted by the King's colonial representatives:

> And whereas great Frauds and Abuses have been committed in purchasing Lands of the Indians, to the Prejudice of our Interests, and to the great Dissatisfaction of the said Indians; In order, therefore, to prevent such Irregularities for the future, and to the end that the Indians may be convinced of our Justice and determined Resolution to remove all reasonable Cause of Discontent, We do, with the Advice of our Privy Council strictly enjoin and require, that *no private Person do presume to make any purchase from the said Indians of any Lands reserved to the said Indians, within those parts of our Colonies where We have thought proper to allow settlement*; but that, if at any time any of the said Indians should be inclined to dispose of the said Lands, *the same shall be purchased only for Us, in our Name, at some public Meeting or Assembly of the said Indians, to be held for that purpose by the Governor or Commander in Chief of our Colony respectively within which they shall lie.* (emphasis added)
> (Reprinted in RSC 1970, Appendices, at pp. 127-29.)

Land transactions involving the Indian nations of what is now Canada have followed the procedures originally set down in the Royal Proclamation of 1763. Indian lands have been surrendered only to the Crown's representatives at public meetings of the tribes in question.

The major pre-Confederation transactions with the Indian people of Upper Canada were the Robinson Treaties of 1850. Earlier treaties in what is now

272

southern Ontario had paved the way for agricultural settlement, but settlement was not the motive behind the Robinson Treaties. In 1846, after the discovery of minerals along the north shores of Lakes Huron and Superior, the local Indian people, familiar with the procedures set down by the Royal Proclamation of 1763, petitioned the Governor General of Canada, asking that no mining development take place until after suitable arrangements had been made with them — the true owners of the land. In September 1850, the Honourable W.B. Robinson met with the Chiefs and "Principal men" of the Ojibway Indians at Sault Ste Marie to negotiate what have since been called the Robinson-Huron and Robinson-Superior Treaties.

The Robinson Treaties were the first with the Indian people of Canada to make specific reference to continued hunting and fishing rights within the ceded territory:

> . . . further to allow the said Chiefs and their tribes the full and free privilege to hunt over the territory now ceded by them, and to fish in the waters thereof, as they have heretofore been in the habit of doing, saving and excepting such portions of the said territory as may from time to time be sold or leased to individuals or companies of individuals and occupied by them with the consent of the Provincial Government.
> (Alexander Morris, *The Treaties of Canada with the Indians*, Facsimile Edition, Coles Publishing Co., 1971, pp. 304-09)

The promise of continued hunting and fishing rights was Robinson's rationale for paying less for Indian land than in previous Treaties; the promise would also prevent the Indian people from claiming "that the Government takes from their usual means of subsistence." (Morris, p. 19)

With Confederation, "Indians, and Lands reserved for the Indians" became a federal responsibility under section 91(24) of the British North America Act. The federal government used this constitutional authority to negotiate, between 1871 and 1921, eleven Treaties with Indian people in the northern and western parts of the Dominion of Canada.

All eleven "numbered" Treaties are in essence the same document. In the words of the Honourable Alexander Morris, who negotiated Treaties 3 through 6:

> The treaties are all based upon the models of that made at the Stone Fort in 1871 and the one made in 1873 at the north-west angle of the Lake of the Woods with the Chippewa tribes, and these again are based, in many material features, on those made by the Hon. W.B. Robinson with the Chippewas dwelling on the shores of Lakes Huron and Superior in 1860 [*sic*].
> (Morris, p. 285.)

Although differing in certain details, the "numbered" treaties contain the same core provisions as the Robinson treaties. In exchange for surrendering "all their right and title" to their lands, the Indian people were to receive annuities in perpetuity and "reserves" for their own use. Treaties Nos. 1 to 7 (1871-77), which were designed to open the West to agricultural settlement, were also to provide tools, livestock, and seed grain to those Indian people who took up farming. (Morris, p. 288)

Treaties 3 through 11 also include a guarantee of hunting and fishing rights, which does not appear in Treaties 1 and 2. This is how the clause first appeared in the North-West Angle Treaty (Treaty 3) of 1873:

> Her Majesty further agrees with her said Indians that they, the said Indians, shall have right to pursue their avocations of hunting and fishing throughout the tract surrendered as hereinbefore described, subject to such regulations as may from time to time be made by her Government of her Dominion of Canada, and saving and excepting such tracts as may from time to time be required or taken up for settlement, mining, lumbering or other purposes, by her said Gov't of the Dominion of Canada, or by any of the subjects thereof duly authorized therefore by the said Government.
> (Morris, p. 323.)

In Treaties 8 through 11 (1899-1921), the clause reads this way:

> And Her Majesty the Queen (His Majesty the King) Hereby Agrees with the said Indians that they shall have the right to pursue their usual vocations of hunting, trapping and fishing throughout the tract surrendered as heretofore described, subject to such regulations as may from time to time be made by the Government of the country, acting under the authority of Here Majesty, and saving and excepting such tracts as may be required or taken up from time to time for settlement, mining, lumbering, trading, or other purposes.

Treaties 1 and 2 covering Southern Manitoba (1871) were negotiated by federal Indian Commissioner Wemyss M. Simpson, with the active assistance of Adams Archibald, Lieutenant Governor of Manitoba. (Morris, pp. 25-43.) Treaties 3 and 6 (1873-76) were negotiated by Archibald's successor as Lieutenant Governor, Alexander Morris. As was noted above, in 1880 Morris stated that all subsequent treaties were based on the Robinson Treaties, Treaty 1 and Treaty 3. Although this clause on hunting and fishing rights is much more tightly worded in the "numbered" treaties than in those of 1850, Morris's interpretation of the clause, given in 1880, is much looser. In fact, his interpretation conforms very closely to the wording of the Robinson Treaties:

> In return for such relinquishment [of their lands], permission [was given] to the Indians to hunt over the ceded territory and to fish in the waters thereof, excepting such portions of the territory as pass from the

Crown into the occupation of individuals or others.
(Morris, pp. 285-86.)

Morris's statement confirms a fact which is evident from published accounts of the various Treaty negotiations — that the restrictions on native fishing and hunting as written into the Treaties were not explained to the Indian people. There is no evidence that the Indian people were told their rights were to be

> . . . subject to such regulations as may from time to time be made by her Government of her Dominion of Canada. . . . (Treaties 3, 5, 6)

> or

> . . . subject to such regulations as may from time to time be made by the Government of the country acting under the authority of Her Majesty. . . . (Treaties 4, 7, 8, 9, 10, 11)

There was a twenty-two year hiatus between the "settlement" treaties, 1 to 7, and those that can best be described as the "northern resource development" treaties (8 to 11). In 1899, three Commissioners were appointed by the federal government to negotiate on behalf of Her Majesty the Queen with the "Cree, Beaver, Chipewyan and other Indians" in the Lesser Slave Lake country. This treaty, called Number 8, was thought necessary because of an influx of miners and "other travellers" into the Yukon and Northwest Territories. The Treaty was identical in form to the earlier seven, except that the Commissioners were empowered to offer reserve lands "in severalty" if the Indian people wished it. It is instructive to note the explanation given to the Indian people in 1899 of the standard hunting and fishing rights clause with its "subject to" and "saving and excepting" restrictions:

> Our chief difficulty was the apprehension that the hunting and fishing privileges were to be curtailed. The provision in the treaty under which ammunition and twine is to be furnished went far in the direction of quieting the fears of the Indians, for they admitted that it would be unreasonable to furnish the means of hunting and fishing if laws were to be enacted which would make hunting and fishing so restricted as to render it impossible to make a livelihood by such pursuits. But over and above the provision, we had to solemnly assure them that only such laws as to hunting and fishing as were in the interest of the Indians and were found necessary in order to protect the fish and fur-bearing animals would be made, and *that they would be as free to hunt and fish after the treaty as they would be if they never entered into it*. (emphasis added) (Quoted by Johnson JA in *R.* v. *Sikyea* (1964) 43 DLR (2d) 150, at 153-54.)

Treaties 10 (1906) and 11 (1921), which cover parts of northern Alberta, Saskatchewan and the Northwest Territories, were also negotiated by federal Commissioners. Once again, they followed the usual form, and their clauses on hunting and fishing rights were identical to that in Treaty 8. The Treaty 10 Commissioner, J.J. McKenna, who had been one of the Treaty 8 Commissioners, explained that provision in the following way:

> The Indians seemed afraid, for one thing, that their liberty to hunt, trap and fish would be taken away or curtailed, but were assured by me that this would not be the case, and the Government will expect them to support themselves in their own way, and, in fact, that more twine for nets and more ammunition were given under the terms of this treaty than under any of the preceding ones; this went a long way to calm their fears. I also pointed out that any game laws made were to their advantage, and, whether they took treaty or not, they were subject to the laws of the Dominion.
> (*R.* v. *Sikyea*, 43 DLR (2d) 150, at pp. 158-59.)

Note

1. The complete texts of Treaties 1 to 7 and adhesions thereto are found in Morris, pp. 313-75. The texts of all the number treaties have been published in booklets by the Queen's Printer, Ottawa.

(b) Treaty No. 9 — A Case Study

(i) The Role of the Government of Ontario

Treaty No. 9 follows the standard model of the other numbered treaties, except for the fact that one of the three commissioners was selected by the provincial government. Like the others, it was drafted in its entirety by the federal government. Ontario took part in the negotiations at the very end; the province's major concern, because of an earlier dispute with the federal government over the provisions of Treaty 3, was with the selection of reserve lands.

One of the immediate consequences of Confederation was a dispute between the Dominion government and the government of Ontario over provincial boundaries. Ontario claimed that its western limit extended to the Lake of the Woods (longitude 95° 13' 48''), and its northern boundary to the Albany River — and this territory was awarded to Ontario in 1884 by the Judicial Committee of the Privy Council. But the Dominion still claimed the natural resources of the disputed lands by virtue of its treaty (No. 3) of 1873 with the Indian people of the region. This argument also went to the Privy Council in the case of the St Catharine's Milling Company, given a Dominion licence to cut timber in the Lake of the Woods area. In 1888, the Judicial

Committee of the Privy Council decided in Ontario's favour (*St Catharine's Milling and Lumber Company* v. *The Queen* (1889) 14 App. Cas. 46). An Imperial Act of 1889 — the Canada-Ontario Boundary Act — confirmed the 1884 Privy Council award to Ontario. (52-53 Vic., Cap. 28.)

Although these awards settled the boundary question, Ontario continued to dispute the status of reserve lands granted to the Indians by the Dominion Commissioner in Treaty 3. On 16 April 1894, pursuant to statutes passed by Canada (1891, 54-55 Vic., Cap. 5) and Ontario (54-55 Vic., Cap. 3), entitled "An Act for the settlement of certain questions between the governments of Canada and Ontario respecting Indian lands," the two governments signed a formal agreement on the subject of Treaty 3 reserves. The sixth clause of the agreement also provided:

> That any future treaties with the Indians in respect of territory in Ontario to which they have not before the passing of the said statutes surrendered their claim aforesaid, shall be deemed to require the concurrence of the government of Ontario.

The question of Indian reserve lands was again the subject of an agreement, in July 1902, between counsel on behalf of the Dominion and Ontario, intervening parties upon the appeal to the Judicial Committee of the Privy Council in *Ontario Mining Company* v. *Seybold et al.*:

> As to all Treaty Indian reserves in Ontario (including those in the territory covered by the Northwest Angle Treaty, which are or shall be duly established pursuant to the statutory agreement of one thousand eight hundred and ninety-four), and which have been or shall be duly surrendered by the Indians to sell or lease for their benefit, Ontario agrees to confirm the titles heretofore made by the Dominion and that the Dominion shall have full power and authority to sell or lease and convey title in the fee simple or for any less estate. . . . The question as to whether other reserves in Ontario include precious metals to depend upon the instruments and circumstances and law affecting each case respectively.
>
> (Treaty 9, pp. 27-28)

The Department of Indian Affairs proposed to negotiate Treaty 9 in the autumn of 1904. On 30 April 1904, the Deputy Superintendent General of Indian Affairs, Frank Pedley, wrote to the Ontario Commissioner of Crown Lands outlining the "main Stipulations upon which the treaty would be based":

> It is proposed to offer the Indians a maximum annuity of $4.00 a head and a gratuity at the first payment of the same amount once and for all. It is further proposed to set apart reserves of sufficient area in localities chosen by the Indians with special regard for their needs, which reserves

should be held in trust by this Department, free of any claims of the Province for timber upon, or base or precious metals in, upon or under the soil. These Reserves should be surveyed and confirmed by the Ontario Government within one year after selection by the Indians or at any time after the expiry of one year upon the request of this Department. It is proposed to provide the ordinary educational facilities afforded by day schools to be established upon Reserves. It is contended that as the entire area of the land will, by this treaty, remain with the Province free for all Indian claims, the financial responsibility, as well as the provisions of reserves, should rest with the Province of Ontario. (Sessional Papers, Vol. XL, Part IX, Fourth Session of Eleventh Legislature of the Province of Ontario, Session 1908, letter, 30 April 1904.)

Aubrey White, Assistant Commissioner of Crown Lands, replied to Pedley on 30 May. The reply, drafted by Sir Aemilius Irving, Counsel to the Province, referred specifically to the Agreement of 16 April 1894, respecting future treaties in Ontario, and to the Agreement of 1902 between counsel for Ontario and the Dominion upon the appeal involving *Ontario Mining Co.* v. *Seybold et al.*:

The Government of Ontario does not concede that without its concurrence (and the tenor of your letter may not so imply), the Department of Indian Affairs can promote a treaty with Indians placing the financial responsibility as well as the providing of reserves upon the Province.
(Letter of 30 May 1904.)

Pedley's answer to White, dated 23 June 1904, stated that the documents quoted by White had "not been overlooked":

With due appreciation of the position of the Province of Ontario . . . the opinion might be advanced that the simple concurrence by the Government of Ontario in the maximum terms to be offered under the new treaty and an extension of good will in carrying out these stipulations would be all that this Government could at present expect.
(Letter of 23 June 1904.)

Pedley stressed the urgency of treating with the Indian people that year, and pointed out the bargain the province would receive:

The terms laid down upon which the treaty might be based are the maximum terms which would, in any event, be offered to the Indians. They are in effect the same as those fixed by the Robinson treaty, *and the Government interested might be considered fortunate to cancel the Indian title at this time by considerations which were thought adequate in the year 1850.* (emphasis added)

The province delayed the matter for almost a year, despite frantic pleas from the Department of Indian Affairs to discuss the "New Indian Treaty" (Telegram of 18 March 1905.) After the exchange of several letters, agreement was finally reached on the terms of the proposed treaty, and on 12 June 1905 the Deputy Superintendent General of Indian Affairs sent A.J. Matheson, the Provincial Treasurer, a draft of the "proposed James Bay Treaty":

> I have to draw your attention specially to the clause with reference to reserves and to ask whether these meet with your approval.
> (Letter of 12 June 1905.)

The draft, which is identical to the final version of the Treaty, reads, on the subject of reserves:

> . . . the location of the said reserves having been arranged between His Majesty's Commissioners and the Chiefs and Headmen as described in the schedule of Reserves hereunto attached.
> (Letter of 12 June 1905.)

The rest of the Treaty followed the format of the other "numbered" treaties. The clause on hunting and fishing rights is exactly the same as that of Treaty 8 of 1899.

The Provincial Treasurer outlined yet another obstacle to the Treaty in a letter dated 23 June 1905:

> The Committee of Council thought it well to take the advice of counsel, and we have been strongly advised that in order to prevent future litigation an agreement should be made between the Dominion and the Province defining the liability of the Province in respect to the Treaty.
>
> I enclose herewith draft of amended Order-in-Council and draft of agreement between the Province and the Dominion.
> (Letter of 23 June 1905.)

The draft agreement stated that the province would pay over to the Dominion the amount of annuities, and would agree to the setting aside of reserves, but that all further payments and expenditures would be at the Dominion's expense. In addition, no site suitable for development of water power exceeding 500 H.P. was to be included within the boundaries of any reserve. And the Dominion was to bear the cost of the Treaty, and was to pay the Ontario Commissioner.

On 26 June 1905, the Dominion government agreed to the provincial stipulations, and settled on a per diem of $10.00 for the Ontario Commissioner. The Agreement between Ontario and the Dominion was formally signed on 3 July 1905, and its text is appended to printed copies of Treaty 9. (Treaty 9, pp. 25-27.)

(ii) The "Negotiation" of Treaty No. 9

Letter of Transmission from Treaty Commissioners to the Superintendent General of Indian Affairs, dated 6 November 1905, in *The James Bay Treaty: Treaty No. 9* (Ottawa: Queen's Printer, 1964), pp. 3-11.

SIR, — Since the treaties known as the Robinson Treaties were signed in the autumn of the year 1850, no cession of the Indian title to lands lying within the defined limits of the province of Ontario had been obtained. By these treaties the Ojibeway Indians gave up their right and title to a large tract of country lying between the height of land and Lakes Huron and Superior. In 1873, by the Northwest Angle Treaty (Treaty No. 3), the Saulteaux Indians ceded a large tract east of Manitoba, part of which now falls within the boundaries of the province of Ontario. The first-mentioned treaty was made by the old province of Canada, the second by the Dominion.

Increasing settlement, activity in mining and railway construction in that large section of the province of Ontario north of the height of land and south of the Albany river rendered it advisable to extinguish the Indian title. The undersigned were, therefore, appointed by Order of His Excellency in Council on June 29, 1905, as commissioners to negotiate a treaty with the Indians inhabiting the unceded tract. This comprised about 90,000 square miles of the provincial lands drained by the Albany and Moose river systems.

When the question first came to be discussed, it was seen that it would be difficult to separate the Indians who came from their hunting grounds on both sides of the Albany river to trade at the posts of the Hudson's Bay Company, and to treat only with that portion which came from the southern or Ontario side. As the cession of the Indian title in that portion of the Northwest Territories which lies to the north of the Albany river would have to be consummated at no very distant date, it was thought advisable to make the negotiations with Indians whose hunting grounds were in Ontario serve as the occasion for dealing upon the same terms with all the Indians trading at Albany river posts, and to add to the community of interest which for trade purposes exists amongst these Indians a like responsibility for treaty obligations. We were, therefore, given power by Order of His Excellency in Council of July 6, 1905, to admit to treaty any Indian whose hunting grounds cover portions of the Northwest Territories lying between the Albany river, the district of Keewatin and Hudson bay, and to set aside reserves in that territory.

In one essential particular the constitution of the commission to negotiate this treaty differed from that of others which undertook similar service in the past. One member* was nominated by the province of

Ontario under the provisions of clause 6 of the Statute of Canada, 54-55 Vic., chap. V., which reads: "That any future treaties with the Indians in respect of territory in Ontario to which they have not before the passing of the said Statutes surrendered their claim aforesaid shall be deemed to require the concurrence of the government of Ontario." The concurrence of the government of Ontario carried with it the stipulation that one member of the commission should be nominated by and represent Ontario.

It is important also to note that under the provisions of clause 6 just quoted, the terms of the treaty were fixed by the governments of the Dominion and Ontario; the commissioners were empowered to offer certain conditions, but were not allowed to alter or add to them in the event of their not being acceptable to the Indians.

After the preliminary arrangements were completed, the commissioners left Ottawa for Dinorwic, the point of departure for Osnaburg, on June 30, and arrived there on July 2.

The party consisted of the undersigned, A.G. Meindl, Esq., M.D., who had been appointed to carry out the necessary work of medical relief and supervision, and James Parkinson and J.L. Vanasse, constables of the Dominion police force. At Dinorwic the party was met by T.C. Rae, Esq., chief trader of the Hudson's Bay Company, who had been detailed by the commissioner of the Hudson's Bay Company to travel with the party and make arrangements for transportation and maintenance en route. Mr Rae had obtained a competent crew at Dinorwic to take the party to Osnaburg. The head man was James Swain, an old Albany river guide and mail-carrier, who is thoroughly familiar with the many difficult rapids of this river.

The party left Dinorwic on the morning of July 3, and after crossing a long portage of nine miles, first put the canoes into the water at Big Sandy Lake. On July 5 we passed Frenchman's Head reservation, and James Bunting, councillor in charge of the band, volunteered the assistance of a dozen of his stalwart men to help us over the difficult Ishkaqua portage, which was of great assistance, as we were then carrying a great weight of supplies and baggage. On the evening of the 5th, the waters of Lac Seul were reached, and on the morning of the 6th the party arrived at Lac Seul post of the Hudson's Bay Company. Here the commission met with marked hospitality from Mr J.D. McKenzie, in charge of the post, who rendered every assistance in his power. He interpreted whenever necessary, for which task he was eminently fitted by reason of his perfect knowledge of the Ojibeway language.

The hunting grounds of the Indians who traded at this post had long ago been surrendered by Treaty No. 3, but it was thought advisable to call at this point to ascertain whether any non-treaty Indians had assembled there from points beyond Treaty No. 3, but adjacent to it. Only one family, from Albany river, was met with. The case was fully investigated and the family was afterwards attached to the new treaty.

The afternoon of the 6th was spent in a visit to the Lac Seul reserve in an attempt to discourage the dances and medicine feasts which were being held upon the reserve. The Indians of this band were well dressed, and for the most part seemed to live in a state of reasonable comfort. Their hunting grounds are productive.

The party left Lac Seul on the morning of July 7, en route for Osnaburg passing through Lac Seul, and reached the height of land, via Root river, on July 10. Thence by the waters of Lake St Joseph, Osnaburg was reached on the 11th.

This was the first point at which treaty was to be made, and we found the Indians assembled in force, very few being absent of all those who traded at the post. Those who were absent had been to the post for their usual supplies earlier in the summer, and had gone back to their own territory in the vicinity of Cat lake.

Owing to the water connection with Lac Seul, these Indians were familiar with the provisions of Treaty No. 3, and it was feared that more difficulty might be met with at that point than almost any other, on account of the terms which the commissioners were empowered to offer not being quite so favourable as those of the older treaty.

The annuity in Treaty No. 3 is $5 per head, and only $4 was to be offered in the present instance. The proposed treaty did not provide for an issue of implements, cattle, ammunition or seed-grain.

As there was, therefore, some uncertainty as to the result, the commissioners requested the Indians to select from their number a group of representative men to whom the treaty might be explained. Shortly after, those nominated presented themselves and the terms of the treaty were interpreted. They were then told that it was the desire of the commissioners that any point on which they required further explanations should be freely discussed, and any questions asked which they desired to have answered.

Missabay, the recognized chief of the band, then spoke, expressing the fears of the Indians that, if they signed the treaty, they would be compelled to reside upon the reserve to be set apart for them, and would be deprived of the fishing and hunting privileges which they now enjoy.

On being informed that their fears in regard to both these matters were groundless, as their present manner of making their livelihood would in no way be interfered with, the Indians talked the matter over among themselves, and then asked to be given till the following day to prepare their reply. This request was at once acceded to and the meeting adjourned.

The next morning the Indians signified their readiness to give their reply to the commissioners, and the meeting being again convened, the chief spoke, stating that full consideration had been given the request made to them to enter into treaty with His Majesty, and they were prepared to sign, as they believed that nothing but good was intended. The money they would receive would be of great benefit to them, and the Indians were all very thankful for the advantages they would receive from the treaty.

The other representatives having signified that they were of the same mind as Missabay, the treaty was then signed and witnessed with all due formality, and payment of the gratuity was at once proceeded with.

The election of chiefs also took place, the band being entitled to one chief and two councillors. The following were elected: Missabay, John Skunk and George Wawaashkung.

After this, the feast which usually accompanies such formalities was given the Indians. Then followed the presentation of a flag, one of the provisions of the treaty; this was to be held by the chief for the time being as an emblem of his authority. Before the feast began, the flag was presented to Missabay the newly elected chief, with words of advice suitable for the occasion. Missabay received it and made an eloquent speech, in which he extolled the manner in which the Indians had been treated by the government; advised the young men to listen well to what the white men had to say, and to follow their advice and not to exalt their own opinions above those of meb who knew the world and had brought them such benefits. Missabay, who is blind, has great control over his band, and he is disposed to use his influence in the best interests of the Indians.

At Osnaburg the civilizing work of the Church Missionary Society was noticeable. A commodious church was one of the most conspicuous buildings at the post and the Indians held service in it every evening. This post was in charge of Mr Jabez Williams, who rendered great service to the party by interpreting whenever necessary. He also gave up his residence for the use of the party.

On the morning of July 13 the question of the location of the reserves was gone fully into, and the Indians showed great acuteness in describing the location of the land they desired to have reserved for them. Their final choice is shown in the schedule of reserves which is annexed to this report.

We left Osnaburg on the morning of July 13, and entered the Albany river, which drains Lake St Joseph, and, after passing many rapids and magnificent lake stretches of this fine river, we reached Fort Hope at 5 o'clock on the afternoon of the 18th. This important post of the Hudson's Bay Company is situated on the shore of Lake Eabamet, and is the meeting point of a large number of Indians, certainly 700, who have their hunting grounds on both sides of the Albany and as far as the headwaters of the Winisk river. The post was in charge of Mr. C.H.M. Gordon.

The same course of procedure was followed as at Osnaburg. The Indians were requested to select representatives to whom the business of the commission might be explained, and on the morning of the 19th the commissioners met a number of representative Indians in the Hudson's Bay Company's house. Here the commissioners had the benefit of the assistance of Rev. Father F.X. Fafard, of the Roman Catholic Mission at Albany, whose thorough knowledge of the Cree and Ojibeway tongues was of great assistance during the discussion.

A more general conversation in explanation of the terms of the treaty followed than had occurred at Osnaburg. Moonias, one of the most influential chiefs, asked a number of questions. He said that ever since he was able to earn anything, and that was from the time he was very young, he had never been given something for nothing; that he always had to pay for everything that he got, even if it was only a paper of pins. "Now," he said "you gentlemen come to us from the King offering to give us benefits for which we can make no return. How is this?" Father Fafard thereupon explained to him the nature of the treaty, and that by it the Indians were giving their faith and allegiance to the King, and for giving up their title to a large area of land of which they could make no use, they received benefits that served to balance anything that they were giving.

"Yesno," who received his name from his imperfect knowledge of the English language, which consisted altogether in the use of the words "yes" and "no," made an excited speech, in which he told the Indians that they were to receive cattle and implements, seed-grain and tools. Yesno had evidently travelled, and had gathered an erroneous and exaggerated idea of what the government was doing for Indians in other parts of the country, but, as the undersigned wished to guard carefully against any misconception or against making any promises which were not written in the treaty itself, it was explained that none of these issues were to be made, as the band could not hope to depend upon agriculture as a means of subsistence: that hunting and fishing, in which occupations they were not to be interfered with, should for very many years prove lucrative sources of revenue. The Indians were informed that by signing the treaty they pledged themselves not to interfere with white men who might come into the country surveying, prospecting, hunting, or in other occupations; that they must respect the laws of the land in every particular, and that their reserves were set apart for them in order that they might have a tract in which they could not be molested, and where no white man would have any claims without the consent of their tribe and of the government.

After this very full discussion, the treaty was signed, and payment was commenced. The payment was finished on the next day, and the Indian feast took place, at which the chiefs elected were Katchange, Yesno, Joe Goodwin, Benj. Ooskinegisk, and George Quisees. The newly elected chiefs made short speeches, expressing their gladness at the conclusion of the treaty and their determination to be true to its terms and stipulations.

It is considered worthy of record to remark on the vigorous and manly qualities displayed by these Indians throughout the negotiations. Although undoubtedly at times they suffer from lack of food owing to the circumstances under which they live, yet they appeared contented, and enjoy a certain degree of comfort. Two active missions are established at Fort Hope, the Anglican, under the charge of Rev. Mr. Richards, who is resident, and the Roman Catholic, under the charge of Rev. Father Fafard, who visits from the mission at Albany.

Fort Hope was left on the morning of July 21, and after passing through Lake Eabamet the Albany was reached again, and after three days' travel we arrived at Marten Falls at 7.35 on the morning of Tuesday, July 25.

This is an important post of the Hudson's Bay Company, in charge of Mr. Samuel Iserhoff. A number of Indians were awaiting the arrival of the commission. The first glance at the Indians served to convince that they were not equal in physical development to those at Osnaburg or Fort Hope, and the comparative poverty of their hunting grounds may account for this fact.

The necessary business at this post was transacted on the 25th. The treaty, after due explanation, was signed and the payment made immediately. Shortly before the feast the Indians elected their chief, Wm. Whitehead, and two councillors, Wm. Coaster and Long Tom Ostamas.

At the feast Chief Whitehead made an excellent speech, in which he described the benefits that would follow the treaty and his gratitude to the King and the government for extending a helping and protecting hand to the Indians.

The reserve was fixed at a point opposite the post and is described fully in the schedule of reserves.

The commodious Roman Catholic church situated on the high bank of the river overlooking the Hudson's Bay Company's buildings was the most conspicuous object at this post.

Marten Falls was left on the morning of Wednesday, July 26. Below this point the Albany flows towards James Bay without any impediment of rapids or falls, but with a swift current, which is a considerable aid to canoe travel.

The mouth of the Kenogami river was reached at 2.45 on the afternoon of July 27. This river flows in with a large volume of water and a strong current. It took two days of heavy paddling and difficult tracking to reach the English River post, which is situated about 60 miles from the mouth of the river and near the Forks. We found many of the Indians encamped along the river, and they followed us in their canoes to the post, where we arrived on the afternoon of July 29.

This is a desolate post of the Hudson's Bay Company, in charge of Mr G.B. Cooper. There are very few Indians in attendance at any time: about half of them were assembled, the rest having gone to "The Line," as the Canadian Pacific railway is called, to trade.

Compared with the number at Fort Hope or Osnaburg, there was a mere handful at English River, and it did not take long to explain to the Indians the reason why the commission was visiting them. As these people cannot be considered a separate band, but a branch of the Albany band, it was not thought necessary to have them sign the treaty, and they were merely admitted as an offshoot of the larger and more important band.

The terms of the treaty having been fully explained, the Indians stated that they were willing to come under its provisions, and they were informed that by the acceptance of the gratuity they would be held to have entered treaty, a statement which they fully realized. As the morrow was Sunday, and as it was important to proceed without delay, they were paid at once.

We left the English River post early on Monday morning, and reached the mouth of the river at 6 p.m. Coming again into the Albany, we met a number of Marten Falls Indians who had not been paid, and who had been camped at the mouth of the river, expecting the commission. After being paid, they camped on the shore near us, and next morning proceeded on their way to Marten Falls, with their York boats laden with goods from Fort Albany. The next day a party of Albany Indians were paid at the mouth of Cheepy river, and the post itself was reached on the morning of August 3, at 9.30. Here the commissioners had the advantage of receiving much assistance from Mr G.W. Cockram, who was just leaving the post on his way to England, and Mr A.W. Patterson, who had just taken charge in his stead.

In the afternoon the chief men selected by the Indians were convened in a large room in the Hudson's Bay Company's store, and an interesting and satisfactory conversation followed. The explanations that had been given at the other points were repeated here, and two of the Indians, Arthur Wesley and Wm. Goodwin, spoke at some length, expressing on their own behalf and on behalf of their comrades the pleasure they felt upon being brought into the treaty and the satisfaction they experienced on receiving such generous treatment from the Crown. Some of the Indians were away at their hunting grounds at Attawapiskat river, and it was thought advisable to postpone the election of chiefs until next year. The Indians were paid on August 4 and 5.

During the afternoon the Hudson's Bay Company's steamer *Innenew* arrived, with the Right Rev. George Holmes, the Anglican Bishop of Moosonee, on board.

On Saturday the Indians feasted and presented the commissioners with an address written in Cree syllabic, of which the following is a translation: —

"From our hearts we thank thee, O Great Chief, as thou hast pitied us and given us temporal help. We are very poor and weak. He (the Great Chief) has taken us over, here in our own country, through you (his servants).

"Therefore from our hearts we thank thee, very much, and pray for thee to Our Father in heaven. Thou hast helped us in our poverty.

"Every day we pray, trusting that we may be saved through a righteous life; and for thee we shall ever pray that thou mayest be strong in God's strength and by His assistance.

"And we trust that it may ever be with us as it is now; we and our children will in the church of God now and ever thank Jesus.

"Again we thank you (commissioners) from our hearts."

Fort Albany is an important post of the Hudson's Bay Company, and here there are two flourishing missions, one of the Roman Catholic and one of the Church of England. Father Fafard has established a large boarding school, which accommodates 20 Indian pupils in charge of the Grey Nuns from the parent house at Ottawa. Here assistance is given to sick Indians in the hospital ward, and a certain number of aged people who cannot travel with their relatives are supported each winter. The church and presbytery are commodious and well built, and the whole mission has an air of prosperity and comfort. The celebration of mass was well attended on Sunday. The Church of England mission is also in a flourishing condition. The large church was well filled for all Sunday services conducted by Bishop Holmes, and the Indians took an intelligent part in the services.

We left Albany on the morning of Monday, August 7, in a sail-boat chartered from the Hudsons' Bay Company, and, the wind being strong and fair, we anchored off the mouth of Moose river at 7 o'clock the same evening. Weighing anchor at daylight on Tuesday morning, we drifted with the tide, and a light, fitful wind and reached Moose Factory at 10.30. We had been accompanied on the journey by Bishop Holmes, who immediately upon landing interested himself with Mr J.G. Mowat, in charge of this important post of the Hudson's Bay Company, to secure a meeting of representative Indians on the morrow.

On the morning of the 9th a meeting was held in a large room placed at our disposal by the Hudson's Bay Company. The Indians who had been chosen to confer with us seemed remarkably intelligent and deeply interested in the subject to be discussed. When the points of the treaty were explained to them, they expressed their perfect willingness to accede to the terms and conditions. Frederick Mark, who in the afternoon was elected chief, said the Indians were all delighted that a treaty was about to be made with them; they had been looking forward to it for a long time, and were glad that they were to have their hopes realized and that there was now a prospect of law and order being established among them. John Dick remarked that one great advantage the Indians hoped to derive from the treaty was the establishment of schools wherein their children might receive an education. George Teppaise said they were thankful that the King had remembered them, and that the Indians were to receive money, which was very much needed by many who were poor and sick. Suitable responses were made to these gratifying speeches by ourselves and Bishop Holmes, and the treaty was immediately signed. Payment commenced next day and was rapidly completed.

It was a matter of general comment that the Moose Factory Indians were the most comfortably dressed and best nourished of the Indians we had so far met with.

On the evening of Thursday the Indians announced that they had selected the following chief and councillors: Frederick Mark, James Job, Simon Quatchequan and Simon Cheena. As they were to have their feast in the evening, it was decided to present the flag to the chief on that occasion. The feast was held in a large workshop placed at the disposal of the Indians by the Company; and before this hall, just as night was coming on, the flag was presented to Chief Mark. In many respects it was a unique occasion. The gathering was addressed by Bishop Holmes, who began with a prayer in Cree, the Indians making their responses and singing their hymns in the same language. Bishop Holmes kindly interpreted the address of the commissioners, which was suitably replied to by Chief Mark. It may be recorded that during our stay at this point a commodious church was crowded every evening by interested Indians, and that the good effect of the ministrations for many years of the Church Missionary Society were plain, not only to Moose Factory but after the immediate influence of the post and the missionaries had been left. The crew from Moose Factory which accompanied the commissioners as far as Abitibi held service every night in camp, recited a short litany, sang a hymn and engaged in prayer, a fact we think worthy of remark, as in the solitude through which we passed this Christian service made a link with civilization and the best influences at work in the world which had penetrated even to these remote regions. On Friday, August 11, the question of a reserve was gone into, and settled to the satisfaction of ourselves and the Indians, or any of them, be entitled to sell or otherwise alienate any of the lands allotted to them as reserves.

During our stay we had the opportunity of inspecting Bishop's Court, at one time the residence of the Bishop of Moosonee, but which the present bishop intends to convert into a boarding school for Indian children. The hospital under the supervision of Miss Johnson was also inspected.

On Saturday, August 12, we left Moose Factory at 12.30. For one week we were engaged with the strong rapids of the Moose and Abitibi rivers, and did not reach New Post, our next point of call, until 12.30 on Saturday, the 19th. New Post is a small and comparatively unimportant post of the Hudson's Bay Company. It is situated on a beautiful bend of the Abitibi river, and commands an excellent hunting country. The post is in charge of Mr S.B. Barrett, and nowhere was the commission received with greater consideration and hospitality than at this place. The New Post Indians, although few in number, are of excellent character and disposition. They met us with great friendliness. The treaty was concluded on Monday, the 21st, and the Indians were at once paid. The reserve question was also discussed, and the location finally fixed as shown by the schedule of reserves. One of the leading Indians, Esau Omakess, was absent from the reserve during the negotiations. He, however, arrived during the time the payments were being made, and signified his approval of the action taken by his fellow Indians. He was subsequently chosen unanimously as chief of the band.

We started for Abitibi on Tuesday morning, August 22. On the previous evening the chief had announced to the commissioners his intention of accompanying the party, with five companions, to assist in passing the difficult series of portages which lie immediately above New Post. One unacquainted with the methods of travel in these regions will not perhaps realize the great assistance this was to the party. At a moderate estimate, it saved one day's travel; and this great assistance was to be rendered, the chief said, without any desire for reward or even for maintenance on the route (they were to bring their own supplies with them), but simply to show their good-will to the commissioners and their thankfulness to the King and the government for the treatment which had been accorded them. They remained with us until the most difficult portages were passed, and left on the evening of August 24, with mutual expressions of good-will. As we ascended the Abitibi evidences of approaching civilization and of the activity in railway construction and surveying, which had rendered the making of the treaty necessary, were constantly met with. Surveying parties of the Transcontinental railway, the Timiskaming and Northern Ontario railway and Ontario township surveyors were constantly met with.

On the morning of August 29 we reached Lake Abitibi, camped at the Hudson's Bay Company's winter post at the Narrows on the same evening, and arrived at Abitibi post the next night at dusk. We did not expect to find many Indians in attendance, as they usually leave for their hunting grounds about the first week in July. There were, however, a few Indians who were waiting at the post in expectation of the arrival of the commission. These were assembled at 2.30 on the afternoon of August 31, and the purpose of the commission was carefully explained to them. Until we can report the successful making of the treaty, which we hope to accomplish next year, we do not think it necessary to make any further comment on the situation at this post. A full list of the Indians was obtained from the officer in charge of the Hudson's Bay Company's post, Mr George Drever. Mr Drever has thorough command of the Cree and Ojibeway languages, which was of great assistance to the commissioners at Abitibi, where, owing to the fact of the Indians belonging to the two provinces, Ontario and Quebec, it was necessary to draw a fine distinction, and where the explanations had to be most carefully made in order to avoid future misunderstanding and dissatisfaction. Mr Drever cheerfully undertook this difficult office and performed it to our great satisfaction.

We left Abitibi on the morning of September 1, with an excellent crew and made Klock's depot without misadventure on Monday, September 4. We reached Haileybury on the 6th and arrived at Ottawa on September 9.

In conclusion we beg to give a short resume of the work done this season. Cession was taken of the tract described in the treaty, comprising about 90,000 square miles, and, in addition, by the adhesion of certain Indians whose hunting grounds lie in a northerly direction from the Albany river, which may be roughly described as territory lying between that river and a line drawn from the north-east angle of Treaty No. 3, along the height of land separating the waters which flow into Hudson Bay by the Severn and Winisk from those which flow into James Bay by the Albany and Attawapiskat, comprising about 40,000 square miles. Gratuity was paid altogether to 1,617 Indians, representing a total population, when all the absentees are paid and allowance made for names not on the list, of 2,500 approximately. Throughout all the negotiations we carefully guarded against making any promises over and above those written in the treaty which might afterwards cause embarrassement to the governments concerned. No outside promises were made, and the Indians cannot, and we confidently believe do not, expect any other concessions than those set forth in the documents to which they gave their adherence. It was gratifying throughout to be met by these Indians with such a show of cordiality and trust, and to be able fully to satisfy what they believed to be their claims upon the governments of this country. The treatment of the reserve question, which in this treaty was most important, will, it is hoped, meet with approval. For the most part the reserves were selected by the commissioners after conference with the Indians. They have been selected in situations which are especially advantageous to their owners, and where they will not in any way interfere with railway development or the future commercial interests of the country. While it is doubtful whether the Indians will ever engage in agriculture, these reserves, being of a reasonable size, will give a secure and permanent interest in the land which the indeterminate possession of a large tract could never carry. No valuable water-powers are included within the allotments. The area set apart is, approximately, 374 square miles in the Northwest Territories and 150 square miles in the province of Ontario. When the vast quantity of waste and, at present, unproductive land, surrendered is considered, these allotments must, we think, be pronounced most reasonable.

We beg to transmit herewith copy of the original of the treaty signed in duplicate, and schedule of reserves.

We have the honour to be, sir,

Your obedient servants,

DUNCAN C. SCOTT,

SAMUEL STEWART,

DANIEL G. MacMARTIN,

Treaty Commissioners.

Notes

1. The Treaty 9 commission continued its work in 1906, when it travelled to northeastern Ontario. For a description of that trip, see the letter of transmission of the treaty commissioners, dated 5 October 1906, in *The James Bay Treaty: Treaty No. 9*, pp. 12-18.

2. For a description of the treaty-making process in the prairies written by one of the Commissioners, see Morris, *supra*.

3. For a complete description of the treaty-making process and the conditions under which the treaties were signed in the North-West Territories, see René Fumoleau, *As Long As This Land Shall Last* (Toronto: McClelland & Stewart Ltd., 1973).

4. Descriptions of the treaty-making process are contained in many of the cases reproduced in this and other chapters.

(iii) The Text of Treaty No. 9

The James Bay Treaty — Treaty No. 9

ARTICLES OF A TREATY made and concluded at the several dates mentioned therein, in the year of Our Lord one thousand and nine hundred and five, between His Most Gracious Majesty the King of Great Britain and Ireland, by His Commissioners, Duncan Campbell Scott, of Ottawa, Ontario, Esquire, and Samuel Stewart, of Ottawa, Ontario, Esquire; and Daniel George MacMartin, of Perth, Ontario, Esquire, representing the province of Ontario, of the one part; and the Ojibeway, Cree and other Indians, inhabitants of the territory within the limits hereinafter defined and described, by their chiefs, and headmen hereunto subscribed, of the other part: —

Whereas, the Indians inhabiting the territory hereinafter defined have been convened to meet a commission representing His Majesty's government of the Dominion of Canada at certain places in the said territory in this present year of 1905, to deliberate upon certain matters of interest to His Most Gracious Majesty, of the one part, and the said Indians of the other.

And, whereas, the said Indians have been notified and informed by His Majesty's said commission that it is His desire to open for settlement, immigration, trade, travel, mining, lumbering, and such other purposes as to His Majesty may seem meet, a tract of country, bounded and described as hereinafter mentioned, and to obtain the consent thereto of His Indian subjects inhabiting the said tract, and to make a treaty and arrange with them, so that there may be peace and good-will between them and His Majesty's other subjects, and that His Indian people may know and be assured of what allowances they are to count upon and receive from His Majesty's bounty and benevolence.

And whereas, the Indians of the said tract, duly convened in council at the respective points named hereunder, and being requested by His Majesty's commissioners to name certain chiefs and headmen who should be authorized on their behalf to conduct such negotiations and sign any treaty to be found thereon, and to become responsible to His Majesty for the faithful performance by their respective bands of such obligations as shall be assumed by them, the said Indians have therefore acknowledged for that purpose the several chiefs and headmen who have subscribed hereto.

And whereas, the said commissioners have proceeded to negotiate a treaty with the Ojibeway, Cree and other Indians, inhabiting the district hereinafter defined and described, and the same has been agreed upon and concluded by the respective bands at the dates mentioned hereunder, the said Indians do hereby cede, release, surrender and yield up to the government of the Dominion of Canada, for His Majesty the King and His successors for ever all their rights titles and privileges whatsoever, to the lands included within the following limits, that is to say: That portion or tract of land lying and being in the province of Ontario, bounded on the south by the height of land and the northern boundaries of the territory ceded by the Robinson-Superior Treaty of 1850, and the Robinson-Huron Treaty of 1850, and bounded on the east and north by the boundaries of the said province of Ontario as defined by law, and on the west by a part of the eastern boundary of the territory ceded by North-west Angle Treaty No. 3; the said land containing an area of ninety thousand square miles, more or less.

And also, the said Indian rights, titles and privileges whatsoever to all other lands wherever situated in Ontario, Quebec, Manitoba, the District of Keewatin, or in any other portion of the Dominion of Canada.

To have and to hold the same to His Majesty the King and His successors for ever.

And His Majesty the King hereby agrees with the said Indians that they shall have the right to pursue their usual vocations of hunting, trapping and fishing throughout the tract surrendered as heretofore described, subject to such regulations as may from time to time be made by the government of the country, acting under the authority of His Majesty, and saving and excepting such tracts as may be required or taken up from time to time for settlement, mining, lumbering, trading or other purposes.

And His Majesty the King hereby agrees and undertakes to lay aside reserves for each band, the same not to exceed in all one square mile for each family of five, or in that proportion for larger and smaller families; and the location of the said reserves having been arranged between His Majesty's commissioners and the chiefs and headmen, as described in the schedule of reserves hereto attached, the boundaries thereof to be hereafter surveyed and defined, the said reserves when confirmed shall be held and administered by His Majesty for the benefit of the Indians free of all claims, liens, or trusts by Ontario.

Provided, however, that His Majesty reserves the right to deal with any settlers within the bounds of any lands reserved for any band as He may see fit; and also that the aforesaid reserves of land, or any interest therein, may be sold or otherwise disposed of by His Majesty's government for the use and benefit of the said Indians entitled thereto, with their consent first had and obtained; but in no wise shall the said Indians, or any of them, be entitled to sell or otherwise alienate any of the lands allotted to them as reserves.

It is further agreed between His said Majesty and His Indian subjects that such portions of the reserves and lands above indicated as may at any time be required for public works, buildings, railways, or roads of whatsoever nature may be appropriated for that purpose by His Majesty's government of the Dominion of Canada, due compensation being made to the Indians for the value of any improvements thereon, and an equivalent in land, money or other consideration for the area of the reserve so appropriated.

And with a view to show the satisfaction of His Majesty with the behaviour and good conduct of His Indians, and in extinguishment of all their past claims, He hereby, through His commissioners, agrees to make each Indian a present of eight dollars in cash.

His Majesty also agrees that next year, and annually afterwards for ever, He will cause to be paid to the said Indians in cash, at suitable places and dates, of which the said Indians shall be duly notified, four dollars, the same, unless there be some exceptional reason, to be paid only to the heads of families for those belonging thereto.

Further, His Majesty agrees that each chief, after signing the treaty, shall receive a suitable flag and a copy of this treaty to be for the use of his band.

Further, His Majesty agrees to pay such salaries of teachers to instruct the children of said Indians, and also to provide such school buildings and educational equipment as may seem advisable to His Majesty's government of Canada.

And the undersigned Ojibeway, Cree and other chiefs and headmen, on their own behalf and on behalf of all the Indians whom they represent, do hereby solemnly promise and engage to strictly observe this treaty, and also to conduct and behave themselves as good and loyal subjects of His Majesty the King.

They promise and engage that they will, in all respects, obey and abide by the law; that they will maintain peace between each other and between themselves and other tribes of Indians, and between themselves and others of His Majesty's subjects, whether Indians, half-breeds or whites, this year inhabiting and hereafter to inhabit any part of the said ceded territory; and that they will not molest the person or property of any inhabitant of such ceded tract, or of any other district or country, or interfere with or trouble any person passing or travelling through the said tract, or any part thereof, and that they will assist the officers of His Majesty in bringing to justice and punishment any Indian offending against the stipulations of this treaty, or infringing the law in force in the country so ceded.

And it is further understood that this treaty is made and entered into subject to an agreement dated the third day of July, nineteen hundred and five, between the Dominion of Canada and Province of Ontario, which is hereto attached.

In witness whereof, His Majesty's said commissioners and the said chiefs and headmen have hereunto set their hands at the places and times set forth in the year herein first above written.

Signed at Osnaburg on the twelfth day of July, 1905, by His Majesty's commissioners and the chiefs and headmen in the presence of the undersigned witnesses, after having been first interpreted and explained.

(Signatures omitted for Osnaburg and other places where the treaty party met the Indians in 1905 and 1906.)

Note

1. In 1912, the boundaries of Ontario were extended to their present northern limits by legislation that specifically required that treaties be made with the Indian inhabitants. (*Ontario Boundaries Extension Act,* SC 1912, c. 45, s. 2(1)-(c).) In 1929 and 1930 adhesions to Treaty 9 were signed by representatives of the Cree and Ojibway people of northern Ontario. See *The James Bay Treaty: Treaty No. 9,* pp. 29-35.

(iv) *R. v. Batisse* (1978), 19 OR (2d) 145, 84 DLR (3d) 377, 40 CCC (2d) 34 (Ontario District Court)

BERNSTEIN DCJ: — The appellant was convicted in Provincial Court of "unlawfully hunting game birds during the closed season" contrary to s. 51 of the *Game and Fish Act*, RSO 1970, c. 186, a legislative enactment of the Province of Ontario. He appeals the conviction on the basis that Indian Treaty No. 9 provides a defence to the charge.

At the outset it was agreed that the appellant is an Indian member of one of the bands subject to Treaty No. 9 and as such is entitled to any defence arising out of the Treaty. The appellant, while hunting within unoccupied Crown land ceded by Treaty No. 9 Indians, shot three ruffed grouse out of season and without a licence. The conviction was proper unless Treaty No. 9 provides him a defence.

The James Bay Treaty — Treaty No. 9 was entered into during the years 1905 and 1906, covering approximately 90,000 square miles of Northern Ontario. Prior to the execution of this treaty there had been no extinguishment of Indian interest in the land. Increased activity in mining and railroad construction caused the senior Governments to make serious efforts to obtain a cession of Indian title, eventually resulting in the treaty presently an issue.

Treaty No. 9 provided that the various Indian tribes inhabiting this vast area:

do cede, release, surrender and yield up to the government of the

> Dominion of Canada, for His Majesty the King and His successors for ever, all their rights titles and privileges whatsoever to the lands . . .

As a part of the *bargain* following term concerning Indian hunting, trapping and fishing rights was inserted:

> And His Majesty the King hereby agrees with the said Indians that they shall have the right to pursue their usual vocations of hunting, trapping and fishing *throughout the tract surrendered* as heretofore described *subject to such regulations as may from time to time be made by the government of the country, acting under the authority of His Majesty*, and saving and excepting such tracts as may be required or taken up from time to time for settlement, mining, lumbering, trading or other purposes. (emphasis mine.)

The issue in this appeal is whether the appellant's treaty right to hunt on unoccupied Crown land is subject to provincial legislation in the form of the *Game and Fish Act*.

Section 88 of the *Indian Act*, RSC 1970, c. I-6 (enacted in 1951, [by c. 29] provides as follows:

> 88. *Subject to the terms of any treaty* and any other Act of the Parliament of Canada, *all laws of general application from time to time in force in any province are applicable to and in respect of Indians in the province*, except to the extent that such laws are inconsistent with this Act or any order, rule, regulation or by-law made thereunder, and except to the extent that such laws make provision for any matter for which provision is made by or under this Act. (emphasis mine.)

There is no doubt that Treaty No. 9 is a "treaty" as referred to in s. 88 of the *Indian Act* or that the *Game and Fish Act* is a law of general application in force in the Province of Ontario. It is now clear that the term "laws" in s. 88 refers to provincial laws and excludes federal legislation: *R.* v. *George*, [1966] 3 CCC 137, [1966] SCR 267, 55 DLR (2d) 386.

A careful examination of the cases dealing with the effect of s. 88 on treaty rights over surrendered Indian lands, establishes, in my view, that such rights as defined in the treaty remain in effect unless federal legislation derogates from those treaty rights: *R.* v. *White and Bob* (1965), 50 DLR (2d) 613, 52 WWR 193; affirmed 52 DLR (2d) 481 [1965] SCR vi (SCC); *R.* v. *George*, *supra*; *Krugers and Manuel* v. *The*

Queen, 1977 (SCC unreported) [since reported 34 CCC (2d) 377, 75 DLR (2d) 434, [1977] 4 WWR 300].

In *R. v. White and Bob* the issue was whether members of a tribe of Indians in British Columbia were subject to the restrictions on hunting outlined in the provincial *Game* Act. The majority of the British Columbia Court of Appeal, after finding on the particular facts of the case that the accused was a member of a tribe which had executed a "treaty" within the meaning of s. 87 (now s. 88) of the *Indian Act*, and that the treaty reserved hunting rights over the ceded lands to the Indians, held that such treaty rights could not be abrogated or abridged by provincial legislation alone and that only Parliament can derogate from those rights. This position was clearly stated by Davey JA, at p. 618, where he stated:

> Legislation that abrogates or abridges the hunting rights reserved to Indians under the treaties and agreements by which they sold their ancient territories to the Crown and to the Hudson's Bay Company for white settlement is, in my respectful opinion, legislation in relation to Indians because it deals with rights peculiar to them. Lord Watson's judgment in *St Catharine's Milling & Lumber Co. v. The Queen* (1888), 58 LJPC 54, if any authority is needed, makes that clear. At p. 60 he observed that the plain policy of the *BNA Act* is to vest legislative control over Indian affairs generally in one central authority. On the same page he spoke of Parliament's exclusive power to regulate the Indians' privilege of hunting and fishing. *In my opinion, their peculiar rights of hunting and fishing over their ancient hunting grounds arising under agreements by which they collectively sold their ancient lands are Indian affairs over which Parliament has exclusive legislative authority, and only Parliament can derogate from those rights.*

(emphasis mine.)

On appeal to the Supreme Court of Canada (1965), 52 DLR (2d) 481n, [1965] SCR vi, Mr Justice Cartwright, for the Court, affirmed the judgment of the majority in the British Columbia Court of Appeal as follows:

> We are all of the opinion that the majority in the Court of Appeal were right in their conclusion that the document, Exhibit 8, was a "treaty" within the meaning of that term as used in s. 87 of the *Indian Act* [RSC 1952, c. 149]. We therefore think that in the circumstances of the case, the operation of s. 25 of the *Game Act* [RSBC 1960, c. 160] was excluded by reason of the existence of that treaty.

It follows of course that s. 51 of the *Game and FIsh Act* (Ontario) is subject to the terms of the James Bay Treaty — No. 9 and counsel for the Crown did not strenuously oppose this proposition.

Rather, the respondent's argument was basically that the treaty itself was entered into by the Indians with the Province of Ontario as well as with the Dominion Government, and that by its terms, provincial regulation was anticipated and provided for by the parties. The learned Provincial Court Judge agreed with this position and hence convicted the appellant. It is indeed clear that one of the Commissioners who was present when the treaty was negotiated and signed was appointed by the Province of Ontario. The opening paragraph describes the parties to the treaty as follows:

> Articles of a Treaty . . . between His Most Gracious Majesty the King of Great Britain and Ireland, by His Commissioners, Duncan Campbell Scott, of Ottawa, Ontario, Esquire, and Samuel Stewart, of Ottawa, Ontario, Esquire; and Daniel George MacMartin, of Perth, Ontario, Esquire, representing the province of Ontario, of the one part; and the Ojibeway, Cree and other Indians . . . of the other part:

With the greatest respect I am unable to agree that the Province of Ontario was a "party" to the Agreement in the usual sense of that term. The Province was not described as a separate party; its nominee was merely identified as such to indicate compliance with an agreement between the Government of Canada and the Province of Ontario as set out in "An Act for the settlement of certain questions between the Governments of Canada and Ontario respecting Indian Lands", 1891 (Can.), c. 5, and 1891 (Ont.), c. 3. By the terms of these Acts (both passed in 1891) both Governments authorized an agreement whereby the Province would have to concur in the location of reserves, etc., and by para. 6 of the Agreement:

> 6.   That any future treaties with the Indians in respect of territory in Ontario to which they have not hitherto surrendered their claim aforesaid, shall be deemed to require *the concurrence* of the government of Ontario.

The practical wisdom of the agreement between the two levels of Government becomes obvious when one considers the implications of the judgment of the Privy Council one year earlier in *St Catharine's Milling & Lumber Co.* v. *The Queen* (1889), 14 App. Cas. 46. This decision held that when Indians surrendered their usufructuary interest in land, the entire beneficial interest in the land, subject to retained privileges, was transmitted to the Province pursuant to s. 109 of the *BNA Act, 1867*. Clearly, therefore, in view of the provincial responsibility to determine future development and use of ceded lands, it was essential that the Province have the right to *concur* with the decisions setting out the size and locations of reserves.

In my view, the Province had no constitutional right to negotiate an Indian treaty as an independent party. Its sole right, in view of the legislation, was to *concur* in a treaty entered into between the Indians and the federal Government. Although the Province could *perhaps* veto a treaty by refusing to concur, the legislation did not purport to give it any more extensive powers over this area of exclusive federal jurisdiction. Indeed para. 1 of the Agreement between the Province and federal Government (attached as a schedule to the two Acts passed in 1891) seems to indicate that the Province's sole concern over the retained hunting and fishing rights was that "they not continue with reference to any tracts which have been, or from time to time may be, required or taken up for settlement, mining, lumbering or other purposes of the Government of Ontario . . .''. In my opinion, the Province was represented during negotiations only because of its concern for future *user* of the land being ceded, and not because there was any intent to assume authority to regulate Indian hunting and fishing rights in general.

The Reports of the Commissioners to the Superintendent-General of Indian Affairs forwarded during negotiations cast further light on the nature of the negotiations and the obvious intent of the parties. Throughout the Reports, the Commissioners comment on the concern the Indians had about their hunting and fishing rights over the ceded lands.

In the report of November 6, 1905, the Commissioners report (in relation to the band at Osnaburg):

> Missabay, the recognized chief of the band, then spoke, expressing the fears of the Indians that, if they signed the treaty, they would be compelled to reside upon the reserve to be set apart for them, and would be deprived of the fishing and hunting privileges which they now enjoy.
>
> *On being informed that their fears in regard to both these matters were groundless*, as their present manner of making their livelihood would in no way be interfered with, the Indians talked the matter over among themselves . . .

Needless to say, this band signed the treaty the next day. Throughout the Reports are numerous examples of the importance which the Indians *and the Commissioners* placed on hunting and fishing rights. That both parties (*i.e.*, the Indians and the Commissioners) felt that the Indians were dealing only with the federal Government was made clear in the

Report of the October 5, 1906 (signed by all three Commissioners, including the provincial nominee). They reported that in relation to negotiations at Fort Abitibi:

> On June 7, the looked-for Indians having arrived, a meeting was called for the afternoon of that day. Some difficulty was anticipated in negotiating the treaty at Abitibi owing to the peculiar position of the Indians who trade at that post. The post is situated a few miles within the province of Quebec, and the majority of the Indians who trade there belong to that province. *It was natural for the Indians to conclude that, as it was the Dominion government and not the provincial government that was negotiating the treaty*, no distinction would be made between those hunting in Ontario and those hunting in Quebec. The commissioners had, however, to state that they had no authority to treat with Quebec Indians . . .

(emphasis mine.)

All of this evidence leads me to the conclusion that Treaty No. 9 was an agreement between the Indians of Northern Ontario and the federal Government and that the Province of Ontario obtained no rights vis-à-vis *the Indians* because of the presence of one of their nominees as a Commissioner.

2. Status of Indian Treaties in Canadian Law

(a) **P.A. Cumming and N.H. Mickenberg (eds.)** *Native Rights in Canada* **2nd ed. (Toronto: General Publishing/Indian-Eskimo Association of Canada, 1972), pp. 54-58.**
   Reproduced in the chapter: *Pre-Confederation Treaties, supra.*

(b) **Delia Opekokew** *The First Nations: Indian Government in the Community of Man* **(Regina: Federation of Saskatchewan Indians, 1982), p. 22.**

But, the international status of the treaties is clearly illustrated by following facts:
1. The British Crown, rather than any department of government or ministry, entered into the treaties;
2. The negotiations leading to the making of the treaties were conducted on the basis of mutual sovereignty;
3. The mutual acceptance of the treaties was in solemn form, accompanied by ceremonies appropriate to the conclusion of international treaties; and

4. There have been formal adhesions to the treaties, this being the appropriate method for later participation by other parties in international treaties. The most recent adhesion was entered into on May 15th, 1970.

At all material times the British Crown acknowledged the title of the Indian bands to the territory they occupied, and at no time claimed that Indian territorial rights were extinguished by occupation or conquest. On the contrary, as declared in the Royal Proclamation of 1763 and subsequent documents, all dealings with the bands were to be on the basis of mutual respect and consent. Indian lands could only be acquired by the British Crown with such consent: without it, no individual subject of the British Crown was to purchase or settle upon or take possession of any Indian land. Provincial governments come within the same ban. At no time did the British Crown express any doubt as to the capacity of the bands to enter into treaties. Indeed, Britain herself chose to call the transactions treaties rather than agreements or contracts.

(c) **Delia Opekokew** *The First Nations: Indian Government and the Canadian Confederation.* **(Saskatoon: Federation of Saskatchewan Indians, 1980), pp. 13 and 16-17.**

The International Status of Indian Treaties

A treaty is a compact or agreement between two or more independent nations, but Canadian governments and courts have used the argument that the Indian treaties were not international treaties, in order to deny Indian nations the right to sovereignty and self-government. European immigrants had to deny the fact that North America was already governed by Indian nations in order to establish their own interest in the land. As this interest developed and expanded over time (from the fur trade, to settlement, to the extraction of resources), official European recognition of Indian title was correspondingly altered and cut back. In the 1971 book *Native Rights in Canada* published by the Indian-Eskimo Association of Canada, the editors state that "it is clear that the agreements entered into with the Indians are neither international treaties nor simple private contracts." Their evidence for that conclusion is coloured by their source. Their sources are Lieutenant Governor Morris' interpretation and the case law that has been built up in the Canadian courts which is based on arguments developed by lawyers, judges, and parliamentarians whose predecessors were the original early "discoverers" of North America. . .

The treaties entered by both the United States and Canada with Indian people are similar, and the treaty-making process outlined in the Royal Proclamation of 1763, applies in both cases, as Mr Chief Justice Marshall expressly relied upon it as an additional ground for his judgment in *McIntosh*. The significant difference is that the United States constitution confirms their international status because the federal power to make treaties was the basis for both international treaties and agreements with the Indians. In other words, the power to make treaties is incorporated into one section of the constitution and that section specifically defines Indian treaties as included. The American constitution was confirmed in 1789 when Indian allies were an important political factor.

In Canada, the conduct of international affairs for the entire empire (including Canada) was still firmly vested in the British (imperial) government, and it was the British government through authorized Commissioners such as the Queen's representative in 1876, Lieutenant Governor Morris, which negotiated, signed and ratified all treaties which applied to the empire or to any part of the empire. For implementation, section 132 of the *BNA Act* provides that,

> The Parliament and government of Canada shall have all powers necessary or proper for performing the obligations of Canada or of any province thereof, as part of the British empire, towards foreign countries, arising under treaties between the empire and such foreign countries.

In *Native Rights in Canada* the following erroneous conclusions are made about Indian treaties,

> The Indian treaties made by Canada and those made by the United States differ in several respects. In the United States, the Federal power to make treaties was the basis for both international treaties and agreements with the Indians. During the treaty-making period, American Indian tribes were described as dependent nationalities, and a tribal Indian was a legal "alien." . . .

In Canada, the power of the Dominion Government to enter into treaties with the Indians does not appear to have been questioned. By virtue of the *British North America Act*, the Federal Government has authority over "Indians and Lands reserved for the Indians." Consequently, there has been no need to justify the Federal authority to engage in agreements with the Indians under its power to enter into international treaties.

The differences identified are:

1.   The ultimate power of the United States as head of state to make both international and Indian treaties whereas the Canadian government made the Indian treaties but did not have international treaty making powers;

2   The Indians were described as dependent nationalities and an Indian was a legal alien in the United States and not Canada.

There are no such differences because the head of state, the Crown, made the Indian treaties in Canada, not the federal government. Under international law, the head of state appoints authorized Commissioners to enter into such treaties on his behalf. The Crown appointed as one of the Commissioners, Lieutenant Governor Alexander Morris. The "executive government" of Canada is vested in the Queen and her powers may be exercised by a Governor General or a Lieutenant Governor, as is the case with the Indian treaties. At the time he was the representative or agent of the Crown and the Dominion Government of Canada did not have any authority over him. Therefore, like the United States, the Indian treaties were dealt with in the same capacity as the international treaties. Furthermore, the Indians were treated as dependent nationalities in both countries and Indians were treated like legal aliens until 1960 when they were recognized as Canadian citizens.

(d) Douglas E. Sanders "Aboriginal Peoples and the Constitution", (1981) 19 *Alta. L. Rev.* 410, at 417-18.

The lack of a clear definition of the status of an Indian treaty in Canadian law is striking. The treaties were not ratified by federal legislation. The Indian Act has only two provisions dealing with treaties. Section 72 provides that treaty annuity payments are to be paid out of the consolidated revenue fund. Section 88 has already been noted.

The most common analysis of the treaties in the case law is to view them as contracts. But courts have been aware of a problem with this analysis. How does it explain the fact that the contract is with a collectivity, the members of which completely alter over time? Does the tribe have a legal entity apart from its individual members? No legislation confers legal status on the tribes. The case law is even equivocal whether bands established under the Indian Act are legal entities. If the treaties are contracts with continuing parties, the tribes must have a legal status arising from the indigenous legal systems. This involves some recognition of the original political separateness of the tribes. The analysis of treaties as contracts, then, leads to a view of treaties as having some international character.

The major alternative theory to the view of treaties as contracts is to deny any legal significance to treaties at all. This analysis suggests that they were politically motivated documents, designed to achieve peaceful relations Governments may have a moral obligation to live up to the treaties, but there is no legal obligation. The case law does not support this view.

A third possibility is to view treaties as a form of subordinate legislation. It has often been asserted that the Royal Proclamation of 1763 has never been repealed and is still in effect. It was the Proclamation which formalized the procedures for treaty-making in Canada. The treaties could derive their authority from the Proclamation, without the need for subsequent ratification or implementation by Parliament. As long as the treaties came within the scope of the Proclamation, they would be valid as subordinate legislation. Like any other form of legislation, they would be subject to repeal, express or implied, by subsequent legislation. The difficulty with this argument is that the Proclamation describes the treaties solely in terms of land purchases, a narrow framework within which to view treaties. A second problem is that the Royal Proclamation would be the source of authority for the treaties in Ontario and the West, but not for the earlier treaties in the Maritime provinces.

Will the new constitutional amendments alter Canadian law on Indian treaties? Treaty rights will be "recognized and affirmed". This would seem to make the question of the original status of the treaties irrelevant. In that sense, it domesticates the treaties in a way that has not fully been done in the past.[35] Now we simply have to focus on the "rights" expressed in the treaties.

3. Lands Surrendered by Treaty

(a) *St Catharine's Milling and Lumber Co.* v. *The Queen* (1888), 14 AC 46 (PC)
Reproduced in the chapter: *Aboriginal Title, supra.*

Note

1. The Indians who signed Treaty 3 were not represented in the *St Catharine's Milling* case, yet it is considered the leading case on post-Confederation treaties.

(b) *Re Paulette's Application*, **[1973] 6 WWR 97 (NWTSC).**

6th September 1973. MORROW J: — On 3rd April 1973 this matter came before me as a result of a Reference under s. 154(1)(*b*) of the Land Titles Act, R.S.C. 1970, c. L-4. The Reference resulted from a purported caveat being presented for registration under s. 132 of the Act which claimed an interest in an area comprising some 400,000 square miles of land located in the western portion of the Northwest Territories. The caveat was based on a claim for aboriginal rights and was signed by 16 Indian chiefs representing the various Indian bands resident in the area covered by the lands referred to in the caveat.

The caveat document follows the form provided for in the Act. The pertinent portion of the caveat is as follows:

"CAVEAT

"TO THE REGISTRAR, Land Titles Office, Yellowknife, Northwest Territories,

"TAKE NOTICE that we Chief Francois Paulette (Fort Smith) . . . [there follow the names of the remaining 15 chiefs] . . . being residents of the Northwest Territories and members of the Indian bands in the Northwest Territories by virtue of Aboriginal Rights in all land in that tract of land in the Northwest Territories within the limits of the land described in Treaties 8 and 11 of 1899 and 1921, respectively, with adhesions of 1900 and 1922, between Her Most Gracious Majesty Queen Victoria and His Most Gracious Majesty King George V, respectively, and the Indian inhabitants of the land described in the said Treaties; which said tract of land may be more particularly described as land included within the following limits:

[Then follows a metes and bounds description covering the lands shown on a map, copy of which was attached to the document.]

"but, SAVING, AND EXCEPTING THERE FROM all lands for which a Certificate of Title in Fee Simple has been issued: FORBID the registration of any transfer affecting such land or the granting of a certificate of title thereto except subject to the claim set forth.

* * *

Counsel for the caveators called expert evidence directed towards the practice followed in the Land Titles Offices both in Yellowknife and in Alberta, to give the Court the observations and opinions of anthropologists with actual experience in the area, and to introduce through another witness, who has been engaged in researching Treaties Nos. 8 and 11, certain documents and opinions from various archives.

In addition, oral evidence from many of the chiefs who had actually signed the caveat, as well as testimony from Indians and others still living who remembered the treaty-making negotiations, was also brought forward. This entailed taking the Court to each of the Indian settlements within the area comprised to record the evidence of some of these old people. In three instances, because of the age and illness of the witnesses, the Court actually attended at the home of the witness and took the evidence there.

While it may not be pertinent to this judgment, I would like to observe that I found this part of the case most interesting and intriguing. I think almost every member of the Court party felt that for a short moment the pages of history were being turned back and we were privileged to relive the treaty-negotiating days in the actual setting. The interest shown by today's inhabitants in each settlement helped to recreate some of the atmosphere. These witnesses, for the most part very old men and women, one of them 101 years old, were dignified and showed that they were and had been persons of strong character and leaders in their respective communities. One cannot but be reminded of the words of Thomas Gray:

> *Full many a gem of purest ray serene*
> *The dark unfathomed caves of ocean bear;*
> *Full many a flower is born to blush unseen,*
> *And waste its sweetness on the desert air.*

There is no doubt in my mind that their testimony was the truth and represented their best memory of what to them at the time must have been an important event. It is fortunate indeed that their stories are now preserved. . .

Chief Baptiste Cazon, Chief of the Fort Simpson Band for some 20 years, explained how the members of the present band at Fort Simpson were all descendants from his greatgrandfather and that, while his people had no written history, as far back as their memories down through each generation could go, his people had made their homes in the general area of Fort Simpson and that such lands had always been considered to be theirs. According to him, for thousands of years, his people had used the land for hunting and fishing, to obtain food and clothing. They roamed all over the country in pursuit of game. He explained that, in his capacity as chief, he considered that he had a responsibility to his people to take the place of their and his ancestors who had signed the treaty. There are still quite a few of his people even at this time who earn their living from the land in the time-honoured way. This witness further explained that before each of the caveators signed the caveat they obtained approval from their people. This witness explained how members from other bands could enter the area normally used by his people. Chief Cazon was a member of the 1959 Commission known as the Nelson Commission.

Alexie Arrowmaker, Chief at Fort Rae, agreed that in following their traditional way of life the Indians, while always working on the land, do not try to extract minerals for money. This chief, as did many others, described how his people have always migrated, and still do, to the east of the area encompassed by the proposed caveat, during certain seasons for the purpose of seeking game, particularly the caribou. Chief Arrowmaker stated that his people, the Dogribs, had never sold their land to anyone. This witness described how in old times his people, living off the land, would as a rule only come to settlements such as Fort Rae for the purpose of exchanging furs for ammunition and supplies but that now, because their children are in schools, the people have for the most part taken up living in the settlement, going out from there during the hunting, fishing and trapping seasons. It is not customary for people of his band to interfere with members of some different band who might come in to their lands to hunt. He agreed that his people did not consider that each of them owned small parcels of land to the exclusion of others.

Louis Norwegian, 64 years of age, was present at Fort Simpson in 1921 when "old" Norwegian, as he describes his grandfather, was leader of the Fort Simpson Band and when treaty was first "paid". He overheard some of the exchange of words between his grandfather and the Government representatives. According to this witness the Commissioner promised a letter on fishing and trapping. When his grandfather, the recognized leader, went home to eat, an Indian by the name of Antoine was left. He took the treaty and became the chief — the white men made him the chief. This man's evidence was to the effect that his grandfather "did not want to take the money for no reason at all". The promises made were that their hunting and fishing would be left to them as long as the sun shall rise and the rivers shall flow. He heard no mention of reserves but he did hear mention that, once they took treaty, the Government would receive the land. His memory was that the purpose of the treaty was to help the Indians live in peace with the whites and that the Indians would receive a grubstake each treaty payment. Once Antoine took the money, this witness testified that the Commissioner said everybody had to take the treaty after that. Antoine was given a medal, the people took the money, and the people — being "kind of scared" — felt that they had to keep Antoine on as chief after that. . .

Those Indians who had either taken part in the treaty negotiations or who had been present while the negotiations were under way and heard parts or all of the conversation, seemed to be in general agreement that their leaders were concerned about what they were giving up, if anything, in exchange for the treaty money, i.e., they were suspicious of something for nothing; that up to the time of treaty the concept of chief was unknown to them, only that of leader, but the Government man was the one who introduced them to the concept of chief when he placed the medal over the Indian's head after he had signed for his people; that they understood that by signing the treaty they would get a grubstake, money, and the promised protection of the Government from the expected intrusion of white settlers. It is clear also that the Indians for the most part did not understand English and certainly there is no evidence of any of the signatories to the treaties understanding English. Some signatures purport to be what one would call a signature, some are in syllabic form, but most are by mark in the form of an "X". The similarity of the "X" 's is suggestive that perhaps the Government party did not even take care to have each Indian make his own "X". Most witnesses were firm in their recollection that land was not to be surrendered, reserves were not mentioned, and the main concern and chief thrust of the discussions centred around the fear of losing their hunting and fishing rights, the Government officials always reassuring them with variations of the phrase that so long as the sun shall rise in the east and set in the west, and the rivers shall flow, their free right to hunt and fish would not be interfered with.

It seems also that very little, if any, reference to a map was made at any of the settlements. In several cases, also, it is apparent that fairly large segments of the Indian community were not present on the occasion of the first treaty, and that the recognized leaders of the respective bands were not always there either. . .

The last witness called was Father R. Fumoleau, who, as a Roman Catholic priest presently living in Yellowknife, has been engaged for some time in researching material in respect of Treaties Nos. 8 and 11 for the purpose of writing a book on the treaties. His research has carried him through material in the Public Archives of Canada, the Provincial Archives, Edmonton, as well as the various Mission Archives located at Ottawa and in Western Canada. Several documents of historical interest and which help to throw light on events both immediately before and shortly after the signing of each treaty were forthcoming through this witness. It is unnecessary here to review his testimony in detail. Suffice to say that requests by Church officials to extend treaty privileges down the Mackenzie to alleviate the poverty and distress of the Indians in that area appeared to arouse no interest in Ottawa until oil was found where Norman Wells is now located. One cannot help but gather that once this event took place the negotiation of a treaty then seemed to acquire a top priority. The urgency to obtain a treaty, the pressure that seemed to be placed on the Indians to enter into a treaty, as the treaty party moved from settlement to settlement, is more easily understood when the above evidence is examined. . .

Counsel for the caveators presented their submissions under six separate headings, so for convience I propose considering them in the same order.

1. *The caveat area has been used and occupied by an indigenous people, Athapascan-speaking Indians, from time immemorial*
2. *From the time of the first non-Indian entry into the caveat area, the land has been occupied by district groups of Indians, organized in societies and using the land as their forefathers had done for centuries . . .*

On the evidence before me I have no difficulty finding as fact that the area embraced by the caveat has been used and occupied by an indigenous people, Athapascan-speaking Indians from time immemorial, that this land has been occupied by distinct groups of these same Indians, organized in societies and using the land as their forefathers had done for centuries, and that those persons who signed the caveat are chiefs representing the present-day descendants of these distinct Indian groups.

3. *An indigenous population have a legal title to land if they were in occupation of that land prior to colonial entry into the area . . .*

From these authorities I conclude that there are certain well-established characteristics of Indian legal title if the Indians or aborigines were in occupation of the land prior to colonial entry. These are.

(1)   Possessory right — right to use and exploit the land.

(2)   It is a communal right.

(3)   There is a Crown interest underlying this title — it being an estate held of the Crown.

(4)   It is inalienable — it cannot be transferred but can only be terminated by reversion to the Crown.

I am satisfied on my view of the facts that the indigenous people who have been occupying the area covered by the proposed caveat come fully within these criteria and that, in the terms of the language of Hall J in the *Calder* case, may therefore be "prima facie the owners of the lands".

4. *The land rights of the caveators have been confirmed or recognized by the Royal Proclamation of 1763, the Imperial Order in Council of 1870 transferring the Northwestern Territory to Canada, the early Dominion Lands Act and by the Government actions relating to Treaty 8 and Treaty 11*

Once it is established, as concluded under heading 3 above, that the Indians may be owners of their lands, it is perhaps unnecessary to examine as to whether this prima facie ownership has enjoyed acceptance from the various levels of Government down through the years. None the less, such an examination may be reassuring, especially when the question of whether such ownership has been extinguished or not has to be looked into as well. . .

Unless, therefore, the negotiations of Treaty No. 8 and Treaty No. 11 legally terminated or extinguished the Indian land rights or aboriginal rights, it would appear that there was a clear constitutional obligation to protect the legal rights of the indigenous people in the area covered by the proposed caveat, and a clear recognition of such rights.

5. *Treaty No. 8 and Treaty No. 11 could not legally terminate Indian land rights. The Indian people did not understand or agree to the terms appearing in the written version of the treaties; only the mutually understood promises relating to wild life, annuities, relief and friendship became legally effective commitments*

Treaty No. 8 contains several recitals of particular significance to the issues under the present heading:

It is not necessary to repeat the equivalent paragraphs contained in Treaty No. 11. It is to be observed that this treaty, which covered all that part of the caveat area not covered by Treaty No. 8, by far the larger part, contained language almost identical in wording.

Treaty No. 8 was netotiated by a Commission made up of three, Treaty No. 11 by a Commission of one.

In the light of the evidence which was adduced during the present hearing it is perhaps of interest to quote H.A. Conroy, the Treaty No. 11 Commissioner, where in his report to his Deputy Superintendent General, Department of Indian Affairs, he said:

"They were very apt in asking questions, and here, as in all the other posts where the treaty was signed, the questions asked and the difficulties encountered were much the same. The Indians seemed afraid, for one thing, that their liberty to hunt, trap and fish would be taken away or curtailed, but were assured by me that this would not be the case."

While the important phrase in respect of surrender of the land is in each case camouflaged to some extent by being included in one of the preambles, none the less the clear intention would seem to be to obtain from the Indians "all their rights, titles and privileges whatsoever, to the lands". The actual words are: "the said Indians DO HEREBY CEDE, RELEASE, SURRENDER AND YIELD UP". Read in conjunction with "all their rights, titles and privileges" it is about as complete and all-embracing language as can be imagined. If one was to stop there, of course, the Indians were left nothing.

It seems to me that there are two possible qualifications:

(1)   That really all the Government did was confirm its paramount title and, by assuring the Indians that "their liberty to hunt, trap and fish" was not to be taken away or curtailed, was in effect a form of declaration by the Government of continuing aboriginal rights in the Indians.

In the present proceedings, I do not have to go so far as to decide whether this is the case or not. In my role as "inquirer" under the Land Titles Act, as I see it, I merely have to ascertain if there is some chance of success by the caveators in this respect.

I am satisfied here that the caveators have an arguable case under this heading and have at least the possibility of persuading the Federal Court, or whichever other court may be called upon to rule, that the two treaties are not effective instruments to terminate their aboriginal rights for the above reason. In other words, the Federal Government sought these treaties to reassure their dominant title only.

(2)   That, unlike perhaps the previous treaties, the manner of negotiation, the "ultimatum" effect of the discussions between the parties in the Northwest Territories was such as to make it possible for the caveators to succeed in persuading a court exercising the final say on these matters that there was either a failure in the meeting of the minds or that the treaties were mere "peace" treaties and did not effectively terminate Indian title — certainly to the extent that it covered what is normally referred to as surface rights — the use of the land for hunting, trapping and fishing.

Under this subheading it is necessary to examine the evidence in somewhat closer detail than has been done heretofore in this judgment.

Throughout the hearings before me there was a common thread in the testimony — that the Indians were repeatedly assured they were not to be deprived of their hunting, fishing and trapping rights. To me, hearing the witnesses at first hand as I did, many of whom were there at the signing, some of them having been directly involved in the treaty-making, it is almost unbelievable that the Government party could have ever returned from their efforts with any impression but that they had given an assurance in perpetuity to the Indians in the Territories that their traditional use of the lands was not affected.

Ted Trindle, present at the signing of Treaty No. 11 at Fort Simpson, said: "Well, they talked about land and the Indians were scared that by taking treaty they would lose all of their rights but the Indians were told not, but if they were taking treaty they would get protection. They were told it was not to get the land but they would still be free to hunt and roam as usual, no interference."

At Fort Wrigley, Phillip Moses remembers that the Commissioner said "nothing would be changed, everything would be the same as way back, and everything would be the same in the future".

Pretty much the same assurance came at Fort Resolution. When Chief Snuff appeared to be holding out, according to Johnny Jean-Marie Beaulieu, who was there, he was told by the treaty party: "We will pay out the treaty to you here and it has no binding on your land or country at all. It has nothing to do with this land."

Almost each Indian witness affirmed how the Indian representatives only signed after being reassured that, as one expressed it, "If you don't change anything, we will take treaty."

As if the above was not enough, further examination of the evidence, including the material from the archives put in through Father Fumoleau, certainly leaves an impression of haste, almost an "ultimatum", as Bishop Breynat later reported. The uneasy feeling that the negotiations were not all as above board as one would have hoped for is enhanced by statements like that of Pierre Michel, who reported that at Fort Providence the Commissioner said, "if didn't take money, there going to be some sort of trouble for the Indian people."

The comments of Mr Harris in his report in 1925 for the Simpson Agency lend some credence to the anxiety. He reports:

"I believe it to be my duty to inform you that I know that certain promises were made these Indians at the first Treaty which in my opinion never should have been made. The Indians at Fort Simpson did not wish to accept the Treaty at first, and I think the wisest course would have been to let them alone till they asked for it themselves, though I do not in any way wish to criticise the action of my superiors in the Department."

Confirmation of haste and perhaps irregularities is easy to find from the suggestion put forth during the hearing that at Fort Simpson, when the Indians led by Old Norwegian (their recognized spokesman) refused to sign and left, the treaty party then appointed Antoine as chief and treaty was signed. Again there is the testimony of Chief Yendo, who is shown as having signed for Fort Wrigly, but who has no memory of having signed and swears that he cannot read or write.

The impracticability of expecting the indigenous peoples with whom the treaties were concerned here to be able to sustain themselves on the area of land each was to receive when reserves came to be allocated and set aside offers one more reason to suspect the bona fides of the negotiations. Perhaps the extreme southwestern area might permit a bare subsistence living to be grubbed from the soil, but most of the area embraced by the treaties is as already described — rock, lake and tundra — with hunting, trapping and fishing offering the only viable method of maintaining life.

In examining agreements such as treaties where, as in the present case, one side, the Indians, were in such an inferior bargaining position, it is perhaps well to remember the cautionary words of Matthews J in *Choctaw Nation* v. *US* (1886), 119 US 1, 7 Supreme Court 75, 30 L. Ed. 306 at 315, where he said:

"The recognized relation between the parties to this controversy, therefore, is that between a superior and an inferior, whereby the latter is placed under the care and control of the former, and which, while it authorizes the adoption on the part of the United States of such policy as their own public interests may dictate, recognizes, on the other hand, such an interpretation of their acts and promises as justice and reason demand in all cases where power is exerted by the strong over those to whom they owe care and protection. The parties are not on an equal footing, and that inequality is to be made good by the superior justice which looks only to the substance of the right, without regard to technical rules framed under a system of municipal jurisprudence, formulating the rights and obligations of private persons, equally subject to the same laws."

Hall J, at p. 73 of the report in the *Calder* case, in discussing onus states:

"It would, accordingly, appear to be beyond question that the onus of proving that the Sovereign intended to extinguish the Indian title lies on the respondent and that intention must be 'clear and plain'. There is no such proof in the case at bar; no legislation to that effect."

With the above principle in mind I conclude under this heading that there is enough doubt as to whether the full aboriginal title had been extinguished, certainly in the minds of the Indians, to justify the caveators attempting to protect the Indian position until a final adjudication can be obtained.

6. *The caveators have a legal title and interest in the lands described in the caveat, which title and interest can be protected by the filing of the caveat in the Land Titles Registry of the Northwest Territories*

This heading of argument was mentioned in my 14th June judgment, supra, but reserved until now. There are two heads of argument here:

(a) *Are aboriginal rights an interest in land that can be protected by caveat?*

(b) *Can the Land Titles Act have application to lands for which no certificate of title has been issued or where no application to register under the Act has been made? . . .*

Under this heading, therefore, I am satisfied that the provisions of the Land Titles Act do permit the filing or registering of a caveat such as is proposed here, and that this applies even in the case of unpatented Crown land. . .

Conclusions

To sum up my conclusions under the Reference:

(1) I am satisfied that those who signed the caveat are present-day descendants of those distinct Indian groups who, organized in societies and using the land as their forefathers had done for centuries, have since time immemorial used the land embraced by the caveat as theirs.

(2) I am satisfied that those same indigenous people as mentioned in (1) above are prima facie owners of the lands covered by the caveat — that they have what are known as aboriginal rights.

(3) There exists a clear constitutional obligation on the part of the Canadian Government to protect the legal rights of the indigenous peoples in the area covered by the caveat.

(4) Notwithstanding the language of the two treaties, there is sufficient doubt on the facts that aboriginal title was extinguished that such claim for title should be permitted to be put forward by the caveators.

(5) The above purported claim for aboriginal rights constitutes an interest in land which can be protected by caveat under the Land Titles Act.

(6) The provisions of the Land Titles Act permit the filing or registering of a caveat such as is presented here even in the case of unpatented land. . .

4. Treaty Annuities

(a) *Attorney General for Canada* v. *Attorney General for Ontario*, [1897] AC 199, 66 LJPC 11 (PC) (Robinson Treaties Annuities Case)

LORD WATSON. In the year 1850 the Ojibeway Indians inhabiting the Lake Huron District, and the Indians of the same tribe inhabiting the Lake Superior District, entered into separate treaties with the Governor of the Province of Canada, acting on behalf of Her Majesty and the

Government of the Province, for the cession of certain tracts of land, which had until that time been occupied as Indian reserves. As considation for these surrenders, a sum of money was immediately paid under each treaty; and a promise and agreement were given by the Governor, as representing the Crown and the provincial Government, to pay a perpetual annuity, in the one case of 600*l.*, and in the other of 400*l.* Both treaties contained the further promise and agreement that, in case the territory ceded should at any future period produce an amount which would enable the Government of the Province, without incurring loss, to increase these annuities, then and in that case the same should be increased from time to time, provided that the amount paid to each individual should not exceed the sum of one pound provincial currency in any one year, or such further sum as Her Majesty might be graciously pleased to order. Provision was also made for a proportional abatement of the annuities, in the event, which has not yet occurred, of the Indian population of either district becoming diminished in number below a specified limit.

The effect of these treaties was, that, whilst the title to the lands ceded continued to be vested in the Crown, all beneficial interest in them, together with the right to dispose of them, and to appropriate their proceeds, passed to the Government of the Province, which also became liable to fulfil the promises and agreements made on its behalf, by making due payment to the Indians of the stipulated annuities, whether original or increased. In 1867, under the Act of Union, the Province of Canada ceased to exist, having been divided by that statute into two separate and independent provinces, Ontario and Quebec. Until the time when that division became operative, the Indian annuities payable under the treaties of 1850 were debts or liabilities of the old province, either present, future or contingent.

There are four sections in the Act of 1867 (ss. 109, 111, 112 and 142) which relate to the incidence, after Union, of the debts and liabilities of the old province. Those clauses contain the whole provisions of the Act upon that subject; and it is upon their construction that the decision of this appeal must ultimately depend. They distribute these debts and liabilities into two classes, the one being payable in the first instance by the Dominion, with a right of indemnity against Ontario and Quebec, and the other being directly chargeable either to Ontario or to Quebec.

Sect. 111 enacts, in general terms, that the Dominion of Canada "shall be liable for the debts and liabilities of each province existing at the Union." Sect. 112 enacts that Ontario and Quebec conjointly shall be liable to the Dominion for the amount (if any) by which the debt of the Province of Canada exceeds at the Union sixty-two million five hundred thousand dollars, and shall be charged with interest at the rate of 5 per cent. per annum thereon. Then, by s. 142, provision is made for the apportionment of the excess of these conjoint liabilities over the sum specified between Ontario and Quebec.

The enactments of s. 109 relate to the lands, mines, minerals, and royalties from which the territorial revenues of the old province were derived. It assigns to Ontario and Quebec, respectively, such of these sources of revenue as are locally situated within the limits of each of these new provinces together with all proceeds thereof which at the date of Union had become due and payable to the Province of Canada. But it is made an express condition of the transfer that the property transferred shall be "subject to any trusts existing in respect thereof, and to any interest other than that of the province (i.e. of Canada) in the same."

The beneficial interest in the territories ceded by the Indians under the treaties of 1850 became vested, by virtue of s. 109, in the Province of Ontario. So far as appears, the perpetual annuities of 600*l.* and 400*l.* were duly paid by the old province; and it was matter of admission, in the course of the argument upon this appeal, that, some time after the Union, the value of these annuities was capitalised, and, with consent of all the parties interested, added to the debts and liabilities which were assumed by the Dominion under the provisions of s. 111. The Indians do not seem to have become aware of the full extent of the rights secured to them by treaty, until the year 1873, when they for the first time preferred against the Dominion a claim for an annual increase of their respective annuities from and after the date of the treaties, upon the ground that, during the whole period which followed, the proceeds of the surrendered lands had been so large as to enable the stipulated increase to be paid without involving loss. The Dominion Government, who maintained then, as they do now, that the Province of Ontario is directly liable to the Indians for any such increase, under the provisions of s. 109, intimated the claim to that province, when its Government admitted that the condition had been satisfied upon which the increased amounts became due and payable, but disputed liability, upon the ground that the claim was one which fell in the first instance upon the Dominion, with recourse against Ontario and Quebec jointly. It was ultimately arranged that the Government of the Dominion should from and after that date and in the meantime continue to pay these increased allowances as they became due to the Indians, until the question of liability was determined.

It appears that many questions have arisen from time to time since that arrangement was made with regard to the debts and liabilities of the Province of Canada at the time of the Union; and these had the effect of delaying the final adjustment of the account contemplated by s. 112, the object of which is to ascertain and fix the precise balance of which Ontario and Quebec are made conjointly liable to relieve the Dominion.

With the view of accelerating that adjustment, three statutes, in terms identical, were in the years 1890 and 1891 passed by the respective Legislatures of Canada, of Ontario, and of Quebec, sanctioning the appointment of three judges as arbitrators for the purpose of finally determining various matters which are therein specified — including all questions which had arisen or might thereafter arise "in the settlement of the accounts between the Dominion of Canada and the provinces of Ontario and Quebec," concerning which no agreement had previously been arrived at.

In terms of, and under the authority of, these statutes a deed of submission was entered into between the Governments of Canada, Ontario, and Quebec, and arbitrators were duly appointed. The Dominion submitted to them a claim against Ontario, (1.) for the increase of Indian annuities (which had not been paid) from the date of Union until 1874, and (2.) for the increased amounts which had been paid to the Indians between 1874 and 1892, with interest from the several dates of disbursement. The claim was urged, mainly upon the ground that the treaty stipulations giving the Indians a right to an increase of annuity either constituted a trust burdening the surrendered lands and their proceeds, within the meaning of s. 109, or created an interest in the same, other than that of the old province, within the meaning of the same section. Quebec, having an obvious interest in the success of the claim, which would exclude any demand against its revenues under s. 112, maintained before the arbitrators the same view which was put forward by the Dominion.

The learned arbitrators, in February, 1895, issued an award, by the 6th article of which they found "that the ceded territory mentioned became the property of Ontario under the 109th section of the British North America Act, 1867, subject to a trust to pay the increased annuities on the happening, after the Union, of the event on which such payment depended, and to the interest of the Indians therein to be so paid. That the ultimate burden of making provision for the payment of the increased annuities in question in such an event falls upon the Province of Ontario; and that this burden has not been in any way affected or discharged." By a clause in the statutes of 1890 and 1891 it is enacted that when the arbitrators proceed on their view of a disputed question of law, the award shall set forth the same at the instance of either party, "and the award shall be subject to appeal so far as it relates to such decision to the Supreme Court, and thence to the Privy Council of England, in case their Lordships are pleased to entertain the appeal." The concluding part of that enactment ignores the constitutional rule that an appeal lies to Her Majesty, and not to this Board; and that no such jurisdiction can be conferred upon their Lordships, who are merely the advisers of the Queen, by any legislation either of the Dominion or of the provinces of Canada. By another clause in these Acts it is provided that, in case of an appeal on a question of law being successful, the matter shall go back to the arbitrators, for making such changes on the award as may be necessary, or an Appellate Court may make any other direction as to the necessary changes.

The learned arbitrators, by a supplementary order dated March 26, 1895, certified and declared that, in respect of the question as to the liability of the Province of Ontario for the increased annuities paid by the Dominion to the Indians since the Union, they proceeded upon their view of a disputed question of law. Their decision upon that point was accordingly brought under the review of the Supreme Court of Canada by an appeal at the instance of Ontario in which the Dominion and Quebec appeared as respondents. The Supreme Court was divided in opinion. Two of the learned judges, Gwynne and King JJ, held that the award ought to be maintained and the appeal dismissed; but the majority, consisting of Strong CJ, with Taschereau and Sedgewick JJ, ordered and adjudged that "the award should be varied by substituting for paragraph 6 thereof the following:

"The ceded territory mentioned became the property of Ontario under the 109th section of the British North America Act, 1867, absolutely and free from any trust, charge or lien in respect of any of the annuities, as well those presently payable as those deferred and agreed to be paid in augmentation of the original annuities upon the condition in the treaties mentioned." The Supreme Court, by the same majority, ordered the award to be further varied by striking out paragraphs 7 and 9; and directed that the respondents should pay his costs to the appellant. Against that judgment, both the Dominion and Quebec have presented appeals which have been admitted by Her Majesty in Council.

The findings which have been substituted, by the order of the Supreme Court for those contained in the 6th paragraph of the award raise the only substantial question which has been presented for their Lordships' decision. The directions to delete paragraphs 7 and 9 of the award are amendments merely consequential upon the previous findings being sustained, and must stand or fall with these findings. In other words, the main and only question between the parties is, whether liability for the increased amount of the Indian annuities stipulated by the treaties of 1850 is so connected with or attached to the surrendered territory and its proceeds, in the sense of the concluding enactments of s. 109, as to follow the beneficial interest, and form a charge upon it in the hands of the province.

The enactments of s. 109, upon which the appellants rely, are to the effect that the beneficial interest in the property held by the Crown of which that section disposes shall belong to the province in which the property is situated, subject always "to any trusts existing in respect thereof, and to any interest other than that of the province in the same." The transfer of beneficial interest which the clause operates is not confined to lands, but extends to all proceeds thereof which had become due and payable to the old province before Union. There is nothing in the Record of these appeals to shew whether any, and, if so, what amount of proceeds were at the time of Union due and payable, and therefore came into the possession of the new Province of Ontario. The claim made by the Dominion, and sustained by the arbitrators, is thefore in substance, that the Indian annuities form a charge upon the lands, and their proceeds arising after Union, with which s. 109 does not deal, except in so far as they are implied or included in the word "lands."

The expressions "subject to any trusts existing in respect thereof," and "subject to any interest other than that of the province," appear to their Lordships to be intended to refer to different classes of right. Their Lordships are not prepared to hold that the word "trust" was meant by the Legislature to be strictly limited to such proper trusts as a court of equity would undertake to administer; but, in their opinion, it must at least have been intended to signify the existence of a contractual or legal duty, incumbent upon the holder of the beneficial estate or its proceeds, to make payment, out of one or other of these, of the debt due to the creditor to whom that duty ought to be fulfilled. On the other hand, "an interest other than that of the province in the same" appears to them to denote some right or interest in a third party, independent of and capable of being vindicated in competition with the beneficial interest of the old province. Their Lordships have been unable to discover any reasonable grounds for holding that, by the terms of the treaties, any independent interest of that kind was conferred upon the Indian communities; and, in the argument addressed to them for the appellants, the claim against Ontario was chiefly if not wholly based upon the provisions of s. 109 with respect to trusts.

Two of the learned arbitrators explained at some length the reasons by which they were influenced in arriving at the conclusions which they embodied in the 6th paragraph of their award. They start from the proposition that the treaties of 1850, being in the nature of international compacts, ought to be liberally construed. That rule when rightly applied, in circumstances which admit of its application, is useful and salutary, but it goes no farther than this, that the stipulations of an international treaty ought, when the language of the instrument permits, to be so interpreted as to promote the main objects of the treaty. Their Lordships venture to doubt whether the rule has any application to those parts, even of a proper international treaty, which contain the terms of an ordinary mercantile transaction, in which the respective stipulations of the contracting parties are expressed in language which is free from ambiguity. Starting from the proposition already stated, Mr Chancellor Boyd arrives, upon equitable and benignant principles, at the conclusion that the treaties of 1850 contain "an implied obligation to pay the increased annuities out of the proceeds of the lands which passes with the lands as a burden to be borne by Ontario." Burbidge J., by a similar process of reasoning, arrived at substantially the same result which was concurred in by Sir Louis Napoleon Casault.

Their Lordships are of opinion that the language of the treaties in question does not warrant the conclusion that payment of the original annuities and of their augmentations was to be derived from different sources, as the learned arbitrators appear to have held. The promise and agreement upon which the obligation for their payment rests is, in both cases, expressed in precisely the same terms. Their Lordships entirely agree with the following observations made by King J, one of the minority in the Supreme Court: "Practically it does not now, and it never did, make any difference to the Indians, whether they were declared to have an interest in the proceeds of the land or not. Their assurance would be equal in either case." Even at the present time, and in view of the change of circumstances introduced by the Act of 1867, their Lordships think it must still be matter of absolute indifference to the Indians whether they have to look for payment to the Dominion, to which the administration and control of their affairs is entrusted by s. 91 (24) of the Act of 1867, or to the Province of Ontario. But it is clear that, for the purposes of the present question, the construction of the treaties must be dealt with on the same footing as if it had arisen between the Indians and the old Province of Canada; and it must be kept in view that, whilst the Indians had no interest in making such a stipulation, an agreement by the province to make a particular debt a charge upon a particular portion of its annual revenues, or an agreement to hold such portion of its revenue in trust for the future payment of that debt, might have occasioned considerable inconvenience to the Government of the province. Why, in these circumstances, a liberal construction should be resorted to for the purpose of raising an equitable right in the Indians which is of no pecuniary advantage to them, and to which the province did not, according to the ordinary and natural construction of the instruments, consent, and cannot with any degree of probability be presumed to have consented, their Lordships are at a loss to understand. The so-called equity appears to have been conjured up for the doubtful purpose of construing the provisions of s. 109 with an amount of liberality which the ordinary canons of construction do not admit of.

It may not be out of place, in this connection, to refer to the general arrangements made by the Government of the Province of Canada for the application of part of its revenues in payment of annuities to the Indian tribes. Before 1850 there had been many cessions of reserved territory by its Indian occupants, in respect of which consideration was due by the province in the shape of annual payments. These annuities, then amounting to 6666*l*. currency, were by the Provincial Act, 9 Vict. c. 114, charged upon the Civil List of the province; and an annual sum of 39, 245*l*. 16*s*. currency was granted to the Crown, which was at that time the administrator of Indians and Indian affairs, out of "the Consolidated Revenue Fund of this province," for the purpose of paying these annuities, and other charges included in Sched. B. of the Act. And there is no evidence to shew that, during the existence of the Province of Canada, the annuities which became payable under the two treaties of 1850 were dealt with on any other footing, or paid out of any other fund than the general revenues of the province.

Their Lordships have had no difficulty in coming to the conclusion that, under the treaties, the Indians obtained no right to their annuities, whether original or augmented, beyond a promise and agreement, which was nothing more than a personal obligation by its governor, as representing the old province, that the latter should pay the annuities as and when they became due; that the Indians obtained no right which gave them any interest in the territory which they surrendered, other than that of the province; and that no duty was imposed upon the province, whether in the nature of a trust obligation or otherwise, to apply the revenue derived from the surrendered lands in payment of the annuities. They will, accordingly, humbly advise Her Majesty that the judgment of the Supreme Court of Canada ought to be affirmed, and both appeals dismissed. Seeing that the substantial question involved in these appeals is that of contract liability for a pecuniary obligation, they are of opinion that the rule followed by them in some really international questions between Canadian Governments ought not to apply here. The appellants must, therefore, pay to the respondent his costs of these appeals.

(b) *Dominion of Canada* v. *Province of Ontario*, [1910] AC 637 (Treaty No. 3 Annuities Case)

By the statement of the Dominion of Canada filed in the Exchequer Court on June 13, 1903, the claimant set forth that by a treaty No. 3, known as the North West Angle Treaty, and dated October 3, 1873, between Her late Majesty Queen Victoria by her Commissioners therein named of the one part, and the Salteaux tribe of the Ojibeway Indians of the other part, the said Indians ceded, released, surrendered, and yielded up to the Government of the Dominion for Her Majesty the Queen and her successors for ever all their rights, titles, and privileges whatsoever to the lands thereinafter mentioned, such lands embracing an area of 55,000 square miles more or less, to hold the same to Her Majesty the Queen and her successors for ever. And Her Majesty the Queen thereby agreed and undertook to lay aside reserves of lands in the territories thereby ceded for the benefit of the Indians as therein mentioned, and further to give to her Indians certain presents of money, and also annually to pay to them certain annuities and to give them certain presents and sums of money for the chiefs and subordinate officers as therein mentioned. And Her Majesty also entered into further agreements with her said Indians as therein mentioned.

The claimant also set forth that in pursuance of the treaty the Dominion had made payments to and for the benefit of the Indians in accordance with its provisions, the details of which were set out in schedules A and B to the said statement, and that the Dominion had also been obliged to make large expenditures of money in making surveys of reserves for the Indians in conducting the necessary business of the administration of the treaty, the details of which expenditure were set forth in schedule C thereto. Also that after the admission into the Union of the Province of Manitoba in the year 1870 a dispute arose between the Dominion and the Province of Ontario as to the correct northern and western boundary of the said Province of Ontario, and that, arbitrators having been appointed to determine the correct boundary, an award was made, by the effect of which out of the 55,000 square miles within the limits of the treaty about 30,000 square miles were found to be within the boundary of the Province of Ontario. Subsequently, in the 1888, in an action brought by the Attorney-General of Ontario against the St Catharine's Milling and Lumber Company, Limited, the Judicial Committee of the Privy Council decided that the portion of the ceded lands found by the Court to be within Ontario formed part of the public domain of Ontario, and were public lands belonging to Ontario by virtue of the provisions of the British North America Act, and the claim that the said lands were the property of the Dominion by reason of the cession of the Indian title to the Dominion was dismissed.

The claim of the Dominion of Canada was for a declaration that (1.) inasmuch as the benefit of the aforesaid surrender accrues to Ontario, that province shall relieve the Dominion of all obligations involving the payment of money which were undertaken by Her Majesty by virtue of the said treaty, and which have been, or may be, fulfilled by the Dominion of Canada; (2.) the Province of Ontario has held, and now holds, the portion of the ceded lands which lie within the province charged with and subject to the payment of a proportion of the annuities and other moneys paid to and for the Indians under the terms and stipulations of the treaty; (3.) the Dominion of Canada is entitled to recover from, and be paid by, the Province of Ontario a proper proportion of annuities and other moneys so paid as aforesaid; (4.) all proper accounts be taken to ascertain the amount payable to the Dominion in respect of the said annuities and other moneys so paid as aforesaid.

By its answer the Province of Ontario denied liability, and, further, counterclaimed in respect of certain revenues received by the Dominion pending a determination of the boundaries of the province and arising out of the lands eventually adjudged to belong to the province.

The judgment of the Judicial Committee in *St Catharine's Milling and Lumber Co.* v. *The Queen* decided that the surrender of so much of the area of 55,000 square miles as was situated in the Province of Ontario enured to transmit to the province in terms of s. 109 of the British North America Act, 1867, the entire beneficial interest in such lands, and in the course of the judgment there occurred this passage: "Seeing that the benefit of the surrender accrues to her, Ontario must of course relieve the Crown and the Dominion of all obligations involving the payment of money which were undertaken by Her Majesty, and which are said to have been in part fulfilled by the Dominion Government."

Burbidge J by his judgment declared the province liable to pay to the Dominion all such sums paid by the Dominion as were referable to the extinguishment of the Indian title, in the proportion which the area of the treaty lands within Ontario bears to the whole treaty area. All other questions, including the question what sums of money so paid by the Dominion were referable to the extinguishment of the Indian title, were reserved for further consideration and adjudication. He considered that, with respect to that portion of the lands surrendered to the Crown which were situated within the province, "the Dominion Government occupied a position analogous to that of a bona fide possessor or purchaser of lands of which the actual title was in another person. The question of the extinguishment of the Indian title in these lands could not with prudence be deferred until such boundaries were determined. It was necessary to the peace, order, and good government of the country that the question should be settled at the earliest possible time. The Dominion authorities held the view that the lands belonged to the Dominion and that they had a right to administer the same. In this they were in a large measure mistaken, but no doubt the view was held in good faith. They proceeded with the negotiations for the treaty without consulting the province. The latter, although it claimed the lands to be surrendered or the greater part thereof, raised no objection and did not ask to be represented in such negotiations. The case bears some analogy to one in which a person in consequence of unskilful survey or in the belief that the land is his own makes improvements in lands that are not his own. In such a case the statutes of the old Province of Canada made, and those of the Province of Ontario make, provision to protect him from loss in respect of such improvements or to give him a lien therefor. The case, however, appears to me to bear a closer analogy to one in which a bona fide possessor or purchaser of real estate pays money to discharge an existing incumbrance or charge upon the estate having no notice of any infirmity in his title. In such a case, as stated by Mr Justice Story in *Bright v. Boyd*, the possessor or purchaser was according to the principles of the Roman law entitled to be repaid the amount of such payment by the true owner seeking to recover the estate from him.'' He also considered that the views expressed in Lord Watson's judgment should be taken as a part or condition of the judgment in favour of the province, and that, although such views found no place in the formal judgment pronounced, it was proper that he should give effect to the view there expressed that the Province of Ontario was liable to indemnify the Dominion against a portion of the expenditure incurred in discharge of the obligations created by the treaty.

The judgment on further consideration (December 4, 1907) referred it to the registrar to take certain accounts necessary to give effect to the declaration.

Both judgments were reversed by the Supreme Court by a majority of one (Idington, Maclennan, and Duff JJ, Girouard and Davies JJ dissenting).

The judgment of the majority dealt first with the scope of the jurisdiction of the Court of Exchequer, to which Court, by identical statutes, the Dominion and the province had committed jurisdiction over controversies between them, and held that the statutes in question required any controversy submitted under them to be determined in accordance with and by the application of legal principles, and not by considerations of mere convenience and propriety.

Idington J. held that there was no foundation in law or fact for the theory that the Dominion acted as an agent for the province, but that the Dominion was impelled to settle with the Indians by virtue of its obligations to the Province of British Columbia, and for other reasons not referable to its wardship over or duties towards such Indians; and that the pronouncement in Lord Watson's judgment in 14 App. Cas. 60 was a mere dictum.

Duff J, with whose opinion Maclennan J concurred, agreed with Idington J as to the motives of the Dominion in making the treaty, and considered that under these circumstances there was no principle on which a Court of Equity could proceed to adjust equitably as between the Dominion and the province the burden of the obligations undertaken by the former; that Lord Watson's remark was a mere dictum, the preferable view of its import being that, upon the facts as they appeared, as a matter of fair dealing Ontario would be expected to assume the obligations in question, but that, in deciding controversies between the two Governments, the Exchequer Court could only apply some appropriate rule or principle of law, and that the pronouncement, even if more than a mere dictum, would not be conclusive of the appeal before them.

* * *

LORD LOREBURN LC   In this appeal the only question argued was whether or not the Dominion of Canada is entitled to recover from the Province of Ontario a proper proportion of annuities and other moneys which the Dominion bound itself in the name of the Crown to pay to an Indian tribe and its chiefs under a treaty of October 3, 1873. There has been marked difference of opinion in the Canadian Courts. Burbidge J decided in favour of the Dominion, but on appeal to the Supreme Court of Canada three out of five learned judges reversed that judgment. The various opinions delivered in both Courts have dealt with the case so exhaustively and so clearly that nothing new really remains to be said, and the matter at issue has been reduced to a simple though extremely important point.

The treaty of 1873 was made between Her late Majesty Queen Victoria, acting on the advice of the Dominion Government, and the Salteaux tribe of the Ojibeway Indians. Its effect was to extinguish by consent the Indian interest over a large tract of land about 50,000 square miles in extent, and in return it secured to the Indians certain payments and other rights agreed to and promised by Her Majesty. At that time it had not been ascertained whether any part of this land was included within the Province of Ontario, but it is now common ground that the greater part of it lies within the Ontario boundaries. In making this treaty the Dominion Government acted upon the rights conferred by the Constitution. They were not acting in concert with the Ontario Government, but on their own responsibility, and it is conceded that the motive was not any special benefit to Ontario, but a motive of policy in the interests of the Dominion as a whole.

When, however, by subsequent decisions it was established that, under the British North America Act of 1867, lands which are released from the overlying Indian interest enure to the benefit, not of the Dominion, but of the province within which they are situated, it became apparent that Ontario had derived an advantage under the treaty. And the principle sought to be enforced by the present appeal is that Ontario should recoup the Dominion for so much of the burden undertaken by the Dominion toward the Salteaux tribe as may properly be attributed to the lands within Ontario which had been disencumbered of the Indian interest by virtue of the treaty.

Their Lordships are of opinion that in order to succeed the appellants must bring their claim within some recognized legal principle. The Court of Exchequer, to which, by statutes both of the Dominion and the province, a jurisdiction has been committed over controversies between them, did not thereby acquire authority to determine those controversies only according to its own view of what in the circumstances might be thought fair. It may be that, in questions between a dominion comprising various provinces of which the laws are not in all respects identical on the one hand, and a particular province with laws of its own on the other hand, difficulty will arise as to the legal principle which is to be applied. Such conflicts may always arise in the case of States or provinces within a union. But the conflict is between one set of legal principles and another. In the present case it does not appear to their Lordships that the claim of the Dominion can be sustained on any principle of law that can be invoked as applicable.

To begin with, this case ought to be regarded as if what was done by the Crown in 1873 had been done by the Dominion Government, as in substance it was in fact done. The Crown acts on the advice of ministers in making treaties, and in owning public lands holds them for the good of the community. When differences arise between the two Governments in regard to what is due to the Crown as maker of treaties from the Crown as owner of public lands they must be adjusted as though the two Governments were separately invested by the Crown with its rights and responsibilities as treaty maker and as owner respectively.

So regarding it, there does not appear sufficient ground for saying that the Dominion Government in advising the treaty did so as agent for the province. They acted with a view to great national interests, in pursuance of powers derived from the Act of 1867, without the consent of the province and in the belief that the lands were not within that province. They neither had nor thought they required nor purported to act upon any authority from the Provincial Government.

Again, it seems to their Lordships that the relation of trustee and cestui que trust, from which a right to indemnity might be derived, cannot, even in its widest sense, be here established. The Dominion Government were indeed, on behalf of the Crown, guardians of the Indian interest and empowered to take a surrender of it and to give equivalents in return, but in so doing they were not under any special duty to the province. And in regard to the proprietary rights in the land (apart from the Indian interest) which through the Crown enured to the benefit of the province, the Dominion Government had no share in it at all. The only thing in regard to which the Dominion could conceivably be thought trustees for the province, namely, the dealing with the Indian interest, was a thing concerning the whole Canadian nation. In truth, the duty of the Dominion Government was not that of trustees, but that of ministers exercising their powers and their discretion for the public welfare.

Another contention was advanced on behalf of the appellants — that this is analogous to the case of a bona fide possessor or purchaser of real estate who pays money to discharge an existing incumbrance upon it without notice of an infirmity of his title. It is enough to say that the Dominion Government were never in possession or purchasers of these lands, that they had, in fact, notice of the claim thereto of the true owner, though they did not credit it, and that they did not pay off the Indian incumbrance for the benefit of these lands, but for distinct and important interests of their own.

This really is a case in which expenditure independently incurred by one party for good and sufficient reasons of his own has resulted in direct advantage to another. It may be that, as a matter of fair play between the two Governments, as to which their Lordships are not called upon to express and do not express any opinion, the province ought to be liable for some part of this outlay. But in point of law, which alone is here in question, the judgment of the Supreme Court appears unexceptionable.

If the opinions of Burbidge J and of the two dissenting judges in the Supreme Court are examined, it will be found that they rely almost entirely upon a passage in the judgment delivered by Lord Watson at this Board in the case of *St Catharine's Milling and Lumber Co.* v. *The Queen*. It must be acknowledged that this passage does give strong support to the view of those who rely upon it, and their Lordships feel themselves bound to regard this expression of opinion with the same respect that has been accorded to it by all the learned judges in Canada. They consider, however, that Idington J and Duff J have stated conclusive reasons against adopting the dictum alluded to as decisive of the present case. The point here raised was not either raised or argued in that case, and it is quite possible that Lord Watson did not intend to pronounce upon a legal right. If he did so intend, the passage in question must be regarded as obiter dictum.

In the course of argument a question was mooted as to the liability of the Ontario Government to carry out the provisions of the treaty so far as concerns future reservations of land for the benefit of the Indians. No such matter comes up for decision in the present case. It is not intended to forestall points of that kind which may depend upon different considerations, and, if ever they arise, will have to be discussed and decided afresh.

Their Lordships will humbly advise His Majesty that this appeal should be dismissed. There will be no order as to costs.

5. Treaty Hunting and Fishing Rights

(a) Application of Federal Laws

(i) *R.* v. *Sikyea*, 43 DLR (2d) 150, [1964] 2 CCC 325, 46 WWR 65 (NWTCA).

JOHNSON JA — The respondent in this case was convicted by a magistrate at Yellowknife upon a charge of unlawfully killing a migratory bird in an area described in Sched. A of the migratory bird regulations at a time not during an open season for that bird in the area, in violation of sec. 5(1)(*a*) of the migratory bird regulations. He was fined $10 and costs, and apparently (although the original conviction is not before us), both the bird and the respondent's gun were seized. The respondent appealed to Sissons, J. and, after a trial *de novo*, (1962-63) 40 WWR 494, that judge set aside the conviction, acquitted the respondent and ordered the return of the gun and the duck to the respondent. From that decision the crown appeals.

On May 7, 1962, not far from Yellowknife airport in the Northwest Territories, the respondent was arrested by a constable of the RCMP shortly after he had shot a female mallard duck. The respondent admitted shooting the duck but stated that he did not know that he was not to shoot ducks out of season.

The respondent is an Indian and a member of band No. 84 under treaty 11. He had contracted tuberculosis in 1959 and had been sent out to Edmonton for treatment. Since his return he had been unable to work and he and his family had been receiving welfare assistance. On this day he was on his way out to the bush to see if he was able to do his customary work. He had taken his tent, gun and muskrat traps and was planning to trap muskrats. He expected to be away two or three weeks. He had taken no food, expecting to shoot game. He shot this duck for food.

The right of Indians to hunt and fish for food on unoccupied crown lands has always been recognized in Canada — in the early days as an incident of their "ownership" of the land, and later by the treaties by which the Indians gave up their ownership right in these lands. McGillivray JA in *Rex* v. *Wesley* [1932] 2 WWR 337, 26 Alta LR

433, 58 CCC 269, discussed quite fully the origin, history and nature of the right of the Indians both in the lands and under the treaties by which these were surrendered and it is unnecessary to repeat what he has said. It is sufficient to say that these rights had their origin in the royal proclamation that followed the *Treaty of Paris* in 1763. By that proclamation it was declared that the Indians

". . . should not be molested or disturbed in the possession of such parts of Our Dominions and Territories as, not having been ceded to or purchased by Us are reserved to them or any of them as their hunting grounds."

The Indians inhabiting Hudson Bay Company lands were excluded from the benefit of the proclamation, and it is doubtful, to say the least, if the Indians of at least the western part of the Northwest Territories could claim any rights under the proclamation, for these lands at the time were *terra incognita* and lay to the north and not "to the westward of the sources of the river which fall into the sea from the west or northwest," (from the 1763 proclamation describing the area to which the proclamation applied). That fact is not important because the government of Canada has treated all Indians across Canada, including those living on lands claimed by the Hudson Bay Company, as having an interest in the lands that required a treaty to effect its surrender.

Two of the earliest treaties (called the "Robinson Treaties" in the book *The Treaties of Canada with the Indians of Manitoba, the Northwest Territories and Kee-Wa-Tin* by *the Hon. Alexander Morris, PC*), entered into in 1850 contained the following:

And the said William Benjamin Robinson of the first part, on behalf of Her Majesty and the Government of this Province, hereby promises and agrees . . . to allow the said Chiefs and their tribes the full and free privilege to hunt over the territory now ceded by them, and to fish in the waters thereof as they have heretofore been in the habit of doing, saving and excepting only such portions of the said territory as may from time to time be sold or leased to individuals, or companies of individuals and occupied by them with the consent of the Provincial Government.

In the North-West Angle treaty of 1873, a clause that became the model for all subsequent treaties appears. By 1877, seven treaties had been signed by which the Indians surrendered most of the arable and grazing lands from the Great Lakes to the mountains. In 1899, by treaty No. 8, the Indians surrendered the Peace River and northern Alberta area. It was not until 1921 that the Indian rights in that part of the Northwest Territories that includes Yellowknife were surrendered by treaty No. 11. As part of the consideration for surrendering their interest in the lands covered by the treaty, the Indians received the following covenant:

And His Majesty the King hereby agrees with the said Indians that they shall have the right to pursue their usual vocations of hunting, trapping and fishing throughout the tract surrendered as heretofore described, subject to such regulations as may from time to time be made by the Government of the Country acting under the authority of His Majesty, and saving and excepting such tracts as may be required or taken up from time to time for settlement, mining, lumbering, trading or other purposes.

This substantially the same covenant as appears in all of the other treaties that I have been able to examine.

From these treaties and from the negotiations preceding the signing of these treaties as reported in *Mr Morris'* book, it is, I think, obvious that while the government hoped that the Indians would ultimately take up the white man's way of life, until they did, they were expected to continue their previous mode of life with only such regulations and restrictions as would assure that a supply of game for their own needs would be maintained. The regulations that "the Government of the Country" were entitled to make under the clause of the treaty which I have quoted, were, I think, limited to this kind of regulation. Certainly the commissioners who represented the government at the signing of the treaties so understood it. For example, in the report of the commissioners who negotiated treaty No. 8, this appears:

Our chief difficulty was the apprehension that the hunting and fishing privileges were to be curtailed. The provision in the treaty under which ammunition and twine is to be furnished went far in the direction of quieting the fears of the Indians, for they admitted that it would be unreasonable to furnish the means of hunting and fishing if laws were to be enacted which would make hunting and fishing so restricted as to render it impossible to make a livelihood by such pursuits. But over and above the provision, we had to solemnly assure them that only such laws as to hunting and fishing as were in the interest of the Indians and were found necessary in order to protect the fish and fur-bearing animals would be made, and that they would be as free to hunt and fish after the treaty as they would be if they never entered into it.

These Indians, as well as all others, would have been surprised indeed if, in the face of such assurances, the clause in their treaty which purported to continue their rights to hunt and fish could be used to restrict their right to shoot game birds to one and one-half months each year. I agree with the view of McGillivray, JA, in the *Wesley* case, *supra*, where he says at p. 352:

> It is true that Government regulations in respect of hunting are contemplated in the treaty but considering that treaty in its proper setting I do not think that any of the makers of it could by any stretch of the imagination be deemed to have contemplated a day when the Indians would be deprived of an unfettered right to hunt game of all kinds for food on unoccupied Crown land.

Discussing the nature of the rights which the Indians obtained under the treaties, Lord Watson, speaking for the judicial committee in *Atty. Gen. for Can.* v. *Atty. Gen. for Ont.; Atty. Gen. for Que.* v. *Atty. Gen. for Ont.* [1897] AC 199, 66 LJPC 11, affirming (*sub nom. Prov. of Ont.* v. *Dom. of Canada; In re Indian Claims*) 25 SCR 434, said at p. 213:

> Their Lordships have had no difficulty in coming to the conclusion that, under the treaties, the Indians obtained no right to their annuities, whether original or augmented, beyond a promise and agreement, which was nothing more than a personal obligation by its governor, as representing the old province, that the latter should pay the annuities as and when they became due;

While this refers only to the annuities payable under the treaties, it is difficult to see that the other covenants in the treaties, including the one we are here concerned with, can stand on any higher footing. It is always to be kept in mind that the Indians surrendered their rights in the territory in exchange for these promises. This "promise and agreement," like any other, can, of course, be breached, and there is no law of which I am aware that would prevent parliament by legislation, properly within sec. 91 of the *BNA Act, 1867*, ch. 3, from doing so.

The government in dealing with the Indians, has, on the whole, treated its obligations under these treaties seriously. This was probably not always the case if we may judge from the remarks of John Beverley Robinson, attorney-general for Upper Canada, in 1824, as quoted in *Sero* v. *Gault* (1921) 50 OLR 27, at pp. 31-32:

> 'To talk of treaties with the Mohawk Indians, residing in the heart of one of the most populous districts of Upper Canada, upon lands purchased for them and given to them by the British Government, is much the same, in my humble opinion, as to talk of making a treaty of alliance with the Jews in Duke street or with the French emigrants who have settled in England:' (Canadian Archives, Q. 337, pt. II, pp. 367, 368).

In refreshing contrast is a speech of lieutenant-governor Morris to the

Indians during the negotiation of the Qu'Appelle treaty as reported in his book (p. 96):

Therefore, the promises we have to make to you are not for to-day only but for to-morrow, not only for you but for your children born and unborn, and the promises we make will be carried out as long as the sun shines above and the water flows in the ocean.

It is interesting to note that when the government of Canada transferred the natural resources within the province of Alberta to that province in 1930 (the *NBA Act, 1930*, ch. 26) the agreement contained the following clause:

12.   In order to secure to the Indians of the Province the continuance of the supply of game and fish for their support and subsistence, Canada agrees that the laws respecting game in force in the Province from time to time shall apply to the Indians within the boundaries thereof, provided, however, that the said Indians shall have the right, which the Province hereby assures to them, of hunting, trapping, and fishing game and fish for food at all seasons of the year on all unoccupied Crown lands and on any other lands to which the said Indians may have a right of access.

Because of the government's concern with the Indians' right to pursue "their usual vocations of hunting, trapping and fishing," and that its obligations under the treaties should be performed, it is difficult to understand why these treaties were not kept in mind when the Migratory Birds Convention was negotiated and when its terms were implemented by the *Migratory Birds Convention Act*, RSC 1952, ch. 179, and the regulations made under that Act.

That Convention was entered into by Great Britain (on behalf of Canada), with the United States in October, 1916, and ratified by both governments in December of that year. Part of the preamble and some of the terms of that Convention should be considered.

In the preamble these paragraphs appear:

Whereas many species of birds in the course of their annual migrations traverse certain parts of the Dominion of Canada and the United States; and

Whereas many of these species are of great value as a source of food or in destroying insects which are injurious to forests and forage plants on the public domain, as well as to agricultural crops, in both Canada and the United States, but are nevertheless in danger of extermination through lack of adequate protection during the nesting season or while on their way to and from their breeding grounds;

His Majesty the King of the United Kingdom of Great Britain and

Ireland and of the British Dominions beyond the seas, Emperor of India, and the United States of America, being desirous of saving from indiscriminate slaughter and of insuring the preservation of such migratory birds as are either useful to man or are harmless, have resolved to adopt some uniform system of protection which shall effectively accomplish such objects, and to the end of concluding a convention for this purpose have appointed as their respective plenipoentiaries . . .

Art. I defines the birds covered by the Convention and among the migratory birds are ''wild ducks.'' Art. II reads:

The High Contracting Powers agree that, as an effective means of preserving migratory birds, there shall be established the following close seasons during which no hunting shall be done except for scientific or propagating purposes under permits issued by proper authorities.

    1.   The close season on migratory game birds shall be between 10th March and 1st September, except that the close of the season on the limicolae or shorebirds in the Maritime Provinces of Canada and in those states of the United States bordering on the Atlantic Ocean which are situated wholly or in part north of Chesapeake Bay shall be between 1st February and 15th August, and that Indians may take at any time scoters for food but not for sale. The season for hunting shall be further restricted to such period not exceeding three and one-half months as the High Contracting Powers may severally deem appropriate and define by law or regulation.

    2.   The close season on migratory insectivorous birds shall continue throughout the year.

    3.   The close season on other migratory nongame birds shall continue throughout the year, except that Eskimos and Indians may take at any season auks, auklets, guillemots, murres and puffins, and their eggs for food and their skins for clothing, but the birds and eggs so taken shall not be sold or offered for sale.

It will be seen from the preamble that the purpose of the convention was to save migratory birds ''from indiscriminate slaughter'' and to assure their preservation. This, it seems to me, would have allowed for exceptions or reservations in favour of the Indians, for there can be no doubt that the amount of game birds taken by the Indians for food during the close season would not have resulted in ''indiscriminate slaughter'' of birds nor would the preservation of those birds have been threatened. We are told that the treaty between the United States and Mexico negotiated in 1936 permits indigent persons in Mexico to take these types of birds for food.

The Migratory Birds Convention Act, 1917, ch. 18, "sanctioned, ratified and confirmed" the Convention. By sec. 4 it provides:

4. (1) The Governor in Council may make such regulations as are deemed expedient to protect the migratory game, migratory insectivorous and migratory nongame birds which inhabit Canada during the whole or any part of the year.

(2) Subject to the provisions of the said Convention, such regulations may provide, —

(*a*) the periods in each year or the number of years during which any such migratory game, migratory insectivorous or migratory nongame birds shall not be killed, captured, injured, taken, molested or sold, or their nests or eggs injured, destroyed, taken or molested;

(*b*) for the granting of permits to kill or take migratory game, migratory insectivorous and migratory nongame birds, or their nest eggs;

(*c*) for the prohibition of the shipment or export of migratory game, migratory insectivorous or migratory nongame birds or their eggs from any province during the close season in such province, and the conditions upon which international traffic in such birds shall be carried on;

(*d*) for the prohibition of the killing, capturing, taking, injuring or molesting of migratory game, migratory insectivorous or migratory nongame birds, or the taking, injuring, destruction or molestation of their nests or eggs, within any prescribed area;

(*e*) for any other purpose which may be deemed expedient for carrying out the intentions of this Act and the said Convention, whether such other regulations are of the kind enumerated in this section or not.

(3) A regulation shall take effect from the date of the publication thereof in the *Canada Gazette*, or from the date specified for such purpose in any regulation, and such regulation shall have the same force and effect as if enacted herein, and shall be printed in the prefix in the next succeeding issue of the Dominion Statutes, and shall also be laid before both Houses of Parliament within fifteen days after the publication thereof if Parliament is then sitting, and if Parliament is not then sitting, within fifteen days after the opening of the next session thereof.

Sec. 5 (1) and (2) of the present regulations provides:

5 (1) Unless otherwise permitted under these Regulations to do so, no person shall

(a) in any area described in Schedule A, kill, hunt, capture, injure, take or molest a migratory bird at any time except during an open season specified for that bird and that area in Schedule A, or

(b) from any area described in Schedule A, kill, hunt, capture, injure, take or molest a migratory birds at any time in another area described in Schedule A except during an open season specified for that birds and both those areas in Schedule A.

(2) Indians and Eskimos may take auks, auklets, guillemots, murres, puffins and scoters and their eggs at any time for human food or clothing, but they shall not sell or trade or offer to sell or trade birds or eggs so taken and they shall not take such birds or eggs within a birds sanctuary.

The "scoter" mentioned in this section and in the Convention is defined in *Murray's New English Dictionary*:

Scoter — (of obscure origin). A duck of the genus Oedemia, esp. nigra, a native of the Arctic regions and common in the seas of Northern Europe and America. Also scoter-duck.

There is no evidence that there are any of these ducks in the Yellowknife area, which is several hundred miles from the sea.

The open season under these regulations for mallard ducks in the Yellowknife area is from September 1 to October 15.

Sissons J in his reasons for judgment, says at p. 504:

There are no express words or necessary intendment or implication in the *Migratory Birds Convention Act* abrogating, abridging, or infringing upon the hunting rights of the Indians.

I have quoted sec. 5(1) of the regulations which says that ". . . no person shall . . . kill . . . a migratory bird at any time except during an open season. . . ." It is difficult to see how this language admits of any exceptions. When, however, we find that reference in the both the Convention and in the regulations to what kind of birds an Indian an Eskimo may "take" at any time for food, it is impossible for me to say that the hunting rights of the Indians as to these migratory birds have not been abrogated, abridged or infringed upon.

It is, I think, clear that the rights given to the Indians by their treaties as they apply to migratory birds have been taken away by this Act and its regulations. How are we to explain this apparent breach of faith on the part of the government, for I cannot think it can be described in any other terms? This cannot be described as a minor or insignificant curtailment of these treaty rights, for game birds have always been a most plentiful, a most reliable and a readily obtainable food in large areas of Canada. I cannot believe that the government of Canada realized that in implementing the Convention they were at the same time breaching the treaties that they had made with the Indians. It is much

more likely that these obligations under the treaties were overlooked —
a case of the left hand having forgotten what the right hand had done.
The subsequent history of the government's dealing with the Indians
would seem to bear this out. When the treaty we are concerned with
here was signed in 1921, only five years after the enactment of *The
Migratory Birds Convention Act*, we find the commissioners who
negotiated the treaty reporting:

> The Indians seemed afraid, for one thing, that their liberty to hunt,
> trap and fish would be taken away or curtailed, but were assured by
> me that this would not be the case, and the Government will expect
> them to support themselves in their own way, and, in fact, that more
> twine for nets and more ammunition were given under the terms of
> this treaty than under any of the preceding ones; this went a long way
> to calm their fears. I also pointed out that any game laws made were
> to their advantage, and, whether they took treaty or not, they were
> subject to the laws of the Dominion.

And there is nothing in this report which would indicate that the
Indians were told that their right to shoot migratory birds had already
been taken away from them. I have referred to Art. 12 of the agreement
between the government of Canada and the province of Alberta signed
in 1930 by which that province was required to assure to the Indians the
right of

> hunting, trapping and fishing game and fish for food at all seasons of
> the year on all unoccupied Crown lands. . . .

The amendment to the *BNA Act, 1930*, that confirmed this
agreement, declared that it should

> have the force of law notwithstanding anything in the British North
> America Act . . . or any Act of the Parliament of Canada. . . .

It is of some importance that while the Indians in the Northwest
Territories continued to shoot ducks at all seasons for food, it is only
recently that any attempt has been made to enforce the Act.

I can come to no other conclusion than that the Indians,
notwithstanding the rights given to them by their treaties, are prohibited
by this Act and its regulations from shooting migratory birds out of
season. Unless one or other of the matters mentioned in the learned trial
judge's reasons for judgment or raised by the respondent's counsel at
the hearing of the appeal is a defence to the charge, the appeal must be
allowed and the conviction sustained. . .

We were invited by counsel for the respondent to apply to the *Migratory Birds Convention Act* those rules which have been laid down for the interpretation of treaties in international law and we have been referred to many authorities on how these treaties should be interpreted. We are not, however, concerned with interpreting the Convention but only the legislation by which it is implemented. To that statute the ordinary rules of interpretation are applicable and the authorities referred to have no application.

The appeal must be allowed and the conviction imposed by the magistrate affirmed. In coming to this conclusion, I regret that I cannot share the satisfaction that was expressed by McGillivray JA in *Rex* v. *Wesley, supra*, when he was writing his judgment dismissing the appeal in that case (at p. 353):

It is satisfactory to be able to come to this conclusion and not to have to decide that 'the Queen's promises' have not been fulfilled. It is satisfactory to think that legislators have not so enacted but that the Indians may still be "convinced of our justice and determined resolution to remove all reasonable cause of discontent.

Note

1. At trial, Sissons held that it had not been proven that the mallard duck killed by Mr. Sikyea was a wild duck. On appeal, Johnson JA held that, in law, it was a wild duck, and thus protected by the *Migratory Birds Convention Act*. The greater part of the decision of the SCC dealt with this issue. On the substantive question, Hall J, giving judgment for the SCC, agreed with the reasons for judgment of Johnson JA. See 49 W.W.R. 306, 44 CR 226, [1964] SCR 642, [1965] 2 CCC 129, 50 DLR (2d) 80.

(ii) *R.* v. *George*, 55 DLR (2d) 386, 47 CR 382, [1966] SCR 267, [1966] 3 CCC 137 (SCC)

CARTWRIGHT J (*dissenting*): — This appeal is brought, pursuant to leave granted by this Court, from a judgment of the Court of Appeal for Ontario dismissing an appeal from an order of McRuer CJHC which dismissed an appeal from an order of Magistrate Dunlap acquitting the respondent on a charge that he did on the 5th day of September 1962, at Kettle Point Indian Reserve unlawfully hunt a migratory bird at a time not during the open season specified for that bird in violation of s. 5(1)(*a*) of the Migratory Bird Regulations thereby committing an offence contrary to s. 12(1) of the *Migratory Birds Convention Act*, RSC 1952, c. 179. Gibson JA, dissenting, would have allowed the appeal.

There is no dispute as to the facts. The respondent is an Indian within the meaning of the *Indian Act*, RSC 1952, c. 149. He is a member of the Chippewa Band residing on the Kettle Point Reserve. On the date stated in the charge he shot two ducks, which were migratory birds, as defined in the *Migratory Birds Convention Act* and the Regulations made thereunder, an area described in Schedule A of the Regulations at a time not during the open season for such birds. The ducks were to be used for food and were not to be sold.

On these facts it would appear that the respondent was guilty of the offence charged unless, because he is an Indian and shot the ducks for food on the reserve on which he resided, he is exempt from the provisions of the *Migratory Birds Convention Act* and *Migratory Bird Regulations* under which he was charged.

The learned Magistrate was of opinion that s. 87 of the *Indian Act* made laws of general application applicable to Indians, subject to the terms of any treaty that the *Migratory Birds Convention Act* was such a law, that the treaty of July 10, 1827, with the Chippewa Indians to be referred to hereafter reserved to them the right to hunt at any time on the lands reserved in that treaty and consequently, that the *Migratory Birds Convention Act* did not apply to the respondent.

McRuer CJHC agreed with the view of the learned Magistrate and was further of opinion that the right of the respondent to hunt for food on Kettle Point Reserve was preserved not only by the treaty of 1827 but also by the proclamation of 1763 and that if it is within the power of Parliament to abrogate that right, a point which the learned Chief Justice left open, that power could be exercised only by legislation expressly and directly extinguishing the right and that it certainly could not be extinguished by order-in-council.

After discussing the case of *Dominion of Canada* v. *Province of Ontario, the learned Chief Justice said:*

> This case clearly recognizes that the 'overlying Indian interest' in the lands reserved to the Indians is not something to be disposed of by any general Act of Parliament applicable to all citizens.

He also said:

> I wish to make it quite clear that I am not called upon to decide, nor do I decide, whether the Parliament of Canada by legislation specifically applicable to Indians could take away their rights to hunt for food on the Kettle Point Reserve. There is much to support an argument that Parliament does not have such power. There may be cases where such legislation, properly framed, might be considered necessary in the public interest but a very strong case would have to be made out that would not be a breach of our national honour.

The judgment of the majority in the Court of Appeal was delivered by Roach JA, with whom Mclennan JA agreed. The learned Justice of

Appeal construed the treaty of 1827, in the light of its historical background including the terms of the Proclamation of 1763, as preserving and confirming to the Indians their right to the use of the lands reserved including those in the Kettle Point Reserve as their "Hunting Grounds". He held that the *Migratory Birds Convention Act* is a law of general application in force in the Province within the meaning of s. 87 of the *Indian Act* so that its application to the respondent is subject to the terms of the treaty. The reasons of Roach JA conclude as follows:

> The treaty does not refer to the Proclamation in terms but historical implication impels the conclusion that what was surrendered and conveyed to the Crown by the treaty were the rights granted to them by the Proclamation to and in respect of the lands described in the treaty as being intended to be thereby conveyed. What was preserved and confirmed to them were those same rights to and in respect of the lands reserved by the treaty and without any time limitation thereon.
>
> Since the *Migratory Birds Convention Act* is subject to the treaty and since the treaty preserved and confirmed to the Indians the *use* of lands, including those in the Kettle Point Reserve, as their 'Hunting Grounds', giving to those words their wide historical significance, it follows that an Indian while hunting on those lands for food is not subject to the restrictions or prohibitions contained in that Act or the regulations.

The essential difference of opinion between Gibson JA and the majority was as to the construction of the treaty of 1827. As to this, after quoting s. 87 of the *Indian Act*, Gibson JA says:

> On behalf of the accused it is argued that the Treaty of 1827 reserved to the Indians the land of the reserve for their "exclusive use and enjoyment", and that by implication that included the perpetual right to fish and hunt on the lands. As I have stated before, nothing contained in the Treaty indicates that questions of hunting and fishing were ever dealt with or considered when the Treaty was entered into.

With the greatest respect to Gibson JA I am unable to accept this view. For the reasons given by Roach JA I agree with his interpretation of the terms of the treaty. I find it impossible to suppose that any of the signatories to the treaty would have understood that what was reserved to the Indians and their posterity was the right merely to occupy the reserved lands and not the right to hunt and fish thereon which they had enjoyed from time immemorial.

The question to be decided is whether the right to hunt on the reserve assured by the treaty to the band of which the respondent is a member has been effectively destroyed by the *Migratory Birds Convention Act* and the *Migratory Bird Regulations* so far as wild ducks are concerned.

Counsel for the appellants submits that this question should be answered in the affirmative on three main grounds, (i) that the point has been decided in favour of the appellant by the decision of this Court in *Sikyea* v. *The Queen*, (ii) that the words "laws of general application from time to time in force in any province" in s. 87 of the *Indian Act* mean provincial laws and not federal laws and (iii) that the treaty of July 10, 1827, did not reserve to the Indians the right to hunt and fish on the reserve I will deal with these three grounds in reverse order.

As to the third ground, counsel for the appellant concedes that the document of July 10, 1827, is a treaty within the meaning of that word as used in s. 87 of the *Indian Act*. I think he was clearly right in making this concession. In my opinion it is the very sort of treaty contemplated by the section. On the question of the true construction of the treaty I have already indicated my agreement with the reasons and conclusion of Roach JA on this branch of the matter. It follows that I would reject this ground of appeal.

As to the second ground, s. 87 of the *Indian Act* reads as follows:

> 87.   Subject to the terms of any treaty and any other Act of Parliament of Canada, all laws of general application from time to time in force in any province are applicable to and in respect of Indians in the province, except to the extent that such laws are inconsistent with this Act or any order, rule, regulation or by-law made thereunder, and except to the extent that such laws make provision for any matter for which provision is made by or under this Act.

The laws of general application in force in the Province of Ontario are made up of the common law, pre-confederation statutes which have not been repealed, Acts of Parliament and Acts of the Legislature. I can find nothing in the words of the section to permit the meaning of the phrase "laws of general application from time to time in force in any province" being restricted to provincial statutes or to laws in relation to matters coming within the classes of subjects assigned to the Legislature by s. 92 of the *British North America Act*. To determine whether any particular law is applicable to an Indian in Ontario only two questions need be answered, (i) is it a law of general application? and (ii) is it in force in the Province? If the answer to both of these questions is in the affirmative the source of the law is of no importance. In my opinion the *Migratory Birds Convention Act* is a law of general application in force in Ontario and applicable to the respondent but by s. 87 its application to him is made subject to the terms of the treaty of July 10, 1827. I would reject this ground of appeal. . .

In order to ascertain whether the question to be decided in the case at bar has been determined in *Sikyea's* case it is necessary to examine the reasons delivered in that case in some detail but before doing so it will be convenient to state in summary form the grounds on which Mr Mackinnon submits that the cases are distinguishable. These are, (i) In *Sikyea* the question was as to the right of Indians to hunt on lands which they had surrendered while in the present case it is as to their right to hunt on lands which they reserved and have never surrendered, (ii) In *Sikyea* the treaty in question was entered into four years after the *Migratory Birds Convention Act* came into force while that in the present case was almost one hundred years earlier, and (iii) the reasons in *Sikyea* give no consideration to the effect of s. 87 of the *Indian Act* which in the present case was held by the Court of Appeal to be decisive. It is to the last of these three grounds of distinction that Mr Mackinnon attaches particular importance. . .

The questions of law decided by Johnson JA (and therefore by this Court since it adopted his reasons as well as his conclusion) in so far as they are relevant to the case at bar were (i) that it is within the power of Parliament to abrogate the rights of Indians to hunt whether arising from treaty or under the Proclamation of 1763 or from user from time immemorial and (ii) that on its true construction the *Migratory Birds Convention Act* shews that it was the intention of Parliament to prohibit Indians from hunting during the closed seasons subject only to the exceptions in their favour set out in the Act as, for example, the right to take scoters for food. I think it clear from reading the whole of the reasons of Johnson JA that he did not direct his mind to the question, so fully argued before us in the case at bar, whether accepting his decision on these two questions the effect of s. 87 of the *Indian Act* was to preserve the Indian's right to hunt notwithstanding the provisions of the *Migratory Birds Convention Act* in so far as that right was assured to them by "any treaty". I think that if the view of the effect of s. 87 which appears to me to be decisive in the case at bar had been considered in the Court of Appeal or in this Court in *Sikyea's* case it would have been examined and dealt with in the reasons delivered. I do not propose to enter on the question, which since 1949 has been raised from time to time by authors, whether this Court now that it has become the final Court of Appeal for Canada is, as in the case of the House of Lords, bound by its own previous decisions on questions of law or whether, as in the case of the Judicial Committee or the Supreme Court of the United States, it is free under certain circumstance to reconsider them. I find it unnecessary to do this. Assuming for the purposes of this appeal that we are governed by the rule of *stare decisis*, it appears to me that the judgment in *Sikyea* falls within one of the exceptions to that rule in that it was given *per incuriam*. . .

I do not suggest that in *Sikyea's* case either the Court of Appeal or this Court was ignorant of the existence of s. 87 of the *Indian Act* but, to use the words of Lord Greene, I am satisfied that that section was not present to the mind of either Court when rendering judgment, although it does appear to have been dealt with in the argument of counsel.

Having reached this conclusion it is not necessary for me to consider the other grounds on which Mr Mackinnon argued that *Sikyea's* case could be distinguished.

In *St Saviour's Southwark (Churchwardens)* case, Lord Coke said:

> If two constructions may be made of the King's grant, then the rule is, when it may receive two constructions, and by force of one construction the grant may according to the rule of law be adjudged good, and by another it shall by law be adjudged bad; then for the King's honour, and for the benefit of the subject, such construction shall be made that the King's charter shall take effect, for it was not the King's intent to make a void grant, and therewith agrees *Sir J. Moleyn's* case in the sixth part of my reports.

We should, I think, endeavour to construe the treaty of 1827 and those Acts of Parliament which bear upon the question before us in such manner that the honour of the Sovereign may be upheld and Parliament not made subject to the reproach of having taken away by unilateral action and without consideration the rights solemnly assured to the Indians and their posterity by treaty. Johnson JA, with obvious regret, felt bound to hold that Parliament had taken away those rights, but I am now satisfied that on its true construction s. 87 of the *Indian Act* shews that Parliament was careful to preserve them. At the risk of repetition I think it clear that the effect of s. 87 is two-fold. It makes Indians subject to the laws of general application in force in the province in which they reside but at the same time it preserves inviolate to the Indians whatever rights they have under the terms of any treaty so that in a case of conflict between the provisions of the laws and the terms of the treaty the latter shall prevail.

For the reasons given by Roach JA and those stated above I would dismiss this appeal costs.

The judgment of Fauteux, Abbott, Martland, Judson, Ritchie and Hall JJ was delivered by

MARTLAND J: — I have had the opportunity to read the reasons stated by my brother Cartwright. The facts giving rise to this appeal are there reviewed and it is unnecessary to repeat them here. With great laws applicable to Indians, so as to preclude any interference with rights respect, I am unable to agree with his interpretation of s. 87 of the *Indian Act*, RSC 1952, c. 149, which provides as follows: [omitted]

I cannot construe this section as making the provisions of the *Migratory Birds Convention Act*, RSC 1952, c. 179, subordinate to the treaty of July 10, 1827. In my opinion, it was not the purpose of s. 87 to make any legislation of the Parliament of Canada subject to the terms of any treaty. I understand the object and intent of that section is to make Indians, who are under the exclusive legislative jurisdiction of the Parliament of Canada, by virtue of s. 91(24) of the *British North America Act, 1867*, subject to provincial laws of general application.

The application of provincial laws to Indians was, however, made subject to "the terms of any treaty *and any other Act of the Parliament of Canada*" (the italics are mine). In addition, provincial laws inconsistent with the *Indian Act*, or any order, rule, regulation or by-law made thereunder, or making provision for any matter for which provision is made under that *Act*, do not apply.

The incorporation in the section of the words italicized to me makes it clear that when the section refers to "laws of general application from time to time in force in any province" it did not include in that expression the statute law of Canada. If it did, the section, in so far as federal legislation is concerned, would provide that the statute law of Canada applies to Indians, subject to the terms of any *Act* of the Parliament of Canada, other than the *Indian Act*. This would be a rather unusual provision, particularly in view of the fact that it did not require any express provision in the *Indian Act* to make Indians subject to the provisions of federal statutes. In my view the expression refers only to those rules of law in a province which are provincial in scope, and would include provincial legislation and any laws which were made a part of the law of a province, as, for example, in the provinces of Alberta and Saskatchewan, the laws of England as they existed on July 15, 1870.

This section was not intended to be a declaration of the paramountcy of treaties over federal legislation. The reference to treaties was incorporated in a section the purpose of which was to make provincial under treaties resulting from the impact of provincial legislation.

Accordingly, in my opinion, the provisions of s. 87 do not prevent the application to Indians of the provisions of the *Migratory Birds Convention Act*. I can see no valid distinction between the present case and that of *Sikyea* v. *The Queen*[1] and, for the reasons given in that case, I think that this appeal should be allowed. The judgment of the learned magistrate should be reversed and a fine of ten dollars be imposed upon the respondent. The Attorney-General of Canada does not ask for costs, and accordingly there should be no costs in this Court or in the Courts below.

(b) Application of Provincial Laws

(i) *R.* v. *White and Bob* (1964), 52 WWR 193, 50 DLR (2d) 613 (BCCA)

DAVEY JA — The crown appeals from the respondents' acquittal by Sweneisky CCJ, on their appeal to him from their summary conviction by Beevor-Potts PM of having game, namely, the carcasses of six deer, in their possession during the closed season without having a valid and subsisting permit under the *Game Act*, RSBC, 1960, ch. 160, contrary to the provisions of that Act.

The crown concedes that if the respondents, who are native Indians, had a legal right to hunt for food for themselves and their families over the lands in question, they were lawfully in possession of the carcasses, no permit was required, and they were not guilty of the offence.

Sec. 18 of the *Game Act* forbids any person to kill deer except in the open season, subject to certain specified exceptions within which the respondents do not fall. They contend that an agreement (Ex. 8) between their ancestors, members of the Saalequun tribe, and Gov. Douglas, dated December 23, 1854, for the sale of the land to the Hudson's Bay Company, gave them the right to hunt for food over the land in question and, alternatively, that as native Indians they possess the aboriginal right to hunt for food over unoccupied land lying within their ancient tribal hunting grounds.

For the purposes of this appeal it must be taken that the respondents are native Indians, members of the Saalequun tribe, and descendants of the members who signed Ex. 8; that they killed the deer on unoccupied land comprised in the sale to the Hudson's Bay Company, and forming part of the ancient hunting grounds of the tribe, for the purpose of providing food for themselves and their families.

It is common ground that Ex. 8 must be taken to include the following clause appearing in all other transfers of Vancouver Island Indian land, which, for reasons that need not be mentioned, does not appear in this instrument:

> The condition of, or understanding of this sale, is this, that our village sites and enclosed fields, are to be kept for our own use, for the use of our children, and for those who may follow after us, and the lands shall be properly surveyed hereafter; it is understood however, that the land itself with these small exceptions, becomes the entire

property of the white people for-ever, it is also understood that we are at liberty to hunt over the unoccupied lands, and to carry on our fisheries as formerly.

The crown does not deny that the respondents are entitled to exercise and enjoy whatever rights or privileges there may be under Ex. 8 until they have been effectively extinguished. It does contend that Ex. 8 conferred no hunting rights and, if it did, that these rights have been extinguished by sec. 87 of the *Indian Act*, RSC, 1952, ch. 149, first enacted in 1951, which the crown says extends in effect the general provisions of the *Game Act* to Indians.

Sec. 87 reads as follows: [omitted]

The crown submits that Ex. 8 does not fall within the prefatory saving clause of sec. 87 because:

(1) Ex. 8 did not create any hunting rights but merely recognized pre-existing privileges; that the alleged hunting rights were mere liberties which formed part of the aboriginal rights of the Indians over the soil, and that they existed when Vancouver Island became British territory, and continued until extinguished or abolished by valid legislation; that the saving clause refers only to rights created by treaties.

(2) That even if Ex. 8 did create or recognize rights that could be the subject of a treaty within the meaning of the saving clause, the document is not such a treaty.

The force of the first argument seems to depend upon the assumption that sec. 87 should be read as if it were subject only to rights created by a treaty; that would remove from the saving clause already in being and excepted from or confirmed by a treaty. That argument fails to accord full meaning to the words, "subject to the *terms* of any treaty. . . ." In my opinion, an exception, reservation, or confirmation is as much a term of a treaty as a grant (I observe parenthetically that a reservation may be a grant) and the operative words of the section will not extend general laws in force in any province to Indians in derogation of rights so excepted, reserved or confirmed.

Counsel for the crown next submits that Ex. 8 is not a treaty. He contends that a treaty within sec. 87 is: (1) A document that on its face is so described or one that uses that word in the text; and (2) Deals with fundamental differences between the parties (*quacre*, political differences?) and not merely with private rights, such as in this case the sale of land; and (3) A formal document in which the terms are set out with some degree of formality; and (4) An agreement to which the crown is a party, or which it has authorized one of the parties to make on its behalf.

Counsel submits that Ex. 8 meets none of these requirements.

It is unnecessary to venture any extended definition of the word "treaty" in this context, but it can be safely said that it does not mean an "executive act establishing relationships between what are recognized as two or more independent states and in sovereign capacities; . . ." *per* Rand J in *Francis* v. *Reg.* [1956] SCR 618, at 625, 56 DTC 1077, affirming [1954] Ex CR 590, 55 DTC 1034. It is also clear, in my opinion, that the word is not used in its widest sense as including agreements between individuals dealing with their private and personal affairs. Its meaning lies between those extremes. Counsel for the crown submits on the authority of Kellock J in *Francis* v. *Reg.*, *supra*, at p. 631, that the word means only those treaties referred to in other sections of the Act, i.e., secs. 11 (*b*), 15 (1) (*b*), 18 (1), 71, 89 (1) (*b*), and 112 (4). Taking the learned judge's remarks in their context, I do not understand him to mean that sec. 87 refers only to those treaties, but that it means treaties of that type, as opposed to solemn, conventions between states, such as the *Jay Treaty*, which was relied upon by Francis in that case.

In considering whether Ex. 8 is a treaty within the meaning of sec. 87, regard ought to be paid to the history of our country; its original occupation and settlement; the fact that the Hudson's Bay Company was the proprietor and, to use a feudal term contained in its charters, the lord of the lands in the Northwest Territories and Vancouver Island; and the part that company played in the settlement and development of this country. In the Charter granting Vancouver Island to the Hudson's Bay Company, it was charged with the settlement and colonization of that island. That was clearly part of the Imperial policy to head off American settlement of and claims to the territory. In that sense the Hudson's Bay Company was an instrument of Imperial policy. It was also the long-standing policy of the Imperial government and of the Hudson's Bay Company that the crown or the company should buy from the Indians their land for settlement by white colonists. In pursuance of that policy many agreements, some very formal, others informal, were made with various bands and tribes of Indians for the purchase of their lands. These agreements frequently conferred upon the grantors hunting rights over the unoccupied lands so sold. Considering the relationship between the crown and the Hudson's Bay Company in the colonization of this country, and the Imperial and corporate policies reflected in those agreements, I cannot regard Ex. 8 as a mere agreement for the sale of land made between a private vendor and a private purchaser. In view of the notoriety of these facts, I entertain no doubt that parliament intended the word "treaty" in sec. 87 to include all such agreements, and to except their provisions from the operative part of the section. That being so, sec. 87 does not extend the general provisions of the *Game Act* to the respondents in the exercise of their hunting rights under Ex. 8 over the lands in question.

We have been referred to no other Act of parliament or the colonial legislature that would have the effect of abrogating or curtailing the respondents' rights under Ex. 8, and the only provincial legislation that might do so is the *Game Act* itself.

Secs. 8 and 15 of the *Game Act* specifically exempt Indians from the operation of certain provisions of the Act, and from that I think it clear that the other provisions are intended to be of general application and to include Indians. If these general sections are sufficiently clear to show an intention to abrogate or qualify the contractual rights of hunting notoriously reserved to Indians by agreements such as Ex. 8, they would, in my opinion, fail in that purpose because that would be legislation in relation to Indians that falls within parliament's exclusive legislative authority under sec. 91 (24) of the *BNA Act, 1867*, 30 & 31 Vict., ch. 3, and also because that would conflict with sec. 87 of the *Indian Act* passed under that authority. Legislation that abrogates or abridges the hunting rights reserved to Indians under the treaties and agreements by which they sold their ancient territories to the crown and to the Hudson's Bay Company for white settlement is, in my respectful opinion, legislation in relation to Indians because it deals with rights peculiar to them. Lord Watson's judgment in *St Catharine's Milling & Lbr. Co.* v. *Reg.* (1888) 14 App Cas 46, 58 LJPC 54, CR [10] AC 13, 4 Cart 107, affirming 13 SCR 577, if any authority is needed, makes that clear. At p. 60 (LJPC) he observed that the plain policy of the *BNA Act* is to vest legislative control over Indian affairs generally in one central authority. On the same page he spoke of parliament's exclusive power to regulate the Indians' privilege of hunting and fishing. In my opinion, their peculiar rights of hunting and fishing over their ancient hunting grounds arising under agreements by which they collectively sold their ancient lands are Indian affairs over which parliament has exclusive legislative authority, and only parliament can derogate from those rights.

In the result, the right of the respondents to hunt over the lands in question reserved to them by Ex. 8 are preserved by sec. 87 and remain unimpaired by the *Game Act*, and it follows that the respondents were rightfully in possession of the carcasses. It becomes unnecessary to consider other aspects of a far reaching argument addressed to us by respondents' counsel.

I would dismiss the appeal.

Notes

1. Sullivan JA concurred with Davey JA. In a frequently quoted judgment, Norris JA

reviewed the pre-Confederation history of British Columbia, aboriginal rights, the Royal Proclamation of 1763, and the rules respecting treaty interpretation. Sheppard JA dissented. Lord JA concurred with Sheppard JA and added reasons of his own.

2. The Supreme Court of Canada agreed with the majority in the BCCA that the document in question was a "treaty" within the meaning of s. 87 of the Indian Act. See (1965), 52 DLR (2d) 481n.

3. *R.* v. *White and Bob* has been followed in many other treaty areas. See, for example, *R.* v. *Taylor and Williams*, *infra*, (hunting — Treaty of 1818 on southern Ontario); *R.* v. *Batisse*, *supra*, (hunting — Treaty 9); *Cheechoo* v. *R.*, [1981] 3 CNLR 45 (Ontario District Court), (trapping — Treaty 9); *R.* v. *Moses*, [1970] 3 OR 314, 13 DLR (3d) 50 (Ontario District Court), (hunting — Robinson-Huron Treaty); *R.* v. *Penasse* (1971), 8 CCC (2d) 569 (Ontario Provincial Court), (fishing — Robinson-Huron Treaty).

(ii) *R.* v. *Taylor and Williams*, 34 OR (2d) 360, 62 CCC (2d) 227, [1981] 3 CNLR 114 (Ontario Court of Appeal)

Reproduced in chapter 4, *Pre-Confederation Treaties*, *supra*.

(iii) *Kruger and Manuel* v. *R.*, [1977] 4 WWR 300, 75 DLR (3d) 434, [1978] 1 SCR 104, 15 NR 495, 34 CCC (2d) 377 (SCC).

DICKSON J: — These appeals raise the question whether provincial game laws apply to non-treaty Indians hunting off a reserve on unoccupied Crown land. They fall to be decided upon a statement of agreed facts. The appellants, Jacob Kruger and Robert Manuel, are Indians living in British Columbia and are members of the Penticton Indian Band. Between 5th September and 8th September 1973, during the closed season for hunting, while hunting for food near Penticton, they killed four deer. The acts of hunting took place upon unoccupied Crown land, which was and is the traditional hunting ground of the Penticton Indian Band. The accused did not have permits issued under The Wildlife Act, 1966 (BC), c. 55, authorizing them to hunt and kill deer for food during the closed season. Such permits were readily obtainable by local native Indians and both appellants had obtained permits in the past.

Appellants were convicted before a Provincial Judge on a charge laid under s. 5(1)(c) [am. 1971, c. 67, s. 3] of The Wildlife Act of unlawfully killing big game during the closed season. Appeals to the County Court [[1974] 6 WWR 206, 19 CCC (2d) 162, 51 DLR (3d) 435] succeeded on the ground that Indian hunting rights fell within the protection of the Royal Proclamation, 1763, and thereby immunized Indians from the reach of The Wildlife Act while hunting for food on unoccupied Crown land. On further appeal to the British Columbia Court of Appeal [[1975] 5 WWR 167, 24 CCC (2d) 120, 60 DLR (3d) 144] the convictions were restored. Robertson JA, who delivered the judgment of the court, was of the view that s. 88 of the Indian Act, RSC

1970, c. I-6, made provincial laws of general application, among which he numbered The Wildlife Act, applicable to Indians. The section reads:

88. Subject to the terms of any treaty and any other Act of the Parliament of Canada, all laws of general application from time to time in force in any province are applicable to and in respect of Indians in the province, except to the extent that such laws are inconsistent with this Act or any order, rule, regulation or by-law made thereunder, and except to the extent that such laws make provision for any matter for which provision is made by or under this Act.

He concluded on the authority of this court's decision in *Regina* v. *George*, 47 CR 382, [1966] SCR 267, [1966] 3 CCC 137, 55 DLR (2d) 386, that s. 4 of The Wildlife Act applied to the appellants unless they could bring themselves within the opening words of s. 88 or under the exceptions spelled out in the latter part of the section. With respect to the opening words of the section, Robertson JA had this to say [p. 170]:

The Proclamation of 1763 was entirely unilateral and was not, and cannot be described as, a treaty. Assuming (without expressing any opinion) that the Proclamation has the force of a statute, it cannot be said to be an Act of the Parliament of Canada: there was no Parliament of Canada before 1867 and by no stretch of the imagination can a proclamation made by the Sovereign in 1763 be said to be an Act of a legislative body which was not created until more than 100 years later.

As to the exceptions, the learned Justice of Appeal said [p. 169]:

There has not been brought to my attention, nor do I know of, any extent to which s. 4 of The Wildlife Act is inconsistent with the Indian Act, or with any Order, Rule, Regulation or bylaw made thereunder. Nor do I know of any provision made by or under the Indian Act with respect to the matters for which provision is made by s. 4 of The Wildlife Act.

It is contended on behalf of the appellants that the British Columbia Court of Appeal erred in three respects, namely:

1. In ruling that the *Wildlife Act*, S.B.C. 1966, Ch. 55, was a law of general application within the meaning of that phrase in s. 88 of the *Indian Act*.

2. In ruling, in effect, that s. 88 of the Indian Act constituted a federal incorporation by reference of certain provincial laws rather than a statement of the general principles relating to the application of provincial laws to Indians.

3.   In ruling, in effect, that aboriginal hunting rights could be expropriated without compensation, and without explicit federal legislation.

The third point can be disposed of shortly. The British Columbia Court of Appeal was not asked to decide nor did it decide, as I read its judgment, whether aboriginal hunting rights were or could be expropriated without compensation. It is argued that absence of compensation supports the proposition that there has been no loss or regulation of rights. That does not follow. Most legislation imposing negative prohibitions affects previously enjoyed rights in ways not deemed compensatory. The Wildlife Act illustrates the point. It is aimed at wildlife management and to that end it regulates the time, place and manner of hunting game. It is not directed to the acquisition of property.

Before considering the two other grounds of appeal, I should say that the important constitutional issue as to the nature of aboriginal title, if any, in respect of lands in British Columbia, the further question as to whether it had been extinguished, and the force of the Royal Proclamation of 1763 — issues discussed in *Calder* v. *AG BC*, [1973] 4 WWR 1, [1973] SCR 313, 34 DLR (3d) 145 — will not be determined in the present appeal. They were not directly placed in issue by the appellants and a sound rule to follow is that questions of title should only be decided when title is directly in issue. Interested parties should be afforded an opportunity to adduce evidence in detail bearing upon the resolution of the particular dispute. Claims to aboriginal title are woven with history legend, politics and moral obligations. If the claim of any band in respect of any particular land is to be decided as a justiciable issue and not a political issue, it should be so considered on the facts pertinent to that band and to that land, not on any global basis. Counsel were advised during argument — and indeed seemed to concede — that the issues raised in the present appeal could be resolved without determining the broader questions I have mentioned.

I

LAWS OF GENERAL APPLICATION

Argument was addressed to the court that The Wildlife Act affects Indian people in a manner quite different from the way in which it affects non-Indian people and for that reason cannot be considered as a law of general application within the meaning of the Indian Act, s. 88. The first thing to notice in this respect is the precise terms of s. 88 itself. It subjects Indians to "*all* laws of general application from time to time *in force in any province*" (the italics are mine). There formerly existed a doubt as to whether s. 88 was restricted to provincially enacted laws but that question has been settled in the affirmative by this court in *Regina* v. *George*, supra. Martland J gave this interpretation to the relevant phrase in s. 88, at p. 281:

> *In my view the expression refers only to those rules of law in a province which are provincial in scope*, and would include provincial legislation and any laws which were made a part of the law of a province, as, for example, in the provinces of Alberta and Saskatchewan, the laws of England as they existed on July 15, 1870.
>
> This section was not intended to be a declaration of the paramountcy of treaties over federal legislation. The reference to treaties was incorporated in a section *the purpose of which was to make provincial laws applicable to Indians, so as to preclude any interference with rights under treaties resulting from the impact of provincial legislation*. (The italics are mine.)

There are two indicia by which to discern whether or not a provincial enactment is a law of general application. It is necessary to look first to the territorial reach of the Act. If the Act does not extend uniformly throughout the territory, the inquiry is at an end and the question is answered in the negative. If the law does extend uniformly throughout the jurisdiction, the intention and effects of the enactment need to be considered. The law must not be "in relation to" one class of citizens in object and purpose. But the fact that a law may have graver consequence to one person than to another does not, on that account alone, make the law other than one of general application. There are few laws which have a uniform impact. The line is crossed, however, when an enactment, though in relation to another matter, by its effect impairs the status or capacity of a particular group. The analogy may be made to a law which in its effect paralyzes the status and capacities of a federal company: see *Great West Saddlery Co.* v. *The King*, [1921] 2 AC 91. Such an act is no "law of general application". See also *Cunningham* v. *Tomey Homma*, [1903] AC 151.

Apply these criteria to the case at bar. There is no doubt that The Wildlife Act has a uniform territorial operation. Similarly it is clear that in object and purpose the Act is not aimed at Indians. Section 4 of The Wildlife Act, under which the accused were charged, commences, "No person shall", and so, on its face, applies to all persons. Subsections (1), (2) and (3) of s. 4 of The Wildlife Act impose licensing requirements on those wishing to hunt, trap or fish. Subsection (4) states that subsections (1), (2) and (3) do not apply to an Indian residing in the province. From this it is clear that the other sections are intended to apply to Indians as well as all other persons within the province.

Provincial game laws, which have as their object the conservation and management of provincial wildlife resources, have been held by this court not to relate to Indians *qua* Indians: *Cardinal* v. *AG Alta.*, [1973] 6 WWR 205, [1974] SCR 695 at 706, 13 CCC (2d) 1, 40 DLR (3d) 553, and *Regina* v. *George*, *supra*. It was long ago decided that provincial laws may affect Indians, insofar as the Act was not in relation to them.

> In other words, no statute of the Provincial Legislature dealing with Indians or their lands as such would be valid and effective; but there is no reason why general legislation may not affect them.

These words of Riddell J in *Rex* v. *Martin* (1917), 41 OLR 79 at 84, 29 CCC 189, 39 DLR 635 (CA), were cited with approval in this court by Martland J in *Cardinal* v. *AG Alta.*, supra, at p. 706. Martland J continued at pp. 213-14:

> The point is that the provisions of s. 12 [of the schedule to The Alberta Natural Resources Transfer Act, 1930 (Alta.), c. 21] were not required to make provincial game laws apply to Indians off the reserve.

The chief justice of this court, then Laskin J, wrote in dissent in *Cardinal*, but on the point of concern in the present inquiry, namely, the applicability of provincial game laws to Indians off reserves, his views seem to accord with those of Martland J. After requiring to the exclusion of reserves from provincial control, he had this to say at p. 224:

> They do not return to that control under s. 12 in respect of the application of provincial game laws. That section deals with a situation unrelated to Indian reserves. It is concerned rather with Indians as such, and with guaranteeing to them a continuing right to hunt, trap and fish for food regardless of *provincial game laws which would otherwise confine Indians in parts of the province that are under provincial administration.* Although inelegantly expressed, s. 12 does not expand provincial legislative power but contracts it. (The italics are mine.)

However abundant the right of Indians to hunt and to fish, there can be no doubt that such right is subject to regulation and curtailment by the appropriate legislative authority. Section 88 of the Indian Act appears to be plain in purpose and effect. In the absence of treaty protection or statutory protection, Indians are brought within provincial regulatory legislation.

Game conservation laws have as their policy the maintenance of wildlife resources. It might be argued that without some conservation measures the ability of Indians or others to hunt for food would become a moot issue in consequence of the destruction of the resource. The presumption is for the validity of a legislative enactment and in this case the presumption has to mean that in the absence of evidence to the contrary the measures taken by the British Columbia legislature were taken to maintain an effective resource in the province for its citizens and not to oppose the interests of conservationists and Indians in such a way as to favour the claims of the former. If, of course, it can be shown in future litigation that the province has acted in such a way as to oppose conservation and Indians' claims to the detriment of the latter — to "'preserve moose before Indians'", in the words of Gordon JA in *Regina* v. *Strongquill*, 8WWR (NS) 247, 16 CR 194, 105 CCC 262, [1953] 2 D.L.R. 264 (Saskatchewan Court of Appeal) — it might very well be concluded that the effect of the legislation is to cross the line demarking laws of general application from other enactments. It would have to be shown that the policy of such an Act was to impair the status and capacities of Indians. Were that so, s. 88 would not operate to make the Act applicable to Indians. But that has not been done here and in the absence of clear evidence the court cannot so presume.

The judgment of this court in *Regina* v. *White and Bob* (1965), 52 DLR (2d) 481n, affirming 52 WWR 193, 50 DLR (2d) 613, is of no assistance to appellants in the present case. In *White and Bob* the accused were charged with having game in their possession during the closed season without having a valid and subsisting permit under The Game Act, RSBC 1960, c. 160 [later repealed by 1966, c. 55, s. 81]. The accused raised the defence that an agreement between their ancestors, members of the Saalequun tribe, and Governor Douglas, dated 23rd December 1854, gave them the right to hunt for food over the land in question and, alternatively, that as native Indians they possessed the aboriginal right to hunt for food over unoccupied land lying within their ancient tribal hunting grounds. The position of the Crown was that the agreement in question conferred no hunting rights and, if it did, these rights were extinguished by s. 87 (now s. 88) of the Indian Act, which the Crown said extended the provisions of The Game Act (the forerunner of The Wildlife Act) to Indians. Davey JA (with whom Sullivan JA concurred) was of the opinion that Parliament intended the word "treaty" in s. 87 to include agreements such as the one in question and to except their provisions from the operative part of the section. He held that, that being so, s. 87 did not extend the general provisions of The Game Act to the respondents in the exercise of their hunting rights under the agreement over the lands in question. The following passage of his judgment is important (p. 198):

Secs. 8 and 15 of the *Game Act* specifically exempt Indians from the operation of certain provisions of the Act, and from that *I think it clear that the other provisions are intended to be of general application and to include* Indians. If these general sections are sufficiently clear to show an intention to abrogate or qualify the contractual rights of hunting notoriously reserved to Indians by agreements such as Ex. 8, they would, in my opinion, fail in that purpose because that would be legislation in relation to Indians that falls within parliament's exclusive legislative authority under sec. 91(24) of the *BNA Act, 1867*, 30 & 31 Vict., ch. 3, and also because that would conflict with sec. 87 of the *Indian Act* passed under that authority.

He concluded (p. 199):

In the result, the rights of the respondents to hunt over the lands in question reserved to them by Ex. 8 are preserved by sec. 87, and remain unimpaired by the *Game Act*, and it follows that the respondents were rightfully in possession of the carcasses. It becomes unnecessary to consider other aspects of a far reaching argument addressed to us by respondents' counsel.

Sheppard JA (with whom JA concurred) dissented. He considered that the agreement was not a treaty and was therefore not within the opening words of s. 87. He said that the section of The Game Act in question was within the legislative jurisdiction of the province and was applicable to Indians not on their reserve. Norris JA wrote separate reasons in which he agreed, substantially for the reasons given by Davey JA, that the agreement was a treaty within the meaning of s. 87 of the Indian Act. He then dealt at length with the matter of aboriginal rights in general and the applicability of the Royal Proclamation of 1763.

As I read the judgments in the Court of Appeal for British Columbia, four of the five judges accepted that the section of The Game Act under which the accused were charged would apply to the accused unless the agreement of 1854 could be said to be a treaty within the opening words of s. 87 of the Indian Act. When the case reached this court, the only question decided was whether or not the agreement constituted such a treaty. At the conclusion of argument for the appellant the court rendered the following oral judgment [p. 481]:

Mr Berger, Mr Sanders and Mr Christie, we do not find it necessary to hear you. We are all of the opinion that the majority in the Court of Appeal were right in their conclusion that the document, Ex. 8, was a "treaty" within the meaning of that term as used in s. 87 of the Indian Act [RSC 1952, c. 149]. We therefore think that in the circumstances of the case, the operation of s. 25 [re-en. 1961, c. 21, s. 10] of The Game Act [RSBC 1960, c. 160] was excluded by reason of the existence of that treaty.

The appeal is accordingly dismissed with costs throughout.

The operation of s. 25 of The Game Act was excluded because the agreement was a "treaty".

It has been urged in argument that Indians having historic hunting rights which they have not surrendered should not be placed in a more invidious position than those who entered into treaties, the terms of which preserved those rights. However receptive one may be to such an argument on compassionate grounds, the plain fact is that s. 88 of the Indian Act, enacted by the Parliament of Canada, provides that "subject to the terms of any treaty" all laws of general application from time to time in force in any province are applicable to and in respect of Indians in the province, except as stated. The terms of the treaty are paramount; in the absence of a treaty provincial laws of general application apply. . . .

On either view of this issue present appellants must fail. If the provisions of The Wildlife Act are referentially incorporated by s. 88 of the Indian Act, appellants, in order to succeed, would have the burden of demonstrating inconsistency or duplication with the Indian Act or any order, rule, regulation or by-law made thereunder. That burden has not been discharged and, having regard to the terms of The Wildlife Act, manifestly could not have been discharged. Accordingly, such provisions take effect as federal legislation in accordance with their terms. Assuming, without deciding, that the theory of aboriginal title as elaborated by Hall J. in *Calder* v. *A.G. B.C.*, [1973] 4 W.W.R. 1, [1973] S.C.R. 313, 34 D.L.R. (3d) 145, is available in respect of present appellants, it has been conclusively decided that such title, as any other, is subject to regulations imposed by validity enacted federal laws: *Derriksan* v. *The Queen*, [1976] 6 W.W.R. 480, 31 C.C.C. (2d) 575. That was also the result in *Regina* v. *George*, supra, *Daniels* v. *White*, 64 W.W.R. 385, 4 C.R.N.S. 176, [1968] S.C.R. 517, [1969] 1 C.C.C. 299, 2 D.L.R. (3d) 1, and *Sikyea* v. *The Queen*, 49 W.W.R. 306, 44 C.R. 266, [1964] S.C.R. 642, [1965] 2 C.C.C. 129, 50 D.L.R. (2d) 80. The latter two cases are instructive as the hunting rights there stood on stronger ground in that they were protected, in the case of *Silyea*, by treaty, and in *Daniels'* case by the Manitoba Natural Resources Agreement. In neither case did the protection prevail against the federal Migratory Birds Convention Act, R.S.C. 1952, c. 179.

If s. 88 does not referentially incorporate The Wildlife Act, the only question at issue is whether the Act is a law of general application.

Since that proposition has not been here negatived, the enactment would apply to Indians ex proprio vigore. It is, therefore, immaterial to the present appeals whether s. 88 takes effect by way of referential incorporation or not. In either case, these appeals must fail.

I would dismiss the appeals.

(c) Effect of the Constitution Act, 1930

Constitution Act, 1930

The Natural Resources Transfer Agreements, subsequently incorporated into the Constitution Act, 1930 (RSC 1970, App. II, No. 25) transferred the beneficial ownership of land and natural resources from the federal government to the governments of Manitoba, Saskatchewan, and Alberta. Each Agreement recognized the obligation of the province to make unoccupied Crown land available to Canada so that Canada could fulfil outstanding land entitlements under treaty. In addition, each contained an identical paragraph recognizing Indian hunting, trapping, and fishing rights:

> In order to secure to the Indians of the Province the continuance of the supply of game and fish for their support and subsistence, Canada agrees that the laws respecting game in force in the Province from time to time shall apply to the Indians within the boundaries thereof, provided, however, that the said Indians shall have the right, which the Province hereby assures to them, of hunting, trapping and fishing game and fish for food at all seasons of the year on all unoccupied Crown lands and on any other lands to which the said Indians may have a right of access.
>
> (Para. 13 of the Canada-Manitoba Agreement, and para. 12 of the Canada-Alberta and Canada-Saskatchewan Agreements.)

Judicial interpretation has limited the hunting rights constitutionally guaranteed by the Natural Resources Transfer Agreements to status Indians and has excluded non-status Indians and Metis from their benefits (See, for example, *R.* v. *Laprise*, [1978] 6 WWR 85; [1978] CNLB (No. 4) 118 (Saskatchewan Court of Appeal), which held that a non-status Indian is not an "Indian" for the purposes of s. 12 of the Natural Resources Transfer Agreement of 1930. The result was that the defendant, a non-status Indian, could not rely on the protection that s. 12 gives to Indian hunting rights.)

(i) *Constitution Act, 1930* and Federal Laws
   (A) *Daniels* v. *White*, [1968] SCR SCR 517, 64 WWR 385, 4 CRNS 176, [1969] 1 CCC 299, 2 DLR (3d) 1 (SCC) (footnotes omitted)

JUDSON J: — The appellant is an Indian within the meaning of para.

(g) of subs. (1) of s. 2 of the *Indian Act*, RSC 1952, c. 149. He was convicted on December 7, 1964, of having in his possession

Migratory Game Birds, during a time when the capturing, killing, or taking of such birds, is prohibited, contrary to the Regulations under the *Migratory Birds Convention Act*, thereby committing an offence under Section 12(1) of the said *Migratory Birds Convention Act*.

On an appeal by way of trial *de novo* his conviction was quashed. On a further appeal to the Court of Appeal of Manitoba, his conviction was restored and the sentence affirmed by a majority judgment. He appeals to this Court with leave.

The issue in this appeal is whether by operation of para. 13 of the agreement made on December 14, 1929, between the Government of the Dominion of Canada and the Government of the Province of Manitoba (hereinafter referred to as ''the agreement'') the appellant was exempted from compliance with the *Migratory Birds Convention Act* and *Regulations* made thereunder bearing in mind that at the relevant time and place he was an Indian who had hunted game for food on land to which he had a right of access.

There can be no doubt that apart from para. 13 of the agreement above quoted the appellant was, in the circumstances of this case, subject to the *Migratory Birds Convention Act and Regulations*. See: *Sikyea* v. *The Queen; The Queen* v. *George; Sigeareak* v. *The Queen*.

Paragraph 13 of the agreement provides:

13. In order to secure to the Indians of the Province the continuance of the supply of game and fish for their support and subsistence, Canada agrees that the laws respecting game in force in the Province from time to time shall apply to the Indians within the boundaries thereof, provided, however, that the said Indians shall have the right, which the Province hereby assures to them, of hunting, trapping and fishing game and fish for food at all seasons of the year on all unoccupied Crown lands and on any other lands to which the said Indians may have a right of access.

Paragraph 13 is part of an agreement dated December 14, 1929, between the government of Canada and the Government of the Province of Manitoba for the transfer to the province from the Dominion of all ungranted Crown lands. This agreement was approved by the Manitoba Legislature and by Parliament. (Statutes of Manitoba, 1930, c. 30; Statutes of Canada, 1930, c. 29.) It was subsequently affirmed by the *British North America Act*, 1930, 20-21 Geo. V., c. 26. Three similar agreements involving Alberta, Saskatchewan and British Columbia were subsequently affirmed.

Section 1 of the *British North America Act* 1930 provides:

1.   The agreements set out in the Schedule to this Act are hereby confirmed and shall have the force of law notwithstanding anything in the *British North America, 1867*, or any Act amending the same, or any Act of the Parliament of Canada, or in any Order in Council or terms or conditions of union made or approved under any such Act as aforesaid.

Prior to the coming into force of the agreement, title to all ungranted Crown lands in the Province of Manitoba was vested in the Dominion. Briefly, the relevant history is that by the *Rupert's Land Act*, 1868, 31-32 Vict., c. 105 (RSC 1952, vol. VI, p. 99) provision was made for the surrender of Rupert's Land by the Hudson's Bay Company and for the acceptance thereof by Her Majesty. Section 3 of the said Act provided:

> that such Surrender shall not be accepted by Her Majesty unti the Terms and Conditions upon which Rupert's Land shall be admitted into the said Dominion of Canada shall have been approved by Her Majesty, and embodied in an address to Her Majesty from both the Houses of the Parliament of Canada in pursuance of the 146th Section of the *British North America Act* 1867.

By Imperial Order in Council of June 23, 1870, Rupert's Land was admitted into and became part of the Dominion of Canada effective July 15, 1870 — RSC 1952, vol. VI, p. 113. By operation of the *Manitoba Act* 1870, 33 Vict., c. 3 (Canada), subsequently affirmed with retrospective effect by the Parliament of the United Kingdom (*BNA Act, 1871*, 34-35 Vict., c. 28, s. 5, RSC 1952, vol. VI, p. 146), the Province of Manitoba was carved out of Rupert's Land and came into being on the same date Rupert's Land entered Confederation. By s. 30 of the *Manitoba Act, 1870*, all ungranted or waste lands in the Province vested in the Crown to be administered by the Government of Canada for the purposes of the Dominion.

The Crown in right of the Dominion being the owner of all Crown lands, including the mines and minerals therein, in the Province of Manitoba that Province, together with Alberta and Saskatchewan, was in a less favourable condition than the other Provinces who by operation of s. 109 of the *British North America Act, 1867*, retained Crown lands upon entering Confederation. The purpose of the agreement was to transfer these lands to Manitoba in order that it might be in the same position as the other provinces under s. 109 of the *British North America Act, 1867*. This is apparent from the preamble to and paragraph 1 of the agreement and from the following cases where the matter was under consideration:

Saskatchewan Natural Resources Reference:

Reference concerning Refunds of Dues paid to the Dominion of Canada in respect of Timber Permits in the Western Provinces;
Anthony v. Attorney General of Alberta;
Attorney General of Alberta v. Huggard Assets Limited:
Western Canadian Collieries Limited v. Attorney General of Alberta.

The whole tenor of the agreement is that of a conveyance of land imposing specified obligations and restrictions on the transferee, not on the transferor. This applies, in particular, to paragraph 13, which makes provincial game laws applicable to Indians in the province subject to the proviso contained therein. That only provincial game laws were in the contemplation of the parties, and not federal enactments, is underscored by the words "which the Province hereby assures to them" in para. 13. As indicated by para. 11 of the agreement and para. 10 of the Alberta and Saskatchewan agreements, Canada, in netotiating these agreements, was mindful of the fact it had treaty obligations with Indians on the Prairies. These treaties, among other things, dealt with hunting by Indians on unoccupied lands. For example, treaties 5 and 6, which cover portions of Manitoba, Saskatchewan and Alberta, provide:

Her Majesty further agrees with Her said Indians, that they, the said Indians, shall have right to pursue their avocations of hunting and fishing throughout the tract surrendered as hereinbefore described, subject to such regulations as may from time to time be made by Her Government of Her Dominion of Canada, and saving and excepting such tracts as may from time to time be required or taken up for settlement, mining, lumbering or other purposes, by Her said Government of the Dominion of Canada, or by any of the subjects thereof duly authorized therefor by the said Government.

Treaty No. 8, which covers portions of Alberta and Saskatchewan, provides:

And Her Majesty the Queen HEREBY AGREES with the said Indians that they shall have right to pursue their usual vocations of hunting, trapping and fishing throughout the tract surrendered as heretofore described, subject to such regulations as may from time to time be made by the Government of the country, acting under the authority of Her Majesty, and saving and excepting such tracts as may be required or taken up from time to time for settlement, mining, lumbering, trading or other purposes.

Treaty No. 7, which covers a portion of Alberta, is to the same effect.

It being the expectation of the parties that the agreement would be given the force of law by the Parliament of the United Kingdom

(Paragraph 25) care was taken in framing para. 13 that the Legislature of the province could not unilaterally affect the right of Indians to hunt for food on unoccupied Crown lands. Under the agreement this could only be done by concurrent Statutes of the Parliament of Canada and the Legislature of the province, in accordance with para. 24 thereof.

The majority opinion in the Manitoba Court of Appeal held that the agreement, affirmed as it was by legislation of all interested governments, could not be reconciled with the *Migratory Birds Convention Act* and that the latter Act must prevail. The *Migratory Birds Convention Act*, being of general application throughout Canada, ought not to be construed as circumscribed by the restricted legislation that is to be found in the *Manitoba Natural Resources Act*. It was desirable that a matter within the legislative responsibility of Parliament and governed by international treaty be uniform in application throughout the country unless specifically provided otherwise.

The dissenting opinion would have held that para. 13 of the agreement should prevail over the *Migratory Birds Convention Act* notwithstanding that such a result gives the Act a different effect in Manitoba from that which it has in other parts of Canada.

The *Migratory Birds Convention Act* was enacted in 1917. It confirms a treaty made between Canada and the United States. The regulations under the Act go back to 1918. (PC 871, April 23, 1918). In my opinion the agreement and the legislation of 1930 confirming it did no more than impose specified obligations and restrictions upon the transferee province. They did not repeal by implication a statute of Canada giving effect to an international convention.

On this subject I adopt the law as stated in 36 Hals., 3rd ed., p. 465:

> Repeal by implication is not favoured by the courts for it is to be presumed that Parliament would not intend to effect so important a matter as the repeal of a law without expressing its intention to do so. If, however, provisions are enacted which cannot be reconciled with those of an existing statute, the only inference possible is that Parliament, unless it failed to address its mind to the question, intended that the provisions of the existing statute should cease to have effect, and an intention so evinced is as effective as one expressed in terms. The rule is, therefore, that one provision repeals another by implication if, but only if, it is so inconsistent with or repugnant to that other that the two are incapable of standing together. If it is reasonably possible so to construe the provisions as to give effect to both, that must be done; and their reconciliation must in particular be attempted if the later statute provides for its construction as one with the earlier, thereby indicating that Parliament regarded them as compatible, or if the repeals expressly effected by the later

statute are so detailed that failure to include the earlier provision amongst them must be regarded as such an indication.

I would dismiss the appeal.

Hall J (dissenting):

The appellant claimed immunity from the provisions of the *Migratory Birds Convention Act* by virtue of the *Manitoba Natural Resources Act*, Statutes of Canada 1930, c. 29, which he contends exempts him from the operations of the *Migratory Birds Convention Act* because he is an Indian residing in the Province of Manitoba.

In the year 1929, some twelve years after the enactment of the *Migratory Birds Convention Act*, the Government of Canada and the Government of Manitoba reached an agreement respecting the transfer to Manitoba of the unalienated natural resources within the Province. The agreement approved by the Parliament of Canada in the *Manitoba Natural Resources Act*, *supra*, and by the Legislature of Manitoba by the *Manitoba Natural Resources Act*, RSM 1954, c. 180. The schedule to both statutes contains the terms of the agreement, in which s. 13 reads as follows:

> In order to secure to the Indians of the Province the continuance of the supply of game and fish for their support and subsistence, Canada agrees that the laws respecting game in force in the Province from time to time shall apply to the Indians within the boundaries thereof, provided, however, that the said Indians shall have the right, which the Province hereby assures to them, of hunting, trapping and fishing game and fish for food at all seasons of the year on all unoccupied Crown lands and on any other lands to which the said Indians might have a right of access.

This section of the agreement was dealt with by this Court in *Prince and Myron* v. *The Queen*, which held that Indians in Manitoba hunting for food on all unoccupied Crown lands and on any other lands to which they may have rights of access were not subject to any of the limitations which the *Game and Fisheries Act* of Manitoba, RSM 1954, c. 94, imposes upon the non-Indian residents of Manitoba. Section 72(1) of *The Game and Fisheries Act*, RSM 1954, c. 94, reads as follows:

> 72(1)   Notwithstanding this Act, and in so far only as is necessary to implement The Manitoba Natural Resources Act, any Indian may hunt and take game for food for his own use at all seasons of the year on all unoccupied Crown lands and on any other lands to which the Indian may have the right of access.

The question which falls to be determined in this appeal is whether the terms of the agreement between the Government of Canada and the Government of Manitoba as ratified by Parliament and by the Legislature of Manitoba and confirmed at Westminster in the *British North America Act* 1930 take precedence over the provisions of the *Migratory Birds Convention Act* and the *Regulations* made thereunder. If full effect is to be given to s. 13 of the agreement in question, it must be held that the provisions of the *Migratory Birds Convention Act* and the *Regulations* made thereunder do not apply to Indians in Manitoba when engaged in hunting migratory birds for food in the areas set out in the section. On the other hand, if the provisions of the *Migratory Birds Convention Act* take precedence, the right of Indians in Manitoba to hunt game for food at all seasons of the year in accordance with said s. 13 is wiped out. Accordingly, the decision must be made as to which legislation is paramount.

Freedman JA, in his dissenting judgment in the Court of Appeal, dealt with the problem as follows:

At first blush it might be though that the reference to Indians and their hunting rights both in the Convention and in the regulations of the *Migratory Birds Convention Act* — under which they are permitted to hunt scoters, auks, auklets, etc. — settles the matter. Obviously such rights are far smaller than the unrestricted right to hunt all game for food, which is provided by Sec. 13 of *"The Manitoba Natural Resources Act"*. The reference to Indians in the Convention and in the regulations is in general terms, no exception being made with regard to Indians of Manitoba or elsewhere. It might accordingly be plausibly argued that the Indians in Manitoba have only such rights with respect to migratory birds as are conferred by the *Migratory Birds Convention Act*. But this is not necessarily so. We must remember that when the Convention of 1917 was entered into, the agreement relating to the transfer of Manitoba's natural resources was not yet in existence nor even in contemplation. Hence no exception with regard to Manitoba Indians could have been expected in the Convention. As for the regulations of 1958, it is true that they were enacted subsequent to *The Manitiba Natural Resources Act* and that they contain no exception in favour of Indians of Manitoba. But the regulations could not enlarge or go beyond the provisions of the statute pursuant to which they were enacted. Rather they would conform to the terms of that statute; so not each exception would be expected in the regulations either.

The parallel argument on the other side appears to me to be far more cogent. The terms of Sec. 13 contained in *The Manitoba*

Natural Resources Act are comprehensive and permit the hunting by Indians of game for food at all seasons of the year. No exception is made with respect to migratory birds, even though the *Migratory Birds Convention Act* had been on the statute books since 1917. Instead of making the provisions of Sec. 13 subject to the terms of the *Migratory Birds Convention Act*, the legislators did quite the opposite. They enshrined the agreement within the Canadian constitutional framework by having it confirmed at Westminster in the *British North America Act, 1930*, and declared it should have the force of law "notwithstanding anything in . . . . any Act of the Parliament of Canada". I believe it should be given that force and not be read as subject to the provisions of the *Migratory Birds Convention Act*.

I am conscious of the fact that this conclusion will give to the *Migratory Birds Convention Act* a different effect in Manitoba (and incidentally in Saskatchewan and Alberta, which have similar provisions to Sec. 13) from that which it has in other parts of Canada. The decision of the Supreme Court of Canada in *Reg.* vs. *Sikyea*, (1964) S.C.R. 642, upheld the application of the *Migratory Birds Act* to an Indian of the Northwest Territories notwithstanding hunting rights contained in treaties. The decision of that Court in *The Queen* vs. *George*, (1966) 55 DLR (2d) 386, came to the same conclusion as regards an Indian in Ontario. In neither case, of course, did Sec. 13 of *The Manitoba Natural Resources Act* apply. If the application of Sec. 13 gives to the *Migratory Birds Convention Act* a disparate result in different parts of Canada, that is simply an unfortunate but inevitable consequence of the conflicting legislation on the subject.

I am in full agreement with Freedman JA and the fact that the conclusion arrived at by him gives the Indians of Manitoba, Saskatchewan and Alberta a latitude while hunting for food on unoccupied crown lands and on other lands to which Indians might have a right of access greater than that possessed by other Indians in Canada is not of itself a reason for putting a strained interpretation on said s. 13 or for failing to give effect to the very plain language in the *British North America Act* 1930. The lamentable history of Canada's dealings with Indians in disregard of treaties made with them as spelt out in the judgment of Johnson JA in *Regina* v. *Sikyea* and by McGillivray JA in *Rex* v. *Wesley* ought in justice to allow the Indians to get the benefit of an unambiguous law which for once appears to give them what the treaties and the Commissioners who were sent to negotiate those treaties promised.

I said at p. 646 of my reasons in *Sikyea* which were concurred in by the six other members of this Court who heard the appeal:

On the substantive question involved, I agree with the reasons for judgment and with the conclusions of Johnson JA in the Court of Appeal, (1964) 2 CCC 325, 43 C.R. 83, 46 WWR 65. He has dealt with the important issues fully and correctly in their historical and legal settings, and there is nothing which I can usefully add to what he has written.

It should be noted that in *Sikyea* the *British North America Act* 1930 had no application because the offence there being dealt with had occurred in the Northwest Territories, an area wholly within the legislative jurisdiction of the Parliament of Canada. Parliament has the power to breach the Indian treaties if it so wills: *Regina* v. *Sikyea*, *supra*. That point is dealt with by Johnson JA at p. 330 as follows:

> Discussing the nature of the rights which the Indians obtained under the treaties, Lord Watson, speaking for the Judicial Committee in *A. G. Can.* v. *A. G. Ont.*, *A. G. Que.* v. *A. G. Ont.*, (1897) AC 199 at p. 213, said:
>
>> Their Lordships have had no difficulty in coming to the conclusion that, under the treaties, the Indians obtained no right to their annuities, whether original or augmented beyond a promise and agreement, which was nothing more than a personal obligation by its governor, as representing the old province, that the latter should pay the annuities as and when they became due . . .
>
> While this refers only to the annuities payable under the treaties, it is difficult to see that the other covenants in the treaties, including the one we are here concerned with, can stand on any higher footing. It is always to be kept in mind that the Indians surrendered their rights in the territory in exchange for these promises. This "promise and agreement", like any other, can, of course, be breached, and there is no law of which I am aware that would prevent Parliament by legislation, properly within s. 91 of the *BNA Act*, from doing so.

However, parliament cannot legislate in contravention of the *British North America Act* and that is why the *British North America Act* 1930 is decisive in this case.

A reading of Johnson JA's historical review in *Sikyea*, particularly at pp. 335-6, where he said:

> It is, I think, clear that the rights given to the Indians by their treaties as they apply to migratory birds have been taken away by this Act and its Regulations. How are we to explain this apparent breach of faith on the part of the Government, for I cannot think it can be described

in any other terms? This cannot be described as a minor or insignificant curtailment of these treaty rights, for game birds have always been a most plentiful, a most reliable and a readily obtainable food in large areas of Canada. I cannot believe that the Government of Canada realized that in implementing the Convention they were at the same time breaching the treaties that they had made with the Indians. It is much more likely that these obligations under the treaties were overlooked — a case of the left hand having forgotten what the right hand had done. The subsequent history of the Government dealing with the Indians would seem to bear this out. When the treaty we are concerned with here was signed in 1921, only five years after the enactment of the *Migratory Birds Convention Act*, we find the Commissioners who negotiated the treaty reporting:

> The Indians seemed afraid, for one thing, that their liberty to hunt, trap and fish would be taken away or curtailed, but were assured by me that this would not be the case, and the Government will expect them to support themselves in their own way, and, in fact, that more twine for nets and more ammunition were given under the terms of this treaty than under any of the preceding ones; this went a long way to calm their fears. I also pointed out that any game laws made were to their advantage, and, whether they took treaty or not, they were subject to the laws of the Dominion.

and there is nothing in this report which would indicate that the Indians were told that their right to shoot migratory birds had already been taken away from them. I have referred to Art. 12 of the agreement between the Government of Canada and the Province of Alberta signed in 1930 by which that Province was required to assure to the Indians the right of "hunting, trapping and fishing game and fish for food at all seasons of the year on all unoccupied Crown lands". (The amendment to the *B.N.A. Act* (1930 (U.K.), c. 26) that confirmed this agreement, declared that it should "have the force of law notwithstanding anything in the British North America Act . . . or any Act of the Parliament of Canada . . .") It is of some importance that while the Indians in the Northwest Territories continued to shoot ducks at all seasons for food, it is only recently that any attempt has been made to enforce the Act.

confirms what I said in *Sikyea* and I am fortified in that view by the judgment of McGillivray JA in *R. v. Wesley*, particularly at pp. 283-4 where, in dealing with s. 12 of the Alberta agreement, identical in effect with s. 13 of the Manitoba agreement, he said:

> In Canada the Indian treaties appear to have been judicially

interpreted as being mere promises and agreements. See *AG Can*. v. *AG Ont*. (Indian Annuities case), (1897) AC 199, at p. 213.

Assuming as I do that our treaties with Indians are on no higher plane than other formal agreements yet this in no wise makes it less the duty and obligation of the Crown to carry out the promises contained in those treaties with the exactness which honour and good conscience dictate and it is not to be thought that the Crown has departed from those equitable principles which the Senate and the House of Commons declared in addressing Her Majesty in 1867, uniformly governed the British Crown in its dealings with the aborigines.

At the time of the making of this Indian Treaty it was of first class importance to Canada that the Indians who had become restless after the sway of the Hodson's Bay Co. had come to an end, should become content and that such title or interest in land as they had should be peacefully surrendered to permit of settlemtn without hindrance of any kind. On the other hand it goes without saying that the Indians were greatly concerned with "their vocations of hunting" upon which they depended for their living.

In this connection it is of historical interest although of no assistance in the interpretation of the treaty, that Governor Laird who with Colonel Macleod negotiated this treaty, said to the Chiefs of the Indian tribes:

> I expect to listen to what you have to say today, but first, I would explain that it is your privilege to hunt all over the prairies, and that should you desire to sell any portion of your land, or any coal or timber from off your reserves, the Government will see that you receive just and fair prices, and that you can rely on all the Queen's promises being fulfilled.

And again he said: "The reserve will be given to you without depriving you of the privilege to hunt over the plains until the land be taken up."

It is true that Government regulations in respect of hunting are contemplated in the Treaty but considering that Treaty in its proper setting I do not think that any of the makers of it could by any stretch of the imagination be deemed to have contemplated a day when the Indians would be deprived of an unfettered right to hunt game of all kinds for food on unoccupied Crown land.

In the case *AG* v. *Metropolitan Electric Supply Co.*, 74 LJ Ch 145, at p. 150, Farwell J said: —

I think it is germane to the subject to consider what the Legislature had in view in making the provisions which I find in the Act of Parliament itself. As Lord Halsbury said in *Eastman Photographic Materials Co.* v. *Comptroller General of Patents, Designs, and Trade Marks*, (1898) AC 571) referring to *Heydons's Case* (1584), (3 CoRep 7a) 'We are to see what was the law before the Act was passed, and what was the mischief or defect for which the law had not provided, what remedy Parliament appointed, and the reason of the remedy.' That is a very general way of stating it, but no doubt one is entitled to put one's self in the position in which the Legislature was at the time the Act was passed in order to see what was the state of knowledge as far as all the circumstances brought before the Legislature are concerned, for the purpose of seeing what it was the Legislature was aiming at.

If as Crown counsel contends, s. 12 taken as a whole gives rise to apparent inconsistency and is capable of two meanings then I still have no hesitation in saying in the light of all the external circumstances relative to Indian rights in this Dominion to which I have alluded, that the law makers in 1930 were in the making of this proviso, aiming at assuring to the Indians covered by the section, an unrestricted right to hunt for food in those unsettled places where game may be found, described in s. 12.

It was argued that para. 13 of the agreement in question is limited in its application solely to provincial laws because of the presence of the clause which the Province hereby assures to them'', in the sentence under consideration. That clause inserted parenthetically between commas cannot derogate from the thrust of the principal clause which contains the specific declaration ''that the said Indians shall have the right . . . of hunting, trapping and fishing game and fish for food at all seasons of the year''. In my view it adds emphasis to the declaration by making manifest the application of the declaration to the Province as though the clause read ''which the Province *also* hereby assures to them''.

If all that s. 13 of the agreement was intended to achieve in 1930 was a declaration by the Province that Indians were to have the right to fish, hunt and trap for food at all seasons of the year, it was, according to that interpretation, an empty, futile and misleading gesture. Either the Indians then had those rights or they did not have them for the *Migratory Birds Convention Act* had been on the statute books since 1917. The only interpretation that makes sense is the one that acknowledges that the right of hunting, trapping and fishing game and fish for food at all seasons of the year existed in 1930 regardless of the *Migratory Birds Convention Act* and the Federal Government wanted those rights to continue notwithstanding the transfer to the Provinces of Manitoba, Saskatchewan and Alberta of the unalienated natural resources withheld when the Provinces were formed. What logic could there have been in having the Provinces assure to Indians non-existing rights?

The Federal authority was already under treaty obligation contained in Treaties 5 and 6 which read:

> Her Majesty further agrees with Her said Indians, that they, the said Indians, shall have right to pursue their avocations of hunting and fishing throughout the tract surrendered as hereinbefore described, subject to such regulations as may from time to time be made by Her Government of Her Dominion of Canada, and saving and excepting such tracts as may from time to time be required or taken up for settlement, mining, lumbering or other purposes, by Her said Government of the Dominion of Canada, or by any of the subjects thereof duly authorized therefor by the said Government.

to preserve the Indians' right to hunt and fish for food at all seasons of the year, and it was merely making certain that the Provinces would accord the same rights when they got control of the unalienated Crown lands. The obligation of Canada to preserve the right to hunt and fish for food at all seasons was an historical one arising out of the rights of Indians as original inhabitants of the territories from which Manitoba, Saskatchewan and Alberta were carved and arising out of the treaties above mentioned. The subject of aboriginal rights as they apply to Indians of Western Canada and the effect of the treaties made with the Indians were dealt with by the Court of Appeal for British Columbia in *Regina* v. *White and Bob*. This Court upheld that decision in an oral judgment as follows:

> Mr Justice Cartwright delivered the following oral judgment:
> "Mr Berger, Mr Sanders and Mr Christie. We do not find it necessary to hear you. We are all of the opinion that the majority in the Court of appeal were right in their conclusion that the document, Exhibit 8, was a 'treaty' within the meaning of that term as used in s. 87 of the *Indian Act* (RSC 1952, c. 149). We therefore think that in the circumstances of the case, the operation of s. 25 of the *Game Act* (RSBC 1960, c. 160) was excluded by reason of the existence of that treaty."

It follows that if Exhibit 8 in *White and Bob* which reads:

> Know all men that we the Chiefs and people of the Sanitch Tribe

who have signed our names and made our marks to this Deed, on the
6th day of February 1852 do consent to surrender entirely and
forever, to James Douglas the Agent of the Hudsons Bay Company,
in Vancouver Island that is to say for the Governor Deputy Governor
and Committee of the same, the whole of the lands situate and lying
between Mount Douglas and Cowitchen Head on the Canal de Arro
and extending thence to the line running through the centre of
Vancouver Island north and south.

The condition of, or understanding of this sale, is this, that our
village sites and enclosed fields, are to be kept for our own use, for
the use of our children, and for those who may follow after us, and
the lands shall be properly surveyed hereafter; it is understood
however, that the land itself with these small exceptions, becomes the
entire property of the white people forever; *it is also understood that
we are at liberty to hunt over the unoccupied lands, and to carry on
our fisheries as formerly*. We have received as payment — Forty one
pounds thirteen shillings, and four pence. — In token whereof we
have signed our names, and made our marks at Fort Victoria, on the
seventh day of February, One thousand eight hundred and fifty two.
(Emphasis added.)

was a treaty within s. 87 of the *Indian Act*, RSC 1952, c. 149, so are
Treaties 5 and 6 aforesaid.

Soon after the agreement in question was entered into, the Court of
Appeal for Saskatchewan in *Rex* v. *Smith*, dealt with the effect of s. 12
of the Saskatchewan agreement which is identical with s. 13 now under
review and in that case Turgeon JA (later CJS) said:

Although this case is of great interest and importance I do not think it
will be necessary in disposing of it to examine minutely the state of
the law existing prior to recent date, nor the Indian treaty or treaties
referred to in the argument. If these treaties, or the various Dominion
or provincial statutes referred to have any present bearing on the case
it is only so far as they may throw some light upon the interpretation
of certain words in the instrument which, in my opinion, now governs
the relations of these Indians with the game laws of Saskatchewan,
and to which I am about to refer.

The 24th enumeration of sec. 91 of the *British North America Act,
1867*, ch. 3, confers upon the parliament of Canada exclusive
jurisdiction upon the subject of "Indians and Lands Reserved for the
Indians," while, on the other hand, the provinces have power to
make laws concerning the hunting, fishing, preservation, etc. of
game in the province. As a result, controversies have arisen in the

past as to the application of provincial game laws to Indians: *Rex* v. *Rodgers* (1923) 2 WWR 353, 33 Man R 139, 40 CCC 51.

But in the years 1929 and 1930 something occurred which, in my opinion, had the effect of recasting the jurisdiction of the province of Saskatchewan in respect to the operation of its game laws upon our Indian population. In December, 1929, an agreement was entered into between the Dominion and the province having for its primary object the transfer from the one to the other of the natural resources within the province. This transfer was accompanied by many terms, some of which had to do with matters pertaining to the Indians. Among these is par. 12 of the agreement, which reads as follows (LR 1929-30, p. 293):

> 12. In order to secure to the Indians of the Province the continuance of the supply of game and fish for their support and subsistence, Canada agrees that the laws respecting game in force in the Province from time to time shall apply to the Indians within the boundaries thereof, provided, however, that the said Indians shall have the right, which the Province hereby assures to them, of hunting, trapping and fishing game and fish for food at all seasons of the year on all unoccupied Crown lands and on any other lands to which the said Indians may have a right of access.

It is admitted in this case that the accused was hunting for food.

This agreement between the Dominion and the province was made "subject to its being approved by the Parliament of Canada and the Legislature of the Province' and also to confirmation by the Parliament of the United Kingdom. Ratification by the Imperial Parliament was necessary in so far at least as the agreement purported to make any change in the constitutional powers of the Dominion or of the province. In a recent decision of this Court, *Rex* v. *Zaslavsky*, ante p. 34, the learned Chief Justice quoted from the remarks of Lord Watson in the course of the argument in *CPR* v. *Notre Dame de Bonsecours Parish* (1899) AC 367, 68 LJPC 54. The statement quoted by the learned Chief Justice may fittingly be repeated here:

> The Dominion cannot give jurisdiction or leave jurisdiction with the province. The provincial Parliament cannot give legislative jurisdiction to the Dominion Parliament. If they have it, either one or the other of them, they have it by virtue of the Act of 1867. I think we must get rid of the idea that either one or other can enlarge the jurisdiction of the other or surrender jurisdiction.

Consequently no legislative jurisdiction can be taken from the Dominion Parliament and bestowed upon a provincial Legislature, or *vice versa*, without the intervention of the parliament of the United Kingdom.

The Imperial statute confirming the agreement is 1930, 20 & 21 Geo. V., ch. 26, sec. 1 of which enacts that the agreement shall have the force of law "notwithstanding anything in the *British North America Act* of 1867 or any Act amending the same," etc. It follows therefore that, whatever the situation may have been in earlier years the extent to which Indians are now exempted from the operation of the game laws of Saskatchewan is to be determined by an interpretation of par. 12, *supra*, given force of law by this Imperial statute. This paragraph says that the Indians are to have the right to hunt, trap and fish for food in all seasons "on all unoccupied Crown lands and on any other lands to which the said Indians may have a right of access".

For the purposes of the present inquiry we can confine ourselves to Crown lands (excluding lands owned by individuals as to which some other question might arise) because this game preserve is Crown land. The question then is (1) is it unoccupied Crown land, or (2) is it occupied Crown land to which the Indians have a right of access? If it is either of these no offence was committed by the accused. (Emphasis added.)

Counsel for the accused, in proposing a test for the meaning which must be given to the word "occupied" and "unoccupied" referred to the treaty made between the Crown and certain tribes of Indians near Carlton, on August 23, 1876, whereby, on the one hand, these Indians consented to the surrender of their title of whatsoever nature in an area of which this game preserve forms part and, on the other hand, the Crown undertook certain obligations towards them and assured them certain rights and privileges. As I have said, it is proper to consult this treaty in order to glean from it whatever may throw some light on the meaning to be given to the words in question. *I would even say that we should endeavour, within the bounds of propriety, to give such meaning to these words as would establish the intention of the Crown and the Legislature to maintain the rights accorded to the Indians by the treaty.* (Emphasis added).

I have already dealt with the meaning of s. 13 of the Manitoba agreement. To me it is clear and unambiguous and by s. 1 of the *British North America Act* 1930 which reads:

1. The agreements set out in the Schedule to this Act are hereby confirmed and shall have the force of law notwithstanding anything in the *British North America Act, 1867*, or any Act amending the same, or any Act of the Parliament of Canada, or in any Order in Council or

terms or conditions of union made or approved under any such Act as aforesaid.

has the force of law, notwithstanding "any Act of the Parliament of Canada". The *Migratory Birds Convention Act* is an Act of the Parliament of Canada. One would suppose that that should end the matter, but it is urged that s. 1 of the *British North America Act* 1930 does not necessarily refer to every provision of the agreement and, in particular, that s. 13 is outside the plain and unambiguous language of the *Act* in that Ottawa and Westminster could not conceivably have intended s. 13 to take precedence over the *Migratory Birds Convention Act* of 1917. One should, I think, be slow to accept the argument that the negotiators of the Manitoba agreement and Parliament at Ottawa were in 1929 and 1930 totally forgetful of the existence of the *Migratory Birds Convention Act* of 1917. Rather is it not more logical that knowing of the solemnity with which the Indian treaties had been negotiated and how highly they were regarded by the Indians, neither the negotiators of the agreement nor the Government at Ottawa had the slightest intention of breaching those treaties.

If it had been intended that the *Migratory Birds Convention Act* should take precedence, it would have been a simple matter to have said so in the agreement or in the *Manitoba Natural Resources Act*. Much would have to be read into s. 13 of the agreement to make it subject to the *Migratory Birds Convention Act*. I am not prepared to add exclusions which Parliament and Westminster did not see fit to do.

It is argued that this is a case for the application of the rule of construction that Parliament is not presumed to legislate in breach of a treaty or in any manner inconsistent with the comity of nations and the established rules of international law. The rule does not, of course, come into operation if a statute is unambiguous for in that event its provisions must be followed even if they are contrary to the established rules of international law. The case of *Inland Revenue Commissioners* v. *Collco Dealings Ltd.* is a case in which this very argument was made. In that case the Court was being asked to read into a section of the *Income Tax Act* 1952 additional words which would enlarge the meaning of the section so as to include persons not included by the precise words of the enactment but which were included under an agreement between the British Government and the Republic of Ireland providing for exemption from tax where the claimant was a resident in the Republic of Ireland and was not a resident in the United Kingdom.

In dealing with the argument, Viscount Simonds said at said at pp. 18 and 19:

It has been urged that the general words of the subsection should be so construed as not to have the effect of imposing or appearing to impose the will of Parliament upon persons not within its jurisdiction. This argument, which had influenced the special commissioners, was not advanced before this House. A somewhat similar argument was, however, pressed upon your Lordships and was perhaps more strongly than any other relied on by the appellant company. It was to the effect that to apply section 4(2) to the appellant company would create a breach of the 1926 and following agreements, and would be inconsistent with the comity of nations and the established rules of international law: the subsection must, accordingly, be so construed as to avoid this result.

My Lords, the language that I have used is taken from a passage at p. 148 of the 10th edition of "Maxwell on the Interpretation of Statutes" which ends with the sentence: "But if the statute is unambiguous, its provisions must be followed even if they are contrary to international law." It would not, I think, be possible to state in clearer language and with less ambiguity the determination of the legislature to put an end in all and every case to a practice which was a gross misuse of a concession. What, after all, is involved in the argument of the appellant? It is nothing else than that, when Parliament said "under any enactment," it meant "any enactment except . . ." But it was not found easy to state precisely the terms of the exception. The best that I could get was "except an enactment which is part of a reciprocal arrangement with a sovereign foreign state." It is said that the plain words of the statute are to be disregarded and these words arbitrarily inserted in order to observe the comity of nations and the established rules of international law. I am not sure upon which of these high-sounding phrases the appellant company chiefly relies. But I would answer that neither comity nor rule of international law can be invoked to prevent a sovereign state from taking what steps it thinks fit to protect its own revenue laws from gross abuse, or to save its own citizens from unjust discrimination in favour of foreigners. To demand that the plain words of the statute should be disregarded in order to do that very thing is an extravagance to which this House will not, I hope, give ear.

I would paraphrase the latter part of this statement as follows in applying it to the Indians of Manitoba, Saskatchewan and Alberta by saying: *But I would answer that neither comity nor rule of international law can be invoked to prevent a sovereign state (Canada) from taking what steps it thinks fit to protect its own aboriginal population (Indians) from being deprived of their ancient rights to hunt and to fish for food assured to them in Treaties 5 and 6 made with them.*

It took those steps when it included s. 13 of the Manitoba toba agreement, confirmed by the *Manitoba Natural Resources Act* and petitioned Parliament at Westminster to enact s. 1 of the *British North America Act* 1930. If there is inconsistency or repugnancy between the *Migratory Birds Convention Act* and the *Manitoba Natural Resources Act* the later prevails over the earlier; *British Columbia Railway Co.* v. *Stewart* and *Summers* v. *Holborn District Board of Works*. It is difficult, I think, to find language more forthright and less ambiguous than s. 1 of the *British North America Act* 1930. To repeat, it reads:

1. The agreements set out in the Schedule to this Act are hereby confirmed and shall have the force of law notwithstanding anything in the *British North America Act, 1867*, or any Act amending the same, or any Act of the Parliament of Canada, or in any Order in Council or terms or conditions of union made or approved under any such Act as aforesaid.

I would, accordingly, allow the appeal and quash the conviction. The appellant is entitled to his costs in this Court and in the Courts below.

Note

1. Fauteux, Abbott, Martland and Pigeon, JJ concurred with Judson J, while Cartwright CJ and Ritchie and Spence JJ concurred with Hall J (dissenting).

(ii) *Constitution Act, 1930* and Provincial Laws

(A) *R.* v. *Sutherland*, [1980] 2 SCR 451, 113 DLR (3d) 374, 35 NR 361, 53 CCC (2d) 289, [1980] 5 WWR 456, [1980] 3 CNLR 21 (SCC).

DICKSON J: — The respondents are treaty Indians, residing on the Peguis Indian Reserve in Manitoba. On the early morning of 2nd October 1976 they were apprehended while hunting deer for food in the Mantagao Lake Wildlife Management Area with the aid of spotlights and, as a result, were charged under s. 19(1) of The Wildlife Act, CCSM, c. W140, with unlawfully at night using lighting or reflecting equipment for the purpose of hunting deer. They were convicted in the Fisher Branch Provincial Judges' Court. They appealed unsuccessfully to the County Court. Both courts relied upon s. 49 of The Wildlife Act, the constitutional validity of which is challenged in the present appeals. The Manitoba Court of Appeal, to which the convictions were further appealed, divided on the outcome [[1979] 2 WWR 552, 45 CCC (2d) 538]. Hall JA, with whom Freedman CJM and O'Sullivan JA concurred, would allow the appeals and direct a verdict of acquittal.

Monnin JA, Guy JA concurring, would have dismissed the appeals. There are two issues raised:

1. A constitutional question, pursuant to the order of Laskin CJC, namely: Is s. 49 of The Wildlife Act ultra vires in whole or in part? The Attorney General of Canada was granted leave to intervene in the appeal and filed a factum in which an affirmative answer to the constitutional question was sought. The Attorneys General of Saskatchewan and Ontario were also granted leave to intervene but withdrew before the hearing.

2. If s. 49 is ultra vires, do treaty Indians have a right of access to Mantagao Lake Wildlife Management Area, for the purpose of hunting game for food, at any time?

I

Section 49 of The Wildlife Act reads in this manner:

49. For all purposes in respect of the hunting or killing of wildlife, land set aside or designated as

(a) a refuge;

(b) a provincial recreation area;

(c) a provincial forest;

(d) a wildlife management area; or

(e) a community pasture;

under this Act or under any other Act of the Legislature shall be conclusively deemed to be occupied Crown lands to which Indians do not have a right of access for purposes of exercising any rights bestowed upon them under paragraph 13 of the Memorandum of Agreement approved under The Manitoba Natural Resources Act.

Land set aside and designated as a wildlife management area is thus conclusively deemed to be occupied Crown land to which Indians have no right of access for purposes of para. 13 of the memorandum of agreement approved under The Manitoba Natural Resources Act, CCSM, c. N30. Paragraph 13 reads:

13. In order to secure to the Indians of the Province the continuance of the supply of game and fish for their support and subsistence, Canada agrees that the laws respecting game in force in the Province from time to time shall apply to the Indians within the boundaries thereof, provided, however, that the said Indians shall have the right, which the Province hereby assures to them, of hunting, trapping and fishing game and fish for food at all seasons of the year on all unoccupied Crown lands and on any other lands to which the said Indians may have a right of access.

By para. 13 the province assures to the Indians the right to hunt game for food at all seasons of the year on (i) all unoccupied Crown lands, and (ii) any other lands to which the Indians may have a right of access. It is readily apparent that the effect of s. 49 of The Wildlife Act, if valid, is thus to proclaim conclusively great tracts of Crown land within the province to be: (i) occupied Crown lands, excluded thereby from the "unoccupied Crown lands" referred to in para. 13; and (ii) lands to which the Indians do not have a right of access, excluded thereby from the "other lands," referred to in para. 13.

I do not think there is any doubt that s. 49 of The Wildlife Act is beyond the constitutional competence of the province of Manitoba and is ultra vires in entirety. The provision cannot purport to be a law of general application. Section 49 has effect only against Indians and its sole purpose is to limit or obliterate a right Indians would otherwise enjoy. Indians are singled out for special treatment. While provincial law may apply to Indians, it can do so only "as long as such laws do not single out Indians nor purport to regulate them *qua* Indians": *Four B Mfg. Ltd.* v. *United Garment Wkrs.* (1979), 102 DLR (3d) 385, 30 NR 421 (Can.). This legislation is clearly "in relation to" one class of citizens in object and purpose and is, therefore, in constitutional derogation of the right of the federal power to legislate in respect of Indians and lands reserved for the Indians under s. 91(24) of the BNA Act, 1867: see *CPR* v. *Notre Dame de Bonsecours*, [1899] AC 367; *Kruger* v. *R.*, [1978] 1 SCR 104, [1977] 4 WWR 300, 34 CCC (2d) 377, 75 DLR (3d) 434, 14 NR 495. As Hall J, speaking for a majority of the Manitoba Court of Appeal in the present case observed: "It is one thing to deem certain lands to be occupied Crown lands to which the public, including Indians, have no right of access: it is quite another thing to deem the same lands to be occupied Crown lands to which Indians have no right of access."

The purpose of any "deeming" clause is to impose a meaning; to cause something to be taken to be different from that which it might have been in the absence of the clause. In the present instance, the patent purpose of s. 49 is to cause certain provincial forests, wildlife management areas, and the like to be regarded as occupied whether or not, on the facts they can properly be said to be occupied.

Section 49 seeks to affect the status of Indians in respect of their constitutionally entrenched right to hunt for food. It is a blatant attempt to un-entrench the concluding words of para. 13 and, by taking lands out of the operation of para. 13, to derogate from rights granted to the Indians by the agreement.

There is a second, equally valid, reason for declaring s. 49 of The Wildlife Act to be *ultra vires*. The province cannot arrogate to itself the right to amend, unilaterally, para. 13 of the memorandum of agreement of 14th December 1929 by giving words a particular interpretation. Paragraph 24 of that agreement makes provision for amendment in these words:

24. The foregoing provisions of this agreement may be varied by agreement confirmed by concurrent statutes of the Parliament of Canada and the Legislature of the Province.

The changes sought to be effected in the agreement by s. 49 of *The Wildlife Act*, were not accompanied either by an amending agreement or by concurrent statutes of the Parliament of Canada and the legislature of Manitoba. A provincial legislature may not pass laws to determine the scope of the protection afforded by the Natural Resources Transfer Agreement. If the laws have the effect of altering the agreement, they are constitutionally invalid; if not, they are mere surplusage.

Gordon JA noted in *R.* v. *Stronquill*, 8 WWR (NS) 247, 16 CR 194, 105 CCC 262, [1953] 2 DLR 264 (Sask. CA), that if the provincial legislature had defined ''game'' as limited to jack rabbits, no one would have had the temerity to suggest that such legislation was not *ultra vires* of the province. In *Strongquill* the Court of Appeal of Saskatchewan dealt with s. 13(2) of The Game Act, SS 1950, c. 76, the purpose and effect of which was similar to s. 49 of The Wildlife Act of Manitoba. Two of the three judges in the majority in the Saskatchewan Court of Appeal, in separate concurring judgmenst, concluded that s. 13(2) of *The Game Act* was *ultra vires*.

I hold that s. 49 of *The Wildlife Act* of Manitoba is wholly *ultra vires*.

II

The second and more difficult question which arises is whether, absent s. 49 of *The Wildlife Act*, the Indians have such right of access as would permit them to hunt game in the Mantagao Wildlife Management Area, at any time, for food.

The constitutional right of a province to enact game laws of general application is undoubted, as is the right, in order to secure the continuance of the supply of game, to set aside reasonable and bona fide areas as game preserves. Although the province may set aside such reserves without breaching para. 13 of the memorandum of agreement, it is only fair to note that land selected for such purpose, habitat where game is to be found, is very land upon which the Indians otherwise could have hunted game for food, without regard to species of game, seasonal restrictions, bag limits, or the like.

Manitoba has set aside large chunks of the province for wildlife management purposes: Reg. 306/74 lists 41 such areas, some of which are of vast size. The Mantagao Lake area is No. 21. It comprises 190 square miles of forest, lake and marsh. There are a few buildings in the area, mainly summer cottages, four or five in number. 325 acres are seeded to alfalfa as forage for the game. The area supports deer, elk, moose, wolves, fur-bearing animals and upland birds. The province has engaged in deer-tagging studies, big game surveys in the winter and an elk restocking program. On 2nd October 1976, in the Mantagao Lake Wildlife Management Area, there was open hunting season for black bear, sharp-tailed grouse, ruffled grouse and spruce grouse. On that date no deer hunting was permitted in the area or elsewhere in Manitoba. The deer hunting season had been closed for three years. In other years, if deer hunting was permitted elsewhere, it was permitted in the area.

There were a number of large signs posted throughout the area bearing such messages as "Elk restocking area", "Hunters be sure to shoot only at legal game" and "Attention big game hunters, snowmobiles prohibited, except for the retrieving of lawfully killed big game animals". It is thus clear that the area was one in which big game, including deer, could legally be hunted and killed from time to time and in which limited hunting for black bear and grouse, though not for deer, was permitted on the day of the alleged offences. Two questions must now be addressed: (i) Was the area unoccupied Crown land? (ii) If not, was it land to which Indians had a "right of access" within the meaning of para. 13 of the memorandum of agreement?

On the question as to whether the area was unoccupied Crown land, we have a finding by Dureault Co. Ct. J. that, quite apart from the deeming provisions of s. 49, the evidence established that the area was occupied Crown land. The Court of Appeal agreed, and I accept the concurrent findings for the purpose of this case.

As occupied Crown lands, what then is the right of access, of the public and of the Indians, to the Mantagao Lake Wildlife Management Area? If the Crown confers upon the public a limited right of access for hunting, do Indians, under para. 13, automatically enjoy *unlimited* hunting rights?

In reasons for judgment recently delivered in *R. v. Mousseau*, [1980] 4 WWR 24, 3 Man R (2d) 338, 31 NR 620, I have expressed the view that "right of access" as used in para. 13 means "access for the purpose of hunting, trapping and fishing game and fish". I would give the phrase a like meaning in the case at bar.

It is arguable that where the Crown has validly occupied lands there is prima facie no right of access, as is the case with land occupied by private owners, save and except that right of access the Crown confers on the public and/or Indians, as occupant of the land. In the management area the Crown has granted public access to hunt, but on certain terms. The province cannot deny access to Indians while granting it to the public, but the province can deny access for purposes of hunting which binds Indians and non-Indians alike. In consonance with this line of argument, the Crown contends that the only lands to which the Indians have right of hunting under the proviso to para. 13 are unoccupied Crown lands and Indian reserves. It is said that *R.* v. *Smith*, [1935] 2 WWR 433, [1935] 3 DLR 703, supports this contention. The Saskatchewan Court of Appeal in that case confirmed the conviction on a charge of carrying a rifle on a game preserve. Turgeon JA said (p. 707):

Any so called "right" of access which the Indians may enjoy in respect to this preserve is, so far as we were shown, merely the privilege accorded to all persons to enter the preserve *without carrying firearms*. We were not told of any special, peculiar right of access to this preserve conferred upon or enjoyed by the Indians.

Martin JA spoke to the same effect (p. 710):

Indians undoubtedly have a right of access to certain reserves set apart for them and upon which they reside, but they have no right of access to game preserves beyond that accorded to all other persons and they are subject, as all persons are, to the provisions of s. 69 of The Game Act.

I am not prepared to accept the argument of the Crown. The Indians' right to hunt for food under para. 13 is paramount and overrides provincial game laws regulating hunting and fishing. The province may deny access for hunting to Indians and non-Indians alike but if, as in the case at bar, limited hunting is allowed, then under para. 13 non-dangerous. (*Myran* v. *R.*, [1976] 2 SCR 137, [1976] 1 WWR 196, 23 CCC (2d) 73, 58 DLR (3d) 1, 5 NR 551) hunting for food is permitted to the Indians, regardless of provincial curbs on season, method or limit: see *R.* v. *Wesley*, [1932] 2 WWR 337, 58 CCC 269, [1932] 4 DLR 774 (Alta. CA); *Prince* v. *R.*, [1964] SCR 81, 46 WWR 121, 41 CR 403, [1964] 3 CCC 1; *R.* v. *McPherson*, [1971] 2 WWR 640 (Man CA). It seems to me that this is the true meaning and intent of para. 13.

Paragraph 13 of the memorandum of agreement will, I think, be better understood if brief reference is made to two treaties — Treaty No. 4 and Treaty No. 5 — which applied to Indians in Manitoba. In *Frank* v. *R.*, [1978] 1 SCR 95, [1977] 4 WWR 294, 34 CCC (2d) 209, 75 DLR (3d) 481, 4 AR 271, 15 NR 487, where consideration was given to para. 12 of the Saskatchewan Natural Resources Transfer Agreement, virtually identical to para. 13 of the Manitoba agreement, this court had this to say at p. 100:

It would appear that the overall purpose of para. 12 of the Natural

Resources Transfer Agreement was to effect a merger and consolidation of the treaty rights theretofore enjoyed by the Indians but of equal importance was the desire to re-state and reassure to the treaty Indians the continued enjoyment of the right to hunt and fish for food. See *R. v. Wesley*; *R. v. Smith*; *R. v. Strongquill, supra*.

By Treaty No. 4, dated 4th September 1870, the Cree and Salteaux tribes ceded, released, surrendered and yielded up to the government of the Dominion of Canada a large part of what is now the province of Manitoba in exchange for reserves (one square mile for a family of five), small cash payments, powder, shot, ball and twine and gardening and carpenters' tools. Of historic interest in the present case is the following provision contained in Treaty No. 4:

> And further, Her Majesty agrees that Her said Indians shall have right to pursue their avocations of hunting, trapping and fishing throughout the tract surrendered, subject to such regulations as may from time to time be made by the Government of the country, acting under the authority of Her Majesty, and saving and excepting such tracts as may be required or taken up from time to time for settlement, mining or other purposes, under grant or other right given by Her Majesty's said Government.

Treaty No. 5 was concluded at Berens River on 20th September 1875 and at Norway House on 24th September 1875 with the Salteaux and Swampy Creek tribes. The Indians surrendered a tract embracing an area of 100,000 square miles in exchange for reserves (160 acres for each family of five), $5 per person, ammunition, twine for nets and tools. The treaty assured the Indians the "right" to pursue their avocations of hunting and fishing throughout the tract surrendered, in terms similar to those found in Treaty No. 4.

Paragraph 13 of the memorandum of agreement, it is true, makes provincial game laws applicable to the Indians within the boundaries of the province, but with the large and important proviso that assures them, *inter alia*, the "right" to hunt game at all seasons of the year for food on lands to which the Indians may have a right of access. This proviso should be given a broad and liberal construction. History supports such an interpretation as do the plain words of the proviso. The right assured is, in my view, the right to hunt game (any and all game) for food at all seasons of the year (not just "open seasons") on lands to which they have a right of access (for hunting, trapping and fishing). An interpretation which would recognize in Indians only the right of access accorded all other persons, in the absence of proof of a "special, peculiar right of access", has the effect of largely obliterating the right of hunting for food provided for in the proviso. The question is not so much one of proving a special right of access, but rather one of deciding what type of hunting is permitted, a right of access (at least for certain purposes) being unquestioned. Is the Indian limited to hunting the game which non-Indians may hunt at the particular time, e.g., black bear and grouse, or may the Indian exercise his right to hunt any type of game for food at any time?

In *R.* v. *Wesley, supra,* Lunney JA considered and rejected the argument that if the proviso had a wide construction it would render nugatory that Indians shall be subject to the game laws of the province. He properly drew a distinction between the sportsman and the man who is seeking food for the sustenance of himself and his family.

McGillivray JA in the same case, in a judgment which has received much favourable comment, adopted the argument of counsel for the accused that "having regard to the proviso at the end of this section (s. 12 of the statutory agreement in The Alberta Natural Resources Act, SA 1930, c. 21) an Indian is entitled to hunt any wild animal of any age at any season of the year in any manner he sees fit provided always that he is hunting for food, on unoccupied Crown lands or other lands to which he has a right of access" (p. 275). At pp. 275-76 of the report the following passage appears which, with respect, I would adopt:

> It seems to me that the language of s. 12 is unambiguous and the intention of Parliament to be gathered therefrom clearly is to assure to the Indians a supply of game in the future for their support and subsistence by requiring them to comply with the game laws of the Province, subject however to the express and dominant proviso that care for the future is not to deprive them of the right to satisfy their present need for food by hunting and trapping game, using the word "game" in its broadest sense, at all seasons on unoccupied Crown lands or other land to which they may have a right of access.

The court's conclusions are found in the following passage, quoted by my brother Martland in *Cardinal* v. *AG Alta.*, [1974] SCR 695, [1973] 6 WWR 205, 13 CCC (2d) 1, 40 DLR (3d) 553, and by Hall J in the earlier case of *Prince and Myron* v. *R.*, *supra* (p.276):

> If the effect of the proviso is merely to give to the Indians the extra privilege of shooting for food "out of season" and they are otherwise subject to the game laws of the Province, it follows that in any year they may be limited in the number of animals of a given kind that they may kill even though that number is not sufficient for their support and subsistence and even though no other kind of game is available to them. I cannot think that the language of the section supports the view that this was the intention of the law makers. I think the intention was that in hunting for sport or for commerce the Indian like the white

man should be subject to laws which make for the preservation of game but in hunting wild animals for the food necessary to his life, the Indian should be placed in a very different position from the white man who generally speaking does not hunt for food and was by the proviso to s. 12 reassured of the continued enjoyment of a right which he has enjoyed from time immemorial.

In the *Strongquill* case, *supra*, the accused, a treaty Indian, hunting for food, killed a moose in the Porcupine Forest Reserve, also known as fur conservation area No. 103, in the province of Saskatchewan, at a time when the hunting and killing of moose was prohibited but the season for hunting of other big game was open. As I read the judgments, a majority of the court held that if the Indians had access to hunt, limitation could not be placed on that access. That is to say, once *any* hunting is allowed, then under para. 13 *all* hunting by Indians is permissible, if hunting for food. Each of the three judges in the majority (Gordon, Procter and McNiven JJA) delivered a separate judgment. Gordon JA distinguished *R. v. Smith*, *supra*, on the ground that in *Smith* the accused Indian was hunting on a game preserve on which all hunting was absolutely prohibited. In setting aside the conviction he said, p. 260 [WWR]: "The accused having the right of access to the forest reserve in question to hunt for big game, I think he had the right to shoot moose provided it was needed for food" and "the Indians should be preserved before moose". The following passage is taken from the reasons of McNiven JA, at pp. 266-67:

The justice of the peace in par. 6 of the stated case has found that "the area known as Porcupine Provincial Forest Reserve and also as fur conservation area No. 103 was open to any visiting hunters who have a licence and they are permitted to hunt over that area which is crown lands." Such being the case Strongquill apart from the other legislation to which I have referred had the same "right of access" to the crown land in the Porcupine Forest Reserve and fur conservation area, No. 103, as the other hunters referred to in par. 6 of the stated case. Having such access to that crown land it was lawful for him to kill the moose for food under the special right reserved to him by par. 12 of the agreement hereinbefore referred to notwithstanding that the killing of moose in the province generally was prohibited.

McNiven JA had this to say, p. 271:

In addition in the stated case there is the fact that the area in question "was open to any visiting hunters who have a licence and they are permitted to hunt over that area which is Crown lands." In my opinion the accused, a treaty Indian, had a right of access to the said land, a right to hunt thereon for and kill the said moose for food irrespective of the provincial Game Act, 1950.

In the case at bar, Hall JA dealt briefly with the point under discussion in these words [p. 554]:

> The evidence establishes that, factually, the area was occupied Crown land to which the Indians had and exercised a right of access. Therefore, but for the deeming provision (s. 49(d)), the conviction cannot be allowed to stand.

If there is any ambiguity in the phrase ''right of access'' in para. 13 of the memorandum of agreement, the phrase should be interpreted so as to resolve any doubts in favour of the Indians, the beneficiaries of the rights assured by the paragraph. Any attempt to construe ''access'' in limited terms as, for example, to hunt the particular type of game which non-Indians could legally hunt at the time, would, it seems to me, run counter to the authorities to which I have referred and so dilute the word ''access'' as to make meaningless the assurance embodied in the proviso to para. 13.

I would dismiss the appeals and answer the constitutional question formulated by the chief justice in this manner: s. 49 of The Wildlife Act is wholly ultra vires. There should be no order as to costs for or against any of the parties or for or against the intervenant Attorney General of Canada.

Appeal dismissed.

(B) *Cardinal* v. *Attorney General of Alberta*, [1974] SCR 695, 13 CCC (2d) 1, 40 DLR (3d) 553, [1973] 6 WWR 205 (SCC).

29th June 1973. MARTLAND J (FAUTEUX CJC, ABBOTT, JUDSON, RITCHIE, and PIGEON JJ concurring): — On 8th December 1970 the appellant, a Treaty Indian, at his home on an Indian reserve, in the Province of Alberta, sold a piece of moose meat to a non-Indian. He was charged with a breach of s. 37 of The Wildlife Act, RSA 1970, c. 391, which provides:

> 37.   No person shall traffic in any big game or any game bird except as is expressly permitted by this Act or by the regulations.

The trial Judge found that the appellant had trafficked in big game within the meaning of this section. The appellant was acquitted on the ground that The Wildlife Act is *ultra vires* of the Alberta Legislature in its application to the appellant as an Indian on Indian reserve. A case was stated on this legal issue, which was considered by a Judge of the Supreme Court of Alberta, who held that the decision was correct. An appeal was taken to the Appellate Division of the Supreme Court of Alberta, which allowed the appeal and overruled the judgment of the Court below [[1972] 1 WWR 536, 17 CRNS 110, 5 CCC (2d) 193 (sub nom. *Regina* v. *Cardinal*), 22 DLR (3d) 716]. The present appeal is brought, with leave, to this Court.

Section 91(24) of the BNA Act, 1867, gives to the Parliament of Canada exclusive authority to legislative in respect of:

> (24)   Indians, and Lands reserved for the Indians.

An Agreement was made between the Government of Canada and the Government of Alberta, dated 14th December 1929, hereinafter referred to as "the Agreement", for the transfer by the former to the latter of the interest of the Crown in all Crown lands, mines and minerals within the Province of Alberta, and the provisions of the Alberta Act, 1905 (Can.), c. 3, were modified as in the Agreement set out.

Sections 10 to 12 inclusive appear in the Agreement [Schedule to The Alberta Natural Resources Act, 1930 (Alta.), c. 21] under the heading "Indian Reserves", and it is ss. 10 and 12 which are of importance in considering this appeal. They provide as follows:

> 10.   All lands included in Indian reserves within the Province, including those selected and surveyed but not yet confirmed, as well as those confirmed, shall continue to be vested in the Crown and administered by the Government of Canada for the purposes of Canada, and the Province will from time to time, upon the request of the Superintendent General of Indian Affairs, set aside, out of the unoccupied Crown lands hereby transferred to its administration, such further areas as the said Superintendent General may, in agreement with the appropriate Minister of the Province, select as necessary to enable Canada to fulfil its obligations, under the treaties with the Indians of the Province, and such areas shall thereafter be administered by Canada in the same way in all respects as if they had never passed to the Province under the provisions hereof . . . .

I now turn to a consideration of the effect of s. 12 of the Agreement.

It has been noted that this section, along with ss. 10 and 11, appears under the heading "Indian Reserves". It begins with the words:

> In order to secure to the Indians of the Province the continuance of the supply of game and fish for their support and subsistence, Canada agrees that the laws respecting game in force in the Province from time to time shall apply to the Indians within the boundaries thereof . . . .

The opening words of the section define its purpose. It is to secure to the Indians of the province a continuing supply of game and fish for their support and subsistence. It is to achieve that purpose that Indians within the boundaries of the province are to conform to provincial game laws subject always to their right to hunt and fish for food. This being the purpose of the section, it could not have been intended that the controls which would apply to Indians in relation to hunting and fishing for purposes other than for their own food should apply only to Indians not on reserves.

Furthermore, if the section were to be so restricted in its scope, it would accomplish nothing towards its purpose. Cases decided before the Agreement, such as *Rex* v. *Martin*, supra, had held that general legislation by a province, not relating to Indians, qua Indians, would apply to them. On their facts, these cases dealt with Indians outside reserves. The point is that the provisions s. 12 were not required to make provincial game laws apply to Indians off the reserve.

In my opinion, the meaning of s. 12 is that Canada, clothed as it was with legislative jurisdiction over "Indians, and Lands reserved for the Indians", in order to achieve the purpose of the section, agreed to the imposition of provincial controls over hunting and fishing, which, previously, the province might not have had power to impose. By its express wording, it provides that the game laws of the province shall apply "to the Indians within the boundaries thereof". To me this must contemplate their application to all Indians within the province, without restriction as to where, within the province, they might be.

This view is supported by an examination of the state of the law, in Alberta, at the time that the Agreement was made. At that time, s. 69 of the Indian Act, RSC 1927, c. 98, provided as follows:

> 69.   The Superintendent General may, from time to time, by public notice, declare that, on and after a day therein named the laws respecting game in force in the province of Manitoba, Saskatchewan or Alberta, or the Territories, or respecting such game as is specified in such notice, shall apply to Indians within the said province or Territories, as the case may be, or to Indians in such parts thereof as to him seems expedient.

The Superintendent General was thus empowered to declare that Alberta laws respecting game should apply to "Indians within the said province" or "in such parts thereof as to him seems expedient". Being a provision of the Indian Act, the section must have contemplated the possible exercise of the power with respect to Indians on reserves when it spoke of "Indians within the said province".

When s. 12 was drafted, it stated its general purpose and then went on to provide that the game laws of the province should apply "to Indians within the boundaries thereof". This is practically the same as the words "Indians within the said province" in s. 69, and, in my opinion, it was intended to have the same meaning and application.

Section 69 ceased to have any effect in Alberta, Saskatchewan and Manitoba after the enactment of the BNA Act, 1930, which gave the Agreements therein mentioned the force of law, notwithstanding anything in the BNA Act, 1867, or any amendments to it, or any Act of the Parliament of Canada. Section 69 disappeared from the Indian Act, 1951 (Can.), c. 29, which then introduced s. 87 (now s. 88) to which reference will be made later, and which provided:

> 87.   Subject to the terms of any treaty and any other Act of the Parliament of Canada, all laws of general application from time to time in force in any province are applicable to and in respect of Indians in the province, except to the extent that such laws are inconsistent with this Act or any order, rule, regulation or by-law made thereunder, and except to the extent that such laws make provision for any matter for which provision is made by or under this Act.

The appellant places emphasis on the words in the proviso to s. 12 of The Agreement, "on any other lands to which the said Indians may have a right of access." The contention is that s. 10 provided for continuance of the vesting of title in Indian reserves in the Federal Crown, as well as for the creation of additional reserves, and that, in these lands, the Indians who reside thereon have an interest considerably greater than a mere "right of access". The use of that phrase, it is submitted, is inconsistent with any reference to reserve lands, and therefore, as the proviso, by the terms used, does not apply to Indian reserves, the section, as a whole, must be taken not to have application to them.

I am unable to agree that the broad terms used in the first portion of s. 12 can be limited, inferentially, in this way. In my view, having made all Indians within the boundaries of the province, in their own interest, subject to provincial game laws, the proviso, by which the province assured the defined rights of hunting and fishing for food, was drawn in broad terms. The proviso assures the right to hunt and fish for food on Indian reserves, because there can be no doubt that, whatever additional rights Indian residents on a reserve may have, they certainly have the right of access to it. This view was expressed by the Saskatchewan Court of Appeal in *Rex* v. *Smith*, [1935] 2 WWR 433, 64 CCC 131, [1935] 3 DLR 703, to which reference has already been made.

For these reasons, I am of the opinion that s. 12 of the Agreement made the provisions of The Wildlife Act applicable to all Indians, including those on reserves, and governed their activities, throughout the province, including reserves. By virtue of s. 1 of the BNA Act, 1930, it has the force of law, notwithstanding anything contained in the BNA Act, 1867, any amendment thereto, or any federal statute.

Having reached this conclusion, it is not necessary, in the circumstances of this case, to determine the meaning and effect of s. 88 (formerly s. 87) of the Indian Act, RSC 1970, c. I-6.

I would dismiss the appeal.

LASKIN J (dissenting) (HALL and SPENCE JJ concurring): . . .

I turn now to the Alberta Natural Resources Agreement which deals separately in its ss. 10 and 12 with reserves and with unoccupied Crown lands and other lands to which Indians may have a right of access. The Alberta Appellate Division simply mentioned and then completely ignored s. 10 in its reasons in this case [[1972] 1 WWR 536, 17 CRNS 110, 5 CCC (2d) 193 (sub. nom. *Regina* v. *Cardinal*), 22 DLR (3d) 716], dealing with it as if the only question was whether lands to which Indians had a right of access included Indian reserves as not being dealt with elsewhere in the Agreement. Even in such a from of reference, I would find it a hardy conclusion to subsume Indian reserves within the phrase "any other lands to which the . . . Indians may have a right of access". It would mean federal adoption of provincial laws for reserves without express mention and in a situation where there was already in existence a federal Indian Act which itself provided for a limited incorporation of provincial law to operate upon and in the reserves.

But the fact is that Indian reserves were specifically dealt with in the Alberta Natural Resources Agreement as they were expressly dealt with in that of Manitoba and in that of Saskatchewan. The words used in the two sections which are directly of concern here are the same in respect of all three provinces.

History, which is highly relevant here, denies the equation of Indian reserves with lands to which Indians may have a right of access. Legal logic also denies the equation in a situation where they are separately dealt with as they are here and in the same document. To treat Indian reserves as coming within the description of "lands to which Indians have a right of access", as did the Alberta Appellate Division, is to describe them in terms of their lowest rather than of their highest legal signification. Indians have at least a right of occupancy of reserves, and this is a larger interest than a mere right of access which, as this Court held in *Prince* v. *The Queen*, [1964] SCR 81, 46 WWR 121, 41 CR 403, [1964] 3 CCC 1, may exist in privately-owned lands. I see no justification for enlarging the category of what I may call, for short, access lands beyond lands which strictly fall within that description and have no higher legal quality. It would be odd, for example, to find the kind of lands considered in *Attorney General of Canada* v. *Giroux* (1916), 53 SCR 172, 30 DLR 123, referred to earlier in these reasons, as being aptly described as access lands; they would be that, of course, but much more besides.

Section 10 of the Alberta Natural Resources Agreement itself negates the view taken by the Court below. All Indian reserves are to continue to be administered by the Government of Canada for the purposes of Canada; there is here no qualification to admit any provincial purpose. Moreover, any further reserves that may be established from unoccupied Crown land transferred to the province are to be administered by Canada in the same way in all respects as if they had never passed to the province. That points clearly to the exclusion of reserves from provincial control.

They do not return to that control under s. 12 in respect of the application of provincial game laws. That section deals with a situation unrelated to Indian reserves. It is concerned rather with Indians as such, and with guaranteeing to them a continuing right to hunt, trap and fish for food regardless of provincial game laws which would otherwise confine Indians in parts of the province that are under provincial administration. Although inelegantly expressed, s. 12 does not expand provincial legislative power but contracts it. Indians are to have the right to take game and fish for food from all unoccupied Crown lands (these would certainly not include reserves) and from all other lands to which they may have a right of access. There is hence, by virtue of the sanction of the BNA Act, 1930, a limitation upon provincial authority regardless of whether or not Parliament legislates. . .

On the facts of this case we are not concerned with the proviso to s. 12 because the accused was not hunting for food, and hence the overriding question is whether provincial game laws apply simply because the reserve where the accused trafficked in big game is in the province. In my opinion, s. 12 does not, either in its generality or in its proviso, cover "Lands reserved for the Indians", which are separately brought under exclusive federal authority under s. 91(24) of the BNA Act; and it does not modify federal power in relation thereto. Even if the words in s. 12, "any other lands to which the said Indians may have a right of access", are taken in a broad general sense as capable, if s. 12 stood alone, of embracing Indian reserves, they must be read to exclude such reserves which are specially dealt with in s. 10. The canon of construction enshrined in the maxim *generalia specialibus non derogant* is particularly apt here.

History, however, is even more telling, and I refer, first, to the canvass by McGillivray JA in *Rex* v. *Wesley,* [1932] 2 WWR 337, 58 CCC 269, [1932] 4 DLR 774. This was a unanimous decision of the Alberta Appellate Division, holding that The Game Act, RSA 1922, c. 70, in force at the time did not apply to a Treaty Indian hunting for food on unoccupied Crown land. After referring to the Royal Proclamation of 1763 which reserved various lands to Indians and enjoined any private purchased thereof from the Indians, McGillivray JA noted that there was excluded from such lands the territory granted to the Hudson's Bay Company in 1670. This territory, later ceded to Canada, included the unoccupied Crown land upon which the accused in *Rex* v. *Wesley* hunted. This land was included in a Treaty of 22nd September 1877 between certain Indian tribes and the Queen under which hunting rights were assured to them in the lands which were the subject of the Treaty upon the surrender of such rights therein as the Indians had.

The Treaty qualified the hunting rights according to such Regulations as might be made by the Government of the country, and saved and excepted such tracts as might be required or taken up for settlement, mining, trading or any other purposes by the Government of Canada. What is particularly significant about this Treaty is a provision therein "that reserves shall be assigned" to the Indians. McGillivray JA adverted in that connection to the fact that the Governor who negotiated the Treaty said at the time to the Indian Chiefs that "it is your privilege to hunt all over the prairies, and that should you desire to sell any portion of your land, or any coal or timber from off your reserves, the Government will see that you receive just and fair prices"; and again, "The reserve will be given to you without depriving you of the privilege to hunt over the plains until the land be taken up". The history recounted in *Rex* v. *Wesley* prompted Lunney JA, who also wrote reasons in that case, to say that "the [Alberta Natural Resources] Agreement did not, nor was there any intention that it should, alter the law applicable to Indians".

I would refer in this connection also to the majority judgment of this Court in *Daniels* v. *White,* [1968] SCR 517, 64 WWR 385, 4 CRNS 176, [1969] 1 CCC 299, 2 DLR (3d) 1 (sub nom. *Daniels* v. *The Queen*), which involved the relationship between s. 13 of the Manitoba Natural Resources Agreement (which is similar to s. 12 of the Alberta Agreement) and the Migratory Birds Convention Act, RSC 1952, c. 179. The question there was whether a Treaty Indian who had shot and killed birds on his reserve for food was protected against culpability under the federal Act by virtue of s. 13 of the Manitoba Agreement. In holding that he was not so protected, Judson J, who spoke for the majority, referred to the Agreement and to the legislation of 1930 confirming it, and stated [p. 526] that "it did no more than impose specified obligations and restrictions upon the transferee province". This accords with the view that I take here that nothing in the Alberta Agreement increases the legislative power of the province in diminution of that of the Parliament of Canada in relation to "Indians, and Lands reserved for the Indians". . .

It is clear from cases like *Rex* v. *Wesley*, supra, and from the *Daniels* case, and from others like *Rex* v. *Smith*, [1935] 2 WWR 433, 64 CCC 131, [1935] 3 DLR 703 (Sask. CA), in which the history of Indian cession Treaties is narrated, that Indians who ceded their lands were assured of hunting privileges over them. I need not consider whether such privileges are themselves property interests of a kind which bring them exclusively within federal jurisdiction under s. 91(24) as coming within the phrase "Lands reserved for the Indians", or whether the jurisdiction attaches because the rights involved are those of Indians: see *Regina* v. *White* (1964), 52 WWR 193, 50 DLR (2d) 613, affirmed 52 DLR (2d) 481n (Can.). What is evident is that the existence of such privileges in such surrendered lands gives subject matter to s. 12 of the Alberta Natural Resources Agreement without compelling the inclusion therein of reserves which are of a different order than lands in respect of which there are only hunting rights or in respect of which hunting rights are assertable by the force of s. 12 alone.

Note

1. This case is known for its discussion of the different theories of how provincial laws are made applicable to Indian reserves. See chapter 7, *Application of Provincial Laws, infra*.

(C) *Myran* v. *R.*, [1976] 1 WWR 196, [1976] 2 SCR 137, 23 CCC (2d) 73, 58 DLR (3d) 1, 5 NR 551 (SCC).

DICKSON J: — The appellants, treaty Indians from the Long Plain Indian Reserve in the Province of Manitoba, were each convicted on the charge of hunting without due regard for the safety of other persons in the vicinity, contrary to the provisions of s. 10(1) of The Wildlife Act, RSM 1970, c. W140, and the convictions were affirmed on appeal by trial de novo in the County Court and by the Court of Appeal for Manitoba. Leave to appeal to this Court was granted on 4th June 1973.

There can be no doubt that the accused were hunting without due regard for the safety of others in the vicinity. They were deer hunting shortly before midnight in an alfalfa field belonging to a farmer who was awakened by the sound of rifle shots and by a light flashing through the window of his bedroom. The range of the weapon was close to two miles; within range were farm houses, highways, railways, pastureland, a town and a breeding station. The convictions were, therefore, properly entered unless it can be said that the accused are immune from prosecution by the terms of para. 13 of the Memorandum of Agreement dated 14th December 1929 as set out in the schedule of The Manitoba Natural Resources Act, RSM 1970, c. N30, which reads:

13   In order to secure to the Indians of the Province the continuance of the supply of game and fish for their support and subsistence, Canada agrees that the laws respecting game in force in the Province from time to time shall apply to the Indians within the boundaries thereof, provided, however, that the said Indians shall have the right, which the Province hereby assures to them, of hunting, trapping and fishing game and fish for food at all seasons of the year on all unoccupied Crown lands and on any other lands to which the said Indians may have a right of access.

Section 46(1) of The Wildlife Act reads:

46   (1)   Nothing in this Act reduces, or deprives any person of, or detracts from, the rights and privileges bestowed upon him under paragraph 13 of the Memorandum of Agreement approved under The Manitoba Natural Resources Act.

The history of para. 13 quoted above and of its Alberta counterpart will be found respectively in the judgment of Judson J in this Court in *Daniels* v. *White*, 64 WWR 385, 4 CRNS 176, [1968] SCR 517, and in the judgment of McGillivray JA in the Appellate Division of the Supreme Court of Alberta in *Rex* v. *Wesley*, [1932] 2 WWR 337, 58 CCC 269, [1932] 4 DLR 774. The case, however, which bears more directly upon the issue raised in the present appeal is *Prince and Myron* v. *The Queen*, 46 WWR 121, 41 CR 403, [1964] SCR 81, [1964] 3 CCC 1. In *Prince and Myron* the appellants, treaty Indians, were charged with unlawfully hunting big game by means of night lights, contrary to The Game and Fisheries Act, RSM 1954, c. 94 and it fell to the Court to consider what was meant by "the right . . . of hunting . . . game . . . for food at all seasons of the year on all unoccupied Crown lands and on any other lands to which the said Indians may have a right of access." It was common ground in that case, as in the instant case, that the accused were hunting for food. The majority position in the Manitoba Court of Appeal was expressed by Miller CMJ, (1962), 40 WWR 234, who said in the course of his judgment at pp. 238-39:

The point is: Just what restrictions in *The Game and Fisheries Act* do apply to Indians? It seems to me that the manner in which they may hunt and the methods pursued by them in hunting must, of necessity, be restricted by the said Act. Mr Pollick, counsel for the Indians, argued that they were only restricted by the provisions of *The Game and Fisheries Act* when hunting for sport or commercial purposes. I can only say that I am unable to read any such provision into sec. 13 of *The Manitoba Natural Resources Act* [RSM 1954, c. 180]. I do not think Indians are debarred from hunting for food during any one of the 365 days of any year, and can hunt for food on all unoccupied crown lands and on any land to which Indians have a right of access. I am of the opinion, though, that they have no right to adopt a method or *manner* of hunting that is contrary to *The Game and Fisheries Act*, because sec. 13 of *The Natural Resources Act* specifically provides that the *Game Act* of the province *shall* apply to Indians in some respect.

Freedman JA, as he then was, giving the reasons for the minority stated at p. 242:

The fundamental fact of this case, as I see it, is that the accused Indians at the time of the alleged offence were hunting for food. It was not a case of hunting for sport or for commercial purposes. By sec. 72(1) of *The Game and Fisheries Act*, and by sec. 13 of *The Manitiba Natural Resources Act*, the special position of the Indian when hunting for food is acknowledged and recognized. The clear purpose of those sections is to secure to the Indians, within certain given territories, the unrestricted right to hunt for game and fish for their support and sustenance. The statement in sec. 13 of *The Manitoba Natural Resources Act* that the law of the province respecting game and fish shall apply to the Indians is, in my view, subordinate in character. Its operation is limited to imposing upon the Indian the same obligation as is normally imposed upon every other citizen, namely, that when he is hunting for sport or commerce he must hunt only in the manner and at the times prescribed by the Act. But the ordinary citizen does not hunt for food for sustenance purposes. The Indian does, and the statute, recognizing his right to sustenance, exempts him from the ordinary game laws when he is hunting for food in areas where he is so permitted.''

The judgment of this Court was delivered by Hall J who adopted the reasons of Freedman JA in his dissenting judgment in the Court of Appeal, and who also adopted the following statement by McGillivray JA in *Rex* v. *Wesley*, supra [p. 344]:

If the effect of the proviso is merely to give to the Indians the extra privilege of shooting for food 'out of season' and they are otherwise subject to the game laws of the province, it follows that in any year they may be limited in the number of animals of a given kind that they may kill even though that number is not sufficient for their support and subsistence and even though no other kind of game is available to them. I cannot think that the language of the section supports the view that this was the intention of the law makers. I think the intention was that in hunting for sport or for commerce the Indian like the white man should be subject to laws which make for the preservation of game but, in hunting wild animals for the food necessary to his life, the Indian should be placed in a very different position from the white man who, generally speaking, does not hunt for food and was by the proviso to sec. 12 [of The Alberta Natural Resources Act, 1930 (Alta.), c. 21] reassured of the continued enjoyment of a right which he has enjoyed from time immemorial.

I think it is clear from *Prince and Myron*, supra, that an Indian of the province is free to hunt or trap game in such numbers, at such times of the year, by such means or methods and with such contrivances as he may wish, provided he is doing so in order to obtain food for his own use and on unoccupied Crown lands or other lands to which he may have a right of access. But that is not to say that he has the right to hunt dangerously and without regard for the safety of other persons in the vicinity. *Prince and Myron* deals with ''method''. Neither that case nor those which preceded it dealt with protection of human life. I agree with what was said in the present case by Hall JA in the Court of Appeal for Manitoba, [1973] 4 WWR 512 at 515-16, 11 CCC (2d) 271, 35 DLR (3d) 473:

In the present case the governing statute is The Wildlife Act and in particular s. 46(1) thereof. Section 10(1), under which the accused were charged, does not restrict the type of game, nor the time or method of hunting, but simply imposes a duty on every person of hunting with due regard for the safety of others. Does that duty reduce, detract or deprive Indians of the right to hunt for food on land to which they have a right of access? If one regards that right in absolute terms the answer is clearly in the affirmative; but is that the case? Surely the right to hunt for food as conferred or bestowed by the Agreement and affirmed by the statute cannot be so regarded. Inherent in the right is the quality of restraint, that is to say, that the right will be exercised reasonably. Section 10(1) is only a statutory expression of that concept, namely, that the right will be exercised with due regard for the safety of others, including Indians.

In my opinion there is no irreconcilable conflict or inconsistency in principle between the right to hunt for food assured under para. 13 of the Memornadum of Agreement approved under The Manitoba Natural Resources Act and the requirement of s. 10(1) of The Wildlife Act that such right be exercised in a manner so as not to endanger the lives of others. The first is concerned with conservation of game to secure a continuing supply of food for the Indians of the province and protect the right of Indians to hunt for food at all seasons of the year; the second is concerned with risk of death or serious injury omnipresent when hunters fail to have due regard for the presence of others in the vicinity. In my view the Court of Appeal for Manitoba properly answered in the negative the question upon which leave to appeal to that Court was granted, namely [p. 513]:

> Did the learned trial judge err in holding that paragraph 13 of the Schedule of the Manitoba Natural Resources Agreement Act, 1930, did not provide immunity to the accused from the restrictions on hunting set out in The Wildlife Act, and specifically section 10(1) thereof.

Another question which arose during argument of this appeal concerns the words "any other lands to which the said Indians may have a right of access" found in para. 13. There may be differing opinions on whether the finding of the trial Judge that the accused had a right of access to the lands upon which they were hunting when apprehended can be impeached in this Court, but the leave to appeal was not limited to the single question before the Court of Appeal and, having regard to the concern among farmers to which, we were told, the majority judgment of the Manitoba Court of Appeal in the earlier case of *Prince and Myron* has given rise, I think it may be opportune and appropriate to make some observations upon the phrase "right of access" on the occasion of, though not as a ground of decision of, the present appeal. The complainant in the present case, Mr Baron, had not given the accused permission to be on his land for hunting or any other purpose; they were not known to him. His lands were not posted. The Wildlife Act, s. 40(1) and (2) [am. 1970, c. 89, s. 27] reads as follows:

> 40 (1) The owner or lawful occupant of land other than Crown land may give notice that the hunting and killing of wildlife or exotic animals is forbidden on or over the land or any part thereof by posting and maintaining signs of at least one square foot in area on or along the boundary of the land facing away from the land at intervals of not more than two hundred and twenty yards with the words "Hunting by Permission Only" or 'Hunting NOT Allowed' or words to the like effect . . .

40 (2) A person who hunts wildlife or exotic animals upon or over any land in respect of which notice is given as prescribed in subsection (1) without the consent of the owner or lawful occupant thereof, is guilty of an offence and is liable, on summary conviction on private prosecution, to a fine not exceeding two hundred dollars or to imprisonment for a term not exceeding one month, or to both such a fine and such imprisonment.

When the charges against the present accused were heard in the first instance, the Magistrate said:

In the instant case there is no evidence before me of any prohibition from hunting upon the land of the complainant and it is my respectful opinion that the four accused persons had a right of access for the purpose of hunting.

On the trial de novo the County Court Judge made no reference to right of access. He considered that there were two issues only: first, hunting, and second, hunting dangerously; and he held against the accused on both issues. In the Court of Appeal Hall JA, on behalf of the Court, said [p. 513]:

Having regard to the limited nature of the appeal we feel bound to accept the implicit findings of the trial Judge that the accused were treaty Indians and that, at the time, they were hunting for food on lands to which they had a right of access.

It would seem that the Magistrate, as a matter of law, found the accused had a right of access to the farm lands upon which they were hunting and that this finding was accepted by the Court of Appeal. The law which supports this position is said to derive from the statement of Miller CJM in *Prince and Myron*, supra; the learned Chief Justice, after quoting s. 76(1) and (2) of The Game and Fisheries Act, the earlier counterpart of s. 40(1) and (2) of The Wildlife Act, continued at p. 238:

I am satisfied that unless notices are posted on the land pursuant to sec. 76(2) a person has access thereto for shooting purposes. It is true that the owner or occupant might specifically warn people off the land and, if this were done, the person intending to shoot, whether he be Indian or not, would be prohibited from going on that land to shoot and would not be deemed to have access thereto, but in the absence of a prohibition, either by notice or otherwise, the Indians would have access to the land upon which they were found hunting. The fact that the land was cultivated does not make any difference. The fact that the common-law rights as to trespass are preserved does not make any difference to the right of access above mentioned.

In this Court there was an admission that the accused Prince and Myron had a right of access to the land in question. Hall JA for the Court, stated at p. 83:

It was admitted in this Court that at the time in question in the charge the appellants were Indians; that they were hunting deer for food for their own use and that they were hunting on lands to which they had the right of access. These admissions are fundamental to the determination of this appeal.

Thus the issue was not argued in this Court and the point was not decided.

It is unnecessary in the present case to express any concluded view on the point, but I must say that if the quoted words of Miller CJM are a correct statement of the law, the results are far-reaching; any person can enter any land in Manitoba which is not posted and hunt thereon without permission of the owner, at least until ordered off; the carrying of a firearm immunizes an act which would otherwise be trespass. I would have grave doubt that this can be the law. Section 40 of The Wildlife Act does not deal with interests in property. It is intended, I would have thought, to create a separate offence under the provincial statute in respect of posted lands and not to confer entry rights in respect of unposted lands. Posting of land and maintaining signs is a tiresome and costly business the purpose of which is to identify the land as private property, to discourage hunters and to underpin a s. 40(2) charge against those who enter without permission. A Manitoba farmer is surely not to be faced, by reason of the enactment of s. 40(1) of The Wildlife Act, with the choice of either posting his land or suffering the entry of those who would hunt his land without permission. With great respect, in my opinion the majority of the Manitoba Court of Appeal in *Prince and Myron* v. *The Queen* may have erred in their view of the import of s. 76 of The Game and Fisheries Act, the antecedent of s. 40, in failing to appreciate the importance of s. 76(4) reading:

76 (4) Nothing in this section limits or affects the remedy at common law of any such owner or occupant for trespass,
strengthened in s. 40(4) of The Wildlife Act to include statutory remedies:

40 (4) Nothing in this section limits or affects any rights or remedies that any person has at common law or by statute for trespass in respect of land.

Miller CJM did recognize that an owner could demand that hunters leave his property. In this way, he acknowledged that the "right of access" was a qualified right, however he would accord to hunters a special status and access rights above and beyond the ordinary trespasser. Although the point does not fall squarely before us for decision in this appeal, I think it can properly be said that there is considerable support for the view that in Manitoba at the present time hunters enter private property with no greater rights than other trespassers; that they have no right of access except with the owner's permission; and, lacking permission, are subject to civil action for trespass and prosecution under s. 2 of The Petty Trespasses Act, RSM 1970, c. P50. The question of right of access will normally have to be decided in each particular case, as a question of fact and not one of law, on the totality of the evidence in the case.

I would dismiss the present appeals.

6. Other Treaty Rights

There are major differences between the written text of the treaties and the Indians' understanding of the agreements they signed. The written text of the treaties included the following rights and benefits to be retained by or given to Indians by treaty.

1.   Reserves were to be established within the territories ceded for the exclusive use and benefit of the Indian bands signing the treaties.

2.   Small cash payments were to be given to the Indians who were parties to the treaty and thereafter annuity payments would be given to them and their descendants.

3.   In the prairie treaties, farming implements and supplies were promised as an initial outlay; thereafter, hunting and fishing materials such as nets and twine were to be furnished annually.

4.   Rights to hunt, fish and trap over the ceded territories were guaranteed.

5.   The government was to establish and maintain teachers and schools on reserves.

6.   Suits of clothing, flags and medals were to be given to the chiefs and headmen of the bands.

7.   In Treaty No. 6, a "medicine chest" for the Indians was promised.

(a) Indian Interpretation of Treaties

(i) D. Opekokew, *The First Nations: Indian Government in the Community of Man, supra*, pp. 16-18.

Indian people entered into a political arrangement with the Crown so that they could live as Indian people forever; that is, retaining their inherent powers. That guarantee is made by a commissioner,

> What I have offered does not take away your way of life, you will have it then as you have it now, and what I offer is put on top of it.

The treaties that were signed by our forefathers confirmed the following principles and guaranteed the following rights in perpetuity:

1. The Indian nations retained sovereignty over their people, lands, and resources, both on and off the reserves, subject to some shared jurisdiction with the appropriate government bodies on the lands known as unoccupied Crown lands. This the foundation of Indian government.
2. By signing the treaties, the Indian nations created an on-going relationship with the Crown in Indian social and economic development in exchange for lands surrendered.
3. The Indian nations established tax revenue sharing between the Crown and the Indian nations.
4. The Indian nations established a political protocol for annual reviews of the progress of the treaties.
5. The Indians' interpretation of the treaties will supersede all other interpretations.

The written treaties do not correspond with the spirit and intent of the treaties as understood by Indian people. There is a disparity, a significant difference between the meaning of treaty as understood from a plain reading of the text of any of the treaties and what Indian persons say it means.

The disparity between our understanding of the treaties and the actual contents of the written documents disappears if the verbal promises, assurances, and guarantees given by the Treaty Commissioners during negotiations are regarded as an integral part of the Treaty agreements.

A study of the elders' understanding of the Treaties has identified these differences:

There is unanimity among the elders that Indian people retained the right to govern themselves. Elders state that white men have usurped this authority and that the Indian Act is purely a white instrument for the purpose of governing Indians and usurping the treaties.

The nature of the land/resources cession is an important topic for which the two sources, treaty text and Indian elders, provide vastly different interpretations. The elders indicate that it was a limited cession. The concept of a limited land cession belies the text of Treaty 4, which states that the Indian signatories "do hereby cede, release, surrender and yield up to the Government of the Dominion of Canada, for Her Majesty the Queen, and Her successors forever, all their rights, titles and privileges whatsoever, to the lands included within the following limits".

The difference between the two interpretations of the land/resources cession is best described by reference to the elders' understanding of their rights with respect to wildlife, subsurface rights, and the status of lands, including waters not utilized for agriculture.

The subject of wildlife, while it has been conventionally phrased in terms of Indian hunting, fishing and trapping "rights", "right-of-access" or "right to use", is discussed here as an element or feature of the land cession because the elders state that the Indian people continue to own or have exclusive use of all wildlife. Specifically, the elders state that wildlife continues to belong to the Indian people as an element in the inventory of unceded resources. It is stated frequently that the Crown assumed a treaty obligation to protect wildlife populations for continuing Indian use.

Subsurface and other non-agricultural resources — The elders indicate that the resources ceded under Treaty 4 were limited and restrictive as some land resources were retained by the Indian people in the ceded lands. The Commissioner stated that the whitemen wanted land to farm only to the depth of a plow, stated most frequently as a depth of six inches. There is an implication that non-agricultural land — mountain country, lakes, other lands unfit for farming — were not requested and not ceded.

The elders state that the Indians were promised Crown protection and assistance to develop and prosper. This promise is described in general terms, with reference to a continuing and comprehensive Crown responsibility, and also in specific terms with respect to economic development assistance and assistance in the event of famine or privation.

(ii) Harold Cardinal, *The Unjust Society* (Edmonton: M.C. Hurtig Ltd., 1969), pp. 28-43.

Reproduced in chapter 4, *Pre-Confederation Treaties, supra*.

Note

1. For an account of the Indian understanding of the treaties covering Alberta, see Richard Price (ed.), *The Spirit of the Alberta Indian Treaties* (Montreal: Institute for Research on Public Policy, 1979).

(b) Judicial Interpretation: The "Medicine Chest" Clause in Treaty No. 6

(i) *Dreaver* v. *R.*, 10 April 1935, unreported, Exchequer Court of Canada.

This was a claim by Chief Dreaver on behalf of the Mistawasis Band of Indians in Saskatchewan for an accounting from the Superintendent General of Indian Affairs for, *inter alia*, moneys deducted from band funds for drugs and medical supplies, certain educational expenses, police services and the salary of a farm instructor. The case examined Treaty No. 6, certain land surrenders and the *Indian Act* (RSC 1906, c. 81 and RSC 1927, c. 98). Although the treaty promise to "maintain schools" was referred to by Angers J, it was not used to determine responsibility for the maintenance of deaf pupils, which was the educational issue in the case. Instead, Angers J based his decision upon the Indian Act and the deeds of surrender.

Angers J:

In virtue of the treaty of 1876 the Plain and Wood Cree Tribes of Indians and all other Indians inhabiting the lands described in the said treaty ceded, released and surrendered to the Government of the Dominion of Canada, for Her Majesty the Queen and Her Successors forever, all their rights, titles and privileges to the said lands as well as to all other lands wherever situated in the North-West Territories or in any other Province or portion of Her Majesty's Dominions situated within the Dominion of Canada.

Her Majesty the Queen, on the other hand, agreed and undertook to lay aside reserves for farming lands, due respect being had to lands then cultivated by the Indians, and other reserves for the benefit of the Indians, to be administered for them by Her Majesty's Government of the Dominion of Canada. A stipulation in the treaty provides that the Chief Superintendent of Indian Affairs shall send a person to "determine and set apart the reserves for each band, after consulting with the Indians thereof as to the locality which may be found to be most suitable for them".

The treaty then contains a proviso reading as follows:

Provided, however, that Her Majesty reserves the right to deal with any settlers within the bounds of any lands reserved for any band as She shall deem fit, and also that the aforesaid reserves of land, or any interest therein, may be sold or otherwise disposed of by Her Majesty's Government for the use and benefit of the said Indians entitled thereto, with their consent first had and obtained . . . .

Then comes a clause relating to schools, which says:

And further, Her Majesty agrees to maintain schools for instruction in such reserves hereby made as to Her Government of the Dominion of Canada may seem advisable, whenever the Indians of the reserve shall desire it.

The next and only other clause in the treaty having any materiality in the present instance is the one dealing with medicines; it is in the following terms:

That a medicine chest shall be kept at the house of each Indian Agent for the use and benefit of the Indians at the direction of such agent.

* * *

We then come to the several charges for drugs, medical supplies or medicines totalling $4,489.95.

As I have previously pointed out, the treaty stipulates that a medicine chest shall be kept at the house of each Indian Agent for the use and benefit of the Indians at the direction of the Agent. This, in my opinion, means that the Indians were to be provided with all the medicines, drugs or medical supplies which they might need entirely free of charge. The proof does not elicit what the medicines, drugs or medical supplies, mentioned in the statement inserted in paragraph 4 of the petition, were nor does it show the reason why they were charged. Do they constitute all the medicines, drugs and medical supplies furnished to the Indians of the Mistawasis Band by the Department of Indian Affairs or do they only represent a part of what was supplied to them, there is nothing in the evidence to indicate it. Be that as it may, I do not think that the Department had, under the treaty, the privilege of deciding which medicines, drugs and medical supplies were to be furnished to the Indians gratuitously and which were to be charged to the funds of the band. The treaty makes no distinction; it merely states that a medicine chest shall be kept at the house of the Indian Agent for the use and benefit of the Indians. The clause might unquestionably be more explicit but, as I have said, I take it to mean that all medicines, drugs or medical supplies which might be required by the Indians of the Mistawasis Band were to be supplied to them free of charge.

The suppliant Dreaver was present when the treaty was signed in 1876; he was then approximately twenty years old. He remembers the conversation between the Commissioners representing Her Majesty the Queen and the Chiefs and Headmen acting for the Indians about medicines and says that it was understood that all medicines were to be supplied free to the Indians (dep. Dreaver, pp. 13, 14, 25 and 26). The witness declares that in fact medicines were supplied gratuitously to the Indians from the date of the treaty until the band surrendered land to the Crown (dep. George Dreaver, p. 14). The date of the surrender is not mentioned, but the first charge for medicines is in 1918-1919; this seems to indicate that the witness was referring to the surrenders made in 1919, to wit exhibits 3 and 4.

The claim of the suppliants with regard to the charges for medicines, drugs and medical supplies is, I think, well founded.

(ii) *R.* v. *Johnston* (1966), 56 DLR (2d) 749 (Sask. CA)

CULLITON, CJS: — This is an appeal by the Attorney-General for Saskatchewan by way of stated case.

The respondent was charged on an information dated March 22, 1965, that he, being a resident of Saskatchewan, did unlawfully fail to pay 1963 tax on or before August 31, 1963, as required by the

Saskatchewan Hospitalization Act, RSS 1953, c. 232 [now RSS 1965, c. 253], and amendments and Regulations thereto. On being arraigned before Judge Policha of North Battleford, a plea of not guilty was entered.

Pursuant to s. 708(5) of the *Criminal Code*, certain facts were admitted by the respondent, namely: that he, Walter Johnston, was a resident of Saskatchewan and that he had not paid the tax as alleged in the information. It was agreed by counsel for the Crown that the respondent was an Indian within the meaning of the *Indian Act*, RSC 1952, c. 149. There was filed by the prosecution a copy of the Regulations issued under the *Saskatchewan Hospitalization Act*. The two pertinent sections of these Regulations [OC 1400/62, 58 Sask. Gaz., p. 861] are as follows:

21.   Where the tax is to be paid by the Government of Canada in accordance with an arrangement to that effect between that Government and the Government of Saskatchewan on behalf of a resident who is an Indian within the meaning of The Indian Act (Canada) and is residing on an Indian reserve or has been residing outside an Indian reserve for less than twelve months, the other provisions of these regulations shall apply to such resident and to the tax payments made on his behalf.

23(1)   Subject to the provisions of section 24 the following classes of persons shall be exempt from taxation:
(iv)   every other person who is entitled to receive general hospital services from the Government of Canada at the beginning of the tax year, to the extent that he continues to be entitled to such general hospital services during the tax year.

Counsel for the prosecution stated that while there was no written agreement, there was an undertaking between the Government of Canada and the government of Saskatchewan that the Government of Canada would pay the hospitalization tax for Indians residing on a reserve or who had been residing outside a reserve for less than 12 months. The evidence established that Johnston had permanent employment in the City of North Battleford and had been residing outside an Indian reserve for more than 12 months.

No evidence was called in defence. There was filed by counsel for the respondent a certified copy of Treaty Number 6 made between Her Majesty the Queen and the Plain and Wood Cree Indians and Other Tribes of Indians at Fort Carlton, Fort Pitt and Battle River with Adhesions and concluded in 1876 [Indian Treaties and Surrenders (1891), vol. 2, No. 157A, p. 35], with special reference to the following clauses in that Treaty:

That a medicine chest shall be kept at the house of each Indian Agent for the use and benefit of the Indians at the direction of such agent. . .

That in the event hereafter of the Indians comprised within this treaty being overtaken by any pestilence, or by a general famine, the Queen, on being satisfied and certified thereof by Her Indian Agent or Agents, will grant to the Indians assistance of such character and to such extent as Her Chief Superintendent of Indian Affairs shall deem necessary and sufficient to relieve the Indians from the calamity that shall have befallen them.

In disposition of the charge, the learned Judge of the Magistrate's Court, in a written judgment, said in part:

Referring to the "medicine chest" clause of Treaty No. 6, it is common knowledge that the provisions for caring for the sick and injured in the areas inhabited by the Indians in 1876 were somewhat primitive compared to present day standards. It can be safely assumed that the Indians had limited knowledge of what provisions were available and it is obvious that they were concerned that their people be adequately cared for. With that in view, and possibly carrying the opinion of Angers J, a step farther, I can only conclude that the "medicine chest" clause and the "pestilence" clause in Treaty No. 6 should properly be interpreted to mean that the Indians are entitled to receive all medical services, including medicines, drugs, medical supplies and hospital care free of charge. Lacking proper statutory provisions to the contrary, this entitlement would embrace all Indians within the meaning of the *Indian Act*, without exception. In my opinion, the accused falls within the exemption from taxation set forth in s. 23(1)(iv) of the Regulations and is not required to pay the tax.

I find the accused not guilty as charged.

In stating the case for the Court, the learned Judge found the facts as I have outlined them, and submitted the following questions:

(1) Was I right in holding that Treaty No. 6 applied to the defendant, Walter Johnston?

(2) Was I right in holding that the clause which reads as follows:

"That a medicine chest shall be kept at the house of each Indian Agent for the use and benefit of the Indians at the direction of such agent"

in Treaty No. 6, covered premiums payable under the Saskatchewan Hospitalization Act by the said defendant. Walter Johnston?

(3)   Was I right in holding that the said defendant, Walter Johnston, is exempt from taxes by virtue of Regulation 23(1)(iv) of the Regulations made pursuant to The Saskatchewan Hospitalization Act, O.C. 1400/62, Saskatchewan Gazette, September 14, 1962, volume 58, No. 37, and thereby not required to pay the said tax?

It was agreed and so found by the trial Judge that the respondent was an Indian as defined in the *Indian Act* and that he was a descendant of the Indians on behalf of whom Treaty Number 6 was made. Treaty Number 6 is, in my opinion, a treaty of the type referred to in s. 87 of the *Indian Act*. He is, therefore, in my opinion, entitled to any rights or immunities under the said Treaty that may have been contemplated by Parliament in enacting s. 87 of the *Indian Act*, unless the claim to such vested rights and immunities is limited to Indians residing on a reserve. Section 87 reads:

87.   Subject to the terms of any treaty and any other Act of the Parliament of Canada, all laws of general application from time to time in force in any province are applicable to and in respect of Indians in the province, except to the extent that such laws are inconsistent with this Act or any order, rule, regulation or by-law made thereunder, and except to the extent that such laws make provision for any matter for which provision is made by or under this Act.

I want to make it perfectly clear that the issue before this Court is not one relating to the general responsibility of the Government of Canada to Indians, but simply whether the learned trial Judge was right in his interpretation of the "medicine chest" and "pestilence" clauses of the Treaty. If I conclude that the learned trial Judge was right in his interpretation, only then would it become necessary to determine whether the respondent, as a non-resident of a reserve, is entitled to the benefits of the terms of the Treaty.

In the interpretation of the clauses of a treaty, one must first look to the words used and give to those words the ordinary meaning that would be attributed to them at the time the treaty was made. To do so, too, it is both proper and advisable to have resourse to whatever authoritative record may be available of the discussions surrounding the execution of the treaty. I agree with the opinion expressed by Norris, JA, in *R.* v. *White and Bob* (1964), 50 DLR (2d) 613, 52 WWR 193 [affd 52 DLR (2d) 481*n*, [1965] SCR vi], when, at p. 629, he said:

The Court is entitled "to take judicial notice of the facts of history whether past or contemporaneous" as Lord du Parcq said in *Monarch*

Steamship Co., Ld. v. *Karlshamns Oljefabriker (A/B)*, [1949] AC 196 at p. 234, [1949] 1 All ER 1 at p. 20, and it is entitled to rely on its own historical knowledge and researches, *Read* v. *Bishop of Lincoln*, [1892] AC 644, Lord Halsbury, LC, at pp. 652-4.

I have perused the treatise entitled *Treaties of Canada with the Indians of Manitoba, North-West Territories, and Kee-Wa-Tin*, by the Honourable Alexander Morris, PC. The learned author, in this work, presents an authoritative record of the negotiations which resulted in the conclusion of a number of treaties, including Treaty Number 6. It is apparent that in the negotiation of Treaty Number 6 the Indians greatly feared both pestilence and starvation. The learned author, at p. 178, says:

> They desired to be fed. Small-pox had destroyed them by hundreds a few years before, and they dreaded pestilence and famine,

and then he went on to say:

> The food question, was disposed of by a promise, that in the event of a *National* famine or *Pestilence* such aid as the Crown saw fit would be extended to them, and that for three years after they settled on their reserves, provisions to the extent of $1,000.00 per annum would be granted them during seed-time.

The undertaking so given was incorporated in the "pestilence" clause of the Treaty. Thus both historically, and on the plain language of the clause, it means no more than it plainly states: the obligation of the Crown in the event of pestilence or general famine, to provide such assistance as the Chief Superintendent of Indians should deem necessary and sufficient to meet the calamity. With every deference to the contrary opinion of the learned Judge of the Magistrate's Court, I do not think this clause of the Treaty has any relevancy in the determination of the question with which he was faced.

There is nothing in Morris' treatise to suggest that any meaning should be given to the words "medicine chest" other than that conveyed by the words themselves in the context in which they are used. The only reference I can find in the treatise is at p. 218, where the author states: " 'A medicine chest will be kept at the house of each Indian agent, in case of sickness amongst you.' " The "medicine chest" clause in the Treaty incorporates this undertaking.

Again, on the plain reading of the "medicine chest" clause, it means no more than the words clearly convey: an undertaking by the Crown to keep at the house of the Indian agent a medicine chest for the use and benefit of the Indians *at the direction of the agent*. (The italics are mine.) The clause itself does not give to the Indian an unrestricted right to the use and benefit of the "medicine chest" but such rights as are given are subject to the direction of the Indian agent. Such limitation would indicate that the obligation was to have physically on the reservations, for the use and benefit of the Indians, a supply of medicine under the supervision of the agent. I can find nothing historically, or in any dictionary definition, or in any legal pronouncement, that would justify the conclusion that the Indians, in seeking and accepting the Crown's obligation to provide a "medicine chest" had in contemplation provision of all medical services, including hospital care.

Mr Justice Angers, of the Exchequer Court of Canada, in an unreported judgment in *Dreaver* v. *The King*, gave an extended interpretation to the "medicine chest" clause of the Treaty when, at p. 20, he said:

> The clause might unquestionably be more explicit but, as I have said, I take it to mean that all medicines, drugs or medical supplies which might be required by the Indians of the Mistawasis Band were to be supplied to them free of charge.

In reaching the foregoing conclusion, the learned Justice appears to have relied on the evidence of the suppliant Dreaver, who testified he was present during the negotiation of the Treaty and that it was understood that all medicines were to be supplied free to the Indian. There appears to be nothing in his evidence to support any wider interpretation of the clause than that given to it by Mr Justice Angers. While I express no opinion as to the correctness of the interpretation of the clause as made by Mr Justice Angers, I do not think, with respect, that the interpretation so given justifies the extended meaning attributed thereto by the learned Judge of the Magistrate's Court.

In light of the conclusion which I have already stated, it is not necessary for me to answer Q. 1 of the stated case, but I must answer "No" to Qq. 2 and 3. I direct that the matter be remitted back to the learned Judge of the Magistrate's Court for disposition.

7. Further Reading

Barkwell, Peter Alan. "The Medicine Chest Clause in Treaty No. 6," [1981] 4 CNLR 1.

Charlton, Linda. "*R.* v. *Sutherland*: A Case Comment," [1981] 2 CNLR 1.

Getty, Ian A.L., and Donald B. Smith, (eds.), *One Century Later: Western Canadian Reserve Indians Since Treaty 7*. Vancouver: University of British Columbia Press, 1978.

Green, L.C. "Legal Significance of Treaties Affecting Canada's Indians," (1972) 1 *Anglo-Am. L. Rev.* 119.

Knoll, David. "Treaty and Aboriginal Hunting and Fishing Rights," [1979] 1 CNLR 1.

Lysyk, Kenneth M. "Indian Hunting Rights: Constitutiona Considerations and the Role of Indian Treaties in British Columbia," (1966) 2 *UBCL Rev.* 401.

——————— . "The Rights and Freedoms of the Aboriginal Peoples of Canada," in Walter S. Tarnopolsky, and G.-A. Beaudoin, (eds.), *The Canadian Charter of Rights and Freedoms: Commentary*, Toronto: Carswell, 1982.

McNeil, Kent. "The Constitutional Rights of the Aboriginal Peoples of Canada," [1982] 4 *Supreme Court LR* 255.

——————— . *Indian Hunting and Fishing Rights in the Prairie Provinces of Canada*. Saskatoon: University of Saskatchewan Native Law Centre, 1983.

Sanders, Douglas E. "Indian Hunting and Fishing Rights," (1973-74) 38 *Sask. L. Rev.* 45.

——————— . "The Rights of the Aboriginal Peoples of Canada" (1983), 61 *CBR* 314.

Zlotkin, Norman K. *Unfinished Business: Aboriginal Peoples and the 1983 Constitutional Conference*. Kingston: Institute of Intergovernmental Relations, Queen's University, 1983.

6. Constitutional Issues in Native Law

NOEL LYON

Section 91(24) of the Constitution Act, 1867 gives the Parliament of Canada exclusive legislative authority over "Indians, and Lands reserved for the Indians." Such authority gives rise to federal questions about the scope of the power so conferred and about the applicability of provincial laws to Indians and on reserve lands. These questions are the easiest to define because they involve the interpretation of a familiar legal text that fits into an established body of interpretative case law.

But the federal division of powers is only one feature of the constitution, however well litigated, and its consideration should be set against a larger view of constitutional law that may disclose other issues. Judicial decisions concerning the nature of aboriginal title or the status of Indian treaties may have been based on questionable assumptions or assertions. The full constitutional basis of native law has, therefore, yet to be established.

The legal position of Aboriginal Peoples is so woven into the constitutional fabric of Canada that all-important issues of native law are constitutional in one sense or another. Questions of aboriginal title take us back to the Royal Proclamation of 1763:

> . . . whereas it is just and reasonable, and essential to our interest, and the security of our colonies, that the several nations or tribes of Indians with whom we are connected, and who live under our protection, should not be molested or disturbed in the possession of such parts of our dominions and territories as, not having been ceded to or purchased by us, are reserved to them or any of them, as their hunting grounds . . . .

Practically every subsequent territorial addition to British North America was accompanied by a recognition of native rights and of the need to settle them fairly when more of the reserved lands were wanted for settlement or for other purposes that were incompatible with their traditional use by indigenous peoples. Did the Parliament of the United Kingdom in 1867 have such absolute authority over these territories that it could confer on the Parliament of Canada a similar absolute authority over Indians and their lands, free of these commitments or of any obligations arising under international law? It is a question we never ask. We have been taught simply to assert the supremacy of Parliament.

Treaties made with Indians raise the question of the position and authority of the Crown in the constitutional hierarchy of British North America. Judicial response to this question has consisted of the simple assertion that these are

408

internal dealings of government and therefore they cannot be real treaties. Like all other agreements made with the Crown, they can be cancelled unilaterally by the government. We have not seriously considered the possibility that at least some of these Indian treaties are real treaties creating obligations under international law; or, alternatively, that they are a distinct genus lying somewhere between a domestic agreement and an international treaty, whose features must be elaborated through an imaginative judicial application of constitutional theory against a background of the relevant principles of international law.

The theory underlying the existing law of Indian treaties is illustrated by the following passage from the judgment in *R.* v. *Syliboy*, [1929] 1 DLR 307 (Nova Scotia County Court):

> Treaties are unconstrained acts of independent powers. But the Indians were never regarded as an independent power. A civilized nation first discovering a country of uncivilized people or savages held such country as its own until such time as by treaty it was transferred to some other civilized nation. The savages' rights of sovereignty even of ownership were never recognized. Nova Scotia had passed to Great Britain not by gift or purchase or even by conquest of the Indians but by treaty with France, which had acquired it by priority of discovery and ancient possession; and the Indians passed with it.

While no Canadian judge would make such a statement today, it reflects a particular view of Indians and confirms a belief that the treaties made with them are not treaties in the international law sense or any variation of that concept. The legal interpretation of Indian treaties that has emerged from this view of Indians is that the treaties are really just contracts, a proposition of law stated most recently by Marceau, J of the Federal Court of Canada in *Pawis* v. *The Queen* (1980), 102 DLR (3d) 602:

> It is obvious that the Lake-Huron Treaty, like all Indian treaties, was not a treaty in the international law sense. The Ojibways did not then constitute an "independent power", they were subjects of the Queen. Although very special in nature and difficult to precisely define, the treaty has to be taken as an agreement entered into by the Sovereign and a group of her subjects with the intention to create special legal relations between them. The promises made therein by Robinson on behalf of Her Majesty and "the principal men of the Ojibewa Indians" were undoubtedly designed and intended to have effect in a legal sense and a legal context. The agreement can therefore be said to be tantamount to a contract, and it may be admitted that a breach of the promises contained therein may give rise to an action in the nature of an action for breach of contract.

If we ask when and how Indians became subjects of the Queen, we are likely to encounter a mixture of questionable international law doctrines, self-serving British colonial law, and dubious evidence of Indian people's submission to the authority of the British Crown.

United States law, on the other hand, has viewed Indian groups as nations within the larger American nation, and has recognized their territorial rights and qualified sovereignty within their lands. Chief Justice Marshall set out the basis on which United States law regards Indian treaties as treaties in the full constitutional sense in the judgment in *Worcester* v. *Georgia*, 31 US (6 Peters) 515 at 559-60:

> The Indian nations had always been considered as distinct, independent political communities, retaining their original natural rights, as the undisputed possessors of the soil, from time immemorial, with the single exception of that imposed by irresistible power, which excluded them from intercourse with any other European potentate than the first discoverer of the coast of the particular region claimed: and this was a restriction which those European potentates imposed on themselves, as well as on the Indians. The very term ''nation,'' so generally applied to them, means ''a people distinct from others.'' The constitution, by declaring treaties already made, as well as those to be made, to be the supreme law of the land, has adopted and sanctioned the previous treaties with the Indian nations, and consequently admits their rank among those powers who are capable of making treaties. The words ''treaty'' and ''nation'' are words of our own language, selected in our diplomatic and legislative proceedings, by ourselves, having each a definite and well understood meaning. We have applied them to Indians, as we have applied them to the other nations of the earth. They are applied to all in the same sense.

Is Canadian law on the nature of Indian treaties so well settled that it is no longer open to the Supreme Court of Canada to adopt the interpretation of the US Supreme Court in *Worcester* v. *Georgia*? *Worcester* was cited with apparent approval by both Judson, J and Hall, J in the *Calder* case on the question of aboriginal title.

Legal questions are seldom so well settled as to be closed to reconsideration. Great cases are great because they give expression to new knowledge and changed standards and perceptions. But more is needed than a rerun of old arguments and received truths; an alternative way of viewing a matter must be offered. Old conceptions of international law as rules for sharing the global spoils among European states, of constitutional law as the justification of state power, and of indigenous peoples as children who are in need of protection because they have no legal rights are all questionable by current standards. And the questions all go to the constitutional basis of distinctive laws that govern those peoples and their rights, which we loosely describe as ''native law.''

In deciding questions of native law, British and Canadian courts have never questioned the absolute power of the Crown and of the British and Canadian parliaments to do as they wish to the Aboriginal Peoples and their rights. Is it really too late to argue before the Supreme Court of Canada that Indian treaties are binding on the Crown in accordance with present-day standards of international law and that aboriginal title is not subject to being extinguished by unilateral legislative action? In the article that follows, Charles Blackmar argues that our tendency to regard these questions as closed by high judicial decision is more a result of legal education than a consequence of any legal or historical inevitability.

1. *He Makes the Best Use of His Opportunities* 21 J Leg Ed 499-512 (1968-69)

Charles B. Blackmar, Professor of Law, St Louis University
(footnotes have been deleted)

A.   The Lawyer's Opportunity for the Future

Just a few months ago I was startled by a headline which announced that the Supreme Court had held that death sentences were invalid under the so-called Lindbergh Kidnapping Law. I thought back to the time, more than ten years ago, when a federal judge had appointed me to represent the defendant in an atrocious kidnap-murder case. My co-counsel and I tried to think of every possible defense. We argued that it was unfair to exclude jurors who admitted that they were conscientiously opposed to capital punishment. We asked the court to charge the jury in terms of the *Durham* rule, in lieu of the *Macnaghten* rule, in defining legal insanity. But, still, another lawyer thought of something that we didn't think of, and he was able to save a client from execution when we were not. One can't help wondering, "Why didn't I think of that?"

This is an illustration of the willingness of courts to reconsider old doctrines and to make changes when they feel that change is in order. Some have argued that a court is guilty of a moral wrong in overruling precedent for other than the most compelling reasons, and that the lawyer who tries to persuade them to depart from precedent may himself be participating in the wrong. I have suggested that a court which paid no attention to precedent invited challenge to its own decisions just as soon as personnel of the court changed, and that if courts become involved in political affairs the other branches of the government may not be willing to accept its pronouncements automatically. But these arguments have nothing to do with the lawyer's duty or with his opportunity. If he thinks that a court is willing to overrule a precedent which conflicts with his clients interest he has the duty to try to get the precedent overruled. Arguments about consistency and stability are for his opponent to make. The lawyer's duty is to his client! So a lawyer no longer abandons his search and his case if he finds that precedent is squarely against him. Nor can he absolutely be sure of success if he finds a case in his favor. The successful lawyer of the future will be one who can argue for changes in rules of long standing.

I am amused at the people who think that there would be a great revolution in the practice of law if more use could be made of computers as an aid in decision-making. Those who think this way apparently believe that the process of judicial decision consists solely of locating and applying the proper authorities, so that if a proper and complete search is made the result will follow automatically. I have no intention of deriding the proper use of computers and I'm all for the most careful and thorough research and for any tool which will save time in researching legal problems. The real work begins, however, only after the precedents have been located. After the lawyer has located the cases in the books, he then has to attack or defend them in their application to the present-day scene. One who thinks that there is any magic in more thorough analysis of cases is not in touch with reality.

The rule that jurors with conscientious scruples against the death penalty could be excluded in capital cases was established at a time when most felonies were punishable under English law by death. The judges felt that a juror who did not believe in capital punishment might vote to acquit a man he believed to be guilty, simply to save him from the gallows. Such a juror could be excluded, just as any other prejudiced juror could. Under modern conditions, however, the death penalty is seldom mandatory. So the Supreme Court finally held that the rule of automatic exclusion is no longer valid. The reason for the initial rule disappeared, but the courts took a long time to change the corollary rule. Surely there are other ancient rules ripe for change.

Let me suggest some instances in which a change in the judicial approach may be predicted with confidence, and in which the resourceful lawyer may achieve spectacular results. . . .

The courts have seen the need for a new approach to products liability problems, and have taken this approach, generally, without legislative sanction. The Supreme Court of New Jersey came to the conclusion that the parties to a contract for the sale of an automobile didn't stand on equal footing. the purchaser probably has to take the car on the dealer's terms, or not at all. The court, therefore, took steps to protect the purchaser against unreasonable provisions of the contract.

A judge of the Supreme Court of Missouri says that the law of charitable exemption from tort liability was made by judges, and should be reconsidered by judges. He does not feel that it is always necessary to wait for the legislature in order to reexamine the existing rules of decision.

It is not my purpose to say that the new course of judicial activism, or judicial iconoclasm, is necessarily good or necessarily bad. I can safely take a middle course in saying that departure from precedent is frequently necessary but that it presents dangers. These problems, however, are not the concern of the lawyer who has a client and a case and is confronted by a rule of law which operates against his client. His duty is to use his resources and imagination to try to get the court to change the law. He doesn't have to argue his opponent's case. In an ever-increasing number of cases furthermore, the lawyer who argues for change will be successful.

B.   Training the Lawyer of the Future

.   .   .

(1)   *How Do We Present the Role of Precedent in our Legal System?*

The common law developed an encapsuled view of the legal system, which is essentially as follows: Courts are called upon to determine disputes between private individuals. They reach conclusions about rights and duties in particular situations. Other courts of equal or subordinate authority are expected to follow these precedents. The basic principles and established doctrines should be changed only by legislative authority. If the courts establish a line of decision, and the legislature makes no change, then this indicates legislative approval and endorsement of the line of decision.

Like most concepts, this one exists more on paper than in actuality. Yet I believe that it accurately represents the conception of the legal system which the average graduate entertains, and the conception held by most judges. If so, it shows what they have gathered from their law teaching.

The legislatures have little time to deal with the intricacies of private law. Such matters as schools, poverty and medicare take up the bulk of their time. Many states limit the length of sessions and the legislatures find it hard to accomplish their work in the time allotted. When changes in the private law are proposed, they often have hard sledding. Many legislators are inherently suspicious of lawyers and of "lawyers bills." If vested interests are disturbed, it is rather easy to secure delays. Anyone who has discussed an evidence code or a proposal for probate reform before a bar association sees the ease with which his colleagues can pick holes in any proposal. The short of it is that most reform in the private law will come about, if at all, through the effort of the courts and of lawyers who argue before the courts.

There are special reasons for adherence to precedent. In some areas, as those involving titles and those outlining procedures to be followed, the public has a right to rely on the continuation of essential precedents.

The process of decision involves considerable judicial time and effort, so that a job once competently done should not have to be redone. Most decisions, furthermore, can be supported by their inherent soundness of reasoning. One who seeks to overturn a precedent has a substantial burden, and properly so, but the doctrine of legislative acquiescence is not a persuasive reason for adhering to precedent, and the court should feel no need to apologize to the legislature if it overrules existing authority. If the court feels that there is error it should make correction. One could argue that a legislature which felt that this process was getting out of hand could amend the overruling precedent just as easily as it could change the decisions which formerly concerned.

The lawyer who is equipped with a realistic view of judicial precedent is better equipped to argue for the change in unsound or outmoded decisions.

(2)   *Courts as Governmental Institutions*

The American courts, state and federal, are directly involved in the political process to a degee not found elsewhere in the world. This is because of the written constitutions which establish government at both levels.

Most instruction in the role of the courts in government has followed the thought of Marshall and Holmes. Marshall emphasized the duty of the courts to find and declare the law. If, in a case properly brought before the court, there was a conflict between the higher law of the constitution and the subordinate law of a statute, the court had to give effect to the former while ignoring the latter. The court, however, was absolutely bound by the work of the framers and of the legislators. It could not exercise its own will.

Holmes accepted Marshall's conception of the role of the court, but took delight in showing colleagues that they were allowing themselves to be influenced by "inarticulate major premises." It was easy for a judge who felt that a statute was very, very unwise to persuade himself that it deprived somebody of liberty or property without due process of law. Holmes asked that his colleagues show greater deference to the legislature and perhaps to allot them some capacity for error in trying to work out solutions to current problems.

The realist sees, however, that the court does operate as a part of the governmental system and that it has been involved in politics from the very beginnings of our government up to the present time. One who suffers disadvantage through governmental action or inaction is privileged to take his case to court. The advocate's first job is to convince the court that there is a wrong which is in need of correction. If he succeeds up to this point the court may often be willing to grant him relief in the face of precedent or convention.

. . . .

For years the rule of *Frothingham* v. *Mellon* stood as an obstacle to any person who wanted to challenge a federal expenditure. It was said that the citizen's interest in federal expenditures was so insignificant that he did not have standing to complain in court. Most law professors simply enunciated this rule of nonreviewability, without questioning it. They must have had some troubles because of the numerous cases permitting challenge to state and local expenditures, for the difference is simply one of degree and it is quite probable that a rich man would have more money involved in a federal appropriation than a poor man would in a local one. And did we show our students that if federal expenditures could not be challenged on constitutional grounds, then there was a possibility for governmental action in stark violation of the constitution. (Especially with regard to the provision relating to "establishment of religion," which is invariably accomplished through some form of expenditures.) When the possibility for constitutional violation was adequately presented to a court sensitive to problems of establishment of religion, it changed the rule of reviewability. This change no doubt came as a surprise to most lawyers and most teachers, yet it shows the willingness to make changes when the need is adequately presented.

The lawyer of course has a better chance for success if he can bring his case within existing authorities. Judges of the first instance are particularly reluctant to engage in pioneering or adventurism. Yet when the precedents are in opposition the lawyer will look to cases in other areas and even when these are not fruitful he might still secure relief through a convincing demonstration of need. . . .

(3) *On the elimination of Mythology*

I have mentioned the young lawyer who felt that he could not, and should not, assail the citadel of negotiability.

In 1927 a man in Kansas City purchased a cashier's check payable to himself. He ventured the instrument, duly endorsed, in a pass of the dice but saw snake eyes staring at him. The winner prevailed upon a merchant to cash the duly endorsed and apparently valid check. The merchant was not allowed to enforce this check against the issuing bank, inasmuch as it had served as consideration for a gambling transaction at a later stage in its history.

This decision knocks the props from under any conventional notion of negotiability. It means that the prospective purchaser is not protected in relying on the credit standing of the prior parties, taking the risk only of the genuineness of the signatures. He must sometimes make further inquiry into the history of the instrument, or else must look primarily to the person who hands it to him. Yet the case involving the gambling transaction is not only refutation of the basic premise of negotiability.

Yet teachers advance the myth, with citation of Lord Mansfield's strictures about the needs and usages of merchants. Contrary decisions are brushed aside as judicial sports. The framers of the Uniform Commercial Code did not tamper with the law of negotiability. The present draft of the Uniform Consumer Credit Code forbids the giving of negotiable instruments in transactions which fall within its provisions, but goes on to provide that if a negotiable instrument is given in violation of the law then it may be enforced by one who can demonstrate that he is a bona fide purchaser without notice. Courts describe the doctrine of negotiability in eloquent terms, and see a solemn duty in denying relief to an aggrieved party if his opponent can qualify as a "holder in due course."

Why not pierce the myth? Why not emphasize the cases in which the prospective purchaser must look primarily to the person with whom he deals, and not to the maker or the prior parties? That the courts have created some exceptions shows that they may consider others. If a negotiable instrument given for gambling consideration is void, why is the same treatment not possible for one which is usurious? If a finance company buys commercial paper from an appliance dealer, it is vain to argue that the purchaser places any reliance at all upon the credit standing or identity of the maker? Might it not be appropriate, then, to make the finance company look first to the dealer from whom it acquired the paper? Might a court not reach such a result if someone would sweep away the cobwebs? And is there any reason to wait for a legislature, especially when the finance companies would have many more lobbyists than the consumers would?

And what about the rule against perpetuities? The rule as initially stated by Professor Gray and refined by the Restatement reads like a statute. Yet it is the result of common-law development extending over more than a century. It was derived by courts to meet specific problems.

Gray exhausted the precedents in the quest for a pure and simple rule, of mathematical exactitude. How he would have welcomed the computer! His work was seized upon by courts anxious to display their erudition. Those which strayed from the straight and narrow path in adopting doctrines of "cy pres" or "wait and see" were criticized for provinciality or softheartedness. Most teachers spoke in favor of the strict application of the rule. It makes intriguing examination questions which are easy to grade. The bar examiners find it helpful. Professor Leach did a service for teachers and students alike by compressing the rule within a nutshell and then revisiting it.

Yet does the rule really do what it is supposed to do? The lawyer intent on doing so can create an interest of extremely long duration. (Compare the English lawyer who had an old formbook, so that he set up a trust measured by the life of the last to die of the 200-odd descendants of Queen Victoria who were alive in the mid-twenties.) At the same time courts have done their solemn duty in striking down interests dependent upon uncertain events which in all probability will occur in 21 years but are not certain to do so. (Compare interests which do not vest "until the gravel pits are worked out" or "until my estate is settled?") So the rule will not always preclude an extremely remote interest, while nonetheless operating as a trap for the careless draftsman of an instrument which consists with every notion of public policy.

One court used the rule against perpetuities to destroy an unconscionable option, renewable annually by the option for a nominal consideration. Should the result have been otherwise if the draftsman had made use of a conventional "saving" clause? Would an instrument containing such a clause be any more consistent with public policy?

So have we told our students the full story about this rule? Might we not suggest the desirability of judicial correction, without waiting for legislatures which have little time and less inclination toward the reform of future interest law?

Conclusion

Courts are receptive to new approaches and new ideas which would not have received the scantiest consideration a short time ago. If it is the lawyer's duty to assert for his client any position which the court might be persuaded to take, then the premium is on an imaginative use of legal talents and resources. The schools must not be found wanting in an area of need.

We must prepare students for both sides of the case. It is proper to defend the existing law, if one's client's interest calls for this. The defense may not be as easy as it has been in the past. Reference to the Restatement or to the black letter or *corpus juris* may not be enough. If we don't equip our students to defend, they may lose cases that should have been won.

The question of how to prepare the lawyer for his new opportunities is not easy to answer. In the process we may destroy the serenity of our students and may deprive them of the sense of symmetry which they so prize. Perhaps my comments will suggest some ideas about how teachers in widely differing areas of the law can help their students to make use of new opportunities.

Professor Blackmar was arguing for a more critical and imaginative use of existing precedent. His urgings are even more appropriate where judges have been given a whole new body of enacted law that is part of the fundamental law and explicitly has been made the supreme law of the land. This is the present situation in Canada, with a new Charter of Rights and Freeedoms that is made the supreme law of Canada by s. 52(1) of the *Constitution Act, 1982*. It will not be a case, therefore, of asking judges to overrule precedent, but rather to perform the duty imposed on them by s. 52(1) to reconsider precedent in the light of its compatibility with the provisions of the new Charter. Even leading cases decided by the Supreme Court of Canada are no longer good authority if they conflict with the Charter, but the likeliest application of the Charter in relation to precedent lies in the guidance it will give to judges when they must choose between two conflicting lines of authority or interpretations of statutory language.

2. The Constitution

(a) The Constitution Act, 1982

S. 35 of the Constitution Act, 1982 provides that

(1) The existing aboriginal and treaty rights of the aboriginal peoples of Canada are hereby recognized and affirmed.
(2) In this Act, "aboriginal peoples of Canada" includes the Indian, Inuit and Metis people of Canada.

S. 52(1) of the Act provides that

The Constitution of Canada is the supreme law of Canada, and any law that is inconsistent with the provisions of the Constitution is, to the extent of the inconsistency, of no force or effect.

Since s. 35 is part of the Constitution of Canada as defined by s. 52(2), it is entrenched law to the extent that the word "affirm" constitutes an incorporation of existing rights into the 1982 Act. While s. 35 does not enjoy the guarantee provided by s. 1 to Charter rights and freedoms, since it is not part of the Charter, its status as part of the supreme law may be even higher than those rights and freedoms, since the Charter's guarantee is subject to "such reasonable limits prescribed by law as can be demonstrably justified in a free and democratic society." The entrenchment, by affirmation, of aboriginal and treaty rights is apparently unqualified.

An example of the kind of argument made possible by s. 52 of the 1982 Act is that the hunting and fishing rights reserved to Indians by the Natural Resource Transfer Agreements of 1929 have become part of the supreme law of Canada and therefore can no longer be subject to federal legislation. In *Daniels* v. *The Queen* (1969), 2 DLR (3d) 1, the Supreme Court decided that those agreements conferred rights only as against the provinces, not as against the government of Canada, as a matter of interpretation of the relevant paragraphs of the agreements. However, if those paragraphs are set in an interpretative framework built around the 1982 Act, a broader interpretation of the hunting and fishing rights may be indicated. The answer to the obvious reply to this argument is that s. 35 entrenches existing rights, not existing precedents and methods of interpretation.

Other treaty rights that can now claim constitutional status, immune from both federal and provincial laws, may include education rights, medical care (based on medicine chest clauses) and immunity from taxation. A thorough discussion of the possibilities can be found in Norman K. Zlotkin, "Unfinished Business: Aboriginal Peoples and the 1983 Constitutional Conference (1983)," a discussion paper published by the Institute of Intergovernmental Relations, Queen's University, Kingston.

These rights are reinforced by the Charter's guarantee of freedom of religion and of the right to life, liberty and security of the person, from which it is not unreasonable to infer, in the case of Indian and Inuit peoples, a constitutional right to cultural survival.

. Following Blackmar's idea, one could argue that section 35 gives to the courts a fresh constitutional mandate, as of 1982, to consider claims of aboriginal and treaty rights, and necessarily to do so in accordance with 1982 standards of constitutional and international law as well as current conceptions of how far and on what kinds of questions domestic tribunals should adopt or consider norms of international law. That is, while no new native rights are created by s. 35, any existing rights are given modern status, which means they are to be considered in the light of current conceptions of state power reflected in such sources as the UN General Assembly's 1960 Declaration on the Granting of Independence to Colonial Countries and Peoples. Political and legal authority that is ultimately based in coercion rather than free and willing participation in political processes may not be adequate to overcome rights that are rooted in an external social order, and assertions of established sovereignty may simply beg the hard questions or deny the existence of international norms.

There is a range of possible aboriginal rights comprehended by s. 35. In addition to title to land and hunting and fishing rights that are already recognized in principle by English and Canadian common law, there are the broader territorial claims like that of the Dene, which amounts to a claim to maintain an Indian nation within the Canadian nation, much like a province. Then there is the claim of a right to live under traditional forms of government which are tribal and quite unlike the band council system prescribed by the Indian Act, and to be governed by customary laws, at least in relation to matters like the family and the control and punishment of anti-social conduct, where cultural values and attitudes may differ from those of the majority. Finally, the increased understanding of the importance of language that has been provided by the Report of the Royal Commission on Bilingualism and Biculturalism suggests that Indian and Inuit claims to language rights are even stronger than those of English and French minorities. Each of these possibilities needs some elaboration.

As to self-government, the Indians and Inuit of North America had functioning communities when the Europeans arrived, some of which were highly developed. For example, the Six Nations Confederacy of the Iroquois had a well-understood system of hereditary chiefs, giving each nation a fixed entitlement to representation in the Confederacy and setting procedures for choosing chiefs and replacing a deceased representative of a nation. Many Iroquois people continue to adhere to the Longhouse tradition of hereditary chiefs and do not recognize the Band Council system of local government imposed by the Indian Act. Self-government according to traditional ways is therefore a feasible alternative, and the argument can be made in constitutional conferences and perhaps even in courts of law that current standards of international law call for a reconsideration of the legitimacy of a system of local government imposed by statute without any real consultation with the Aboriginal Peoples.

In approaching this question, we must overcome the tendency to regard sovereignty in absolute terms and consider the possibility that Aboriginal Peoples are entitled either by law or constitutional concession to a limited sovereignty sufficient to give them autonomy in local government. The conventional assumption required of Canadian judges by their conditioning to an absolute doctrine of sovereignty clearly underlies the judgment of the Supreme Court of Canada in *Davey* v. *Isaac* (1977), 77 DLR (3d) 481. The Court in that case disposed of the claim made by the hereditary chiefs of the Six Nations Reserve to exercise the powers of local government in place of the elected band council, without even considering the possibility that some limited sovereignty had survived the European occupation and could prevail even in the face of federal legislation imposing a band council system of local government. It was assumed that the authority of Parliament over Indians and reserved lands, under s. 91(24) of the 1867 Act, is absolute, so that once the Court rejected the hereditary chiefs' argument that the members of the reserve do not constitute a band within the meaning of the Indian Act, the application of the band council system prescribed by the Indian Act was automatic.

In pursuing the legal inquiry on this point, indigenous peoples are entitled to insist that we apply modern conceptions and standards of sovereignty recognized by international law, not the self-serving notions applied by courts established by the "discovering" or "conquering" European states. The force of this claim is increased by the fact that native systems of government build on family organization by clans. To suppress tribal councils and their authority is to suppress the full expression of familial ties and, thus, is arguably contrary to public policy and — more important for legal purposes — may be repugnant to the right to liberty entrenched by s. 7 of the Canadian Charter of Rights and Freedoms. That is: liberty carries a right to choose a system of local government, either directly or through a representative legislature, rather than having an alien system imposed without consultation or consent. Section 7 of the Charter gives the Supreme Court an opportunity to reconsider the question of Indian and Inuit sovereignty in the light of the different approach taken by the US Supreme Court in *Worcester* v. *Georgia*, seen against the standards of international law appropriate to a constitution enacted in 1982. The US law supporting tribal sovereignty and self-government is described in Felix S. Cohen's *Handbook of Federal Indian Law*, 1982 Edition, Chapter 4, "The Source and Scope of Tribal Authority in Indian Affairs."

The right to be governed by customary law, or tribal law, on matters affecting the distinctiveness of native cultures, is at least a moral right enforceable in the political domain through constitutional or legislative enactment. The Quebec Act, 1774 is the best example of this right being respected, that Act having restored to the French subjects of the Brisish monarch their right to be governed by their traditional laws in matters of property and civil rights. In the case of Indians and Inuit, it has been doctrinal rigidity and ignorance of tribal laws that has led to the suppression of those laws. Transplanted English judges and their Canadian successors naturally assumed that any gaps left by legislation are filled by the common law. It seems never to have been seriously considered as a general proposition that matters not covered by the Indian Act are subject to tribal law, which is the appropriate equivalent of the common law for matters that go to cultural differences. Only in matters relating to the family — marriage, adoption, divorce, child welfare and estates — have the courts recognized customary Indian and Inuit law, a tendency documented by Morse in "Indian and Inuit Family Law and the Canadian Legal System," (1980) 8 *American Indian Law Review*, 199-257. Family law is probably the field where cultural differences are most important for the law, although a powerful case is made for modifying at least the application of criminal law, if not the standards, by Mr Justice Sissons in his autobiographical *Judge of the Far North*. The practice of ignoring tribal law has been reinforced by the enactment of s. 88 of the Indian Act, which induces the belief that gaps in Indian law no longer exist because provincial law has filled them all, either through adoption by Parliament or by means of the strange constitutional doctrine that legislative gaps cannot exist in a federal system.

Again, the new Charter can be invoked to support a legal claim to observe tribal law on matters going to cultural differences. Section 1 of the Charter speaks of a free and democratic society, while section 7 specifies the right to liberty and security of the person. Suppression of customary law with no apparent reason beyond ignorance, the pursuit of uniformity for its own sake, and doctrinal rigidity on questions of sovereignty and authority, may be a denial of liberty and personal security as those rights are understood in a free and democratic society.

Finally, there is the question of language, whose importance to cultural integrity was brought home to us by the Report of the Royal Commission on Bilingualism and Biculturalism, especially in the General Introduction to Book I (1967). We have given elaborate constitutional expression to this fact in the new Charter of Rights and Freedoms, but only as to the two "founding peoples" of Canada. The pre-founding peoples have not had their language rights expressly entrenched in the new constitution and it remains to be seen whether this will prove to be one of the rights that is recognized and affirmed by s. 35 of the Constitution Act, 1982. Among the various reports and position papers on the constitution that were published between 1967 and 1981, only that of the Quebec Liberal Party proposed entrenching the language rights of the original peoples of Canada. It recommended that native peoples' right to federal government services and education in their own languages be enshrined in the proposed Charter. But this was not done, and so language rights remains as one of the unresolved issues for the agenda of the continuing process of definition and implementation of aboriginal and treaty rights that was put in motion at the Constitutional Conference of March 1983.

Native languages are still very much alive in Canada. Band Council meetings and other community activities, as well as much of the social discourse among Indians and Inuit, are conducted in their own tongues. In Quebec, the language problem is complicated by the fact that the Indians and Inuit of northern Quebec have until recently had close contact with Hudson Bay Company employees and Anglophone missionaries, rather than with representatives of the province of Quebec. Consequently, they find themselves bilingual Cree-English or Inuit-English persons in a province whose sole official language is French.

There remains the question of the meaning of the word "existing" in s. 35; this word was inserted in the provision at the insistence of some of the provinces. It might be argued that the word limits the scope of the section to rights which have been established through court decisions. Such an interpretation, however, would credit judicial decision with the creation of rights, whereas it is a basic tenet of our legal system that courts do not create rights but simply declare them to exist and provide remedies when existing rights are violated. A more likely explanation is that since one theory of aboriginal rights is that there must be some act of recognition of them by the Crown before they can be declared or enforced by the courts, it was necessary to specify existing rights to avoid the claim that s. 35 itself constitutes an act of recognition that gives legal status to otherwise inchoate aboriginal claims.

The new Charter contains, in s. 25, a disclaimer of any intention adversely to affect native rights by not including them among the guaranteed rights and freedoms:

25.   The guarantee in this charter of certain rights and freedoms shall not be construed so as to abrogate or derogate from any aboriginal, treaty or other rights or freedoms that pertain to the aboriginal peoples of Canada including

(a)   any rights or freedoms that have been recognized by the Royal Proclamation of October 7, 1763; and

(b)   any rights or freedoms that may be acquired by the aboriginal peoples of Canada by way of land claims settlement.

It is clear that s. 25 creates no new rights. It merely prevents adverse inferences being drawn from the absence of native rights from the guaranteed list. It is not so clear, however, that this provision has no effect on the status of existing native rights. Their inclusion here, even in a negative way, in addition to their recognition in Part II of the Act, suggests they are of a fundamental character. They are not just ordinary legal rights.

What can we make of the fact that s. 25 is part of the Charter while s. 35 is not? The general significance of inclusion in the Charter is the entrenchment of any rights and freedoms set out in the section. This is the effect of s. 1, the "guarantee" clause, taken in conjunction with the supremacy clause in s. 52. But s. 25 does not set out any substantive rights or freedoms. It simply enacts protection of all rights that pertain to Aboriginal Peoples against the inference that their non-inclusion in the Charter indicates an intention to abrogate them. What s. 25 might do is support an inference that these rights are considered fundamental but have not been set out in the Charter, probably because they are even more complex and unexplored than were language rights twenty years ago and would be difficult or impossible to formulate. On this analysis, the important effect of s. 25 would be to give these rights the status of fundamental law and, therefore, make them of the same order of importance as the rights and freedoms that *are* set out in the Charter. Section 52 of the 1982 Act — the supremacy clause — supports this view when it is applied to s. 35 of the Act.

The argument for a broader approach to aboriginal rights is strengthened by section 27 of the Charter, which directs that

This Charter shall be interpreted in a manner consistent with the preservation and enhancement of the multicultural heritage of Canadians.

The Constitution Act of 1982 is the first legal enactment that has ever accorded the status of fundamental rights to the aboriginal and treaty rights of native peoples. Native rights were not perceived by judges as having this status when the existing precedents about aboriginal and treaty rights were established. This recognition of the special status of aboriginal and treaty rights gives further support to the claim that the courts have a mandate, if not an obligation, to reconsider the constitutional foundation on which the precedents rest. These rights have been seen as the residue of traditional practices that remains after the many encroachments of British, Canadian and provincial laws. By giving them a contemporary reference point, the Charter may have freed aboriginal and treaty rights from a residual, subordinate status.

The question of what rights have been preserved or affirmed by sections 25 and 35 of the Constitutional Act, 1982 would have to await judicial interpretation were it not for section 37 of the same Act. This section mandated a constitutional conference within one year of 17 April 1982, the date of proclamation of the Act, at which conference matters directly affecting the Aboriginal Peoples were required to be considered, including "the rights of those peoples to be included in the Constitution of Canada." Indian, Inuit and Metis representatives were to be invited.

The inference to be drawn from this provision is that those who agreed to the "patriation package" acknowledged an obligation to specify aboriginal rights and possibly to entrench some or all of them but were unwilling to delay patriation to do it. The task is obviously complex and will take time, given the dispersal of the Aboriginal Peoples and the diversity of their positions, some of them conflicting on questions like the proper fate of Indian women who marry outside their cultural group.

This inference is confirmed by the fact that the most important point of agreement reached at the conference of March 1983 was the establishment of an continuing process. Another constitutional conference is to be held within a year of this first one, and a further two constitutional conferences within the eight years following the proclamation of the Canada Act (the British statute that gave the force of law to the Joint Resolution of the Senate and House of Commons that embodied the Constitution Act, 1982).

The first conference was apparently a major advance for Indians, Inuit and Metis, in that it established their right to participate in the process of establishing their places in the Canadian constitutional order and of indentifying and securing their fundamental rights, both as peoples and as individuals, within that order. The conference, broadcast live on national television, led to two important clarifications of the claims being made by Aboriginal Peoples. First, they want fair settlements of outstanding land claims, not title to all of Canada. Second, their claim to sovereignty is not one of independence from Canada, but rather one of self-government within the Canadian political system. For example, the Dene claim, if successful, would see a Dene territory established along the Mackenzie Valley, with a Dene-Metis government and system of local laws.

The conference of March 1983 produced the following accord, which was signed on behalf of all delegations except Quebec (that province was unwilling to take any step that could be seen as accepting the legitimacy of the Constitution Act, 1982):

(b) 1983 Constitutional Accord on Aboriginal Rights

Whereas pursuant to section 37 of the *Constitution Act, 1982*, a constitutional conference composed of the Prime Minister of Canada and the first ministers of the provinces was held on March 15 and 16, 1983, to which representatives of the aboriginal peoples of Canada and elected representatives of the governments of the Yukon Territory and the Northwest Territories were invited;

And whereas it was agreed at that conference that certain amendments to the *Constitution Act, 1982* would be sought in accordance with section 38 of that Act;

And whereas that conference had included in its agenda the following matters that directly affect the aboriginal peoples of Canada:

AGENDA

1. Charter of Rights of the Aboriginal Peoples (Expanded Part II)
   Including:
   — Preamble
   — Removal of "Existing", and Expansion of Section 35 to Include Recognition of Modern Treaties, Treaties signed Outside Canada and Before Confederation, and Specific Mention of "Aboriginal Title" Including the Rights of Aboriginal Peoples of Canada to a Land and Water Base (including Land base for the Metis)
   — Statement of the Particular Rights of Aboriginal Peoples
   — Statement of Principles
   — Equality
   — Enforcement
   — Interpretation
2. Amending Formula Revisions, Including:
   — Amendments on Aboriginal Matters not to be Subject to Provincial Opting Out (Section 42)
   — Consent Clause
3. Self-Government
4. Repeal of Section 42(1)(e) and (f)
5. Amendments to Part III, Including:
   — Equalization   )
   — Cost-Sharing   )   Resourcing of
   — Service Delivery   )   Aboriginal Governments
6. Ongoing Process, Including Further First Ministers Conferences and the Entrenchment of Necessary Mechanisms to Implement Rights

And whereas that conference was unable to complete its full consideration of all the agenda items;

And whereas it was agreed at that conference that future conferences be held at which those agenda items and other constitutional matters that directly affect the aboriginal peoples of Canada will be discussed;

NOW THEREFORE the Government of Canada and the provincial governments hereby agree as follows:

1. A constitutional conference composed of the Prime Minister of Canada and the first ministers of the provinces will be convened by the Prime Minister within one year after the completion of the constitutional conference held on March 15 and 16, 1983.

2. The conference convened under subsection (1) shall have included in its agenda those items that were not fully considered at the conference held on March 15 and 16, 1983, and the Prime Minister of Canada shall invite representatives of the aboriginal peoples of Canada to participate in the discussions on those items.

3. The Prime Minister of Canada shall invite elected representatives of the governments of the Yukon Territory and the Northwest Territories to participate in the discussions on any item on the agenda of the conference convened under subsection (1) that, in the opinion of the Prime Minister, directly affects the Yukon Territory and the Northwest Territories.

4. The Prime Minister of Canada will lay or cause to be laid before the Senate and House of Commons, and the first ministers of the provinces will lay or cause to be laid before their legislative assemblies, prior to December 31, 1983, a resolution in the form set out in the Schedule to authorize a proclamation issued by the Governor General under the Great Seal of Canada to amend the *Constitution Act, 1982*.

5. In preparation for the constitutional conferences contemplated by this Accord, meetings composed of ministers of the governments of Canada and the provinces, together with representatives of the aboriginal peoples of Canada and elected representatives of the governments of the Yukon Territory and the Northwest Territories shall be convened at least annually by the government of Canada.

6. Nothing in this Accord is intended to preclude, or substitute for, any bilateral or other discussions or agreements between governments and the various aboriginal peoples and, in particular, having regard to the authority of Parliament under Class 24 of section 91 of the *Constitution Act, 1867*, and to the special relationship that has existed and continues to exist between the Parliament and government of Canada and the peoples referred to in that Class, this Accord is made without prejudice to any bilateral process that has been or may be established between the government of Canada and those peoples.

7. Nothing in this Accord shall be construed so as to affect the interpretation of the Constitution of Canada.

SCHEDULE

Motion for a Resolution to authorize His Excellency the Governor General to issue a proclamation respecting amendments to the Constitution of Canada

Whereas the *Constitution Act, 1982* provides that an amendment to the Constitution of Canada may be made by proclamation issued by the

Governor General under the Great Seal of Canada where so authorized by resolutions of the Senate and House of Commons and resolutions of the legislative assemblies as provided for in sections 38 and 41 thereof;

And Whereas the Constitution of Canada, reflecting the country and Canadian society continues to develop and strengthen the rights and freedoms that it guarantees;

And Whereas, after a gradual transition of Canada from colonial status to the status of an independent and sovereign state, Canadians have, as of April 17, 1982, full authority to amend their Constitution in Canada;

And Whereas historically and equitably it is fitting that the early exercise of that full authority should relate to the rights and freedoms of the first inhabitants of Canada, the aboriginal peoples;

Now Therefore the [Senate] [House of Commons] [legislative assembly] resolves that His Excellency the Governor General be authorized to issue a proclamation under the Great Seal of Canada amending the Constitution of Canada as follows:

PROCLAMATION AMENDING THE CONSTITUTION OF CANADA

1.   Paragraph 25(b) of the *Constitution Act, 1982* is repealed and the following substituted therefore:

"(b)   any rights or freedoms that now exist by way of land claims agreements or may be so acquired."

2.   Section 35 of the *Constitution Act, 1982* is amended by adding thereto the following subsections:

"(3)   For greater certainty, in subsection (1) "treaty rights" includes rights that now exist by way of land claims agreements or may be so acquired."

"(4)   Notwithstanding any other provision of this Act, the aboriginal and treaty rights referred to in subsection (1) are guaranteed equally to male and female persons."

3.   The said Act is further amended by adding thereto, immediately after section 35 thereof, the following section

35.1   The government of Canada and the provincial governments are committed to the principle that, before any amendment is made to Class 24 of section 91 of the *Constitution Act, 1867*, to section 25 of this Act or to this Part,

(*a*)   a constitutional conference that includes in its agenda an item relating to the proposed amendment, composed of the Prime

Minister of Canada and the first ministers of the provinces, will be convened by the Prime Minister of Canada, and

(*b*) the Prime Minister of Canada will invite representatives of the aboriginal peoples of Canada to participate in the discussions on that item.''

4. The said Act is further amended by adding thereto immediately after section 37 thereof the following Part

PART IV.1

CONSTITUTIONAL CONFERENCES

17.1(1) In addition to the conference convened in March 1983, at least two constitutional conferences composed of the Prime Minister of Canada and the first ministers of the provinces shall be convened by the Prime Minister of Canada, the first within three years after April 17, 1982 and the second within five years after that date.

(2) Each conference convened under subsection (1) shall have included in its agenda constitutional matters that directly affect the aboriginal peoples of Canada, and the Prime Minister of Canada shall invite representatives of those peoples to participate in the discussions on those matters.

(3) The Prime Minister of Canada shall invite elected representatives of the governments of the Yukon Territory and the Northwest Territories to participate in the discussions on any item on the agenda of a conference convened under subsection (1) that, in the opinion of the Prime Minister, directly affects the Yukon Territory and the Northwest Territories.''

(4) Nothing in this section shall be construed so as to derogate from subsection 35(1).

5. The said Act is further amended by adding thereto, immediately after section 54 thereof, the following section:

"54.1 Part IV.1 and this section are repealed on April 18, 1987.''

6. The said Act is further amended by adding thereto the following section:

"6.1 A reference to the *Constitution Acts, 1867 to 1982* shall be deemed to include a reference to the *Constitution Amendment Proclamation, 1983*''.

7. This Proclamation may be cited as the *Constitution Amendment Proclamation, 1983*.

3. Who Is An Indian?

Section 2 of the *Indian Act* defines Indian to mean "a person who pursuant to this Act is registered as an Indian or is entitled to be registered as an Indian". That is a statutory definition enacted by Parliament, and since we are asking who is an Indian in order to determine the scope of Parliament's legislative authority, that definition provides no answer. It is for the courts, not the legislatures, to interpret the Constitution Act , 1867 in order to mark out the limits of legislative powers: *BC Power Corp. Ltd.* v. *BC Electric Co.* (1962) 34 DLR (2d) 196 (Sup. Ct. Can.).

The Supreme Court of Canada has decided, on a reference by the federal cabinet, that the Inuit come within the term "Indians" in S. 91(24): *Re Eskimos*, [1939] 2 DLR 417. The case is interesting for its study of usage of the word "Indian" in relevant documents at the time of Confederation and before. It is also the main basis of Chartier's conclusion, in an article entitled "Indian': An Analysis of the Term as Used in Section 91(24) of the British North America Act, 1867" (1978-79) 43 *Saskatchewan Law Review*, 37, that Metis are also included within the term.

If Metis come within s. 91(24), the question arises whether their exclusion from status under the Indian Act simply because they took scrip or land rather than treaty may be unconstitutional. As "Indians" they could claim, as a matter of constitutional law, a right to status or at least to be governed by federal law to some extent as long as they choose to adhere to traditional culture rather than assimilate. This need not imply the right to use reserves or even to be on a band list or the general list. Those are particular devices of existing Indian law. What Metis might successfully claim is that, as members of a cultural group committed to the legislative authority of Parliament, they are entitled to be governed by *some* federal laws so as not to be completely subject to provincial laws in matters of property, civil rights and the family.

The key factor may be the free choice of persons who are "Indians". If their status carries a right to be legally treated as part of a native community, then only they can surrender that right, and Parliament may not completely deny them, against their will, the corollary right to live under distinct laws enacted for Aboriginal Peoples. If this interpretation is applied to all of s. 91(24), it could lead to the conclusion that both Indian status and aboriginal title may be lost only through voluntary surrender.

The proposition can be tested against the case of Mrs Lavell, who lost her status under the Indian Act when she married a non-Indian. Section 12(1)(b) of the Act made this the legal effect of the marriage irrespective of Mrs Lavell's choice (*Lavell* v. *A-G Canada* (1974), 38 DLR (3d) 481). Assuming Mrs Lavell is a full-blooded Indian, there is no question she is an "Indian" within the meaning of s. 91(24). This brings her, as a matter of constitutional law, under the exclusive legislative authority of Parliament. As long as Parliament maintains special laws for Indians, Mrs Lavell and others like her are entitled to live under those laws. This does not mean that she must be treated in exactly the same way as all other Indians, but rather that as long as she chooses Indian culture and society she is entitled to be governed by those federal laws that enable Indians to remain Indians. The only plausible answer to this claim is that marrying outside the cultural group amounts to renunciation of the constitutional status of "Indian".

The challenge to s. 12(1)(b) of the Indian Act that was made in the *Lavell* case was based on a claim of repugnancy to the Canadian Bill of Rights. Neither before nor since *Lavell* has there been a test of that subsection on the ground that it is *ultra vires* because it amounts to a restrictive interpretation of the word "Indian" in s. 91(24), that is, an indirect attempt to amend the Constitution Act, 1867.

Apart from *Re Eskimos*, then, there has been no judicial interpretation to define who is an Indian within s. 91(24), nor is there any precedent on the question of whether Parliament can exclude persons who come within the definition from the application of all laws relating to Indians when their preference is to be governed by those laws. In the reference *Re Eskimos*, the Supreme Court of Canada had only historical usage to assist it. Now there has been added the definition of Aboriginal Peoples in s. 35 of the Constitution Act, 1892 as including Indian, Inuit and Metis peoples. While perhaps not conclusive, this is strong evidence that the word "Indian" in s. 91(24) of the Constitution Act, 1867 should be interpreted by judges, as of 1982, as a reference to all Aboriginal Peoples, including those of mixed blood whose primary communities adhere to native rather than European customs and loyalties.

This new constitutional definition of Aboriginal Peoples should be given greater weight than statutory definitions, at least for purposes of determining what persons are within the exclusive federal legislative competence conferred by s. 91(24) of the Constitution Act. Until now the judicial tendency has been to treat statutory definitions as conclusive on this question. For example, in *R. v. Laprise*, [1977] 3 WWR 379 a non-treaty Indian was denied the special exemption enacted for Indians in the Saskatchewan Game Act because the Indian Act distinguishes between "Indians" and "non-treaty Indians". Yet the issue in *Laprise* was what persons enjoy the privilege conferred by s. 12 of the Saskatchewan Natural Resources Act, 1930, which was given constitutional status by the Constitution Act, 1930. Since it was s. 91(24) of the Constitution Act, 1867 that gave the federal government authority to negotiate the agreement that was the substance of the Act, the relevant inquiry was the scope of 91(24) rather than the scope of the exemption enacted by the province of Saskatchewan in its game legislation. Does the definition of aboriginal peoples in s. 35 of the 1982 Act nullify the decision in *Laprise*?

The *Laprise* case, which raises the general question of whether statutory definitions can limit the rights of persons who are "Indians" within the meaning of s. 91(24), is the subject of a comment by A. Jordan in (1977) 1 *Canadian Native Law Reporter* 22.

4. What Laws Apply to Indians?

One option for Parliament in exercising its legislative powers under s. 91(24) was to enact a comprehensive code of distinct laws for Aboriginal Peoples so that Indians would never be subject to provincial laws. This is obviously an impractical alternative since Aboriginal Peoples are not peoples apart, living their entire lives in separate territories. Reserves are situated in provinces, and Indians themselves move freely about the country in places and activities having nothing to do with native culture. Separate federal laws governing Indians in these places and activities would probably by *ultra vires* anyway since their application to Indians would not by itself give them the character of "Indian" laws. Separate traffic laws for Indians on provincial roads, for example, would make no constitutional sense.

It follows that Indians have no immunity from provincial laws when they are in these situations. But does the absence of some federal Indian law on a subject necessarily mean that provincial law applies? Only if we assume that existing Indian law exhausts the possibilities of s. 91(24). Other conclusions are possible: that Parliament has deliberately left Indians free of legal regulation, or that Parliament has left the matter to tribal or customary law, the Indians' equivalent of the common law.

The difficulty is that, unique among the heads of legislative authority, s. 91(24) must have its scope determined largely by a legislative judgment as to how much distinctive Indian law is necessary or appropriate at any given time. If Parliament were to repeal the Indian Act and all other special laws for Indians, this would signal a judgment that distinctive laws are no longer needed, and as long as this judgment could be reasonably justified by the circumstances and did not represent abdication of responsibility, no court would be likely to question it.

So it turns out that the scope of s. 91(24) is largely a matter for Parliament rather than the courts, which explains why the Indian Act as it exists from time to time is taken by courts as a fair reflection of that scope.

The practical response to this federal question has been the enactment of s. 88 of the Indian Act, which states

> Subject to the terms of any treaty and any other Act of the Parliament of Canada, all laws of general application from time to time in force in any province are applicable to and in respect of Indians in the province, except to the extent that such laws are inconsistent with this Act or any order, rule, regulation or bylaw made thereunder, and except to the extent that such laws make provision for any matter for which provision is made by or under this Act.

Does s. 88 simply amount to a recognition of the constitutional fact that Indians are not immune from provincial laws? Is it an attempt by Parliament to fill the gaps in its code of Indians laws by referential incorporation of provincial laws? Or is it a mixture of the two?

The question came before the Supreme Court of Canada in the *Natural Parents* case, reproduced below.

(a) *Natural Parents* v. *Superintendent of Child Welfare, et al.* (1976), 60 DLR (3d) 148

LASKIN, C.J.C.: — The question in this appeal concerns the validity of an adoption order made in respect of a male Indian child in favour of a non-Indian couple who had provided a foster home for the child. The child's natural parents, who were registered members of a band under the *Indian Act*, R.S.C. 1970, c. I-6, he too being entitled to registration thereunder, objected to the adoption, but it was held at first instance that their consent should be dispensed with. No objection is taken to the regularity of the adoption proceedings, but a constitutional question was raised in respect of the *Adoption Act*, RSBC 1960, c. 4, and, more particularly, in respect of that Act as amended by the addition thereto of s. 10(4a) by 1973 (B.C.) (2nd Sess.), c. 95, s. 1. Connected to this question is the effect of s. 88 of the *Indian Act*.

The Judge at first instance, although satisfied on the merits that an adoption order should be made without the consent of the natural parents, held that there was an inconsistency between the *Adoption Act* and the *Indian Act* which precluded such an order. In his opinion, the *Indian Act* clothed those within its terms with a certain status from which alone certain rights arose, and that status would be obliterated by the operation of the *Adoption Act*. The British Columbia Court of Appeal was unanimously of the opinion that Indian status survived despite adoption. It held that the *Adoption Act*, as a provincial statute of general application, applied to the adoption of Indian children, and was blunted only to the extent of inconsistency with the *Indian Act*. The addition of s. 10(4a) to the *Adoption Act*, between the date of the judgment at first instance and the hearing of the appeal, reinforced the view that there was no impingement on matters within the *Indian Act*. The *Indian Act* would prevail if there was an inconsistency but that was no reason to hold that the *Adoption Act* could not apply at all to Indians.

The British Columbia Court of Appeal also reached and rejected an issue as to the application of the *Canadian Bill of Rights* by holding (1) that s. 88 of the *Indian Act* did not referentially incorporate the *Adoption Act* so as to make it federal legislation for the purposes of the *Canadian Bill of Rights*, and (2) that even if there was referential incorporation, there was no violation of the *Canadian Bill of Rights*, either by way of discrimination on account of race or by way of inequality before the law, especially in the light of the concession by counsel for the natural parents that the *Indian Act* was valid federal legislation that did not in its relevant terms contravene the *Canadian Bill of Rights*. In the result, the British Columbia Court of Appeal concluded that the *Adoption Act*, applied to Indians, subject to the provisions of the *Indian Act*, and that an order of adoption should be made.

The legislative provisions particularly germane to the disposition of this appeal are s. 10 of the *Adoption Act*, as amended, and s. 88 of the *Indian Act*, and they read as follows:

Adoption Act, s. 10, as amended

10(1)   For all purposes an adopted child becomes upon adoption the child of the adopting parent, and the adopting parent becomes the parent of the child, as if the child had been born to that parent in lawful wedlock.

(2)   For all purposes an adopted child ceases upon adoption to be the child of his existing parents (whether his natural parents or his adopting parents under a previous adoption), and the existing parents of the adopted child cease to be his parents.

(3)   The relationship to one another of all persons (whether the adopted person, the adopting parents, the natural parents, or any other persons) shall be determined in accordance with subsections (1) and (2).

(4)   Subsections (2) and (3) do not apply, for the purposes of the laws relating to incest and to the prohibited degrees of marriage, to remove any persons from a relationship in consanguinity which, but for this section, would have existed between them.

(4a)   The status, rights, privileges, disabilities, and limitations of an adopted Indian person acquired as an Indian under the *Indian Act* (Canada) or under any other Act or law are not affected by this section.

(5)   This section is to be read subject to the provisions of any Act which distinguishes in any way between persons related by adoption and persons not so related.

(6)   This section does not apply to the will of a testator dying before or to any other instrument made before the seventeenth day of April, 1920.

(7)   This section applies to adoptions made by the Court or by the Provincial Secretary under legislation heretofore in force.

(8)   For the purpose of this section, "child" includes a person of any age, whether married or unmarried [enacted 1973, c. 2, s. 3]

Indian Act, s. 88

> 88. Subject to the terms of any treaty and any other Act of the Parliament of Canada, all laws of general application from time to time in force in any province are applicable to and in respect of Indians in the province, except to the extent that such laws are inconsistent with this Act or any order, rule, regulation or by-law made thereunder, and except to the extent that such laws make provision for any matter for which provision is made by or under this Act.

I refer also to s. 2(1) of the *Indian Act* in which "child" is defined to include "a legally adopted Indian child" (in the French version "un enfant indien légalement adopté") and s. 48(16) defining "child", for the purpose of that section (being a section respecting distribution of property on an intestacy), to include "a legally adopted child and a child adopted in accordance with Indian custom". These provisions show that adoption is within the scope of the Act, albeit that the general definition in s. 2 is confined to adoption of an Indian child and, in my view, in any context involving parental relationship it would be limited to an Indian child of Indian parents.

The submissions of the appellants against the validity of the adoption order are based on a series of related propositions which I may summarize as follows. The *Indian Act*, which, as enacted in its present form in 1951 by 1951 (Can.), c. 29, and which introduced at that time the Indian register and as well s. 88, makes the original family tie the essence of Indian status and keeps the child in that status (at least until enfranchisement as provided in s. 109). Since adoption under the *Adoption Act* by non-Indian persons would obliterate the family ties and hence destroy the status, the Act cannot of its own force apply to status Indians and, indeed, would be an encroachment on federal legislative power in relation to Indians under s. 91(24) of the *British North America Act, 1867*. If the provincial *Adoption Act* applies at all, it can only apply through referential incorporation under s. 88 of the *Indian Act*, but it cannot be squared with s. 88 because of irreconcilable inconsistency. However, if it does so apply and can operate consistently to some degree, this can only be if it is restricted to the adoption of a status Indian child by status Indians. Appellants went on to contend that if there was no such limitation to the force of the *Adoption Act*, it would run foul of the *Canadian Bill of Rights* because there would be discrimination on account of race and inequality before the law.

The respondents, whose counsel also appeared for the Attorney-General of British Columbia, were supported in this appeal by the Attorney-General of Canada and the Attorneys-General of Saskatchewan, Ontario and Alberta. The main thrust of their submissions was to assert that the *Adoption Act* applied *ex proprio vigore* to the adoption of Indian children and hence no question arose under the *Canadian Bill of Rights*. An alternative submission, made particularly by the respondents' counsel, was that even if the *Adoption Act* applied through referential incorporation, there was nothing inconsistent in giving force to that Act and still recognizing the survival of the Indian status of the adopted child under the *Indian Act*.

This Court did not call upon the respondents or the intervenors to make submissions on the *Canadian Bill of Rights*, being of the opinion that, on the assumption that the *Adoption Act*, by referential incorporation, is federal legislation, there was nothing in it to bring any of the prescriptions of the *Canadian Bill of Rights* into play. I would in this connection adopt the remarks of the British Columbia Court of Appeal on this issue.

I do not, however, agree with the British Columbia Court of Appeal that there was no referential incorporation in this case. Whether there was or was not depends not only on the meaning and scope of the phrase "all laws of general application from time to time in force in any province" in s. 88 of the *Indian Act*, but, as well and priminarily, on the relation between so-called provincial laws of general application and federal legislative powers in relation to matters that, absent federal legislation, are alleged to be governed by those provincial laws in some of their aspects. In this connection I draw attention to the judgment of this Court in *R. v. George* (1966), 55 DLR (2d) 386 at pp. 397-8, [1966] SCR 267 at pp. 280-1, [1966] 3 CCC 137, in which Martland, J., pointed out that the now s. 88 (it was then s. 87) in speaking of "laws of general application from time to time in force in any province" referred to "those rules of law in a Province which are provincial in scope", including laws of England adopted as part of provincial law.

There was no challenge in this Court to the general and long-established proposition found in *Union Colliery Co. of British Columbia, Ltd. v. Bryden*, [1899] AC 580 at p. 588, that:

> The abstinence of the Dominion Parliament from legislating to the full limit of its powers, could not have the effect of transferring to any provincial legislature the legislative power which had been assigned to the Dominion by s. 91 of the Act of 1867.

It cannot be said therefore that because a provincial statute is general in its operation, in the sense that its terms are not expressly restricted to matters within provincial competence, it may embrace matters within exclusive federal competence. Thus, to take an example, it has been held by this Court that general mechanics' lien legislation of a Province could not be enforced against the property of an interprovincial pipe line: *Campbell-Bennett Ltd.* v. *Comstock Midwestern Ltd. et al.*, [1954] 3 DLR 481, [1954] SCR 207, 71 CRTC 291. Again, provincial minimum wage legislation was held inapplicable to the employees of an interprovincial communications enterprise: see *Commission du Salaire Minimum* v. *Bell Telephone Co. of Canada* (1966), 59 DLR (2d) 145, [1966] SCR 767, and, similarly, inapplicable to employees of a local contract postmaster: see *Reference re Minimum Wage Act of Saskatchewan*, [1948] 3 DLR 801, 91 CCC 366, [1948] SCR 248. This is because to construe the provincial legislation to embrace such activities would have it encroaching on an exclusive federal legislative area. On the other hand, provincial hours of work legislation was held applicable to employees of a hotel owned and operated by a railway company but not as an integral part of its transportation system: see *CPR* v. *A-G BC et al.*, [1950] 1 DLR 721, [1950] AC 122, [1950] 1 WWR 220 *sub nom. Reference re Application of Hours of Work Act (BC), etc.*

Ex facie, and apart from the amendment of 1973 introducing s. 10(4a), the *Adoption Act* did not purport to extend to areas of exclusive federal competence, *e.g.*, Indians. It could only embrace them if the operation of the Act did not deal with what was integral to that head of federal legislative power, there being no express federal legislation respecting adoption of Indians. It appears to me to be unquestionable that for the provincial *Adoption Act* to apply to the adoption of Indian children of registered Indians, who could be compelled thereunder to surrender them to adopting non-Indian parents, would be to touch "Indianness", to strike at a relationship integral to a matter outside of provincial competence. This is entirely apart from the question whether, if referentially incorporated, the *Adoption Act* could have any force in the face of various provisions of the *Indian Act*, securing certain benefits for Indians.

Counsel for the respondents cited a number of cases holding Indians to be subject to provincial legislation. Among them was *R.* v. *Hill* (1907), 15 OLR 406, and *R.* v. *Martin* (1917), 39 DLR 635, 41 OLR 79. These, and other like cases, are simply illustrative of the amenability of Indians off their reservations to provincial regulatory legislation, legislation which, like traffic legislation, does not touch their "Indianness". Such provincial legislation is of a different class than adoption legislation which would, if applicable as provincial legislation *simpliciter*, constitute a serious intrusion into the Indian family relationship. It is difficult to conceive what would be left of exclusive federal power in relation to Indians if such provincial legislation was held to apply to Indians. Certainly, if it was applicable because of its so-called general application, it would be equally applicable by expressly embracing Indians. Excusive federal authority would then be limited to a registration system and to regulation of life on a reserve.

The fallacy in the position of the respondents in this case and, indeed, in that of all the intervenors, including the Attorney-General of Canada, is in the attribution of some special force or special effect to a provincial law by calling it a "provincial law of general application", as if this phrase was self-fulfilling if not also self-revealing. Nothing, however, accretes to provincial legislative power by the generalization of the language of provincial legislation if it does not constitutionally belong there.

This is, no doubt, overly obvious, but it is compelled by the nature of the submissions made in this case by the respondents and the intervenors. If the phrase "provincial laws of general application" has any source, it is in the "federal company" cases, involving the relationship of general companies legislation of a Province to federally incorporated companies. Thus, in *John Deer Plow Co.* v. *Wharton* (1914), 18 DLR 353 at p. 362, [1915] AC 330 at pp. 342-3, 7 WWR 635, 706, Viscount Haldan, LC, commented as follows:

> It is true that even when a company has been incorporated by the Dominion Government with powers to trade, it is not the less subject to provincial laws of general application enacted under the powers conferred by sec. 92.

The history of this matter is well-known because from the very beginning of its concern with the *British North America Act, 1867* the Privy Council drew a distinction between authority to incorporate companies and to prescribe their powers and their corporate structure and the internal relationship to shareholders and directors and authority to regulate the activities or enterprises in which the companies are engaged. It was in this connection that Lord Haldane made the observation above-quoted. Yet in the very case in which he made it, the Privy Council concluded that it was not open to a Province under its general companies legislation to require a licence of a federally incorporated company as a condition of carrying on business *qua* company because this would in effect prevent it from exercising the powers with which it was endowed by federal authority. *A-G Man* v. *A-G Can.*, [1929] 1 DLR 369, [1929] AC 260, [1929] 1 WWR 136, and *Lymburn et al.* v. *Mayland et al.*, [1932] 2 DLR 6, [1932] AC 318, 57 CCC 311, are two contrasting cases in which the principle of *John Deere Plow*, seen in later cases like *Great West Saddlery Co.* v. *The King* (1921), 58 DLR 1, [1921] 2 AC 91, [1921] 1 WWR 1034, was applied to provincial legislation which was alleged to put federally incorporated companies at the mercy of the Province in respect of the sale of their shares. The particular results in those two cases are of no direct relevance here, but simply illustrate the care that must be taken in the analysis of the issues and of the provincial legislation before subjecting federally incorporated companies to general provincial companies legislation. I cannot believe that any less care should be taken in analysis before subjecting Indians, coming as they do within a specific head of exclusive federal jurisdiction, to general provincial legislation, unless the inclusion of Indians within the scope of the provincial legislation touches them as ordinary persons and in a way that does not intrude on their Indian character or their Indian identity and relationship.

I would add that to give a primary effect to so-called "provincial laws of general application", in the face of s. 88 of the *Indian Act*, is to fall into the same trap that was noted by Judson J., in *A-G Can.* v. *Nykorak* (1962), 33 DLR (2d) 373, [1962] SCR 331, 37 WWR 660. The fact is that we are concerned here with a federal enactment which would be robbed of any meaning if the respondents' and intervenors' submissions went as far as they appeared to carry them. When s. 88 refers to "all laws of general application from time to time in force in any province" it cannot be assumed to have legislated a nullity but, rather, to have in mind provincial legislation which, *per se*, would not apply to Indians under the *Indian Act* unless given force by federal reference.

I am fully aware of the contention that it is enough to give force to the several opening provisions of s. 88, which, respectively, make the "provincial" reference subject to the terms of any treaty and any other federal Act and subject also to inconsistency with the *Indian Act* and orders, rules, regulations or by-laws thereunder. That contention would have it that s. 88 is otherwise declaratory. On this view, however, it is wholly declaratory save perhaps in its reference to "the terms of any treaty", a strange reason, in my view, to explain all the other provisions of s. 88. I think too that the concluding words of s. 88, "except to the extent that such laws make provision for any matter for which provision is made by or under this Act" indicate clearly that Parliament is indeed effecting incorporation by reference. To hold otherwise would be to reject the proposition quoted earlier from the *Union Colliery Co.* case and to treat the distribution of legislative powers as being a distribution of concurrent powers.

In the view I take, I find it immaterial that the provincial Legislature introduced s. 10(4a) into the *Adoption Act*. It may properly be considered as an abjuring provision, but there is the point, which was raised during the hearing, that if the Province does indeed claim that its Act applies to interfere in Indian family relationships, s. 10(4a) may be constitutionally suspect. I do not find it necessary to pursue this point.

Treating the *Adoption Act* as referentially incorporated, the central question in this case becomes one of the extent to which that Act is inconsistent with the *Indian Act*. Certainly, there would be no problem of consistency or inconsistency if, as the appellants urge, the incorporation was limited to adoption of Indian children by Indians. Whether it should be so limited depends on the effect of adoption under the incorporated Act upon the position of an Indian child under the *Indian Act*. For this purpose, I am not concerned with the actual administration of the incorporated legislation, that is with whether a case for adoption of the particular child by the particular applicants is made out and whether the case is one where the consent of the natural parents should be dispensed with. Assumptions to these ends must be made to focus on the issue of consistency.

In view of the effect of s. 10 of the *Adoption Act* (as an incorporated provision in the *Indian Act*) upon parentage, is it open to say that notwithstanding adoption by non-Indians the Indian child still has entitlement to be or to continue to be registered as an Indian under s. 11 of the *Indian Act*? This, in my view, is the key provision going to consistency or inconsistency, since "Indian" is defined in the *Indian Act* as "a person who pursuant to this Act is registered as an Indian or is entitled to be registered as an Indian". Section 11, so far as relevant, reads as folllws:

11(1)   Subject to section 12, a person is entitled to be registered if that person

(*a*) on the 26th day of May 1874 was, for the purposes of *An Act providing for the organization of the Department of the Secretary of State of Canada, and for the management of Indian and Ordinance Lands*, being chapter 42 of the Statutes of Canada, 1868, as amended by section 6 of chapter 6 of the Statutes of Canada, 1869, and section 8 of chapter 21 of the Statutes of Canada, 1874, considered to be entitled to hold, use or enjoy the lands and other immovable property belonging to or appropriated to the use of the various tribes, bands or bodies of Indians in Canada;

(*b*) is a member of a band

(i) for whose use and benefit, in common, lands have been set apart or since the 26th day of May 1874, have been agreed by treaty to be set apart, or

(ii) that has been declared by the Governor in Council to be a band for the purposes of this Act;

(*c*) is a male person who is a direct descendant in the male line of a male person described in paragraph (*a*) or (*b*)

(*d*) is the legitimate child of

(i) a male person described in paragraph (*a*) or (*b*), or

(ii) a person described in paragraph (*c*);

I may say here that s. 12 of the *Indian Act*, mentioned in the opening words of s. 11 above, does not have any bearing here.

It has not been contested that the Indian child in this case comes within s. 11(1)(*d*) unless the effect of an adoption order would be to remove him from that classification. Section 10(2) of the *Adoption Act*, previously quoted, apeaks of a cessation, upon adoption of the relationship of the child to his natural parents and of the natural parents to the child "for all purposes". These quoted words do not destroy entitlement to registration under s. 11(1)(*d*) of the *Indian Act*. They would equally be involved if the adoption of the Indian child was by Indian adopting parents, and yet counsel for the appellants did not urge that there was complete inconsistency in that situation. There may, indeed, be some situations under the *Indian Act* with which an adoption order and the effect given to it may not be squared. That, however, should not exclude adoption *per se* through the incorporating effect of s. 88, since adoption legislation is ruled out only to the extent that it is inconsistent.

I do not find that on the key issue of registrability there is inconsistency between the *Adoption Act* and the *Indian Act*. I would be loathe to give such a wide construction (and it is construction only with which we are here concerned) to the incorporated s. 10(2) of the *Adoption Act* as to create incompatibility with the continuing effect of s. 11(1)(*d*) of the *Indian Act*. This would result in excluding Indian children from possible adoption (save perhaps by Indian custom as mentioned in s. 48(16)) outside of the Indian community, a result to which I would not come unless clearly compelled to do so by unambiguous legislation.

For these reasons, differing somewhat from those of the British Columbia Court of Appeal, I would dismiss the appeal. This is not a case for costs in any Court.

MARTLAND, J:

[After setting out the relevant provisions of the BC Adoption Act and the findings of fact set out in the judgment at trial, Martland J dealt with the question of the proper legal basis for applying provincial adoption laws to Indian children.]

. . . the first question which requires consideration is as to whether the adoption which is under consideration here could properly be authorized by provincial legislation. There is no question as to the power of a provincial Legislature to legislate concerning the subject-matter of adoption. There is also no question that the *Adoption Act* is a statute of general application applying to all residents of British Columbia. It did not purport to affect Indians, *qua* Indians, in a manner different from its effect on all other persons in the Province. The only reference in the Act to Indians, as such, appears in s. 10(4a), enacted in 1973 [2nd Sess., c. 95, s. 1], which sought to provide that s. 10 of the Act should not affect the status of an adopted Indian person acquired as an Indian under the *Indian Act*. It is also clear that the *Indian Act* contains no procedure of its own for the adoption of Indian children.

The only references to adoption in that Act are:

2(1)   In this Act

. . . . .

"child" includes a legally adopted Indian child;

. . . . .

DISTRIBUTION OF PROPERTY ON INTESTACY
48(16)   In this section "child" includes a legally adopted child and a child adopted in accordance with Indian custom.

No other provision is made in this Act with regard to the legal effect or consequences of adoption.

It is contended, however, that, notwithstanding the absence of federal legislation on the subject, to the extent that the *Adoption Act* might purport to govern the adoption of Indian children it would constitute an encroachment upon the exclusive federal jurisdiction, under s. 91(24) of the *British North America Act, 1867*, to legislate on the subject of "Indians, and Lands reserved for the Indians".

Subsection (24) of s. 91 is unlike the other subsections of that section (other than s-s. (25)) in that it confers legislative jurisdiction on the Parliament of Canada in relation to a specified group of people. The ambit of that authority is uncertain, in that it has not been positively defined by the Courts. Within certain limits this includes the power to define Indian status, and this power has been exercised by Parliament by the enactment of the *Indian Act*. In my opinion it does not mean that Parliament alone can enact legislation which may affect Indians. It does not mean that Indians are totally exempted from the application of provincial laws. A number of cases dealing with the application of provincial laws to Indians were mentioned in the judgment of this Court to *Cardinal* v. *A-G Alta.* (1973), 40 DLR (3d) 553, 13 CCC (2d) 1, [1974] SCR 695, [1973] 6 WWR 205. The extent to which provincial legislation could apply to Indians was stated to be that the legislation must be within the authority of s. 92 of the *British North America Act, 1867* and that the legislation must not be enacted in relation to Indians. Such legislation, generally applicable throughout the Province, could affect Indians.

In the present case we have provincial social legislation, applicable throughout British Columbia, dealing with the subject of the adoption of children. Is the scope of s. 91(24) such that it makes it impossible for an Indian child to be adopted under the provisions of the *Adoption Act*? In support of the proposition that s-s. (24) has that effect, it is argued that the *Adoption Act* can compel Indian parents to surrender their child to non-Indian parents. But, under the provision of the *Adoption Act*, no Indian child could be adopted by anyone without the parents' consent unless the child had been made a permanent ward of the Superintendent of Child Welfare, or of a children's aid society, or unless consent of the parents is dispensed with because the child has been abandoned or deserted, or because of failure to contribute to the child's support, or because the parent is a person whose consent, in the opinion of the Court, in all the circumstances of the case, ought to be dispensed with.

These exceptions to the general rule requiring the consent of a child's natural parents to an adoption are all cases in which the child is in need of protection.

The *Protection of Children Act*, RSBC 1960, c. 303, as amended, makes provision for the committal of children in need of protection to the custody of the Superintendent of Child Welfare or to a children's aid society, and for the placement of such children in a foster home. The Indian child in the present case was a ward of the Superintendent of Child Welfare and had been placed in the custody of the petitioners on an official foster home basis.

Both the *Protection of Children Act* and the Adoption Act are designed for the protection, custody and care of children in the Province of British Columbia. In my opinion the power given to Parliament, under s. 91(24), to legislate on the subject-matter of "Indians, and Lands reserved for the Indians" does not make such legislation inapplicable to Indian children, in the absence of federal legislation dealing with the matter, merely because the designated authorities under those statutes might consider it appropriate, in certain circumstances, in the child's interest, to entrust custody of such child to a foster home, or to parents by adoption, who were not themselves Indians. I do not interpret s. 91(24) as manifesting an intention to maintain a segregation of Indians from the rest of the community in matters of this kind, and, accordingly, it is my view that the application of the *Adoption Act* to Indian children will only be prevented if Parliament, in the exercise of its powers under that subsection, has legislated in a manner which would preclude its application.

There have been cases in which it has been held that some provincial legislation of general application would not be applicable to a corporation or institution subject to exclusive federal control. In *Campbell-Bennett Ltd.* v. *Comstock Midwestern Ltd. et al.*, [1954] 3

DLR 481, [1954] SCR 207, 71 CRTC 291, it was held that a federally incorporated company which was incorporated for the purpose of transporting oil by means of interprovincial and international pipe lines, and thus was a work or undertaking within the exclusive jurisdiction of Parliament, was not subject to a mechanics' lien registered under provincial legislation, because such legislation would permit the sale of the undertaking piecemeal and thus nullify the purpose for which it was incorporated.

The case of *Commissioners du Salaire Minimum* v. *Bell Telephone Co. of Canada* (1966), 59 DLR (2d) 145, [1966] SCR 767, held that a company which had been declared to be a work for the general advantage of Canada was not subject to having its employer-employees relationships affected by a provincial minimum wage statute. Similarly, in *Reference re Minimum Wage Act of Saskatchewan*, [1948] 3 DLR 801, 91 CCC 366, [1948] SCR 248, it was decided that provincial minimum wage requirements would be inapplicable to an employee who was a part of the postal service.

McKay v. *The Queen* (1965), 53 DLR (2d) 532, [1965] SCR 798, held that a municipal zoning regulation governing the erection of signs on residential properties could not preclude the erection of a sign to support a candidate in a federal election.

Each of these cases was concerned with a particular statute which had the effect of restricting an enterprise or activity within exclusive federal jurisdiction. The *Adoption Act* is not legislation of this kind. It does not restrict the rights of Indians. It makes it possible for Indian children to have the same right to become adopted as that of all other children in the Province. If the contention of the appellants were to prevail it would mean that the parents of an Indian child who desired that the child be adopted by non-Indian adoptive parents would not be able to accomplish that end under the provisions of the provincial legislation, despite their consent.

I do not find any conflict between the provisions of the *Adoption Act* and the *Indian Act*. I agree with the view expressed in the Court of Appeal that the words "for all purposes" in s-ss. (1) and (2) of s. 10 of the *Adoption Act* must be taken to refer to all purposes within the competence of the British Columbia Legislature. Section 10, even prior to the enactment of s-s. (4a), did not purport to deprive the child of any status or rights which he possessed under the *Indian Act* at the time of his adoption, and it is clear that no provincial legislation could deprive him of such rights.

With respect to the constitutional validity of s-s. (4a) of s. 10 of the *Adoption Act*, it is my view that the purpose of this amendment to s. 10 was merely to make it clear that the Legislature did not intend that the *Adoption Act* should be construed as encroaching upon a legislative area which was beyond its competence. If it purported to have any effect beyond that it would be *ultra vires* of the Legislature as being legislation in relation to Indians. I do not propose to deal with the matter further, because the views which I have so far expressed are not in any way based upon s-s. (4a).

I now propose to consider the impact of s. 88 of the *Indian Act* upon the circumstances of this case. I do not regard s. 88 as intending to incorporate, as part of federal legislation in respect of Indians, all provincial laws of general application. To adopt this view would be to say that, in respect of one class of persons, *i.e.*, Indians, only federal law should apply to them, and subject to federal enforcement. It would mean that Parliament, by enacting s. 88, had caused valid provincial legislation, properly applicable to Indians, to cease to have effect as provincial legislation, by incorporating it as federal legislation into the *Indian Act*. The wording of s. 88 does not purport to incorporate the laws of each Province into the *Indian Act* so as to make them a matter of federal legislation. The section is a statement of the extent to which provincial laws apply to Indians. I agree with the view expressed by the Court of Appeal with respect to the meaning of this section, which is cited earlier in these reasons.

For the foregoing reasons, I would dispose of this appeal in the manner proposed by the Chief Justice.

Justices Ritchie, Pigeon and de Grandpré agreed with Martland's view that there was no referential incorporation of provincial law through section 88 and that the law of British Columbia applied of its own force. Ritchie, J, in a separate judgment, gave this clear explanation of his opinion:

> As will hereafter appear, I am satisfied that the *Adoption Act* is not a statute enacted in relation to Indians "under the *Indian Act*" and that its provisions, including those of s. 10, do not affect the "status, rights, privileges, disabilities, limitations . . . acquired as an Indian under the *Indian Act*". The *Adoption Act* only applies to Indians by reason of their character as citizens of the Province of British Columbia and I can find no conflict between that statute and the *Indian Act*.

Justices Judson, Spence and Dickson concurred with Chief Justice Laskin.

Beetz, J, in a separate judgment, concluded that he need not decide whether the provincial law applied on its own or by virtue of referential incorporation. In his opinion, the absence of adoption laws in the Indian Act left provincial law as the only option. He went so far as to state that the provincial law would apply even if the result were loss of Indian status for the adopted child, the silence of the Indian Act on adoption giving no basis for repugnancy. He concluded by holding *ultra vires* s. 10(4a) of the BC Adoption Act on the ground that it is exclusively for Parliament to determine the effects of adoption on the status, rights, privileges, disabilities and limitations acquired by an Indian under the Indian Act.

The appeal was therefore dismissed and the adoption of the Indian child permitted to go ahead.

The dominant view in the Supreme Court — that provincial laws apply of their own force without the need of federal adoption as laws of Canada — denies federal status to any feature of native culture. No native interests are held subject to being affected only by federal law. Thus, in *Kruger & Manuel* v. *The Queen* (1977) 75 DLR (3d) 434, the Supreme Court allowed aboriginal hunting rights to be curtailed by provincial game laws. In the course of delivering the unanimous judgment of the Court, Mr Justice Dickson commented as follows on s. 88 of the *Indian Act*:

II
Referential incorporation

There is in the legal literature a juridical controversy respecting whether s. 88 referentially incorporates provincial laws of general application or whether such laws apply to Indians *ex proprio vigore*. The issue was considered by this Court in *Natural Parents* v. *Superintendent of Child Welfare et al.* (1975), 60 DLR (3d) 148, [1976] 2 SCR 751, [1976] 1 WWR 699. The question in that appeal concerned the validity of an adoption order made in respect of a male Indian child in favour of a non-Indian couple. The Chief Justice (Judson, Spence and Dickson, JJ, concurring, de Grandpré, J., concurring in the result) rejected the submission that the *Adoption Act*, RSBC 1960, c. 4, applied *ex proprio vigore* to the adoption of Indian children and, treating the *Adoption Act* as referentially incorporated, considered whether and to what extent that Act was inconsistent with the *Indian Act*. Mr Justice Martland (with whom Pigeon, J, concurred) was of the opinion that the ambit of authority conferred on the Parliament of Canada by s. 91(24) to legislate on the subject of "Indians and Lands reserved for the Indians" was not such that Parliament alone could enact legislation which might affect Indians: it was not such that Indians were totally exempted from the application of provincial laws. After referring to the *Cardinal* case, Mr Justice Martland said, p. 163:

> The extent to which provincial legislation could apply to Indians was stated to be that the legislation must be within the authority of s. 92 of the *British North America Act, 1867* and that the legislation must not be enacted in relation to Indians. Such legislation, generally applicable throughout the Province, could affect Indians.

Mr Justice Ritchie, considering s. 88, said, p. 170:

> In my view, when the Parliament of Canada passed the *Indian Act* it was concerned with the preservation of the special status of Indians

and with their rights to Indian lands, but it was made plain by s. 88 that Indians were to be governed by the laws of their Province of residence except to the extent that such laws are inconsistent with the *Indian Act* or relate to any matter for which provision is made under that Act.

Mr Justice Beetz did not find it necessary to express an opinion on the purview of s. 88 of the *Indian Act*. In the result four members of the Court, less than a majority, adopted the position that the section is a referential incorporation of provincial legislation which takes effect under the section as federal legislation.

On either view of this issue present appellants must fail. If the provisions of the *Wildlife Act* are referentially incorporated by s. 88 of the *Indian Act*, appellants, in order to succeed, would have the burden of demonstrating inconsistency or duplication with the *Indian Act* or any order, Rule, Regulation or by-law made thereunder. That burden has not been discharged and, having regard to the terms of the *Wildlife Act*, manifestly could not have been discharged. Accordingly, such provisions take effect as federal legislation in accordance with their terms. Assuming, without deciding, that the theory of aboriginal title as elaborated by Hall, J, in *Calder et al.* v. *A-G BC* (1973), 34 DLR (3d) 145, [1973] SCR 313, [1973] 4 WWR 1, is available in respect of present appellants it has been conclusively decided that such title, as any other, is subject to Regulations imposed by validly enacted federal laws: *Noll Derriksan* v. *The Queen* (a recent decision of this Court not yet reported). That was also the result in *R.* v. *George*, [1966] 3 CCC 137, 55 DLR (2d) 386, [1966] SCR 267; *Daniels* v. *The Queen*, [1969] 1 CCC 299, 2 DLR (3d) 1, [1968] SCR 517, and *Sikyea* v. *The Queen*, [1965] 2 CCC 129, 50 DLR (2d) 80, [1964] SCR 642. The latter two cases are instructive as the hunting rights there stood on stronger ground in that they were protected, in the case of *Sikyea*, by treaty, and in *Daniels'* case by the Manitoba Natural Resources Agreement. In neither case did the protection prevail against the federal *Migratory Birds Convention Act*, RSC 1952, c. 179.

If s. 88 does not referentially incorporate the *Wildlife Act*, the only question at issue is whether the Act is a law of general application. Since that proposition has not been here negatived, the enactment would apply to Indians *ex proprio vigore*. It is, therefore, immaterial to the present appeals whether s. 88 takes effect by way of referential incorporation or not. In either case, these appeals must fail.

One would think that aboriginal rights are among the matters that certainly come within the exclusive authority of the Parliament of Canada by reason of s. 91(24), requiring that the corresponding limit on provincial authority be read down, making the BC Wildlife Act not applicable to the exercise of aboriginal hunting rights, *unless* s. 88 is a valid adoption by Parliament of that Act as part of federal Indian law.

The acceptance of s. 88 as providing the test for applicability of provincial laws avoids the constitutional question of whether a province can limit aboriginal rights and suggests that if the Court intends to preserve any exclusive character for s. 91(24), it will have to accept the referential incorporation theory of s. 88. This leads to the further question of whether such an uncritical, wholesale adoption of provincial laws amounts to an unconstitutional delegation of legislative power to the provinces or, alternatively, is a serious infringement of Indians' right to equality before the law by way of consistent national standards governing the exercise of aboriginal rights. In any case, the decision in *Kruger and Manuel* may now be trumped by ss. 37 and 52 of the Constitution Act, 1982.

5. What Are "Lands Reserved for the Indians" and What Laws Apply on Those Lands?

The theory that reserves under the *Indian Act* are enclaves of federal territory where provincial laws cannot apply at all was rejected by a majority in the Supreme Court of Canada in *Cardinal* v. *A-G Alberta* (1974), 40 DLR (3d), 553. Cardinal was convicted of selling moose meat contrary to the Alberta Wildlife Act; the Supreme Court of Canada upheld his conviction even though he was an "Indian" and the sale took place on a reserve. The important point of the case is that s. 91(24) confers no proprietary rights, just legislative authority, and what it reserves to Parliament is the making of laws that relate to reserved lands. That is, various kinds of land laws.

The effect of *Cardinal* is that the applicability of provincial laws to Indians that was settled by the *Natural Parents* case is not affected in principle by whether an Indian is on or off a reserve. It would, however, be affected in fact because of the much greater number of federal Indian laws in force on a reserve than elsewhere in a province.

Cardinal resolved only the question of what laws apply on a reserve as defined by the Indian Act. It was common ground among the judges in that case that provincial laws cannot apply *to* Indian reserves. If they did, they would obviously become to that extent laws in relation to lands reserved for the Indians. Provincial land and land-use laws are therefore taken by judges not to be intended to apply to reserves. This is simply an application of the basic judicial presumption in favour of validity of legislation. The really complex questions are just starting to emerge with respect to the broader category of "lands reserved for the Indians" used in s. 91(24) to define the area of exclusive federal competence.

Until quite recently, the law was thought to be settled by the decision in *St Catharine's Milling and Lumber Company* v. *The Queen* (1889), 14 AC 46, in the following passage from Lord Watson's judgment:

The enactments of sect. 109 are, in the opinion of their Lordships, sufficient to give to each Province, subject to the administration and control of its own Legislature, the entire beneficial interest of the Crown in all lands within its boundaries, which at the time of the union were vested in the Crown, with the exception of such lands as the Dominion acquired right to under sect. 108, or might assume for the purposes specified in sect. 117. Its legal effect is to exclude from the "duties and revenues" appropriated to the Dominion, all the ordinary territorial revenues of the Crown arising within the Provinces. That construction of the statute was accepted by this Board in deciding *Attorney-General of Ontario* v. *Mercer*, where the controversy related to land granted in fee simple to a subject before 1867, which became escheat to the Crown in the year 1871. The Lord Chancellor (Earl Selborne) in delivering judgment in that case, said (2): "It was not disputed, in the argument for the Dominion at the bar, that all territorial revenues arising within each Province from 'lands' (in which term must be comprehended all estates in land), which at the time of the union belonged to the Crown, were reserved to the respective Provinces by sect. 109; and it was admitted that no distinction could, in that respect, be made between lands then ungranted and lands which had previously reverted to the Crown by escheat. But it was insisted that a line was drawn at the date of the union, and that the words were not sufficient to reserve any lands afterwards escheated which at the time of the union were in private hands, and did not then belong to the Crown. Their Lordships indicated an opinion to the effect that the escheat would not, in the special circumstances of that case, have passed to the Province as "lands;" but they held that it fell within the class of rights reserved to the Provinces as "royalties" by sect. 109.

Had its Indian inhabitants been the owners in fee simple of the territory which they surrendered by the treaty of 1873, *Attorney-General of Ontario* v. *Mercer* might have been an authority for holding that the Province of Ontario could derive no benefit from the cession, in respect that the land was not vested in the Crown at the time of the union. But that was not the character of the Indian interest. The Crown has all along had a present proprietary estate in the land, upon which the Indian title was a mere burden. The ceded territory was at the time of the union, land vested in the Crown, subject to "an interest other than that of the Province in the same," within the meaning of sect. 109; and must now belong to Ontario in terms of that clause, unless its rights have been taken away by some provision of the Act of 1867 other than those already noticed.

In the course of the argument the claim of the Dominion to the ceded territory was rested upon the provisions of sect. 91(24), which in express confer upon the Parliament of Canada power to make laws for

"Indians, and lands reserved for the Indians." It was urged that the exclusive power of legislation and administration carried with it, by necessary implication, any patrimonial interest which the Crown might have had in the reserved lands. In reply to that reasoning, counsel for Ontario referred us to a series of provincial statutes prior in date to the Act of 1867, for the purpose of shewing that the expression "Indian reserves" was used in legislative language to designate certain lands in which the Indians had, after the royal proclamation of 1763, acquired a special interest, by treaty or otherwise, and did not apply to land occupied by them in virtue of the proclamation. The argument might have deserved consideration if the expression had been adopted by the British Parliament in 1867, but it does not occur in sect. 91(24), and the words actually used are, according to their natural meaning, sufficient to include all lands reserved, upon any terms or conditions, for Indian occupation. It appears to be the plain policy of the Act that, in order to ensure uniformity of administration, all such lands, and Indian affairs generally, shall be under the legislative control of one central authority.

Their Lordships are, however, unable to assent to the argument for the Dominion founded on sect. 92(24). There can be no à priori probability that the British Legislature in a branch of the statute which professes to deal only with the distribution of legislative power, intended to deprive the Provinces of rights which are expressly given them in that branch of it which relates to the distribution of revenues and assets. The fact that the power of legislating for Indians, and for lands which are reserved to their use, has been entrusted to the Parliament of the Dominion is not in the least degree inconsistent with the right of the Provinces to a beneficial interest in these lands, available to them as a source of revenue whenever the estate of the Crown is disencumbered of the Indian title.

By the treaty of 1873 the Indian inhabitants ceded and released the territory in dispute, in order that it might be opened up for settlement, immigration, and such other purpose as to Her Majesty might seem fit, "to the Government of the Dominion of Canada," for the Queen and Her successors for ever. It was argued that a cession in these terms was in effect a conveyance to the Dominion Government of the whole rights of the Indians, with consent of the Crown. That is not the natural import of the language of the treaty, which purports to be from beginning to end a transaction between the Indians and the Crown; and the surrender is in substance made to the Crown. Even if its language had been more favourable to the argument of the Dominion upon this point, it is abundantly clear that the commissioners who represented Her Majesty, whilst they had full authority to accept a surrender to the Crown, had neither authority nor power to take away from Ontario the interest which had been assigned to that province by the Imperial Statute of 1867.

This decision seemed to establish as a general proposition that when land in a province is surrendered by Indians it ceases to be Indian land and becomes unencumbered provincial land. This may have been so when Indians used lands in Indian ways and surrenders were made to open up lands for settlement or other non-Indian uses. However, lands surrendered in trust to the Crown for the purpose of leasing them for the benefit of the surrendering band or its members are in a different category. While they are not reserves, they remain "lands reserved for the Indians" within s. 91(24) and therefore subject exclusively to federal land and land-use laws: *Corporation of Surrey* v. *Peace Arch Enterprises Ltd.* (1970), 74 WWR 380 (BCCA). Today Indian bands no longer authorize 999-year, 10 dollar-a-year leases, preferring to develop their lands themselves as commercial or residential properties, and the Indian Act's requirement that the Crown be interposed between Indians and those who rent these properties has led to a new class of surrenders in which the Crown is just a "front" for the corporations set up by Indians themselves to develop and manage their lands.

Do provincial land laws apply to lands which have been surrendered to the Crown in order to be developed as revenue properties? Because a number of Alberta bands are proceeding with this kind of land development, the Alberta government referred the question to that province's Court of Appeal in *Re Proposed Development of Land in the Stoney Plain Indian Reserve No. 135* (1982), 130 DLR (3d) 636. The questions referred to the Court run to some length but the Court's opinion can be simply stated: as long as the lands surrendered are held in trust for the benefit of the surrendering band, they remain "lands reserved for the Indians" within s. 91(24) and are subject only to Indian land laws enacted by Parliament. Again, it should be noted that in *Cardinal* the Supreme Court decided that provincial laws will apply *on* these lands, to Indians and to others. It is only provincial *land* laws that cannot apply *to* the lands. The Court further concluded that the Indian Act would apply on developed Indian lands held by a corporation, as though the lands were a reserve because of s. 36 of the Act:

SPECIAL RESERVES

36.   Where lands have been set apart for the use and benefit of a band and legal title thereto is not vested in Her Majesty, this Act applies as though the lands were a reserve within the meaning of this Act.

The meaning of "lands reserved for the Indians" in s. 91(24) is carefully considered in relation to northern land claims by R.D.J. Pugh in an article entitled "Are Northern Lands Reserved for the Indians?" (1982) 60 *Can. B. Rev.* 36, at p. 66 ff.

Even where surrendered lands are not held in trust for the benefit of Indians, there remains the question of the status of those lands between the time of surrender and their disposition by the Crown to achieve the purpose for which the surrender was obtained.

This issue came up for decision in *The Queen* v. *Smith* (1981) 113 DLR (3d) 522 (Fed. CA) when Smith, a squatter on lands surrendered in 1895 to be sold to squatters but never actually sold to them, claimed a right by adverse possession. Although no part of the surrendered lands was made into a reserve, the Court concluded that they were "lands reserved for the Indians" within the meaning of s. 91(24) of the Constitution Act, 1867 as long as the Crown had not disposed of them. This gave the Crown a right of possession sufficient to enable it to discharge its responsibilities arising from federal legislative authority over the lands in question.

The Court went on to find that adverse possession for sixty years had not been proved by Smith but that he was entitled to compensation in respect of improvements he had made to the land, given the long period of apparent acquiescence in his occupation. This finding, however, was altered on appeal by the Supreme Court of Canada (see further discussion in Chapter 8, *Reserve Lands, infra*.

References

Norman K. Zlotkin, *Unfinished Business: Aboriginal Peoples and the 1983 Constitutional Conference* (Institute of Intergovernmental Relations, Queen's University, 1983).

Felix S. Cohen, *Handbook of Federal Indian Law*, 1982 Edition.

Bradford W. Morse, "Indian and Inuit Family Law and the Canadian Legal System" (1980) 8 *American Indian Law Review*, 199.

Report of the Royal Commission on Bilingualism and Biculturalism, Book I (1967).

Clem Chartier, " 'Indian': An Analysis of the Term as Used in Section 91(24) of the British North America Act, 1867," (1978-79) 43 *Saskatchewan Law Review*, 37.

A. Jordan, "Comment on *R.* v. *Laprise,* (1977) 1 *Canadian Native Law Reporter* 22.

R.D.J. Pugh, "Are Northern Lands Reserved for the Indians?" (1982) 60 *Canadian Bar Review*, 36.

6. Further reading

K.M. Lysyk, "The Unique Constitutional Position of the Canadian Indian" (1967) 45 *Canadian Bar Review*, 513.

K.M. Lysyk, "Constitutional Developments Relating to Indians and Indian Lands: An Overview," (1978) *Law Society of Upper Canada Special Lectures*, 201.

K.M. Lysyk, "The Rights and Freedoms of the Aboriginal Peoples of Canada," in Tarnopolsky and Beaudouin, *The Canadian Charter of Rights and Freedoms* (1982), at p. 467.

L.C. Green, "Canada's Indians: Federal Policy, International and Constitutional Law," (1970-71) 4 *Ottawa Law Review*, 101.

7. The Application of Provincial Laws

DOUGLAS SANDERS

Federal jurisdiction over "Indians, and Lands reserved for the Indians" both permits federal legislative action and excludes the application of certain provincial laws. In Canadian constitutional law, provincial laws can be held inapplicable to a federal subject matter in two different situations: (1) if the provincial law is in conflict with valid federal legislation, and (2) if the provincial law affects the character of the federal subject. This second proposition is put in differing ways in the cases: does the provincial law affect Indians "as" Indians? Does the provincial law affect the "status" and capacity" of the federal entity or subject matter? A value judgment is made by the courts on whether the provincial law has a tolerable impact on the federal subject matter. If a provincial law picked out the federal subject matter for special and discriminatory treatment, clearly the result would be intolerable. But, as well, a general provincial law may affect a federal railway or an Indian reserve in a manner which interferes with its normal and proper function. That too is intolerable.

Section 91(24) of the Constitution Act meant federal jurisdiction over two subjects: Indians and Indian lands. Some cases did not distinguish clearly between these two and either limited the federal jurisdiction to Indians on Indian lands or envisaged a more than cumulative effect when the two subjects came together. In 1979 the Supreme Court of Canada in *Four B* v. *United Garment Workers* (1980), 102 DLR (3d) 385, criticized those views and confirmed that the two subjects must be treated separately.

The federal status of Indians and Indian lands has few analogies in Canadian law. Aliens, too, were placed under special federal jurisdiction, but no special legal regime exists for them. Federally incorporated companies were another group of federal "persons" and some of the Indian cases use terminology developed in relation to them. In sum, the cases on aliens and federal companies indicated that provincial laws generally applied to federal persons (in the absence of special federal legislation). The cases on the immunities of interprovincial railways from provincial laws dealt with a land based system and, for that reason, had direct analogies to questions about Indian reserves. But those cases have been of very limited help. Only one line of non-Indian cases has paralleled an Indian issue sufficiently closely to practically determine the outcome: decisions permitting provincial taxation of non-governmental occupiers of federally owned lands have been applied to allow provincial taxation of non-Indian occupiers of Indian reserve lands.

The cases over the last two decades seem to establish the following propositions about federal jurisdiction:

1.   Provincial laws apply to Indians, so long as they do not discriminate against them and unless they are in conflict with federal Indian legislation. This asserts that "Indians" fall into a "double aspect" area in which provincial laws will always apply in the absence of special federal legislation. No case states this proposition quite this bluntly. Chief Justice Laskin's concurring judgment in *Natural Parents* v. *Superintendent of Child Welfare* (1975), 60 DLR (3d) 148 is in conflict with the proposition, for he reasoned that provincial adoption laws (which affect kinship relations) could not of their own force apply to Indians. His view was not the majority view; indeed, in this badly fragmented judgment, there was no majority view on exactly why the provincial adoption law applied to Indians. Yet all the judges agreed that the provincial law applied. In *Regina* v. *Kruger and Manuel,* [1978] 1 SCR 104, the Supreme Court of Canada applied provincial hunting laws to Indians hunting off reserves in non-treaty areas of Canada. Hunting laws, apparently, did not affect Indians as Indians. And, of course, it is a continuing reality that no immunity from provincial laws is recognized for the Inuit and non-status Indians who come within the constitutional category of Indians in section 91(24) but who are excluded from the Indian Act.

2.   Provincial laws apply to Indian reserve lands if they do not directly affect the use of land, do not discriminate against them and are not in conflict with federal Indian legislation. This asserts that some legislation will fall within an "exclusive" federal sphere in which provincial laws will not apply even in the absence of federal legislation. The leading example of this proposition is *Municipality of Surrey* v. *Peace Arch* (1970), 74 WWR 380, in which the British Columbia Court of Appeal ruled that provincial zoning and health legislation governing the use of land could not apply on lands reserved for Indians, even in the absence of federal provisions on the same matters.

1. A Review of the Cases

In 1870 in *R. ex rel. Gibb* v. *White* (1870), 5 PR 315, an Ontario court ruled that an Indian could be elected in a local election off a reserve if the Indian otherwise met the qualifications of provincial law. Indians were held to be subjects, not aliens. Quebec courts in 1878 upheld the federal exemptions of Indian property located on a reserve from seizure under provincial law: *Durand* v. *Sioui* (1878), 4 QLR 93; *Lepage* v. *Watzo* (1878), 8 RL 596; *Hannis* v. *Turcotte* (1878), 8 RL 708. An Ontario court recognized in 1884 that a local law about animals running at large would not apply on Indian reserve lands: *Re Milloy* (1884), OR 573. In 1889 an Ontario court held that the province could not grant timber rights on reserve lands: *Attorney General of Ontario* v. *Francis*, The Empire Newspaper, Toronto, 21 January 1889.

Federal legislation about Indian wills was upheld in Ontario in *Johnson* v. *Jones* (1895), 26 OR 109.

In 1907, in *R*. v. *Hill*, 15 OLR 11, the Ontario Court of Appeal ruled that the Ontario Medical Act, creating an offence for the unlicenced practice of medicine, applied to an Indian. the case is unsatisfactory in two ways. There is no indication whether the Indian was practicing traditional medicine or western medicine. Apparently, the offence took place off the reserve, although that factor is not commented on in the judgment. Would it have been important if the Indian was serving other Indians or holding himself out to non-Indians as well? The case has been frequently cited and is one of the foundations for the general principle that provincial laws apply to Indians unless there is a conflict with federal Indian legislation.

In 1915 a British Columbia court, in *R*. v. *Jim*, 26 CCC 236, held that provincial hunting laws did not apply to an Indian on a reserve. Two years later, an Ontario court, in *R*. v. *Martin*, 39 DLR 635, convicted an Indian under the provincial Temperance Act. The decision has been subsequently cited for the general proposition that provincial laws apply to Indians. It is not a good example of the principle, for the legislative field was occupied, for Indians, by the Indian Act.

In *Re Caledonia Milling* v. *Johns* (1918), 42 DLR 338, an Ontario court declared that an Indian, being a ward of the federal government, could not be imprisoned under provincial laws. This decision was followed in New Brunswick in *Ex Parte Tenasse* [1931] 1 DLR 806 and in Nova Scotia in *Re Kane*, [1940] 1 DLR 390. The proposition was rejected in *Campbell* v. *Sandy* (1956), 4 DLR (2d) 754 by an Ontario county court, which relied on a new section in the Indian Act introduced in 1951. This doctrine was the only judicially constructed exemption of Indians from provincial laws that did not have an explicit federal legislative base.

The inapplicability of provincial game laws to Indians on reserves, upheld in British Columbia in 1915, was applied by the Manitoba Court of Appeal to Indian trappers in *R*. v. *Rodgers,* [1923] 3 DLR 414. Did this mean that provincial hunting laws had no application on reserves? In peculiar companion cases in British Columbia, an Indian agent and his hunting companion, a white lawyer, were both convicted under provincial laws for hunting on an Indian reserve: *R*. v. *McLeod,* [1930] 2 WWR 37; *R*. v. *Morley*, [1931] 4 DLR 483. This confused the questions of jurisdiction over Indians and jurisdiction over reserve lands, and the authority of the decisions is doubtful.

In *City of Vancouver* v. *Chow Chee,* [1941] 1 WWR 72, the British Columbia of Appeal allowed the province to tax non-Indian occupiers of reserve lands on the basis of the assessed value of the lands and improvements, although the tax could not be realized against the land. As was noted earlier, the decision was based on previous caselaw on the tax status of federal crown lands. It has been followed in *Provincial Municipal Assessor* v.

Harrison, [1971] 3 WWR 735; *Sammartino* v. *Attorney General of British Columbia,* [1972] 1 WWR 24.

In *John Murdock* v. *La Commission des Relations Ouvrières,* [1956] Quebec CS 30, the Quebec Superior Court ruled that Indian employees should be included in any bargaining unit under provincial labour relations law.

In the 1960s a major series of Indian hunting and fishing rights cases began. They upheld Indian hunting rights against provincial laws in two situations. Indian hunting rights guaranteed in the prairie provinces by the Natural Resources Transfer Agreements and the British North America Act of 1930 were upheld against provincial laws: *R.* v. *Prince,* [1964] SCR 81. Secondly, treaty protected hunting rights were upheld against provincial laws with the aid of section 88 of the Indian Act: *R.* v. *White and Bob* (1965), 52 DLR (2d) 481. Provincial hunting laws applied to Indians off reserves in all other situations: *R.* v. *Kruger and Manuel,* [1978] 1 SCR 104. In result, the courts upheld federal legislative power over Indians hunting off reserves, but ruled that Indians were not exempt from provincial laws unless federal legislation gave them exemption.

A series of cases began in the 1970s on the application of provincial laws on reserves. In *Municipality of Surrey* v. *Peace Arch* (1970), 74 WWR 380, the British Columbia Court of Appeal ruled that provincial health and zoning laws did not apply to a development on leased reserve lands, for such laws would affect the use of land. Other decisions have applied provincial laws on minimum wages (*R.* v. *Baert Construction* (1974), 19 CCC (2d) 304), rent control (*Park* v. *Lee Greely* (1978), 85 DLR (3d) 618), automobile insurance (*R.* v. *Twoyoungmen* (1979), 101 DLR (3d) 618) and builders' liens (*Western* v. *Sarcee* (1979), 98 DLR (3d) 424). Provincial laws have been held not to apply on reserves when they deal with hunting (*R.* v. *Isaac* (1976), 13 NSR (2d) 460), the physical requirements for a mobile home park (*Milbrook* v. *Northern* (1978), 84 DLR (3d) 174), fire permits (*R.* v. *Sinclair,* [1978] 6 WWR 37) or a tax on the purchase of property by an Indian (*Brown* v. *Attorney General of British Columbia,* BCCA, 4 December 1979).

Two cases on the application of provincial laws on Indian reserves have gone to the Supreme Court of Canada. The decision in *Cardinal* v. *Attorney General of Alberta,* [1974] SCR 695, turned on a very narrow point. Provincial laws relating to game (in this case, the sale of wild meat) which did not affect the right of Indians to hunt and fish for food, applied to Indians as a result of the provisions of the Natural Resources Transfer Agreements. The significance of the case lies not in the actual decision but in the language used by the majority and minority judgments. The majority judgment rejected the notion that reserves were "enclaves" beyond the reach of provincial laws, while conceding that certain provincial laws would not apply on reserves. The minority asserted that reserves were "enclaves," while conceding that certain provincial laws would apply on them. The decision of the Supreme Court of Canada in *Four B* v. *United Garment Workers* (1979), 102 DLR (3d) 385, is much clearer. The court applied provincial labour relations laws to an Indian-owned business, located on reserve lands with a majority of Indian employeees. The Supreme Court found nothing inherently Indian about the operation and noted that there was no federal legislation asserting jurisdiction over the labour relations in question.

2. The Question of Section 88

There have been varying opinions on the meaning of section 88 of the Indian Act. It reads:

> Subject to the terms of any treaty and any other Act of the Parliament of Canada, all laws of general application from time to time in force in any province are applicable to and in respect of Indians in the Province, except to the extent that such laws are inconsistent with this Act or any order, rule, regulation or bylaw made thereunder, and except to the extent that such laws make provision for any matter for which provision is made by or under this Act.

The section, by its terms, only refers to the application of provincial laws to "Indians". It does not purport to deal with the application of provincial laws on Indian reserves. Opinion has been divided on whether section 88 is simply a restatement of existing constitutional rules or whether the section has the effect of making certain provincial laws apply to Indians which would otherwise not apply to them. In *Natural Parents* v. *Superintendent of Child Welfare* (1975), 60 DLR (3d) 148, the Supreme Court of Canada divided equally on this question, with one judge making no comment on the issue. A workable resolution of the question would be to regard the legislative field in relation to Indians as a double aspect area. All provincial laws that do not discriminate against Indians will apply to Indians unless they are in conflict with federal legislation. Section 88, in this analysis, is not important in defining what provincial laws apply to Indians, but in defining what provincial laws do not apply to Indians. In stating that provincial laws do not apply where there are federal legislative provisions or any regulation or bylaw enacted under the authority of the Indian Act, the section is simply stating the normal constitutional rules about the occupation of the field in a double aspect area. In only one way does section 88 extend the federal occupation of the field: by its reference to treaties. The operative part of section 88 is its provision that provincial laws of general application do not apply to Indians when they are in conflict with the provisions of a treaty. This is an unusual kind of occupation of the field, but there is no reason to question its effectiveness.

3. Recent Family Law Cases

Only one case on the application of provincial laws to Indians has gone to the

THE APPLICATION OF PROVINCIAL LAWS   457

Supreme Court of Canada. The question in *Natural Parents* v. *Superintendent of Child Welfare* (1975), 60 DLR (3d) 148, was whether provincial adoption laws could apply to a status Indian child. Four judges ruled that the provincial law affected Indians as Indians and therefore could apply to them only if the provincial law had been adopted by federal legislation and made to apply to Indians. They ruled that section 88 of the Indian Act had so adopted the provincial adoption law. Three other judges held that the Indian Act, by referring to adoption, implicitly intended that provincial adoption laws would apply to Indians. Two judges ruled that a provincial adoption law did not affect Indians as Indians and, at least in the absence of federal legislation on the question, such a law would apply to Indians. This four to three to two ruling produced no majority reasoning on the question.

Other family law questions have arisen. An Alberta court ruled in *Black Plume* v. *Black Plume* (1970), 4 RFL 149, that provincial laws on maintenance applied to Indians, in spite of minor provisions in the Indian Act on the same question. More serious issues emerged in relation to provincial laws relating to on-reserve marital property. In *Re Bell and Bell* (1977), 16 OR (2d) 197, the Ontario Supreme Court ruled that the provincial Partition Act could be applied to the on-reserve property of an Indian couple, subject to sections 24 and 25 of the Indian Act (which provide that no transfer of on-reserve property is valid without the approval of the Minister of Indian Affairs). But in *Sandy* v. *Sandy* (1979), 27 OR (2d) 248, the Ontario Court of Appeal ruled that the Ontario Family Law Reform Act on the division of marital property could not apply to on-reserve real property. In *Re Hopkins and Hopkins* (1980), 29 OR (2d) 24, the Ontario County Court ruled that an order could be made under the Family Law Reform Act granting exclusive possession of the matrimonial home to the wife. This court cited and distinguished the *Sandy* decision.

The application of provincial laws has also come up in the context of the membership sections of the Indian Act:

(a) Re Ranville et al. and Attorney General of Canada, [1979] 4 CNLR 65 (Ontario County Court)

HUDSON, CO. CT. J.: — On April 3, 1978, the Registrar under the *Indian Act*, RSC 1970; c. I-6, declared the protestor infants Sean Gerald Ranville and Danielle Winona Ranville not to be Indians and deleted their names from the Fort Alexander Band list in purported accordance with the provisions of s. 7(1) of the *Indian Act*.

This deletion has been referred to this Court for review pursuant to the provisions of s. 9(3) [am. 1974-75, c. 48, s. 25(1); 1978-79, c. 11, s. 10(1)] of the *Indian Act*.

The facts are not in dispute. Sean and Danielle were born on February 1, 1971, and September 24, 1972, respectively.

Their mother Myrelene Ranville (nee Henderson) was an Indian within the meaning of the *Indian Act* and was so registered as No. 1542 on the Fort Alexander Band list in the Province of Manitoba.

Myrelene Ranville was not married when Sean and Danielle were born. The two infants were accordingly registered on the Fort Alexander Band list on March 4, 1971, and December 4, 1972, respectively, in accordance with the provisions of s. 11(1)(*e*) of the *Indian Act*.

No protest to the addition of the names of the infants to the Fort Alexander Band list was made in accordance with s. 12(2), or any other section, of the *Indian Act*.

The mother, Myrelene Ranville, married the father of the infants, Brian Gerald Ranville, on March 2, 1974.

The father was never a person entitled to be registered under the *Indian Act*. Therefore, the infants would not have been entitled to be registered under the *Indian Act* if their parents had been married at the time of their births.

The *Indian Act* does not define "legitimate" or "illegitimate".

The *Indian Act* does not provide for the legitimation of a child by the marriage of his parents after his birth.

The *Indian Act* does not specify whether or not a child, once registered pursuant to s. 11(1)(*e*) of the *Indian Act*, is entitled to remain registered after the marriage of his or her mother to a "non-Indian" father.

The disposition of this reference depends upon the effect to be properly given to s. 2(1) of the *Legitimacy Act*, 1962 (Man.) c. 38, as amended [now s. 2(1) of RSM 1970, c. L130] and s. 88 of the *Indian Act*.

The *Legitimacy Act*, s. 2(1), as amended:

2(1) Where, before or after the first day of July, 1962, and after the birth of a person, his parents have intermarried or intermarry, he is legitimate from birth for all purposes of the law of Manitoba.

Indian Act, s. 88 (in so far as it is applicable):

88. . . . all laws of general application from time to time in force in any province are applicable to and in respect of Indians in the province, except to the extent that such laws are inconsistent with this Act . . .

If the *Legitimacy Act* of Manitoba is not a law of general application in the Province then it does not affect Indians.

However, the *Legitimacy Act* extends uniformly throughout the Province and is not in relation to one class of citizen. Therefore, I am of the view that it is a law of general application and we must consider its effect on the status of the two infants.

The Full Court of the Supreme Court of Canada had to consider the combined effect of the *Adoption Act*, RSBC 1960, c. 4, and the *Indian Act* in *Natural Parents* v. *Superintendent of Child Welfare*, [1976] 2 SCR 751, 60 DLR (3d) 148, [1976] 1 WWR 699.

In that case, two non-Indian residents of British Columbia wished to adopt an Indian child.

The Chief Justice (Judson, Spence and Dickson, JJ., concurring) treated the *Adoption Act* as referentially incorporated into the *Indian Act* by virtue of s. 88 of the *Indian Act*, and considered whether and to what extent the *Adoption Act* was inconsistent with the *Indian Act*. At the bottom of p. 760 SCR, p. 154 DLR:

> It appears to me to be unquestionable that for the provincial *Adoption Act* to apply to the adoption of Indian children of registered Indians, who could be compelled thereunder to surrender them to adopting non-Indian parents, would be to touch "Indianness", to strike at a relationship integral to a matter outside of provincial competence. This is entirely apart from the question whether, if referentially incorporated, the *Adoption Act* could have any force in the face of various provisions of the *Indian Act*, securing certain benefits for Indians.
>
> Counsel for the respondents cited a number of cases holding Indians to be subject to provincial legislation. Among them was *Rex* v. *Hill* and *Rex* v. *Martin*. These, and other like cases, are simply illustrative of the amenability of Indians off their reservations to provincial regulatory legislation, legislation which, like traffic legislation, does not touch their "Indianness". Such provincial legislation is of a different class than adoption legislation which would, if applicable as provincial legislation *simpliciter*, constitute a serious intrusion into the Indian family relationship. It is difficult to conceive what would be left of exclusive federal power in relation to Indians if such provincial legislation was held to apply to Indians. Certainly, if it was applicable because of its so-called general application, it would be equally applicable by expressly embracing Indians. Exclusive federal authority would then be limited to a registration system and to regulation of life on a reserve.

Further, at the top of p. 763 SCR, pp. 155-6 DLR, the Chief Justice said:

> I cannot believe that any less care should be taken in analysis before subjecting Indians, coming as they do within a specific head of exclusive federal jurisdiction, to general provincial legislation, unless the inclusion of Indians within the scope of the provincial legislation touches them as ordinary persons and in a way that does not intrude on their Indian character or their Indian identity and relationship.

Mr Justice Martland (Pigeon J, concurring) considered that the meaning and effect of s. 88 of the *Indian Act* was that the provincial *Adoption Act* applied *ex proprio vigore* to the adoption of Indian children. Section 91(24) of the *British North America Act, 1867* conferred exclusive legislative authority on the Parliament of Canada on the subject of "Indians, and Lands reserved for the Indians". Notwithstanding s. 91(24) of the *British North America Act, 1867*, Mr Justice Martland did not believe that only the Parliament of Canada could enact legislation which might affect Indians. However, he had this to say at the middle of p. 775 SCR, pp. 165-6 DLR:

> . . . the words "for all purposes" in subss. (1) and (2) of s. 10 of the *Adoption Act* must be taken to refer to all purposes within the competence of the British Columbia Legislature. Section 10, even prior to the enactment of subs. (4a), did not purport to deprive the child of any status or rights which he possessed under the *Indian Act* at the time of his adoption, and it is clear that no provincial legislation could deprive him of such rights.

In my view it is immaterial whether or not the *Legitimacy Act* is referentially incorporated into the *Indian Act*.

In *Natural Parents* v. *Superintendent of Child Welfare* the Chief Justice held that the words "for all purposes" in s. 10(2) of the *Adoption Act* did not destroy Indianness and entitlement to registration under s. 11(1)(*d*) of the *Indian Act*.

In my opinion, the words "for all purposes" in s. 2(1) of the *Legitimacy Act* are equally incapable of destroying Indianness and entitlement to registration under s. 11(1)(*c*) of the *Indian Act*.

Further, if the *Legitimacy Act* is referentially incorporated then, in my opinion, the words in s. 2(1) limiting its effect to "the law of Manitoba" must by necessary construction exclude the *Indian Act* which is part of the law of Canada and not just one Province.

If not referentially incorporated then, in the words of Mr. Justice Martland, the quoted words do "not purport to deprive the child of any status or rights which he possessed under the *Indian Act* at the time of his" parents' marriage, "and it is clear that no provincial legislation could deprive him of such rights".

Furthermore, the status of Indian carries with it valuable rights not enjoyed by non-Indians. There would need to be clear, unambiguous language to persuade me that it was the intention of the Parliament of Canada to deprive a child of such status because of the subsequent marriage of his parents.

Therefore, in my opinion, the Registrar was in error and it is my decision that Sean Gerald Ranville and Danielle Winona Ranville are

entitled to have their names included in the Fort Alexander Band list.
Decision accordingly.

The Federal Court of Appeal, [1982] 4 CNLR 80, and the Supreme Court of Canada, [1983] 1 CNLR 12, refused to review Judge Hudson's decision. See, as well, *Martin* v. *Chapman*, [1980] 1 FC 72, which was reversed by the Supreme Court of Canada, [1983] 2 CNLR 76.

4. Non-Indians on the Reserve

The earlier case law did not give clear guidelines on the factors that the courts would consider important in applying or refusing to apply provincial laws on reserves. One factor that seemed to play a role in decision making was whether the person to whom the particular laws to be applied was an Indian or a non-Indian. The decisions in *Carter* v. *Nichol*, [1911] 1 WWR 392 (provincial fire control laws), *R.* v. *McLeod*, [1930] 2 WWR 37 and *R.* v. *Morley*, [1931] 4 DLR 483 (provincial game laws), *R.* v. *Gullberg*, [1933] 3 WWR 639 (restaurant licence), *R.* v. *Superior Concrete*, (unreported, Judge Swencisky, Vancouver County Court, 16 May 1966, involving a provincial anti-noise bylaw), *R.* v. *Baert Construction* (1974), 19 CCC (2d) 304 (minimum wage laws), *Park Mobile Home* v. *Le Greely* (1978), 85 DLR (3d) 618 (rent control laws), *Western Industrial Contractors* v. *Sarcee Developments* (1979), 98 DLR (3d) 424 (builders liens), and *Four B Manufacturing* v. *United Garment Workers* (1979), 102 DLR (3d) 385 (labour relations laws), could all be explained on the basis that the provincial laws were being applied to non-Indians on the reserve. Only one of the cases cited, however, explicitly says that the fact that the person is a non-Indian is an important factor (*R.* v. *Superior Concrete*) and the reasoning in the decision is unimpressive. In contrast, the decision of the British Columbia Court of Appeal in *Corporation of Surrey* v. *Peace Arch* (1970), 74 WWR 380, a decision which has been uniformly cited favourably since it was rendered, refused to apply provincial laws to a non-Indian enterprise on reserve lands on the basis that they directly affected the use of land. The notion that the status of the individual on the land might be decisive has now been rejected by the Supreme Court of Canada in *Four B Manufacturing* v. *United Garment Workers* (1979), 102 DLR (3d) 385:

> S. 91.24 of the *British North America Act, 1867* assigns jurisdiction to Parliament over two distinct subject matters, Indians *and* Lands reserved for the Indians, not Indians *on* Lands reserved for the Indians. The power of Parliament to make laws in relation to Indians is the same whether Indians are on a reserve or off a reserve. It is not reinforced because it is exercised over Indians on a reserve any more than it is weakened because it is exercised over Indians off a reserve.

Equally, jurisdiction over reserves would be the same whether the person on the land is an Indian or a non-Indian.

One aspect of the question of non-Indians on reserve lands is the status to be attributed to a company that is wholly owned by Indians or wholly owned by an Indian Band. In *Western Industrial Contractors Ltd.* v. *Sarcee Developments* (1979), 98 DLR (3d) 424 and *Four B Manufacturing* v. *United Garment Workers* (1979), 102 DLR (3d) 698, provincial laws were sought to be applied to such companies functioning on reserve lands. In both cases the company was treated as a non-Indian. In *Re Kinookimaw Beach Association* (1978), 91 DLR (3d) 698, the Saskatchewan Court of Queen's Bench ruled that an Indian-owned company could be considered an Indian for the purposes of tax exemption provisions found in the Indian Act. That decision was reversed on appeal to the Saskatchewan Court of Appeal: (1979) 102 DLR (3d) 333. Leave to appeal to the Supreme Court of Canada has been refused. While the result may be criticized or regretted (it creates a disincentive for Indians to use modern forms of commercial organization), the authorities on the point are uniform.

5. The Factor of Surrendered Lands

There is limited case law on the consequences of surrendering reserve lands. The earlier pattern was that a surrender would be followed by a sale. In that context, issues arose about provincial powers in relation to the land between the point of surrender and agreement for sale and final transfer of title by the issuance of letters patent to the new owner. After the issuance of letters patent (or a deed) to the new owner, there would be no question but that provincial laws applied.

A more recent series of cases has involved surrendered lands. The British Columbia Court of Appeal in the leading decision of *Corporation of Surrey* v. *Peace Arch* (1970), 74 WWR 380, dealt with a situation where reserve lands had been specifically surrendered for lease. The surrender only enabled a specific lease, which has already been negotiated, to be granted to a specific non-Indian lessee. The Court described the surrender as "qualified or conditional". Mr Justice Maclean stated:

> Under this form of surrender, "in trust" and for a particular purpose that is "to lease the same" it seems to me that it cannot be said the tribal interest in these lands has been extingusihed. In my respectful opinion the learned Judge below was in error when he held that the surrender was an "unconditional" one.

> The subject of "surrender" under the *Indian Act* was dealt with in *St Ann's Island Shooting & Fishing Club Ltd.* v. *Rex.* [1950] SCR 211, (1950) 2 DLR 225, affirming (1949) 2 DLR 17, where Rand J said at p. 219:

"I find myself unable to agree that there was a total and definitive surrender. What was intended was a surrender sufficient to enable a valid letting to be made to the trustees 'for such term and on such conditions' as the Superintendent General might approve. It was at most a surrender to permit such leasing to them as might be made and continued, even though subject to the approval of the Superintendent General, by those having authority to do so. It was not a final and irrevocable commitment of the land to leasing for the benefit of the Indians, and much less to a leasing in perpetuity, or in the judgment of the Superintendent General, to the club. To the Council, the Superintendent General stood for the government of which he was the representative. Upon the expiration of the holding by the Club, the reversion of the original privileges of the Indians fell into possession."

In my view the "surrender" under the *Indian Act* is not a surrender as a conveyancer would understand it. The Indians are in effect forbidden from leasing or conveying the lands within an Indian reserve, and this function must be performed by an official of the Government if it is to be performed at all: See sec 58(3) of the *Indian Act*. Further, it is to be noted that the surrender is in favour of Her Majesty "in trust". This obviously means in trust for the Indians. The title which Her Majesty gets under this arrangement is an empty one. . . .

In my opinion the land in question is still within the category of lands described in sec. 91(24) of the *BNA Act, 1867*, i.e., "lands reserved for the Indians." This land was reserved for the Indians in 1887, and the Indians still maintain a reversionary interest in it.

Near the end of his judgment, Mr Justice Maclean stated:

It might well be (but it is not necessary for me to decide) that if an absolute surrender were made by the Indians under the *Indian Act*, and this surrender was followed by a conveyance from the Government to a purchaser the land would cease to be a reserve under the *Indian Act* and would also cease to be "lands reserved for the Indians" under sec. 91(24) of the *BNA Act, 1867*, but that is not the case here.

This statement was clearly made out of an abundance of caution. The factor isolated by Mr Justice Maclean earlier in his judgment — the retention of an Indian reversionary interest in the land — would end with a conveyance of title to a new owner. At that point federal jurisdiction would end. Before that point, according to the earlier authorities, federal jurisdiction would continue. The relevant event is not an unconditional surrender (as opposed to the conditional surrender in the *Peace Arch* case), but the conveyance of title.

In 1974 the Sarcee Indian Band in southern Alberta surrendered certain reserve lands. By the surrender document, the land was to be leased to Sarcee

Developments, which was described as a wholly band-owned enterprise. The land was leased to Sarcee Developments for a period of 75 years, with provision that the land and improvements would revert at the end of the term to "Her Majesty the Queen in the Right of Canada for the use and benefit of the Sarcee Band." This surrender and lease featured in two cases; *Palm Dairies* v. *The Queen,* [1979] 1 FC 531 (Federal Court, Trial Division), and *Western Industrial Contractors* v. *Sarcee Developments Ltd.* (1979), 98 DLR (3d) 424 (Alberta Supreme Court, Appellate Division). Both cases concerned the question of whether a builder's lien, authorized under provincial law, could be filed against surrendered lands. The Federal Court decision dealt with the question of whether the lien could be filed in the surrendered lands registry maintained by the Department of Indian Affairs under section 55 of the Indian Act. The court ruled that it could not be so filed. The decision of the Alberta Supreme Court, Appellate Division, ruled that it could be filed in the land titles office maintained under provincial law, though any transfer of the leasehold interest could not occur without the consents necessary under the provisions of the Indian Act. We are concerned, at this point, with any rulings in these cases about the status of surrendered lands.

In the *Palm Dairies* case, Mr Justice Primrose followed the decision in the *Peace Arch* case and ruled at page 540:

> I accept the argument that the lands continue to be reserved for the Indians within the meaning of *The British North America Act, 1867*, and exclusive legislative jurisdiction remains in the Parliament of Canada, so that provincial legislation which might lay down rules as to how these lands are to be used is inapplicable. See also *Gauthier* v. *The King*, (1918) 56 SCR 176.

However, Mr Justice Morrow, giving the majority decision in *Western Industrial Contractors* v. *Sarcee Developments Ltd.*, ruled that as long as the Indian reversion was protected, provincial builder's liens could be applied to the leashold interest. He stated at p. 441:

> In the present situation, the whole purpose of the exercise, the whole thrust of the surrender and of the resultant lease with the tenant or lessee being incorporated under provincial legislation is, in my opinion, to encourage and to assist the participants as a development company (as a non-Indian) to take part in commercial, agricultural, industrial, housing and recreational purposes. The conditions in the surrender and the many protections afforded to the lessor, the Crown, in the lease protect the Sarcee Band and their reversionary land interest from any intrusion by the provincial statute.

Mr Justice Prowse, in a dissenting judgment, took a more orthodox view of the problem. Following the *Peace Arch* decision, he ruled that the lands remained under federal legislative jurisdiction and that the provincial law in question affected the land even more directly than the legislation that had been considered in *Peace Arch*. As a result, it could not apply to the surrendered lands.

In *Four B Manufacturing* v. *United Garment Workers* (1979), 102 DLR (3d) 385 (SCC), an Indian-owned company established its business operations on a reserve through the use of a three-year permit, issued by the Minister of Indian Affairs with the consent of the Band Council under section 28(2) of the Indian Act. This gives a new dimension to the "surrendered lands" problem. There is more than one way to validate non-Indian use of reserve lands under the Indian Act. The permit is one option and was described by Mr Justice Beetz in *Four B* as creating no tenancy and being subject to cancellation at the discretion of the Minister of Indian Affairs (concepts apparently deriving from the wording of the permit, for they are not found in the wording of the Indian Act or in judicial decision). A third method of validating non-Indian use of reserve lands is through a lease between an Indian in possession of specific reserve lands (by an allottment of the land to the Indian) and a non-Indian when the lease has received the approval of the Minister of Indian Affairs, as provided for in section 58(3) of the Indian Act. There are, then, three methods in the Indian Act to validate the non-Indian use of reserve lands. The sale of reserve lands can be accomplished only by the first method examined, that of surrender by the band. Business enterprises have been established on reserve lands by the use of all three methods, with the relative rights of the non-Indian enterprise and the band being, in practice, much the same.

Mr Justice Beetz in the *Four B* case simply commented that he attached "little importance to the permit under which *Four B* occupies the premises." In other words, the established occupancy of reserve lands by a non-Indian company under a permit did not itself affect the question of whether provincial laws would or would not apply. There is no logical reason to distinguish between a lease following a surrender and a permit. In both situations non-Indian occupancy of reserve lands has been legally established for a term, after which band rights to the land can be fully resumed.

In *The Queen* v. *Smith*, a decision of the Federal Court of Appeal, [1980] 4 CNLR 29, Mr Justice Le Dain took the orthodox view of jurisdiction over surrendered lands:

> It remains to be considered whether the Crown in right of Canada may bring an action for the possession of surrendered lands based on the continuing jurisdiction and responsibility of the federal government with respect to such lands under the *Indian Act*. In my opinion, the answer to this question must be in the affirmative. I agree with the conclusion of the British Columbia Court of Appeal in the *Peace Arch* case that, whether or not surrendered lands remain part of the reserve as defined by the *Indian Act*, they remain, until finally disposed of, lands reserved for the Indians within the meaning of s. 91(24) of the *BNA Act*,

and as such within federal legislative jurisdiction. The category of surrendered lands is a category created by Parliament in the exercise of its exclusive legislative jurisdiction with respect to lands reserved for the Indians. Because of the federal government's continuing responsibility for the control and management of such land until its final disposition in accordance with the terms of a surrender, surrendered land must remain within federal legislative and administrative jurisdiction. It is land that is still held for the benefit of the Indians, although they have agreed to accept the proceeds of sale of it in place of their right of occupation.

Although this decision was reversed by the Supreme Court of Canada, [1983] 3 CNLR 161, this point was not altered.

It is submitted that the result of the case law is to sustain federal legislative jurisdiction over surrendered lands down to the point of "final disposition" (in the words of *The Queen* v. *Smith*) or down to the issuance of letters patent, or full title to a new owner (in line with the early authorities quoted at the beginning of this section). This conclusion is in harmony with the *Peace Arch* decision, which in recent case law has clearly been regarded as the governing decision on the question. It is not consistent with the ruling in *Western Industrial Contractors Ltd.* v. *Sarcee Developments*, though the majority judgment attempted to present their conclusions as not being in conflict with the *Peace Arch* ruling.

8. Reserve Lands

RICHARD H. BARTLETT

1. Object

"In [Lower Canada] the native tribes had, from a period as remote as the middle of the 17th Century up to the Conquest, been under the especial care and direction of the Jesuit Missionaries, who collected some of them in settlements which now exist, obtained grants of land for them from the French Crown, to be applied to their education and civilization, and became themselves their instructors in so much of the knowledge and arts of life as they thought it advisable to impart to them."

1845 Report on Indian Affairs

In 1829 the need in Upper Canada was suggested:

1. To collect the Indians in considerable numbers, and to settle them in villages with due portion of land for their cultivation and support.
2. To make such provision for their religious improvement, education and instruction in husbandry, as circumstances may from time to time require.
3. To afford them such assistance in building their houses, rations, and in procuring such seed and agricultural implements as may be necessary, commuting where practicable, a portion of their presents for the latter . . .

PAC RG 10 Vol. 5, Kempt to Colbourne, 16 May 1829.

The suggestions have been described as "the essence of the Indian reserve policy begun in Upper Canada" which had the object of transforming the Indian from a "migrant or semi-migrant to a settled, civilized Christian, equipped with all the moral and mechanical skills necessary to compete in the European world of Upper Canada."

R.J. Surtees, "Development of an Indian Reserve Policy in Canada", *Ontario History*, Vol CXI, pp. 87, 92.

The Robinson Treaties in Ontario and the "numbered" treaties of the Prairies provided for the establishment of reserves. Treaty Commissioner Alexander Morris described the objectives of such reserves in the following terms:

The allotment of lands to the Indians, to be set aside as reserves for them for homes and agricultural purposes, and which cannot be sold or alienated without their consent, and then only for their benefit; the extent of lands thus set apart being generally one section for each family of five. I regard this system as of great value. It at once secures to the Indian tribes tracts of land, which cannot be interfered with, by the rush of immigration, and affords the means of inducing them to establish homes and learn the arts of agriculture. I regard the Canadian system of allotting reserves to one or more bands together, in the localities in which they have had the habit of living, as far preferable to the American system of placing whole tribes, in large reserves, which eventually become the object of cupidity to the whites, and the breaking up of which, has so often led to Indian wars and great discontent even if warfare did not result. The Indians, have a strong attachment to the localities, in which they and their fathers have been accustomed to dwell, and it is desirable to cultivate this home feeling of attachment to the soil. Moreover, the Canadian system of band reserves has a tendency to diminish the offensive strength of the Indian tribes, should they ever become restless, a remote contingency, if the treaties are carefully observed. Besides, the fact of the reserves being scattered throughout the territories, will enable the Indians to obtain markets among the white settlers, for any surplus produce they may eventually have to dispose of. It will be found desirable, to assign to each family parts of the reserve for their own use, so as to give them a sense of property in it, but all power of sale or alienation of such lands should be rigidly prohibited. Any premature enfranchisement of the Indians, or power given them to part with their lands, would inevitably lead to the speedy breaking up of the reserves, and the return of the Indians to their wandering mode of life, and thereby to the re-creation of a difficulty which the assignment of reserves was calculated to obviate.

Morris pp. 287-88

The Federation of Saskatchewan Indians has asserted:

When we signed treaties, our ancestors held back or "reserved" certain lands for our own people. Canada did not give those lands to us because the land was not Canada's to give. It was, and still is, our land.

Also at the time of Treaty-making, our ancestors held back or "reserved" certain rights and powers of Indian Governments. These are not mentioned in the Treaty Articles, because they were not subject to negotiation. They were, and they remain, our inalienable rights. Among these are the *inherent sovereignty of Indian nations*, the *right to self-government*, *jurisdiction over our lands* and citizens and power to enforce the terms of the Treaties.

"Principles of Indian Government",
1977, Prince Albert, Saskatchewan

2. The Establishment of Reserves

No common form or authority was employed in the establishment of Indian reserves. Each reserve possesses a distinct history and form of creation which entails distinct legal consequences, e.g., as to the nature of the provincial and the Indian interest. A general classification would indicate that reserves have been created by Crown grant to religious communities and missions, by federal purchase of private lands, by executive action setting apart public lands, and by treaty and modern agreements. The establishment of reserves by treaty is only predominant on the Prairies and in Ontario. In British Columbia and the Maritimes many reserves were set apart by executive action under public lands legislation. In Southern Ontario and Quebec a variety of forms and authority are evident.

The Indian Act has never provided for the establishment of Indian reserves. Through most of its history it did, however, define a ''reserve'' as:

. . . any tract or tracts set apart by treaty or otherwise for the use and benefit of or granted to a particular band of Indians, of which the legal title is in the Crown, but which is unsurrendered and includes all the trees, wood, timber, soil, stone, minerals, metals or other valuables thereon or therein . . .

[SC 1876, c. 18, s. 3]

(a) In *Town of Hay River* v. *The Queen and Chief Daniel Sonfrere* (1979), 101 DLR (3d) 184, [1979] 2 CNLR 101, the Federal Court considered the authority under which a reserve was set apart in the area subject to Treaty #8:

MAHONEY, J: The issue is the legality of the creation of Hay River Indian Reserve No. 1, comprising some 52 square miles bounded on the north by the southerly shore of Great Slave Lake and on the west by the right bank of the Hay River, all in the Northwest Territories. Some of the land comprised in the reserve was within the corporate limits of the Town of Hay River when, by Order in Council 1974-387, dated February 26, 1974, it was set apart as a reserve in fulfilment of obligations of the Government of Canada under Treaty No. 8. The reserve is within the territory ceded by the Indians to Her Majesty under Treaty No. 8 and legal title to all the land in hte reserve, both within and without the Plaintiff's boundaries, was, when set apart, vested in Her Majesty in right of Canada. The Plaintiff is a municipal corporation duly incorporated under the laws of the Northwest Territories.

At the trial, the Plaintiff abandoned the causes of action raised in paragraphs 6 and 7 of the Statement of Claim. These related, respectively, to the alleged invalidity of the provisions of Treaty No. 8 respecting the establishment of reserves and to the alleged violation of the Canadian Bill of Rights by the creation of a privileged group of inhabitants within the municipality. In the result, the Plaintiff relied entirely on the alleged failure of Her Majesty to observe and follow the requirements of Treaty No. 8 in a number of respects. The Defendants challenge the Plaintiff's *locus standi* to sue on that cause of action. The Plaintiff says that compliance with the requirements of the Treaty by Her Majesty is not merely a private obligation to Indians but is made public by paragraph 19(d) of the *Territorial Lands Act*.

> 19.   The Governor in Council may
>
> . . .
>
> (d)   set apart and appropriate such areas or lands as may be necessary to enable the Government of Canada to fulfil its obligations under treaties with the Indians and to make free grants or leases for such purposes, and for any other purpose that he may consider to be conducive to the welfare of the Indians;

Only the first of the three purposes stipulated in paragraph 19(d) is in play.

The entire text of the Order in Council, exclusive of the Schedule, follows:

> Whereas the lands described in Part 1 of the Schedule are Territorial Lands within the meaning of the Territorial Lands Act;
>
> And whereas the said lands are required for the purpose of enabling the Governments of Canada to fulfil its obligations under Treaty No. 8 with respect to the Hay River Band of Indians.

Therefore, His Excellency the Governor General in Council, on the recommendation of the Minister of Indian Affairs and Northern Development, is pleased hereby,

> (1)   pursuant to section 19 of the Territorial Lands Act, to revoke Orders in Council P.C. 1973-2238 of 24th July, 1973, and P.C. 1973-2213 of 24th July, 1973, and to set apart and appropriate the said lands, including all mines and minerals, for the purpose aforesaid.
>
> (2)   pursuant to the Indian Act, to set apart the said lands for the use and benefit of the Hay River Band of Indians as Hay River Indian Reserve No. 1, subject to the existing rights and privileges described in Part 2 of the Schedule, any proceeds of which shall be credited to the revenue monies of the Hay River Band of Indians.

The authority of the Governor in Council under paragraph 19(d) of the *Territorial Lands Act* to "set apart and appropriate such areas or lands as may be necessary to enable the Government of Canada to fulfil its obligations under treaties with the Indians" is not the source of authority to set apart Crown lands as a reserve in that part of Canada to which the Act applies, i.e. the Yukon and Northwest Territories. It is, rather, the authority to create a land bank for that purpose. The *Indian Act* defines "reserve" but nowhere deals with the creation of a reserve. Notwithstanding the words "pursuant to the Indian Act" in paragraph (2) of the Order in Council, the authority to set apart Crown lands for an Indian reserve in the Northwest Territories appears to remain based entirely on the Royal Prerogative, not subject to any statutory limitation. I therefore conclude that, the cause of action being limited to Her Majesty's alleged failure to observe and follow the requirements of Treaty No. 8, the objection that the Plaintiff is without *locus standi* to maintain the action is well taken.

It is not necessary, for this purpose, to attempt a comprehensive definition of the legal nature of Treaty No. 8. Clearly, it is not a concurrent executive act of two or more sovereign states. Neither, however, is it simply a contract between those who actually subscribed to it. It does impose and confer continuing obligations and rights on the successors of the Indians who entered into it, provided those successors are themselves Indians, as well as on Her Majesty in right of Canada. It confers no rights on strangers to the Treaty such as the Plaintiff.

If I am wrong in the foregoing conclusion, then the only particular of non-observance alleged, in respect of which the Plaintiff has a peculiar or special interest beyond that of the general public, is that to the extent that the lands set aside were within its municipal boundaries, they were not suitable for selection. The other particulars of non-observance were:

1.   that the Indians having, by the Treaty, ceded all their right to the lands specifically covered by the Treaty and "to all other lands wheresoever situated in the Northwest Territories", Her Majesty had no right to create the Reserve without prejudice to the band's or band members' right to participate in any future overall settlement of Indian land claims in the Northwest Territories;
2.   the failure to offer individual band members 160 acres each, an option provided by the Treaty to Indians who "may prefer to live apart from band reserves";
3.   the failure to contact each individual band member in the consultative process leading up to selection of the reserve lands, which was conducted with the band council in meetings open to all members.

None of these, if indeed they give rise to a cause of action, are causes of action that could properly be advanced by the Plaintiff.

The Treaty does require, *inter alia*, that the land set apart be selected after consulting with the Indians concerned as to the locality which may be found suitable and open for selection.

The Plaintiff does not contend that, by reason of their being within its municipal boundaries, the lands selected were not open for selection; only that they were not suitable because:

1. they were within an established municipality;
2. they were already occupied by "numerous non-band members";
3. they are "not contiguous but contain large parcels of privately owned land";
4. they are not intended to be used by the band for settlement but rather the band intends to derive revenue from leasing them;
5. they are intended to be used for harbours and public works "which should not form part of the reserve".

While no evidence was, in fact, adduced in support of points 4 and 5, it is clear that they reflect the real reason for this action. The Plaintiff, understandably, wants the entire control and benefit of future development within its boundaries and particularly that on the river front. That development, no doubt, appeared both imminent and substantial when the action was commenced in view of the prospect of construction of a natural gas pipeline and associated works along the Mackenzie River valley and the town's location as a highway, rail and waterway terminus. That said, I have no basis, in the absence of evidence, for concluding that lands suitable for the purposes mentioned in items 4 and 5 are not suitable within the contemplation of the Treaty.

As to non-members of the band the evidence is that, as of December 31, 1977, 15 non-treaty Indians and 14 treaty Indians not of the Hay River Band resided within the limits of the reserve along with 123 band members. The "large parcels of privately owned land" within the global boundaries of the Reserve, but excluded from it, aggregate something under 250 acres most of which is made up of parcels patented to the Hudson's Bay Company and the Roman Catholic and Anglican churches. None of the non-members or private owners complain and the Plaintiff, by the mere fact of it being the municipality in which they reside or their land is located, has no right to bring this action for them.

The only basis for complaint in which the Plaintiff might conceivably have *locus standi* flows from the fact that lands within its boundaries were chosen at all. This is based on the notion that the provisions of the Municipal Ordinance, on the one hand, and the *Indian Act*, on the other, dealing with such matters as the legislative authorities vested in the band council and municipal council, the obligation to provide services and liability to and exemption from property taxes are incompatible. I accept that co-existence of a municipality and Indian reserve over the same territory could prove vexing to all concerned but that is not necessarily to say that the arrangement would render the lands unsuitable as a reserve.

The Town of Hay River has a population of about 3,500. Its geographic area, as appears from Exhibit P-8, is only slightly less than that of the reserve. Between a quarter and a third of each is within the limits of the other. The reserve includes all that portion of the town, other than some private property, east of the river as well as a 15 acre island in the river. Except when frozen over, the river must be crossed by private boat or a bridge seven miles upstream. The municipal services actually provided to the portion of the Town within the Reserve were, prior to its creation, minimal and have since been reduced to the level of nonexistence. Municipal facilities within the developed town site, to which reserve residents have access, are heavily subsidized by senior governments. It is fortunate that, whatever the situation might be in theory, in fact the coincidence of municipality and reserve, in this instance, results in no significant burden on the municipal ratepayers.

The pertinent provision of the Treaty requires that the location selected be suitable to the Indians and to Her Majesty. If its suitability to either can be brought into issue by a municipality within whose limits the lands lie, which I doubt, the duty of one or the other to take the municipality's interests into account would have to be based on a far more substantial real municipal interest in the lands than is established here.

The action is dismissed with costs.

The text of Treaty #8 provides:

And Her Majesty the Queen hereby agrees and undertakes to lay aside reserves for such bands as desire reserves, the same not to exceed in all one square mile for each family of five for such number of families as may elect to reside on reserves, or in that proportion for larger or smaller families; and for such families or individual Indians as may prefer to live apart from band reserves, Her Majesty undertakes to provide land in severalty to the extent of 160 acres to each Indian, the land to be conveyed with a proviso as to non-alienation without the consent of the Governor General in Council of Canada, the selection of such reserves, and lands in severalty, to be made in the manner following, namely, the Superintendent General of Indian Affairs shall depute and send a suitable person to determine and set apart such reserves and lands, after consulting with the Indians concerned as to the locality which may be found suitable and open for selection.

Provided, however, that Her Majesty reserves the right to deal with any settlers within the bounds of any lands reserved for any band as She may see fit;

The area subject to Treaty #8 consists in the Peace River region of British Columbia, the Northern half of Alberta, North-Western Saskatchewan, and the North-West Territories south-west of Great Slave Lake.

The selection, establishment and development of Indian reserves in Saskatchewan has been described by Stewart Raby:

> With the onset of agricultural settlement in Saskatchewan, the Canadian government set about pursuing its policy of setting up supervised, self-supporting reserves for the Indian populations. These, it was thought, would serve as a mechanism for transforming the Indians from nomadic hunters of the prairies into farmers or labourers living in stabilized communities. Though three reserves in the extreme south-east of the province were included in Treaty No. 2 (1871), it was not until 1874-76 that Treaties Nos. 4 and 6 were concluded; these pertained to the majority of Saskatchewan's Indian peoples, those of the Qu'Appelle and Saskatchewan River Valleys and the Assiniboine bands of the south-west. Reserves were set up on the basis of approximately one square mile of inalienable territory for each family of five. The land was chosen by the Indians themselves, government surveyors helping only to ensure that they had a reasonably well-balanced array of natural resources such as land, timber and water. This is an important reason why, aside from security, they were generally located or relocated away from the semi-arid south-western part of the province. The transfer of agricultural equipment and stock, annual payments and the provision of educational facilities were also agreed upon. The administration of Indians in the area that was to become Saskatchewan was achieved through the North-West Superintendency, whose agents and agricultural instructors resided in their respective groups of individual reserves. In many cases small areas of hay land and fishing stations, separate from the reserves proper, were made available.
>
> Problems were initially encountered in inducing the Indian groups to settle upon their chosen reserves, especially since the presence and rumour of buffalo were inclined to work against such attempts in the plains area. Once established, reserves were by no means fixed in location, since both Indian demands for alternative allocations and the amalgamation of declining bands led to changes in the reserve pattern at the same time as surveys of new reserves were in progress further north. Thus, two reserves, Pheasant Rump and Ocean Man, to the west of White Bear and covering over 73 square miles, were surrendered in March, 1901 and the area sold for $58,000 through public competition. In total, almost one-third of the reserve lands in Assiniboia in 1885 have since been ceded. Settlement was dispersed over some reserves, partly to stimulate private ownership and economic emulation within bands, though this was also found impractical when the benefits of close supervision and centralized education became apparent.
>
> The uprising of 1885 brought in its immediate wake both destruction

and the interruption of that steady improvement confidently anticipated by the Government's employees. Dissident Indians were gradually taken back into Treaty since they were judged willing to settle the reserves and to learn farming. Remarkedly quickly the balance in the plains area between agricultural enterprises and the more traditional fishing and hunting was changed, though as an interim measure there continued the rationing out of supplies by the Government, notably of flour, tea and bacon, and of increasing quantities of fresh beef. Not all the territory granted through reserves was amenable to grain farming; this encouraged expansion into livestock production, an emphasis which is still evident in several agencies. Mixed farming was further stimulated by discouraging setbacks from the natural environment during the drought of the early 1890's. Whilst the grain harvest on Assiniboian reserves increased sixfold between 1886-91 to almost 40,000 bushels, it had fallen to 5,000 bushels by 1894, the trough of that particular climatic cycle. Out-migration in times of hardship, a recourse for white settlers, was not a possible alternative for the Indians.

Some two thousand square miles were included in reserves by the turn of the century. By 1906, treaties had been concluded for all lands in Saskatchewan and the majority of the Plains Indian population had changed over to a mixed farming economy. This was supplemented by the increasing opportunities for wage-labour as the railways and settlement moved in and by assistance from the government and the churches; these were accompanied by declining outputs from hunting and fishing.

In line with most of the populations of the Indian groups on the reserves of the Great Plains, those in Saskatchewan fell during the period up to about 1905, after which they steadily increased to the present. Thus, the reserve Cree population of the six major agencies fell from over 6,200 in 1884 to approximately 4,800 in 1904, when approximately 6,500 treaty Indians, in total, were resident in the province. The crude death rates were high and did not fall consistently below 50 per thousand people until after the latter date. By that time the disastrous tuberculosis epidemic was well past its 1890 peak of over 135 deaths per thousand population in the reserves around Qu'Appelle. . .

The halting, gradual expansion in the base of the reserve economies has not kept pace with this continuing natural increase, which itself has not been offset by any major expansion in permanent out-migration from the reserves. In 1961, the total Indian income from sales of commodities and wages was about $3.4 millions, providing a per capita average of $143 for the 24,180 Indians resident on Saskatchewan reserves in that year. Federal subventions equalized the inter-agency variations and raised the total per capita income to $347. When correlated with the locations of the agencies, the regional variations in the economies which contribute to these outputs are quite clear, reflecting the natural resources and wage labour opportunities in the different sections of the province. But even among the bands with higher annual incomes, which approach $500 per capita, these compare unfavourably with the overall provincial average of over twice that amount. . .

Most reserve areas in the southern agencies have insufficient land for adequate self-supporting agrarian economies. In any case, existing resources are not fully utilized, partly as a result of a shortage of capital. Alternative employment is hampered by limited rural industrialization, the underemployed white population and high competition for urban jobs. Further north there are even fewer opportunities to engage in agriculture, and despite efforts both at conservation and marketing, the fur catch appears to have attained a maximum of some $350 per annum for each trapper. Consequently, dependence on relief has increased, a trend reinforced by the poor prospects for employment and income from fishing. Employment in mining is limited both by the Indians' lack of training and the small number of active mines, though the improving prospects in forestry industries deserve note.

> J.H. Richards and K.I. Fung, *Atlas of Saskatchewan*, University of Saskatchewan, 1969, p. 174.

In 1980, it was recorded that 70% of the 300,000 status Indians in Canada lived on reserves. There are 2,242 separate tracts of reserve land totalling 10,021 square miles, which comprises 0.28% of the land area of Canada, and 0.48% of the land area of the provinces of Canada. There are Indian reserves in every jurisdiction except Newfoundland. The per capita acreage of reserve land is approximately 34 acres, varying between 8 acres per capita in Quebec and the Atlantic Provinces and 80 acres per capita in Alberta (excluding the Yukon and North West Territories). Forest lands cover 44% of the total area of Indian Reserves.

Inuit, Indians, non-status Indians and Metis are estimated to number between 600,000 and 1.2 million, that is between 2.4% and 4.8% of the total population of Canada.

In Australia, a country with similarly large areas of unworkable agricultural land, reserves and aboriginal land comprise 10.28% of the total land area. As at 31 December 1981 the Aboriginal population of Australia numbered 181,300, comprising 1.2% of the country's population.

Unfulfilled reserve land entitlement, as distinct from land claims founded upon aboriginal occupancy, continues to exist in the Prairie Provinces. The failure to fulfil treaty land entitlement was recognized in 1930 in the Natural Resource Transfer Agreements. The Agreements with Alberta, Manitoba and Saskatchewan each require that:

. . . the Province will from time to time, upon the request of the Superintendent General of Indian Affairs, set aside out of the unoccupied Crown lands hereby transfered to its administration, such further areas as the said Superintendent General may, in agreement with the appropriate Minister of the Province, select as necessary to enable Canada to fulfil its obligations under the treaties with the Indians of the Province, and such areas shall thereafter be administered by Canada in the same way in all respects as if they had never passed to the Province under the provisions hereof.

Alberta SC 1930, c. 3, s. 10, Saskatchewan SC 1930 c. 41, s. 10, Manitoba SC 1930 c. 29, 11

Final settlement of treaty land entitlement has yet to be achieved in the Prairies. In Saskatchewan thirty bands claim entitlement to be outstanding. The federal and Saskatchewan governments have acknowledged the validity of the claim of fifteen. The Government and the bands agreed in 1977 that the bands were entitled, in accord with the Treaty, to one square mile per family of five (128 acres per band member) using the band population figure of 31 December 1976. The area of land the bands had already received would be subtracted from such entitlement. No such agreement has been reached in Alberta or Manitoba. The Saskatchewan government described its position on "Indian Lands and Canada's Responsibility" in 1979:

Saskatchewan Indian Land Entitlements

The British North America Act, 1867 placed the responsibility for "Indians and the Lands Reserved for Indians" squarely upon the federal government. The Treaties defined those responsibilities further and the Indian Act provided the working rules. When the Province was formed in 1905, Canada retained administration of land and resources. The national settlement program was not interrupted.

From 1890 to 1930 over 79 million acres in the Saskatchewan area were surveyed in the search for agricultural land suitable for settlement. Title was alienated completely for over 61 million acres, with 14 million of the total remaining being considered suitable only for forest production and/or grazing. 30 million acres were homesteaded, the railroads got 15 million acres in the form of land grants, and the Hudson's Bay Company received 3.3 million. The Indians of the territory were allocated 1.5 million acres. By 1930, most of the agricultural land in the West had been disposed of in meeting the "purposes of the Dominion", and the natural resources were transferred from federal to provincial jurisdiction. Section 10 of The Resources Transfer Agreement required the Province to make unoccupied Crown land available to Canada so that Canada could fulfil any outstanding land entitlements that may have been overlooked. It appeared that only those Bands living in the northern part of the Province had not requested specific Reserves, and there was plenty of vacant land to meet their needs.

In 1975, Saskatchewan was informed by Canada that research into the Treaties found outstanding land entitlements for some Bands in Saskatchewan, and a request was made by the federal minister to honor these entitlements as provided under Section 10 of The Resources Transfer Agreement. Most vacant lands in Saskatchewan had limited possibilities and Saskatchewan offered all its Crown lands, occupied or vacant, under the following conditions: a) that the federal government make its lands available on the same basis; b) where occupied Crown lands were selected, the lessees' interests be satisfactorily discharged, through compensation, or other arrangement; c) acreage for the settlement of Treaties would be based on the Band population as established at December 31, 1976.

At present, research into the various Treaties has revealed that over 1 million acres is still outstanding for 15 Indian Bands in the Province, with over half of the acreage for Bands situated in the agricultural area. Saskatchewan will be hard pressed to find this amount of suitable land in all the Crown holdings occupied or vacant. But this is a legitimate debt which should not be allowed to continue. Saskatchewan people recognize this and are prepared through co-operation and adjustment to find a satisfactory settlement.

A reasonable start has been made with those Bands living in Northern Saskatchewan, where, in spite of mineral exploration, mining leases and licences, well over 100,000 acres are to be transferred to Indian Bands. A far more difficult problem exists in the agricultural area of the Province, where well established agricultural production by individual farmers may be affected.

In summary, less than 1% of the total agricultural acreage of the Province will be needed to satisfy all entitlements. This is an area less than the size of the Prince Albert National Park. Both Canada and Saskatchewan must make sure that the debt is paid. At the same time it cannot be expected that anyone affected by land transfer should be forced to assume the full impact of it. It is an outstanding debt of all society and should be assumed and resolved by governments.

In 1979 it was reported that the Manitoba government was prepared to transfer 70,000 acres of unoccupied Crown land for reserve land. The Manitoba Indian Brotherhood claimed entitlement to an acreage in excess of half a million acres.

In 1982, the newly elected Saskatchewan government announced that it was reviewing the 1977 "agreement" respecting outstanding treaty land entitlement. This review was not completed as of mid-1984.

Further Reading

R.H. Bartlett, ''Establishment of Indian Reserves on the Prairies,'' 3 [1980] CNLR 3.

R.J. Surtees, ''Development of Indian Reserve Policy in Canada,'' *Ontario History*, Vol. CXI, p. 87.

Department of Indian Affairs, *Indian Conditions: A Survey*, 1980, Ottawa.

3. The Provincial Interest in Reserve Lands

(a) *Seybold* and *Star Chrome Mining*

(i) In 1888, the Privy Council held in *St Catharine's Milling and Lumber Co. v. The Queen* (1888), 14 AC 46 that under the British North America Act, section 109, the title to lands in Ontario, reserved to the Indians under the Royal Proclamation of 1763, was vested in the Crown in the right of the province subject to the Indian interest. Upon the surrender of such lands by treaty, the entire beneficial interest vested in the Crown in the right of the province. The decision suggested difficulties for the federal government in the establishment of reserves following a surrender of the Indian title by treaty and also in the disposition of reserves upon surrender under the Indian Act. These difficulties were considered in *Ontario Mining Company v. Seybold,* [1903] AC 73 by the Privy Council in a dispute between a claimant relying upon letters patent issued by Canada and a claimant relying upon letters patent issued by Ontario. The land had been surrendered by the Indians under Treaty #3, set apart as reserve land and then surrendered for sale under the Indian Act for the benefit of the Indians. The Privy Council upheld the letters patent issued by Ontario and observed:

> LORD DAVEY:
>
> Their Lordships agree with the Courts below that the decision of this case is a corollary from that of the *St Catharine's Milling Co. v. Reg*. The argument of the learned counsel for the appellants at their Lordships' bar was that at the date of the letters patent issued by the Dominion officers to their predecessors in title the land in question was held in trust for sale for the exclusive benefit of the Indians, and the province of Ontario. This argument assumes that the Reserve 38 B was rightly set out and appropriated by the Dominion officers as against the Government of Ontario, and ignores the effect of the surrender of 1873 as declared in the previous decision of this Board. By s. 91 of the British North America Act, 1867, the Parliament of Canada has exclusive legislative authority over ''Indians and lands

reserved for the Indians.'' But this did not vest in the Government of the Dominion any proprietary rights in such lands, or any power by legislation to appropriate lands which by the surrender of the Indian title had become the free public lands of the province as an Indian reserve, in infringement of the proprietary rights of the province. Their Lordships repeat for the purposes of the present argument what was said by Lord Herschell in delivering the judgment of this Board in the *Fisheries Case* as to the broad distinction between proprietary rights and legislative jurisdiction. Let it be assumed that the Government of the province, taking advantage of the surrender of 1873, came at least under an honourable engagement to fulfil the terms on the faith of which the surrender was made, and, therefore, to concur with the Dominion Government in appropriating certain undefined portions of the surrendered lands as Indian reserves. The result, however, is that the choice and location of the lands to be so appropriated could only be effectively made by the joint action of the two Governments.

In 1920, the Privy Council was required to consider the title to lands set apart for the use of the Indians in Quebec pursuant to an 1851 statute and subsequently surrendered for sale pursuant to the Indian Act for the benefit of the Indians. Canada argued that title under the 1851 statute vested in the Commissioner of Indian Lands, who held the entire beneficial interest for the Indians. Canada accordingly argued that title did not vest in the province under section 109 of the British North America Act.

(ii) *Attorney General of Quebec and Star Chrome Mining* v. *Attorney General of Canada*, [1921] 1 AC 401.

DUFF J:

The first question which arises concerns the effect of the deed of surrender of April 3, 1882 — whether, that is to say, as a result of the surrender, the title to the lands affected by it became vested in the Crown in right of the Dominion, or, on the contrary, the title, freed from the burden of the Indian interest, passed to the Province under s. 109 of the British North America Act.

The claim of Quebec is based upon the contention that at the date of Confederation the radical title in these lands was vested in the Crown, subject to an interest held in trust for the benefit of the Indians, which, in the words used by Lord Watson, in delivering judgment in *St Catharine's Milling and Lumber Co.* v. *The Queen*, was only ''a personal and usufructuary right dependent upon the goodwill of the Sovereign.'' On behalf of the Dominion it is contended that the title, both legal and beneficial, was held in trust for the Indians.

In virtue of the enactment of s. 91, head 24, of the British North America Act, by which exclusive authority to legislate in respect of lands reserved for Indians is vested in the Dominion Parliament, it is not disputed that that Parliament would have full authority to legislate in respect of the disposition of the Indian title, which, according to the Dominion's contention, would be the full beneficial title. On the other hand, if the view advanced by the Province touching the nature of the Indian title be accepted, then it follows from the principle laid down by the decision of this Board in *St Catharine's Milling and Lumber Co.* v. *The Queen* (supra) that upon the surrender in 1882 of the Indian interest the title to the lands affected by the surrender became vested in the Crown in right of the Province, freed from the burden of that interest.

The answer to the question raised by this controversy primarily depends upon the true construction of two statutes passed by the Legislature of the Province of Canada in 1850 and 1851 (13 & 14 Vict. c. 42 and 14 & 15 Vict. c. 106). The last-mentioned statute is entitled, "An Act to authorise the setting apart of lands for the use of certain Indian tribes in Lower Canada," and, after reciting that it is expedient to set apart certain lands for such use," it enacts that tracts not exceeding 230,000 acres may, under the authority of Orders in Council, be described, surveyed and set out by the Commissioner of Crown Lands, and that "such tracts of land shall be and are hereby respectively set apart and appropriated to and for the use of the several Indian tribes in Lower Canada, for which they shall be respectively directed to be set apart . . . . and the said tracts of land shall accordingly, by virtue of this Act . . . . be vested in and managed by the Commissioner of Indian Lands for Lower Canada, under" the statute first mentioned, 13 & 14 Vict. c. 42.

This statute (13 & 14 Vict. c. 42) is entitled "An Act for the better protection of the lands and property of the Indians in Lower Canada," and, following upon a recital that it is expedient to make better provision in respect of "lands appropriated to the use of Indians in Lower Canada," enacts (by s. 1) as follows: "That it shall be lawful for the Governor to appoint from time to time a Commissioner of Indian Lands for Lower Canada, in whom and in whose successors by the name aforesaid, all lands or property in Lower Canada which are or shall be set apart or appropriated to or for the use of any tribe or body of Indians, shall be and are hereby vested, in trust for such tribe or body, and who shall be held in law to be in the occupation and possession of any lands in Lower Canada actually occupied or possessed by any such tribe or body in common, or by any chief or member thereof or other party for the use or benefit of such tribe or body, and shall be entitled to receive and recover the rents, issues and profits of such lands and property, and shall and may, in and by the name aforesaid, but subject to the provisions hereinafter made, exercise and defend all or any of the rights lawfully appertaining to the proprietor, possessor or occupant of such land or property." And by s. 3: "That the said Commissioner shall have full power to concede or lease or charge any such land or property as aforesaid and to receive or recover the rents, issues and profits thereof as any lawful proprietor, possessor or occupant thereof might do, but shall be subject in all things to the instructions he may from time to time receive from the Governor, and shall be personally responsible to the Crown for all his acts, and more especially for any act done contrary to such instructions, and shall account for all moneys received by him, and apply and pay over the same in such manner, at such time, and to such person or officer, as shall be appointed by the Governor, and shall report from time to time on all matters relative to this office in such manner and form, and give such security, as the Governor shall direct and require; and all moneys and movable property received by him or in his possession as Commissioner, if not duly accounted for, applied and paid over as aforesaid, or if not delivered by any person having been such Commissioner to his successor in office, may be recovered by the Crown or by such successor, in any Court having civil jurisdiction to the amount or value, from the person having been such Commissioner and his sureties, jointly and severally."

The rival views which have been advanced before their Lordships touching the construction of these enactments have already been indicated.

In support of the Dominion claim it is urged that, as regards lands "appropriated" under the Act of 1851, the words "shall be and are hereby vested in trust for" the Indians, create a beneficial estate in such lands, which by force of the statute is held for the Indians, and which could not lawfully be devoted to any purpose other than the purposes of the trust, and indeed is equivalent to the beneficial ownership.

While the language of the statute of 1850 undoubtedly imports a legislative acknowledgment of a right inherent in the Indians to enjoy the lands appropriated to their use under the superintendence and management of the Commissioner of Indians Lands, their Lordships think the contention of the Province to be well founded to this extent, that the right recognized by the statute is a usufructuary right only and a personal right in the sense that it is in its nature inalienable except by surrender to the Crown.

By s. 3 the Commissioner is not only accountable for his acts, but is subject to the direction of the Governor in all matters relating to the trust; the intent of the statute appears to be, in other words, that the rights and powers committed to him are not committed to him as the delegate of the Legislature, but as the officer who for convenience of administration is appointed to represent the Crown for the purpose of managing the property for the benefit of the Indians. If this be the correct view, then, whatever be the nature or quantum of the Commissioner's interest, it is held by him in his capacity of officer of the Crown and his title is still the title of the Crown; and this, it may be observed, is apparently the view upon which the Dominion Government proceeded in accepting the surrender of 1882, the lands surrendered being treated (and their Lordships think rightly treated) for the purposes of that transaction as a "Reserve" within the meaning of the Act of 1882 — in other words, as lands "the legal title" to which still remained in the Crown (s. 2, sub-s. 6). It is not unimportant, however, to notice that the term "vest" is of elastic import; and a declaration that lands are "vested" in a public body for public purposes may pass only such powers of control and management and such proprietary interest as may be necessary to enable that body to discharge its public functions effectively: *Tunbridge Wells Corporation* v. *Baird*, an interest which may become devested when these functions are transferred to another body. In their Lordships' opinion, the words quoted from s. 1 are not inconsistent with an intention that the Commissioner should possess such limited interest only as might be necessary to enable him effectually to execute the powers and duties of control and management, of suing and being sued, committed to him by the Act.

In the judgment of this Board in the *St Catharine's Milling Co.'s Case* already refered to, it was laid down, speaking of Crown lands burdened with the Indian interest arising under the Proclamation of 1763, as follows: "The Crown has all along had a present proprietary estate in the land, upon which the Indian title was a mere burden. The ceded territory was, at the time of the union, land vested in the Crown, subject to 'an interest other than that of the Province in the same,' within the meaning of s. 109; and must now belong to Ontario in terms of that clause, unless its rights have been taken away by some provision of the Act of 1867 other than those already noticed." And their Lordships said: "It appears to them to be sufficient for the purposes of this case that there has been all along vested in the Crown a substantial and paramount estate, underlying the Indian title, which became a plenum dominium whenever that title was surrendered or otherwise extinguished."

The language of the statutes of 1850 and 1851 must, therefore, be examined in light of the circumstances of the time and of the objects of the legislation as declared by the enactments themselves, for the purpose of ascertaining whether or not the Crown retained in lands appropriated for the use of an Indian tribe a "paramount title" upon which the Indian interest was a mere "burden" in the sense in which these phrases are used in these passages.

The object of the Act of 1850, as declared in the recitals already quoted, is to make better provision for preventing encroachments upon the lands appropriated to the use of Indian tribes and for the defence of their rights and privileges, language which does not point to an intention of enlarging or in any way altering the quality of the interest conferred upon the Indians by the instrument of appropriation or other source of title; and the view that the Act was passed for the purpose of affording legal protection for the Indians in the enjoyment of property occupied by them or appropriated to their use, and of securing a legal status for benefits to be enjoyed by them, receives some support from the circumstance that the operation of the Act appears to extend to lands occupied by Indian tribes in that part of Quebec which, not being within the boundaries of the Province as laid down in the Proclamation of 1763, was, subject to the pronouncements of that Proclamation in relation to the rights of the Indians, a region in which the Indian title was still in 1850, to quote the words of Lord Watson, "a personal and usufructuary right dependent upon the good-will of the Sovereign." It should be noted also that the Act of 1851, under which the lands in question were set apart, is plainly an Act passed with the object of setting lands apart "for the use" of Indian tribes, and that by the same Act the powers of the Commissioner of Indian Lands under the Act of 1850 are referred to as "powers of management."

Their Lordships do not find it necessary to enter upon a consideration of the precise effect of the words of s. 3, investing the Commissioner with power to "concede," "lease" or "charge" lands or property affected by the statute. It is sufficient to say that, having regard to the recitals of the same statute and the language of the Act of 1851 just referred to, as well as to the policy of successive administrations in the matter of Indian affairs which, to cite the judgment of the Board in the *St Catharine's Milling Co.'s Case* had been "all along the same in this respect, that the Indian inhabitants have been precluded from entering into any transaction with a subject for the sale or transfer of their interest in the land, and have only been permitted to surrender their rights to the Crown by a formal contract, duly ratified at a meeting of their chiefs or head men convened for the purpose," their Lordships think these words ought not to be construed as giving the Commissioner authority to convert the Indian interest into money by sale or to dispose of the land freed from the burden of the Indian interest, except after a surrender of that interest to the Crown.

It results from these considerations, in their Lordships' opinion, that the effect of the Act of 1850 is not to create an equitable estate in lands set apart for an Indian tribe of which the Commissioner is made the recipient for the benefit of the Indians, but that the title remains in the Crown and that the Commissioner is given such an interest as will enable him to exercise the powers of management and administration committed to him by the statute.

The Dominion Government had, of course, full authority to accept the surrender on behalf of the Crown from the Indians, but, to quote once more the judgment of the Board in the *St Catharine's Milling Co.'s Case*, it had "neither authority nor power to take away from Quebec the interest which had been assigned to that Province by the Imperial statute of 1867." The effect of the surrender would have been otherwise if the view, which no doubt was the view upon which the Dominion Government acted, had prevailed — namely, that the beneficial title in the lands was by the Act of 1850 vested in the Commissioner of Indian Lands as trustee for the Indians with authority, subject to the superintendence of the Crown, to convert the Indian interest into money for the benefit of the Indians. As already indicated, in their Lordships' opinion, that is a view of the Act of 1850 which cannot be sustained.

The appeal should, therefore, be allowed and the action remitted to the Superior Court to give judgment against the respondent Dame Rosalie Thompson for the amount of the purchase money and of the damages which, if any, she shall be found liable to pay to the appellants, the Star Chrome Mining Co., and their Lordships will humbly advise His Majesty accordingly.

The respondent Dame Rosalie Thompson will pay the costs of the Star Chrome Mining Co. here and in the Courts below. There will be no order as to the costs of other parties.

The reasoning of *St Catharine's Milling*, *Ontario Mining*, and *Star Chrome Mining* was recently applied to reserve lands surrendered for sale in New Brunswick: *Smith* v. *The Queen*, [1983] 3 CNLR 161 (Supreme Court of Canada).

(b) Quebec

The 1850 Act for the Better Protection of the Lands and Property of the Indians in Lower Canada applied "to any lands in Lower Canada now held by the Crown in trust for or for the benefit of any such tribe or body of Indians." (SC 1850, c. 42, 13 and 14 Vic.) Such lands were vested in the Commissioner of Indian Lands. The 1850 Act included all the reserves established in Quebec before that time, except for that at Oka (SC 1841, 3 & 4 Vict. c. 30). In 1851 the Act to Authorize the Setting Apart of Lands for the use of Indian Tribes in Lower Canada (SC 1851, 14 & 15 Vict. c. 106) authorized the setting apart of 230,000 acres. The acreage was set apart by 1854. The 1851 statute directed that the lands be vested in the Commissioner of Indian Lands established under the 1850 legislation. The conclusion of the Privy Council in the *Star Chrome Mining Case* — that title, and upon surrender the "plenum dominum'' vested in the Crown in the right of the Province — is applicable to all the reserves that vested in the Commissioner of Indians Lands.

In 1922, immediately after the decision in *Star Chrome*, Quebec enacted an Act respecting Lands set apart for Indians (SQ 1922, c. 37, now RSQ 1964, c. 92, ss. 65-67).

1.   The Lieutenant-Governor in Council may reserve and set apart, for the benefit of the various Indian tribes of this Province, the usufruct of public lands described, surveyed and classified for such purpose by the Minister of Lands and Forests.

The extent of such public lands shall not exceed, in all, three hundred and thirty thousand acres in superficies.

The usufruct of the lands described, surveyed and classified by the Minister of Lands and Forests shall be transferred, gratuitously and on the conditions be may determine, by the Lieutenant-Governor in Council to the Government of Canada to be administered by it in trust for the said Indian tribes.

Such usufruct shall be inalienable, in whole or in part, and the lands subjected thereto shall return to the Government of this Province, without any formality whatsoever, from and after the day when the Indians to whom they have been assigned in usufruct by the Government of Canada cease to occupy them as usufructuaries.

Mining rights shall not be included in such concession, notwithstanding the absence of any mention to this effect.

Nor shall any such reserve be granted or taken out of any territory under license to cut timber, unless the consent of the license-holder shall be first obtained.

The legislation sought, of course, to codify the *Star Chrome* decision. The 1922 legislation authorized the setting apart of 330,000 acres. Only 14,000 acres have been set apart under such authority.

The federal government has generally not been prepared to purchase lands of the Crown in the right of Quebec for the establishment of reserves. With respect to privately owned land, however, the federal government has been willing to purchase small areas for those bands with a traditional association with the land sought. Such purchases occurred in 1891 and 1892 and periodically between 1945 and 1968. The Oka reserve was the subject of the largest purchase — in 1945 from the Sulpician Order. There is, of course, no interest in the Quebec government in such lands.

Quebec has resisted entering into any general agreement with the federal government providing for the Indian interest in all reserve lands and their proceeds. Indeed, as a result of the *Star Chrome* decision, the Quebec government sought to recover proceeds of the sale of *all* surrendered reserve lands in Quebec. In 1933, $140,959.37 was paid to the Quebec government in full payment of such proceeds.

In the late 1970s, a federal-provincial agreement was reached with respect to lands set apart as category I lands under the James Bay and Northern Quebec Agreement (1975) and the Northeastern Quebec Agreement (1978). The provisions of the Agreements reflect the analysis of the Privy Council in *Star Chrome Mining*. Under the terms of those agreements no category I or category I-N lands "may be sold or otherwise ceded except to the Crown in the right of Canada." And with respect to category IA and 1A-N the Agreements specifically provide that Quebec retains "bare ownership of the land", albeit such lands are recognized as being subject to the jurisdiction of and administration by the Government of Canada.

It is apparent that it is only rarely that there is no provincial interest in Indian reserves in Quebec as declared in *Star Chrome*.

Further Reading

R.H. Bartlett, "Indian Reserves in Quebec", unpublished.

W. Henderson, *Canada's Indian Reserves: The Usufruct in Our Constitution*, Department of Indian Affairs, February 1980.

F.G. Stanley, "First Indian Reserves in Canada" (1950) IV *Revue d'Histoire de L'Amerique Francaise*, 178.

Rapport de la Commission D'étude sur l'integrité du Territoirre du Quebec, Le Domaine Indien (*Dorion Report*) May 1973.

4. The Federal-Provincial Agreements Respecting Indian Reserve Lands

The effect of the Privy Council decision in *Ontario Mining* and *Star Chrome Mining* was, *inter alia*, to inhibit the establishment of reserves by the federal government and to preclude the surrender of such lands for the benefit of the Indians. It was sought by agreement between the federal and provincial governments to remove such impediments.

(a) Ontario

An Act for the settlement of certain questions between the Governments of Canada and Ontario respecting Indian Reserve Lands. SC 1924, c. 48.

CHAP. 48

An Act for the settlement of certain questions between the Governments of Canada and Ontario respecting Indian Reserve Lands.

[Assented to 19th July, 1924.]

HIS Majesty, by and with the advice and consent of the Senate and House of Commons of Canada, enacts as follows: —

1. The agreement between the Dominion of Canada and the Province of Ontario, in the terms set out in the schedule hereto, shall be as binding on the Dominion of Canada as if the provisions thereof had been set forth in an Act of this Parliament, and the Governor in Council is hereby authorized to carry out the provisions of the said agreement.

SCHEDULE.

MEMORANDUM OF AGREEMENT made in triplicate this 24th day March 1924.

BETWEEN the Government of the Dominion of Canada, acting herein by the Honourable Charles Stewart, Superintendent General of Indian Affairs, of the first part,

AND the Government of the Province of Ontario, acting herein by the Honourable James Lyons, Minister of Lands and Forests, and the Honourable Charles McCrea, Minister of Mines, of the second part.

WHEREAS from time to time treaties have been made with the Indians for the surrender for various considerations of their personal and usufructuary rights to territories now included in the Province of Ontario, such considerations including the setting apart for the exclusive use of the Indians of certain defined areas of land known as Indian Reserves;

AND WHEREAS, except as to such Reserves, the said territories were by the said treaties freed, for the ultimate benefit of the Province of Ontario, of the burden of the Indian rights, and became subject to be administered by the Government of the said Province for the sole benefit thereof;

AND WHEREAS the surrender of the whole or some portion of a Reserve by the band of Indians to whom the same was allotted has, in respect of certain Reserves in the Provinces of Ontario and Quebec, been under consideration in certain appeals to the Judicial Committee of the Privy Council, and the respective rights of the Dominion of Canada and the Province of Ontario, upon such surrenders being made, depend upon the law as declared by the Judicial Committee of the Privy Council and otherwise affecting the Reserve in question, and upon the circumstances under which it was set off;

AND WHEREAS on the 7th day of July, 1902, before the determination of the last two of the said appeals, it had been agreed between counsel for the Governments of the Dominion of Canada and the Province of Ontario, respectively, that, as a matter of policy and convenience, and without thereby affecting the constitutional or legal rights of either of the said Governments, the Government of the Dominion of Canada should have full power and authority to sell, lease and convey title in fee simple or for any less estate to any lands forming part of any Reserve thereafter surrendered by the Indians, and that any such sales, leases or other conveyances as had theretofore been made by the said Government should be confirmed by the Province of Ontario, the Dominion of Canada, however, holding the proceeds of any lands so sold, leased or conveyed subject, upon the extinction of the Indian interest therein and so far as such proceeds had been converted into money, to such rights of the Province of Ontario as might exist by law;

AND WHEREAS by the said agreement it was further provided that, as to the Reserves set aside for the Indians under a certain treaty made in 1873 and recited in the Schedule to the Dominion Statute, 54-55 Victoria, chapter 5, and the Statute of the Province of Ontario, 54 Victoria, chapter 3, the precious metals should be considered to form part thereof and might be disposed of by the Dominion of Canada in the same way and subject to the same conditions as the land in which they existed, and that the question whether the precious metals in the lands included in Reserves set aside under other treaties were to be considered as forming part thereof or not, should be expressly left for decision in accordance with the circumstances and the law governing each;

NOW THIS AGREEMENT WITNESSETH that the parties hereto, in order to settle all outstanding questions relating to Indian Reserves in the Province of Ontario, have mutually agreed subject to the approval of the Parliament of Canada and the Legislature of the Province of Ontario, as follows: —

1. All Indian Reserves in the Province of Ontario heretofore or hereafter set aside, shall be administered by the Dominion of Canada for the benefit of the band or bands of Indians to which each may have been or may be allotted; portions thereof may, upon their surrender for the purpose by the said band or bands, be sold, leased or otherwise disposed of by letters patent under the Great Seal of Canada, or otherwise under the direction of the Government of Canada, and the proceeds of such sale, lease or other disposition applied for the benefit of such band or bands, provided, however, that in the event of the band or bands to which any such Reserve has been allotted becoming extinct, of if, for any other reason, such Reserve, or any portion thereof is declared by the Superintendent General of Indian Affairs to be no longer required for the benefit of the said band or bands, the same shall thereafter be administered by, and for the benefit of, the Province of Ontario, and any balance of the proceeds of the sale or other disposition of any portion thereof then remaining under the control of the Dominion of Canada shall, so far as the same is not still required to be applied for the benefit of the said band or bands of Indians, be paid to the Province of Ontario, together with accured unexpended simple interest thereon.

2. Any sale, lease or other disposition made pursuant to the provisions of the last preceding paragraph may include or may be

limited to the minerals (including the precious metals) contained in or under the lands sold, leased or otherwise disposed of, but every grant shall be subject to the provisions of the statute of the Province of Ontario entitled "The Bed of Navigable Waters Act", Revised Statutes of Ontario, 1914, chapter thirty-one.

3.   Any person authorized under the laws of the Province of Ontario to enter upon land for the purpose of prospecting for minerals thereupon shall be permitted to prospect for minerals in any Indian Reserve upon obtaining permission so to do from the Indian Agent for such Reserve and upon complying with such conditions as may be attached to such permission, and may stake out a mining claim or claims on such Reserve.

4.   No person not so authorized under the laws of the Province of Ontario shall be given permission to prospect for minerals upon any Indian Reserve.

5.   The rules governing the mode of staking and the size and number of mining claims in force from time to time in the Province of Ontario or in the part thereof within which any Indian Reserve lies shall apply to the staking of mining claims on any such Reserve, but the staking of a mining claim upon any Indian Reserve shall confer no rights upon the person by whom such claim is staked except such as may be attached to such staking by the Indian Act or other law relating to the disposition of Indian Lands.

6.   Except as provided in the next following paragraph, one-half of the consideration payable, whether by way of purchase money, rent, royalty or otherwise, in respect of any sale, lease or other disposition of a mining claim staked as aforesaid, and, if in any other sale, lease or other disposition hereafter made of Indian Reserve lands in the Province of Ontario any minerals are included, and the consideration for such sale, lease or other disposition was to the knowledge of the Department of Indian Affairs affected by the existence or supposed existence in the said lands of such minerals, one-half of the consideration payable in respect of any such other sale, lease or other disposition, shall forthwith upon its receipt from time to time, be paid to the Province of Ontario; the other half only shall be dealt with by the Dominion of Canada as provided in the paragraph of this agreement numbered 1.

7.   The last preceding paragraph shall not apply to the sale, lease or other disposition of any mining claim or minerals on or in any of the lands set apart as Indian Reserves pursuant to the hereinbefore recited treaty made in 1873, and nothing in this agreement shall be deemed to detract from the rights of the Dominion of Canada touching any lands or minerals granted or conveyed by His Majesty for the use and benefit of Indians by letters patent under the Great Seal of the Province of Upper Canada, of the Province of Canada or of the Province of Ontario, or in

any minerals vested for such use and benefit by the operation upon any such letters patent of any statute of the Province of Ontario.

8. No water-power included in any Indian Reserve, which in its natural condition at the average low stage of water has a greater capacity than five hundred horsepower, shall be disposed of by the Dominion of Canada except with the consent of the Government of the Province of Ontario and in accordance with such special agreement, if any, as may be made with regard thereto and to the division of the purchase money, rental or other consideration given therefor.

9. Every sale, lease or other disposition heretofore made under the Great Seal of Canada or otherwise under the direction of the Government of Canada of lands which were at the time of such sale, lease or other disposition included in any Indian Reserve in the Province of Ontario, is hereby confirmed, whether or not such sale, lease or other disposition included the precious metals, but subject to the provisions of the aforesaid statute of the Province of Ontario entitled "The Bed of Navigable Waters Act", and the consideration received in respect of any such sale lease or other disposition shall be and continue to be dealt with by the Dominion of Canada in accordance with the provisions of the paragraph of this agreement numbered 1, and the consideration received in respect of any sale, lease or other disposition heretofore made under the Great Seal of the Province of Ontario, or under the direction of the Government of the said Province, of any lands which at any time formed part of any Indian Reserve, shall remain under the exclusive control and at the disposition of the Province of Ontario.

10. Nothing herein contained, except the provision for the application of "The Bed of Navigable Waters Act" aforesaid, shall affect the interpretation which would, apart from this agreement, be put upon the words of any letters patent heretofore or hereafter issued under the Great Seal of Canada or the Great Seal of the Province of Ontario, or of any lease or other conveyance, or of any contract heretofore or hereafter made under the direction of the Government of Canada or of the Province of Ontario.

IN WITNESS WHEREOF these presents have been signed by the parties thereto the day and year above written.

(b) The Prairie Provinces

The Crown in the right of Canada retained titled to the public lands in the Prairie Provinces until 1930. Up until that time, the Government of Canada was not inhibited in providing for Indian reserves by any title in the provinces of Alberta, Manitoba or Saskatchewan. In 1930, title to the public lands in the provinces was transferred to the Crown in the right of the provinces. Such transfer necessitated an agreement respecting title to and administration of

Indian reserves. The Natural Resources Agreements made between Canada and Alberta, Manitoba and Saskatchewan contain identical provisions governing Indian reserves:

INDIAN RESERVES

10. All lands included in Indian reserves within the Province, including those selected and surveyed but not yet confirmed, as well as those confirmed, shall continue to be vested in the Crown and administered by the Government of Canada for the purposes of Canada, and the Province will from time to time, upon the request of the Superintendent General of Indian Affairs, set aside, out of the unoccupied Crown lands hereby transferred to its administration, such further areas as the said Superintendent General may, in agreement with the appropriate Minister of the Province, select as necessary to enable Canada to fulfil its obligations under the treaties with the Indians of the Province, and such areas shall thereafter be administered by Canada in the same way in all respects as if they had never passed to the Province under the provisions hereof.

11. The provisions of paragraph one to six inclusive and of paragraph eight of the agreement made between the Government of the Dominion of Canada and the Goverment of the Province of Ontario on the 24th day of March, 1924, which said agreement was confirmed by statute of Canada, fourteen and fifteen George the Fifth chapter forty-eight, shall (except so far as they relate to the *Bed of Navigable Waters Act*) apply to the lands included in such Indian reserves as may hereafter be set aside under the last preceding clause as if the said agreement has been made between the parties hereto, and the provisions of the said paragraphs shall likewise apply to the lands included in the reserves heretofore selected and surveyed, except that neither the said lands nor the proceeds of the disposition thereof shall in any circumstances become administrable by or be paid to the Province.

> Alberta SC 1930, c. 3, ss. 10 and 11
> Saskatchewan SC 1930, c. 41, ss. 10 and 11
> Manitoba SC 1930, c. 29, ss. 11 and 12

(c) British Columbia

Treaties entered into upon the settlement of Vancouver Island provided that "our village sites and enclosed fields are to be kept for our own use, for the use of our children, and for those who may follow after us." The treaties were confined to the area immediately surrounding Victoria. No further treaties were entered into in British Columbia, except with respect to the Peace River area which was subject to Treaty #8. Reserves were thereafter established by executive action. The size of such reserves varied but was often as little as ten acres per family.

On 20 July 1871 British Columbia became part of the Dominion of Canada. A term of the admission of British Columbia provided:

13. The charge of the Indians, and the trusteeship and management of the lands reserved for their use and benefit, shall be assumed by the Dominion Government, and a policy as liberal as that hitherto pursued by the British Columbia Government shall be continued by the Dominion Government after the Union.

To carry out such policy, tracts of land of such extent as it has hitherto been the practice of the British Columbia Government to appropriate for that purpose, shall from time to time be conveyed by the Local Government to the Dominion Government in trust for the use and benefit of the Indians on application of the Dominion Government; and in case of disagreement between the two Governments respecting the quantity of such tracts of land to be so granted, the matter shall be referred for the decision of the Secretary of State for the Colonies.

The British Columbia and Canadian governments were unable to agree upon the provision of reserve lands as required by the Terms of Admission. In 1912 an Agreement was reached upon proposals to settle the differences between the governments:

AGREEMENT

MEMORANDUM OF AN AGREEMENT ARRIVED AT BE-TWEEN J.A.J. McKENNA, SPECIAL COMMISSIONER AP-POINTED BY THE DOMINION GOVERNMENT TO INVESTI-GATE THE CONDITION OF INDIAN AFFAIRS IN BRITISH COLUMBIA, AND THE HONOURABLE SIR RICHARD McBRIDE, AS PREMIER OF THE PROVINCE OF BRITISH COLUMBIA.

"Whereas it is desirable to settle all differences between the Governments of the Dominion and the Province respecting Indian lands and Indian Affairs generally in the Province of British Columbia, therefore the parties above named, have, subject to the approval of the Governments of the Dominion and of the Province, agreed upon the following proposals as a final adjustment of all matters relating to Indian Affairs in the Province of British Columbia: —

1. A Commission shall be appointed as follows: Two Commissioners shall be named by the Dominion and two by the Province. The four Commissioners so named shall select a fifth Commissioner, who shall be the Chairman of the Board.

2.   The Commission so appointed shall have power to adjust the acreage of Indian Reserves in British Columbia in the following manner:

(*a*)   At such places as the Commissioners are satisfied that more land is included in any particular Reserve as now defined than is reasonably required for the use of the Indians of that tribe or locality, the Reserve shall, with the consent of the Indians, as required by the Indian Act, be reduced to such acreage as the Commissioners think reasonably sufficient for the purposes of such Indians.

(*b*)   At any place at which the Commissioners shall determine that an insufficient quantity of land has been set aside for the use of the Indians of that locality, the Commissioners shall fix the quantity that ought to be added for the use of such Indians. And they may set aside land for any Band of Indians for whom land has not already been reserved.

3.   The Province shall take all such steps as are necessary to legally reserve the additional lands which the Commissioners shall apportion to any body of Indians in pursuance of the powers above set out.

4.   The lands which the Commissioners shall determine are not necessary for the use of the Indians shall be subdivided and sold by the Province at public auction.

5.   The net proceeds of all such sales shall be divided equally between the Province and the Dominion, and all moneys received by the Dominion under this Clause shall be held or used by the Dominion for the benefit of the Indians of British Columbia.

6.   All expenses in connection with the Commission shall be shared by the Province and Dominion in equal proportions.

7.   The lands comprised in the Reserves as finally fixed by the Commissioners aforesaid shall be conveyed by the Province to the Dominion with full power to the Dominion to deal with the said lands in such manner as they may deem best suited for the purposes of the Indians, including a right to sell the said lands and fund or use the proceeds for the benefit of the Indians, subject only to a condition that in the event of any Indian tribe or band in British Columbia at some future time becoming extinct, then any lands within the territorial boundaries of the Province which have been conveyed to the Dominion as aforesaid for such tribe or band, and not sold or disposed of as hereinbefore mentioned, or any unexpended funds being the proceeds of any Indian Reserve in the Province of British Columbia, shall be conveyed or repaid to the Province.

8.   Until the final report of the Commission is made, the Province shall withhold from pre-emption or sale any lands over which they have a disposing power and which have been heretofore applied for by the Dominion as additional Indian Reserves or which may during the sitting

of the Commission, be specified by the Commissioners as lands which should be reserved for Indians. If during the period prior to the Commissioners making their final report it shall be ascertained by either Government that any lands being part of an Indian Reserve are required for right-of-way or other railway purposes, or for any Dominion or Provincial or Municipal Public Work or purpose, the matter shall be referred to the Commissioners who shall thereupon dispose of the question by an Interim Report, and each Government shall thereupon do everything necessary to carry the recommendations of the Commissioners into effect.

Signed in duplicate at Victoria, British Columbia, this 24th day of September, 1912.

The McKenna-McBride Commission reported in 1916. An Indian agent described the reaction of the Indians:

The Indians see nothing of real value for them in the work of the Royal Commission. Their crying needs have not been met. The Commissioners did not fix up their hunting rights, fishing rights, and land rights, nor did they deal with the matter of reserves in a satisfactory manner. Their dealing with reserves has been a kind of maniuplation to suit the whites, and not the Indians. All they have done is to recommend that about 47,000 acres of generally speaking good lands be taken from the Indians, and about 80,000 acres of generally speaking poor lands, be given in their place. A lot of the land recommended to be taken from the reserves has been coveted by whites for a number of years. Most of the 80,000 acres additional lands is to be provided by the Province, but it seems that the Indians are really paying for these lands. Fifty percent of the value of the 47,000 acres to be taken from the Indians is to go to the Province, and it seems this amount will come to more than the value of the land the Province is to give the Indians. The Province loses nothing, the Dominion loses nothing, and the Indians are the losers. They get fifty percent on the 47,000 acres, but, as the 47,000 acres is much more valuable land than the 80,000 they are actually losers by the work of the Commission.

> F.E. LaViolette, *The Struggle for Survival*, University of Toronto Press, 1961, p. 135.

In 1919 the Lieutenant-Governor in Council for British Columbia and in 1920 the Governor in Council for the Dominion were empowered to do such acts and things as were necessary for the carrying out of the agreement of 12 September 1912. (Indian Affair Settlement Act, SCC 1919, c. 32; British Columbia Indian Lands Settlement Act, SC 1919-1920, c. 51.)

In 1924 the Report, by Provincial and Dominion order in council, was "approved and confirmed as constituting *full and final adjustment and settlement* of all differences in respect thereto between the Governments of the Dominion and the Province, in fulfillment of the said Agreement of the 24th day of September 1912, and also of section 13 of the Terms of Union," except as to the Peace River area, [O/C 26, July 1923, BC; PC 1265, 19 July, 1924].

In 1929, an Agreement was entered into by the Province and the Dominion respecting the form of the conveyance of Indian reserves by the Province to the Dominion, and providing with respect to reserves in the Peace River Area:

> 6.   Regarding Indian Reserves in the Railway Belt and Peace River Block, we have agreed that the Indian Reserves set apart by the Dominion Government in the Railway Belt and in the Peace River Block (as shown in Schedule hereto annexed), and also the Indian Reserves set apart before the transfer of the Railway Belt and the Peace River Block by the Province to the Dominion shall be excepted from the re-conveyance of the Railway Belt and the Peace River Block, and shall be held in trust and administered by the Dominion under the terms and conditions set forth in the Agreement dated 24th September, 1912, between Mr J.A.J. McKenna and the Hon. Sir Richard McBride (as confirmed by Dominion Statute, Chapter 51 of the Statutes of 1920, British Columbia Statute, Chapter 32 of the Statutes of 1919) in the Dominion Order-in-Council Number 1265, approved 19th July, 1924, and Provincial Order-In-Council Number 911, approved 26th of July, 1923, and in the form of conveyance marked "A" of the Indian Reserves outside the Railway Belt and the Peace River Block.

The Agreement was approved by Dominion Order in Council in 1930 (P.C. 208). The terms of the Agreement with respect to the Peace River area were entrenched in the 1930 British North America Act whereby Canada re-transferred the lands in the Railway Belt and the Peace Block to the Province. Clause 13 of the Agreement provided:

> 13.   Nothing in this agreement shall extend to the lands included within Indian reserves in the Railway Belt and the Peace River Block, but the said reserves shall continue to be vested in Canada in trust for the Indians on the terms and conditions set out in a certain order of the Governor General of Canada in Council approved on the 3rd day of February 1930 (P.C. 208).

The form of conveyance was approved by Provincial Order in Council in 1938 (OC 1036, 29 July).

RECOMMEND: —

THAT under authority of Section 93 of the "Land Act", being Chapter 144, "Revised Statutes of British Columbia, 1936", and

Section 2 of Chapter 32, "British Columbia Statutes", being the "Indian Affairs Settlement Act", the lands set out in schedule attached hereto be conveyed to His Majesty the King in the right of the Dominion of Canada in trust for the use and benefit of the Indians of the Province of British Columbia, subject however to the right of the Dominion Government to deal with the said lands in such manner as they may deem best suited for the purpose of the Indians including a right to sell the said lands and fund or use the proceeds for the benefit of the Indians subject to the condition that in the event of any Indian tribe or band in British Columbia at some future time becoming extinct that any lands hereby conveyed for such tribe or band, and not sold or disposed of as heretofore provided, or any unexpended fund being the proceeds of any such sale, shall be conveyed or repaid to the grantor, and that such conveyance shall also be subject to the following provisions: —

PROVIDED NEVERTHELESS that it shall at all times be lawful for Us, Our heirs and successors, or for any person or persons acting in that behalf by Our or their authority, to resume any part of the said lands which it may be deemed necessary to resume for making roads, canals, bridges, towing paths, or other works of public utility or convenience; so, nevertheless that the lands so to be resumed shall not exceed one-twentieth part of the whole of the lands aforesaid, and that no such resumption shall be made of any lands on which any buildings may have been erected, or which may be in use as gardens or otherwise for the more convenient occupation of any such buildings:

PROVIDED also that it shall be lawful for any person duly authorized in that behalf by Us, Our heirs and successors, to take and occupy such water privileges, and to have and enjoy such rights of carrying water over, through or under any parts of the hereditaments hereby granted, as may be reasonably required for mining or agricultural purposes in the vicinity of the said hereditaments, paying therefor a reasonable compensation:

PROVIDED also that the Department of Indian Affairs shall through its proper officers be advised of any work contemplated under the preceding provisoes that plans of the location of such work shall be furnished for the information of the Department of Indian Affairs, and that a reasonable time shall be allowed for consideration of the said plans and for any necessary adjustments or arrangements in connection with the proposed work:

PROVIDED also that it shall be at all times lawful for any person duly authorized in that behalf by Us, Our heirs and successors, to take from or upon any part of the hereditaments hereby granted, any gravel, sand, stone, lime, timber or other material which may be required in the construction, maintenance, or repair of any roads, ferries, bridges, or other public works. But nevertheless paying therefor reasonable compensation for such material as may be taken for use outside the boundaries of the hereditaments hereby granted:

PROVIDED also that all travelled streets, roads, trails, and other highways existing over or through said lands at the date hereof shall be excepted from this grant.

In 1961, "full and final settlement" of the provision of reserve lands in the area subject to Treaty #8 was declared by Provincial Order in Council No. 2995 (28 November 1961). It recommended that:

. . . pursuant to Section 65(1) of the Land Act, being Chapter 206, Revised Statutes of British Columbia, 1960 and Sections 2 and 3 of the Indian Affairs Settlement Act being Chapter 32, Statutes of British Columbia, 1919, the lands approximately outlined in red on the maps hereunto attached, which, in aggregate, shall not exceed a total of 24,448 acres, and when surveyed at the expense of the Department of Citizenship and Immigration under instructions of the Surveyor-General of the Province of British Columbia, be conveyed to her Majesty the Queen in the Right of Canada in trust for the use and benefit of the Indians of British Columbia, subject however, to the right of Canada to deal with the said lands in such manner as Canada may deem best suited for the purpose of the Indians including a right to sell the said lands and fund or use the proceeds for the benefit of the Indians, and on the condition that in the event of any Indian tribe or band in British Columbia becoming extinct at some future date, any lands hereby conveyed for such tribe or band and not sold or disposed of as hereinbefore provided, or any unexpended fund being the proceeds of any such sale, shall be conveyed or repaid to the Province of British Columbia, and on the condition, also, that the conveyance to Canada herein authorized shall be subject to the provisions and reservations set forth in Form No. 12 of the Schedule to the Land Act, and shall also be subject to rights acquired prior to the date of this Minute under the provisions of the Petroleum and Natural Gas Act.

The Order in Council reserved title to all minerals to the Province. In 1969, the provincial order in council No. 1036 and No. 2995 were amended to provide for the deletion of the condition respecting the entitlement of the province in the event that a tribe or band became extinct. (O/C No. 1555 13 May 1969).

The validity of the Order in Council promulgated to provide for the agreement respecting Indian reserves in British Columbia was considered in *Moses* v. *The Queen in Right of Canada*, [1977] 4 WWR 474 (British Columbia Supreme Court). The Chief and Council of the Lower Nicola Band alleged that the province had trespassed on reserve land by entering to widen a road without the consent of the band or the Dominion. The province asserted such right upon the basis of the right of resumption of one-twentieth of the area of reserve lands declared in P.C. 208 and O.C. 1036. Andrews J concluded at p. 490-91:

> The British Columbia Indian Lands Settlement Act (Canada) and the Indian Affairs Settlement Act (British Columbia) gave the Governor in Council and the Lieutenant-Governor of British Columbia in Council, respectively, broad powers for the purpose of settling all differences between the governments of the Dominion and the province respecting Indian lands and Indian affairs in the province. Privy Council O. 208 and order in council 1036 were validly made pursuant to the authority established by these two statutes.
>
> In my view, the sections of the Indian Act then in force regarding taking lands for public purposes and alienating lands had no application to the provisions of Privy Council O. 208. The draft form of conveyance approved by Privy Council O. 208 established the terms on which Indian lands in the province were to be held by the Dominion and in this regard provided for a reservation to the province of a right to resume possession of a portion of each reserve for purposes of public works. The reservation of such a right to the province did not constitute a taking of lands or an alienation of lands, as provided for in the Indian Act (RSC 1927, c. 98, ss. 48 and 50).
>
> Neither does the present exercise of this right come within s. 35(1) of the Indian Act now in force, regarding the taking of lands for public purposes pursuant to statutory powers, or s. 37 of the Act, requiring a surrender of lands before they may be alienated or otherwise disposed of.
>
> In my view, the province must be allowed, pursuant to its right of resumption, to enter upon the reserves in order to ascertain what land is required to accommodate the building of highways or the improvement of existing highways and to conduct proper surveys. This is necessary to enable the province to advise the Department of Indian Affairs of work contemplated and to furnish plans of the location of such work for the information of the Department of Indian Affairs. Only then can the department consider such plans and make representations regarding adjustments in connection with the proposed work.

The decision was affirmed by the British Columbia Court of Appeal [1979] 5 WWR 100, [1979] 4 CNLR 61.

In 1969, the Government of Canada acknowledged that in order to fulfil the Agreement of 1912, the consent of the Indians to any reduction of acreage or "cut-off" was required, and that it had not been obtained. In February 1982, the Penticton band settled its claim with respect to such a cut-off: 4,800 hectares were returned to the band, the federal government agreed to pay 13.2

million dollars with respect to 730 hectares of alienated land, and the province agreed to pay 1 million dollars with respect to land which it wished to retain. In November 1982, the Osoyoos Band settled its claim with respect to 28.7 hectares which had been cut-off. The federal government agreed to pay $634,908 for 23 hectares of the land which had been alienated, and the province $360,000 for the remainder of the lands which it wished to retain.

For further discussion, see, Chapter 10, *infra*.

Further Reading

Cumming and Mickenberg, *Native Rights in Canada*, 2d ed, Chapter 17.

(d) The Atlantic Provinces

Reserves were set apart for the use of Indians in New Brunswick and Nova Scotia under legislation governing the administration of Crown Lands. There was no provision by treaty or agreement for the surrender of Indian title to the Crown and, accordingly, no agreed provision for the establishment of reserves.

It was considered that title, subject to the Indian interest, to the reserves was vested in the Crown in the right of the Provinces pursuant to section 109 of the British North America Act. See *R. v. Smith*, [1983] 3 CNLR 161 (Supreme Court of Canada). In 1959, agreements between Canada and Nova Scotia (SC 1959, c. 50), and Canada and New Brunswick (SC 1959, c. 4), were ratified and confirmed. The Agreements contain identical terms:

> An Act to confirm an Agreement between the Government of Canada and the Government of the Province of Nova Scotia respecting Indian Reserves.
>
> *[Assented to 18th July, 1959.]*

HER Majesty, by and with the advice and consent of the Senate and House of Commons of Canada, enacts as follows:

1.   The Agreement between the Government of Canada and the Government of the Province of Nova Scotia, set out in the Schedule, is ratified and confirmed, and it shall take effect according to its terms.

SCHEDULE.

MEMORANDUM OF AGREEMENT MADE THIS 15TH DAY OF APRIL, 1959

>   BETWEEN

>>   THE GOVERNMENT OF CANADA, hereinafter referred to as "Canada",

of the first part,

AND

THE GOVERNMENT OF THE PROVINCE OF NOVA SCOTIA, hereinafter referred to as "Nova Scotia",

of the second part.

WHEREAS since the enactment of the British North America Act, 1867, certain lands in the Province of Nova Scotia set aside for Indians have been surrendered to the Crown by the Indians entitled thereto;

AND WHEREAS from time to time Letters Patent have been issued under the Great Seal of Canada purporting to convey said lands to various persons;

AND WHEREAS two decisions of the Judicial Committee of the Privy Council relating to Indian lands in the Provinces of Ontario and Quebec lead to the conclusion that said lands could only have been lawfully conveyed by authority of Nova Scotia with the result that the grantees of said lands hold defective titles and are thereby occasioned hardship and inconvenience;

NOW THIS AGREEMENT WITNESSETH that the parties hereto, in order to settle all outstanding problems relating to Indian reserves in the Province of Nova Scotia and to enable Canada to deal effectively in future with lands forming part of said reserves, have mutually agreed subject to the approval of the Parliament of Canada and the Legislature of the Province of Nova Scotia as follows:

1. In this agreement, unless the context otherwise requires,
   (a) "Province means the Province of Nova Scotia;
   (b) "reserve lands" means those reserves in the Province referred to in the appendix to this agreement;
   (c) "patented lands" means those tracts of land in the Province in respect of which Canada accepted surrenders of their rights and interests therein from the Indians entitled to the use and occupation thereof and in respect of which grants were made by Letters Patent issued under the Great Seal of Canada;
   (d) "minerals" includes salt, oil, natural gas, infusorial earth, ochres or paints, the base of which is found in the soil, fire clays, carbonate of lime, sulphate of lime, gypsum, coal, bituminous shale, albertite and uranium, but not sand, gravel and marl;
   (e) "Indian Act" means the Indian Act, Revised Statutes of Canada 1952, cap. 149, as amended from time to time and includes any re-enactment, revision or consolidation thereof;
   (f) "surrender" means the surrender for sale of reserve lands or a portion thereof pursuant to the Indian Act but does not include

a surrender of rights and interests in reserve lands for purposes other than sale; and

(g) "public highways" means every road and bridge in reserve lands, constructed for public use by and at the expense of the Province or any municipality in the Province and in existence at the coming into force of this agreement.

2. All grants of patented lands are hereby confirmed except insofar as such grants purport to transfer to the grantees any minerals and said minerals are hereby adknowledged to be the property of the Province.

3. Nova Scotia hereby transfers to Canada all rights and interests of the Province in reserve lands except lands lying under public highways and minerals.

4. (1) In the event that a band of Indians in the Province becomes extinct, Canada shall revest in the Province all the rights and interests transferred to it under this agreement in the reserve lands occupied by such band prior to its becoming extinct.

(2) For the purpose of subparagraph (1) a band does not become extinct by enfranchisement.

5. The mining regulations made from time to time under the Indian Act apply to the prospecting for, mining of or other dealing in all minerals in unsurrendered reserve lands and all minerals reserved in the grants referred to in paragraph 2, and any payment made pursuant to such regulations whether by way of rent, royalty, or otherwise, shall be paid to the Receiver General of Canada for the use and benefit of the Indian band of Indians from whose reserve lands such monies are so derived.

6. (1) Canada shall forthwith notify Nova Scotia of any surrender and Nova Scotia may within thirty days of receiving such notification elect to purchase the surrendered lands at a price to be agreed upon.

(2) If Nova Scotia fails to elect within such thirty-day period, Canada may dispose of the surrendered lands without further reference to Nova Scotia.

(3) Where a surrender is made under the condition that the surrendered lands be sold to a named or designated person at a certain price or for a certain consideration, Nova Scotia shall exercise its election subject to that price or consideration.

(4) Subject to subparagraph (3) of the paragraph, should Canada and Nova Scotia be unable, within thirty days of the date of an election to purchase being made, to reach agreement on the price to be paid by Nova Scotia for any surrendered lands, the matter shall be referred to arbitrators as follows:

(a) Canada and Nova Scotia shall each appoint one arbitrator, and the two arbitrators so appointed shall appoint a third arbitrator;

(*b*) the decision of the arbitrators as to the price to be paid by Nova Scotia for the surrendered lands shall be final and conclusive; and

(*c*) the costs of arbitration shall be borne equally by Canada and Nova Scotia.

IN WITNESS WHEREOF the Honourable Ellen L. Fairclough, Minister of Citizenship and Immigration, has hereunto set her hand on behalf of the Government of Canada and the Honourable R. Clifford Levy, Minister of Lands and Forests, has hereunto set his hand on behalf of the Government of the Province of Nova Scotia.

In *Smith* v. *Queen*, [1983] 3 CNLR 161 (Supreme Court of Canada), Estey J, for the Supreme Court of Canada, observed with respect to the Canada-New Brunswick Agreement:

What then is the effect in law of the 1958 agreement approved legislatively, as has been seen, by both Canada and New Brunswick? The recited purpose of the agreement was to make good defective titles created by grants made of those Indian lands by the Government of Canada after surrender by the Indians, but only with reference to surrendered lands which had been set aside in the Province of New Brunswick and where the title has remained in the Province. Indeed, the recitals refer to decisions of the Privy Council which no doubt is a reference to the *St Catharine's* case which indicated that the title remained in the Province and that the only effect of the surrender was to remove from the title to those lands the burden arising under 91(14) upon the lands being set aside for Indian purposes. The agreement then goes on to establish that the parties had entered into it with a view:

a) to settling "all outstanding problems relating to Indian Reserves in the Province; and,

b) "to enabl[ing] Canada to deal effectively in future with lands forming part of the said Reserves".

It follows from both the recitals and the asserted purpose of the entry into the agreement that the agreement does not relate to the said lands:

a) because they were surrendered without any subsequent patent issued to the defendant or to any one else, and hence no defective paper title had been created; and

b) since these lands had been surrendered, they were not comprised in "Indian Reserves in the Province" so as to require any future dealing therein by Canada.

Section 2 of the agreement is a joint confirmation by the federal and provincial governments of grants theretofore made by Canada. This section of course does not relate to the said lands. Section 3 of the agreement "hereby transfers to Canada all rights and interests of the Province in Reserve lands . . . ." By s. 1(b), Reserve lands are defined as those Reserves in the Province referred to in the appendix to the agreement. The appendix refers to Red Bank Reserves Nos. 4 and 7. The said lands are clearly not included in those Reserves, and in any event could not be included in Reserve lands because all parties have agreed that the said lands had been surrendered and no longer formed part of the lands set aside for the benefit of Indians under s. 91(24).

In *R.* v. *Marshall* (1979), 31 NSR (2d) 30, [1979] 4 CNLR 113, the Nova Scotia Court of Appeal upheld a conviction under the provincial Motor Vehicles Act against a member of the Eskasoni Indian Band for illegally parking on a public highway running through the reserve. The Court held that, pursuant to the Canada-Nova Scotia Agreement, title to the highway was vested in the province and accordingly the Motor Vehicles Act applied.

In *R.* v. *Nicholas* (1978), 39 APR 285, [1979] 1 CNLR 69, (NB Prov. Ct.), it appears to have been held that the Canada-New Brunswick Agreement confirmed all grants of patent land prior thereto; the argument that the land in question had never been properly surrendered was accordingly rejected.

5. The Indian Band Interest in Reserve Lands

The Indian interest in reserve lands is subject to any restrictions or reservations vested in others. Such interests may arise from the conveyance of privately owned land in which the transferor does not own the entire interest, e.g. mineral reservations in Quebec; from the conveyance of Provincial Crown Land subject to specified reservations, e.g. 1922 legislation respecting setting apart of reserves in Quebec (see RSQ 1964, c. 92, s. 65-67); or from the nature of a Federal-Provincial Agreement respecting the reserve land.

Subject to such limitations, the Indian interest in reserve lands must be determined by the terms of the Indian Act. In the *Star Chrome Mining* case, the Privy Council declared that the Indian interest in reserve lands administered under the 1850 Act for the Better Protection of the Lands and Property of Indians in Lower Canada consisted in "a usufructuary right only, and a personal right in the sense that it is in its nature inalienable except by surrender to the Crown". The 1850 Act contained provisions respecting management and administration not dissimilar from the modern form of the Indian Act. The Privy Council suggested that the legislature had not intended to "enlarge" or in any way "alter the quality of the interest conferred upon the Indians by the instrument of appropriation or other source of title". The reserve lands had been set apart "for the use" of the Indians pursuant to the 1851 Act to Authorize the Setting Apart of Lands for the Use of Certain Tribes in Lower Canada. The Privy Council (in characterizing the Indian interest) referred to the "policy of successive administrations in the matter of Indian affairs". The Privy Council drew no distinction between Indian title at common law and the Indian interest in reserve lands. Such approach and the characterization of the Indian interest has been followed in obiter remarks of several courts. The Ontario Court of Appeal declared in *Isaac* v. *Davey* (1975) 5 OR (2d) 610, that land vested in the Crown "subject to the exercise of traditional Indian rights". Arnup, JA declared at p. 620,

> For the purposes of this case, it is sufficient to say that Indian title in Ontario has been "a personal and usufructuary right, dependent upon the good will of the sovereign.

The Supreme Court expressly refused to make a "final decision on the matter of title to the lands". [1977] 2 SCR 897, 902, per Martland J.

In Nova Scotia, the Chief Justice of the Court of Appeal declared in *R.* v. *Isaac* (1976), 9 APR 460, 469 and 478:

> I conclude that Indians on Nova Scotia reserves have a usufructuary right in the reserve land, a legal right to use that land and its resources, including, of course, the right to hunt on that land. In my opinion that right arises in our customary or common law, was confirmed by the *Royal Proclamation* of 1763 and other authoritative declarations, was preserved in respect of reserve lands when they were originally set apart for the Indians, and is implicit in the *Indian Act* which continues reserves "for the use and benefit of the respective bands" (s. 18(1)). That legal right is possibly a supervening law which in itself precludes the application of provincial game laws in a reserve, but it is, I think, more properly considered as an "Indian land right" which is inextricably part of the land to which the provincial game law cannot extend.
>
> That right, sometimes called "Indian title" is in interest in land akin to a *profit a prendre*. It arose long before 1867 but has not been extinguished as to reserve land and, being still an incident of the reserve land, can be controlled or regulated only by the federal government. This stresses legalistically the perhaps self-evident proposition that hunting by an Indian is traditionally so much a part of his use of his land and its resources as to be for him, peculiarly and specially, integral to that land.

Also Cooper, JA at 497, and Macdonald, JA at 499.

The Federal Court of Appeal expressly followed the *Star Chrome* case when, in obiter, considering the Indian interest in reserve lands in New Brunswick. The Court declared in *R.* v. *Smith*, [1980] 4 CNCR 29, 51 (Fed. CA):

> The legal title to land in an Indian reserve is in the Crown, with the beneficial interest, in the absence of an agreement such as that which was entered into in the present case in 1958, belonging to the province

in which the land is located by virtue of section 109 of the *BNA Act*. The Crown's title is subject to the Indian right or interest (sometimes referred to as the "Indian title") which has been characterized as personal and usufructuary in nature. When the Indian title is extinguished, the beneficial interest in the land reverts to the province in the absence of an agreement that has transferred that interest to Canada.

On appeal in *Smith* v. *The Queen*, [1983] 3 CNLR 161 (Supreme Court of Canada), Estey, J observed:

> The right of the Indians to the lands in question was described by Lord Watson in *St Catharine's* at p. 54 as "a personal and usufructuary right". The latter term is defined as follows:
>
> *Usufruct*
>
> 1. *Law*. The right of temporary possession, use, or enjoyment of the advantages of property belonging to another, so far as may be had without causing damage or prejudice to it.
> 2. Use, enjoyment, or profitable possession (of something) 1811.
>
> *Usufructuary*
>
> 1. *Law*. One who enjoys the usufruct of a property, etc.
>
> *The Shorter Oxford English Dictionary* 1959, p. 2326.
>
> The release, therefore, is of a personal right which by law must disappear upon surrender by the person holding it; such an ephemeral right cannot be transferred to a grantee, be it the Crown or an individual. The right disappears in the process of the release, and a release couched in terms inferring a transfer cannot operate effectively in law on the personal right any more than an express transfer could. In either process, the right disappears.

The British Columbia Court of Appeal observed in *Joe* v. *Findlay*, [1981] 3 WWR 60, [1981] 3 CNLR 58, 60, per Carrothers, JA:

> The legal title to the reserve lands vests in Her Majesty the Queen in right of Canada. By virtue of the interpretation of s. 2 and s. 18 of the *Indian Act*, RSC 1970, c. I-6, the use and benefit of reserve lands accrues to and comes into existence as an enforceable right (subject to the consent of the Minister of Indian Affairs and Northern Development, hereinafter called the Minister) vested in the entire band for which such reserve lands have been set apart. . . . This statutory right of use and benefit, often referred to in the cases as a usufruct (not a true equivalent borrowed from Roman law), is a collective right in common conferred upon and accruing to the band members as a body and not to the band members individually. For a discussion on the nature of this possessory right see *St Catharine's Milling and Lumber Company* v. *The Queen* (1888), 14 A.C. 46.

Lord Denning, in *The Queen* v. *Secretary of State for Foreign and Commonwealth Affairs, Indian Association of Alberta et al.*, [1981] 4 CNLR 86, in the English Court of Appeal observed:

> Apart from the ceded lands — ceded under the treaties — there were Indian reserves — not ceded to the Crown — in which the Indian peoples still retained their "personal and usufructuary right" to the fruits and produce of the lands and to hunt and fish thereon.

Doug Sanders has commented:

> Most questions of band rights to reserve lands have been effectively subsumed into the administrative regime for reserve lands set out in the *Indian Act*. As a result general discussions of theories of ownership of reserves (as between the band and the Crown) have little practical application. For most purposes, the nature of band rights and the nature of federal government rights are found in the detailed provisions of the *Indian Act*, not in traditional property law concepts or alternative theoretical models of property relationships.

Legal Aspects of Economic Development on Reserve Lands, Department of Indian Affairs, 1976.

Berger J in the British Columbia Supreme Court in *Mathias* v. *Findlay*, [1978] 4 WWR 653, [1978] 4 CNLR 130, rejected the traditional approach. The Band Council sought an injunction to restrain a member of the band from residing on the reserve. His application to reside in a trailer on a special development area on the reserve had been rejected by the Council. The Council had a waiting list of applicants who wished to live in houses on the reserve. In order to secure an injunction in trespass, it was necessary to show that the band had a right to possession. Berger J declared:

> Counsel relies on the judgment of Armour J. of the High Court of Ontario in *Point* v. *Dibblee Const. Co.*, [1934] OR 142, [1934] 2 DLR 785. He said at p. 793:
> "The legal title to the land set apart by treaty or otherwise for the use or benefit of a particular band of Indians is in the Crown. The tenure of the Indians is a personal and usufructuary right, dependent upon the good will of the Sovereign. They have no equitable estate in the lands".
> That was a case where an Indian sued the defendant, a construction company, for trespass to reserve lands. The defendant held a licence from the Crown. It was held that the plaintiff could not succeed against the Crown, so he could not succeed against a licensee of the Crown; in either case he would not have the requisite possession to sue for ejectment.

The views of Armour J must be regarded today as unsound. The idea that Indian title to land could be comprehended by the application of the Roman notion of the usufruct appears often in the cases: see the judgment of the Privy Council in *St Catharine's Milling & Lbr. Co.* v. *R.* (1888), 14 App. Cas. 46 at 54-55. But it may be taken to have been rejected by the Supreme Court of Canada in *Calder* v. *AG BC*, [1973] SCR 313, [1973] 4 WWR 1, 34 DLR (3d) 145. Judson J said at p. 328 that it was not helpful. The judgment of Hall J proceeds on the footing that Indian title depends upon an examination of indigenous concepts of ownership. As for the statement that the tenure of the Indians was ''dependent upon the good will of the Soverign'', this is simply to assert what was never in dispute, that is, that Indian title could be extinguished by competent legislative authority. And see Professor Kenneth Lysyk's article on the *Calder* case: ''The Indian Title Question in Canada: An Appraisal in the Light of Calder'' (1973), 51 Can. Bar. Rev. 450.

In any event, even before the judgment in the *Calder* case, the idea of the usufruct was used to define Indian title only by virtue of aboriginal occupation or by treaty. Except for *Point* v. *Dibblee Const. Co.* it was never regarded as a means for defining, even by analogy, the tenure of Indian bands to reserve lands. That must depend, in the final analysis, upon the provisions of the Indian Act.

Seymour Reserve No. 2 is an Indian reserve. The legal title to the reserve is vested in the Crown. The land comprising the reserve is set aside for the use and benefit of the Indian band. Section 2(1) of the Indian Act defines a reserve in this way:

> 'reserve' means a tract of land, the legal title to which is vested in Her Majesty, that has been set apart by Her Majesty for the use and benefit of a band.

This implies that possession is in the band. The matter is placed beyond doubt by s. 20(1) of the Act, which says:

> 20. (1) No Indian is lawfully in possession of land in a reserve unless, with the approval of the Minister, possession of the land has been allotted to him by the council of the band.

If the band can allot possession to an Indian, then the band must have possession in the first instance. The defendant has no allotment from the council. Thus he is not in lawful possession of the land that he is occupying. Possession is in the band and not in the Crown, the band can sue in this court, and the provisions of the Federal Court Act do not apply. The scheme of the Act for the management of reserve lands by Indian bands would be impeded if such a fundamental legal remedy as ejectment were not available to the band suing in its own behalf before the ordinary courts of the province.

6. Trusteeship of Reserve Lands

Extract from D. Sanders, ''The Friendly Care and Directing Hand of the Government Trusteeship of Indians in Canada'', 1977.

By 1867 it was common to use the term "trust" in legislation dealing with Indian reserves. Additionally, the idea of protection had been established both conceptually and in the language of legislation. As suggested earlier, the rationale behind the assignment of legislative jurisdiction over Indians and Indian lands to the federal Parliament in 1867 appears to have been the protection of Indians from local competing settler interests. While the British North America Act itself does not use the term "trust" in relation to reserves, trusteeship terminology occurred in later constitutional documents. In 1871 the Terms of Union of British Columbia and Canada provided:

> The charge of the Indians, and the trusteeship and management of the lands reserved for their use and benefit, shall be assumed by the Dominion Government. . . .

In 1912 lands were added to both the provinces of Quebec and Ontario. The transfers were effected by joint federal-provincial legislation. In each case the legislation provided:

> That the trusteeship of the Indians in the said territory, and the management of any lands now or hereafter reserved for their use, shall remain in the Government of Canada subject to the control of Parliament.

There is an odd divergence in this language. In the British Columbia case, "trusteeship" was of the lands reserved for Indian use and benefit. In the Quebec legislation, "trusteeship" was of the Indians. In both wordings, "management" of the lands is with the federal government.

The first federal Indian legislation after 1867 was the Act establishing the Department of the Secretary of State in 1868. It repeated the language already quoted from sections 2, 3 and 8 of the pre-Confederation legislation of 1860. It provided that the Secretary of State shall be the Superintendent General of Indian Affairs and as such shall have

> . . . the control and management of the lands and property of the Indians in Canada.

The legislation of 1868 was concerned with consolidating the various pre-Confederation Indian affairs systems under a new and unified administration. There were other federal enactments in the following few years, but the first comprehensive federal Indian legislation was enacted in 1867. The 1867 legislation defined reserves in the following ways:

> 3. (6) The term "reserve" means any tract or tracts of land set apart by treaty or otherwise for the use or benefit of or granted to a

particular band of Indians, of which the legal title is in the Crown, but which is unsurrendered, and includes all the trees, wood, timber, soil, stone, minerals, metals, or other valuables thereon or therein.

3. (7) The term "special reserve" means any tract or tracts of land and everything belonging thereto set apart for the use or benefit of any band or irregular band of Indians, the title of which is vested in a society, corporation or community legally established, and capable of suing and being sued or in a person or persons of European descent, but which land is held in trust for, or benevolently allowed to be used by, such band or irregular band of Indians.

3. (8) The term "Indian Lands" means any reserve or portion of a reserve which has been surrendered to the Crown.

The Act repeats the language of 1860 and 1868:

4. All reserves for Indians or for any band of Indians, or held in trust for their benefit, shall be deemed to be reserved and held for the same purposes as before the passing of this Act, but subject to its provisions.

The concern with "special reserves" is indicated by sections 21 and 22. Section 21 enables the Crown to proceed against trespassers and squatters although legal title to the reserve may not be vested in the Crown.

21. In all cases of encroachment upon, or of violation of trust respecting any special reserve, it shall be lawful to proceed by information in the name of Her Majesty, in the superior courts of law or equity, notwithstanding the legal title may not be vested in the Crown.

22. If by the violation of the conditions of any such trust as aforesaid, or by the breaking up of any society corporation, or community, or if by the death of any person or persons without a legal succession of trusteeship, in whom the title to a special reserve is held in trust, the said title lapses or becomes void in law, then the legal title shall become vested in the Crown in trust, and the property shall be managed for the band or irregular band previously interested therein, as an ordinary reserve.

Special reserves, under this legislation (and under section 36 of the present *Indian Act*) are primarily those reserves in southern Quebec under ancient grants to Catholic religious orders. In addition there is privately granted reserve land in Prince Edward Island. Problems with these anomolous early reserves are best symbolized by the litigation in relation to the Oka "reserve", *Corinthe* v. *Seminary of St Sulpice*, (1912) 5 DLR 263 (Judicial Committee of the Privy Council). In this case, title to certain lands had been granted to a Catholic order for the purposes of an Indian mission. In a dispute between the Indians and the order, the Judicial Committee held that title was clearly in the religious order. The Judicial Committee felt unable to say whether it was held under a charitable trust or not without having heard arguments in relation to charitable trusts in the province of Quebec. The Indians had argued that they held title to the lands (not that the Order held the lands in trust).

The 1876 Act, section 29, provided that surrendered lands shall be

. . . managed, leased and sold as the Governor in Council may direct, subject to the conditions of surrender, and to the provisions of this Act.

The Indian Act of 1880 repeated the provisions already noted for the Indian Act of 1876. The Indian Act of 1880 remained basically unchanged until 1951.

In summary, the federal Indian Acts of 1876 and 1880 used the term "trust", but in a more limited way than the pre-Confederation legislation. In the 1876 and 1880 statutes, only "special reserves" (where title is not in the Crown) are described as held in trust.

In the 1951 Indian Act the category of "special reserves" was dropped from the definition section. "Reserve" is defined as

. . . a tract of land, the legal title to which is vested in Her Majesty, that has been set apart by Her Majesty for the use and benefit of a band.

While "special reserve" is not a separate category in the definition section, the anomolies of certain of the older reserves required a section under the heading "special reserves":

36. Where lands have been set apart for the use and benefit of a band and legal title thereto is not vested in Her Majesty, this Act applies as though the lands were a reserve within the meaning of this Act.

By this section "special reserves" are now defined without using the word "trust". The key wording for both "reserves" and "special reserves" is that these lands have been set aside for the *use and benefit* of a band. The wording "use and benefit" is repeated in section 18 (1):

Subject to this Act, reserves are held by Her Majesty for the use and benefit of the respective bands for which they were set apart; and subject to this Act and to the terms of any treaty or surrender, the Governor in Council may determine whether any purpose for which lands in a reserve are used or are to be used is for the use and benefit of the band.

and in section 37:

> Except where this Act otherwise provides, lands in a reserve shall not
> be sold, alienated, leased or otherwise disposed of until they have
> been surrendered to Her Majesty by the band for whose use and
> benefit in common the reserve was set apart.

By section 53(1) the Minister or his delegate can manage surrendered
lands:

> The Minister or a person appointed by him for the purpose may
> manage, sell, lease or otherwise dispose of surrendered lands in
> accordance with this Act and the terms of the surrender.

Sections 61 to 69 deal with the management of Indian monies.

What is striking (in the context of this study) about all the sections of
the Indian Act of 1951 is the fact that the terms "trust" and "trustee"
are nowhere used. It is clear that, in law, the avoidance of the term
"trust" does not preclude the establishment of a trust. It is the writer's
view that the use of a concept that one group (an Indian band) are
entitled to the use and benefit of certain lands (a reserve) but that the
management of the lands is in the hands of another person (the Minister
or the Crown) is sufficient to establish a trust relationship. The three
elements of a trust have been defined: the trustee, the beneficiary and
the trust property. The same is true in relation to band funds.

Extract from R. Bartlett, "Indian and Native Law," (1983) 15 *Ottawa Law
Review 431, 461.*

In *Kruger* v. *Queen* (1982), 125 DLR (3d) 513, [1982] 1 CNLR 50
(FCtTD) the Penticton band asserted that the Crown "failed to exercise
the degree of care, stewardship and prudent management required of a
trustee in the management of trust assets" upon the expropriation of
reserve lands for the construction of Penticton airport. The lands were
expropriated in 1940 and 1943 under what is now section 35 of the
Indian Act against the wishes of the band members. The compensation
paid was so low as to be described as "ridiculous" from the "vantage
point of 1981" by Mahoney J of the Federal Court. Section 35 provides
for expropriation of reserve lands for public works upon the consent of
the Governor in Council. The learned judge held that such power to
expropriate is not subject to the surrender provisions of the Indian Act.
Mahoney J offered a definitive statement of the trusteeship of the
Crown:

> I accept that the defendant held title to the Reserve in trust and that
> the Band was beneficiary of that trust. I further accept that the trust
> was a legally enforceable trust, or "true trust", not a "political
> trust", whatever that may be, nor a trust to be executed by the

defendant in an uncontrolled exercise of the royal prerogative. The defendant was required to execute the trust with the high degree of honour, care, prudence and business efficiency required of any trustee, subject to the terms of the trust.

The learned judge determined, however, that the Governor in Council could not have been intended under what is now section 35 to act as trustee in the expropriation of reserve lands. Mahoney, J concluded that the officials of the Indian Affairs Department had not acted in breach of trust because they had sought additional compensation and to avoid expropriation. The decision of the Governor in Council to consent to the expropriation defeated their efforts but was not in breach of trust nor caused their actions to be so.

The conclusion that reserve lands are held upon an express trust by the Crown for the benefit of the Indians is not without contrary authority. In *Attorney General of Quebec* v. *Attorney General of Canada* ("the Star Chrome Case"), [1921] AC 401, the Privy Council considered that the effect of the 1850 Act for the Better Protection of the Lands and Property of the Indians in Lower Canada "is not to create an equitable estate in lands set apart for an Indian tribe of which the Commissioner is made the recipient for the benefit of the Indians but that the title remains in the Crown and that the Commissioner is given such an interest as will enable him to exercise the powers of management and administration committed to him by the statute." Five years previously, however, the Supreme Court of Canada had declared the Secretary of State under the 1868 legislation (SC, c. 42) to be "the trustee of the Indian title". *Attorney General of Canada* v. *Giroux* (1916), 53 SCR 172 per Duff J.

On 10 December 1982 the Federal Court of Appeal rendered judgment in *Queen* v. *Guerin*, [1983] 1 CNLR 20. The Musqueam Band had brought an action for breach of trust in the leasing of reserve lands surrendered for that purpose. On appeal it was argued that a trust was imposed on the Crown by the provisions of the Indian Act with respect to the management and disposition of reserve land. The Court determined that "there must be clear evidence of an intention to make the Crown a trustee". The Court also concluded that the Indian interest in a reserve was in "the nature of a right of property" which "could be the subject of a trust". The Court, however, rejected the existence of a trust enforceable in law against the Crown with respect to the reserve land. Le Dain J declared for the Court:

> *Kinlock*, *Tito* v. *Waddell* and *Town Investments Ltd.* indicate that in a public law context neither the use of the words "in trust" nor the fact that property is to be held or dealt with in some manner for the benefit of others is conclusive of an intention to create a true trust. The respondents insisted that the facts in *Kinlock*, *The Hereford Railway* and *Tito* v. *Waddell* are quite different and distinguishable from the facts in

the present case. There can be no doubt of that, but the distinction that is affirmed in those cases and the policy considerations which underly it are relevant to the issue in the present case.

The appellant laid particular stress on the discretion conferred on the government by section 18 of the *Indian Act* as indicating that it could not have been intended to create an equitable obligation, enforceable in the courts, to deal with the reserve land in a particular manner. Section 18 provides, as we have seen, that "subject to this Act and to the terms of any treaty or surrender, the Governor in Council may determine whether any purpose for which lands in a reserve are used or are to be used is for the use and benefit of the band." Discretion, it will be recalled, was a significant factor in *Kinlock*, *The Hereford Railway*, and *Tito* v. *Waddell* as indicating, in the opinion of the courts, an intention to exclude the equitable jurisdiction of the courts. In *Kinloch* it was the authority conferred on the Secretary of State to determine questions of doubt touching the distribution of the booty in a final and conclusive manner, subject to it being ordered otherwise by Her Majesty. In *The Hereford Railway* it was the discretion as to whether to grant a subsidy for railway construction. In *Tito* v. *Waddell* it was the proviso in the 1928 mining ordinance that the obligation or duty of the Resident Commissioner was "subject to such directions as the Secretary of State for the Colonies may from time to time give." In my opinion the discretionary authority conferred by section 18 on the Governor in Council, or government, to determine whether a particular purpose for which land in a reserve is to be used is one for the use and benefit of the band indicates, much as the discretion that was conferred on the Secretary of State in *Kinloch*, that it is for the government and not the courts to determine what is for the use and benefit of the band. That provision is incompatible, in my opinion, with an intention to impose an equitable obligation, enforceable in the courts, to deal with the land in the reserve in a certain manner, and particularly, an obligation to develop or exploit the reserve so as to realize its potential as a source of revenue for the band, which is in essence the obligation that is invoked in the present case.

The respondents, as did the Trial Judge, stressed the importance of the words "use and benefit" in section 18(1), as it was during the relevant period: "Subject to the provisions of this Act, reserves shall be held by Her Majesty for the use and benefit of the respective bands for which they were set apart . . . ." The words "use and benefit" appear in several definitions and other sections of the Act. A "reserve" defined in section 2 as "a tract of land, the legal title to which is vested in Her Majesty, that has been set apart by Her Majesty for the use and benefit of a band." A "band" means a body of Indians "for whose use and benefit in common, lands, the legal title to which is vested in Her

Majesty, have been set apart before, on or after the 4th day of September 1951.'' ''Surrendered lands'' means ''a reserve or part of a reserve or any interest therein, the legal title to which remains vested in Her Majesty, that has been released or surrendered by the band for whose use and benefit it was set apart.'' Section 36 provides: ''Where lands have been set apart for the use and benefit of a band and legal title thereto is not vested in Her Majesty, this Act applies as though the lands were a reserve within the meaning of this Act.'' Section 37 provides: ''Except where this Act otherwise provides, lands in a reserve shall not be sold, alienated, leased or otherwise disposed of until they have been surrendered to Her Majesty by the band for whose use and benefit in common the reserve was set apart.'' The words ''use and ''benefit'' in these provisions simply refer to the nature or purpose of the executive act by which lands are reserved for the Indians — they are set apart for their use and benefit. This is the sense, in my opinion, in which these words are used in section 18(1). Although the legal title in land is vested in the Crown, and the federal government has a power of control and management over the reserve by virtue of its constitutional jurisdiction with respect to lands reserved for the Indians, the land is to be held by the Crown (that is, controlled and managed) as a reserve (that is, for the use and benefit of the Indians). To the extent that section 18(1) implies any obligation at all it is an obligation to make the reserve available for the exercise and enjoyment of the Indian right of occupation or possession, but not an obligation to deal with the land in the reserve in any particular manner. There are other indications in the Act besides the discretionary authority conferred on the Governor in Council by section 18 that the responsibility for a reserve is governmental in character. The Act confers on the Minister, the Governor in Council, and the Band Council certain powers of a local government nature for the management of the reserve. See, for example, sections 18(2), 19, 57, 58, 73(1), and 81. The Governor in Council has a discretionary authority under section 60(1) to ''grant to the band the right to exercise such control and management over lands in the reserve occupied by that band as the Governor in Council considers desirable.'' All of this, it seems to me, clearly excludes an intention to make the Crown a trustee in a private law sense of the land in a reserve. How the government chooses to discharge its political responsibility for the welfare of the Indians is, of course, another thing. The extent to which the government assumes an administrative or management responsibility for the reserves of some positive scope is a matter of governmental discretion, not legal or equitable obligation. I am, therefore of the opinion that section 18 of the *Indian Act* does not afford a basis for an action for breach of trust in the management or disposition of reserve lands.

This case was subsequently appealed to the Supreme Court of Canada.

Further Reading

D. Sanders, "The Friendly Care and Directing Hand of the Government: A Study of Government Trusteeship of Indians in Canada," 1977.

R. Bartlett, "The Existence of an Express Trust derived from the Indian Act in respect of Reserve Lands," 1979.

D.M. Brans, "The Trusteeship Role of the Government of Canada," Indian Claims Commission, 1971.

D.R. Lowry, "The Position of the Govenrment of Canada as Trustee for Indians, a Preliminary Analysis."

Above papers are unpublished but are held, *inter alia*, in the Native Law Centre Library, University of Saskatchewan.

7. The Management of Reserve Lands

The Indian Act provides for the administration and management of reserve lands. Look at the following sections of the Act and consider what powers are possessed by the band council and what powers are possessed by the Minister.

(a) *Reserves*
— sections 18, 19, 20, 24, 28(2), 31, 34, 49, 57, 58, 60, 71, 73, 81, 93.

(b) *Surrendered Lands*
— sections 53(1), 57.

(c) *Indian Monies*
— sections 61, 64, 65, 66, 69.

What body or person is empowered to manage a reserve?

"management of the reserve and monies arising therefrom is the prerogative of the Minister of Indian Affairs, albeit the consent of the band council is required in specified instances.

The Minister may direct the use of reserve lands for schools, administration burial grounds, health projects, and with the consent of the band council, for any other purpose for the general welfare of the band. He may survey and subdivide the land, and direct the construction of roads that the band must maintain in accordance with his instructions. If land is uncultivated on a reserve, the Minister may direct its cultivation by lease or otherwise with the consent of the band council — no such consent is necessary for the operation of farms on the reserve by the Minister.

Recognition of the management prerogative of the Minister is manifest in section 60 of the Indian Act, which provides:

(1) The Governor in Council may at the request of a band grant to the band the right to exercise such control and management over lands in the reserve occupied by that band as the Governor in Council considers desirable.

(2)   The Governor in Council may at any time withdraw from a band a right conferred upon the band under subsection (1).

The only significant power of the band council under the Act with respect to reserve land is the power to allot possession of that land to band members. Such allotments are, however subject to the approval of the Minister. The Minister issues a Certificate of Possession when approval is given and a Certificate of Occupation when the approval given is conditional. Particulars of the Certificates are entered in a Reserve Land Register maintained by the Department of Indian Affairs. An Indian may also transfer a right to possession to another member of the band subject, of course, to the Minister's approval.

1.   *Surrendered lands*. Surrender is the mechanism by which Indian bands dispose of reserve lands to the remainder of Canadian society. A surrender must be made to the Crown and assented to by the majority of electors, or a majority of those voting at a second election if a majority of electors do not vote at the initial election. The Minister is empowered to "manage, sell, lease or otherwise dispose of surrendered lands" in accordance with the terms of surrender. Minerals on reserve lands must be surrendered in order to be disposed of by a band. Although the band may specify the terms of a surrender, the Minister administers the disposition of such terms.

The nature of surrenders is derived from the concept of aboriginal title recognized by Canadian jurisprudence — Indian title precludes any alienation of the reserve land base of the band without a surrender to the Crown. The Indian Act has introduced deviations from this traditional principle, however, since the Minister may lease, upon request, an individual Indian's reserve land of which he is lawfully in possession or authorize by permit the use of reserve land by any person.

2.   *Indian moneys*. Indian moneys refers to money held by the Crown for the use and benefit of Indians or bands. Such money includes revenue from the sale of surrendered lands, including minerals, and other capital assets of the band. Indian moneys are managed and expended by the Minister, usually with the consent of the band council. This consent may be dispensed with in an emergency, for example, in order to pay compensation, and to suppress unsanitary conditions, diseases or overcrowding, or, to finance programs established by Governor in Council regulations. The Governor in Council may, however, under section 69, permit a band to "control, manage and expend in whole or in part its revenue moneys."

3.   *Estates*. In order to ensure management and disposition of reserve lands in accord with federal objectives "all jurisdiction and authority in relation to matters and causes testamentary with respect to deceased Indians is vested exclusively in the Minister." Provincial courts may only exercise jurisdiction with the consent of the Minister.

In *Attorney General of Canada* v. *Canard*, [1976] 1 SCR 170 (1975), the appointment of an administrator by the Minister was upheld as valid notwithstanding that the widow had obtained letters of administration from the Provincial Surrogate Court. The exclusive jurisdiction of the Minister also extends to estates of mentally disordered and infant Indians. No band council or tribal court has any jurisdiction over estates governed by the Indian Act.

The provisions of the Indian Act clearly indicate the managerial prerogative of the Minister of Indian Affairs over reserves and band resources. The denial of self-government inflicted by such provisions is compounded by the denial of any legal remedy. Regarding reserves, section 18(1) provides: ". . . Subject to this Act and to the terms of any treaty or surrender, the Governor in Council may determine whether any purpose for which lands in a reserve are used or are to be used is for the use and benefit of the band." A similar provision applies to Indian moneys. The provisions deny any action for breach of trust by the Minister. Thus the Indian Act classically seeks to confer on the Minister "power without responsibility for exercise of this power."

R. Bartlett: "Indian Act of Canada,"
University of Saskatchewan Law
Centre, 1980, pp. 21-24; 27 *Buffalo
Law Review* 581, 600-603 (1979).

8. Possession of Reserve Lands

(a) Indian Possession of Reserve Lands

Indian possession of reserve lands is regulated by sections 20-27 of the Indian Act. It has previously been suggested that the "only significant power of the band council under the Act with respect to reserve land is the power to allot possession of that land to land members." Such allotments are subject to ministerial approval, as are subsequent transfers of such right to possession. The Minister issues a Certificate of Possession when approval is given. The "right to possession" reverts to the band in the event that an Indian ceases to be entitled to reside on the reserve and fails to transfer such right.

The Indian Act does not make clear the character of the right that attaches to a Certificate of Possession, and in particular, whether or not it may be revoked at will by the band council or the Minister. Section 24 provides that a right to possession may be transferred back to the band only with the approval of the Minister. Section 27 provides for the cancellation of Certificates of Possession in the event of clerical error or fraud.

In *Lindley* v. *Derrickson*, [1978] 4 CNLB 75 (British Columbia Supreme Court) the defendant holder of a Certificate of Possession with respect to a lot on the reserve agreed in writing with the band to exchange his land for three other parcels on the reserve, subject to a condition that he would not be required to give up his lot until construction upon it was commenced by the band. The defendant executed a transfer of the lot. The transfer was registered following its approval by the Minister pursuant to secction 24. The Minister issued a Certificate of Possession with respect to the land to the band. No construction was commenced on the lot in question but the band council brought an action requiring the defendant to give up possession of the land. The Court refused any such order. It held that the agreement was contrary to sections 20-27 of the Indian Act and was therefore void. The Court concluded that the Ministerial approval was ineffective when only the transfer was submitted to him for approval and the condition of such transfer was not disclosed to him. The Court ordered that the lot be returned to the exclusive possession of the defendant. The decision suggests that the band council cannot by resolution revoke the right to possession of a band member.

The respective rights to possession of the band and a band member with regard to unallocated land were examined in *Joe* v. *Findlay*, [1981] 3 WWR 60, [1981] 3 CNLR 58 (BCCA).

CARROTHERS, JA: The appellant, aged in his middle thirties, with a wife and three children, is a registered member of the Squamish Indian Band, which has the right of use and benefit of 24 separate reserves, aggregating some 6,000 acres, in the North Shore-Howe Sound area near Vancouver, British Columbia, including Seymour Indian Reserve No. 2, which is situate along the banks of the Seymour River within the boundaries of the district of North Vancouver. The Squamish Indian Band consists of approximately 1,200 members of which upwards of 800 reside on various of the reserves of the band. Others of the reserves of that band are undeveloped and unoccupied. In January of 1978, the appellant, not having by then succeeded in getting the Squamish Band Council to assign him a home site within the band reserve lands, proceeded to clear brush and establish himself and his family in a mobile home which he installed on a previously unoccupied parcel of land between the bank of the Seymour River and Seymour Boulevard, within the said Seymour Indian Reserve No. 2.

In June of 1978, the respondents, who are members of the Squamish Indian Band Council, joined by the Attorney General of Canada, brought a representative action in the Supreme Court of British Columbia against the appellant seeking a declaration that the appellant's possession of that parcel of land was unlawful and constituted a trespass [[1981] 2 CNLR 58, [1980] 5 WWR 121, 109 DLR (3d) 747]. The respondents also sought damages and to restrain such possession. The appellant defended his action primarily on the basis of lawful justification, which defence became the principal ground of appeal and upon which I shall presently elaborate. . .

As a member of the Squamish Indian Band, the appellant claims a fundamental right in common with all other members of that band to the use and benefit of that band's reserve lands, including, in the absence of designiation of a home site to the appellant by the band council with the consent of the Crown, what might be termed squatter's rights over unoccupied band reserve lands. This common right of a band member to squat on band reserve lands is asserted by the individual band member and is held out as the lawful justification which avoids the trespass in this case.

That right to squat exercised individually and unilaterally by a band member can not be sustained by authority. The legal title to the reserve lands vests in Her Majesty the Queen in right of Canada. By virtue of the interpretation of s. 2 and s. 18 of the *Indian Act*, RSC 1970, c. I-6, the use and benefit of reserve lands accrues to and comes into existence as an enforceable right (subject to the consent of the Minister of Indian Affairs and Northern Development, hereinafter called the Minister) vested in the entire band for which such reserve lands have been set apart. In that statute, band is a noun singular in form used with a plural implication and in a context which admits only of a plural use and application. This statutory right of use and benefit, often referred to in the cases as a usufruct (not a true equivalent borrowed from Roman law), is a collective right in common conferred upon and accruing to the band members as a body and not to the band members individually. For a discussion on the nature of this possessory right see *St Catharine's Milling and Lumber Company* v. *The Queen* (1888), 14 A.C. 46.

This right of the entire band in common may be exercised for the use and benefit of an individual member of the band by the band council, with the approval of the Minister, allotting to such individual member the right to possession of a given parcel of reserve lands: see *Indian Act*, *supra*, s. 20.

The subsequent provisions of the statute relating to improvements on reserve lands and transfer of possession of reserve lands are consistent only with this right of use and benefit being exercised by the individual band member through an allotment to that individual band member of reserve land on the part of the band council, with the approval of the Minister. I emphasize that we are considering merely the right to possession or occupation of a particular part of the reserve lands, which right is given by statute to the entire band in common, but which can, with the consent of the Crown, be allotted in part as aforesaid to individual members, thus vesting in the individual member all the incidents of ownership in the allotted part with the exception of legal title to the land itself, which remains with the Crown: *Brick Cartage Limited* v. *The Queen*, [1965] ExCR 102. In the absence of such allotment by the band council there is no statutory provision enabling the individual band member alone to exercise through possession the right of use and benefit which is held in common for all band members. . .

The appellant also argued with considerable force and authority that a tenant-in-common of a right to possession of certain land can not commit a trespass thereon short of ouster of a co-tenant in common lawfully in possession of that same land, and applied this argument to the appellant's occupation, as a member of the Squamish Indian Band, of unalloted reserve land of the band. In my view this argument breaks down simply because, as I have indicated earlier, until allotment by the band council with Crown consent in his favour (or alternatively his acquisition by devise, descent or purchase) the appellant does not have by mere membership in the band the essential present entitlement to possession of the land in question to establish in him the tenancy-in-common which could absolve him from the trespass.

The establishment or creation of a tenancy-in-common requires each of the tenants-in-common to have a distinct and several (but not necessarily equal) entitlement or interest. Here the appellant's entitlement to possession of a given parcel of reserve lands of the band is inchoate, not perfected and contingent upon a prerequisite allotment or other acquisition.

D. Sanders has commented on the practice in the Prairie Provinces with respect to allotment of lands to band members.

> Many bands, particularly on the Prairies, choose not to use Certificates of Possession or any of the *Indian Act* provisions for internal Indian land holding on reserves. They follow what may be called "custom" or "traditional" land allotment patterns, in contrast with those found in the *Indian Act*. They allot land to individual band members, but do so at the discretion of the band council. They avoid any Ministerial validation of the allotment. The allottee, in law, has no more security of tenure than the band council, from time to time, is prepared to permit. In practice, on some reserves, the custom system is considered by the band council as being as sacrosanct as a fee simple system.
>
> D. Sanders, *Legal Aspects of Economic Development on Reserve Lands,* Department of Indian Affairs, 1976, p. 5.

(b) Entry on and possession of Reserve Lands by Non-band Members

A band member with a right to possession of reserve lands may invite non-band members to visit or attend the person's home on the reserve despite resolutions of the band council to the contrary.

(i) *Gingrich* v. *The Queen* (1959), 29 WWR 471 (Alberta Court of Appeal).

FORD, CJA: This appeal is from a conviction under s. 30 of the *Indian Act,* RSC 1952, c. 149, for trespassing on the Blood Indian Reserve on Sunday March 16, 1958, and comes to this Division by way of a stated case from the Magistrate. The appeal was allowed and the conviction quashed at the conclusion of the hearing. Our reasons for judgment follow.

The salient facts are that the appellant, who is a missionary, and has during the period from 1952 to 1957 been permitted to go on the Reserve to minister to members of the tribe, was refused a permit to do so by the council of the band after it had set up a system of permits in the autumn of 1957. He twice requested a permit but it was declined, and he was duly advised by the superintendent of each refusal. Members of the tribe or band continued to intite him to visit their homes situated on the Reserve, and on the Sunday in question he was invited to the home of one Margaret Davis on the Reserve, for the purpose of holding a service for various members of the band congregated there. Shortly after his arrival he was arrested, and charged as above.

The authority or powers of the council of the band, in so far as the question under consideration on this appeal is concerned, are to be found in s. 80 of the *Indian Act.* Among the express powers to make by-laws, not inconsistent with the Act, or any Regulation made by the Governor in Council, or the Minister, is that contained in s-s. (*p*) which reads: "The removal and punishment of persons trespassing upon the reserve or frequenting the reserve for prescribed purposes." No other subsection of s. 80 affects the question, except as it may help to interpret this particular subsection. That is also true of several other sections of the Act, which have been considered, and which will be referred to so far only as they are of assistance in determining the question in issue.

It will be seen at once that as the Act does not define "trespassing" one must look to the common law for a definition of the term, as it is quite clear that the powers of the council are not to decide what constitutes trespassing, but are limited to removing and punishing persons who are found trespassing upon the Reserve. In other words the council cannot by establishing a system of permits to be given to individual persons to go on the Reserve, create the offence of trespass by those who enter the Reserve without such a permit. There must first be a trespass before the power of the council to remove and punish can be exercised.

The definition of common law trespass varies as stated by different authorities, but it clearly involves the entering upon another's land without lawful justification. See Salmond on Torts, 11th ed., p. 227: "The wrong of trespass to land consists in the . . . . entering upon land in the possession of the plaintiff . . . . without lawful justification." Other writers of authority define it in different terms but with the same content.

The appellant in this appeal entered upon the Reserve for the purpose of holding a religious meeting at the invitation of the Indian woman, a member of the band, but without the permit of the council, and the question resolves itself into one of justification that was lawful, or no justification at all.

It was said in argument by counsel for the respondent that the land constituting the Reserve is held by the Crown for the use and benefit of the band in common, and that an individual member or members of the band had no right to invite the appellant to visit her or them in their homes on the Reserve for any purpose, however lawful or necessary it might be; as for example in the case of medical services that might be necessary. Probably the question is more accurately put by stating that if the Crown is right, no person would be justified in entering upon the Reserve in response to an invitation unless he held the permit of the council to do so. As I understood the argument, it was incumbent on the Crown to go that far in order to maintain its position.

On the other hand it was argued on behalf of the appellant that an Indian, although living on the Reserve, is a British subject, and subject to curtailment by statute, has all the rights of a British subject and Canadian citizen. Authority for this was cited: See *Sanderson* v. *Heap* (1909), 11 WLR 238, and *Prince* v. *Tracey* (1913), 13 DLR 818. Indeed, this view of the law is accepted by council for the Crown in his factum, but he goes on to say that the *Indian Act* restricts in a variety of ways rights and privileges which those who are not subject to its jurisdiction ordinarily enjoy, and that this is particularly true of rights relating to land. He illustrates this by pointing out that an Indian on a Reserve cannot deal with his land by alienation, charge or mortgage, except as provided by ss. 87-89 of the *Indian Act*. But that is not the question here.

It may help if s. 87 dealing with the legal right of Indians on the Reserve be referred to. This section expressly states that all laws *of general application from time to time in force in any Province are applicable to and in respect of Indians in the Province* subject to the terms of any Treaty and any other Act of the Parliament of Canada and the other exceptions therein stated. The italics are mine. This supports the view that the rights of an Indian on a Reserve are those of a resident of Alberta, except where curtailed by Treaty or Act of Parliament, or Regulations made thereunder.

One of these rights is that of religious freedom with the qualifications or restrictions attendant on the exercise thereof. That an Indian on a Reserve may exercise this right is further secured by [*Rectories Act*] 14 & 15 Vict. (Statutes of the Province of Canada), 1851, c. 175, proclaimed June 9, 1852, which in referring to the then Provinces of Canada enacted — "That the free exercise and enjoyment of Religious Profession and Worship, without discrimination or preference, so as the same be not made an excuse for acts of licentiousness, or a justification of practices inconsistent with the peace and safety of the Province, is by the constitution and laws of this Province allowed to all Her Majesty's subjects within the same".

By virtue of the *BNA Act*, 1867, s. 129, and the *Alberta Act*, 1905 (Can.), c. 3, ss. 3 and 16, the above enactment has been incorporated into the laws of Canada and Alberta.

The right to preach and teach the gospel, as well as to hear it preached and taught, is recognized in a free society. It is also clearly inferred from the last-mentioned enactment of 14 & 15 Vict. In my opinion this includes the right of one who preaches or teaches to accept an invitation for this purpose from a person or persons, who desire to hear and learn, to visit him or them in their residences, and to enter upon the land occupied by their residences in order to do so. It is understood, of course, that the regularly used means of ingress and egress to the dwellings be used, as was done here, by the person who is responding to the invitation. One need go no further in deciding this case.

It is, however, of interest to note that the *Indian Act* provides for the establishment, operation and maintenance of schools for Indian children on a Reserve, and every Indian child who has attained the age of 7 years is required to attend school with certain exceptions. Although the Minister may make regulations *inter alia* with respect to teaching, education, inspection and discipline in connection with schools, there are no provisions with respect to the right of a teacher or inspector, or other official of the school, to enter upon the Reserve to carry out his duties as such. Could it be said that without a permit of the council of the band he would be a trespasser when doing so? In my opinion the provisions in respect of the operation of schools throw considerable light on how to interpret the *Indian Act* as to who would or would not be a trespasser on the Reserve.

I do not think it necessary to add any further reasons in support of the judgment quashing the conviction.

Appeal allowed.

Section 28(1) of the Indian Act declares void any agreement by which "a band or a member of a band purports to permit a person other than a member of that band to occupy or use a reserve or to reside or otherwise exercise any rights on a reserve''; for instance, occupation of a lot on a band-operated trailer park, *Attorney General of Nova Scotia and Millbrook Indian Band* (1978), 92 DLR (3d) 230, [1979] 4 CNLR 59 (Nova Scotia Court of Appeal), farming of reserve land, *Queen* v. *Devereux,* [1965] SCR 567. Section 28(2) allows the Minister to "authorize any person for a period not exceeding one year, or with the consent of the band for any longer period, to occupy or use a reserve or to reside or otherwise exercise rights on a reserve". The Minister may also, with the consent of the band council under section 58(1), lease uncultivated or unused reserve land to any person, or, under section 58(3), with the consent of the band member, lease the reserve land to which he is entitled to possession. No surrender is required for such possession of reserve land by non-band members. In the absence of such right to possession, a band may secure an injunction restraining the trespass.

(ii) *Johnson* v. *British Columbia Hydro* (1981), 27 BCLR 50, [1981] 3 CNLR 63 (British Columbia Supreme Court).

MURRAY J: This is a representative action brought on behalf of the Mowachaht Indian Band against a crown corporation incorporated under a special act of the British Columbia legislature. The action arises out of the erection by the defendant about the month of July, 1971 of a power transmission line across the Suewoa Indian Reserve (No. 6) which is located between the towns of Gold River and Tahsis on Vancouver Island. The main items of relief asked by the plaintiffs are damages for trespass and a mandatory injunction directing removal of the power transmission line.

In the fall of 1970 the defendant had entered into a contract with the Tahsis Company Ltd. for the construction of a power transmission line from Gold River to Tahsis and had surveyed the route between the two towns. There was a deadline of November or December, 1971 for completion of the line. The Sucwoa Indian Reserve (No. 6) at that time was not occupied by any members of the band but members of the band had used the area for many years for fishing, hunting and picking berries and had plans to eventually construct a resort and marina on the land.

Prior to the construction of the transmission line employees of the defendant had approached band representatives for an easement across the reserve and the defendant was aware that a resolution of the band would be required for the grant of the easement. Such a resolution has never been passed, but in spite of that fact and without the knowledge or consent of the band the defendant proceeded to erect the transmission line. That this was an unwarranted trespass appears from the diary of the defendant's negotiator, one Kibblewhite, dated September 10th, 1971, where the following passage occurs:

The situation is therefore that we are legally in trespass. The mitigating circumstances of prolonged negotiations would have no bearing in law for the actions I am taking in crossing without permission.

From that time until the 22nd of August, 1979 negotiations took place between the band and the defendant as to what compensation was to be paid to the band in respect of the trespass to its property and for an easement across the land. No agreement as to amount was ever arrived at, and on August 22nd, 1979 the band, having received legal advice for the first time, demanded removal of the transmission line and threatened legal action. Several more unsuccessful attempts were made to negotiate a settlement and on February 15th, 1980 the writ in this action was issued.

The first defence advanced by the defendant in this case is that the plaintiffs lack the capacity to bring this action. Counsel for the defendant argues that the action should have been brought by the Attorney General of Canada. In my view this submission is answered by the decision of Wallace J in the case of *Joe et al.* v. *Findlay et al.* (1980), 109 DLR (3d) 747, [1981] 2 CNLR 58. I need quote no more than the headnote as follows:

An Indian Band has sufficient interest in unallotted reserve lands to maintain an action in trespass against a band member who is unlawfully claiming possession or a right of occupation thereof. The action need not be brought by the Attorney General of Canada but may be brought by the band by way of a representative action on behalf of its members.

Even if I am wrong in my conclusion that the action is properly constituted, I would, out of an abundance of caution, grant leave and would add the Attorney General of Canada as a party plaintiff. I am convinced that in view of the circumstances of this case the Attorney General would be under a duty to consent to be added and would in fact give his consent.

The next defence advanced is that the band has acquiesced in the defendant's occupation of the land in question and by so doing, it has granted the defendant a licence to occupy the land and that licence has not been revoked. In support of that proposition the defendant relies primarily on the decision of the Judicial Committee of the Privy Council in *Canadian Pacific Railway Company* v. *The King*, [1931] AC 414. In that case the Canadian Pacific Railway Company had erected certain telegraph poles on the roadway of a Canadian government railway and was admittedly originally a trespasser thereon. It was held that many years of acquiescence and a claim to the payment of rent had long since prevented the Canadian Pacific Railway Company from being regarded as a trespasser and that it had acquired a licence which could only be revoked by a notice terminating the licence on a definite date. I think that case is clearly distinguishable from the case at bar.

In that case the contest was between a very large corporation and the federal government with both parties to the litigation being advised through the negotiations by their very large legal departments. In the case at bar the British Columbia Hydro and Power Authority has a large and able legal department. On the other hand the evidence is clear that the Mowachaht Indian Band received no legal advice at all until 1979. To compare a contest between the C.P.R. and the federal government to a contest between British Columbia Hydro and Power Authority and the Mowachaht Indian Band seems to me to be an attempt to equate a contest between two great white sharks with a contest between a great white shark and a minnow.

As I have already indicated the band had no knowledge of its legal rights until 1979. The defence of acquiescence accordingly fails.

The only other defence advanced by the defendant in this case is that this action is barred by various statutory limitations.

[The Court held (a) that the defendants were estopped from raising this defence because they had encouraged the plaintiff to undertake negotiation.

(b) it was doubtful that provincial statutory limitations could run against the Attorney General of Canada,

(c) the defendants were engaged in a continuing trespass.]

Having held that all defences advanced by the defendant fail I turn next to the question of damages. Insofar as general damages are concerned it is clear from the evidence that the defendant was prepared to expend the sum of $17,000.00 in the form of constructing a distribution line to the Tahsis Reserve. In so doing I consider they have adequately assessed the measure of general damages with the exception of a yearly award for continuing occupation which I would fix at $150.00 per acre per year on seven acres of the reserve. Over a period of ten years this amounts to the sum of $10,500.00. I accordingly assess general damages as the total sum of $27,500.00.

The plaintiffs have also claimed punitive damages and I consider that the conduct of the defendant was so arrogant, callous and indifferent that it deserves to be punished by an award of exemplary damages. Here I need only refer to such cases as *Sulisz* v. *Flin Flon*, [1979] 3 WWR 728; *Barthropp* v. *Corporation of the District of West Vancouver* (1980), 17 BCLR 202 and the recent unreported decision of the British Columbia Court of Appeal in *Vancouver Block Ltd.* v. *Empire Realty Col. Ltd.* (CA780018). Exemplary damages are hereby fixed at the sum of $15,000 . . .

The plaintiffs will accordingly recover the total sum of $42,500.00 from the defendant and in addition the plaintiffs are entitled to a mandatory injunction directing that the power transmission line which is the subject of this action be removed by the defendant from the plaintiff's land by June 30th, 1981.

Johnson v. *BC Hydro* was approved by the Saskatchewan Court of Appeal in *Custer and Morin* v. *Hudson's Bay Company*, [1983] 1 CNLR 1 reversing [1982] 4 WWR 139 (Sask. Q.B.).

(iii) In *The Queen* v. *Smith,* [1980] CNLR 29 (Federal Court of Appeal) the applicability of provincial statutes of limitations was rejected in a case where a non-Indian asserted a right of adverse possession of reserve land dating back to 1838.

LE DAIN J:

The right to possession of land that forms part of a reserve or surrendered lands within the meaning of the *Indian Act* falls in my opinion within exclusive federal legislative jurisdiction with respect to lands reserved for the Indians under s. 91(24) of the *BNA Act*. It is of the very essence of this jurisdiction. The so-called Indian title or right of occupation is really a right of possession. This is recognized by the provisions of the *Indian Act* (now sections 20 and following under the heading "Possession of Lands in Reserves") which prescribe the manner in which "possession" of land in a reserve may be allotted to individual Indians and the circumstances under which the right to possession of land may revert to the band. The right of the Crown in right of Canada to claim the possession of land that is part of a reserve or of surrendered lands within the meaning of the *Indian Act* exists, as an incident of the federal government's power of control and management of such land, for the protection of the Indian interest in the land. While the land is under federal legislative and administrative jurisdiction, it is the Crown in right of Canada that must act for the protection of that interest, whether it consists of the right of occupation or possession itself, or the "Indian moneys" (see section 62 of the Act) which are to be accepted in return for its surrender. Indeed, it would appear that so long as the land is under federal legislative and administrative jurisdiction, the Crown in right of the province in which the underlying legal title to the land is vested would not have the right to claim the possession of it. On this view of the matter, I am of the opinion that the provincial law respecting the limitation of actions for the recovery of land could not constitutionally apply so as to give the respondent or his predecessors in occupation a possessory title good against either the Indian right of occupation or the right of the federal Crown to claim possession for the protection of the Indian interest.

What is really involved is the existence of land as part of a reserve or surrendered lands within the meaning of the *Indian Act*. If provincial law respecting the limitation of actions could apply so as to have the effect of extinguishing the Indian title or the right of the federal Crown to recover possession of land for the protection of the Indian interest, it could have a dismembering effect analogous to that which was held in the *Campbell* v. *Bennett* case to be beyond provincial legislative competence. It would have the effect of destroying or eliminating a part of the very subject-matter of federal jurisdiction. If provincial legislation of general application cannot constitutionally apply to restrict the use of land reserved for the Indians within the meaning of s. 91(24) of the *BNA Act*, as was held in the *Peace Arch* case (a conclusion that appears to have been impliedly approved by the Supreme Court of Canada in the *Cardinal* case), then *a fortiori* must this be true of legislation that would have the effect of extinguishing the right to possession of such land.

Such an effect would also be in conflict with or repugnant to the legislative scheme which has existed from the earliest federal enactment for the protection of the Indian interest. There have been three fundamental features of this scheme: the provision that the Indian right of occupation or possession can only be validly given up or lost by surrender to the Crown in accordance with the formalities prescribed by the *Indian Act*; the provision that any agreement made by the Indians to permit the occupation of Indian land by non-Indians is void; and the prohibition of the unauthorized occupation of or trespass on Indian land by non-Indians, with special recourses for its suppression. These provisions vary somewhat in their particular form or expression through the successive versions of the *Indian Act* but they remain in substance as a central feature of the legislation. They exhibit a special regime for the protection of the Indian interest from the impact of the ordinary law of contract and property. The Indians are not permitted to become divested of their rights in a reserve by the ordinary legal methods applicable to other individuals. This characteristic of the legislation was emphasized by Judson J in the *Devereux* case, *supra*, when he said, "The scheme of the *Indian Act* is to maintain intact for bands of Indians, reserves set apart for them regardless of the wishes of any individual Indian to alienate for his own benefit any portion of the reserve of which he may be a locatee."

The Supreme Court of Canada allowed the appeal, [1983] 3 CNLR 161. Estey J, for the court, declared:

I must with all deference therefore conclude, contrary to the Court of Appeal, that an absolute surrender of lands by Indians for whose benefit the lands were set aside, leaves no retained or other interest in the Crown enabling the Government of Canada to retain the surrendered lands within the federal jurisdiction under s. 91(24), and therefore ''under the *Indian Act* until finally disposed of''. To conclude otherwise would be to allow the federal authority to extend its limited relationship to these lands at the expense of the provincial title in fee simple by the simple device of an 'absolute surrender' coupled with a 'directive' to sell the lands and to hold the proceeds of sale for the benefit of he who has surrendered his personal possessory right to these lands . . .

By reason of the surrender of these lands in 1895 the burden of s. 91(24) disappeared and the legal and beneficial interest, unencumbered thereby, continued in the Province of New Brunswick. The Federal Government thereafter had no interest in the said lands legislatively under s. 91(24), and of course the Crown in the right of Canada at no time had a beneficial interest in the ownership of the said lands, nor did that government hold any right to dispose of the said lands. The ownership of the Province in these lands was in no way affected by the agreement of 1958, nor did the Federal Government acquire any interest therein under that agreement.

It therefore follows that in 1973 Her Majesty the Queen in right of Canada had no enforceable interest in or in relation to the said lands and had no connection therewith which afforded a status to commence the action which gave rise to these proceedings.

Whether or not any such status might exist to raise the question, the answer must be that the action should be dismissed. It is therefore unnecessary to determine whether any proscriptive legislation, either federal or provincial, can operate against the usufructory rights under s. 91(24). Unless the surrender document of 1895 is ineffective, the courts are not concerned with the operation of provincial statutes prescribing the rights of prescription and limitation periods for the bringing of actions. It may well be that s. 38 of the *Federal Court Act* has incorporated by reference the applicable provincial limitation statutes, but again this need not be here decided. It may of course be that the appellant has acquired proscriptive rights under the applicable New Brunswick statutes, but again this question must remain for decision in any action which might be brought against the Province, and/or others, under the appropriate legislation.

(iv) Section 31 of the Indian Act empowers the Attorney General of Canada to claim relief from trespassing by a non-Indian on reserve lands in the Federal Court. The operation of the section was considered in *Queen* v. *Devereux,* [1965] SCR 567.

The judgment of Taschereau CJ and of Martland, Judson and Hall JJ was delivered by

JUDSON J: — The judgment of the Exchequer Court[1] from this appeal as taken rejects the Crown's claim for possession of a farm of

225 acres which is part of the Six Nations Indian Reserve in the County of Brant, Ontario. The action was brought under s. 31(1) of the Indian Act, R.S.C. 1952, c. 149, which reads:

> 31. (1) Without prejudice to section 30, where an Indian or a band alleges that persons other than Indians are or have been
> (*a*) unlawfully in occupation or possession of,
> (*b*) claiming adversely the right to occupation or possession of, or
> (*c*) trespassing upon
> a reserve or part of a reserve, the Attorney General of Canada may exhibit an Information in the Exchequer Court of Canada claiming, on behalf of the Indian or the band, the relief or remedy sought.

The defendant, Harry Devereux, is not an Indian. He has assisted in the working of this farm since 1934, when he entered into a leasing agreement with Rachel Ann Davis, the widow of a member of the Six Nations Band. This private arrangement was void under s. 34(2) of the Indian Act, RSC 1927, c. 98, now RSC 1952, c. 149, s. 28(1), but at the request of Mrs. Davis and the defendant, the Crown granted to the defendant a lease of the farm for a term of ten years commencing December 1, 1950. This lease expired on November 30, 1960. On the expiry of the lease, two successive permits were granted to the defendant under s. 28(2) of the Indian Act, RSC 1952, c. 149, allowing him to use and occupy the lands for agricultural purposes. The second of these permits expired on November 30, 1962. The defendant nevertheless still remains in possession of the lands. He claims his rights by devise under a will of Rachel Ann Davis, dated November 19, 1953, and admitted to probate in the Surrogate Court of the County of Brant on May 30, 1958. Rachel Ann Davis died on April 25, 1958.

In November 1962, the band council notified the defendant to vacate the property at the expiration of his permit, and in January, 1963, the Indian Superintendent at Brantford notified him to vacate on or before January 31, 1963.

On July 4, 1963, the band council passed a resolution alleging that the defendant was still unlawfully in possession of the lands and asking that the Attorney General of Canada bring this action.

It is clear that subsequent to November 30, 1962, the defendant can point to no applicable provision of the *Indian Act* which gives him the right to possess or use the lands in question.

When Mrs. Davis died in 1958, her title was that of locatee under s. 20, subs. (1), of the *Indian Act*, RSC 1952, c. 149. She held a certificate of possession dated February 28, 1954, issued under s. 20, subs. (2) of the Act. The rights of the defendant after the expiry of his permit on November 30, 1962, which was four years after the death of Mrs. Davis are governed by s. 50 of the Act:

50.   (1)   A person who is not entitled to reside on a reserve does not by devise or descent acquire a right to possession or occupation of land in that reserve.

(2)   Where a right to possession or occupation of land in a reserve passes by devise or descent to a person who is not entitled to reside on a reserve, that right shall be offered for sale by the superintendent to the highest bidder among persons who are entitled to reside on the reserve and the proceeds of the sale shall be paid to the devisee or descendant, as the case may be.

(3)   Where no tender is received within six months or such further period as the Minister may direct after the date when the right to possession or occupation is offered for sale under subsection (2), the right shall revert to the band free from any claim on the part of the devisee or descendant, subject to the payment, at the discretion of the Minister, to the devisee or descendant, from the funds of the band, of such compensation for permanent improvements as the Minister may determine.

(4)   The purchaser of a right to possession or occupation of land under subsection (2) shall be deemed not to be in lawful possession or occupation of the land until the possession is approved by the Minister.

The procedure laid down by this section has been followed and the only rights of the defendant are now to receive the proceeds of the sale. This sale is not a cash transaction. The proceeds will be payable over a period of years.

The Exchequer Court, in dismissing the action, held, in effect, that in respect of land allocated to an individual Indian, an action under s. 31 above quoted would lie only at the instance of the individual Indian locatee and not at the instance of the band. In so holding I think there was error. I do not think that s. 31 requires that an action to put a non-Indian off a reserve can only, in respect of lands allocated to an individual Indian, be brought on behalf of that particular Indian. The terms of the section to me appear to be plain. The action may be brought by the Crown on behalf of the Indian or the band, depending upon who makes the allegation of wrongful possession or trespass.

The judgment under appeal involves a serious modification of the terms of s. 31(1). Instead of reading "Where an Indian or a band" alleges unlawful possession by a non-Indian, it should be understood to read "Where an Indian *in respect of land allocated to him* or a band *in respect of unallocated land*" makes the allegation of unlawful possession. I think that this interpretation is erroneous and that its acceptance would undermine the whole administration of the Act by enabling an Indian to make an unauthorized arrangement with a non-Indian and then, by refusing to make an individual complaint, enable the non-Indian to remain indefinitely.

The scheme of the *Indian Act* is to maintain intact for bands of Indians, reserves set apart for them regardless of the wishes of any individual Indian to alienate for his own benefit any portion of the reserve of which he may be a locatee. This is provided for by s. 28(1) of the Act. If s. 31 were restricted as to lands of which there is a locatee to actions brought at the instance of the locatee, agreements void under s. 28(1) by a locatee with a non-Indian in the alienation of reserve land would be effective and the whole scheme of the Act would be frustrated.

Reserve lands are set apart for and inalienable by the band and its members apart from express statutory provisions even when allocated to individual Indians. By definition (s. 2(1) (o)) ''reserve'' means

a tract of land, the legal title to which is vested in Her Majesty, that has been set apart by Her Majesty for the use and benefit of a band.

By s. 2(1) (a), ''band'' means a body of Indians

(i)   for whose use and benefit in common, lands, the legal title to which is vested in Her Majesty, have been set apart . . .

By s. 18, reserves are to be held for the use and benefit of Indians. They are not subject to seizure under legal process (s. 20). By s. 37, they cannot be sold, alienated, leased or otherwise disposed of, except where the Act specially provides, until they have been surrendered to the Crown by the band for whose use and benefit in common the reserve was set apart. There is no right to possession and occupation acquired by devise or descent in a person who is not entitled to reside on the reserve (s. 50, subs. (1)).

One of the exceptions is that the Minister may lease for the benefit of any Indian upon his application for that purpose, the land of which he is lawfully in possession without the land being surrendered (s. 58(3)). It was under this section that the Minister had the power to make the ten-year lease to the defendant which expired on November 30, 1960.

Under this Act there are only two ways in which this defendant could be lawfully in possession of this farm, either under a lease made by the Minister for the benefit of any Indian under s. 58(3), or under a permit under s. 28(2).

Evidence was given of attempted arrangements between the defendant and the purchaser and the assignee of the purchaser under s. 50(2) which would have enabled the defendant to remain in possession at a rental which would have made it possible for the purchaser to make his instalment payments. The Crown took the position that these attempted arrangements were irrelevant, the Department not having consented to any further lease or permit. This objection was properly taken and the attempted arrangements do not assist in any way the defendant's claim to remain in possession. He also says that as an unpaid vendor who has not contracted to give up possession, he is entitled to remain in possession until he receives the full proceeds of the sale by the Superintendent made under s. 50 of the Act. He has no such right. He must give up possession and his right is limited by s. 50 to the receipt of the proceeds.

There should, therefore, be judgment for Her Majesty on behalf of the Six Nations Band of Indians that vacant possession of the lands be delivered with costs in this Court and in the Exchequer Court.

CARTWRIGHT J *(dissenting)*: — The facts and statutory provisions relevant to the solution of the questions raised on this Appeal are set out in the resaons of my brother Judson and in those of Thurlow J.

On the argument of the appeal we were told by counsel that the respondent is still in actual occupation of the lands in question. For the purposes of the appeal I am prepared to assume that the respondent has not shown any right to remain in possession of these lands.

The action was commenced by an Information in which "Her Majesty the Queen on the Information of the Deputy Attorney General of Canada" is plaintiff and the respondent is defendant. The Information does not in terms allege that the Six Nations Band of Indians, hereinafter sometimes referred to as "the Band" is entitled to possession of the lands but does state that the Band has demanded vacant possession of the lands from the defendant and that he has refused to vacate the same. The prayer for relief so far as relevant reads:

> The Deputy Attorney General of Canada, on behalf of Her Majesty, claims as follows: —
>
> (a) vacant possession of the said lands on behalf of the Six Nations Band of Indians.

It will be observed that possession is not claimed by Her Majesty in her own right but only on behalf of the Band. This is in accordance with the provisions of s. 31 of the *Indian Act* which so far as relevant reads:

> 31. (1) Without prejudice to section 30, where an Indian or a band alleges that persons other than Indians are or have been
>
> (a) unlawfully in occupation or possession of . . . . a reserve or part of a reserve, the Attorney General of Canada may exhibit an Information in the Exchequer Court of Canada claiming, on behalf of the Indian or the band, the relief or remedy sought.

I can find no ambiguity in this section. It contemplates, as do many other provisions of the Act, that the right to possession of a parcel of land in a reserve may belong to the Band or to an individual Indian. The claim for possession is to be made either on behalf of the Band if it is entitled to possession or on behalf of the individual Indian if he is so entitled.

I agree with Thurlow J that the evidence shews that the right to possession of the lands in question is vested in Hubert Clause or in Arnold and Gladys Hill, all of whom are Indians and members of the Band, and not in the Band.

I also agree with Thurlow J when he says:

When a member of a band obtains lawful possession of land in a reserve the right which the band would otherwise have to possession of that land is at an end, though circumstances may arise in which the band may once again have a right of possession either by purchase of the individual members' right or on reversion of the right to the band under ss. 25(2) or 50(3). The statutory scheme accordingly in my opinion contemplates a statutory right of possession of any part of a reserve being vested in an individual member of a band, or in the band itself, but not in the band when it is vested in the individual member.

The applicable principle of law is accurately stated in the passage from Williams and Yates on Ejectment, 2nd ed., page 1 et seq, quoted and adopted by Thurlow J., and particularly the following sentences:

To entitle a plaintiff to bring an action for the recovery of possession of land he must have a right of entry either legal or equitable. A right of entry means a right to enter and take actual possession of lands, tenements, or hereditaments, as incident to some estate or interest therein.

The right of entry must be a right to the immediate possession of the property. A reversionary or other future estate is not sufficient until it has become an estate in possession.

I can find nothing in the *Indian Act* to alter these well settled rules as to actions for the possession of the land.

For the reasons briefly stated above and for those given by Thurlow J., with which I am in full agreement, I would dismiss the appeal with costs.

Appeal allowed, CARTWRIGHT J *dissenting*

In *Mathias* v. *Findlay*, [1978] 4 WWR 653, [1978] 4 CNLB 130 (British Columbia Supreme Court), Berger J observed with respect to section 31:

Whether this provision should be regarded as precluding the right of an Indian or a band to sue for trespass in such a case [alleged trespass by a non-Indian] remains to be seen: see *D'Ailleboust* v. *Bellefleur* (1918), 25 RLNS 50.

The Saskatchewan Court of Appeal held that section 31 does not preclude an action by an Indian or the band with respect to trespass in *Custer and Morin* v. *Hudson's Bay Company*, [1983] 1 CNLR 1, overturning [1982] 4 WWR 139 (Saskatchewan Queen's Bench). To similar effect, see, *R.* v. *Crosby* (1980), 54 CCC (2d) 497 (Ontario Court of Appeal).

There is no jurisdiction in the Federal Court to hear claims with respect to possession of reserve lands where the action is not brought by the Attorney General of Canada: *Piche* v. *Cold Lake Transmission*, [1981] 3 CNLR 78 (Fed. Ct. T.D.). A band may bring such actions in the provincial courts: *Mathias* v. *Findlay*, [1978] 4 WWR 653, [1978] 4 CNLB 130 (British Columbia Supreme Court), *Joe* v. *Findlay*, [1981] 3 CNLR 58 (British Columbia Court of Appeal).

Further Reading

Trespass on Indian Reserves, University of Saskatchewan Native Law Centre, Legal Information Services, Report No. 4 (1980).

D. Sanders, *Economic Development on Reserve Lands*, Department of Indian Affairs, 1976.

9. Mineral Rights on Reserve Lands

In 1979-80, mineral revenues from reserve lands exceeded 200 million dollars; practically all the revenue was derived from reserves in Alberta and was almost entirely obtained from sales of oil and gas. The Department of Indian Affairs observed in 1980:

> The mineral potential of reserve lands is not confined to oil and gas. A mineral inventory prepared by DIAND estimates that 15 to 20 per cent of reserves in most provinces have good to excellent potential mineral development of metallic (e.g. iron), non-metallic (e.g. asbestos) and structural (e.g. sand and gravel) resources.''
>
> *Indian Conditions: A Survey*, 1980, DIAND

(a) Ownership and Beneficial Entitlement to Minerals

The extent to which Indians own or are entitled to the benefit of minerals located in reserve lands is subject to the extent to which the provinces retain an interest therein and the degree of recognition accorded Indian mineral rights by the Indian Act. The determination of Indian mineral rights is merely another aspect of the larger question of the Indian interest in reserve lands, which was considered above.

The agreements reached between Canada and Ontario, Alberta, Manitoba, Saskatchewan, British Columbia, Nova Scotia and New Brunswick with respect to reserve lands and minerals thereon were arrived at after consideration of the concept of the usufruct, the Crown prerogative with respect to precious metals, and the promises made by treaty.

(i) The Usufruct

The Privy Council in *Attorney General of Quebec* v. *Attorney General of Canada,* [1921] AC 601 (Star Chrome Mining) described the Indian interest in reserve lands set apart before 1867 in Quebec as a personal usufructuary right. Such a characterization has been applied to reserves set apart in the other provinces that were parties to Confederation and to reserves set apart in British Columbia. Any reversionary or residual interest in the reserve lands was vested in the provinces by section 109, British North America Act 1867. The concept of the usufruct was significant in determining the form of the agreements made between the federal and provincial governments as to reserve lands. In the absence of such an agreement in Quebec, the content of the usufruct retains a contemporary importance. The significance of the concept with respect to mineral rights derives from the argument that the usufruct does not extend to minerals, which are accordingly vested in the provinces.

The concept of a usufructuary right is derived from Roman Law. It was described by Chief Justice Mackeighan in the Nova Scotia Court of Appeal in *R.* v. *Isaac* (1976), 9 APR 460, 478:

A "usufructuary right" to land is, of course, merely a right to use that land and its "fruit" or resources, It certainly must include the right to catch and use the fish and game and other products of the streams and forests of that land. For the primitive, nomadic Micmac of Nova Scotia in the 18th Century, no other use of land was important.

A contrary emphasis is evident in a study prepared for the Dorion Report in Quebec:

Before the Mines Act of 1880 mining rights had always been considered as belonging to the owner of the surface or as attached to the surface. The Indians as usufructuaries of the earth could exploit them . . . .

> Vol. 4.3, P. Grant *Les Reserves In-*
> *diennes*, 129 at 147, translation.

United States jurisprudence establishes the right to the commercial exploitation of the natural resources of reserve lands including minerals, in so far as "the right of perpetual and exclusive occupancy of the land is not less valuable than full title in fee": *United States* v. *Shoshone* (1938), 304 US 111, 116, 82 L. Ed. 1213, 1219.

In Canada it is difficult not to conclude as declared by the Quebec Court of

Appeal in *James Bay Development Corporation* v. *Chief Robert Kanatewat* (21 November 1974):

> The Indian right has never been defined in a clear fashion.

(ii) Precious Metals

The provinces asserted the right to the precious metals of gold and silver in reserve lands. Such claim was upheld and explained in Ontario in *Ontario Mining* v. *Seybold* (1900), 31 OR 386, 399-400, affirmed (1901), 32 SCR 1:

> According to the law of England and of Canada, gold and silver mines, until they have been aptly severed from the title of the Crown are not regarded as *partes soli* or as incidents of the land in which they are found. The right of the Crown to waste lands in the colonies and the baser metals therein contained is declared to be distinct from the title which the Crown has to the precious metals which rests upon the royal prerogative. Lord Watson has said in *Attorney-General of British Columbia* v. *Attorney-General of Canada* (1889), 14 App. Cas., at pp. 302, 303, the seprerogative revenues differ in legal quality from the ordinary territorial rights of the Crown.

Chancellor Boyd declared that the precious metals passed to Ontario under section 109 of the British North America and observed:

> Now with these royal mines, the Indians had no concern. Whatever their claim might be to the waste lands of the Crown, and hunting and fishing thereon, it was never recognized that they extended to the gold and silver of the country.
>
> Having no interest in the gold and silver they could surrender nothing. The Dominion Government in dealing with these particular Indians in 1873, had no proprietary interest in the gold and silver and could make no valid stipulation on that subject with the Indians which would affect the rights of Ontario.
>
> The Indians are not in any way represented in this litigation, and I do not and could not prejudice their claims against any government by what I now decide.
>
> The stipulations on the face of the treaty do not deal with the precious metals, but even if it is competent to go behind the treaty, still it remains that the Indians had no interest, and the Dominion had no competence *quaad* these royal mineral rights.

Were the Indians promised the gold and silver on the reserves in the treaties?

(iii) The Treaties

The written texts of the treaties do not generally refer to mineral rights in reserve lands. Exceptions are provided by the Robinson Treaties of 1850 with

respect to the lands upon the northern shores of Lakes Huron and Superior.
The treaties provide:

> . . . and should the said Chiefs and their respective Tribes at any time
> desire to dispose of any mineral or other valuable productions upon the
> said reservations, the same will be at their request sold by order of the
> Superintendent General of the Indian Department for the time being, for
> their sole use and benefit, and to the best advantage.

The Robinson Treaties, like many of the succeeding treaties, were the result
of "the discovery of minerals". [A. Morris, *Treaties of Canada with the
Indians*, p. 16].

Treaty Commissioner Morris reported this exchange in the discussion
preceding Treaty #3 (1873):
Fort Francis Chief:

> Should we discover any metal that was of use, could we have the
> privilege of putting our own price on it?

Governor Morris:

> If any important minerals are discovered on any of their reserves the
> minerals will be sold for their benefit with their consent, but not on any
> other land that discoveries may take place upon. (Morris, *Treaties of
> Canada with the Indians*, p. 76)

The understanding of the Indians with respect to the number treaties appears
to have been that they "owned the land right down", including the mineral
rights. Such is in accord with the definition of "reserve" adopted in 1886
revision of the Indian Act (RSC 1886, c. 43). The definition included all
"stone, minerals, metals and other valuables thereupon or therein".

The definition of "reserve" in the Indian Act today refers to "land"
without specific reference to minerals. Section 18 declares that such land is
"held for the use and benefit of the respective bands for which" the reserves
were set apart. Section 18 is a statutory declaration that the entire beneficial
interest created upon the establishment of the reserve, including such mining
rights as are not retained by the provinces, are held for the benefit of the
Indians.

(iv) The Federal-Provincial Agreements

(A) Ontario

The Agreement (*supra*, SC 1924, c. 48) with Ontario declares that all
reserves in Ontario shall be administered by the Dominion for the benefit of
the bands for which the lands were set apart, but that one half of the
"consideration payable, whether by way of purchase money, rent, royalty or
otherwise" in respect of any mining disposition shall be paid to the Province

of Ontario. The entitlement of the Province to one half of the consideration payable with respect to minerals was expressly declared not to extend to reserves set apart pursuant to Treaty #3 (1873).

(B) The Prairie Provinces

The Natural Resources Agreements (*supra*, SC 1930, c. 3, SC 1930, c. 41, SC 1930, c. 29) expressly apply the terms of the Ontario Agreement to reserves in the Prairies, but declare that with respect to reserves "heretofore selected and surveyed . . neither the said lands nor the proceeds of disposition shall in any circumstances become administerable by or be paid to the Province." The Provinces are not entitled to share in any consideration arising from mineral dispositions with respect to reserves set apart before 1930.

(C) British Columbia

British Columbia and Canada reached an Agreement with respect to the development of mineral resources on reserve lands in 1943 (SC 1943, c. 19). The Agreement provided that one half of the revenues derived from mineral dispositions on all reserves in the Province should be retained by the Province and the other half remitted to the Dominion "for the benefit of the Indians". In 1980 the entitlement of the Indians of the Fort Nelson Indian Band to one half of the consideration payable with respect to mineral dispositions was agreed with respect to lands set apart and transferred in 1961 pursuant to Treaty #8 and Order in Council No. 2995 (Fort Nelson Indian Reserve Minerals Revenue Sharing Act, SC 1980-81-82, c. 38).

(D) The Atlantic Provinces (Nova Scotia and New Brunswick

The Agreements with Nova Scotia (SC 1959, c. 50) and New Brunswick (SC 1959, c. 47) declared that ownership of minerals on reserve lands was vested in the provinces. The Agreements also provided, however, that any consideration received with respect to a mineral disposition on reserve lands or with respect to surrendered reserve lands should be paid to Canada "for the use or benefit of the Indian band or Indians from where reserve land such monies are so derived."

(b) Locating Reserves Where There Are No Minerals

In 1880 Treaty Commissioner Morris urged that "no patents should be issued, or licences granted, for mineral or timber lands, or other lands, until the question of the reserves has first been adjusted." (Morris, *Treaties*, p. 52).

It has often been suggested that reserve lands were set apart so as to deny valuable mineral lands to the Indians. The following comments were made with respect to reserves set apart in Saskatchewan:

The setting aside of reserve lands pursuant to treaty was accomplished by survey of the Department of the Interior in consultation with the Indians concerned. Upon such survey the land might be withdrawn from the *Dominion Lands Act* and thus not be open for settlement. Such withdrawal was, however, subject to "existing rights", including mineral disposition pursuant to regulations promulgated under the Act. The traditional lands of an Indian band and its accompanying mineral wealth might accordingly be denied the band in favour of a prospector. The policy is described and explained in these communications from the Department of Indian Affairs concerning the establishment of the Lac La Ronge reserve:

> . . . I am directed to enclose you herewith a blue print of Lac La Ronge, showing the country around it and the names of the several mineral claims for which entries have been granted in the vicinity as well as the approximate positions of such claims, and the name of the registered owner thereof. In this connection, I am to notify you that your surveyor must not on any account include any of these mineral claims within tracts of land which you may set apart in connection with the Indian Reserves in that locality. (Assistant Secretary, Department of Indian Affairs, March 11, 1909.)

> . . . until your department has completed the survey of the proposed Indian Reserves, so that the same may be noted in our records, there is no provision whereby the Department may prevent prospectors from locating Mining Claims within the tract nor refuse to grant entry for such claims, if staked in accordance with the regulations, unless the Reserve is defined in some way on the ground. (Assistant Secretary, Department of Indian Affairs, March 26, 1912.)

The Department of the Interior was encouraged in this policy by the Government of Saskatchewan. The text of the following letter from the Premier of Saskatchewan in 1925 demonstrates the concern the provincial government has historically maintained for mineral development in the North albeit denying any entitlement therein to the Indian and native inhabitants.

> Mr D.A. Hall, M.L.A., for Cumberland, our most northerly constituency, has requested me to write to you regarding the matter of Indian Reserves at Lac La Ronge.

> He states that he believes there are some thirty odd square miles still due the Indians of the band at Lac La Ronge. At present, he says, there are some five, or six Reserves close to Lac La Ronge and also states that he is positive that not ten per cent of the Indians are living on them.

> The Indians are apparently aware of the activities of prospectors and others interested in the development of mineral claims and are

anxious to prevent further developments of any kind and Mr Hall states they have applied to Ottawa to have all the territory in the vicinity of the mineral claims made into a Reserve.

The land in the section referred to, is all very hilly, rocky, broken country, quite unsuitable, according to Mr Hall, for an Indian Reserve. He says, there are many other places in that section of the country, much more suitable for Reserves and strongly recommends that the Dominion Government have a geological survey made this year, and that nothing be done until this survey has been completed. It would then be an easy matter for the Minister to decide the most suitable lands to be given to the Indians.

It seems to me, highly desirable that no action should be taken which would have the effect of throwing mineralized sections of our northern country into Indian Reserves, if it can be avoided, and I strongly endorse Mr Hall's suggestion that a geological survey be made before a decision is reached to comply with the request of the Indians.

If mineralized sections are kept out of Indian Reserves, as far as possible, there is a chance for their development in the future. The placing of them within the borders of the Reserves would hamper development very materially.

Hoping that you will give consideration to this matter and with kind regards, . . .

Premier of Saskatchewan to the Minister of the Interior
Feb. 18, 1925

The location of mineral and uranium deposits outside the boundaries of reserves appears as government policy rather than careless selection. Except for recent exploration developments at Fond du Lac and Stony Rapids there had never been any mineral development upon reserve lands in Northern Saskatchewan. Such state of affairs caused the Aski-Puko Report upon the Churchill River Project for the Peter Ballantyne and Lac La Ronge Bands to observe:

> In total, four mining companies have taken the largest part of $2 billion in wealth from the area, with no significant benefit for the North or for Northern natives.

The Provincial Government of recent years has repeatedly urged the fulfilment of outstanding treaty land entitlement and acknowledged it as a "debt" of the provincial and federal governments. The Province has not, however, deviated from that position first put forth by Liberal Premier Dunning in 1925. In a perhaps unrealized affirmation of that pre-Depression government's position on dealings with Indians Premier Blakeney has declared that once exploration permits are issued in respect of Crown lands they are considered occupied and not open for Indian land selection. Fifteen bands have been recognized in Saskatchewan by the Federal and Provincial governments as possessing outstanding treaty land claims totalling over one million acres. The suggestion that mere exploration pursuant to provincial permit can "occupy" the land under the terms of the Natural Resources Transfer Agreement would stifle the bands' claims and violate the intent of the treaties.

> R. Bartlett, "Indian and Native Rights in Uranium Development in Northern Saskatchewan," (1980) 45 *Saskatchewan Law Review* 13, 24-26.

(c) Management and Control of Mineral Development on Reserve Lands

Management and control of mineral development on reserve lands is subject to a division of jurisdiction between the federal and provincial governments and to the administration declared by the Indian Act and the Indian Oil and Gas Act.

(i) Federal and Provincial Jurisdiction

(A) Ontario and the Prairie Provinces

The Canada-Ontario Agreement of 1924 provides that only those persons authorized under the provincial mining legislation may prospect or explore for minerals on Indian reserves. But such persons must first obtain "permission to do so from the Indian Agent for such Reserve". The Indian Agent, accordingly possesses a veto on exploration on Indian reserves. The staking out of a mining claim upon compliance with the provincial mining legislation does *not* confer a right to a mining lease as it would off the reserve. The holder of a mining claim on a reserve is entitled only to such rights "as may be attached to such staking by the Indian Act . . . ." The Agreement provides that the federal government shall administer and dispose of minerals on the reserve.

The Natural Resources Agreements of 1930 with Alberta, Manitoba and Saskatchewan apply the regime established by the 1924 Ontario Agreement to those provinces.

(B) British Columbia

The Canada-British Columbia Agreement of 1943 provides for provincial administration and disposition of minerals on reserve lands. A veto over exploration and mining is conferred upon the "Indian Agent" of the reserve.

British Columbia Indian Reserves Mineral Resource Act SC 1943, c. 19: Schedule:

1. Subject as hereinafter in this Agreement provided, the Indian Reserves in the Province of British Columbia shall continue to be administered in accordance with the legislation and agreements now in force.

2. The administration, control and disposal of all minerals and mineral claims, both precious and base, in, upon or under all Indian Reserves in the said Province shall be subject to the laws of the Province which shall apply to the prospecting, staking, recording, developing, leasing, selling or otherwise disposing of or dealing with all such minerals and mineral claims;

Provided, however, that any leases now existing by virtue of subsection (2) of Section 50 of the Indian Act shall not be affected hereby;

And provided further that no prospecting or right of entry on the said Indian Reserve shall be authorized or permitted until permission so to do has been obtained from the Indian Agent for such Reserve; such permission shall be subject to such terms and conditions as the said Indian Agent may specify and shall be granted only to such persons whose application for permission has been approved by the Gold Commissioner for the Mining Division of the Province in which such Reserve is situated;

And provided further that base minerals and mineral right shall only be subject to this agreement upon being surrendered pursuant to the Indian Act.

3. The term ''mineral'' shall mean and include gold, silver, and all naturally occurring useful minerals, but shall not include peat, coal, petroleum, natural gas, bitumen, oil shales, limestone, marble, clay, gypsum, or any building stone when mined for building purposes, earth, ash, marl, gravel, sand or any element which forms part of the agricultural surface of the land.

The Fort Nelson Indian Reserve Minerals Revenue Sharing Act, SC, 1980-81-82, c. 38 applied such principles to mineral dispositions, including natural gas, on the reserve.

(C) The Atlantic Provinces (Nova Scotia and New Brunswick)

The Canada-Nova Scotia and Canada-New Brunswick Agreements of 1959 provide that prospecting, mining and disposition of minerals on reserve land is subject to regulation and administration under the Indian Act. The Agreements recognize federal control of mineral development on reserve lands. There is no provincial control in the form recognized in the Agreements entered into with respect to Ontario, the Prairie Provinces, and British Columbia.

(D) Quebec

There is no Canada-Quebec Agreement providing for the development of minerals on Indian reserves in Quebec, other than the James Bay and Northern Quebec Agreement (1975) and the Northeastern Quebec Agreement (1978). Those Agreements apply provincial mining legislation to mineral development on Category I lands, but no exploration or mining may take place, except with respect to pre-existing interests, without the consent of the particular community and compensation for surface rights.

Title to most reserves in Quebec is in the province. Upon surrender of minerals on such reserves, the beneficial interest vests in the province. The development of minerals upon such reserves is subject to administration under the Indian Act, but interest of the province presents difficulties in its application. The Indian Act does, of course, recognize a veto in the band over mineral development in so far as a surrender of the minerals is required.

(ii) Federal Administration

Except in British Columbia, administration and disposition of minerals on reserve lands is subject to the Indian Act and the Indian Oil and Gas Act.

> R. Bartlett, "Indian and Native Rights in Uranium Development in Northern Saskatchewan" (1980) 45 *Saskatchewan Law Review* 13, 31.

Minerals upon reserve lands must be surrendered under sections 37-39 of the *Indian Act* prior to disposition. A valid surrender requires the assent of the majority of the band to the terms thereof and the acceptance of the Governor in Council. Historically a surrender has not always been considered necessary. In 1919 the *Indian Act* was amended to provide for the "issuance of leases for surface rights . . . for the mining of precious metals", *without* surrender purportedly to enable the British Columbia government to exercise its rights upon reserve lands to precious metals (gold and silver). The Annual Report of the Department of Indian Affairs of 1920 observed:

> Owing to local conditions, misapprehension or hostility on the part of a band, it is not always possible to secure a surrender for mining rights. This obstacle has been effectively overcome by the amendment.

The absence of any reference in the Act or amendment to sub-surface rights caused the Justice Department to question the validity of oil and gas disposition regulations purportedly promulgated pursuant to the amendment. As the Federal Minister of Mines and Resources candidly observed:

At the time the regulations were passed, or indeed at the time the provision was inserted in the *Indian Act*, it was not expected that developments of minerals or coal or of oil so far as Alberta is concerned would take place on Indian reserves, located as they were mostly in the northern part of the province. The opinion of the Justice department is that the power of the Governor in Council to make these regulations does not extend to the subsurface rights.

In 1938 the Act was amended to provide for the disposition, upon surrender, of sub-surface rights and without surrender, of surface rights in respect of all minerals. In 1951 the Act was amended to its present form. Upon surrender the Minister "may manage, sell, lease or otherwise dispose of surrendered lands in accordance with the Act and terms of surrender." The Governor in Council is authorized to make regulations "providing for the disposition of surrendered mines and minerals underlying lands in a reserve". Surface rights in respect of surrendered minerals may be obtained by Ministerial permit for one year, or longer with the consent of the band council.

The requirement of a surrender prior to the disposition of mineral rights confers an absolute veto upon band members with respect to mineral development on reserve lands. Such veto may be contrasted with the provisions in Australia of the Aboriginal Land Rights (Northern Territory) Act 1976, c. 191 (C'th), s. 50(1):

> 40. (1)   A mining interest in respect of Aboriginal land shall not be granted unless —
> (a)   both the Minister and the Land Council for the area in which the land is situated have consented, in writing, to the making of the grant; or
> (b)   the Governor-General has, by Proclamation, declared that the national interest requires that the grant be made.

The mining industry in Australia has long and loudly protested the control over mineral development conferred upon Aborigines by the Act. In 1979 the Australian Mining Industry Council declared:

> On the question of mineral rights, the Council believes it to be in both the national interest and the interests of the Aborigines themselves that they not be given any special privileges. In particular, access by the Community to Crown owned minerals in Aboriginal land must be maintained.

The Indian Oil and Gas Act, SC 1974-75-76, c. 15 was enacted "for greater certainty" to authorize the making of the Indian Oil and Gas Regulations, which had been expressed to have been made pursuant to section

57(c) of the Indian Act. The Indian Oil and Gas Regulations, c. 963 provide for the disposition of oil and gas rights. The Indian Mining Regulations provide for the disposition of other mineral rights. The Regulations require compliance with provincial laws respecting exploration, development, production and treatment except where inconsistent with the Regulations themselves. The Indian Oil and Gas Regulations also require compliance with provincial laws respecting the environment and,

> 45. To the extent that it is practicable and consistent with reasonable efficiency, safety and economy, every person conducting exploratory work, drilling or production operations under these Regulations shall give employment to persons resident on the Indian lands within which the operations are conducted.

The Indian Mining Regulations contain no such requirements.

The Indian Oil and Gas Regulations provide for royalties at levels similar to those established by the provinces. A difficulty that has arisen in Saskatchewan is the imposition of the levy under the provincial Freehold Oil and Gas Production Tax Act, SS 1982, upon oil and gas production from wells on Indian reserves. Subject to agreement, the Indian Mining Regulations set a royalty rate of 5 per cent.

Further Reading

R. Bartlett, "Indian and Native Rights in Uranium Development in Northern Saskatchewan," (1980) 45 *Saskatchewan Law Review*, 13.
Cuming and Mickenberg, *Native Rights in Canada*, 2d ed, Chapter 21.

10. Water Rights

R. Bartlett, "Indian Water Rights on the Prairies," (1980) 11 *Manitoba Law Journal* 59, 67-68.

Indian bands may claim water rights on the basis of both treaty and ownership of riparian land. The treaty right to water is an ill-defined right to use of water for the development of reserve lands. Riparian rights have been classified by LaForest as follows:

1) right of access to water
2) rights of drainage
3) rights relating to flow of water
4) rights relating to quality of water
5) rights relating to use of water
6) right of accretion.

The right to flow and quality of water has been classically described as the entitlement of the riparian owner to have the flow of water reach his lands "without sensible alteration in its character or quality." At common law, the riparian owner did not, of course, own the water, but might make use of it for domestic purposes without incurring liability to other owners. Extraordinary use of the water, for example, for irrigation or driving a mill, was only permissible if reasonable and if the water was restored to the stream substantially undiminished in quality and quantity. It is submitted that Indian treaty right to water is considerably in excess of that permitted upon the basis of riparian ownership of land.

It appears that riparian rights or their equivalent in Civil Law of Indian bands have remained largely undisturbed in Ontario, Quebec, and New Brunswick. In Nova Scotia and British Columbia the statutory vesting of the property in and the right to use water in the Crown in the right of the provinces suggests that such common law rights are denied Indian bands: (See *Western Canada Ranching* v. *Department of Indian Affairs* (1921) 2 WWR 836 (British Columbia Court of Appeal)). The 1959 Canada-Nova Scotia Agreement does not provide for such rights. In British Columbia the form of transfer of reserve lands by the province to the Dominion reserved to the province the right "to take and occupy such water privileges and to have and enjoy such rights of carrying water over, through or under any parts of the hereditaments hereby granted, as may be reasonably required for mining or agricultural purposes in the vicinity of the said hereditaments, paying therefor a reasonable compensation."

With respect to the Prairie Provinces it has been observed:

Under neither the common law nor Indian traditional law were bodies of water regarded as the subject of ownership, rather mere rights of use might attach to them. The treaties with the Indians of the Prairie Provinces recognized such rights and assured the Indian bands of their right to use such waters for the development of their reserves. In the 1894 *Irrigation Act* the Federal Government broke faith with the treaties and declared the ownership and power of disposition of water rights to reside solely in the Crown. Treaty rights to water use were confiscated. The same statute also sought to deny any entitlement to the water-bed arising thereafter. The furtherance of irrigation and water use policy appears to have been developed entirely without regard for the Indian people or the treaty promises made to them.

Upon the transfer of the natural resources of Alberta, Manitoba and Saskatchewan to the administration of the provinces the abrogation and confiscation of Indian water rights is no longer within the administering government's competence. The provinces are not empowered to deny Indian reserve property interests. The provinces have, however, and continue to deny the water rights of Indian bands on outstanding reserve land entitlement. The provinces cannot vary the obligation imposed upon them to set aside lands and associated water rights to fulfill the treaty obligations of the Government of Canada.

R. Bartlett, "Indian Water Rights", p. 90.

Further Reading

G.V. LaForest, "Water Law in Canada — The Atlantic Provinces," 1973, *Canadian Environmental Law,* Vol. I, Butterworths.

11. Surrender

Sections 37-41 of the Indian Act provide for the surrender of reserve lands. Section 37 prohibits the disposition of reserve lands, except as elsewhere provided by the Act, until they have been surrendered. A surrender is void unless it is made to Her Majesty, assented to by a majority of the electors of the land, and it is accepted by the Governor in Council. The assent of the majority of those voting is sufficient where the Minister calls a second meeting, which he may do if a majority of the election did not vote at the initial meeting. *Logan* v. *Styres* (1954), 20 DLR (2d) 416 (Ontario High Court) describes the acceptance of a surrender where only 54 of 3,600 electors voted; the remainder refused to recognize the form of government laid down by the Indian Act. Upon surrender, the Minister is empowered to "manage, sell, lease or otherwise dispose of surrendered lands" in accordance with the terms of the surrender. A surrender may be absolute or qualified, conditional or unconditional.

(a) The origin of the requirement of a surrender is considered in *Easterbrook* v. *The King,* [1931] SCR 210.

The judgment of the court was delivered by

NEWCOMBE J. — The Attorney-General of Canada, by Information filed in the Exchequer Court of Canada, seeks to recover, as ungranted Crown lands reserved for the Indians, the possession of the lands hereinafter described, situate on Cornwall Island, in the River St Lawrence, opposite the town of Cornwall. The island is said to be five miles long; to average in width three-quarters of a mile, and to comprise 3,500 acres. There is in proof a report of Mr Davidson, an Indian Agent, dated 3rd June, 1878, wherein it is stated that this island is exclusively occupied by Indians, except the Chesley farm (the subject of this action), containing about 200 acres, and that there are thirty-seven houses on the island, inhabited by about forty families. It is shewn elsewhere that the farm extends across the island from one side to the other, thus dividing into two sections the lands which remain in the possession of the Indians. The dichotomy is explained by the circumstances in which the claim has its origin.

There is in evidence a document, dated 10th March, 1821, executed at Cornwall

By and between the British Indian Chiefs of St Regis, in the Province of Lower Canada, of the first part and Solomon Youmans Chesley, of the said Town of Cornwall, gentleman, of the second part;

Whereby the said Indian Chiefs, for themselves and on behalf of their tribe (whom they represent) for and in consideration of the sum of One Hundred Dollars to them in hand paid by the said Solomon Youmans Chesley, before the signing, sealing and delivering of these presents as well as the rents and covenants hereinafter mentioned do by these presents lease, convey and to farm let unto the said Solomon Y. Chesley, his heirs and assigns all and singular that certain parcel of land and premises situated on Cornwall Island in the River St Lawrence and being composed of that portion of it which lies immediately south and in front of the said Town of Cornwall containing by admeasurement one hundred and ninety-six acres more or less which piece or parcel of land and tenement is butted and bounded as follows, viz: — Commencing at the water's edge on the north side of said Cornwall Island nearly opposite to the Court House in said Town and at the mouth of a ravine or gully immediately below Nett Point where a white ash post is planted and running south ten degrees east fifty-two chains more or less across said Island to the south bank thereof, thence following the water's edge downwards a distance at a right angle from the base line of forty-five chains to a white oak post, thence northward on a line parallel to said base line across said Island to the water's edge on the north side thereof, thence following the water's edge upward or against the current to the place of beginning. To have and to hold the said land and premises with all and singular its appurtenances unto him the said Solomon Y. Chesley, his heirs and assigns for and during the full end and term of ninety-nine years to be fully ended and completed and at the expiration thereof for another and further like period of ninety-nine years and so on until the full end and term of nine hundred and ninety-nine years shall be fully ended and completed. He, the said Solomon Y. Chesley, his heirs and assigns yielding and paying therefor to the said Chiefs of St Regis and their successors yearly and every year on the tenth day of February, the sum or rent of ten dollars of lawful money of Canada, and the said Chiefs do hereby covenant with the said Solomon Y. Chesley, his heirs and assigns, that they are the representatives of the said tribe of St Regis as well as trustees of their estate and as such that they have a perfect right to make, execute and deliver this lease in good faith upon the terms and, conditions herein already expressed.

And there are covenants on the part of Mr Chesley with the Indian Chiefs, expressed as follows:

And the said Solomon Youmans Chesley, for himself, his heirs and assigns doth hereby covenant and agree to and with the said Indian Chiefs of St Regis and with their successors in manner and form following, that is to say: that he the said Solomon Y. Chesley being put into peaceable and quiet possession of aforesaid described lands and premises shall and will on the tenth day of February, one thousand eight hundred and twenty-two, pay unto the said Indian Chiefs or their successors, the sum or rent of ten dollars, at the Town of Cornwall aforesaid and in like manner, so long as he the said Solomon Y. Chesley, his heirs and assigns shall be kept and assured in peaceable and undisturbed possession of said lands and premises, so long as he, his heirs and assigns continue to pay the said annual sum at rent of ten dollars on the tenth day of February in each succeeding year to the end and term of nine hundred and ninety-nine years.

And further that should he the said Solomon Y. Chesley, his heirs and assigns allow the said rent of ten dollars to remain unpaid by the space of one month after the same shall have been due in any year to come and after the same may have been legally demanded, he and they shall renounce the said land and premises and return the same to the said Indian Chiefs or their successors.

The original document is not produced upon this appeal; but it purports, so it is said, to be executed under seal, on behalf of the parties of the first part, by nine individuals, said to be Indian Chiefs, and by Mr Chesley, the party of the second part. There is no evidence whatever as to what were the powers or authority of the British Indian Chiefs of St Regis, but it is admitted that the premises, being Crown Lands, had not been ceded or surrendered to the Crown by the Indians; and, therefore, as a matter of law, the Chiefs could not dispose of the reserve or any part of it, or of any estate therein. *St Catharine's Milling and Lumber Company* v. *The Queen*. And there is an additional reason in this case why the alleged lease, in the absence of proof to the contrary, should be regarded as invalid, seeing that the Chiefs, whatever powers they may have possessed during their tenure of office, profess to grant an estate in the land, to commence at a time ninety-nine years after the date of the instrument. It is very carefully stated that the term is to endure for

ninety-nine years to be fully ended and completed and at the expiration thereof for another and further like period of ninety-nine years and so on until the full end and term of nine hundred and ninety-nine years shall be ended and completed.

Strong J, who certainly did not speak without information as to the facts, tells us in his dissenting judgment in the *St Catharine's Milling* case, that

> the control of the Indians and of the lands occupied by the Indians had, until a comparatively recent period, been retained in the hands of the Imperial Government; for some fifteen years after local self government had been accorded to the Province of Canada the management of Indian Affairs remained in the hands of an Imperial officer, subject only to the personal direction of the Governor General, and entirely independent of the local government, and it was only about the year 1855, during the administration of Sir Edmund Head and after the new system of Government had been successfully established, that the direction of Indian affairs was handed over to the Executive authorities of the late Province of Canada.

There is no evidence that either the Imperial Superintendent of Indian Affairs or the local government was, at the time, consulted or became in anywise party to or concerned in, or even informed as to the transaction of 1821 between the Chiefs and Mr Chesley, which certainly was brought about in breach of the prohibition expressed, and repeated more than once by the proclamation of 1763, as essential to the interest of the British Crown and the security of its colonies. The governors and commanders-in-chief in America are forbidden to grant warrants of survey, or to pass any patents upon any lands whatever which, not having been ceded to or purchased by the Crown, are reserved to the Indians, or any of them; and all British subjects are strictly forbidden, on pain of the royal displeasure,

> from making any purchases or settlements whatsoever, or taking possession of any of the lands above reserved (which include the lands now in question), without our special leave and licence for that purpose first obtained.

Also, it is provided that:

> And We do further strictly enjoin and require all persons whatsoever, who have either wilfully or inadvertently seated themselves upon any lands within the countries above described, or upon any other lands which, not having been ceded to or purchased by Us, are still reserved to the said Indians as aforesaid, forthwith to remove themselves from such settlements.

Moreover the policy of the Crown is further emphasized by the following injunction:

> And whereas great frauds and abuses have been committed in the

purchasing lands of the Indians, to the great prejudice of Our interests and to the great dissatisfaction of the said Indians; in order, therefore, to prevent such irregularities for the future, and to the end that the Indians may be convinced of Our Justice and determined resolution to remove all reasonable cause of discontent, We do, with the advice of Our Privy Council, strictly enjoin and require that no private person do presume to make any purchase from the said Indians of any lands reserved to the said Indians within those parts of Our colonies where We have thought propèr to allow settlement; but that, if at any time any of the said Indians should be inclined to dispose of the said lands, the same shall be purchased only for Us, in Our name, at some public meeting or assembly of the said Indians, to be held for that purpose by the Governors or Commander-in-Chief of Our colony respectively, within which they shall lie.

These provisions have persisted, both under British and Colonial administration; and there is in evidence an Order in Council of the Lieutenant-Governor of Upper Canada, dated 10th November, 1802, and certified for publication, which comes out of the custody of the Dominion Archives, and reads as follows:

His Excellency the Lieutenant-Governor in Council hereby gives notice, to all whom it may concern, That no leases which have been, or shall be Granted, or pretended to be Granted, by or under the authority of any Indian Nation, will be admitted or allowed — And this Public Notice is given in order that No person may pretend ignorance of the same.

See the clauses relating to Indian lands in the Consolidated Statutes of Upper Canada, 1859, chap. 82, secs. 21 *et seq.*; also the *Indian Act* as enacted by the Dominion, RSC, 1886, chap. 43, secs. 38-41 inclusive, and in the subsequent revisions.

Looking at the provisions of the lease itself, which have been fully quoted above, it is difficult to avoid a reasonable inference that Mr Chesley was fully aware of the precarious nature of the estates evidenced by the instrument of 10th March, 1821. It will be perceived that he paid the chiefs $100 in hand; and, beyond that, the consideration on his part for the valuable concession which he stipulated for consists only of the annual rent of $10. It is not suggested that there was any meeting of the band to authorize or approve the grant; and Mr Chesley's security, *quantum valeat*, consists in the covenant of the chiefs, "that they are the representatives of the said tribe of St Regis as well as trustees of their estate and as such that they have a perfect right to make, execute and deliver this lease in good faith upon the terms and conditions herein already expressed." Mr Chesley, upon his part, covenants for payment of the rent to the chiefs at Cornwall "so long as he the said Solomon Y. Chesley, his heirs and assigns shall be kept and assured in peaceable and undisturbed possession of said lands and premises"; and, finally, it is provided that if he, Mr Chesley, his heirs and assigns, "allow the said rent of ten dollars to remain unpaid by the space of one month after the same shall have been due in any year to come and after the same may have been legally demanded, he and they shall renounce the said land and premises and return the same to the said Indian Chiefs or their successors."

It would seem not improbable that the lease first came to the knowledge of the Department of Indian Affairs when, on 18th February, 1875, Mitchell Benedict, an Indian of the St Regis settlement, wrote to the Superintendent General, or the Deputy Superintendent General, presumably making enquiries about the validity of Mr Chesley's title. Immediately following this letter, on 24th February, 1875, the lease was registered at the Department, as certified by the initials of Mr Van Koughnet, the Assistant Superintendent General; and a letter was written to Benedict on 26th *idem*, signed, as I infer, by Mr Van Koughnet, and saying:

> I have to state in reply to your letter of the 18th inst., that the lease to Mr Chesley of 196 acres of land on Cornwall Island in the St Lawrence River is dated March 10th, 1821, and is for 99 years, renewable at the end of each such period until the full term of 999 years has expired on payment of the annual rental of $10.00. Mr Chesley has complied with the terms of his lease, and has a right to sublet the land as he has been in the habit of doing for years.

A memorandum, written by Mr Chesley, is also introduced by the defendant, which reads as follows:

> In reply to a letter from Mitchell Benedict an Indian of Cornwall Island addressed to the Indian Department under date the 18th February, 1875, enquiring whether the ownership and possession of a farm on Cornwall Island by Solomon Y. Chesley was known to me and recognized by the said Department. A letter was addressed to the said Benedict by direction of Mr Laird the Superintendent General, under date the 24th February, 1875, stating that Mr Chesley held a lease for 196 acres of land on Cornwall Island dated 10th March, 1821, to run 999 years from date at a rental of $10 per annum. That Mr Chesley having fulfilled his engagements under said Lease he had a right to said land and to sublet same as heretofore.

The said lease is registered in the Book of the office of the Indian Department on the 24th February, 1875, as appears indorsed on the back thereof. Certified by the initials of lawrence Van Koughnet, Asst. Supt. Genl.

But there seems to be some confusion about the minutes relating to this subject, because it is stated by counsel for the defendant, and admitted by counsel for the Crown, that

> the endorsement upon our original lease at Cornwall shows that the late Mr. Van Koughnet made a memorandum on the back of the lease that it was originally in the Department on the 24th September 1875.

It is admitted, in the following terms, that Mr Chesley entered into possession on or about 10th March, 1821, and that

> the present defendant is in possession as assignee of whatever rights Solomon Y. Chesley had under that original lease. There is a chain of assignments but they admit that they have been in possession.

Then, immediately following,

> The Crown admits that during that period rents were paid by the occupant and received by the Crown, or the Department of Indian Affairs, for the benefit of the Indians.

And this, as I interpret it, is intended to mean that during the period of the defendant's possession, the rent, instead of being paid directly to the Indian Chiefs, as it was at the beginning, was paid to the Department for the benefit of the Indians, although there is evidence in another place that the first payment of rent to the Department was made in 1877, three years before the defendant was born.

The defendant continued to pay the rent until the expiry of the term of ninety-nine years provided for by the lease; and there are Admissions:

> That all rents provided by the lease in question herein have been paid by the original lease and successive occupants to 10th March 1920, since which time the Respondent (the Crown) has refused to accept further rents.

> That the Respondent served Appellant with Notice to Quit and demand for possession in due time prior to the expiration of the first 99 year period of the lease in question herein.

> That the Appellant has remained in possession of the lands described in said lease since the 10th March, 1920, and is still in possession of same.

> That the Appellant is the successor in title to such rights as the original lessee from the Indian Chiefs may have had and has been in continuous possession thereof since on or about the 28th October, 1904.

The facts are not set out or introduced in a very orderly fashion and the reader is left in some perplexity to ascertain precisely the order of events and what the truth is; but nevertheless, it seems to be clear enough that although the lease was ineffective and void at law, by reason of the absence of any authority on the part of the grantors to make it, and for non-compliance with the peremptory requirements of the proclamation, which have the force of statute, an officer of the Department, constituted after the union of the provinces in 1867 for the administration of Indian Affairs, registered the lease, not earlier than 1875; and, from that time until the expiration in 1920 of the demised term of ninety-nine years, received, for the Indians, the annual rent of $10, as it accrued from year to year. But the Department then ceased to tolerate the defendant's possession and gave notice to quit in a manner which, it is admitted, satisfied the requisites, as in the case of a tenant from year to year; refusing to receive any further rent, or in any manner to recognize a tenancy. And so the case passed to the Attorney-General, who filed his Information on 18th October, 1921; but the defendant remained in possession, and, pending the litigation, has enjoyed the benefit of the use and occupation.

The defendant alleges four grounds of appeal: first, that the alleged lease was not void *ab initio*; secondly, that the learned judge erred in holding "that the appellant was not entitled as of right to compensation for permanent improvements"; thirdly, he denies that the proclamation of 1763 affects the transaction; and, fourthly, he denies that the Crown is entitled to $400 a year for the occupation of the premises after 10th March, 1920.

The learned judge found no difficulty in disposing of the case, and I have no doubt that his conclusions must be maintained. By the formal judgment he declared that the lease of 10th March, 1821, was and is null and void *ab initio*, and that the King was entitled to recover forthwith the possession of the lands described with their appurtenances. He found the value of the defendant's use and occupation, computed from 10th March, 1920, until delivery of the possession, to be at the rate of $400 per annum; and, moreover, he held that the defendant's claim for compensation for improvements made by him or his predecessors should be dismissed.

There is some conflict of opinion as to the annual value of the premises, but the evidence certainly preponderates in favour of an estimate not less than that found by the learned judge; and, therefore, his finding in that particular ought not to be disturbed.

As to the defendant's claim for compensation for the improvements to which he asserts a right, there is no statutory liability upon the Crown; and I agree with the learned judge that the defendant has entirely failed to establish any act or representation, for which the Crown is responsible, whereby he was misled to believe that he had a title which could be vindicated in competition with that of the Crown. There is no claim to recover compensation for the use of the premises during the period of the first term, which, in the words of the instrument, is "fully ended and completed"; and, to that extent, the defendant has profited by the unauthorized and illegal transaction. The learned judge refers to the leading case of *Ramsden* v. *Dyson*; and I cannot avoid the conclusion that the defendant and his predecessors were not, at any time, in ignorance of the infirmity of the title which they claim to have derived from the Indians; and, certainly, they knew that there had been no surrender, and that they had no grant from the Crown. The law, as applicable in such cases, is very aptly stated by Lord Wensleydale at page 168, where he says:

> If a stranger build on my land, supposing it to be his own, and I, knowing it to be mine, do not interfere, but leave him to go on, equity considers it to be dishonest in me to remain passive and afterwards to interfere and take the profit. But if a stranger build knowingly upon my land, there is no principle of equity which prevents me from insisting on having back my land, with all the additional value which the occupier has imprudently added to it. If a tenant of mine does the same thing, he cannot insist on refusing to give up the estate at the end of his term. It was his own folly to build.

The letter from the Indian, Mitchell Benedict, is not produced, and without it one cannot interpret the reply with certainty; moreover the introduction of secondary evidence by Mr Chesley's memorandum, admitted to be inaccurate in a material particular, does not add to the proof. Whether Mr Laird or Mr Van Koughnet was the writer, he was evidently under an utter misapprehension if he intended to assure the Indian of the validity of the Chesley lease, and these gentlemen should have sought the advice of the law officers; but, anyhow, Mr Chesley was not a party to the correspondence, and it contains no representation by which the Crown is bound to him. If he were looking for an assurance from the Indian Department to strengthen his title, why did he not approach the competent authorities in a straightforward manner? Neither the Crown, as to its title, nor the Indians, as to their burden upon the lands, are to suffer deprivation by the facts which this incident discloses or suggests.

It is true that, during the latter part of the term of ninety-nine years, the annual rent of $10 was received at the Department of Indian Affairs, and presumably distributed as belonging to the income of the band or the Indians of the reserve; but that circumstance could not serve to validate a lease which was void at law, nor even to create a tenancy from year to year under conditions which the law prohibited. In any event, the defendant and his predecessors have had the full benefit of possession for the term during which the rent was paid; and, for the period which has since elapsed, and for the future, the Crown has not, so far as I can perceive, incurred any obligation, legal or equitable, to recognize the defendant's possession or right to compensation.

I would dismiss the appeal with costs.

Appeal dismissed with costs.

SC 1926-27, c. 37

(b) An Act to provide for special control by the Superintendent General of Indian Affairs of certain islands in the St Lawrence river being part of the St Regis Indian reservation.

[Assented to 31st March, 1927.]

WHEREAS the St Regis band of Indians situated at the village of St Regis, in the township of Dundee, county of Huntingdon, in the province of Quebec, hold certain islands in the river St Lawrence, between the town of Prescott and the village of Lancaster, as part of their Reserve; and whereas over a century ago the chiefs and headmen of the said band purported to grant leases of a number of the said islands, or portions of islands, in consideration of a nominal rental, for terms of ninety-nine years with covenants for renewals of the said leases for further periods of ninety-nine years; and whereas in the interest of the Indians of the said band, the Crown has taken action in courts to have these alleged leases declared null and void and has already succeeded in recovering what are known as Lewis island, Snyder island and Thompson or Macmaster island; and whereas actions are still pending in respect of Thomas or Hamilton island, and what is known as the Easterbrook farm on Cornwall island; and whereas it is considered that the revenues to be derived from these islands maintained in their scenic beauty and leased for summer resorts or agricultural purposes, would be of much greater benefit to the band than they would derive from having these islands thrown open to the Indians generally resulting in the groves of timber being cut down and removed for firewood, as has happened with many other islands, rendering them non-productive as summer resorts: Therefore His Majesty, by and with the advice and consent of the Senate and House of Commons of Canada, enacts as follows:

1.   This Act may be cited as the *St Regis Islands Act*.

2.   Notwithstanding the provisions of the *Indian Act* to the contrary, the Superintendent General of Indian Affairs shall have full power to deal with the said Thompson or Macmaster Island, Lewis Island, Snyder Island, also Thomas or Hamilton Island and the Easterbrook farm, in the event of the leases under which they are held being declared by the courts to be null and void, and also any other island or islands belonging to the St Regis band which are not held under location ticket or under any recognized interest by individual members of the band, in any way that may be deemed to be in the best interests of the band, and may for such purpose grant leases, licences or other concessions without the necessity of obtaining a surrender of the said islands from the band.

3. No Indian or other person shall without the consent of the Superintendent General, expressed in writing, use or occupy any part of the said islands or cut, carry away or remove from the said islands any of the trees, saplings, shrubs, underwood or other material whatsoever.

4. Any one violating the provisions of the preceding section shall be liable on summary conviction to a term of imprisonment not exceeding six months nor less than one month, or to a fine not exceeding two hundred dollars with costs of prosecution and in default of immediate payment to a term of imprisonment not exceeding three months.

The written terms of the "numbered" treaties contained a provision:

. . . that the aforesaid reserves of land, or any part thereof, or any interest or right therein, or appointment thereto, may be sold, leased or otherwise disposed of by the said Government for the use and benefit of the said Indians, with the consent of the Indians entitled thereto first had and obtained . . . .

It is not evident that this term was explained or discussed with the Indians. In the introduction to the treaties, the Treaty Commissioner invariably observed:

. . . the promises we have to make to you are not for today only but for tomorrow, not only for you but for your children born and unborn, and the promises we make will be carried out as long as the sun shines above and the water flows in the ocean.

A. Morris, *Treaties with the Indians*, p. 96.

(c) Surrenders of Indian reserve land have been extensive. It has often been suggested that surrenders were invalid or improper. The following indicates the degree of surrender for sale of reserve land in Saskatchewan:

SURRENDERS FOR SALE IN SASKATCHEWAN

BAND	RESERVES		DATE	ACRES SURRENDERED
YORKTON DISTRICT				
Cote	(Kamsack Townsite)	#64	21 June 1904	242
			20 June 1907	10,740
			20 November 1913	10,422
			29 April 1914	164
	(some land was returned — total lost was 16,240			

SURRENDERS FOR SALE IN SASKATCHEWAN

BAND	RESERVES		DATE	ACRES SURRENDERED

YORKTON DISTRICT (Continued)

BAND	RESERVES		DATE	ACRES SURRENDERED
Cowessess		#73	29 January 1907	20,704
			13 November 1908	350
Kahkewistahaw		#72	28 January 1907	33,281
		#72A	4 July 1944	68
Keeseekoose		#66	15 May 1909	7,600
Key		#65	18 May 1909	11,775
Ochapawace		#71	30 June 1919	18,333
Sakimay	Little Bone (Leech Lake)	#73A	6 July 1907	6,976
White Bear	Ocean Man	#69	21 March 1901	23,680
	Pheasant's Rump	#68	21 March 21 1901	23,424

TOTAL SURRENDERED ACREAGE FOR SALE   416,870

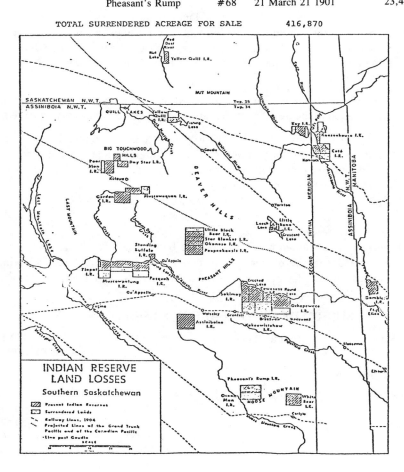

INDIAN RESERVE
LAND LOSSES
Southern Saskatchewan

SURRENDERS FOR SALE IN SASKATCHEWAN

BAND	RESERVES		DATE	ACRES SURRENDERED

TOUCHWOOD FILE HILLS QU'APPELLE DISTRICT

BAND	RESERVES		DATE	ACRES
Carry the Kettle		#76	26 April 1905	5,760
Fishing Lake		#89	1907	13,025
Gordon	(Anglican Church)	#86	25 November 1925	8
Last Mountain Lake	(Fishing Station)	#80A	23 March 1918	1,408
Little Black Bear		#84	30 June 1928	12,408
Muscowpetung		#80	4 January 1909	17,600
Muskowekan	(Lestock)	#85	7 March 1910	160
			14 October 1920	7,485
Pasqua		#79	5 June 1906	16,077
Piapot		#75	28 May 1918	2,180
			10 July 1919	15,360
Poorman		#88	18 April 1918	8,080
Standing Buffalo	(Road R/W)	#78	12 January 1897	2
Wood Mountain		#160	12 May 1919	4,960

NORTH BATTLEFORD DISTRICT

BAND	RESERVES		DATE	ACRES
Moosomin		#112	7 May 1909	14,729
		#112A	7 May 1909	640
Mosquito	Grizzly Bear's Head	#110	19 May 1905	14,400
	Lean Man	#111		
Saulteaux		#159	25 January 1960	207
Thunderchild		#115	27 August 1908	15,360
		#115A	27 August 1908	5,538
		#112A	27 August 1908	640

SASKATOON DISTRICT

BAND	RESERVES		DATE	ACRES
	Chacostapasin	#98	23 June 1897	15,360
Mistawasis		#103	20 March 1911	1,666
			8 August 1919	15,900
Muskeg Lake		#102	25 September 1919	8,960
One Arrow	(Road R/W)	#95	9 October 1894	30

SHELLBROOK AGENCY

BAND	RESERVES		DATE	ACRES
Big River		#118A	9 August 1919	980
Young Chipewayon	Stony Knoll	#107	(relinquished by Order in Council — 1897)	19,200

MEADOW LAKE DISTRICT

BAND	RESERVES		DATE	ACRES
Island Lake	Ministikwan	#161	('eliminated' by Order in Council — 1916)	10,279
Loon Lake	Makwa Lake (townsite)	#129B	9 February 1932	28
	(hospital)	#129B	15 October 1938	2

SURRENDERS FOR SALE IN SASKATCHEWAN

BAND	RESERVES		DATE	ACRES SURRENDERED
MEADOW LAKE DISTRICT (Continued)				
	(townsite)	#129B	17 August 1938	17
	(School Unit)	#129B	27 November 1954	67
Meadow Lake		#105	10 November 1960	3.5
PRINCE ALBERT DISTRICT				
Cumberland House		#20	3 August 1893	640
James Smith	Cumberland	#100A	24 July 1902	22,080
Shoal Lake	(exchanged)	#28A	18 June 1927	640
	(exchanged)	#28B	5 December 1935	640
Sturgeon Lake	(exchanged)	#101	17 December 17 1913	2,145

(d) The requirement that a surrender ''be assented to by a majority of the male members of the band of the full age of twenty-one years, at a meeting or council thereof summoned for that purpose . .'' under section 49(1) of the Indian Act RSC 1906, c. 81 was considered in *Cardinal* v. *The Queen* (1982), 41 NR 300 (Supreme Court of Canada).

On April 5, 1982, ESTEY, J delivered the following judgment for the Supreme Court of Canada:

ESTEY J: On the 13th of May, 1908, a meeting was held of the male members of the Enoch Band of Indians of Alberta to determine whether or not to surrender certain Indian lands. A majority of those present at the meeting and who voted cast their vote in favour of the surrender but the number so giving their assent did not represent a majority of all male members of the Enoch Band at the time. . .

Subsection (1) of s. 49 may be capable of at least five interpretations (assuming always a validly called meeting regularly held).

1. A majority of all eligible voters in the band must attend a meeting and that same absolute majority must assent to the surrender.

2. A majority of all eligible voters in the band must attend a meeting and a majority of those present must assent to the surrender.

3. A majority of all eligible voters in the band must attend a meeting and a majority of those present and voting must assent to the surrender.

4. A simple majority of eligible voters who attend the meeting assent to the surrender.

5. A simple majority of all eligible voters who attend and vote must vote in favour of the surrender.

The learned trial judge found that the surrender in 1908 was valid stating:

> A majority of their number attended the meeting or council of May 13, 1908. That was clearly a quorum; perhaps fewer than a majority would also have been but I do not have to decide that. A majority of that quorum approved the surrender. The act of that majority was the act of the band . . .

If the critical words of s. 49(1) appeared in the reserve order so that it read "unless assented to at a meeting of members summoned for that purpose by a majority of the male members of the band", the result would be clear. In that case the key to the subsection would be found in the reference to the majority of all members of the band. In the subsection as it is written, however, the prescribed requirement of a majority would appear more logically to refer to the quorum which must be present to give validity to the assent given at the meeting. That portion of the subsection after the comma then is given a full and sensible meaning, in my view, as being merely an assignment or a prescription of a requirement that the assent be taken at a meeting. Thus when read together the requirement is that there be a meeting of eligible members of the band and that in attendance at that meeting there must be a majority of male members of the full age of 21. As already said, we do not, on the facts in this appeal, need to determine whether such majority need be computed with reference to s. 49(2).

There only remains to determine the requirement for the expression of assent in the sense of that term in s. 49(1) at the meeting attended by the prescribed majority. In the common law, and indeed in general usage of the language, a group of persons may, unless specially organized, express their view only by an agreement by the majority. A refinement arises where all members of a defined group present at a meeting do not express a view. In that case, as we shall see, the common law expresses again the ordinary sense of our language that the group viewpoint is that which is expressed by the majority of those declaring or voting on the issue in question. Thus, by this rather simple line of reasoning, the section is construed as meaning that an assent, to be valid, must be given by a majority of a majority of eligible band members in attendance at a meeting called for the purpose of giving or withholding assent . . .

It has also been argued that the interpretation which is now being considered is one which exposes the membership of the band to a risk of loss of property and other rights contrary to the general pattern and spirit of the *Indian Act*. It is perhaps well to observe in this connection that there are precautions built into the procedures of Part I of the Act dealing with surrender. Firstly, the meeting must be called to consider the question of surrender explicitly. It may not be attended to at a regular meeting or one in respect of which express notice has not been given to the band. Secondly, the meeting must be called in accordance with the rules of the band. Thirdly, the chief or principal men must certify on oath the vote and that the meeting was properly constituted. Fourthly, only residents of the reserve can vote by reason of the exclusionary provisions of subs. (2) of s. 49. Fifthly, the meeting must be held in the presence of an officer of the Crown. And sixthly, even if the vote is in the affirmative, the surrender may be accepted or refused by the Governor in Council. It is against this background of precautionary measures that one must examine the manner in which the assent of eligible members of the band is to be ascertained under s. 49

. . .

I therefore come to the conclusion that of the five possible interpretations which might be placed upon s. 49(1) the plain meaning of the section as applied to the facts on this appeal is that a majority of the majority of the male members of the band of the full age of 21 is sufficient to produce a valid consent and accordingly the question is answered in the negative and I would dismiss the appeal with costs.

Appeal dismissed.

In the Federal Court of Appeal, Heald J dissented, (1980) 109 DLR (3d) 366.

I have concluded that, reading the words in s. 49(1) in their entire context in their grammatical and ordinary sense harmoniously with the scheme of the Act, the objects of the Act and the intention of Parliament, the interpretation urged on us by the appellants is the correct one, notwithstanding that the result is a requirement for an absolute majority of the eligible voters. Breaking up a reserve or a part of a reserve is a serious matter with serious consequences not only for the eligible voters but for all the other members of the band as well. In my view, Parliament in using the words of s. 49(1) clearly intended to provide a high standard of protection for these bands.

Can the giving of assent *follow* the disposition of the reserve lands?

(e) *Ports Franks Properties* v. *The Queen* (1979), 99 DLR (3d) 28, (1981) 3 CNLR 86 (FCTD).

LIEFF DJ:

The plaintiff's second submission is, namely, that there is a fatal flaw in the Crown's legal title because in the surrender and conveyance of Indian lands the procedure set out in the *Indian Act* was not followed properly. This contention is not tenable for reasons which I shall now discuss.

Section 50 of the *Indian Act* [RSC 1927, c. 98] provides that there can
be no conveyance of an Indian reserve or a portion thereof until it has
been released or surrendered to the Crown. It reads as follows:

> 50. Except as in this Part otherwise provided, no reserve or portion
> of a reserve shall be sold, alienated or leased until it has been released
> or surrendered to the Crown for the purposes of this Part;

In the case at bar the "consent" meeting of the band was held on 18
October 1928; the land was conveyed to Scott on 27 June 1929, and the
surrender was accepted in a resolution of the Privy Council on 7 August
1929. The deed was registered a short time thereafter. The plaintiff
argued that because the deed was given prior to the acceptance of the
surrender by the Governor in Council such deed purported to convey
unsurrendered land and was thus void ab initio.

No effective conveyance of lands on a reserve can be made until these
lands have been surrendered to the Crown. Clearly, a surrender is not
valid or binding unless all of the necessary procedures set out in s. 51
are performed. What is not clear, upon a plain reading of s. 51, is
whether all of these acts must be completed prior to the date of
conveyance in order to make it a valid convenance.

In *St Ann's Island Shooting & Fishing Club Ltd.* v. *The King*, [1950]
2 DLR 225, [1950] SCR 211 (SCC); affirming [1949] 2 DLR 17, [1950]
Ex.C.R. 185 (Ex. Ct.), the appellant sought a declaration of a right to a
renewal of a lease of surrendered Indian lands. In 1880, the appellant
secured a lease of part of the reserve for five years, to shoot and fish the
leased area. Further leases were entered into between 1884 and 1925.
The 1925 lease contained somewhat different conditions and provided
for a term of 20 years with the right of renewal. In 1944 the
Solicitor-General refused to grant such renewal or to admit that the
lessee was entitled thereto. The Exchequer Court and the Supreme
Court of Canada refused the appellant's action for a declaration of right
of renewal. The Courts held that the original lease, having been
approved by Order in Council, was a valid one but such approval
terminated with the said lease. The subsequent leases lacked the
authorization by Order in Council and consequently were void. What is
interesting about the case as far as the case at bar is concerned is that the
lease was entered into on May 30, 1881, pursuant to a resolution by the
Council of Indians authorizing the lease dated 18 March 1880. No
formal surrender of the leased lands was made until 1882.

The sequence of events is set out as follows at pp. 226-7 DLR, p. 215
SCR:

> Following the execution of this lease, the officers of the Club raised
> certain questions as to the validity of the lease, and more particularly
> as to whether there had been a surrender of the lands as required by

the *Indian Act*, 1880 (Can.), c. 28, an acceptance thereof by the Governor-General in Council, and finally, an Order in Council authorizing the lease. A further meeting of the Indians was therefore held in February, 1882, and a formal surrender was executed in due form, and on February 24th of that same year, the Indian Superintendent at Sarnia wrote to the Club that for the purpose of the lease, a formal surrender had been given, and that the defect in the preliminary proceedings had been remedied. In April, 1882 Order in Council P.C. 529 was passed purporting to accept the surrender, and on April 18th, the Department again advised the Club that the surrender had been accepted, and that the lease had been confirmed by the said Order in Council.

There is no suggestion in that case that the proceedings described above were not sufficient to validate the lease.

It appears that a lease of part of a reserve is valid if approximately one year after the granting of the lease the Indians make a formal surrender of the said lands and an Order in Council is passed approving the surrender and confirming the lease. In light of this, it does not seem to be fatal that the surrender of the Stoney Point Indian Reserve was not accepted by the Governor in Council until one and a half months after the land was conveyed to Scott.

Consequently, I find that the defendant has established that it has valid legal title to the property in question in this action.

Quaere whether the Supreme Court of Canada in *St Ann's* considered whether the "original lease" was valid? The validity of the "original lease" was not material to the proceedings in the case. With respect to the result in *St Ann's* consider section 124, Indian Act.

Section 37 of the Indian Act, RSC 1970, c. I-60 is worded differently from section 50 of the Indian Act, RSC 1927, c. 98 and the result in *Ports Franks Properties* might not be repeated upon a surrender after the enactment of the section.

Section 37 has been considered in the context of surrenders of reserve land provided by way of outstanding treaty land entitlement in Saskatchewan:

> R. Bartlett, "Indian and Native Rights in Uranium Development in Northern Saskatchewan," (1980) 45 *Saskatchewan Law Review* 13, 31-32.

The requirement of a surrender has posed difficulties in the selection of lands pursuant to Indian treaty land entitlement subject to existing exploration permits. Such permits provide an option to enter into mineral lease arrangements with the Province. In order to protect the interest of the exploring corporations it has been necessary to conduct surrenders of minerals contemporaneously with the acceptance by the band of the land entitlement. The Agreement in respect of Stony Rapids land entitlement provided:

> And whereas by a vote held on February 18, 1980 . . . the Band did approve the transfer of the entitlement lands by Saskatchewan to Canada in fulfilment of the band's treaty land entitlement and did also approve the surrender of the minerals within the reserve . . .

The band members were required to vote upon the question "Do you approve of fulfillment of your treaty land entitlement in the manner proposed and described in the notices posted on January 17, 1980?" The notices contained a description of the entitlement lands and copies of the communities to explain the mineral lease and its effects and translated video-tape recordings of the negotiations were provided to the communities.

Legislative provisions have always sought to protect Indians and their lands from private purchase and government grant by barring any disposition without a surrender. Section 37, as did its predecessor provisions, operates only upon reserve lands and bars any disposition "*until* they have been surrendered". Section 37 assumes, as any purposive construction of the Act would suggest, a time lapse will occur after the creation of the reserve and prior to its surrender. It is suggested that a "surrender" conducted *prior* to or *contemporaneously* with the existence of a reserve is not effective to validate any disposition — section 37 would bar any such disposition. Such conclusion is, of course, in accord with the history and intent of the provision which sought to prevent advantage being taken of Indians in respect to their lands.78 A vote upon a surrender in respect of land with mineral deposits upon a condition that they may only be selected if the vote is favourable seems to entail the taking of such an advantage.

(f) The Effect of a Surrender

The significance of a surrender may be examined by determining if the reserve status of the land under the Indian Act is thereby terminated and considering whether or not surrendered lands are "lands reserved for Indians" within section 91(24) British North America Act. The Federal Court of Appeal in *The Queen* v. *Smith*, [1980] 4 CNLR 29 determined that land surrendered for sale was no longer reserve land within the meaning of the Indian Act.

LE DAIN J (for the Court)

> Further to the application of section 31 of the *Indian Act*, there is also in my opinion a serious question as to whether the Land remains part of the reserve as defined by the Act, or put another way, whether the word

"reserve" in section 31 includes "surrendered lands" within the meaning of the Act. The relevance of this question is that section 31 contemplates an encroachment on the "reserve" and by implication the recovery of possession of land in a reserve.

From 1876 the federal Indian legislation has distinguished between the "reserve", as defined by the Act, and surrendered land in a reserve, formerly known as "Indian lands" and now known as "surrendered lands". The definitions of "reserve" and "Indian lands" in *The Indian Act, 1876*, SC 1876, c. 18, s. 3(6) and (8), were as follows:

> 6.   The term "reserve" means any tract or tracts of land set apart by treaty or otherwise for the use or benefit of or granted to a particular band of Indians, of which the legal title is in the Crown, but which is unsurrendered, and includes all the trees, wood, timber, soil, stone, minerals, metals, or other valuables thereon or therein.
>
> 8.   The term "Indian lands" means any reserve or portion of a reserve which has been surrendered to the Crown.

These were the definitions of "reserve" and "Indian lands" in *The Indian Act*, 1880 (43 Vict. c. 28, s. 2(6) and (8)). In *The Indian Act*, RSC 1886, c. 43, which applied when the surrender of 1895 took place, the express exclusion of surrendered land was removed from the definition of "reserve" in s. 2(k) which read as follows:

> (k)   The expression "reserve" means any tract or tracts of land set apart by treaty or otherwise for the use or benefit of or granted to a particular band of Indians, of which the legal title is in the Crown, and which remains a portion of the said reserve, and includes all the trees, wood, timber, soil, stone, minerals, metals and other valuables thereon or therein.

The express exclusion of surrendered land was restored to the definition of "reserve" in the *Indian Act*, R.S.C. 1906, c. 81, s. 2(i) which read as follows:

> (i)   "reserve" means any tract or tracts of land set apart by treaty or otherwise for the use or benefit of or granted to a particular band of Indians, of which the legal title is in the Crown, and which remains so set apart and has not been surrendered to the Crown, and includes all the trees, wood, timber, soil, stone, minerals, metals and other valuables thereon or therein.

This was the definition of "reserve" in the *Indian Act*, RSC 1927, c. 98, s. 2(j), which remained in force until the present *Indian Act* was adopted in 1951.

The expression of opinion, express or implied, in the *Giroux* case, *supra*, at pp. 176, 199 and 201, that the surrendered land had ceased to be part of the reserve was based on the definition of "reserve" in the Act of 1876. In the *St Ann's* case, at pp. 212 and 215 there was a similar expression of opinion based on the definition of "reserve" in the Act of 1906.

The definitions of "reserve" and "surrendered lands" in s. 2 of the present Act are as follows:

> "reserve" means a tract of land, the legal title to which is vested in Her Majesty, that has been set apart by Her Majesty for the use and benefit of a band;
>
> "surrendered lands" means a reserve or part of a reserve or any interest therein, the legal title to which remains vested in Her Majesty, that has been released or surrendered by the band for whose use and benefit it was set apart.

There is not doubt that the Land falls within the definition of "surrendered lands". It will be noted that the definition of "reserve" does not expressly exclude surrendered land as it did until 1951. This might appear to decide the question. Moreover, the definition of reserve might be read so as to mean that, so long as land has in the past been set aside for the use and benefit of a band and the legal title to it remains vested in Her Majesty, it remains part of the reserve as defined by the Act. "Surrendered lands", which are defined as "a reserve or part of a reserve . . . the legal title to which remains vested in Her Majesty . . ." would in effect be merely a particular part of a reserve as defined by the Act. This view is, however, excluded in my opinion by other provisions of the Act which indicate that when the Act uses the word "reserve" alone, as in section 31, it does not intend to refer to surrendered lands as well as to the unsurrendered part of a reserve. I draw this conclusion from the provisions of the Act in which the words "surrendered lands" are used in addition to the words "reserve" or "reserve lands". See, for example, section 2(2) — "The expression 'band' with reference to a reserve or surrendered lands means the band for whose use and benefit the reserve or the surrendered lands were set apart"; section 4(2)(b) — "any reserve or any surrendered lands or any part thereof"; section 57(a) — "authorizing the Minister to grant licences to cut timber on surrendered lands or, with the consent of the council of the band, on reserve lands"; section 59(a) — "reduce or adjust the amount payable to Her Majesty in respect of a sale, lease or other disposition of surrendered lands or a lease or other disposition of lands in a reserve"; section 64(b) — "water courses on the reserves or on surrendered lands"; section 64(i) — "the management of lands on a reserve, surrendered lands and any band property"; section 87(a) — "the interest of an Indian or a band in reserve or surrendered lands." The administrative authority with respect to reserve and surrendered lands is separately provided for in the Act: see sections 18 and 53. Section 21, under the heading "Possession of Lands in Reserves", provides that "There shall be kept in the Department a register to be known as the Reserve Land Register in which shall be entered particulars relating to Certificates of Possession and Certificates of Occupation and other transactions respecting lands in a reserve." Section 55(1), under the heading "Management of Reserves and Surrendered Lands", provides that "There shall be kept in the Department a register, to be known as the Surrendered Lands Register, in which shall be entered particulars in connection with any lease or other disposition of surrendered lands by the Minister or any assignment thereof." In view of this use of the expressions "reserve" and "surrendered lands" in the Act, I find the conclusion unavoidable that when the Act uses the word "reserve" in section 31 it does not include surrendered lands.

The result is that the appellant's recourse cannot rest on section 31, both because the Land is not part of the reserve within the meaning of the Act, and because the Band does not have a right to the occupation or possession of the Land.

On appeal, Estey J, for the Supreme Court of Canada, [1983] 3 CNLR 161, commented:

Some confusion results in the inclusion of surrendered lands in the reserve by reason of the above definition of surrendered lands. The question, therefore, is whether Parliament, by adopting such a definition, may have sought thereby to retain legislative control of the use of such surrendered lands as being Indian lands under s. 91(24), in the fact of its constitutional position as settled in *St Catharine's* and subsequent decisions.

The reference from the first *Indian Act* onwards in the definition of "reserve lands", and in later statutes in the definition of "surrendered lands", to the requirement that "title [be] vested in Her Majesty" is also a source of confusion in that the right of the Crown in respect of which the land is held remains unspecified. The definition of "Her Majesty" in the *Interpretation Act* of Canada, s. 28, is of no assistance in determining on whose behalf, federal or provincial, the lands so defined are held.

By reason of the strictures placed upon disposition of the Indians' interest in these lands, it is not surprising to find, from the earliest version of the *Indian Act* down to the provisions of that statute as it existed at the time of the commencement of these proceedings in 1973, a detailed procedure for the surrender of these lands by the Indians. The surrender procedures are found in s. 37 *et seq.* and expressly require that a surrender may only be to Her Majesty together with an express prohibition against the sale of lands in a reserve. Section 37 provides:

> Except where this Act otherwise provides, lands in a reserve shall not be sold, alienated, leased or otherwise disposed of until they have been surrendered to Her Majesty by the band for whose use and benefit in common the reserve was set apart.

The comparable term in the Royal Proclamation of 1763 stated:

> And We do hereby strictly forbid, on Pain of our Displeasure, all our loving Subjects from making any Purchases or Settlements whatever, or taking Possession of any of the Lands above reserved, without our special leave and Licence for that Purpose first obtained.

Section 37, of course, in light of the aforementioned cases, must be read as meaning that the right of the Indians may not be sold or otherwise dealt with prior to surrender to Her Majesty in the manner prescribed by the statute, but cannot be read as establishing a right in Her Majesty in the right of Canada to sell or otherwise dispose of the fee in these lands either before or after surrender. The inferential power to lease by the Crown after surrender relates, in my view, as can be seen in some of the cases already reviewed, to leasing as one of the ways in which the lands may be made use of by the Indians in whom reposes the possessory title. Section 37, therefore, is but an exercise of the legislative authority under s. 91(24). Because there is no question here but that the procedure for surrender has been fully complied with, it is not necessary to examine these detailed provisions.

A later segment of the statute under the heading Management of Reserves and Surrendered Lands'', commencing with s. 53, deals with the power of the Minister to sell, lease or otherwise dispose of surrendered lands. Section 53(1) of the present *Indian Act* provides:

> 53(1). The Minister or a person appointed by him for the purpose may manage, sell, lease or otherwise dispose of surrendered land in accordance with this Act and the terms of the surrender.

If these lands are indeed held by Her Majesty in the right of the Province, as has long since been determined, then the question immediately arises as to what further legislative interest Parliament may have in such lands. The confusion continues in subs. (2) of s. 53 where provision is made for a confirming grant of surrendered lands to the heirs and devisees of the original purchaser of these lands from the Crown. It may be that reference is here made to lands where, as we have seen in the case of New Brunswick lands covered in the 1958 agreement, the title is held by the Crown in the right of Canada. Otherwise, the power of disposition purported to be granted by s. 53 offends the rights of the provinces in these lands after their surrender.

The reference to leasing the lands is of course capable of innocent interpretation, namely that the Crown in the right of Canada pursuant to authority granted by Parliament under s. 91(24) may manage the Indians' interest in these lands by the leasing thereof for the benefit of the Indians. Examples of this we have seen in some of the cases already reviewed. Other sections of the currently applicable statute provide for the possession of lands in reserves by Indians (s. 20); for the transfer of possessory rights by Indians (s. 24); and for the enforcement of the possessory right in s. 31, which is the section under which these proceedings were launched.

It is interesting to note that in s. 35 provision is made for the expropriation of the Indian interest by either level of government with the proceeds received therefrom being held by the Receiver General of Canada for the benefit of the Indians whose possessory title has been removed. This procedure is of course consistent with the constitutional position of the Government of Canada and the provinces under the authorities. Similarly, provisions relating to the management of Indian moneys (defined as "all moneys collected, received or held by Her Majesty for the use and benefit of Indians or Bands") are found in the statute as an exercise of the supervisory authority under the federal constitutional powers (see s. 61, *et seq.*). Section 53(1), *supra*, would therefore appear to have been based upon an assumption that after the surrender of lands set aside for Indians under s. 91(14), some interest therein remains in the Government of Canada; or alternatively, that a facilitative surrender has been taken so as to enable the Crown to manage the lands for the continued use and benefit by and of the Indians. The *St Catharine's*, of course, has long since decided otherwise when the surrender of the usufructuary interest is complete. It may be that s. 53 and like provisions in the *Indian Act* are predicated upon the assumption that lands comprised in the Indian Reserves have been conveyed by the Province to the Federal Government. Since these lands would then become public lands of the Government of Canada, Parliament could validly make provision for their continued use under s. 91(14). However, insofar as s. 53(1) purports to affect lands held by the province, it would be *ultra vires*.

A different result was suggested with respect to land surrendered for leasing in *Surrey* v. *Peace Arch Enterprises* (1970), 74 WWR 380 (British Columbia Court of Appeal); *Western Industrial Contractor* v. *Sarcee Developments*, [1979] 3 WWR 631, [1979] 2 CNLR 107 (Alberta Court of Appeal). These conclusions were affirmed in *Re Stony Plain Indian Reserve No. 35*, [1982] 1 WWR 302 (Alberta Court of Appeal).

Jurisdiction with respect to surrendered lands is further examined in Chapter 6, *supra*.

(g) Compliance with Terms of Surrender

The great majority of surrenders of Indian reserves took place in an era when the Department of Indian Affairs exercised both protection and control with respect to the lands. An era when, to quote Collier, J in *Guerin* v. *The Queen,* [1982] 2 CNLR 83 (FCTD), "a great number of Indian Affairs personnel, vis-à-vis Indian bands, and Indians, took a paternalistic, albeit well-meaning attitude: the Indians were children or wards, father knew best". It was the disposition of surrendered lands under such administration that was the subject of litigation in *Guerin*. In 1957, the Musqueam band surrendered 162 acres of prime land in Vancouver.

> in trust to lease the same to such person or persons, and upon such terms as the Government of Canada may deem most conducive to our welfare and that of our people.

The band brought an action in 1975 asserting a breach of trust in the eventual leasing of the lands in January 1958. . .

Mr. Justice Collier concluded that the Crown was the trustee of the surrendered lands for the benefit of the band. It was not a mere "political trust" or "governmental" responsibility. He determined that the Crown acted in breach of trust when it entered into a 75-year lease upon terms and conditions substantially different from those discussed with the band prior to and contemporaneously with the surrender. The terms of the lease were not discussed with the band after the surrender. The Department did not attempt to secure a lease from any other interested parties than that originally contemplated, and the evidence did not explain why a rent lower than that suggested by outsider advisers to the Department was accepted. Collier J expressly asserted that there was a *duty* on the Crown as trustee to lease in accordance with the terms discussed with and contemplated by the band and to secure band approval with respect to any changes to such terms.

The learned judge rejected a defence founded on the provincial statute of limitations because of "concealment amounting to equitable fraud" by the Department in failing to indicate that the terms of the lease were different from those originally contemplated by the band, the conclusion that there was no lack of reasonable diligence by the band in ascertaining the terms of the lease, and the finding that the "band and its members were not aware of the actual terms of the lease, and therefore of the breach of trust until March of 1970." Upon such conclusions, the learned judge concluded that there was "no inequity in permitting the plaintiff's claim to be enforced" and rejected the plea of laches.

Actual damages were assessed at ten million dollars. Collier J rejected a claim for exemplary damages because, whatever the nature of the paternalistic conduct of the officials of the Department of Indian Affairs, it could not be described as "oppressive or arbitrary".

An appeal of the decision in *Guerin* in the Federal Court of Appeal was argued in the summer of 1982. A decision is awaited.

> R. Bartlett, "Indian and Native Law (1983), 15 *Ottawa Law Review* 431.

The Federal Court of Appeal rendered judgment on the appeal in *The Queen* v. *Guerin* on 10 December 1982, [1983] 1 CNLR 20. The Court accepted the argument of the Crown that the terms of any trust found to exist could not be the oral terms found by Collier J, but must be the written terms contained in the surrender document. The Court then went on to deny the existence of any trust with respect to the surrendered lands. The Court had earlier rejected the assertion of a trust enforceable in law with respect to reserve lands. Le Dain J for the Court, declared:

> Upon a surrender, which is the giving up of the Indian title or interest in reserve land, the land becomes surrendered land, as defined by the Act, and subject to the continuing control and management of the federal government in accordance with the terms of the Act and the surrender. Section 53(1) of the Act, under the heading "Management of Reserves and Surrendered Lands", provides: "The Minister or a person appointed by him for the purpose may manage, sell, lease or otherwise dispose of surrendered lands in accordance with this Act and the terms of the surrender." This provision confirms in my opinion that a conditional surrender for the purpose of leasing land in a reserve is intended to confer an authority to lease and not to impose an obligation or duty to do so. The surrender is made conditional upon the making of a lease in accordance with its terms, but it cannot have been intended that the Crown should have a trustee's duty or equitable obligation to make a lease. It cannot have been intended that a surrender, which is part of the statutory scheme, should make such a fundamental change in the nature of the Crown's responsibility for the management and disposition of land in a reserve.
>
> The words "in trust" have been used in surrenders for well over one hundred years. They have been in general use with reference to the governmental responsibility for Indian lands. As we have seen, they appear in Term 13 of the Terms of Union upon which British Columbia was admitted into Canada, in section 93 of the *Land Act*, RSBC 1936, c. 1 pursuant to which the Musqueam Reserve was conveyed by the province to the Dominion, and in the provincial order in council which conveyed the reserve. The words used in the three provisions are "in trust for the use and benefit of the Indians." The words "in trust" add little to the words "for the use and benefit of" as descriptive of the

purpose for which a reserve is set aside, except possibly to emphasize the importance of the political or governmental responsibility for such land. They could not have been intended to make the Crown in right of the Dominion a trustee, in the private law sense, of the land in the reserve. As in section 18 of the *Indian Act*, the provincial order in council expressly provides for the discretionary authority of the Dominion Government to determine what use of the land is in the interest of the Indians. Within this context of statute and intergovernmental agreement it is my opinion that the words "in trust" in the surrender document were intended to do no more than indicate that the surrender was for the benefit of the Indians and conferred an authority to deal with the land in a certain manner for their benefit. They were not intended to impose an equitable obligation or duty to deal with the land in a certain manner. For these reasons I am of the opinion that the surrender did not create a true trust and does not, therefore, afford a basis for liability based on a breach of trust.

This decision has since been appealed to the Supreme Court of Canada and a decision is awaited.

12. Exemption from Seizure

Provisions protecting reserve lands from imposition and abuse were introduced into the earliest legislation respecting Indians and Indian lands. The first consolidation of legislation respecting Indians, the Indian Act 1876, maintained such protection. Section 8 of Indian Act, SC 1876, c. 18 declared that the conferring of a location ticket "shall not have the effect of rendering the land covered thereby subject to seizure under legal process." Section 66 of the same Act prohibited the taking of any security or otherwise obtaining "any lien or charge, whether by mortgage, judgment or otherwise" upon real property of an Indian in a reserve.

In *Diabo* v. *Rice,* [1942] CS 418 (Quebec Supreme Court) it was sought to seize and hold a sheriff's sale of real property on a reserve in satisfaction of a judgment debt. Archambault J declared:

Any sale of the property under seizure would be a violation of the provisions of the Indian Act. It is, therefore, impossible to give any legal effect to the sheriff's sale as required by arts. 778 to 783 C.P. If this Court ordered the sale of the property herein to be proceeded with, such judgment would virtually mean that the Superior Court recognized the right of the sheriff to sell property on an Indian Reserve without complying with the formalities and requirements demanded by said public Act;

The Indian Act now provides:

s. 29   Reserve Lands are not subject to seizure under legal process.

s. 89(1) Subject to this Act, the *real* and personal property of an Indian

or a band situated on a reserve is not subject to charge, pledge, mortgage, attachment, levy, seizure, distress or execution in favour or at the instance of any person other than an Indian.

It has been suggested that such provisions have "frustrated many attempts by individual Indians and band councils to provide a satisfactory security for loans from financial lending institutions" ("Legal Aspects relative to on-reserve financing", prepared for Saskatchewan Indian Agricultural Program Inc. by P. Paulowicz, [1979] 4 CNLR).

It is to be observed that section 29 has been held to be no bar to the filing of a builders' lien against the interest of a lessee of reserve lands surrendered for lease: *Western International Contractor* v. *Sarcee Developments*, [1979] 7 WWR 631, [1979] 2 CNLR (Alberta Court of Appeal), Morrow J (Haddad J concurring):

If a lien is to be enforced, such enforcement can only be exercised and carried out against the Sarcee Development's interest and in no way against the lessor's or the band's interest.

13. Conclusion

The ascertainment of rights in Indian reserve lands is a complex task requiring resolution of federal, provincial and Indian claims and entailing recourse to statutes, judicial decisions, the royal prerogative, treaties, and federal-provincial agreements. All must be examined in the context and the history of the particular reserve under consideration. The generalizations that follow are accordingly necessarily suspect. In every province in which there are reserves, the province claims a property interest or entitlement of some kind therein. Title resides in the Crown, usually in the right of Canada. The Indian interest in the property and management of reserves is all too often that element that remains after providing for the federal and provincial governments.

In the future, the Indian interest in reserve lands must be reshaped to accord to the promises made by Treaty and otherwise. The Indians must be accorded full ownership of the lands with powers of self-government with respect thereto. This will necessitate constitutional agreements to which the Indians should be a party.

Claims of misappropriation in the past remain to be resolved. Many depend upon the notion that reserve lands were held 'on trust' by the Crown for the benefit of the Indians. The Supreme Court of Canada will have an opportunity to consider the question in the Guérin case. The decision will indicate judicial attitudes to the degree to which the Crown should be held accountable for the past.

14. Questions

Q. Why were Indian reserves established? What did the Indians consider to be the object of the reserves at the time of Treaty? Why were reserves not generally set aside for the Metis? Why should the area set aside for reserves be so small in Canada compared to Australia?

Q. What property interest do the provinces have in Indian reserves? What is the origin of such interest? What are the objects of the Federal-Provincial Agreements respecting Indian reserve lands? Why is there no general Agreement respecting reserves in Quebec and what difference does it make? Why and how does the provincial interest in reserves in British Columbia differ from that in Nova Scotia?

Q. What are the property rights of an Indian band in a reserve? Do they and should they differ depending upon where a reserve is located?

Q. What is a trust? Do you consider that reserve lands are held ''in trust'' by the Crown? What is the significance of reserve lands being held ''in trust''?

Q. What body or person governs and manages reserve lands in law? Who should?

Q. What rights does a non-Indian have to enter and occupy a reserve? When and how might such a person be removed?

Q. Who owns the minerals located on a reserve? Does such ownership include the oil and gas, and the gold and silver? What did the treaties promise with respect to minerals? Who controls the development of minerals: the federal government, the provincial governments, or the Indians?

Q. What is the object of the surrender provisions of the Indian Act? What is their origin? What is the consequence of an invalid surrender? May the Indians recover the land? Why were lands surrendered in such substantial amounts in the first part of the twentieth century?

Q. Do you think that the ''reasonable person'' could follow, understand or agree with the decision of the Supreme Court of Canada in *Cardinal* v. *The Queen*? Do you think that the Court arrived at the ''plain meaning''?

Q. Are surrendered lands held on trust? What is the obligation of the Crown to the Indian band with respect to surrendered lands? What are the reasons of the Federal Court of Appeal for its decision in *Queen* v. *Guerin*? What distinguishes a ''political trust'' from a ''true trust''?

Q. Why are reserve lands exempt from seizure? Can they be mortgaged?

15. Further Reading

R.H. Bartlett, ''Establishment of Indian Reserves on the Prairies'' 3 [1980] CNCR 3.

R.H. Bartlett, "Indian and Native Law", (1983) 15 *Ottawa Law Review*, 431.

R.H. Bartlett, "Indian Act of Canada", Native Law Centre, University of Saskatchewan, 1980; reprinted from 27 *Buffalo Law Review*, 581 (1979).

R.H. Bartlett, "Indian and Native Rights in Uranium Development in Northern Saskatchewan" (1980) 45 *Saskatchewan Law Review* 13.

R.H. Bartlett, "Indian Water Rights on the Prairies" (1980) 11 *Manitoba Law Journal* 59.

P. Cumming and N. Mickenberg, *Native Rights in Canada*, 2d ed.

W. Henderson, *Canada's Indian Reserves: The Usufruct in Our Constitution*, Dept. of Indian Affairs.

Dept. of Indian Affairs, *Indian Conditions: A Survey*, 1980, Ottawa.

A. Morris, *Treaties of Canada with the Indians*, Coles Canadiana Collection.

Native Law Centre, University of Saskatchewan, "Trespass on Indian Reserves" Legal Information Service, Report #4, 1980.

P. Paulowicz, "Legal Aspects Relative to On-Reserve Financing" [1979] 4 CNLR

Rapport de la Commission D'etude sur l'integrite du Territoire du Quebec, Le Domaine Indien (Dorion Report) 1973.

D. Sanders, *Legal Aspects of Economic Development on Reserve Lands* 1976, Dept. of Indian Affairs.

D. Sanders, "The Friendly Care & Directing Hand of the Government; a Study of Government Trusteeship of Indians in Canada", 1977, unpublished.

Government of Saskatchewan, "Indian Lands and Canada's Responsibility", 1979.

F.C. Stanley, "First Indian Reserves in Canada" (1950) IV *Revue d'Histoire de L'Amerique Francaise* 178.

R.J. Surtees, "Development of an Indian Reserve Policy in Canada" *Ontario History*, Vol. CXI, p. 87.

9. Taxation

RICHARD H. BARTLETT

The material in this chapter examines the powers of an Indian band to levy taxation and the extent to which Indians are subject to taxation under federal or provincial authority. Neither the Inuit nor the Metis are generally possessed of power to impose taxation or to be exempt therefrom.

The significance of the power to tax should be clear. In modern society it is an essential attribute of government, without which policies of social and economic development cannot be pursued. The denial of the ability of *other* governments to tax a community, such as an Indian band, may secure the self-government of that community. Irrespective of the powers of government possessed by a community, an exemption from taxation will encourage economic development thereof.

1. Indian Power to Tax

The Federation of Saskatchewan Indians declared in 1977:

Indian tribes and subsequently Indian Bands are qualified to exercise powers of self-government because they are independent political groups. Among the inherent powers of Indian government are the power to:
a) determine the form of government;
b) define conditions for membership in the nation;
c) regulate the domestic relations of its members;
d) levy and collect taxes.

"Indian Government", Prince Albert, Saskatchewan

Federal legislation has acknowledged only the most limited power to levy taxes, and has never contemplated inherent powers approaching that described above. In 1884 the Indian Advancement Act, which sought to replace government by chiefs in council with government by a form of municipal council, provided that bands considered "fit" might assess and tax "lands of Indians enfranchised, or in possession of lands by location ticket in the reserve subject to the approval and confirmation of the Superintendent General." S.C. 1884, c. 28, s. 10(11) The revenue might only be expended on matters in respect of which the council might pass bylaws. This provision remained unchanged until 1951. No Indian band in Western Canada was considered "fit" to exercise the power conferred in 1884. In 1951 the modern form of the provision was adopted. It is now section 83 of the Indian Act:

83. (1) Without prejudice to the powers conferred by section 81, where the Governor in Council declares that a band has reached an advanced stage of development, the council of the band may, subject to the approval of the Minister, make bylaws for any or all of the following purposes, namely
(a) the raising of money by
    (1) the assessment and taxation of interests in land in the reserve of persons lawfully in possession thereof, and
    (ii) the licensing of businesses, callings, trades and occupations;
(b) the appropriation and expenditure of moneys of the band to defray band expenses;
(c) the appointment of officials to conduct the business of the council, prescribing their duties and providing for their remuneration out of any moneys raised pursuant to paragraph (a);
(d) the payment of remuneration, in such amount as may be approved by the Minister, to chiefs and councillors, out of any moneys raised pursuant to paragraph (a);
(e) the imposition of a penalty for non-payment of taxes imposed pursuant to this section, recoverable on summary conviction, not exceeding the amount of the tax or the amount remaining unpaid;
(f) the raising of money from band members to support band projects; and
(g) with respect to any matter arising out of or ancillary to the exercise of powers under this section.
(2) No expenditure shall be made out of moneys raised pursuant to paragraph (1)(a) except under the authority of a bylaw of the council of the band.
Subparagraph 83(1)(f) was added in 1956.

The imposition of real property taxes is confined to "persons lawfully in possession" of reserve lands. Such persons may only be those members of a band to whom "possession of the land has been allotted . . . by the council of the band" in accordance with section 20(1) of the Indian Act. A contrary opinion would extend such power to all those persons, including non-Indians, in possession of reserve lands under any provision of the Indian Act: see D. Sanders, *Legal Aspects of Economic Development on Indian Reserve Lands*, Department of Indian Affairs, 1976. A denial of the power to tax non-Indian property interests on a reserve would bar valuable revenue to the band in the economic development of a reserve and encourage the imposition of provincial property taxes. Of perhaps greater significance than the "municipal" property taxing and licensing powers declared in section 83(1)(a) is the power described in 83(1)(f), which was added by amendment in 1956.

(f) the raising of money from band members to support band projects.

No explanation for the amendment is evident in the *Debates in Parliament* or the Annual Report of the Indian Affairs Branch.

Many bands, particularly in Ontario and British Columbia, have been declared to have reached "an advanced stage of development". Some bands, e.g. Saugeen and Walpole Island in Ontario and Squamish in British Columbia, raise substantial sums under bylaws made under section 83(1)(a)(i) with which to provide services to the taxpayers.

Section 85 provides:

> The Governor in Council may revoke a declaration made under section 83 whereupon that section no longer applies to the band to which it formerly applied, but any bylaw made under the authority of that section and in force at the time the declaration is revoked shall be deemed to continue in force until it is revoked by the Governor in Council.

The exemption from taxation declared in section 87 is "subject to section 83" and thus would not be effective to preclude a band council imposing a full range of taxes upon its members in the furtherance of self-government and economic development. The introduction of taxing bylaws under section 83 would be effective, however, to bar the imposition of provincial taxes upon reserve interests if "such laws are inconsistent" (Sec. 88) with the bylaw. If the imposition of income taxation or the taxation of non-Indian property interests upon reserves was considered a valid exercise of power within section 83, such inconsistency *may* be denied in accordance with the constitutional principle that "two taxations . . . can stand side by side without interfering." *Lachine* v. *Montreal Light, Heat and Power* (1932), 70 CS 442 (Quebec Superior Court), *Re Silver Bros.,* [1932] ACS 14.

In the absence of band bylaws imposing taxes upon non-Indian interests on reserves, the provinces may authorize municipal taxation of such interests. Such taxes are construed as a tax upon the occupier's interest, not the land itself: *City of Vancouver* v. *Chow Chee,* [1941] 1 WWR 72 (British Columbia Court of Appeal). Alberta, Ontario and Saskatchewan have, however, barred municipal taxation of non-Indian occupants of reserve lands. Provincial taxation of non-Indian interests on reserve lands may be challenged as invading exclusive federal jurisdiction within section 91(24).

2. The History of the Exemption from Taxation

(a) The Treaties

The texts of the treaties entered into by Canada do not refer specifically to taxation. The Indians understood, however, they were not to be subject to taxation. In 1885 a member of the Mohawk band of the Bay of Quinte was quoted in the House of Commons:

In a recent interview with one of their intelligent young men, he stated that his people did not want the franchise on the basis of tribal lands. These lands are secured to them by treaty with the Crown, free from all taxation — a perpetual inheritance. He said they considered this attempted legislation as being part of a scheme to place their reserve under ordinary municipal control and taxation, and finally to deprive them or their children of their birthright.

House of Commons Debates, 26 May 1885, p. 2125.

The only specific reference to taxation in official reports of the treaties and their negotiation is contained in the report of the Treaty Commissioner in respect of Treaty #8, 1899. [Northern Alberta, the Peace River District of British Columbia, North West Saskatchewan, and the North West Territories, south-west of Great Slave Lake.]

There was expressed at every point the fear that the making of the Treaty would be followed by the curtailment of the hunting and fishing privileges, and many were impressed with the notion that the Treaty would lead to taxation and enforced military service.

We assured them that the Treaty would not lead to any forced interference with their mode of life, that it did not open the way to the imposition of any tax, and that there was no fear of enforced military service.

It is, of course to be observed that the promises of goods, services, and land made to the Indians in the Treaties did not refer to the imposition of any charge or levy with respect to such items. Taxation may accordingly be considered inconsistent with such promises: see *R. v. Johnston* (1966), 56 WWR 565 (Saskatchewan Court of Appeal), *infra*.

(b) The Franchise

Until 1885, federal elections were governed by existing provincial statutes. In 1885 the Conservative government of Sir John A. Macdonald passed the Electoral Franchise Act to provide for federal elections. The franchise was extended to Indians in the East possessed of real property on a reserve valued in excess of $150 and not otherwise qualified. The Six Nations Indians were concerned about the implications of the extension of the franchise. Chief Jones wrote to the Prime Minister:

Many of the Indians on the Grand River Reservation have been told, that in case they received the right to vote, then *Treaty Rights* with the Government would not be able to compel the Government to observe and carry out the treaties.

They have also been told that the granting of the Franchise to them, was a scheme of the Government with the object of imposing direct *taxation* upon them.

These two subjects are being used successfully in many cases to induce the Indians to either vote against your government or not to vote at all. Kindly give us your opinion upon these two subjects immediately and oblige.

> Public Archives of Canada M.G. 26A, Vol. 428, p. 209783, 8 August 1886.

Sir John A. Macdonald wrote to Chief Johnson of Desoranto as follows:

I am informed that your are under the impression that if an Indian on a reserve should exercise the franchise under the late act it would render him liable to pay additional taxes. This is altogether a mistake. The Grits who did all they could to deprive the Indians of the right of voting are spreading that falsehood in order to prevent the original proprietors of the soil of this country from standing on a footing of equality with the white men who have come into it. I can assure you that an Indian will not increase his liability, his burdens, or his duties as a subject or citizen by voting at the election. He will stand exactly in the same position in all respects the hour after he may vote as he stood the hours before he voted.

> Macdonald Papers, M.G. 26A, Vol. 436, p. 214108-6, 7 July 1887.

The Liberals were returned to power in 1896 and the Franchise Act of 1898 eliminated the separate federal franchise. In 1920 the federal franchise was re-established, but it excluded Indians ordinarily resident on a reserve. The anxiety of the Six Nations, expressed sixty-five years before, proved well founded when in 1950 the franchise was extended to those Indians who:

[e]xecuted a waiver, in a form prescribed by the Minister of Citizenship and Immigration, of exemptions under the *Indian Act* from taxation on or in respect of personal property, and subsequent to the execution of such waiver a writ has issued ordering an election in any electoral district . . . .

The franchise granted to the Eskimos in that year was not subject to any conditions. The Minister of Citizenship and Immigration explained that "the Eskimo, not being exempt from taxation, may vote" (June 1950. *House of Commons Debates*, p. 3812, per Harris MP) It was not until 1960 that the federal franchise was finally extended to Indians upon the same conditions as other citizens of Canada. The restriction upon the franchise requiring a waiver of the taxation exemption was repealed.

Note

1. *Eligibility to vote in provincial election*

> The Western provinces of Alberta, British Columbia, Manitoba and Saskatchewan disqualified "Indians" from voting, with exceptions in the case of the latter three provinces for those who served in the armed forces. The franchise was granted in British Columbia in 1949, in Manitoba in 1952, in Saskatchewan in 1960, and in Alberta in 1965. The Eastern provinces of Ontario, New Brunswick, Prince Edward Island and Quebec disqualified "Indians resident on a reserve" from voting, with the exception in the case of the first three provinces of those who had served in the armed forces. The franchise was granted in Ontario in 1954, in New Brunswick and Prince Edward Island in 1963, and in Quebec in 1969.

Although there was never a specific exclusion from the franchise of Indians in Nova Scotia or the Yukon, prerequisites relating to the place of residence and the holding of property appeared to deny the vote until the middle of this century. The franchise was extended to Indians in the North West Territory in 1960. Indians in Newfoundland have been entitled to vote since the province joined Confederation in 1949.

(c) The Indian Acts

In 1850 the Province of Canada passed "An Act for the protection of Indians in Upper Canada from imposition, and the property occupied or enjoyed by them from trespass and injury." Section four provided:

> That no taxes shall be levied or assessed upon any Indian or any person inter-married with any Indian for or in respect of any of the said Indian lands, nor shall any taxes or assessments whatsoever be levied or imposed upon any Indian or any person intermarried with any Indian so long as he, she or they shall reside on Indian lands not ceded to the Crown, or which having been so ceded may have been again set apart by the Crown for the occupation of Indians.

The 1876 Indian Act modified the ambit of the exemption from taxation. Sections 64 and 65 provided:

> 64.   No Indian or non-treaty Indian shall be liable to be taxed for any real or personal property, unless he holds real estate under lease or in fee simple, or personal property, outside of the reserve or special reserve, in which case he shall be liable to be taxed for such real or personal property at the same rate as other persons in the locality in which it is situated.
>
> 65.   All land vested in the Crown, or in any person or body corporate, in trust for or for the use of any Indian or non-treaty Indian, or any band or irregular band of Indians or non-treaty Indians shall be exempt from taxation.

The exemption remained almost unaltered until 1951. In that year it was rewritten in the following form, now embodied in section 86 of the Act:

87. (1) Notwithstanding any other Act of the Parliament of Canada or any Act of the legislature of a province, but subject to subsection (2) and to section 83, the following property is exempt from taxation, namely,

(a) the interest of an Indian or a band in reserve or surrendered lands, and

(b) the personal property of an Indian or band situated on a reserve,

and no Indian or band is subject to taxation in respect of the ownership, occupation, possession or use of any property mentioned in paragraph (a) or (b) or is otherwise subject to taxation in respect of any such property; and no succession duty, inheritance tax or estate duty is payable on the death of any Indian in respect of any such property or the succession thereto if the property passes to an Indian, nor shall any such property be taken into account in determining the duty payable under the *Dominion Succession Duty Act* on or in respect of other property passing to an Indian.

(2) Subsection (1) does not apply to or in respect of the personal property of an Indian who has executed a waiver under the provisions of paragraph (e) of subsection (2) of section 14 of the *Canada Elections Act*, 1951.

90. (1) For the purposes of sections 87 and 89, personal property that was

(a) purchased by Her Majesty with Indian moneys or moneys appropriated by Parliament for the use and benefit of Indians or bands, or

(b) given to Indians or to a band under a treaty or agreement between a band and Her Majesty, shall be deemed always to be situated on a reserve.

Subsection 87(2) was repealed in 1960.

3. Provincial Taxation Subject to the Terms of any Treaty

The application of provincial laws of general application to Indians is expressed by section 88 of the Indian Act to be "subject to the terms of any treaty". It was argued in *R. v. Johnston* (1966), 56 WWR 565 (Saskatchewan Court of Appeal) that the imposition of hospitalization tax was contrary to the terms of Treaty #6. Treaty #6 contained, *inter alia*, the following terms:

That a medicine chest shall be kept at the house of each Indian Agent for the use and benefit of the Indians at the direction of such agent.

> That in the event hereafter of the Indians comprised within this treaty being overtaken by any pestilence, or by a general famine, the Queen, on being satisfied and certified thereof by Her Indian Agent or Agents, will grant to the Indians assistance of such character and to such extent as her Chief Superintendent of Indian Affairs shall deem necessary and sufficient to relieve the Indians from the calamity that shall have befallen them.

The magistrate had determined:

> Referring to the 'medicine chest' clause of Treaty No. 5, it is common knowledge that the provisions for caring for the sick and injured in the areas inhabited by the Indians in 1876 were somewhat primitive compared to present day standards. It can be safely assumed that the Indians had limited knowledge of what provisions were available and it is obvious that they were concerned that their people be adequately cared for. With that in view, and possibly carrying the opinion of Angers, J a step farther, I can only conclude that the "medicine chest" clause and the "pestilence" clause in Treaty No. 6 should properly be interpreted to mean that the Indians are entitled to receive all medical services, including medicines, drugs, medical supplies and hospital care free of charge. Lacking proper statutory provisions to the contrary, this entitlement would embrace all Indians within the meaning of The Indian Act, without exception.

Chief Justice Culliton declared, for the Saskatchewan Court of Appeal:

> It was agreed and so found by the trial judge that the respondent was an Indian as defined in the *Indian Act* and that he was a descendant of the Indians on behalf of whom treaty 6 was made. Treaty 6 is, in my opinion, a treaty of the type referred to in sec. 87 of the *Indian Act*. He is, therefore, in my opinion, entitled to any rights or immunities under the said treaty that may have been contemplated by parliament in enacting sec. 87 of the *Indian Act*, unless the claim to such vested rights and immunities is limited to Indians residing on a reserve. Sec. 87 reads:
>
> > 87. Subject to the terms of any treaty and any other Act of the Parliament of Canada, all laws of general application from time to time in force in any province are applicable to and in respect of Indians in the province, except to the extent that such laws are inconsistent with this Act or any order, rule, regulation or by-law made thereunder, and except to the extent that such laws make provision for any matter for which provision is made by or under this act.
>
> I want to make it perfectly clear that the issue before this court is not

one relating to the general responsibility of the government of Canada to Indians, but, simply, whether the learned trial judge was right in his interpretation of the "medicine chest" and "pestilence" clauses of the treaty. If I conclude that the learned trial judge was right in his interpretation, only then would it become necessary to determine whether the respondent, as a non-resident of a reserve, is entitled to the benefits of the terms of the treaty.

In the interpretation of the clauses of a treaty, one must first look to the words used and give to those words the ordinary meaning that would be attributed to them at the time the treaty was made. To do so, too, it is both proper and advisable to have recourse to whatever authoritative record may be available of the discussions surrounding the execution of the treaty. I agree with the opinion expressed by Norris, JA in *Reg.* v. *White and Bob* (1965) 52 WWR 193, affirmed (1965) 52 DLR (2d) 481n, when he said at p. 210:

> The court is entitled "to take judicial notice of the facts of history whether past or contemporaneous" as Lord du Parcq said in *Monarch Steamship Co.* v. *A/B Karlshamns Oljefabriker* [1949] AC 196, at 234, [1949] LJR 772, [1949] 1 All ER 1, at 20, and it is entitled to rely on its own historical knowledge and researches: *Read* v. *Lincoln (Bp.)* [1892] AC 644, 62 LJPC 1, *per* Lord Halsbury, L.C. at pp. 652-4.

I have perused the treatise entitled *The Treaties of Canada with the Indians of Manitoba, The North-West Territories, and Kee-Wa-Tin*, by the Hon. Alexander Morris, PC. The learned author, in this work, presents an authoritative record of the negotiations which resulted in the conclusion of a number of treaties, including treaty 6. It is apparent that in the negotiation of treaty 6 the Indians greatly feared both pestilence and starvation. The learned author says at p. 178:

> They desired to be fed. Small-pox had destroyed them by hundreds a few years before, and they dreaded pestilence and famine.

And then he went on to say:

> The food question, was disposed of by a promise, that in the event of a *National* famine or *pestilence* such aid as the Crown saw fit would be extended to them, and that for three years after they settled on their reserves, provisions to the extent of $1,000.00 per annum would be granted them during seed-time."

The undertaking so given was incorporated in the "pestilence" clause of the treaty. Thus, both historically, and on the plain language of the clause, it means no more than it plainly states: The obligation of the crown in the event of pestilence or general famine, to provide such assistance as the chief superintendent of Indians should deem necessary and sufficient to meet the calamity. With every deference to the contrary opinion of the learned judge of the magistrate's court, I do not think this clause of the treaty has any relevancy in the determination of the question with which he was faced.

There is nothing in Morris' treatise to suggest that any meaning should be given to the words "medicine chest" other than that conveyed by the words themselves in the context in which they are used. The only reference I can find in the treatise is at p. 218 where the author states:

A medicine chest will be kept at the house of each Indian agent, in case of sickness amongst you.

The "medicine chest" clause in the treaty incorporates this undertaking.

Again, on the plain reading of the "medicine chest" clause, it means no more than the words clearly convey: An undertaking by the crown to keep at the house of the Indian agent a medicine chest for the use and benefit of the Indians *at the direction of the agent*. [The italics are mine.] The clause itself does not give to the Indian an unrestricted right to the use and benefit of the "medicine chest" but such rights as are given are subject to the direction of the Indian agent. Such limitation would indicate that the obligation was to have physically on the reservations, for the use and benefit of the Indians, a supply of medicine under the supervision of the agent. I can find nothing historically, or in any dictionary definition, or in any legal pronouncement, that would justify the conclusion that the Indians, in seeking and accepting the crown's obligation to provide a "medicine chest" had in contemplation provision of all medical services, including hospital care.

Angers, J of the Exchequer Court of Canada, in an unreported judgment in *Dreaver* v. *Reg.*, gave an extended interpretation of the "medicine chest" clause of the treaty when he said at p.   :

The clause might unquestionably be more explicit but, as I have said, I take it to mean that all medicines, drugs or medical supplies which might be required by the Indians of the Mistawasis Band were supplied to them free of charge.

In reaching the foregoing conclusion, the learned justice appears to have relied on the evidence of the suppliant, Dreaver, who testified he was present during the negotiation of the treaty and that it was understood that all medicines were to be supplied free to the Indian. There appears to be nothing in his evidence to support any wider interpretation of the clause than that given to it by Angers, J. While I express no opinion as to the correctness of the interpretation of the clause as made by Angers, J, I do not think, with respect, that the interpretation so given justifies the extended meaning attributed thereto by the learned judge of the magistrate's court.

The Court remitted the matter back to the magistrate's court for disposition in accordance with its ruling.

R. v. *Johnston* was followed in *R.* v. *Swimmer*, [1971] 1 WWR 756 (Saskatchewan Court of Appeal).

The meaning of "treaty" for the purposes of section 88 has been examined elsewhere. It is to be observed that in *R.* v. *Francis*, [1956] SCR 618, 631, it was held that an international treaty, such as the Jay Treaty, was not contemplated by the section. Accordingly, section 88 could not be relied on in that case to resist the imposition of customs and sales tax.

4. Who is Exempt?

Section 87 of the Indian Act exempts from taxation prescribed property of an "Indian or band". It appears that the ambit of the terms "Indian" and "band" in section 87 are governed by the meanings thereof provided elsewhere in the Act. Thus, it does not appear that the Inuits, Metis or non-status Indians may benefit from the exemption by reference to some broader definition.

In *Boadway* v. *Minister of National Revenue,* 80 DTC 1231, [1981] 2 CNLR 31 an Indian woman who married a non-Indian claimed to be exempt from income tax until her name was removed from the band list nine months after marriage. The Tax Review Board held:

> This case is more a question of law than a question of fact because, apparently, according to the evidence adduced, the facts are admitted.
>
> The main question is to decide whether the registration or the fact that the appellant remained registered on the list made it possible for her to keep the status as an Indian.
>
> There is no doubt in my mind that the mere registration does not create the law. It is well defined in the *Indian Act* at Section 12(1):

> > The following persons are not entitled to be registered, namely.
> >
> > (b)   a woman who marries a person who is not an Indian . . .

> Furthermore, the Supreme Court decision in *AG of Canada* v. *Lavell*, [1974] SCR 1349, decided that point.
>
> Therefore, whether the appellant's name remained on the list or not is immaterial in the present case. The list is only for administration purposes.
>
> I refer also to Section 2(1) of the *Indian Act*, and I quote:

> > "Indian" means a person who pursuant to this Act is registered as an Indian or is entitled to be registered as an Indian.

According to the evidence adduced, the appellant was not entitled to be registered as an Indian, and as such she is subject to taxation under the *Income Tax Act*.

What of the possibility of exemption of "Indian corporations"? In *Kinookimaw Beach Association* v. *The Queen in Right of Saskatchewan*, [1979] 6 WWR 84 (Saskatchewan Court of Appeal), the application of taxation to a non-profit corporation formed by seven Indian bands as equal shareholders for the development of reserve lands as a golf, tennis and beach resort was considered. The Saskatchewan Board of Revenue Commissioner "with regret" held that the corporation was liable to pay a provincial sales tax (termed "education and hospitalization tax") upon capital purchases. The Board acknowledged that if the seven bands had joined together in an organization other than a corporate body, they would have enjoyed the benefit of the exemption under section 87. This observation is to be considered in the light of the Department of Indian Affairs' policy of insisting upon Indian band economic development taking place through corporations. Upon appeal to the Saskatchewan Queen's Bench Court, it was argued "that this was an appropriate case for the corporate veil to be lifted". Upon an examination of the inconclusive jurisprudence in this area, Chief Justice Johnson declared:

It seems that if the corporate veil can be lifted to prevent taxpayers from avoiding the payment of taxes, it may also be lifted to give taxpayers the benefit of tax exemptions in a case such as this where such exemption is specially granted to a particular group or class of people for whose care and assistance the legislation is designed as is the Indian Act. This would lead to "the just and equitable enforcement of a tax law" in the words of Culliton CJS. This Act is designed to ensure that the Indian people are specially cared and provided for by the government of Canada. It is notorious that dozens of projects by the federal government to enable the Indian people to help themselves as a step in their upward development and growth, and I can take judicial notice that the project of the appellant falls within the class of these works. It would be completely incongruous and anomalous for public funds to be expended by one government to assist Indian peoples if another government were permitted to assess taxes payable by Indians ultimately which would not be assessable if the corporate structure were not the vehicle for carrying out their project.

Accordingly, I am of the view that in this case the lifting of the corporate veil is justified and, having done that, I find that the appellant association is owned and controlled by Indians bands and carries out the works of the association on an Indian reserve. These Indian bands are, accordingly, entitled to the benefit of the tax exemption.

[1978] 7 WWR 749, 751 (Saskatchewan Queen's Bench)

This reasoning was rejected by the Chief Justice of the Court of Appeal, who asserted that:

> . . . the autonomous and independent existence of the corporate structure must be accepted and respected unless it can be shown that such structure is being deliberately used to defeat the intent and purpose of a particular law, or is intended to or does convey a false picture of independence between one or more corporate entities which, if recognized, would result in the defeat of a just and equitable right. . .
>
> To grant to the Association the exemption from taxation provided for in Section 87 of the *Indian Act*, *supra*, would be to destroy the legal obligations of the Association as an independent corporate entity and to determine its obligations by the character of its shareholders.

Leave to appeal to the Supreme Court of Canada was denied on 6 November 1979.

Whatever the merits of the decision of the Saskatchewan Court of Appeal, it is in accord with the announced practice of the Department of National Revenue in the collection of income tax. The Department has offered its opinion that:

> Although "person" is defined for purposes of the *Income Tax Act* to include any body corporate or public, a corporation cannot meet the definition of "Indian" in the *Indian Act* and its income is not exempted from tax by these provisions, even where its only shareholders are Indians, its head office and physical assets are on a reserve and all of its business is carried on there.
>
> I.T-62, 18 August 1972.

5. Income Taxation

(a) Income as a Form of Property Exempt from Taxation

The current practice of the Department of National Revenue has been explained as follows:

> 3. The Income Tax Act does not specifically refer to Indians but paragraph 81(1)(a) exempts from taxation "an amount that is declared to be exempt from income tax by any other enactment of the Parliament of Canada."
>
> 5. While the exemption in the *Indian Act* refers to "property" and the tax imposed under the *Income Tax Act* is a tax calculated on the income of a person rather than a tax in respect of his property, it is considered that the intention of the *Indian Act* is not to tax Indians on income earned on a reserve. Income earned by an Indian off a reserve,

however, does not come within this exemption, and is therefore subject to tax under the *Income Tax Act*.

Interpretation Bulletin IT-62.

The practice of the Department may be ascribed to a series of cases which established that income constituted personal property and was exempt under section 89(1) *Indian Act* or its predecessor, if situated on a reserve, from "charge, pledge, mortgage, attachment, levy, seizure, duties or excution" by a non-Indian. In *Simkevitz* v. *Thompson* (1910), 16 OWR 865 (Ontario County Court), it was first acknowledged that income might be regarded as a debt, and accordingly as a form of personal property to which the protection of the exempting provision could extend. Such conclusion was confirmed in *Petersen* v. *Cree* (1941), 79 CS 1 (Quebec Superior Court), wherein the creditor sought to attach the wages of a member of the Oka Band of Indians whose domicile was on the reserve, but who resided and worked in Montreal. MacKinnon J held the wages attachable and declared that "personal property means all property not immovable and includes chose-in-action".

In recent years the arguments of Indian organization and the practice of the Department of National Revenue have been fundamentally questioned by the Federal Court of Appeal. On 19 April 1979, in *Snow* v. *The Queen*, [1979] CTC 227 (Federal Court of Appeal), the Court declared that income taxation was not subject to the exemption of section 87.

Such a position was judicially evident in 1956 in the decision of the Supreme Court of Canada in *Francis* v. *The Queen*, [1956] SCR 618. All members of the Court rejected any notional concept of the situs of personal property and in doing so doubted the application of section 87 to intangible property such as income. Rand J (Cartwright J concurring) observed with respect to that section's predecessor:

> To be taxed as by s. 102 "at the same rate as other persons in the locality" refers obviously and only to personal or real property under local taxation.[124]

The learned judge was clearly of the opinion that the ambit of that exemption was confined to local property taxation.

In 1972 Russell Snow, a member of the Caughnawaga Indian band, challenged the imposition of taxation upon income earned off the reserve. Roland St Onge, QC, in November 1974, for the Tax Review Board suggested that there was no exemption from income taxation conferred by section 87 irrespective of where the income was earned.

> Because the *Income Tax Act* taxes all the residents of Canada and does not exclude the Indian as an actual taxpayer, and as the *Indian Act* is completely silent on this important matter of income tax, it is

self-evident that an Indian falls under the *Income Tax Act*, especially when his income is earned outside the Reserve.

[1974] CTC 2327 (TRB)

In *The Queen* v. *National Indian Brotherhood*, decided four months later, A.J. Frost, for the Tax Review Board applied the exemption of section 87 to income taxation and offered his explanation of his resolution of the dilemma:

Statutory law exempting Indians from taxation preceded, by many years, the *Income Tax Act*, and established the broad principle that all property of an Indian situated on a reserve is exempt from taxation, thereby raising a presumption in law that the Income Tax Act cannot be taken to apply to the property of Indians on a reserve unless it is spelled out in clear unambiguous language and there is no conflict. Although the language of the *Indian Act* and the *Income Tax Act* appear to be repugnant in respect to taxation, it cannot be supposed that Parliament intended to contradict itself by exempting Indians under the earlier legislation and then tearing up the earlier statutes by imposing liabilities on them under the *Income Tax Act*. Besides the question of repugnancy, the *Indian Act* is a special Act which tends to be derogatory of the *Income Tax Act*, which is a general taxing Act. To avoid collision between these two statutes, the logical construction is simply that the *Income Tax Act* as a general statute applies to Indians only in respect of those areas of taxation wherein the *Indian Act* is silent. The *Indian Act*, however, is not silent but speaks with rather a loud voice, on the subject of taxability of Indians. The appropriate sections read as follows: [sections 87 and 90 are recited]

The language of the above provisions is broad and speaks to exclude all other tax legislation, and thereby constitutes special legislation overriding the *Income Tax Act*. It is only where the *Indian Act* is silent that other statutes can affect the rights of unenfranchised Indians.

[1975] CTC 2112 (TRB)

Upon appeal of both cases to the Federal Court Trial Division, argument was confined to the question of situs of the income and the Court was able, in the language of Thurlow ACJ in *The Queen* v. *National Indian Brotherhood*, [1978] CNLR 107 to "assume that the taxation imposed by the Income Tax Act is taxation in respect of individuals in respect of property and that a salary or a right of salary is property". Shortly before this, a fellow judge of the Trial Division had found that a scholarship did constitute "property" within the exemption conferred by section 87, in the face of argument that "the Income Tax Act levies a tax on persons, not on property". Mahoney J, in

Greyeyes v. *The Queen* (1978), 84 DLR (3d) 146 (FCTD), refused to accept the soundness of the Crown's position in citing *Sura* v. *MNR*, [1962] SCR 65, wherein Mr Justice Taschereau for the Supreme Court of Canada observed:

> Nothing in subsequent amendments of the [Income Tax] Act changes the rule that it is not ownership of property which is taxable, but that tax is imposed on a taxpayer . . . .
>   . . . as Mignault J. in *McLeod* v. *Minister of Customs*: "All of this is in accord with the general policy of the Act which imposes the Income Tax on the persons and not on the property."

The Federal Court of Appeal was not as reticent as the Trial Division. In *MNR* v. *Iroquois of Caughnawaga*, [1977] CTC 49, Chief Justice Jackett (Pratte J and Hyde DJ concurring on this matter) declared that the obligation of an employer to pay statutory unemployment insurance premiums is not 'taxation or property' within the ambit of section 87''. The Chief Justice commented:

> From one point of view, all taxation is directly or indirectly taxation on property; from another point of view, all taxation is directly or indirectly taxation on persons. It is my view, however, that when section 87 exempts "personal property of an Indian or band situated on a reserve" from "taxation", its effect is to exempt what can properly be classified as direct taxation on property. The courts have had to develop jurisprudence as to when taxation is taxation on property and when it is taxation on persons for the purposes of subsection 92(2) of the British North America Act, 1867, and there would seem to be no reason why such jurisprudence should not be applied to the interpretation of section 87 of the *Indian Act*. See, for example, with reference to subsection 92(2), *Provincial Treasurer of Alberta* v. *Kerr*.

The Chief Justice asserted that the exemption conferred by section 87 should be confined to indirect taxation.

The Federal Court of Appeal delivered the following judgment in *Snow* v. *The Queen*, [1979] CTC 277:

> We are all of the view that the appeal must be dismissed on the ground that the tax imposed on the appellant under the *Income Tax Act*, is not taxation in respect of personal property within the meaning of section [87] of the *Indian Act*. In our opinion section [87] contemplates taxation in respect of specific personal property *qua* property and not taxation in respect of taxable income as defined by the *Income Tax Act*, which, while it may reflect items that are personal property, is not itself personal property but an amount to be determined as a matter of calculation by application of the provisions of the Act.

An appeal to the Supreme Court of Canada was abandoned when it was learned that arrangements were being made for the hearing of *Nowegijick* v. *The Queen* by that Court. The practice of the Department of National Revenue did not change pending the decision of the Supreme Court.

(i) *Nowegijick* v. *The Queen*

Judgment in *Nowegijick* v. *The Queen*, [1983] 2 CNLR 89 was pronounced by the Supreme Court of Canada on 25 January 1983. Dickson J delivered judgment on behalf of a unamimous Court.

The question is whether the appellant, Gene A. Nowegijick, a registered Indian, can claim by virtue of the *Indian Act*, RSC 1970 c. I-6, an exemption from income tax for the 1975 taxation year.

I

The Facts:

The facts are few and not in dispute. Mr Nowegijick is an *Indian* within the meaning of the *Indian Act* and a member of the Gull Bay (Ontario) Indian Band. During the 1975 taxation year Mr Nowegijick was an employee of the Gull Bay Development Corporation, a company without share capital, having its head office and administrative offices on the Gull Bay Reserve. All the directors, members and employees of the Corporation live on the Reserve and are registered Indians.

During 1975 the Corporation in the course of its business conducted a logging operation 10 miles from the Gull Bay Reserve. Mr Nowegijick was employed as a logger and remunerated on a piece-work basis. He was paid bi-weekly by cheque at the head office of the Corporation on the Reserve.

During 1975, Mr Nowegijick maintained his permanent dwelling on the Gull Bar Reserve. Each morning he would leave the Reserve to work on the logging operations, and return to the Reserve at the end of th working day.

Mr Nowegijick earned $11,057.08 in such employment. His assessed taxable income for the 1975 taxation year was $8,698.00 on which he was assessed tax of $1,965.80. By Notice of Objection he objected to the assessment on the basis that the income in respect of which the assessment was made is the "personal property of an Indian . . . situated on a reserve" and thus not subject to taxation by virtue of s. 87 of the *Indian Act*.

Mr Nowegijick also brought an action in the Federal Court, Trial Division to set aside the Notice of Assessment. Mr Justice Mahoney of that Court ordered that Mr Nowegijick's 1975 income tax return be referred back to the Minister of National Revenue for re-assessment on the basis that the wages paid him by the Gull Bay Development

Corporation were wrongly included in the calculation of his taxable income.

The Crown appealed the decision of Mr Justice Mahoney. The Federal Court of Appeal allowed the appeal and restored the original assessment.

The proceedings have reached this Court by leave. The Grand Council of Crees of Quebec, three Cree organizations, eight Cree bands and their respective Chiefs have intervened to make common cause with Mr Nowegijick.

II

The Legislation

Mr Nowegijick, in his claim for exemption from income tax, relies upon s. 87 of the *Indian Act* . . .

We need not speculate upon parliamentary intention, an idle pursuit at best, since the antecedent of s. 87 of the *Indian Act* was enacted long before income tax was introduced as a temporary war-time measure in 1917.

One point might have given rise to argument. Was the fact that the services were performed off the reserve relevant to *situs*? The Crown conceded in argument, correctly in my view, that the *situs* of the salary which Mr Nowegijick received was sited on the reserve because it was there that the residence or place of the debtor, the Gull Bay Development Corporation, was to be found and it was there the wages were payable. See Cheshire, *Private International Law* (10th ed.) pp. 536 *et seq* and also the judgment of Thurlow ACJ in *R.* v. *National Indian Brotherhood*, [1979] 1 FC 103, particularly at pp. 109 *et seq*.

III

The Federal Court Judgments

I turn now to the conflicting views in the Federal Court. The opinion of Mr Justice Mahoney at trial was expressed in these words:

> The question is whether taxation of the Plaintiff in an amount determined by reference to his taxable income is taxation "in respect of" those wages when they are included in the computation of his taxable income. I think that it is.
>
> The tax payable by an individual under the *Income Tax Act* is determined by application of prescribed rates to his taxable income calculated in the prescribed manner. If his taxable income is increased by the inclusion of his wages in it, he will pay more tax.

The amount of the increase will be determined by direct reference to the amount of those wages. I do not see that such a process and result admits of any other conclusion than that the individual is thereby taxed in respect of his wages.

The Federal Court of Appeal concluded that the tax imposed on Mr Nowegijick under the *Income Tax Act* was not taxation in respect of personal property within the meaning of s. 87 of the *Indian Act*. The Court, speaking through Mr Justice Heald, said:

We are all of the view that there are no significant distinctions between this case and the *Snow* case (*Russell Snow* vs *The Queen*, [1979] CTC 227) where this Court held: ''Sec. 86 of the *Indian Act* contemplates taxation in respect of specific personal property *qua* property and not taxation in respect of taxable income as defined by the *Income Tax Act*, which, while it may reflect items that are personal property, is not itself personal property but an amount to be determined as a matter of calculation by application of the provisions of the *Act*''.

IV

Construction of Section 87 of the *Indian Act*

Indians are citizens and, in affairs of life not governed by treaties or the *Indian Act*, they are subject to all of the responsibilities, including payment of taxes, of other Canadian citizens.

It is legal lore that, to be valid, exemptions to tax laws should be clearly expressed. It seems to me, however, that treaties and statutes relating to Indians should be liberally construed and doubtful expressions resolved in favour of the Indian. If the statute contains language which can reasonably be construed to confer tax exemption that construction, in my view, is to be favoured over a more technical construction which might be available to deny exemption. In *Jones* v. *Meehan*, 175 US 1, it was held that ''Indian treaties must be construed, not according to the technical meaning of their words, but in the sense in which they would naturally be understood by the Indians''.

Administrative policy and interpretation are not determinative but are entitled to weight and can be an ''important factor'' in case of doubt about the meaning of legislation: per de Grandpré J. *Harel* v. *The Deputy Minister of Revenue of the Province of Quebec*, [1978] 1 SCR 851 at p. 859. During argument in the present appeal the attention of the Court was directed to Revenue Canada Interpretation Bulletin IT-62 dated 18 August 1972, entitled: ''Indians''. Paragraph 1 of the Bulletin reads:

This bulletin does not represent a change in either law or assenting policy as it applies to the taxation of Indians but is intended as a statement of the Department's interpretation and policies that have been established for several years.

Paragraph 5 reads:

While the exemption in the Indian Act refers to "property" and the tax imposed under the Income Tax Act is a tax calculated on the income of a person rather than a tax in respect of his property, it is considered that the intention of the Indian Act is not to tax Indians on income earned on a reserve. Income earned by an Indian off a reserve, however, does not come within this exemption, and is therefore subject to tax under the Income Tax Act.

Counsel for the Crown said the Bulletin was simply "wrong".

The prime task of the Court in this case is to construe the words "no Indian . . . is subject to taxation in respect of any such [personal] property". Is taxable income personal property? The Supreme Court of Illinois in the case of *Bachrach* v. *Nelson* (1932), 182 NE 909 considered whether "income" is "property" and responded:

The overwhelming weight of judicial authority holds that it is. The cases of *Eliasberg Bros. Mercantile Co.* v. *Grimes*, 204 Ala. 492, 86 So. 56, 11 ALR 300, *Tax Commissioner* v. *Putnam*, 227 Mass. 522, 116 NE 904, LRA 1917F, 806, *Stratton's Independence* v. *Howbert*, 231, US 399, 34 S Ct 136, 58 L Ed 285, *Doyle* v. *Mitchell Bros. Co.*, 247 US 179, 38 S Ct 467, 62 L Ed 1054, *Board of Revenue* v. *Montgomery Gaslight Co.*, 64 Ala. 269, *Greene* v. *Knox*, 175 NY 432, 67, NE 910, *Hibbard* v. *State*, 65 Ohio St. 574, 64 NE 109, 58 LRA 654, *Ludlow-Saylor Wire Co.* v. *Wollbrinck*, 275 Mo. 339, 205 SW 196, and *State* v. *Pinder*, 7 Boyce (30 Del.) 416, 108 A. 43, define what is personal property and in substance hold that money or any other thing of value acquired as gain or profit from capital or labor is property, and that, in the aggregate, these acquisitions constitute income, and, in accordance with the axiom that the whole includes all of its parts, income includes property and nothing but property, and therefore is itself property. (at p. 914).

I would adopt this language. A tax on income is in reality a tax on property itself. If income can be said to be property I cannot think that taxable income is any less so. Taxable income is by definition, s. 2(2) of the *Income Tax Act*, "his income for the year minus the deductions permitted by Division C." Although the Crown in paragraph 14 of its factum recognizes that "salaries" and "wages" can be classified as "personal property" it submits that the basis of taxation is a person's "taxable" income and that such taxable income is not "personal property" but rather a "concept", that results from a number of operations. This is too fine a distinction for my liking. If wages are personal property it seems to me difficult to say that a person taxed "in respect of" wages is not being taxed in respect of personal property. It is true that certain calculations are needed in order to determine the quantum of tax but I do not think this in any way invalidates the basic proposition.

The words "in respect of" are, in my opinion, words of the widest possible scope. They import such meanings as "in relation to", "with reference to" or "in connection with". The phrase "in respect of" is probably the widest of any expression intended to convey some connection between two related subject matters.

Crown counsel submits that the effect of s. 87 of the *Indian Act* is to exempt what can properly be classified as "direct taxation on property" and the judgment of Jackett CJ in *Minister of National Revenue* v. *Iroquois of Caughnawaga (Caughnawaga Indian Band)*, [1977] 2 FC 269 is cited. The question in that case was whether the employer's share of unemployment insurance premiums was payable in respect of persons employed by an Indian band at a hospital operated by the band on a reserve. It was argued that the premiums were "taxation" on "property" within s. 87 of the *Indian Act*. Chief Justice Jackett held that even if the imposition by statute on an employer of liability to contribute to the cost of a scheme of unemployment insurance were "taxation" it would not, in the view of the Chief Justice, be taxation on "property" within the ambit of s. 87. The Chief Justice continued:

> From one point of view, all taxation is directly or indirectly taxation on property; from another point of view, all taxation is directly or indirectly taxation on persons. It is my view, however, that when section 87 exempts "personal property of an Indian or band situated on a reserve" from "taxation", its effect is to exempt what can properly be classified as direct taxation on property. The courts have had to develop jurisprudence as to when taxation is taxation on property and when it is taxation on persons for the purposes of section 92(2) of *The British North America Act, 1867*, and there would seem to be no reason why such jurisprudence should not be applied to the interpretation of section 87 of the *Indian Act*. See, for example, with reference to section 92(2), *Provincial Treasurer of Alberta* v. *Kerr*, [1933] AC 710. (at p. 271) . . .

With all respect for those of a contrary view, I cannot see any compelling reason why the jurisprudence developed for the purpose of resolving constitutional disputes or for determining the tax implications of Quebec's communal property laws, or for interpreting the phrase "unascertained persons or persons with contingent interests" in the *Income War Tax Act* should be applied to limit the otherwise broad sweep of the language of s. 87 of the *Indian Act*.

With respect, I do not agree with Chief Justice Jackett that the effect of s. 87 of the *Indian Act* is only to exempt what can properly be classified as direct taxation on property. Section 87 provides that "the personal property of an Indian . . . on a reserve" is exempt from taxation; but it also provides that "no Indian . . . is . . . subject to taxation in respect of any such property". The earlier words certainly exempt certain property from taxation; but the latter words also exempt certain persons from taxation in respect of such property. As I read it, s. 87 creates an exemption for both persons and property. It does not matter then that the taxation of employment income may be characterized as a tax on persons, as opposed to a tax on property.

We must, I think, in these cases, have regard to substance and the plain and ordinary meaning of the language used, rather than to forensic dialectics. I do not think we should give any refined construction to the section. A person exempt from taxation in respect of any of his personal property would have difficulty in understanding why he should pay tax in respect of his wages. And I do not think it is a sufficient answer to say that the conceptualization of the *Income Tax Act* renders it so.

I conclude by saying that nothing in these reasons should be taken as implying that no Indian shall ever pay tax of any kind. Counsel for the appellant and counsel for the intervenants do not take that position. Nor do I. We are concerned here with personal property situated on a reserve and only with property situated on a reserve.

I would allow the appeal, set aside the judgment of the Federal Court of Appeal and reinstate the judgment in the Trial Division of that Court. Pursuant to the arrangement of the parties the appellant is entitled to his costs in all courts to be taxed as between solicitor and client. There should be no costs payable by or to the intervenors.

(b) Situs of Income

The Department of National Revenue has announced the following practice with respect to the situs of income:

(g)   The key factor in determining whether or not a specific item of income received by an Indian is taxable or exempt is the location where the income is earned. Income earned on a reserve by an Indian is considered exempt. Income earned away from the reserve is taxable.

(h)   Different types of income have different criteria for establishing whether they are on or off the reserve. Some of the types of income may be classified as follows:

(i)   Salary and wages are considered to be earned where the services are performed. for an office worker this is the office at or out of which his duties are performed; for a construction worker employed on a project it is the job-site; for a teacher it is the school and so on. The principal office of his employer, the location where he is paid or from which the pay is issued are not usually relevant in determining the location of income from an office or employment. In some cases it will be found that employment is partly on and partly off the reserve. In these cases a reasonable allocation must be made between exempt and taxable income, based on the facts of the particular case.

(ii) Business income is normally allocable to the permanent establishment. For example, for a self-employed merchant it would be at his store.

(iii) Rental income is earned at the location of the property rented.

(iv) Interest on a bank account is earned at the location at which the funds are on deposit, to the specific bank branch address.

(v)   Dividends on shares from a company whose head office, principal business activity and share-register are on a reserve will normally be considered to be earned on the reserve.

(vi) Income from other sources is generally considered to be located at the payer's principal place of business for purposes of determining whether or not it is on a reserve. This general rule will apply to such amounts as annuity payments, unemployment insurance benefits, old age security payments and supplement, scholarships, bursaries, pension and Canada Pension plan benefits.

Interpretation Bulletin IT-62.

The learned judge in *Petersen* v. *Cree* adopted the analysis of the British Columbia Court of Appeal in *Avery* v. *Cayuga* (1913), 13 DLR 275 in identifying the situs of the income. The Court of Appeal had cryptically observed that "it seems not to be open to question" that a bank deposit was "property situated outside of the reserve" and therefore not exempt. The Court recited the leading Privy Council cases in the establishment of situs of personalty for the purpose of succession and stamp duties.

The applicable principles respecting situs were examined by Thurlow ACJ of the Federal Court in *Queen* v. *National Indian Brotherhood*, [1979] 1 FC 103, 109-110:

The question then is whether the salaries here in question, which were paid to the employees in Ottawa by cheque drawn on an Ottawa bank by a corporation with its head office in Ottawa and resident there, can be regarded as situate on a reserve, that is to say, the reserve of the individual Indian entitled to the salary.

A chose in action such as the right to a salary in fact has no situs. But where for some purpose the law has found it necessary to attribute a situs, in the absence of anything in the contract or elsewhere to indicate the contrary, the situs of a simple contract debt has been held to be the residence or place where the debtor is found. See Cheshire, *Private International Law*, seventh edition, pp. 420 *et seq*.

In *Commissioner of Stamps* v. *Hope*, Lord Field, speaking for the Privy Council, said:

> Not a debt per se, although a chattel and part of the personal estate which the probate confers authority to administer, has, of course, no absolute local existence; but it has been long established in the Courts of this country, and is a well-settled rule governing all questions as to which Court can confer the required authority, that a debt possess an attribute of locality, arising from and according to its nature, and the distinction drawn and well settled has been and is whether it is a debt by contract or a debt by specialty. In the former case, the debt being merely a chose in action — money to be recovered from the debtor and nothing more — could have no other local existence than the personal residence of the debtor, where the assets to satisfy it would presumably be, and it was held therefore to be bona notabilia within the area of the local jurisdiction within which he resided; but this residence is of course of a changeable and fleeting nature, and depending upon the movements of the debtor, and inasmuch as a debt under seal or specialty had a species of corporeal existence by which its locality might be reduced to a certainty, and was a debt of a higher nature than one by contract, it was settled in very early days that such a debt was bona notabilia where it was "conspicuous," i.e., within the jurisdiction within which the specialty was found at the time of death: see Wentworth on the Office of Executors, ed. 1763, pp. 45, 47, 60(1) [*sic*].

In *New York Life Insurance Company* v. *Public Trustee*, [1924] 2 Ch. 101 at page 119, Atkin LJ put the matter thus:

> The question as to the locality, the situation of a debt, or a chose in action is obviously difficult, because it involves consideration of what must be considered to be legal fictions. A debt, or a chose in action, as a matter of fact, is not a matter of which you can predicate position; nevertheless, for a great many purposes it has to be ascertained where a debt or chose in action is situated, and certain rules have been laid down in this country which have been derived from the practice of the ecclesiastical authorities in granting administration, because the jurisdiction of the ecclesiastical authorities was limited territorially. The ordinary had only a jurisdiction within a particular territory, and the question whether he should issue

letters of administration depended upon whether or not assets were to be found within his jurisdiction, and the test in respect of simple contracts was: Where was the debtor residing? Now, one knows that, ordinarily speaking, according to our law, a debtor has to seek out his creditor and pay him; but it seems plain that the reason why the residence of the debtor was adopted as that which determined where the debt was situate was because it was in that place where the debtor was that the creditor could, in fact, enforce payment of the debt. I think that is a very material consideration. The result is that in the case of an ordinary individual by that rule for a long time the situation of a simple contract debt under ordinary circumstances has been held to be where the debtor resides; that being the place where under ordinary circumstances the debt is enforceable, because it is only by bringing suit against the debtor that the amount can be recovered.

The decision of Collier J in *Snow* v. *The Queen* 78 DTC 6335 and of the case which he followed, *i.e.*, *Petersen* v. *Cree and Canadian Pacific Express Co.* (1941) 79 CS (Que.) 1, appear to me to proceed on that rule. *Avery* v. *Cayuga* (1913) 13 DLR 275, as well, proceeds on that rule. There, a deposit belonging to an Indian resident on a reserve in a bank not situated on a reserve was held to be not situated on the reserve, Meredith CJO saying at page 276:

> That the deposit is property situate outside of the reserve, within the meaning of sec. 99, seems not to be open to question: *Commissioner of Stamps* v. *Hope*, [1891] AC 476, 481-2; *Lovitt* v. *The King*, 43 Can. SCR 106; *The King* v. *Lovitt* (1911), 28 Times LR 41.

> There are expressions of opinion to the contrary in *Armstrong Growers' Ass'n* v. *Harris* [1924] 1 DLR 1043 and *Crepin* v. *Delorimier* (1930) 68 CS (Que.) 36, but I do not think they can prevail over the authorities cited.

> As the salaries in question of the individual Indians until paid were simple contract debts owed by a corporation not resident on a reserve, it is my view that they were not "situated on a reserve" within the meaning of subsection 87(1).

Such portion of the judgment of Thurlow ACJ was cited with approval by Dickson J for the Supreme Court of Canada in *Nowegijick* v. *The Queen*.

In *The Queen* v. *National Indian Brotherhood* (1975), CTC 2112 it had been argued that the employees of the Indian organization employed at the head office in Ottawa were exempt. A.J. Frost declared for the Tax Review Board:

> . . . in the present case, the facts are somewhat extraordinary, and quite different from the *Snow* case referred to by counsel for the respondent.

Here a number of unenfranchised Indians temporarily leave their reserve to join the staff of the appellant, an organization of a purely non-commercial nature acting on behalf of Indians and in respect of purely Indian affairs, and financed by moneys appropriated for the Indian cause by Parliament. Their domicile is their reserve and they were certainly employed as members of their band. In no way do I consider these people as having left the reserve to seek their fortune and earn a living in the non-Indian society. One could consider them as an extended arm of their bands, operating in Ottawa at the convenience of Indian and non-Indian parties concerned with the well-being and interests of unenfranchised Indians. It seems to me that the *Indian Act* should be interpreted and applied in a flexible way which does justice to the underlying philosophy of the Act.

The Federal Court Trial Division decisively rejected such an approach. Thurlow ACJ asserted:

There is no legal basis not withstanding the history of the exemption, and the special position of Indians in Canadian society, for extending it by reference to any notional extension of reserves or what may be considered as being done on reserves.

[1979] 1 FC 103, 108.

In 1951, Section 90 was introduced into the Indian Act. It deems the situs of certain forms of personal property to be located on a reserve.

In *The Queen* v. *National Indian Brotherhood*, it was contended that, as the funding of the defendant's operation was largely provided from appropriations by Parliament for the use and benefit of Indians, paragraph 90(1)(a) applied to the salaries of the defendants' Indian employees so to deem them to be property situated on a reserve, from which it would follow that the individual Indian would be exempt from taxation in respect of his salary.

Thurlow ACJ rejected the argument:

In my opinion, it is not possible to regard the salaries here in question as "personal property that was purchased by Her Majesty" within the meaning of paragraph 90(1)(a) and I am unable to accept counsel's submission that the paragraph should be interpreted as if it read "personal property that was . . . moneys appropriated by Parliament" as I think that grammatically the words "purchased by Her Majesty with" govern the whole of the remainder of the paragraph. The provision therefore cannot apply.

An appeal in *Queen* v. *National Indian Brotherhood* has been filed in the Federal Court of Appeal, but has yet to be heard.

The "numbered" treaties between the Indians of Western Canada and the Crown provided that "Her Majesty agrees to maintain schools for instruction in such reserves". Indian organizations have argued that such terms and the oral assurances accompanying them place an obligation upon the Crown to support Indian students in all forms of education. The Crown has provided such support pursuant to agreements between the Department of Indian Affairs and Indian bands. In *Greyeyes* v. *The Queen* (1978), 84 DLR (3d) 196, the Federal Court Trial Division held that a scholarship paid to an Indian student by the Department of Indian Affairs to attend a university off reserve lands was deemed "situate on a reserve" by the operation of the provisions of section 90(1)(b) and was accordingly not taxable. The statement of agreed facts provided that "the said funds . . . were given to her pursuant to an agreement and treaty between the plaintiff's band and Ottawa and specifically pursuant to an agreement to assist band members in their education in compliance with the obligations of the Federal Government under Treaty #6."

6. Sales Tax and Customs Duty

(a) *Francis* v. *The Queen*, [1956] SCR 618, (1956) 3 DLR 641. Rand J (Cartwright J concurring)

The appellant, Louis Francis, is an Indian within the definition of that word in the *Indian Act*, RSC 1952, c. 149, s. 2(1)(*g*) and resides on the St Regis Indian Reserve in Quebec. The latter is part of a larger settlement of the St Regis Tribe extending into the United States and is bounded on the south by the international boundary between the two countries. Between 1948 and 1951 Francis purchased an electric washing machine, a second-hand oil burner or heater and an electric refrigerator in the United States; two of these were brought over or from the international boundary to his home in the Reserve by Francis and the other delivered by the seller. They were not reported at the customs office for the district and some time later were seized and held until the duty amounting to $123.66 was paid. The petition of right was thereupon brought for the return of these moneys.

The claim is based first on that clause of Article III of the Jay Treaty between Great Britain and the United States of 1794 which stipulates: "No duty on entry shall ever be levied by either party on peltries brought by land or inland navigation into the said territories respectively, nor shall the Indians passing or repassing with their own proper goods and effects of whatever nature, pay for the same any impost or duty whatever. But goods in bales, or other large packages, unusual among Indians, shall not be considered as goods belonging bona fide to Indians."

And on the 9th Article of the Treaty of Ghent, 1814 [Treaties, Conventions, International Acts, etc. 1910, vol. 1, p. 618], between the same states which, as regards Great Britain, reads: "And His Britannic Majesty engages, on his part, to put an end immediately after the ratification of the present treaty to hostilities with all the tribes of nations of Indians with whom he may be at war at the time of such ratification, and forthwith to restore to such tribes or nations respectively all the possessions, rights and privileges which they may have enjoyed or been entitled to in one thousand eight hundred and eleven, previous to such hostilities: Provided always that such tribes or nations shall agree to desist from all hostilities against his Britannic Majesty, and his subjects, upon the ratification of the present treaty being notified to such tribes or nations, and shall so desist accordingly."

The contention is put as follows: Article III effects the enactment of substantive law not requiring statutory confirmation as being a provision in a treaty of peace, the making of which is in the exercise of the prerogative including, here, a legislative function; on the true interpretation of the treaty the article was intended to be perpetual and was not affected by the war of 1812; in any event it was restored by the 9th Article of 1814.

A second ground is that the appellant is exempted from liability for the duties by s. 102 of the *Indian Act*, RSC 1927, c. 98, and by s. 86(1) of RSC 1952, c. 149. [Now s. 87(1) RSC 1970 c. I-6]. . . .

Except as to diplomatic status and certain immunities and to belligerent rights, treaty provisions affecting matters within the scope of municipal law, that is, which purport to change existing law or restrict the future action of the Legislature, including, under our Constitution, the participation of the Crown, and in the absence of a constitutional provision declaring the treaty itself to be law of the state, as in the United States, must be supplemented by statutory action. An instance of the joint involvement of executive, legislative and judicial organs is shown by the provisions of the Treaty of 1783 respecting the holding of lands in the United States by subjects of Great Britain, including their heirs and assigns, and *vice versa*. These were supplemented by 37 Geo. III., c. 97, which was declared to continue so long as the treaty should do so and no longer. In *Sutton* v. *Sutton*, 1 Russ. & M. at p. 676, Sir John Leach M.R. held that this provision was not annulled by the war of 1812, that so far the statute remained in force and that "the heirs and assigns of every American who held lands in Great Britain at the time mentioned in the Act of 37 G. 3, are, so far as regards those lands, to be treated, not as aliens, but as native subjects."

To the enactment of fiscal provisions, certainly in the case of a treaty not a peace treaty, the prerogative does not extend, and only by legislation can customs duties be imposed or removed or can the condition under which goods may be brought into this country be affected. I agree, therefore, with Cameron J in holding that legislation was necessary to bring within municipal law the exemption of the clause in question. Legislation to that effect was enacted, in Upper Canada by 41 Geo. III., c. 5, s. 6, repealed by 4 Geo. IV., c. 11; in Lower Canada by the enabling statute, 36 Geo. III., c. 7, and the ordinance of 1796 made thereunder, the former having been continued by annual renewals up to January 1, 1813, when it lapsed. No legislation is suggested to have been passed by any other Province. For over a century, then, there has been no statutory provision in this country giving effect to that clause of the article.

The particular privilege law within a structure of settled international relations between sovereign states and from its nature was not viewed as intended to be perpetual. Following the treaty of 1783 large scale transfers of Indians belonging to the Six Nations and more western tribes took place from the United States to lands north of Lake Erie. This was a major step which was bound to affect materially the circumstances instigating the clause.

But the Indians north of the boundary were not confined to the district between Montreal and Detroit: they inhabited also the eastern maritime Provinces and the territories to the west of central Canada; these were within the general language but there has been no suggestion that the treaty was significant to them, much less that they have ever claimed its privilege . . .

Indian affairs generally, therefore, have for over a century been the subject of expanding administration throughout what is now the Dominion, superseding the local enactments following the treaty designed to meet an immediate urgency. In the United States the last statutory provision dealing with duties on goods brought in by Indians was repealed in 1897. This appears from the case of *United States* v. *Garrow* (1937), 88 Fed. (2d) 318 at p. 321. In that case, also, it was pointed out that under the Ghent treaty the contracting parties merely "engaged" themselves to restore by legislation the "possessions, rights and privileges" of the Indians enjoyed in 1811 but that no such enactment had been passed. The article itself was held to have been abrogated by the war of 1812: *Karnuth* v. *United States* (1928), 279 US 231. In the last decade of the 18th century peace had been reached between the United States and the tribes living generally between Lake Champlain and the Mississippi river. There followed the slow but inevitable march of events paralleled by that in this country; and today there remain along the border only fragmentary reminders of that past. The strike had waged over the free and ancient hunting grounds and their fruits, lands which were divided between two powers, but that life in its original mode and scope has long since disappeared.

These considerations seem to justify the conclusion that both the Crown and Parliament of this country have treated the provisional accommodation as having been replaced by an exclusive code of new and special rights and privileges. Appreciating fully the obligation of good faith toward these wards of the state, there can be no doubt that the conditions constituting the *raison d'être* of the clause were and have been considered such as would in foreseeable time disappear. That a radical change of this nature brings about a cesser of such a treaty provision appears to be supported by the authorities available: McNair, *The Law of Treaties*, 1938, pp. 378-381. Assuming that Art. 9 of the Treaty of Ghent extended to the exemption, it was only an "engagement" to restore which, by itself, could do no more than to revive the clause in its original treaty effect, and supplementary action was clearly envisaged. Whether, then, the time of its expiration has been reached or not it is not here necessary to decide; it is sufficient to say that there is no legislation now in force implementing the stipulation.

There remains the question of exemption under s. 102 of RSC 1927, c. 98, and s. 86(1) of RSC 1952, c. 149, the former of which was repealed as of June 20, 1951 [proclaimed September 4, 1951]. I can find nothing in these provisions that assists the appellant. To be taxed as by s. 102 "at the same rate as other persons in the locality" refers obviously and only to personal or real property under local taxation; it cannot be construed to extend to customs duties imposed on importation.

Similarly in 86(1), property "situated on a reserve" is unequivocal and does not mean property entering this country or passing an international boundary. On the argument made, the exemption would be limited to situations in which that boundary bounded also the Reserve and would be a special indulgence to the small fraction of Indians living on such a Reserve, a consequence which itself appears to me to be a sufficient answer.

The appeal must therefore be dismissed and with costs if demanded.

Kellock J (Abbott J concurring), after quoting what was then section 86(1) Indian Act [now section 87(1)], concluded:

Before the property here in question could become situated on a Reserve, it had become liable to customs duty at the border. There has been no attempt to impose any other tax.

The learned judge then quoted what was then section 89 [now section 90].

It is quite plain from this section that the actual situation of the personal property on a Reserve is contemplated by s. 86 and that any argument suggesting a notional situation is not within the intendment of that section. . . .

In my opinion the provisions of the *Indian Act* constitute a code governing the rights and privileges of Indians, and except to the extent that immunity from general legislation such as the *Customs Act* or the *Customs Tariff Act* is to be found in the *Indian Act*, the terms of such general legislation apply to Indians equally with other citizens of Canada.

Kerwin CJC (Taschereau and Fauteux JJ concurring)

The Jay Treaty was not a treaty of peace and it is clear that in Canada such rights and privileges as are here advanced of subjects of a contracting party to a treaty are enforceable by the Courts only where the treaty has been implemented or sanctioned by legislation. . . .

I agree with Cameron J that cl. (*b*) of s. 86(1) of the *Indian Act* does not apply, because customs duties are not taxes upon the personal property of an Indian situated on a Reserve but are imposed upon the importation of goods into Canada.

(b) The exemption was applied in *Lillian Brown* v. *The Queen in the Right of British Columbia*, [1979] 3 CNLR 67 (BCCA).

This appeal is from a judgment dismissing an action brought by the appellant Lillian Brown against the respondents for a declaration, with consequential relief, that social services tax purportedly imposed and collected under the *Social Services Tax Act*, 1960 RSBC, Ch. 361, as amended (the "Tax Act") on the purchase price of electricity sold and delivered to her, an Indian, at her home on an Indian reserve, was unlawful. The appellant sued on her own behalf and on behalf of other Indians in like position.

The trial proceeded on an agreed statement of facts and on an agreed question posed. This disclosed (*inter alia*) that the appellant was an Indian within the definition of the *Indian Act* (Canada) 1970 RSC, Ch. I-6 (the "Indian Act") and maintained a residence and lived on an Indian reserve as defined and provided for in that statute. The respondent British Columbia Hydro and Power Authority ("Hydro"), which carried on the business of generating, distributing and supplying electricity, delivered (presumably through transmission and distribution lines) electricity to the appellant at the residence on the reserve for domestic use. The specific period of delivery set out for the purposes of the trial was between October 12, 1976 and December 9, 1976. The appellant was charged for the electricity purchased and used by her and also under the provisions of the *Tax Act* for a percentage tax (for the period amounting to $4.38) on the purchase price of the electricity. The appellant paid to Hydro the purchase price and the tax imposed, and Hydro remitted the tax portion collected to the Crown in the provincial right as provided in the *Tax Act*.

The specific question posed to the trial Judge was

> Is Lillian Brown properly liable for $4.38 or part thereof, social services tax in respect of the electricity purchased from British Columbia Hydro and Power Authority between October 13, 1976 and December 9, 1976?

Basically, the position taken by the appellant, both in the court below and before us, was that as an Indian she was exempt from the tax by reason of the provisions of section 87 of the *Indian Act* because the electricity delivered to her at her home on the reserve was "personal property situated on the reserve".

On the other hand, the respondents asserted that section 87 did not so exempt as:

  (i) the electricity so purchased and delivered, although by definition included as tangible personal property in the *Tax Act*, was not personal property
    (a) at common law or within the meaning of the section, or
    (b) situated on a reserve;
 (ii) the tax was not on the electricity but on a transaction of sale; and
(iii) in any event, if the tax came with the terms of section 87 under its true construction then, to the extent it purported to exempt personal property from validity imposed provincial direct taxation, it was *ultra vires* the Parliament of Canada . . .

The question to be answered was whether electricity is "personal property" within the meaning of section 87 of the *Indian Act*. The learned trial Judge held it is not because properly construed the words "personal property" do not include intangible property which is other than a chose in action and which is not capable of being subject to succession. The Judge concluded this because of the explicit references in the latter part of the section to succession, inheritance and estate taxes. He therefore decided that electricity is not personal property included in the exemption from taxation under section 87.

The appellant argued that the Judge's conclusions were based on too narrow a view and that he put an unmerited weight on those provisions in the latter part of the section. I agree with that view and am of the opinion that personal property as used in section 87 should not be held to be so limited in scope. It is to be noted that the general exemption against taxes set out in the first part of the section refers to property of all kinds, both real and personal, of an Indian or a band situated on the reserve. The last part, following a semi-colon, dealing with succession, inheritance and estate taxes, refers only to a different situation, namely, where property passes on the death of an Indian. The provision was required to maintain the exemption in certain cases after an Indian's death. In my view, those provisions stand by themselves as appropriate adjuncts to the exemption and should not be used to govern or limit the general words "personal property" in the section.

Accordingly, I find the trial Judge erred in concluding for the reasons he outlined, that electricity was not included in the words "personal property" in section 87(b).

But the respondents submitted two other grounds upon which the trial Judge's finding that electricity was not covered by the exemption could, and should, be supported.

The first was that the exemption by its terms covered the Indian's personal property when it was "situated on a reserve". It was argued that electricity by its very nature was not and could not be so situated. It was said that electricity has no "situs". Even if it could be said to have situs it would be a mere fleeting one with no permanency. Reliance was placed on four authorities, viz. . . . .

> *The Queen* v. *National Indian Brotherhood* (1978) 92 DLR (3d) 333, (Federal Court);
> *Norwegijick* v. *The Queen* (1979) 79 DTC 5115 (Federal Court);
> *Snow* v. *The Queen* (1979) 79 CTC 227, and
> *Anderson* v. *Canadian Mercantile Insurance Co.* (1965) 51 WWR (NS) 129, affirmed (1965) 53 WWR 446.

. . . I think the first mentioned cases are quite distinguishable. The decision in *Anderson* depended on the terms and purpose of the particular provision of the policy of insurance in which the word was found, and, in my view, is of no assistance in the case at bar. As to the suggestion that the word "situated" as used in section 87 means that there must be some degree of permanence to the occurrence of electricity on the reservation, my opinion is that the word "situated" is not used in that sense but rather in the sense of "located". I therefore consider that the electricity was clearly delivered to and situated on the reserve.

The second submission of the respondents was that the tax levied on the appellant under the *Tax Act*, was not a tax on electricity itself as personal property within the meaning of section 87, but a tax on a transaction of purchase. It was pointed out that section 3(1) of the *Tax Act* reads:

> Every purchaser shall pay to Her Majesty in the right of the Province at the time of making the purchase, a tax at the rate of 7% of the purchase price of the property purchased.

In other words, the tax was on the purchase price and not on the property itself, and so, the exemption of section 87 did not come into play. In my view, the submission of the respondents cannot be supported in view of the wording of that section. There might be some merit if only the first part of the section were looked at, that is, the part that provides that no Indian is subject to taxation "in respect of the ownership, occupation, possession or use" of any personal property situated on a reserve. It is quite arguable that the social services tax is not levied on any of those enumerated characteristics. However, the argument falls to the ground by reason of the later words which provide exemption from taxation "in respect of any such property", namely, the personal property situated on the reserve. Accepting the respondents' submission that the tax was on the purchase rather than on the electricity itself (which I do not find necessary to accept) I am of the opinion that the tax was "taxation with respect to" the electricity. I must, therefore, reject this submission of the respondents.

Having thus come to the conclusion that the electricity purchased by the appellant Indian was personal property situated on a reserve and that the tax levied thereon by the *Tax Act* was in respect of that property to the end that she was entitled to the exemption from the tax under section 87(b) of the *Indian Act*, it remains only to be determined whether that section, insofar as it purported to give her the exemption claimed, was *ultra vires* the Parliament of Canada which enacted it. If *intra vires* the appellant must be successful in her suit . . .

If matters testamentary referred to in *Canard*, *supra*, were validly included in federal legislation in the *Indian Act* notwithstanding that the subject matter would normally be within general provincial competency and legislation, I cannot but find that even more adhesive to the power to deal or, "to do", with Indians given by section 92(24) of the *BNA Act* are provisions exempting them (while living on a reserve) from the incidents of taxation including properly enacted provincial tax legislation applying generally to all persons in the Province. In my view, such an exemption from taxation should be considered, having regard to the exclusive nature of Parliament's competency given by the *BNA Act* and the obvious purpose thereof to provide for the protection, welfare and guidance of Indians, to be almost essential legislation.

It follows that I am unable to accede to the respondents' submissions that the exemption from taxation on, or in respect of, personal property

of an Indian situated on a reserve as provided in section 87(2) of the
Indian Act, is *ultra vires*. In my view the section, validly enacted, has in
effect ousted that part of the *Tax Act* levying the Social Services Tax on
the electricity sold to the appellant, and section 87(2) of the *Indian Act*
overrides. . .

(c) Compare *R*. v. *Simon* (1977), 34 NSR (2d) (NSCCJ), where the accused
was charged with unlawfully using marked gasoline contrary to the
Gasoline and Diesel Oil Tax Act, RSNS 1967, c. 116. The accused's
vehicle was on an Indian reserve at the time and the accused was an Indian
within the meaning of the Indian Act.

McLELLAN CCJ:

Broadly stated, it is said on behalf of the defendant that as an Indian he
is not subject to a taxing statute of the Province of Nova Scotia and that
the *Gasoline and Diesel Oil Tax Act* is *ultra vires* the Province of Nova
Scotia to the extent that it purports to impose a tax on the personal
property of Indians. If I were satisfied that the purpose and effect of the
Gasoline and Diesel Oil Tax Act was to impose a tax on the personal
property of Indians in Nova Scotia I would agree with this submission
but I believe that on analysis the purpose and effect of the latter act is
quite different.

In the first place it is quite obvious that the subject of Indians and
lands reserved for Indians is assigned exclusively to the Parliament of
Canada as a field of legislative competence by the *BNA Act*. But by the
Indian Act (supra) it is provided that all laws of general application in a
province are applicable to Indians except to the extent that such laws are
inconsistent with any federal laws relating to Indians (s. 88). Becoming
more specific it is provided by s. 87 of the *Indian Act* that the personal
property of an Indian or band situated on a reserve is exempt from
taxation. This cannot mean that such property is exempt from all
taxation at every stage of its existence from production to consumption.
I think it must refer to the personal property of an Indian after he
acquires title to it, and I think it was intended to prevent municipal
taxation of the personal property of Indians on reserves.

I think there is merit on the Crown's submission that the *Gasoline and
Diesel Oil Tax Act* provisions are aimed at taxation of the two sources of
energy generally and the particular *Regulation* referred to in the
information is one which regulates use of gas on which a tax has not
been paid. Continuing the argument, an inspector under the latter act
does not say to an individual who has been found to be using marked gas
contrary to the regulations, "You owe so much tax," he says, "You are
using that gas unlawfully."

Again, the object of the *Gasoline and Diesel Oil Tax Act* and the manner in which it is achieved can be seen from the following. While there may be a levy or tax imposed on gasoline generally, regardless of who owns it, there is no tax or levy on a particular kind of gasoline, namely, marked gas. Any person may purchase it, but he is limited in the way in which he may use it.

Both counsel referred to *R.* v. *Isaac* (1976), 13 NSR (2d) 460; 9 APR 460, for an extensive review of the constitutionality of provincial laws relating to Indians. That case held that hunting on a reserve was a use of reserve lands, and that the *Lands and Forests Act of Nova Scotia*, RSNS 1967, c. 163, could not regulate hunting on Indian reserve lands. Both that case and this are concerned with use of property, but of different kinds and for different purposes.

I am not satisfied that the decision of the learned judge in the summary conviction is one which should be set aside on the ground that it was wrong on a question of law or that there was any miscarriage of justice (See s. 613(1), Criminal Code)''

Sales taxes were introduced by the provinces in the Depression and have generally been levied by legislation or administrative practice so as to exempt Indian ''purchases for consumption or use on a reserve''. The legislation and regulations that have been introduced in Manitoba (1974), New Brunswick (1974), Nova Scotia (1973), Ontario, Prince Edward Island (1978) and Quebec (1974) have all followed such an approach. Section five of the Ontario Retail Sales Act, RSO 1980 c. 454, exempts:

73. tangible personal property situated on a reserve, as defined by the *Indian Act* (Canada) or by the Minister when purchased by an Indian, and tangible personal property purchased by an Indian off the reserve when delivered to the reserve for consumption or use by an Indian;

74. taxable services used on a reserve as defined by the *Indian Act* (Canada) or by the Minister, when purchased by an Indian;

Saskatchewan, which has not legislated upon the subject, exempts purchases by Indians on or off the reserve, irrespective of the place of delivery. By contrast, British Columbia, which also has no legislation specifically concerned with the exemption of Indians, has by administrative practice exempted only sales made by an Indian purchaser at a store located on a reserve. No exemption for sales off a reserve for delivery to a reserve has been allowed.

Sales taxes are levied upon all forms of tangible and intangible personal property by the provinces. The provinces have not, however, applied the exemption demanded by section 87 to a similar degree. In the main, liquor, tobacco, gasoline, electricity and telephone services are excluded from the exemption, as in Alberta, Manitoba, Prince Edward Island and Quebec. Saskatchewan and New Brunswick differ only in including telephone services within the exemption liquor, tobacco, telephone services and electricity, but exempts liquor, and gasoline delivered to a reserve. Nova Scotia includes within the exemption liquor, tobaccc, telephone services and electricity, but not gasoline. At the other extreme Manitoba denies the application of the exemption to motor vehicles and commercial property. The varieties of property considered by the provinces to be excluded from section 87 are clearly not dictated by the language of that section or the judgments of the members of the Supreme Court in *Francis* v. *The Queen*.

7. Conclusion

Indian bands are possessed of a limited power to impose taxation upon interests in reserve lands. The power may extend to interests held by non-Indians. It does not as yet extend to the power to impose taxation upon the income of non-Indians doing business on a reserve. The provinces have been allowed to tax non-Indians on reserves and to impose taxation upon Indians off reserves for objects, such as education, which were assured them by the spirit of the treaties. The exemption from taxation may receive a broader construction in the future. Dickson J in *Nowegijick* v. *The Queen* for the Supreme Court of Canada, observed "that treaties and statutes relating to Indians should be liberally construed and doubtful expressions resolved in favour of the Indians." Such a rule of construction will assist the resolution of the confused state of provincial taxes applied to Indians and allow effective income tax-planning so as to encourage economic development of reserves. It will not assist the claims of the Metis or the Inuit to a similar exemption from taxation. The exemption of the Metis and the Inuit must depend upon the terms of any land claims settlements that are arrived at.

8. Questions

1. What is the ambit of Indian band councils' power to impose taxation? Does it extend to non-Indians? Does it extend to income taxation? What kinds of tax may band councils levy and upon whom? To what extent are such powers invaded by the provinces? What is the significance of the band council's power to levy taxes?
2. Why are Indians exempted from various forms of taxation? Are Indians entitled to an exemption irrespective of the provisions of the Indian Act?
3. Are the Inuit exempt from any form of taxation? Should Indian corporations be exempt from taxation?
4. Is income within the exemption from taxation conferred by section 87 of the Indian Act? What is the significance of the decision of the Supreme Court of Canada in *Nowegijick* v. *The Queen*?
5. Advise an Indian band upon whether the exemptions from taxation extends

to (i) interest on a bank accoaunt in a bank in a town off a reserve, (ii) dividends paid by an Indian corporation located on a reserve, (iii) salaries paid by an Indian corporation located on a reserve with respect to work conducted off a reserve.

What advice would you give an Indian band with respect to the organization of a lumber business on a reserve, assuming Indian employees would work on and off the reserve?

6. Why are Indians exempt from sales tax? Why are Indians exempt from sales tax on motor vehicles in Saskatchewan but not in Manotiba?

9. Further Reading

R.H. Bartlett, "Indians and Taxation in Canada", University of Saskatchewan, Native Law Centre, 1980.

D. Sanders, *Legal Aspects of Economic Development on Indian REserve Lands,* Department of Indian Affairs and Northern Development, 1976.

R.H. Bartlett, "Citizens Minus: Indians and The Right to Vote" (1979) 44 *Saskatchewan Law Review* 163.

J.V. White, *Taxing those they found here; an examination of the tax exempt status of the American Indian,* 1972 Washington, Institute for Development of Indian Law.

10.   The Resolution of Land Claims

BRADFORD W. MORSE

1. Introduction

It should be clear from the preceding chapters that the indigenous people were the sole original owners and occupants of what is now known as Canada. English common law has recognized the validity of this ownership for some three centuries, acknowledging that it gave rise to a legally recognized interest in the land possessed by the individual Indian nation or Inuit community. This interest has been generally described as "aboriginal title" and has been defined as analogous to a usufructuary interest in land.

British recognition of aboriginal title resulted in the necessity for purchasing this interest, which was done in reference to large parts of the country through treaties and land surrenders. Nevertheless, the Imperial, colonial and Dominion governments neglected to complete this process of land acquisition in the Maritimes, Quebec, Newfoundland, British Columbia and the North. The Aboriginal Peoples of these regions have consistently asserted their continuing ownership to their lands and deprecated the lack of recognition and attention given to their claims.

Those Indian and Metis people who have signed treaties, and other Metis who signed half-breed adhesions, are not without complaints. Many of the promises made in the treaties have not been kept or were never initially fulfilled. Hunting and fishing rights have been overriden by general federal legislation in the form of the Migratory Birds Convention Act and the Fisheries Act. The purchase price that was originally paid under these agreements was frequently well below the fair market value and might be regarded as so inadequate as to be unconscionable consideration.

In addition, Indian reserve lands have sometimes been expropriated without adequate or indeed any compensation, have been illegally sold, have been lost through moving boundaries or by redefinition, have been sold below fair market value, and have been mismanaged by Indian agents. Bands have also had their funds lost, stolen, and mismanaged. All of these events form the basis for claims.

Indian bands and associations have presented petitions, memorials, and submissions to the Queen and to the Government of Canada on numerous occasions throughout the history of Indian-white relations in Canada. Generally, these presentations have fallen on deaf ears.

2. The Development of a Federal Policy, and Indian Reactions

After intensive consultations across the country between Indian bands and the Department of Indian Affairs and Northern Development, the federal government issued its ill-fated White Paper on Indian Policy in 1969. It was designed to eliminate the special status of Indians through the repeal of the Indian Act and termination of the unique tenure of reserve lands so as to promote equality with other Canadians. The removal of special status was thought to assist registered Indians by eliminating the disadvantages and advantages flowing from their unique constitutional and legal position.

(a) Statement of the Government of Canada on Indian Policy, 1969

. . . Canada is richer for its Indian component, although there have been times when diversity seemed of little value to many Canadians.

But to be a Canadian Indian today is to be someone different in another way. It is to be someone apart — apart in law, apart in the provision of government services and, too often, apart in social contacts.

To be an Indian is to lack power — the power to act as owner of your lands, the power to spend your own money and, too often, the power to change your own condition . . . .

To be an Indian must be to be free — free to develop Indian cultures in an environment of legal, social and economic equality with other Canadians . . . .

The policies proposed recognize the simple reality that the separate legal status of Indians and the policies which have flowed from it have kept the Indian people apart from and behind other Canadians. The Indian people have not been full citizens of the communities and provinces in which they live and have not enjoyed the equality and benefits that such participation offers.

The treatment resulting from their different status has been often worse, sometimes equal and occasionally better than that accorded to their fellow citizens. What matters is that it has been different . . . .

THE NEW POLICY

True equality presupposes that the Indian people have the right to full and equal participation in the cultural, social, economic and political life of Canada.

The government believes that the framework within which individual Indians and bands could achieve full participation requires:

that the legislative and constitutional bases of discrimination be removed;

that there be positive recognition by everyone of the unique contribution of Indian culture to Canadian life;

that services come through the same channels and from the same government agencies for all Canadians;

that those who are furthest behind be helped most;

that lawful obligations be recognized;

that control of Indian bands be transferred to the Indian people.

The Government would be prepared to take the following steps to create this framework;

Propose to Parliament that the Indian Act be repealed and take such legislative steps as may be necessary to enable Indians to control Indian lands and to acquire title to them.

Propose to the governments of the provinces that they take over the same responsibility for Indians that they have for other citizens in their provinces. The take-over would be accompanied by the transfer to the provinces of federal funds normally provided for Indian programs, augmented as may be necessary.

Make substantial funds available for Indian economic development as an interim measure.

Wind up that part of the Department of Indian Affairs and Northern Development which deals with Indian Affairs. The residual responsibilities of the Federal Government for programs in the field of Indian Affairs would be transferred to other appropriate federal departments.

In addition, the Government will appoint a Commissioner to consult with the Indians and to study and recommend acceptable procedures for the adjudication of claims . . . .

Claims and Treaties

LAWFUL OBLIGATIONS MUST BE RECOGNIZED

Many of the Indian people feel that successive governments have not dealt with them as fairly as they should. They believe that lands have been taken from them in an improper manner, or without adequate compensation, that their funds have been improperly administered, that their treaty rights have been breached. Their sense of grievance influences their relations with governments and the community and limits their participation in Canadian life.

Many Indians look upon their treaties as the source of their rights to land, to hunting and fishing privileges, and to other benefits. Some believe the treaties should be interpreted to encompass wider services and privileges, and many believe the treaties have not been honoured. Whether or not this is correct in some or many cases, the fact is the treaties affect only half the Indians of Canada. Most of the Indians of Quebec, British Columbia, and the Yukon are not parties to a treaty.

The terms and effects of the treaties between the Indian people and the Government are widely misunderstood. A plain reading of the words used in the treaties reveals the limited and minimal promises which were included in them. As a result of the treaties, some Indians were given an initial cash payment and were promised land reserved for their exclusive use, annuities, protection of hunting, fishing and trapping privileges subject (in most cases) to regulation, a school or teachers in most instances, and, in one treaty only, a medicine chest. There were some other minor considerations such as the annual provision of twine and ammunition.

The annuities have been paid regularly. The basic promise to set aside reserve land has been kept except in respect of the Indians of the Northwest Territories and a few bands in the northern parts of the Prairie Provinces. These Indians did not choose land when treaties were signed. The government wishes to see these obligations dealt with as soon as possible.

The right to hunt and fish for food is extended unevenly across the country and not always in relation to need. Although game and fish will become less and less important for survival as the pattern of Indian life continues to change, there are those who, at this time, still live in the traditional manner that their forefathers lived in when they entered into treaty with the government. The Government is prepared to allow such persons transitional free hunting of migratory birds under the Migratory Birds Convention Act and Regulations.

The significance of the treaties in meeting the economic, educational, health and welfare needs of the Indian people has always been limited and will continue to decline. The services that have been provided go far beyond what could have been foreseen by those who signed the treaties.

The Government and the Indian people must reach a common understanding of the future role of the treaties. Some provisions will be found to have been discharged; others will have continuing importance. Many of the provisions and practices of another century may be considered irrelevant in the light of a rapidly changing society, and still others may be ended by mutual agreement. Finally, once Indian lands are securely within Indian control, the anomaly of treaties between groups within society and the government of that society will require that these treaties be reviewed to see how they can be equitably ended.

Other grievances have been asserted in more general terms. It is possible that some of these can be verified by appropriate research and may be susceptible of specific remedies. Others relate to aboriginal claims to land. These are so general and undefined that it is not realistic to think of them as specific claims capable of remedy except through a policy and program that will end injustice to Indians as members of the Canadian community. This is the policy that Government is proposing for discussion . . . .

The Government had intended to introduce legislation to establish an Indian Claims Commission to hear and determine Indian claims. Considerations of the questions raised at the consultations and the review of Indian policy have raised serious doubts as to whether a Claims Commission as proposed to Parliament in 1965 is the right way to deal with the grievances of Indians put forward as claims.

The Government has concluded that further study and research are required by both the Indians and the Government. It will appoint a Commissioner who, in consultation with representatives of the Indians, will inquire into and report upon how claims arising in respect of the performance of the terms of treaties and agreements formally entered into by representatives of the Indians and the Crown, and the administration of moneys and lands pursuant to schemes established by the legislation for the benefits of Indians may be adjudicated.

The Commissioner will also classify the claims that in his judgment ought to be referred to the courts or any special quasi-judicial body that may be recommended . . . .

The Indian reaction to this policy was swift and clear — total rejection. Almost every Indian association prepared a rebuttal to the White Paper, denouncing it as a fraud for not reflecting the Indian views that were put forward during the consultations, for having been prepared before the conclusion of the consultations, and for counteracting Indian objectives. The best known of these positions was the one prepared by the Indian Chiefs of Alberta, *Citizens Plus*, that has often been called the Red Paper.

(b) Citizens Plus, 1970

(from Waubageshig, ed., *The Only Good Indian* (Toronto: New Press, 1970), pp. 5-40).

"Indians should be regarded as 'Citizens Plus'; in addition to the normal rights and duties of citizenship, Indians possess certain additional rights as charter members of the Canadian community."

The Hawthorn Report

A. THE PREAMBLE

To us who are Treaty Indians there is nothing more important than our Treaties, our lands and the well-being of our future generation. We have studied carefully the contents of the Government White Paper on Indians and we have concluded that it offers despair instead of hope. Under the guise of land ownership, the government has devised a scheme whereby within a generation or shortly after the proposed Indian Lands Act expires our people would be left with no land and consequently the future generation would be condemned to the despair and ugly spectre of urban poverty in ghettos . . . .

In his White Paper, the Minister said, "This review was a response to things said by Indian people at the consultation meetings which began a year ago and culminated in a meeting in Ottawa in April." Yet, what Indians asked for land ownership that would result in Provincial taxation of our reserves? What Indians asked that Treaties be brought to an end? What group of Indians asked that aboriginal rights not be recognized? What group of Indians asked for a Commissioner whose purview would exclude half of the Indian population in Canada? The answer is no Treaty Indians asked for any of these things and yet through his concept of "consultation," the Minister said that his White Paper was in response to things said by Indians . . .

The White Paper Policy said "that the legislative and constitutional bases of discrimination should be removed."

We reject this policy. We say that the recognition of Indian status is essential for justice.

Retaining the legal status of Indians is necessary if Indians are to be treated justly. Justice requires that the special history, rights and circumstances of Indian People be recognized. The Chrétien Policy says, "Canada cannot seek the just society and keep DISCRIMINATORY legislation on its statute books." That statement covers a faulty understanding of fairness.

The legal definition of registered Indians must remain. If one of our registered brothers chooses, he may renounce his Indian status, become "enfranchised," receive his share of the funds of the tribe, and seek admission to ordinary Canadian society. But most Indians prefer to remain Indians. We believe that to be a good useful Canadian we must first be a good, happy and productive Indian . . . .

Channels for Services

The White Paper Policy says "that services should come through the same channels and from the same government agencies for all Canadians."

We say that the Federal Government is bound by the British North America Act, Section 91, Head 24, to accept legislative responsibility for "Indians and Indian lands." Moreover in exchange for the lands which the Indian people surrendered to the Crown the treaties ensure the following benefits:

(a) To have and to hold certain lands called "reserves" for the sole use and benefit of the Indian people forever and assistance in the social, economic and cultural development of the reserves.
(b) The provision of health services to the Indian people on the reserve or off the reserve at the expense of the Federal government anywhere in Canada.
(c) The provision of education of all types and levels to all Indian people at the expense of the Federal Government.
(d) The right of the Indian people to hunt, trap and fish for their livelihood free of governmental interference and regulation and subject only to the proviso that the exercise of this right must not interfere with the use and enjoyment of private property.

These benefits are not "handouts" because the Indian people paid for them by surrendering their lands. The Federal Government is bound to provide the actual services relating to education, welfare, health and economic development . . . .

Lawful Obligations

The White Paper Policy says "that lawful obligations should be recognized." If the Government meant what it said we would be happy. But it is obvious that the Government has never bothered to learn what the treaties are and has a distorted picture of them.

The government shows that it is willfully ignorant of the bargains that were made between the Indians and the Queen's Commissioners.

The Government must admit its mistakes and recognize that the treaties are historical, moral and legal obligations. The redmen signed them in good faith, and lived up to the treaties. The treaties were solemn agreements. Indian lands were exchanged for the promises of the Indian Commissioners who represented the Queen. Many missionaries of many faiths brought the authority and prestige of whiteman's religion in encouraging Indians to sign.

In our treaties of 1876, 1877, 1899 certain promises were made to our people; some of these are contained in the text of the treaties, some in the negotiations, and some in the memories of our people. Our basic view is that all these promises are part of the treaties and must be honoured.

Modernize the Treaties

The intent and spirit of the treaties must be our guide, not the precise letter of a foreign language. Treaties that run forever must have room for the changes in the conditions of life. The undertaking of the Government to provide teachers was a commitment to provide Indian children the educational opportunity equal to their white neighbors. The machinery and livestock symbolized economic development.

The White Paper Policy says "a plain reading of the words used in the treaties reveals the limited and minimal promises which were included in them . . . and in one treaty only a medicine chest." But we know from the Commissioners' Reports that they told the Indians that medicine chests were included in all three.

Indians have the right to receive, without payment, all health-care services without exception and paid for by the Government of Canada.

The medicine chests that we know were mentioned in the negotiations for Treaties Six, Seven and Eight mean that the Indians should now receive free medical, hospital and dental care — the same high quality services available to other Canadians . . . .

The Indian people see the treaties as the basis of all their rights and status. If the Government expects the co-operation of Indians, in any new policy, it must accept the Indian viewpoint on treaties. This would require the Government to start all over on its new policy.

Indian Control of Indian Lands

The White Paper Policy says "that control of Indian lands should be transferred to Indian people."

We agree with this intent but we find that the Government is ignorant of two basic points. The Government wrongly thinks that Indian Reserve lands are owned by the Crown. The Government is, of course, in error. These lands are held in trust by the Crown but they are Indian lands.

The Indians are the beneficial (actual) owners of the lands. The legal title has been held for us by the Crown to prevent the sale or breaking up of our land. We are opposed to any system of allotment that would give individuals ownership with rights to sell.

According to the Indian Act RSC 1952 the land is safe and secure, held in trust for the common use and benefit of the tribe. The land must never be sold, mortgaged or taxed.

The second error the Government commits is making the assumption in the way that ordinary property is owned. The Government should either get some legal advice or get some brighter legal advisers. The advice we have received is that the Indian Act could be changed to give Indians control of lands without changing the fact that the title is now held in trust.

Indian lands must continue to be regarded in a different manner than other lands in Canada. It must be held forever in trust of the Crown because, as we say, "The true owners of the land are not yet born."

C. IMMEDIATE REQUIREMENTS

Recognize the Treaties

The Government must declare that it accepts the treaties as binding and must pledge that it will incorporate the treaties in updated terms in an amendment to the Canadian Constitution. The preamble or introduction to this amendment should contain a reaffirmation of the treaties and an undertaking by the Government to abide by the treaties.

When this declaration is given, Indians will be prepared to consider some specific details of policy changes.
The treaties could be clarified in several ways:

(a) The Government should appoint a Permanent Standing Committee of the House of Commons and Senate with members from all parties to deal only with registered Indians and their affairs.

(b) The Treaties could be referred to the Court of Canada with the understanding that the Court will examine all supporting evidence and not merely the bare treaty.

(c) We would agree to referring the interpretation of the treaties to an impartial body such as the International Court of Justice at the Hague.

When the Government applies the same intent to the treaties as our forefathers took them to mean, the Government must enact the provisions of the treaties as an Act of the Canadian Parliament. We would regard this Act as an interim and temporary measure indicating good faith. Then with the consent of the Provinces, the Government of Canada should entrench the treaties in the written Constitution . . . .

Indian Claims Commission

The White Paper Policy said: "In addition, the Government will appoint a Commissioner to consult with the Indians and to study and recommend acceptable procedures for the adjudication of claims."

We reject the appointment of a sole Commissioner because he has been appointed without consultation and by the Government itself. He is not impartial and he has no power to do anything but a whitewash job.

What a Claims Commission Would Be

A Claims Commissioner would be established by consultation with the Indians. the Commissioners would be impartial. The Commission would have the power to call any witness the Indians or the Commission wanted or any documents that either wanted. The Commission would make binding judgments.

What Would a Claims Commission Do?

The Claims Commission could:

(a) Help modernize the treaties.

(b) Award compensation to aboriginal peoples who are registered

Indians who have no treaties. The Royal Proclamation of 1763 issued following the acquisition of Canada by the British provided that no Indian could be dispossessed of his land unless with his consent and the consent of the Crown. This common consent was given in the treaties under which Indians were to be compensated for giving up their title to the lands.

(c) Examine the boundaries of reservations and recognize the need to include as a part of reserves the lakes that are on the edge of the reserves.

(d) Prepare draft legislation to overcome the bad effects of the Migratory Birds Convention Act and other improper restrictions on Indians fishing in lakes and rivers.

(e) Hear all other claims that Indian persons or tribes want to have heard . . . .

E. CONCLUSION

If the Federal Government accepts its well-established obligations and seeks to honor them fully and enthusiastically, there is good reason to believe that consultation and progress are possible.

But in the case of grave social wrongs and deeply felt concerns, time is of the essence. The Indian leadership today is accustomed to the honorable and peaceful discussion and eventual solution, of the rights and needs and aspirations of our people.

But if for much longer the rights are not noticed, needs not met, or aspirations not fulfilled, then no one — especially having regard to developments all over the globe — can be assured that the rank and file will continue to accept such pacific conduct from its leaders.

Some reserves now have an agricultural-economic base adequate to support only one sixth the Indian population and the prediction is that by 1980 the base will support only one tenth the Indian population. Thus the problems are urgent.

The Government of Canada ultimately recognized that its new proposed policy was unacceptable to the status Indian population. Therefore, the White Paper was officially shelved by the government as being unworkable without Indian co-operation and acceptance. Nevertheless, certain aspects of the White Paper were actually implemented, and an Indian Economic Development Fund and Indian Claims Commission were established. In addition, the federal government continually encouraged provincial governments to offer their services and programmes to status Indians on and off reserves.

The statements in the White Paper regarding treaty and aboriginal rights of status Indians became the cornerstone of the federal land claims policy; that is, that "lawful obligations must be recognized". This, however, did not refer in any way to aboriginal claims, which were described as being "so general and undefined that it is not realistic to think of them as specific claims capable of remedy." In other words, treaty rights to hunt and fish would be respected, although they were viewed as "less and less important for survival" and would only continue to be necessary during a transitional period.

The Government of Canada also realized that some treaty promises to set aside reserve land had not been kept, which would have to be rectified. The Department of Indian Affairs and Northern Development (DIAND) only believed that this was a problem "in respect of the Indians of the Northwest Territories and a few bands in the northern parts of the Prairie Provinces." As later discussion will indicate, this was a serious underestimation of the scope of outstanding treaty land entitlement claims.

The federal government generally did not place great importance upon the treaties themselves and treaty rights. This is evident in the White Paper's description where it is stated that a "plain reading of the words used in the treaties reveals the limited and minimal promises which were included in them." Therefore, the government viewed the real claims, or "grievances" as they were generally referred to, as relating to the maladminstration of band funds or the improper taking of reserve lands. In other words, the claims were small and specific in nature.

On this basis, the government thought that the appointment of one person as an Indian Claims Commissioner would be sufficient to remedy and remove these "minor" claims. Dr Lloyd Barber was appointed on 19 December 1969 under Part I of the federal Inquiries Act to investigate claims relating to treaties and those that refer to the administration of lands and moneys under the Indian Act. He was given no authority to hear and decide any claims submitted to him; rather, he was "to receive and study the grievances" and "to recommend measures to be taken by the Government of Canada" to provide for adjudication of the claims received" that he thought warranted special action (PC 1969-2405).

As the Red Paper indicates, this approach was not viewed positively by Indian people. Dr Barber's appointment occurred without consultation, his mandate expressly excluded aboriginal title claims, and his authority was severely restricted. As a result of these inadequacies, very few Indian bands or associations presented their cases to his Commission. The atmosphere improved somewhat after Dr Barber was able to persuade the Prime Minister in August 1971 to expand his terms of reference so as to at least be able to study aboriginal rights issues and to make recommendations concerning federal policy on these matters.

Nevertheless, few results were demonstrated by this Commission other than in terms of research that it fostered or conducted directly. The Commissioner did play a very important role in educating government officials and the public at large through his many and varied speaking engagements.

The Commissioner was successful in obtaining compensation of approximately $250,000 for a breach of Treaty No. 7 regarding the provision of ammunition annually to the treaty signatories. Dr Barber described this event in a presentation to the Standing Committee on Indian Affairs and Northern Development in March of 1973 in these words:

> There are many Indian groups that wish to have immediate action on certain claims. In several cases I have responded to such groups and asked the Department of Indian Affairs and Northern Development to provide information and negotiate settlements. The example of the Treaty No. 7 ammunition allowance will illustrate the procedure I have followed in these cases.
>
> Treaty No. 7 covers all five bands of southern Alberta: the Blackfeet, Stony, Sarcee, Piegan and Blood. The treaty states:
>
> > Further, Her Majesty agrees that the sum of two thousand dollars shall hereafter every year be expended in the purchase of ammunition for distribution among the said Indians; Provided that if at any future time ammunition become comparatively unnecessary for said Indians, Her Government, with the consent of said Indians, or any of the Bands thereof, may expend the proportion due to such Band otherwise for their benefit.
>
> About fourteen years ago the Blackfeet prepared a petition for the Exchequer Court. Included in the petition was a claim that the ammunition provision of Treaty No. 7 had not been fulfilled. The petition was not acted upon and shortly after my appointment, at the Indians' request, I agreed to examine the situation to determine what contribution I might make. About one year ago I met in Calgary with representatives of all five bands of Treaty No. 7 regarding the ammunition provision of their treaty. The band representatives claimed at the meeting that their ammunition allowance had, at best, been provided only in a very few years and that they had no record or recollection of consenting to expenditures for their benefit in lieu of receipt of ammunition. They requested that I pursue the ammunition question with a view to settlement.
>
> When I received the request I was thinking a great deal about the efficacy of the negotiation process for the settlement of this type of claim. It seemed to me that if a prima facie case could be developed through examination of the records, long, costly and emotionally wasteful court or tribunal proceedings could be avoided were the Government simply to agree to negotiate a settlement based on the prima facie case. Accordingly, I recommended two things to the Government: first, that records about the ammunition provision of

Treaty No. 7 be collected, made available and examined by the Indians and Government; and second, that if the records bore out the contention of the bands that ammunition had not been provided and consent had not been obtained for alternative expenditures, the Government should negotiate a settlement with the people concerned.

Last fall the records, about a foot and a half of them, were made available. The evidence provided was relatively inconclusive, but the Government could not prove from the records that ammunition had been provided regularly or that consent had been obtained for alternative expenditures. Negotiations began.

Several meeting were held. The Government's position essentially was that they would pay two thousand dollars for 80 of the 96 years of the treaty, for a total of $160,000. The Indian position was that in addition to this sum an interest and inflation factor should be added and that costs incurred by the Indians to mount their case should be paid. Accordingly, they countered with an offer of $631,000. At a meeting in Calgary on March 1st this difference was reconciled and agreement reached on settlement.

The federal policy continued to be generally unsatisfactory and resulted in little progress towards the settlement of thousands of specific claims or towards the resolution of the major aboriginal title claims. The position changed dramatically with the decision of the Supreme Court of Canada in January 1973 in *Calder* v. *Attorney General of British Columbia*, [1973] SCR 313. Although the claim brought on behalf of the Nishga Indians was rejected by a bare majority of the Court, six of the seven judges supported the argument that aboriginal title was recognized by the common law of Canada.

This decision forced the federal government to develop a new land claims policy. The Minister of Indian Affairs and Northern Development, Jean Chrétien, issued a new policy on 8 August 1973.

(c) Claims of Indian and Inuit People, 1973

Many Indian groups in Canada have a relationship with the Federal Government which is symbolized in Treaties entered into by those people with the Crown in historic times. As the Government pledged some years ago, lawful obligations must be recognized. This remains the basis of Government policy.

The Federal Government's commitment to honour the Treaties was most recently restated by Her Majesty the Queen, when speaking to representatives of the Indian people of Alberta in Calgary on July 5. She said: "You may be assured that my Government of Canada recognizes the importance of full compliance with the spirit and terms of your Treaties."

This assurance and the present policy statement signify the Government's recognition and acceptance of its continuing responsibility under the British North America Act for Indians and lands reserved for Indians. The Government sees its position in this regard as an historic evolution dating back to the Royal Proclamation of 1763, which, whatever differences there may be about its judicial interpretation, stands as a basic declaration of the Indian people's interests in land in this country . . . .

The present statement is concerned with claims and proposals for the settlement of long-standing grievances. These claims come from groups of Indian people who have not entered into Treaty relationship with the Crown. They find their basis in what is variously described as "Indian Title" , "Aboriginal Title", "Original Title", "Native Title", or "Usufructuary Rights". In essence, these claims relate to the loss of traditional use and occupancy of lands in certain parts of Canada where Indian title was never extinguished by treaty or superseded by law . . . . The lands in question lie in British Columbia, Northern Quebec, the Yukon and Northwest Territories . . . .

The Government has been fully aware that the claims are not only for money and land, but involve the loss of a way of life. Any settlement, therefore, must contribute positively to a lasting solution of cultural, social and economic problems that for too long have kept the Indian and Inuit people in a disadvantaged position within the larger Canadian society.

It is basic to the position of the Government that these claims must be settled and that the most promising avenue to settlement is through negotiation. It is envisaged that by this means agreements will be reached with groups of the Indian and Inuit people concerned and that these agreements will be enshrined in legislation, enacted by Parliament, so that they will have the finality and binding force of law.

The Government is now ready to negotiate with authorized representatives of these native peoples on the basis that where their traditional interest in the lands concerned can be established, an agreed form of compensation or benefit will be provided to native peoples in return for their interest.

Not all of the lands in question are the sole concern of the Federal Government. In the Yukon and Northwest Territories, the Government has authority, to be exercised in full consultation with the Territorial Governments, to deal with interests in land. But for claims arising in the provinces concerned, provincial lands are involved and so are rights of Canadians living in those provinces. Settlements with Indian and Inuit groups in those provinces can only be satisfactorily reached if the provinces concerned participate along with the Government of Canada in the negotiation and settlement.

It is in the interest of those provinces and their residents that claims respecting land in the provinces be settled, and it is, therefore, reasonable to expect that provincial governments should be prepared to provide compensation. The Government has informed the provincial governments concerned of its position and urged them to take part in the negotiations envisaged . . . .

There are other areas of the country where no treaties of surrender were entered into, such as southern Quebec and the Atlantic provinces. The Government's view is that land claims in these areas are of a different character from those referred to earlier in this statement. The Indian people have submitted claims respecting their interests in land in these areas and the Government is examining them. The Government is providing funds to enable them to undertake the necessary research . . . .

This major development did suffer, however, from a critical defect. It divided aboriginal title claims expressly into two categories. Those claims which came from British Columbia, Northern Quebec, the Yukon, and the Northwest Territories (they were called "comprehensive claims") would receive a more favourable reaction than those stemming from southern Quebec and the four Atlantic provinces, which were claims of "a different character". This latter concept was never defined in this policy nor does it appear ever to have been described in greater detail subsequently. The policy also ignored the possibility of aboriginal title claims arising anywhere else in Canada.

The title is also interesting in that it specifically refers to the claims of the Inuit, yet the policy statement only makes passing references to their claims and never discusses those of the Metis.

The 1973 policy also reaffirmed the government's continued willingness to settle its outstanding "lawful obligations" to Indian people. This position was intended to encompass those grievances referred to in the policy statement as "specific claims", which included governmental maladministration of Indian lands and other assets under the various Indian Acts and Regulations enacted over the years, as well as those claims that exist with regard to the non-fulfilment of promises made within treaties and disagreements concerning the proper interpretation and scope of treaties or other agreements and proclamations.

The policy clearly indicated that the federal government preferred to address both comprehensive and specific claims through direct negotiation between DIAND and the claimants. DIAND has provided funding to Indian and Inuit associations to research and develop their claims leading to the submission of formal claims to the Minister. Additional grants and loans are then made available for the purposes of negotiating the claims. The Department does not generally give money for litigation.

The 1973 policy statement indirectly gave birth to a claims negotiation process. The rationale for this process was threefold. It was designed to provide an alternative to the courts of any other legal institution which might hear and decide upon the validity of specific or comprehensive claims. This meant that the parties themselves would actively participate in negotiating settlements of claims, rather than put them in the hands of a third party. It also allowed greater flexibility concerning the use of historical documentation and other evidence that might not be admissible in a court of law, yet could be very important in demonstrating the basis, or lack thereof, of individual claims.

A second important consideration from the federal standpoint was to

> . . . provide a forum which will take into account the interests of non-claimant groups in the area that may be affected by a claim settlement. Settlement of the claim must accommodate these interests, else settlement will merely give rise to another set of grievances. The involvement of the provincial or territorial governments is essential to ensure this accommodation. In the case of claims arising in the provinces, provincial participation is particularly necessary because lands and resources which may form part of a settlement are under provincial jurisdiction.[1]

The last main purpose particularly related to comprehensive claims in that the process was intended to

> . . . translate the concept of "aboriginal interest" into concrete and lasting benefits in the context of contemporary society. Such benefits can be many and varied. They can include lands; hunting, fishing and trapping rights; resource management; financial compensation; taxation; native participation in government structures; and native administration of the implementation of the settlement itself. Final settlement confirms these benefits in legislation, to give them the stability and binding force of law. The significance of the element of finality is that negotiations on the same claim cannot be reopened at some time in the future. It is recognized, however, that the relationship between native people and the Government is a dynamic one and must be allowed to evolve over time. Final agreements must provide for change as circumstances may require in the future.[2]

In order to implement this claims negotiation process, DIAND established the Office of Native Claims (ONC) in July 1974 to handle all claims on behalf of the Minister that were submitted to the Government of Canada. It is ONC which reviews and analyzes all claim submissions, does further research from a governmental perspective, communicates with any other relevant federal department or agency, and discusses the substance and foundation of the claim with the claimant band or association. The Office is also involved in negotiating any compensation that pertains to the settlement of specific and comprehensive claims. Finally, it advises the Minister concerning further developments in the federal claims policy. ONC has specifically described its role and responsibilities in the following circular, which was last revised in July 1980:

1. To receive comprehensive and specific claims from native groups and associations which are referred to Office by Minister of Indian and Northern Affairs. ''Comprehensive claims'' are based on loss of ''native interest'' in areas of Canada where it has not been extinguished by treaty or superseded by law; ''specific claims'' are based on government's alleged maladministration of Indian assets under treaties or Indian Act, or failure to fulfill provisions of treaties and Indian Act relating to specific bands.

2. To represent Minister of Department of Indian and Northern Affairs (DINA) in discussions with native groups and associations concerning validity of their claims; to act as representative of Minister and Federal Government in negotiation of claims which are accepted, and to develop advice concerning their resolution or other dispositions.

3. To identify potential policy issues and to advise of further development of policy relating to both comprehensive and specific claims, including policy on funding of claims research, development and negotiations and other related activities.

4. To advise on overall strategy for dealing with comprehensive and specific claims, whether through negotiations or other means that may evolve, with view to ensuring coordination and consistency in government's total approach to claims settlement.

5. To be responsible for carrying out analysis and such further supplementary research as may be necessary for discharge of foregoing responsibilities and to maintain liaison with native groups and associations, federal department, provincial and territorial governments, and any special agency, commission or body that may be established from time to time and which may have an interest in native claims.

6. To maintain close liaison with other sections of DINA concerning claims processes, revision of Indian Act, and other policy developments relating to claims.

7. To initiate, assist with and monitor as required the implementation of claims settlements by Programs in DINA and other departments, governments and agencies, within their respective areas of competence.

8. To provide public information concerning native claims, including all material on native claims for public statements by Minister and government.

The actual process in handling claims has been described by ONC in these terms:

> When comprehensive or specific claims are referred to the Office, the first step is a careful analysis by ONC staff. Included in this analysis is an examination of the supporting documentation submitted by the claimant group and of the results of the Office's own research on the claim. In cases where clarification is needed on some of the elements of the claim, the Office arranges for meetings to be held with the claimant group to discuss the issues. The claim is also referred to the Department of Justice for a legal review and analysis, and to other departments that may be involved, for their comments. The last step in the process is reference of the documentation to the Minister of Indian Affairs, for a formal response to the claim on behalf of the Government of Canada. If the evidence produced by the claimant group substantiates the claim, the Office of Native Claims initiates negotiations under the Minister's direction. Where the findings do not substantiate the claim, the claimants are so advised and are provided with copies of the key documents used by the Government in rendering its opinion on the merits of the claim. In some cases, the findings may reveal insufficient grounds for negotiation, but the claim may be capable of redress through existing programs of the department or the government. In addition, the Government has reviewed claims that had previously been rejected, in cases where new evidence has been found which might support them.
>
> Although the process has been seen as an alternative to the courts, the validity of a claim is determined by the Department of Justice according to its view of the application of the existing common law and legislation. Notions of morality, fairness, and unconscionable dealings does not enter into such an analysis.

The Metis have largely been excluded from this process since the Government of Canada has taken the view that they have no land claims. This position has been most recently reiterated by the Minister of Justice, Jean Chrétien, despite the passage of the Constitution Act with its reference to the aboriginal rights of all Aboriginal Peoples, including the Metis.

The Indian and Inuit people have been dissatisfied with the federal claims policy. Even the Minister of Indian Affairs and Northern Development, John Munro, stated in the Spring of 1982 that

> To date progress in resolving specific claims has been very limited indeed. Claimants have felt hampered by inadequate research capabilities and insufficient funding; government lacked a clear, articulate policy. The result, too often, was frustration and anger. This could not be allowed to continue.

Only one significant comprehensive claim has been settled, resulting in the James Bay and Northern Quebec Agreement, along with its subsequent addition in the form of the Northeastern Quebec Agreement. Although negotiations have been conducted regularly regarding other comprehensive claims, alleged deficiencies in the federal policy has rendered settlements unobtainable elsewhere.

It must be realized that dissatisfaction with the federal land claims policy and process has not occurred in isolation. The Metis and non-status Indians have continually objected to the federal government's position that these people are not 91(24) BNA Act Indians and therefore have no unique constitutional rights. As a result of this opinion, Metis and non-status Indians do not benefit from any special legislation nor do they receive any services directly from DIAND.[3]

The Inuit, who have been judicially defined as s. 91(24) BNA Act Indians, have also felt frustrated by the lack of federal legislation which would protect their aboriginal rights and implement their special constitutional status. In addition, they have been disappointed with the quality and quantity of social and economic assistance they have received over the years from DIAND.

Status Indians have been the most vociferous regarding the paternalistic and inadequate response of DIAND to their needs (as described in Chapter One). Furthermore, they have objected to many aspects of the Indian Act which have retarded their development while simultaneously permitting their aboriginal and treaty rights to be infringed.

A mechanism was established in October 1974 to address the wide variety of concerns of Indian people with the federal government. A joint committee consisting of the leadership of the National Indian Brotherhood (NIB) and members of Cabinet was struck to discuss Indian complaints in broad terms, while a sub-committee of three pertinent Ministers and three Indian leaders of NIB met to negotiate solutions about specific problems. In order to facilitate this process, an independent entity, entitled the Canadian Indian Rights Commission (CIRC), was eventually established by the Privy Council on 17 March 1977 to act as a secretariat, to chair the meetings and to categorize and make an inventory of Indian land claims. The CIRC consisted of the former executive director of the Indian Claims Commission, Brian Pratt, and a member of the Supreme Court of Ontario, Mr Justice E.P. Hartt. The Indian Claims Commission was dissolved and its former Commissioner, Dr Lloyd Barber, was appointed by the Privy Council with powers under Part I of the federal Inquiries Act to collect evidence from Indian elders concerning land claims.

The NIB publicly withdrew from the Joint NIB-Cabinet Committee on 13 April 1978 in protest for its lack of progress, the absence of federal commitment to this process, and because of the Brotherhood's feeling that "the government was purposefully eroding Indian rights and attempting to implement its 1969 White Paper."[4] This meant a cessation of the joint federal-Indian initiative to revise the government's claims policy. It also left the Canadian Indian Rights Commission without a real function to fulfil in the claims field other than the development of an inventory of known, outstanding claims. It later disbanded upon completion of that project for the Ontario region.

The four Ontario Indian Associations were unwilling to give up completely on this type of format for political consultation and negotiation. Therefore, they approached the Minister of Indian Affairs and Northern Development with a proposal to create a new structure that would apply only to Indians in Ontario. The Minister then sought and obtained the approval and participation of the provincial government. In the summer of 1978 a Tripartite Council was established, comprised of federal and provincial ministers and the leaders of the Indian Associations through their joint organization, the Chiefs of Ontario.

The Indian commission of Ontario (ICO) was constituted on 28 September 1978 to facilitate these tripartite discussions at political and technical levels. Mr Justice Hartt was appointed as the sole Commissioner to continue the role he had played with the CIRC in assisting the parties to maintain a forum for dialogue and in making progress on issues of mutual interest. One of these common interests concerned the settlement of certain identified specific claims in Ontario.

Many Indian associations and bands have developed position papers or submissions for DIAND in which their objections to the federal claims policy are discussed and proposals for reform are made. Although these positions have tended to focus primarily upon that aspect of the federal claims policy that has the greatest impact upon their region of the country — namely, on comprehensive or specific claims or claims of a different character — the content of the criticisms concerning the claims process and the role of ONC is largely the same.

Three Indian associations in Ontario — the Association of Iroquois and Allied Indians, Grand Council Treaty #3, and the Union of Ontario Indians — developed a joint position, which was presented to the Minister of Indian Affairs on 11 April 1981. It, perhaps, best typifies the level and nature of Indian concerns regarding the federal claims policy. It also represents the views of Indian people who have made numerous efforts to work within the boundaries of the federal policy while attempting to broaden its scope. These associations have had the added experience of the special claims process that has existed in Ontario since the initiation of the ICO.

(d) A New Proposal for Claims Resolution in Ontario, 1981
Association of Iroquois and Allied Indians, Grand Council
Treaty #3, and Union of Ontario Indians

INADEQUACIES OF THE PRESENT SYSTEM

1. *The Department of Indian Affairs as judge and defendant*

When an Indian claimant presents a claim to the Federal Government, it is always referred to the Office of Native Claims (ONC) for review and research. The ONC statement of facts regarding the claim is then sent to Justice lawyers for their opinion as to whether the government has a "lawful obligation" (see below). Finally, a claim with ONC and Justice opinions attached is sent to the Minister for final acceptance or rejection. Only then will a band or Indian claimant be told if their claim is accepted for negotiation on compensation. In this way, the Department acts as judge of the claim, usually against itself.

In negotiating an agreement with an Indian claimant for compensation, the Department is placed in a position of defending the federal government's authority and purse. On the other hand, it is generally recognized that the federal government has a trust relationship under s. 91(24) of the BNA Act to protect "Indians and lands reserved for Indians".

2. *Government policy to "honour lawful obligations"*

In 1973, Hon. Jean Chrétien, Minister of Indian Affairs, declared the policy of the federal government to "honour lawful obligations". No one since — or before — has taken the time to define what this phrase means. Recent experience with ONC has indicated that the phrase is interpreted to mean that, if in the opinion of a Justice lawyer, the government could lose a case, if an Indian claimant went to court, then the government has a "lawful obligation". However. the judgement on the "validity" of a claim is made usually by one lawyer within the Department of Justice, often on facts presented and arranged by the Department not by the Indian claimant.

Due to the inconsistent application of this policy, there is confusion across Canada over what claims the Department is willing to negotiate. "Lawful Obligations" standard is often used to refuse responsibility toward 'moral' obligations of the government. The lawyer's opinion may be based on strict legal liability, depending on technical rules of evidence or limitation periods to reject a claim. The whole policy is "general and undefined" and tends to be too legalistic to permit just and equitable settlements.

3. *Research Categories*

The Department of Indian Affairs has stated there are four types of claims. Specific Claims relate to failure to live up to the terms of the treaties or mismanagement under successive Indian Acts. Comprehensive claims refer to those based on traditional use and occupancy of the land if Indian interest has not been "extinguished by treaty" nor "superseded by law". It is debatable in many areas of the country if Indian people would see their interest extinguished or rather recognized through treaty. The Department fails to define what is meant by "superseded by law" but decides to apply this label to areas of contention. For example, the aboriginal rights claim of Nova Scotia Indians was rejected as being "superseded by law", yet the same federal government is willing to negotiate British Columbia Indian claims which that provincial government argues have been "superseded by law".

In effect, the government is agreeing to a policy of "expropriation without compensation". The fourth undefined category are "claims of a different character; which the 1973 Policy says refer to the Atlantic region and Quebec, but which remain vague notions against which Indian claimants are told they have no defence.

The labels and divisions between claims invented by the Department do not reflect reality and have even created problems.

Throughout Ontario, there are aboriginal rights cases existing along with specific claims against the government for mismanagement. One 'type' is not exclusive of another. Yet, the Department requires a different standard of proof of each. If a comprehensive claim, evidence is presented on the basis of traditional use and occupancy and does not have to prove a "lawful obligation" on the part of the government that a specific claim does.

4. *Research Funding*

The Department of Indian Affairs Corporate Policy Branch has two committees dealing with claims, the Claims Policy Committee which ONC sits on with Research Funding and other Directors, and Research Funding, which ONC also sits on. Thus, the branch which reviews the claim and advises the Minister on acceptance also has a say in how much money each region will receive to research and document specific claims . . . .

Allocations are made on a year to year basis, thereby preventing long term planning and hiring commitments. There has been no increase in the past four years.

Funding policy clearly states that research funds cannot be used for litigation. Departmental policy will not support defences of charges against status Indians when a right is being defended. They will only consider litigation funding at an appeal level.

Treasury Board has been reluctant to increase funding because no claims have been settled. Organizations are reluctant to present claims to ONC because the process is not fair and not working. ONC recommends no increases in funding because no claims are being presented and settled. A 'Catch-22' situation has developed.

5. *Access to Documents*

Indian organizations have encountered difficulties in obtaining uncensored, fully intact files regarding band claims. Particularly at the regional level, documents are lifted from files 'screened' before the Organization researcher sees the file . . . .

In Ontario, we also have the *Office of Indian Resource Policy* which was established in 1976 to review Indian claims against the province. The main criticism is that this branch wields authority but operates in secret. There is no information regarding how claims are judged or processed, and no involvement of Indian people in developing policy. However, the OIRP operates within the Ministry of Natural Resources, judged by most Indian people to be the provincial department most in the forefront in denying Indian rights.

In Ontario, there also exists the Indian Commission of Ontario. The ICO was developed with advice from the Chiefs of Ontario and acts to facilitate the working of the tripartite forum (Canada-Ontario-Chiefs of Ontario). The ICO also seeks to facilitate claims resolution and has made some inroads in gaining OND's acceptance of developing a joint statement of facts to be argued upon before being sent to Justice. However, the ICO has no powers of coercion to force the parties to meet deadlines, share information or make progress . . . .

[The paper then proceeds to discuss the advantages and disadvantages of settling claims through the courts, independent commissions, and legislated settlements based upon the experience of Indian Inuit people in North America.]

PRINCIPLES OF CLAIMS RESOLUTION:

STANDARDS AND PROCEDURES

SUMMARY:

1. The goal of any claims resolution process or standards must be the fair and permanent resolution of the claims.
2. The standard of "lawful obligations" now used by the Government of Canada is in fact one of "legal" obligations with a political review or veto. It owes more to the statutes and precedents of the law ("if this went to court, is it likely that we would be found liable?") than to the principles of the law that the word "lawful" implies.

3. "Lawful obligations" could be defined more precisely through the passing of a statute that clarifies that the "governmental obligations" of the Government of Canada to Indian groups are both "lawful" and enforceable.

4. The nature of the trust relationship between Canada and the Indian peoples requires more study and definition, but this should not prevent the clarification through statute that the "governmental obligations" are enforceable ones, included in the definition of "lawful obligations".

5. "Validation" and "compensation" are separate phases of the resolution process and can be accomplished through separate methods, if desirable.

6. The Indian governments always retain the rights to select other domestic or international forums for settling their claims. The introduction of new processes should not close the door on older ones, which may remain appropriate in certain cases. No method of dispute resolution should ever be imposed upon the Indian claimants at anytime. A final and binding decision making alternative can only be utilized when the claimants agree to choose this option.

7. The success of any process is totally dependent on the degree of commitment to it by the participants. Commitment includes dedication of effort and resources, and good faith.

8. The existing Indian Affairs process is not acceptable to claimants in most situations. The courts are generally inappropriate for the resolution of Indian claims.

9. Other issues require decisions of principle, though the decisions should not block decisions on standards and processes: divisions of claims into categories; pre-Confederation responsibility of the Crown; funding of claimants . . . .

A NEW VALIDITY STANDARD FOR INDIAN CLAIMS

Government commitment to honour only its "lawful obligations" respecting Indian claims has been a primary cause of failure of recent claims processes. Government has not defined the phrase and has in practice interpreted it narrowly and technically. It is essential that any new claims process set out, as precisely as possible, what standard or standards are to be applied.

It is proposed that a new validity standard for Indian claims be incorporated in the mandate, statutory or otherwise, of the proposed new resolution mechanism. The standard would be structured as and found within a listing of the types of grievances or disputes which would give rise to valid claims. One of these types (#9 on the following list) would define the *concept* of "lawful obligations", and breach by government of that *concept*, even without reference to the more straightforward types of claims also included in the list, would be sufficient to establish the validity of a claim.

The proposed list is as follows:

Claims by Indians based upon and establishing any one or more of the following shall be valid.

1. Breach by government or the Crown of any Treaty or agreement between Indians and the Crown or representatives of the Crown.
2. Breach by government or the Crown of any obligation arising out of the Indian Act, regulations thereunder, or any statute or regulation pertaining directly or indirectly to Indians or Indian lands, as have been in force from time to time.
3. Breach by government or the Crown of any obligation arising out of the Royal Proclamation of 1763.
4. Breach by government or the Crown of any obligation to Indians arising out of the sale or other disposition of Indian lands.
5. Breach by government or the Crown of any obligation to Indians arising out of government management of Indian funds or assets.
6. Invalidity of any surrender of Indian land or rights, including claims arising out of the making of any Treaty.
7. Failure of government or the Crown to provide compensation, or adequate compensation, for lands owned and occupied by Indians and taken, damaged or adversely affected by any government or agency of government or any private individual or corporation pursuant to legislation or pursuant to any authority from any government or with the knowledge of any government.
8. Denial or derogation by government or the Crown of any rights or benefits due to individual Indians; or mismanagement by government or the Crown of any assets of individual Indians.
9. Breach by government or the Crown of any lawful obligation to Indians, including legal obligations, governmental obligations or obligations arising out of a trust in the higher sense, and obligations arising out of any unconscionable dealings or unjust enrichment of which government or the Crown was, or should have been, on notice.

> For purposes of this paragraph, legal obligations shall include any duty to Indians lying in law or equity; whether or not such duty may be enforceable in a court of law by reason of technical rules of law including limitations periods, the doctrine of laches and perpetuities, or for any other reason; and whether or not such duty may have been repealed or superseded by subsequent law.
>
> For purposes of this paragraph, the Crown as trustee for Indians

is under a governmental obligation or an obligation arising out of a trust in the higher sense when the Crown or its officers discharges a duty to the Indians, which duty is a function belonging to the perogative of authority of the Crown, and whether or not discharge of that duty would be one out of which obligations in a court of law would arise.

For purposes of this validity standard, all instruments and agreements entered into by Indians shall be interpreted according to common law and equitable rules of interpretation; and shall be interpreted largely and liberally and in a manner consistent with the Indian interpretation of such instruments and agreements as understood by Indians at the time of making of such instruments and agreements; and shall be interpreted in a manner consistent with, or incorporating, any oral promises and representations which may have been made at the time of making of such instruments and agreements; and silence of any such instruments or agreements as to any matter or particular shall not be construed as evidence of lack or relinquishment of any Indian right.

For purposes of this validity standard, the Government of Canada shall be deemed to have assumed all obligations of pre-Confederation governments, and all obligations of the Imperial Crown and of any agencies of the Crown whether the same came into existence before or after Confederation.

For purposes of this validity standard, Indian lands shall be deemed to include waters and resources.

THE PROCESS

Our proposal includes the creation of a new method of settling outstanding claims. This method is strictly intended to lead to the establishment of a new approach to resolving Indian grievances. It must *not* be viewed as being the only avenue available to Indian governments who wish to settle their claims, but instead be seen as a new alternative. Existing options within Canada, such as the courts, and outside Canada, such as the United Nations or international tribunals, must and will continue to be open to Indian governments.

The overall proposal is to establish a representative, yet independent, commission to function within a newly created claims resolution process. Negotiations should commence forthwith concerning this proposal and its specific terms. It is our recommendation that a memorandum of agreement be developed and signed between the provincial Indian association(s), the federal government and the provincial government. This agreement should then be incorporated within legislation as an appendix thereto, which is concurrently enacted as a statute by both governments and by the Indian association(s). This general approach has been used on many occasions over the years in relation to other international treaties and federal-provincial agreements. The agreement would delineate the legislative mandate of the claims commission, the non-binding intervenors, and the binding dispute resolution mechanism as well as clearly defining the standards of validity to be used in assessing claims.

A refusal by any particular province to agree would not jettison this scheme, but would instead cause only a bilateral arrangement to be possible between the federal and Indian governments. In this situation, Indian governments would merely be able to pursue claims against the federal government under this new system.

The function envisioned for this proposed claims commission is as follows:

(a) It would develop a roster of expert mediators, conciliators and arbitrators for the use of the parties. The commission would recruit promising candidates and provide them with a training program on land claims and the skills necessary to act as third party intevenors. Indian participation must be included in the development of the training program and in its implementation;

(b) It would receive formal requests from the parties for its assistance in selecting external intervenors and would provide a secretariat function to the persons selected;

(c) It would also have a quasi-judicial function in receiving complaints alleging a breach of the duty to bargain in good faith. This duty would be a statutory one imposed on all sides through the agreement and its enabling legislation. Alleged violations of this duty could be brought before the commission upon a motion of any party seeking a resolution to their complaint of a breach. A full hearing would be held in which all pertinent evidence would be introduced, followed by arguments based upon the parameters of the duty and its application to the facts would be submitted to the commission. The commissioners would then deliver their ruling and grant the remedy sought by the applicant, if the complaint is upheld. The commission should be given the power to grant declarations or remedial orders. The latter should range from an order to furnish relevant information to the applicant, an order to convene negotiation meetings, or an order directing the violator to agree to the provision of a specific form of non-binding intervention. The applicant would indicate the specific remedy it desired; and the order would be binding upon the parties and enforceable as an order of the Supreme Court of Ontario;

(d) It may be engaged in educating the public at large on land claims and the settlement thereof; and it may assist in allaying any fears of owners of land within a claimed area; and

(e) It may provide general information upon request to any of the three parties on: land claims research, how to research and develop a claim, and the specific options available for resolving the claim.

The proposed commission's mandate would largely reflect a merger of the responsibilities of human rights commissions and labour relations boards across Canada. It would have a supportive function in assisting the parties through its role in training and providing third party intervenors as well as through the provision of general assistance. It would also have a quasi-judicial function in handling alleged violations of the duty to bargain in good faith . . . .

The commission must be constituted and it is recommended that it be comprised of nominees of the different sides and a neutral chairperson. The government nominees would be representatives of the Crown directly rather than of the specific governments. This is to ensure that the Crown in all its constituent parts is being properly represented so that all forms of Crown liability can be addressed. The Indian nominees would be on the commission as representatives of all the Indian people within that province as opposed to just reflecting the interests of a particular association.

For a province in which the provincial government agrees to participate, the commission would be constituted as follows: 1 Federal government nominee; 1 Provincial government nominee; 2 Indian government nominees; and 1 Chairperson.

Where the provincial government refuses to participate, the commission would be comprised solely of three members as follows: 1 Federal government nominee; 1 Indian government nominee; and 1 Chairperson. In either situation, the chairperson would be selected by way of unanimous agreement of all the parties concerned. This type of approach is based on the model of tripartite labour-management arbitration boards and it ensures that the commission will be knowledgeable, representative and independent. . . .

The claimant band is initially in control of the process directed towards the settlement of its claim. Only the band determines when a claim is fully researched and ready for submission to the relevant governments. Once the claim has been presented, however, it will then proceed on the basis of agreement through negotiations and non-binding intervention. The band cannot unilaterally demand that the other side submit to one of the various forms of outside assistance. If any government does refuse to respond to a suggestion made by the claimant, then the only remedy for the band within this process is to apply to the commission for a decision on its allegation of bad faith bargaining.

The only subsequent decision which a claimant can impose upon the federal and/or provincial Crown is the decision to go to binding arbitration. It is our expectation that the federal and provincial governments will be sufficiently interested in resolving claims that they will readily agree to engage in binding arbitration. If this should not transpire, then it is recommended that the claimant have the sole authority to impose arbitration upon the other parties, as it can decide to pursue the resolution of its grievance through other domestic or international channels.

The agreement to refer the claim to arbitration should specifically determine what is being referred. That is, arbitration could be used to decide only the validity or invalidity of the claim, with the issue of compensation for valid claims being left to the parties for a negotiated settlement or another series of steps up the ladder. Alternatively, arbitration could be used as a last stage solely to settle the quantum of compensation that is appropriate. It also would be possible to refer both issues to the same arbitration board simultaneously for a binding decision on both. We recommend that the two issues be completely severed, as they are at present, to avoid confusion and potentially unnecessary effort as compensation is only relevant once it has been agreed that the claim is a valid one . . . .

[The paper continues to discuss this process in greater detail].

In summary, we are proposing what we believe to be a comprehensive and workable system for resolving Indian land claims in Canada. It has been designed to be as equitable and flexible as possible, while at the same time maximizing the abilities of the parties to maintain control over the process. It, as with any system of dispute resolution, is predicated upon the good will and good faith of the different sides of the disputes. It is to be hoped that the necessary degree of these characteristics is present, for without them no system can function.

In general, the Minister of Indian Affairs and Northern Development responded positively to this presentation. The Executive Director of the ONC was instructed to pursue talks with the three associations using their proposal as a basis for the development of a new specific claims policy. A number of meetings were held with the staff of these associations in the spring of 1981. At the same time, the ONC was holding discussions with all other Indian associations in Canada regarding the federal government's willingness to revise its policy for all claims as a result of its lack of success to date. The Indian associations were given the impression that the Government of Canada understood the defects in its claims policy and was prepared to transform it completely. This, however, did not happen.

3. The New Federal Claims Policy

The Minister of Indian Affairs released a booklet in December 1981 that was designed to reflect the position of Cabinet on comprehensive claims after it had reviewed the 1973 policy on this matter. *In All Fairness* briefly describes the government's early policy concerning aboriginal title, the background to the development of a new policy statement in 1973, and how that policy has been implemented. It indicates how the government had reviewed the experiences of some other countries in dealing with comprehensive land claims and rejected those alternatives in favour of the negotiation process. It further states as basic guidelines that:

> When a land claim is accepted for negotiation, the government requires that the negotiation process and settlement formula be thorough so that the claim cannot arise again in the future. In other words, any claims settlement will be final. The negotiations are designed to deal with non-political matters arising from the notion of aboriginal land rights such as lands, cash compensation, wildlife rights, and may include self-government on a local basis.
>
> The thrust of this policy is to exchange undefined aboriginal land rights for concrete rights and benefits. The settlement legislation will guarantee these rights and benefits.[5]

After discussing each form of possible compensation in a settlement, the policy goes on to say that the same "practices in relation to determining the validity of claims will continue to be used."[6] In other words, the government would continue to analyze the validity of a particular claim based upon its view of the prevailing law and would continue to require the involvement of provincial governments before negotiating claims within southern Canada.

In May of 1982, the federal government released another publication, *Outstanding Business*, as a result of its review of the specific claims area. It also briefly reviews the pertinent history, this time in relation to treaties, the Indian Act, and the policy of honouring Canada's lawful obligations to Indian people outlined in the 1969 White Paper and the 1973 policy statement on land claims. It then summarizes common positions of Indian organizations as follows:

> In the first instance Indian groups have complained that the lawful obligation criterion has been too narrow to permit their claims to be dealt with fairly and hence has been an inhibiting factor in their resolution. They believe that claims should be based on moral and equitable grounds as well as lawful obligation and these should be clearly set out. They also wish to ensure that the lawful obligation criterion is not interpreted as only allowing for claims that originated after Confederation. In all cases it was the view that treaty rights respecting land, hunting, fishing and trapping should be met and should

be fairly interpreted. Moreover, it was contended that the federal government has had an historical trust responsibility for Indian bands and their assets, and that particular actions taken by the government over the years have breached such responsibility.

With regard to the assessment of claims, Indian representatives stated that rules of evidence, time limitations and other procedural defences should be relaxed or eliminated. They added that oral tradition should be accepted as evidence. It was further stated that Indians should have access to Department of Justice opinions so that adequate responses could be prepared.

In terms of process it was held that the department should actively assist in the preparation of claims, making internal documents more easily available and generally acting in a supporting role. The Office of Native Claims should either be disbanded or given a more liberal mandate to settle claims. It was also held that the government should not unilaterally assess the validity of a claim but rather that greater efforts should be made at reaching consensus on facts and merits. Independent third parties should be used to facilitate settlements especially in the role of mediator. The use of courts for certain claims may be desirable but, in the Indian view, government should provide funding for court action and be prepared to negotiate while claims are under litigation. Furthermore, funding assistance should be increased in amount and extended as accountable contributions to all phases of the claims process.

In the area of compensation, the general view expressed was that bands should be restored to positions held before loss. Many of the bands view claims not only as a means to restore or improve their land base but to obtain necessary capital for socio-economic development. Where non-Indians are occupying claimed lands, such lands should be returned to the bands concerned and, if necessary, the former occupants compensated by the government.

Indian representatives all stated, in the strongest of terms, that Indian views must be considered in the development of any new or modified claims policy. It was also pointed out, in nearly every case, that any national policy for claims resolution should take account of regional variations in the nature of claims and in the circumstances lying behind them.

All of these views have been taken into consideration by the government in developing new policy initiatives as outlined in the next section. The policy as now adopted by the government, while not meeting in full the wishes of the Indian people in the area of specific claims, will clarify procedures and liberalize past practice. In effect, the government has done its best to meet the aspirations of the Indians, while maintaining the required degree of fiscal responsibility.

Moreover, the government will continue to fund the specific claims process through both contributions and loans, assist in the provision of documentation and enter into negotiations in a spirit of good faith.[7]

After reading such a relatively thorough summary of the broad perceptions of Indian people concerning the federal specific claims policy, one would expect to see major changes in the policy. This reaction is further promoted by the statement's use of language such as

Together with this effort at meeting the concerns of Indian people . . . .[8]

The policy . . . while not meeting in full the wishes of the Indian people . . . will . . . liberalize past practice.[9]

The government has clearly established that its primary objective with respect to specific claims is to discharge its lawful obligations as determined by the courts if necessary. Negotiation, however, remains the preferred means of settlement . . . . In order to make this process easier, the government has now adopted a more liberal approach eliminating some of the existing barriers to negotiations.[10]

Outstanding Business, however, then describes the gist of the federal policy as follows:

1) Lawful Obligation

The government's policy on specific claims is that it will recognize claims by Indian bands which disclose an outstanding "lawful obligation", i.e., an obligation derived from the law on the part of the federal government.
A lawful obligation may arise in any of the following circumstances:

  (i)   The non-fulfilment of a treaty or agreement between Indians and the Crown.
  (ii) A breach of an obligation arising out of the *Indian Act* or other statutes pertaining to Indians and the regulations thereunder.
  (iii) A breach of an obligation arising out of government administration of Indian funds or other assets.
  (iv) An illegal disposition of Indian land.

2) Beyond Lawful Obligation

In addition to the foregoing, the government is prepared to acknowlege claims which are based on the following circumstances:

  (i)   Failure to provide compensation for reserve lands taken or damaged by the federal government or any of its agencies under authority.
  (ii) Fraud in connection with the acquisition or disposition of Indian

reserve land by employees or agents of the federal government, in cases where the fraud can be clearly demonstrated.

3) Statutes of Limitation and the Doctrine of Laches

Statutes of Limitation are federal or provincial statutes which state that if one has a legitimate grievance, yet fails to take action in the courts within a prescribed length of time, the right to take legal action is lost. The right to take action on a valid civil claim, therefore, will expire after a certain length of time unless legal proceedings have been started.

The doctrine of laches is a practice which has come into observance over the years. It is, therefore, a common law rule as opposed to a specific piece of legislation passed in Parliament. The doctrine is based on actual cases whereby people lose certain rights and privileges if they fail to assert or exercise them over an unreasonable period of time.

With respect to Canadian Indians, however, the government has decided to negotiate each claim on the basis of the issues involved. Bands with longstanding grievances will not have their claims rejected before they are even heard because of the technicalities provided under the statutes of limitation or under the doctrine of laches. In other words, the government is not going to refrain from negotiating specific claims with Native people on the basis of these statutes or this doctrine. However, the government does reserve the right to use these statutes or this doctrine in a court case.

What the government has basically done, then, is to clarify the phrase "lawful obligation" by giving several concrete examples of types of claims which would give rise to legal liability in the courts if the Crown in right of Canada were to be sued by an Indian band. Although two additional headings of claims have been classified as going "beyond lawful obligation," this is not completely accurate since they both can form the basis for legal liability under the general law and have been previously accepted as such by the ONC and the Minister. This, then, does not liberalize or change the former policy; it merely describes the standard emanating from the 1969 White Paper more fully. This last extract also restates what had been recent federal practice regarding technical defences. That is, although a claim will be evaluated on its merits within the negotiation process, these defences may be relied upon in opposing any litigation initiated by a claimant.

The policy statement also outlines the process for resolving specific claims. It simply describes the pre-existing process established in 1974, without any reference to the possibility for flexibility in this process or for developing innovative alternatives. In doing so, it does not exclude the creation of new options; however, neither does it suggest any federal interest in considering variations to this process. This is somewhat surprising since the publication also mentions that only 250 specific claims for all of Canada had been presented to DIAND by December 1981, when over 400 claims for Ontario alone had been identified by the CIRC in a partial inventory in 1978. By December 1981 out of the 250 claims presented, only 12 had been settled and 17 rejected. Two additional claims were settled in early 1982, however, in both cases the staff of ONC indicated that the legal opinion from the Department of Justice was negative and that they could not have been resolved under this new policy because of its emphasis upon standards of legal liability and the importance placed upon the legal opinion of the Department of Justice.

Outstanding Business then contains guidelines regarding the process of submitting and assessing specific claims as well as standards for determining appropriate levels of compensation. These guidelines are stated as forming an "integral part of the government's policy".

Submission and Assessment of Specific Claims

Guidelines for the submission and assessment of specific claims may be summarized as follows:

1) Specific claims shall be submitted by the claimant band to the Minister of Indian Affairs and Northern Development.
2) The claimant bringing the claim shall be the band suffering the alleged grievance, or a group of bands, if all are bringing the same claim.
3) There shall be a statement of claim which sets out the particulars of the claim, including the facts upon which the claim is based.
4) Each claim shall be judged on its own facts and merits.
5) The government will not refuse to negotiate claims on the grounds that they are submitted too late (statutes of limitation) or because the claimants have waited too long to present their claims (doctrine of laches).
6) All relevant historic evidence will be considered and not only evidence which, under strict legal rules, would be admissible in a court of law.
7) Claims based on unextinguished native title shall not be dealt with under the specific claims policy.
8) No claims shall be entertained based on events prior to 1867 unless the federal government specifically assumed responsibility therefor.
9) Treaties are not open to renegotiation.
10) The acceptance of a claim for negotiation is not to be interpreted as an admission of liability and, in the event that no settlement is reached and litigation ensues, the government reserves the right to plead all defences available to it, including limitation periods, laches and lack of admissible evidence.

Compensation

The following criteria shall govern the determination of specific claims compensation:

1) As a general rule, a claimant band shall be compensated for the loss it has incurred and the damages it has suffered as a consequence of the breach by the federal government of its lawful obligations. This compensation will be based on legal principles.

2) Where a claimant band can establish that certain of its reserve lands were taken or damaged under legal authority, but that no compensation was ever paid, the band shall be compensated by the payment of the value of these lands at the time of the taking or the amount of the damage done, whichever is the case.

3) (i) Where a claimant band can establish that certain of its reserve lands were never lawfully surrendered, or otherwise taken under legal authority, the band shall be compensated either by the return of these lands or by payment of the current, unimproved value of the lands.

   (ii) Compensation may include an amount based on the loss of use of the lands in question, where it can be established that the claimants did in fact suffer such a loss. In every case the loss shall be the net loss.

4) Compensation shall not include any additional amount based on "special value to owner," unless it can be established that the land in question had a special economic value to the claimant band, over and above its market value.

5) Compensation shall not include any additional amount for the forcible taking of land.

6) Where compensation received is to be used for the purchase of other lands, such compensation may include reasonable acquisition costs, but these must not exceed 10% of the appraised value of the lands to be acquired.

7) Where it can be justified, a reasonable portion of the costs of negotiation may be added to the compensation paid. Legal fees included in those costs will be subject to the approval of the Department of Justice.

8) In any settlement of specific native claims the government will take third party interests into account. As a general rule, the government will not accept any settlement which will lead to third parties being dispossessed.

9) Any compensation paid in respect to a claim shall take into account any previous expenditure already paid to the claimant in respect to the same claim.

10) The criteria set out above are general in nature and the actual

amount which the claimant is offered will depend on the extent to which the claimant has established a valid claim, the burden of which rests with the claimant. As an example, where there is doubt that the lands in question were ever reserve land, the degree of doubt will be reflected in the compensation offered.

CONCLUSION

The Government of Canada is committed to resolving specific claims in a fair and equitable manner. At the same time it recognizes that over the years the existing process has not been effective in resolving them in any significant degree. The new policy initiatives outlined in this publication are meant to correct this situation. The injection of new resources for research, development and the processing of claims is a measure of the depth of this government's commitment.

The thrust of this policy, then, is towards the final redress of particular Indian specific claims, each of which will be evaluated "on its own facts and merits". A formal release will be required from the claimants upon settlement so that the matter can not be reopened in the future. The claimant band will have to research its claim in full so that it can make a case under prevailing legal standards, disregarding technical defences, that a lawful obligation exists upon the Crown which must be honoured through compensation. Political and legal assertions were made by federal representatives in the Parliaments of Canada and the United Kingdom, as well as by barristers representing the Government of Canada before the English courts[11] during the process of patriating the Constitution, that all Crown liability for Indian claims resided in Canada. Nevertheless, *Outstanding Business* indicates that the federal government will not acknowledge any pre-Confederation claims unless it can be proven that the "federal government specifically assumed responsibility therefor." This will apparently exclude dozens, if not hundreds, of claims stemming from the colonial era in southern Ontario, Quebec, the Maritimes, and southern British Columbia.

On the positive side, the policy statement reiterates the federal commitment to meet its lawful obligations and does give some definition and substance to what those obligations are. The government has clarified the policy that it has been following for some years by describing the process more fully and by elaborating the principles it will rely upon in developing compensation offers. In addition, the government has substantially increased its financial contribution to Indian bands and associations for the purposes of researching their claims while simultaneously increasing the resources allocated to the ONC so that it can respond more quickly to those claims which are submitted for assessment or compensation.

An indication of the Indian reaction to the federal policy on specific claims is evident in the following article written by a research director of one Indian association.

Dean Jacobs, "Betrayed," (1982) 1 *Strength in Unity*, No. 3, pp. 33 and 36.

Minister of Indian Affairs, John Munro, announced the long awaited federal specific claims policy on May 13, 1982. The policy came out in the form of a flashy three-part pamphlet entitled, *Outstanding Business — A Native Claims Policy*. The policy statement, designed primarily for the general public, covers the background of Native Claims, attempts to clarify the policy standards, outlines the process of handling claims and describes the guidelines to be used in the assessment of claims. Because of the policy's major significance and the active involvement in direct discussions, with the Department of Indian Affairs (DIA) representatives, in the development of the policy statement, the Association of Iroquois and Allied Indians (AIAI) and other native groups were particularly anxious. Our apprehensions seemed to be well founded. As we reviewed "Outstanding Business" our initial utterances were shock and dismay. Upon further analysis, our thoughts became more bitter, we felt used and betrayed.

From the opening foreword the federal policy begins to crystalize, evidenced by the statement that Indian claims "now must be settled without further delay". This political will resulted in the Federal government enunciating major policies dealing with comprehensive and specific claims within a six month period (Dec. 81-May 82). New claims funding were attached to the "new" policies and have been made available to both Natives and the federal Office of Native Claims (ONC). The ONC has already expanded their operations in anticipation that the "new" federal claims policy would precipitate a flood of Indian claim submissions. An immediate onslaught of claims is not likely as the federal policy has not changed substantially. It is basically the same old policy, which is that the government will recognize claims based on an outstanding lawful obligation which is defined as an obligation derived from law. This policy rules out any serious consideration for grievances based on governmental/political responsibilities and moral obligations. The federal governments reliance solely on legal principles threatens the entire resolution process of Indian claims in Canada.

Already there exists a ground swelling Native boycott of the ONC and its lawful obligation policy. Many Native organizations have voiced their objections and have denounced the specific claims policy and rejected it in its entirety. The reasons are clear. Although Native associations were "consulted" during the process of the new policy development, their views were not taken seriously nor were they properly addressed in the new policy. In part one, the "Indian Views" section is a token attempt and pays lip service to Indian concerns. Although this section is quite accurate in reflecting Indian statements, these views unfortunately were not fully considered when developing the new policy initiatives. For example, views were expressed that the old policy was too narrow in terms of its reliance on legal principles, the new policy categorically states that the policy basis is derived from law. Another Indian view cited was the real concern that an arbitrarily determined claims cut-off date not be set. In response, the new policy dictates that "No claims shall be entertained based on events prior to 1867 . . ." and goes to say "unless the federal government specifically assumed responsibility therefore." In effect, pre-1867 Indian claims are being used as a political football. The Canadian government rejects pre-1867 liability and the British Courts have ruled that all their responsibilities to Indian people have been transferred to Canada.

The "Indian Treaties" section provides basic background information but often is incorrect and at best misleading. For example, early Upper Canada land transactions were made with Indian *Nations* and were for the purpose of opening lands for non-Indian occupation settlement and cultivation and not for the surrender of Indian *peoples'* interest in the land. Initially these deals involved a one-time payment in *goods,* not one-time *cash* payments. In the Robinson Treaties of 1850 the *Indians* and not the Crown undertook to set aside reserves. "*As far back as* the Royal Proclamation of 1763, the British sovereign recognized an Indian interest in the lands occupied by various Tribes . . ." should have been simply stated "historically the British Crown recognized the sovereignty of Indian Nations . . .."

Part II deals specifically with the policy. Lawful Obligation is narrowly defined to arise only in three circumstances described briefly as follows:

a) non-fulfillment of a treaty or agreement.
b) breach of an obligation arising out of the Indian Act, other statutes and administration [of] other assets.
c) Illegal disposition of Indian land.

In an attempt to step beyond Lawful Obligation, claims may be acknowledged based on:

a) Failure to provide compensation for reserve lands taken or damaged;
b) Fraud; both a&b bear close resemblance to the existing legal process. The policy concludes with a warning to Indian claimants. In determining whether or not to negotiate a claim based on an outstanding lawful obligation, the Federal government will not use the technical defence of statutes of limitation or the doctrine of laches. However, the feds will use these arguments in a court case. This warning goes without saying, as the defences are legal in nature and are unenforceable in any other setting, so why the statement, the only plausible explanations are

to force Indian claimants into an unacceptable resolution process and secondly, to give the impression that the big-hearted government is making a major concession in land claims negotiations.

The process remains essentially unchanged. What is unsaid is more important. There is no mention of alternative processes such as the moderately successful Indian Commission of Ontario (ICO) established through tripartite negotiations. There is no indication of the Minister's privilege of accepting a claim for negotiation based on merits other than legal, seemingly precluding the Minister's political prerogative. In the event a claim hurdles all the policy obstructions and is accepted as valid, settlement negotiations are commenced. Any compensation arrived at will be based on legal principles. Compensation is further determined by the strength of the claim, it seems that each claim upon acceptance as an outstanding lawful obligation will then be assigned a degree of strength or doubt factor which will be reflected in the compensation offered.

Part III covers guidelines to assist claimants in preparing submissions. A ten point check list is provided summarizing the submission and assessment guidelines for specific claims. Included is the blatant statement that treaties are not open to renegotiation and the face saving disclaimer that the acceptance of a claim for negotiation is not to be interpreted as an admission of liability.

The conclusion recognizes previous policies were ineffective in resolving claims and that the "new" policy initiatives are meant to correct this situation in a fair and equitable manner.

The Minister correctly points out that the claims resolution task is enormous, complex and time consuming. Unfortunately, the "new" policy has become more restrictive and any previous room for interpretation has been further narrowed in favour of the federal government. So much so, that DIA officials openly challenge Indian claimants to take the federal government to court if you are not satified with the "new" specific claims policy.

The fundamental differences of opinion as well as the crux of the matter and which the policy fails to grasp is that the governments tend to view Native claims in terms of extinguishment. Settlement is to be once and for all time.

Indian people look to claim settlement not as an assimilation policy but as a foundation to be built upon, especially in the recognition of their inherent rights to political, economical, cultural, and spiritual self-determination.

There are however some good points to mention about the policy. The policy has finally been released, we are no longer kept in limbo, and in all its inadequacies the policy was made public, we no longer have to make guesses as to the policy.

The questions of where do we go from here and what are the implications of Canada's Constitution and Native claims must now be contemplated carefully by Native people

The success of this policy in resolving outstanding claims can only be assessed after it has been in place for several years. The lack of results under the former policy and its close similarity with the new one does, however, indicate that one should not expect major advancement to occur in the near future under this approach to settling claims.

4. An Overview of Settled and Outstanding Claims

(a) Claims Resolved

The only success in the settlement of comprehensive claims to date has been restricted to the James Bay and Northern Quebec Agreement of 1975 and the supplementary Northeastern Quebec Agreement of 1978. Since these agreements will be discussed in greater detail in a subsequent chapter, only the highlights will be noted here.

The James Bay Agreement affects approximately 6,500 Cree and 4,200 Inuit who have released their aboriginal title to the Crown for the benefit of Quebec over 379,400 square miles in Northern Quebec in return for money, some land and certain special rights. They are to receive 225 million dollars over a twenty-year period. The Crees retain ownership and control over 2,095 square miles for their eight communities (Category Ia and b lands) along with exclusive hunting, fishing and trapping rights over a further 25,130 square miles (Category II lands). The Inuit receive 3,250 square miles for their fourteen communities and a further 33,400 square miles over which they possess exclusive hunting, fishing, and trapping rights. All of these lands can be expropriated by Quebec for public purposes, subject to the payment of compensation, and the province has all mineral rights to these lands. The agreement also provides for the establishment of local and regional governments, environmental committees, health and social services boards, school boards, separate police forces and economic development committees in which the Cree or Inuit participate actively or control. Special provisions have also been included to provide some income security for hunters and trappers. This agreement was brought into force on 31 October 1977 with the proclamation of corresponding federal and provincial legislation.

The Naskapis de Schefferville, a band of some 400 Indians living within the territory covered by the James Bay Agreement, negotiated their own settlement in 1978; except for certain modifications, it adopts the language and provisions of the James Bay Agreement.

Although these two agreements have sparked bitter complaints and condemnation for their shortcomings and the environment in which they were negotiated, nevertheless they are the broadest and most exhaustive land claim settlement involving indigenous peoples anywhere in the world. If the federal and provincial governments honour the commitments they have made, then the agreements could represent a new starting point in Indian and Inuit history in northern Quebec. The James Bay Agreement could be seen as an intergovernmental agreement providing for the dramatic transfer of power and legal authority over many issues fundamental to the lives of the indigenous signatories. Whether it will become a bold new charter governing the future relations among the federal, provincial and Aboriginal governments remains to be seen. Initial experience indicates dissatisfaction and more broken promises.

Under provisions contained in the treaties covering the three Prairie Provinces, reserve lands were to be set aside for all the Indian bands who signed. Many bands, however, did not receive their full land entitlement. This situation was recognized in the individual Natural Resources Transfer Agreements, which form part of the Canadian Constitution, between Canada and these provinces in which Alberta, Saskatchewan and Manitoba agreed to transfer whatever lands were necessary to enable the federal government to honour its treaty obligations in return for obtaining practically all unalienated federal Crown land and ownership of all natural resources. On 24 August 1977, a tripartite agreement was reached by the Federation of Saskatchewan Indians, the Province of Saskatchewan and the Government of Canada in which a formula for settlement was established. The first land transfers occurred in 1979 and the Stony Rapids Band became the first band to have its entitlement completely fulfilled in 1981. Over one million acres of land will ultimately be transferred to reserve status.

On 16 December 1977, the Manitoba Northern Flood Agreement was signed by Canada, the Province of Manitoba, Manitoba Hydro and the five bands whose reserve lands were to be flooded by two major hydroelectric projects planned for northern Manitoba. The Agreement provided for an exchange of four acres for each acre flooded, the expansion and protection of hunting, fishing and trapping rights, five million dollars over five years for economic development projects, job opportunities, water level guarantees, and future participation in wildlife management, resource development and environmental concerns in that part of the province.

Outstanding Business indicates that fourteen specific claims have been settled as of spring 1982 involving cash payments of 17.9 million dollars and 12,000 acres of land.[12] According to DIAND's latest status report, this consists of the Saskatchewan treaty land entitlement and the following:

1. Wagmatcook, Nova Scotia. A claim was presented in 1973 alleging the improper alienation of 3,800 acres of reserve land and was settled on 27 March, 1982 for $1.2 million.
2. Batchewana, Ontario. The Ontario government paid $65,000 in

October 1974 as compensation for a highway right-of-way over unsold surrendered lands.

3. Osnaburg, Ontario. The band was paid $16,000 by the province in December 1975 for damages caused by the construction of a highway.

4. Canoe Lake, Saskatchewan. The band was paid $4,366.17 in December 1976 by DIAND as a result of being paid for treaty ammunition since 1962 on the wrong scale.

5. Nikaneet, Saskatchewan. Band members were reinstated on the treaty annuity lists in 1976.

6. Penticton, British Columbia. The band received $13.2 million from the federal government and $1 million and 12,000 acres from the provincial government in March 1982 as settlement for its claim. It and twenty-one other bands claimed that land was cut off from 34 reserves in British Columbia as a result of the 1920 Federal British Columbia Indian Land Settlement Act without their consent, notwithstanding the Royal Commission recommendations of 1916 that assured that Indian consent would be obtained.

7. Kitsumkalum Band, British Columbia. The band was paid $9,357 compensation in December 1974 as a result of earlier compensation being inadequate regarding reserve lands that were used for a National Defence road.

8. Treaty 7 Ammunition Claim, Alberta. Five bands were paid $250,000 in December 1974 due to failure to provide ammunition to each band under Treaty 7 as required.

Unfortunately, the data in *Outstanding Business* is not equivalent to the information contained in *Specific Claims in Canada: Status Report*, which was published by DIAND on 7 April 1982 and used as background briefing on the release of the former. The latter includes some additional settlements, but it should be noted that most of these settlements were minor in nature and occurred before 1976.

In addition, the Whitedog Indian Band of Northwestern Ontario successfully concluded two claims agreements in 1982 and 1983. After twenty years of seeking compensation for the flooding of reserve lands by hydro dams, it reached an agreement with Ontario Hydro for $1.5 million and 1,700 hectares of land as a settlement for the claim. Agreement was also reached with the Government of Canada in 1982 for $2.3 million and with the Government of Ontario on 28 January 1983 for additional compensation to resolve the economic and health problems caused by mercury poisoning of the English-Wabigoon River system. Another nearby reserve, of the Grassy Narrows Indian Band, has also suffered from the effects of pollution from the same paper mill. Negotiations are still continuing as the Band is seeking other forms of compensation beyond money. The Government of Canada agreed to provide $4.4 million of recovery funding on June 27, 1984, but agreements with Ontario, Ontario Hydro and the polluter have not yet been reached.

The Osoyoos Band of British Columbia settled its "cut-off" claim in Novenber 1982. It received almost $1 million dollars in compensation for about 29 hectares of land removed from the reserve in 1916 under the McKenna-McBride Commission.

A further "cut-off" claim in British Columbia was settled by the Clinton Band in March 1983. They regained almost 69 hectares of land out of the original 90 hectares severed from the reserve in 1916 plus $150,500. The Chemainus Band settled its "cut-off" claim in June of 1984 in which it received $575,000 from the federal government for the loss of 12.69 hectares of land and the return of 23.9 hectares from the Province along with $124,200.

A number of other cut-off claims are nearing completed settlements with the federal and provincial governments. The Parliament of Canada also enacted special legislation to give the present and future settlements the force of law in early 1984. Companion legislation was passed by the British Columbia government.

The Oromocto Band of New Brunswick signed a claim settlement agreement for $2.55 million in July of 1983 with the federal government. This claim was for approximately 29 hectares of land which had been improperly surrendered in 1953 to the Government of Canada and subsequently used as part of Camp Gagetown.

The Long Lake Indian Band of Ontario settled its claim for the loss of 43 hectares of reserve land to the construction of a highway for $192,466 in April of 1984. The same month witnessed the agreement to compensate the Blackfoot Band of Alberta for cattle promised but never delivered under Treaty 7 by way of a cash payment of $1,675,000.

A number of other claims are in the final stages of negotiation.

(b) Outstanding Claims

Seventeen further specific claims have been suspended by the claimants. In addition, 80 claims are under government review to assess their validity, twelve have been filed in court, 55 others have been referred for an administrative remedy and 73 are in the negotiation process.[13]

These claims, and many others which have yet to be filed with the Minister, generally relate to one of the following types of complaints: provisions contained in treaties have not been fulfilled or have been violated; treaty payments constituted unconscionable consideration as being far below the value of the land relinquished to the Crown; reserve land that was surrendered improperly and later sold; reserve land that was surrendered for the purpose of sale but was never sold; reserve land was sold improperly or for less than its market value; reserve lands have been damaged or illegally expropriated;

squatters are residing on reserve lands; mismanagement of Indian funds or non-payment of sale proceeds; and alleged breach of trust responsibilities by the Crown and its agents.

Comprehensive claims are still unresolved throughout the four Atlantic Provinces, southern Quebec, some parts of Ontario, most of British Columbia, and in both Territories. *In All Fairness* summarizes the present situation as follows:

> An Agreement-in-Principle, signed in 1978 with the Committee for Original Peoples' Entitlement (COPE), representing approximately 2,500 Inuit of the Western Arctic region was to have had a final agreement by October 31, 1979. Negotiations were delayed as a result of the 1979 general election, but the way was cleared for intensive discussions with the appointment of a new chief government negotiator in June 1980. After several months of unsuccessful negotiations, meetings were suspended in December 1980. It is hoped that negotiations translating the Agreement-in-Principle into a Final Agreement will resume in the near future.
>
> In the Yukon, as a result of fresh initiatives, including the appointment of a new chief government negotiator, in May 1980, considerable progress is being made in the negotiations with the Council for Yukon Indians (CYI) which represents 5,000-6,000 Status and non-Status Indians. The goal here is to finalize an Agreement-in-Principle by the summer of 1982.
>
> In 1977 the Inuit Tapirisat of Canada (ITC) submitted, on behalf of some 13,500 Inuit in the Central and Eastern Arctic of the Northwest Territories, a proposal for a new territory of Nunavut, to encompass all lands north of the treeline. The proposal contained provisions respecting land, wildlife, compensation and other elements of a claim. Until late 1980 little progress was made, since government policy distinguished between the process of constitutional change and the negotiated settlement of a claim. Late in 1979, the ITC agreed to separate the claims and constitutional processes; and in August 1980, a chief government negotiator — a new position — was appointed to conduct negotiation of the claims elements. Negotiation from late 1980 until late October 1981 has resulted in the initialing, in Frobisher Bay, of an agreement-in-principle on wildlife harvesting rights. Negotiations on the claims elements continue, in tandem with efforts on both sides to resolve the question of political development.
>
> The Dene Nation and the Metis Association of the Mackenzie Valley, NWT presented separate claims in 1976 and 1977 respectively, but since the two claims did not reflect the actual degree of mutual interest among the native population, negotiation did not commence, and loan funding for research and development pertaining to claims was suspended by government between October 1978 and April 1980.

In April 1980 funding was resumed on the understanding that the Dene Nation would represent all the native beneficiaries during negotiation of the claims. In April 1981, a chief government negotiator was appointed and several negotiation sessions have been held to clarify principles.

In British Columbia, the potential for negotiating the Nishga claim is tenuous due primarily to the apprehension with which the provincial government approaches the possibility of unextinguished Native title within the province, and the doubt which the province has as to whether it should accept any responsibility to compensate Native people for the loss of use and occupancy of traditional lands. Nevertheless in June of this year a fulltime chief government negotiator was appointed by the Minister to negotiate a settlement and the province has agreed to participate in the negotiations. Preliminary negotiations with the Nishga Tribal Council got underway earlier this fall.

The federal government has also accepted claims for negotiation from, the Association of United Tahltans, the Gitksan-Carrier Tribal Council, the Kitwancool Band and the Kitamaat Village Council. These claims will be negotiated once the implications of the Nishga claim negotiations are apparent. Claims from the Nuu-Chah-Nulth, Haida and Heiltsuk are presently under review.

Claims on behalf of Naskapi-Montagnais Indians and the Inuit in Labrador were accepted for negotiation by the federal government in 1978. The Province of Newfoundland confirmed its willingness to participate in tripartite negotiations of these claims in September 1980. Bilateral discussions are planned to clarify the role and responsibilities that each government will assume in these negotiations.

The claim of le Conseil Attikamek-Montagnais, representing Montagnais and Attikamek bands living on the north shores of the St Lawrence and St Maurice rivers, was accepted by the federal government in October 1979, and has been met by a willingness to participate in negotiations by the provincial government. The claim will be negotiated in a tripartite forum. Le Conseil Attikamek-Montagnais is currently completing its research with the view to entering early negotiations.

The COPE claim has since reached the Final Agreement stage and been ratified by Cabinet and the Inuvialuit. The CYI claim has advanced to a signed Agreement-in-Principle approved by Cabinet and a majority of the communities in the Yukon. Progress on the other claims is continuing slowly.

The claims of the Metis have not been resolved nor has the federal government displayed any intention to discuss them seriously, except in the Yukon and the Northwest Territories.

5. Australian and American Experience

(a) American Efforts at Resolving Claims

The high degree of attention given to treaty-making in the United States tends to lead Canadians, along with many Americans, into believing that the United States government consistently maintained the British colonial policy of obtaining land through negotiations with the Indian nations who owned that land. This, however, is far from the truth, since well over one half of the USA, amounting to over one billion acres, was either confiscated by express federal actions without compensation or was assumed without consideration for the existence of aboriginal title. This process left the original inhabitants with less than two percent of the land mass of the United States or under 100 acres per capita. It also destroyed tribal economies to such an extent that in 1980 the Bureau of Indian Affairs had an annual budget of over $1,000,000,000 while the federal government was spending over 3 billion dollars, or $5,000 per capita, on services and programs for Indians.

The unfairness and illegality of this massive land theft has not only embittered the Indian population but has also generated continuous pressure for redressing these injustices through settling land claims. Once Congress terminated the President's authority to enter into Indian treaties in 1871, the indigenous peoples were left without remedy, since they could not sue the federal government because of its ability to invoke the cloak of sovereign immunity. The Indian governments were also expressly excluded from litigating their claims before the only court with jurisdiction over lawsuits against the US government, the Court of Claims.

Commencing in 1881, Congress initiated a policy of providing individual exceptions to this jurisdictional obstacle by enacting the first of almost one hundred special statutes expressly referring specific tribal complaints to the Court of Claims. Of course, it was an extremely arduous process for a tribal government to persuade Congress to pass a statute for its individual grievance. Even if it was successful in obtaining such an act, the tribe was confronted with a vigorous defence by the Department of Justice and a court that tended towards highly technical rulings and which was exceedingly unsympathetic to the merits of the claim. Out of the 135 cases brought before the Court of Claims, 103 were dismissed. The Court had the authority only to award monetary compensation and thus was unable to meet the real goals of the Indian people. Even with this limitation, the claimants received only a little over 53 million dollars of the 1.7 billion dollars claimed. These awards were further reduced by the deduction of 19 million dollars, representing all "gratuitous" payments spent by the federal government on behalf of the successful litigants.

The net effect of this experience was to leave thousands of substantial and minor claims outstanding by the end of World War II. In order to resolve this situation, and to pay tribute to the contributions of Indian soldiers in the war, it was decided that a specialized administrative tribunal should be established to review all claims without requiring individual jurisdictional statutes.

(i) The Indian Claims Commission

Congress passed the *Indian Claims Commission Act* in 1946 to authorize claims to the Indian Claims Commission.

> Kenneth Lysyk, "The United States Indian Claims Commission" in Peter A. Cumming and Neil H. Mickenberg, eds., *Native Rights in Canada*, 2d ed., General Publishing Co., 1972, p. 243, 246-248.

4. *Types of Claims.* The bulk of the claims brought before the Commission are land claims. These relate to the terms of Indian land cessions to the United States by treaty, or to lands taken pursuant to statute or otherwise. The majority of these land claims fall into the category of "treaty takings," and the typical claim is that compensation paid to the Indians for land ceded in this way was so low as to be "unconscionable."

Section 2 of the Act provides for five categories of claims:

(1) claims in law or equity arising under the Constitution, laws, treaties of the United States, and Executive orders of the President;

(2) all other claims in law or equity, including those sounding in tort, with respect to which the claimant would have been entitled to sue in a court of the United States if the United States was subject to suit;

(3) claims which would result if the treaties, contracts, and agreements between the claimant and the United States were revised on the ground of fraud, duress, unconscionable consideration, mutual or unilateral mistake, whether of law or fact, or any other ground cognizable by a court of equity;

(4) claims arising from the taking by the United States, whether as the result of a treaty or cession or otherwise, of lands owned or occupied by the claimant without the payment of such lands of compensation agreed to by the claimant; and

(5) claims based upon fair and honourable dealings that are not recognized by any existing rule of law or equity.

Clauses (1) and (2) authorize claims which can be based on ordinary doctrines of law or equity or of constitutional law, and remove the obstacle of the doctrine of sovereign immunity. These clauses do not represent a new departure; their counterparts may be found in the special jurisdictional acts employed to vest jurisdiction in the Court of Claims.

Clause (3) provides, in effect, for the reopening of Indian treaties. The Commission is to entertain claims based on grounds which affect the validity of contracts in private law — fraud, duress, mutual or unilateral mistake of law or fact, or any other grounds on which a court of equity would grant relief — with one particularly important additional basis for revision of the treaty, namely, that the consideration paid to the Indians thereunder was so low as to be "unconscionable."

Clause (4) covers claims for lands owned or occupied by the claimant and taken by treaty or otherwise without payment of compensation agreed to by the claimant. It will be noted that this category embraces lands taken otherwise than by treaty. For some time there was doubt as to whether the Commission had jurisdiction to entertain claims based on aboriginal (or Indian) title, as opposed to "recognized title." (The former is based on actual and exclusive occupation for a long period of time, whereas the latter rests on recognition by treaty or other Congressional action. The distinction is further discussed elsewhere in this chapter.) The Commission took the view that it possessed jurisdiction to entertain claims based on aboriginal title, and that position has been sustained by the courts.

Clause (5) contains the "fair and honourable dealings" clause conferring jurisdiction to entertain claims not recognized by existing legal doctrine. While the clause is commonly understood to embrace purely moral claims, the Commission has had little occasion to define its scope more precisely. Typically, the "fair and honourable dealings" clause is pleaded as an altenative, or in supplement, to one of the other clauses. Both plaintiff's attorneys and the Commission tend to rely on the more concrete bases set out in the first four categories.

As noted at the outset, the Commission has been concerned almost exclusively with land claims. The potential for non-land claims has been reduced by the fact that the jurisdiction of the Commission has been limited to tribal or group claims, as opposed to individual claims. Thus the Commission would not, for example, grant relief in respect of injuries that might have been suffered by indivuduals during displacement by United States military forces, and the like. Other claims, though not individual claims, might be rejected essentially on the ground that the nature of the alleged grievance was not such as to admit of assessment and compensation; an example might be the destruction of the buffalo.

It may be noted that while Indian claims before the Commission will not be barred by laches or by statutes of limitation, all other defences are available to the United States as defendant (s. 2).

The Act relates only to claims which arose prior to the date it came into force, namely August 13, 1946 (s. 2). Jurisdiction to hear Indian claims accruing after that date has been vested in the Court of

Claims, but the jurisdiction so authorized is not as broad as that exercised by the Indian Claims Commission. The types of claims that may be brought in the Court of Claims under this provision are limited to those arising "under the Constitution, laws or treaties of the United States, or Executive orders of the President," or which would otherwise be cognizable if the claimant was not an Indian tribe, band, or group. Finally, it may be noted that the jurisdiction of the Indian Claims Commission is to hear claims against the United States — that is, the Federal government only — and does not extend to claims for what was done by way of extinguishment of Indian title, and the like, either by European governments or by colonial governments prior to Union. Nor has jurisdiction been extended to hear claims respecting actions taken by state governments. Federal responsibility in some form is a prerequisite to proceeding before the Commission . . . .

Russel Barsh, "Indian Land Claims Policy in the United States", (1982), 58 *North Dakota Law Review* 7 at pp. 12, 13, 15-19, 22, 23 and 32-34.

Disposition of claims was now to be complete and final, joining every conceivable tribal grievance. The Bureau of Indian Affairs was directed to notify all tribes of the creation of the Indian Claims Commission, and all claims were to be filed with the Commission within five years of its establishment. The Senate, over the opposition of the Justice Department, expressed its understanding that the Indian Claims Commission Act authorized reopening of dockets dismissed by the Court of Claims on purely jurisdictional or procedural grounds. Moreover, in cases in which the Court of Claims had denied tribal claimants interest on the principal amount of an award, entitlement to the added interest could be relitigated before the Commission . . . .

National "morality" in no way contemplated tribes' right of political or cultural self-determination. On the contrary, Congress and the Administration agreed on settling tribal claims because they believed it would hasten tribes' assimilation and dispersal . . . .

Settlement also would spur many tribes to be economically self-sustaining. In other words, the Government believed claims settlement payments would be small, and would be used to pay for, or eliminate the need for reservation programs otherwise paid out of federal funds . . . .

In several significant areas, the Indian Claims Commission failed to meet the expectations either of tribes or of Congress. Most obvious was its failure to complete its work in ten years, as Congress originally had intended. Although Administration spokesmen were confident in 1946 that ten years would be adequate, the Commission had finally disposed of only a little more than half of its caseload twenty-five years later.

"You won't get it done in 100 years," Oklahoma Senator Burdick complained to the Commission Chairman Kuykendall in 1971, "Do you have any idea how many Indians have died in those 25 years, and will never see any money?"

Commission staff identified three main sources of delay. First, even with its eighteen staff attornies, the Justice Department's Indian Claims unit found itself overwhelmed with the task of defending the United States; in one eighteen-month period, government defense lawyers requested 6,451 days of delays. Second, staff shortages also limited the General Accounting Office's ability to provide the Commission audits of tribal funds and property held by the United States. Finally, complicating the sheer volume of work involved in reconstructing transactions stretching back a century or more was the "chaotic" state of Bureau of Indian Affairs records reported by other contemporary investigators.

The Commission also faulted tribes' lawyers, in part, for trial delays, but recognized that tribes' ability to promptly prosecute complex cases has been limited by lack of funds for expert witnesses . . .

After repeated extensions, the Commission was permitted to expire in 1978, and its remaining caseload was transferred to the Court of Claims.

Notwithstanding thirty-two years of litigation, the Commission failed to achieve Congress's goal of a thorough and final settlement of tribal grievances. In at least one instance, a tribe was not notified of the Commission's establishment early enough to file its claims within the five-year statutory deadline. Congress in 1980 enacted a special jurisdictional bill to refer this case to the Court of Claims. The Sioux and as many as six other tribes whose pre-1946 petitions were dismissed by the Court of Claims on procedural or technical grounds tried unsuccessfully to relitigate their cases under the Indian Claims Commission Act. Despite Congress's apparent desire that such cases be reopened, the Commission dismissed all of them as res judicata . . .

The Commission's measure of damages in most claims was the market value of the land at the time of taking, without interest or adjustment for inflation. One 1860 dollar had the buying power of about fifteen 1980 dollars — leading some representatives of the Cowlitz tribe to demand payment of their claim judgment in gold and silver coins of the year their land was lost. Moreover, one 1860 dollar, with interest, would have earned about sixty-four dollars by 1980, causing many tribes, generally without success, to demand the payment of interest on their claims judgments. Lastly, it is noteworthy that the market value of tribal lands at the time of nineteenth-century transactions often has to be guessed at or based on the federal resale rate of a dollar or two per acre, because prior to the treaty or taking in issue, no land in the area had been bought or sold privately. Consequently, Commission awards frequently represented less than one percent of the real value of the damages suffered by tribal claimants.

Interest was not paid on any claims against the United States until 1925, and not ordinarily on any tribal claims against the United States until 1935. Thereafter, the Court of Claims adopted the rule, observed also by the Indian Claims Commission, "that interest is not allowed unless title to the land has already been recognized by the United States. Further, the land must have been taken without the tribe's consent, and the taking must have been ratified by Congress." When those criteria were met, the taking was deemed to have been made in accordance with the fifth amendment, hence subject to the requirement of "just compensation" with interest. Federal confiscation of "unrecognized" or "aboriginal" lands (lands immemorially occupied by a tribe but never reserved expressly for the tribe's use by treaty) was deemed to raise at best a "moral" right to restitution, without interest. These distinctions worked two inequities, from tribes' point of view. Several tribes won judgments in the Court of Claims before that court began to allow tribes interest on takings of "recognized" title, then were barred from seeking the added interest before the Indian Claims Commission. Other tribes lost out on interest merely because their ancient landholdings had never been mentioned in federal laws or treaties.

Tribes also found fault with the Commission's handling of "gratuitous" offsets. The United States often sought to count as "gratuities" services paid for with the tribal claimant's own funds, and in at least one instance succeeded. The United States also sought to deduct the cost of grants and contracts awarded to tribes under recent laws such as the Indian Self-Determination Act of 1975, which were intended to strengthen tribal self-government . . . .

Tribal claimants manifestly were more successful in the Commission than in previous litigation before the Court of Claims, winning more than twenty times as many dollars, although 200 of 484 dockets were dismissed. On the other hand, the Commission was costly both to tribes and to the Government, since the adversary proceedings required the participation of scores of lawyers, judges, accountants, and clerks for more than three decades. Overall, the Commission awarded tribes roughly the amount of money the Bureau of Indian Affairs spends in a single fiscal year, at an efficiency of about sixteen percent — sixteen cents cost for every dollar received by tribes . . . .
Approximately 11.25 percent of the tribe's recovery, then, was paid to counsel and to the United States prior to distribution . . . .

After thirty years of continuous litigation, tribal claimants had won the equivalent of about 1,000,000,000 1978 dollars at a cost of more than 1,200,000,000 1978 dollars to the United States. Thus, tribes would have been as well off financially had the United States simply transferred $150,000,000 to their trust accounts in 1946, and allowed them to reap thirty years' intervening interest . . . .

It is noteworthy, however, that in all areas except "legal assistance," judgment funds have been used to pay for programs for which federal grants-in-aid and contracts are available. This reinforces the likelihood that judgment funds have been used to substitute for federal financing to which the tribes would otherwise have been entitled, leaving them with no net fiscal gain. Most plans provide, moreover, that actual disbursements will be subject to Departmental approval, the tribe may have no choice but to spend judgment funds allocated to "education" or "land acquisition" exactly as the Department directs. Furthermore, unexpended "programmed" judgment funds ordinarily remain in Interior Department investment management rather than in accounts directly accessible to the tribes. Exceptions have been made only when the Department believes that a tribe's officers "are capable of managing their own affairs." Departmental portfolios themselves leave much to be desired, however. Interest rates are often low and aggregate rates differ significantly from tribe to tribe. One tribe has sued the United States successfully for breach of trust in management of recent investments.

Most judgment funds have been paid per capita in one form or another. No complete accounting for these funds has been published, but congressional committee reports for the period 1972-1980 offer a sample of thirty-one planned distributions with actual or estimated per capita shares. Share size ranged from $55 to $7,050 with an average of $1,375 . . . .

As a general rule, special distribution legislation exempted per capita shares from state and federal income taxes, a policy incorporated in section 7 of the Distribution of Judgment Funds Act. Until 1973, however per capita distributions often resulted in payees' loss of eligibility under the Social Security Act. For this reason, many judgments resulted in no net gain to tribal members and no net loss to the United States . . . .

The American experience with the Indian Claims Commission has been widely seen as unsatisfactory. It has been criticized for being unnecessarily legalistic, complicated and time-consuming. The settlements were far too small to represent a complete compensation to the tribes for what they lost as well as being insufficient to generate economic revitalization of reservation life. Furthermore, it did nothing to meet the real demand of Indian people — the return of at least some of their own land. The United States has, however, transferred more than 500,000 acres of federal land to tribes since 1970 for socio-economic purposes unrelated to land claims. Even putting the Commission in the best possible light still means that it was unsuccessful in meeting Congress's objective of final settlement of all Indian claims. Nearly

100 dockets were still pending before the Commission upon its expiry and had to be referred to the Court of Claims for resolution.

In addition, a further 10,000 claims had been identified by the Bureau of Indian Affairs by 1979. These claims are similar to what have been labelled "specific claims" in Canada since they involve disputes, unauthorized use of timber, water, and other resources in reservations, breaches of fishing rights, state tax foreclosures of tax-exempt lands, damage to reservation lands, and breaches of trust responsibility.

(ii) The Alaskan Settlement

Treaties were never negotiated with the Indian, Inuit and Aleut populations of Alaska largely as a result of lack of interest in their traditional lands by the US government. Various federal statutes over the years simply made exceptions to the general law in recognition of the continued occupation of most of the land by these three peoples. Upon statehood in 1959, Alaska was required to disclaim any interest in Native lands.

This inaction and indifference was to change suddenly upon the discovery of major petroleum reserves in the Arctic Slope and the subsequent plans for a pipeline across the state. Since only seven percent of Alaska was privately or state-owned in 1970, there was considerable concern that assertions of continuing aboriginal title could play havoc with the multibillion dollar development plans of the oil industry.

The state appointed a task force which recommended in 1968 that a settlement should be negotiated with the indigenous peoples, including 40 million acres and royalty rights. In 1969 the Secretary of the Interior froze all further selection and conveyance of federal lands in Alaska. This action, when combined with intense lobbying by environmentalists, the petroleum industry, the state, and the Alaskan Natives, forced Congress to readdress the issue.

Various different bills to settle the claim were debated in Congress during 1970 and 1971 and led to a number of compromises. Although the Indian, Inuit and Aleut populations appeared before congressional committees and actively lobbied in the halls of Congress, they did not actually negotiate or have any control over the terms of the final settlement.

Russel Barsh, "Indian Land Claims Policy in the United States," (1982) 58 *North Dakota Law Review* 7 at pp. 48, 49, and 61.

> As enacted in 1971, the Alaska Native Claims Settlement Act (ANCSA) tempered the major features of the Harris-Kennedy plan with occasional deference to Senator Jackson's wishes. Natives receive nearly $1,000,000,000, $462,500,000 contributed by federal taxpayers, and $500,000,000 generated by a two percent temporary royalty on federal and state development of Alaska lands. Natives also select 40,000,000 acres: 22,000,000 for villages at a rate of approximately 400 acres per village; 16,000,000 for regional corporations allocated by regions' geographic areas, together with the subsurface rights to village

selections; and 2,000,000 for individuals and groups not sharing in village entitlements. Village land selections are to be patented by the Secretary of the Interior "immediately" after setting aside reasonably sufficient rights-of-way for public users. Villages themselves are responsible for reconveying land to individual Natives and, "as necessary for community expansion," to any existing municipalities.

By eliminating statewide organizations, ANCSA's distribution hierarchy agrees more closely with Native wishes than either the Harris-Kennedy or Jackson approaches. Settlement funds are distributed directly to regional corporations in proportion to their populations. Regionals remit ten percent of these funds directly, to Native shareholders, and fifty percent of all regional revenues to village corporation and nonvillage (''at large'') shareholders. Regionals also are required to share with one another seventy percent of "all revenues received by them" from timber and subsurface development — in effect a perpetual Native royalty on other Natives' lands.

In addition to twelve geographical regional corporations for "Natives having a common heritage and sharing common interest," there is a thirteenth regional corporation for Natives who did not elect or qualify to enroll in the other twelve. To qualify for ANCSA benefits, villages must satisfy the Secretary of the Interior that they have at least twenty-five residents, the majority of them Natives, and that they are not of a modern and urban character.

ANCSA compromises the protectiveness of the Harris-Kennedy proposal with Jackson's goal of rapid legal assimilation. Redistribution of settlement funds among Native corporations and their shareholders is permanently tax-exempt, and cannot be considered as income in computing eligibility for federal grants and transfer payments. Native lands are taxable at the end of twenty years, however, and land revenues are taxable at once. All Native corporations must be organized under Alaska state law, although they remain exempt from federal securities laws for twenty years. During this period of immunity, Natives' shares are inheritable, but voting rights can be exercised only by Native heirs, and shares cannot be sold. All "trust" restrictions, reservation land withdrawals, and allotment laws are terminated. BIA responsibility for services remains, by implication of ANCSA's silence and Natives' inclusion in subsequent federal Indian legislation, but approval of village corporate charters and village expenditures of settlement funds is now the responsibility of regional corporations.

However well-intentioned and generous, by historical standards, ANCSA never worked quite the way it was planned. Implementation was entangled from the start in costly federal administrative "white tape," suspending Native rights while ANCSA's time limits ran out. The complex hierarchy of new organizations designed to facilitate

Native economic growth were embroiled in overlapping and conflicting responsibilities and competing interests. Natives' chief concern throughout the settlement planning process, control of land for both subsistence and growth, now appears unlikely. Four principal problems of federal law and administration have been encountered: administrative discretion; delays in land management; taxation of Native lands; and alienability of shares. Additionally, there are four organizational problems: overlapping local organizations; village-region conflicts; conflict among regions; and elites and value conflicts. These have resulted in internal conflict and merit particular attention . . . .

Some Alaska Native groups did indeed initially regard the settlement proposal as "terminationist," but were persuaded to throw their support to the more moderate Harris-Kennedy plan. Fears of termination were revived after ANCSA implementation began, leading the American Indian Policy Review Commission in 1977 to advise Congress that the special political status of Alaska Natives had survived the settlement. Judging from the growth in federal grants-in-aid to Native villages' tribal councils over the past decade, Congress and the Administration share the Commission's view. As a political settlement, then, ANCSA merely increased the variety and wealth of Native organizations.

ANCSA was little more successful in bringing closure to Native claims for land, resource rights, and damages for historical trespass. Although section 4(a) of the law declares it to be a "full and final settlement" of all claims based on land use or ownership, its application to offshore marine and coastal rights, among others, remains unclear . . . .

(iii) The Eastern Claims

The most recent American experience in land claims is back where it all began with the initial colonization of the Atlantic seaboard. These claims raise many parallels to the situation in eastern and central Canada where the historical background is very similar indeed. The Indian nations in what is now the USA frequently had treaty relations with Britain and her colonies and were included within the terms of the Royal Proclamation of 1763. Some of the Indian nations had agreed to the reserve system while many others consented only to entering military alliances through treaties of peace and friendship.

Congress maintained the British policy of recognition of aboriginal title after independence. One of its first legislative acts after the institution of the US Constitution was the passage of the Trade and Intercourse Act in 1790. Not only did it regulate all commercial dealings with the Indian nations, it also invalidated all land sales or treaties by Indians with the states or private individuals. Nevertheless, most of the eastern states continued to buy land from the Indian peoples or simply took it despite this Act.

As the events which give rise to these claims are basically those of the states and private parties, lawsuits would not lie before the Indian Claims Commission or the Court of Claims. Therefore, several of the claimants went to court to seek to compel the federal government as trustee to sue the states and private landholders on behalf of the tribes.

Russel Barsh, "Indian Land Claims Policy in the United States," (1982) 58 *North Dakota Law Review* 7 at pp. 63-66.

The first eastern claim to be prosecuted and the most successful in terms of dollars, was initiated in 1972 by the Passamaquoddy and Penobscot tribes of Maine. According to the tribes, 12,500,000 acres worth more than $25,000,000,000 had been acquired by the State and its citizens in violation of the Indian Trade and Intercourse Act. Since the land never had been acquired lawfully, the tribes demanded repossession rather than compensation. Failing to persuade the Administration to file suit on their behalf, the tribes successfully brought an action against the Secretary of the Interior, as "trustee," to compel his cooperation. In 1977 the Attorney General agreed to sue the State of Maine for tribal lands, but refused to join small private landowners as defendants on the grounds that they were "completely innocent of any wrongdoing."

Pendency of the suit threw a cloud on title over a large part of the state and impaired municipalities' ability to float revenue bonds, resulting in congressional and Presidential pressure for a prompt, negotiated settlement. In 1977 the tribes and the State rejected a Presidential mediator's suggestion of 25,000,000 federal dollars and 100,000 acres of state lands in satisfaction of tribal claims. A proposal for $50,500,000 and 300,000 acres to be acquired for $5.00 per acre at federal expense was rejected the following year. Acknowledging that further litigation, even if successful, would cost at least $1,000,000 and jeopardize land transactions for five or more years, Maine State Attorney General Richard Cohen won state agreement to a third compromise plan and, in 1980, a tribal-state agreement was submitted for congressional approval.

The "Maine Indian Claims Settlement Act" ratifies all land transactions previously made in that State in contravention of the Indian Trade and Intercourse Act. As compensation, tribes may use $54,500,000 to purchase 300,000 acres, and the income from a $27,000,000 trust fund for other purposes. Neither fund is to be considered in determining the eligibility of the State, tribes, or tribal members for federal financial assistance. The Secretary of the Interior manages both funds and supervises the tribes' purchase, development, and use of reacquired lands. No part of the cost of settlement is borne by the State, on the theory that past state expenditures for the benefit and support of the tribes were substantial and gratuitous.

At first blush, this settlement for the equivalent of approximately

$25,000 and 275 acres per capita appears generous compared to the results of Indian Claims Commission Act litigation. The Passamaquoddy and Penobscot tribes paid a considerable political price, however, agreeing in exchange for compensation to place themselves for most purposes under state governance and jurisdiction. "Except as otherwise provided" by the State's claims settlement implementing act, "all Indians, Indian nations, and tribes and bands of Indians in the State and any lands or other natural resources owned by them . . . shall be subject to the laws of the State and to the civil and criminal jurisdiction of the courts of the State to the same extent as any other person or lands or other natural resources therein." The tribes reserve exclusive legislative authority and jurisdiction only over "internal tribal matters" such as membership, tribal government organization, and the "right to reside" on tribally owned lands. Tribal courts retain original forum jurisdiction over juvenile matters, domestic relations, and small claims involving only tribal matters, but must apply Maine laws. Tribal authority to regulate hunting and fishing is subject to state approval, and may not discriminate against nonmenbers. On all other matters, tribes have the same legislative powers as Maine's non-tribal municipalities, but must prosecute ordinance violations by nonmenbers in state courts.

Reacquired lands are subject to state taxes, although there can be no foreclosure for nonpayment. Reacquired lands can be lost by the State's exercise of eminent domain when there is no "reasonably feasible alternative," however, leaving the affected tribe two years to apply any compensation to the purchase of substitute acreage. Tribes' sovereign immunity is waived in effect, if not in principle, by provision for paying money claims against the tribes out of the settlement trust fund. As explained by Maine Attorney General Cohen, the settlement plan is "based on the principle that all Maine laws must apply to all lands and citizens within the State and that we all must live under one system of law which governs us all." As such, that settlement gained for the State a measure of control over Indian lands unlike that in any other state."

A similar yet smaller claim was settled in Rhode Island in 1978: the Narragansett tribe received 900 acres of land from the state (worth an estimated $2,700,000) and $3,500,000 from the US to purchase an additional 900 acres on the open market. Since the Narragansetts had lost all of its territory through a sale to Rhode Island in 1880, it no longer functioned as a tribal government and was content to accept a corporate structure to hold the land subject to all state laws.

The Mashpee, Chappaquiddick, Catowka, and Oneida Indians all are negotiating their land claims, although the former two have lost their initial court cases; the latter two have been successful and have forced the federal government to exercise its trust responsibility by acting on their behalf.

That these eastern settlements have been larger than ANCSA or the Indian

Claims Commission awards is due in part to the effects of inflation and partly to their success in the courts. It must be remembered, however, that the lands they have relinquished are far more valuable and they have suffered from dispossession for many more years. They have also voluntarily surrendered most aspects of residual sovereignty and self-government. Furthermore, the settlements represent approximately one percent of the current value of the land released, not counting loss of use and accrued interest.

(b) The Australian Experience

The first point that must be realized about land rights in Australia is that aboriginal title has yet to be recognized by the courts. Early decisions categorically rejected the argument that the Aboriginal people had any form of government, any laws of their own or any sovereignty. Recent decisions have altered this position somewhat by indicating that the Aborigines did have a highly evolved and complex legal system with clear connections to defined territories. Nevertheless, the Northern Territory Supreme Court denied that the Australian version of the common law included any recognition of aboriginal title in the Gove Land rights case, *Mathaman* v. *Nabalco Pty. Ltd.* (1969), 14 FLR 10; and *Milirrpum* v. *Nabalco Pty. Ltd. and the Commonwealth of Australia* (1971), 17 FLR 141, (For further information see J. Hookey, ''The Gove Land Rights Case: A Judicial Dispensation for the Taking of Aboriginal Lands in Australia?'' (1972), 5 FLR 85; P. Chartrand, ''The Status of Aboriginal Land Rights in Australia'', (1981) 19 *Alberta law Review* 436), while the High Court rejected any continuing sovereignty in *Coe* v. *Commonwealth of Australia* (1977), 18 ALR 592; (1979) 24 ALR 118. It should be noted, however, that a major new test case is before the High Court which may definitively resolve this issue (*Mabo* v. *Government of Queensland and the Commonwealth*).

Despite these judicial setbacks, Aboriginal land rights are receiving considerable public and governmental attention in all parts of Australia. The present government in office in Queensland has completely rejected Aboriginal rights, although the Queensland government has offered fifty year grants of deeds in trust to communities for their reserve land, but the pressure against this policy is increasing. New South Wales tabled a draft land rights settlement act in December 1982 which was passed in early 1983 under protest by Aboriginal associations. The Victoria government has been considering its own bill since April of 1982 and a draft statute was released for consideration in 1983. The Tasmanian government has also drafted legislation which recognizes a very small amount of land as being under Aboriginal ownership. The new Labour government in Western Australia completed an independent review in 1984 of the means to implement land rights after deciding politically that it would do so.

The most significant actions have transpired in the Northern Territory (NT) and South Australia. After receiving reports from an inquiry in 1974 on land rights, the then federal Labour government introduced legislation in 1975 to transfer all reserves in the NT to Aboriginal ownership and to establish a land commission to hear and report on all Aboriginal claims in that territory. The subsequent Liberal government passed a modified version of the earlier bill, which immediately vested 249,013 square kilometers of reserve land, or about 18 percent of the NT, in Aboriginal Land Councils.

The Aboriginal Land Rights (Northern Territory) Act of 1976 addresses issues relating to managing the land conveyed and its future development. It also establishes the position of Aboriginal Land Commmmissioner to receive all claims for additional land. After exhaustive hearings, he issues a report with conclusions regarding the validity of the claim and recommendations concerning what land should be granted if the claim is upheld. The ultimate decision is in the hands of the Minister of Aboriginal Affairs.

The Commissioner considers the following criteria in the 1976 Act, as amended, in assessing the validity of the claim:

50.(1) The functions of the Commissioner are—
(a) on an application being made to the Commissioner by or on behalf of Aboriginals claiming to have a traditional land claim to an area of land, being unalienated Crown land or alienated Crown land in which all estates and interests not held by the Crown are held by, or on behalf of, Aboriginals —
   (i) to ascertain whether those Aboriginals or any other Aboriginals are the traditional Aboriginal owners of the land; and
   (ii) to report his findings to the Minister and to the Administrator of the Northern Territory, and, where he finds that there are Aboriginals who are the traditional Aboriginal owners of the land, to make recommendations to the Minister for the granting of the land or any part of the land in accordance with sections 11 and 12;
(b) to inquire into the likely extent of traditional land claims by Aboriginals to alienated Crown land and to report to the Minister and to the Administrator of the Northern Territory, from time to time, the results of his inquiries;
(c) to establish and maintain a register of the traditional land claims referred to in paragraph (b);
(d) to advise the Minister in connexion with any other matter relevant to the operation of this Act that is referred to the Commissioner by the Minister, and
(e) to advise the Minister and the Administrator of the Northern Territory in connexion with any other matter relating to land in the Northern Territory that is referred to the Commissioner by the Minister with the concurrence of the Administrator of the Northern Territory.

(1A) For the purposes of sub-section (1), land in the Alligator Rivers Area (No. 3) that is alienated Crown Land in which all estates and interests not held by ther Crown are held by the Director shall be deemed to be unalienated Crown land.

(2) The Commissioner may, with the approval of the Minister, perform any function that may be conferred on him by a law of the Northern Territory.

(3) In making a report in connexion with a traditional land claim the Commissioner shall have regard to the strength or otherwise of the traditional attachment by the claimants to the land claimed, and shall comment on each of the following matters:

(a) the number of Aboriginals with traditional attachments to the land claimed who would be advantaged, and the nature and extent of the advantage that would accrue to those Aboriginals, if the claim were acceded to either in whole or in part;

(b) the detriment to persons or communities including other Aboriginal groups that might result if the claim were acceded to either in whole or in part;

(c) the effect which acceding to the claim either in whole or in part would have on the existing or proposed patterns of land usage in the region; and

(d) where the claim relates to alienated Crown land — the cost of acquiring the interests of persons (other than the Crown) in the land concerned.

(4) In carrying out his functions the Commissioner shall have regard to the following principles:

(a) Aboriginals who by choice are living at a place on the traditional country of the tribe or linguistic group to which they belong but do not have a right or entitlement to live at that place ought, where practicable, to be able to acquire secure occupancy at that place;

(b) Aboriginals who are not living at a place on the traditional country of the tribe or linguistic group to which they belong but desire to live at such a place ought, where practicable, to be able to acquire secure occupancy of such a place.

As of mid-1982, a further 157,535 square kilometers was being vested in Aboriginal Land Trusts under the management of Aboriginal Land Councils as a result of the claims process. Aborigines now own 30 percent of the Northern Territory, which is an area one and a half times the size of the United Kingdom. Approximately another 20 percent of the NT is under claim as still being "unalienated Crown land" within the terms of the Act. The Aboriginal Land Rights (NT) Act does not, however, provide any mechanism for granting compensation to the Aborigines for loss of use of the land over the years, damage to land which is conveyed, or for the land which has already been alienated by the Crown. As the Aboriginal people have received no money under the claims process, they are forced to rely upon mining royalties or federal grants from the Aboriginal Development Commission to engage in economic enterprises and community development projects as alternatives to the welfare system.

The other major settlement occurred in South Australia: the state passed the Pitjantjatjara Land Rights Act, 1981 after over three years of discussions with the Pitjantjatjara Land Council. Under this statute, freehold title far over 100,000 square kilometers of traditional land in the far north-west, comprising approximately 10 per cent of South Australia, was vested in an Aboriginal corporation. The people also have the right to control entry to the land and negotiate any development agreements that they choose. The Act does not provide any form of compensation beyond the land transfer. A second major settlement has been completed in South Australia transferring a further 10% into Aboriginal hands to the Maralinga people.

Although the struggle for land rights in Australia has a long way to go before it is completely successful, the experiences in the Northern Territory and South Australia regarding the quantum and manner of land transfers, the way in which land is vested, and the approach to mining development should be given serious consideration by Canadians. New proposals by the Commonwealth Government (federal) deserve detailed review.

6. Conclusion

Commissioner Barber of the Indian Claims Commission analyzed the various approaches to settling claims and the inherent difficulties in this area in a presentation to the Joint NIB-Cabinet Committee in April 1975:

Commissioner on Indian Claims — *A Report: Statements and Conclusions*, 1977, pp. 38-41.

> Over the years very little has been done to deal effectively with fundamental Indian grievances. The courts have reviewed some issues, but usually in a patchwork manner and often without the benefit of direct representation on the Indians' behalf. In general, judgments have tended to be negative although, in some instances, and particularly in recent years, the courts have supported Indian contentions. The problem is that the issues commonly transcend strictly legal criteria. While there are aspects of law which support Indian claims, there are others, often procedural, which tend to fortify an opposite viewpoint and, while some claims may be recognized by the courts, legal remedies may not exist. Furthermore, the problems are frequently much too complex to be dealt with fully through a purely legal apparatus. While the courts will

undoubtedly continue to be used, they cannot be expected to play the primary role. Special claims mechanisms must be created to resolve the issues.

The are two basic forms of claims process available: adjudication and negotiation. The former provides a rational, orderly method of resolving claims. Arguments are presented by the interested parties and there is usually a concerted effort to ensure that the procedure is fair and that justice is seen to be done. Some serious objections to this method, however, have caused both the Indians and the Federal Government to seek alternatives.

The major difficulty is that, like the courts, adjudicatory bodies tend to be restrictive. They operate within a carefully defined set of rules and their ability to commit a government is usually so circumscribed that they are unable to consider broader political and moral issues. Their power to redress grievances is characteristically limited to monetary compensation; they are thus ill-equipped to encompass the many-faceted questions of resource allocation which lie at the root of most claims. They tend to approach issues in terms of rights and to concern themselves with the validity of the claimant's case. To make decisions in this way they require direction as to the nature of the rights in question, in the same way that the courts review issues in relation to established law. This creates substantial problems since the definition of Indian rights is usually the chief point in dispute. Until these questions of rights are resolved, adjudicatory bodies cannot deal satisfactorily with most Indian claims. Taken in isolation, they are certainly handicapped in their ability to alleviate the sense of grievance which created the claim.

In addition, adjudicatory processes have operational disadvantages. Their formal approach is time-consuming and costly. They tend to rely on representation through lawyers and on the testimony of expert witnesses, thus denying Indian people any direct role in claims settlement. Further, many contentions cannot be effectively treated without provincial involvement, and it is doubtful that the provinces would submit to an adjudicatory mechanism which would make binding judgments in relation to provincial land and other resources.

The method of negotiation, on the other hand, appears to offer more promise. Through it, the Government and Indians might work towards comprehensive agreements encompassing forms of redress other than simple monetary settlements. Such agreements could accommodate future needs as well as past grievances and, what is more important, would involve mutual acceptability, a result which adjudication by a third part could not achieve. Indians, through their leaders, would participate directly, a feature of clear importance to Indian people. Thus, while adjudication may have some place in resolving claims, negotiation is inherently superior. Both the Federal Government and Indian leaders appear to concur on this point.

There are, however, problems with such negotiations which must be faced. The countervailing power that exists in many dispute settings, for example in labour relations is not present in this situation. Labour disputes are negotiated with the knowledge that each party can do economic harm to the other; a strike, the result of a breakdown in negotiations, is economic. warfare fought on the assumption that power is reasonably equally distributed. Native people do not have any such direct economic threat and the Government, of course, has the ability to legislate its will unilaterally. Indians, therefore, are ultimately left with only the opportunity to engage in moral suasion and political argument, and they are a small minority. This might suggest that it would be impossible to achieve fair, effective negotiations.

Yet, an important offsetting factor is the Federal Government's own special responsibility for Indians. This should reduce the tendency towards viewing negotiations as a power struggle, and create a situation where both parties should be concerned with the interest of the Indians. Even so, the inherent adversary element in any such negotiations will make this difficult. While native people look to the Government as a trustee, there is no avoiding the fact that their claims are against this same trustee and often centre on the very nature of the Government's trust responsibility. Moreover, whatever Indians gain through negotiations, other Canadians may lose. The Government must necessarily be conscious of these political ramifications.

If negotiations on the key issues are to be fruitful, I am convinced that they must directly involve members of the Cabinet. There are a number of reasons for this conclusion. Indians have a special constitutional status in relation to the Federal Government, and essential questions about their rights and their relationship with the Government merit the quality of attention from Ministers that, for example, federal-provincial matters receive.

Although such an avenue has always been extended through the Minister in charge of Indian Affairs, that method presents some fundamental problems. Many of the claims are being pressed against the Department of Indian Affairs, and Indians feel strongly that there would be an intolerable conflict of interest if the Department alone were to assess their claims. This concern does not apply to the Minister himself, whom they regard as their current trustee; they value their relationship with him a great deal and do not want him to be cast as their adversary. On the contrary, to the extent that there are both adversary and protective elements in the situation, they would prefer that he be as free as possible to concern himself with the protective aspects, in particular the Government's trust responsibility.

Most importantly, the direct involvement of Cabinet Ministers would help reduce the very serious differences of perception which plague the field of Indian affairs. Appointed people, this Commissioner included, may be able to assist, but can never effectively communicate across the social and cultural gap existing between Indians and non-Indians. The mutual understanding crucial to resolving these issues can only be achieved through direct dialogue between Indian leaders and the politicians who have the standing requisite to respond authoritatively. Indian people should not be expected to pass their vital concerns through appointed "interpreters" to remote decision-makers. There are enough problems without adding the distortions which are inevitable when Indians try to communicate through a series of officials with conflicting fundamental viewpoints. The essential questions, in any event, are almost entirely political, and Ministers must be involved if negotiations are to be productive.

Despite such arguments, the Government may be reluctant to dedicate the time of busy Cabinet Ministers to this task. Doubtless other groups in society will feel they should be given similar attention, but this situation is truly exceptional. We are dealing here with a heritage of over one hundred years of political grievances. With the increasing awareness and rising expectations and frustrations of the Indians, the so-called "Indian problem" today has bcome critical. If a base is not properly laid now, there is little hope for the future.

The intervening years have done little to minimize the problems; in fact, the social and economic difficulties faced by the Aboriginal People have increased, while their longstanding political, moral and legal grievances have continued unresolved.

The required degree of commitment and mutual understanding which is essential for the settlement of land claims does not yet appear to be present. Continuing domestic and international pressure combined with the impact of the new Canadian Constitution may well change this situation. Dissatisfaction with the federal policy may encourage further use of international fora to seek the resolution of claims[14] or litigation in the Canadian courts due to the presence of s. 35 of the Constitution Act.

Endnotes

1. Office of Native Claims, *Native Claims: Policy, Processes and Perspectives* (Ottawa: Supply and Services Canada, 1978), p. 4.
2. *Ibid.*
3. V.F. Valentine, "Native Peoples and Canadian Society: A Profile of Issues and Trends" in *Cultural Boundaries and the Cohesion of Canada* (Montreal: The Institute for Research on Public Policy, 1980).
4. J.R. Ponting and R. Gibbins, *Out of Irrelevance: A Socio-Political Introduction to Indian Affairs in Canada* (Toronto: Butterworths and Company, 1980), p. 265.

5. Department of Indian Affairs and Northern Development, *In All Fairness — A Native Claims Policy — Comprehensive Claims* (Ottawa: Supply and Services Canada, 1981), p. 19.
6. *Ibid.*, p. 27.
7. Department of Indian Affairs and Northern Development, *Outstanding Business — A Native Claims Policy — Specific Claims* (Ottawa: Supply and Services Canada, 1982), pp. 15-16.
8. *Ibid.*, p. 3.
9. *Ibid.*, p. 16.
10. *Ibid.*, p. 19.
11. See e.g., *R.* v. *Secretary of State for Foreign and Commonwealth Affairs, ex parte Indian Association of Alberta and Others*, [1982] 2 All E.R. 118 (C.A.), in Chapter Four.
12. *Ibid.*, pp. 13-14.
13. *Ibid.*
14. See the last chapter for a greater discussion of these options; and R.L. Barsh and J.Y. Henderson, "Aboriginal Rights, Treaty Rights and Human Rights: Indian Tribes and Constitutional Renewal", (1982) 17 *J. Can. Studies*, No. 2, pp. 55-81.

7. Questions

1. What are the advantages and disadvantages of the various claims processes and settlements reached in Australia, Canada and the United States? Which approach do you favour and why?
2. Why have the land portion of settlements in Australia been larger than those in Canada despite the non-recognition of aboriginal title by Australian courts?
3. What have been the repercussions of land settlements upon indigenous peoples and the general society over the years?
4. Why have the comprehensive claims settlements in Canada been broader and more far-reaching on matters other than land and money than the Australian and American experience? What advantages or disadvantages does the Canadian approach provide?
5. What changes would you make in Canadian claims policy? Why?
6. What has occurred after settlements that have been viewed as unsatisfactory by the claimants?
7. What changes would you make in Canadian land claims settlements? Why?

8. Further Reading

Barsh, Russel L., "Indian Land Claims Policy in the United States", (1982) 58 *N. Dak. L. Rev.* 7.

Berger, Justice Thomas R., *Northern Frontier, Northern Homeland*, Vol. 1, 1977, Ottawa, Government Printer.

Brown, George and Ron Maguire, *Indian Treaties in Historical Perspective*, 1979, Ottawa, Department of Indian and Northern Affairs.

Canada, Indian Claims Commission, *Indian Claims in Canada*, 1975, Ottawa, Government Printer.

Chartrand, Philip E., "The Status of Aboriginal Land Rights in Australia", (1981) 19 *Alta. L.R.* 436.

Cohen, Felix S., "Original Indian Title" and "Indian Claims" in L.K. Cohen, ed., *The Legal Conscience*, 1960, New Haven, Yale University Press.

Colvin, Eric, *Legal Process and the Resolution of Indian Claims*, Saskatoon, University of Saskatchewan Native Law Centre, 1981.

Daniel, Richard C., *A History of Native Claims Processes in Canada 1867-1979*, Ottawa; Treaties and Historical Research Centre, Department of Indian and Northern Affairs, 1980.

Daniels, Harry W., *We Are the New Nation — The Metis and National Native Policy*, Ottawa; Native Council of Canada, 1979.

—————————, ed., *The Forgotten People — Metis and non-status Indian Land Claims*, Ottawa; Native Council of Canada, 1979.

Harris, Stewart, *It's Coming Yet . . . An Aboriginal Treaty within Australia between Australians*, 1979, Canberra, Aboriginal Treaty Committee.

Hocking, Barbara, "Does Aboriginal Law Now Run in Australia", (1979) 10 *Fed. L. Rev.* 161.

Hookey, John, "The Gove Land Rights Case: a Judicial Dispensation for the Taking of Aboriginal Lands in Australia", (1972) 5 *Fed. L. Rev.* 85.

La Rusic, Ignatius E., et al., *Negotiating a Way of Life: Initial Cree Experience with the administrative structure arising from the James Bay Agreement, 1979* (Available from Department of Indian and Northern Affairs).

Lester, Geoffrey and Graham Parker, "Land Rights: the Australian Aborigines Have Lost a Legal Battle, But . . .", (1973) 11 *Alta. L.R.* 189.

Lysyk, Kenneth, "Approaches to Settlement of Indian Title Claims: The Alaskan Model", (1973) 8 *U.B.C. Law Rev.* 321.

—————————, "The United States Indian Claims Commission", in Peter Cumming and Neil Mickenberg, eds., *Native Rights in Canada*, 2d ed., 1972, Toronto, General Publishing Co.

Mickenberg, Neil H., "Aboriginal Rights in Canada and the United States", (1971) 9 *Osgoode Hall L.J.* 119.

Morse, Bradford W., ed., *Indian Land Claims in Canada*, 1981 (Available from Department of Indian and Northern Affairs).

Native Council of Canada, *Native People and the Constitution of Canada — The Report of the Metis and Non-Status Indian Constitutional Review Commission*, Ottawa; Mutual Press, 1981) (Available from the Native Council of Canada).

New South Wales, *Green Paper on Aboriginal Land Rights in New South Wales*, 1982, Sydney, Government Printer.

Price, Monroe, ''A Moment in History: The Alaska Native Claims Settlement Act'', (1979) 8 *U.C.L.A. — Alaska L.R.* 89.

Redbird, Duke, *We Are Metis — A Metis View of the Development of a Native Canadian People,* Willowdale, Ont.; Ontario Metis and Non Status Indian Association, 1980.

Richardson, Boyce, *Strangers Devour the Land*, 1975, Toronto, Macmillan.

Vance, John, ''Indian Claims — The U.S. Experience'', (1973-74), 38 *Sask. Law Rev.* 1.

11. The Implementation of the James Bay and Northern Quebec Agreement

WENDY MOSS

The federal policy of settling outstanding native claims based on Indian title and Aboriginal rights has, since it was announced in 1973, produced only one significant concluded settlement — the James Bay and Northern Quebec Agreement.[1] Although the James Bay Agreement is essentially a modern version of the treaties concluded one hundred years ago between the Government of Canada and the prairie Indian peoples, it is otherwise an unprecedented chapter in Indian-government relations in Canada. For example, unlike the older treaties, the James Bay Agreement unquestionably has the legal status of a contract, and most — if not all — of its provisions have the force of law as a result of federal and provincial enactments ratifying and implementing its provisions.[2] In addition, there are several unique features to the rights granted to the native parties. For example, section 30 establishes an income security programme for Cree hunters and trappers; the first such programme anywhere in Canada. Sections 22 and 23 provide for the first environmental impact review and assessment procedure in the province of Quebec, as part of a general environmental regime.

The catalytic event leading to negotiations and eventually to settlement was the James Bay Hydroelectric Project, which the Quebec government began to construct in 1971 in an area not yet ceded and which was still used by native people engaged in a traditional hunting economy. This enormous project involved the damming and diversion of several major rivers flowing into James Bay and the flooding of several thousand acres of land. In the process, the livelihood of a good many native people (Cree and Inuit) in northern Quebec would be destroyed. No consultation or negotiation of land claims had been anticipated by the Quebec government, even though the province had a statutory obligation, under the Boundary Extension Acts of 1912, to deal with the Indian title of those native people living in the newly added territory.[3] The land in question was part of a tract comprising approximately 410,000 square miles that had been transferred by the federal government to the province of Quebec on condition,

> That the province of Québec will recognize the rights of the Indian inhabitants in the territory above described to the same extent, and will obtain surrenders of such rights in the same manner, as the Government of Canada has heretofore recognized such rights and has obtained

surrender thereof, and the said province shall bear and satisfy all charges and expenditures in connection with or arising out of such surrenders.[4]

Requests by the Cree and the Inuit to negotiate a cession of their property interest, as well as some form of compensation for the loss of hunting and other economic rights, were ignored by the provincial government. Consequently, the Cree and the Inuit instituted legal proceedings against Quebec and its Crown corporation, the James Bay Development Corporation, for the purpose of securing an injunction prohibiting construction until the native interests had been dealt with. At trial, an interim injunction to halt the project was granted by Mr Justice Malouf.[5] This decision was overturned by the Quebec Court of Appeal[6] and, before the appeal to the Supreme Court of Canada was heard, a settlement was reached in the form of the James Bay and Northern Quebec Agreement. In addition to the native parties (the Grand Council of the Cree (of Quebec); the Northern Québec Inuit Association; the Inuit of Quebec; and the Inuit of Port Burwell), and the two levels of government, three corporate business entities were parties to the Agreement: the James Bay Development Corporation, the James Bay Energy Corporation and Hydro-Quebec. The inclusion of business interests in a land claims settlement is another distinctive feature of the Agreement.

The James Bay Agreement, comprising some 450 pages, was negotiated under the heavy pressure of a rigid time deadline set by all the parties. Lawyers and various technical consultants played major roles in the negotiations, as is evidenced by the highly technical and legally complex nature of the Agreement. An immense administrative structure has been created for the application of its provisions, and the employment of legal and other consultants continues to be an essential way of ensuring that the Agreement is adequately carried out. The complexity of the Agreement is one of many features that have been attacked by other native groups, which, without exception, severely criticized the Agreement at its signing.[7] Of primary concern was the legislative extinguishment of all native interest to the territory covered by the Agreement, by virtue of subsection 3(3) of the James Bay and Northern Québec Native Claims Settlement Act.[8] This, it was said, set an undesirable precedent for other negotiations elsewhere in the country being conducted by groups that advocated the retention of some form of legal right to or interest in traditional native lands even after settlement was reached. Other Aboriginal groups also took objection to the significant amount of legislative and administrative jurisdiction over Indians and Inuit transferred by the federal government to the province in regard to the provision of health services and education. Although the federal government is often considered to be derelict in its responsibilities towards indigenous people, native groups generally hold an even deeper mistrust of how much a provincial government would exert itself on behalf of an Indian or Inuit population. Criticism was also made of the cash settlement of $75 million (as part of the total monetary compensation of $225 million) given in place of royalties from the development of the region's natural resources.

The Cree and Inuit still maintain that the Agreement is satisfactory in its terms, even though both groups have been very unhappy about the performance of both governments on certain aspects of it. Under the Agreement, the Cree and the Inuit were promised a number of rights, benefits and services in exchange for the extinguishment of their Indian title; the cessation of legal proceedings regarding the James Bay Hydroelectric Project (and a promise not to institute future proceedings regarding that particular development project); and the renouncing of any right to royalties and so on from resource development. The Agreement established a land regime[9] dividing the territory into three categories of land, by which are determined the kind and nature of native property rights and hunting rights throughout the territory. Native hunting rights are set out in detail in section 24 of the Agreement (and later by An Act respecting hunting and fishing rights in the James Bay and New Québec Territories[10]). In Category 1 and 2 lands for example, the Cree and the Inuit have the exclusive right to hunt, fish and trap. Regional and local governments run by the Cree and the Inuit, with jurisdiction over Category 1 lands, have been created in the conventional form of municipal governments, although these governments do possess a few limited but extraordinary powers (for example, over hunting and fishing rights and over the environment).

However, the local and regional government systems provided for the Cree and the Inuit are not the same. While the Inuit are completely within provincial jurisdiction as far as the Agreement is concerned,[11] the Cree have retained some federal jurisdiction by splitting their Category 1 lands into 1A lands (under federal jurisdiction) and 1B lands (under provincial jurisdiction).[12] As a result, there now are (on passage of the Cree-Naskapi (of Quebec) Act, Bill C-46, which was passed in June 1984 and replaces the Indian Act in the James Bay Region) two sets of municipal corporations providing local government to the Cree communities. Since all the Cree communities live on 1A lands, the membership of the 1B municipal councils is essentially the same as the Band Councils which presently have jurisdiction over the 1A lands. Federal Band Corporations will succeed the present Band Councils as the local government power in 1A lands. Provincial legislation has already created Cree village municipalities with jurisdiction over the 1B lands.[14] The 1B lands, like the Inuit Category 1 lands, are completely owned by the native people through land-holding corporations.[15] In the case of the 1A lands, however, "bare ownership" rests with Quebec; "administration, management and control" lie with Canada; and the "exclusive use and benefit" lie in the Cree local government.[16]

Category 2 is composed of public lands governed by the James Bay Regional Zone Council,[17] three of whose six members are appointed by the

Cree. As in Category 1, the Cree have *exclusive* rights   1) to hunt, fish and trap; 2) to commercial fisheries; 3) to determine if and under what conditions non-native people may hunt and fish (and may pass bylaws in this regard); 4) to establish and operate outfitting operations; 5) to soapstone and other traditional materials for arts and crafts.

In Category 3 lands, native people may continue to hunt, fish and trap without licences, but these activities are subject to the right of the provincial government, the James Bay Energy Corporation, Hydro-Quebec and the James Bay Development Corporation and any other authorized persons to develop these lands. The Cree nevertheless have the exclusive right to some species of fish and the right of first refusal over the issuance of outfitting licenses.

The major feature of the Agreement in the eyes of the Cree are the provisions designed to preserve as much of their traditional hunting life as possible. To this end, section 24 sets out a detailed hunting regime and section 30 provides for an income security programme for Cree hunters and trappers and an environmental regime is set out in section 22. The integrity of native cultures are also to be protected by special provisions regarding education (sections 16 and 17) and the administration of justice (sections 18, 19, 20 and 21).

Sections 28 and 29 impose joint obligations on the federal and provincial governments to correct the displacement of native people from their hunting economies as a result of industrial and commercial development, by providing various programs and services that will contribute to the economic and social development of both native groups. Reassured by the success of the hunting regime and the income security programme, the Cree are now concentrating their efforts on the implementation of section 28, a kind of catch-all section for a variety of things they wanted but which could not be subsumed under the other headings such as hunting or education. Because of the way it was negotiated section 28 will probably be the most difficult to implement; since agreement was very difficult to achieve, its provisions were purposely left uncertain and ambiguous. Section 28 requires both levels of government to provide training programs and assistance in job placement so that the Cree will be filling a significant number of the permanent jobs created by the James Bay Development Project. Assistance is also to be given to Cree entrepreneurs and the Cree will be given priority in respect to any projects undertaken by either government in the region. Community services — essential sanitation services, fire protection, economic development agents, community workers and community centres — are to be provided by both governments. Section 28 also provides for the creation of the James Bay Native Development Corporation,[18] which has proven to be a major disappointment to the Cree, who feel that it does not adequately fulfil its mandate: to help finance Cree businesses.

Section 8 of the Agreement, which sets out the technical conditions for the construction of the James Bay Project, also provides for remedial works to offset, as much as is possible and practical, the negative effects of industrial commercial development upon wildlife and upon the environment. In accordance with the Agreement, a public corporation was created by special provincial legislation[19] to carry out these remedial works; it is financed to the extent of $30 million.

Last but not least, the Cree and the Inuit were together paid $225 million for the loss of the use their lands and for relinquishing the right to royalties from resource development. This money is disbursed according to a schedule set out in the Agreement and is paid to the native legal entities created by the Agreement. It is to be invested; the revenue and interest obtained is to be used to assist in the economic and social development of the beneficiaries (e.g., financial assistance to native entrepreneurs).

1. Implementation Problems

The primary difficulties to implementing the Agreement have been the lack of financial and overall planning by the federal government and the reluctance of both federal and provincial governments fully to recognize the extent of their obligations in a period of economic crisis. The federal government has been hard-pressed to find the funds to meet its obligations to provide the programmes and services specified in the Agreement, partly because it failed to cost the Agreement at the time of signing. Furthermore, there is no single body responsible for coordinating and planning the Agreement's implementation. Consequently, intergovernmental and interdepartmental disputes over which department or government is to do what are common occurrences. Another major factor contributing to arguments between the native people and the governments has been the uncertain language of certain provisions, particularily those that outline programme and service obligations. Sections like 28 and 29, which cover native economic and social development, contain many provisions which qualify government obligations in an unclear manner and thereby set up uncertain standards of expected performance. The ambiguity found in these sections are a sharp contrast to the specific descriptions of the parties' duties in the hunting regime (section 24) and section 30, which sets out the provisions governing the income security programme for Cree hunters and trappers. Both of these sections are considered to be have been successfully implemented to date and this success is partly attributable to the precise language used in these sections.

These problems were recognized by the Cree negotiators at the time the Agreement was drafted. The decision was taken, nevertheless, to settle for a general description of obligations with numerous qualifications of an ambiguous nature and to continue the fight to delineate the obligations more precisely *after* the Agreement had been signed. The reason for adopting this strategy was that both governments, but especially the federal government, were very much against having anything in the Agreement relating to socio-economic development; this appeared to be the only way to wring any promises out of them on this question. The federal government thought it had covered itself by introducing qualifications that would limit its obligations to whatever programmes and services it normally ran from time to time and that the services promised to the Cree and Inuit were to come out of the regular yearly departmental budgets. The Cree and Inuit, however, interpreted sections 28 and 29 as committing the governments to achieving the social and economic objectives specified; they argued that if the funds could not be found in regular departmental budgets, the governments were obligated to obtain the necessary funding through special appropriations. Both parties were eager to meet the deadlines they had set for themselves and both felt that they "had" the other by the time agreement was reached on the social and economic development sections. The process of negotiating the content of government obligations in sections 28 and 29 is still continuing. The Cree negotiators remain convinced that the shorter the time spent negotiating, the better the chances are of obtaining the best deal possible from government parties.

Particular problems with the Quebec government can be attributed to the inability of SAGMAI (Secretariat des Activités Gouvernmentales en Milieu Amerindien et Inuit), the provincial coordinating agency for native affairs, to understand and therefore communicate effectively with its native consti- tuency. At this writing the Inuit still appear to be dealing with the agency, but the Cree will have nothing to do with it, preferring, instead, to speak directly to the various provincial departments just as other citizens of Quebec do.

The danger of transferring jurisdiction over native affairs to a provincial government has become evident. Quebec has often tied proper performance of its obligations to a reduction of remaining federal jurisdiction over Quebec Cree communities and a recognition by the Cree of Quebec's sovereignty in the region. For example, section 28 provides that Canada and Quebec jointly provide essential sanitation services to the Cree communities. No distinction is drawn between the Cree 1A and 1B lands, but the provincial government has refused to extend its municipal services programme to the Cree communities or otherwise supply this essential infrastructure, on the ground that the Crees implicitly disqualified themselves from the programme by insisting on federal jurisdiction for the 1A lands. Cree applications to participate in other programmes provided by Quebec's Municipal Affairs Ministry have also been rejected. However, in 1982 there was a significant change in Cree-provincial relations, and negotiators now feel that a new phase has begun and that present implementation problems stand a good chance of being resolved to the satisfaction of both parties.

2. The Implementation Process

Immediately upon signing the Agreement, the Cree and the Inuit were faced with the huge task of recruiting and training native administrators, managers and staff for the dozens of new bodies created and called for by the Agreement. The Crees, for example, needed people to fill positions on more than thirty statutory bodies, committees and boards. Although some of these vacancies could wait until provincial legislation formally created bodies such as the landholding corporations, there were many sections that called for interim entities to begin work in the period before the proper statutory bodies (the Regional Health Boards, for instance) were created. The impressive speed and efficiency with which this was done is characteristic of the dogged determination both native groups have applied to the enormous challenge of making the Agreement work. Neither the Cree nor the Inuit have been fully reimbursed for the costs of financing these transitional measures nor for the costs of negotiating the Agreement and its implementing legislation. These expenses have caused a corresponding and permanent reduction in the native compensation funds.

Several sections of the Agreement specifically call for provincial legislation to confirm and further specify their provisions. The process of consultation and negotiation between the native representatives and the provincial and federal governments regarding these enactments created the suspicion that it provided an opportunity for the government to surreptitiously renegotiate the terms of the Agreement. The Cree feel that they have so far successfully resisted any such attempts.

With the necessary provincial legislation in place, the Cree and the Inuit became fully occupied with the never ending task of obtaining and overseeing the proper implementation of the Agreement. This stage provides yet another opportunity for the government parties to renegotiate the Agreement, since the translation of its terms into action by the federal and provincial bureaucracies necessarily involves an interpretative function. It is at this stage that the most bitter disputes between the governments and the native groups have occurred.

By 1980, the James Bay and Northern Quebec Agreement had reached a critical point in its brief history. Certain key sections had barely been acted upon, but the Cree and the Inuit seemed unable to elicit any concern in either Ottawa or Québec City. Both native groups found it hard to convince government officials and leaders that the successful implementation of the Cree hunter income security programme and other sections of the Agreement had been overshadowed by the poor performance of Quebec and Canada in regard to health and social services (sections 14 and 15), economic and social development (sections 28 and 29) and education (sections 16 and 17).

Prior to the Agreement, health and social services were provided only by the federal government and even these were inadequate. Sections 14 and 15 provided for a gradual transfer of jurisdiction over health services to the Quebec government, but any improvement in the quality of services was far from meeting essential needs in the Cree and Inuit communities. Health conditions in the region have been exacerbated and are clearly linked to the negligible performance of the obligations jointly imposed upon Canada and

Quebec to provide basic community infrastructure and municipal services such as access roads, airstrips, water and sewage systems, fire protection, and housing. By the spring of 1982, many of the eight Cree communities could say that their living conditions had not improved since the Agreement has been signed; the Inuit claim that, in their communities, conditions have significantly and steadily deteriorated.[20]

Each year the Cree have had to face crisis after crisis: epidemics of gastroenteritis among pre-school children has led to several deaths; outbreaks of tuberculosis; severe housing shortages; a poor supply of electricity in some communities has caused water services to be disrupted and schools to be closed. The federal government acknowledges that the poor state of native health may be attributed to the lack of water and sewer systems, the lack of community infrastructure, overcrowding in housing and generally inadequate health services.

Forced into a continual state of "crisis management," the Cree have had little opportunity since signing the Agreement to engage in long-term socio-economic planning. Indeed, all the revenue and interest earned by the Cree on their compensation monies up to the fiscal year 1981/82 — some $30 million was to be applied to socio-economic development for future generations — has been spent trying to remedy some of the conditions brought about by years of government neglect and government non-performance of contractual and statutory obligations. The Inuit, too, have spent the revenue from their compensation monies and a significant portion of the capital. (The Cree have also spent some of their capital, but not to the same degree as the Inuit).

The Agreement was clearly in danger of failing to meet several of its most important objectives. However, in the ten years since the first court action, the Cree and the Inuit have learned that in order to obtain what they believe is justly theirs, they must apply constant pressure on the two governments, through the bureaucracy, the courts, the House of Commons, or all three. The Cree, in particular, have taken this lesson to heart. Since 1980 they have mounted and maintained an intensive and well-organized lobby in Ottawa, across the nation and even overseas (at the United Nations, and at the World Health Organization in Geneva) to enlist support and to exert as much pressure as possible upon both levels of government but particularly upon the federal government. This pressure led to an unprecedented action by the House of Commons Indian Affairs Committee after they had heard testimony from the Cree and the Inuit last year. The Committee endorsed the native statements alleging government failures in implementation and called on the necessary government departments to meet federal obligations under the James Bay Agreement. This in turn prompted the Department of Indian Affairs to undertake an implementation review to determine whether the federal government has respected the spirit as well as the legal letter of the Agreement. While insisting that there has been no legal breach of the

Agreement, the "Tait Report" acknowledged that its spirit has frequently been violated and acknowledged the federal government's poor performance on several aspects. The conclusions of its own civil service and the efforts of the Cree and Inuit lobbies led the federal Cabinet in July 1982 to decide that further monies were to be granted to both groups to compensate for past transgressions and to remedy present problems. The sum of $32.34 million has been allocated to the Cree over the next five years for: "past and present construction of infrastructure to improve essential sanitation services, for construction of electric supply facilities, for construction of houses in Cree communities, for repayment to the Crees of certain health care expenditures, for CORE funding for the Cree Regional Authority and for certain aspects of the implementation of the Agreement by the Crees." A little more than $29 million has been allocated to the Inuit for similar purposes. Although both groups were happy to receive these amounts of money in a time of economic restraint, the allocations represent a fraction of what the native representatives estimated was required under the Agreement and as a result of subsequent letters of undertaking made by the federal government. The challenge of making the James Bay Agreement work has in no way diminished. As the federal government is well aware, the fate of the James Bay Agreement has become critically important because of the influence it will have on land claims negotiations elsewhere in Canada. Should the implementation of the Agreement come to be seen as a failure (when its terms are already regarded as undesirable), other native groups will be demanding proof and assurance that negotiated rights and benefits exchanged for aboriginal title (or for the right to develop on native lands) will not be undermined.

Endnotes

[1.] *The James Bay and Northern Quebec Agreement*, Editeur officiel du Quebec, 1976.

[2.] See *Appendix 1*, for a list of ratifying and implementing legislation.

[3.] An Act respecting the extension of the Province of Quebec by the annexation of Ungava, Que. 2 Geo. V C. 7 (1912), s. 2 of the Schedule. Quebec Boundaries Extension Act, 1912 Can. 2 Geo. V, c. 45, s. 2.

[4.] *Ibid.* Among other conditions relating to the native population — no surrender could be obtained of Indian lands without the approval of the Governor-in-Council and, further, the trusteeship of the Indians and management of lands reserved to them was to remain in the Government of Canada subject to the control of Parliament.

[5.] *Kanatewat et al.* v. *James Bay Development Corporation et al.*, [1974] RP 38 (Quebec Supreme Court).

[6.] *James Bay Development Corporation et al.* v. *Kanatewat et al.*, [1975] CA 166, (Quebec Court of Appeal).

[7.] It should be noted that the Cree, for example, are keenly aware of their reliance on white consultants. Whenever they are able to, it is their policy to replace white consultants with Cree.

[8.] The James Bay and Northern Quebec Native Claims Settlement Act, 25-26 Eliz. II, c. 32 (Statutes of Canada 1976-77).

[9.] An Act respecting the land regime in the James Bay and New Quebec Territories, Statues of Quebec 1978, c. 93.

[10.] An Act respecting hunting and fishing rights in the James Bay and New Quebec Territories, Statutes of Quebec 1978, c. 92.

[11.] Loi concernant les villages nordiques et l'administration régionale Kativik, LRQ, c. V-6.1. Loi concernant les villages nordiques et l'administration régionale Kativik, 1978, LQ c. 87.

[12.] *Supra*, note 9.

[13.] Indian Act, RSC 1970, c. I-6.

[14.] The Cree Villages Act, Statutes of Quebec 1978, c. 88.

[15.] Ownership by letters patent is vested in Cree landholding corporations created by An Act respecting the land regime in the James Bay and New Quebec Territories, Statutes of Quebec 1978, c. 93.

[16.] *Supra*, note 9.

[17.] An Act to establish the James Bay Regional Zone Council, Statutes of Quebec 1978, c. 90.

[18.] This was accomplished by An Act to incorporate the James Bay Native Development Corporation, Statutes of Québec 1978, c. 96.

[19.] An Act to create the La Grande Complex Remedial Works Corporation, Statutes of Quebec 1978, c. 95.

[20.] From excerpts of Inuit testimony on deteriorating conditions before the House of Commons, Minutes of Proceedings and Evidence of the Standing Committee on Indian Affairs and Northern Development, Issue No. 52, Wednesday 19 May 1982.

3. Appendix I
A List of Federal and Provincial Enactments Ratifying and Implementing the James Bay and Northern Quebec Agreement

1. Loi approuvant la Convention de la Baie James et du Nord québécois, 1977, LRQ, c. C-67

2. Loi amendée ré émission d'obligations, 1977, LQ, c. 15

3. Loi sur le règlement des revendications des autochtones de la Baie James et du Nord québécois, 1976-77, SC c. 32

4. Loi sur l'instruction publique, 1977, LRQ c. I-14
   (non refondu, 1978, LQ, c. 78)

5. Loi concernant les villages nordiques et l'administration régionale Kativik, LRQ, c. V-6.1

6. Loi concernant les villages nordiques et l'administration régionale Kativik, 1978, LQ, c. 87

7. Loi de la qualité de l'environnement, LRQ c. Q-2
   amendement 1978, LQ, c. 94

8. Loi constituant la Société des travaux de correction du Complexe La Grande, 1978, LQ, c. 95

9. Loi constituant la Société de développement autochtone de la Baie James, 1978, LQ, c. 96

10. Loi concernant les autochtones cris, inuit et naskapis, LRA, c. A-33.1

11. Loi approuvant la Convention du Nord-Est québécois, 1978, LQ, c. 98

12. Loi sur la sécurité du revenu des chasseurs et piégeurs cris bénéficiaires

de la Convention de la Baie James et du Nord québécois, 1979, LQ, c. 16

13. Loi concernant les villages cris, 1978, LQ, c. 88

14. Loi concernant l'administration régionale crie, 1978, LQ, c. 89

15. Loi constituant le conseil régional de zone de la Baie James, 1978, LQ, c. 80

16. Loi constituant la Société Makivik, 1978, LQ, c. 91

17. Loi concernant les droits de chasse et de pêche dans les territoires de la Baie James et du Nouveau-Québec, 1978, LQ, c. 92

18. Loi concernant le régime des terres dans les territoires de la Baie James et du Nouveau-Québec, 1978, LQ, c. 93

19. Loi concernant les dispositions législatives prévues par la Convention du Nord-Est québécois et modifiant d'autres dispositions législatives 1979, LQ, c. 25 (projet de loi 26).

12. Canada's North and Native Rights

PETER CUMMING

1. Canada as a Nation State and How This Relates to Northern Development

Canada is at least the equal of any of the advanced societies in the world. It has all the technological benefits of the industrial society with the attendant high standards of living. This growth has meant that the public sector has been able to provide Canadians with all kinds of social services. However, the growth of the Canadian industrial state has not yet so changed the social and physical environment as to compromise traditional values. Canada is a free society with the traditional core values and institutions remaining intact.

True, the forces of significant economic and cultural change constitute a threatening challenge to Canada. How does Canada go forward, maximizing the advantages of an industrial and free society, yet maintaining a high standard of living?

Compare Canada's position with those nations with which Canada has significant ties. Britain and France, the charter cultures of Canada, may maintain their quality of life, but one must question the strength of their economies. Canada's economy and culture can never escape the enveloping shadow of its all-powerful neighbour to the south. Yet while the United States may continue to have a robust economy, one can argue that the country no longer has a maintainable quality of life.

Clearly, Canada does not want to follow the examples of Britain, France, or the United States. Canada is the world's second largest country in size (after the USSR) with only 25 million people, with a Gross National Product of $350 billion, and abundant natural resources. It has the cultural heritage, industrial capacity, and social and physical environment to become a model society.

Canada's North constitutes a major factor in realizing that promise. However, since less than one-third of one per cent of the country's population lives in the North, and less than five per cent of Canadians have ever been there, few of them appreciate the magnitude of its unique potential or the problems it faces.

What are the present problems faced by Canada, and how they affect northern development?

A fundamental problem of advanced, industrial democratic society is the growth of monolithic institutions — big cities, bureaucracies, corporations, and trade unions. These necessary and often beneficial institutions have grown to the point where the checks and balances of the former frontier society are no longer present. They continue to serve the legitimate needs of the institutional self-interest, but they tend to get out of control. This phenomenon is exacerbated by the fact that the institutions are intertwined. Self-interested and unchecked growth of any institution becomes counter-productive to the larger public interest.

The result is continuing quantitative development, often accompanied by a qualitative deterioration. Paradoxically, as society grows, many of its services disintegrate. This is not to argue for no growth. We must have industrial growth. But if Canadians are to have a "quality" society, growth must be balanced by having due regard to all factors relevant to the public interest.

2. Northern Development and Institutions in Decision-making

Turning to northern development, let us consider a few examples. With respect to the development of petroleum and natural gas, the competitive market system worked well in the 1950s and 1960s, with the result that the price of oil and gas actually fell between 1950 and 1970. However in 1973, because of the external OPEC cartel and an insufficient domestic supply to meet demand, the price of oil and gas increased dramatically. Government intervention was necessary to ensure that the domestic price was kept lower than the international price, to appropriate the windfall profits to the public sector, and to ensure that the profits went to exploration and development in the higher cost frontier areas. Maximization of profit — a corporate self-interest — had to be subordinated to the public interest.

Another example is the natural resources sector of public policy-making. There is a need for new public agencies in respect of both the policy advisory and the regulatory functions. The National Energy Board (NEB), a quasi-independent public agency, acts in both an advisory and regulatory capacity on important national energy questions. It is a mistake to marry these functions. During the critical period of decision-making in respect of northern development, between 1968 and 1972, the chairman of the NEB was a member of the intra-governmental advisory committee on northern development policy. The principal objective of policy development at that time was to do everything possible to guarantee Canadian oil, thought to be in great surplus, access to US markets in the face of threatened competition from the discovery of reserves at Prudhoe Bay, Alaska in February 1968. The NEB would hardly provide alternative policy suggestions, or criticism, to such a policy.[1]

For most of the last hundred years Canada has been very much a frontier society. Moreover, its proximity to the United States has easily led a willing Canada to be a mirror-image society. Given a strong industrial base coupled with post-war opportunity, it was inevitable that in both societies the development and consumer ethic would dominate all other considerations over the past thirty years.

Being a branch-plant, limited market economy, with supposedly unlimited natural resources,[2] it was both necessary and easy to sell natural resources to generate the foreign exchange necessary to support the trading deficit in the consumer goods sector.[3] The effort of government in the development of the minerals industry was premised upon the desirability of growth and exports. That was the intuitively perceived public interest. Thus, the "northern vision" of Prime Minister Diefenbaker, a manifestation of the growth ethic, had immense appeal to an electorate, which in 1958 gave him the largest election victory in Canada's history. Growth on any terms was seen as inevitable progress, and the north was considered a hinterland supportive of the southern, urban metropolis.

Exploration permits for northern Canada were made available in the 1960s on easier terms than anywhere else in the world, and without any prior land use planning or environmental regulation.[4]

Moreover, with the Prudhoe Bay oil discovery in February 1968, policy-makers at both the federal and provincial levels of government[5] were gripped with near hysteria. Canadian petroleum had to be assured of an American market, in the face of the threat of a glut of American oil and gas from Prudhoe Bay. Canadian exports would be assured by facilitating American use of Prudhoe Bay through allowing oil and natural gas to be transported across Canada to the United States. Canada would strive for a continental energy policy, if not stated or recognized as such, with northern pipelines serving to link Canada's petroleum reserves into the American market more closely, thus enhancing the possibility for continuing and increasing Canadian exports. How times change! Only five years later, in October 1973, Canada and the rest of the world were to experience the energy crisis.

3. The Northwest Territories and Yukon Territory as Jurisdictions, and the Decision-Making Process

Since the Northwest Territories and Yukon Territory are federal jurisdictions,[6] there is no check upon the federal use of power by a provincial government in these jurisdictions. The Territorial governments are weak, derivative governments, beholden to Ottawa.[7] They have no role in non-renewable resource management. This means there is no check upon federal decision-making by another level of government.

Moreover, within the structure of the federal government, the Northern Affairs Branch of the Department of Indian and Northern Affairs (DINA)[8] traditionally had a decision-making power unconstrained in any significant way by other branches or other departments. Northern native peoples' affairs have been dealt with by the same branch in which the development interest has been paramount.[9] Similarly, the conservation interest, represented by the National Parks Branch, was submerged as well within the same department, DINA, until its recent transfer to the Department of the Environment (DOE) in 1979. Although the conflict between the interest of northern native peoples, the conservation interest and the northern development interest is obvious, generally it has been submerged and controlled at the bureaucratic level. In fact, as between these competing interests, the northern development interest has been the dominant one in policy formulation, and in northern jurisdictional control. The Northern Affairs Branch has controlled the issuance of exploration permits,[10] and initiated, administered and enforced the regulations for environmental protection.[11]

However, after the introduction of the National Energy Program on 28 October 1980, and the subsequent Canada Oil and Gas Act,[12] as of 1982 the Department of Energy, Mines and Resources (EMR) has been chiefly responsible for oil and gas development on federal lands. It is to be hoped that this will lead to greater interdepartmental checks and balances, with DINA representing Aboriginal Peoples' interests, the DOE representing the conservation and recreation interest, and EMR representing the development interest.

Although the interdepartmental struggle for jurisdictional control was not predicated upon achieving checks and balances, but rather largely as simply bureaucratic quests for power, it may well be that far better policy-making, administration and regulation of the north will result, since three ministries with separate, identifiable interests are in control. At the same time, while the territorial governments do not have authority over non-renewable resource development, they are evolving as politically stronger institutions whose voice must be heard.

However, the federal government itself is often now the developer through Panarctic Oils Ltd. and Petro-Canada.[13] When the government becomes the developer, the regulated becomes the regulator. The board of directors of Petro-Canada and Panarctic have included civil servants who have had to administer the regulations constraining development.

The overall effect is that, at least up to the present, the Arctic has been largely a monolithic jurisdiction effectively controlled by a federal bureaucracy whose central and declared goal is development. The policy advisory, regulatory, and developer roles have been largely within a single bureaucracy with no significant checks upon it, nor any balancing factors. The branch within DINA which has the goal of northern development has had the power to submerge and defeat the competing Aboriginal Peoples' and conservation interests. Because there have not been checks and balances, the consequences has been inadequate planning, ineffective control, and failure to ensure that the other aspects of the general public interest have been properly considered in decision-making. This may change in the future, as DINA's responsibility focuses more upon just the Aboriginal Peoples' interest, EMR handles the development interest, and DOE looks after the conservation and recreational interest. However, at the same time, the federal government, through Crown corporations, will itself become the prime explorer and developer in the Arctic. With the Crown being the developer, and the frontier regions holding the only real promise for Canada to achieve oil self-sufficiency, it is probable that the development interest will remain paramount in northern policy formulation and decision-making.

The policy process has been largely secret, with access to the critical information limited to government, and industry with the consent of the government. The history of northern development in Canada demonstrates how government has paid lip-service to native peoples' and environmentalists' concerns, while all the time pressing relentlessly forward for resource development.

One could give many examples of early decisions on matters to do with the development of the North which may have been different had the decision-making process allowed for all the necessary consultation.

On 16 April 1976, the federal Cabinet decided to allow drilling for oil and gas in the Beaufort Sea, that part of the Arctic Ocean along the coast of the western part of the Northwest Territories, and the coast of the Yukon and the Alaskan North Slope; the drilling was to take place about fifty miles off the Canadian coast. The only drilling in the Beaufort Sea to that time had been from artificial islands constructed in shallow water close to the Mackenzie Delta.

In July 1973 Dome Petroleum Ltd. had received approval in principle to a drilling program from the federal Cabinet, after private meetings between exploration companies and government officials. This was done without consulting the Inuit, who use the area for hunting and fishing, and notwithstanding the fact that no government agency had studied the environmental hazards, even though the Beaufort Sea represents an ecologically sensitive area. Indeed, the memorandum to Cabinet prepared by the Department of Indian and Northern Affairs said that the environmental risk was low. The Department had done no research and proposed no research.

However, the Aboriginal Peoples and environmentalists learned of the plans and protested. The matter came before the Cabinet, which, to its credit, in giving approval required an in-house environmental research program conducted jointly by the Department of the Environment and by industry to determine the possible environmental impact of the drilling. Initially, most observers described the study as mere window-dressing. However, the resulting report was sufficiently sceptical that the Minister of the Environment opposed the drilling. The report indicated that the presence of sea ice means operations in the Beaufort Sea differ significantly from those in other climates. If there were to have been an oil blowout (the chance of which was estimated by the report as being somewhere between one in 1,000 and one in

10,000) it might well have been impossible to drill a relief well to stop the spill before the fall pack ice moves in, about mid-October. It might have been impossible to drill a relief well for many months, during which time the blow-out would continue to be out of control. Some scientists predicted that such a blow-out would constitute one of the world's worst ecological disasters.

Even the US State Department requested that approval be delayed because of the need to assess further the potential environmental impact , and because of the danger to adjacent Alaskan waters and shores. Moreover, Canada's willingness to run undue risk in offshore exploration seemed inconsistent with Canada's assertions at the same time at the Law of the Sea Conference for the right of a coastal country (Canada has the longest coastline in the world) in international law to declare an international economic zone extending 200 nautical miles off its coasts, in which the coastal country has jurisdiction to prevent pollution.[14]

The permits affording Dome exploration rights had been issued in 1969, and approval in principle to drilling had been given by the Cabinet in July 1973. When final approval was sought from Cabinet, and given in April 1976, one argument in favour of it was that Dome had vested rights and had then put some $150 million into drilling ships which were almost ready to embark for the Arctic. Indeed, if the drilling program was not approved there was a suggestion that legal action might be taken for detrimental reliance. Thus, at the very least, the unchecked bureaucratic northern development interest had created a situation which made it very difficult to further postpone drilling in the Beaufort Sea. Since that time, drilling has taken place each summer, with significant discoveries and, fortunately, only minor mishaps.[15] Moreover, the Beaufort Sea, together with the development of Hibernia offshore Newfoundland, hold the only significant hope for achieving domestic oil self-sufficiency, and Crown corporations, particularly Petro-Canada, have taken a lead role in exploration.[16]

4. Arctic Native Peoples and Land Claims

Aboriginal and treaty rights have already been considered in earlier chapters. Let us now look at these topics as they relate to the Arctic, after briefly reviewing the historical policy toward native peoples in Canada.

The sovereignty of New France passed to Britain by conquest in 1760, and was followed by the Royal Proclamation of 1763,[17] which affirmed Indian property rights under British sovereignty. The centralization of authority through the Royal Proclamation to deal with the native peoples and their property rights was continued in the constitutional framework at Confederation, the authority to deal with "Indians, and Lands reserved for the Indians" being given to the federal Parliament by s. 91(24) of the British North America Act,[18] now the Constitution Act 1867.

The treaty-making process intended by the Royal Proclamation for the surrender of Indian property rights accelerated after Confederation, culminating in land cession Treaty No. 11 in 1921, which covered the MacKenzie River Valley in the Northwest Territories. Today, about 150,000 Indians are descendants of those Indian nations entering into treaties. Land cession treaties cover about one-third of Canada. The limited case law in Canada in respect of the legal nature of these Indian treaties has held them to have only a legal status equivalent to that of ordinary contracts, and hence they have been subject to unilateral abrogation by Parliament.[19] Perhaps protection is now offered to such rights by reason of sections 35 and 52 of the Constitution Act 1982?

The more general question of Indian sovereignty has not received much analysis in Canadian law. British, and subsequent Canadian sovereignty is assumed in all discussions of the recognition of native rights by English and Canadian law. The only legislation enacted by Parliament under its constitutional authority has been the Indian Act[20] (which had its genesis in pre-Confederation legislation), but this special legislation significantly affects the lives of the 300,000 status[21] (treaty and non-treaty) Indians. The historical twin policy goals of the Indian Act, being protection and integration into the dominant society through the mechanism of rigorous paternalism paradoxically have been a main contributing cause of the Indian plight, namely, the loss of identity and pride, living in a state of debilitating dependence, and being in a resultant disadvantageous economic, educational and social position. The social pathology of Indian and Metis in southern Canada can be understood only by realizing the impact of this invidious piece of legislation for more than a century, upon a defenseless people.

In recent years, provisions of the Indian Act have been tested before the courts[22] as being discriminatory and thus in conflict with the federal Canadian Bill of Rights, enacted in 1960.[23] This Act recognizes and is protective of fundamental individual freedoms of intrinsic value to the whole of Canadian society. In this sense, the Canadian Bill of Rights is protective only of the values of the dominant society, and its language is not necessarily protective of the values of minority group rights. Moreover, at least one of the lower court decisions interpreting the Bill of Rights took an egalitarian approach.[24] Because the Indian Act sets apart one racial group, it was found that it was thereby inherently discriminatory and in conflict with the Bill of Rights. However, the courts have never been confronted with the question of special legislation premised on a policy of protection and enhancement of minority rights as a group. Undoubtedly, this issue will be considered in the future under the Charter of Rights and Freedom in the Constitution Act 1982. Presumably, group "rights" within the Indian Act are protected by s. 25 of the Constitution Act, being "other rights or freedoms" saved from the otherwise levelling effect of the various provisions of the Charter, section 15 in particular.

The end of treaty-making in 1923 was followed by nearly forty years of quietude until the 1960s, when Parliament's unilateral abrogation of treaty rights, in particular hunting and fishing rights guaranteed by the treaties, became a dominant issue.[25] In June 1969, the federal government's White Paper[26] asserted that special laws for Indians were inherently discriminatory, that egalitatianism was the path to progress, and that the government should not respect unsurrendered native land rights. The White Paper was emphatically rejected by native peoples[27].

In 1973, a case in the Northwest Territories[28] raised for the first time the fundamental question of whether the literal words of the treaties are in fact representative of the true understanding of the Indian people at the time of treaty-making. The Supreme Court of Canada dealt with the issue before it on a technicality, leaving unresolved the fundamental issue as to whether there truly was a legally effective surrender of native title by Treaty No. 11.

5. Northern Development Projects 1968-84

In the past sixteen years, with the explosive northward expansion of the dominant society pursuing the exploitation of natural resources, the question of Indian title in the Mackenzie Valley area (being 400,000 square miles and purportedly surrendered under Treaties #8 and #11) and Indian or Inuit title in non-treaty areas (the balance of the Northwest Territories, the Yukon Territory, and Arctic Quebec) has become a focal point in the subject area of native rights in Canada.[29] In Canada's north, native peoples constitute a significant percentage of the population (in some areas a majority), and the people continue to use their traditional land base with the consciousness of a food gathering tribal society. One particular land use and occupancy study sets forth comprehensively that the 20,000 Inuit in the Northwest Territories still use and occupy 1.23 million square miles (866,600 of land, 371, 000 of water).[30]

In the Northwest Territories, about 10,000 status (non-treaty) Indians and perhaps 8,000 non-status Indians and Metis live along the MacKenzie River Valley, and some 20,000 Inuit (who never signed treaties and who cannot have status under the Indian Act). In the Yukon Territory, there are about 4,000 status Indians and perhaps an equal number of non-status Indians. Arctic Quebec is the home of about 7,000 status (but non-treaty) Indians and 4,000 Inuit. There are about 2,000 Inuit in the Labrador part of Newfoundland.

With the competing land uses of exploration for petroleum and natural gas, or other minerals, or hydroelectric projects, the land base of all these people has been endangered, suggesting the urgency of fair, legislated land claims settlements in the Northwest Territories and Yukon Territory.

A land claims settlement was made in November 1975 in respect of Indian and Inuit claims in Arctic Quebec, where the James Bay hydroelectric project was under construction.[31] An Agreement in Principle was signed on 31

October 1978, between the Committee for Original Peoples' Entitlement and the federal government, settling the Inuvialiut land rights' claims in the western Arctic. Native land rights and northern development continue to be a major source of friction between native and non-native societies in Canada. A Final Agreement has since been negotiated. A further Agreement in Principle was reached with the Council of Yukon Indians, the Yukon Territorial Government and the Government of Canada in December of 1983.

There are two major resource projects: in the North the $13.6 billion James Bay hydroelectric project, recently completed, and the now apparently indefinitely postponed $50 billion Alcan natural gas pipeline.

However, it was the Mackenzie Valley gas pipeline, proposed in 1975 but rejected by the National Energy Board in July 1977, that was the early focal point for conflict.

The Mackenzie Valley natural gas pipeline controversy involved the largest then projected commitment of private capital in Canadian history. Debate about this project covered a broad range of matters, including native land claims, environmental protection, existing gas supply and a gas export policy, and the economic impact. Four proposals were considered.

The first was the application before the NEB of Canadian Arctic Gas to build a 48-inch, $8.4 billion pipeline extending from the 49th parallel north and thence two spurs to the Mackenzie Delta and to Prudhoe Bay in Alaska. The applicant contended that the gas supply from Alaska alone would provide the threshold volumes of natural gas necessary to achieve an economic link with the very limited proved reserves of the Mackenzie Delta, and that without using Alaskan gas, such access to Canadian supplies in the western Arctic would be prejudiced for many years. Thus, the Canadian Arctic Gas proposal would have used the same pipeline facility to bring gas from Alaska and the Mackenzie Delta to southern Canada and the United States, each country receiving the quantity of gas it contributed at source.

The second applicant, Foothills Pipeline Limited, proposed a "Maple Leaf Project". This $3.06 billion project conceived a smaller, lower pressure 42-inch pipeline from the Mackenzie Delta to the northern perimeter of the Province of Alberta, where it would connect with the existing Alberta gas trunk line facilities to deliver western Arctic gas to points west, south, and east in Canada. Foothills argued that an Alaskan link was unnecessary, and that regulatory approval of its proposal would catalyze sufficient exploratory activity that the necessary threshold reserves would soon be found in the Mackenzie Delta area. Foothills also disputed the contention that the Canadian Arctic Gas 48-inch system offered economies-of-scale that could improve upon the proven efficiency of the 42-inch system.

The third proposal was for what was called the "Alcan Route". This undertaking was supported by Foothills, and consisted of Alberta Gas Trunkline, West Coast Transmission, and Pacific Northwest Pipelines. It proposed bringing Alaskan gas south by means of a gas line extending from

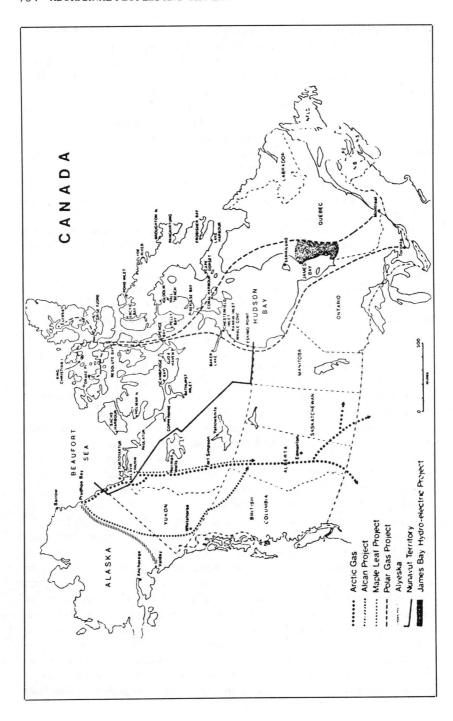

Prudhoe Bay to Fairbanks and thence to northern British Columbia and Alberta via the Alaska Highway right-of-way, and then to the north-western USA by way of existing pipeline systems.

Acceptance of this third "Alcan" proposal defeated the Canadian Arctic Gas application, and there is a slight chance that an Alcan pipeline may result in the Foothills Project, once greater gas reserves in the western Canadian Arctic become established, and the threshold in reserves is reached to make the Foothills pipeline economic. If such reserves in the western Arctic are not sufficient to support the Foothills pipeline, then a "Dempster link" with the Alcan pipeline is also contemplated.

In further opposition to Canadian Arctic Gas was a US entity, El Paso, which had applied before the American regulatory authorities to construct a natural gas pipeline to carry Prudhoe Bay gas across Alaska following the Alyeska oil pipeline route; the gas would then be liquefied and shipped by tanker, probably to California. With the Alcan proposal accepted by Canada, the higher-cost El Paso proposal was eventually rejected in the United States.

With the approval of the Alcan proposal, some parts of the pipelines now have 'pre-built' in Canada, but as of the spring of 1982, private financing of the main, American, sections of the pipeline, has proved impossible, with the result that construction of the Alcan natural gas pipeline is at present postponed indefinitely. Underlying the postponement is the fact that the energy crisis of 1973 and 1978 have waned, with falling international energy prices and economic recession, with the result that there is an abundance of gas supplies to the southern 48 states of the US, and Alaskan natural gas is simply not needed for the forseeable future.

Another development project, the Polar Gas Project, in the future may apply to the NEB for the necessary authority to construct a more than $10 billion natural gas pipeline from the Arctic Islands. This pipeline would move natural gas 3,200 miles southwards and across up to 170 miles of Arctic Ocean channels with some depths for crossings exceeding 600 feet. While there are two other routes, the probable one would be down the west side of Hudson Bay through Manitoba and Ontario (rather than the east side through Quebec), with a possible connecting link from the Mackenzie Delta area. This project remains very doubtful at present, given its high cost, and the large natural gas surplus in southern Canada.

Imperial Oil is in the process of expanding its producing oil field at Norman Wells on the Mackenzie River. This field was first discovered in 1921 and was the impetus for the federal government seeking to obtain Treaty No. 11 that year. The oil was transported by pipeline to Whitehorse, Yukon Territory, and then transported to the south. The latest plan is to transport the oil to Alberta via a new pipeline along the Mackenzie River, with construction beginning in 1984.

Finally, the Arctic Pilot Project, involving a consortium including Petro Canada, Nova, an Alberta corporation, and Dome Petroleum, propose to bring liquefied natural gas from the high Arctic (Bridport Inlet on Melville Island) by tanker down the east coast to New Brunswick or Nova Scotia, where the liquefied gas would be regasified and used on the east coast. This proposal is currently being considered by the NEB. Recently, the Arctic Pilot Project has suggested it may seek to transport its liquefied natural gas to Europe rather than to southern Canada. This proposal, however, appears to be dormant as agreements with U.S. buyers expired in mid-1984.

6. Northern Land Claims

Underlying the specific concerns about land and treaty rights is the more pervasive claim by all native peoples in Canada for their realization of more basic human rights — that is, true general equality of opportunity so that native peoples will be able to gain the self-expression and self-realization of other Canadians.[32]

Northern land claims settlements offer the opportunity of a significant mechanism whereby native cultural identity can be retained, so far as is realistically possible in present-day society, and at the same time equality of opportunity can be effectuated within an integrated, emerging northern industrial society. At the same time, it is critical to engage the northern peoples in all aspects of decision-making so that they can influence the nature of northern development. It will be a better Canada, for both northern peoples as well as for the larger, non-native society, if common objectives can be achieved.

Given the competing cultures of northern Canada — a dominant society that values the vast northern land base primarily for its exploitative, development potential, and minority native peoples whose consciousness and lifestyle are rooted in an autochthonous culture — is there any realistic hope that there can be any northern land claims settlement, or more general Aboriginal Peoples' policy, which truly meets the criteria of fairness to Aboriginal Peoples as well as to the general Canadian public interest? This is the continuing major question for public policy formulation in respect of Canada's North.

7. Recent Court Developments in respect of the Question of Aboriginal Title, and Related Political Developments

The federal government expressly stated in the 1969 White Paper that native land rights, apart from those that are part of treaty rights, would no longer be recognized. The Aboriginal Peoples, in seeking redress for the loss of their lands and their traditional rights in the early 1970s, had to pursue their claims through the only forum available, the courts. It is useful to review briefly four major court cases.

As was discussed in an earlier chapter, the non-treaty Indian Nishga nation of northwestern British Columbia took court action in 1968 to seek a declaration that their aboriginal title to a large area of land in the Nass River Valley of British Columbia had never been extinguished. The Nishga Indians lost in the trial court;[33] on appeal, the British Columbia Court of Appeal held that the Royal Proclamation of 1763 did not apply to British Columbia and, further, that there could be no judicial recognition of aboriginal title.[34] The Nishgas appealed to the Supreme Court of Canada and a decision was rendered 31 January 1973.[35] The court held for the defendant, British Columbia. However, due to the nature of the judgments rendered, there was not a decision for the defendant on the merits.

The Nishga case has been the most important court decision to date in respect of aboriginal title. It was heard by only seven justices, rather than the full nine member court usual in a case of such importance. Mr Justice Hall, with Justices Laskin and Spence concurring, decided on the merits in favour of the Indians. Mr Justice Judson, with Justices Martland and Ritchie concurring, found on the merits for the defendant, British Columbia, but the operative reason was that any aboriginal title had been extinguished. The seventh Justice, Mr Justice Pidgeon, held for the defendant, but simply on a procedural basis.

As a result, the substantive issue of whether the Nishgas have aboriginal title remains unresolved by the court, as it does for all Aboriginal Peoples in Canada pursuing such claims.[36] However, six members of the Supreme Court of Canada recognized that an aboriginal title had existed in British Columbia, although they disagreed on the secondary question of extinguishment. Thus, aboriginal title may exist where there has not been any land cession treaty, and this would include the traditionally used and occupied areas of the approximately 20,000 Inuit and the areas of the 16,000 non-treaty Indians in the Northwest Territories and the Yukon Territory. It would also include the areas of the approximately 10,000 treaty Indians in the Northwest Territories, if they can still assert an unsurrendered native title, that is, if Treaty No. 11 is not effective in extinguishing aboriginal title.

The controversy first ensuing from this decision often missed the point that the court is the least appropriate forum for dealing with aboriginal title. Litigation is expensive, time-consuming, and abounds with technical uncertainties. Even if the Nishgas were successful in their court action, further litigation would have been necessary. First, it would have been required to resolve the question of the precise incidents of aboriginal title, since the question of the legal content of native title has not been resolved by the courts in Canada, and the Nishgas' action sought only a declaration that aboriginal title exists. Second, litigation could easily have ensued to settle the conflicts as between aboriginal title and other, competing land users. Third, there would have to have been litigation to determine if compensation was payable in those instances where aboriginal title existed but had been extinguished by legislation.

It seems obvious that these issues are best determined and resolved by legislation rather than by litigation.[37] The questions cannot be answered by a yes or no, which is the only approach a court can take. The issues are such that they only can be resolved to the reasonable satisfaction of all through a negotiated settlement. To accomplish this, the government must recognize aboriginal rights and provide for a legislated settlement. Following the Nishga decision, individual members of Parliament for the opposition parties took a strong position in favour of recognition, and given the fact of a Liberal minority government, the administration was under considerable pressure.

On 14 February 1973, the Yukon Native Brotherhood presented its proposal[38] to the prime minister for negotiation and settlement of the land claims of the non-treaty Indians and non-status Indians of the Yukon Territory. Mr Trudeau, whose representatives had met with Indian leaders and had considered the proposal privately during the preceding week, warmly embraced the proposal and agreed to set up the requested negotiating committee "with great haste".[39]

Thus, on 14 February 1973, the government, to its credit, in effect reversed its position with respect to aboriginal title, although without any formal recognition thereof. Although the Yukon proposal did not specifically ask for a settlement of its claims on a basis of aboriginal title, this was implicit to the proposal. A tentative settlement of the claims of the Yukon Aboriginal Peoples was reached and initialled by the negotiators in December of 1983. However, whatever the legal niceties, the simple agreement to negotiate implied a recognition of some rights on the part of the Aboriginal Peoples, and a fair and reasonable settlement of claims based upon those rights.

Why the government refused to recognize aboriginal rights before February 1973 remains unclear. There had been nebulous references to the view that such recognition might amount to "giving the country back to the Indians." Perhaps Mr Trudeau's concern stemmed from his fear of assisting separatism in Québec, for he had said: ". . . some of us are also sorry about the Plains of Abraham but we don't ask for compensation about that . . . ."[40] If this is so, he failed to realize that the aboriginal rights question, in its proper context, is not one of sovereignty. Moreover, at the time of the fall of New France, the British recognized the property rights of French settlers, as well as the property rights of the Aboriginal Peoples, through the Royal Proclamation of 1763.[41] In any event, since Parliament has control of any legislative settlement of a native title claim, nothing is being given away through the political recognition of such rights and the negotiation of a fair settlement. This assertion omits for the moment the question of possible constraints imposed upon Parliament by sections 35 and 52 of the Constitution Act 1982, which will be discussed *infra*. The discussion to this point assumes that Parliament has the sovereign power to expropriate aboriginal title, like the power within its jurisdiction under the distribution of constitutional powers to expropriate the property rights of any citizen or group of citizens if this is seen to be in the national interest and Parliament is acting within a power conferred by the Constitution Act 1867.

There have been three other important cases before the courts in recent years which relate to the question of aboriginal title.

In 1972, the 10,000 treaty Indians of the Northwest Territories, the Dene, sought to lodge a *caveat*, with respect to lands traditionally used and occupied, with the Registrar of Titles of the Land Titles Office for the Northwest Territories. The Indians asserted that the literal wording of the treaties did not accord with the true agreement or understanding reached at the time of the signing of the treaties and that there has not been any legally effective surrender of their title.

In a decision given on 6 September 1973,[42] the Supreme Court of the Northwest Territories held in favour of the Indians. Mr Justice Morrow said:[43]

> That notwithstanding the language of the two treaties there is sufficient doubt on the facts that aboriginal title was extinguished that such claim for title should be permitted to be put forward by the Caveators.

However, the court stayed the filing of the *caveat* pending a possible appeal. The decision was reversed on appeal, and a further appeal by the Dene was subsequently dismissed in the Supreme Court of Canada, but on technical grounds.[44]

The Superior Court of Québec, in a decision by Malouf J on November 1973[45] allowed petitioners representing the 10,000 Inuit and Cree Indians of the James Bay area of Québec an interlocutory order of injunction against the James Bay Development Corporation and others. On 22 November 1973, the Court of Appeal for Québec suspended the lower court's injunction until determination of the appeal in respect thereof.[46] On 21 December 1973, the Supreme Court of Canada (by a 3:2 decision) refused leave to appeal to the petitioners with respect to the suspension order.[47]

An agreement-in-principle on a settlement was signed between the Indian and Inuit peoples and the federal and provincial governments on 15 November 1974, and this ended the court action. However, the Court of Appeal shortly thereafter gave its judgment reversing Malouf J's decision on the merits.[48] Because of the agreed-to settlement, that decision was not appealed further to the Supreme Court of Canada.

If the Québec Indians and Inuit had been successful in court, undoubtedly the Government of Québec would have expropriated, probably through a specific piece of legislation. This might have resulted in further court action on the assertion that the Province of Québec does not have the constitutional power to expropriate aboriginal title.[49] Again, there could have been a multiplicity of court actions, including a petition for an interlocutory order of injunction in the first instance. If the complex constitutional issue had been decided in favour of the native peoples, the federal government would then have had to decide whether it would meet Québec demands upon the federal government to expropriate and, if so, on what terms. Finally, even if the federal government did expropriate, there is a possible argument that native title in the James Bay area had received recognition and protection by the British North America Act of 1870-71[50] and, therefore, even the federal government could not pass expropriating legislation that sought to deny that there is any native title.[51] Therefore, further court action could have resulted from an attempted expropriation by the federal government. Certainly, as of passage of the Constitution Act 1982, either provincial or federal expropriation legislation would be challenged as being inconsistent with aboriginal title and therefore of no force or effect, given section 35 coupled with section 52 of the Constitution Act, 1982. It is a moot point whether aboriginal title was "existing" in northern Quebec in 1975, and, if so, whether such aboriginal title would have protection from expropriation by such constitutional provisions if they had then been in force?

In 1978, the hamlet of Baker Lake in the Northwest Territories, the Baker Lake Hunters and Trappers Association, the Inuit Tapirisat of Canada, and various individual Inuit living in the Baker Lake area, sought various forms of relief, including an injunction and a declaration that an area near Baker Lake was subject to the aboriginal title of the Inuit residents, in order to restrain mining activities that would impinge upon such title — specifically their rights to hunt caribou.

In *Hamlet of Baker Lake* v. *Minister of Indian Affairs*, Mahoney J held, *inter alia*, that the aboriginal rights of the Inuit had not been extinguished by surrender, or by general legislation, and therefore still exist.[52] On this basis, Mahoney J found that the plaintiffs were entitled to a declaration that the area in question is subject to their aboriginal rights to hunt and fish. However, he also held that the claim that the intended mining activities would interfere with the hunting of caribou was not established and so, except for the declaration, the action was dismissed. This decision was helpful to the Inuit because of the court's recognition of an aboriginal right at common law; on the other hand, it was unhelpful because of the finding that the aboriginal right was a severely limited one, a mere personal right to simply hunt and fish. The existence of an aboriginal right was recognized, but the nature or content of the right was seen as being a limited one, and the court further held that where the existence of the aboriginal right of occupancy is inconsistent with statutory law, then that aboriginal right has been extinguished, and that such extinguishment can be effectuated by legislation without Parliament ever having addressed itself expressly to the point.

This chapter does not deal with the many complex legal issues, and provides only a brief synopsis of the major recent cases. However, three points are obvious from this analysis. First, in *Calder* there was a recognition of the existence of a native title, and in both the *caveat* case in the Northwest Territories and the James Bay case, the trial courts' decisions (although both turn directly upon subsidiary or preliminary issues) suggest the petitioning native peoples may well have successful claims to native title on the merits. The Baker Lake case also recognizes an aboriginal right, albeit a very limited one.

Second, although the path of litigation was the only recourse open to the native peoples in the early 1970s, it is a complex and unsuitable means of dealing with their fundamental problems and concerns. Even with successful litigation, the government has had the power to expropriate, although nice constitutional questions will now arise in this regard given sections 35 and 52 of the Constitution Act 1982. Third, the only fair and ultimately successful approach to the root problems and concerns can come about through a political and legislative solution.

There are many reasons compelling a political and legislative solution to each of the land claims of the several northern native groups. Some of the reasons have already been identified, but it is useful to discuss three main reasons, before considering further possible political/legislative approaches to land claims settlements.

First, the historical legal theory and practice of the British in North America, and of Canada, establish a strong argument that northern native peoples are owners of traditionally used and occupied lands. There is a legal basis to land claims. Secondly, there is a moral basis to land claims. Thirdly, the settlement of land claims is a practical and desirable public policy.

8. Historical Legal Theory and Practice with Respect to Native Title

We have already considered "aboriginal" title in earlier chapters, but the legal and historical theory and practice with respect to the recognition of native title[53] can be briefly considered again. There are two distinguishable, but overlapping, theories.

First, there is the historical legal theory of English common law (also found in international law[54] and continental law, going back to Roman law) regarding the rules of law applicable to the acquisition of new territories. Upon the acquisition of a new territory by the English sovereign, the local customary law (*lex loci*) of the inhabitants in the acquired territory is recognized, protected, and incorporated by English law until the English sovereign authority (the Crown's prerogative or the legislative authority, depending upon the nature of the acquisition and the time in history) changes that local law.[55] Thus, aboriginal rights are those rights which are inherent to Aboriginal Peoples by reason of their simply having the status of being Aboriginal Peoples. In contrast, treaty rights are conferred by the government upon a native signatory group, as consideration for the surrender of one incident of their general aboriginal rights, that of aboriginal title.

Thus, the local customary law of native peoples in North America as to property rights would, at least in theory, be recognized and protected by

English and later by Canadian common law. Mahoney J, in the *Baker Lake* case, put the proof requirement for the existence of aboriginal title at common law as:

1. That they and their ancestors were members of an organized society.
2. That the organized society occupied the specific territory over which they assert the aboriginal title.
3. That the occupation was to the exclusion of other organized societies.
4. That the occupation was an established fact at the time sovereignty was asserted by England.[56]

Such rights can be altered only by the sovereign, which power now rests with Parliament. Historically, the native peoples have been considered to be British subjects, with full rights and privileges. Their property rights receive full protection from Crown interference. Assuming that it can be established that the local customary law of the native peoples recognized property rights, then these property rights were recognized and protected within British law, and the essential question then really becomes: Has Parliament terminated the native title for a given geographical area? Looking to expropriation law, it seems arguable that Parliament does not terminate that title without expressly doing so, especially if compensation is not payable,[57] although the court in Baker Lake was of a different view. The Canadian Bill of Rights with its due process provisions, might also be seen to apply. However, in *National Capital Commission* v. *Lapointe,*[58] it was held that "due process" means a guarantee only of natural justice and other safeguards, not of fair compensation.

Moreover, under the Charter of Rights in the Constitution Act 1982, no explicit protection is offered regarding property rights, nor is any explicit protection of due process extended with respect to expropriations. However, these concerns may be answered in part by section 26, which says:

The guarantee in this Charter of certain rights and freedoms shall not be construed as denying the existence of any other rights or freedoms that exist in Canada.

Therefore, a legal basis of the Inuit claim (the Inuit never having signed treaties) in the Northwest Territories is that they have a customary system of tenure, that is, an organized and systematic use and occupation of their traditional lands and waters, and that under Canadian law this is a right of property. The Inuit Land Use and Occupancy Study provides the extensive factual data to support the legal argument of the Inuit. As the argument then goes, before the Crown can legally interfere with Inuit property rights, it has either to obtain their consent, or else properly compensate them for an expropriation of their lands.

The Inuit assert that their rights extend to all the renewable and non-renewable resources. They argue that any territory that belongs to them by reference to their own customary system of tenure also belongs to them under Canadian law. This means that their claims to ownership extend to the sea ice adjacent to the continent and offshore islands. The conclusion, if this historical legal theory is accepted, is that the federal government has no legal right to alienate lands in respect of which the Inuit have property rights, without first obtaining the consent of the Inuit, or alternatively, at the least, following expropriation procedures under Parliamentary authority. Moreover, with the passage of the Constitution Act 1982, for such "existing" aboriginal title there is now an additional argument that sections 35 and 52 protect such title from inconsistent legislative encroachment. This shall be discussed *infra*.

The second approach of historical legal theory is to look simply at British colonial practice. In North America, in part for the expedient reason of maintaining the peace with the native peoples, the British expressly recognized native property rights in the Royal Proclamation of 1763 (which now has constitutional force in Canada, by virtue of the Constitution Act 1982). This expedient historical policy of political recognition ripened into recognition by both the common law and a good many statutory enactments (for example, the Manitoba Act of 1870[59] and the Québec Boundaries Extension Act, 1912).[60] Under the 1763 Proclamation, procedures were provided so that a surrender of native property rights could be obtained. As already discussed, the treaty-making process for land cessions by the native peoples lasted up to sixty years ago, about one-third of Canada being dealt with through this process. The treaties quite clearly employ the language of a purchase and transfer of property rights. Thus, it can be said that from colonial practice itself evolved a firm legal basis for native property rights in Canada.

An outline[61] of some of the leading authorities from Confederation to the present will serve to support the argument that the property rights of northern native peoples have been conceded historically and that those rights may not be interfered with, without both consent and compensation:

1869-70 — The purchase of the Hudson's Bay Company's territories and the acquisition of the North-western Territory. The Federal Government accepted responsibility for any land claims.[62]

1870 — The *Manitoba Act* granted land to settle the Metis' aboriginal claims.[63]

1871-1930 — The numbered treaties and their adhesions speak of the Indians conveying land to the Crown. As the Order-in-Council for Treaty No. 10 demonstrates, the treaty-making was done with a concept of aboriginal title clearly in mind.

On a report dated 12th July, 1906 from the Superintendent General of Indian Affairs, stating that the aboriginal title has not been extinguished in the greater portion of that part of the Province of Saskatchewan which lies north of the 54th parallel of latitude and in a small adjoining area in Alberta . . . that it is in the public interest that the whole of the territory included within the boundaries of the Provinces of Saskatchewan and Alberta should be relieved of the claims of the aborigines; and that $12,000.00 has been included in the estimates for expenses in the making of a treaty with Indians and in settling the claims of the Half-breeds and for paying the usual gratituities to the Indians."[64]

1872 — Section 42 of the first *Dominion Act* dealing with the sale of Crown land stated:

"None of the provisions of this Act respecting the settlement of Agricultural lands, or the lease of Timber lands, or the purchase and sale of Mineral lands, shall be held to apply to territory the Indian title to which shall not at the time have been extinguished."[65]

This provision remained in the various Dominion Lands Acts until 1908.

1875 — The Federal Government disallowed "An Act to Amend and Consolidate the Laws Affecting Crown Lands in British Columbia" stating "There is not a shadow of doubt, that from the earliest times, England has always felt it imperative to meet the Indians in council, and to obtain surrenders of tracts of Canada, as from time to time such were required for the purposes of settlements."[66]

1876 — A speech of Governor-General Dufferin in Victoria strongly upheld the concept of Indian title and criticized the British Columbia Government.[67]

1879 — The *Dominion Lands Act* authorized the granting of land in the Northwest Territories to satisfy "any claims existing in connection with the extinguishment of the Indian title, preferred by half-breeds. . ."".[68]

1888 — In the St Catharine's case the Federal Government argued that it obtained a full title to land from the Indians by Treaty No. 3.[69]

The Federal-Provincial Agreements which followed the decision in the St Catharine's case sometimes employed the following "whereas" clause (taken from the 1924 Ontario Agreement):

"Whereas from time to time treaties have been made with the Indians for the surrender for various considerations of their personal and usufructuary rights to territories now included in the Province of Ontario. . . ."[70]

1889 — The Federal Government disallowed the *Northwest Territories Game Ordinance* because it violated Indian treaty hunting rights.[71]

1912 — In the boundaries extension legislation for both Ontario and

Quebec, the Federal Government made a special provision requiring treaties with the Indians.[72]

1930 — A Constitutional enactment transferred the ownership of natural resources from the Federal Government to the prairie provinces. In each of the provinces the Indians are protected in their right "of hunting, trapping and fishing game and fish for food at all seasons of the year on all unoccupied Crown lands and on any other lands to which the said Indians may have a right of access."[73]

1946 — Mr R.A. Hoey, Director of the Indian Affairs Branch, May 30, 1946, before the Joint Committee of the Senate and House of Commons, stated:

"From the time of the first British settlement in New England, the title of the Indians to lands occupied by them was conceded and compensation was made to them for the surrender of their hunting grounds . . . this rule, which was confirmed by the Royal Proclamation of October 7, 1763, is still adhered to."[74]

1946 — The evidence of Mr T.R.L. MacInnes, Secretary, Indian Affairs Branch, June 4, 1946 stated:

"Now it remained for the British to recognize an Indian interest in the soil to be extinguished only by bilateral agreement for a consideration. That practice arose very early in the contracts between the British settlers and the aborigines in North America, and it developed into the treaty system which has been the basis of Indian policy both in British North America and continuing on after the revolutionary war in the United States."[75]

1966 — *The Canadian Indian*, a pamphlet published by the Department of Indian Affairs, stated:

"Early in the settlement of North America, the British recognized Indian title or interests in the soil to be parted with or extinguished by agreement with the Indians and then only to the Crown."[76]

1971 — The Dorion Commission Report expressly recognized aboriginal rights in Québec, urged an expansive view of the content of aboriginal title and acknowledged the need to compensate native peoples for the extinguishment of their native rights.[77]

1973 — *Calder* v. *Attorney General of British Columbia* an inconclusive decision, provided strong *dicta* in support of the judicial recognition of native title.[78]

The Government of Canada's Statement of August 8, 1973 agreed to negotiate a settlement of native land claims.[79]

1974 — The James Bay case — a strong decision at the trial level recognized native title (reversed on appeal, but not appealed to the Supreme Court of Canada due to settlement of the dispute).[80]

1975 — The Northwest Territories Indian caveat case[81]— a decision at the trial level supported recognition of native title (reversed on appeal, but not on the issue of native title, in the Supreme Court of Canada).

1975 — The James Bay land claims settlement is signed (with supportive legislation,[82] subsequently passed by Parliament and Québec.)

1977 — Mackenzie Valley Pipeline Inquiry — Mr Justice Berger recommended a 10 year moratorium on pipeline development and that the settlement of native claims should precede any pipeline construction.

1978 — The *Baker Lake*[83] case affirms an aboriginal right, albeit limited to a hunting and fishing right.

1978 — A comprehensive Agreement-in-Principle is signed October 31, 1978, between the Committee for Original Peoples' Entitlement and the Government of Canada for the settlement of Inuvialuit land rights in the Western Arctic.

1981 — DIAND releases "In All Fairness", a restatement of native claims policy with its implicit recognition of aboriginal title (to those areas of Canada where there have not been land cession treaties).

1982 — The Constitution Act, 1982 recognizes and affirms existing aboriginal and treaty rights, but the identification and definition of those rights awaits later determination, as well as the extent of entrenched protection.

9. The Moral Reasons for Land Claims Settlement in the North

There are moral reasons for a settlement of northern land claims. First, even if northern native peoples are considered not to have a legal basis for their claims, the undisputed fact is that they use and occupy the lands as claimed. With respect to the 20,000 Inuit of the Northwest Territories, the Inuit Land Use and Occupancy Report suggests that current land use and occupancy amounts to some 1.23 million square miles (866,600 of land and 371,000 of water).

Parliament has the power, of course, to change the law and give northern native peoples property rights which are fully recognized and protected by law. Because of the inevitable diminution of the traditional pursuits of hunting, fishing and trapping due to the competing, conflicting uses for native lands through non-renewable resource development, and hydroelectric projects,[84] it is only fair that native peoples not be displaced from their lands, but rather that they retain an extensive interest, recognized and protected by

Canadian law. They should not lose their extensive property usage, and that which is the essence of their cultural identity, without receiving in exchange property rights recognized by law.

With respect to the Dene people, it seems clear that Treaty No. 11 was at the worst a fraud or forgery, at the least a unilateral imposition of a forced purchase by the government upon a people who did not understand what they were signing and certainly did not understand the ramifications thereof. Moreover, the reserves to be set aside by the federal government as a provision of Treaty No. 11 were never in fact conferred upon the Indians historically, and now would be understandably refused by the Dene if offered for the reason that the small land base constituted by the promised reserves would be an unacceptable exchange for their aboriginal title. Quite sensibly, the Government of Canada has been negotiating a settlement of Dene claims on the basis that an aboriginal title to the Mackenzie Valley exists, and not simply very limited treaty rights. This does not imply the renegotiation of other treaties. Treaty No. 11 is unique, given the geographical area it pertains to and the fact that reserves were never set aside by virtue of the treaty. The Treaty has not been substantially acted upon even by the federal government.

Second, there are immense social and human costs associated with the transition from a traditional society to the new, industrial society of the north. It is unfair for the Aboriginal Peoples to be the ones who bear the brunt of the social costs of change. As the first and continuing land users, they have a moral claim to benefit through non-renewable resource development as it comes to the Arctic, particularly because they will have to cope with tremendous social changes.

10. Social Policy Through Land Claims Settlements

With significant resource development already under way in northern Canada, it is clear that government must deal with the social problems of the local, native peoples arising from such development. Canadians are familiar with the inadequacy of governmental policy over the last one hundred years towards the Indian peoples in southern Canada. Not only are they the most socially debilitated of all Canadians, their plight imposes a continuing economic burden to the country. Canadians must learn from past mistakes in devising a new social policy for northern native peoples within Canadian society, and in formulating a humane and effective social policy for Arctic Canada. Land claims settlements offer a unique opportunity for a new, effective and progressive, yet less costly, social policy to meet the foremost problem of northern development — the relationship of the native peoples to that development.

11. The Prospects and Principles with respect to a Settlement of Land Claims in Canada's North

On 8 August 1973 the federal government issued a new and encouraging policy statement saying that it was "prepared to negotiate" with non-treaty Indians and Inuit on the basis of their "traditional interest in lands".[85] Given the unique nature of Treaty No. 11, this document has been a basis for negotiating with the Indian people (the Dene) on the basis of their traditional interest in lands, ignoring the Treaty. Since 1972, the government has also been providing substantial funding to northern native organizations to research and advance their claims.

In December 1981, *In All Fairness — A Native Claims Policy* was published. It sets forth three government objectives with respect to native claims:

1. To respond to the call for recognition of Native land rights by negotiating fair and equitable settlements;
2. To ensure that settlement of these claims will allow Native people to live the way they wish;
3. That the terms of settlement of these claims will respect the rights of all other people.[86]

This document emphasizes that native rights be recognized and tolerated unless they impede the "rights of all other people". Such an approach begs the question as to what are "the rights of all other people". If a settlement is to be based on the recognition of the existence of aboriginal rights, then those rights must be recognized as having a certain priority over competing, interfering claims. A fair resolution through a negotiated settlement involves compromises on both sides, with the best possible reconciliation of conflicting claims in the national interest.

It is the responsibility of the federal government, as negotiator, and ultimately Parliament as the final sovereign authority, to achieve land claim settlements that are in the national interest. This will mean, for example, that some existing rights to non-renewable resources will have to be terminated. This should be done with fairness and with compensation to developers, although the federal government and Parliament have themselves recently departed from these values through section 27 of the Canada Oil and Gas Act,[87] whereby there is expropriation of existing oil and gas rights of developers without the payment of adequate compensation.

The essential question is: What is the extent of native property rights? Once this is determined, then such rights imply that other people cannot have competing, interfering property rights, subject to the general sovereign power to expropriate peoples' property rights — in this instance, the property rights of native peoples. To insist, then, that native claims be satisfied only until the rights of others are affected is a denial of any true meaning to aboriginal title and serves to detract from the negotiation of a fair settlement.

The December 1981 government policy statement briefly discusses other approaches. It says that, negotiation is the clear choice of the government because when a settlement is reached, after mutual agreement between the parties, a claim can then be dealt with once and for all. Once this is achieved, the claim is nullified.[88]

Specific reference is made to lands, wildlife, subsurface rights, monetary compensation, corporate structures, taxation, and programs with no new elements being introduced beyond the 1973 policy paper. Self-government continues to be considered appropriate on a local basis.

The paper has been received with a general lack of enthusiasm by the native community, who suspect its stated approach of "fairness".

It is obvious the so-called "new" policy has been written as much for non-native people as for native people. Given that the statement is entitled *In All Fairness*, Canadians have every right to ask the question "to whom"?[89]

What are the prospects of a land claims settlement in the North? Few Canadians realize that many native people are experiencing within a single lifetime the tremendous cultural transformation from a tribal community to an industrial society. The far North is being radically changed because of the dictates of non-native society. The first phase of economic activity arising from outside influence was the 19th-century whaling industry, which ended about 1910. The fur economy then came into full bloom, but the era of the fur trader has now ended. With the discovery of oil in Prudhoe Bay in February 1968, and the subsequent exploration in the Mackenzie Delta and the Arctic Islands, a third phase of economic change has been initiated by non-native society. The assimilation of the North into the national industrial economy is fast approaching.

It is not intended that this brief and simplified view of the far North should overlook the impact on this society and culture of other important forces, such as Christianity, the Distant Early Warning (DEW) Line in the 1950s and, recently, the non-native educational and television system, which has been available via satellite since 1975. These influences continue to have a profound effect on cultural transformation. However, the incipient industrial era will have as traumatic an impact on native society as the collective influence of all these forces.

The industrial economy is bringing profound changes. At the Inuit Arctic Coppermine Conference in July 1970, the central issue was the intended exploration activity upon Banks Island. This was the first national conference of Inuit from across the Far North, and everyone sensed the magnitude of the forces being thrust upon this vast region: for the first time, the land base, the integral element of the Inuit culture, was significantly threatened. It is essential for the non-native person to realize that the unique, essential element of native culture is the intense group and personal relationship to the natural environment and, to the extent that such a relationship lessens, there is a corresponding diminution of identity.

Exploration and development is changing Canada's North very quickly. Ideally, there would have been a temporary freeze (which the government always refused) upon exploration activities and development until facets of development could have been comprehensively planned; not only land rights, but land-use planning, ecological and game preserves, national parks, and related vital questions such as the fiscal regime to govern exploration activities, and a national energy policy. The latter two elements are now in place with the National Energy Program of October 1980, and the consequential Canada Oil and Gas Act, enacted on March, 1982.

Given the fact of no land cession treaties in the Yukon and Northwest Territories (except for Treaty No. 11 in 1921 with the Indians in the Mackenzie River Valley, which has a peculiar history and is of doubtful validity) or northern Québec, with northward expansion in the 1970s of southern technology in pursuit of non-renewable resources and hydroelectric power, an intense conflict over land once again emerged between native peoples and the dominant society.

This conflict mirrored what happened in southern Canada with the westward expansion of settlers in the 19th century. The Riel uprising of 1869, which led to the creation of the province of Manitoba, was due primarily to a similar conflict over Indian and Metis property rights. The McDonald government, in fostering settlement westward of Ontario in anticipation of the transfer of Rupert's Land to Canada, had sent out government officials in 1869 who simply ignored the property rights of the native people. The later Riel Rebellion of 1885 in the Northwest Territory (in what is now Saskatchewan) also was due in part to the federal government ignoring the Metis claim to any significant property base in the face of rapidly expanding western settlement accompanying the fulfilment of "the national dream", the construction of the Canadian Pacific Railway which had begun in 1871.

The Inuit and Dene insist on maintaining their close relationship with the lands and waters that they have traditionally used and occupied. At the same time, rapid changes are being forced upon them and considerable development is going to take place. This poses the question: How can the Aboriginal People influence the form of development, and to what extent can they control their destiny? At the same time, how can they retain the closest possible relationship to their land in the midst of this development and change?

To the extent that change is inevitable and that development is taking place, it is clear that the Aboriginal People should be involved in that development in both an ownership and management capacity. The people are not prepared to be just employees taking direction from non-natives; they cannot simply be labourers or welfare recipients. Until 1973, the federal government's policy on northern development had been limited mainly to pursuing the few employment opportunities for Aboriginal Peoples.[90] As we have seen, the government did announce a new policy on 8 August 1973, saying that it would negotiate land claims settlements, and this policy was re-emphasized in the December 1981, policy statement. Prime Minister Trudeau summed up the federal government's position on 28 April 1980:

> During the course of the 1970s, we changed our minds on aboriginal rights. With the help of your educational efforts and some judicial examination of the issue, the government accepted the concept of land rights accruing without treaties to the original inhabitants of this country. We began negotiating land claims arising from those rights, acquired through the traditional use and occupancy of the land.

We shall now examine land claims negotiations from the announcement of the 8 August 1973 policy, to the present.

A recent Annual Report of Indian and Northern Affairs Canada sets forth succinctly the federal government's view on "comprehensive claims".

> The 1973 policy statement on native claims indicated the government's willingness to negotiate settlements with the Inuit and the Indian people who had not entered into treaty relationships with the crown. The purpose of these negotiations would be to deal with their long-standing grievances relating to the loss of their traditional use and occupancy of lands in those parts of Canada where any native rights based on traditional use and occupancy had not been extinguished by treaty nor superceded by law. Although this use and occupancy (variously described as "aboriginal interest," "native interest," "native title") had never been definitively recognized or expressed in Canadian law, the 1973 policy statement recognized that non-native occupancy of land had not taken the aboriginal interest into account, had not provided compensation for its gradual erosion, and had generally excluded native people from benefiting from development that might have taken place as a result of non-native settlement. Claims made on this basis are termed comprehensive claims.[91]

The map on the next page illustrates the locale of these claims.

12. Recent Practice with Respect to the Settlement of Northern Land Claims — The James Bay Land Claims Settlement of 1975

The James Bay land claims settlement of November 1975 allows the Inuit and Cree Indians in the area to retain the ownership of about 1.3% of the traditionally used lands which are ceded and surrendered.[92] The other major element of the settlement is the transfer, over several years, of $225 million to the 10,000 native people.[93] Discounting for inflation, the *per capita* present value of a share in these monies could be as little as $7,000.

This land/money formula[94] is not unlike the historical land cession treaties in southern Canada. Indeed, the comparative value of southern reserve lands

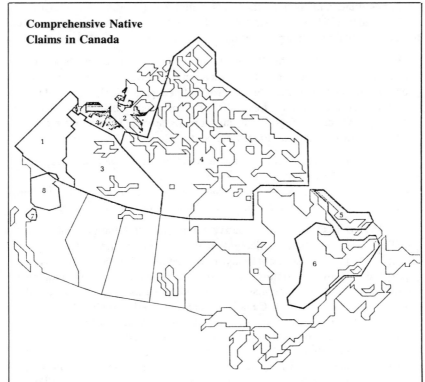

Comprehensive Native Claims in Canada

Legend:

The areas indicated on this map represent only approximate boundaries of the areas in which the various native associations have claimed an interest. The precise delineation of these areas for each claimant group will be determined as negotiations proceed on the separate claims settlements. All comprehensive native claims are not indicated on the map.

1 Yukon Claim: Council for Yukon Indians

▲ Proposed national wilderness park, northern Yukon.

2 Western Arctic: Committee for Original Peoples Entitlement [COPE] land areas selected pursuant to the COPE agreement-in-principle.

3 Mackenzie Valley: Dene and Métis claim.

4 Central and Eastern Arctic: Inuit Tapirisat of Canada.

5 Labrador: Labrador Inuit Association.

6 St Lawrence North Shore: Conseil Attikamek-Montagnais.

7 Nass River Valley: Nishga Tribal Council.

8 British Columbia West Coast: Association of United Tahltans.

From Annual Report, Indian and Northern Affairs Canada, 1980-81, p. 48.

retained, and annuities received, through a land cession treaty (say, for example, in 1873, when Treaty No. 3 was signed in northwestern Ontario in respect of the Lake of the Woods region) would be greater than those under the present James Bay 'treaty'. The James Bay settlement is simply a forced purchase, an 'offer that could not be refused' in the sense that no other offer would be made. Construction on the hydroelectric project went on throughout the negotiations. All provincial political parties supported the hydroelectric scheme, the largest development project in Canada's history. A major installation was proposed near the Cree Indian Community of Fort George on La Grande River, and a major inducement to the Indians to enter into the agreement-in-principle was the government's undertaking to move this installation thirty-two miles away. The federal government was not prepared, and indeed was politically unable, to exert any pressure upon the Quebec government. It was the provincial government that negotiated this settlement.

The only bargaining lever of the Cree and Inuit arose from the interim injunction against the project that they had succeeded in obtaining in November 1973 on the basis of aboriginal title. Although the injunction was removed by the Québec Court of Appeal a week later, the temporary success afforded a psychological advantage to the Aboriginal People, and the chance of success through an eventual appeal to the Supreme Court of Canada did give them some leverage.

However, perhaps they should have continued their court action rather than accept the settlement they were offered. If they had been ultimately successful before the Supreme Court of Canada, as was certainly possible, partial expropriation would have followed quickly, but it is probable there would have been a much more favourable settlement. Even if they had lost in court, it is probable that they still would have been able to get at least the settlement they eventually did, since they deserved some consideration on a moral basis, even if their rights might not be enforceable through court action. Finally, one might argue that, from the standpoint of social policy, no settlement at all would have been better than the settlement achieved.

By settling, the public assumes that justice has been done. The problems of the Cree and Inuit are forgotten. But as the traditional hunting and trapping identity inevitably disappears, and the James Bay native realizes that he is not part of the new identity of his surrounding society, he will lose his self-esteem and become frustrated and even hostile. Canadians may well see the experience of the southern Canadian Indian repeated in Arctic Québec in the coming years, and the loss in both human and economic terms will far outweigh what a fair settlement would have cost in 1975.

One can see some rationale behind the historical land cession treaties. They afforded a peaceful colonization with the westward expansion of Canada. The Canadian policy was clearly preferable to the American practice of sending in the cavalry, or giving Indians gifts of blankets laced with smallpox germs. The treaty-making process did seek to effectuate a social policy, misguided as it may have been. The benefits retained or given to the Indians were an attempt to make them farmers, part of a policy of assimilating them into the lifestyle and values of the white colonizer. This policy failed, but at least the land cession treaties were founded upon a discernible, if naive, social policy which at the time was honestly viewed by government as being both possible and desirable.

In contrast, the James Bay settlement appears to have few positive features for the Cree and Inuit. It seems not to deal with the two essential requirements in a land claims settlement in Arctic Canada. On the one hand, it fails to do anything significant effectively to preserve the traditional identity. In surrendering their land rights, the people are removed from their traditional identity; they retain only a surface title to about 1.3% of traditional lands.[95] On the other hand, the settlement does not provide a means of integrating the people into Arctic Québec's emerging industrial society. They will not be the owners of sufficient lands to make them effective participants in non-renewable resource development. They have no equity or managerial role in non-renewable resource development.

The unwitting public believes that fairness has been done and will not readily respond to complaints of the Inuit and Cree. Finally, the native peoples themselves may well eventually become despondent and hard on themselves because they settled (if only in the sense that they agreed to an offer they could not refuse) and yet they received nothing substantial in return.

The federal government obligated itself through the settlement only to the extent of $40 million. Perhaps this is why the federal government with its short-term perspective, could hail the settlement as a "bench-mark" for the future.

The northern Aboriginal Peoples' culture and identity is based upon an intimate relationship with their lands and waters. They are truly part of the very lands they occupy. These lands are not regarded by them as a marketable commodity simply because they provided them with their traditional livelihood, with a cash payment through a sale seen as providing a substitute for physical needs. Their lands and waters are an integral part of their being. To the extent that this relationship is compromised, they lose their identity. Given the values and perceived needs of the dominant society, this loss of identity is to some extent inevitable. But they do not want to sell their lands, and thus themselves and their heritage, for money. They do not want to give up their lands as part of a settlement. On the other hand, a considerable part of the traditional land bases will be used for non-renewable resource development. Is there room for a compromise that will meet the interests of both native peoples and non-native peoples?

13. The Alaska Land Claims Settlement of December 1971

In Alaska, the 70,000 native people received a legislated settlement in 1971[96] whereby they retained a full *fee simple* title to forty million acres of land (about 11 percent of Alaska) and received $962.5 million as compensation for the taking of the remainder. However, the peoples' shares in the corporations which own the retained lands can be sold to non-natives, and the lands can be taxed, after twenty years. By then, many of the native peoples may be well-to-do Alaskans, although they will have lost a great deal of their identity as native people. Their lifestyle will be that of the wage economy and industrial society — the antithesis of the autochthonous culture.

Perhaps such *realpolitik* is the best possible solution in that the new land use and development makes the traditional society impossible in the long term. For example, a James Bay trapper who uses more than 50 square miles of land is inevitably compromised by non-renewable resource development. However, the Alaskan settlement, unlike the James Bay settlement, is premised upon a policy of settling land claims within a context of discernible social policy. The United States' Congress realized that the historical governmental policy of paternalism toward the native person had failed. Accordingly, the new policy sought to give Alaskan native peoples the means to grow within the context of a changing Alaska.

There is no question that the Alaskan settlement is a policy of assimilation. It does not recognize special rights. Perhaps the reason for this was threefold. First, Congress viewed special rights as being inegalitarian. Second, special rights and racially defined institutions were regarded as tending to isolate the native peoples from the mainstream of society; this was thought to be counter-productive, being seen in part as a primary cause of the problem. Finally, perhaps Congress thought it unrealistic to think that there could be any retention of other than a few vestiges of the native culture in moving into the industrial society. After all, the native culture is a land-rooted culture and that land base is somewhat lost with non-renewable resource development. Thus, it is possible that the view was that once the decision to have extensive non-renewable resource development has been made, the integral element of the culture is substantially diminished, and only other cultural elements, such as language and art, can survive in the new order over the long term. Moreover, the Alaskan native retains the same scope for hunting, fishing and trapping that the James Bay native supposedly retains through his land claims settlement. The point is, in both Alaska and James Bay traditional pursuits will remain only to the extent that non-renewable resource development proceeds without interference. In reality, the James Bay native has no greater protection than the Alaskan native.

Be that as it may,[97] the Alaskan settlement did at least seek to give the means to native Alaskans to participate in industrial society. Without implying that the Alaska settlement was sufficient and fair, the point for the purpose of this discussion is that the Alaskan natives received more in the way of *ownership* of land than did the James Bay native peoples under their land claims settlement. It is still too early, and too much of a generalization, to say whether the Alaska settlement is working. All that can be said is that the results are very mixed, indeed.

However, on the North Slope, there is positive social change with the Inupiat (Eskimos). The North Slope Regional Corporation, adjacent to Prudhoe Bay, owns sizeable tracts of good lands for development. This amounts to about 2¼ square miles (surface and subsurface interest) on a *per capita* basis.[98] In contrast, on a *per capita* basis an Inuk in James Bay received less than one square mile, with no subsurface interest. The Inupiat are actively involved in the development of the region. They are engaged in joint ventures in exploration for petroleum and natural gas with the multinational petroleum corporations. Moreover, they control the local government, the North Slope Borough, which encompasses Prudhoe Bay.

The North Slope Regional Corporation has formed several business corporations to administer work construction and sub-contract work on the Alyeska oil pipeline. A cadre of strong and discerning leaders is appearing, increasingly well-versed in non-native business skills. They have even engaged in such relatively esoteric corporate experiences as proxy-fights. However, the greater participation of the Inupiat has also modified the nature of development. Holidays are geared to the hunting seasons, seismic work is restricted when the caribou are migrating, and so on.

The point is that the land claims settlement of the Inupiat on the North Slope of Alaska is at least attempting to provide a means to a new identity. However, the Alaskan Native Land Claims Settlement may well be insufficient in providing this means (and this seems so for many of the groups encompassed by the settlement, who do not have the resource rich lands of the Inupiat) and the harshly assimilative approach of the Alaskan settlement is undesirable. On the other hand, it may well be that the James Bay settlement will serve only to further alienate the native people of northern Québec, while at the same time offering no effective mechanism to gain a new identity within the emergent industrial society. The major flaw of the James Bay settlement is the absence of a sufficiently large land base *owned* by the native peoples, such that they will necessarily and effectively be involved in future non-renewable resource development.

14. The Abortive Yukon Land Claims Settlement of 1976

In May 1976, a draft "Agreement-in-Principle" was drawn up by a negotiating committee on behalf of the 8,500 Yukon Indians (status and non-status) and a negotiating team acting on behalf of the Government of Canada. Apparently the document received approval by the federal Cabinet, but was repudiated, along with the Indian negotiators, by the membership of the Yukon Indian organization. Under the draft agreement, the *fee simple* (Category I lands) retention was to have been 128 acres *per capita*, the identical *per capita* land retention under most of the land cession numbered Treaties in southern Canada a century before! This would have resulted in a total of about 2,200 square miles with 8,500 people participating, the lands to be chosen by mutual agreement. By subsection 7(2) of the Agreement-in-Principle, there were no subsurface mineral rights given in respect of any lands. Category II lands were to have been 17,000 square miles in extent, upon which there was to be exclusive hunting, fishing and trapping. This provision did not give anything at all except "exclusivity". As development took place, and the wildlife diminished, exclusivity would become worthless, although a nebulous provision on compensation was included in the agreement.

Negotiations between the Council for Yukon Indians (CYI) and the federal and Yukon governments were resumed in 1980. Agreement was reached by the negotiators in late 1983 and initialled in December of that year. It consists of over 40 specific sub-agreements on hunting, fishing and trapping rights, quantities and location of lands, resources, financial compensation, and governmental entities. The agreement is to be ratified by all Yukon Indian communities and the Government of Canada.

15. Inuit Claims in the Northwest Territories

In February 1976 the Inuit Tapirisat of Canada (ITC) presented a claim to the federal government entitled "Nunavut", on behalf of all the Inuit of the Northwest Territories. This proposal was withdrawn in the fall of 1976, because of internal political conflicts, but a revised claim was presented in December 1977 on behalf of the Inuit of the central and eastern Arctic. Negotiating sessions have taken place since then, with an agreement-in-principle on wildlife issues being signed on 28 October 1981.

With the withdrawal of the ITC of the original Nunavut proposal, the Committee for Original Peoples' Entitlement determined in December 1976 to negotiate a separate claim on behalf of the 2,500 Inuvialuit of the Western Arctic. They presented their proposal, entitled *Inuvialuit Nunangat*, to the federal government in March 1977. The ensuing negotiations led to an agreed-upon detailed Joint Position Paper on 13 July 1978, approved by both the federal Cabinet and the Inuvialuit, through a plebiscite in the Inuvialuit communities of the Western Arctic. An Agreement-in-Principle ensued from the Joint Position Paper, signed on 31 October 1978.

Numerous negotiating sessions have followed since then, in an attempt to complete a Final Agreement, which would be implemented by settlement legislation. A Final Agreement has been achieved, but enabling legislation has not yet been enacted. The "Inuvialuit Land Rights Settlement Agreement-In-Principle" (hereafter called the "COPE Agreement") is in itself an extensive, detailed document of 180 pages, with final agreement on all of the most critical aspects of the intended settlement, including quantity of lands, nature of title, hunting, fishing and trapping rights, and financial compensation. Indeed, 85 per cent of the lands to be selected by the Inuvialuit have in fact been selected, and put aside by Cabinet order-in-council.

Inuvialuit Nunangat was, in essence, a Western Arctic regional version of the 1976 ITC Nunavut Proposal, and the COPE Agreement is the result of the negotiations ensuing from Inuvialuit Nunangat. The COPE Agreement sets forth four basic principles of the Inuvialuit land rights settlement:

(1) To preserve Inuvialuit cultural identity and values within a changing northern society
(2) To enable Inuvialuit to be equal and meaningful participants in the northern and national economy and society
(3) To provide specific rights, benefits, and compensation to the Inuvialuit in exchange for any Inuvialuit land rights that now exist; and
(4) To protect and preserve the Arctic wildlife, environment, and biological productivity.

The most critical element of any northern land claims settlement is the obtaining of *fee simple* title to large tracts of land, including subsurface interests. The COPE Agreement provides for the Inuvialuit to obtain title to the surface and all minerals in 5,000 square miles, being a selected 700 square mile block near each of the six communities, and an 800 square mile block in Cape Bathurst, proximate to Tuktoyaktuk. The selected lands have a high value from both the standpoint of Inuvialuit traditional interests and non-renewable (petroleum and natural gas) resource potential. These selections, for the most part, are subject to existing alienations by way of permits to explore for petroleum and natural gas, but the Inuvialuit step into the shoes of the Crown in receiving the economic rents the Crown would otherwise have received in respect of such third-party rights.

In addition, the Inuvialuit receive *fee simple* title to 32,000 square miles, less minerals. Although this title includes the residual property interest to such lands (that is, everything except most minerals), it is commonly referred to as a "surface title".

Furthermore, Part 12 of the COPE Agreement commits the federal government to the dedication of not less than the most northern 5000 square miles of Yukon Territory as a "National Wilderness Park for the purpose of wildlife protection and wilderness conservation," with the Inuvialuit having hunting, fishing and trapping rights to this area. The north slope of the Yukon is an area of traditional and continuing current hunting, fishing and trapping use by the Inuvialuit. There were large settlements of these people in the area at the turn of the century, but they were decimated by smallpox epidemics. In settling their claim, the Inuvialuit would have dedicated such area for the purposes of wildlife protection and wilderness conservation even if they had title, but during the negotiations the government precluded them from selecting title.

Thus, for 37,000 square miles the Inuvialuit are to be *fee simple* owners, with at least a further 5000 square miles dedicated in the public interest in a manner that accords precisely with the Inuvialuit self-interest. In addition, the COPE Agreement contemplates other areas being dedicated for wildlife protection and conservation, and some areas of restricted development activities. The onshore lands traditionally used and occupied by the Inuvialuit amount to approximately 65,000 square miles, with an additional 90,000 square miles in the offshore Beaufort Sea. Thus, the Inuvialuit have title, or a dedication for conservation purposes, to more than half of the onshore lands that they traditionally used and occupied.

Moreover, where there are existing third-party subsurface rights in Inuvialuit lands, or third-party subsurface rights arise in the future in those Inuvialuit lands where the Inuvialuit have only a surface title, the Agreement provides that explorers and developers shall enter into "participation agreements" with the Inuvialuit, which shall provide for not only rent and compensation for access, but also for "terms and conditions with respect to employment, service contracts, education and training, to reflect the nature of the land use for which access is being sought."

Part 14 of the COPE Agreement seeks first, "an integrated result of wildlife management and land management" and "that critical wildlife is [to be] protected," with "effective integration of the Inuvialuit into all structures, functions and decisions pertaining to wildlife management and land management in the Western Arctic Region". Second, Part 14 of the Agreement provides for extensive harvesting rights, exclusive to some species and in some areas, and otherwise preferential, throughout the Western Arctic Region.

16. The Nishgas' Claim

Negotiations have taken place intermitently over the years since the *Calder* decision in 1973, regarding the Nishgas' claim to the lands and resources in the Nass River valley of northwestern British Columbia. A continuing, major stumbling block is that the federal government insists that the British Columbia government play the lead role, but the province has not wished to do this and, accordingly, tripartite negotiations have been ineffective.

17. The Claims of the Dene and Metis of the Northwest Territories

The claim submitted to the Government of Canada by the Indian Brotherhood of the Northwest Territories on 26 October 1976, proposing an Agreement-in-Principle between the "Dene Nation and Her Majesty The Queen In Right of Canada," included the following principles as premises to resolve land claims:

1. The Dene have the right to recognition, self-determination, and ongoing growth and development as a People and as a Nation.

2. The Dene, as aboriginal people, have a special status under the Constitution of Canada.
3. The Dene, as aboriginal people, have the right to retain ownership of so much of their traditional lands, and under such terms, as to ensure their independence and self-reliance, traditionally, economically and socially, and the maintenance of whatever other rights they have, whether specified in this agreement or not.

Their "Dene Declaration" states that "the Dene . . . insist on the right to be regarded . . . as a nation." Referring to "colonialism and imperialism," the document says the Government of Canada was "imposed upon the Dene," and although it is "forced to submit to [the reality of] the existence of a country called Canada," demands for the Dene "the right to self-determination as a distinct people and the recognition of the Dene Nation", seeking "independence and self-determination within the country of Canada . . . [through] a just land settlement."

The claim submitted to the Government of Canada by the Metis Association of the Northwest Territories, on 28 September 1977, names as two of its fundamental objectives:

Objective 1 To secure the ownership and use and enjoyment of the lands needed by the aboriginal peoples for preserving, protecting and enhancing the native traditional lifestyle and land economy; such lands to be known as "Aboriginal Lands".

Objective 3 To develop political institutions for the effective participation of aboriginal peoples in governing "Aboriginal Lands".

The government responded to the Dene and Metis with its own "Proposals for Discussion" on 24 January 1978. On the critical issues of land and political structures, this document stated:

1. LAND
   Lands in the area of 30,000 to 50,000 square miles will be selected for a number of distinct purposes:
   — *community use:* lands in and around existing native communities;
   — *traditional use:* lands over which native people would have preferential use for hunting, fishing and trapping. Non-native hunting, fishing and trapping would be restricted in these areas;
   — *economic use:* lands with potential for renewable resource development, tourism, recreation, etc.

5. POLITICAL STRUCTURES

The Federal Government is prepared to discuss measures to secure greater participation by native people in government structures; and to explore new institutional arrangements at the territorial, regional and community levels that will enable native people, in a democratic manner, to further their interests in such areas as education, game management, land use control, renewable resource development. . . .

The management structures for implementation of claims settlement and the assurance of more effective native participation in the decisions pertaining to the North will affect not only the native people, but also the existing political structures, the federal and territorial governments, and all territorial residents. To review the existing political structures and to assist in the resolution of the conflicting political demands, the Prime Minister nominated Mr. Drury as his Special Representative.

In 1978, problems developed because the Dene nation and Metis Association of the Northwest Territories could not agree upon a mechanism for conducting joint negotiations, but by 1981 negotiations were again taking place intermittently, with some limited apparent progress to date.

18. The Constitution Act 1982 and Northern Land Claims

The Constitution Act 1982 contains four main provisions to consider with respect to aboriginal rights, sections 25, 35, 37 and 52. Section 25 states that:

The guarantee in this charter of certain rights and freedoms shall not be construed so as to abrogate or derogate from any aboriginal, treaty or other rights or freedoms that pertain to the aboriginal peoples of Canada including:

(a) any rights or freedoms that have been recognized by the Royal Proclamation of October 7, 1763; and

(b) any rights or freedoms that may be acquired by the aboriginal peoples of Canada by way of land claims settlement.

Part II, subsection 35(1) states:

(1) The existing aboriginal and treaty rights of the aboriginal peoples of Canada are hereby recognized and affirmed.

"Aboriginal peoples" is subsequently defined in subsection 35(2):

In this act, "aboriginal peoples' of Canada" includes the Indian, Inuit and Metis peoples of Canada.

On the face of it, subsection 35(1) appears at least innocuous, and perhaps positively beneficial. Section 37 states:

(1) A constitutional Conference composed of the Prime Minister of Canada and the first ministers of the provinces shall be convened by the Prime Minister of Canada within one year after this part comes into force.

(2) The conference convened under subsection (1) shall have included in its agenda an item respecting constitutional matters that directly affect the aboriginal people of Canada, including the identification and definition of the rights of those peoples to be included in the Constitution of Canada, and the Prime Minister of Canada shall invite representatives of those peoples to participate in the discussions on that item;

It is a paradox that section 25 offers protection from infringement by the Charter in respect of aboriginal and treaty rights, and subsection 35(1) recognizes and affirms "existing aboriginal treaty rights," which protection and affirmation took effect upon proclamation of the Act on 17 April 1982; yet the content of the protected rights will have to be defined retroactively (s. 37). On the face of it, there might be an inherent unconstitutionality: if the rights have been protected, and a subsequent asserted definition can be shown (by the courts) to abrogate or derogate, then the definition process would have to be seen as infringing upon constitutionally recognized rights. These, and other issues await consideration by future constitutional conferences and the many interested participants.

Section 25 affords protection to the referred to special native rights from attack on the basis of possibly infringing other provisions of the Charter of Rights and Freedoms. The protected rights are those possessed by the Aboriginal Peoples of Canada by virtue of the special status of that group, not enjoyed by other Canadians. The reference is to "aboriginal, treaty or other rights or freedoms that pertain to the aboriginal peoples of Canada." An obvious example would be the special hunting and fishing rights extended by the land cession treaties. Historically, these rights could not be circumscribed by provincial game laws, which would apply to all other Canadians.

Section 25 goes further and protects "rights or freedoms that have been recognized by the Royal Proclamation of October 7, 1763." That document expressly provided for special rights for Indian people. Furthermore, "rights or freedoms" are extended to include those by way of land claims settlement. In both the James Bay Agreement and the Inuvialuit Agreement-in-Principle — the two comprehensive land claims settlements to date — special hunting, fishing and trapping rights are provided to the native signatories. Such special native rights, but for section 25, might arguably be in conflict with the equality rights of section 15 of the Charter.

The protection in section 25 relates simply to protection from the other provisions of the Charter, and not from the effects of the ordinary statutory or common laws. However, a broader range of rights is protected than in section 35, and the rights protected are not qualified by the word "existing," as in section 35.

The extent of the breadth of the range of rights protected by section 25 is uncertain, other than with respect to the category of "rights or freedoms . . . acquired . . . by way of land claims settlement." Clearly, these would be contractual and legislated rights of the aboriginal group, and not "aboriginal" rights. Moreover, although the negotiated agreement settling a modern comprehensive land claim might notionally and functionally be seen as the equivalent of the historical land cession treaty (that is, the agreement is a modern treaty and section 25 does not employ the qualifying word "existing" in respect of "treaty . . . rights"), it seems that through the express reference to "treaty . . . rights" and also "rights . . . by way of land claims settlement," the latter rights cannot be characterized as also "treaty . . . rights" in interpreting section 25.

However, apart from rights arising from a land claims settlement, at first glance it is difficult to think of concrete examples of rights that are not embraced by "aboriginal [or] treaty . . . rights". Moreover, the "rights" recognized by the Royal Proclamation of 1763 also seem to be "aboriginal . . . rights". The phrase "other rights or freedoms" presumably refers to rights conferred under legislation: for example, the Indian Act provides that reserve lands are exempt from taxation.

It seems as a matter of interpretation that future and past land claims settlements are embraced by the language of section 25 through the use of the words "any rights or freedoms that may be acquired".

Sections 35 and 37, are of course, outside the Charter of Rights and Freedoms, in a special Part II with the heading "Rights of the Aboriginal Peoples of Canada". Placing it here has several advantages. First, by section 33, Parliament or a provincial legislature may opt out of section 2 or sections 7 and 15 of the Charter for five-year periods. Second, the rights and freedoms protected by the Charter are subject to the concluding language of section 1:

1. The Canadian Charter of Rights and Freedoms guarantees the rights and freedoms set out in it subject only to such *reasonable limits prescribed by law as can be demonstrably justified in a free and democratic society.* [emphasis added]

Rights protected by section 35 are not subject to this limitation. We have seen that section 25 protects native rights only from other provisions of the Charter, but not from the effects of ordinary laws. The force of subsection 35(1) is determined by section 52:

(1) The Constitution of Canada is the supreme law of Canada, and any law that is inconsistent with the provisions of the Constitution is, to the extent of the inconsistency of no force or effect.

(2) The Constitution of Canada includes:
   (a) the Canada Act, including this Act;
   (b) the Acts and orders referred to in Schedule 1:
   and
   (c) any amendment to any Act or order referred to in paragraph (a)
   or (b).

(3) Amendments to the Constitution of Canada shall be made only in accordance with the authority contained in the Constitution of Canada.

The effect of subsection 52(1) is to give legal paramountcy to the Constitution, including section 35 of the Constitution Act, 1982, over federal and provincial statutes and the common law. Subsection 52(1) operates for the past as well as for the future. Indeed, pre-Confederation statutes by both Canadian legislative assemblies and those by Britain that applied to British North America, seem to be covered. Subsection 52(1) has no temporal restrictions.

Leaving aside for the moment any consideration of the qualifying word "existing," section 35, coupled with section 52, has the apparent effect of giving legal paramountcy to aboriginal and treaty rights that have a factual basis and in spite of inconsistent common law or statutory law.

Let us consider an example. Practically every land cession treaty expressly affirmed hunting and fishing rights for food upon both reserve lands and also unoccupied Crown lands within the traditionally used and occupied land mass of the Indian group in question. However, the federally enacted Migratory Birds Convention Act, 1917 abridged those rights, by confining them to certain species, numbers, and time periods, and the Supreme Court of Canada has upheld the statutory law's abridgment of these historical treaty rights. Now, given Constitutional affirmation and paramountcy to such treaty rights (and leaving aside for the moment any constraining effect by the word "existing"), does this mean that the inconsistent provisions of the Migratory Birds Convention Act would be "of no force or effect"? In most treaties, the hunting and fishing rights were made subject to "federal regulations". However, for some treaties (for instance, Robinson Huron Treaty, 1850) there was no such qualification: the treaty right was literally unfettered.

Section 35 embraces "aboriginal" as well as "treaty" rights. The latter category consists of those benefits arising from promises made by the Crown in exchange for promises by an Indian group, usually including the surrender of aboriginal title. Thus, the major historical treaties are referred to as land cession treaties. In exchange for the surrender of aboriginal title, the Indian nation received promises from the Crown, including the establishment of reserve lands, annuity monies for members, monies and benefits in kind to assist in becoming farmers, and the aforementioned hunting and fishing rights. Thus, treaty rights refer to undertakings made by the Crown. In contrast, aboriginal rights refer to those rights that inhere to Canada's indigenous peoples because of that special status. Both international and

British law recognized that these independent indigenous peoples had rights, including rights to the lands in their possession and control, and although sovereignty passed with conquest, remaining rights continued until they were displaced by effective domestic law. "Aboriginal rights" is a broad phrase encompassing customs (*lex loci*) of the native group, and this may include such aspects as customary adoptions, language rights, and rights to some degree of local self-government. The scope of "aboriginal rights" is uncertain, but it is clear that it includes, at the least, rights in respect of lands traditionally used and occupied. The content of this right is very uncertain, and may consist of a full property interest in traditional lands, subject only to a burden of the Crown's underlying title, or a property right of exclusive occupancy, or a personal right of occupancy until encroachment by the Crown, or perhaps merely a limited personal right to hunt and fish upon unoccupied Crown lands. Whatever the content of aboriginal or native title, it is clear that it is, at least at present, the principal component of the broader phrase "aboriginal rights".

Returning to section 35, it is arguable that where the factual basis to aboriginal title continues to exist as of 17 April, 1982 — the factual basis being a present continuation of the traditional use and occupancy, then section 35, coupled with section 52, affords constitutional primacy to those rights. Thus, the argument goes, though there may be (purported) expropriation of that title by provincial or federal legislation in the past, such inconsistent legislation would be of no force or effect.

The above argument as to the possible impact of section 35 coupled with section 52 seems to be strongest with respect to aboriginal rights and treaty rights that have not been infringed upon by either the common law or statutory law pre-passage of the Constitution Act 1982.

However, the important question remains as to the effect of the word "existing" in section 35. Does this word restrict the rights recognized and affirmed by section 35?

First, it seems that "existing" refers to the date of proclamation of the Constitution Act 1982. Therefore, any rights arising subsequent to 17 April 1982, would not be protected, for example, if a new treaty was entered into. Moreover, recall that section 25, in contrast, has no temporal restrictions, which is particularly obvious by the clear reference to future rights in the inclusion of "any rights or freedoms that may be acquired . . . by way of land claims settlement." A modern agreement to settle land claims may be a "treaty", and rights by way of land claims settlement are not expressly referred to in section 35, in contrast to section 25. Does "treaty" in s. 35 encompass past land claims settlements, i.e., the James Bay settlement of 1975?

Thus, if a "treaty" were entered into subsequent to 17 April 1982, such "treaty" might not be protected by section 35. On the other hand, the James Bay Agreement, which clearly is given force by federal and provincial legislation (and there is not any inconsistent law), if it can be characterized as a "treaty," would be protected by section 35 as it existed before 17 April 1982. This possible situation was viewed as unsatisfactory and was resolved by a proposed amendment agreed to at the Constitutional Conference of March 1983 and implemented in 1984.

The impact of "existing," in protecting only rights as of 17 April 1982, is important, but by far the major question is whether "existing" also means that aboriginal and treaty rights that have a continuing factual basis but which have been subject to inconsistent laws before 17 April 1982, have been compromised or removed by such laws.

To return to our example of the Migratory Birds Convention Act of 1917, given that its legal effect, as determined by Canada's highest court, has been to mean that aboriginal and treaty rights to hunt and fish have been abridged since 1917 to the extent of the inconsistent provisions of the statute, does this mean that such rights (historically existing) have not existed since 1917? That is, given that such rights did not exist in law from 1917 to 17 April, 1982, are they then not "existing" rights within the meaning of section 35? Alternatively, given their clear historical existence, and indeed, the continuing literal, but legally ineffective, promises contained in the treaties, can it be said that the rights continue to exist on a factual basis, and this is enough to mean they are "existing" rights within the ambit of section 35. Then, as section 52 has no temporal restrictions in extending legal paramountcy, such "existing" rights within section 35 could not be compromised by inconsistent laws. Therefore, to continue with our example, the Migratory Birds Convention Act would be of no force or effect with respect to aboriginal and treaty rights.

In support of this interpretation, one can point to the concluding five words of subsection 35(1) which say that aboriginal and treaty rights "are *hereby* recognized and affirmed." The provision seems to be intended to be remedial, and restorative of rights that have a factual basis but which have been compromised or abrogated by laws. To choose a contrary interpretation is to give only hortatory significance to the word "hereby," and is to reduce the protective scope of section 35 to simply those scraps of aboriginal and treaty rights that might remain after a century of abuse.

One recalls that the addition of the word "existing" came at the final hour of constitutional negotiations, at the initiative of the Saskatchewan and Alberta Governments, and with the stated assurance by federal officials to native groups that it had no significant impact.

It would do much to redress the historical grievances of Aboriginal Peoples to interpret section 35 as intended to have a remedial effect. It practically emasculates the provision to interpret it as only protecting those rights that have survived the encroachment by the dominant society's laws over the past 100 years. The example of hunting rights is an apt one. The federal Government even signed one major treaty, Treaty No. 11 in the Northwest

Territories (in 1921), that expressly promised unfettered hunting and fishing rights four years *after* the Migratory Birds Convention Act had been passed (in 1917) that restricted those rights severely in law, and removed them in effect, for at the time of year of the limited hunting season allowed by the *Act*, no migratory birds remain in the Territories.

However, to interpret section 35 liberally, such that pre-17 April, 1982 inconsistent laws have no force or effect, would cause many practical problems.

There have been many specific breaches of treaties over the years, particularly, before the growing consciousness of the 1960s with respect to minority rights. These breaches would include the non-transmittal of monies or other benefits promised by some historical treaties. There have been unlawful expropriations, expropriations without fair compensation, and, arguably, breaches of trust by the government in respect of the administration of Indian lands and monies. Are treaty rights that have been so compromised "recognized and affirmed" as of 17 April 1982?

Suppose, for example, the federal government expropriated a reserve tract of land, given pursuant to a treaty, in 1940 for national defence purposes, without the consent of the Indian band. Subsequently, after the war, the lands were transferred to the province in which they were situated, and various interests were then transferred by the province over the years to third party purchasers. Such purchasers might include subdivision lots, or interests in producing petroleum and natural gas fields. The province and the third parties would take title without notice of any outstanding Indian claim, and provincial property laws would protect the titles now held. Are these "inconsistent" provincial laws now of "no force or effect"? Is the injustice of the past remedied by a provision that would render havoc upon present citizens? Obviously, in such a situation, fair compensation (whether lands or monies or both) should be paid to the aggrieved Indian band in respect of the breach of treaty, but present innocent holders of title should not be placed in jeopardy. Historical injustices are remedied by negotiated, fair settlements, not by enacting a constitutional provision that retrospectively removes the offending laws, but ignores the social impact.

The above example is not realistic in southern Canada because the *factual basis* of aboriginal title would have been removed by the expropriation. Once the *factual basis* for aboriginal title is removed, the legal rights fall away so that there are no longer "aboriginal rights" for any purpose, including for the purpose of section 35 of the Constitution Act 1982.

However, if a group of native peoples such as the Inuit in the Northwest Territories, is in factual possession of lands traditionally used and occupied, and has never surrendered their aboriginal title, do their aboriginal rights receive protection by section 35, notwithstanding any inconsistent laws?

What if they will not agree to a land claims settlement? If the liberal, remedial interpretation is given to section 35 then the expropriation power of

Parliament is removed, for the Inuit would have "rights" protected by s. 35, given the continuing factual basis to support aboriginal title. In *Calder*, where three justices of the Supreme Court of Canada found that legislation had extinguished aboriginal title, such legislation would now be of no force or effect given the continuing factual basis to the Nishga's claim of aboriginal title to much of their traditionally used territory.

Thus, it seems, section 35 is a very unsatisfactory approach to the legal aspects of aboriginal and treaty rights. Depending upon the interpretation given to the combined effect of sections 35 and 52, either no, or very few, rights are given constitutional protection, in which case the provision is a sham; or alternatively, protection is given to native peoples at the expense of the general society, inasmuch as Parliament has lost its sovereign power to act in the national interest.

Subsection 35(2) defines "aboriginal peoples of Canada" as including "Indian, Inuit and Metis people" and this definition applies to all pertinent constitutional provisions. However, the definition necessarily begs the question as to who is an Indian, Inuit or Metis. Is the test an ancestral (blood lineage) standard? If so, what degree of Indian ancestry makes one an Indian 50%?, 25%?, 5%?, 1%? Alternatively, is the test a cultural one? Is one an Indian even though one's ancestors became enfranchised and thus became non-status, no longer receiving treaty benefits? A person might be of Metis ancestry (an identification at a particular point in history) and yet a status Indian for purposes of the *Indian Act*. Is such a person a "Metis" or "Indian" within the meaning of subsection 35(2)? If the person is both, and different rights accrue to him depending upon which group he falls within, how is the question decided? The problem of deciding who were to be the aboriginal persons entitled to participate in the two northern land claims settlements to date was solved by allowing the negotiating native organizations to determine eligibility.

Endnotes

1 See, generally, E. Dosman, *The National Interest* (Toronto: McClelland & Stewart, 1975).
2 Thus, given this very tenuous premise, the Government stated in June 1973: "Thus, present indications of Canada's oil and gas potential suggest that there is probably more than enough energy resources to meet domestic requirements until at least the year 2050 with a possibility of substantial amounts of oil and gas being available for export." *An Energy Policy For Canada Phase I,* (Ottawa: Queen's Printer, 1973), p. 12.
3 *An Energy Policy for Canada Phase I, supra,* note 2, pp. 35-36, which indicates the impact of the petroleum industry on Canada's foreign reserves.
4 Thompson and Crommelin, "Canada's Petroleum Leasing Policy — A Cornucopia for Whom?", in *Canada's Petroleum Leasing Policy* (Ottawa: Papers presented to CARC, 22 March, 1973), p. 1.
5 See, generally Dosman, *Supra*, note 1, pp. 1-84.

[6] Northwest Territories Act, RSC 1970, c. N-22; Yukon Act, RSC 1970, c. Y-2.

[7] See, generally, J. Lotz, *Northern Realities — The Future of Northern Development in Canada* (Toronto: New Press, 1970), and *Report of the Advisory Commission on the Development of Government in the Northwest Territories,* (Ottawa: Queen's Printer, 1966) — Carrothers Report.

[8] See generally, Annual Report, Indian and Northern Affairs Canada, 1980-1981, pp. 28, 29.

[9] In the early 1970s, what is now the "Northern Affairs Branch" was actually named the "Northern Development Branch".

[10] Except for Hudson Bay and Hudson Straight in respect to which the issuance of permits is controlled by the Department of Energy, Mines and Resources — a Department with an obvious bias in favour of development. This Department also issues permits for the offshore areas of the east and west coasts.

[11] See, generally, P. Usher, "Land Use Regulations: A Conflict of Interests", in *Northern Perspectives* (Ottawa: Canadian Arctic Resources Committee, March, 1973), pp. 1-4.

[12] Canada Oil and Gas Act, 1981. The Canada Gazette, Part III, Vol. 6 No. 12, c. 81.

[13] Panarctic Oils Ltd. is now a subsidiary of Petro-Canada.

[14] See, generally, B. Buzan and B. Johnson, *Canada at the Third Law of the Sea Conference: Policy, Rule, and Prospects* (Kingston, R.I., Law of the Sea Institute, 1975).

[15] This discussion in respect to drilling in the Beaufort Sea is for the purpose of illustrating the inadequacies of the northern development decision-making process. There were many arguments put forward in favour of drilling, not discussed here. Given the lack of Canadian self-sufficiency in oil supplies, the lack of proven natural gas reserves at this point to justify the proposed Gas Arctic pipeline, and the fact that the Beaufort Sea has a large potential for oil and natural gas, an early start to drilling in the Beaufort Sea was favoured by many in Government. Moreover, in giving approval to drilling the Government did impose conditions to seek to ensure environmental protection. Two drilling operations commenced in August, 1976, but in mid-September there was a water blowout in one well (from an underground lake below the ocean floor) necessitating the abandonment of this site. There was a discovery of gas at the other drilling site. As to drilling in the Beaufort Sea, see generally, Pimlott, Brown and Sam, *Oil Under the Ice* (Ottawa: Canadian Arctic Resources Committee, 1976) at 41-50.

[16] By s. 27 of the Canada Oil and Gas Act, the Crown receives a 25% carried interest in all federal lands. This provision, in effect, an expropriation (without meaningful compensation) applies to all lands, including the Hibernia field, not in production as of the time of passage of the legislation, March 1982.

[17] Reproduced in R.S.C. 1970, Appendices, 123-29.

[18] The British North America Act, 1867, 30 & 31 Vict. c. 3, (U.K.) now the Constitution Act, 1867. The word "Indians" in the Constitution has been interpreted to include Inuit. *Re Eskimos,* [1939] S.C.R. 104. See also *Sigeareak E1-53* v. *The Queen,* [1966] S.C.R. 645, 57 D.L.R. (2d) 536.

[19] *Attorney-General of Canada* v. *Attorney-General of Ontario,* [1897] A.C. 199 (P.C.); and *R.* v. *Wesley,* [1932] 4 D.L.R. 774; [1932] 2 W.W.R. 337 (Alta. App. Div.) constitute authority for the proposition that Indian treaties are of a contractual nature. *R.* v. *Sikyea,* [1964] S.C.R. 642; (1965), 44 C.R. 266, *aff'g* (1964), 43 D.L.R. (2d) 150; 46 W.W.R. 65 (N.W.T.C.A.) is a leading case which deals with a conflict between hunting rights given under a treaty and the terms of the Migratory Birds Convention Act, (R.S.C. 1970, c. M-12). There the Supreme Court of Canada held that Parliament had the power to abrogate treaty agreements through its legislation.

[20] R.S.C. 1970, c. I-6.

[21] The word "status" means that the person is registered or has "status" under the Indian

Act. Of the possible 900,000 Indian people in Canada, some 300,000 are "status" Indians. This figure includes the 150,000 treaty Indians.

22 *R.* v. *Drybones,* [1970] S.C.R. 282; 9 D.L.R. (3d) 473; *Attorney-General of Canada* v. *Lavell* (1974), 38 D.L.R. (3d) 481; 23 C.R.N.S. 197 (S.C.C.); *rev'g (sub nom. Bedard* v. *Isaac),* [1972] 2 O.R. 391 (Ont. H.C.) and *(sub nom. Re Lavell and Attorney-General of Canada),* [1972] 1 O.R. 396; 22 D.L.R. (3d) 188 (Fed. C.A.) *which reversed,* [1972] 1 O.R. 390; 22 D.L.R. (3d) 182 (Cty. Ct.); *Canard* v. *Attorney-General of Canada,* [1973] 3 W.W.R. 1 (S.C.C.); *rev'g* (1973), 30 D.L.R. (3d) 9; [1972] 5 W.W.R. 678 (Man. C.A.); *Isaac* v. *Davey* (1975), 5 O.R. (2d) 610 (Ont. C.A.); *rev'g,* [1973] 3 O.R. 677 (Ont. H.C.); *Davey et al.* v. *Isaac et al.,* [1977] 2 S.C.R. 897, 77 D.L.R. (3d) 481.

23 R.S.C. 1970, Appendices, 457-60.

24 See *Isaac* v. *Davey,* [1973] 3 O.R. 667 (Ont. H.C.) at 690-91 *per* Osler, J.; *rev'd* on appeal, (1975), 5 O.R. (2d) 610 (Ont. C.A.); *Davey et al.* v. *Isaac et al.,* [1977] 2 S.C.R. 897, 77 D.L.R. (3d) 481.

25 This is illustrated in several cases: for example, *R.* v. *Sikyea, supra,* note 19; *R.* v. *White and Bob* (1965), 50 D.L.R. (2d) 613; 52 W.W.R. 193 (B.C.C.A.); *The Queen* v. *George,* [1966] S.C.R. 267; 55 D.L.R. (2d) 386; *R.* v. *Cooper* (1969), 1 D.L.R. (3d) 113 (B.C.S.C.); *Daniels* v. *The Queen,* [1968] S.C.R. 517; (1969), 2 D.L.R. (3d) 1.

26 Department of Indian Affairs and Northern Development, *Statement of the Government of Canada on Indian Policy* (Ottawa: 1969). (hereinafter referred to as the White Paper on Indian Policy).

27 See, generally, H. Cardinal, *The Unjust Society* (Edmonton: M.G. Hurtig, 1969).

28 *Re Paulette et al and Registrar of Titles (No. 2) Re Paulette's Application to file a Caveat,* [1976] 2 W.W.R. 193 (N.W.T.C.A.); *rev'g* (1974), 42 D.L.R. (3d) 8; [1973] 6 W.W.R. 97, 115; *Paulette et al.* v. *The Queen,* [1977] 2 R.S.C. 628.

29 *Id.* See, also, *Kanatewat* v. *James Bay Development Corporation,* [1975] 1 S.C.R. 48; (1974), 41 D.L.R. (3d) 1.

30 Done by Milton Freeman Research Ltd., for the Inuit Tapirisat of Canada and the Government of Canada (1976).

31 S.C. 1977, c. 32 (James Bay and Northern Quebec Native Claims Settlement Act); S.Q. 1976, c. 46.

32 Although Canada is a rich and progressive country, the native peoples are at a distinct disadvantage, economically and socially, when compared with non-native society. This is illustrated by E.R. McEwen in *Rights of Canada's First Citizens — The Indian & Eskimo,* a Resource Paper prepared for the World Council of Churches Consultation on Racism, London, England, 1969 (Toronto: Indian-Eskimo Association of Canada, 1969) at 7-8. He cites statistics indicating that over 40% of Canada's native peoples are on relief, with 75% of Indian families earning less than $2,000 a year. The infant mortality rate among the Inuit and Indian people is twice the national average, while the average life expectancy is from one-third to one-half of that of the average Canadian. The levels of educational achievement are very low; for example, approximately 50% of Indian students do not go beyond Grade VI and about 61% fail to reach Grade VIII. Although these statistics were given in 1969, there is little indication that the situation in 1983 is significantly different.

Chief George Manuel, President of the National Indian Brotherhood, in his submission in 1976 to the Mackenzie Valley Pipeline Inquiry (called the Berger Inquiry, after Mr Justice Thomas Berger who conducted the Inquiry) in Appendix "B" thereof ("Economic and Social Conditions of Canadian Indians") stated that infant mortality is four times higher among Indians, 62.12 per 1,000, compared with 15.3 for all infants in Canada (1973 figures), and that the mortality rate for status Indians was 8.32 per 1,000 in 1973 compared to 7.42 per 1,000 for other Canadians (p. 1). Chief Manuel stated that a 1975 survey indicated that the average income earned by the Indian labour force was $730.00 (p. 2). He cited figures from 1973-74 indicating that the school drop-out rate for

Indians was 84% compared to the national rate of 12% (to the end of Grade 12). (p. 2). Chief Manuel stated that 41% of the native people were receiving welfare, compared to the national rate of 3.7% (p. 2). For further information, see, Chapter 1.

[33] *Calder* v. *Attorney-General* (1970), 8 D.L.R. (3d) 59; 71 W.W.R. 81 (B.C.S.C.).

[34] *Calder* v. *Attorney-General* (1971), 13 D.L.R. (3d) 64; (1970), 74 W.W.R. 481 (B.C.C.A.).

[35] *Calder* v. *Attorney-General,* [1973] S.C.R. 313.

[36] See, generally, K. Lysyk, "The Indian Title Question in Canada: An Appraisal in the Light of Calder" (1973), 51 *Can. Bar. Rev.* 450.

[37] See generally, P. Cumming, "Native Rights and Law in an Age of Protest" (1973), 11 *Alta. L. Rev.* 238 at 256.

[38] Yukon Native Brotherhood, *Together Today for Our Children Tomorrow: A Statement of Grievances and an Approach to Settlement by the Yukon Indian People* (Whitehorse: Prepared for the Commissioner on Indian Claims and the Government of Canada, 1973).

[39] Referred to in an article by P. Cumming, Toronto *Globe & Mail,* February 21, 1973, p. 8.

[40] Speech given in Vancouver, British Columbia, August 8, 1969.

[41] It appears that there was a concerted effort, at the time of the conquest, to preserve the property rights of the French-Canadian colonists. British leaders, such as Attorney-General Edward Turlow and Solicitor-General Alexander Wedderburn, made statements to the effect that the colonists should be able to maintain their own laws to the greatest extent possible. The Quebec Act of 1774 permitted the retention of French civil law, and thus "embodied a new sovereign principle of the British Empire: the liberty of non-English people to be themselves". See, I. Burt, *The Old Province of Quebec* (Toronto: McClelland & Stewart, 1968), pp. 166-181.

[42] *Re Paulette et al and Registrar of Titles* (1974), 42 D.L.R. (3d) 8; [1973] 6 W.W.R. 97 at 115 (N.W.T.S.C.). In a decision rendered in June 1973, Morrow, J. had held the Supreme Court of the NWT had jurisdiction to hear the case: 38 D.L.R. (3d) 45.

[43] *Id.* at 40 and 148.

[44] See, *supra*, note 28.

[45] *Chief Robert Kanatewat et al.* v. *The James Bay Development Corporation et. al., supra,* note 29.

[46] Unreported: Case No. 09-000890-73.

[47] *Kanatewat* v. *James Bay Development Corporation, supra,* note 29.

[48] Unreported.

[49] By s. 91(24) of the B.N.A. Act the Federal Government has the competence to legislate in respect to "Indians, and Lands reserved for the Indians". The question then is, can a province expropriate property interests falling within a federal sphere of power, for purposes within the legislative competence of a province by s. 92 of the *B.N.A. Act,* when the expropriation would affect the very status of the native peoples, as they have an autochthonous culture, that is, their identity is intimately tied to the lands and waters they have traditionally used and occupied? Two of the many cases pertinent to this question of overlapping jurisdiction are *Charlie Cardinal* v. *The Attorney-General of Alberta,* [1974] S.C.R. 695; (1974), 13 C.C.C. (2d) 1; *aff'g* 5 C.C.C. (2d) 193; 22 D.L.R. (3d) 716; and *British Columbia Power* v. *A.-G. of B.C.* (1965), 47 D.L.R. (2d) 633. For a discussion of the last mentioned case, and of the issue generally, see, G. La Forest, *Natural Resources and Public Property Under the Canadian Constitution* (Toronto, Univ. of Toronto Press, 1969) at 174-182.

[50] British North America Act, 1871. Now sections 35 and 52 of the *Constitution Act,* 1982, would also have to be considered. Does section 35 entrench aboriginal title from attack by federal and provincial expropriation legislation?

[51] See the reasons for judgment of Morrow, J. in the Northwest Territories Caveat case, *supra* note 42, where he discusses the unique history of Rupert's Land and the transfer

thereof by the Hudson's Bay Company to Canada. Justice Morrow's remarks are pertinent as well with respect to the James Bay area as this territory historically was also part of Rupert's Land.

[52] [1979] 3 C.N.L.R. 1, at p. 17, (F.C.T.D.).

[53] For a good discussion of this topic see the testimony of Douglas Sanders to the Berger Inquiry April 15, 1976. See, generally, Cumming and Mickenberg, eds., *Native Rights in Canada,* 2d ed. (Toronto: General Publishing Co. and the Indian Eskimo Association of Canada, 1972).

[54] See, generally, *Native Rights in Canada, supra,* note 53 and Chapter 2, *supra.*

[55] *Calvins Case,* [1608] 7 Co. Rep. 1a; 2 Howell St. Tr. 559; 77 E.R. 377 (K.B.); *Campbell* v. *Hall* (1974), 1 Cowp. 204; 98 E.R. 1045 (K.B.); *Amodu Tijani* v. *Secretary, Southern Nigeria,* [1921] 2 A.C. 399.

[56] *Supra,* note 53, p. 49.

[57] *Native Rights in Canada, supra,* note 53, pp. 46, 47.

[58] [1972] F.C. 568, 29 D.L.R. (3d) 376.

[59] S.C. 1870, c. 3, s. 31.

[60] S.C. 1912, c. 45, s. 2(c).

[61] This outline is taken largely from *Native Rights in Canada, supra,* note 53, pp. 276-278.

[62] The deed of surrender is reprinted in R.S.C. 1970, Appendices, pp. 257-77. In the December, 1867, Address to Her Majesty the Queen from the Senate and House of Commons of the Dominion of Canada upon the transference of Rupert's Land to Canada, it was stated: "And furthermore that, upon the transference of the territories in question to the Canadian Government, the claims of the Indian tribes to compensation for lands required for purposes of settlement will be considered and settled in conformity with the equitable principles which have uniformly governed the British Crown in its dealings with the aborigines." Reprinted in R.S.C. 1970, Appendices, at 264. Transfer Order now in Constitution Act, 1982.

[63] S.C. 1870, c. 3, s. 31.

[64] *Treaty No. 10 and Reports of Commissioners* (Ottawa: Queen's Printer, 1966), p. 3.

[65] S.C. 1872, c. 23.

[66] W.E. Hodgins, *Dominion and Provincial Legislation,* 1867-1895 (Ottawa: Government Printing Bureau, 1896), p. 1026.

[67] The speech may be found in G. Stewart, *Canada under the Administration of the Earl of Dufferin* (Toronto: Rose-Belford Publishing Co., 1879), pp. 491-93.

[68] S.C. 1879, c. 31, s. 125(e).

[69] *St. Catharine's Milling and Lumber Co.* v. *The Queen,* (1889), 14 A.C. 46, at 54.

[70] S.C. 1924, c. 48, s. 1.

[71] Reprinted in S.C. 1891, p. 1xi.

[72] S.C. 1912, c. 40, s. 2(a) (Ontario); S.C. 1912, c. 45, s. 2(c) (Quebec).

[73] British North America Act, 1930, R.S.C. 1970, Appendices, pp. 371, 380-81, and 388-89.

[74] Minute No. 1, p. 31.

[75] Joint Committee of the Senate and House of Commons, Minute No. 2, p. 54.

[76] Department of Indian Affairs and Northern Development, *The Canadian Indian* (Ottawa: Queen's Printers, 1966), p. 3.

[77] H. Dorion, *Commission of Inquiry on the Territorial Integrity of Quebec,* Rapport 4: le domaine Indian (Quebec: 1971) pp. 389-97.

[78] [1973] S.C.R. 313.

[79] Department of Indian Affairs and Northern Development, *Statement on Claims of Indian and Inuit People* (Ottawa: Queen's Printer, 1973).

[80] *Kanatewat* v. *James Bay Development Corporation, supra,* note 29.

[81] *Supra,* note 28.

[82] *Supra*, note 31.

[83] *Supra*, note 52.

[84] The fifth of five "energy targets" of the Government of Canada in *An Energy Strategy for Canada: Policies for Self-Reliance* (Ottawa: Minister of Energy, Mines & Resources, 1976), p. 6 is expressed as being: "doubling at a minimum, exploration and development activity in the frontier regions of Canada over the next three years, under acceptable social and environmental conditions."

[85] Department of Indian Affairs and Northern Development, *Statement on Claims of Indian and Inuit People* (Ottawa: Queen's Printer, 1973).

[86] Department of Indian Affairs and Northern Affairs, *In All Fairness — A Native Claims Policy* (Ottawa: Queen's Printer, 1981).

[87] Canada Oil and Gas Act, 1981. The Canada Gazette, Part III, Vol. 6, No. 12, c. 81.

[88] *Id.*, p. 21.

[89] M. Angus, "In Fairness To Whom" in *Newsletter Project North*, vol. 6, no. 1, p. 3.

[90] See, generally, the brief of the Inuit Tapirisat of Canada to the Government of Canada in response to the Government of Canada's *Guidelines for Northern Pipelines* (1972).

[91] Annual Report, Indian and Northern Affairs Canada, 1980-1981, QS-3217-000-BB-A1; Catalogue No. R1-1981; ISBN 0-662-51604-4, p. 44.

[92] The Agreement provided the following allocations:

Crees: Category I — 2,158 square miles.

II — 25,130 square miles (hunting, fishing and trapping rights).

Inuit: Category I — 3,250 square miles.

Category II — 35,000 square miles (hunting, fishing and trapping rights).

The Cree and Inuit receive a surface title ownership to Category I lands, plus 50% of any subsurface development benefits. They receive hunting, fishing and trapping rights to Category II lands, but not ownership.

The land settlement covers a total area of some 410,000 square miles (the areas added to the province of Quebec in 1899 and 1912 — see section 1.16 of the Agreement), and it seems the native peoples' position that this entire area comprised traditionally used and occupied lands was not challenged by the Government. Thus, some 10,000 people will own (collectively) 5,408 square miles. Not being owners of Category II lands (upon which there are hunting, fishing and trapping rights), development is permitted and will over time diminish the traditional form of livelihood.

[93] This figure is approximate, and at the time of the settlement in 1975 was based upon 6,500 Cree Indians and 3,500 Inuit. Quebec Government figures in 1975 suggested about 9,600 native persons while native organizations referred to about 10,050.

[94] This analysis deals only with those lands retained by the native peoples as *owners*, and the amount and form of monetary compensation through settlement. The settlement did provide for many other things, however, they may be inconsequential in the long term, or amount to rights extended which are simply those rights other citizens ordinarily have. Moreover, the 'ownership of land' is the essential element in a northern land claims settlement, and therefore, this criticism centres upon this aspect of the settlement. On the James Bay settlement, see generally J. Ciaccia, "Native Claims — the James Bay Settlement," Canadian Bar Association Annual Meeting, August 31, 1976.

[95] The Inuit retention as owners works out to slightly less than one square mile (about 601.6 acres) *per capita*. The Inuit usage for hunting, fishing and trapping works out to about 50 square miles *per capita*.

[96] Alaska Native Claims Settlement Act, 85 Stat. 688 (1971); 43 U.S.C. #1601-1628 (1973).

[97] Perhaps the most significant special right is hunting and fishing. In the writer's conversations with native leaders in Alaska during a visit in June, 1974, they stated that they considered special hunting and fishing rights as still being a question for discussion

with government, and that it was not dealt with at the time of the land claims settlement because there was not sufficient time to consider all aspects of the issue.

[98] Traditionally used lands for the 3,900 Inupiat (of the North Slope area) was 56.5 million acres. They received 5.5 million acres in the settlement. This works out to about 1,510 acres *per capita* or almost 2-¼ square miles *per capita*. Ownership of the land is on a *fee simple* basis: that is, ownership includes the subsurface mineral interests, although existing alienations at the time of the land claims settlement remain. Title is held collectively through use of the corporate entity.

Note that 70% of all revenues from timber and subsurface resources in the region's lands must be divided equally among the 12 regional corporations, on a relative population basis. Thus the Inupiat, through their Arctic Slope Regional Corporation will be allowed to retain only a total of about 35% of its timber and subsurface income: 30% due to the location of resources in its region, and approximately 5% because of its relatively small population.

This analysis is taken largely from *The Alaska Native Claims Settlement: A Report on a Trip to Alaska by Representatives of the Inuit Tapirisat of Canada* (Ottawa: Inuit Tapirisat of Canada, June 1974).

13. Aboriginal Rights in International Law: Human Rights

MAUREEN DAVIES

1. Introduction

Since World War II, the community of nations has become increasingly concerned with developing standards of conduct in the field of human rights to which all nations aspire. This concern has been manifested in the Charter of the United Nations, the International Bill of Rights, and an ever increasing number of conventions, declarations and covenants. In addition to the activities of the United Nations, regional systems have established codes of conduct and legal machinery to deal with violations of human rights. There can be no doubt that human rights considerations have become a legitimate concern of the World Community legally, morally and politically.

The particular concerns of aboriginal peoples throughout the world have long been on the periphery of these developments, but this situation, at last, is changing. The decades ahead portend that the rights of aboriginal peoples will assume a prominent place on the world's agenda:

> By our own efforts, over the last decade, we have successfully reasserted our sovereignty as Indian Nations in our own homelands and have begun to re-establish our international personality in the courts and political assemblies of the world.
>
> But there is much work to be done. While we have been trussed up and gagged in Canada for the better part of this century, the international community of nations has been restructured and a body of international law, which is not yet sensitive to our Indian concepts of nationhood, has come into use. In our enforced absence from world forums, nobody spoke for us and nobody contradicted Canada's definition of us as an insignificant and disappearing ethnic minority.
>
> In the thirty-five years since the Second World War, Britain and the other European powers dismantled their colonial empires and, with the United States, sought a new world order. The integrity of every nation, however poor or small, would be protected by universal observance of international law based on common respect for fundamental human rights, including the right to self-determination.[1]

These developments have a specific relevance for indigenous peoples, both as individuals and as nations.

The following chapter provides a brief survey of the factors that are of particular concern to aboriginal peoples:

1. The United Nations:

(a) The Charter
(b) The International Bill of Rights
(c) Self-determination
(d) The Convention on the Prevention and Punishment of the Crime of Genocide
(e) The International Convention on the Elimination of all Forms of Racial Discrimination

2. International Labour Organization Convention 107.
3. The Inter-American System.

The exploitation of these fora is in a state of infancy. International redress of violations of human rights on the whole is not really practical or effective. Nevertheless, it is important to make use of all possible avenues, if only to provide a balance to the otherwise bleak alternative of the classic "domestic jurisdiction" position.

2. The United Nations

(a) The Charter

(i) The Preamble

WE THE PEOPLES OF THE UNITED NATIONS DETERMINED
> to save succeeding generations from the scourge of war, which twice in our lifetime has brought untold sorrow to mankind, and
> to reaffirm faith in fundamental human rights, in the dignity and worth of the human person, in the equal rights of men and women and of nations large and small, and
> to establish conditions under which justice and respect for the obligations arising from treaties and other sources of international law can be maintained, and
> to promote social progress and better standards of life in larger freedom,

AND FOR THESE ENDS
> to practise tolerance and live together in peace with one another as good neighbours, and
> to unite our strength to maintain international peace and security, and
> to ensure, by the acceptance of principles and the institution of

methods, that armed force shall not be used, save in the common interest, and

to employ international machinery for the promotion of the economic and social advancement of all peoples.

HAVE RESOLVED TO COMBINE OUR EFFORTS TO ACCOMPLISH THESE AIMS

Although the preamble, in common with the other articles in the Charter, does not refer specifically to aboriginal peoples, it is nonetheless applicable. In general, the preamble to a treaty is used to outline the intentions of the parties thereto and, while it does not define the parties' obligations, it can be, and often is, referred to in the interpretation of subsequent articles.

Thus references to the "[reaffirmation of] faith in fundamental human rights, in the dignity and worth of the human person . . . and of nations large and *small* . . ." are important principles that give sustenance to the subsequent provisions of Articles 1 and 55.[2]

(ii) Chapter I. Purposes and Principles

Article 1

The Purposes of the United Nations are:

1. To maintain international peace and security, and to that end: to take effective collective measures for the prevention and removal of threats to the peace, and for the suppression of acts of aggression or other breaches of the peace, and to bring about by peaceful means, and in conformity with the principles of justice and international law, adjustment or settlement of international disputes or situations which might lead to a breach of the peace;

2. To develop friendly relations among nations based on respect for the principle of equal rights and self-determination of peoples, and to take other appropriate measures to strengthen universal peace;

3. To achieve international co-operation in solving international problems of an economic, social, cultural, or humanitarian character, and in promoting and encouraging respect for human rights and for fundamental freedoms for all without distinction as to race, sex, language, or religion; and

4. To be a centre for harmonizing the actions of nations in the attainment of these common ends.

One of the significant principles from the perspective of indigenous peoples is contained in Article 1 (2). Reference to "respect for the principles of equal rights and self-determination of peoples" is an important precursor to similar provisions in the "International Bill of Rights". The inclusion of self-determination in Article 1 (2) reflects the fundamental importance of the concept that "territorial changes [ought] to accord with the freely expressed wishes of the peoples concerned to choose the form of government under which they will live."[3]

No attempt has been made to define the terms used, and there have been problems of interpretation over the meaning of "nations," "peoples" and "states" as well as with the term "self-determination" itself. Within the context of the Charter, various interpretations are tenable. The two prevailing views characterize "self-determination" as either essentially a legal right giving rise to concomitant legal claims and obligations, or as a political principle with considerations of relevant phenomena in terms of applicability.[4] Subsequent developments which have helped to give more definition to the concept are considered in more detail below. It is clear that "self-determination" was considered an important element in the attempt to put an end to the practice of colonialism.[5]

There is also a conflict of opinion on the nature of the obligations contained in Article 1 (3). One view suggests that there is no legal obligation to respect particular rights in the absence of specific undertakings so to do, and that the United Nations has no authority to involve itself in alleged violations of human rights. States proposing this interpretation rely on Article 2 (7), claiming that such matters are "essentially within the domestic jurisdiction" of that state. The opposing viewpoint suggests that Article 1 (3), when read together with Articles 55 and 56, does impose obligations with regard to human rights and fundamental freedoms, which the General Assembly has authority to consider.

Article 2 (7) states:

> Nothing contained in the present Charter shall authorize the United Nations to intervene in matters which are essentially within the domestic jurisdiction of any state or shall require the members to submit such matters to settlement under the present Charter; but the principle shall not prejudice the application of enforcement measures under Chapter VII.

States have attempted to rely on this article to shirk accountability for violations of human rights. Interpretative roadblocks have been raised with reference to what constitutes "intervention" and as to what falls within the "domestic jurisdiction" of the state. In UN practice, merely placing an issue on the agenda for consideration does not by itself constitute intervention."[6] With regard to considerations of human rights *vis-à-vis* the "domestic jurisdiction" argument, subsequent developments, in particular the International Bill of Rights, have made this an increasingly untenable position for states to take.[7]

Attempts to limit considerations of human rights relating to indigenous populations living within the borders of member states to the domestic level are similarly unacceptable.

(iii) Chapter IX. International Economic and Social Cooperation
Article 55

> With a view to the creation of conditions of stability and well-being which are necessary for peaceful and friendly relations among nations based on respect for the principle of equal rights and self-determination of peoples, the United Nations shall promote:
> (a) higher standards of living, full employment, and conditions of economic and social progress and development;
> (b) solutions of international economic, social, health, and related problems; and international cultural and educational cooperation; and
> (c) universal respect for, and observance of, human rights and fundamental freedoms for all without distinction as to race, sex, language, or religion.

Article 56

> All Members pledge themselves to take joint and separate action in cooperation with the Organization for the achievement of the purposes set forth in Article 55.

Articles 55 and 56 provide a more positive platform for action than Article 1, which emphasizes "cooperation". Here we find an even clearer commitment to take a more active role in achieving the general aims which have been outlined, as well as a clearer definition of what those aims are. Once again there is a firm commitment to the principle of self-determination. The term "promote" used in Article 55 has led to a number of important developments. Through the General Assembly and the Economic and Social Council resolutions intended to influence public opinion as well as governments have been adopted, international instruments have been drafted for specific adoption and ratification by member states, together with various educational endeavours, including the provision of information relating to the observance of human rights.[8] Perhaps the most profound of these developments was the adoption of the Universal Declaration of Human Rights in 1948.

The Economic and Social Council, pursuant to Articles 62 and 68, has been instrumental in initiating many important studies and reports.[9] It has established commissions and sub-commissions, and appointed ad hoc bodies and rapporteurs.[10] Furthermore, the Council is responsible for the International Bill of Rights.

Among the important contributions made by this body has been the establishment of the Human Rights Commission, and its sub-commissions, which includes the Sub-Commission on the Prevention of Discrimination and the Protection of Minorities.

The Commission and Sub-Commission include among their duties responsibility for dealing with "particular situations which reveal a consistent pattern of gross and reliably attested violations of human rights."

Complaints of this kind may be launched by adopting the "1503" procedure. This can be done by (a) individuals or groups who are victims of this type of violation, (b) by individuals, or groups who have direct and reliable knowledge of such violations, (c) by non-governmental organizations with such knowledge or (d) by individuals, who though possessing only second-hand knowledge, are able to supply clear evidence.[11] Indigenous peoples have recently begun to make use of this procedure. In March 1980, for example, a complaint was filed with the Commission and Sub-Commission by the Seminoles, the Houdenousaunee, the Hopi, the Western Soshone, the Lakota Nations and the Mohawk People claiming violation by the United States of America of adequate and equal legal protection to land belonging to American Indian peoples. In support of this claim, they cite violation of Article 17 (1) of the Universal Declaration of Human Rights, Articles (2) and (5)(d)(V) of the International Convention on the Elimination of All Forms of Racial Discrimination, and Articles 21(1) and 24 of the American Convention on Human Rights, Articles 1 and 55 of the Charter of the United Nations, Article 26 of the International Covenant on Civil and Political Rights, and Basket 1, Principle VII of the Helsinki Final Act:

> The existence of a rule of law within the legal system of the United States which allows the United States government to expropriate the ancestral lands of American Indian peoples without legal liability to pay compensation and without other legal restrictions constitutes a flagrant violation of all these international commitments. This rule of law, most clearly stated by the United States Supreme Court in 1955, declares that Indian people do not possess a legal right to the land they and their ancestors have lived on for centuries.

> The lack of legal protection given to Indian land interests is in sharp contrast to the protection afforded non-Indian land owners by the Constitution of the United States and other legal principles of United States law. Non-Indian property may not be taken by the government without according the owners "due process," meaning notice of the proposed action and an opportunity to be heard, and "just compensation" meaning the fair market value of the land plus interest from the time of taking. Finally, the government must show the acquisition of the land is for a public purpose before it can be taken. By contrast, the United States may expropriate Indian land for any purpose and on any terms it seems desirable without providing an opportunity to contest the

taking in a fair and impartial hearing. Stated another way, the interest Indian people have in their lands does not constitute a "property right" as that phrase is understood in American law. Because their lands are not protected against arbitrary government action, Indian peoples face destruction of their communities and of their way of life.[12]

Similar communications have also been submitted alleging violations of the principle of self-determination. It is probable that indigenous groups both within and outside the United States will be resorting to the 1503 procedure alleging similar as well as additional violations. The Sub-Commission's power to redress such grievances is limited to focussing attention on the problem and to stimulating action.[13] Both the proceedings and the decisions of the Commission and Sub-Commission are confidential and remain so until such time as the Commission decides to make a recommendation to the Economic and Social Council, a fact which tends to limit its effectiveness as a means of influencing public opinion. Another negative feature of this procedure is that the complainants take no part in the process beyond the written submission. There is not even provision for reporting the progress of the complaint to the parties involved.

In furtherance of the objectives contained in the Charter, the Sub-Commission has sponsored a "study of the Problem of Discrimination Against Indigenous Populations" by special rapporteur Martinez Cobo.

The undertaking is a formidable one, surveying worldwide the *de jure* and *de facto* position of indigenous peoples. The study has been in progress for ten years and has produced several preliminary reports, and more recently, a number of the chapters of the final report. Consideration has been given to such questions as basic legal status, measures undertaken for the prohibition, prevention and elimination of discrimination, and issues related to indigenous languages. The following excerpts give an indication of the nature of the rapporteur's findings:

A. *Preliminary observations*

It must be stated from the outset that in all countries, whether developed or developing, unitary or federal and wherever they may be located and whatever their background may be, there is discrimination in fact even when full equality may have been formally proclaimed in law. To be sure, there are varying degrees and different characteristics in the incidence of this phenomenon, but, everywhere the *de facto* situation is at variance with the *de jure* situation. Actual behaviour is often very far from what has been foreseen in juridicial norms. Regardless of the best of intentions and of the most generous ideals that may have inspired the adoption of legal provisions, their actual workings may have ended up producing unwanted results. Unfavourable distinctions affecting indigenous populations are, of course, not seldom based on intentional and very realistic oppressive or repressive actions or practices specifically designed to bring about freely chosen effects to the detriment of indigenous populations. Existing discriminatory patterns have also, by way of reaction, produced defensive attitudes or conduct against them, or against proposed ways of preventing them or the enactment of provisions seeking their elimination. Everywhere legal norms have been elaborated to cope with existing discriminatory acts or practices by prohibiting them and declaring them to be punishable, establishing ways or procedures to avoid or overcome them, or else to punish those responsible for and remedy the effects of these actions or practices.

B. *Re: Languages*

Before concluding this introduction, the Special Rapporteur should point out that the policies followed by many States have consistently been based on the assumption that indigenous populations, cultures and languages would either die out naturally or be absorbed by other population groups and "national cultures". It was hoped that perhaps even before that, the indigenous languages would die out as a result of the pressure, quality and attractiveness of the official languages — international languages which were supposed to have advantages of all kinds, both real and imaginary, and to be particularly well suited to science, technology, art and civilization. Little emphasis was therefore placed on State plans for the teaching of indigenous languages and their use as languages of instruction in the early stages of education. That was thought to be contrary to the best interests of society because it might endanger national unity and it was feared that it would inevitably lead to linguistic isolation and to excessive social and political fragmentation. It is now believed that such policies, which, in some cases were followed for centuries, were, to judge by the facts, ill-founded. Although some peoples and their languages have died out for various reasons, most of them have survived. The presence of indigenous peoples and languages is strongly felt in many parts of the world. These groups are defending their languages with determination and tenacity. The linguistic deadlock is practically the same as before. In addition, many contemporary experts question and deny the supposedly undesirable effects — namely, insularity and competing micronationalism — of promoting indigenous languages. It is now being affirmed that diversity in itself is not contrary to unity. It is also said that uniformity does not necessarily produce the desired unity. Indeed, artificially produced uniformity may be a source of weakness and hostility, while there may be strength in coordinated diversity within a multifaceted but harmonious whole, based on respect for the particular characteristics of each component.[14]

The recent establishment of a UN Working Group on Indigenous Populations is further evidence of the concern felt about the problems faced by indigenous people.

1. The creation of the Working Group on Indigenous Populations was proposed by the Sub-Commission on Prevention of Discrimination and Protection of Minorities in its resolution 2 (XXXIV) of 8 September 1981, endorsed by the Commission on Human Rights in its resolution 1982/19 of 10 March 1982 and authorized by the Economic and Social Council in its resolution 1982/34 of 7 May 1982. In that resolution the Council authorized the Sub-Commission to establish annually a Working Group on Indigenous Populations which shall meet for up to five working days before the annual sessions of the Sub-Commission in order to:

(a) review developments pertaining to the promotion and protection of human rights and fundamental freedoms of indigenous populations, including information requested by the Secretary-General annually from governments, specialized agencies, regional intergovernmental organizations and non-governmental organizations in consultative status, particularly those of indigenous peoples, to analyse such materials, and to submit its conclusions to the Sub-Commission, bearing in mind the report of the Special Rapporteur of the Sub-Commission;

(b) give special attention to the evolution of standards concerning the rights of indigenous populations, taking account of both the similarities and the differences in the situations and aspirations of indigenous populations throughout the world.

62. With a view to strengthening the implementation of existing standards and to formulating others in consultation with indigenous representatives the Working Group agreed on the principle of participation of organizations of indigenous populations in the deliberations of the Working Group, as observers.

63. The members of the Working Group took as their starting point the fact that the general provisions on human rights, found in the main international instruments on human rights, were applicable equally to members of indigenous populations and to other groups. In practice, however, it was not advisable to rely solely on principles such as equality of opportunity, equal right to work, equal right to education, for in their passive form they would not give protection but could have adverse effects on indigenous populations, who for historical reasons were disadvantaged in society. A member therefore argued that affirmative action must be taken in regard to indigenous populations, in order to bridge the gap between them and other members of society.

64. A government observer referred to affirmative action as a positive policy step for the protection of indigenous populations, while an indigenous representative objected to this policy on the grounds that fair play was not the rule in the application of the legislation and that it

might be only a way of simulating a participation in decision making.

71. The members of the Working Group agreed that particular attention should be given to the implementation of the Convention on the Prevention and Punishment of the Crime of Genocide; and to the examination of gross violations of human rights in various areas.

72. The representatives of several organizations stressed the importance of self-determination as the key to the implementation of solutions for the indigenous populations problems. Self-determination would allow those groups to freely decide how to solve their own problems and how to develop their own culture, their own resources and their own way of life. It was emphasized that self-determination did not necessarily equate to separatism. In connection with self-determination, other specific rights were also stressed: the right to lands and to the mineral resources it contained; the right to develop their own culture and education; the right to enjoy religious and political rights and to be consulted and to participate in national development processes.

73. Most representatives of NGOs and of Indigenous Populations as well as some government observers stressed the importance of consultation in formulating and implementing national and international standards. It was suggested that to determine the range of aspirations of Indigenous Populations was a step in establishing the meaning of the right to self-determination.

Areas of concern

74. During the debate, representatives of indigenous organizations and other NGOs expressed their concern in relation to certain aspects which the indigenous populations perceive as the main areas of concern affecting their human rights or their specific rights as indigenous populations. Those areas of concern would provide the basis for the development of standards.

75. The Working Group encouraged the indigenous representatives, the observers of Governments and organizations, and the experts who attended its meetings to express their views on the main areas of concern as regards the question of indigenous populations, with a view to the adoption of standards which would help to improve the respect for and effective recognition of the rights of indigenous peoples.

76. The main areas of concern mentioned were:

(a) *Right to life, to physical integrity and to security of the indigenous populations.*

77. Several indigenous groups and NGOs stated that the right to life, a

basic human right recognized in several international declarations and instruments, was repeatedly violated with respect to indigenous peoples. Furthermore, some also alleged that genocide was being committed against indigenous peoples in Central and South America. Statements concerning what they called genocidal actions against the indigenous populations of Guatemala and El Salvador were made by representatives of indigenous organizations and of several NGOs who contended that massacres of entire indigenous communities took place in those countries, due to the action of regular army units as well as para-military groups used by the Governments.

78. The Working Group brought to the attention of the participants the definition of "genocide" as established in the Convention on the Prevention and Punishment of the Crime of Genocide of 9 December 1948 and indicated that the definition did not apply to other cases which had also been presented as such. It was indicated that the word ethnocide would be more appropriate to describe certain situations. The word ethnocide meant, according to the Conference of UNESCO in San José in 1981, the violation of the right of an ethnic group to develop its own culture.

79. It was also emphasized that the right to life could also be violated by depriving the indigenous peoples of their lands or their natural resources and so subjecting those peoples to hunger, disease, suffering and death. The case of Bangladesh was mentioned in that regard.

80. Representatives of indigenous groups alleged that in the parts of the world where they came from indigenous populations were subjected to different forms of violations of their right to life, poisoned food, clothes contaminated with viruses, fire set to their houses and lands, persecution by Governments or other groups. According to those statements, indigenous persons who were active in the promotion of the respect of human rights and specific indigenous rights were usually harassed and subjected to serious violations of human rights. A NGO requested that an investigation be carried out on military and paramilitary abuses committed against indigenous peoples, including the killing of tribal leaders. The representative of another NGO expressed that, even though national security was a legitimate concern, and one which was shared by the indigenous peoples, it should not be used by Governments as a pretext for depriving or restricting basic human rights and so committing serious violations of those rights. That was alleged to occur in several countries where considerations of national security were given paramount importance.

81. Considering the extremely serious situation existing in Guatemala, where the genocide of the indigenous peoples was alleged by all of the

indigenous representatives and by most of the NGOs that spoke in that connection, the Working Group decided to reflect the concern of these observers by transmitting to the Sub-Commission the draft resolution concerning the Guatemalan people, which had been submitted by the International Indian Treaty Council and was supported by all the indigenous organizations and most of the NGOs present at the meeting. (See paragraphs 77 above and 109 below).

(b) *The right to self-determination. The right to develop their own culture, traditions, language and way of life*

82. The question of self-determination of the indigenous populations was brought up in various statements and members of the Working Group sought clarification from the NGOs and representatives of indigenous peoples who had raised the problem. Some indigenous observers argued that distinctions should be made between minorities and peoples. While minorities were constituted by persons who had accepted to be incorporated within existing States, peoples were collective entities requiring self-determination. In the first case elimination of discrimination was particularly valuable, whereas as regards the latter self-determination was the key issue. It was suggested that the situation varied from group to group, from country to country, and that the question of self-determination was varied in content and approach, leaving a kaleidoscope of positions in between, including the mere participation in decisions concerning their status in the country where the indigenous people lived, through self-government arrangements establishing different forms of autonomy within the State. It had individual and collective aspects, internal and external dimensions ranging from individual dignity, autonomy in different forms, to the establishment of an independent State. It was expressed that the indigenous peoples should have the right to self-determination, that is, to possess in their territories whatever degree of self-government they wished to choose.

83. Furthermore, the observers from those organizations stated that the question of self-determination was linked to a number of rights whose recognition was vital to the survival of an indigenous population, such as the right to develop its own culture, its own language, its own traditions and its own way of life. They added that the denial of those rights might result in the destruction or disintegration of the cultural and political integrity of the indigenous group, even creating situations of ethnocide. (see paras. 52, 77 and 78 above).

84. In connection with the right to self-determination several NGOs and indigenous representatives emphasized the need for consultation

with the indigenous populations before making decisions that might affect the rights to their lands, to their natural resources and to develop their natural environment within the framework of their traditional way of life, as well as any decision concerning their status or other matters of their concern.

85. Several cases related to the non-recognition by States of the right to self-determination of the indigenous populations were reported, as well as the institutional arrangements which created the illusion of self-determination while being, in fact, other ways of imposing the will of the dominant society. It was also stated that the right to self-determination was indissolubly linked to the right to land, as the territorial base of the existence of the indigenous groups as such.

(c) *The right to freedom of religion and traditional religious practices*

86. Some indigenous representatives reported alleged violations to the right to freedom of religion and traditional religious practices. Particularly, the Lakota reported the deprivation of the Black Hills, part of their ancestral territory which was considered sacred by several indigenous groups in the United States of America. That sacred area had been confiscated by the Government many years ago. Recently, compensation had been offered instead of the return of the area to its rightful owners.

87. In that respect, the observer of the United States of America said that the Indian nations which had participated in the United States court proceedings concerning the Black Hills case, had been awarded approximately 110 million dollars in compensation. Indigenous representatives pointed out that not all Indian people had accepted the money, since to them the Black Hills were sacred and ceremonial land and that no amount of money would ever compensate for the loss of such places.

88. Several organizations stressed that indigenous populations should not be subjected to systematic campaigns of forced conversion, and that measures should be taken to prevent any act or practice of interference, disruption or prohibition of indigenous religious rites, practices and ceremonies.

(d) *The right to land and to natural resources*

89. Problems concerning land tenure, deprivation of the land belonging to indigenous populations and their natural resources were brought to the attention of the Working Group by several indigenous and NGO organizations. Alleged violations of those rights in numerous countries

were reported during the session of the Working Group. In most of the cases mentioned, the dispossession of lands was linked to development projects which were being carried out by multinationals or governmental activities for the exploitation of indigenous lands and resources.

90. Some government observers also contended that the right to land was also closely linked to the right to develop their own indigenous culture and way of life. It was reported that the enforced division of indigenous lands, as well as the enforced displacements of the communities from their ancestral land to another area destroyed the integrity of the indigenous community and forced the indigenous peoples to accept unfavourable labour practices as well as face new conditions in areas different from their natural environment.

91. Several representatives of NGOs and indigenous populations organizations made statements of concern regarding what they alleged to be gross and systematic violation of human rights in some places. Particular reference was made to land rights, deprivation of land and individualization of indigenous land property. Examples of alleged violations of existing norms in various countries were given: annexation of indigenous land without compensation under the Indian Act (1951) of Canada and the Black Hills in the United States of America. In that connection, emphasis was put by several speakers on the requirement of consent, as indispensable in cases of annexations or appropriations of land of the indigenous populations.

92. The impact of multinationals and governmental activities upon the exploitation of indigenous lands and natural resources was also discussed. Uranium exploitation in Canada, the United States and Australia and the mining of nickel in Guatemala were mentioned by way of examples. In other countries, certain development projects, carried out by national Governments, with technical and financial assistance from international development and financial agencies such as the World Bank and the International Development Bank, were said to result in many cases in the fragmentation of indigenous lands and forests, the disintegration of indigenous cultural centres and societies, and in the creation of up-rooted social groups which were forced to change their way of life (either by migrating or becoming sedentary). Mention was made of five projects aiming at colonizing forests in Peru, the policy of inviting European immigrants from southern Africa to take over Indian land in Bolivia, the role played by transnational companies, banks and churches in the annexation of indigenous lands, the constitution of reserves, the policy of dual standards, and forced relocation of indigenous populations.

93. A case of relocation in the United States of America was mentioned by several representatives of indigenous organizations. They said that this was being done in order to take over the mineral resources in the area; they also stated that a Bill now pending before Congress would legalize actions which had resulted or might result in compulsory relocations. The observers of the United States said that the case of relocation mentioned was due to a long-standing dispute between the Navajo and the Hopi.

94. One speaker made special reference to the social and economical impact of copper project in Cerro Colorado, Panama, upon the Guaymi people's land and their cultural way of life. Another speaker made reference to the hydroelectric project in the Chittagong Hills district of Bangladesh, without the indigenous people being consulted. It was contended that the project resulted in the loss of agriculturally productive land, the displacement of the people and rapid environmental degradation.

95. It was also expressed by some NGOs and indigenous organizations that in some countries, the exploitation of the resources of the land belonging to indigenous communities was carried out by utilizing the indigenous labor force, with low levels of pay, violations of trade-union rights and of many other civil, political, economic and social rights. The situation of indigenous peoples in the Philippines was mentioned in this regard.

96. Some indigenous representatives contended that respect for the natural environment, as it is conceived by the indigenous peoples, should not be disrupted by actions which involve the pollution of land, air and water or the destruction of the natural environment, lands, wildlife and other natural resources.

97. The role of the international and national development agencies such as the World Bank, the International Development Bank, AID and other banks and organizations was considered as a negative one with respect to the indigenous populations, because of their financial support for government development projects which affected unfavourably the rights of the indigenous populations. It was recommended that international development agencies should be invited by the Working Group to discuss the impact of their action on the rights of the indigenous peoples, in particular the negative aspects thereof.

98. Indigenous and NGO representatives expressed the view that the right to land should include full ownership, not merely the right to use the land. Respect should be paid to the existing patterns of communal ownership of land. Transformation to individual ownership was, in

most cases, not desirable. Any modification in the legal status of land and land areas should be made only with the consent of the indigenous group concerned and only after a thorough and public discussion involving those populations had been held. Development projects within the areas settled by indigenous populations should also be initiated only with their consent, and they should be given their rightful share in the profits obtained through such projects.

99. Some organizations criticized the "reservation policy" on the grounds that it was being used to abrogate drastically the traditional land rights of the indigenous peoples in order to use the lands for commercial exploitation, without consultation with the indigenous communities. Others criticized certain national legislations permitting government authorities to remove the indigenous populations from the lands they occupy. The legislation mentioned allegedly gave the authorities a discretional power over lands that had neither been ceded nor seized, for determining the use and disposition of those lands, still occupied by indigenous groups. It was said that such situations existed almost everywhere; as an example one speaker made special mention of certain provisions and practices in Canada.

(e) *Civil and political rights*

100. The observers of some of the Governments present at the meeting argued that specific international standards must be developed. They also pointed out that existing international instruments applied to indigenous peoples and alleged that they were implemented in their countries to ensure the full enjoyment of the human rights, encompassed in those texts, by members of indigenous populations. It was proposed, as one of the tasks of the Working Group, to study the degree of protection that those instruments in fact provided to the indigenous populations.

101. Several representatives of indigenous organizations said that there was little or no recognition of the political rights of the indigenous populations. It was alleged that in some countries, indigenous peoples were equated to minors at law; in others, they were categorized into groups; in some systems there were provisions whereby it was necessary to be able to read and write in order to exercise the right to vote; in some states indigenous persons were obliged to vote or to decide according to the modalities established by the dominant society, or their "representatives" who were chosen by the Government, while the real leaders were not recognized or consulted. One government observer argued that the application of the general principles of election to public office was the most appropriate for indigenous communities which had opted for elective forms of government.

102. It was also alleged that indigenous populations were usually deprived of their lands and resources through the use of ''legal'' means by the dominant society, because they ignored or rejected the rules of profit and those of civil or commercial negotiations.

103. It was further alleged that indigenous peoples were generally considered as culturally backward, they were seen as children, incompetent, less than human. So, without any consultation the indigenous peoples concerned were displaced, deprived of their lands, houses and resources or forced to accept rules which were alien to them and their culture.

104. Several representatives of indigenous and non-governmental organizations alleged that, in most countries, national agencies dealing with tribes and minorities had a paternalistic approach. It was also alleged that those agencies were more often concerned with counter insurgency warfare and techniques than with promotion of the indigenous communities' rights; high ranking military personnel allegedly occupied prominent positions in those agencies, which in certain cases, were under the Ministry of Defence.

105. In connection with the enjoyment of the civil and political rights, it was stressed that the respect for the forms of autonomy required by indigenous peoples was the necessary condition for ensuring those rights, since their specific forms of internal organization constituted an essential consideration for any arrangement aimed at securing appropriate participation by indigenous groups in all affairs which affected them. The guarantee of the enjoyment of civil and political rights was thus closely linked to the self-determination of the indigenous populations.

106. It was alleged, in several statements by indigenous representatives, that treaties that recognized the right of indigenous populations to the enjoyment of lands or natural resources had been broken, often very soon after their conclusion. The need was stressed for respect of treaties or other agreements, which should not be subject to unilateral abrogation. It was also expressed that the municipal law of any State should not serve as a defense for the failure to adhere to and implement the terms of treaties and agreements concluded with indigenous peoples.

(f) *The right to education*

107. Some of the participants expressed the need to guarantee indigenous persons access to public education of all kinds and at all levels, but felt that such education should not be aimed at the integration of the indigenous peoples into the dominant society, and at the deprivation of the indigenous people's own traditions. The indigenous

populations should enjoy the right to structure, conduct and control their own educational systems with complete autonomy, so that education could be a way of developing indigenous culture and traditions and not embody forms of aggression against their own culture and lifestyle.

(g) *Other rights mentioned*

108. In different statements and interventions by members of the Working Group, specialized agencies, NGOs and indigenous organizations, mention was made of other civil, political, economic and social rights, in the enjoyment of which the indigenous populations were subjected to different degrees of discrimination. The rights included the following: right of association, right to social security and labour protection, right to legal assistance and protection in administrative and judicial affairs, right to trade and to maintain economic, technological, cultural and social relations and exchange with other indigenous or non-indigenous communities. Representatives of some Governments made statements on their national constitutions and legislation which provided for non-discrimination, and aimed at ensuring the enjoyment of civil, political, economic and social rights by indigenous populations, as well as the protection of or the effective exercise of those rights and the development of the indigenous populations.

109. The Working Group decided to transmit to the Sub-Commission together with its report, a statement submitted by the World Council of Indigenous Peoples and a document mentioned in that statement entitled "Principles for guiding the deliberations of the Working Group on Indigenous Populations", submitted by the Indian Law Resource Center. Both texts had been unanimously supported by the indigenous groups and NGOs participating in the debates of the Working Group. The Working Group also decided to forward to the Sub-Commission, together with its report, a draft resolution concerning the Guatemalan people, that had been submitted by the International Indian Treaty Council. [See paragraphs 77 and 81 above.]

CONCLUDING REMARKS

110. *The Working Group did not want, at this first and explorative session, to adopt firm recommendations to the Sub-Commission. Nevertheless, it has found it desirable to highlight some of the recommendations presented during the session, without necessarily endorsing those recommendations by the Working Group as such:*

Principles to guide the Working Group

111. In fulfilment of its mandate, the Working Group should be open

and accessible to representatives of indigenous populations, as well as to non-governmental organizations with consultative status, to intergovernmental agencies and to Governments. The Working Group should encourage a dialogue between all of these in order to advance, as a collective enterprise, the evolution of and respect for standards safeguarding the reasonable concerns of indigenous populations.

112. The Working Group should encourage wide participation by representatives of indigenous peoples and encourage the establishment of a fund to make such participation possible.

113. The Working Group should endeavour to hold some of its sessions away from Geneva, in regions where many indigenous populations can be found.

114. The Working Group should not become a quasi-judicial body or a "chamber of complaints" but should examine developments pertaining to indigenous populations in order to elucidate whether existing or emerging standards are adhered to.[15]

(b) The International Bill of Rights

One of the greatest achievements in the field of Human Rights is the "International Bill of Rights". This term has been used to refer collectively to the Universal Declaration of Human Rights, the Covenant on Civil and Political Rights, and the Covenant on Economic, Social and Cultural Rights.

(i) *The Universal Declaration of Human Rights Preamble*

Whereas recognition of the inherent dignity and of the equal and inalienable rights of all members of the human family is the foundation of freedom, justice and peace in the world,

Whereas disregard and contempt for human rights have resulted in barbarous acts which have outraged the conscience of mankind, and the advent of a world in which human beings shall enjoy freedom of speech and belief and freedom from fear and want has been proclaimed as the highest aspiration of the common people,

Whereas it is essential, if man is not to be compelled to have recourse, as a last resort, to rebellion against tyranny and oppression, that human rights should be protected by the rule of law,

Whereas it is essential to promote the development of friendly relations between the nations,

Whereas the peoples of the United Nations have in the Charter reaffirmed their faith in fundamental human rights, in the dignity and worth of the human person and in the equal rights of men and women and have determined to promote social progress and better standards of life in larger freedom,

Whereas Member States have pledged themselves to achieve, in cooperation with the United Nations, the promotion of universal respect for and observance of human rights and fundamental freedoms.

Whereas a common understanding of these rights and freedoms is of the greatest importance for the full realization of this pledge.

Now, Therefore,

THE GENERAL ASSEMBLY

proclaims

This universal declaration of human rights as a common standard of achievement for all peoples and all nations, to the end that every individual and every organ of society, keeping this Declaration constantly in mind, shall strive by teaching and education to promote respect for these rights and freedoms and by progressive measures, national and international, to secure their universal and effective recognition and observance, both among the peoples of Member States themselves and among the peoples of territories under their jurisdiction.

Article 1

All human beings are born free and equal in dignity and rights. They are endowed with reason and conscience and should act towards one another in a spirit of brotherhood.

Article 2

Everyone is entitled to all the rights and freedoms set forth in this Declaration, without distinction of any kind, such as race, colour, sex, language, religion, political or other opinion, national or social origin, property, birth or other status.

Furthermore, no distinction shall be made on the basis of the political, jurisdictional or international status of the country or territory to which a person belongs, whether it be independent, trust, non-self-governing or under any other limitation of sovereignty.

Article 25

1. Everyone has the right to a standard of living adequate for the health and well-being of himself and of his family, including food, clothing, housing and medical care and necessary social services, and the right to

security in the event of unemployment, sickness, disability, widow-hood, old age or other lack of livelihood in circumstances beyond his control.

Article 26

1. Everyone has the right to education. Education shall be free, at least in the elementary and fundamental stages. Elementary education shall be compulsory. Technical and professional education shall be made generally available and higher education shall be equally accessible to all on the basis of merit.

2. Education shall be directed to the full development of the human personality and to the strengthening of respect for human rights and fundamental freedoms. It shall promote understanding, tolerance and friendship among all nations, racial or religious groups, and shall further the activities of the United Nations for the maintenance of peace.

3. Parents have a prior right to choose the kind of education that shall be given to their children.

Article 27

1. Everyone has the right freely to participate in the cultural life of the community, to enjoy the arts and to share in scientific advancement and its benefits.

2. Everyone has the right to the protection of the moral and material interests resulting from any scientific, literary or artistic production of which he is the author.

Adopted unanimously by the UN General Assembly in December, 1948, the Universal Declaration of Human Rights (UDHR) embodies in a more specific form some of the general principles asserted in the Charter.

In spite of the fact that it was never intended to be a binding instrument, the UDHR has been accorded a degree of recognition which leads many to suggest that it has attained the force of customary international law.[16]

The Declaration has been the inspiration for a great number of constitutions and Charters of Human Rights and has provided a much needed focal point for the expression of certain fundamental ideals. It has also served as a basis for many international treaties, covenants and conventions and has been cited in numerous court decisions. Whether or not the Declaration has now attained customary international legal status, it provides an important contextual framework for aboriginal as well as for other rights.

In view of the ever-increasing importance of the Declaration in international law, it is clear that the potential exists for its fruitful application to the problems facing indigenous peoples. Yet its usefulness in this regard has scarcely been explored.

For those who are concerned with aboriginal rights, among its more important provisions relate to issues of egalitarianism and to adequate standards of living. The rights contained in Articles 26 and 27, however, raise some difficult questions of interpretation. For example, does the parent's right to choose the kind of education that a child shall receive conflict with the state's duty to provide compulsory elementary education? What alternatives are to be made available to the parents? Consider, for example, the difficulties that stem from the forced removal of aboriginal children to residential schools, a practice adopted by several countries. What the the linguistic, religious and cultural implications?

The guarantees relating to participation in the cultural life of the community raise the question of whether this right extends only to the majority or dominant culture.

In spite of the difficulties that inevitably must be encountered when interpreting such clauses, the Declaration remains a dynamic and vital yardstick against which nations may measure their human rights records.

(ii) *The Covenants*

The two covenants that round out the "International Bill of Rights" did not appear until 1966, almost twenty years after the Declaration had been adopted; the legal implications of ratification of the covenants account in part for the long delay. [17] Even after the covenants had been adopted, ratifications were slow in materializing, so that it was not until 1976 that they actually came into force. (Canada ratified both covenants in 1976.)

The covenants, which are international instruments of a binding legal nature, give definition to the rights contained in the Declaration.

(A) **International Covenant on Civil and Political Rights**

Preamble

The States Parties to the present Covenant,

Considering that, in accordance with the principles proclaimed in the Charter of the United Nations, recognition of the inherent dignity and of the equal and inalienable rights of all members of the human family is the foundation of freedom, justice and peace in the world,

Recognizing that these rights derive from the inherent dignity of the human person,

Recognizing that, in accordance with the Universal Declaration of Human Rights, the ideal of free human beings enjoying civil and political freedom and freedom from fear and want can only be achieved if conditions are created whereby everyone may enjoy his civil and political rights as well as his economic, social and cultural rights,

Considering the obligation of States under the Charter of the United Nations to promote universal respect for, and observance of, human rights and freedoms,

Realizing that the individual, having duties to other individuals and to the community to which he belongs, is under a responsibility to strive for the promotion and observance of the rights recognized in the present Convenant,

Agree upon the following articles:

PART 1

Article 1

1. All peoples have the right of self-determination. By virtue of that right they freely determine their political status and freely pursue their economic, social and cultural development.

2. All peoples may, for their own ends, freely dispose of their natural wealth and resources without prejudice to any obligations arising out of international economic cooperation, based upon the principle of mutual benefit, and international law. In no case may a people be deprived of its own means of substance.

3. The States Parties to the present Covenant, including those having responsibility for the administration of Non-Self-Governing and Trust Territories, shall promote the realization of the right of self-determination, and shall respect that right, in conformity with the provisions of the Charter of the United Nations.

PART II

Article 2

1. Each State Party to the present Covenant undertakes to respect and to ensure to all individuals within its territory and subject to its jurisdiction the rights recognized in the present Covenant, without distinction of any kind, such as race, colour, sex, language, religion, political or other opinion, national or social origin, property, birth or other status.

2. Where not already provided for by existing legislative or other measures, each State Party to the present Covenant undertakes to take the necessary steps, in accordance with its constitutional processes and with the provisions of the present Covenant, to adopt such legislative or

other measures as may be necessary to give effect to the rights recognized in the present Covenant.

3. Each State Party to the present Covenant undertakes:
   (a) To ensure that any person whose rights or freedoms as herein recognized are violated shall have an effective remedy, notwithstanding that the violation has been committed by persons acting in an official capacity;
   (b) To ensure that any person claiming such a remedy shall have his right thereto determined by competent judicial, administrative or legislative authorities, or by any other competent authority provided for by the legal system of the State, and to develop the possibilities of judicial remedy;
   (c) To ensure that the competent authorities shall enforce such remedies when granted.

Article 3

The States Parties to the present Covenant undertake to ensure the equal right of men and women to the enjoyment of all civil and political rights set forth in the present Covenant.

Article 18

1. Everyone shall have the right to freedom of thought, conscience and religion. This right shall include freedom to have or to adopt a religion or belief of his choice, and freedom, either individually or in community with others and in public or private, to manifest his religion or belief in worship, observance, practice and teaching.

2. No one shall be subject to coercion which would impair his freedom to have or to adopt a religion or belief of his choice.

3. Freedom to manifest one's religion or beliefs may be subject only to such limitations as are prescribed by law and are necessary to protect public safety, order, health, or morals or the fundamental rights and freedoms of others.

4. The States Parties to the present Covenant undertake to have respect for the liberty of parents and, when applicable, legal guardians to ensure the religious and moral education of their children in conformity with their own convictions.

Article 26

All persons are equal before the law and are entitled without any discrimination to the equal protection of the law. In this respect, the law shall prohibit any discrimination and guarantee to all persons equal and effective protection against discrimination on any ground such as race, colour, sex, language, religion, political or other opinion, national or social origin, property, birth or other status.

Article 27

In those States in which ethnic, religious or linguistic minorities exist, persons belonging to such minorities shall not be denied the right, in community with the other members of their group, to enjoy their own culture, to profess and practise their own religion, or to use their own language.

A number of provisions of the Covenant on Civil and Political Rights are of direct concern to indigenous peoples. Although this covenant is specifically directed toward the rights of individuals rather than groups, it does enshrine, in Article 1, recognition of the fundamental right of all *peoples* to self-determination. An identical provision appears in the Covenant on Economic, Social and Cultural Rights. There was a substantial divergence of opinion on whether to include this particular Article, but the view that, in the final analysis, the rights of individuals, depended upon recognition of this fundamental right proved to be persuasive.[18]

The Covenant on Civil and Political Rights and its Optional Protocol exhibit several important features regarding the practical application of the rights it enumerates. The emphasis in this, as in other international human rights instruments, is on implementation at the national level. Article 2 of the covenant provides that each state ensure that adequate domestic remedies exist, and that the state take legislative action where necessary to ensure that the municipal law gives effect to those rights.[19] National remedies may, of course, be ineffective and the covenant therefore provides in Article 28 for the establishment of the Human Rights Committee, consisting of eighteen members serving in their personal capacities. The committee has several functions. Article 40 of the convenant requires state parties to submit progress reports on measures they have adopted which give effect to the rights contained in the covenant.[20] In addition, provision is made for the initiation of a complaint by one state party against another. Perhaps the most important function of the committee, however, is its power to hear petitions brought by individuals.[21]

Traditionally, states, not individuals, have been the key actors at the international level. Since violation of an individual's rights is normally the result of acts directly or indirectly attributable to the state itself, it is essential for the individual to have access to international fora for the protection of those rights. This fact was recognized by providing for an Optional Protocol to the Covenant on Civil and Political Rights, which affords the right of individual petition to the citizens of states that are party to the covenant.

Although states parties to the covenant are under no obligation to accede to the Optional Protocol, several countries, including Canada, have done so. The case of Sandra Lovelace demonstrates the usefulness of the Protocol.

Sandra Lovelace is a Maliseet Indian, resident in Canada, who lost her Indian status because of her marriage to a non-Indian. Section 12(1)(b) of Canada's Indian Act provides that female status Indians who marry Non-Indians forfeit their rights under the Act (this disability also extends to the children of the marriage). The provision does not pertain with respect to male status Indians or their children in the same circumstance.

In her submission to the Human Rights Committee, dated 29 December 1977, Lovelace claimed that as a result of S 12(1)(b) of the Indian Act Canada was in violation of rights concerning the family, equal protection before the law and minority rights.

In its final decision, dated 31 July 1981, the majority of the committee stated that it could not rule on the issue relating to discrimination on the basis of sex, since the marriage took place in 1970 and Canada was not a party to the covenant at that time:

10. *The Human Rights Committee,* in the examination of the communication before it, has to proceed from the basic fact that Sandra Lovelace married a non-Indian on 23 May 1970 and consequently lost her status as a Maliseet Indian under Section 12(1)(b) of the Indian Act. This provision was — and still is — based on a distinction *de jure* on the ground of sex. However, neither its application to her marriage as the cause of her loss of Indian status nor its effects could at that time amount to a violation of the Covenant, because this instrument did not come into force for Canada until 19 August 1976. Moreover the Committee is not competent, as a rule, to examine allegations relating to events having taken place before the entry into force of the Covenant and the Optional Protocol. Therefore, as regards Canada it can only consider alleged violations of human rights occurring on or after 19 August 1976. In the case of a particular individual claiming to be a victim of a violation, it cannot express its view on the law in the abstract, without regard to the date on which this law was applied to the alleged victim. In the case of Sandra Lovelace it follows that the Committee is not competent to express any view on the original cause of her loss of Indian status, i.e. the Indian Act as applied to her at the time of her marriage in 1970.

However, the committee went on to make a determination based on Article 27, the potential effect on which is perhaps of even greater significance for Aboriginal Peoples:

13.1 The Committee considers that the essence of the present complaint concerns the continuing effect of the Indian Act, in denying Sandra Lovelace legal status as an Indian, in particular because she cannot for this reason claim a legal right to reside where she wishes to, on the Tobique Reserve. This fact persists after the entry into force of the Covenant, and its effects have to be examined, without regard to their original cause. Among the effects referred to on behalf of the author, the greater number relate to the Indian Act and other Canadian rules in fields which do not necessarily adversely affect the enjoyment of rights protected by the Covenant.

In this respect the significant matter is her last claim, that "the major loss to a person ceasing to be an Indian is the loss of the cultural benefits of living in an Indian community, the emotional ties to home, family, friends and neighbours, and the loss of identity".

13.2 Although a number of provisions of the Covenant have been invoked by Sandra Lovelace, the Committee considers that the one which is most directly applicable to this complaint is article 27, which reads as follows:

In those States in which ethnic, religious or linguistic minorities exist, persons belonging to such minorities shall not be denied the right, in community with the other members of their group, to enjoy their own culture, to profess and practise their own religion, or to use their own language.

It has to be considered whether Sandra Lovelace, because she is denied the legal right to reside on the Tobique Reserve, has by that fact been denied the right guaranteed by article 27 to persons belonging to minorities, to enjoy their own culture and to use their own language in community with other members of their group.

14. The rights under article 27 of the Covenant have to be secured to "persons belonging" to the minority. At present Sandra Lovelace does not qualify as an Indian under Canadian legislation. However, the Indian Act deals primarily with a number of privileges which, as stated above, do not as such come within the scope of the Covenant. Protection under the Indian Act and protection under article 27 of the Covenant therefore have to be distinguished. Persons who are born and brought up on a reserve, who have kept ties with their community and wish to maintain these ties must normally be considered as belonging to that minority within the meaning of the Covenant. Since Sandra Lovelace is ethnically a Maliseet Indian and has only been absent from her home reserve for a few years during the existence of her marriage, she is, in the opinion of the Committee, entitled to be regarded as "belonging" to this minority and to claim the benefits of article 27 of the Covenant. The question whether these benefits have been denied to her, depends on how far they extend.

15. The right to live on a reserve is not as such guaranteed by article 27

of the Covenant. Moreover, the Indian Act does not interfere directly with the functions which are expressly mentioned in that article. However, in the opinion of the Committee the right of Sandra Lovelace to access to her native culture and language ''in community with the other members'' of her group, has in fact been, and continues to be interfered with, because there is no place outside the Tobique Reserve where such a community exists. On the other hand, not every interference can be regarded as a denial of rights within the meaning of article 27. Restrictions on the right to residence, by way of national legislation, cannot be ruled out under article 27 of the Covenant. This also follows from the restrictions to article 12(1) of the Covenant set out in article 12(3). The Committee recognizes the need to define the category of persons entitled to live on a reserve, for such purposes as those explained by the Government regarding protection of its resources and preservation of the identity of its people. However, the obligations which the Government has since undertaken under the Covenant must also be taken into account.

16. In this respect, the Committee is of the view that statutory restrictions affecting the right to residence on a reserve of a person belonging to the majority concerned, must have both a reasonable and objective justification and be consistent with the other provisions of the Covenant, read as a whole. Article 27 must be construed and applied in the light of the other provisions mentioned above, such as articles 12, 17 and 23 in so far as they may be relevant to the particular case, and also the provisions against discrimination, such as articles 2, 3 and 26, as the case may be. It is not necessary, however, to determine in any general manner which restrictions may be justified under the Covenant, in particular as a result of marriage, because the circumstances are special in the present case.

17. The case of Sandra Lovelace should be considered in the light of the fact that her marriage to a non-Indian has broken up. It is natural that in such a situation she wishes to return to the environment in which she was born, particularly as after the dissolution of her marriage her main cultural attachment again was to the Maliseet band. Whatever may be the merits of the Indian Act in other respects, it does not seem to the Committee that to deny Sandra Lovelace the right to reside on the reserve is reasonable, or necessary to preserve the identity of the tribe. The Committee therefore concludes that to prevent her recognition as belonging to the band is an unjustifiable denial of her rights under article 27 of the Covenant, read in the context of the other provisions referred to.

18. In view of this finding, the Committee does not consider it

necessary to examine whether the same facts also show separate breaches of the other rights invoked. The specific rights most directly applicable to her situation are those under article 27 of the Covenant. The rights to choose one's residence (article 12), and the rights aimed at protecting family life and children (articles 17, 23 and 24) are only indirectly at stake in the present case. The facts of the case do not seem to require further examination under those articles. The Committee's finding of a lack of a reasonable justification for the interference with Sandra Lovelace's rights under article 27 of the Covenant also makes it unnecessary, as suggested above (paragraph 12), to examine the general provisions against discrimination (articles 2, 3, and 26) in the context of the present case, and in particular to determine their bearing upon inequalities predating the coming into force of the Covenant for Canada.

19. Accordingly, the Human Rights Committee, acting under article 5(4) of the Optional Protocol to the International Covenant on Civil and Political Rights, is of the view that the facts of the present case, which establish that Sandra Lovelace has been denied the legal right to reside on the Tobique Reserve, disclose a breach by Canada of article 27 of the Covenant.[22]

The decision is a promising one for a number of reasons. First, the committee showed a welcome flexibility in interpreting the "exhaustion of domestic remedies" rule. In petitioning the committee, Lovelace relied on the decision of the Supreme Court of Canada in the *Lavell* case, ([1974] 38 DLR (3d) 481), a decision which did not address the issues raised by Article 27 of the covenant.

In addition, the interpretation of Article 27, based on considerations of "reasonable and objective justification in line with the spirit of the Covenant as a whole," gives rise to some optimism for future petitions based on other articles.

One of the unfortunate drawbacks of the committee process is the time lapse between the initial complaint and the ultimate determination. (In common with other UN institutions, the Human Rights Committee is hampered, among other things, by its relatively short and infrequent sittings; it is not a "full-time" body, and so it faces an ever-increasing workload.) Moreover, the committee possesses no powers of enforcement, and so the petitioner must rely on the effectiveness of adverse publicity on the state to effect a practical redress of the particular grievance. It should be noted that Lovelace decision appears to have had a direct impact on government policy: protecting Indian women against discrimination on the basis of sex was included on the agenda for the Constitutional Conference on Aboriginal Rights held in Ottawa on 15 and 16 March 1983.

On the whole, then, while this particular process concentrates on the rights of the individual, clearly there are implications for the protection of certain key rights which affect indigenous peoples as groups. It is also apparent that the Human Rights Committee is prepared to function in a way that is consistent with the spirit as well as the letter of the Covenant.

The Covenant on Civil and Political Rights and its Optional Protocol promise to provide a useful context for the clarification of basic aboriginal rights. In addition, there exists a potential for influencing states party thereto.

(B) The Covenant on Economic, Social and Cultural Rights

Rounding out the International Bill of Rights is the Covenant on Economic, Social and Cultural Rights.

Unlike the Covenant on Civil and Political Rights, and its Optional Protocol, the Covenant on Economic, Social and Cultural Rights does not contain provisions for individual petition. This fact, together with the much vaguer concepts employed in the covenant, render it, in the short run, a less fruitful source for complaints regarding the violation of indigenous rights. As was indicated above, however, both covenants declare in alluringly simple terms the fundamental importance of the right of all peoples to self-determination. That the concept is a critical one in terms of aboriginal rights is unquestioned; that it is fraught with difficulties in terms of interpretation and application is equally clear.

(c) Self-Determination

"Self-determination," as set out in the Charter and Covenants, raises a number of important questions. Who are the "peoples" entitled to self-determination? How is this "determination" to manifest itself? Does the concept necessarily include the ultimate option of secession? Does the concept refer to colonial situations only (external) or does it apply in so-called metropolitan areas as well (internal)?

Of course, the idea of self-determination is not a new one. Its history in modern terms can be traced back more than two centuries. Developments following the two world wars, however, are primarily responsible for the current prominence of the concept.

Following World War I, Woodrow Wilson's desire to promote recognition of the ideal of self-determination led to the setting up of the mandate system under the supervision of the League of Nations. Under this system, the Allies were to administer the mandated territories on the basis that the territory in question would ultimately exercise its right to self-determination.[23] After World War II the United Nations adopted a similar approach and provided in its Charter for a trusteeship system (Articles 75-91).

In addition, Article 73 of the Charter refers to a "sacred trust" imposed on members of the United Nations in this regard.

Chapter XI. Declaration Regarding Non-Self-Governing Territories

Article 73

Members of the United Nations which have or assume responsibilities for the administration of territories whose peoples have not yet attained a full measure of self-government recognize the principle that the interests of the inhabitants of these territories are paramount, and accept as a sacred trust the obligation to promote to the utmost, within the system of international peace and security established by the present Charter, the well-being of the inhabitants of these territories, and to this end:

(a) to ensure, with due respect for the culture of the peoples concerned, their political, economic, social and educational advancement, their just treatment, and their protection against abuses;

(b) to develop self-government, to take due account of the political aspirations of the peoples, and to assist them in the progressive development of their free political institutions, according to the particular circumstances of each territory and its peoples and their varying stages of advancement;

(c) to further international peace and security;

(d) to promote constructive measures of development, to encourage research, and to cooperate with one another and, when and where appropriate, with specialized international bodies with a view to the practical achievement of the social, economic, and scientific purposes set forth in this Article; and

(e) to transmit regularly to the Secretary-General for information purposes, subject to such limitation as security and constitutional considerations may require, statistical and other information of a technical nature, relating to economic, social, and educational conditions in the territories for which they are respectively responsible other than those territories to which Chapters XII and XIII apply.

Disagreements as to the application of this section led in 1960 to the adoption by the General Assembly of Resolution 1541(xv), which interpreted the Article as applying to territories that are geographically separate and ethnically or culturally distinct.[24]

The controversy which led to the adoption of the resolution basically involved polarisation of the colonial powers and the third world nations into opposite camps over a proposal known as the "Belgian thesis." According to this thesis, Chapter XI ought to apply to "primitive" communities living within various states, since the situation in these cases amounted to "colonization" no less than if it involved an overseas territory. The fear articulated most strenuously by the South American delegates was that to accept the thesis would bring practically every nation within its ambit and thereby pose a real threat to "sovereignty" and the integrity of the state.

Ultimately, for reasons that were primarily political, the Belgian thesis failed. However, even the clear requirement of geographical separation in theory is not so clear in practice:

> Firstly it is strongly arguable that indigenous groups who are isolated from the rest of the nation by vast tracts of unoccupied land, as for example are the Eskimos of Northern Canada, must on any rational basis be regarded as "geographically separate." Secondly there are many island communities which, although not normally described as colonial peoples, are nevertheless 'geographically separate" from the mainland. . . .[25]

Further invocation of the principle is found in Resolution 1514(xv) (December 1960) — "Declaration on the Granting of Independence to Colonial Countries and Peoples."

> 1. The subjection of peoples to alien subjugation, domination and exploitation constitutes a denial of fundamental human rights, is contrary to the Charter of the United Nations and is an impediment to the promotion of World peace and cooperation.
>
> 2. All peoples have the right to self-determination; by virtue of that right they freely determine their political status and freely pursue their economic, social and cultural development.

This resolution stresses "national unity" and "territorial integrity" (Clause 6),[26] and further resolutions reaffirm and amplify the principle.[27]

The 1975 decision of the International Court of Justice in the *Western Sahara* case (ICJ Report 1975, p. 122) sheds further light on the issue of self-determination. The opinion of the court affirms the right of the people of the territory to political self-determination. The opinion of Judge Dillard in this regard is worth noting:

> It seemed hardly necessary to make more explicit the Cardinal restraint which the legal right of self-determination imposes. That restraint may be captured in a single sentence. It is for the people to determine the destiny of the territory and not the territory the destiny of the people.

There exists a growing conviction, particularly among Western writers, that the concept is now entrenched and has therefore acquired universality of application:

> . . . it seems to me, that the original impulse of the doctrine of self-determination, what led to its formation as a principle, has to do with a basic affirmation of respect for the inherent dignity of individuals and groups, and that fundamentally the internal application of the doctrine of self-determination is a human rights claim, a human rights claim that can draw a number of legal sources. . . .[28]

Certainly the inclusion of self-determination in the Covenant on Civil and Political Rights, in particular, lends support to this point of view.

The covenant ties the fundamental rights of individuals with the underlying right of self-determination. There is no indication in either covenant that it is to be confined to external application only. In fact, references to responsibility by states parties to "promote the realization of the right to self-determination" appear to be a clear undertaking to apply the principle internally.

Perhaps the most significant recent development in terms of the evolution of the concept can be seen in the Helsinki Final Act. Signed on 1 August 1975 by 33 European nations, the United States and Canada, the Helsinki Final Act covers a number of important fields. Part I is concerned with "Questions Relating to Security in Europe" and includes a declaration setting out ten guiding principles, dealing among other things with sovereign equality, human rights and self-determination.

VII. Respect for human rights and fundamental freedoms, including the freedom of thought, conscience, religion or belief

The participating States will respect human rights and fundamental freedoms, including the freedom of thought, conscience, religion or belief, for all without distinction as to race, sex, language or religion. . . . The participating States on whose territory national minorities exist will respect the right of persons belonging to such minorities to equality before the law, will afford them the full opportunity for the actual enjoyment of human rights and fundamental freedoms and will, in this manner, protect their legitimate interests in this sphere. . . .

In the field of human rights and fundamental freedoms, the participating States will act in conformity with the purposes and principles of the Charter of the United Nations and with the Universal Declaration of Human Rights. They will also fulfill their obligations as set forth in the international declarations and agreements in this field, including inter alia the International Covenants on Human Rights, by which they may be bound.

VIII. Equal rights and self-determination of peoples

The participating States will respect the equal rights of peoples and their right to self-determination, acting at all times in conformity with the purposes and principles of the Charter of the United Nations and with the relevant norms of international law, including those relating to territorial integrity of States.

By virtue of the principle of equal rights and self-determination of peoples, all peoples always have the right, in full freedom, to determine, when and as they wish, their internal and external political status, without external interference, and to pursue as they wish their political, economic, and social and cultural development.

The participating States reaffirm the universal significance of respect for an effective exercise of equal rights and self-determination of peoples for the development of friendly relations among themselves or among all States; they also recall the importance of the elimination of any form of violation of this principle.

Part II of the Final Act is concerned essentially with cooperation in economics, science, technology and the environment. Part III refers to cooperation in humanitarian and other fields.

It seems that the Helsinki Final Act provides at the very least an important reinterpretation of the concept of self-determination. Reference in the covenants to self-determination, as discussed above, appears to imply recognition of its internal application, but this interpretation has by no means been universally accepted.

Attempting to confine self-determination as contained in the Helsinki Final Act to an "external" interpretation seems to be more difficult. To begin with, the signatories to the Act do not conform to the classic colonial models envisaged by the "external" interpretation. For the most part, the type of situation to which the concept would be applicable is subsumed under the "internal" application:

> The logical conclusion should be that, to a very great extent, the principle of external and internal self-determination has already been realized in Europe (as well as in the United States and Canada) and that, therefore, it would be pointless to codify and reaffirm it in some sort of regional European instrument. Yet situations exist in Europe which come within the purview of a broader concept of self-determination . . . [e.g.] the German nation . . . the Irish people. . . ."

In addition, principle VIII enforces the standard reference to "all peoples" by adding the word "always" and the phrase "when and as they wish," thus indicating emphatically that the right is a continuing one. There is no clear indication in the text as to whether the right extends to minority groups within the sovereign state, but appears that minorities were not envisaged as possessing this right.[30] Nevertheless, a strong argument may be made that a number of indigenous peoples do not fall within this traditional "minority" category since, as peoples, they have never voluntarily given up their original status and do *not* identify themselves with the nation-state within whose borders they may live:

> In general, all indigenous peoples are entitled to self-determination and to recognition as nations. . . . Therefore, indigenous peoples ought not to be considered as minorities or social classes. . . .[31]

The Helsinki Final Act, then, may be viewed as an important development in the evolution of the concept of self-determination. From the perspective of the indigenous peoples living in the states that are signatories to the instrument, it might be argued that this definition provides an authoritative interpretation of the concept as contained in the charter and covenants to which Canada is a signatory. Therefore, whatever the exact legal status of the Final Act itself may be, the clarification of the concept of self-determination acknowledged by states signatories to the Final Act might be applicable to the concepts set out in the covenants which *are* legally binding.[32]

An overriding concern of states, as evidenced in all the relevant instruments, is "territorial integrity" and "national unity". The concern here is with the political results that flow from the practical application of the principle. Many political leaders fear that recognizing the right of indigenous groups to self-determination would inevitably result in the session of these peoples from the state. In fact, of course, the political manifestations of the application of the principle are almost limitless. The essential significance of the concept for indigenous peoples is the right to autonomy over political, social and cultural development. The exact nature of the political arrangement for the relevant group depends on the exigencies of the particular circumstance:

> . . . it is important to understand that claims for control over national development and for autonomy are to be appropriate to the circumstance of the dependent people. What is their circumstance? How much autonomy do they need in order to safeguard their cultural integrity.[33]

In most instances one would expect that recognition of the fundamental right to determine the use of tribal lands and development of natural resources would be essential.[34] The most immediate problem faced by many indigenous groups is, of course, the onslaught of industrialization and exploitation of resources by the state within whose boundaries they find themselves.[35] At least one writer has suggested that while the principle of control by indigenous peoples in this regard ought to be recognized, "the right to decide whether industrial or other development should be permitted on aboriginal lands [might] be subject . . . to the government of the day having the power to override that decision where satisfied that the national interest genuinely requires it."[36] Such an exception would, *prima facie*, divest the principle of its value in practical terms, in view of the fact that similar arguments already provide the basis for many governmental claims to indigenous resources:

> If the indigenous people were accorded the genuine exercise of their right of self-determination they would be able to live in their lands and feed their people in accordance with their own traditions, technology and culture, which are in harmony with the natural environment. Indigenous delegates stressed that complete control over the resources within their territories is essential to their right to self-determination and that the decision whether to develop their resources is their own.[37]

But in the New World the Native peoples have not fared so well. Even in countries in South America where the Native peoples are the vast majority of the population there is not one country which has an Amerindian government for the Amerindian peoples.

Whatever the ultimate evolution of the principle of self-determination may prove to be, it is a concept which at this time is both legal and political in nature and one which is being asserted with vigour by indigenous peoples, as the following examples illustrate.

International Covenant on the Rights of Indigenous Peoples:[38] April 1981

Part I
Self-Determination

Article 1. All peoples have the right to self-determination. By virtue of that right Indigenous Peoples may freely determine their political status and freely pursue their economic, social and cultural development.

Article 2. The term Indigenous People refers to a people (a) who lived in a territory before the entry of a colonizing population, which colonizing population has created a new state or states or extended the jurisdiction of an existing state or states to include the territory, and (b) who continue to live as a people in the territory and who do not control the national government of the state or states within which they live.

Article 3. One manner in which the right of self-determination can be realized is by the free determination of an Indigenous People to associate their territory and institutions with one or more states in a manner involving free association, regional autonomy, home rule or associate statehood as self-governing units. Indigenous People may freely determine to enter into such relationships and to alter those relationships after they have been established.

Article 4. Each state within which an Indigenous People lives shall recognize the population, territory and institutions of the Indigenous People. Disputes about the recognition of the population, territory and institutions of an Indigenous People shall initially be determined by the state and the Indigenous People. Failing agreement, such questions may be determined by the Commission of Indigenous Rights and the Tribunal of Indigenous Rights, as subsequently provided.

Excerpt from the Dene Declaration[39]

. . . . the African and Asian peoples — the peoples of the Third World — have fought for and won the right to self-determination, the right to recognition as distinct peoples and the recognition of themselves as nations.

But in the New World the Native peoples have not fared so well. Even in countries in South America where the Native peoples are the vast majority of the population there is not one country which has an Amerindian government for the Amerindian peoples.

Nowhere in the New World have the Native peoples won the right to self-determination and the right to recognition by the world as a distinct people and as Nations.

While the Native people of Canada are a minority in their homeland, the Native people of the Northwest Territories, the Dene and the Inuit, are a majority of the population of the Northwest Territories.

The Dene find themselves as part of a country. That country is Canada. But the Government of Canada is not the government of the Dene. These governments were not the choice of the Dene, they were imposed upon the Dene.

What we the Dene are struggling for is the recognition of the Dene nation by the governments and peoples of the world.

And while there are realities we are forced to submit to such as the existence of a country called Canada, we insist on the right to self-determination as a distinct people and the recognition of the Dene Nation. We the Dene are part of the Fourth World. And as the peoples and Nations of the world have come to recognize the existence and rights of those peoples who make up the Third World the day must come and will come when the nations of the Fourth World will come to be recognized and respected. The challenge to the Dene and the world is to find the way for the recognition of the Dene Nation.

Our plea to the world is to help us in our struggle to find a place in the world community where we can exercise our right to self-determination as a distinct people and as a nation.

What we seek then is independence and self-determination within the country of Canada. This is what we mean when we call for a just land settlement of the Dene Nation.

(d) Convention on the Prevention and Punishment of the Crime of Genocide[40]

Among the other instruments of potential benefit to indigenous groups is the Genocide Convention. Originally adopted as a resolution of the General

Assembly of the United Nations in 1948, it came into force in 1961 and has since attracted a sizeable number of ratifications. Under the convention, genocide is defined so as to include:

> . . . any of the following acts committed with intent to destroy, in whole or in part, a national, ethnical, racial or religious group, as such:
> (a) Killing members of the group;
> (b) Causing serious bodily or mental harm to members of the group;
> (c) Deliberately inflicting on the group conditions of life calculated to bring about its physical destruction in whole or in part;
> (d) Imposing measures intended to prevent births within the group;
> (e) Forcibly transferring children of the group to another group.[41]

The convention makes genocide a crime under international law, whether committed in time of peace or war, and parties undertake "to provide effective penalties for persons guilty of genocide. . . ."[42] While the definition is a very useful one, reliance in the Convention on state enforcement of the provisions or voluntary submission to the jurisdiction of an international penal tribunal robs it of effectiveness. For the most part, the perpetrators of the crime in cases involving indigenous populations is the state itself. Clearly a state is going to be reluctant to indict itself. Nevertheless, as a standard by which the world may judge a state's treatment of its indigenous population, the convention does serve a useful purpose.

(e) International Convention on the Elimination of all Forms of Racial Discrimination[43]

Adopted on the 21 December 1965 by the UN General Assembly, the International Convention on the Elimination of All Forms of Racial Discrimination came into force in 1969.

The convention consists of three major divisions and deals with substantive issues, such as defining "racial discrimination" and outlining the specific obligations undertaken by the parties. Special measures taken to advance certain groups of individuals "requiring such protection as may be necessary in order to ensure such groups or individuals equal enjoyment or exercise of human rights"[44] are not to be deemed discriminatory.

States undertake to eliminate racial discrimination by all available appropriate means. These are to include positive measures that are "immediate and effective . . . particularly in the fields of teaching, education, culture and information with a view to combating prejudices which lead to racial discrimination. . ."[45] In addition, the convention provides that states parties provide "within their jurisdiction effective protection and remedies through the competent national tribunals and other State institutions. . . ."[46] The convention also establishes a Committee on the Elimination of Racial Discrimination, consisting of eighteen experts appointed in their personal capacity.[47] This committee reviews reports submitted by states parties on their progress in implementing the provisions of the convention, as well as being empowered to make suggestions and recommendations on the basis of those reports. The committee may also hear interstate complaints and submit these to an "ad hoc conciliation Commission" provided for in the convention.[48] The committee may also in certain circumstances be empowered to deal with individual complaints"[49] and is the "expert body" reviewing complaints from individuals of trust, non-self-governing and dependent territories.[50]

Some interesting interpretations have been suggested of the convention's effect on indigenous peoples,[51] but overall the convention is more useful as an ideal standard of achievement than as a practical mechanism for redress. Although the convention does not deal specifically with indigenous peoples, the World Conference to Combat Racism and Racial Discrimination, held in Geneva in 1978 and attended by 125 member states, discussed the case of indigenous peoples.

Among the proposals emanating from the conference were the following:

[The Conference] . . . endorses the right of indigenous peoples to maintain their traditional structure of economy and culture, including their language, and also recognizes the special relationship of indigenous peoples to their land, land rights and natural resources should not be taken away from them.

. . . [States are urged to] . . . recognize the following rights of indigenous peoples:

(a) To call themselves by their proper name and to express freely their ethnic, cultural and other characteristics;
(b) To have an official status and to form their own representative organization;
(c) To carry on within their areas of settlement their traditional structure of economy and way of life; this should in no way effect their right to participate freely on an equal basis in the economic, social and political development of the country;
(d) To maintain and use their own language, wherever possible, for administration and education;
(e) To receive education and information in their own language, with due regard to their needs as expressed by themselves, and to disseminate information regarding their needs and problems.

and in addition:

. . . to allow indigenous peoples within their territories to develop cultural and social links with their own kith and kin everywhere with strict respect for the sovereignty, territorial integrity and political independence and non-interference in the internal affairs of those countries in which the indigenous peoples live.[52]

Two international Conferences of non-Governmental Orgnaizations on Discrimination Against Indigenous Populations in the Americas have been held in Geneva, the first in 1977, and the second in 1981. The 1977 Conference drafted a Declaration that includes a number of important provisions:

DECLARATION OF PRINCIPLES FOR THE DEFENSE OF THE INDIGENOUS NATIONS AND PEOPLES OF THE WESTERN HEMISPHERE (September 1977)

PREAMBLE:

Having considered the problems relating to the activities of the United Nations for the promotion and encouragement of respect for human rights and fundamental freedoms,

Noting that the Universal Declaration of Human Rights and related international covenants have the individual as their primary concern, and

Recognizing that individuals are the foundation of cultures, societies, and nations, and

Whereas, it is a fundamental right of any individual to practice and perpetuate the cultures, societies and nations into which they are born, and

Recognizing that conditions are imposed upon peoples that supress, deny, or destroy the cultures, societies, or nations in which they believe or of which they are members,

Be it affirmed, that,

1. RECOGNITION OF INDIGENOUS NATIONS

Indigenous peoples shall be accorded recognition as nations, and proper subjects of international law, provided the people concerned desire to be recognized as a nation and meet the fundamental requirements of nationhood, namely:

a. Having a permanent population
b. Having a defined territory
c. Having a government
d. Having the ability to enter into relations with other states.

2. SUBJECTS OF INTERNATIONAL LAW

Indigenous groups not meeting the requirements of nationhood are hereby declared to be subjects of international law and are entitled to the protection of this Declaration, provided they are identifiable groups having bonds of language, heritage, tradition, or other common identity.

3. GUARANTEE OF RIGHTS

No indigenous nation or group shall be deemed to have fewer rights, or lesser status for the sole reasons that the nation or group has not entered into recorded treaties or agreements with any state.

4. ACCORDANCE OF INDEPENDENCE

Indigenous nations or groups shall be accorded such degree of independence as they may desire in accordance with international law.

5. TREATIES AND AGREEMENTS

Treaties and other agreements entered into by indigenous nations or groups with other states, whether denominated as treaties or otherwise, shall be recognized and applied in the same manner and according to the same international laws and principles as the treaties and agreements entered into by other states.

6. ABROGATION OF TREATIES AND OTHER RIGHTS

Treaties and agreements made with indigenous nations or groups shall not be subject to unilateral abrogation. In no event may the municipal law of any state serve as a defense to the failure to adhere to and perform the terms of treaties and agreements made with indigenous nations or groups. Nor shall any state refuse to recognize and adhere to treaties or other agreements due to changed circumstances where the change in circumstances has been substantially caused by the state asserting that such change has occurred.

7. JURISDICTION

No state shall assert or claim or exercise any right or jurisdiction over any indigenous nation or group or the territory of such indigenous nation or group unless pursuant to a valid treaty or other agreement freely made with the lawful representatives of the indigenous nation or group concerned. All actions on the part of any state which derogate from the indigenous nations' or groups' rights to exercise self-determination shall be the proper concern of existing international bodies.

8. CLAIMS TO TERRITORY

No state shall claim or retain, by right of discovery or otherwise, the territories of an indigenous nation or group, except such lands as may have been lawfully acquired by valid treaty or other cession freely made.

9. SETTLEMENT OF DISPUTES

All states in the Western Hemisphere shall establish through negotiation or other appropriate means of procedure for the binding settlement of disputes, claims, or other matters relating to indigenous nations or groups. Such procedures shall be mutually acceptable to the parties, fundamentally fair, and consistent with international law. All procedures presently in existence which do not have the endorsement of the indigenous nations or groups concerned shall be ended, and new procedures shall be instituted consistent with this Declaration.

10. NATIONAL AND CULTURAL INTEGRITY

It shall be unlawful for any state to take or permit any action or course of conduct with respect to an indigenous nation or group which will directly or indirectly result in the destruction or disintegration of such indigenous nation or group or otherwise threaten the national or cultural integrity of such nation or group, including, but not limited to the imposition and support of illegitimate governments and the introduction of non-indigenous religions to indigenous peoples by non-indigenous missionaries.

11. ENVIRONMENTAL PROTECTION

It shall be unlawful for any state to make or permit any action or course of conduct with respect to the territories of an indigenous nation or group which will directly or indirectly result in the destruction or deterioration of an indigenous nation or group through the effects of pollution of earth, air, water, or which in any way depletes, displaces or destroys any natural resource or other resources under the dominion of, or vital to the livelihood of an indigenous nation or group.

12. INDIGENOUS MEMBERSHIP

No state, through legislation, regulation, or other means, shall take actions that interfere with the sovereign power of an indigenous nation or group to determine its own membership.

All rights and obligations declared herein shall be in addition to all rights and obligations existing under international law.

3. International Labour Organization: Convention 107

Interest in the situation of aboriginal peoples was manifested by the ILO as early as 1921. In 1926 its governing body set up a committee of experts on native labour with a mandate to "[frame] international standards for the protection of indigenous workers." As a result of the committee's work, a number of conventions were drafted, including the Forced Labour Convention 1930; the Recruiting of Indigenous Workers Convention 1936; the Contracts of Employment (Indigenous Workers) Convention 1939; and The Penal Sanctions (Indigenous Workers) Convention 1939.

In 1957, in consultation with various United Nations organizations, the ILO drafted a more comprehensive convention, the Indigenous and Tribal Populations Convention (No. 107) and the Indigenous and Tribal Populations Recommendation (No. 104). This last is intended to provide more detailed guidance to governments and is not binding. Unfortunately, the Convention itself suffers from some serious defects and, in spite of its adoption with a very promising vote (179 to 8 with 45 abstentions), the subsequent ratification by only 27 states failed to fulfil early expectations.

The convention has been criticized on a number of grounds. Indeed, it has been rejected by the World Council of Indigenous Peoples in view of the emphasis it places on integration. In addition, a discernible note of paternalism pervades several of the provisions, which undermine in a general way the benefits which might otherwise be derived from the mere existence of such a convention as a declaration of principles.

Specific problems exist with regard to the identification and definition of indigenous groups, the reconciling of tribal custom with national legal systems (particularly in the area of crime) and with the "duties of citizenship" generally.

Perhaps the most positive contribution of the convention is in the field of land rights:

> Aboriginal title by virtue of immemorial possession per se or contingent upon official recognition? In countries untrammelled by judicial precedents, the courts must be urged to accept the patient justice of the aboriginal claim and to place that claim on its only logical basis — that of simple possession. To those which are inclined to favour the Nabalco doctrine, however, an argument could well be addressed on Article 11 of the 107 Convention. (This requires ratifying States to recognize their indigenous populations' rights of ownership in their traditional lands, and is analysed in detail below.) Not even the Australian judiciary has suggested that the allegedly prerequisite "Crown grant" must assume a particular form; indeed, in parts of his judgment Mr Justice Blackburn appeared to accept that a grant might be properly inferred from a course of executive conduct. It is therefore submitted that in those countries whose government delegates voted in support of the Convention at the 1957 International Labour conference, and whose national legislatures subsequently approved the ratification of the Convention, aboriginal litigants should be permitted to rely upon these actions as evidence of an

implied grant which is admissible in the municipal courts.

The Convention should also prove helpful in another respect, for it envisages proprietary rights of a higher order than those normally included in the notion of aboriginal title.[53]

A further difficulty exists with regard to subsequent ratifications. Among those who have failed to ratify the convention are Australia, Canada and the USSR; of those states which have done so, five have no aboriginal populations. With regard to the remaining states, it appears that ratification has had little effect on the governments relations with their aboriginal populations.

Whether, in all the circumstances, it is worthwhile to try to revitalise the convention is a debatable question. It is clear, however, that at present it offers little promise for the fulfilment of aboriginal aspirations.

4. The Inter-American System

In 1948, some seven months before the adoption of the UDHR by the United Nations, the Western Hemisphere evidenced a similar concern with human rights when it adopted the American Declaration of the Rights and Duties of Man, along with the Charter of the Organization of American States (OAS).

In August 1959, in the "Declaration of Santiago," provision was made for the establishment of an Inter-American Commission of Human Rights which gradually gained in influence and authority so that it has become one of the "principle organs" of the OAS.[54]

The Commission consists of seven members serving in their personal capacity and has authority to hear individual complaints, to prepare and publish reports on individual member states within the OAS, and to make recommendations to individual states regarding violations of human rights.[55]

In 1969 the American Convention on Human Rights was opened for signature and entered into force in 1978. The Convention provides for the establishment of an Inter-American Court of Human Rights consisting of seven judges with contentious as well as advisory jurisdiction. Although the court as an institution is in its infancy, it has already been seized of several matters, including requests for advisory opinions by the government of Peru and by the Inter-American Commission.

The Commission has actively investigated and reported complaints. But practical impact of such reports and condemnations has been disappointing to say the least. The record of violations by members of the OAS against indigenous nations living within their jurisdiction is dismal. Charges of genocide have justifiably been levelled at several member countries. The Commission has declared that "special protection for indigenous populations constitute a sacred commitment"[56] of the member states of the OAS. This "commitment" has been honoured more in the breach than in the observance.

The potential usefulness of the Inter-American apparatus for redress of human rights complaints by indigenous peoples remains to be demonstrated. At present the situation gives little cause for optimism.

5. Conclusion

This brief survey indicates a number of the avenues that are open to indigenous peoples at the international level. Each of these fora, individually, provide to a greater or lesser degree inadequate mechanisms for the redress of grievances. The combined power of these mechanisms lies in general in the raising of the level of awareness of world opinion, thereby creating a climate of influence which may be conducive to the realization of Aboriginal aspirations. The inadequacies of mechanisms for the enforcement of international law is a well-known flaw of the system.

> There has been much publicity recently about the Lovelace case, which involved a claim to an international authority by an Indian woman to obtain in effect the reversal of the Supreme Court of Canada's decision in *Lavell*. (1) The international decision-maker was the Human Rights Committee, set up to secure the implementation of the International Convenant on Civil and Political Rights, which Canada ratified in 1976, and the claim was brought through the modality of the right of individual petition to the Committee provided for by the Optional Protocol to the Covenant. The culmination of this process, which took more than three years, was the expression by the Committee of "its views" to the petitioner and the Canadian government. (2) The Committee's "decision" in this case did not bind the government, which had in any event in effect previously admitted the violation. However, *Lavell* is still the law in Canada (though perhaps not for much longer). My point is not to deny the value of the Covenant and the Optional Protocol as important milestones in the international protection of human rights, but rather to demonstrate how international measures enabling an individual to remedy human rights violations, of which the Optional Protocol is in many ways the most promising, (3) leave much to be desired, particularly in terms of such factors as ease of access and ultimate effectiveness.[58]

Nevertheless, if any significant protection at the domestic level is to occur it will come about to a large degree as a result of recognition of certain factors at the international level.

This position has been increasingly adopted by the "Fourth World" itself. International coalescence of aboriginal peoples both regionally and universally is a very significant development in this regard. In 1982, an important international meeting took place in Regina. The World Assembly of First Nations met with a view to providing a unified indigenous voice in world affairs:

Political influence and international diplomacy appear to be the only means of pressuring for the development of standards and, more importantly, their enforcement and supervision. Indigenous people will need allies from both the member states and the non-governmental organizations to advance their interests through political influence and diplomacy.

Indigenous people must depend on one another to promote our common concerns. We must learn of each other's positions and organize to express our ideas and concerns to the world community.[59]

The formation of the World Council of Indigenous People, the International Indian Treaty Council, and the Consejo Indio de Sud America, together with events such as the World Assembly of First Nations and the Inuit Circumpolar Conference, are indications that indigenous peoples will no longer be confined within the context of "domestic jurisdiction".

Developments at the United Nations and in other spheres indicate a responsiveness to these approaches, albeit tentative at this stage.

The process is clearly an evolutionary one, the outcome of which will ultimately depnd on the actual commitment of all parties to principles already firmly in place.

Endnotes

[1] Chief S. Sanderson (Federation of Saskatchewan Indians Nations' Chiefs Council), "The International Rights of Indian Nations," in D. Opekokew: *The First Nations: Indian Governments in the Community of Man.*

[2] Note in this regard reference to the preamble in the "Final Report (First Part) of the Study of the Problem of Discrimination against Indigenous Populations" by special Rapporteur, Jose-R. Martinez Cobo for the Commission on Human Rights Sub-Commission on Prevention of Discrimination and Protection of Minorities. E/CN. 4/sub. 2/476/Add .4 30 July 1981.

[3] M.N. Bentwich, *A Commentary on the Charter of the United Nations* (Routledge and Kegan Paul (New York: Ltd., 1969), p. 7.

[4] L.M. Goodrich, *Charter of the United Nations: Commentary and Documents,* (New York: Columbia University Press, 1969), pp. 30-31.

[5] Id.

[6] Ibid., p. 67.

[7] Note the Comments of L. Henkin in *The International Bill of Rights* (New York: Columbia University Press, 1981), pp. 14-15.

The United States Charter made human rights a legitimate subject for discussion and recommendation by the Assembly and its sub-organs. Human rights may also properly come into the ken of the Security Council when it implicates peace and security, e.g., in South Africa. By discussing human rights the General Assembly does not intervene in matters "which are essentially within the domestic jurisdiction of any state" (Article 2(a)). Intervention, strictly, means dictatorial interference by force, and there have been no UN military interventions in support of human rights; discussion and recommendation are a matter of international concern, not essentially within any state's domestic jurisdiction. Enforcement measures by the Security Council are in any event exempted from Article 2(7).

Article 2(7) speaks only to intervention by the UN, not by member states, but most challenges to activities by states on behalf of human rights as "intervention" are equally unfounded. Peaceful objections by states to human rights violations by other states are not interventions. Generally, human rights are no longer within a state's domestic jurisdiction. That which is governed by international law or agreement is *ipso facto* and by definition a matter of international concern, not a matter of any state's domestic jurisdiction. Certainly, any state that adheres to an international human rights agreement has made the subject of that agreement a matter of international concern. It has submitted its performance to scrutiny and to appropriate, peaceful reaction by other parties, and to any special procedures or machinery provided by the agreement for its implementation.

[8] Goodrich, *supra*, note 4, p. 377.

[9] For examples, see Bentwich, *supra*, note 3, pp. 129-31.

[10] Goodrich, *supra,* note 4, p. 415.

[11] See T. Van Boven, "Human Rights Fora at the United Nations," in Tuttle, *International Human Rights Law and Practice* (American Bar Association, March 1978).

[12] Excerpt from complaint filed in March 1980.

[13] *Supra,* note 15, p. 88.

[14] Final Report (First Part), "Study of the Problem of Discrimination Against Indigenous Populations." E/CN. 4/Sub. 2/476/Add.4 30 July 1981. p. 14.

[15] "Study of the Problem of Discrimination Against Indigenous Populations," E/CN.4/Sub. 2/1982/33, 25 August 1982.

[16] Note the comments of J. Humphrey, in B.G. Ramcharan, *Human Rights: Thirty Years After the Universal Declaration* (The Hague: Nijhoff, 1979), pp. 4-5, when he suggests that the UDHR has attained customary international legal status:

> In resolution after resolution the UN has used the declaration to interpret human rights provisions of the Charter which nowhere catalogue or define the human rights and fundamental freedoms to which it refers. When, for example, the General Assembly condemns South Africa for violating the human rights provisions of the Charter in a resolution in which reference is also made to the Declaration it is obvious that it is using the latter to interpret the former. If this is so and there is a logical necessity about the proposition that cannot be denied the achievement of 10 Dec. 1948, is a far greater one than anyone could have imagined at that time. It is also of the greatest practical importance; for whereas the covenants are and will be binding only on those states which ratify them, the Declaration is binding on all states.

[17] In addition to this aspect, factors such as the increasing number of states and ideological divisions contributed to the long delay.

[18] For discussion of this debate, see Pechota, "The Development of the Covenant on Civil and Political Rights," in L. Henkin, *supra*, note 7, p. 32.

[19] For a discussion of the direct application fo the covenant in domestic fora, see O. Schacter, "Obligation to Implement the Covenant in Domestic Law," in Henkin, *supra*, note 7, p. 311.

[20] The initial report is to be submitted within one year of the entry into force of the covenant for the state party and thereafter whenever the committee so requests.

[21] See A.H. Robertson, "Implementation System: International Measures," in Henkin, *supra*, note 7, p. 332.

[22] See "Selected Documents in the Matter of Lovelace versus Canada Pursuant to the International Covenant on Civil and Political Rights," September 1981.

[23] See J. Crawford, *The Creation of States in International Law* (Oxford: Clarendon Press, 1979), p. 84.

[24] See G. Bennett, *Aboriginal Rights in International Law* (London: Survival International, 1978), pp. 12-13.

[25] Ibid., p. 13.

[26] 3. Inadequacy of political, economic, social or educational preparedness should never serve as a pretext for delaying independence.

    4. All armed action or repressive measures of all kinds directed against dependent peoples shall cease in order to enable them to exercise peacefully and freely their right to complete independence, and the integrity of their national territory shall be respected.

    5. Immediate steps shall be taken, in Trust and Non-Self-Governing Territories or all other territories which have not yet attained independence, to transfer all powers to the peoples of those territories, without any conditions or reservations, in accordance with their freely expressed will and desire, without any distinction as to race, creed or colour, in order to enable them to enjoy complete independence and freedom.

    6. Any attempt aimed at the partial or total disruption of the national unity and the territorial integrity of a country is incompatible with the purposes and principles of the Charter of the United Nations.

    7. All States shall observe faithfully and strictly the provisions of the Charter of the United Nations, the Universal Declaration of Human Rights and the present Declaration on the basis of equality, non-interference in the internal affairs of all States, and respect for the sovereign rights of all peoples and their territorial integrity.

[27] See J. Crawford, *supra*, note 23, pp. 89-90. Also note, in particular, *Declaration on Principles of International Law Concerning Friendly Relations and Cooperation Among States*, October 1970, UNGA Res. 2625 (xxv).

[28] Falk, Berger, *The Report of the Mackenzie Valley Pipeline Inquiry*, 6 UNCIO Doc. 396.

[29] A. Cassese, "The Helsinki Declaration and Self-Determination," in Buergenthal, T. *Human Rights, International Law and the Helsinki Accord* (New York: Landmark Studies, 1977), p. 94.

[30] Ibid., p. 101.

[31] International NGO conference on Indigenous Peoples and the Land, Report of the Legal Commission, September 1981, p. 1. See also Paragraph 82 Report of the Working Group on Indigenous Populations, *infra*, p. xxx.

[32] See Buergenthal, *supra*, note 29. Note in particular Chapter 1, p. 9. M.F. Dominick, *Human Rights and the Helsinki Accord* (Nashville: Hein, 1981), and *Proceedings of the Seventh Annual Conference on International Law*, Canadian Council on International Law, October 25-28, 1978.

[33] *Supra*, note 28.

[34] Articles 1 of the Covenants and Principle VIII of the Helsinki Final Act refer to control over natural resources.

[35] Note, for example, the plight of the Sami, the Dene, and the Cree.

[36] Bennett, *supra*, note 24, p. 51.

[37] *Supra*, note 31, p. 2.

[38] World Council of Indigenous Peoples, Melbourne, Australia, April 1981.

[39] Dene Declaration, Statement of Rights, 19 July 1975.

[40] Adopted by the UN General Assembly, 9 December 1948. Entered into force, 12 January 1961. 78 UNTS 277.

[41] Article II.

[42] Article V. See also Article IV.

[43] Opened for signature, 7 March 1966. Entered into force, 4 January 1969. 660 UNTS 195.

[44] Part I. Article 1(4).

[45] Part I, Article 2.

[46] Part I, Article 6.

[48] Id.

[49] Ibid., Article 14. As of 31 December 1981, only eight states had made such declarations.

[50] That is, to which the Declaration on the Granting of Independence to Colonial Countries

and Peoples applies. At the meetings of the committee, the indigenous populations of some of the countries which are states parties to the convention have been studied. These include: Argentina, Australia, Brazil, Canada, Chile, Costa Rica, Denmark, Ecuador, Finland, India, Mexico, New Zealand, Norway, Panama, Peru, Philippines, Sweden, and Venezuela.

[51] See Bennett, *supra*, note 24, pp. 54-55.
[52] Cobo, *supra*, note 14, pp. 31-32.
[53] Bennett, *supra*, note 24, p. 32.
[54] Tittle, *supra*, note 11, p. 49.
[55] Id.
[56] Bennett, *supra*, note 24, p. 61.
[57] Note Report e/CN.4/Sub.2/1982/2/ Add.2, Chapter III of the Cobo Report, for detailed analysis.
[58] J. Claydon, ''The International Law of Human Rights and the Canadian Courts,'' Proceedings of the 1981 Conference of the Canadian Council on International Law, p. 2.
[59] Opekokew, *supra*, note 1, p. 44.

6. Questions

Consider the Following Questions

1. Are indigenous peoples ''minorities'' for purposes of international human rights considerations?
2. What role should indigenous nations or peoples play in the world community in general, and at the UN in particular?
3. When indigenous customs conflict with the norms of international human rights, which ought to prevail? How and by whom should conflicts be resolved?
4. What criteria ought to be applied to indigenous peoples in determining whether or not they are ''appropriate'' units for purposes of ''statehood''?
5. Is the WCIP draft covenant likely to be adopted by the UN in its present form?

7. Further Reading

(a) Books

G. Alfredsson, *Greenland and the Right to External Self-Determination*, SJD Dissertation, Harvard 1982.

R. Arens, *Genocide in Paraguay,* Philadelphia; Temple University Press, 1976.

M.N. Bentwich, *Commentary on the Charter of the United Nations.* New York, Routledge and Kegan Paul Ltd., 1969.

T. Buergenthal, *Human Rights, International Law and the Helsinki Accord,* New York, Landmark Studies, 1977.

L.M. Goodrich, *Charter of the United Nations: Commentary and Documents,* 3d rev. ed., New York and London, Columbia University Press, 1969.

L. Henkin, *The International Bill of Rights,* New York, Columbia University Press, 1981.

D. Opekokew, *The First Nations: Indian Goverments in the Community of Man, Regina,* Federation of Saskatchewan Indian Nations, 1982.

(b) Articles

G. Alfredsson, "International Law, International Organizations and Indigenous Peoples," 36 *Journal of International Affairs*, No. 1, 1982, 113.

T. Buergenthal, "The Inter-American Court of Human Rights," (1982) 76 *AJIL*.

T. Buergenthal, "Implementing the UN Racial Convention," (1977) 12 *Texas International Law Journal*.

International Work Group for Indigenous Affairs (IWGIA), Newsletters and Documents, c/o Fiolstraede 10 DK-1171 Copenhagen K, Denmark

D. Knight, "Identity and Territory: Geographical Perspectives on Nationalism and Regionalism," *Annals of the Association of American Geographers,* 72(4) 1982, 514.

Supplement to the Revised First Edition

Litigation has occurred at a phenomenal rate over the last five years as Aboriginal people turned to the courts in unprecedented numbers to assert their special legal rights. It is only possible here, however, to include a few of the most significant judicial pronouncements. This collection begins with the Supreme Court of Canada decision in *Guerin* v. *The Queen* in which the Court rendered a landmark decision by declaring the Crown to constitute a fiduciary in relation to its administration of reserve lands on behalf of status Indians. This case is also extremely important for its analysis of aboriginal title and the classification of Indian legal matters as being both unique and incapable of fitting within other existing legal categories.

The second decision, *Simon* v. *The Queen*, is also from the Supreme Court. This time the Court was addressing the alleged extinguishment of pre-Confederation treaty rights. Not only did the decision conclusively settle that these treaties have the full force of law, but the judges also clarified the legal rules for treaty interpretation and suggested that any descendant of the original treaty beneficiaries may qualify for the rights contained therein.

Section 35 of the *Constitution Act, 1982* has given rise to broadly different possible interpretations of its meaning and its consequences for existing federal and provincial legislation. As the Supreme Court of Canada has yet to provide a definitive statement on the impact of this section, this Supplement contains three appellate decisions reflecting quite different opinions. The caselaw segment concludes with *Manitoba Métis Federation* v. *A.G. of Canada*, which is the first time that the constitutionality of various statutes enacted between 1871 and 1886 have been challenged for allegedly being designed to undermine the land rights guaranteed to the Métis by the *Manitoba Act*.

The materials also contain the final Federal and Aboriginal proposals regarding a constitutional amendment on self-government that were tabled and debated at the 1987 First Ministers' Conference. Numerous proposals on self-government were developed over several years of meetings of senior officials and ministers as well as the 1983, 1984 and 1985 First Ministers' Conferences by many of the 17 parties to these negotiations. Although neither of the two proposals received sufficient support, they represent the differing perspectives as well as the continuing chasm that exists between the Aboriginal peoples' desires on the one hand, and the limits of current government flexibility on the other.

The supplement concludes with the latest amendments to the *Indian Act* which are not yet included in the office consolidations that are available from the Federal Government.

The existing office consolidation does include the dramatic changes that occurred in 1985 through Bill C-31. As of June 30, 1989, the Department of Indian Affairs had received 66,760 applicants for registration involving

118,420 people (as minors may be included on adult applications). A total of 60,624 people had been registered as status Indians while 14,056 individuals have been rejected and the remaining 43,740 people are awaiting the processing of their applications. In addition, a large number of First Nations have developed their own membership codes and formally assumed control over their Band Lists (which identify the members) such that the rules governing registration as a status Indian and entitlement to band membership may differ significantly.

There are numerous other decisions of major importance that the reader should be aware of, including: *Canadian Pacific Ltd.* v. *Paul*, [1989] 1 C.N.L.R. 47 (S.C.C.); *Attorney General for Ontario* v. *Bear Island Foundation*, [1989] 2 C.N.L.R. 73 (Ont. C.A.); *R.* v. *Ashini*, [1989] 2 C.N.L.R. 119 (Nfld. Prov. Ct.); *Roberts* v. *Canada*, [1989] 2 C.N.L.R. 146 (S.C.C.); *R.* v. *Jimmy*, [1987] 3 C.N.L.R. 77(B.C.C.A.); *Sioui* v. *Attorney General for Quebec*, [1987] 4 C.N.L.R. 118 (Que. C.A.); *MacMillan Bloedel Ltd.* v. *Mullin*, [1985] 3 W.W.R. 577 (B.C.C.A.); *Ominayak* v. *Norcen Ltd.*, [1985] 3 W.W.R. 193 (Alta. C.A.); and *Saanichton Marina Ltd.* v. *Claxton* (1989), 36 B.C.L.R.(2d) 79(B.C.C.A.) among others.

Guerin v. The Queen
(1985) 13 D.L.R. (4th) 321 (S.C.C.)

Ed. Note: The essential facts in this case centre around a lease of 162 of the 416.53 acres of the Musqueam Indian Reserve adjacent to Vancouver in 1958 to the Shaughnessy Heights Golf Club by the federal Crown for a term of up to 75 years on terms significantly different from those disclosed to the Band by the District Superintendent of Indian Affairs prior to its surrender of the land to the Crown for leasing in 1957. The governmental officials further failed to adhere to several of the essential preconditions to the surrender established by the Band Council or advise the Council of their inability to negotiate a lease in accordance with this direction. The net result was that the actual lease offered far less to the Musqueam people than they had anticipated. The facts also indicate that they were unable to obtain a copy of the lease, despite repeated requests, until 1970 such that they were unaware of the full extent of the changes made to their demands until 12 years after the fact. The evidence also demonstrated that the land was perhaps the most valuable in the city at that time with other more lucrative developments possible.

DICKSON J.: — The question is whether the appellants, the chief and councillors of the Musqueam Indian Band, suing on their own behalf and on behalf of all other members of the band, are entitled to recover damages from the federal Crown in respect of the leasing to a golf club of land on the Musqueam Indian Reserve. Collier J., of the Trial Division of the Federal Court, declared that the Crown was in breach of trust [[1982] 2 F.C. 385,

[1982] 2 F.C. 445 (supplementary reasons)]. He assessed damages at $10,000,000. The Federal Court of Appeal allowed a Crown appeal, set aside the judgment of the Trial Division and dismissed the action [143 D.L.R. (3d) 416, [1983] 2 F.C. 656.

1. General

Before adverting to the facts, reference should be made to several of the relevant sections of the *Indian Act*, R.S.C. 1952, c. 149, as amended. Section 18(1) provides in part that reserves shall be held by Her Majesty for the use of the respective Indian bands for which they were set apart. Generally, lands in a reserve shall not be sold, alienated, leased or otherwise disposed of until they have been surrendered to Her Majesty by the band for whose use and benefit in common the reserve was set apart (s.37). A surrender may be absolute or qualified, conditional or unconditional (s.38(2)). To be valid, a surrender must be made to Her Majesty, assented to by a majority of the electors of the band, and accepted by the Governor in Council (s.39(1)).

2. The Facts

The Crown does not attack the findings of fact made by the trial judge. The Crown simply says that on those facts no cause of action has been made out . . .

3. Assessment at Trial and on Appeal of the Legal Effect of the Facts as Found

The plaintiffs based their case on breach of trust. They asserted that the federal Crown was a trustee of the surrendered lands. The trial judge agreed.

The Crown attempted to argue that if there was a trust it was, at best, a "political trust", enforceable only in Parliament and not a "true trust", enforceable in the courts. This distinction was recognized in two leading English cases dealing with the position of the Crown as trustee: *Tito* v. *Waddell (No. 2)*, [1977] 3 All E.R. 129; *Kinloch* v. *Secretary of State for India in Council* (1882), 7 App. Cas. 619.

In *Kinloch* Lord Selbourn L.C. said at pp. 625-6:

Now the words "in trust for" are quite consistent with, and indeed are the proper manner of expressing, every species of trust—a trust not only as regards those matters which are the proper subjects for an equitable jurisdiction to administer, but as respects higher matters, such as might take place between the Crown and public officers discharging, under the directions of the Crown, duties or functions belonging to the prerogative and to the authority of the Crown. In the lower sense they are matters within the jurisdiction of, and to be administered by, the ordinary Courts of Equity; in the higher sense they are not. What their sense is here, is the question to be determined, looking at the whole instrument and at its nature and effect.

Counsel for the band objected to any argument on the "political trust" defence because the Crown had failed to plead it. Collier J. gave leave, on terms, to amend the defence to raise the point but the Crown chose not to take advantage of the opportunity to amend. Collier J. therefore refused to consider the point.

The Crown then argued that if there were a legally enforceable trust its terms were those set out in the surrender document, permitting it to lease the 162 acres to anyone, for any purpose, and upon any terms which the Crown deemed most conducive to the welfare of the band. In the Crown's submission the surrender document imposed on it no obligation to lease to the golf club on the terms discussed at the surrender meeting; nor did it impose any duty on the Crown to obtain the approval of the band in respect of the terms of the lease ultimately entered into.

The trial judge rejected these submissions. He held, citing the *Tito* case, *supra*, that the Crown can, if it chooses, act as a trustee. He held also that the surrender of October 6, 1975, imposed on the Crown, as trustee, a duty as of that date, to lease the surrendered land to the golf club on the conditions contemplated by the band. Substantial changes were made to these conditions, in respect of which no instruction or authorization was sought by the Crown, as trustee, from the members of the band, the *cestuis que trust*. The judge found the Crown liable for breach of trust.

In respect of damages, there was a great deal of evidence at trial, most of it by experts. Citing *Fales et al.* v. *Canada Permanent Trust Co.*; *Wohlleben* v. *Canada Permanent Trust Co.* (1976), 70 D.L.R. (3d) 257 at pp. 271-2, the judge held that the measure of damages is the actual loss which the acts or omissions have caused to the trust estate, the plaintiffs being entitled to be placed in the same position so far as possible as if there had been no breach of trust. The judge proceeded on the basis that the band would not have agreed to the terms of the lease as signed and the club would not have agreed to a lease on the terms found by the judge to be the terms of the trust. Therefore it would have been possible for the band at some point to have leased the land for residential purposes on a 99-year leasehold basis on extremely favourable terms. In quantifying the award, the judge confessed to being unable to set out a precise rationale or approach, mathematical or otherwise. He said that the award was obviously a "global" figure: a considered reaction based on the evidence, the opinions, the arguments and, in the end, his own conclusions of fact. The judge assessed the plaintiffs' damages at $10,000,000.

The Federal Court of Appeal, speaking through Mr. Justice Le Dain, proceeded on the premise that the case presented on behalf of the band rested on the existence of a statutory trust in the private law sense based primarily on the terms of s.18(1) of the *Indian Act*. Section 18(1) reads:

18(1) Subject to the provisions of this Act, reserves shall be held by Her Majesty for the use and benefit of the respective bands for which they were set apart; and subject to this Act and to the terms of any treaty or surrender, the Governor in Council may determine whether any purpose for which lands in a reserve are used or are to be used is for the use and benefit of the band.

Le Dain J. scrutinized this section and concluded that it was not consistent with a "true trust" in the sense of an equitable obligation enforceable in a court of law. Especially telling, in his opinion, was the discretion vested by s.18(1) in the Governor in Council to determine whether a particular purpose to which reserve land is being put, or is proposed to be put, is "for the use and benefit of the band". In his view this discretion indicated it was for the government, not the courts, to determine what was for the use and benefit of the band. Such a discretion, in his opinion, was incompatible with an intention to impose an equitable obligation, enforceable in court, to deal with the land in a certain manner. Section 18(1) was therefore incapable of making the Crown a true trustee of those lands [at p. 469 D.L.R.]:

> The extent to which the government assumes an administrative or management responsibility for the reserves of some positive scope is a matter of governmental discretion, not legal or equitable obligation. I am, therefore, of the opinion that s. 18 of the *Indian Act* does not afford a basis for an action for breach of trust in the management or disposition of reserve lands.

Le Dain J. also rejected the alternative contention on behalf of the band that a trust was created by the terms of the surrender document, especially the words "in trust to lease the same", and that the Crown was in breach of that trust by its alleged failure to exercise ordinary skill and prudence in leasing the land [at pp. 470-71]:

> . . . it is my opinion that the words "in trust" in the surrender document were intended to do no more than indicate that the surrender was for the benefit of the Indians and conferred an authority to deal with the land in a certain manner for their benefit. They were not intended to impose an equitable obligation or duty to deal with the land in a certain manner. For these reasons, I am of the opinion that the surrender did not create a true trust and does not, therefore, afford a basis for liability based on a breach of trust.

Even if he had been able to find a "true trust", Le Dain J. would have refused to follow Collier J. in concluding that the terms of such a trust were defined by the Indians' understanding of conditions the Crown was to secure in the lease. These conditions did not appear in the surrender document and they did not comply with ss. 37 to 41 of the *Indian Act*, governing the conditions of a surrender [at pp. 452-3]:

> From these provisions it is argued that the conditions of a surrender, in order to be valid, must be voted on and approved by a majority of the electors of a band, be certified by the superintendent or other officer who

attended the meeting and by the chief or a member of the council of the band, and be submitted to and approved by the Governor in Council, all of which presuppose that the conditions will be in written form. I agree with these contentions. These solemn formalities have been prescribed as a matter of public policy for the protection of a band and the proper discharge of the government's responsibility for the Indians. They are also important as ensuring certainty as to the effect of a surrender and the validity of a subsequent disposition of surrendered land. It is to be noted that they are the only provisions of the Act excluded from the power of the Governor in Council under s. 4(2) to declare by proclamation that particular provisions of the Act shall not apply in certain cases. The oral terms found by the trial judge were not voted on and approved by a majority of the band. They were deduced by the trial judge from the testimony of three members of the band and a former official of the Indian Affairs branch as to what was said at the meetings, and in some cases as to what was not said. The oral terms of the surrender found by the trial judge were not accepted by the Governor in Council, as required by the Act. What was accepted by Order in Council P.C. 1957-1060 of December 6, 1957, was the "attached surrender dated the sixth day of October, 1957". It was an unqualified acceptance of the written surrender, with no reference, express or implied, to other terms or conditions.

Le Dain J. concluded that the oral conditions of the surrender found by the trial judge could not afford a basis in law for finding liability and awarding damages.

Having found no basis for the trust alleged, the Federal Court of Appeal allowed the Crown's appeal.

4. Fiduciary Relationship

The issue of the Crown's liability was dealt with in the courts below on the basis of the existence or non-existence of a trust. In dealing with the different consequences of a "true" trust, as opposed to a "political" trust, Le Dain J. noted that the Crown could be liable only if it were subject to an "equitable obligation enforceable in a court of law". I have some doubt as to the cogency of the terminology of "higher" and "lower" trusts, but I do agree that the existence of an equitable obligation is the *sine qua non* for liability. Such an obligation is not, however, limited to relationships which can be strictly defined as "trusts". As will presently appear, it is my view that the Crown's obligations *vis-à-vis* the Indians cannot be defined as a trust. That does not, however, mean that the Crown owes no enforceable duty to the Indians in the way in which it deals with Indian land.

In my view, the nature of Indian title and the framework of the statutory scheme established for disposing of Indian land places upon the Crown an equitable obligation, enforceable by the courts, to deal with the land for the benefit of the Indians. This obligation does not amount to a trust in the private law sense. It is rather a fiduciary duty. If, however, the Crown breaches this fiduciary duty it will be liable to the Indians in the same way and to the same extent as if such a trust were in effect.

The fiduciary relationship between the Crown and the Indians has its roots in the concept of aboriginal, native or Indian title. The fact that Indian bands have a certain interest in lands does not, however, in itself give rise to a fiduciary relationship between the Indians and the Crown. The conclusion that the Crown is a fiduciary depends upon the further proposition that the Indian interest in the land is inalienable except upon surrender to the Crown.

An Indian band is prohibited from directly transferring its interest to a third party. Any sale or lease of land can only be carried out after a surrender has taken place, with the Crown then acting on the band's behalf. The Crown first took this responsibility upon itself in the Royal Proclamation of 1763 (R.S.C. 1970, App. II, No. 1). It is still recognized in the surrender provisions of the *Indian Act*. The surrender requirement, and the responsibility it entails, are the source of a distinct fiduciary obligation owed by the Crown to the Indians. In order to explore the character of this obligation, however, it is first necessary to consider the basis of aboriginal title and the nature of the interest in land which it represents.

(a) The Existence of Indian Title

In *Calder et al.* v. *A.-G. B.C.* (1973), 34 D.L.R. (3d) 145, this court recognized aboriginal title as a legal right derived from the Indians' historic occupation and possession of their tribal lands. With Judson and Hall JJ. writing the principal judgments, the court split three-three on the major issue of whether the Nishga Indians' aboriginal title to their ancient tribal territory had been extinguished by general land enactments in British Columbia. The court also split on the issue of whether the Royal Proclamation of 1763 was applicable to Indian lands in that province. Judson and Hall JJ. were in agreement, however, that aboriginal title existed in Canada (at least where it has not been extinguished by appropriate legislative action) independently of the Royal Proclamation of 1763. Judson J. stated expressly that the Proclamation was not the "exclusive" source of Indian title (at pp. 152-3, 156 D.L.R.). Hall J. said (at p. 200 D.L.R.) that "aboriginal Indian title does not depend on treaty, executive order or legislative enactment". . . .

In recognizing that the Proclamation is not the sole source of Indian title the *Calder* decision went beyond the judgment of the Privy Council in *St. Catherine's Milling & Lumber Co.* v. *The Queen* (1888), 14 App. Cas. 46. In that case Lord Watson acknowledged the existence of aboriginal title but said it had its origin in the Royal Proclamation. In this respect *Calder* is consistent with the position of Chief Justice Marshall in the leading American cases of *Johnson and Graham's Lessee* v. *M'Intosh* (1823), 8 Wheaton 543, 21 U.S.

240, and *Worcester* v. *State of Georgia* (1832), 6 Peters 515, 31 U.S. 530, cited by Judson and Hall JJ. in their respective judgments.

In *Johnson* v. *M'Intosh* Marshall C.J., although he acknowledged the Royal Proclamation of 1763 as one basis for recognition of Indian title, was nonetheless of the opinion that the rights of Indians in the lands they traditionally occupied prior to European colonization both predated and survived the claims to sovereignty made by various European nations in the territories of the North American continent. The principle of discovery which justified these claims gave the ultimate title in the land in a particular area to the nation which had discovered and claimed it. In that respect at least the Indians' rights in the land were obviously diminished; but their rights of occupancy and possession remained unaffected. Marshall C.J. explained this principle as follows, at pp. 573-4:

> The exclusion of all other Europeans, necessarily gave to the nation making the discovery the sole right of acquiring the soil from the natives, and establishing settlements upon it. . . . It was a right which all asserted for themselves, and to the assertion of which, by others, all assented.
>
> Those relations which were to exist between the discoverer and the natives, were to be regulated by themselves. The rights thus acquired being exclusive, no other power could interpose between them.
>
> In the establishment of these relations, the rights of the original inhabitants were, in no instance, entirely disregarded; but were necessary, to a considerable extent, impaired. *They were admitted to be the rightful occupants of the soil, with a legal as well as just claim to retain possession of it*, and to use it acording to their own discretion; but their rights to complete sovereignty, as independent nations, were necessarily diminished, and their power to dispose of the soil at their own will, to whomsoever they pleased, was denied by the original fundamental principle, that discovery gave exclusive title to those who made it. (Emphasis added.)

The principle that a change in sovereignty over a particular territory does not in general affect the presumptive title of the inhabitants was approved by the Privy Council in *Amodu Tijani* v. *Secretary, Southern Nigeria*, [1921] 2 A.C. 399. That principle supports the assumption implicit in *Calder* that Indian title is an independent legal right which, although recognized by the Royal Proclamation of 1763, none the less predates it. For this reason *Kinloch* v. *Secretary of State for India, supra*; *Tito* v. *Waddell, supra*, and the other "political trust" decisions are inapplicable to the present case. The "political trust" cases concerned essentially the distribution of public funds or other property held by the government. In each case the party claiming to be beneficiary under a trust depended entirely on statute, ordinance or treaty as the basis for its claim to an interest in the funds in question. The situation of the Indians is entirely different. Their interest in their lands is a pre-existing legal right not created by Royal Proclamation, by s. 18(1) of the *Indian Act*, or by any other executive order or legislative provision.

It does not matter, in my opinion, that the present case is concerned with the interest of an Indian band in a reserve rather than with unrecognized aboriginal title in traditional tribal lands. The Indian interest in the land is the same in both cases: see *A.-G. Que.* v. *A.-G. Can.* (1920), 56 D.L.R. 373 at pp. 378-9 (the *Star Chrome* case). It is worth noting, however, that the reserve in question here was created out of the ancient tribal territory of the Musqueam band by the unilateral action of the Colony of British Columbia, prior to Confederation.

(b) The Nature of Indian Title

In the *St. Catherine's Milling* case, *supra*, the Privy Council held that the Indians had a "personal and usufructuary right" [p. 54] in the lands which they had traditionally occupied. Lord Watson said that "there has been all along vested in the Crown a substantial and paramount estate, underlying the Indian title, which became a *plenum dominium* whenever the title was surrendered or otherwise extinguished" (at p. 55). He reiterated this idea, stating that the Crown "has all along had a present proprietary estate in the land, upon which the Indian title was a mere burden" (at p. 58). This view of aboriginal title was affirmed by the Privy Council in the *Star Chrome* case. In *Amodu Tijani*, *supra*, Viscount Haldane, adverting to the *St. Catherine's Milling* and *Star Chrome* decisions, explained the concept of a usufructuary right as "a mere qualification of or burden on the radical or final title of the Sovereign" (p. 403). He described the title of the Sovereign as a pure legal estate, but one which could be qualified by a right of "beneficial user" that did not necessarily take the form of an estate in land. Indian title in Canada was said to be one illustration "of the necessity for getting rid of the assumption that the ownership of land naturally breaks itself up into estates, conceived as creatures of inherent legal principle" [p. 403]. Chief Justice Marshall took a similar view in *Johnson* v. *M'Intosh*, *supra*, saying, "All our institutions recognize the absolute title of the Crown, subject only to the Indian right of occupancy" (p. 588).

It should be noted that the Privy Council's emphasis on the personal nature of aboriginal title stemmed in part from constitutional arrangements peculiar to Canada. The Indian territory at issue in *St. Catherine's Milling* was land which in 1867 had been vested in the Crown subject to the interest of the Indians. The Indians' interest was "an interest other than that of the Province", within the meaning of s. 109 of the *Constitution Act, 1867*. Section 109 provides:. . .

When the land in question in *St. Catherine's Milling* was subsequently disencumbered of the native title upon its surrender to the federal government by the Indian occupants in 1873, the entire beneficial interest in the land was held to have passed, because of the personal and usufructuary nature of the Indians' right, to the Province of Ontario under s. 109 rather than to Canada.

The same constitutional issue arose recently in this court in *Smith et al.* v. *The Queen* (1983), 147 D.L.R. (3d) 237, in which the court held that the Indian right in a reserve, being personal, could not be transferred to a grantee, whether an individual or the Crown. Upon surrender the right disappeared "in the process of release".

No such constitutional problem arises in the present case, since in 1938 the title to all Indian reserves in British Columbia was transferred by the provincial government to the Crown in right of Canada.

It is true that in contexts other than the constitutional the characterization of Indian title as "a personal and usufructuary right" has sometimes been questioned. In *Calder, supra*, for example, Judson J. intimated at p. 156 D.L.R. that this characterization was not helpful in determining the nature of Indian title. In *A.-G. Can.* v. *Giroux* (1916), 30 D.L.R. 123, Duff J., speaking for himself and Anglin J., distinguished *St. Catherine's Milling* on the ground that the statutory provisions in accordance with which the reserve in question in *Giroux* had been created conferred beneficial ownership on the Indian band which occupied the reserve. In *Cardinal* v. *A.-G. Alta.* (1973), 40 D.L.R. (3d) 553, Laskin J., dissenting on another point, accepted the possibility that Indians may have a beneficial interest in a reserve. The Alberta Court of Appeal in *Western Industrial Contractors Ltd.* v. *Sarcee Developments Ltd.* (1979), 98 D.L.R. (3d) 424, accepted the proposition that an Indian band does indeed have a beneficial interest in its reserve. In the present case this was the view as well of Le Dain J. in the Federal Court of Appeal. See also the judgment of Kellock J. in *Miller* v. *The King*, [1950] 1 D.L.R. 513, in which he seems implicitly to adopt a similar position. None of these judgments mentioned the *Star Chrome* case, however, in which the Indian interest in land specifically set aside as a reserve was held to be the same as the "personal and usufructuary right" which was discussed in *St. Catherine's Milling*.

It appears to me that there is no real conflict between the cases which characterize Indian title as a beneficial interest of some sort, and those which characterize it a personal, usufructuary right. Any apparent inconsistency derives from the fact that in describing what constitutes a unique interest in land the courts have almost inevitably found themselves applying a somewhat inappropriate terminology drawn from general property law. There is a core of truth in the way that each of the two lines of authority has described native title, but an appearance of conflict has none the less arisen because in neither case is the categorization quite accurate.

Indians have a legal right to occupy and possess certain lands, the ultimate title to which is in the Crown. While their interest does not, strictly speaking, amount to beneficial ownership, neither is its nature completely exhausted by the concept of a personal right. It is true that the *sui generis* interest which the Indians have in the land is personal in the sense that it cannot be transferred to a grantee, but it is also true, as will presently appear, that the interest gives rise upon surrender to a distinctive fiduciary obligation on the part of the Crown to deal with the land for the benefit of the surrendering Indians. These two aspects of Indian title go together, since the Crown's original purpose in declaring the Indians' interest to be inalienable otherwise than to the Crown was to facilitate the Crown's ability to represent the Indians in dealings with third parties. The nature of the Indians' interest is therefore best characterized by its general inalienability, coupled with the fact that the Crown is under an obligation to deal with the land on the Indians' behalf when the interest is surrendered. Any description of Indian title which goes beyond these two features is both unnecessary and potentially misleading.

(c) The Crown's Fiduciary Obligation

The concept of fiduciary obligation originated long ago in the notion of breach of confidence, one of the original heads of jurisdiction in chancery. In the present appeal its relevance is based on the requirement of a ''surrender'' before Indian land can be alienated.

The Royal Proclamation of 1763 provided that no private person could purchase from the Indians any lands that the Proclamation had reserved to them, and provided further that all purchases had to be by and in the name of the Crown, in a public assembly of the Indians held by the governor or commander-in-chief of the colony in which the lands in question lay. As Lord Watson pointed out in *St. Catherine's Milling, supra*, at p. 54, this policy with respect to the sale or transfer of the Indians' interest in land has been continuously maintained by the British Crown, by the governments of the colonies when they became responsible for the administration of Indian affairs, and, after 1867, by the federal government of Canada. Successive federal statutes, predecessors to the present *Indian Act*, have all provided for the general inalienability of Indian reserve land except upon surrender to the Crown, the relevant provisions in the present Act being ss. 37-41.

The purpose of this surrender requirement is clearly to interpose the Crown between the Indians and prospective purchasers or lessees of their land, so as to prevent the Indians from being exploited. This is made clear in the Royal Proclamation itself, which prefaces the provision making the Crown an intermediary with a declaration that ''great Frauds and Abuses have been committed in purchasing Lands of the Indians, to the great Prejudice of our Interest and to the great Dissatisfaction of the said Indians . . .''. Through the confirmation in the *Indian Act* of the historic responsibility which the Crown has undertaken, to act on behalf of the Indians so as to protect their interests in transactions with third parties, Parliament has conferred upon the Crown a discretion to decide for itself where the Indians' best interests really lie. This is the effect of s. 18(1) of the Act.

This discretion on the part of the Crown, far from ousting, as the Crown contends, the jurisdiction of the courts to regulate the relationship between the Crown and the Indians, has the effect of transforming the Crown's obligation into a fiduciary one. Professor Ernest Weinrib maintains in his article "The Fiduciary Obligation", 25 U.T.L.J. 1 (1975), at p. 7, that the "hallmark of a fiduciary relation is that the relative legal positions are such that one party is at the mercy of the other's discretion". Earlier, at p. 4, he puts the point in the following way:

> [Where there is a fiduciary obligation] there is a relation in which the principal's interests can be affected by, and are therefore dependent on, the manner in which the fiduciary uses the discretion which has been delegated to him. The fiduciary obligation is the law's blunt tool for the control of this discretion.

I make no comment upon whether this description is broad enough to embrace all fiduciary obligations. I do agree, however, that where by statute, agreement, or perhaps by unilateral undertaking, one party has an obligation to act for the benefit of another, and that obligation carries with it a discretionary power, the party thus empowered becomes a fiduciary. Equity will then supervise the relationship by holding him to the fiduciary's strict standard of conduct.

It is sometimes said that the nature of fiduciary relationships is both established and exhausted by the standard categories of agent, trustee, partner, director, and the like. I do not agree. It is the nature of the relationship, not the specific category of actor involved that gives rise to the fiduciary duty. The categories of fiduciary, like those of negligence, should not be considered closed: see, *e.g.*, *Laskin* v. *Bache & Co. Inc.* (1971), 23 D.L.R. (3d) 385 at p. 392 (C.A.); *Goldex Mines Ltd.* v. *Revill et al.* (1974), 54 D.L.R. (3d) 672 (C.A.) at p. 680.

It should be noted that fiduciary duties generally arise only with regard to obligations originating in a private law context. Public law duties, the performance of which requires the exercise of discretion, do not typically give rise to a fiduciary relationship. As the "political trust" cases indicate, the Crown is not normally viewed as a fiduciary in the exercise of its legislative or administrative function. The mere fact, however, that it is the Crown which is obligated to act on the Indians' behalf does not of itself remove the Crown's obligation from the scope of the fiduciary principle. As was pointed out earlier, the Indians' interest in land is an independent legal interest. It is not a creation of either the legislative or executive branches of government. The Crown's obligation to the Indians with respect to that interest is therefore not a public law duty. While it is not a private law duty in the strict sense either, it is none the less in the nature of a private law duty. Therefore, in this *sui generis* relationship, it is not improper to regard the Crown as a fiduciary.

Section 18(1) of the *Indian Act* confers upon the Crown a broad discretion in dealing with surrendered land. In the present case, the document of surrender, set out in part earlier in these reasons, by which the Musqueam band surrendered the land at issue, confirms this discretion in the clause conveying the land to the Crown "in trust to lease . . . upon such terms as the Government of Canada may deem most conducive to our Welfare and that of our people". When, as here, an Indian band surrenders its interest to the Crown, a fiduciary obligation takes hold to regulate the manner in which the Crown exercises its discretion in dealing with the land on the Indians' behalf.

I agree with Le Dain J. that before surrender the Crown does not hold the land in trust for the Indians. I also agree that the Crown's obligation does not somehow crystallize into a trust, express or implied, at the time of surrender. The law of trusts is a highly developed, specialized branch of the law. An express trust requires a settlor, a beneficiary, a trust corpus, words of settlement, certainty of object and certainty of obligation. Not all of these elements are present here. Indeed, there is not even a trust corpus. As the *Smith* decision, *supra*, makes clear, upon unconditional surrender the Indians' right in the land disappears. No property interest is transferred which could constitute the trust *res*, so that even if the other *indicia* of an express or implied trust could be made out, the basic requirement of a settlement of property has not been met. Accordingly, although the nature of Indian title coupled with the discretion vested in the Crown are sufficient to give rise to a fiduciary obligation, neither an express nor an implied trust arises upon surrender.

Nor does surrender give rise to a constructive trust. As was said by this court in *Pettkus* v. *Becker* (1980), 117 D.L.R. (3d) 257 at p. 273: "The principle of unjust enrichment lies at the heart of the constructive trust." See also *Rathwell* v. *Rathwell* (1978), 83 D.L.R. (3d) 289. Any similarity between a constructive trust and the Crown's fiduciary obligation to the Indians is limited to the fact that both arise by operation of law; the former is an essentially restitutionary remedy, while the latter is not. In the present case, for example, the Crown has in no way been enriched by the surrender transaction, whether unjustly or otherwise, but the fact that this is so cannot alter either the existence or the nature of the obligation which the Crown owes.

The Crown's fiduciary obligation to the Indians is therefore not a trust. To say as much is not to deny that the obligation is trust-like in character. As would be the case with a trust, the Crown must hold surrendered land for the use and benefit of the surrendering band. The obligation is thus subject to principles very similar to those which govern the law of trusts concerning, for example, the measure of damages for breach. The fiduciary relationship between the Crown and the Indians also bears a certain resemblance to agency, since the obligation can be characterized as a duty to act on behalf of the Indian bands who have surrendered lands, by negotiating for the sale or lease of the land to third parties. But just as the Crown is not a trustee for the Indians, neither is it their agent; not only does the Crown's authority to act on the band's behalf lack a basis in contract, but the band is not a party to the ultimate sale or lease, as it would be if it were the Crown's principal. I repeat, the fiduciary obligation which is owed to the Indians by the Crown is *sui generis*. Given the unique character both of the Indians' interest in land and of their historical relationship with the Crown, the fact that this is so should occasion no surprise.

The discretion which is the hallmark of any fiduciary relationship is capable of being considerably narrowed in a particular case. This is as true of the Crown's discretion *vis-à-vis* the Indians as it is of the discretion of trustees, agents, and other traditional categories of fiduciary. The *Indian Act* makes specific provision for such narrowing in s. 18(1) and 38(2). A fiduciary obligation will not, of course, be eliminated by the imposition of conditions that have the effect of restricting the fiduciary's discretion. A failure to adhere to the imposed conditions will simply itself be a *prima facie* breach of the obligation. In the present case both the surrender and the Order in Council accepting the surrender referred to the Crown leasing the land on the band's behalf. Prior to the surrender the band had also been given to understand that a lease was to be entered into with the Shaughnessy Heights Golf Club upon certain terms, but this understanding was not incorporated into the surrender document itself. The effect of these so-called oral terms will be considered in the next section.

(d) Breach of the Fiduciary Obligation

The trial judge found that the Crown's agents promised the band to lease the land in question on certain specified terms and then, after surrender, obtained a lease on different terms. The lease obtained was much less valuable. As already mentioned, the surrender document did not make reference to the "oral" terms. I would not wish to say that those terms had none the less somehow been incorporated as conditions into the surrender. They were not formally assented to by a majority of the electors of the band, nor were they accepted by the Governor in Council, as required by s. 39(1)(b) and (c). I agree with Le Dain J. that there is no merit in the appellants' submission that for purposes of s. 39 a surrender can be considered independently of its terms. This makes no more sense than would a claim that a contract can have an existence which in no way depends on the terms and conditions that comprise it.

Nonetheless, the Crown, in my view, was not empowered by the surrender document to ignore the oral terms which the band understood would be embodied in the lease. The oral representations form the backdrop against which the Crown's conduct in discharging its fiduciary obligation must be measured. They inform and confine the field of discretion within which the Crown was free to act. After the Crown's agents had induced the band to surrender its land on the understanding that the land would be leased on certain terms, it would be unconscionable to permit the Crown simply to ignore those terms. When the promised lease proved impossible to obtain, the Crown, instead of proceeding to lease the land on different, unfavourable terms, should have returned to the band to explain what had occurred and seek the band's counsel on how to proceed. The existence of such unconscionability is the key to a conclusion that the Crown breached its fiduciary duty. Equity will not countenance unconscionable behaviour in a fiduciary, whose duty is that of utmost loyalty to his principal.

While the existence of the fiduciary obligation which the Crown owes to the Indians is dependent on the nature of the surrender process, the standard of conduct which the obligation imports is both more general and more exacting than the terms of any particular surrender. In the present case the relevant aspect of the required standard of conduct is defined by a principle analogous to that which underlies the doctrine of promissory or equitable estoppel. The Crown cannot promise the band that it will obtain a lease of the latter's land on certain stated terms, thereby inducing the band to alter its legal position by surrendering the land, and then simply ignore that promise to the band's detriment: see, *e.g.*, *Central London Property Trust Ltd.* v. *High Trees House Ltd.*, [1947] 1 K.B. 130; *Robertson* v. *Minister of Pensions*, [1949] 1 K.B. 227 (C.A.).

In obtaining without consultation a much less valuable lease than that promised, the Crown breached the fiduciary obligation it owed the band. It must make good the loss suffered in consequence.

6. Limitation of Action and Laches

The Crown contends that the band's claim is barred by the *Statute of Limitations*, R.S.B.C. 1960, c. 370, because it was not filed by January 22, 1964, six years from the date the lease was signed. The trial judge, however, found that the band and its members were not aware of the actual terms of the lease, and therefore of the breach of fiduciary duty, until March of 1970. This was not for lack of effort on the band's part. The Indian Affairs Branch, in conformity with its then policy, had refused to give a copy of the lease to the band, despite repeated requests.

It is well established that where there has been a fraudulent concealment of the existence of a cause of action, the limitation period will not start to run until the plaintiff discovers the fraud, or until the time when, with reasonable diligence, he ought to have discovered it. The fraudulent concealment necessary to toll or suspend the operation of the statute need not amount to deceit or common law fraud. Equitable fraud, defined in *Kitchen* v. *Royal Air Force Ass'n et al.*, [1958] 1 W.L.R. 563 at p. 573, as "conduct which, having regard to some special relationship between the two parties concerned, is an unconscionable thing for the one to do towards the other", is sufficient. I agree with the trial judge that the conduct of the Indian Affairs Branch toward the band amounted to equitable fraud. Although the branch officials did not act dishonestly or for improper motives in concealing the terms of the lease from the band, in my view their conduct was nevertheless unconscionable, having regard to the fiduciary relationship between the branch and the band. The limitations period did not therefore start to run until March, 1970. The action was thus timely when filed on December 22, 1975.

Little need be said about the Crown's alternative contention that the band's claim is barred by laches. Since the conduct of the Indian Affairs Branch personnel amounted to equitable fraud; since the band did not have actual or constructive knowledge of the actual terms of the golf club lease until March, 1970; and since the Crown was not prejudiced by reason of the delay between March, 1970, until suit was filed in December, 1975, there is no ground for application of the equitable doctrine of laches.

7. Measure of Damages

In my opinion the quantum of damages is to be determined by analogy with the principles of trust law: see, *e.g.*, *West of England and South Wales District Bank, Ex p. Dale & Co.* (1879), 11 Ch. D. 772 at p. 778. Reviewing the record it seems apparent that the judge at trial considered all the relevant evidence. His judgment, as I read it, discloses no error in principle. I am content to adopt the quantum of damages awarded by the judge, rejecting, as he did, any claim for exemplary or punitive damages.

I would therefore allow the appeal, set aside the judgment in the Federal Court of Appeal and reinstate without variation the trial judge's award, with costs to the present appellants in all courts.

. . . . .

WILSON J.: — . . .

In any case of alleged breach of trust the facts are extremely important and none more so than in this case. We are fortunate, however, in having very careful and extensive findings by the learned trial judge and, although counsel on both sides roamed at large through the transcript for evidence in support of their various propositions, I have considered it desirable to confine myself very closely to the trial judge's findings.

2. *Section 18 of the Indian Act*

The appellants contend that the Federal Court of Appeal erred in failing to find that s. 18 of the *Indian Act* imposed on the Crown a fiduciary obligation enforceable in the courts. The section reads as follows: . . .

Mr. Justice Le Dain, after concluding on the authorities that there was nothing in principle to prevent the Crown from having the status of a trustee in equity, found that s. 18 nevertheless did not have that effect. It merely imposed on the Crown a governmental obligation of an administrative nature. It was a public law obligation rather than a private law obligation. Section 18 could not therefore afford a basis for an action for breach of trust.

While I am in agreement that s. 18 does not *per se* create a fiduciary obligation in the Crown with respect to Indian reserves, I believe that it recognizes the existence of such an obligation. The obligation has its roots in the aboriginal title of Canada's Indians as discussed in *Calder et al.* v. *A.-G.*

B.C. (1973), 34 D.L.R. (3d) 145. In that case the court did not find it necessary to define the precise nature of Indian title because the issue was whether or not it had been extinguished. However, in *St. Catherine's Milling & Lumber Co. v. The Queen* (1888), 14 App. Cas. 46, Lord Watson, speaking for the Privy Council, had stated at p. 54 that "the tenure of the indians [is] a personal and usufructuary right". That description of the Indian's interest in reserve lands was approved by this court most recently in *Smith et al.* v. *The Queen* (1983), 147 D.L.R. (3d) 237. It should be noted that no constitutional issue such as arose in the *St. Catherine's* and *Smith* cases arises in this case since title to Indian reserve land in British Columbia was transferred to the Crown in right of Canada in 1938: see British Columbia Orders in Council 208 and 1036 passed pursuant to art. 13 of the Terms of Union of 1870 (see R.S.C. 1970, App. II, No. 10).

I think that when s. 18 mandates that reserves be held by the Crown for the use and benefit of the bands for which they are set apart, this is more than just an administrative direction to the Crown. I think it is the acknowledgment of a historic reality, namely, that Indian bands have a beneficial interest in their reserves and that the Crown has a responsibility to protect that interest and make sure that any purpose to which reserve land is put will not interfere with it. This is not to say that the Crown either historically or by s. 18 holds the land in trust for the bands. The bands do not have the fee in the lands; their interest is a limited one. But it is an interest which cannot be derogated from or interfered with by the Crown's utilization of the land for purposes incompatible with the Indian title unless, of course, the Indians agree. I believe that in this sense the Crown has a fiduciary obligation to the Indian bands with respect to the uses to which reserve land may be put and that s. 18 is a statutory acknowledgment of that obligation. It is my view, therefore, that while the Crown does not hold reserve land under s. 18 of the Act in trust for the bands because the bands' interests are limited by the nature of Indian title, it does hold the lands subject to a fiduciary obligation to protect and preserve the bands' interests from invasion or destruction.

The respondent submits, however, that any obligation imposed on the Crown by s. 18(1) of the *Indian Act* is political only and unenforceable in courts of equity. Section 18, he says, gives rise to a "trust in the higher sense" as discussed in *Kinloch* v. *Secretary of State for India in Council* (1882), 7 App. Cas. 619 (H.L.), and *Tito* v. *Waddell (No. 2)*, [1977] 3 All E.R. 129 (Ch.). Mr. Justice Le Dain, delivering the judgment of the Federal Court of Appeal, adopted this approach. He expressed the view [at p. 467 D.L.R.] that these cases indicate that "in a public law context neither the use of the words 'in trust' nor the fact that the property is to be held or dealt with in some manner for the benefit of others is conclusive of an intention to create a true trust". He found that the discretion conferred on the Crown by s. 18(1) evidenced an intention to exclude the equitable jurisdiction of the courts.

With respect, while I agree with the learned justice that s. 18 does not go so far as to create a trust of reserve lands for the reasons I have given, it does not, in my opinion, exclude the equitable jurisdiction of the courts. The discretion conferred on the Governor in Council is not an unfettered one to decide the use to which reserve lands may be put. It is to decide whether any use to which they are proposed to be put is "for the use and benefit of the band". This discretionary power must be exercised on proper principles and not in an arbitrary fashion. It is not, in my opinion, open to the Governor in Council to determine that a use of the land which defeats Indian title and affords the band nothing in return is a "purpose" which could be "for the use and benefit of the band". To so interpret the concluding part of s. 18 is to deprive the opening part of any substance.

Moreover, I do not think we are dealing with a purely public law context here. Mr. Justice Le Dain agrees that a band has a beneficial interest in its reserve. I believe it is clear from s. 18 that that interest is to be respected and this is enough to make the so-called "political trust" cases inapplicable.

In *Kinloch, supra*, in which Lord Selborne L.C. first advanced the idea of the political trust, the issue was whether a royal warrant that "granted" booty of war to the respondent Secretary of State for India "in trust" for the officers and men of certain forces created a trust enforceable in the courts. It was held that it did not, the effect of the warrant being to constitute the Secretary of State an agent of the Crown for the distribution of the booty rather than a trustee. In *Civilian War Claimants Ass'n Ltd.* v. *The King*, [1932] A.C. 14, the plaintiffs, as the assignees of civilian claimants who had suffered loss at the hands of the Germans during World War I, alleged *inter alia*, that money received by the Crown as war reparations from Germany pursuant to treaty was being held for the claimants on trust. Their claim was rejected by the House of Lords. In *Hereford R. Co.* v. *The Queen* (1894), 24 S.C.R. 1, money alleged by the plaintiff railway to have been granted by the Legislature as a subsidy was held not to be subject to a trust enforceable in the courts. In all these cases the funds at issue were the property of the Crown (or, at least, as in *Kinloch*, in the possession of the Crown) and none of those laying claim to them as beneficiaries could show a right to share in the funds independent of the treaty, statute or other instrument alleged to give rise to an enforceable trust.

In *Tito* v. *Waddell, supra*, the plaintiff Banaban Islanders asserted that certain royalties payable to the local government commissioner as a result of mining operations on their land gave rise to trusts in their favour. In rejecting their claims on the basis of a number of different considerations, Megarry V.-C. found at pp. 225-6 that there was not a sufficient relationship between the land on which the mining operations took place and the royalties to give rise to a fair inference that a true trust of the royalties was intended. The royalties were exclusively Crown property and the fact that the Banaban Islanders owned the land did not give them an interest in the royalties. I believe it is implicit in Megarry V.-C.'s reasons that if the Banaban Islanders could have shown an interest in the royalties themselves, a stronger case would have arisen in favour of a trust.

It seems to me that the "political trust" line of authorities are clearly distinguishable from the present case because Indian title has an existence apart altogether from s. 18(1) of the *Indian Act*. It would fly in the face of the clear wording of the section to treat that interest as terminable at will by the Crown without recourse by the band.

Continuing with the analysis of s. 18, it seems to me clear from the wording of the section that the Governor in Council's authority to determine in good faith whether any purpose to which reserve lands are proposed to be put is for the use and benefit of the band is "subject . . . to the terms of any treaty or surrender". I take this to mean that if a band surrenders its beneficial interest in reserve lands for a specific purpose, then the Governor in Council's authority under the section to decide whether or not the purpose is for the use and benefit of the band is pre-empted. The band has itself agreed to the purpose and the Crown may rely upon that agreement. It will be necessary to consider this in greater detail in connection with the surrender which in fact took place in this case.

3. *The failure to plead the defence of "political trust"*

The second ground of appeal put forward by the appellants concerns the fact that the defence of "political trust", which was accepted by the Federal Court of Appeal and formed the basis of its decision, was not specifically pleaded as required by Rule 409 of the *Federal Court Rules*.

I need say very little about this ground since I think the case falls to be decided on the substantive rather than the procedural issues. However, I agree with the appellants' submission that the Crown's tactics in this regard left a lot to be desired. It is quite apparent that when the trial judge indicated a willingness to permit an amendment at trial but went on to order discovery on the issue, the Crown renounced the defence both at trial and through ministerial statements made out of court. It nevertheless went ahead and sought and obtained leave to raise it in the Federal Court of Appeal. Even although, as the Court of Appeal pointed out, the defence is a strictly legal one and the band was probably not prejudiced by the absence of discovery, the Crown's behaviour does not, in my view, exemplify the high standard of professionalism we have come to expect in the conduct of litigation.

4. *The surrender*

Reference has already been made to the language of s. 18 and in particular to the fact that the Crown's fiduciary duty under it is "subject . . . to the terms of any . . . surrender". The implications of this have to be considered in the context of the learned trial judge's finding that the band surrendered the 162 acres to the Crown for lease to the golf club on specific terms which were not obtained. The trial judge found that the surrender itself created a trust relationship between the Crown and the band. The subject of the trust, the trust *res*, was not the band's beneficial interest in the land but the land itself. The

Crown prior to the surrender had title to the land subject to the Indian title. When the band surrendered the land to the Crown, the band's interest merged in the fee. The Crown then held the land free of the Indian title but subject to the trust for lease to the golf club on the terms approved by the band at its meeting on October 6, 1957. This trust was breached by the Crown when it leased the land to the club on terms much less favourable to the band.

It was submitted on behalf of the Crown that even if the surrender gave rise to a trust between the Crown and the band, the terms of the trust must be found in the surrender document and it was silent both as to the lessee and the terms of the lease. Indeed, it expressly gave the government complete discretion both as to the lessee and the terms of the lease and contained a ratification by the band of any lease the government might enter into.

I cannot accept the Crown's submission. The Crown was well aware that the terms of the lease were important to the band. Indeed, we have the trial judge's finding that the band would not have surrendered the land for the purpose of a lease on the terms obtained by the Crown. It ill becomes the Crown, therefore, to obtain a surrender of the band's interest for lease on terms voted on and approved by the band members at a meeting specially called for the purpose and then assert an overriding discretion to ignore those terms at will: see *Robertson* v. *Minister of Pensions*, [1949] 1 K.B. 227; *Lever Finance Ltd.* v. *Westminster (City) London Borough Council*, [1971] 1 Q.B. 222 (C.A.). It makes a mockery of the band's participation. The Crown well knew that the lease it made with the golf club was not the lease the band surrendered its interest to get. Equity will not permit the Crown in such circumstances to hide behind the language of its own document.

I return to s. 18. What effect does the surrender of the 162 acres to the Crown in trust for lease on specific terms have on the Crown's fiduciary duty under the section? It seems to me that s. 18 presents no barrier to a finding that the Crown became a full-blown trustee by virtue of the surrender. The surrender prevails over the s. 18 duty but in this case there is no incompatibility between them. Rather the fiduciary duty which existed at large under the section to hold the land in the reserve for the use and benefit of the band crystallized upon the surrender into an express trust of specific land for a specific purpose.

There is no magic to the creation of a trust. A trust arises, as I understand it, whenever a person is compelled in equity to hold property over which he has control for the benefit of others (the beneficiaries) in such a way that the benefit of the property accrues not to the trustee, but to the beneficiaries. I think that in the circumstances of this case as found by the learned trial judge the Crown was compelled in equity upon the surrender to hold the surrendered land in trust for the purpose of the lease which the band members had approved as being for their benefit. The Crown was no longer free to decide that a lease on some other terms would do. Its hands were tied.

What then should the Crown have done when the Golf Club refused to enter into a lease on the approved terms? It seems to me that it should have returned to the band and told them. It was certainly not open to it at that point of time to go ahead with the less favourable lease on the basis that the Governor in Council considered it for the benefit of the band. The Governor in Council's discretion in that regard was pre-empted by the surrender. I think the learned trial judge was right in finding that the Crown acted in breach of trust when it barrelled ahead with a lease on terms which, according to the learned trial judge, were wholly unacceptable to its *cestui que trust*.

5. *The claim of deceit*

The appellants base their claim against the Crown in deceit as well as in trust. They were unsuccessful on this aspect of their claim at trial but have raised it again on appeal to this court. While the learned trial judge found that the conduct of the Indian Affairs personnel amounted to equitable fraud, it was not such as to give rise to an action for deceit at common law. He found no dishonesty or moral turpitude on the part of Mr. Anfield, Mr. Arneil and the others. Their failure to go back to the band and indicate that the terms it had approved were unobtainable, their entry into the lease on less favourable terms and their failure to report to the band what those terms were, all flowed, he found, from their paternalistic attitude to the band rather than from any intent to deceive them or cause them harm.

Nevertheless, there was a concealment amounting to equitable fraud. It was "conduct which, having regard to some special relationship between the two parties concerned, is an unconscionable thing for the one to do towards the other": *Kitchen* v. *Royal Air Force Ass'n et al.*, [1958] 1 W.L.R. 563, *per* Lord Evershed M.R. at p. 573. The effect of the finding of equitable fraud was to disentitle the Crown to relief for breach of trust under s. 98 of the *Trustee Act*, R.S.B.C. 1960, c. 390 (now R.S.B.C. 1979, c. 414). A trustee cannot be exonerated from liability for breach of trust under that section unless he has acted "honestly and reasonably".

The trial judge's findings on this aspect of the band's claim are, I believe, sufficient to dispose of this ground of appeal.

.   .   .   .   .

Disposition

For the reasons given, I would allow the appeal, set aside the judgment of the Federal Court of Appeal and reinstate the judgment of the learned trial judge. I would award the appellants their costs both here and in the Federal Court of Appeal.

> Editor: Mr. Justice Estey concurred in the result but relied solely on agency principles. Three judges concurred in the opinion of Dickson J. while two judges concurred with Wilson J. resulting in no clear majority decision despite the unanimous finding for the Plaintiff.

Simon v. The Queen
(1986) 24 D.L.R. (4th) 390 (S.C.C.)

Ed. Note: Mr. Simon was charged with violating a provincial statute by having a rifle and shotgun shells in his possession during a closed season. He was arrested while driving on a public road adjacent to the Reserve of the Shubenacadie Band, of which he was a member. He was convicted at trial and lost on appeal.

The judgment of the court was delivered by

DICKSON C.J.C.: — This case raises the important question of the interplay between the treaty rights of native peoples and provincial legislation. The right to hunt, which remains important to the livelihood and way of life of the Micmac people, has come into conflict with game preservation legislation in effect in the province of Nova Scotia. The main question before this Court is whether, pursuant to a Treaty of 1752 between the British Crown and the Micmac, and to s. 88 of the *Indian Act*, R.S.C. 1970, c. I-6, the appellant, James Matthew Simon, enjoys hunting rights which preclude his prosecution for offences under the *Lands and Forests Act*, R.S.N.S. 1967, c. 163. . . .

Although all essential elements of the charges were admitted by Simon, it was argued on his behalf at trial that the right to hunt set out in the Treaty of 1752, in combination with s. 88 of the *Indian Act*, offered him immunity from prosecution under s. 150(1) of the *Lands and Forests Act*. . . .

The Treaty of 1752, the relevant part of which states at art. 4 that the Micmacs have "free liberty of hunting and Fishing as usual", provides: [see Chapter 4, pp. 189-191]

II

Lower court judgments

Nova Scotia provincial court

For the purposes of his decision, Judge Kimball assumed that the 1752 document was a valid treaty and that the appellant was entitled to claim its protection as a direct descendant of the original Micmac Indian Band. Nevertheless, he convicted the appellant. His conclusion, based largely upon *R. v. Isaac* (1975), 13 N.S.R. (2d) 460 (N.S.S.C.A.D.), is best summarized in his own words:

I am satisfied that any right which the defendant may have to hunt off the reserve is not applicable to the area where the offence took place. It is my opinion that any right which the defendant may have to hunt on that said land has been extinguished "by Crown grant to others or by occupation by the white man." . . . I am prepared to take judicial notice of the fact that the area is made up of land where the right to hunt no longer exists because the land has been settled and occupied by the white man for purposes of farming and that the Crown grants have been extended to farmers for some considerable length of time so that any right which might have at one time existed to the defendant or his ancestors, to use or occupy the said lands for purposes of hunting, has long since been extinguished.

Nova Scotia Supreme Court, Appellate Division

. . . . .

MacDonald J.A. (Hart J.A. concurring) rejected, on three grounds, the appellant's argument that the Treaty of 1752 was a treaty within s. 88 of the *Indian Act*, thus rendering the appellant immune from the provisions of the *Lands and Forests Act*.

First, he concluded that the Treaty of 1752 provided no positive source of protection for hunting rights. On this point, MacDonald J.A. cited *R. v. Cope* (1981), 132 D.L.R. (3d) 36 (N.S.S.C.A.D.), where MacKeigan C.J.N.S. found that the clause recognizing the liberty to hunt and fish in the Treaty of 1752 was [at p. 42 D.L.R.] "very far short in words and substance from being a grant by the Crown of a special franchise or privilege replacing the more nebulous aboriginal rights" and that the document could not "be considered a treaty granting or conferring new permanent rights".

Secondly, MacDonald J.A. held that even if the treaty were valid at one time, it was effectively terminated in 1753 when the Micmac chief, Major Jean Baptiste Cope, and his band killed six Englishmen at Jeddore. MacDonald J.A. noted that the treaty was one of peace and that the resumption of hostilities by the Indians in Nova Scotia terminated automatically, and for all time, any obligations to them under the treaty.

Finally, MacDonald J.A. stated that even if he were wrong in his conclusion that the treaty was terminated by the actions of the Indians, the appellant could not, in any event, claim the protection of the treaty because he had not established any connection by "descent or otherwise" with the original group of Indians.

In a concurring judgment, Jones J.A. added that it was clear from the case-law, in particular *R. v. Isaac, supra*, that any rights of Indians to hunt and fish under the terms of "any treaty or otherwise" had been restricted to reserve lands. Furthermore, Jones J.A. held that, in claiming the exemption from the application of the general laws of the province under s. 88 of the *Indian Act*, the burden was on the appellant to show that he was exercising a right to "hunt . . . as usual" under the treaty. This, in his view, had not been done.

The appeal was accordingly dismissed and the convictions were affirmed.

III

The issues

This appeal raises the following issues:

1. Was the Treaty of 1752 validly created by competent parties?
2. Does the treaty contain a right to hunt and what is the nature and scope of this right?
3. Has the treaty been terminated or limited?
4. Is the appellant covered by the treaty?
5. Is the treaty a "treaty" within the meaning of s. 88 of the *Indian Act*?
6. Do the hunting rights contained in the treaty exempt the appellant from prosecution under s. 150(1) of the *Lands and Forests Act*?

. . . . .

In his factum, the appellant asks this Court to dispose of the appeal on the sole basis of the effect of the Treaty of 1752 and s. 88 of the *Indian Act*. Therefore, if the treaty does not exempt the appellant from s. 150(1) of the *Lands and Forests Act*, he requests that the appeal be dismissed without prejudice to the Micmac position based on other treaties and aboriginal rights. The respondent agreed with this approach. I will, therefore, restrict my remarks to the Treaty of 1752 and s. 88 of the *Indian Act*. It will be unnecessary to deal with aboriginal rights, the Royal Proclamation of 1763, or other treaty rights.

IV

Was the Treaty of 1752 validly created by competent parties?

The respondent raised the issue of the capacity of the parties for two reasons which are stated at p. 8 of the factum:

> The issue of capacity is raised for the purpose of illustrating that the Treaty of 1752 was of a lesser status than an International Treaty and therefore is more easily terminated. The issue is also raised to give the document an historical legal context as this issue has been raised in previous cases.

The question of whether the Treaty of 1752 constitutes an international-type treaty is only relevant to the respondent's argument regarding the appropriate legal tests for the termination of the treaty. I will address this issue, therefore, in relation to the question of whether the Treaty of 1752 was terminated by hostilities between the British and the Micmac in 1753.

The historical legal context provided by the respondent consists primarily of the 1929 decision of Judge Patterson in *R.* v. *Syliboy*, [1929] 1 D.L.R. 307 (Co. Ct.) and the academic commentary it generated immediately following its rendering. In the *Syliboy* case Judge Patterson addressed the question of the capacity of the parties to enter into a treaty at pp. 313-4 D.L.R.:

> Two considerations are involved. First, did the Indians of Nova Scotia have status to enter into a treaty? And second, did Governor Hopson have authority to enter into one with them? Both questions must I think be answered in the negative.
>
> (1) "Treaties are unconstrained Acts of independent powers". But the Indians were never regarded as an independent power. A civilized nation first discovering a country of uncivilized people or savages held such country as its own until such time as by treaty it was transferred to some other civilized nation. The savages' rights of sovereignty even of ownership were never recognized. Nova Scotia had passed to Great Britain not by gift or purchase from or even by conquest of the Indians but by treaty with France, which had acquired it by priority of discovery and ancient possession; and the Indians passed with it.
>
> Indeed the very fact that certain Indians sought from the Governor the privilege or right to hunt in Nova Scotia as usual shows that they did not claim to be an independent nation owning or possessing their lands. If they were, why go to another nation asking this privilege or right and giving promise of good behaviour that they might obtain it? In my judgment the Treaty of 1752 is not a treaty at all and is not to be treated as such; it is at best a mere agreement made by the Governor and council with a handful of Indians giving them in return for good behaviour food, presents, and the right to hunt and fish as usual — an agreement that, as we have seen, was very shortly after broken.
>
> (2) Did Governor Hopson have authority to make a treaty? I think not. "Treaties can be made only by the constituted authorities of nations or by persons specially deputed by them for that purpose." Clearly our treaty was not made with the constituted authorities of Great Britain. But was Governor Hopson specially deputed by them? Cornwallis' commission is the manual not only for himself but for his successors and you will search it in vain for any power to sign treaties.

It should be noted that the language used by Patterson J., illustrated in this passage, reflects the biases and prejudices of another era in our history. Such language is no longer acceptable in Canadian law and, indeed, is inconsistent with a growing sensitivity to native rights in Canada. With regard to the substance of Judge Patterson's words, leaving aside for the moment the question of whether treaties are international-type documents, his conclusions on capacity are not convincing.

No court, with the exception of the Nova Scotia Supreme Court, Appeal Division in the present case, has agreed explicitly with the conclusion of Judge Patterson that the Indians and Governor Hopson lacked capacity to enter into an enforceable treaty. The Treaty of 1752 was implicitly assumed to have been validly created in *R*. v. *Simon* (1958), 124 C.C.C. 110 (N.B.S.C.A.D.); *R*. v. *Francis*, [1970] 3 C.C.C. 165 (N.B.S.C.A.D.); *R*. v. *Paul* (1980), 54 C.C.C. (2d) 506 (C.A.); *R*. v. *Cope, supra*; *R*. v. *Atwin and Sacobie*, [1981] 2 C.N.L.R. 99 (N.B. Prov. Ct.); *R*. v. *Secretary of State for Foreign and Commonwealth Affairs, Ex p. Indian Ass'n of Alberta et al.*, [1982] 2 All E.R. 118 (C.A.); *R*. v. *Paul and Polchies* (1984), 58 N.B.R. (2d) 297 (Prov. Ct.). In *R*. v. *Isaac, supra*, Cooper J.A., after noting Judge Patterson's conclusions on the validity of the Treaty of 1752, expressed doubt as to their correctness, at p. 496:

> The *Treaty of 1752* was considered in *Rex* v. *Syliboy*. . . . It was there held by Patterson, Acting C.C.J., that it did not extend to Cape Breton Indians and further that it was not in reality a treaty. I have doubt as to the second finding and express no opinion on it, but I have doubt as to the correctness of the first finding.

N.A.M. MacKenzie, in "Indians and Treaties in Law", 7 Can. Bar. Rev. 561 (1929), disagreed with Judge Patterson's ruling that the Indians did not have the capacity, nor the Governor the authority, to conclude a valid treaty. MacKenzie stated at p. 565:

> As to the capacity of the Indians to contract and the authority of Governor Hopson to enter into such an agreement, with all deference to His Honour, both seem to have been present. Innumerable treaties and agreements of a similar character were made by Great Britain, France, the United States of America and Canada with the Indian tribes inhabiting this continent, and these treaties and agreements have been and still are held to be binding. Nor would Governor Hopson require special "powers" to enter into such an agreement. Ordinarily "full powers" specially conferred are essential to the proper negotiating of a treaty, but the Indians were not on a par with a sovereign state and fewer formalities were required in their case. Governor Hopson was the representative of His Majesty and as such had sufficient authority to make an agreement with the Indian tribes.

The treaty was entered into for the benefit of both the British Crown and the Micmac people, to maintain peace and order as well as to recognize and confirm the existing hunting and fishing rights of the Micmac. In my opinion, both the Governor and the Micmac entered into the treaty with the intention of creating mutually binding obligations which would be solemnly respected. It also provided a mechanism for dispute resolution. The Micmac Chief and the three other Micmac signatories, as delegates of the Micmac people, would have possessed full capacity to enter into a binding treaty on behalf of the Micmac. Governor Hopson was the delegate and legal representative of His Majesty the King. It is fair to assume that the Micmac would have believed that Governor Hopson, acting on behalf of His Majesty the King, had the necessary authority to enter into a valid treaty with them. I would hold that the Treaty of 1752 was validly created by competent parties.

V

Does the treaty contain a right to hunt and what is the nature and scope of this right?

Article 4 of the Treaty of 1752 states, "it is agreed that the said Tribe of Indians shall not be hindered from, but have free liberty of hunting and Fishing as usual . . .''. What is the nature and scope of the "liberty of hunting and Fishing" contained in the treaty?

The majority of the Nova Scotia Court of Appeal seemed to imply that the treaty contained merely a general acknowledgement of pre-existing non-treaty aboriginal rights and not an independent source of protection of hunting rights upon which the appellant could rely. In my opinion, the treaty, by providing that the Micmac should not be hindered from but should have free liberty of hunting and fishing as usual, constitutes a positive source of protection against infringements on hunting rights. The fact that the right to hunt already existed at the time the treaty was entered into by virtue of the Micmac's general aboriginal right to hunt does not negate or minimize the significance of the protection of hunting rights expressly included in the treaty.

Such an interpretation accords with the generally accepted view that Indian treaties should be given a fair, large and liberal construction in favour of the Indians. This principle of interpretation was most recently affirmed by this Court in *Nowegijick* v. *The Queen* (1983), 144 D.L.R. (3d) 193. I had occasion to say the following at p. 198 D.L.R.:

> It is legal lore that, to be valid, exemptions to tax laws should be clearly expressed. It seems to me, however, that treaties and statutes relating to Indians should be liberally construed and doubtful expressions resolved in favour of the Indian . . . In *Jones* v. *Meehan* (1899), 175 U.S. 1, it was held that
>
> > "Indian treaties must be construed not according to the technical meaning of their words, but in the sense that they would naturally be understood by the Indians."

Having determined that the treaty embodies a right to hunt, it is necessary to consider the respondent's contention that the right to hunt is limited to hunting for purposes and by methods usual in 1752 because of the inclusion of the modifier "as usual" after the right to hunt.

First of all, I do not read the phrase "as usual" as referring to the types of weapons to be used by the Micmac and limiting them to those used in 1752. Any such construction would place upon the ability of the Micmac to hunt an unnecessary and artificial constraint out of keeping with the principle that Indian treaties should be liberally construed. Indeed, the inclusion of the phrase "as usual" appears to reflect a concern that the right to hunt be interpreted in a flexible way that is sensitive to the evolution of changes in normal hunting practices. The phrase thereby ensures that the treaty will be an effective source of protection of hunting rights.

Secondly, the respondent maintained that "as usual" should be interpreted to limit the treaty protection to hunting for non-commercial purposes. It is difficult to see the basis for this argument in the absence of evidence regarding the purpose for which the appellant was hunting. In any event, art. 4 of the treaty appears to contemplate hunting for commercial purposes when it refers to the construction of a truck house as a place of exchange and mentions the liberty of the Micmac to bring game to sale: see *R.* v. *Paul, supra*, at p. 519 C.C.C., *per* Ryan J.A., dissenting in part.

It should be clarified at this point that the right to hunt to be effective must embody those activities reasonably incidental to the act of hunting itself, an example of which is travelling with the requisite hunting equipment to the hunting grounds . . . In my opinion, it is implicit in the right granted under art. 4 of the Treaty of 1752 that the appellant has the right to possess a gun and ammunition in a safe manner in order to be able to exercise the right to hunt. Accordingly, I conclude that the appellant was exercising his right to hunt under the treaty.

VI

Has the treaty been terminated or limited?

(a) *Termination by hostilities*

In accordance with the finding of the Nova Scotia Court of Appeal, the Crown argued that the Treaty of 1752 was terminated and rendered unenforceable when hostilities broke out between the Micmac and the British in 1753. The appellant maintained that the alleged hostilities were sporadic and minor in nature and did not, therefore, nullify or terminate the treaty. It was further argued by the appellant, relying on L.F.S Upton, *Micmac and Colonists: Indian — White Relations in the Maritimes 1713-1867* (1979), that the English initiated the hostilities and that, therefore, the Crown should not be permitted to rely on them to support the termination of the treaty. Finally, the appellant submitted that, even if the Court finds that there were sufficient hostilities to affect the treaty, at most it was merely suspended and not terminated.

In considering the impact of subsequent hostilities on the peace Treaty of 1752, the parties looked to international law on treaty termination. While it may be helpful in some instances to analogize the principles of international treaty law to Indian treaties, these principles are not determinative. An Indian treaty is unique; it is an agreement *sui generis* which is neither created nor terminated according to the rules of international law. *R.* v. *White and Bob* (1964), 50 D.L.R. (2d) 613 at pp. 617-8 (B.C.C.A.); affirmed (1965), 52

D.L.R. (2d) 481n (S.C.C.); *Francis* v. *The Queen* (1956), 3 D.L.R. (2d) 641 at p. 652; *Pawis* v. *The Queen and three other actions* (1979), 102 D.L.R. (3d) 602 at 607 (F.C.T.D.).

It may be that under certain circumstances a treaty could be terminated by the breach of one of its fundamental provisions. It is not necessary to decide this issue in the case at bar since the evidentiary requirements for proving such a termination have not been met. Once it has been established that a valid treaty has been entered into, the party arguing for its termination bears the burden of proving the circumstances and events justifying termination. The inconclusive and conflicting evidence presented by the parties makes it impossible for this Court to say with any certainty what happened on the eastern coast of Nova Scotia 233 years ago. As a result, the Court is unable to resolve this historical question. The Crown has failed to prove that the Treaty of 1752 was terminated by subsequent hostilities.

I would note that there is nothing in the British conduct subsequent to the conclusion of the Treaty of 1752 and the alleged hostilities to indicate that the Crown considered the terms of the treaty at an end. Indeed, His Majesty's Royal Instructions of December 9, 1761, addressed, *inter alia*, to the Governor of Nova Scotia, declared that the Crown "was determined upon all occasions to support and protect the . . . Indians in their just rights and possessions and to keep inviolable the treaties and compacts which have been entered into with them . . .". These royal instructions formed the basis of the proclamation issued by Jonathan Belcher, Lieutenant-Governor of Nova Scotia on May 4, 1762, which also repeated the above words.

I conclude from the foregoing that the Treaty of 1752 was not terminated by subsequent hostilities in 1753. The treaty is of as much force and effect today as it was at the time it was concluded.

(b) *Termination by extinguishment*

The respondent's argument that the Treaty of 1752 has been extinguished is based on *R.* v. *Isaac, supra*, at pp. 476, 479; *Calder et al.* v. *A.-G. B.C.* (1973), 34 D.L.R. (3d) 145 at p. 151; *United States* v. *Sante Fe Pacific Ry. Co.* (1941), 314 U.S. 339 at p. 347; *Johnson and Grahams Lessee* v. *McIntosh* (1823), 21 U.S. 543 at pp. 586-8, and *Worcester* v. *Georgia* (1832), 31 U.S. 515. The respondent submits that absolute title in the land covered by the treaty lies with the Crown and, therefore, the Crown has the right to extinguish any Indian rights in such lands. The respondent further submits, based on *Isaac*, that the Crown, through occupancy by the white man under Crown grant or lease, has, in effect, extinguished native rights in Nova Scotia in terrritory situated outside of reserve lands. As the appellant was stopped on a highway outside the Shubenacadie Reserve, the respondent argues that the Treaty of 1752 affords no defence to the appellant regardless of whether the treaty is itself valid.

In my opinion, it is not necessary to come to a final decision on the respondent's argument. Given the serious and far-reaching consequences of a finding that a treaty right has been extinguished, it seems appropriate to demand strict proof of the fact of extinguishment in each case where the issue arises. As Douglas J. said in *United States* v. *Sante Fe Pacific Ry. Co.*, *supra*, at p. 354, "extinguishment cannot be lightly implied".

The respondent tries to meet the apparent right of the appellant to transport a gun and ammunition by asserting that the treaty hunting rights have been extinguished. In order to succeed on this argument it is absolutely essential, it seems to me, that the respondent lead evidence as to where the appellant hunted or intended to hunt and what use has been and is currently made of those lands. It is impossible for this Court to consider the doctrine of extinguishment "in the air"; the respondent must anchor that argument in the bedrock of specific lands. That has not happened in this case. In the absence of evidence as to where the hunting occurred or was intended to occur, and the use of the lands in question, it would be impossible to determine whether the appellant's treaty hunting rights have been extinguished. Moreover, it is unnecessary for this Court to determine whether those rights have been extinguished because, at the very least, these rights extended to the adjacent Shubenacadie reserve. I do not wish to be taken as expressing any view on whether, as a matter of law, treaty rights may be extinguished.

VII

Is the appellant an Indian covered by the treaty?

The respondent argues that the appellant has not shown that he is a direct descendant of a member of the original Micmac Indian Band covered by the Treaty of 1752. The trial judge assumed that the appellant was a direct descendant of the Micmac Indians, parties to the treaty. The Nova Scotia Supreme Court, Appellate Division, on the other hand, relied on the decision of the New Brunswick Court of Appeal in *R.* v. *Simon*, *supra*, and held that the appellant had not established any connection by "descent or otherwise" with the original group of Micmac Indians inhabiting the eastern part of Nova Scotia in the Shubenacadie area.

With respect, I do not agree with the Appellate Division on this point. In my view, the appellant has established a sufficient connection with the Indian band, signatories to the Treaty of 1752. . . .

This evidence alone, in my view, is sufficient to prove the appellant's connection to the tribe originally covered by the treaty. True, this evidence is not conclusive proof that the appellant is a *direct* descendant of the Micmac Indians covered by the Treaty of 1752. It must, however, be sufficient, for otherwise no Micmac Indian would be able to establish descendancy. The Micmacs did not keep written records. Micmac traditions are largely oral in nature. To impose an impossible burden of proof would, in effect, render nugatory any right to hunt that a present-day Shubenacadie Micmac Indian would otherwise be entitled to invoke based on this treaty.

The appellant, Simon, as a member of the Shubenacadie Indian Brook Band of Micmac Indians, residing in Eastern Nova Scotia, the area covered by the Treaty of 1752, can therefore raise the treaty in his defence.

VIII

Is the treaty a "treaty" within the meaning of s. 88 of the Indian Act?

. . . . .

The majority of the Appellate Division held that it was extremely doubtful whether the Treaty of 1752 was a "treaty" within the meaning of s. 88, primarily because it was merely a general confirmation of aboriginal rights and did not grant or confer "new permanent rights". MacDonald J.A. also concluded that the 1752 document could not be considered a "treaty" under s. 88 because it was made by only a small portion of the Micmac Nation and it did not define any land or area where the rights were to be exercised. The respondent urges these views upon this Court. The respondent further submits that the word "treaty" in s. 88 of the *Indian Act* does not include the Treaty of 1752 even under the extended definition of "treaty" enunciated in *R. v. White and Bob*, *supra*, because the treaty did not deal with the ceding of land or delineation of boundaries.

Most of these arguments have already been addressed in this judgment and can be dealt with briefly at this point. To begin, the fact that the treaty did not *create* new hunting or fishing rights but merely *recognized* pre-existing rights does not render s. 88 inapplicable. On this point, Davey J.A. stated in *R. v. White and Bob*, *supra*, at p. 616:

> The force of the first argument seems to depend upon the assumption that s. 87 [now s. 88] should be read as if it were subject only to rights created by a Treaty; that would remove from the saving clause rights already in being and excepted from or confirmed by a Treaty. That argument fails to accord full meaning to the words, "subject to the *terms* of any treaty . . ." *In my opinion an exception, reservation, or confirmation is as much a term of a Treaty as a grant*, (I observe parenthetically that a reservation may be a grant), and the operative words of the section will not extend general laws in force in any Province to Indians in derogation of rights so excepted, reserved or confirmed. (Emphasis added.)

This holding was followed by the New Brunswick Court of Appeal in *R. v. Paul*, *supra*: see also *R. v. Polchies and Paul* (1982), 43 N.B.R. (2d) 449 at p. 453 (C.A.). As I concluded earlier, the treaty was validly created by representatives of the Micmac people and it covers the territory of concern in this appeal.

With respect to the respondent's submission that some form of land cession is necessary before an agreement can be described as a treaty under s. 88, I can see no principled basis for interpreting s. 88 in this manner. I would adopt the useful comment of Norris J.A. of the British Columbia Court of Appeal in *R.* v. *White and Bob*, *supra*, affirmed on appeal to this Court. In a concurring judgment, he stated at pp. 648-9:

> The question is, in my respectful opinion, to be resolved not by the application of rigid rules of construction without regard to the circumstances existing when the document was completed nor by the tests of modern day draftsmanship. In determining what the intention of Parliament was at the time of the enactment of s. 87 [now s. 88] of the *Indian Act*, Parliament is to be taken to have had in mind the common understanding of the parties to the document at the time it was executed. In the section "Treaty" is not a word of art and in my respectful opinion, it embraces all such engagements made by persons in authority as may be brought within the term "the word of the white man" the sanctity of which was, at the time of British exploration and settlement, the most important means of obtaining the goodwill and co-operation of the native tribes and ensuring that the colonists would be protected from death and destruction. On such assurance the Indians relied.

In my view, Parliament intended to include within the operation of s. 88 all agreements concluded by the Crown with the Indians that would otherwise be enforceable treaties, whether land was ceded or not. None of the Maritime treaties of the eighteenth century cedes land. To find that s. 88 applies only to land cession treaties would be to limit severely its scope and run contrary to the principle that Indian treaties and statutes relating to Indians should be liberally construed and uncertainties resolved in favour of the Indians.

Finally, it should be noted that several cases have considered the Treaty of 1752 to be a valid "treaty" within the meaning of s. 88 of the *Indian Act* (for example, *R.* v. *Paul* and *R.* v. *Atwin and Sacobie*). The treaty was an exchange of solemn promises between the Micmacs and the King's representative entered into to achieve and guarantee peace. It is an enforceable obligation between the Indians and the white man and, as such, falls within the meaning of the word "treaty" in s. 88 of the *Indian Act*.

IX

Do the hunting rights contained in the treaty exempt the appellant from prosecution under s. 150(1) of the Lands and Forests Act?

As a result of my conclusion that the appellant was validly exercising his right to hunt under the Treaty of 1752 and the fact he has admitted that his conduct otherwise constitutes an offence under the *Lands and Forests Act*, it must now be determined what the result is when a treaty right comes into conflict with provincial legislation. This question is governed by s. 88 of the *Indian Act*, which, it will be recalled, states that "Subject to the terms of any treaty, all laws of general application . . . in force in the province are applicable to . . . Indians".

It is now clear that the words "all laws" in s. 88 refer to provincial legislation and not federal legislation. In *R. v. George*, [1966] 3 C.C.C. 137 at p. 151, Martland J. stated the following with respect to s. 88:

> This section was not intended to be a declaration of the paramountcy of treaties over Federal legislation. The reference to treaties was incorporated in a section the purpose of which was to make *provincial* laws applicable to Indians, *so as to preclude any interference with rights under treaties resulting from the impact of provincial legislation.* (Emphasis added.)

Under s. 88 of the *Indian Act*, when the terms of a treaty come into conflict with federal legislation, the latter prevails, subject to whatever may be the effect of s. 35 of the *Constitution Act, 1982*. It has been held to be within the exclusive power of Parliament under s. 91(24) of the *Constitution Act, 1867*, to derogate from rights recognized in a treaty agreement made with the Indians: see *R. v. Sikyea*, [1964] 2 C.C.C. 325; *R. v. George, supra*; *R. v. Cooper* (1968), 1 D.L.R. (3d) 113; *R. v. White and Bob*.

Here, however, we are dealing with provincial legislation. The effect of s. 88 of the *Indian Act* is to exempt the Indians from provincial legislation which restricts or contravenes the terms of any treaty. In *Frank v. The Queen* (1977), 75 D.L.R. (3d) 481 at p. 484, the Court held:

> The effect of this section is to make applicable to Indians except as stated, all laws of general application from time to time in force in any province, including provincial game laws, but subject to the terms of any treaty and subject also to any other Act of the Parliament of Canada.

Similarly, in *Kruger and Manuel v. The Queen* (1977), 75 D.L.R. (3d) 434 at p. 439, the Court held:

> However abundant the right of Indians to hunt and to fish, there can be no doubt that such right is subject to regulation and curtailment by the appropriate legislative authority. Section 88 of the *Indian Act* appears to be plain in purpose and effect. In the absence of treaty protection or statutory protection, Indians are brought within provincial regulatory legislation.

and at p. 441 D.L.R., the Court held in reference to Indian treaties and s. 88: "The terms of the treaty are paramount; in the absence of a treaty, provincial laws of general application apply."

Therefore, the question here is whether s. 150(1) of the *Lands and Forests Act*, a provincial enactment of general application in Nova Scotia, restricts or contravenes the right to hunt in art. 4 of the Treaty of 1752. If so, the treaty right to hunt prevails and the appellant is exempt from the operation of the provincial game legislation at issue. . . .

In my opinion, s. 150 . . . restricts the appellant's right to hunt under the treaty. The section clearly places seasonal limitations and licensing requirements, for the purposes of wildlife conservation, on the right to possess a rifle and ammunition for the purposes of hunting. The restrictions imposed in this case conflict, therefore, with the appellant's right to possess a firearm and ammunition in order to exercise his free liberty to hunt over the lands covered by the treaty. As noted, it is clear that under s. 88 of the *Indian Act* provincial legislation cannot restrict native treaty rights. If conflict arises, the terms of the treaty prevail. Therefore, by virtue of s. 88 of the *Indian Act*, the clear terms of art. 4 of the treaty must prevail over s. 150(1) of the provincial *Lands and Forests Act*.

Several cases have particular relevance. These also deal with charges similar to those in the present case where Indians were accused of unlawful possession of certain objects without the permit required under provincial legislation. In each case, the accused Indians raised their treaty rights in defence and it was held that they should be acquitted because they were not bound by the terms of the provincial statutes: see *R. v. White and Bob, supra*; *R. v. Paul, supra*; *R. v. Atwin and Sacobie, supra*; *R. v. Paul and Polchies, supra*; *R. v. Batisse* (1978), 19 O.R. (2d) 145 (Dist. Ct.); *R. v. Taylor and Williams* (1981), 62 C.C.C. (2d) 227 (Ont. C.A.); *R. v. Moses*, [1970] 5 C.C.C. 356 (Ont. Dist. Ct.); *R. v. Penasse and McLeod* (1971), 8 C.C.C. (2d) 569 (Ont. Prov. Ct.); *Cheeco v. The Queen*, [1981] 3 C.N.L.R. 45 (Ont. Dist. Ct.).

I conclude that the appellant has a valid treaty right to hunt under the Treaty of 1752 which, by virtue of s. 88 of the *Indian Act*, cannot be restricted by provincial legislation. It follows, therefore, that the appellant's possession of a rifle and ammunition in a safe manner, referable to his treaty right to hunt, cannot be restricted by s. 150(1) of the *Lands and Forests Act*.

I would accordingly quash the convictions and enter verdicts of acquittal on both charges. . . .

Conclusions

To summarize:

1. The Treaty of 1752 was validly created by competent parties.
2. The treaty contains a right to hunt which covers the activities engaged in by the appellant.
3. The treaty was not terminated by subsequent hostilities in 1753. Nor has it been demonstrated that the right to hunt protected by the treaty has been extinguished.
4. The appellant is a Micmac Indian covered by the treaty.
5. The Treaty of 1752 is a "treaty" within the meaning of s. 88 of the *Indian Act*.

6. By virtue of s. 88 of the *Indian Act*, the appellant is exempt from prosecution under s. 150(1) of the *Lands and Forests Act*.
7. In light of these conclusions, it is not necessary to answer the constitutional question raised in this appeal.

I would, therefore, allow the appeal, quash the convictions of the appellant and enter verdicts of acquittal on both charges.

Regina v. Eninew; Regina v. Bear
(1984) 10 D.L.R. (4th) 137 (Sask. C.A.)

Ed. Note: The following two cases were heard together and treated as one by the Saskatchewan Court of Appeal due to the similarities. Eninew was convicted of hunting migratory birds out of season while Bear was convicted of possessing two ducks out of season, both actions contrary to the federal *Migratory Birds Convention Act*. Each lost their separate appeals and appealed again. Both were status Indians with Eninew benefitting from Treaty No. 10 while Bear was entitled to rights under Treaty No. 6.

. . . . .

The judgment of the court was delivered by HALL J.A.

The appellants contend that they are not subject to the *Migratory Birds Convention Act* and the regulations passed there under because of s. 35 of the *Constitution Act, 1982*, which reads:. . . .

It is common ground that prior to the enactment of the *Constitution Act, 1982* the appellants, as treaty Indians, did not have the right to hunt contrary to the *Migratory Birds Convention Act*. This follows from such cases as *Sikyea* v. *The Queen*, [1965] 2 C.C.C. 129; *R.* v. *George*, [1966] 3 C.C.C. 137; *Daniels* v. *The Queen*, [1969] 1 C.C.C. 299; *R.* v. *Settee*, [1981] 2 W.W.R. 85; affirmed [1981] 4 W.W.R. 377.

The thrust of the appellants' argument is that the enactment of s. 35(1) of the *Constitution Act, 1982* made such cases inapplicable to this situation. They contend that the rights given by the respective treaties must stand as they did when the treaty was concluded, unmodified by subsequent jurisprudence.

At trial, it was held that the word "existing" as it appears in s. 35(1) of the *Constitution Act, 1982* has the effect of limiting the rights of the appellants to those which they actually enjoyed at the time when the *Constitution Act, 1982* came into effect, namely, April 17, 1982.

The pertinent clause of Treaty No. 6 reads as follows:

Her Majesty further agrees with her said Indians that they, the said Indians, shall have the right to pursue their avocations of hunting and fishing throughout the tract surrendered as hereinbefore described, subject to such regulations as may from time to time be made by Her Government of Her Dominion of Canada and saving and excepting such tracts as may from time to time be required or taken up for settlement, mining, lumbering or other purposes by Her said Government of the Dominion of Canada, or by any of the subjects thereof, duly authorized therefor by the said Government;

The corresponding clause in Treaty No. 10 reads:

And His Majesty the King hereby agrees with the said Indians that they shall have the right to pursue their usual vocations of hunting, trapping and fishing throughout the territory surrendered as heretofore described, subject to such regulations as may from time to time be made by the government of the country acting under the authority of His Majesty and saving and excepting such tracts as may be required or as may be taken up from time to time for settlement, mining, lumbering, trading or other purposes.

In one case, the word "avocations" is used and in the other, the word "vocations". In my opinion, nothing turns upon the differences in terms. The effect of each clause is the same.

In Eninew's case, it was agreed that his alleged offence took place on the tract surrendered pursuant to Treaty No. 10. No similar admission is made in the case of the appellant Bear. I will assume, however, for the purposes of this appeal that his alleged offence occurred on the tract surrendered under Treaty No. 6.

The facts do not establish whether either appellant was actually pursuing the "avocation" or the "vocation" of hunting. Again for the purposes of this appeal, I will assume that they were doing so.

In my opinion, it makes no difference to the outcome whether the reasons followed in the trial courts are adopted or whether, as the appellant contends, s. 35(1) of the *Constitution Act, 1982* recognizes and affirms the treaty rights as originally set out in the respective treaties. The rights so given were not unqualified or unconditional. In each case the right to pursue the avocation of hunting was subject to such regulations as may from time to time be made by the Government of Canada. Regulations made under the *Migratory Birds Convention Act* are the type of regulations which were contemplated in Treaties Nos. 6 and 10. The purpose of the *Migratory Birds Convention Act* is to conserve and preserve migratory birds, including mallard ducks. That purpose is of benefit to the appellants. Indeed, it was said that the Indians in general, and the appellants in particular, are concerned with and practise conservation. They would not hunt ducks during the summer nesting season. They would be affected by the regulations only during the "spring fly-in". They would accept as reasonable regulations such as those aimed at preserving the existence of the whooping crane.

It follows that the treaty rights can be limited by such regulations as are reasonable. The *Migratory Birds Convention Act* and the regulations made pursuant to it, based as they are on international convention, are reasonable, desirable limitations on the rights granted. That, in effect, is what was held in *Sikyea* v. *The Queen* and the other cases above noted.

The result is that the enactment of s. 35(1) of the *Constitution Act, 1982* does not exempt the appellants in this case from the operation of the *Migratory Birds Convention Act*.

The appeals are therefore dismissed.

Ed. Note: This decision was not appealed. For contrary conclusions see *R.* v. *Flett*, [1987] 3 C.N.L.R. 70 (Man. Prov. Ct.) and *R.* v. *Arcand*, [1989] 2. C.N.L.R. 110 (Alta. Q. B.).

Regina v. Sparrow
(1987) 36 D.L.R. (4th) 246 (B.C.C.A.)

Ed. Note: Mr. Sparrow, a member of the Musqueam Indian Band near Vancouver, was charged under s. 61(1) of the federal *Fisheries Act* for fishing with a drift net longer than that permitted by the Band's Indian food fishing licence on May 25, 1984. He admitted the actions that constitute the offence but asserted that the restriction violated his aboriginal right to fish as protected by s. 35(1) of the *Constitution Act, 1982* such that the limitation was of no force and effect. He was convicted by the Provincial Court and his appeal was dismissed by the County Court resulting in a further appeal. Expert evidence was adduced which indicated that the Coast Salish people had lived in this territory for at least 1500 years and that the salmon fishery had occupied a special position in that society not only as an important source of food but also as a central component in their system of beliefs and ceremonies.

BY THE COURT: — Before April, 12, 1982, it was clearly the law that fishing by Indians, even if in exercise of an aboriginal right to fish, was subject to any controls imposed by the *Fisheries Act*, R.S.C. 1970, c. F-14, and the regulations made thereunder. The issue on this appeal is whether that power to regulate is now limited by s. 35(1) of the *Constitution Act, 1982*:. . .

In this court, counsel for the Attorney-General for British Columbia appeared in support of the federal Crown on the constitutional question whether s. 35(1) limits the federal power to regulate Indian fishing. The several tribal councils and bands named in the style of cause were permitted to intervene to make submissions on that question in support of the appellant. . .

The statutory scheme

The licences were issued under the authority of the *Fisheries Act*, s. 34 of which confers a broad power to make regulations for carrying out the purposes and provisions of the Act. The Act makes no reference to Indians or to aboriginal rights to fish although s. 34.5, dealing with marine plants, provides:

34.5 Nothing in sections 34.1 and 34.4 shall be construed to prevent traditional harvesting of marine plants by aborigines for their use as food.

The regulations relevant to this case are the *British Columbia Fishery (General) Regulations*, SOR/84-248. The most relevant regulation is:

Indian Food Fishing

27(1) In this section "Indian food fish licence" means a licence issued by the Minister to an Indian or a band for the sole purpose of obtaining food for that Indian and his family or for the band.

(2) No Indian shall, while fishing or transporting fish caught under the authority of an Indian food fish licence, fail to carry with him and produce on the demand of a fishery officer or fishery guardian

  (a) his Indian food fish licence; or

  (b) where the Indian food fish licence is issued to a band,

      (i) a copy thereof endorsed by him and by the council of the band, or

      (ii) a signed document from the council of the band that authorizes him to engage in fishing thereunder.

(4) No person other than an Indian shall have in his possession fish caught under the authority of an Indian food fish licence.

The significance of licences in the statutory scheme is shown by this regulation:

4(1) Unless otherwise provided in the Act or in any Regulations made thereunder in respect of the fisheries to which these Regulations apply or in the *Wildlife Act* (British Columbia), no person shall fish except under the authority of a licence or permit issued thereunder. . .

History of regulation

The history of regulation of Indian fishing is set out in some detail in the judgment of Dickson J. (now C.J.C.) in *Jack et al.* v. *The Queen* (1979), 48 C.C.C. (2d) 246. The facts of that case were in many respects similar to those in the present one. Jack, and other members of the Cowichan Band, were convicted of fishing for salmon during a prohibited period. The prohibition was effected by an order made under the *British Columbia Fishing Regulations*. The defence was that the prohibition was invalid on a constitutional ground, *viz.* that art. 13 of the Terms of Union upon which British Columbia entered confederation had "sanctified" a colonial policy of permitting Indians to fish for food without regulation; and that it was therefore not competent to the federal government to regulate that right except for the purpose of conserving the fishery. The judgment of Laskin C.J.C., joined in by five other members of the court, held against that contention on the basis that it was not supported by the language of art. 13. Laskin C.J.C. found it unnecessary to review the history as it emerged from the evidence. The only member of the court to accept the position of the Indians with respect to art. 13 was Dickson J. He held that the right to fish was protected by art. 13, although he joined in dismissing the appeal on the ground that the specific prohibition complained of was for a conservation purpose and therefore one which could lawfully be imposed. In the course of his judgment, he extensively reviewed the history of dealings between the Indians and the colonial, federal and provincial governments. The following outline is based on that review.

There was little or no regulation of fishing before the province entered confederation in 1871 and no federal regulation of it until the first federal *Fisheries Act* was enacted in 1876 [see 1868 (Can.), c. 60]. The first *Salmon Fishery Regulations for British Columbia* were adopted in 1878. The first reference to Indians is to be found in the regulations of 1888 which provided [see *Jack* v. *The Queen, supra,* p. 258 C.C.C.]:

> "Fishing by means of nets or other apparatus without leases or licences from the Minister of Marine and Fisheries is prohibited in all waters of the Province of British Columbia.

> "Provided always that Indians shall, at all times, have liberty to fish for the purpose of providing food for themselves but not for sale, barter or traffic, by any means other than with drift nets, or spearing."

The regulations were amended in 1900 and again in 1917 when regulations substantially similar to those now in effect were enacted. The 1917 regulations empowered the chief inspector to limit or fix the waters in which, the means by which, and the time in which, such fish might be caught. Dickson J. summed up the development of the regulations at p. 259 C.C.C.:

> The federal Regulations became increasingly strict in regard to the Indian fishery over time, as first the commercial fishery developed and then sport fishing became common. What we can see is an increasing subjection of the Indian fishery to regulatory control. First, the regulation of the use of drift nets, then the restriction of fishing to food purposes, then the requirement of permission from the Inspector and, ultimately, in 1917, the power to regulate even food fishing by means of conditions attached to the permit.

It is that power to regulate fishing by means of conditions attached to the permit which is in issue here. What has changed since 1917 is the coming into force of s. 35 of the *Constitution Act, 1982.* The question is whether it has limited the power to regulate so as to render unenforceable the condition that the Musqueam, in fishing for food, cannot use nets longer than 25 fathoms.

The evidence

. . . . .

The evidence relating to the net length reduction was more contentious and gave rise to issues of fact which remain unresolved. At the opening of trial, Mr. Storrow took the position, on the basis of American authorities which will be referred to later, that the Crown must assume the burden of establishing that its regulation was intended to and did serve a valid conservation purpose and, if that burden was not discharged, that the regulation should be held invalid. The issue thus raised appears to be one of first impression in Canadian courts. . .

On the view of the law taken by both the trial judge and the appeal court judge, they found it unnecessary to deal with the evidence. So the conflicts were not resolved and, because the appeal to this court is on questions of law alone, cannot be resolved here. Nevertheless, reference to the evidence is necessary in order to place these novel issues in a factual context. . .

The policy of issuing annual licences to the Musqueam Band began in 1978. The stated policy of the Department of Fisheries and Oceans is that the reasonable food fish requirements of Indians should rank second in priority only to conservation. In other words, the policy is to accord priority to Indian food fishing over the interests of the other principal "user groups", *i.e.*, commercial and sports fishermen. The latter groups do, of course, include Indians. Mr. Sparrow, for instance, is a licenced commercial fisherman. But neither he nor other Indians are entitled to priority in the commercial and sports fishery because of their race.

Fishing under the licences is carried out under direct supervision by a fisheries patrol vessel which is present to guard against infractions and to keep a record of the number of fish caught. In 1978, the recorded catch by the Musqueam was under 5,000. The numbers rose modestly in 1980 and 1981 but, in 1982, rose dramatically to over 58,000. The total number of band members including men, women and children, is about 420. Divided equally, the 1982 catch would have given each member about 138 fish averaging about five pounds (undressed) yielding about three pounds dressed.

It is that drastic rise in 1982 which led to the net length reduction imposed in March, 1983. There are, on the Fraser River, 91 other bands which are regarded by the department as having equal entitlement to the "Indian food fishery". They all live upriver from the Musqueam. Their members, in total, number about 20,000. The annual licence issued to the Musqueam beginning in 1978 was an experiment by the department in the management of the Indian food fishery which was intended to be less confining than the previous system of daily licences. . .

In 1983, the recorded catch declined to something over 11,000 salmon. Again, discussions took place in early 1984 as to what conditions should be set out in the next licence. By this time, feelings were running high. The band took the position that no restrictions should be imposed but suggested that, if there were any, the net length should be fixed at 50 fathoms. . .

It is part of the case for Sparrow that a catch in the order of 57,000 salmon is necessary in order for the band to meet its reasonable food requirements . . . Other evidence casts doubt on the reliability of that estimate which includes 12,000 fish (more than the total catch in any year except 1982) to be used in potlatches and other social and cultural events. That would leave for ordinary food purposes 45,000 salmon, or something over 100 fish per year for each man, woman and child . . . The number of fish which would meet the reasonable food requirements of the members of the Musqueam band remains an unresolved factual issue in this case.

It should be noted that 1982 was an unusual year because the number of fish entering the Fraser River as part of the "Adams River run" was far in excess of any number recorded in any other year in recent memory. The appellant says that the department failed to give appropriate weight to that factor in deciding to restrict the net length the following year.

What emerges most clearly from the competing expert evidence is that fish stock management is an uncertain science, that conclusions must be reached on uncertain evidence, and that the issues are not well adapted to being resolved in court. The conflicts in the evidence cannot, in any event, be resolved in this court. . .

The judgment at trial

The Provincial Court judge held that s. 35(1) of the *Constitution Act, 1982* did not apply to Mr. Sparrow's case. In reaching that conclusion he referred firstly to the decision of the Supreme Court of Canada in *R.* v. *Derriksan* (1976), 31 C.C.C. (2d) 575n. That case, which concerned a member of the Okanagan Band of Indians, was markedly similar in its facts to this one. Derriksan was convicted of catching salmon in breach of the *Fisheries Act* in that he did not possess a permit as required by the regulations. The judgment of the Supreme Court was given orally by Laskin C.J.C. who said:

> On the assumption that Mr. Sanders is correct in his submission (which is one which the Crown does not accept) that there is an aboriginal right to fish in the particular area arising out of Indian occupation and that this right has had subsequent reinforcement (and we express no opinion on the correctness of this submission), we are all of the view that the Fisheries Act, R.S.C. 1970, c. F-14, and the Regulations thereunder which, so far as relevant here, were validly enacted, have the effect of subjecting the alleged right to the controls imposed by the Act and Regulations. . .

The trial judge considered and rejected the submission that s. 35(1) required a different result. He held that Sparrow could possess no aboriginal right to fish. That conclusion was not based upon any consideration of the evidence in this case but upon his view that he was bound by the decision of this court in *Calder et al.* v. *A-G. B.C.* (1970), 13 D.L.R. (3d) 64 (B.C.C.A.), affirmed 34 D.L.R. (3d) 145. On that basis, he found himself bound to hold that:

. . . unless an Indian in British Columbia can invoke any special treaty, or proclamation or contract in support, he cannot claim what is called aboriginal or Indian title to bring himself within the scope of s. 35 of the *Constitution Act, 1982*.

He went on to conclude that it would be inappropriate for him to deal with the evidence called in support of a claim for aboriginal rights because: "They can only be declared to exist by a court not bound by *Calder*. Meanwhile s. 35 of the *Constitution Act, 1982* does not apply to him."

The judgment on appeal

The reasons of the County Court Judge for dismissing Sparrow's appeal are to much the same effect. He considered himself bound by the decision of this court in *Calder* to hold that "aboriginal rights no longer exist in this province". He went on to consider whether s. 35 grants or revives aboriginal rights and held that it does not. He then went on to hold that, even if aboriginal rights exist, they exist subject to the *Fisheries Act* and regulations. He based that conclusion on *R.* v. *Derriksan, supra*, which was decided before s. 35(1) came into force.

What was decided by Calder et al. v. *A.-G. B.C.?*

Both the trial judge and the appeal court judge decided the case on the primary ground that he was bound by the decision of this court in *Calder* to hold that Sparrow can have no aboriginal right to fish. That is an error for two reasons:

(a) The judgment of this court in *Calder* has not, since the pronouncement of the judgment of the Supreme Court of Canada in the same case, been binding on anyone;

(b) The nature of the claim put forward in *Calder*, and the facts of the case, differ in fundamental respects from those of this case. Not even this court's judgment in *Calder* supports the conclusion that the Musqueam do not have an existing aboriginal right to fish.

The view that the decision of this court in *Calder* continues to be binding on lower courts is one which has had surprising vitality in British Columbia. It has been put forward in other cases since the coming into force of the *Constitution Act, 1982*: see, *e.g.*, *Peters* v. *The Queen in right of British Columbia et al.* (1983), 42 B.C.L.R. 373. In the *Meares Island* case, it formed one of the grounds for refusing an interlocutory injunction in the first instance. Because of the apparently wide acceptance of the fallacy, it may be worth making a further effort to lay it to rest, notwithstanding that no counsel attempted to support it before us in this case and notwithstanding that by clear implication, it was rejected by this court in *Meares Island* [see *MacMillan Bloedel Ltd.* v. *Mullin et al.*] The decision is reported at [1985] 3 W.W.R. 577 . . . All members of the court clearly regarded the Supreme Court judgments as controlling.

The fallacy arises from the somewhat unusual division amongst the seven judges who sat on *Calder* in the Supreme Court of Canada. The action was brought by the Nishga Indians seeking a declaration that they hold aboriginal title to the very large area of the province in which they have always lived. The trial judge dismissed the claim and his decision was upheld by all three judges who sat in this court. The division of opinion in the Supreme Court on the substantive issues was summed up by Dickson J. in *Guerin et al.* v. *The Queen, supra*, p. 335 D.L.R.:

> In *Calder et al.* v. *A.-G. B.C.*, this court recognized aboriginal title as a legal right derived from the Indians' historic occupation and possession of their tribal lands. With Judson and Hall JJ. writing the principal judgments, the court split three-three on the major issue of whether the Nishga Indians' aboriginal title to their ancient tribal territory had been extinguished by general land enactments in British Columbia. The court also split on the issue of whether the Royal Proclamation of 1763 was applicable to Indian lands in that province. Judson and Hall JJ. were in agreement, however, that aboriginal title existed in Canada (at least where it has not been extinguished by appropriate legislative action) independently of the Royal Proclamation of 1763, Judson J. stated expressly that the Proclamation was not the "exclusive" source of Indian title. Hall J. said that "aboriginal Indian title does not depend on treaty, executive order or legislative enactment".

Pigeon J. did not deal with the substantive issues. He held that the action must be dismissed because no fiat had been obtained. Judson J. agreed with that and so that finding became, strictly speaking, the *ratio* of the decision.

On the substantive issue, the basis of decision by Judson J. was essentially the same as that of the trial judge, Gould J., and the alternative ground of decision by the judges of this court. That is that the aboriginal title of the Nishga had been extinguished by general land legislation before British Columbia entered confederation. That, of course, was not a finding that no aboriginal title could exist. There cannot be extinguishment of something which never existed.

The primary ground of decision in the Court of Appeal was different. In the words of Davey C.J.B.C., it was: "In each case it must be shown that the aboriginal rights were ensured by prerogative or legislative act, or that a course of dealing has been proved from which that can be inferred".

That view was not accepted in the Supreme Court. Hall J., particularly at pp. 200-1 D.L.R., set out in detail his reasons for holding that aboriginal title does not depend on treaty, executive order or legislative enactment. Judson J., at least by implication, expressed the same view. . .

The view that the decision of this court remains binding is apparently based on a misapplication of the rule that, where a court composed of an even number of judges divides equally on the question whether the appeal should be allowed, the judgment of the final court is one dismissing the appeal. So the result is that the judgment of the lower court is upheld. It does not follow that, where the judges in the highest court divide equally in their reasons for judgment, those reasons are to be treated as if they did not exist. Even less can the equal division on certain issues justify ignoring the agreement of a majority in rejecting a conclusion of the lower court. Six judges of the Supreme Court having joined in rejecting the view that aboriginal title can exist only if conferred by a treaty, statute or agreement, there can be no justification for continuing to treat that view as binding.

The second error in relation to *Calder* is in failing to have regard to the fundamental distinctions in the facts. The claim in *Calder* was not particularized but clearly the essence of it was a broadly based claim affecting title to land. The right to fish may have been an aspect of the claim but was so incidental an aspect as to be given virtually no attention in any of the judgments. . .

Even in dealing with a similar claim to aboriginal title to land, regard must be had to the facts of the particular case. Dickson J. (now C.J.C.), in giving the judgment of the court in *Kruger and Manuel* v. *The Queen* (1977), 34 C.C.C. (2d) 377 at p. 380 said:

> Before considering the two other grounds of appeal, I should say that the important constitutional issue as to the nature of aboriginal title, if any, in respect of lands in British Columbia, the further question as to whether it had been extinguished, and the force of the Royal Proclamation of 1763 — issues discussed in *Calder et al.* v. *A.-G. B.C.* (1973), 34 D.L.R. (3d) 145, [1973] S.C.R. 313, [1973] 4 W.W.R. 1 — will not be determined in the present appeal. They were not directly placed in issue by the appellants and a sound rule to follow is that questions of title should only be decided when title is directly in issue. Interested parties should be afforded an opportunity to adduce evidence in detail bearing upon the resolution of the particular dispute. Claims to aboriginal title are woven with history, legend, politics and moral obligations. *If the claim of any Band in respect of any particular land is to be decided as a justiciable issue and not a political issue, it should be so considered on the facts pertinent to that Band and to that land, and not on any global basis.* (Emphasis added.)

The claim put forward in this case is much further removed from the claim in *Calder* than is any claim in respect of land. What is claimed here by the Musqueams is their right to fish for food in their traditional fishing grounds. That general type of right has always been recognized; and continues to be recognized today in the regulations under the *Fisheries Act.* The specific right to fish in Canoe Passage is recognized by the licences issued under those regulations. So, even if the law laid down by this court in *Calder* was binding, this claim would seem to meet the test of having been incorporated into the municipal law. What possible reason can there be for the continuous regulation for a century of Indian fishing except recognition of an aboriginal right? Counsel for the federal Crown, in seeking to provide some other explanation for the existence of a regulation based on a racial distinction, offered the suggestion that it is "affirmative action" under s. 15(2) of the *Canadian Charter of Rights and Freedoms*. That answer does not lend itself to serious discussion. No other was suggested.

There is an existing aboriginal right to fish

The trial judge said in his reasons: "I have no difficulty finding as a fact, that Mr. Sparrow was fishing in ancient tribal territory where his ancestors had fished from time immemorial in that part of the mouth of the Fraser River for salmon . . .". That conclusion is supported by the evidence and, taken with the other circumstances, should have led to the conclusion that Sparrow was at the relevant time exercising an existing aboriginal right.

The only submission that the right is not an existing one was that of counsel for the federal Crown who put forward the doctrine, apparently propounded in this case for the first time, of "extinguishment by regulation". The major premise is that the aboriginal right to fish was unrestricted. The minor premise is that, over the past century or so, restrictions have been imposed by both federal and provincial fisheries legislation. So, it is said, whatever right to fish is retained by Indians cannot be an aboriginal right because it has been restricted. No logical basis is suggested for the proposition that a right which is restricted ceases to be a right. The result is said to somehow follow from the decisions in *R.* v. *Derriksan, supra*, and *Kruger and Manuel* v. *The Queen, supra*. Those cases provide no support for the proposition. *Derriksan* makes it clear that, before April 17, 1982, rights to fish, even if they were aboriginal rights, were subject to regulation. It decides nothing about extinguishment and nothing about the effect of constitutional recognition of aboriginal rights. *Kruger* established that an Indian's right to hunt in British Columbia is subject to regulation by the provincial *Wildlife Act* in so far as it is a "law of general application". Mr. Kruger therefore could be convicted of hunting without the permit required by that act, even if he was hunting on land which was the traditional hunting ground of his band. Again, the case was not about extinguishment or the effect of constitutional recognition of aboriginal rights. On the other hand, the language of Dickson J. quoted earlier, referring to aboriginal title, is inconsistent with the notion that regulation of the kind dealt with in that case could have had the effect of extinguishing aboriginal rights.

In our view, the "extinguishment by regulation" proposition has no merit. The short answer to it is that regulation of the exercise of a right presupposes the existence of the right. If Indians did not have a special right in respect of the fishery, there would have been no reason to mention them in the regulations. The regulations themselves, which have consistently recognized the Indian right to fish, are strong evidence that the right does exist. It is clear that here was an aboriginal right. It is equally clear that such right has not been extinguished, either expressly (as Hall J. would require) or by implication (as Judson J. held).

It follows that the judgment appealed from was wrong in holding that no aboriginal rights can exist in British Columbia, and in failing to hold that Sparrow at the relevant time was exercising an existing aboriginal right. In this case, the Musqueam assert no right to catch fish for other than food purposes. So no issue arises as to whether the aboriginal right to take fish for other purposes has been extinguished.

The effect of s. 35(1) of the Constitution Act, 1982

Before April 17, 1982, the federal power to regulate the Indian fishery and the provincial power to regulate it by laws of general application were upheld in many cases including *Derriksan, Kruger, Jack, Sikyea* v. *The Queen*, [1965] 2 C.C.C. 129, and *R.* v. *Billy*, [1982] 1 C.N.L.R. 99 (B.C.C.A.). In this case we are concerned only with the federal power to regulate. The issue is whether the coming into force of s. 35(1) has the effect of limiting that power and, if it does, in what respect.

On this issue, several different positions were put forward by the parties. The position which would most broadly limit the power of regulation is that put forward by Mr. Pape on behalf of the intervenors. He says that any regulation under the *Fisheries Act* which interferes with, rather than protects, the right to fish is inconsistent with s. 35(1) and therefore of no force or effect. Specifically, he submits, regulations governing the kind of gear which may be employed are inconsistent with the aboriginal right.

Mr. Storrow for the appellant supports Mr. Pape's submission but puts forward a less sweeping alternative. He says that a regulation which restricts an aboriginal fishing right is thus *prima facie* inconsistent with s. 35. But it may nevertheless be valid if the Crown demonstrates by clear and convincing evidence that the restriction is reasonably necessary for the purpose of conserving the fishery. That is the position stated on behalf of the appellant at the opening of trial and in respect of which evidence was called at trial. Mr. Storrow submits that the Crown failed on that issue and that the regulation should therefore be held invalid.

Counsel for the federal Crown does not, in his submissions, deal directly with this issue. He puts his whole case on the ground that, if there ever was an aboriginal right to fish, it was extinguished by the fisheries regulations and no longer exists. We have already rejected that view.

Mr. Edwards for the provincial Crown, on the other hand, starts with the assumption (not admission) that the Musqueam have an existing aboriginal right to fish. His submission that s. 35 does not affect the power to regulate is put on two alternative grounds. The first is that s. 35 has no effect on aboriginal or treaty rights; that it is merely a kind of preamble to the parts of the *Constitutional Act, 1982*, which deal with aboriginal rights. This contention rests most strongly upon s. 37 of the *Constitution Act, 1982* (repealed and replaced by s. 37.1 in 1983), which provided for a conference to be convened to, *inter alia*, identify and define the rights of aboriginal peoples "to be included in the constitution of Canada". On this view, s. 35 is an assurance of good intentions but not a provision which can have any effect on any specific aboriginal right unless and until that right has been identified and defined as contemplated by s. 37 and its successor sections.

The alternative contention is that, even if s. 35 has the effect of constitutionally protecting the Musqueam's right to fish, it protects only the right as it existed before April 17, 1982, *i.e.*, subject to whatever regulation or curtailment parliament sees fit to impose.

The submission that s. 35 is merely a kind of preamble to s. 37 and that no aboriginal rights can be legally enforceable unless and until identified and defined under s. 37.1 may, as Mr. Storrow submits, be met completely by s. 37.1(4) which reads:

> 37.1(4) Nothing in this section shall be construed so as to derogate from subsection 35(1). [New, *Constitution Amendment Proclamation, 1983.*]

However, the words which are submitted to derogate from s. 35(1) are not in "this section" but are the words "identify" and "define" in the now repealed s. 37. So s. 37.1(4) may not entirely meet the argument. It is unnecessary to pursue that question because the argument is, on broader grounds, an untenable one. Section 37 provided for the identification and definition of aboriginal rights by the essentially political process of conventions. In so doing, it recognized what is obviously the fact — many aboriginal rights are inadequately identified and defined. It made provision for resolving those doubts by a course of compromise and negotiation rather than the "win or lose" process of litigation. But it did not say or imply that no aboriginal rights can be enforced before being identified and defined by the convention process.

This submission gives no meaning to s. 35. If accepted, it would result in denying its clear statement that existing rights are hereby recognized and affirmed, and would turn that into a mere promise to recognize and affirm those rights sometime in the future; or perhaps never if the convention process fails to produce a final answer. To so construe s. 35(1) would be to ignore its language and the principle that the constitution should be interpreted in a liberal and remedial way. We cannot accept that that principle applies less strongly to aboriginal rights than to the rights guaranteed by the Charter, particularly having regard to the history and to the approach to interpreting treaties and statutes relating to Indians required by such cases as *Nowegijick* v. *The Queen et al.* (1983), 144 D.L.R. (3d) 193.

We hold therefore that the right to fish asserted by the appellant, being one which has already been identified and which can be adequately defined, is one entitled to constitutional protection. The more difficult issue is whether that protection extends so far as to preclude regulation of the exercise of that right. The specific restriction in issue here is that as to the length of net which can be used. But the submission, in its broadest form, is that it is not competent to the federal government to impose restrictions and, in its narrower form, is that it is not competent to impose restrictions except for specific and quite limited purposes.

It is clear from the *Derriksan* line of cases that before April 17, 1982, the aboriginal right to fish was subject to regulation by legislation; and that it was subject to extinguishment. The question whether there is now a power to extinguish does not arise in this case but it is relevant to observe that extinguishment and regulation are essentially different concepts. Even if there cannot now be extinguishment, it would not follow that there cannot be regulation. It may be that a power to extinguish is necessarily inconsistent with the recognition and affirmation of aboriginal right in s. 35(1). There is no necessary inconsistency with a power to regulate.

That is illustrated by some of the authorities referred to by Mr. Pape in reply to Mr. Kier's submission of extinguishment by regulation. On that issue, Mr. Pape relied on the authorities which establish that regulatory legislation may affect or interfere with the enjoyment of common law property rights, but that the result is not to extinguish the right. Examples of such authorities are *Toronto* v. *Presswood*, [1944] 1 D.L.R. 569, and *Canadian Petrofina Ltd.* v. *Martin and St. Lambert*, [1959] S.C.R. 453.

In submitting that regulation of the right to fish is inconsistent with the constitutional status accorded it by s. 35(1), Mr. Storrow and Mr. Pape place considerable emphasis on the nature of the right as described in the evidence. The salmon fishery is important to the Musqueam, not only as a source of food for subsistence, but as an integral part of their distinctive culture. The evidence supports the contention that the traditional Indian fishery has significant social and cultural aspects which make the claims of the Indian people to the fishery different in kind and quality from those of other groups. . .

The gist of the argument as it bears upon the present issue is that regulation of the method of fishing is an inherent aspect of the aboriginal right to fish. If the right is to be kept intact, the regulation must be by the possessors of the right, in this case, the band. It is submitted that there would continue to be consultation between the band and the fisheries authorities. What will be different will be that, where no agreement is reached, the final word will rest with the band. That situation might be modified in the future because it is anticipated that, as part of the process contemplated by s. 37.1, agreements will be entered into which will more completely identify and define the right including providing machinery for regulation.

Mr. Pape lays some stress on the authorities which illustrate that such deference to the possessors of an aboriginal right would be no new thing. He points particularly to the cases which arose under what is now the *Constitution Act, 1930*, which gave constitutional recognition to Indian hunting rights in the three prairie provinces. The most significant of those cases are: *R.* v. *Wesley*, [1932] 2 W.W.R. 337; *Prince and Myron* v. *The Queen*, [1964] S.C.R. 81; reversing [1963] 1 C.C.C. 129; *R.* v. *Sutherland, Wilson and Wilson*, [1980] 2 S.C.R. 451. Those cases concern the construction to be given the language of the clause which appeared as s. 12 of the statutory agreement between the Parliament of Canada and the Legislature of Alberta, and s. 13 of the equivalent agreement between Canada and Manitoba. Those agreements were confirmed by the *Constitution Act, 1930*, an Act of the United Kingdom Parliament, and thus had constitutional effect. The language which had to be construed was this:

> In order to secure to the Indians of the Province the continuance of the supply of game and fish for their support and subsistence, Canada agrees that the laws respecting game in force in the Province from time to time shall apply to the Indians within the boundaries thereof, provided however, that the said Indians shall have the right, which the Province hereby assures to them, of hunting, trapping, and fishing game and fish for food at all seasons of the year on all unoccupied Crown lands and on any other lands to which the said Indians may have a right of access.

It was decided in *R.* v. *Wesley* and *Prince and Myron* v. *The Queen* that the Indian food hunting guaranteed by that provision was not subject to provincial game legislation controlling such matters as the hunting methods that could be used. In *R.* v. *Sutherland*, it was held that it was not competent to the province to limit the effect of s. 13 by a restricted definition of "right of access". . . .

The *R.* v. *Wesley* line of cases deal with the construction to be given the specific language of the 1930 agreements and also, in *Prince and Myron* v. *The Queen*, the similar language incorporated in s. 72(1) of the *Game and Fisheries Act* to give effect to the 1930 agreement. That basis of decision has no direct application to the issues here. Those cases do not decide that regulation is necessarily inconsistent with a constitutionally entrenched right to hunt (or fish). Rather, they decide that the particular language by which the right was entrenched precludes, as a matter of construction, regulation of the kind imposed by the provincial legislation.

That line of cases is nevertheless significant in relation to the question as to what limitation is placed upon the power of regulation by constitutional entrenchment of the right. In identifying the evil sought to be avoided by the constitutional provision, *R.* v. *Wesley* suggests a basis for limiting the power to regulate. In the passage quoted by Hall J., McGillivray J.A. said that if the Indians were otherwise subject to provincial game laws " . . . in any year they may be limited in the number of animals of a given kind that they may kill even though that number is not sufficient for their support and subsistence and even though no other kind of game is available to them''. The same evil need not follow from regulations, such as those in question here, which are specifically directed to Indian fishing. In such a case, the principle can be served by limiting the power to regulate so that it cannot limit the number of fish to be taken to one insufficient for support and subsistence.

Somewhat similar considerations provide an answer to the submission that the cultural aspects of the Indian salmon fishery preclude government regulation. It must be borne in mind that what is recognized and affirmed by s. 35(1) is the "existing" right. In 1982, the Indian right to fish existed in circumstances profoundly different from those prevailing before or in the early years of white settlement when the fishery was thought to be "inexhaustible": see Dickson J. in *Jack et al.* v. *The Queen*, *supra*, p. 309 S.C.R. The constitutional recognition of the right to fish cannot entail restoring the relationship between Indians and salmon as it existed 150 years ago. The world has changed. The right must now exist in the context of a parliamentary system of government and a federal division of powers. It cannot be defined as if the Musqueam Band had continued to be a self-governing entity, or as if its members were not citizens of Canada and residents of British Columbia. Any definition of the existing right must take into account that it exists in the context of an industrial society with all of its complexities and competing interests. The "existing right" in 1982 was one which had long been subject to regulation by the federal government. It must continue to be so because only government can regulate with due regard to the interests of all.

Mr. Storrow accepts that there continues to be a power to regulate. But it is, he says, a power subject to narrow limits imposed by s. 35(1) and s. 52. The suggested limits are based upon the rules developed in the United States and, in particular, those which have defined the extent of the power of the States of Washington and Oregon to regulate salmon fishing by Indians whose right to fish arises under treaties entered into between their tribes and the government of the United States in the 1850s when territorial status was first accorded. We are particularly referred to four cases: *Tulee* v. *Washington* (1942), 86 L. Ed. 1115; *Puyallup Tribe* v. *Department of Game* (1973), 38 L. Ed. 2d 254; *Sohappy* v. *Smith* (1969), 302 F. Supp. 899; and *United States* v. *Washington* (1974), 384 F. Supp. 312 affirmed 520 F. 2d 674 (9th Cir.), *certiorari* denied 96 S. Ct. 877.

The treaties entered into with the various tribes all had wording to the effect that they granted ''the right of taking fish, at all usual and accustomed grounds and stations . . . in common with all citizens of the Territory''. In the *Tulee* case the issue was whether treaty Indians could be required to obtain a licence to fish. It was held that they could not. The court held that the states' power to regulate treaty Indians was confined to imposing upon them, equally with others, such restrictions of a purely regulatory nature concerning the time and manner of fishing as are necessary for the reconservation of fish. The *Puyallup* case concerned the question whether a prohibition against the use of set nets in a certain area could be enforced against treaty Indians. The Supreme Court upheld the decision of the Court of Appeal which had referred the matter back to the trial court to determine whether that prohibition was a reasonable and necessary conservation measure.

The *Sohappy* case was one brought by certain tribes in Oregon to obtain a declaration defining the scope of permissible restriction of their treaty right of taking fish "at all the usual and accustomed places" on the Columbia River. Belloni D.J. held that the language of the Supreme Court, in holding that the restrictions must be necessary for conservation, was speaking of " . . . conservation in the sense of perpetuation or improvement of the size and reliability of the fish runs and not endorsing any program which took into account allocation of fish amongst the user groups". He held that the state must establish before regulation that the proposed regulation is both necessary and reasonable for conservation and at p. 908:

> To prove necessity, the state must show there is a need to limit the taking of fish and that the particular regulation sought to be imposed upon the exercise of the treaty right is necessary to the accomplishment of the needed limitation. This applies to regulations restricting the type of gear which Indians may use as much as it does to restrictions on the time at which Indians may fish.

U.S. v. *Washington*, which had many parties, is often called the "Boldt case", the reference being to the name of the trial judge. It was brought by the federal government and the treaty tribes against the State of Washington and those who supported the state's power of regulation. The case laid down sweeping limitations on that power. It was held that the state could regulate fishing rights guaranteed to the Indians only to the extent necessary to preserve a particular species in a particular run. It was also held that, in order to ensure a fair share of the catch to the treaty Indians, they must have the opportunity to catch one-half of all the fish which, if there were no fishing activities by other citizens, would pass their traditional fishing grounds.

The appellant submits that the general rules developed in those cases should be adopted in Canada as the basis for restricting the power to regulate the now constitutionally protected right to fish. It is pointed out that there is a close geographical and historical link between the circumstances of the tribes in the two states and those of the Musqueam Indians. What is different, however, is the constitutional framework which gave rise to the issues; and the breadth of the right granted by the treaties. It is out of that framework, and the specific language of the treaties, that those rules developed. The differences are so much more significant than the similarities that those decisions have limited, if any, application to our situation. We may, in the end, adopt somewhat similar rules. But the content of our rules must be determined by our own factual and legal circumstances.

The appellant also relies upon the language of Dickson J. (now C.J.C.) in

Jack et al. v. *The Queen.* Having held that art. 13 of the Terms of Union imposed a constitutional limitation on the federal power to regulate, Dickson J. went on to say at p. 313 S.C.R.:

> Conservation is a valid legislative concern. The appellants concede as much. Their concern is in the allocation of the resource after reasonable and necessary conservation measures have been recognized and given effect to. They do not claim the right to pursue the last living salmon until it is caught. Their position, as I understand it, is one which would give effect to an order of priorities of this nature: (i) conservation; (ii) Indian fishing; (iii) non-Indian commercial fishing; or (iv) non-Indian sports fishing; the burden of conservation measures should not fall primarily upon the Indian fishery.
>
> I agree with the general tenor of this argument . . .

That conclusion, however, rests on a fundamentally different basis from that established by s. 35(1). As Dickson J. pointed out at p. 312 S.C.R.:

> The appellants' argument rests not upon any "right" derived from treaty or aboriginal title that can be invoked against federal legislation, rather upon a constitutional limitation of that very federal power to legislate in respect of Indians in British Columbia, a limitation imposed upon the federal government in the Terms of Union.

The constitutional limitation referred to in that passage was, of course, found by the majority of the court not to exist. So the observations of Dickson J. as to the priority to be accorded Indian fishing, while entitled to respectful consideration, are far from being a binding authority.

Mr. Edwards, in the submissions outlined earlier in these reasons, submits that s. 35(1) provides no basis for restricting the federal power to regulate. In support of that submission, he refers to two appellate decisions which have considered the effect of s. 35(1) on hunting and fishing rights.

The first is *R.* v. *Eninew* (1984), 10 D.L.R. (4th) 137 (Sask. C.A.); affirming 1 D.L.R. (4th) 595. That case dealt with the issue whether the restrictions on hunting imposed by the *Migratory Birds Convention Act* applied to treaty Indians. Both the trial judge and the Court of Appeal held that, notwithstanding the enactment of s. 35(1), the Act continued to apply and the regulations enacted before April 17, 1982, continued to be effective. Mr. Edwards relies particularly on the statement of Hall J.A. who, in giving the judgment of the Court of Appeal, said at p. 140 D.L.R., that " . . . the treaty rights can be limited by such regulations as are reasonable". Mr. Edwards relies on that passage as stating a general rule that rights recognized by s. 35(1) can be limited by such regulations as are reasonable. That language, however, must be read in light of the facts of the case and in particular the language of the treaties which granted to the Indians the right to hunt "subject to such regulations as may from time to time be made . . .". The decision is of little assistance in resolving the issues before us.

The second case is *R.* v. *Hare and Debassige* (1985), 20 C.C.C. (3d) 1, a decision of the Ontario Court of Appeal. The issue was whether the *Ontario Fishery Regulations* made under s. 34 of the Fisheries Act, which prohibited taking fish other than by angling, applied to Hare and Debassige who were members of a band entitled to the benefit of the Manitoulin Island Treaty which granted certain rights and privileges in respect of the taking of fish in certain waters. On the first appeal, the District Court judge set aside the convictions on several grounds, one of which was that s. 35 "removes any doubt as to the validity and efficacy" of treaties with the Indians. The Court of Appeal restored the convictions. On the s. 35 point, it found that that section could have no application because the offences took place in 1980.

That case also has limited application to the issues before us. It deals with an asserted right based on treaty and does not involve a new restriction or regulation imposed after the coming into force of s. 35(1). There are, however, in the judgment of Thorson J.A. for the court, certain observations which are of general application to the questionf the extent of the power to regulate aboriginal rights to fish. At p. 17 C.C.C., he said:

> Since 1867 and subject to the limitations thereon imposed by the Constitution, which of course now includes s. 35 of the *Constitution Act, 1982*, the constitutional authority and responsibility to make laws in relation to the fisheries has rested with Parliament. Central to Parliament's responsibility has been, and continues to be, the need to provide for the proper management and conservation of our fish stocks, and the need to ensure that they are not depleted or imperilled by deleterious practices or methods of fishing.
>
> The prohibitions found in ss. 12 and 20 of the Ontario regulations clearly serve this purpose. Accordingly it need not be ignored by our courts that while these prohibitions place limits on the rights of all persons, they are there to serve the larger interest which all persons share in the proper management and conservation of these important resources.

Of particular interest in that passage is the emphasis upon the need to give priority to measures directed towards the proper management and conservation of fish stocks. There is, on that point, a significant degree of unanimity on the part of all those who have considered the status of aboriginal or treaty rights to take fish.

We conclude that none of the submissions made to us as to the effect of s. 35(1) upon the power to regulate is entirely right but that the correct position lies between that put forward by the appellant and that put forward by the provincial Crown. There continues to be a power to regulate the exercise of fishing by Indians even where that fishing is pursuant to an aboriginal right but there are now limitations on that power.

Section 35(1) and the regulation of the fisheries

Parliament has the constitutional authority and responsibility under head 12 of s. 91 of the *Constitution Act, 1867*, to make laws in relation to sea-coast and inland fisheries. Indians share with other Canadians the need for reasonable regulations to ensure the proper management and conservation of this resource. The regulations made pursuant to the *Fisheries Act* place limits on the rights of all persons including Indians.

Parliament has the constitutional authority and responsibility under head 24 of s. 91 of the *Constitution Act, 1867*, to make laws in relation to Indians and lands reserved to Indians.

Section 35(1) of the *Constitution Act, 1982*, does not purport to revoke the power of Parliament to act under heads 12 or 24. The power to regulate fisheries, including Indian access to the fisheries continues, subject only to the new constitutional guarantee that the aboriginal rights existing on April 17, 1982, may not be taken away.

The aboriginal right which the Musqueam had was, subject to conservation measures, the right to take fish for food and for the ceremonial purposes of the band. It was in the beginning a regulated, albeit self-regulated, right. It continued to be a regulated right, and on April 17, 1982, it was a regulated right. It has never been a fixed right, and it has always taken its form from the circumstances in which it has existed. If the interests of the Indians and other Canadians in the fishery are to be protected then reasonable regulations to ensure the proper management and conservation of the resource must be continued.

What can be said with certainty in this case is that there is a right in the Musqueam to take salmon from Canoe Passage and Ladner Reach, the waters referred to in the licence. It is necessary to distinguish between a right and the method by which the right may be exercised. The aboriginal right is not to take fish by any particular method or by a net of any particular length. It is to take fish for food purposes. The breadth of the right should be interpreted liberally in favour of the Indians. So ''food purposes'' should not be confined to subsistence. In particular, this is so because the Musqueam tradition and culture involves a consumption of salmon on ceremonial occasions and a broader use of fish than mere day to day domestic consumption.

The general power to regulate the time, place and manner of all fishing, including fishing under an aboriginal right, remains. The essential limitation upon that power is that which is already recognized by government policy as it emerges from the evidence in this case. That is, in allocating the right to take fish, the Indian food fishery is given priority over the interest of other user groups. What is different is that, where the Indian food fishery is in the exercise of an aboriginal right, it is constitutionally entitled to such priority. Furthermore, by reason of s. 35(1) it is a constitutionally protected right and cannot be extinguished.

Those regulations which do not infringe the aboriginal food fishery, in the sense of reducing the available catch below that required for reasonable food and societal needs, will not be affected by the constitutional recognition of the right. Regulations which do bear upon the exercise of the right may nevertheless be valid, but only if they can be reasonably justified as being necessary for the proper management and conservation of the resource or in the public interest. These purposes are not limited to the Indian food fishery.

Is the net length restriction valid?

The trial judge found against the accused on the ground that, as a matter of law, he could have no aboriginal right and that, in any event, the federal power to regulate in the field of fisheries continued to be unfettered. He found it unnecessary to consider the evidence in any detail but did make this observation regarding the case for the defence:

> A major issue at trial, at least from the point of view of the defence, is its attack on the validity of the regulation which imposed on the defendant the restriction as to the length of his net. The evidence called by the defendant casts some doubt as to whether the restriction was necessary as a conservation measure. More particularly, it suggests that there were more appropriate measures that could have been taken if necessary; measures that would not impose such a hardship on the Indians fishing for food. That case was not fully met by the Crown.

Accepting those observations as findings of fact, they are insufficient to lead to an acquittal. The "case" which was not fully met by the Crown was based on the American authorities and the evidence of Dr. Walters. The rules laid down by the American authorities do not apply. The evidence of Dr. Walters on the subject of conservation may be premised on the view that conservation should be defined as the preservation of fish stocks from extinction. There are, as noted earlier in these reasons, several unresolved conflicts in the evidence, not the least important of which is with respect to the question whether some change in the fishing conditions was necessary to reduce the catch to a level sufficient to satisfy reasonable food requirements, as well as for conservation purposes.

The conviction was based on an erroneous view of the law and therefore cannot stand. The facts relevant to the defence not having been determined, the appropriate order is one setting aside the conviction and directing a new trial. It is so ordered.

Appeal allowed; new trial ordered.

[Ed. Note: Mr. Sparrow appealed to the Supreme Court of Canada and the Crown cross-appealed. The appeal was heard on November 3, 1988. The decision was reserved and was pending at the time of publication.]

R. v. Agawa
[1988] 3 CNLR 73 (Ont. C.A.)

Ed. Note: The respondent was a member of the Batchawana Indian Band which was a signatory to the Robinson Huron Treaty of 1850, which promised the right "to fish in the waters thereof as they have heretofore been doing . . .". The Band had received a fishing licence annually from 1950 to 1983 but chose not to apply for one in 1984 in order to test the scope of s. 35(1) of the *Constitution Act, 1982*. He was convicted at trial on six charges of fishing with a gill net without a licence in violation of s. 12(1) of the *Ontario Fishery Regulations* enacted pursuant to the federal *Fisheries Act*. The Crown appealed the subsequent quashing of the convictions. The respondent was a commercial fishermen who had caught approximately 8000 pounds of fish over the 6 months covered by the charges which he had sold for over $12,000.

BLAIR J.A.:. . .

The evidence established that Indians in the area occupied by the Batchawana Indian Band habitually fished with gill nets for their own consumption and for commercial purposes when the treaty was executed. Dr. Charles E. Cleland, Professor of Anthropology and Curator of Anthropology at Michigan State University and an expert on Indians in the area, testified that from the time of Christ Indians were heavily dependent upon fish for their livelihood. The use of gill nets by the ancestors of the band can be traced back to 800 A.D. . .

Two questions are raised in this appeal. The first is whether the *Ontario Fishery Regulations* prevail over the respondent's treaty rights. If the first question is answered in the affirmative, the second question is whether the legal position is changed by s. 35(1) of the *Constitution Act, 1982*.

Treaty Rights and Section 88 of the Indian Act

Canadian Indian treaties were described by Chief Justice Dickson as *sui generis* in *Simon v. The Queen*, [1985] 2 S.C.R. 387 at 404. They are not the same as treaties between independent countries: see *Simon*, at p. 404 S.C.R. and *Horse v. The Queen*, [1988] 2 W.W.R. 289 at 300 (S.C.C.). Indian treaties are, however, similar in one respect to Canada's international treaties. They are not self-executing and can acquire the force of law in Canada only to the extent that they are protected by the Constitution or by statute. Some marginal constitutional protection was provided before 1982 by the Terms of Union with British Columbia of 1870 and the agreement transferring jurisdiction over natural resources to the three prairie provinces incorporated in the *Constitution Act, 1930*: see as to British Columbia *Jack v. The Queen*, [1980] 1 S.C.R. 294 and as to the prairie provinces *R. v. Sutherland*, [1980] 2 S.C.R. 451 at 461, and *Moosehunter v. The Queen*, [1981] 1 S.C.R. 282 at 285.

In practical terms, however, the only effective protection of Indian treaty rights until 1982 was provided by the *Indian Act*, R.S.C. 1970, c. I-6, enacted by the Parliament of Canada pursuant to its power under s. 91(24) of the *Constitution Act, 1867* to make laws in relation to "Indians and lands reserved for Indians". Section 88, which was only inserted in the Act in 1951 (1951 S.C., c. 29, s. 87), provides:

The Supreme Court of Canada has established that the phrase "all laws of general application . . . in force in any province" in s. 88 refers only to provincial laws and not federal laws. The result is that, in the event of conflict Indian treaty rights prevail over provincial legislation: *R. v. White and Bob* (1966), 52 D.L.R. (2d) 481; *Simon v. The Queen*, supra. Where, however, treaty rights conflict with federal legislation, the federal law prevails as the Supreme Court of Canada held in *Sikyea v. The Queen*, [1964] S.C.R. 642 and *R. v. George*, [1966] S.C.R. 267. Martland J. in *George* said at p. 281 S.C.R.:

> This section was not intended to be a declaration of the paramountcy of treaties over federal legislation. The reference to treaties was incorporated in a section the purpose of which was to make provincial laws applicable to Indians, so as to preclude any interference with rights under treaties resulting from the impact of provincial legislation.

R. v. George, was applied by this court in *R. v. Hare and Debassige*, [1985] 3 C.N.L.R. 139.

In the present case, the learned summary conviction appeal court judge treated the *Ontario Fishery Regulations* as if they were provincial laws subject to Indian treaty rights because they are administered by provincial officials. The delegation of administrative authority over the *Ontario Fishery Regulations* is a proper exercise of Parliament's legislative authority and does not alter their status as federal laws: see *Re: Shoal Lake Band of Indians No. 39 et al. and The Queen in right of Ontario* (1979), 25 O.R. (2d) 334. The respondent conceded that the summary conviction appeal court judge had erred but, nevertheless, invited this court to hold that, even before s. 35(1) took effect, Indian treaty fishing rights should not have been restricted by the *Ontario Fishery Regulations*.

This court is not at liberty to depart from the rule established by the Supreme Court of Canada that valid federal legislation prevails over the terms of Indian treaties unless that rule is changed by s. 35(1) of the *Constitution Act, 1982*. This is a possibility which was contemplated by Chief Justice Dickson in *Simon v. The Queen*, supra, when he observed at p. 411 S.C.R.:

> Under s. 88 of the *Indian Act*, when the terms of a treaty come into conflict with federal legislation, the latter prevails, subject to whatever may be the effect of s. 35 of the *Constitution Act, 1982*.

The Effect of Section 35 of the Constitution Act, 1982

Three provisions of the *Constitution Act, 1982* deal with the rights of aboriginal peoples. The first is s. 25, which is part of the *Canadian Charter of Rights and Freedoms* forming Part I of the Act, and reads as follows:. . .

Paragraph (b) was added by the *Constitution Amendment Proclamation, 1983*. This section confers no new rights but rather shields the treaty and other rights of aboriginal people from interference from other Charter provisions.

The second and main provision dealing with aboriginal and treaty rights is s. 35 which constitutes all of Part II of the *Constitution Act, 1982* and provides:. . .

Sub-sections (3) and (4) were added by the *Constitution Amendment Proclamation, 1983*. Because s. 35 is in Part II of the *Constitution Act, 1982* and not Part I, which comprises the Charter, the rights protected by s. 35 cannot be limited under s. 1, overridden under s. 33, or enforced under s. 24 of the Charter. Laws contravening s. 35 can, however, be set aside under s. 52(1) of the *Constitution Act, 1982* which provides:

> 52.(1) The Constitution of Canada is the supreme law of Canada, and any law that is inconsistent with the provisions of the Constitution is, to the extent of the inconsistency, of no force or effect.

The third set of provisions dealing with aboriginal peoples occurs in Parts IV (now repealed) and IV.1 entitled Constitutional Conferences which are not relevant to this appeal.

Section 35(1), for the first time, entrenches aboriginal and treaty rights in the constitution by recognizing and affirming "existing aboriginal and treaty rights of the aboriginal peoples". Aboriginal rights are not involved in this case. The issue in this appeal comes down to the meaning to be given to the words "existing treaty rights" in s. 35(1) and, in particular, the significance of the inclusion of the word "existing" in this phrase. There are two alternatives. Do the words mean the rights established by a treaty at the time the treaty was executed? Or do they mean only those treaty rights which could be exercised after restriction or limitation by federal law on April 17, 1982 when the *Constitution Act, 1982* came into force?

How s. 35 came to be incorporated in the *Constitution Act, 1982* is described in contemporary accounts of the evolution of the Act from the initial proposal made by the Government of Canada in 1978 for a Charter of Rights and patriation of the constitution. Originally no significant protection of aboriginal rights was proposed. It was not until the process was well advanced and being considered by a Joint Parliamentary Committee that the Government of Canada, on January 30, 1981, amended its proposal to include a clause identical with the present s. 35(1) except for the absence of the word "existing". The negotiations which followed between the federal and provincial governments resulted in the deletion of the clause in the inter-governmental agreement known as the "Accord" of November 5, 1981. There were protests against this deletion which led to further federal-provincial discussions. The final result was an agreement on November 23, 1981, to re-insert s. 35(1) in the proposal with the addition of the word "existing". It is generally believed that the word was added to provide some restriction on the concept of aboriginal rights which native organizations claim included the right of self-government. The inclusion of the word "existing" allayed the fears of some provinces as to the section's impact on their jurisdiction: see Romanow, Whyte and Leeson, *Canada . . . Notwithstanding, The Making of the Constitution 1976-1982*, (1984), at pp. 121-22, 209, 212-14 and 268-69; K.M. Lysyk, "The Rights and Freedoms of the Aboriginal Peoples of Canada", Tarnopolsky and Beaudoin eds., *The Canadian Charter of Rights and Freedoms* (1982), at p. 477; Douglas Sanders, "Prior Claims: Aboriginal People in the Constitution of Canada" *op. cit.*, at pp. 228-237; and Douglas Sanders, "The Indian Lobby", Banting and Simeon eds., *And No One Cheered, Federalism, Democracy and the Constitution Act* (1983); Douglas Sanders, "The Rights of Aboriginal Peoples of Canada" (1983), 61 Can. Bar Rev. 314 at pp. 330-31.

Courts are entitled to take notice of the evolution of clauses in pre-Charter discussions just as references to the pre-Confederation discussions leading to the *Constitution Act, 1867* have been accepted as an aid in interpreting that Act. . .

Professor Lysyk, as he then was, stated that, in the House of Commons, "the Ministers of Justice and of Indian and Northern Affairs expressed the view that the addition of the word 'existing' carried no legal consequences": *op. cit.*, p. 478. the Minister of Justice said that it only made explicit what was already implicit in the section: see House of Commons Debates, November 24, 1981, pp. 13203-13206. However, while it is permissible to refer to the reports of pre-Charter discussions to trace the evolution of s. 35(1) and to ascertain when and in what circumstances the word "existing" was inserted, they are of little assistance in establishing its meaning. In *Re B.C. Motor Vehicle Act*, [1985] 2 S.C.R. 486, Lamer J. observed that speeches made in Parliament, while admissible, should be given minimal weight in the interpretation of Charter provisions. . .

The statutory history of s. 35(1) is thus of little assistance in determining its meaning and effect and no consensus has yet emerged from the judicial decisions and academic articles in which it has been considered and to which I will now refer.

Judicial Opinion of Section 35

In *R. v. Hare and Debassige*, supra, the offence of fishing by means of a gill net without a licence contrary to s. 12(1) of the *Ontario Fishery Regulations* was committed prior to the proclamation of the *Constitution Act, 1982*. This court followed *R. v. George*, supra, in holding that Indian treaties were subject to valid federal legislation. The Court also stated that s. 35(1) did not apply to a pre-proclamation offence. Nevertheless, Thorson J.A. expressed, in *obiter*, the opinion that s. 35(1) protected only those treaty rights which had not been "lost by operation of federal legislation". He said at p. 155:

The offences in this case occurred in October, 1980. Quite apart from that, as I read s. 35, any treaty right for which protection may be claimed thereunder must have been in existence on April 17, 1982, when the *Constitution Act, 1982* was proclaimed in force, and if any such right had become extinguished before that date, s. 35 does not have the effect of reviving it. In this I agree with the interpretation of s. 35 favoured by Professor P.W. Hogg in *Canada Act 1982 Annotated* (1982), at p. 83, that these rights have been

> . . . "constitutionalized" prospectively, so that past (validly enacted) alterations or extinguishments continue to be legally effective, but future legislation which purports to make any further alterations or extinguishments is of no force or effect.

In this case, as earlier concluded, whatever right the respondents' forefathers may once have enjoyed under Treaty No. 94 in relation to fishing by means of gill-nets had become lost by operation of federal legislation well before the charges were brought. One may leave to another occasion any speculation on what effect s. 35 might have on any right enjoyed by the respondents in common with all other persons to fish by a means that had not become unlawful before April 17, 1982, but which is thereafter sought to be made unlawful for all persons by an amendment to the regulations promulgated after that date.

He also emphasized that the reason for limitation of treaty rights was conservation and the proper management of fish and wildlife resources when he said at p. 156:. . .

The same interpretation was placed on s. 35(1) in two decisions of the Saskatchewan Court of Queen's Bench which precede *Hare*. In *R. v. Eninew* . . . the accused argued that s. 35(1) invalidated the restrictions in the *Migratory Bird Regulations*, C.R.C. 1978, c. 1035, s. 5(4) as they applied to Indians and restored to Indians an unfettered right to hunt. This argument was rejected by Gerein J. who said at pp. 598-99:

> What then is the effect of the word "existing"? In my opinion, it circumscribes the rights of the aboriginal peoples of Canada. It limits the rights of those peoples to those rights which were in being or which were in actuality at the time when the *Constitution Act, 1982* came into effect, namely, April 17, 1982. Were it to be otherwise, Parliament would have used the word "original" or some like word or would have utilized some other device such as a date.
>
> As of April 17, 1982, and more particularly as of April 29, 1982, when the offence was committed, Indians did not enjoy an unrestricted right to hunt. As stated earlier, this treaty right had been abridged by a regulation of Parliament acting within its authority. The *Constitution Act, 1982* did not have the effect of repealing the regulation or rendering

it invalid. Rather the *Constitution Act, 1982* only recognized and secured the *status quo*. What might be the fate of any future legislation similar to the regulation herein is another matter to be dealt with at another time. . .

An identical decision was rendered on the same facts by Milliken J. in *R.* v. *Bear*, [1983] 3 C.N.L.R. 57. The decision of Gerein in *Eninew* was followed by the New Brunswick Court of Queen's Bench in *R.* v. *Martin* (1985), 65 N.B.R. (2d) 21 and in *R.* v. *Paul*, released March 15, 1988, unreported.

In *R.* v. *Eninew*; *R.* v. *Bear*, [1984] 2 C.N.L.R. 126, the Saskatchewan Court of Appeal dismissed appeals from the above Queen's Bench decisions but for different reasons. The treaty right of the appellant, Bear, to hunt and fish was "subject to such regulations as may from time to time be made by Her Government of Her Dominion of Canada". The appellant Eninew's treaty right to pursue hunting, trapping and fishing was "subject to such regulations as may from time to time be made by the government of the country acting under the authority of His Majesty". Since the treaty rights were subject to regulation, the Court held that it made no difference to the outcome which view of the treaty rights was adopted. . .

He held that the treaty rights could be limited by reasonable regulations and said at p. 129 C.N.L.R.:

It follows that the treaty rights can be limited by such regulations as are reasonable. The *Migratory Birds Convention Act* and the regulations made pursuant to it, based as they are on international convention, are reasonable, desirable limitations on the rights granted . . . .

Re Steinhauer and The Queen, [1985] 3 C.N.L.R. 187 (Alta. Q.B.) and *R.* v. *Sundown*, released February 11, 1988, (Sask. Q.B.) unreported, followed *Eninew* and *Bear*, supra.

A different approach to s. 35(1) was taken in *Sparrow* v. *The Queen* (1987), 36 D.L.R. (4th) 246 where the British Columbia Court of Appeal dealt with an amendment to the *British Columbia Fishery Regulations* made after the *Constitution Act, 1982* was proclaimed . . . The court held, in a by-the-court decision, that s. 35(1) protected aboriginal fishing rights from extinguishment but not regulation under valid federal legislation enacted after the *Constitution Act, 1982* took effect. The court stated at p. 269 D.L.R.:

. . . [T]hat before 17th April 1982, the aboriginal right to fish was subject to regulation by legislation; and that it was subject to extinguishment. The question whether there is now a power to extinguish does not arise in this case but it is relevant to observe that extinguishment and regulation are essentially different concepts. Even if there cannot now be extinguishment, it would not follow that there cannot be regulation. It may be that a power to extinguish is necessarily inconsistent with the recognition and affirmation of aboriginal right in s. 35(1). There is no necessary inconsistency with a power to regulate.

The court had earlier rejected the doctrine of "extinguishment by regulation" when it said at p. 265 D.L.R.:. . .

The court rejected the Crown's argument that the decisions in *R.* v. *Eninew*; *R.* v. *Bear* and *R.* v. *Hare*, supra, supported the argument that s. 35(1) provided no basis for restricting its power to regulate. *R.* v. *Eninew*; *R.* v. *Bear* was said to be of little assistance because the treaty provisions themselves made hunting and fishing rights subject to future regulation. *R.* v. *Hare* was described as of limited application because it dealt with an offence which occurred before s. 35(1) came into effect and did not involve regulations imposed afterwards.

The court had no difficulty in holding that aboriginal fishing rights were subject to regulation where it was demonstrated that restriction was necessary for the conservation of the fishery. This principle was conceded by counsel for the appellant who argued that the Crown had failed to demonstrate the necessity of the reduction in net size. The importance of conservation was recognized by the court by quoting the passage in the judgment of Thorson J.A. in *Hare*, supra, referred to above and by adding a further observation at p. 272 D.L.R.:. . .

Although *Sparrow* was concerned with aboriginal and not treaty rights, its conclusions can properly be considered in this case. It rejected the two extreme views that under s. 35(1) aboriginal rights could either not be interfered with or were defined by fishing regulations in existence when the section came into force. The court found a compromise between these extremes by approving restrictions on fishing rights which could be justified under s. 35(1) as conservation measures. It concluded at p. 276 D.L.R.:

> We conclude that none of the submissions made to us as to the effect of s. 35(1) upon the power to regulate is entirely right but that the correct position lies between that put forward by the appellant and that put forward by the provincial Crown. There continues to be a power to regulate the exercise of fishing by Indians even where that fishing is pursuant to an aboriginal right but there are now limitations on that power.

A new trial was ordered in *Sparrow* because the trial judge had misdirected himself in holding that there were no aboriginal fishing rights in British Columbia. As a consequence, he had not properly considered whether the reduction of the additional net size was required to conserve fish stocks. The decision is now under appeal to the Supreme Court of Canada.

Sparrow was followed and applied in two Manitoba provincial court decisions: *R.* v. *Flett*, [1987] 5 W.W.R. 115 and *R.* v. *Stevenson*, released January 27, 1988, unreported, as well as in an Alberta provincial court decision in *R.* v. *Arcand*, released February 23, 1988, unreported.

Academic Comment on Section 35(1)

The effect of s. 35(1) has been carefully examined by scholars concerned with the rights of aboriginal peoples in Canada. They are almost unanimous in their view that a treaty right, which has not been extinguished but merely limited or restricted by federal legislation, is an existing treaty right within the meaning of s. 35(1). Only a treaty right which has been extinguished is incapable of revival. A representative statement of this view is provided by Professor Kent McNeil in "The Constitutional Rights of the Aboriginal Peoples of Canada" (1982), 4 Sup. Ct. L. Rev. 255. Professor McNeil adopts the approach of distinguishing between "sleeping" rights, which can be protected under s. 35(1) and "dead" rights, which are incapable of revival. He wrote at pp. 257-58:

> While it may be conceded that section 35(1) probably does not revive rights previously abrogated by legislation, it is suggested that different considerations apply to rights that were merely restricted but not extinguished. Thus, where aboriginal title to land had been extinguished by legislation, that title would no longer have been in existence on April 17, 1982 and therefore would not have been revived by section 35(1). Aboriginal or treaty rights to hunt, trap and fish that have been limited by federal or provincial legislation, on the other hand, continue to exist even though their exercise has been restricted. *A workable test that might be applied to determine whether a particular right has been extinguished or merely rendered unexercisable would be to ask whether the right would be restored if the legislation affecting it was repealed. If the answer is no, then the right must have been extinguished; if yes, it must still exist and therefore is entitled to constitutional protection under section 35(1).* [Emphasis added.]

Professor Norman K. Zlotkin, in "Unfinished Business: Aboriginal Peoples and the 1983 Constitutional Conference" (1983) (Institute of Intergovernmental Relations, Queen's University, Discussion Paper No. 15), approved the test proposed by Professor McNeil to distinguish rights that have been extinguished from those that have merely been limited. The test was also approved by Professor Brian Slattery in his article "The Constitutional Guarantee of Aboriginal and Treaty Rights" (1983), 8 Queen's L.J. 232 where he wrote at p. 264:. . .

Professor Douglas Sanders, in "The Rights of the Aboriginal Peoples of Canada", Beck and Bernier eds., *Canada and the New Constitution, The Unfinished Agenda*, Vol. 1 (1983), distinguishes consensual extinguishment of treaty rights, which removes them from the protection of s. 35(1), from non-consensual limitation which does not deprive them of the protection of the section. Rights which were extinguished ceased to exist but rights which had been merely limited continued in existence as he explained at p. 331:

The consensual loss of treaty rights (as occurred with valid surrenders of reserve lands) would be confirmed, but the non-consensual loss (as in the example of hunting and fishing rights) would not be.

The literature is reviewed by Professor W.F. Pentney in *The Aboriginal Rights Provisions in the Constitution Act, 1982*, (Saskatoon: University of Saskatchewan, Native Law Centre, 1987). His views are summarized at pp. iii and iv of the preface.

Section 35 of the Constitution Act, 1982, is an independently enforceable guarantee of "existing aboriginal and treaty rights." The word "existing" is interpreted in this thesis to mean "not extinguished" rather than "not subject to any restriction." Section 35, therefore, protects any rights which have not previously been lawfully extinguished. An analysis of the scholarly commentary and the cases on section 35 reveals a divergence of opinion on this point, but a principled analysis of the provision supports the view advanced in this thesis.

The divergence of opinion referred to by Professor Pentney is illustrated by the caution expressed by Professor Lysyk that the insertion of the word "existing" in s. 35(1) might have a limiting effect. In his article, referred to above, he said, *op. cit.*, at pp. 485-86:

> . . . [F]ederal enactments have paramount effect over treaty rights and the latter must yield to the extent of any conflict. It has been suggested above that prior to insertion of the word "existing" in what is now subs. 35(1) of the Constitution Act a strong argument would have been available to the effect that the constitutional recognition and affirmation of treaty rights was intended to accord primacy to treaty rights against all federal, as well as against all provincial, legislation. The present formulation, however, expressed in terms of "existing" treaty rights, suggests an entrenchment of, not a change in, existing law.

Professor D. Sanders, also recognized the problems of interpretation created by s. 35(1). In "The Renewal of Indian Special Status", Bayefsky and Eberts eds., *Equality Rights and The Canadian Charter of Rights and Freedoms* (1985), he wrote at pp. 554-55:. . .

Section 35(1) has been the subject of less extensive comment in general textbooks on Canadian constitutional law. Although the authors take note of some of the literature referred to above, they conclude, without the same detailed analysis, that the section only protects treaty rights as limited by federal legislation when the *Constitution Act, 1982* was proclaimed. The conclusion of Professor Hogg in *Canada Act 1982 Annotated* (1982) was approved by Thorson J.A. in *Hare*, supra. It is repeated in his *Constitutional Law of Canada*, 2nd ed. (1985), at p. 566. The same view is expressed in *Laskin's Canadian Constitutional Law*, Vol. 1, 5th ed. (1988) at p. 659 and

Magnet, *Constitutional Law of Canada*, Vol. II, 3rd ed. (1987) at p. 974 where he wrote:

> It seems most likely that "existing" adds nothing to section 35(1). With or without the word, the section was never intended to revive aboriginal or treaty rights which had been legally ended in the past. Therefore, treaty protected hunting rights will continue to be subject to the Migratory Birds Convention Act, R.S.C. 1970, c. M-12 as held in various pre-1982 cases beginning with *R. v. Sikyea* . . . .

Some academic commentators have raised a further problem which cannot be ignored. The *Ontario Fishery Regulations* contain detailed rules which vary for different regions in the province. Among other things, the regulations specify seasons and methods of fishing, species of fish which can be caught and catch limits. Similar detailed provisions apply under the comparable fisheries regulations in force in other provinces. These detailed provisions might be constitutionalized if it were decided that the existing treaty rights referred to in s. 35(1) were those remaining after regulation at the time of the proclamation of the *Constitution Act, 1982*. This, it is argued, might necessitate reading what Professor Slattery has termed the "myriad of regulations" in existence on April 17, 1982 into the treaty rights protected by s. 35. Logically it might seem to follow that even a minor variance of the regulations affecting Indian treaty fishing rights might possibly require a constitutional amendment: see also McNeil *op. cit.*, at p. 258.

This problem is confronted by Professor Slattery in a recent article, "Understanding Aboriginal Rights" (1986), 66 Can. Bar. Rev. 727. He recognizes the need for greater flexibility in changing legislation and regulations in the future to conserve wildlife resources and protect endangered species from extinction. Although his article deals with aboriginal rights, his observations, in my opinion, apply equally to treaty rights. Like other authors referred to above, he regards the words "existing rights" as meaning "unextinguished rights". But he recognizes that even though these rights may be "unextinguished", the question remains as to the degree to which they may be subject to regulations or limitations either in place at the proclamation of the *Constitution Act, 1982* or enacted thereafter. Professor Slattery envisions a number of possible solutions. The first is to read into the aboriginal or treaty rights the "myriad of regulations" in existence on April 17, 1982. An alternative is to recognize unextinguished aboriginal rights in their original form unrestricted by subsequent regulation. Professor Slattery rejects both suggestions and proposes a compromise at p. 782:

> The desirable solution, then, lies between these two extremes. *It is submitted that section 35(1) permits a court to uphold certain regulations in existence at the commencement date, while striking down others, and allows legislatures a limited power of regulation in the future.* The

governing criteria should be worked out on a case by case basis. But, at the least, the following sorts of regulations would be valid: (1) regulations that operate to preserve or advance section 35 rights (as by conserving a natural resource essential to the exercise of such rights); (2) regulations that prevent the exercise of section 35 rights from causing serious harm to the general populace or native peoples themselves (such as standard safety restrictions governing the use of fire-arms in hunting); and (3) regulations that implement state policies of overriding importance to the general welfare (as in times of war or emergency). [Emphasis added.]

This approach would import a justificatory process, comparable to that provided in s. 1 of the Charter, to assess the validity of past, present and future limitations on Indian fishing treaty rights. This approach avoids the rigidity of definitions of Indian treaty rights in terms of what they were at the time treaties were executed or as they had been restricted when the *Constitution Act, 1982* was proclaimed.

Conclusion

Although great respect is due to the dicta pronounced by this court in *Hare*, supra, and the views of other courts, it must be recognized that there is no decision binding on this court and no judicial or academic consensus on the meaning of the words "existing treaty rights" in s. 35(1). It is arguable that the phrase refers either to rights created by Indian treaties or to only such of those rights as were legally exercisable on April 17, 1982. Which of these two views should prevail depends upon the proper construction of the phrase "existing treaty rights". This cannot be undertaken as an arid semantical exercise concentrating on the meaning of particular words and especially the word "existing". Rather, the phrase "existing treaty rights" must be interpreted in its context in s. 35(1) which includes the principles governing the status and interpretation of Indian treaty rights in Canada.

Two principles governing the interpretation of Indian treaties and statutes apply equally, in my opinion, to the interpretation of s. 35(1). The first was stated by Dickson J. in *Nowegijick* v. *The Queen* [1983] 1 S.C.R. 29 where he said at p. 36 S.C.R.:

. . . [T]reaties and statutes relating to Indians should be liberally construed and doubtful expressions resolved in favour of the Indians.

This principle was applied to the interpretation of aboriginal rights in s. 35(1) by the British Columbia Court of Appeal in *Sparrow* v. *The Queen*, supra, at p. 268 D.L.R.

The second principle was enunciated by the late Associate Chief Justice MacKinnon in *R.* v. *Taylor and Williams* (1981), 34 O.R. (2d) 360. He emphasized the importance of Indian history and traditions as well as the perceived effect of a treaty at the time of its execution. He also cautioned against determining Indian rights "in a vacuum". The honour of the Crown is involved in the interpretation of Indianreaties and, as a consequence, fairness to the Indians is a governing consideration. He said at p. 367 O.R.:

> The principles to be applied to the interpretation of Indian treaties have been much canvassed over the years. In approaching the terms of a treaty quite apart from the other considerations already noted, the honour of the Crown is always involved and no appearance of "sharp dealing" should be sanctioned.

This view is reflected in recent judicial decisions which have emphasized the responsibility of Government to protect the rights of Indians arising from the special trust relationship created by history, treaties and legislation: see *Guerin* v. *The Queen*, [1984] 2 S.C.R. 335.

While it is consistent with authority to dispose of this appeal by resolving any ambiguity in s. 35(1) in favour of the Indian band, I consider that there is a more positive justification for the continuing exercise of Indian treaty rights to fish. In this case, it seems to me that it is impossible to say that this right does not exist. It has not been extinguished. At most, it has been restricted by the requirement that Indians be licensed before exercising it. What is at stake is not the existence of the Indians' treaty right to fish but whether that right can properly be restricted by the licensing requirement.

In addressing this question it must be borne in mind that not all Indian treaty rights are absolute and immutable. While Indian property rights derived from treaties may remain virtually unqualified, hunting and fishing rights cannot be divorced from the realities of life in present-day Canada. Much has changed since the treaty was executed in 1850. At that time, fish and game may have been regarded as limitless resources. They are no longer. Conservation and management of fish and game resources are required if they are to be protected from extinction and preserved for the benefit of Indians as well as other Canadians. This fact is recognized in the extracts quoted earlier form the judgments of this court in *Hare*, supra, and the British Columbia Court of Appeal in *Sparrow*, supra. It has also been recognized by the Supreme Court in *Jack* v. *The Queen*, [1980] 1 S.C.R. 294 where Dickson J. said at p. 313 S.C.R., "Conservation is a valid legislative concern". Professor Slattery, *op. cit.*, also suggests that aboriginal rights must be properly restricted for other reasons of overriding importance to the general welfare, such as public health and safety.

In this respect, Indian treaty rights are like all other rights recognized by our legal system. The exercise of rights by an individual or group is limited by the rights of others. Rights do not exist in a vacuum and the exercise of any right involves a balancing with the interests and values involved in the rights of others. This is recognized in s. 1 of the *Canadian Charter of Rights and Freedoms* which provides that limitation of Charter rights must be justified as reasonable in a free and democratic society. In the United States the rights proclaimed by the *Bill of Rights* are not qualified by a provision similar to s. 1 of the Charter, yet they have been subjected, nonetheless, to reasonable limitation by judicial decisions.

This test of reasonableness has been applied to Indian treaty and aboriginal rights. The Saskatchewan Court of Appeal in *R. v. Eninew*; *R. v. Bear*, supra, applied the same principle to provisions in Indian treaties, making them subject to governmental regulation. It held that restrictions on hunting and fishing rights must be shown to be reasonable for the purpose of conservation. In *Sparrow*, supra, the British Columbia Court of Appeal held that restrictions on aboriginal fishing rights must also be reasonably justified as conservation measures.

Conservation, in my view, is manifestly the purpose of the licensing provisions in the Regulations. At first instance, the learned justice of the peace found that:

> The purpose of the Fisheries Act and Regulations made thereunder, although binding upon all persons, is not to abolish the rights to fish of all persons, but to monitor and regulate, so that the fisheries resource will provide an adequate supply of fish now, and in the future.

On a fair reading of the reasons of the learned summary conviction appeal court judge those findings were, in my opinion, approved and affirmed by him . . .

These concurrent findings were not disputed by counsel for the respondent who stated, as noted above, that the purpose of the challenge to the *Ontario Fishery Regulations* was to test Indian rights under s. 35(1) of the *Constitution Act, 1982*. Since s. 12(1) of the Regulations, which requires a licence for gill net fishing and applies to all residents of Ontario, serves a valid conservation purpose, it constitutes a reasonable limitation on the Batchawana Band's treaty right to fish and, therefore, does not infringe s. 35(1) of the *Constitution Act, 1982*. From this, it follows that the appeal must succeed.

It is almost unnecessary to add that this decision is based upon the facts established in this case. Counsel for the respondent did not pursue in argument the submission made in his factum that Indian fishing rights constitute a prior claim on fishery resources. In support of this argument that factum quoted a passage from the judgment of Dickson J. in *R. v. Jack, supra*, at p. 313 S.C.R. where he said that he agreed with "the general tenor of the argument" that "the burden of conservation measures should not fall primarily upon the Indian fishery". The adjustment of priorities, where required in appropriate cases, between Indian fishermen based on their treaty rights and other fishermen must be left for another day.

For the foregoing reasons, I would grant leave to appeal, allow the appeal, set aside the order of the summary conviction appeal court judge and restore the conviction.

Manitoba Métis Federation Inc. v.
Attorney General of Canada
[1988] 3 CNLR 39 (Man. C.A.)

Ed. Note: The plaintiffs (Manitoba Métis Federation and various individual Métis) sued for a declaration that a number of federal and provincial statutes and orders-in-council passed between 1871 and 1886 were unconstitutional because their effect was to deprive many people of land to which they were entitled under the *Manitoba Act*. The purpose for this lawsuit was to strengthen their position in seeking a negotiated land settlement. Before the matter could go to trial against both the Governments of Canada and Manitoba, the federal Justice Department sought to strike out the statement of claim on the basis that (a) it revealed no cause of action; (b) the plaintiffs did not have legal standing to sue; and (c) the claim disclosed no justiciable issue. The Court of Queen's Bench rejected this motion and the federal Attorney General appealed.

TWADDLE J.A. (with 3 judges concurring): The plaintiffs challenge the constitutional validity of several pieces of federal legislation enacted between 1871 and 1886. They say the legislation was unconstitutional because it altered provisions of the *Manitoba Act*, S.C. 1870, c. 3, contrary to the prohibition against such alteration contained in the *Constitution Act, 1871* (U.I. c. 28). The Attorney General of Canada seeks to abort the challenge on the ground, amongst others, that the validity of the impugned legislation is a matter of academic interest only.

Rupert's Land was granted to the Hudson's Bay Company by Charles II in 1670. By 1867, the effective authority of the Company in Rupert's Land was on the decline. The United Kingdom Parliament was thus able to foresee, and provide for, the eventual union of Rupert's Land with Canada. Provisions for this union are to be found in the *Constitution Act, 1867* and the *Rupert's Land Act, 1868*.

Included in Rupert's Land was the territory which was to become Manitoba. Many of those who lived in the territory in the years immediately preceding union were persons of mixed native and European blood, their European ancestors having come to North America after 1670. These persons were then known as "half-breeds". Some half-breeds occupied small areas of land and all used unoccupied land freely. The area of land used by them lacked definition.

In anticipation of the union of Rupert's Land with Canada, the Parliament of Canada enacted the *Rupert's Land Act*, S.C. 1869, c. 3, by which it made provision for the future government of the territory. Also in anticipation of the union, the Government of Canada sent survey teams into the territory.

In August, 1869, a number of half-breeds, fearful of the effect the proposed union would have on their use of land, opposed the making of surveys. What followed was, from Canada's viewpoint, rebellion. A number of local inhabitants openly disputed Canada's right to annex the territory, although others were anxious for union. A state of unrest prevailed. The authority of the Company had been weakened by its own inaction. In the absence of an effective ruling power, a provisional government was formed by some of the people.

The Provisional Government (as it styled itself) sent delegates to Ottawa to negotiate the terms on which the territory might be united with Canada. A draft bill resulted from the negotiations. Before its enactment as the *Manitoba Act*, it was approved by what was known as the Assembly of the Provisional Government. This Act, assented to in May, 1870, preceded the effective date on which legislative authority for the government of the territory was vested in the Parliament of Canada by the Order of Her Majesty in Her Imperial Council dated June 23, 1870.

Land rights within the province were provided for in ss. 30, 31 and 32 of the *Manitoba Act*, in these terms:

30.   All ungranted or waste lands in the Province shall be, from and after the date of the said transfer, vested in the Crown, and administered by the Government of Canada for the purposes of the Dominion, subject to, and except and so far as the same may be affected by, the conditions and stipulations contained in the agreement for the surrender of Rupert's Land by the Hudson's Bay Company to Her Majesty.

31.   And whereas, it is expedient, towards the extinguishment of the Indian Title to the lands in the Province, to appropriate a portion of such ungranted lands, to the extent of one million four hundred thousand acres thereof, for the benefit of the families of the half-breed residents, it is hereby enacted, that, under regulations to be from time to time made by the Governor General in Council, the Lieutenant-Governor shall select such lots or tracts in such parts of the Province as he may deem expedient, to the extent aforesaid, and divide the same among the children of the half-breed heads of families residing in the Province at the time of the said transfer to Canada, and the same shall be granted to the said children respectively, in such mode and on such conditions as to settlement and otherwise, as the Governor General in Council may from time to time determine.

32.   For the quieting of titles, and assuring to the settlers in the Province the peaceable possession of the lands now held by them, it is enacted as follows:

[Subsections 1 to 3 guarantee freehold title to all occupants who possessed an interest in land from the Hudson's Bay Company.]

4.   All persons in peaceable possession of tracts of land at the time of the transfer to Canada, in those parts of the Province in which the Indian Title has not been extinguished, shall have the right of pre-emption of the

same, on such terms and conditions as may be determined by the Governor in Council.

5.   The Lieutenant-Governor is hereby authorized, under regulations to be made from time to time by the Governor General in Council, to make all such provisions for ascertaining and adjusting, on fair and equitable terms, the rights of Common, and rights of cutting Hay held and enjoyed by the settlers in the Province, and for the commutation of the same by grants of land from the Crown.

Doubts having been expressed as to the authority of the Parliament of Canada to establish the Province of Manitoba, the United Kingdom Parliament enacted the *Constitution Act, 1871*, which retroactively validated the *Manitoba Act*. Section 6 of the *Constitution Act, 1871* provided:

6.   Except as provided by the third section of this Act, it shall not be competent for the Parliament of Canada to alter the provisions of the last-mentioned Act of the said Parliament in so far as it relates to the Province of Manitoba, . . .

Subsequent legislation enacted by the Parliament of Canada and by the Governor General in Council regulated the allocation of land to half-breed children and the making of claims to land under s. 32 of the *Manitoba Act*. The plaintiffs allege that the subsequent legislation went beyond mere regulation. They say that it altered or embellished the original statutory provisions. They also say that this alteration or embellishment was contrary to the provisions of s. 6 of the *Constitution Act, 1871*.

I must say that, when I read the impuged legislation, I do not find provisions which can readily be regarded as alterations to the original enactment. Indeed, one of the impugned statutes actually conferred additional rights on individual half-breeds (S.C. 1874, c. 20). I do not find it necessary, however, to decide this appeal on the basis that the plaintiffs do not have a reasonable cause of action. It is my view that this appeal can be decided on the question of whether the issue which the plaintiffs wish to raise is justiciable.

Before turning to that question, let me make it clear that, for the purpose of this appeal, I assume the truth of all allegations of fact contained in the statement of claim. Those allegations include the allegation that all half-breeds of 1870 were "Métis"; that the Métis of 1870 were a distinct people; and that all their descendants are included within the undefined group of persons constitutionally recognized today as "the Métis people." These allegations which I assume as true also include the allegation that some half-breeds of 1870 did not receive, or were deprived of, constitutionally entrenched rights and the allegation that their loss of those rights was a result of the impugned legislation.

The plaintiffs do not assert any rights of their own. They acknowledge, at least in argument, that the land of which their forebears were deprived cannot be restored to them and that they, the plaintiffs, have no legal right to compensation for the loss. What they seek is a declaration that the impugned legislation was invalid. They seek this declaration not to establish rights arising from that loss, but for a collateral purpose. That purpose is stated in the statement of claim in these terms:

> [I]t would be greatly to the advantage of the Métis, in seeking to achieve a land claims agreement pursuant to s. 35(3) of the *Constitution Act*, 1982, as amended, to obtain a declaration that the federal . . . statutes and orders-in-councils . . . were unconstitutional measures that had the purpose and effect of stripping the Métis of the land base promised to them under sections 31 and 32 of the *Manitoba Act*, 1870.

The land claims agreement which the Métis seek is being sought extra-judicially. The land claim is rooted in the aboriginal status of the Métis people, a status recognized by s. 35 of the *Constitution Act, 1982*. Section 35 of that enactment provides: . . .

The Constitution was further amended by Proclamation in 1984 when subsection (3) was added to s. 35. It provides: . . .

The fact that the Métis might acquire a community of interest in land under a land claims agreement does not mean that the plaintiffs are claiming that such an interest in the land was given to half-breeds by the *Manitoba Act*. I can find no allegation in the statement of claim which suggests that the plaintiffs are asserting in this action a community of interest in any land.

Any doubt as to what the plaintiffs are alleging is removed when one reads para. 13 of the statement of claim. It reads in part:

> Approximately 85% of Métis persons entitled to rights under sections 31 and 32 of the Manitoba Act failed to receive or were deprived of such rights by reason of the unconstitutional . . . legislation. . . .

It must follow that some 15 percent of Métis retained their rights. Such a result is totally inconsistent with a collective grant to a community of persons. Such a grant must stand or fall as an entirety.

It is, in any event, impossible to construe s. 31 of the *Manitoba Act* as conferring on half-breed children generally a community of interest in the 1,400,000 acres appropriated for the benefit of the families of half-breed residents. The section makes it quite clear that the land was to be divided "among the children of the half-breed heads of families residing in the Province" and "granted to the said children respectively."

The plaintiffs argue that, by reason of the loss of individual land rights, their forebears were unable to assemble the land which should have been theirs into townships. The argument proceeds on the notion that, but for the impugned legislation, individual titles to land within the townships would have been handed down from one generation to the next so that the present generation of Métis people would not only have enjoyed land rights inherited by them as individuals, but would also have enjoyed the social and economic benefits to be derived from belonging to an integrated community. That argument is purely speculative of what might have been. It offers no justification for a finding that the plaintiffs have a community of interest in some unspecified land or that their own rights are at issue.

What the court is being asked to consider in this case is the constitutional validity of spent legislation which does not affect anyone's current rights. The rights affected by the impugned legislation were the statutory rights of individuals who are now deceased. These rights are not being pursued individually by the legal representatives of the persons whose rights they were, but generally by descendants whose degree of relationship is not even stated.

The courts can determine the constitutional validity of legislation no matter how old it is. Thus, in *Attorney General of Manitoba* v. *Forest*, [1979] 2 S.C.R. 1032, the Supreme Court of Canada held that the *Official Language Act*, S.M. 1890, c. 14, was inoperable although it had been enacted almost 90 years before. The differences in that case from this are, however, quite significant. The language rights conferred by the *Manitoba Act* were conferred on the public generally. They were conferred not only on persons then alive, but also on all future generations.

The plaintiffs are not entitled to a declaration merely for the purpose of demonstrating that their forebears were deprived of their rights unconstitutionally. It is a well-established principle that a declaration is not available as a cure for past ills. Dickson J. (as he then was) used that language in his reasons for judgment in *Solosky* v. *The Queen*, [1980] 1 S.C.R. 821 in which he also said (at p. 832):

> It is clear that a declaration will not normally be granted when the dispute is over and has become academic.

The dispute to which Dickson J. was referring in *Solosky* was the defended claim by a prison inmate that he had been denied his right to receive uncensored correspondence from his solicitor. The Supreme Court disposed of the claim on its merits, but only because the declaration sought would also have affected the right of the inmate to receive uncensored correspondence in the future.

The rationale for the grant of a declaration in this case can only be its potential utility to the parties in the resolution of the Métis land claim. The granting of a declaration in aid of an extra-judicial claim is illustrated by a number of cases including *Merricks* v. *Nott-Bower*, [1964] 1 All E.R. 717, *Landreville* v. *The Queen* (1973), 41 D.L.R. (3d) 574 and *Kelso* v. *The Queen*, [1981] 1 S.C.R. 199 . . .

Although the court could not provide a legal remedy in any of these three cases, it could decide an issue the resolution of which was essential to the settlement of an extra-judicial claim. The settlement of the extra-judicial claim would thus be promoted by the court deciding the entitlement of the plaintiff or the plaintiffs to the declaration sought.

As I have already said, the declaration sought in the present case can only have utility if it has the potential of promoting a settlement of the Métis land claim. It is therefore necessary to examine the basis of that claim and the factors which likely will influence the parties in their settlement negotiations.

The *Constitution Act, 1982* recognized the Métis as an aboriginal people. The enactment also recognized the existing aboriginal rights of the Métis, whatever they were. The Proclamation of 1984 recognized the future rights which the Métis might acquire by way of a land claims agreement. The federal government has expressed a willingness to negotiate a settlement of the claim. Once it has been settled, the rights which the agreement confers on the Métis will be part of the Constitution of Canada. Until then, the federal government is obliged to do no more than negotiate with the Métis in good faith.

The legal basis of the land claim is a matter of great uncertainty. Unlike the Nishga Indian Tribe in *Calder* v. *Attorney-General of British Columbia*, [1973] S.C.R. 313, 34 D.L.R. (3d) 145, the Métis people did not occupy a clearly defined area of land and only on one side of their families can they show descent from persons who inhabited the land from time immemorial. Even if they had aboriginal rights prior to July 15, 1870, these rights may have been extinguished by the *Manitoba Act* or its subsequent validation. The issue of extinguishment divided the Supreme Court of Canada in the *Calder* case. It cannot be assumed that it will be resolved in favour of the Métis.

The federal government will be influenced in its negotiations with the Métis by many considerations. As well as by the Métis claim to legal rights, the federal government will be influenced by social and political considerations and by the historical circumstances which have resulted in the Métis being an aboriginal people without a land base. Those historical circumstances include the effects of the impugned legislation on the land holdings of individual Métis. The federal government will be able to consider those effects regardless of the legislation's constitutional validity.

The constitutional validity of the impugned legislation is certainly an issue of academic interest. The question is, however, whether a decision on the issue has the potential of being useful to the parties in the course of negotiating a political settlement to the Métis land claim. Unlike the declarations sought in *Merricks* v. *Nott-Bower, Landreville* and *Kelso*, all supra, the declaration sought in this case will not decide an issue essential to the resolution of the extra-judicial claim. The settlement of the Métis claim will not be promoted in any real sense by the making of the declaration sought by the plaintiffs.

For these reasons, I am of the opinion that the appeal should be allowed, the order made in Motions Court set aside and an order made striking out the plaintiffs' claim against the Attorney General of Canada. . . .

O'SULLIVAN J.A. (dissenting):

Lawyers trained in the British tradition tend to look on rights as either private or public. If private, they must be asserted by persons who claim a property interest in the rights. If public, the rights must be asserted by an Attorney

General or on the relation of an Attorney General. In extraordinary cases, it is conceded that individual persons may be granted special status to assert public rights. See, for example, *Thorson* v. *A.G. Canada*, [1975] 1 S.C.R. 138, and *Minister of Justice* v. *Borowski*, [1981] 2 S.C.R. 575.

At the hearing before us, counsel for the appellant were asked to show what title or interest individual half-breeds claim to land denied them by the impugned statutes. It was accepted that any individual who asserts a claim in himself, and who can show a claim of title or right of inheritance, may be able to secure relief by suing on his own behalf but it is disputed whether anyone is capable of asserting in our municipal courts rights belonging to a people.

It is difficult for common lawyers to understand what the rights of "a people" can mean. Indeed, at a hearing before a parliamentary committee on the 1987 Constitution Accord (of Meech Lake) held August 27, 1987, the distinguished constitutional expert, the Right Honourable Pierre Elliott Trudeau said:

> In my philosophy, the community, an institution itself, has no rights. It has rights by delegation from the individuals. You give equality to the individuals. Then they will organize in societies to make sure those rights are respected.

This is an approach with deep roots in the British tradition and was probably the outlook adopted by the legislators who, following 1870, interpreted s. 31 of the *Manitoba Act* as establishing individual rights in the immense tract of land referred to in the section. Indeed, it seems clear that the authorities of the time took painstaking care to count the individuals with rights under the section and did their best to see to it that each claimant received, so far as practicable, his aliquot share of the tract.

True, there were undoubtedly some abuses in the acquisition by unscrupulous persons of the share of individual claimants. Such abuses have always been regretted and, even at this late date, I am sure that if any person could show that he or his ancestors were deprived of this or that particular share in the allotment, the courts would be astute to find him a remedy and, if through effluxion of time it was no longer possible to give effect to his claim, he could rely on the British sense of fair play to ensure that what he was deprived of is restored to him.

But, as far as I can see, what we have before us in court at this time is not the assertion of bundles of individual rights but the assertion of the rights and status of the half-breed people of the western plains.

The problem confronting us is how can the rights of the Métis people as a people be asserted. Must they turn to international bodies or to the conscience of humanity to obtain redress for their grievances as a people, or is it possible for us at the request of their representatives, to recognize their people claims as justiciable?

Whatever may have been the case prior to 1982, I think it is indisputable that the Canadian Constitution recognizes the existence of aboriginal peoples of

Canada and that the Métis are an aboriginal people. Section 35 of the *Constitution Act, 1982* reads as follows: . . .

I know there is a school of thought that says that the framers of the Constitution were of the view that the Métis people as such had no rights and that a cruel deception was practised on them and on the Queen whose duty it is to respect the treaties and understandings that she has entered into with her Métis people. But I do not subscribe to this school of thought.

In my opinion, it is impossible in our jurisprudence to have rights without a remedy and the rights of the Métis people must be capable of being asserted by somebody. If not by the present plaintiffs, then by whom?

It must be noted that the existence of the Métis people is asserted in the Constitution as of the present, not simply as of the past. Each individual plaintiff can, I think, prove indisputably his membership in the Métis nation. Their genealogical records are unparalleled in modern societies. See Sprague and Frye, *The Genealogy of the First Métis Nation* (1983). In any event, the question of their membership in this nation should not be called into question at the preliminary stage of a motion to strike out.

I may say in parenthesis that I find it most extraordinary that as I understand it the federal government should be funding a lawsuit which the government's Attorney General is simultaneously attempting to kill at birth.

One of the difficulties in enforcing the rights of native peoples is that they are difficult to define in common-law terms. Even the question of membership in a people may provide perplexing issues. But that a half-breed people existed as a people in the western plains of British North America in 1869 can hardly be doubted by those familiar with the history of this country. The half-breeds formed the overwhelming majority of the population of the Red River colony and had achieved such a degree of self-awareness as a people that with the acquiescence of Donald A. Smith and under the chairmanship of Judge Black they were able to form a provisional government which maintained law and order for many months in 1870. This provisional government may not have been recognized by some of the Canadian settlers in Ruperts' land, but it was recognized by the British government which entered into negotiations with delegates appointed by the convention that sanctioned and elected the provisional government.

The *Manitoba Act* sanctioned by Imperial legislation, is not only a statute; it embodies a treaty which was entered into between the delegates of the Red River settlement and the Imperial authority. Although some historians have suggested that concessions made to the Métis were "granted" by Macdonald, the truth is that the negotiations proceeded in the presence of Imperial delegates.

One of the key questions in dispute among historians and that arises in the case before us is what terms were agreed on between the representatives . . .

This one-sided view of history, shared by many English-speaking historians, looks on the Manitoba settlement as one of concession on the part of

Sir John A. Macdonald but the facts of history, in my opinion, demonstrate that the agreement was between representatives of the settlers and British representatives and not merely Macdonald alone. Note the important role played by Sir Clinton Murdoch who was sent by the Imperial authorities to help settle the affairs of the northwest.

It must be remembered that in 1869 and 1870 the Queen recognized the aboriginal titles in the land theretofore governed by the Hudson's Bay Company. This was acknowledged by Sir John A. Macdonald himself when he said in the House of Commons on May 2, 1870: . . .

The aboriginal titles so recognized were honoured by the whole of the civilized people of Europe at lease since the Papal bull Sublimis Deus issued by the Pope in 1537 which said in part:

> Desiring to provide ample remedy for these evils, we define and declare . . . the said Indians and all the people who may later be discovered by the Christians, are by no means to be deprived of their liberty or the possession of their property, even though they may be outside the faith of Jesus Christ, and that they may and should, fully and legitimately, enjoy their liberty and the possession of their property; nor should they in any way be enslaved; should the contrary happen it shall be null and of no effect.

See, on aboriginal titles generally, the authorities collected in *Aboriginal Peoples and the Law: Indian, Métis and Inuit Rights in Canada*, edited by Bradford W. Morse (Ottawa 1984), passim.

It has been accepted by everyone that the aboriginal rights could not be lost save by the consent of those who enjoyed them. If the Métis people did not give up their aboriginal rights by agreeing to accept the provisions of the *Manitoba Act* in lieu thereof, then the aboriginal rights of this people must still subsist.

But when they state the rights given to them under the *Manitoba Act* were given to them as a people and not simply as individuals, they are met with incomprehension.

As I understand the claim of the plaintiffs they say that the rights which the Métis were led to expect they had as a result of their agreement to give up their aboriginal titles were never honoured and they are seeking in a variety of ways to assert their grievances as a result.

One of the things which stands in the way of their claim is that the federal and provincial legislatures and governments have passed a series of statutes and regulations which were designed to have the effect, and did have the effect, of rendering nugatory the scheme which the Métis representatives had negotiated.

That scheme envisioned the developing of tracts of land en bloc to the extent of 1,400,000 acres in Manitoba. The people say they expected to have the land surveyed and allotted in such a way as to enable the half-breeds to continue their way of life which was not to live in isolated square sections, but in communities with community resources, with provision not only for individual cultivation but also for common pasturage and hunting . . .

The governments knew well how to allot land in such a way as to enable a community to live as such. They were able to accommodate the Mennonites by the eastern reserve and the western reserve and they were able to accommodate the French-Canadians on Pembina mountain. There, settlers were not given land at random; land was allotted only to persons who shared common values. . . .

The *British North America Act, 1871* (now the *Constitution Act*, 1871, 34 & 35 Vict., c. 28 U.K.) was an Imperial Act which confirmed the *Manitoba Act*. Section 6 of this Act specifically made the Act creating the province unalterable by the Parliament of Canada. An exception was created allowing the provincial legislature to make laws with respect to the qualifications of members of the legislature and elections within the province. The plaintiffs allege that the restrictions imposed on the federal Parliament and the provincial legislature were never adhered to.

The policy of land distribution spelled out in the *Manitoba Act* was amended by ancillary enactments on at least eleven occasions between 1873 and 1884. According to the plaintiffs, by 1884 the original legislation had been reduced to a hollow shell . . .

In my opinion, the plaintiffs are suitable persons to assert the claims of the half-breed people and their suit should be allowed to go forward with such suitable amendments as may be sought to conform with the evidence and materials to be introduced in the course of a trial. I would dismiss the application to strike out the statement of claim . . .

Nevertheless, I think it is important to accept that the claims asserted by the plaintiffs in the present action are justiciable and not merely political. The plaintiffs have status to assert their claims in the Court of Queen's Bench. I am sure the judge assigned to try the case will have a difficult time and will have to be able to adapt the process of the court to suit the nature of the case. But, in the end, in my opinion it is in the development of law to deal with claims of "peoples" that lies the best hope of achieving justice and harmony in a world full of minority groups.

Ed. Note: The plaintiffs have obtained leave to appeal this decision to the Supreme Court of Canada.

. . . . .

Ed. Note: The following two documents represented the final proposals from the Government of Canada and the national Aboriginal organizations presented on the last day of the 1987 First Ministers' Conference. Although numerous other drafts had been officially tabled and unofficially circulated by various parties during the numerous ministerial and senior officials' meetings held in preparation for the First Ministers' Conference (FMC), as well as on the opening day of the FMC, none gained the requisite level of support necessary to support a constitutional amendment, namely, seven provinces, the federal government and the Aboriginal groups. These two drafts became the final subjects for debate. The federal draft could only muster tentative support from five provinces while the Aboriginal draft did not obtain a "roll call" vote, however, it clearly did not receive the endorsement of the majority of the provinces or the federal government. As a result, the Prime Minister adjourned the FMC early on the second day after an in-camera meeting was unsuccessful in causing a significant shifting of positions.

First Ministers' Conference on Aboriginal Constitutional Matters
March 26-27, 1987
Federal Draft
Schedule
Amendment to the Constitution of Canada

1.   The *Constitution Act, 1982*, is amended by adding thereto, immediately after section 35 thereof, the following sections:

Right to self-government

*35.01 (1) The aboriginal peoples of Canada have the right to self-government within the context of the Canadian federation.

Jurisdiction etc., of bodies exercising right

(2) The jurisdiction, legislative powers, proprietary rights and other powers, rights and privileges of bodies or institutions exercising the right to self-government referred to in subsection (1) shall be determined and defined through agreements described in section 35.03.

Scheduling, nature and scope of negotiations

35.02 (1) The government of Canada and the provincial governments are committed to discussing with representatives of aboriginal people the scheduling, nature and scope of negotiations to be undertaken pursuant to subsection (2) and to providing to all aboriginal peoples of Canada equitable access to those discussions and to the process of negotiation.

Request for negotiations

(2) Any identifiable group of aboriginal people living in a particular community or region may request the government of Canada, and the government of any province in which the community or region is located, to negotiate an agreement relating to self-government.

Commitment to negotiate

(3) Where the government of Canada and the provincial governments of any province have received a request to negotiate an agreement pursuant to subsection (2), those governments shall negotiate with representatives of the group that made the request for the purpose of concluding an agreement that is appropriate to the circumstances of that group.

Agenda for negotiations

(4) Negotiations pursuant to subsection (3) may relate to any matter respecting self-government including, where appropriate, jurisdiction, powers, lands, resources, funding and preservation and enhancement of language and culture.

Participation of territories

(5) The government of Canada may invite elected representatives of the government of the Yukon Territory or the Northwest Territories to participate in discussions referred to in subsection (2) and negotiations referred to in subsection (3), where the negotiations relate to communities or regions within the Yukon Territory or the Northwest Territories, as the case may be.

Deemed treaty rights where legislatures approve

35.03 Self-government rights that are set out in any agreement concluded with aboriginal people living in a particular community or region that

(a) includes a declaration to the effect that this section applies in respect of those rights, and

(b) is approved by an Act of Parliament and an Act of the Legislature of each province in which that community or region is located

are deemed to be treaty rights for the purposes of section 35.

Application of the Charter

35.04 (1) The *Canadian Charter of Rights and Freedoms* applies, to the extent that its application is appropriate in the circumstances, to all legislative or governmental bodies or institutions exercising the right to self-government in respect of all matters within their authority.

Application of section 33 of the Charter

(2) For greater certainty, section 33 of the *Canadian Charter of Rights and Freedoms* applies, with such modifications as the circumstances require, in respect of enactments of bodies or institutions referred to in subsection (1).

Non-derogation of rights of aboriginal peoples

35.05 Nothing in sections 35.01 to 35.03 abrogates or derogates from any rights of the aboriginal peoples of Canada.

Non-derogation of legislative powers, etc. of government

35.06 Nothing in subsections 35.01(1) aborgates or derogates from the jurisdiction, legislative powers, proprietary rights or any other rights or privileges of Parliament or the government of Canada, or the legislature or government of a province, except in accordance with agreements described in 35.03.

2. Section 61 of the said Act is repealed and the following substituted therefor:

References

"61. A reference to the *Constitution Act, 1982*, or a reference to the *Constitution Acts 1867 to 1982*, shall be deemed to include a reference to any amendments thereto."

Constitutional conference

3. (1) A constitutional conference composed of the Prime Minister of Canada and the first ministers of the provinces shall be convened by the Prime Minister of Canada within ten years after his Amendment comes into force.

Review of this amendment

(2) The conference convened under subsection (1) shall have on its agenda a review of the provisions of this Amendment and its implication.

Participation of aboriginal peoples and territories

(3) The Prime Minister of Canada shall invite representatives of the aboriginal peoples of Canada and elected representatives of the governments of the Yukon Territory and the Northwest Territories to participate in the conference convened under subsection (1).

Citation

(4) This Amendment may be cited as the *Constitution Amendment*, year of proclamation (*Aboriginal peoples of Canada*).

Notes

1* This could be drafted as additional subsections to section 35.

1987 First Ministers' Conference on Aboriginal Constitutional Matters

Joint Aboriginal Proposal for Self-Government

Assembly of First Nations
Native Council of Canada
Métis National Council
Inuit Committee on National Issues

Statement of the Right to Self-Government

35(5)(a) For greater certainty, the inherent right of self-government and land of all the Indian, Inuit, and Métis peoples of Canada is recognized and affirmed in subsection (1).

The Commitment to Negotiate

35(5)(b)(i) Upon the request of an aboriginal people of a community or region, the government of Canada shall negotiate agreements relating to the matters referred to in (iii);

35(5)(b)(ii) the government of a province shall participate in the negotiations, to the extent of its jurisdiction, if so requested by the aboriginal people concerned; and

35(5)(b)(iii) the agreements referred to in this subsection shall be negotiated in good faith by all parties, and without limiting their scope, the negotiations shall include such matters as self-government, lands, resources, economic and fiscal arrangements, education, preservation and enhancement of language and culture and equity of access, as may be requested by the aboriginal people concerned.

35(5)(b)(iv) For greater certainty, and without prejudice to the rights to any aboriginal peoples of a community or region, or its negotiation of agreements, all the aboriginal peoples of Canada are guaranteed equitable access to the processes and resources by which agreements will be negotiated pursuant to this section.

Negotiations Will Not Prejudice Other Programs

35(5)(c) No program, service, financial arrangement, claims or other process available to the aboriginal peoples of Canada, shall be prejudiced by reason of the fact that negotiations have been entered into pursuant to this section.

Rights in Agreements shall be Treaty Rights

35(5)(d) For greater certainty, the rights of aboriginal people set forth in agreements reached pursuant to paragraph (b) shall be ''treaty rights'' within the meaning of subsections (1) and (3).

Economic and Fiscal Arrangements

35(6)(a) Parliament and the government of Canada and, to the extent provided by agreements and other treaties referred to in this Part, the legislatures and the governments of the province, are committed to:

35(6)(a)(i) ensuring that aboriginal governments have the legislative authority and other powers necessary to raise revenues and derive benefits by taxation and otherwise, within their territories or regions subject to their jurisdictions; and

35(6)(ii) providing aboriginal governments with sufficient fiscal resources in the form of direct payments and other fiscal arrangements, to govern their affairs to maintain and develop aboriginal cultures, to promote economic development and employment opportunities, and to provide services of reasonable quality and at levels reasonably comparable to those available to all Canadians.

35(6)(b) For the purposes referred to in this Part, Parliament and the government of Canada have the primary financial responsibility concerning aboriginal peoples.

Commitment to the Principles of Promoting Self-Government and Self-Reliance

35(7) To the extent that each has jurisdiction, Parliament and the provincial legislatures, together with the government of Canada and the provincial governments, are committed to the principle of promoting self-government and self-reliance among aboriginal peoples in communities or regions in Canada, in co-operation with them.

Treaty Process

35(8)(a) Parliament and the government of Canada are committed to fulfilling the spirit and intent of each treaty made between aboriginal people and the Crown.

35(8)(b) In order to fulfill the spirit and intent of treaties, the government of Canada is committed to clarify, rectify, renovate or implement those treaties as may be requested by the aboriginal peoples concerned.

35(8)(c) The results of the negotiations contemplated in paragraph (b) shall be set out in

(a) an amendment to a treaty

(b) an adhesion to a treaty, or

(c) a new treaty,

as determined by the aboriginal peoples concerned.

35(8)(d) At the request of the Indian, Inuit or Métis peoples concerned, the government of a province is committed to participate in the negotiations contemplated in paragraph (b) to the extent of its jurisdiction, in a manner that does not abrogate or derogate from the role and authority of the government of Canada to conclude treaties with any of the aboriginal peoples of Canada.

35(8)(e) For the purpose of this subsection, references to "treaties" includes "land claims agreements" subject to paragraph (f).

35(8)(f) Notwithstanding paragraph (d), a government of a province is committed to participate in negotiations contemplated in paragraph (b) for the purposes stated therein with respect to land claims agreements to which it is a party.

Interpretation

35(9)(a) The rights of the aboriginal peoples of Canada shall be interpreted in a broad and liberal manner, so as to promote the preservation and enhancement of the heritage and cultures of the aboriginal peoples.

35(9)(b) Without limiting the generality of subsection (a), treaty rights of the aboriginal peoples of Canada shall be interpreted in accordance with the spirit and intent of the specific treaties including land claims agreements concerned.

Non-Derogation

35(10) Nothing in subsections (5) to (8) abrogates or derogates from any rights or freedoms of the aboriginal peoples of Canada.

Legislative Powers Not Extended

35(11) Nothing in this subsection extends the legislative powers of Parliament or a provincial legislature.

BILL C-115: An Act to amend the Indian Act
(designated lands), S.C. 1988

1. (1) The definition "reserve" in subsection 2(1) of the *Indian Act* is repealed and the following subsituted therefor:

" "reserve"

(a) means a tract of land, the legal title to which is vested in Her Majesty, that has been set apart by Her Majesty for the use and benefit of a band, and

(b) except in subsection 18(2), sections 20 to 25, 28, 36 to 38, 42, 44, 46, 48 to 51, 58, 60 and 124 and the regulations made under any of those provisions, includes designated lands;''

(2) Subsection 2(1) of the said Act is further amended by adding thereto, in alphabetical order within the subsection, the following definition:

" "designated lands" means a tract of land or any interest therein the legal title to which remains vested in Her Majesty and in which the band for whose use and benefit it was set apart as a reserve has, otherwise than absolutely, released or surrendered its rights or interests, whether before or after the coming into force of this definition;"

2. The heading preceding section 37 and sections 37 and 38 of the said Act are repealed and the following substituted therefor:

"SURRENDERS AND DESIGNATIONS

37. (1) Lands in a reserve shall not be sold nor title to them conveyed until they have been absolutely surrendered to Her Majesty pursuant to subsection 38(1) by the band for whose use and benefit in common the reserve was set apart.

(2) Except where this Act otherwise provides, lands in a reserve shall not be leased nor an interest in them granted until they have been surrendered to Her Majesty pursuant to subsection 38(2) by the band for whose use and benefit in common the reserve was set apart.

38. (1) A band may absolutely surrender to Her Majesty, conditionally, or unconditionally, all of the rights and interests of the band and its members in all or part of a reserve.

(2) A band may, conditionally or unconditionally, designate by way of a surrender to Her Majesty that is not absolute, any right or interest of the band and its members in all or part of a reserve, for the purpose of its being leased or a right or interest therein being granted."

3. Subsections 39(1) to (3) of the said Act are repealed and the following substituted therefor:

"**39.** (1) An absolute surrender or designation is void unless

(a) it is made to Her Majesty;

(b) it is assented to by a majority of the electors of the band

   (i) at a general meeting of the band called by the council of the band,

   (ii) at a special meeting of the band called by the Minister for the purpose of considering a proposed absolute surrender or designation, or

   (iii) by a referendum as provided in the regulations; and

(c) it is accepted by the Governor in Council.

(2) Where a majority of the electors of a band did not vote at a meeting or referendum called pursuant to subsection (1), the Minister

may, if the proposed absolute surrender or designation was assented to by a majority of the electors who did vote, call another meeting by giving thirty days notice thereof or another referendum as provided in the regulations.

(3) Where a meeting is called pursuant to subsection (2) and the proposed absolute surrender or designation is assented to at the meeting or referendum by a majority of the electors voting, the surrender or designation shall be deemed, for the purposes of this section, to have been assented to by a majority of the electors of the band.''

4. Sections 40 and 41 of the said Act are repealed and the following substituted therefor:

''**40.** A proposed absolute surrender or designation that is assented to by the band in accordance with section 39 shall be certified on oath by the superintendent or other officer who attended the meeting and by the chief or a member of the council of the band and then submitted to the Governor in Council for acceptance or refusal.

41. An absolute surrender or designation shall be deemed to confer all rights that are necessary to enable Her Majesty to carry out the terms of the surrender or designation.''

5. (1) The heading preceding section 53 and subsection 53(1) of the said Act are repealed and the following substituted therefor:

''MANAGEMENT OF RESERVES AND SURRENDERED AND DESIGNATED LANDS

53. (1) The Minister or a person appointed by the Minister for the purpose may, in accordance with this Act and the terms of the absolute surrender or designation, as the case may be,

(a) manage or sell absolutely surrendered lands; or
(b) manage, lease or carry out any other transaction affecting designated lands.''

(2) Subsection 53(3) of the said Act is repealed and the following substituted therefor:

''(3) No person who is appointed pursuant to subsection (1) or who is an officer or servant of Her Majesty employed in the Department may, except with the approval of the Governor in Council, acquire directly or indirectly any interest in absolutely surrendered or designated lands.''

6. Section 54 of the said Act is repealed and the following substituted therefor:

''**54.** Where absolutely surrendered lands are agreed to be sold and letters patent relating thereto have not issued, or where designated lands are leased or an interest in them granted, the purchaser, lessee or other person who has an interest in the absolutely surrendered or designated lands may, with the approval of the Minister, assign all or part of that interest to any other person.''

7. (1) Subsection 55(1) of the said Act is repealed and the following substituted therefor:

"**55.** (1) There shall be kept in the Department a register, to be known as the Surrendered and Designated Lands Register, in which shall be entered particulars in connection with any transaction affecting absolutely surrendered or designated lands.''

(2) The Surrendered Lands Register kept in the Department before coming into force of this Act constitutes, on the coming into force of this Act, the Surrendered and Designated Lands Register.

8. (1) Subsection 58(3) of the said Act is repealed and the following substituted therefor:

"(3) The Minister may lease for the benefit of any Indian, on application of that Indian for that purpose, the land of which the Indian is lawfully in possession without the land being designated.''

(2) All that portion of subsection 58(4) of the said Act preceding paragraph (a) thereof is repealed and the following substituted therefor:

"(4) Notwithstanding anything in this Act, the Minister may, without an absolute surrender or designation''

9. Paragraph 59(a) of the said Act is repealed and the following substituted therefor:

"(a) reduce or adjust the amount payable to Her Majesty in respect of a transaction affecting absolutely surrendered lands, designated lands or other lands in a reserve or the rate of interest payable thereon; and''

10. (1) All that portion of subsection 83(1) of the said Act preceding paragraph (b) thereof is repealed and the following substituted therefor:

"**83.** (1) Without prejudice to the powers conferred by section 81, the council of a band may, subject to the approval of the Minister, make by-laws for any or all of the following purposes, namely,

(a) subject to subsections (2) and (3), taxation for local purposes of land, or interests in land, in the reserve, including rights to occupy, possess or use land in the reserve;

(a.1) the licensing of businesses, callings, trades and occupations;''

(2) Paragraph 83(1)(e) of the said Act is repealed and the following substituted therefor:

'' (e) the enforcement of payment of amounts that are payable pursuant to this section, including arrears and interest;

(e.1) the imposition and recovery of interest on amounts that are payable pursuant to this section, where those amounts are not paid before they are due, and the calculation of that interest;''

(3) Subsection 83(2) of the said Act is repealed and the following substituted therefor:

''(2) An expenditure made out of moneys raised pursuant to subsection (1) must be so made under the authority of a by-law of the council of the band.

(3) A by-law made under paragraph (1)(a) must provide an appeal procedure in respect of assessments made for the purposes of taxation under that paragraph.

(4) The Minister may approve the whole or a part only of a by-law made under subsection (1).

(5) The Governor in Council may make regulations not consistent with this section respecting the exercise of the by-law making powers of bands under this section.

(6) A by-law made under this section remains in force only to the extent that it is consistent with the regulations made under subsection (5).''

11. Section 85 of the said Act is repealed.

12. Subsection 89(1) of the said Act is repealed and the following substituted therefor:

''89. (1) Subject to this Act, the real and personal property of an Indian or a band situated on a reserve is not subject to charge, pledge, mortgage, attachment, levy, seizure, distress or execution in favour or at the instance of any person other than an Indian or a band.

(1.1) Notwithstanding subsection (1), a leasehold interest in designated lands is subject to charge, pledge, mortgage, attachment, levy, seizure, distress and execution.''

BILL C-150: An Act to amend the
Indian Act (death rules)., S.C. 1988

1. Paragraph 6(3)(b) of the *Indian Act* is repealed and the following substituted therefor:

''(b) a person described in paragraph 1(c), (d), (e) or (f) or subsection (2) who was no longer living on April 17, 1985 shall be deemed to be entitled to be registered under that provision.''

2. Subsection 11(3) of the said Act is repealed and the following substituted therefor:

"(3) For the purposes of paragraph 1(d) and subsection (2),

(a) a person whose name was omitted or deleted from the Indian Register or a band list in the circumstances set out in paragraph 6(1)(c), (d) or (e) who was no longer living on the first day on which the person would otherwise be entitled to have the person's name entered in the Band List of the band of which the person ceased to be a member shall be deemed to be entitled to have the person's name so entered; and

(b) a person described in paragraph (2)(b) shall be deemed to be entitled to have the person's name entered in the Band List in which the parent referred to in that paragraph is or was, or is deemed by this section to be, entitled to have the parent's name entered."

3. This Act shall be deemed to have come into force on April 17, 1985.

THE CARLETON LIBRARY SERIES

CARLETON CONTEMPORARIES

AN INDEPENDENT FOREIGN POLICY FOR CANADA? Edited by
Stephen Clarkson
THE DECOLONIZATION OF QUEBEC: AN ANALYSIS OF LEFT-WING
NATIONALISM by Henry Milner and Sheilagh Hodgins Milner
THE MACKENZIE PIPELINE: ARCTIC GAS AND CANADIAN ENERGY
POLICY Edited by Peter H. Pearse
CONTINENTAL COMMUNITY? INDEPENDENCE AND
INTEGRATION IN NORTH AMERICA Edited by W.A. Axline, J.E.
Hyndman, P.V. Lyon and M.A. Molot
THE RAILWAY GAME: A STUDY IN SOCIO-TECHNOLOGICAL
OBSOLESCENCE by J. Lukasiewicz
FOREMOST NATION: CANADIAN FOREIGN POLICY AND A
CHANGING WORLD Edited by N. Hillmer and G. Stevenson
TAKING SEX INTO ACCOUNT: THE POLICY CONSEQUENCES OF
SEXIST RESEARCH Edited by Jill McCalla Vickers

GENERAL LIST

1. DICCIONARIO DE REFERENCIAS DEL "poema de mio cid", compiled
   and arranged by José Jurado
2. THE POET AND THE CRITIC: A Literary Correspondence Between D.
   C. Scott and E. K. Brown, edited by Robert L. McDougall